COVER: Geber86/Getty Images

mheducation.com/prek-12

Send all inquiries to:
McGraw-Hill Education
8787 Orion Place
Columbus, OH 43240

ISBN: 978-0-02-140110-9
MHID: 0-02-140110-1

Printed in the United States of America.

3 4 5 6 7 8 9 QVS 21 20 19 18 17 16

Glencoe

Marketing
Essentials

Lois Schneider Farese

Grady Kimbrell

Dr. Carl A. Woloszyk

Mc
Graw
Hill
Education

Lois Schneider Farese is a nationally recognized secondary marketing educator and DECA advisor from New Jersey. She has been involved in organizing and running New Jersey regional and state DECA conferences and has also participated as series director and event manager at state and national DECA conferences. The State Officer Action Team presented Farese with the Outstanding Service Award for her dedication, professionalism, and commitment to New Jersey DECA in 1993, 1996, and 1999, as well as with the Honorary Life Membership Award in 1990 for setting a new level of professionalism for local advisors. She was inducted into the DECA Hall of Fame in 1996. Farese was named "Teacher of the Year" in 1981 by the Marketing Education Association of New Jersey. In 1993 and 1999, the University of Richmond recognized Farese for her contributions to the intellectual growth and achievement of students who graduated from her marketing program. In 2000 Farese was the nominee from Northern Highlands Regional High School for the Princeton Prize for Distinguished Secondary School Teaching. Farese holds a bachelor's degree in business and distributive education and two master's degrees from Montclair State University in New Jersey.

Grady Kimbrell, a nationally recognized author and consultant on career education, began his career in education teaching high school business in Kansas. After relocating to Southern California, Kimbrell taught business courses and coordinated students' in-class activities with their on-the-job experience. He later directed the work experience program for the high schools of Santa Barbara, California. A pioneer in the use of computers as a tool for educational research, Kimbrell has assisted school districts with a wide variety of research and evaluation activities. Kimbrell has served on numerous state instructional program committees and writing teams, designed educational computer programs, and produced educational films. Kimbrell holds degrees in business administration, educational psychology, and business education.

Carl A. Woloszyk is a professor emeritus from Western Michigan University with an extensive background in marketing education. He has served as a state department of education consultant for marketing and cooperative education, DECA and Delta Epsilon Chi state advisor, a career and technical administrator for a regional education service agency, and a secondary marketing teacher-coordinator. As a secondary marketing teacher-coordinator, he taught beginning and advanced marketing courses. His students have received numerous awards at district, state, and national DECA conferences. Woloszyk has served on the board of directors for DECA; he has been president of the Marketing Education Foundation and of the ACTE Cooperative Work Experience Education Association. He is a board member of the Michigan Marketing Educators' Association. He has received the Marketing Education Professional Award from the national Marketing Education Association for Exemplary Service to Marketing Education. Woloszyk holds a master's degree from Eastern Michigan University and an educational specialist degree in occupational education from the University of Michigan. He received his doctorate in business and distributive education from Michigan State University.

REVIEWERS AND CONTRIBUTORS

Priscilla McCalla
Professional Development Director (retired)
National DECA
Reston, VA

Jennifer Allen
Marketing Teacher
Wilson Central High School
Lebanon, TN

Shauna Binkerd
Business/Marketing Educator
Springville High School
Springville, UT

Rose M. Blevins
DECA Advisor/SkillsUSA Advisor
Kecoughtan High School
Hampton, VA

Diana Canton
Marketing Education Teacher/DECA Advisor
Cigarroa High School
Laredo, TX

Tracy Conley
Coolidge High School
Coolidge, AZ

Ron Cooper
Advisor Development
Washington DECA
Seattle, WA

Alana Eaton
Business Education Teacher
Kennard-Dale High School
Fawn Grove, PA

Michelle Gilbert
Marketing DECA Coordinator
Justin F. Kimball High School
Dallas, TX

Cassandra Jones
Marketing Education Teacher-Coordinator
Allen High School
Allen, TX

Shanna LaMar
Executive Director
Washington DECA
Seattle, WA

Ariana Langford
Har-Ber High School
Springdale, AR

Kit Lynch
Marketing Instructor
Gahanna Lincoln High School
Gahanna, OH

Michelle Stortzum
Marketing Instructor / LHS DECA Advisor
Lindbergh High School
St. Louis, MO

Shelly Stanton
Billings West High School
Billings, MT

James Walker Todd
Douglas MacArthur High School
San Antonio, TX

TABLE OF CONTENTS

TABLE OF CONTENTS

TABLE OF CONTENTS

TABLE OF CONTENTS

TABLE OF CONTENTS

Ingram Publishing

TABLE OF CONTENTS

Lane Oatey/Blue Jean Images/Getty Images

TABLE OF CONTENTS

Robert Churchill/Getty Images

FEATURES TABLE OF CONTENTS

Project-Based Learning

These project-based features will help you get involved in the world of marketing. Each project includes a related worksheet activity and a rubric you can use to evaluate your work.

Marketing Internship Project

Discovery Project

Marketing in the Real World

It is important to know how marketing concepts actually work in business and global economies. These features will show you how real companies faced marketing challenges and how the economies in different countries and cultures can affect people around the world.

MARKETING CASE STUDIES

WORLD MARKET

FEATURES TABLE OF CONTENTS

Marketing with DECA

DECA prepares emerging leaders and entrepreneurs in marketing, finance, hospitality and management in high schools and colleges around the world. These features can help you prepare for DECA events and interact with other students.

DECA Connection Role Play

  Online Connection!

Visit connectED.mcgraw-hill.com for more DECA Role Plays.

What Do You Want to Be?

The world of marketing is a gateway to many different careers. These features allow you to learn about many different marketing-related careers and the skills and education you will need to get them.

Career Chatroom

 connectED.mcgraw-hill.com

Learn more about these careers and complete a Career Exploration Activity.

FEATURES TABLE OF CONTENTS

Improve Your Marketing Skills

Do you know how to properly use social media for marketing? Can you promote products and services using green methods? These features will help you improve your digital and green marketing skills.

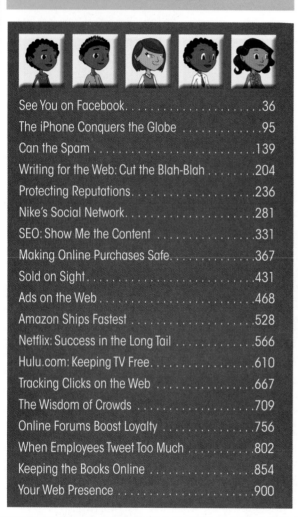

DIGITAL NATION

The GREEN Marketer

Thinking Creatively

Marketing professionals must be able to think creatively to solve problems. These Hot Topic features will help improve your understanding of important marketing concepts.

What is DECA?

DECA is a national association for students of marketing. It was formed in 1946 to improve the education of students in business subject areas, in particular marketing, entrepreneurship, and management.

DECA, which stands for the Distributive Education Clubs of America, offers students the opportunity to develop their leadership and professional skills. This is done through on-the-job experience, activities and projects sponsored by individual schools or chapters, and a series of competitive events in specific occupational areas. All activities apply the concepts of marketing to real-life situations. It is likely that DECA will be an integral part of your learning experience as you explore the world of marketing.

What is DECA's mission statement?

The mission of DECA is to enhance the co-curricular education of students with interests in marketing, management, and entrepreneurship. DECA helps students develop skills and competence for marketing careers, build self-esteem, experience leadership, and practice community service. DECA is committed to the advocacy of marketing education and the growth of business and education partnerships.

How can DECA help me?

Even though some activities may take time outside of school, DECA should be considered a co-curricular activity instead of an after-school activity. The basis for the projects and events will come from your classroom learning. Information from events that you take back to the classroom will enhance not only your learning experience, but that of your classmates as well. DECA also offers scholarships and other recognition awards to exceptional students. In general, success in DECA events is a positive addition to your résumé or portfolio.

DECA can help you:

- Develop strong leadership skills
- Understand the importance of making ethical decisions in your personal life and future career
- Focus on enhancing effective public speaking and presentation skills
- Understand the need for diversity in the global marketplace
- Enhance skills needed for a career in marketing or as an entrepreneur
- Increase your self-confidence when presenting or speaking in public
- Investigate career opportunities available in the marketing field
- Develop good social and business etiquette

What is DECA's mission statement?

Marketing Essentials is designed to prepare you for a career or further study in marketing. It is also helpful in preparing for DECA activities. You will notice that the DECA logo and DECA-approved activities are prominently featured throughout your book. The DECA Connection feature is modeled after DECA individual or team projects. It will help you apply knowledge learned in your marketing class. DECA activities can also enhance your classroom learning by helping you develop stronger communication and analytical skills.

DECA sponsors competitive events in 30 occupational areas, including:

- Apparel and Accessories Marketing Series
- Advertising Campaign Event
- Automotive Services Marketing Series
- Business Services Marketing Series
- E-Commerce Management Team Decision-Making Event
- Food Marketing Series, AL
- Financial Analysis Management Team Decision-Making Event
- Food Marketing Series, ML
- Full Service Restaurant Management Series
- Hospitality Services Management Team Decision-Making Event
- Hospitality and Recreation Marketing Research Event
- Marketing Management Series
- Quick Serve Restaurant Management Series
- Restaurant and Food Service Management Series
- Retail Merchandising Series
- Sports and Entertainment Marketing Series
- Sports and Entertainment Marketing Management Team Decision-Making Event
- Travel and Tourism Marketing Management Team Decision-Making Event
- Technical Sales Event

THE WORLD OF MARKETING

Marketing Internship Project

SWOT Analysis

Essential Question How do businesses find out their strengths and weaknesses in the marketplace?

In order to sell products, marketers must learn about and analyze the strengths and weaknesses of their products as well as the opportunities and threats in the market. How do they get this information? One way is through a SWOT analysis. SWOT stands for strengths, weaknesses, opportunities, and threats. Even the best companies have internal weaknesses and external threats that they must face. A SWOT analysis helps a company determine how to lessen the impact of these factors. Similarly, the results of a SWOT analysis can help a company think of ways to enhance its strengths and take advantage of new opportunities in the market. It is especially important for a new company to conduct a SWOT analysis before it enters the market.

Project Goal

In the project at the end of this unit, you will conduct a SWOT analysis to market a new business.

Prepare for the Project

As you read this unit, use this checklist to prepare for the Marketing Internship Project at the end of this unit:

- Conduct research on beverage retailers.
- Make a list of large and small competitors.
- Consider the marketing mix of these competitors.

 connectED.mcgraw-hill.com

Worksheet Activity
Complete a worksheet activity about conducting a SWOT analysis.

 AMERICAN **MARKETING** ASSOCIATION

Marketing is no longer a function—it is an educational process.

MARKETING CORE FUNCTIONS IN THIS UNIT

- Marketing Information Management
- Market Planning
- Pricing
- Promotion
- Selling

A Taste of Dawn
African Sunrise Tea Latte

With our new African Sunrise Tea Latte, experience the delicate blend of steamed milk and the flavors of the coastal regions of South Africa, a fullbodied blend of African honeybush and orange peel with a sweet creamy aroma, balanced by hints of vanilla and citrus.

New from *The Coffee Bean & Tea Leaf*®

www.coffeebean.com.ph

Taste Matters.

SHOW WHAT YOU KNOW

Visual Literacy
Before this business designed its print ad to appeal to customers, it performed a SWOT analysis that included researching the target market, or customers. *How would you describe the customer targeted by this ad?*

3

Chapter 1

Section 1.1
Marketing and the
Marketing Concept

Section 1.2
The Importance of
Marketing

Section 1.3
Fundamentals of
Marketing

marketing is all around us

SHOW WHAT YOU KNOW

Visual Literacy Whenever you see advertising in print, online, or on the street, marketing is in action. When you go shopping, marketing is present in displays. When you go on the Internet, marketing pops up in front of you. When you see trucks hauling products, marketing is taking place. All these activities are aspects of marketing. *What other activities have you observed that are part of marketing? How would you define marketing?*

Ilene MacDonald/Alamy

Discovery Project

Keeping Customers

Essential Question How do businesses keep their customers?

Project Goal
Work with a partner to identify two businesses that cater to teenagers. One business should sell goods and the other services. Use the seven marketing functions—Channel Management, Marketing Information Management, Market Planning, Pricing, Product/Service Management, Promotion, and Selling—to explain how each business caters to its customers. How effective are those businesses in satisfying their customers' needs and wants? Develop a rating scale to present your findings.

Ask Yourself...
- Which two businesses will you study?
- How will you use the marketing functions to evaluate each business?
- How will you devise a rating scale?
- How will you present your findings?

 Analysis and Interpretation Why is it important for businesses to follow the marketing functions?

 connectED.mcgraw-hill.com

Activity
Get a worksheet activity about keeping customers.

Evaluate
Download a rubric that you can use to evaluate your project.

DECA Connection

DECA Event Role Play
Concepts in this chapter are related to DECA competitive events that involve either an interview or role play.

Performance Indicators The performance indicators represent key skills and knowledge. Your key to success in DECA competitive events is relating them to the concepts in this chapter.

- Explain the concept of marketing strategies.
- Explain the concept of markets and market identification.
- Explain the importance of promotion in the marketing mix.
- Describe marketing functions and related activities.
- Determine economic utilities created by business activities.

DECA Prep
Role Play Practice role playing with the DECA Connection competitive-event activity at the end of this chapter. More information about DECA events can be found on DECA's Web site.

READING GUIDE

Before You Read

Connect When have you been influenced by marketing?

Objectives

- **Describe** the scope of marketing.
- **Describe** each marketing core function.
- **Explain** the marketing concept.

The Main Idea

To be a successful marketer, you need to understand the marketing skills, marketing core functions, and basic tools of marketing.

Vocabulary

Content Vocabulary
- marketing
- goods
- services
- marketing concept

Academic Vocabulary

You will find these words in your reading and on your tests. Make sure you know their meanings.
- create
- conduct

Graphic Organizer

Draw or print this umbrella graphic organizer to take notes about the marketing core functions.

 connectED.mcgraw-hill.com

Print this graphic organizer.

MARKETING CORE FUNCTION

Market Planning

 # Marketing and the Marketing Concept

THE SCOPE OF MARKETING

You have been a consumer for many years, and you have made decisions about products you liked and did not like. As you study marketing, you will analyze what businesses do to influence consumers' buying decisions. That knowledge will help you begin to think like a marketer.

According to the American Marketing Association (AMA), "**marketing** is the activity, set of institutions, and processes for creating, communicating, delivering, and exchanging offerings that have value for customers, clients, partners, and society at large." It involves the process of planning, pricing, promoting, selling, and distributing ideas, goods, or services to **create** exchanges that satisfy customers. Note that marketing is a process. The AMA reviews the definition of marketing on a regular basis to make sure it conforms to current marketing practices. Thus, marketing is ongoing, and it changes. As a marketer, you need to keep up with trends and consumer attitudes.

As You Read

Connect Marketers track trends and consumer attitudes. What trends have you noticed in your experience as a teenager?

IDEAS, GOODS, AND SERVICES

Ideas, goods, and services are offerings. Politicians, for example, offer voters their platform or ideas in hopes of getting votes. **Goods** are tangible items that have monetary value and satisfy your needs and wants, such as cars, furniture, televisions, and clothing. Intangible items that have monetary value and satisfy your needs and wants are **services**. Intangible means you cannot physically touch an item.

Services involve a task, such as cooking a hamburger or cutting hair. Banks, dry cleaners, and accounting offices all provide economic services.

> ❝ **You already know a lot about marketing because it is all around you.** ❞

Every time someone sells or buys something, an exchange occurs in the marketplace. The marketplace is the commercial environment where exchanges occur. It is the world of shops, Internet stores, financial institutions, catalogs, and more.

SKILLS AND KNOWLEDGE

Marketing is one career cluster in business administration. The practice of marketing depends on many key areas of skill and knowledge. These areas are listed in the Marketing Core image on page 2 that introduces Unit 1. Many of the topics that you will study in *Marketing Essentials* are based on these areas of skill and knowledge:

- ▶ Business Law
- ▶ Communications
- ▶ Customer Relations
- ▶ Economics
- ▶ Emotional Intelligence
- ▶ Entrepreneurship
- ▶ Financial Analysis
- ▶ Human Resource Management
- ▶ Information Management
- ▶ Operations
- ▶ Professional Development
- ▶ Strategic Management

The GREEN Marketer

Trustmarks:
Green Seals of Approval

More and more companies are using trustmarks, packaging symbols that suggest that a product is greener or healthier than the competition.

The three most recognized trustmarks are the recyclable symbol, the Energy Star label, and the USDA Organic seal. Energy Star and USDA Organic are awarded by the federal government, while the use of the recycling symbol is not regulated by law. That means anyone can use it to promote a product.

Nonprofit organizations award many other trustmarks, such as the Rainforest Alliance Certified seal, in exchange for a fee. Each of these trustmarks tells consumers about the product's benefits.

Social Studies
Discuss Some trustmarks, such as the Smart Choices Program for healthy foods, are created by industry groups. Would you trust a seal created by the companies that use it on their products? Why or why not? Discuss your responses with a partner.

connectED.mcgraw-hill.com

Get an activity on green marketing.

SEVEN MARKETING CORE FUNCTIONS

The marketing core includes seven functions. The image here also includes these functions. These functions define all the aspects that are part of the practice of marketing.

CHANNEL MANAGEMENT

Channel management, or distribution, is the process of deciding how to get goods into customer's hands. Physically moving and storing goods is part of distribution planning. The main methods of transportation are by truck, rail, ship, or air. Some large retail chains store products in warehouses for later distribution. Distribution also involves the systems that track products.

Companies may decide on several different channels of distribution, depending on whether the product is sold to individuals or businesses. The goal is to find the best way to get the product into the customer's hands based on his or her purchasing methods.

MARKETING INFORMATION MANAGEMENT

Good business and marketing decisions rely on good information about customers, trends, and competing products. Gathering this information, storing it, and analyzing it are all part of marketing information management. Companies **conduct** research so they can be successful at marketing and selling their products. They need to get information about their customers, their habits and attitudes, where they live, and trends in the marketplace. Marketers can use this information to create a marketing plan for their products.

MARKET PLANNING

Market planning involves understanding the concepts and strategies used to develop and target specific marketing strategies to a select audience. This function requires an in-depth knowledge of activities that involve determining information needs, designing data-collection processes, collecting data, analyzing data, presenting data, and using that data to create a marketing plan. The plan will include methods for reaching different types of customers.

U.S. Department of Agriculture

PRICING

Pricing decisions dictate how much to charge for goods and services in order to make a profit. Pricing decisions are based on costs and on what competitors charge for the same product or service. To determine a price, marketers must also determine how much customers are willing to pay.

PRODUCT/SERVICE MANAGEMENT

Product/service management is obtaining, developing, maintaining, and improving a product or a product mix in response to market opportunities. Marketing research guides product/service management toward what the consumer needs and wants. New technology and trends influence product/service management as well.

PROMOTION

Promotion is the effort to inform, persuade, or remind current and potential customers about a business's products or services. Television and radio commercials, and online ads are forms of promotion. This type of promotion is called advertising.

Promotion is also used to improve a company's public image. A company can show social responsibility by recycling materials or cleaning up the environment. Promotion concepts and strategies can help to achieve success in the marketplace.

SELLING

Selling provides customers with the goods and services they want. This includes selling in the retail market to you, the customer, and selling in the business-to-business market to wholesalers, retailers, or manufacturers.

Selling techniques and activities include determining client needs and wants and responding through planned, personalized communication. The selling process influences purchasing decisions and enhances future business opportunities.

Reading Check

Compare and Contrast What is the difference between goods and services?

HOT TOPIC

Pricing Microbanks are banks that loan very small amounts of money to people who are poor so they can purchase everyday goods or fund projects.

Products Help Consumers Go Green

The Pompeian® olive oil company uses methods that help reduce greenhouse gases by reducing fuel costs through shipping in bulk and switching to recyclable bottles. *How can green initiatives like these help a business's profits as well as the environment?*

"We're using a sea of blue to become a lot greener"

Bill Monroe, CEO of Pompeian
"King of All Olive Oil"

What we've been doing for a century is actually great for reducing greenhouse gases.

Our trained, expert purveyors seek the best olive oil throughout the Mediterranean and use the deep blue sea to ship it to our state-of-the-art facility in Baltimore, Maryland. Pompeian is the only leading brand to import its product in bulk and pack it daily in the USA. This reduces the use of fuel by not shipping excess packaging weight across the ocean.

By packing our olive oil fresh daily, we guarantee the best tasting product and high levels of healthy polyphenols.

But we didn't stop there. To further reduce greenhouse emissions, Pompeian switched to lightweight PET bottles

so when our product is distributed to our retailers, we once again conserve fuel. Preferred by consumers and retailers, our PET bottles are 100% recyclable as well as free of worrisome BPA and phthalates.

Not only are our bottles environmentally friendly, but they look great too. Our award-winning packaging was designed to move off your shelf. You'll discover how going green with Pompeian will mean more green at retail!

Contact Bob Eckhoff, VP Sales via email:
VPsales@pompeian.com

POMPEIAN

Profit from the taste of success!
www.pompeian.com

THE MARKETING CONCEPT

The **marketing concept** is the idea that a business should strive to satisfy customers' needs and wants while generating a profit for the business. The focus is on the customer. After all, if customers do not buy a company's products, then it will go out of business.

The marketing concept holds that the desires and needs of the target market must be determined, anticipated, and satisfied in order to successfully achieve the goals of the producer. The best way to satisfy customers' needs is to stay in touch with them and monitor their purchasing behavior. The marketing concept is a philosophy. It makes the customer, and the satisfaction of his or her needs, the focal point of all business activities.

For an organization to be successful, all seven marketing core functions need to support the marketing concept. There are methods of satisfying customers' needs with regard to each marketing core function.

The people who are responsible for the marketing core functions must understand the marketing concept and reach for the same goal in order to send a consistent message to the customer. The message is that customer satisfaction is most important. Everyone in an organization needs to recognize that repeat customers keep a company in business. It is much more profitable for a company to hold on to existing customers than to search for new ones.

MARKETING CASE STUDY

Johnson & Johnson: Target Marketing

Research indicates that moms go online to get information about their newborn babies. Research also found that babies who are Hispanic represent more than 25 percent of babies born in the United States.

Media to Reach Moms

After analyzing these facts, Johnson & Johnson saw an opportunity to reach out to mothers who are Hispanic to sell its baby products. The company decided to create a Web site completely in Spanish, offering educational Webisodes that address concerns mothers have regarding their newborns. A few topics address the importance of touch in bonding with a newborn.

The product being introduced during this campaign was baby lotion. The message offers the benefits of touch in the development of a healthy baby.

To coordinate the campaign, Johnson & Johnson turned to Univision, a Spanish-language media company. It placed banner video ads on Univision's Web site, as well as ads on a variety of shows airing on its television network. A similar program was established in English so that mothers who are Hispanic could have a choice in language.

Social Studies

Math If Johnson & Johnson sold $12,949,847 of hand lotion in 2009 and $3,150,367 of that money was spent by mothers of children who are Hispanic, what percentage of Johnson & Johnson's profits were due to mothers who are Hispanic? Round to the nearest tenth.

CUSTOMER RELATIONSHIP MANAGEMENT

In the 21st century marketplace, a company's relationship with its customers is most important. It may be the main factor that determines whether a company is successful. Customer relationship management (CRM) is an aspect of marketing that combines customer information (through database and computer technology) with customer service and marketing communications. This combination allows companies to serve their customers as efficiently as possible.

By using CRM, companies are better able to understand their customers' purchasing patterns and demographics. An understanding of who its customers are and what they want to buy helps a company satisfy its customers' needs, optimize revenue, and generate more profit.

Computer databases contain information about customers who have purchased products from a company. Information from these databases is shared with the company's marketing professionals. Marketers analyze and interpret the information and search for trends and patterns in the data. These trends and patterns can serve as a company's inspiration to create new products or offer new services to meet customer needs.

Marketing professionals can also use forms of digital communication as part of CRM. A company can send emails or Tweets via Twitter® or use posts on social networking sites like Facebook® to notify customers of new promotions and events that the company offers. Customers can also use live chats or email to contact the company with comments and questions about products and services. Effective communication between a company and its customers helps to keep customers satisfied and increase profits.

 After You Read | **Section 1.1**

Review Key Concepts

1. **Explain** why the definition of marketing changes over time.
2. **Identify** an example of an economic good and an economic service.
3. **Describe** how Customer Relationship Management helps businesses employ the marketing concept.

Practice Academics

English Language Arts

4. What would be the ramifications if marketers did not conduct business with the marketing concept in mind?

Mathematics

5. A customer purchases two chairs at $249.99 each and would like them to be delivered. Your company charges $60 for delivery, and the state imposes a 6 percent sales tax on furniture, but not on the delivery charge. What is the total amount due from the customer?

Math Concept **Problem Solving** Think about which operations to use.

Starting Hints Use addition to calculate the sum for both chairs, which is the subtotal. To find the sales tax amount, multiply the subtotal by the tax percentage. Add the sales tax amount to the delivery charge to find the total amount due.

 **connectED.mcgraw-hill.com**

Check your answers.

For help, go to the Math Skills Handbook located at the back of this book.

READING GUIDE

Connect What promotions did you see the last time you went shopping? How did these promotions affect your decision to buy?

Objectives

- **Describe** the benefits of marketing.
- **Explain** the concept of utility.
- **Cite** examples of types of utilities.

The Main Idea

Marketing supports competition and offers benefits to consumers.

Vocabulary

Content Vocabulary
- utility

Academic Vocabulary

You will find these words in your reading and on your tests. Make sure you know their meanings.
- impact
- benefits

Graphic Organizer

Draw or print the figure below. Take notes about the benefits of marketing and list the five utilities.

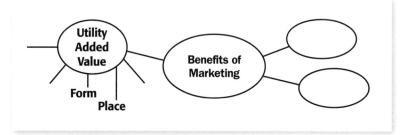

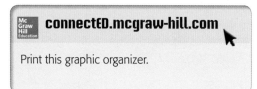
Print this graphic organizer.

MARKETING CORE FUNCTION

Market Planning

The Importance of Marketing

ECONOMIC BENEFITS OF MARKETING

The **impact** of marketing affects the economy and standard of living in countries around the world. Marketing is a global force. Marketing plays an important role in an economy because it provides the means for competition to take place. In a competitive marketplace, businesses try to create new or improved products at lower prices than their competitors. Those efforts force them to be efficient and responsive to consumers. In addition, businesses look for ways to add value to a consumer's shopping experience. There are many economic **benefits** of marketing to an economy and to consumers.

As You Read

Reflect How have you benefited from marketing?

NEW AND IMPROVED PRODUCTS

Marketing generates competition, which fosters new and improved products. Businesses always look for ways to satisfy customers' wants and needs to keep customers interested. This creates a larger variety of goods and services. For example, cell phones have become "smart phones." Their capabilities have evolved from simple to complex.

> 66 **Through the study of marketing, you will understand the importance of marketing and how much it affects you and other consumers.** 99

LOWER PRICES

Marketing activities increase demand, and this helps to lower prices. When demand is high, manufacturers can produce products in larger quantities. This reduces the unit cost of each product. This is because the fixed costs (such as the rent on a building) remain the same whether the company produces 1,500 units or 15,000 units. When a company produces a larger quantity of a product, it spends less per unit on fixed costs. The company can charge a lower price per unit, sell more units, and make more money.

Here is an example using a fixed cost of $300,000:

Scenario 1

1,500 units with $300,000 fixed costs

$300,000 ÷ 1,500 units = $200 per unit

Scenario 2

15,000 units with $300,000 fixed costs

$300,000 ÷ 15,000 units = $20 per unit

In Scenario 2, the fixed cost per unit is reduced by $18 ($20 – $2). If the original price was $95, the new price to customers would be $77.

In addition, when products become popular, more competitors enter the marketplace. To remain competitive, marketers find ways to lower their prices. Consider the personal computer market where computers have become smaller, lighter, more powerful, and a lot less expensive.

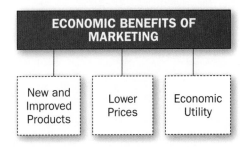

ECONOMIC BENEFITS OF MARKETING

New and Improved Products | Lower Prices | Economic Utility

ECONOMIC UTILITY

The functions of marketing add value to a product. This added value in economic terms is called **utility**. Utilities are the attributes of goods or services that make them capable of satisfying consumers' wants and needs.

There are five economic utilities involved with all products: form, place, time, possession, and information. Although form utility is not directly related to marketing, much of what goes into creating new products, such as marketing research and product design, makes it an integral part of the marketing process.

FORM UTILITY

Form utility involves changing raw materials into usable goods or putting parts together to make them more useful. The manufacturing of products involves taking things of little value by themselves and putting them together to create more value. If you consider a zipper, a spool of thread, and several yards of cloth, each would have some value. However, the value would be greater if you put all three together to make a jacket.

Form utility involves making products that consumers need and want. Special features or ingredients in a product add value and increase its form utility. For example, electronic controls on the steering wheel of an automobile add value to the final product.

PLACE UTILITY

Place utility involves having a product where customers can buy it. Businesses study consumer shopping habits to determine the most convenient and efficient locations to sell products. Some businesses use a direct approach by selling products through catalogs or the Internet. Other businesses rely on retailers to sell their products at a physical store.

TIME UTILITY

Time utility is having a product or service available at a certain time of year or a convenient time of day. For example, some banks are open seven days a week with extended hours for drive-through operations. Some gas stations are open 24 hours a day. Retailers often have extended shopping hours during special promotions or holiday seasons. Marketers increase the value of products by having them available when consumers want them.

New Products

One of the major economic benefits of marketing is the proliferation of new and improved products. *Why is it important for marketers to constantly update and improve their products?*

POSSESSION UTILITY

The exchange of a product for money is possession utility. Retailers may accept alternatives to cash, such as personal checks or debit cards, in exchange for their merchandise. They may even offer installment or layaway plans (delayed possession in return for gradual payment). In business-to-business situations, companies also grant credit to their customers. They may give them a certain period (for example, 30 days) to pay a bill. This adds value to the products they sell.

Possession utility is involved every time legal ownership of a product changes hands. Possession utility increases as purchase options increase. That is, the choice between using cash, credit, check, or another form of payment increases possession utility. The Internet also provides consumers with options to pay by providing secure sites where credit cards are accepted.

INFORMATION UTILITY

Information utility involves communication with the consumer. Salespeople provide information to customers by explaining the features and benefits of products. Displays communicate information, too. Packaging and labeling inform consumers about qualities and uses of a product. The label on a frozen food entrée tells you the ingredients, nutritional information, directions for preparation, and any safety precautions needed. Advertising informs consumers about products, tells where to buy products, and sometimes tells how much products cost.

Many manufacturers provide owners' manuals that explain how to use their products. Businesses also have Web sites where they provide detailed information about their companies and their products for customers.

 After You Read | **Section 1.2**

Review Key Concepts

1. **Explain** the role that marketing plays in an economy.
2. **How** does increased demand for a product help lower its price to consumers?
3. **Describe** how form utility is not explicitly related to marketing.

Practice Academics

English Language Arts

4. How has technology changed the toy industry over the past ten years? How has marketing helped new high-tech toys to be more prevalent?

Mathematics

5. In a business-to-business transaction, the seller offers the buyer a 2 percent discount for paying a bill early. If the buyer takes advantage of this offer, how much would be discounted on a $12,000 invoice?

> **Math Concept** **Number and Operations: Percents** A percent is a ratio comparing a number to 100. To convert percents to decimals, move the decimal point two places to the left.

Starting Hints Convert the percent to a decimal number. Multiply that decimal number by the invoice amount to find the discount amount.

 **connectED.mcgraw-hill.com**

Check your answers.

For help, go to the Math Skills Handbook located at the back of this book.

READING GUIDE

Before You Read

Connect What markets are you a part of?

Objectives

- **Describe** how marketers use knowledge of the market to sell products.
- **Compare and Contrast** consumer and organizational markets.
- **Explain** the importance of target markets.
- **Explain** how each component of the marketing mix contributes to successful marketing.

The Main Idea

The term *market* refers to all the people who might buy a product. The marketing mix is a combination of elements used to sell a product to a specific target market.

Vocabulary

Content Vocabulary

- market
- consumer market
- organizational market
- market share
- target market
- customer profile
- marketing mix

Academic Vocabulary

You will find these words in your reading and on your tests. Make sure you know their meanings.

- similar
- elements

Graphic Organizer

Draw or print these two diagrams. In the first diagram, write four terms about the concept of market. In the second diagram, write the four Ps of the marketing mix.

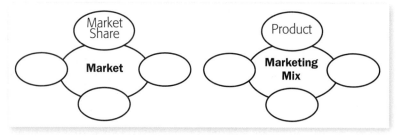

connectED.mcgraw-hill.com

Print this graphic organizer.

MARKETING CORE FUNCTION

Market Planning

Fundamentals of Marketing

MARKET AND MARKET IDENTIFICATION

Remember these terms so you can use them correctly when discussing marketing principles and practices. These terms are used throughout this textbook. It is essential to learn the language that marketers use to communicate with each other.

Marketers design products to satisfy customers' needs and wants. They know not all customers may want their product or service. So they identify those people who want their product and who have the ability to pay for their product. All people who share **similar** needs and wants and who have the ability to purchase a given product are a **market**.

You could be part of the market for video games, but not be part of the market for an expensive car. Even though you may want an expensive car, you may not have the means to buy one. If you liked video games and had the resources to buy or rent them, you would be part of the video game market.

As You Read

Predict How do you think marketers decide where to sell their products?

CONSUMER VERSUS ORGANIZATIONAL MARKETS

There are different types of markets. A market can be described as a consumer market or an organizational market.

The **consumer market** consists of consumers who purchase goods and services for personal use. Consumers' needs and wants generally fall into a few categories that reflect their lifestyles. For the most part, consumers are interested in products that will save them money, make their lives easier, improve their appearance, create status in the community, or provide satisfaction.

The **organizational market** or business-to-business (B2B) market includes all businesses that buy products for use in their operations. This market includes transactions among businesses. The goals and objectives of business firms are somewhat different from those in the consumer market. Most goals and objectives relate to improving profits. Companies want to increase productivity, increase sales, decrease expenses, or increase efficiency.

> **" The marketing terminology in this section is the foundation for future work and study in marketing. "**

Companies that produce goods and services for sale in the consumer market consider the reseller of their products to be part of the organizational market. The wholesaler who sells to the retailer is part of the organizational market. Therefore, the company needs to create two distinct marketing plans to reach each market.

MARKET SHARE

A market is further described by the total sales in a product category. Examples of categories are video games, televisions, cameras, ice cream, or soft drinks. For example, the smartphone market (e.g., iPhones, Droids, and Blackberrys) could have sales of $15 billion, and the market for Blu-Ray DVD players could have total sales of $1.2 billion. The smartphone or DVD player market includes sales through electronic or appliance stores, computer or office superstores, mass merchandisers, the Internet, and through catalog mail order.

A company's **market share** is its percentage of the total sales volume generated by all companies that compete in a given market. It may be represented in dollars or units. Knowing market share helps companies analyze their competition as well as their status in a given market. (See **Figure 1.1**.)

Market shares change all the time as new competitors enter the market and as the size of the market increases or decreases in volume. A company with a large market share can afford to take risks that other companies cannot. For example, it can develop new products that are more adventurous than its competitors because of its large market share.

MARKET SEGMENTATION

Businesses look for ways to sell their products to different consumers who may be potential customers. This involves segmenting, or breaking down, the market into smaller groups that have similar characteristics. Market segmentation is the process of classifying customers by specific characteristics. Marketers know that groups of people often buy the same products. They use this information to fine tune their approach to selling in that market.

TARGET MARKETS

The goal of market segmentation is to identify the group of people most likely to become customers. The group that is identified for a specific marketing program is the **target market**.

Target markets are very important because all marketing strategies are directed to them. When a business does not identify a target market, its marketing plan has no focus. Identifying the target market correctly is an important key to success.

FIGURE 1.1   Market Share

Who Leads in This Market? A company's percentage of total sales in a given market, such as the smartphone market, is its market share. *What could cause a business's market share to change?*

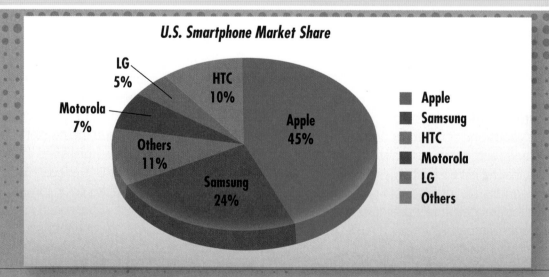

Target Markets

The Campbell Soup company manufactures a variety of soups to meet the needs of different target markets. The Chicken Noodle soup ad on the right is targeting moms with small children, while the other ad targets health-conscious adults who are looking for low-sodium soups. *Why are target markets so important in marketing?*

Surprise. It's lower sodium.

Campbell's® *Healthy Request*® Soups
— all 25 choices —
have our lower sodium natural sea salt
added for taste you can actually taste.

Today's lunch forecast:
sunny, warm and very noodly.

Kids love the delicious fun. Moms love that we make it with fresh noodles.

M'm! M'm! Good!®
POSSIBILITIES

© 2008 CSC Brands LP

Sun representative of a child's imagination

For example, consider the market for shoes. Everyone needs shoes for comfort and protection. Some people need shoes for athletics, work safety, or special occasions. There are also different shoe sizes for women, men, girls, and boys. If a company tries to sell the same type of shoe to all of these people, it will not be successful. It has not identified a target market.

MULTIPLE TARGET MARKETS

A product may have more than one target market. For example, manufacturers of children's cereal know that they need to target children and parents differently. They have two target markets: one is the children (consumers) who will be asking for the cereal and eating it; the other is the parents (customers) who need to approve of it and will be buying it. To reach the children, marketers might advertise on Saturday morning television programs specifically designed for children. The advertising message might be how much fun it is to eat this cereal. To reach parents, print advertising in magazines, such as *Family Circle* or *Parenting*, might be used, and the ad message might stress health benefits.

CUSTOMER PROFILES

To develop a clear picture of their target market, businesses create a customer profile. A **customer profile** lists information about the target market, such as age, gender, income level, marital status, ethnic background, geographic residence, attitudes, lifestyle, and behavior. Marketers spend a lot of money and time on research to collect data so that they understand the characteristics of their target market's customer profile.

Reading Check

Respond How can you use a customer profile to learn about a business's target market?

MARKETING MIX

An easy and fun way to understand customer profiles of a target market is to look at magazines. If you thumb through a magazine's articles and advertisements, you will know who reads the publication. To see if you are correct about the target market, check out the magazine's Web site and view its media kit where you will find the reader profile. Magazines use the reader profile of its target market to convince advertisers that the customer profile matches their product's target market. As you can see, target markets are very important in marketing.

The **marketing mix** includes four basic marketing strategies called the four Ps: product, place, price, and promotion. Marketing professionals or businesses use these elements to communicate with and reach their intended target market. Marketers control decisions about each of the four Ps and base their decisions on the people they want to win over and make into customers. Because of the importance of customers, some would add a fifth "P" to the list: people. Marketers must first clearly define each target market before they can develop marketing strategies.

Advertising in the Consumer Market

This ad suggests that consumers should consider using State Farm insurance policies. *How different would this ad look if the company were advertising insurance policies in the business market?*

You know where **DUDE** meets **DAD?** I'M THERE

Whoa, that happened fast, didn't it?
The next 18 years will zip right by, too.
So don't wait until Junior
is a senior to figure out how
much life insurance is enough
to protect your new family.
Let State Farm® help. Call, click or visit a
State Farm Agent today, because **Like a good neighbor,**
State Farm is there.®

 State Farm
statefarm.com

The importance of the target market (people) cannot be overemphasized. Marketers make decisions for the other four **elements** of the marketing mix based on the target market. They are interconnected. Each strategy involves making decisions about the best way to reach, satisfy, and keep customers and the best way to achieve the company's goals.

Let's look at what each marketing mix element involves, using a specific target market—the first "P" in the marketing mix. The target market is health-conscious adults who do not get their daily requirement of vegetables. Follow **Figure 1.2** (on page 22) to see each of the other Ps illustrated and explained for a vegetable/fruit juice.

PRODUCT

Product decisions begin with choosing what products to make and sell. Much research goes into product design. A product's features, brand name, packaging, service, and warranty are all part of the development. Companies also need to decide what to do with products they currently sell. In some cases, those products require updating or improvements to be competitive. By developing new uses or identifying new target markets, a company can extend the life of a product. V8 V-Fusion juice is a product developed for adults who do not like the taste of the original V8 juice, which is still on the market and has been for more than 75 years. The company developed flavors, such as Pomegranate Blueberry, Peach Mango, and Strawberry Banana, to reach out to the specific target market that wanted a tasty alternative to the original V8 juice. Package design included 46-ounce and 12-ounce bottles with bright colors that matched the juices' flavors.

PRICE

Price is what is exchanged for the product. Price strategies should reflect what customers are willing and able to pay. To that end, marketers must consider the price they will charge their organizational customers, including resellers. Pricing decisions also consider prices that the competition charges for comparable products.

Price strategies, therefore, include arriving at the list price or manufacturer's suggested retail price, as well as discounts, allowances, credit terms, and payment period for organizational customers. Originally, the manufacturer's suggested retail price for the V8 V-Fusion 46-ounce bottle was $3.89; and $1.79 for the 12-ounce size.

On occasion, a company may use special promotional pricing that would adjust the suggested retail price. Companies frequently use this technique to launch new products.

FIGURE 1.2 | Marketing Mix for a New Juice

V8 V-Fusion's Marketing Mix The Campbell Soup Company introduced V8 V-Fusion Vegetable-Fruit juice to appeal to health-conscious men and women who do not get their daily requirement of fruits and vegetables in the foods they eat. This target market (people) was the focus for all marketing mix decisions: product, place, price, and promotion. *Assume the company wanted to market a new vegetable-fruit juice for teenagers. What suggestions would you give the company with regard to its marketing strategies for the four Ps of the marketing mix?*

Product

Product decisions are based on how best to meet the target market's needs through product development, packaging, and naming the product. V8 V-Fusion provides 100 percent of daily fruit and vegetable requirements, and it contains antioxidants A, C, and E with no sugar added. It comes in variety of flavors, such as Strawberry Banana, Peach Mango, Tropical Orange, Pomegranate Blueberry, and Acai Mixed Berry. Bottle sizes are 46 oz. and 12 oz.

Place

The parent company, Campbell's Soup, wanted V8 V-Fusion juices to be available in as many outlets as possible, including convenience, grocery, and mass merchandise stores, as well as vending machines.

Target Market

Health Conscious Men and Women

Price

The suggested retail prices for V8 V-Fusion Juices were $1.79 for the 12 oz. bottle and $3.89 for the 46 oz. bottle.

Promotion

V8 V-Fusion juices were advertised in magazines and on television, as well as the Internet through its own Web site and on social networking sites, such as Facebook. "I could have had a V8" tagline was used to reinforce the theme of consuming vegetables as part of a healthy diet.

WE LOVE FRUIT SO MUCH WE MARRIED IT.

PLACE

The means of getting the product into the customer's hands is the place element of the marketing mix. Knowing where one's customers shop helps marketers make the place decision. Place strategies determine how and where a product will be distributed. For global companies, it may mean making decisions about which products will be sold in which countries and which retail outlets or other means of selling the product will best reach the customer. Marketers need to determine whether the product can be sold directly to the customer, over the Internet, through catalogs, or through a reseller. Other place decisions include deciding which transportation methods and what stock levels are most effective.

PROMOTION

Promotion refers to activities related to advertising, personal selling, sales promotion, and publicity. Today many companies include social media in a product's promotional mix. Promotional strategies deal with how marketers tell potential customers about a company's products. Strategies include the message, the media selected, special offers, and the timing of the promotional campaigns. The Campbell Soup company decided to capitalize on its original V8 juice brand recognition in its ad message.

Place Interactive kiosks have replaced brick-and-mortar stores as places to rent and return DVDs for home viewing.

 After You Read | **Section 1.3**

Review Key Concepts

1. **Identify** a market in which a business would consider you a potential customer.
2. **Contrast** What is the main difference between consumer and organizational markets?
3. **Connect** How are market segmentation, target markets, and customer profiles related?

Practice Academics

English Language Arts

4. Write a paragraph to explain the importance of the target market (people) in the marketing mix for a product of your choice. Address all four marketing mix elements in your answer.

Mathematics

5. If total sales in the cereal market were $6.5 billion and Kellogg's® sales were $2,850,475,620 what would be its market share? Round your answer to the tenth decimal place.

Math Concept **Number and Operations: Fractions, Decimals, and Rounding** Think of market share as a fraction of a whole market that converts to a percentage.

Starting Hints Write total sales, $6.5 billion, as a number in standard form. Divide Kellogg's sales by the total sales. Round to the tenth decimal place.

 connectED.mcgraw-hill.com

Check your answers.

For help, go to the **Math Skills Handbook** located at the back of this book.

Marketing Is All Around Us

The benefits of marketing are new and improved products, lower prices, and increased economic utility. The five economic utilities are form, place, time, possession, and information.

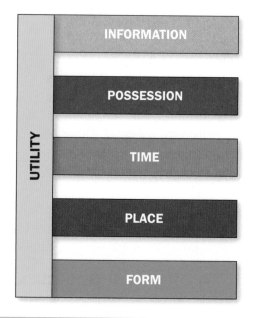

There are four elements of the marketing mix: product, place, price, and promotion. All four marketing mix elements are strategized to appeal to the target market (people), which some refer to as the fifth P.

Review and Activities

Written Summary

- Marketing is the process of creating, communicating, delivering, and exchanging ideas, goods, and services that are valuable to consumers.
- There are seven marketing core functions.
- The marketing concept is a focus on customers' needs and wants while generating a profit.
- Three benefits of marketing are new and improved products, lower prices, and added value (utility).
- Five economic utilities are form, place, time, possession, and information.
- A market is all the people who share similar needs and wants and who have the ability to purchase given products.
- Market share is a firm's percentage of total sales of all competitors in a given market.
- The four Ps of the marketing mix are product, place, price, and promotion.
- Marketing decisions and strategies for the four Ps are based on the target market.

Review Content Vocabulary and Academic Vocabulary

1. Write your own definition for each content and academic vocabulary term.

Content Vocabulary
- marketing (p. 7)
- goods (p. 7)
- services (p. 7)
- marketing concept (p. 10)
- utility (p. 14)
- market (p. 17)
- consumer market (p. 17)
- organizational market (p. 17)
- market share (p. 18)
- target market (p. 18)
- customer profile (p. 20)
- marketing mix (p. 20)

Academic Vocabulary
- create (p. 7)
- conduct (p. 8)
- impact (p. 13)
- benefits (p. 13)
- similar (p. 17)
- elements (p. 21)

Assess for Understanding

2. **Imagine** How would the world be different if marketing did not exist?
3. **Explain** How is customer satisfaction central to the marketing concept?
4. **Discuss** What are some ways marketing benefits customers?
5. **Describe** What are the five types of utility? (Describe them in terms of a single product.)
6. **Connect** How does the importance of target markets connect to the use of a customer profile?
7. **Reflect** How does price relate to successful marketing?
8. **Contrast** How is time utility different from information utility?
9. **Role Play** Imagine you are a marketer who is telling a customer about a new product. How will you address the customer's questions about the four Ps for your product?

21st  Century Skills

Teamwork Skills

10. Target Markets Work with a partner to demonstrate the importance of target markets. Prepare a customer profile for a product of your choice. Change the customer profile (age, income level, gender) to target a different audience. Explain all the changes that must be made in the marketing mix (product, place, price, and promotion) for the new target market (people). Prepare a written report and an oral presentation using presentation software.

Financial Literacy Skills

11. Business Loans A company took out a $9,000 loan in order to create a Web site. The interest on the loan is 5 percent for one year. The Web site generated enough business to pay back the loan in 9 months. What is the total amount of the check the owner will prepare to pay back the loan with interest?

Everyday Ethics

12. Calling on Youth Hello Kitty products are very popular with young girls. British retailer WH Smith and Sanrio, owner of Hello Kitty, want to find out how popular they are with young women. They have begun marketing the phones to women in their 20s and 30s. The problem is some advocates object to promoting adult products to children. They argue that all Hello Kitty products target 6- to 7-year-olds. Some believe that marketing products directly to children is unethical. What is your opinion on this topic? Discuss your response as a class and be sure to distinguish between customers and consumers.

e-Marketing Skills

13. Social Media Marketing Help a local business utilize social media to better communicate with its customers. Design an e-mail program or use other social media platforms to share new promotions and offerings with customers. Present your ideas in a written and an oral report.

Build Academic Skills

English Language Arts

14. The Marketing Concept Write a memo to the staff of a computer customer service center explaining the marketing concept. Stress their role in keeping customers satisfied. Be sure to use the correct format and check your grammar, spelling, and punctuation.

Science

15. Scientific Inquiry Describe market share by conducting a survey of the cell phone service providers of 25 teens. Follow the procedures used for an experiment. Calculate the percentages and draw a pie chart to show the results of your survey. What do your findings suggest about the respective companies' market shares?

Mathematics

16. Calculating Market Share Calculate Panasonic's market share if total sales in the HD television market are $4,865,375,550 and Panasonic's sales are $1,798,450,782. Round your answer to the nearest tenth decimal place.

Math Concept **Computing Percentages** To solve this problem, use the following formula:

Company's Sales/Whole Market's Sales = Company's Market Share

For help, go to the **Math Skills Handbook** located at the back of this book.

Standardized Test Practice

Directions Read the following questions. On a separate sheet of paper write the best possible answer for each one.

1. In addition to people (target market), what are the elements of the marketing mix?

   A. product, place, advertising, and sales

   B. goods, services, ideas, and promotion

   C. product, place, price, and promotion

   D. form, place, time, and possession

2. True or False? All people who share similar needs and wants and who have the ability to purchase a given product are called a market.

   T

   F

3. Form, place, time, possession, and information are types of economic _____.

Test-Taking Tip

When you sit down to take a math test, jot down important equations or formulas on scrap paper. This way, you will not forget them during the test.

DECA Connection Role Play

Employee Cleaning Service

Situation Assume the role of employee of a recently opened cleaning service business. You have solid business experience and are experienced in the services provided by your new employer. The business provides a wide assortment of cleaning services targeted to a broad variety of businesses. The business offers cleaning services ranging from display window cleaning to daily interior cleaning and trash disposal. The business has been open for one month. Business has been good and cleaning contracts have exceeded the plan.

The business owner has asked you to help prepare a newspaper advertisement for the business. The purpose of the advertisement is to announce the opening of the business and the services your business provides. A fellow employee (judge) who has little business experience asks you why the business is planning an advertisement when the business is doing well.

Activity You are to briefly explain to the employee (judge) the role of advertising and promotion and the role they play in a business's overall marketing strategy. You are also to explain the role of marketing in general.

Evaluation You will be evaluated on how well you meet the following performance indicators:

1. Explain the concept of marketing strategies.

2. Explain the concept of market and market identification.

3. Explain the importance of promotion in the marketing mix.

4. Describe marketing functions and related activities.

5. Determine economic utilities created by business activities.

 connectED.mcgraw-hill.com

Download the Competitive Events Workbook for more Role-Play practice.

the marketing plan

SHOW WHAT YOU KNOW

Visual Literacy Marketers want to know what products teens buy, how much they spend, and where they shop. They use this information to create the marketing mix as part of their marketing plans. *Why is this target market of consumers important to marketers?*

Discovery Project

The Right Mix

Essential Question How do stores use the four Ps to create an effective marketing mix?

Project Goal

Work with a partner to identify and visit three different specialty stores where you and other teenagers shop. Create a marketing mix report for each store by describing the 4 Ps: product (type and quality of products), price (cost, discount, and member rewards), place (type of location), and promotion (in-store and media advertising). For example, for "product," you might identify teen apparel or electronic games. Describe each store's marketing mix and discuss whether it is effective in a report to the class.

Ask Yourself...

- Which stores will you select?
- How will you share your findings with the class?
- How will you organize your report?
- How will you make your presentation effective?

 Synthesize and Present Research Synthesize your research by describing whether each store's marketing mix is effective for selling to teens.

 connectED.mcgraw-hill.com

Activity
Get a worksheet activity about creating a marketing mix.

Evaluate
Download a rubric you can use to evaluate your project.

DECA Connection

DECA Events

Concepts in this chapter are related to DECA competitive events that involve either an interview or role play.

Performance Indicators The performance indicators represent key skills and knowledge. Your key to success in DECA competitive events is relating them to the concepts in this chapter.

- Explain the nature of marketing plans.
- Explain the nature of marketing planning.
- Explain the nature of sales forecasts.
- Explain the concept of marketing strategies.
- Prepare simple written reports.

DECA Prep

Role Play Practice role-playing with the DECA Connection competitive-event activity at the end of this chapter. More information about DECA events can be found on DECA's Web site.

READING GUIDE

Before You Read

Connect Suppose you had to market yourself as a student. What are your strengths?

Objectives

- **Learn** how to conduct a SWOT analysis.
- **List** the three key areas of an internal company analysis.
- **Identify** the factors in a PEST analysis.
- **Explain** the basic elements of a marketing plan.

The Main Idea

A company looks at itself and the world around it to create a marketing plan for reaching goals.

Vocabulary

Content Vocabulary

- SWOT analysis
- PEST analysis
- marketing plan
- executive summary
- situation analysis
- marketing strategy
- sales forecasts
- performance standard

Academic Vocabulary

You will find these words in your reading and on your tests. Make sure you know their meanings.

- factors
- technology

Graphic Organizer

Draw or print a two-column chart to identify the seven elements of a marketing plan.

connectED.mcgraw-hill.com

Print this graphic organizer.

Marketing Plan	
Element	**Analysis**
1.	
2.	
3.	
4.	
5.	
6.	
7.	

MARKETING CORE FUNCTION

 Market Planning

Section 2.1

Marketing Planning

SWOT ANALYSIS

The **SWOT analysis** is an assessment that lists and analyzes the company's strengths and weaknesses. It also includes the opportunities and the threats that surround it. In other words, this analysis lists everything that can foster the business's success and what could make it fail. The acronym for strengths, weaknesses, opportunities, and threats is also the name of this process: SWOT analysis.

This internal and external awareness will help a business identify weaknesses and prepare for handling threats such as competition or a changing marketplace. An accurate analysis will also help a company be more competitive because it provides guidance and direction. The company will develop strategies around the SWOT analysis.

As You Read

Predict How can a business use a SWOT analysis to assess its place in the market?

INTERNAL STRENGTHS AND WEAKNESSES

Strengths and weaknesses are both internal **factors** that affect a business's operation. The internal analysis centers around three Cs: company, customers, and competition. It is important to review these factors objectively and fairly.

COMPANY ANALYSIS

Questions that are part of a company's internal analysis are about what a company does well (core competencies) and what areas are weak. This includes a review of the staff, the company's financial situation, its production capabilities, and each aspect of the marketing mix (product, promotion, place, and pricing). Here are a few sample questions:

Staff-Related Questions

▶ What is the company's mission statement? Is everyone on staff following it?

▶ How experienced are the company executives? What have they accomplished?

▶ Does the company have too much or not enough staff to provide the quality of service it should? Should staff be re-assigned?

▶ What is the quality of the staff? Are there training and assessment programs?

▶ How effective is the sales force?

> **"** **Good marketing relies on good plans and accurate analysis. "**

Financial Questions

▶ Has the company been profitable? In which areas and why?

▶ Are there enough financial resources to achieve the company's goals?

▶ What is the company's sales history? Are sales increasing or decreasing?

Production Capability Questions

▶ How are adjustments made in production due to an increase or decrease in the company's sales orders?

▶ Has the research and development (R&D) department created any successful new products?

▶ What percentage of sales come from products that are five years or older?

▶ What changes in **technology** are required to remain competitive?

Marketing Mix (Four Ps) Questions

Remember that a business's marketing mix includes product, price, place, and promotion. These factors influence how customers respond to a business. Therefore, when analyzing the four Ps of the marketing mix, it is also important to see if they are properly coordinated with one another and with the target market. Any P not focused completely on the potential or current customer would be a reason for review and adjustment.

MARKETING MIX		
P PRODUCT	**P** PLACE	
P PRICE	**P** PROMOTION	

P PRODUCT

- What new products have been successful and why?
- Does the company own a patent on any of those products?
- Are any patents expiring in the future?

P PRICE

- What are the present pricing strategies?
- Are the pricing strategies working?

P PLACE

- Do products easily reach customers?
- Who helps the company with distribution?

P PROMOTION

- How is the company positioned in the marketplace?
- What are the promotional strategies and have they been successful?
- What is the company's reputation and image among consumers?

The answers to these questions might reveal such strengths (or core competencies) as talented and well-trained employees, quality workmanship, and excellent service records.

CUSTOMER ANALYSIS

Customers are a great source of information. Studying their buying habits reveals patterns that offer insights into product offerings and pricing strategies. These questions can be used to analyze customers.

- Who are the customers?
- How do groups of customers differ from one another?
- What, when, where, and how much do they buy?

Customer Analysis

Companies likes Vans® conduct research about customers before making marketing mix decisions. *What questions would you ask to find out about the customers of the product featured in this ad?*

Horizon Organic

- How do customers rate the company on quality, service, and value?
- Is your customer base increasing or decreasing? Why?

Catalog companies use database technology to analyze buying patterns, which allow them to produce interest-specific catalogs. Companies with this technology have a major advantage over their competitors because they can structure their product selection, pricing, and promotional messages to very specific targeted audiences.

To monitor customer satisfaction, many firms ask customers to complete a survey or questionnaire after making a purchase. Data from this research help companies pinpoint areas that need improvement. That is, monitoring customer satisfaction can reveal useful information about both the strengths and weaknesses of a company's products and services. For example, customers may indicate their interest in a product because it is useful, but they may also want it to be sold for a lower price.

COMPETITIVE POSITION

A company may find that it has certain strengths and weaknesses when compared to its competitors. A company's market share may be greater than its competitors', which would be a major strength. If a company loses market share to competitors, it would be a weakness. Questions that help a company analyze its internal competitive position might include the following:

- What is the company's market share?
- What advantages does the company have over its competitors?
- What core competencies does the company possess? A better reputation? A patent? Special resources? Better distribution?
- Are competitors taking business away? Why?

EXTERNAL OPPORTUNITIES AND THREATS

Companies must always look for opportunities to create competitive advantage due to external factors.

MARKETING CASE STUDY

Refocusing Nikon Cameras

More than 6 out of 10 people in the United States own a digital camera. These cameras are easy to use, and more users are able to upload and share photos online—plus, digital cameras have become less expensive.

With its 90-year history, Nikon® created some of the first digital single lens cameras for NASA. Today, its COOLPIX® line has become popular with consumers who prefer a compact camera.

As Seen on TV, Print, and Web Ads

To promote the COOLPIX line, Nikon focused on the image of style and fun. Television commercials were directed by an Emmy awardwinning director. To target a broader and youthful audience, a young star was signed as spokesperson. The TV spots served as the basis for Web video and banner ads, as well as print ads in magazines.

Social Studies

Ask Discuss this question with a partner: How does the price of Nikon's cameras determine how they are promoted through TV, print, and Web ads and then distributed to customers?

FIGURE 2.1 | Plan Success With SWOT Analysis

Planning with SWOT The SWOT analysis helps a business and its employees organize factors that influence its success. *What factor is the successful marketing of a competitor's product?*

SWOT	INTERNAL		EXTERNAL	
	STRENGTHS	**WEAKNESSES**	**OPPORTUNITIES**	**THREATS**
	▪ large market share ▪ reputation for quality ▪ creative product developers	▪ low profit ▪ few employees	▪ competitors going out of business ▪ strong economy ▪ few direct competitors	▪ legal issues ▪ decreasing amounts of natural resources

COMPETITION

To stay competitive, companies need to know what their competitors are doing at all times. Changes in a competitor's financial situation and problems in the marketplace can provide opportunities. For example, Starbucks became the largest coffee company in the world, but it relied heavily on U.S. sales. However, in 2008, due to a slowdown in consumer spending, consumers sought coffee at less expensive competitors.

Companies that conduct a SWOT analysis (See **Figure 2.1**) on an ongoing basis are in a better position to react and make adjustments to their marketing mix. To assist in this process, companies must continually scan the external environment.

PEST ANALYSIS

A **PEST analysis** is the scanning of outside influences on an organization. This is a methodical look at the world that typically includes four factors: political, economic, socio-cultural, and technological. Understanding how each of these areas is changing or is likely to change can lead to a better appreciation of potential opportunities or threats for the firm. An alert business owner may use a change in one of these four influences as an opportunity to be first to market products customers want.

POLITICAL ISSUES

Political issues center around government involvement in business operations. Companies must be alert to changes in laws and regulations that affect their industries. Global companies need to understand the political structure and regulations of each foreign country in which they conduct business. To assess potential political risks and new opportunities, it is important to see what changes are likely in the laws governing a business operation, as they will have an impact on marketing plans.

Here are a few examples of issues regulations in the United States that may affect certain industries in a positive way (opportunity) or in a negative way (threat):

▶ **Do Not Call Registry** This legislation requires telemarketers to drop from their lists home and cell phone numbers of registered consumers. This regulation forced many businesses to rethink their marketing strategies. Telemarketing companies had to adjust data files to comply with the law.

▶ **Downloading Music from the Internet** Illegal downloading of music created an industry of companies that provide legal downloading of music for a fee. This reduced revenue for traditional music stores, but has become an opportunity for other Internet retailers.

ECONOMIC FACTORS

The current state of the economy is of interest to all businesses: If the economy is robust, businesses are more likely to invest in new products and markets. An economy that is in a recession or slowing down sends a completely different message to the company's decision makers.

Upcoming marketing programs may be altered or scrapped altogether in a weak economy. Factors such as the unemployment rate, inflation, retail sales figures, productivity, and consumer confidence are tools to estimate the current status of the economy. The value of the dollar in relation to foreign currencies affects imports and exports. Import and export prices affect how a company buys and sells its products in the global market. It is necessary for companies to analyze the economy from local, national, and international perspectives. That way, they can adapt to changes in their local market as well as those in markets all over the world. Here are some economic factors marketers would consider as opportunities or threats:

▶ **Recession** An economy in recession poses a threat to nearly all companies. Most companies slow or stop plans for new facilities and often reduce research and development (R&D) efforts.

▶ **Unemployment** If unemployment figures decrease and consumer confidence increases, companies may see an opportunity to grow their businesses.

▶ **Currency Rates** Changes in foreign currency rates could be seen as a threat or an opportunity depending on whether this makes the company's products or services cheaper or more expensive in their foreign target market.

▶ **Import Pricing** Illegal dumping (selling imported products at a very low price) in a given market is a threat to all businesses in that industry.

▶ **Trade Restrictions** Changes in trade restrictions, such as lowering or raising tariffs (taxes) on imported goods, could be considered a threat or an opportunity, depending on where a company does business.

Companies cannot control these economic factors, so they must react to them in ways that create opportunities and diminish threats. For example, a company may develop a less expensive line of goods during a recession. It may also offer special promotions and discounts to attract customers to its business. It may also focus more on online retail opportunities when consumers are less willing to travel to shop.

When laws began to prohibit most free downloading of music, new businesses developed for legal music downloading. *What products have become popular as a result of the downloading laws?*

i Opportunity

SOCIO-CULTURAL FACTORS

A socio-cultural analysis is based on customers and potential customers. Changes in their attitudes, lifestyles, and opinions provide a multitude of opportunities and threats. Socio-cultural analysis examines changes in all demographic factors, such as age, income, occupation, education level, and marital status. Here are two examples of such changes:

▶ **Diversity** The United States is becoming a more ethnically and racially diverse country. Marketing plans need to meet this change.

▶ **Health** Obesity has become an issue in the United States, as it causes many health problems. Consumer advocates for healthier eating habits criticize fast food.

TECHNOLOGY

Changing technology may be a threat for one industry or company, but an opportunity for others. A perfect example is digital photography. To be competitive, traditional photo companies such as Canon® look for ways to adapt to this new technology. Camera companies are making more digital cameras. Other companies are seizing the opportunity to capitalize on this new technology by developing products to support it. Printer companies like Epson® and Hewlett-Packard® have developed products to make it easy for consumers to print their own digital photographs.

EPSON®
EXCEED YOUR VISION

Companies that keep abreast of the newest technological breakthroughs, such as computer animation and satellite technology, can use that knowledge to be more competitive.

✔ Reading Check

Recall What is a SWOT analysis?

WRITING A MARKETING PLAN

Marketing is a complicated activity that relies on many different tasks. For this reason, marketers create a marketing plan. A **marketing plan** is a formal, written document that directs a company's activities for a specific period of time. It details analysis and research efforts and provides a road map for how a product will enter the market, be advertised, and sold.

A marketing plan also communicates the goals, objectives, and strategies of a company's management team. The specifics let managers know their responsibilities, budget, and timelines for completion. A plan helps a company monitor a company's performance. A small retail business may develop a simple marketing plan for a year, but a large manufacturer would prepare a marketing plan that covers five years.

ELEMENTS OF A MARKETING PLAN

Marketing plans may differ from company to company. However, there are some basic elements that will be found in all marketing plans. Those elements include an executive summary, a situation analysis, marketing goals/objectives, marketing strategies, and implementation, as well as a system for evaluation and control. See **Figure 2.2** on page 38 for a complete outline of a marketing plan.

EXECUTIVE SUMMARY

An **executive summary** is a brief overview of the entire marketing plan. It briefly addresses each topic in the plan and gives an explanation of the costs involved in implementing the plan. The executive summary may also be used to provide information to people outside the organization, such as investors or business consultants.

SITUATION ANALYSIS

Situation analysis is the study of the internal and external factors that affect marketing strategies. The situation analysis takes stock of where the company or product has been, where it is now, and where it is headed. It also considers the external factors and trends that affect a company. The information from a company's SWOT and PEST analyses creates the basis for this portion of the marketing plan. The situation analysis can be done for a whole company, a business unit, a product line, or an individual product.

OBJECTIVES

Objectives let everyone know what the marketing plan will accomplish. They are based around the company's mission statement. To be useful, an objective must be single-minded (meaning it has only one topic for each objective), specific, realistic, measurable, and have a time frame.

- ▶ **Single-Minded** For example, you cannot include increasing sales and increasing profits in the same objective. Each topic needs to be a separate objective.

- ▶ **Specific** Specific means that the objective provides enough detail that there can be no misunderstanding. You cannot use, "to be better than a competitor" as an objective because what is "better" is vague.

- ▶ **Realistic** Realistic means the goal can be achieved by the company. It must take both its strengths and weaknesses into account.

- ▶ **Measurable** Measurable means that the objective includes a way to measure or evaluate the results. You cannot simply say you want to increase sales. You need to identify the percentage increase in dollar or unit sales to make that objective measurable. So, you could state, "to increase dollar sales by 15 percent as compared to the same time last year."

- ▶ **Time Framed** Finally, you must include a time frame, such as in six months, or as compared to last year's sales. You need a time frame to know if an objective was actually reached.

Marketing Mix Businesses use social networking sites to promote their products and research new ones.

FIGURE 2.2 **The Marketing Plan**

Elements of a Marketing Plan A marketing plan is an essential planning tool for a company. This outline lists the basic elements found in a marketing plan. *How can a small company benefit from writing a marketing plan?*

Marketing Plan Outline

I.   EXECUTIVE SUMMARY

II.   SITUATION ANALYSIS

      A. SWOT Analysis
      B. Environmental Scan

III.   OBJECTIVES

      A. Company's Mission
      B. Marketing Objectives
      C. Financial Objectives

IV.   MARKETING STRATEGIES

      A. Positioning and Points of Difference
      B. Marketing Mix (four Ps)
         1. Product
         2. Price
         3. Place (distribution)
         4. Promotion

V.   IMPLEMENTATION

      A. Organization
      B. Activities and Responsibilities
      C. Timetables

VI.   EVALUATION AND CONTROL

      A. Performance standards and measurements
         1. Marketing Objectives
         2. Financial Objectives
         3. Marketing Mix Strategies
      B. Corrective Action

VII.   APPENDIX

A company's mission statement provides the focus for a firm's goals with its explanation of the company's core competencies, values, expectations, and vision for the future.

Marketing objectives must be in line with the organization's goals and mission. If an organization's goal is to double its business in five years, marketing objectives must coincide with that goal and provide the means to reach it.

When writing objectives, the need for specific and measurable goals is important. For example, if a marketing objective involves increasing a company's market share by a certain percentage, then a corresponding financial objective would provide an increase in sales to achieve that market share. The use of objectives helps a company determine if it has met its goals.

MARKETING STRATEGIES

A **marketing strategy** identifies target markets and sets marketing mix choices that focus on those markets. All strategies need to take the customer's needs and wants into account, as well as the objectives of the marketing plan.

A company's or product's position in the marketplace determines the appropriate marketing strategy. The positioning of the product or service will drive decisions for each of the four Ps.

An effective marketing strategy should be focused on the key points of difference. The key point of difference is the advantage a company, a product, or service has over its competition. The point of difference could be any of the following factors:

▶ The quality of the product
▶ A superior distribution system
▶ A more creative ad campaign
▶ A more competitive pricing structure

This competitive advantage is what will make the company successful. The marketing mix elements can help create points of difference with respect to competition.

Notice how each of these factors relates to one of the four Ps of the marketing mix. The company assesses whether to adjust each or every element of the marketing mix to emphasize its points of difference.

The results of both the situation analysis and the SWOT analysis should provide enough information to identify the specific target market and to suggest ideas to create the necessary point(s) of difference for the product to be competitive.

IMPLEMENTATION

Implementation is putting the marketing plan into action and managing it. This means obtaining the financial resources, management, and staffing necessary to put the plan into action. A timetable shows when each part goes into play.

This part of the marketing plan outlines a schedule of activities, job assignments, **sales forecasts** (the projection of probable, future sales in units or dollars), budgets, details of each activity, and who will be responsible for each activity.

This phase of the plan requires excellent communication among members of the management team so that tasks are completed on a timely basis.

EVALUATION AND CONTROL

In the evaluation section of the marketing plan, measures that will be used to evaluate the plan are discussed. It is important to explain exactly how a specific objective will be measured and who will be responsible for providing that evaluation.

PERFORMANCE STANDARDS AND EVALUATION

A **performance standard** is an expectation for performance that reflects the plan's objectives. Performance standards are the measuring stick. These performance standards can help assess marketing objectives, financial objectives, and marketing mix strategies. As part of the planning process, the control section suggests actions that should be considered if objectives are not met. In the control phase, the company's goal is to reduce the gap between the planned performance standards and the actual performance.

Let's say sales did not reach the sales forecast numbers. One reason could be recent changes in economic conditions. In such a situation, a company may take corrective action and revise its sales forecast to be more realistic.

APPENDIX

The appendix is the section of the marketing plan that includes supplemental materials such as financial statements, sample ads, and other materials that support the plan.

Implementing a marketing plan requires communication and teamwork. *How do sales forecasts relate to a marketing plan's budget?*

Making It Happen

©Ariel Skelley/Blend Images LLC

MARKETING AUDIT

The marketing process is ongoing. You can think of it as a circular pattern that continues through the three phases of the marketing process of planning, implementation, and control. The key question at the end of the process is, "Did we accomplish the objectives listed in the marketing plan within the boundaries of the plan?"

If the objectives are met, then the marketing plan can be deemed a success. If the answer to that question is that the objectives were not accomplished, then a company must determine the reasons and make adjustments.

This evaluation at the end of the marketing process is called a marketing audit. A marketing audit evaluates a company's marketing objectives, strategies, budgets, organization, and performance. It identifies problem areas in marketing operations as well as areas that proved to be successful in meeting objectives. Most companies typically conduct a formal marketing audit at least once every year, but informal reviews of the marketing plan happen on a continual basis. Because of the important feedback that a marketing audit provides, a company that regularly conducts marketing audits can be more flexible and responsive than a competitor that reviews its processes only every now and then.

 After You Read   **Section 2.1**

Review Key Concepts

1. **Explain** the four aspects of a SWOT analysis and tell how it fits into a marketing plan.
2. **List** the four areas that are investigated in PEST analysis and explain why the knowledge gained can be valuable to a company.
3. **Describe** how the marketing mix relates to the implementation of a marketing plan.

Practice Academics

English Language Arts

4. One of the statements below represents a goal that a company has established. The other represents an objective. Tell which is which and write a sentence or two explaining your choices.
   - To increase by one-third the amount of paper waste each store recycles within eight months.
   - To become a strong advocate for the environmental concerns of our customers and employees.

Mathematics

5. A company's sales revenue at year end is $1,386,000. If the company's objective is to increase sales by 10 percent in the next year, what is its new sales goal in dollars?

   Math Concept **Ways of Representing Numbers** An increase in a number can be represented by a percent greater than 100.

   Starting Hints Think of next year's sales goal as 110 percent of this year's sales. Convert 110 percent to a decimal by moving the decimal point two places to the left. Multiply that decimal number by this year's sales revenue to find next year's sales goal in dollars.

 **connectED.mcgraw-hill.com**

Check your answers.

For help, go to the **Math Skills Handbook** located at the back of this book.

READING GUIDE

Before You Read

Connect Think of all the ways a marketer might describe you as a consumer. Begin with your age and gender, then get more specific about your shopping requirements.

Objectives

- **Explain** the concept of market segmentation.
- **Analyze** a target market.
- **Differentiate** between mass marketing and market segmentation.

The Main Idea

The key to marketing is to know your customer or target market. Market segmentation helps identify the target market.

Vocabulary

Content Vocabulary
- market segmentation
- demographics
- disposable income
- discretionary income
- geographics
- psychographics
- mass marketing

Academic Vocabulary

You will find these words in your reading and on your tests. Make sure you know their meanings.
- ranges
- attitudes

Graphic Organizer

Draw or print this chart to list different ways to segment markets and the reason each is used.

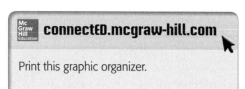
connectED.mcgraw-hill.com

Print this graphic organizer.

Market Segmentation	
Methods of Segmentation	**Reasons for Use**

MARKETING CORE FUNCTION

 Market Planning

IDENTIFYING AND ANALYZING MARKETS

The surest way for businesses to make a connection with customers is to know these people well. This means knowing where they live, their income level, age, ethnic background, activities, values, and interests. Such information can help identify groups of people who have many things in common.

As You Read

Predict How do you think marketers identify their customers?

MARKET SEGMENTATION

Marketers analyze groups of customers to see if any of them can be further broken down into smaller, more precise clusters. The process of classifying people who form a given market into even smaller groups is called **market segmentation**.

Let's look at the market for jeans. A marketer might ask, "Who buys jeans? At what price? What special features do they want?" Depending on the answers to these questions, the market for jeans could be segmented by these characteristics:

▶ **Age:** jeans for kids, teens, and adults.

▶ **Price:** reach different income levels (socio-economic groups).

▶ **Desired features:** tight fit, comfortable fit, newest fashion, or a unique design.

To meet the needs of the different market segments, jeans manufacturers develop a unique marketing mix, including different products, promotions, stores for distribution, and price points. For example, Levi's® jeans are available in relaxed fit, regular fit, 501 original, loose straight, loose boot cut, low-rise straight, and low-rise boot cut.

The next question marketers ask is: "Which of these segments should we target?" It is usually too costly to target all the potential target markets. So, it is very important to identify those markets in which the company has an advantage that enables it to survive against its competition over a long period of time. Marketers call this situation a sustainable competitive advantage.

GATHERING DATA

Companies study data generated by governments, private research firms, trade associations, and their own research to determine if a given target market is large enough to justify the expense.

> **Businesses look for ways to connect with current and potential customers. The surest way to make that connection is to know these people well.**

For example, U.S. census data might reveal that there are enough teenagers to justify making jeans for that segment of the market. Additional research into teenagers would reveal more about this market segment. Their buying behavior, interests, activities, opinions about fashion, values, status, household income levels, ethnic background, and any other factor might help marketers create a customer profile. These factors help marketers gather demographic, geographic, psychographic, and behavioral information about each market segment.

Reading Check

Recall What sources do marketers use to find data for their research?

Teens buy jeans, but so do many other people. *How might a jeans ad for a teenager differ from a jeans ad for an adult?*

Just for You

TYPES OF SEGMENTATION

The data marketers gather can be used to segment the market in various ways. There are four ways to segment the market. Customers can be segmented into groups based on demographics, geographics, psychographics, and behavioral characteristics.

DEMOGRAPHICS

Demographic factors help define a target market for a company wanting to sell its products. **Demographics** refer to statistics that describe a population in terms of personal characteristics such as age, gender, income, marital status, ethnic background, education, and occupation. See **Figure 2.3**.

AGE

Marketers can easily use age to segment the market by creating age **ranges**. The United States census provides information that might help in deciding on the age categories. Here are common labels used to segment the population by generation:

▶ **Baby Boom Generation** The 76 million babies born in the United States between 1946 and 1964 are known as the baby boomers. As baby boomers get older, their income and spending power increase. So, they are targets for all types of products, such as technological gadgets, cosmetics, and products to enhance lifestyle.

▶ **Generation X** (or the Baby Bust Generation) They followed the Baby Boom Generation. Most members of Generation X are children of dual-career households or divorced parents. They have been bombarded with media from an early age. They are savvy purchasers and skeptical consumers. To reach this group, marketers must use interesting images, hip music, and a sense of humor.

▶ **Generation Y** They are the sons and daughters of the later baby boomers. Generation Y is also known as the Echo Boomers or Millennium Generation. According to the U.S. Census, this group is more racially and ethnically diverse with spending power. Fashions and information get passed along via the Internet.

GENDER

Gender helps to create market segments as well. Jockey®, at one time a men's underwear company, doubled its sales when it entered the women's market with Jockey underwear for women. Products such as safety razors are also segmented by gender. The razors women use often have longer handles than those used by men. Electric razors are different for each gender as well. These differences are due to the different uses of razors by each gender, which means marketers need to have a different approach for men and women.

INCOME

Marketers want to know how much money people have to spend on different products. For this reason, they look at two types of income measurement: disposable income and discretionary income. **Disposable income** is the money left after taking out taxes. Marketers who produce and distribute products that are necessities are interested in changes in consumers' disposable income. **Discretionary income** is the money left after paying for basic living necessities such as food, shelter, and clothing. Marketers who sell luxury and premium products are interested in changes in consumers' discretionary income. During tough economic times, people have less discretionary income, so it is harder to market luxury items.

MARITAL STATUS

The U.S. Census indicates that there is currently a lower percentage of married couples in the United States compared to the percentage in the 1950s. Reasons for this reduction in married couples can be attributed to several factors. People are older when they get married for the first time.

They are also living longer, divorcing more, and remarrying less. All of this information is useful to marketers. They can decide whether to market their products to married couples with children, single adults living together, or adults who live alone. You may have seen family-sized or individual-sized boxes of food at the grocery store. This product packaging is a result of demographic segmentation. Since parents need to provide food for their children, marketers created boxes that have more servings of food. Adults who live alone must buy smaller portions of perishable foods. They will not be able to eat all of their food before it spoils, so their buying patterns are different from families with children.

ETHNIC BACKGROUND

The U.S. population is becoming more multicultural and ethnically diverse, mainly due to increased immigration. The Caucasian population is declining relative to African-American, Hispanic, and Asian-American populations. It is essential for marketers to be aware of the multicultural nature of the modern United States.

FIGURE 2.3 Demographic Characteristics

Targeting a Market Demographic information relates to personal characteristics, such as age, gender, income, marital status, ethnic background, education, and occupation. Marketing plans are customized for the target market. *Think of your demographic profile. What products would a marketer try to sell to you?*

By Age Marketers use age to segment and define the target market. They use age ranges, such as ages 15 to 18. Certain products are designed and marketed specifically to children, teens, or adults.

By Gender Many products are made for both men and women. However, products such as clothing and shoes are designed specifically by gender.

By Ethnicity With a diverse and multicultural population, the United States has many different ethnic market segments.

GEOGRAPHICS

The term **geographics** refers to segmentation of the market based on where people live. To segment a market geographically, you can refer to local, state, regional, national, or even global markets. Geographic segmentation can also include population density (urban vs. suburban areas) and climate (warm vs. cold). It is well known that people who reside in a certain area generally share similar demographic characteristics, such as income, ethnic background, and education. Thus, geographic segmentation is often combined with demographic data to provide marketers with the information they need to make marketing decisions.

LOCAL, STATE, AND REGIONAL GEOGRAPHICS

A small independent restaurant segments its market on a local basis. It knows the geographic area from which it attracts most of its customers. The restaurant may very well have customers who dine there so frequently that they become known as regulars. Such a level of familiarity with customers allows the business owner to gain a detailed view of the restaurant's primary demographic. The restaurant can create menu offerings and set prices based on the known preferences of people who live nearby. This information can help the business provide the greatest appeal to its most likely customers.

Local and state geographics also play a very significant role in political campaigns. Politicians who want to reach their constituents know exactly where their voters live and what those voters' communities are like. Their campaigns compile data on the demographics of particular areas in order to learn the issues that matter most to the voters who live there. Political consultants conduct research to learn the income and education levels of their constituents, their ethnic and religious backgrounds, their average age, and how various segments of the population tended to vote in previous elections. Politicians can use this data to target the specific needs and interests of residents of the geographic areas they hope to represent.

Regional geographics can influence the way regional banks do business. Banks may study the geographical area to identify possible new branch sites. Demographic information, such as income levels in an area, helps in that decision-making process. Also, knowing the population of a certain geographic area helps banks develop correct marketing messages and staffing levels.

Food manufacturers and retailers have learned that people in certain geographic areas share similar tastes and may even use different terms to describe the same product. A sausage company had to change its ingredients to cater to both northeastern tastes and southeastern tastes. A slight change in its spices did the trick. Carbonated drinks may be referred to as either "pop" or "soda." Certain regions of a country may have different climates. A snowblower manufacturer would segment the market geographically to the northern region of the United States. Manufacturers and retailers of surfboards would segment their markets geographically around the nation's coasts. Another example involves cultural and language differences that require employees and advertisements to be bilingual.

NATIONAL AND GLOBAL GEOGRAPHICS

Large national and global companies create divisions within their organization in order to segment their markets geographically. If you visit a global company's Web site, like Unilever® or Pepsico®, you will be able to see the corporate subdivisions of the global company. For example Unilever's Web site has five regional divisions: Africa, Americas, Asia Pacific, Europe, and Middle East. Within those divisions, you can select specific countries. The language for each country is provided on its Web site, making it easy for its customers to research its products and services. It is interesting to note that products are developed for specific geographic areas. For example, Pepsico has several brands of potato chips to cater to specific geographic regions. You will find Lay's® brand potato chips in North America. In its international market you will find Walkers® Potato Crisps brand and Sabritas® brand of potato chips.

PSYCHOGRAPHICS

Psychographics involves grouping people with similar attitudes, interests, and opinions, as well as lifestyles and shared values. Consumer lifestyles include how people spend their time and money. Attitudes, values, and opinions require research to learn more about a group's personality traits and motivation. When psychographics is coupled with demographics, marketers can create a comprehensive customer profile. Its marketing programs can be tailored to reach the inner-most consumer motivations that influence purchases.

These characteristics require marketers to use special research techniques. They need to learn more about each group's personality traits and motivation. One special method involves hiring a marketing research firm to conduct research in small groups called focus groups. Sessions with these groups are recorded. This process allows researchers to study responses to questions and the interaction among participants. This method lends itself to in-depth analysis.

ATTITUDES AND OPINIONS

Consumers' **attitudes** and opinions are often created by changing times and personal experiences. Marketers study trends that evolve from these shared attitudes. Clothing manufacturers capitalize on fashion trends. Going "green" to save the environment is a trend that businesses have utilized to create new products and packaging.

Taking responsibility for one's health, eating healthier, and becoming physically fit are trend-setting issues for businesses. Food marketers are increasingly revamping their offerings to include more reduced-fat selections. Food manufacturers are also displaying lower calorie counts on their packaging. Small 100-calorie count packages of cookies and other treats help consumers control their calorie intake. Fast-food chains have created healthier menu options. The dairy industry capitalized on this trend by promoting skim milk and water instead of soda and other drinks high in sugar content in an ad campaign to help combat childhood obesity.

Marketers must also exercise caution when segmenting by psychographics. It is often difficult to predict whether new opinions, interests, and attitudes in the marketplace will result in short-lived fads or long-lasting trends. Due to the possibility of quickly changing consumer values and lifestyles, it is especially important for marketers to be sure of their market before they respond to every new shift in their customers' attitudes or opinions.

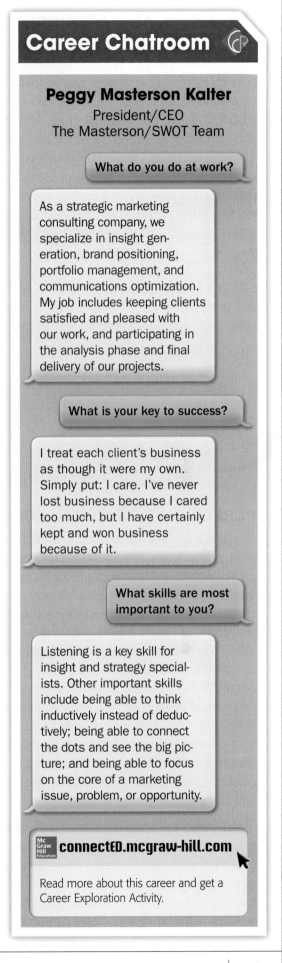

Career Chatroom

Peggy Masterson Kalter
President/CEO
The Masterson/SWOT Team

What do you do at work?

As a strategic marketing consulting company, we specialize in insight generation, brand positioning, portfolio management, and communications optimization. My job includes keeping clients satisfied and pleased with our work, and participating in the analysis phase and final delivery of our projects.

What is your key to success?

I treat each client's business as though it were my own. Simply put: I care. I've never lost business because I cared too much, but I have certainly kept and won business because of it.

What skills are most important to you?

Listening is a key skill for insight and strategy specialists. Other important skills include being able to think inductively instead of deductively; being able to connect the dots and see the big picture; and being able to focus on the core of a marketing issue, problem, or opportunity.

connectED.mcgraw-hill.com

Read more about this career and get a Career Exploration Activity.

INTERESTS AND ACTIVITIES

If you made a list of all your present activities and interests, you would come to realize just how many market segments can be identified by psychographics. Visit the magazine section of a bookstore. For each interest group and activity, you will find at least one magazine that represents a market segment. People who share common interests and activities often purchase similar products and services. In a fashion magazine, you will find advertisements for clothing, cosmetics, and accessories. Similarly, in a music magazine, you will find advertisements for albums, music players, and concerts or festivals. Use an Internet search engine to see consumer, trade, industry, and professional magazines to grasp the extent of interest groups available for market segmentation.

Shifting Psychographics
Magazines are becoming less prevalent so marketers must use digital content to reach their customers.

PERSONALITIES AND VALUES

More advanced study of psychographics includes the study of personality characteristics and values. Abraham Maslow created a hierarchy of needs that helps define the personality and values of individuals at each stage of development. The five stages of needs are the following: survival, safety, love and belonging, esteem, and self-actualization. Marketers use those innermost desires in the hierarchy to sell their products. Ads for financial institutions offer individuals the means to retire and have enough money to realize their life's dreams (self-actualization). Certain clothing brands promote the need for belonging or self esteem. Greeting cards address the need for love and caring. Tires promise safety.

An offshoot of Maslow's hierarchy of needs is a research tool called VALS™. VALS identifies types of consumers based on their motivations (thinkers, achievers, experiencers, believers, strivers, and makers) and resources (innovators vs. survivors). This research helps businesses create consumer profiles.

BEHAVIORAL CHARACTERISTICS

Segmenting the market based on purchasing-related behavior involves analyzing your customers with regard to sales generated, shopping patterns, and purchase decision-making processes. Companies classify their customers according to the percentage of sales each group generates. Many businesses find that the 80/20 rule applies. The 80/20 rule means that 80 percent of a company's sales are generated by 20 percent of its loyal customers. This information helps businesses decide how to allocate their resources to each market segment. Some companies use loyalty programs to ensure that their customers keep buying the company's products. This method helps companies retain the customers that generate the most sales.

Astute marketers study consumer shopping patterns to determine usage rates. For example, Jupiter Research, a market research company, has determined that most teenagers spend about $50 a month on entertainment and that teenage girls spend 15 percent more on music than teenage boys spend. A company that markets products to teenagers might use this research to target more of their advertising toward teenage girls.

Companies have found that many consumers research products on the Internet before making a final purchase. As more and more consumers connect with others via social media and the Internet, marketers follow suit by utilizing that media to stay close to their customers. They recognize the need to create a presence in places where consumers look for product information. Also, this shift in decision-making means that companies need to make sure they offer helpful information about their products on the Internet. Often this can take the form of product reviews by customers themselves. Companies that have easy-to-use Web sites or interesting online promotions will be more likely to stay close to their customers.

 Reading Check

Recall What are four types of market segmentation?

MASS MARKETING VS. SEGMENTATION

When products have universal appeal and few features to differentiate them from competitors, mass marketing is used. **Mass marketing** involves using a single marketing strategy to reach all customers.

An advantage of mass marketing is economies of scale. Companies can produce more products at lower costs because their product, promotion, pricing, or distribution does not change. The marketing plan is simplified. A disadvantage is competitors can identify specific unmet needs and wants of customers, and then steal those customers. Some marketers think mass marketing does not even exist any longer. They say it is more important to focus on various market segments. This type of broad approach ensures that a company can reach as many customers as effectively as possible. A mass marketing approach may reach all customers in a market, but it may not be as effective as segmented marketing.

NICHE MARKETING

Since most products can be segmented by demographics, psychographics, geographics, and behavioral characteristics, mass marketing is not as popular as it once was. One advantage of market segmentation is the ability to identify and target a very specific audience. Niche marketing narrows and defines a market with extreme precision, which increases the chances of a product's success. A disadvantage of niche marketing is the cost involved. Research is needed to identify target markets and develop different marketing strategies. For example, milk can have a number of target markets. The "Got Milk" campaign targets different segments with different themes through various media, including print ads, television spots, and Internet banners. If a particular product has multiple varieties and many target markets, then the production, packaging, and advertising of that product becomes more expensive.

 After You Read | Section 2.2

Review Key Concepts

1. **Explain** how market segmentation can help a company increase its market share.
2. **Define** the four factors that are used to describe a target market.
3. **List** the advantages and disadvantages of niche marketing.

Practice Academics

English Language Arts

4. Identify the prefixes in demographics, geographics, and psychographics. Define each prefix in a sentence, and list two other words that use them.

Social Studies

5. How do marketers use the group and cultural influences of a market to sell their products?

 connectED.mcgraw-hill.com

Check your answers.

For help, go to the Math Skills Handbook located at the back of this book.

The Marketing Plan

The SWOT analysis helps create a marketing plan that includes an executive summary, a situation analysis, marketing goals, marketing strategies, implementation, evaluation and control, and an appendix.

Companies need to know about their customers. Market segmentation identifies customers with shared characteristics.

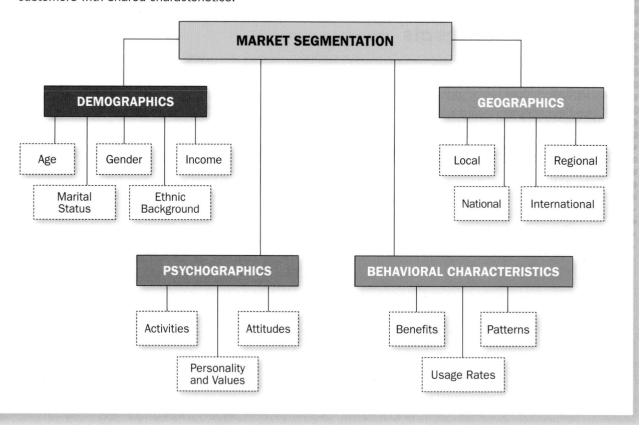

Review and Activities

Written Summary

- A SWOT analysis identifies a company's internal strengths and weaknesses, as well as external opportunities and threats.
- Internal strengths and weaknesses involve analysis of the company, its customers, and its competitive position.
- External opportunities and threats include competitive, as well as political, economic, socio-cultural, and technological factors.
- A marketing plan is a written document that directs the marketing activities of a company for a specific period of time.
- A marketing plan includes an executive summary, situation analysis, marketing goals, marketing strategies, implementation, evaluation and control, and an appendix.
- Marketing segmentation classifies people in a given market into smaller groups.
- Four methods of segmenting are demographics, geographics, psychographics, and behavioral characteristics.

Review Content Vocabulary and Academic Vocabulary

1. Find a visual example in the textbook or bring one in from home of each of these content vocabulary words.

Content Vocabulary
- SWOT analysis (p. 31)
- PEST analysis (p. 34)
- marketing plan (p. 37)
- executive summary (p. 37)
- situation analysis (p. 37)
- marketing strategy (p. 39)
- sales forecasts (p. 40)
- performance standard (p. 40)

- market segmentation (p. 43)
- demographics (p. 44)
- disposable income (p. 45)
- discretionary income (p. 45)
- geographics (p. 46)
- psychographics (p. 47)
- mass marketing (p. 49)

Academic Vocabulary
- factors (p. 31)
- technology (p. 31)
- ranges (p. 44)
- attitudes (p. 47)

Assess for Understanding

2. **Connect** How does a SWOT analysis relate to the goals of a marketing plan?
3. **Discuss** Why must the objectives of a marketing plan be single-minded, specific, realistic, measurable, and time-framed?
4. **Compare and Contrast** How are the uses of demographic segmentation different from or similar to the uses of geographic segmentation?
5. **Analyze** Based on your activities, interests, and attitudes, what is your psychographic profile?
6. **Evaluate** What are the benefits and risks of using mass marketing in a market that has a variety of potential customers?
7. **Discuss** How might marketers use information from the U.S. Census or World Factbook to help them segment a market?
8. **Assess** Why is it important to monitor customer satisfaction and competitors' products in a market?
9. **Create** What questions will help a company complete a PEST scan?

21st  Century Skills

Teamwork Skills

10. SWOT Analysis Work with a partner to select a company that interests you or that you know something about. It should be one that you can find information about on the Web or through observation at stores or in business magazines. Conduct a SWOT analysis. Then prepare a chart that depicts the results of the analysis. With your partner, present your findings to the class.

Financial Literacy Skills

11. Transportation Costs Consumers who buy online might pay about 10 percent of the cost of an item for shipping and handling. These charges are not included when a customer buys the same item at a store. However, the customer does pay for his or her own transportation costs separately. If it costs you 38 cents per mile to drive your car, what are the transportation costs for a 15-mile trip to the store?

e-Marketing Skills

12. E-Returns Imagine that you are in charge of Customer Service for a large e-marketing firm such as Amazon.com. Investigate the process for returning defective merchandise by logging on to a large online store.

- List the steps a consumer must take in order to return merchandise and get a refund.
- What problems does returning defective merchandise present for customers who purchase products online?
- What are some ways you could make returning defective merchandise easy for online customers?
- Create a step-by-step guide for customers to use when they are returning defective merchandise. Be sure to consider factors such as shipping costs, packaging materials, insurance issues, and other issues that may arise.
- Share your guide with the class.

Build Academic Skills

Social Studies

13. Economics In recent years trade has expanded among the nations of the world. Research the effects of increased world trade. Describe a situation in which this represents an opportunity and a threat.

Science

14. Scientific Inquiry Conducting a SWOT analysis is like conducting a scientific inquiry or experiment. Research online or at the library how to properly design and execute a scientific experiment. Identify the scientific procedures and principles that apply to marketing research and SWOT analysis.

Mathematics

15. The 80/20 Rule Here are the sales figures of ten customers: (1) $75,000; (2) $700,000; (3) $815,000; (4) $70,000; (5) $60,000; (6) $30,000; (7) $25,000; (8) $53,750; (9) $40,000; and (10) $25,000. Explain the 80/20 rule using these figures.

Math Concept **Understanding Ratios** The 80/20 rule states that the top 20 percent of customers generates 80 percent of a company's sales. In this case, total sales is $1,893,750 from 10 customers.

For help, go to the **Math Skills Handbook** located at the back of this book.

Standardized Test Practice

Directions Read the following questions. On a separate piece of paper, write the best possible answer for each one.

1. What is 150 percent of 44?

    A. 80   **C.** 66

    B. 50   **D.** 88

2. True or false? The 20 in the 80/20 rule represents 20 percent of a company's sales.

    T

    F

3. Demographic characteristics help define a _____ market.

Test-Taking Tip

When you first sit down to take a math test, jot down important equations or formulas on scrap paper. This will help you to remember them during the test.

DECA Connection Role Play

Assistant Manager Children's Clothing Store

Situation Your store is located in a strip mall in a family-focused suburban area. The strip mall is five miles from the nearest regional shopping mall. That mall has three department stores that carry children's clothing and shoes, a specialty children's store that also carries children's shoes—and a children's shoe store.

Your store carries clothing and accessory items for infants, toddlers, girls, and boys. The clothing lines range from casual to dressy. The accessory items include baby blankets, hair accessories for girls, and neckties and bowties for boys. Your store does not currently carry children's shoes.

The store's owner (judge) has decided to expand the store's merchandise lines to include a children's shoes department. The store's owner (judge) has asked for your help in creating a marketing plan for the new department. The owner believes she is not as knowledgeable about marketing plans as she would like to be. So, she has asked you to explain the parts of a marketing plan.

Activity Prepare an outline that will include the parts of a marketing plan. You will then use your outline to explain each part of a marketing plan to the store's owner (judge) in a meeting that will take place later today.

Evaluation You will be evaluated on how well you meet these performance indicators:

1. Explain the nature of marketing plans.
2. Explain the nature of marketing planning.
3. Explain the nature of sales forecasts.
4. Explain the concept of marketing strategies.
5. Prepare simple written reports.

 connectED.mcgraw-hill.com

Download the Competitive Events Workbook for more Role-Play practice.

McGraw-Hill Education/Joe Polillio

SWOT Analysis
for a Coffee and Tea Chain

Competition in the specialty coffee and tea market is hot. Is it too late for a new competitor to break into this lucrative market?

Scenario

An Italian coffee and tea chain is considering entering the specialty coffee market in the United States. Before making that investment, our client would like our firm to conduct a SWOT analysis. The Italian coffee chain has been successful in European and Asian markets because it has used its strengths and taken advantage of opportunities in these markets.

Each café's interior design is upscale with comfortable seating, artwork, and designer plates and cups. Exotic teas and specialty coffee offerings are priced in line with and below current competitors' offerings. Only high-grade coffee beans from selected coffee bean growers are used. The Italian cafés are trying to create a unique experience in coffee and tea drinking: coffee and tea should be savored.

The Skills You'll Use

Academic Skills Reading, writing, social studies, and researching

Basic Skills Speaking, listening, thinking, and interpersonal

Technology Skills Word processing, telecommunication, and Internet

Your Objective

Analyze the current specialty coffee and tea market in order to help a client decide whether or not to enter the market.

STEP 1 Do Your Research

Go to the Internet or your school library. Find out about the coffee and tea specialty market in restaurants, cafés, and similar outlets in the United States.

As you conduct your research, answer these questions:

- Is the market growing or shrinking and why?
- What economic, political, socio-cultural or technological factors affect this market?
- Who makes up the target market of U.S. coffee drinkers and tea drinkers in terms of demographic, psychographic, geographic, and behavioral factors?
- How successful are the marketing mixes of competitors such as Starbucks®, Dunkin Donuts®, and McDonald's®?
- What are the strengths, weaknesses, opportunities, and threats for our client in the United States coffee and tea specialty market?

Write a summary of your research.

STEP 2 Plan Your Project

Now that you have completed your research, you need to begin planning your project.

- Conduct a SWOT analysis for the Italian café chain.
- Identify a potential target market in the United States for the Italian café chain.
- Write a report summarizing your SWOT analysis, identifying your target market, and explaining why you have chosen this target market.
- Suggest a marketing mix for the Italian café chain.
- Determine whether that market segment is big enough to support the Italian café chain.

STEP 3 | Connect with Your Community

- Test your conclusions by conducting interviews with trusted adults in your community that match the target market you have identified. Ask questions about their habits.
- Take notes during the interviews, and transcribe your notes after the interviews.
- Observe customers in the competition's places of business and note how long they wait for service, how long they sit and drink their beverages, and what else they might be doing while drinking their beverages.

STEP 4 | Share What You Learn

Assume your class is the committee from the Italian café chain.

- Share your findings in an oral presentation to your class. Be prepared to answer questions.
- Explain how businesses find out their strengths and weaknesses in the marketplace.
- Explain how businesses react to opportunities and threats in the marketplace.
- Make your recommendation and provide rationale for your decision.
- Use software to create a slide presentation to accompany your oral report. Include one slide in your presentation for each key topic in your written report.

STEP 5 | Evaluate Your Marketing and Academic Skills

Your project will be evaluated based on the following:

- Knowledge of the specialty coffee and tea market
- Comprehensive SWOT analysis
- Proper use of marketing terminology
- Rationale for recommendation
- Organization and continuity of presentation
- Mechanics—presentation and neatness
- Speaking and listening skills

MARKETING CORE FUNCTIONS

 Market Planning

Pricing

Marketing Internship Project Checklist

Plan

✓ Research current market conditions in the industry.

✓ Assess the strengths, weaknesses, opportunities, and threats a new competitor would face in this market.

✓ Identify a location to use as a test market for the new competitor.

Write

✓ Describe current market conditions in the industry.

✓ Explain how the results of the SWOT analysis help the new competitor understand the risks involved in the market.

Present

✓ Present the results of your SWOT analysis and justify your chosen location for the new competitor.

✓ Respond to questions posed by the audience.

✓ Consider the needs and experiences of the audience as you present research to your class.

 connectED.mcgraw-hill.com

Evaluate Download a rubric you can use to evaluate your final project.

my marketing portfolio

Internship Report When you have completed your Marketing Internship Project and oral presentation, put your written report and printouts of key slides from your oral presentation in your marketing portfolio.

Analyze a Different Market and Company Select a different market (e.g., sports equipment, ice cream, cell phones, bicycles, vitamin-enriched water) and a company of your choice in that market. Conduct a SWOT analysis of that company. How effective is that company in following the marketing concept? Should that company pull out of that market or remain? If it should remain, make recommendations with regard to the company's marketing mix (product, place, price, and promotion). Prepare a written report and an oral presentation.

ECONOMICS

Marketing Internship Project

A Marketing Plan

Essential Question How can a marketing plan help a company meet the needs of consumers during a recession?

Some say that toys are recession-proof. However, TB Toys, a toy retailer, went bankrupt and closed its doors during the 2008 recession. In China, 4,000 toy manufacturers also closed. Even though some toy manufacturers and retailers may have weathered the recession, overall toy sales declined. It is apparent that to be successful, toy companies must innovate and be sensitive to the financial burdens consumers face at any time. In a global recession, toy companies around the world feel the effects of fewer dollars available for toy purchases. Some major toy manufacturers like Mattel® and Hasbro® rely on between 40 and 50 percent of sales from outside the United States. So, how is a global toy company to survive in difficult economic times?

Project Goal

In the project at the end of this unit, you will create a marketing plan for a toy company so it can survive a recession.

Prepare for the Project

As you read this unit, use this checklist to prepare for the Marketing Internship Project at the end of this unit:

- Consider how a global recession affects the toy industry.
- Recall some toys that have remained successful during economic downturns.
- Think of some marketing strategies that might work during a recession.

 connectED.mcgraw-hill.com

Project Activity
Complete a worksheet activity about creating a marketing plan.

The world and business will move on without you if you're not constantly innovating.

MARKETING CORE FUNCTIONS IN THIS UNIT

 Market Planning

 Pricing

 Product/Service Management

Promotion

LEGO CREATOR

LET YOUR CHILD BE A LEGO® CREATOR

3 IN 1

7-12
5891

www.Creator.LEGO.com

Remember what it was like playing with LEGO® bricks as a child? With the new Apple Tree House set from LEGO Creator, you can give your child the classic LEGO experience in an exciting, up-to-date version.

Build the Apple Tree House and enjoy all its great details: the mailbox with letters inside, the satellite dish on the roof and the neat little lawnmower. When your LEGO creator decides it's time to relocate, he or she can rebuild the Apple Tree House into a tall townhouse or a summer house for a relaxing vacation. Building instructions for all three models are included in the set.

Three houses in one – build your favourite. This is what the LEGO Creator series is all about.

SHOW WHAT YOU KNOW

Visual Literacy
Since the 1940s, LEGO® products have been popular with children and adults around the world. Licensed themes, video games, and social networking help LEGO® stay connected with consumers. *Why do you think LEGO® has maintained its popularity?*

political and economic analysis

SHOW WHAT YOU KNOW

Visual Literacy The stock market reacts to changes in economic and political conditions. Investors watch economic indicators and government policies to determine when to buy and when to sell stocks and bonds. *Why do different countries have their own stock markets?*

Discovery Project

Risks and Rewards

Essential Question How will you invest the money you have saved?

Project Goal
Work with a partner to study economic indicators, such as unemployment rate, Consumer Price Index, and Gross Domestic Product to determine the current state of the United States economy. Study any pending government actions that may affect the economy in the near future. Then decide how you would invest $100,000. Conduct a SWOT analysis to determine which company or companies you think will be successful. Provide rationale for your decisions.

Ask Yourself...
- Where will you find information on the economy and government policies?
- Where will you find information on companies that may be successful?
- How will you use this information to help you decide how to invest your money?
- How will you present your investment decisions with supporting rationale?

 Critical Thinking How does the economy affect government policies and personal financial decisions?

 connectED.mcgraw-hill.com

Activity
Get a worksheet activity about economic risks and rewards.

Evaluate
Download a rubric you can use to evaluate your project.

DECA Connection

DECA Event Role Play
Concepts in this chapter are related to DECA competitive events that involve either an interview or role play.

Performance Indicators The performance indicators represent key skills and knowledge. Your key to success in DECA competitive events is relating them to the concepts in this chapter.

- Explain the concept of economic resources.
- Explain the types of economic systems.
- Examine the relationship between government and business.
- Discuss the role government agencies play in the food marketing industry.
- Determine the impact of business cycles on business activities.

DECA Prep
Role Play Practice role playing with the DECA Connection competitive-event activity at the end of this chapter. More information about DECA events can be found on DECA's Web site.

READING GUIDE

Before You Read

Connect How do economic decisions and policies affect your daily life?

Objectives

- **Explain** the concept of an economy.
- **Discuss** how scarcity and factors of production affect the economy.
- **Compare and contrast** how traditional, market, command economies answer the three basic economic questions.
- **Explain** why most economies are mixed.
- **Identify** examples of different political and economic philosophies.

The Main Idea

An economy is a nation's method for making economic choices that involve how it will use its resources to produce and distribute goods and services to meet the needs of its population.

Vocabulary

Content Vocabulary

- economy
- resources
- factors of production
- infrastructure
- entrepreneurship
- scarcity
- traditional economy
- market economy
- command economy

Academic Vocabulary

You will find these words in your reading and on your tests. Make sure you know their meanings.

- approaches
- theory

MARKETING CORE FUNCTION

Market Planning

Graphic Organizer

Draw or print a diagram like this to record similarities and differences among market and command economies.

 connectED.mcgraw-hill.com

Print this graphic organizer.

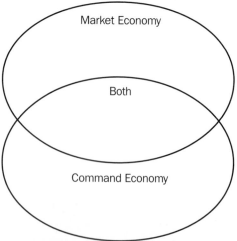

Market Economy

Both

Command Economy

What Is an Economy?

WHAT CREATES AN ECONOMY?

An **economy**, or economic system, is the organized way a nation provides for the needs and wants of its people. Countries with different economic systems have different **approaches** when making choices. A country's economic resources determine economic activities, such as manufacturing, buying, selling, transporting, and investing. Broad categories of economic resources that are common to all nations affect how business is done across the world.

As You Read

Predict How are products manufactured and transported through the economy?

ECONOMIC RESOURCES

Economic **resources** are all the things used in producing goods and services. Economists use the term **factors of production** when they talk about these resources. Factors of production are comprised of land, labor, capital, and entrepreneurship. Tangible economic resources include land and capital. Intangible economic resources include labor and entrepreneurship.

LAND

Land includes everything contained in the earth or found in the seas. Coal and crude oil are natural resources. So is a lake and all of the living things in it. Trees and plants, as well as the soil in which they grow, are natural resources. These natural resources are used as the raw material for making goods and creating services. Some countries' climate and geography are perfect for attracting tourists. Switzerland is a destination for skiing and mountain landscapes. So, the tourist trade is a viable industry that helps support its economy.

> " **A nation chooses how to use its resources to** produce and distribute goods and services. "

LABOR

Labor refers to all the people who work. Labor includes full- and part-time workers, managers, and professional people in both the private and public sectors. Companies may spend a lot of money training employees because a well-trained labor force is an asset to a company. Economies with well-educated and well-trained labor have an advantage. A country with such a labor force can use its own citizens for jobs. It does not have to search for employees in other countries.

CAPITAL

Capital includes money to start and operate a business. It also includes the goods used in the production process. Factories, office buildings, computers, and tools are all considered capital resources. Raw materials that have been processed into a more useful form (such as lumber or steel) are considered capital. Without capital, a business would not have the funds or the resources needed to develop, to advertise, and to transport goods. Capital includes **infrastructure**, which is the physical development of a country. This includes its roads, ports, sanitation facilities, and utilities, especially telecommunications. These things are necessary for the production and distribution of goods and services in an economy. For example, an international business needs dependable phone and Internet service. Companies that ship goods need to be able to reach their customers.

ENTREPRENEURSHIP

Entrepreneurship refers to the skills of people who are willing to invest their time and money to run a business. Entrepreneurs organize factors of production to create the goods and services that are part of an economy. They are the employers of a population.

People who are constantly thinking of new ideas can be good entrepreneurs. It takes more than a good idea, though. An entrepreneur must also have the skills needed to run a business. A good imagination and a capacity for hard work are the qualities all entrepreneurs have.

Entrepreneurs can make major contributions to the economy. Innovations in transportation and communications led to much of the growth and change in the U.S. during the twentieth century.

Entrepreneurship With consumers wanting cheaper, greener fuel, an entrepreneur is marketing machines to convert garbage into auto fuel in minutes at home.

SCARCITY

Different economies have different amounts of economic resources. The United States has an educated labor force, a great deal of capital, an abundance of entrepreneurs, and many natural resources. Most underdeveloped nations are not that fortunate. They might have natural resources to spare but not the capital or the skilled labor to develop them.

Even the United States, with its wealth of economic resources, cannot meet the needs and wants of all its citizens. Many citizens live below poverty level. Businesses go bankrupt on a regular basis. It is apparent that nations have unlimited wants and needs for growth and development but limited resources to meet them. The difference between wants and needs and available resources is called **scarcity**. Scarcity forces nations to make economic choices. For example, entrepreneurs in underdeveloped nations may not have much money or resources. They will need capital or raw materials so they can start a business. The scarcity in their country can make it hard to be successful.

 Reading Check

Recall What are the four economic resources?

Small business owners are employers for a majority of workers in the United States. *How do small business owners use economic resources aside from entrepreneurship?*

Small Business Owners and the Economy

Image Source

TYPES OF ECONOMIC SYSTEMS

Nations must answer these three basic economic questions about how to use limited economic resource to get the goods and services the country needs.

1. **What** goods and services should be produced?

2. **How** should the goods and services be produced?

3. **For whom** should the goods and services be produced and distributed?

Economists have studied the way nations answer the three basic economic questions and have classified economic systems into three broad categories: traditional, market, and command economies. However, no economy is purely traditional, market, or command. Elements of all three systems are found in all economies. Learning the characteristics of the pure form of each economic system will make it easier to classify and categorize information about them.

TRADITIONAL ECONOMIES

In a **traditional economy**, habits, traditions and rituals answer the basic questions of what, how, and for whom. The answers are often based on cultural or religious practices and ideals that have been passed from one generation to the next. Typically, these activities involve subsistence farming, animal gathering, tool making, and other activities used to provide food, shelter, and clothing.

1. What? In a traditional economy there is little choice about what to produce. People produce what they need to survive. They use the natural resources in their habitat to do so.

2. How? Traditional societies are underdeveloped. They produce what they need with simple, handmade tools and their ingenuity. People use the techniques they learned from their ancestors.

3. For whom? Traditional economic systems have a sense of community. Any excess food or other items that are made are traded among the residents.

MARKET ECONOMIES

In a pure **market economy**, there is no government involvement in economic decisions. Individuals and companies own the means of production and businesses compete for consumers. The government lets the market answer the three basic economic questions.

1. What? Consumers decide what should be produced in a market economy through the purchases that they make. Products that do not satisfy consumers' needs are not purchased and are not successful. They are no longer sold.

2. How? Businesses in a market economy decide how to produce goods and services. They must produce quality products at lower prices than their competitors. It is necessary for them to find the most efficient way to produce their goods and services and the best way to encourage customers to buy these products.

3. For whom? In a market economy, the people who have more money are able to use it as a medium of exchange to buy more goods and services. To obtain money, people are motivated to work and invest the money they make.

Tourism Contributes to an Economy

A country's natural economic resources can help build its economy through tourism. *Choose a country and explain the economic resources or factors of production that make it a good vacation spot or site for opening a business.*

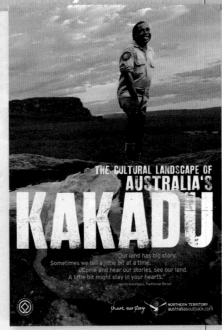

THE CULTURAL LANDSCAPE OF AUSTRALIA'S KAKADU

"Our land has big story. Sometimes we tell a little bit at a time. Come and hear our stories, see our land. A little bit might stay in your hearts."
Jacob Nayinggul, Traditional Owner

NORTHERN TERRITORY
australiasoutback.com

Natural Economic Resources

Countries with the right mix of sun and fertile ground have many farms. In the United States, California's natural resources are perfect for farming fruits, vegetables, nuts, and grapes. *How do your state's economic resources benefit its economy?*

BIGGER, BETTER BERRIES.

Recognized Worldwide For Superior Berries.

Grown under the golden California sun, Well·Pict berries grow big as all outdoors thanks to the fertile valleys and cool coastal breezes our West Coast fields offer all year round. Known around the globe for their bigger-than-life taste, color and aroma, Well·Pict's sizeable flavor is unmatched in the industry. Just one bite, and your customers are sure to leave their heart with Well·Pict.

WELL·PICT
BERRIES

www.wellpict.com   USA 831-722-3871

In 2008, Hugo Chavez, the past President of Venezuela, nationalized foreign oil companies. He also nationalized telephone, electricity, steel, and cement companies during his regime. Chavez used the revenue generated from these companies to support government-sponsored programs.

DEVELOPING ECONOMIES

Developing economies are mostly poor countries with little industrialization. They are trying to become more prosperous and develop their infrastructure. Much of their success depends on improving the education levels of their labor force.

Directing and using foreign investments efficiently will also contribute to their success.

Chad, a country in central Africa, is a good example of a developing economy. It is a traditional economy based on agriculture and livestock farming. Cotton, cattle, and gum arabic are its primary exports. However, with an oil field and pipeline project paid for by foreign investors, Chad has begun to develop its oil reserves for export. This investment will help generate much-needed funds for this poor nation to use to improve its infrastructure and develop its labor resources.

After You Read | Section 3.1

Review Key Concepts

1. **Define** *economy* and explain the three questions it seeks to answer.
2. **Explain** the relationship between economic resources and the concept of scarcity.
3. **Compare and contrast** privatization and nationalization. Which political and economic philosophy would most likely be prevalent when a country decides on privatization? On nationalization? Explain.

Practice Academics

English Language Arts

4. Write a paragraph to explain and provide examples of why most economies are considered mixed economies.

Mathematics

5. In socialist countries taxes are higher than in capitalist countries. If income taxes were 33 percent of a person's income in a capitalist country and 55 percent in a socialist country, how much more disposable income would a person have in a capitalist country when compared to a socialist country if their respective incomes were $150,000 a year?

Math Concept **Ways of Representing Numbers** A decrease in a number can be represented by a percent less than 100.

Starting Hints Subtract the lower percentage from the higher percentage to determine the difference in percent of disposable income (33 percent from 55 percent). Convert the resulting percentages to decimals by moving the decimal point two places to the left. Multiply that decimal number by $150,000 (annual income) to determine the additional disposable income a person would have in a capitalistic system.

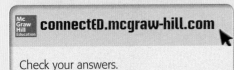
connectED.mcgraw-hill.com

Check your answers.

For help, go to the **Math Skills Handbook** located at the back of this book.

READING GUIDE

Before You Read

Connect How do your actions affect the economy?

Objectives

- **List** the goals of a healthy economy.
- **Explain** how an economy is measured.
- **Analyze** the key phases of the business cycle.

The Main Idea

Aspects of an economy such as consumers, businesses, and governments affect the economy and marketing decisions.

Vocabulary

Content Vocabulary
- productivity
- gross domestic product (GDP)
- gross national product (GNP)
- inflation
- consumer price index (CPI)
- producer price index (PPI)
- business cycle
- expansion
- recession
- depression
- recovery

Academic Vocabulary

You will find these words in your reading and on your tests. Make sure you know their meanings.
- invest
- method

Graphic Organizer

Draw or print this figure. Use it to identify the key economic measurements.

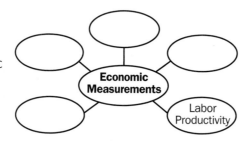

Economic Measurements

Labor Productivity

 connectED.mcgraw-hill.com

Print this graphic organizer.

 MARKETING CORE FUNCTION

Market Planning

THE ECONOMY AND MARKETING

An understanding of how to measure an economy and what factors contribute to economic strength or weakness is essential. It is only then that you can appreciate how the economy, consumers, businesses, and government influence each other.

As You Read

Evaluate What effect do your actions have on the economy?

GOALS OF A HEALTHY ECONOMY

A healthy economy has three goals: increase productivity, decrease unemployment, and maintain stable prices. All nations analyze their economies to keep track of how well they are meeting these goals. This analysis allows businesses, consumers, and governments to make appropriate economic decisions.

Goals of a Healthy Economy

Increase Productivity — Decrease Unemployment — Maintain Stable Prices

ECONOMIC MEASUREMENTS

Accurate information about an economy is essential to determining whether it is meeting its goals. The key economic measurements that nations routinely use to analyze their economic strength are labor productivity, gross domestic product, standard of living, inflation rate, and unemployment rate.

LABOR PRODUCTIVITY

Productivity is output per worker hour that is measured over a defined period of time, such as a week, month, or year. Businesses can increase their productivity in a number of ways. They can **invest** in new equipment or facilities that allow their employees to work more efficiently. Providing additional training or financial incentives can also boost staff productivity. Businesses can also reduce their work force and increase the responsibilities of the workers who remain. This makes an organization more financially efficient and more effective. Higher productivity improves a company's profit.

> **"** If you want to perform a useful SWOT analysis, you need to consider the economic measures that will influence your market planning. **"**

Specialization and division of labor are key concepts related to increasing productivity. An assembly line is an example of specialization and division of labor whereby each part of a finished product is completed by a person who specializes in one aspect of its manufacturing. The theory behind this **method** of production is that the work can be completed faster and more efficiently when people specialize in certain areas. This method also makes it easier for companies to identify issues with their products. They know where and how each part of the product is made. They can use this information to find out what went wrong when the product was made.

GROSS DOMESTIC PRODUCT

Most governments study productivity by keeping track of an entire nation's production output. Today the principal way of measuring that output in the United States is gross domestic product. **Gross domestic product (GDP)** is the output of goods and services produced by labor and property located within a country. The U.S. Bureau of Economic Analysis publishes a report on the United States' GDP.

The GDP is made up of private investment, government spending, personal spending, net exports of goods and services, and change in business inventories (see **Figure 3.1**). Private investment includes spending by businesses for things like equipment and software. It also includes home construction. Government spending includes money spent by local, state, and federal governments. This money is spent on social services and also construction projects. Personal spending includes all the money consumers spend on goods and services for their own use.

Expanding inventories show that businesses are producing goods that are being stored in their warehouses—that adds to the GDP. Inventories that are shrinking indicate that people are buying more than what was actually produced, so you subtract that figure from the GDP.

As a review, here is the calculation for GDP: Add private investment, government spending, and personal spending. Then either add a trade surplus or subtract a trade deficit. After that, add expanding inventories or subtract shrinking inventories.

Since 1991, the United States has been using GDP as its primary measurement of productivity. Before 1991, it used a measurement called gross national product. **Gross national product (GNP)** is the total dollar value of goods and services produced by a nation, including goods and services produced abroad by U.S. citizens and companies. There is a significant difference between GNP and GDP. The GNP counts the country responsible for production. With GDP, the country where the production takes place is more important.

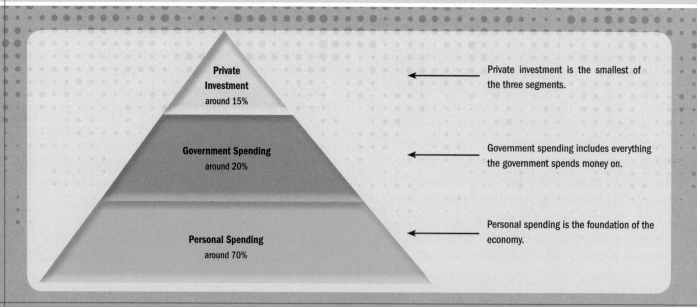

FIGURE 3.1 Gross Domestic Product

Here is a look at what makes up the United States' GDP. These numbers vary year to year and do not add up to 100% because two items shrink the economy's total production. When we import more than we export, the resulting trade deficit is subtracted from the GDP. Expanding inventories add to the GDP. Shrinking inventories subtract from the GDP. *Of what significance is GDP when evaluating the health of a country's economy?*

Private Investment
around 15%

Government Spending
around 20%

Personal Spending
around 70%

Private investment is the smallest of the three segments.

Government spending includes everything the government spends money on.

Personal spending is the foundation of the economy.

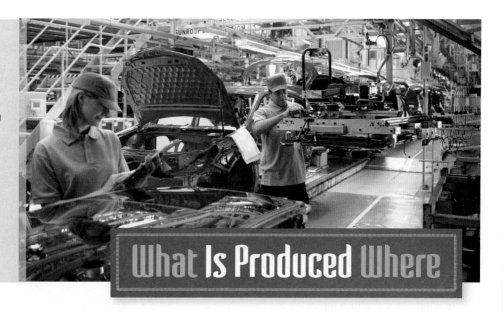

BMW®, a German car manufacturer, produces cars in Germany that are exported and sold in the United States. BMW has also built factories in North America. *If you buy a car manufactured by BMW in South Carolina, is this car part of the U.S. GDP? Is the same car also part of the U.S. GNP?*

What Is Produced Where

For example, Ford® is a U.S. corporation. It has a plant in England that produces cars. The portion of Ford's production that occurs in England is included in the U.S. GNP, but not in its GDP. The portion of Ford's production that occurs in England is part of England's GDP, but not its GNP.

STANDARD OF LIVING

A country's standard of living is a measurement of the amount and quality of goods and services that a nation's people have. It is a number that reflects their quality of life. To calculate the standard of living, you divide the GDP or GNP of a country by its population. This calculation gives you the amount of GDP or GNP per person. (Rates measured per person are also known as per capita measurements.) Most industrialized nations enjoy a high standard of living because they have a high level of production.

Some marketers also look at additional factors to get a broader picture of a nation's standard of living. Some countries provide more social services for their citizens. Social benefits, such as free education and health care provided by the government, may be reviewed. The number of households per 1,000 inhabitants with durable goods, such as washing machines, refrigerators, dishwashers, and autos, can be included in the analysis. High levels of social services and durable goods mean that a country has a high standard of living.

INFLATION RATE

Inflation refers to rising prices. A low inflation rate (1 to 5 percent each year) is good because it shows that an economy is stable. Double-digit inflation (10 percent or higher) hurts an economy. When inflation is that high, money loses its value. The period from the mid-1960s to the early 1980s was a highly inflationary period. Prices tripled in the United States during that time. People who live on a fixed income such as a monthly Social Security check are especially hurt by high inflation.

Controlling inflation is one of a government's major goals. When inflation starts to go up, many governments raise interest rates to discourage borrowing money. The result is slower economic growth, which helps to bring inflation down. Two measures of inflation used in the United States are the consumer price index and the producer price index. The **consumer price index (CPI)** measures the change in price over a period of time of 400 specific retail goods and services used by the average urban household. It is also called the cost of living index. Food, housing, utilities, transportation, and medical care are a few of its components. The CPI excludes food and energy prices, which tend to be unpredictable. The **producer price index (PPI)** measures wholesale price levels in the economy. Producer prices generally get passed along to the consumer. When there is a drop in the PPI, it is generally followed by a drop in the CPI.

Monty Rakusen/Getty Images

UNEMPLOYMENT RATE

All nations chart unemployment, or jobless rates. The higher the unemployment rate, the greater the chances are of slow economic times. The lower the unemployment rate, the greater the chances are of an economic expansion. This is true because when more people work, there are more people spending money and paying taxes. Businesses and government both take in more money. The government does not have to provide as many social services.

Unemployment High unemployment does not always mean that there are no jobs available. Rather, many workers may not be qualified for the jobs that are available.

OTHER ECONOMIC INDICATORS AND TRENDS

The Conference Board provides additional indicators to help economists evaluate the performance of the U.S. economy. The Conference Board is a private business research organization that is made up of businesses and individuals who work together to assess the state of the economy. Three Conference Board indicators are the consumer confidence index, the consumer expectations index, and the jobs index. The jobs index measures consumers' perceptions regarding the number of jobs available. Consumers are polled to see how they feel about personal finance, economic conditions, and buying conditions. Retail sales are studied to see whether consumer confidence polls match consumer actions in the marketplace. Along those same lines, the rate of housing starts is reviewed, as are sales of trucks and autos. These are big purchases that tend to be affected by the economy and interest rates.

Wages and new payroll jobs provide additional information about the strength of the economy at any given point in time. When everyone is employed, supply and demand theory predicts that wages should increase due to the shortage of workers. Economists study these factors, because they may affect inflation and other economic indicators.

✓ Reading Check

Identify What are the key economic measurements?

THE BUSINESS CYCLE

History shows that sometimes an economy grows, which is called expansion, and at other times it slows down, which is called contraction. These recurring changes in economic activity are called the **business cycle** (see **Figure 3.2**). The business cycle includes the following key phases: expansion, recession, trough, and recovery. After recovery, expansion begins again.

Expansion is a time when the economy is flourishing. It is sometimes referred to as a period of prosperity. Across the nation, there is low unemployment. More goods and services are produced and purchased. Consumers spend a lot of money that fuels the economy. An expansion is a good time for new businesses to start up or expand their operations. Expansion continues until it reaches a peak. A peak signifies the end of expansion and the beginning of a recession.

A **recession** is a period of economic slowdown that lasts for at least two quarters of a year, or six months. Financial experts call periods of three months "quarters." The National Bureau of Economic Research (NBER) defines a recession as a significant decline in activity spread across the economy. To be considered a recession, this decline must last more than a few months.

During a recession, companies reduce their workforces and consumers have less money to spend. A reduced workforce results in higher unemployment. When more consumers are out of work, they have less money to spend. Since consumers are spending less, producers respond by making fewer goods and services. Companies cut back on research and development (R&D) of new products. Future plans for expanding business operations are generally put on hold.

FIGURE 3.2 **The Four Key Phases of the Cycle**

Throughout history, economies have followed a pattern of expansion and contraction called the business cycle. There are four phases in the business cycle: expansion (ended by a peak), recession, trough, and recovery. The length and intensity of each of the phases depends on many factors such as wars, natural disasters, and industrial innovation. *In which phase is the United States today?*

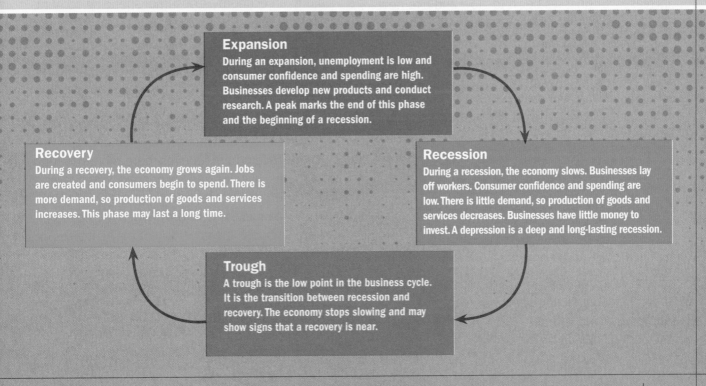

Expansion
During an expansion, unemployment is low and consumer confidence and spending are high. Businesses develop new products and conduct research. A peak marks the end of this phase and the beginning of a recession.

Recovery
During a recovery, the economy grows again. Jobs are created and consumers begin to spend. There is more demand, so production of goods and services increases. This phase may last a long time.

Recession
During a recession, the economy slows. Businesses lay off workers. Consumer confidence and spending are low. There is little demand, so production of goods and services decreases. Businesses have little money to invest. A depression is a deep and long-lasting recession.

Trough
A trough is the low point in the business cycle. It is the transition between recession and recovery. The economy stops slowing and may show signs that a recovery is near.

Recessions can end relatively quickly or last for a long time. According to the NBER, a recession begins immediately after the economy reaches a peak of activity. It ends as the economy reaches its trough. A trough is when the economy reaches the lowest point in a recession. After this point is reached, economic activity begins to rise. The NBER studies indicators in the economy to determine the start of a recession. However, it is not always easy to identify when an economy has moved out of the trough.

A **depression** is a period of prolonged recession. During a depression, it becomes nearly impossible to find a job, and many businesses are forced to shut down. During a depression, consumer spending is very low, unemployment is very high, and production of goods and services is down significantly. Poverty results because so many people are out of work and cannot afford to buy food, clothing, or shelter. The Great Depression of the early 1930s best illustrates this aspect of the business cycle.

Recovery is the term that signifies a period of renewed economic growth following a recession or depression. This is where the cycle begins again with economic expansion. The GDP begins to increase. During this stage, business picks up, people find jobs, and the demand for goods increases. As more goods are needed, production increases. Businesses begin to grow and hire new employees. As jobs increase, consumers have more money to spend, furthering recovery with an upward economic climb. Recovery is characterized by reduced unemployment, increased consumer spending, and moderate expansion by businesses. Periods of recovery differ in length and strength.

FACTORS THAT AFFECT BUSINESS CYCLES

Business cycles are affected by the actions of businesses, consumers, and the government. In turn, businesses, consumers, and the government are affected by business cycles. Businesses tend to react to business cycles by expanding their operations during periods of recovery or expansion. They may also react by cutting back their operations during periods of recession.

During an expansion businesses may invest in new properties, equipment, and inventories, and hire more employees.

Economists study indicators to identify the changing phases of the economy's business cycle. Theses indicators help the government and businesses predict the future of the economy. The predictions are used to make business and economic decisions.

When the economy moves into a recession, businesses may lay off employees. Businesses also cut back inventories to match lowered demand for products in a recession or depression. This has a ripple effect in the economy as business suppliers lose revenue.

During a period of recession, consumers' biggest fear is losing their jobs. Another big fear is a decrease in wages. These fears result in a loss of consumer confidence in the economy. This change reduces consumer spending. Reduced consumer spending causes businesses to reduce their operations in response to lower demand.

The opposite is true during periods of prosperity and recovery. During those periods, consumers are more optimistic. They spend more money on material goods and luxury items. Businesses will also respond by producing more goods. This cycle shows how important consumers are to an economy. Consumer spending accounts for more than-two thirds of the U.S. GDP.

GOVERNMENT'S INFLUENCE ON BUSINESS CYCLES

A government influences business cycles through its policies and programs. Taxation has a strong effect on what happens in an economy. As the government requires more money to run programs, higher taxes are needed. When taxes are raised, businesses and consumers have less money to fuel the economy. When the economy needs a boost, the government may cut taxes or reduce interest rates. Lower taxes and interest rates give businesses and consumers more money to spend and invest. The government may also use tax money to fund various programs. Government spending can help spark a depressed economy in which other activity is very slow.

When an economy worsens, the Federal Reserve generally responds by lowering interest rates. This practice makes borrowing money more affordable, which encourages businesses and consumers to spend. Mortgage rates are affected because the commercial banks' prime lending rate reflects the Federal Reserve's funding rate. For example, when the federal funds rate was at one percent, the prime lending rate was around four percent. At the same time, mortgage rates were between five and six percent. Lower mortgate rates serve as an incentive for consumers to buy homes and borrow money for other major purchases. If inflation becomes a problem, interest rates might be increased to discourage buying on credit.

Other actions governments can take to spark economic growth are illustrated by efforts in the United States in 2008–2009. Under President George W. Bush in 2008, the government issued tax rebates to taxpayers to encourage consumer spending. His administration also enacted the Emergency Economic Stabilization Act of 2008 to help troubled banks. The following year, President Barack Obama signed the American Recovery and Reinvestment Act of 2009, which was a $787 billion economic stimulus package. The U.S. government took these dramatic actions to try to spur consumption and shore up the financial sector. The goal was to revive an economy that was in its worst recession in 70 years.

 After You Read | **Section 3.2**

Review Key Concepts

1. **Explain** how monitoring economic measures help economists achieve the three goals of a healthy economy.
2. **Describe** the effect of high unemployment on a nation's economy.
3. **Describe** what happens to an employee in each phase of the business cycle.

Practice Academics

Social Studies

4. Compare the financial crisis of 2008 with that of the Great Depression (1929–1933). What effect did each crisis have on individuals and on business?

Mathematics

5. Productivity is output per worker hour that is measured over a defined period of time. Determine the monthly labor productivity for a widget company that produced 864,000 widgets with 100 employees that worked 40 hours a week for four weeks.

   Math Concept **Ways of Representing Numbers** Numbers can be represented as numerals, words that stand for numerals, or words that describe quantity.

   Starting Hints Determine total working hours (100 employees × 40 hours a week × 4 weeks). Divide the resulting number (total workers' hours) into 864,000 widgets to determine monthly productivity for the widget company.

connectED.mcgraw-hill.com

Check your answers.

For help, go to the Math Skills Handbook located at the back of this book.

Political and Economic Analysis

Economic resources are four factors of production: land, labor, capital, and entrepreneurship.

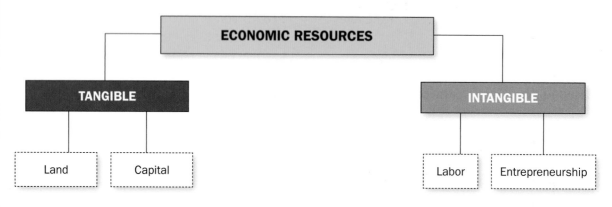

Economic indicators such as productivity, gross domestic product (GDP), gross national product (GNP), and unemployment rates can measure an economy.

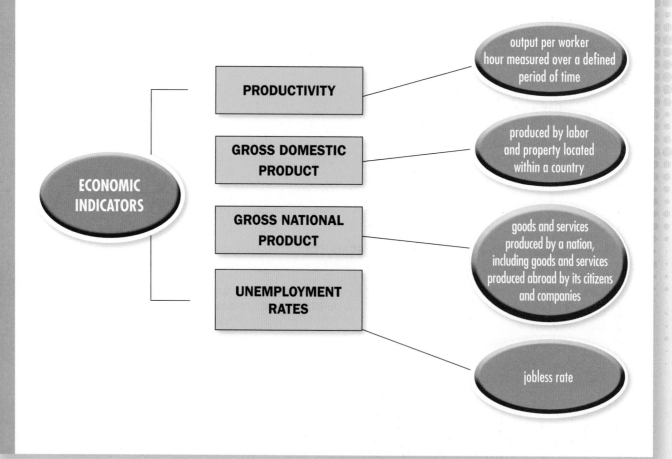

Review and Activities

Written Summary

- An economy is how a nation chooses to use its resources to produce and distribute goods and services to provide for the needs and wants of its people.
- Due to the possibility of scarcity, all nations must answer three fundamental economic questions: what will be produced, how will it be produced, and who should get what is produced.
- Traditional, market, and command economies answer these economic questions in different ways.
- Capitalism, socialism, and communism encourage different economic philosophies.
- Most economies are mixed because the idealized forms of these economic philosophies do not exist in the real world.
- The characteristics of a healthy economy are high productivity, stable prices, and low unemployment.
- Economic indicators include productivity, gross domestic product (GDP), gross national product (GNP), standard of living, consumer price index (CPI), consumer confidence, and unemployment rates.
- The key phases of the business cycle are expansion, recession, trough, and recovery.

Review Content Vocabulary and Academic Vocabulary

1. Create multiple-choice test questions for each content and academic vocabulary term.

Content Vocabulary

- economy (p. 61)
- resources (p. 61)
- factors of production (p. 61)
- infrastructure (p. 61)
- entrepreneurship (p. 62)
- scarcity (p. 62)
- traditional economy (p. 63)
- market economy (p. 63)
- command economy (p. 64)
- productivity (p. 71)
- gross domestic product (GDP) (p. 72)
- gross national product (GNP) (p. 72)
- inflation (p. 73)
- consumer price index (CPI) (p. 73)
- producer price index (PPI) (p. 73)
- business cycle (p. 75)
- expansion (p. 75)
- recession (p. 75)
- depression (p. 76)
- recovery (p. 76)

Academic Vocabulary

- approaches (p. 61)
- theory (p. 65)
- invest (p. 71)
- method (p. 71)

Assess for Understanding

2. **Explain** How are two of the factors of production related?
3. **Compare and Contrast** How are the three basic economic questions answered in a traditional economy, in a market economy, and in a command economy?
4. **Provide** What are examples of countries that use the three different political and economic philosophies?
5. **Explain** How are Gross Domestic Product (GDP) and the Consumer Price Index (CPI) used in a market economy for analysis and marketing decisions?
6. **Identify** What is the current phase of the business cycle? What evidence shows this phase?
7. **Describe** What are two ways governments influence business cycles?
8. **Explain** How does the concept of economic resources relate to the economy of your state?
9. **Compare and Contrast** How is the role of a worker in a traditional economy different from the role of a worker in a command economy?

Teamwork Skills

10. Analyze Government Policies Work with a team to analyze the impact of the current U.S. government's monetary and fiscal policies on businesses and consumers. Prepare a written report using a word processing program and an oral report using presentation software.

Communication Skills

11. Specialized and Organized Labor Debate Research labor unions in the United States. Debate the advantages and disadvantages of specialized and organized labor.

Everyday Ethics

12. Economic Judgments In 2008, three auto company executives flew to Washington, D.C., to ask for government funding during a recession. These executives were criticized for using company-owned jets instead of the cars their companies manufacture. When they returned to Washington, D.C., for a second time, all three executives drove in company autos. Other criticism during the recession involved companies that paid excessive executive salaries and bonuses with federal funds. So, in 2009, legal safeguards limited executive salaries and bonuses for companies that received new government funding. Investigate government limits on executive compensation. Write a paragraph on your opinion about that policy.

e-Marketing Skills

13. Government Web Sites Research United States government Web sites to determine the current phase of the business cycle. Search sites that provide information on U.S. productivity, balance of trade, inflation, and unemployment. Based on your findings, would you suggest that marketers invest more or less money on product expansion; increase or decrease prices; and increase or decrease research and development?

Build Academic Skills

Social Studies

14. Economic Analysis Use the U.S. Bureau of Economic Analysis Web site to find information on the GDP. Chart the percentage of GDP attributed to government spending over the past ten years in the United States. Use your chart to make a statement about how government spending has changed in this period. Explain your statement to demonstrate your understanding of different political and economic systems.

Science

15. Natural Resources Explore the natural resources in a developing country to determine how those resources are being used for its population. Discuss your findings with a partner.

Mathematics

16. Inflation and Deflation During inflationary periods the cost of living is higher than during a deflationary period. During a stable price period, assume the weekly food bill was $125. If inflation goes up to 15 percent, what would be the weekly food bill? If deflation occurred by the same 15 percent what would be the weekly food bill?

> **Math Concept** **Understanding Percentages** Multiply the $125 food bill by 115 percent to determine the weekly food bill during an inflationary period.

For help, go to the **Math Skills Handbook** located at the back of this book.

Standardized Test Practice

Directions Read the following questions. On a separate sheet of paper write the best possible answer for each one.

1. What are recurring changes in economic activity called?
   A. expansion
   B. recession
   C. business cycle
   D. depression
2. True or false? Privatization is the same as nationalization.
   T
   F
3. The output per worker hour defined over a measure of time is _____.

Test-Taking Tip

When answering multiple-choice questions, ask yourself if each option is true or false.

DECA. Connection Role Play

Retail Store Manager Food Store Chain

Situation You are a retail store manager for a food store chain. The corporate office is reviewing all stores due to the current recession. The community serviced by this store has an unemployment rate that is higher than the national rate. Consumer confidence is down. The demographics of the customer base have changed with a greater influx of lower income families, many of whom receive government subsidies. Based on the current measures of the economy and your store's particular situation, what changes in product selection or store policy do you recommend?

The corporate office is sending a representative (judge) to your store to meet with you regarding your store's operation.

Activity Prepare a report noting recommendations you believe would be helpful in making your store more profitable during this economic recession. Use that report when meeting with the representative from the corporate office (judge).

Evaluation You will be evaluated on how well you meet these performance indicators:
- Explain the concept of economic resources.
- Explain the types of economic systems.
- Examine the relationship between government and business.
- Discuss the role government agencies play in the food marketing industry.
- Determine the impact of business cycles on business activities.

  connectED.mcgraw-hill.com

Download the Competitive Events Workbook for more Role-Play practice.

global analysis

Visual Literacy Globalization has created new markets for all products. It has also changed how business is done. *What challenges and opportunities do you see for global businesses?*

SHOW WHAT YOU KNOW

Discovery Project

Marketing in an Emerging Country

Essential Question
How would you select an emerging country to market a product and what marketing strategy would you use?

Project Goal

Select a product to sell in an emerging nation. An emerging nation is a country that is developing into an industrialized nation. Conduct a PEST analysis on a minimum of two countries to determine which country is better suited for the product. Provide rationale for your selection and note any problems you may have to address. Prepare an advertising message and explain your plan for marketing the product in that country. Use a word processing program to prepare a written report. Use presentation software to prepare visuals for your oral presentation to the class.

Ask Yourself...

- What products do consumers need in emerging countries?
- In which nation would you have a chance of success?
- How will you address differences in language and culture in your marketing plan?
- How will you decide on what to include in the advertising message?
- What marketing strategy should you use?

 Think Critically What opportunities and threats are apparent in emerging countries as a market for consumer products?

 connectED.mcgraw-hill.com

Activity
Get a worksheet activity about globalization.

Evaluate
Download a rubric you can use to evaluate your project.

DECA Connection

DECA Event Role Play

Concepts in this chapter are related to DECA competitive events that involve either an interview or role play.

Performance Indicators The performance indicators represent key skills and knowledge. Your key to success in DECA competitive events is relating them to the concepts in this chapter.

- Explain the nature of global trade.
- Discuss the impact of cultural and social environments on global trade.
- Assess global trends and opportunities.
- Discuss the global environment in which businesses operate.
- Identify considerations in implementing international marketing strategies.

DECA Prep

Role Play Practice role-playing with the DECA Connection competitive-event activity at the end of this chapter. More information about DECA events can be found on DECA's Web site.

READING GUIDE

Before You Read

Connect What international products do you consume?

Objectives

- **Describe** the benefits of international trade.
- **Discuss** the balance of trade.
- **Compare and Contrast** three types of trade barriers.
- **Discuss** three significant trade agreements and alliances.

The Main Idea

Nations rely on each other to provide goods and services. This interdependence creates a global marketplace.

Vocabulary

Content Vocabulary
- international trade
- imports
- exports
- balance of trade
- free trade
- tariff
- quota
- embargo
- protectionism
- World Trade Organization (WTO)
- North American Free Trade Agreement (NAFTA)
- European Union (EU)

Academic Vocabulary
You will find these words in your reading and on your tests. Make sure you know their meanings.
- potential
- infrastructure

Graphic Organizer

Draw or print this chart to help you organize key concepts related to international trade.

MARKETING CORE FUNCTION

Market Planning

Balance of Trade | Trade Barriers | Trade Agreements

connectED.mcgraw-hill.com

Print this graphic organizer.

 International Trade

NATURE OF INTERNATIONAL TRADE

The global marketplace exists because countries need to trade with one another. It continues to expand because of the reduction of trade restrictions throughout the world. This new global marketplace makes all people and businesses in the world not only **potential** customers but also potential employees or employers.

International trade is the exchange of goods and services among nations. **Imports** are goods and services purchased from other countries. Conversely, **exports** are goods and services sold to other countries. These exchanges occur between businesses, but they are controlled by the governments of the countries involved.

 As You Read

Consider How would your life be different if countries did not exchange products?

INTERDEPENDENCE OF NATIONS

Most countries do not produce or manufacture all the goods and services they need. They get some of their goods and services from other nations. This economic interdependence happens because each country possesses unique resources and capabilities. The principle of economic interdependence is fundamental to marketing in a global environment.

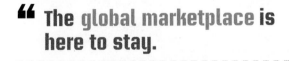

" **The global marketplace is here to stay.** "

ABSOLUTE ADVANTAGE AND COMPARATIVE ADVANTAGE

Some nations tend to specialize in certain areas. They specialize in products that they can produce most efficiently due to available resources in their countries.

ABSOLUTE ADVANTAGE

An absolute advantage occurs when a country has economic resources that allow it to produce a product at a lower unit cost than any other country. For example, Brazil has an absolute advantage in coffee over most other countries. In this case, it is clear that Brazil will export its coffee to other countries in the global marketplace.

COMPARATIVE ADVANTAGE

Some countries have an absolute advantage in more than one product. They must compare the unit cost of each product. Then they decide which ones to produce and which ones to import.

The United States has a comparative advantage in producing high-tech products because of its **infrastructure**, raw materials, and educated work force. Products include airplanes, computers, high-tech machinery, entertainment, and telecommunications.

Some emerging nations have large, unskilled labor forces available at low costs. Labor-intensive industries—ones that rely on labor as opposed to machinery—do well in these countries. Emerging nations can produce labor-intensive toys, clothing, and shoes at a lower unit cost than most industrialized nations. They have a comparative advantage when manufacturing these goods. It is more cost-effective for high-wage countries like the United States to buy those items from emerging nations.

BENEFITS OF INTERNATIONAL TRADE

Consumers, producers, workers, and nations benefit from international trade in different ways. Consumers benefit from the competition that the foreign companies offer. This competition encourages the production of high-quality goods with lower prices. The variety of goods increases as more producers market their goods in other countries. Individuals have more options when making purchasing decisions.

Many producers today expand their business by conducting operations in other countries. Hewlett-Packard®, IBM®, and H.J. Heinz® report that over 50 percent of their sales are made overseas. About one-third of the profits of U.S. businesses come from international trade and foreign investments. As a result, businesses that want to be successful should consider using international trade. Even small businesses sell products that are used all over the world.

Workers also benefit from international trade. Increased trade leads to higher employment rates both at home and abroad. For example, according "to Toyota®, a Japanese company, more than 30,000 Americans are employed by this company in the United States. Thousands of U.S. manufacturing firms employ workers because they have a strong export business.

Nations as a whole benefit from international trade. Increased foreign investment in a country often improves the standard of living for that country's people. Individuals have more options to choose from when making purchasing decisions. Economic alliances among nations often solidify political alliances that foster peace.

> ### ✓ Reading Check
>
> **Contrast** What is the difference between absolute advantage and comparative advantage?

Brazil is the largest producer of coffee in the world, so it has an absolute advantage over all other countries. China produces rice. *Does China have an absolute advantage or comparative advantage over the United States in the production of rice?*

BRAZIL

Absolute Advantage

David Freund/Getty Images

GOVERNMENT INVOLVEMENT IN INTERNATIONAL TRADE

All nations control and monitor their trade with businesses in other countries. The U.S. government monitors imports through the customs division of the U.S. Treasury Department. All goods that enter the United States from another country are subject to search and review by U.S. customs officials. Other countries also check incoming goods. All U.S. citizens and businesses must meet the customs requirements of foreign countries when exporting goods.

BALANCE OF TRADE

Nations must keep track of their international trade to be aware of their economic status. The difference in value between exports and imports is called **balance of trade**. A trade surplus occurs when a nation exports more than it imports.

A negative balance of trade, or trade deficit, occurs when a nation imports more than it exports.

TRADE DEFICIT

The large U.S. trade deficit may seem surprising because the United States is the world's biggest exporter. Some analysts believe this situation exists because Americans purchase more goods and services than do people of other nations. Others believe that the United States is now focusing more on providing services, making it more economical to import goods that were once domestically manufactured. The textile trade is a perfect example of this trend. Most apparel sold in the United States is imported from foreign countries, many of which are located in Asia. For example, the United States has a huge trade deficit with China in the area of textiles.

MARKETING CASE STUDY

Global Philanthropists

A global nonprofit venture capital firm called Acumen Fund is helping people in developing nations. It finds out what small villagers need and then researches a simple solution. The problems generally fall into three categories: health, water, and housing. Acumen uses the donations it receives to invest and loan money to companies in those developing countries. Then the companies can produce the needed products and services.

Global Solutions

In Africa, malaria is a major health problem. Acumen financed an existing business: A to Z Textile Mills of Tanzania. This helped the company create a specially designed bed net with an insecticide. The insecticide kills mosquitoes that spread malaria.

In India, where water is scarce, an inexpensive drip-irrigation kit was designed to help farmers. An Indian company started with Acumen financing was created to help provide information to poor rural residents about health, pensions, and government resources. The business model consists of information-hub kiosks equipped with computers, modems, digital cameras, and fax machines. Villagers pay a small fee for each transaction. They can apply for loans or look for jobs. These information kiosks can now be found all over India's countryside.

English Language Arts/Writing

Investigate Research developing countries around the world and select one country to support. Write a letter to Acumen recommending a specific project the company should consider.

CDC/James Gathany

Ancient Seasoning

From the Old English *garleac*, meaning "spear leek," garlic originated in Central Asia some 6,000 years ago. Worshipped by pharaohs and used as protection against vampires, this small white bulb eventually found its way into world cuisine. Garlic reached America in the 1700s, but was not appreciated by gourmets until the 1940s.

Garlic Showdown China has cornered the garlic market, supplying 75 percent of the world's garlic. "We can meet any specifications," promises one Chinese farmer. Consumers can buy garlic fresh or frozen, in flakes, paste, or granules, and in decorated braids with colors ranging from white to purple.
All of this worries U.S. growers. The U.S. garlic industry peaked in 1999 and now ranks fifth in sales. "We're going to fight," says a farmer from California where 90 percent of U.S. garlic is grown.

English Language Arts/Writing

Report Research the differences between the U.S. and Chinese garlic industries and write a short editorial that weighs the benefits of purchasing each type of garlic.

Here are some entry-level phrases that are used in conversations about marketing all over the world.

English	Chinese
Hello	ni hao
Goodbye	zai jian
How are you?	ni hao ma?
Thank you	xie xie
You're welcome	bu ke qi

TRADE AGREEMENTS AND ALLIANCES

Governments make agreements with each other to establish guidelines for international trade and to set up trade alliances. Some milestones in the progress toward worldwide free trade are formation of the World Trade Organization, the North American Free Trade Agreement, and the European Union. To view specific United States trade agreements visit the *United States Trade Representative* Web site.

THE WORLD TRADE ORGANIZATION

The **World Trade Organization (WTO)** is a global coalition of nations that make the rules governing international trade. The WTO was formed in 1995 as the successor to the General Agreement on Tariffs and Trade (GATT). GATT was an international trade agreement designed to open markets and promote global free trade. It reduced tariffs and created a common set of trading rules. GATT had no enforcement power, so it created the WTO to police the agreement and resolve disputes among nations. For example, in 2009, the WTO ruled in favor of the United States, which had alleged that European countries subsidize Airbus.

The WTO also manages world trade by studying important trade issues and evaluating the health of the world economy. It deals with activities that GATT was unable to address, including intellectual property rights, investments, and services.

THE WTO, FOR OR AGAINST?

Supporters of the WTO and free trade stress that globalization and the expansion of trade have created enormous wealth in both rich and previously poor countries.

Free trade supporters believe global prosperity can be maintained and expanded only through a borderless economy. This requires a set of rules that is universally accepted. Advocates argue that such a system is the only way to ensure fairness and avoid damaging trade wars.

Critics of the WTO raise concerns about democracy, labor rights, and the environment. They charge that the WTO makes decisions affecting all of society on a commercial basis. They do not like giving a nonelected body the power to overrule the government on issues of environmental protection and labor rights. Some of the more radical critics want the organization disbanded. Others want to transform it into a body that addresses social and environmental concerns as well as economic ones.

Image Source

NORTH AMERICAN FREE TRADE AGREEMENT

The **North American Free Trade Agreement (NAFTA)** is an international trade agreement among the United States, Canada, and Mexico. It went into effect on January 1, 1994. The principal benefit of NAFTA is increased trade with Mexico.

The main goal of NAFTA was to abolish all trade barriers and investment restrictions among the three countries by 2009. Tariffs were eliminated immediately on thousands of goods traded between Mexico and the United States, including food, clothing, and automobiles.

EUROPEAN UNION

The **European Union (EU)** is Europe's trading bloc. In 1992, the Maastricht Treaty created the EU and established free trade among its member nations. The treaty also created a single European currency (the euro) and a central bank. The euro replaced such national currencies as the French franc and the German mark.

Other provisions of the Maastricht Treaty relate to fair competitive practices, environmental and safety standards, and security matters. To be considered part of the European Union, all countries had to conform to the EU's political, economic, and legal standards.

 After You Read | **Section 4.1**

Review Key Concepts

1. **Explain** how countries benefit from international trade.
2. **Distinguish** between tariffs, quotas, and embargoes.
3. **Describe** the common goal or purpose of WTO, NAFTA, and the EU trade agreements.

Practice Academics

Social Studies

4. What are the pros and cons of United States protectionism during difficult economic times? Identify them and then take a position, pro or con, on the issue. Write a brief statement of your position and share it with your classmates.

Mathematics

5. If a Japanese company reported a 5.3 percent increase in trade surplus from last year's 160 billion yen, what would be this year's net profit in yen?

   Math Concept **Numbers and Operations: Percent Increase** A percent increase can be calculated in one step by multiplying the original amount by a percent greater than 100.

   Starting Hints To solve the problem think of this year's trade surplus as 105.3 percent of last year's. Convert the percent to a decimal number. Multiply that decimal number by 160 billion yen, last year's trade surplus, to find the dollar amount of this year's trade surplus.

 **connectED.mcgraw-hill.com**

Check your answers.

For help, go to the Math Skills Handbook located at the back of this book.

READING GUIDE

Before You Read

Prior Knowledge How does a PEST analysis help a company assess its place in the market?

Objectives

- **List** forms of international trade.
- **Identify** political, economic, socio-cultural, and technological factors that affect international business.
- **Understand** global marketing strategies.

The Main Idea

Besides language barriers, there are many other factors that must be considered for doing international business.

Vocabulary

Content Vocabulary
- licensing
- contract manufacturing
- joint venture
- foreign direct investment (FDI)
- multinationals
- mini-nationals
- globalization
- adaptation
- customization

Academic Vocabulary

You will find these words in your reading and on your tests. Make sure you know their meanings.
- proprietary
- corporate

Graphic Organizer

Draw or print this chart to list factors that affect international businesses.

International Business	Global Environmental Scan	Market Strategies
_____	_____	_____
_____	_____	_____
_____	_____	_____
_____		

connectED.mcgraw-hill.com

Print this graphic organizer.

MARKETING CORE FUNCTION

Market Planning

The Global Marketplace

DOING BUSINESS INTERNATIONALLY

The global marketplace has been growing with the increased acceptance of capitalism around the world, advances in technology such as Internet connections, and the reduction of trade barriers. Global news coverage is instantaneous, connecting people throughout the world. These factors have encouraged businesses to venture into foreign countries. In this section, you will see what it takes for a business to become a global player.

Trade agreements by governments set the guidelines for businesses to operate in the global marketplace. Getting involved in international trade can mean importing, exporting, licensing, contract manufacturing, joint ventures, or foreign direct investment. Each of these options offers a different level of risk and control. **Figure 4.1** (page 94) shows how the profit potential increases as the level of financial commitment, risk, and marketing control increase for each market entry option.

As You Read

Connect What risks are involved in trying to learn a new skill?

IMPORTING

Importing involves purchasing goods from a foreign country. A domestic company that wants to expand its product selections can begin importing goods. Products imported for the U.S. market must meet the same standards as domestic products, including those imposed by the Food and Drug Administration. If these standards are met, most products can be imported without prior government approval.

A quota can limit entry of certain goods into the country. Quotas exist on agriculture, food products, and other merchandise.

Once a quota is reached for a certain item, no more of that item may enter the country. Any shipment in excess of the quota is quarantined by U.S. Customs. Because understanding importing policies can be difficult, U.S. businesses usually hire customs brokers—specialists licensed by the U.S. Treasury Department. Customs brokers know the laws, procedures, and tariffs governing imports. They handle over 90 percent of all imports because of the complex procedures involved.

> **❝ What does it take to become a global player? ❞**

EXPORTING

A domestic company that wishes to enter into the global marketplace with minimal risk and control might consider exporting. Domestic companies that want to export their goods and services can get help from the United States government through its Internet export portal and at its BuyUSA Web site.

LICENSING

Licensing involves letting another company, or licensee, use a trademark, patent, special formula, company name, or some other intellectual property for a fee or royalty. This type of market entry has its pros and cons. With licensing, a foreign company makes the product using the information or guidelines provided by the licensor. If the product is a success in the foreign country, the licensor has gained entry with minimal risk. If the product fails, the licensor will have a harder time trying to enter the market in the future.

A special type of licensing is franchising. In a franchise agreement, a franchisor grants the franchisee the rights to operate under the company name. The agreement involves following specific guidelines for operation to foster a unified image of the franchisor. Many fast-food chains, like McDonald's®, Wendy's®, and Burger King®, have franchised operations in foreign countries. Even though these companies are operating in different countries, there are elements of their stores, menus, and service that are the same.

CONTRACT MANUFACTURING

Contract manufacturing has become popular as emerging countries offer facilities, know-how, and inexpensive labor. **Contract manufacturing** involves hiring a foreign manufacturer to make products according to a company's specifications. The finished goods are either sold in that country or exported. Many U.S. companies that sell clothing, toys, golf clubs, and computers use contract manufacturers in emerging countries to manufacture their products.

The major benefit is lower wages, which allow companies to be more competitive in their pricing. One of the pitfalls of contract manufacturing is that **proprietary** information must be given to these companies. Golf clubs are an example. In China, molds of new golf club heads have been stolen by workers and sold to counterfeiters. The counterfeit clubs are then sold as copies or knockoffs in the United States and abroad for much less than the brand-name clubs.

JOINT VENTURES

A **joint venture** is a business enterprise that a domestic company and a foreign company undertake together. In some countries, foreign investors are not permitted to own 100 percent of a business. If a company wants to conduct business in those countries, it must find a local business partner, thus creating a joint venture. This is often a good idea even when it is not mandated by law. Domestic business partners know the market and procedures for conducting business in their own country.

FIGURE 4.1 | **Doing Business Internationally**

Level of Risk and Control International trade includes importing, exporting, licensing, contract manufacturing, joint ventures, and foreign direct investment. Each of these options involves a different level of risk and control. *What advice would you give to a small or medium-sized company interested in international trade?*

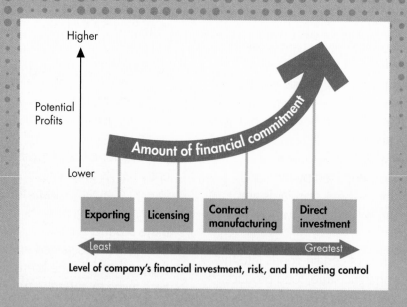

As an example of a joint venture, consider Viacom, Inc.® It owns CBS, Nickelodeon, and MTV, and it has a minority share in a joint venture with Shanghai Media Group. That means Viacom has operations in both the United States and China.

FOREIGN DIRECT INVESTMENT

All the joint ventures described above are considered foreign direct investments. A **foreign direct investment (FDI)** is the establishment of a business in a foreign country. It can take many forms and is used for many purposes.

Sometimes that may involve no more than setting up an office with a staff to maintain a presence in that country. Higher levels of direct investment involve acquisitions of existing foreign companies and construction of facilities such as manufacturing plants and retail stores. Honda®, a Japanese company, has invested in several countries. It has foreign direct investment of approximately $9 billion in North America. In the United States, Honda has eight manufacturing plants and several other related businesses in various states.

MULTINATIONALS AND MINI-NATIONALS

Multinationals are large corporations that have operations in several countries. About one-third of the world's private-sector assets are controlled by more than 37,000 transnational corporations. These corporations have more than 170,000 foreign affiliates. The affiliates are companies that do business in international markets.

Apple® Inc., Procter and Gamble®, Unilever®, Nike®, PepsiCo®, and Coca Cola® are multinational firms. Nike has manufacturing operations in more than 50 countries. The products from these operations are sold in more than 160 countries. **Mini-nationals** are midsize or smaller companies that have operations in foreign countries.

Multinationals and mini-nationals are different from domestic businesses because of how they generate revenue. Multinationals make their money from foreign investments in factories, offices, and other facilities abroad. All these investments are referred to as FDIs. The difference between multinationals and mini-nationals is their size.

Reading Check

Contrast How is franchising different from foreign direct investment?

DIGITAL NATION

The iPhone Conquers the Globe

Apple® Computers launched the iPhone to long lines and big headlines in the U.S. on June 29, 2007. Within a year the product was available in 27 countries, including Australia, Japan, and Mexico, and had sold over 14 million units.

International Challenges

When it introduced the iPhone on the international market, Apple set up exclusive distribution deals with a single cell carrier in each country. Then legislation in several nations forced a halt to such exclusive deals.

The company quickly switched its strategy. Apple began to distribute the iPhone through a variety of cell carriers, which boosted sales. By 2010 the iPhone dominated the smart phone market everywhere except Asia and Africa. International sales are growing faster than U.S. sales.

Social Studies

Collaborate Discuss with your class how Apple was able to effectively analyze and evaluate the way its technology was used in the international market.

 connectED.mcgraw-hill.com

Get a Digital Nation activity.

GLOBAL ENVIRONMENTAL SCAN

Recall the factors involved in a PEST analysis (See Chapter 2). These factors can be used to evaluate a country's marketing opportunities and threats in the international market. A global environmental scan includes analysis of political and economic factors, socio-cultural differences, and technological levels.

POLITICAL FACTORS

Political factors include a government's stability, its trade regulations and agreements, and any other laws that impact a company's operation.

GOVERNMENT STABILITY

A government's stability is an important factor when considering international business operations. If there are changes in the government, investors become wary. For example, when Luiz Inacio Lula da Silva, a left-wing politician, won Brazil's presidential election in 2002, stock prices plunged. Stocks regained strength when businesses saw that President Da Silva supported continued economic reform.

TRADE REGULATIONS AND LAWS

A business must keep abreast of new trade regulations, which can force companies to reconsider doing business in a country. Changes in trade regulations include review of trade agreements, tariffs, and laws to protect intellectual property rights and foreign direct investment. For example, on January 1, 2004 the United States-Chile Free Trade Agreement went into force. Under this agreement, Chile must adopt stronger standards for the protection of intellectual property rights. This means that Chile must adopt rules similar to those in the United States for copyrights, trademarks, patents, and trade secrets.

Domestic laws must be followed by foreign marketers. For example, Sweden does not permit advertising to children, and war toys cannot be advertised in Greece. These regulations are important for toy retailers, such as Toys "R" Us®.

Microlending

The concept of microlending is a growing field of interest in international business. Premal Shah founded Kiva, a company that facilitates investors' lending small amounts of money to people in emerging countries to help them get their businesses up and running. *How might the practice of microlending be incorporated into a global PEST scan?*

Premal Shah
President, Kiva.org
Micro-loans in developing countries

Ask Premal Shah Why He Loves His BlackBerry

"Our website, Kiva.org, lets people make low interest micro-loans to the working poor in developing countries. A little seed capital can buy a sewing machine, a rickshaw—the means to self-sufficiency. My BlackBerry® is the tool I use to constantly check how we're progressing. Kiva is growing so fast, it's nonstop interaction with people all over the world. At any moment, I need to know what's going on, and be able to respond quickly and creatively. My BlackBerry is a liberating phenomenon."

Find out why people love BlackBerry, or tell us why you love yours, at www.blackberry.com/ask.

::: BlackBerry

ECONOMIC FACTORS

Key economic factors relevant to starting a business in another country include infrastructure, the quality and cost of labor, employee benefits, taxes, the standard of living, and foreign exchange rates. In addition, economic stability of that nation should be considered.

INFRASTRUCTURE

Things like undependable telephone service or inadequate roads would rule out a location for some businesses. Yet these same infrastructure factors would be an opportunity for companies involved in building roads, energy plants, and tele-communications systems. For example, Poland and the Czech Republic had to carry out environmental cleanup to meet the entry requirements for membership in the European Union. U.S. companies that have expertise in that area could partner with companies in Poland and the Czech Republic to help them with these projects.

LABOR FORCE

The quality and cost of a labor force is another important element in the decision to enter the market in another country. The educational and skill levels of the workers, as well as the customary wages and employment laws are important pieces of information. For example, India has been supporting technology education and now has a pool of highly qualified workers whose wages are lower than those for similar workers in the United States. U.S. companies like AOL®, Yahoo!®, and Google® have recognized this opportunity. They now look to India for computer programming and other computer-related expertise.

EMPLOYEE BENEFITS

In most countries, employers must pay for mandated employee benefits in addition to employees' wages. Many companies do not invest in France because of its labor policies. France restricts the work week to 35 hours and requires companies to consult with employees before downsizing or restructuring. Payroll taxes and employee benefits are high. The cost of hiring a new employee is higher in France than in many countries.

TAXES

Other costs include taxes on property and profits. Countries that want to attract foreign investment may offer reduced taxes for a period of time as an incentive.

Switzerland has been known for its low **corporate** taxes since 1997. In 2008 additional tax incentives were introduced. As a result of these tax breaks, Switzerland has experienced a significant growth in foreign direct investment. Some large companies, like Procter & Gamble®, McDonalds®, Kraft Foods®, Nissan®, Starbucks®, and Google®, have their European headquarters in Switzerland.

STANDARD OF LIVING

Standard of living can be a consideration if a business is considering a country as a market.

When Honda entered China's consumer market, it recognized that most Chinese people could not afford cars. The company targeted the motorcycle market instead and was very successful.

The number of middle-income workers is increasing in poorer nations. This increases the demand for all types of ordinary consumer goods. U.S. products like soaps, detergents, breakfast cereals, snack foods, cell phones, and soft drinks are gaining popularity among consumers in emerging nations.

FOREIGN EXCHANGE RATE

The foreign exchange rate is the price of one country's money currency if purchased with another country's currency. Exchange rates vary every business day. The exchange rate for a nation's currency based on the U.S. dollar is an important factor to consider.

Changes in a nation's currency exchange affect businesses that sell abroad. If the dollar strengthens in value against other currencies, that means it costs more yen, euros, or pesos to buy one dollar. It also means it costs more yen, euros, or pesos to buy one dollar's worth of U.S.-made products. If the U.S. dollar is devalued, U.S. products are more attractive in the global marketplace.

ECONOMIC INDICATORS

Economic indicators used to evaluate a country's economic stability are the same for all nations. You can study inflation, unemployment, and business failure rates to determine how stable a nation's economy is. Interest rate data and retail sales figures also offer information on economic stability.

SOCIO-CULTURAL FACTORS

Before conducting business in a foreign country, a cross-cultural analysis should be performed. It should include socio-cultural factors such as language, symbols, holidays, religious observances, and social and business etiquette.

Differences in language and customs make international trade more challenging than doing business domestically. Cultural symbols are often different. In the United States, the number 13 is considered unlucky. In China and Japan, the number four is unpopular because it relates to death. Marketers should consider such symbols.

Holidays and religious observances are part of a country's culture too. In India, the cow is sacred, so no beef is sold there. Marketers must heed these cultural differences when creating, naming, packaging, and advertising products.

Social and business etiquette is critical when doing business abroad. A common practice in one nation may take on a different meaning elsewhere.

Gift giving is another area of concern. A gift may be considered part of business etiquette in some countries. However, it might be considered an illegal bribe in the United States.

TECHNOLOGICAL FACTORS

Technology is changing the ways that businesses can get involved in international trade. Studying a country's technology means taking into consideration even the most basic factors such as measurement systems and electric voltage standards.

It is important to take a thorough look at the use of computers, faxes, voicemail, wireless phones, and the Internet. A visit to the CIA's *World Fact Book* Web site provides information about the number of telephones (land lines and mobile), radio and television broadcast stations, and Internet users in a given country. These facts must be considered if a company is trying to do business in another country.

Reading Check

Interpret How can infrastructure be an opportunity as well as a threat to foreign investment?

Insuring Business in another Country

This ad suggests that businesses need to consider buying insurance to cover risks in a foreign country. *What kinds of risks might a company encounter in a foreign country?*

Zurich HelpPoint

One global insurance program
for your expanding business.
Even for places you've never been.

Zurich HelpPoint is here when you need more than just insurance. So we offer the Zurich Multinational Insurance Proposition (MIP)®. It helps you keep global insurance programs compliant when you expand your business to a new market and expose yourself to new risks. The strength of Zurich MIP lies in a transparent and thorough set of solutions for writing and maintaining global insurance programs in over 170 countries. Our game-changing solution can help you sleep better at night, no matter the time zone. For more details about Zurich HelpPoint, visit www.zurich.com

Here to help your world.

 ZURICH

Because change happenz.

In the United States, coverages are underwritten by member companies of Zurich in North America, including Zurich American Insurance Company. Certain coverages not available in all states. Some coverages may be written on a non-admitted basis through licensed surplus lines brokers. Risk engineering services are provided by Zurich Services Corporation. *patent pending

GLOBAL MARKETING STRATEGIES

In planning and making decisions about the four Ps (see Chapter 1) of the marketing mix, global marketers need to consider all the factors that were analyzed as part of the PEST analysis. There are three marketing strategies marketers can use when selling abroad. **Globalization** means complete standardization. New product development and complete customization are also options. **Figure 4.2** (p. 100) shows examples of the global marketing strategies for product and promotion decisions.

GLOBALIZATION

Globalization is selling the same product and using the same promotion methods in all countries. Globalization is mass marketing on a global scale. Very few products can use this marketing strategy.

HOW GLOBALIZATION WORKS

Companies can use the same product and same promotion if they have found a common need across cultures. Benefits of globalization are global brand recognition and reduced marketing costs. A company only has to design one logo and one ad campaign. A challenge is that it is difficult to translate words and phrases so they have the same intended meaning in different countries.

GLOBALIZATION EXAMPLES

Coca-Cola® and other soft drink companies can use a globalization marketing strategy by offering the same version of their products. They can use the same advertising message in countries around the world. Another example of a company that answers common needs across the globe is Microsoft®. Users need computer programs to function in different languages, but the basic applications remain the same. This is also true of Internet search engines.

The success of e-commerce has increased the power of globalization in some instances, particularly where technology is involved.

ADAPTATION

Companies study the characteristics of a country and find ways to target consumers with similar needs and wants. That often requires adapting their products or promotions. Sometimes only the product is changed, while in other cases, only the promotion is changed. **Adaptation** is a company's use of an existing product or promotion from which changes are made. These changes better suit the characteristics of a country or region. This type of market segmentation has the advantage of addressing very specific cultural tastes and interests, which makes market acceptance more reliable. When compared to globalization there is a slight increase in marketing costs. There is also an increase in research and development, which may be considered a disadvantage.

PRODUCT ADAPTATION

Changing a product to meet different consumer needs or to reflect the cultural differences in a foreign market is product adaptation. In some cases, a product's brand name is changed. For example, Unilever's® Sunsilk hair products are called Seda (which means silk) in Latin America. In addition, Sunsilk's ingredients are formulated to match consumers' needs (in this case, typical hair types and styles) in different countries.

PROMOTION ADAPTATION

A promotion adaptation strategy involves changing the advertising message to reflect the values, familiar images, and cultural differences in a foreign market. The change may be as simple as using a popular model or star from a respective country in the different ads. In some cases, the advertising is changed in order to adhere to specific government regulations. For example, McDonald's must use adults in its advertising in Sweden, where advertising to children is prohibited.

FIGURE 4.2 | Global Marketing Strategies

Marketing Abroad When marketing products in foreign countries, companies must make product and promotion decisions. Some create completely new products for specific countries (customization), while others use the same products and promotions for every country (globalization). Between these two extremes are companies that keep their products' brand names but vary their products and/or promotions enough to meet local tastes. Here are some examples of each strategy. *How do companies reach customers around the world?*

GLOBALIZATION Häagen-Dazs® ice cream uses the same logo, product packaging, and promotional messages around the world. The name Häagen Dazs is not derived from any language. It is simply two words that were made up by company founder Reuben Mattus. Mattus created a unique and original name that evokes the spelling systems used in several European countries. This is an example of foreign branding, a term describing the implied superiority of products and services with foreign or foreign-sounding names.

CUSTOMIZATION This global marketing strategy involves specially designed products for certain countries or regions. By customizing a product, it can reach a very specific market with new products and promotions. For example, Nestle's® developed custom packaging with a soccer player's image for its Milo drink mix product specifically for the South African market. In South Africa, soccer (known as "football") is one of the country's most popular sports.

PRODUCT ADAPTATION The William Underwood® Company began exporting its spreadable deviled ham to Venezuela in 1896. Since 1961, the product has been produced in Venezuela. With product adaptation, the company keeps the same product but changes the name of the product to Diablitos Jamon Endiablado and the language on the packaging to Spanish.

PROMOTION ADAPTATION Promotion adaptation involves changing some part of the promotional message or visuals used in the promotional campaigns for different markets. Advertisements for McDonald's use the same promotional message (in different languages) and format but different visuals and promotional messages to appeal to customers from different countries.

CUSTOMIZATION

Customization involves creating specially designed products or promotions for certain countries or regions. Each geographical area where a product is sold or a service is offered becomes a unique market segment. For example, Coca-Cola® has partnered with the China Academy of Chinese Medical Sciences to create drinks solely for the Chinese market. Its first drink was called Yuan Ye ("Original Leaf"), which is a ready-to-drink tea. The goal of the partnership is to incorporate herbs often used in Chinese medicine into drinks for the Chinese market. The company decided that it was worthwhile to change its products for this market.

Customization is the optimized form of market segmentation. That means companies spend a lot of time researching demographic, geographic, psychographic, and behavioral characteristics.

As a result, customization has the advantage of reaching a very specific market target with new products and promotions. The excitement and interest generated by the new product is an advantage to a company. The disadvantage is the increased cost involved. Educating the new market about the benefit of a new product is more costly than introducing a brand extension of an existing product. New promotions are equally costly and risky. Once the product catches on, the company can determine whether it was a good investment.

After You Read   Section 4.2

Review Key Concepts

1. **Describe** an example of a political factor that could discourage a business from engaging in international trade with a given country.
2. **Identify** the socio-cultural factors that make doing business abroad difficult. Cite an example.
3. **Name** and give an example of three different global marketing strategies.

Practice Academics
Social Studies

4. Translate a magazine ad or advertising slogan into a foreign language you are studying. What problems did you encounter with the translation? Suggest any changes and present your new ad or slogan in class.

Mathematics

5. Assume the currency exchange rate between the United States and Canada is $1.10, which means $1 in U.S. currency is equal to $1.10 in Canadian currency. If a sweater costs $50 at a Gap store in Montreal, how much should it cost at a Gap in Detroit?

   Math Concept **Numbers and Operations: Exchange Rates** Exchange rates are decimal numbers that represent the value of one currency in relation to another.

   Starting Hint To solve this problem, divide the amount the sweater costs in Canadian currency by the exchange rate.

 connectED.mcgraw-hill.com

Check your answers.

For help, go to the Math Skills Handbook located at the back of this book.

Global Analysis

A global environmental scan analyzes political, economic, socio-cultural, and technological factors.

GLOBAL PEST SCAN

Political

- Government Stability
- Trade Regulations
- Trade Agreements
- Laws

Economic

- Infrastructure
- Quality And Cost Of Labor
- Employee Benefits
- Taxes
- Standard Of Living
- Foreign Exchange Rates

Socio-cultural

- Language
- Symbols
- Holidays
- Religious Observances
- Social Etiquette
- Business Etiquette

Technological

- Measurement Systems
- Electronic Voltage Standards
- Use Of Computers
- Number Of Telephones, Radios, And Television Stations

Review and Activities

Written Summary

- International trade is necessary because of the interdependence of nations.
- Customers, workers, and countries benefit from international trade because of competition, increased employment, and higher standards of living.
- Currently, the United States has a trade deficit, which means it imports more than it exports.
- Trade agreements and alliances, such as the WTO, NAFTA, and the EU aim to establish guidelines for international trade.
- Three types of trade barriers are tariffs, quotas, and embargoes.
- Businesses can get involved in international trade through importing, exporting, licensing, contract manufacturing, joint ventures, and foreign direct investments.
- A global environmental scan analyzes political, economic, socio-cultural, and technological factors.
- Global marketing strategy options include globalization, adaptations of product and promotion, and customization.

Review Content Vocabulary and Academic Vocabulary

1. Arrange the vocabulary terms below into groups of related words. Explain why you put the words together.

Content Vocabulary
- international trade (p. 85)
- imports (p. 85)
- exports (p. 85)
- balance of trade (p. 87)
- free trade (p. 88)
- tariff (p. 88)
- quota (p. 89)
- embargo (p. 89)
- protectionism (p. 89)
- World Trade Organization (WTO) (p. 90)
- North American Free Trade Agreement (NAFTA) (p. 91)
- European Union (EU) (p. 91)
- licensing (p. 93)
- contract manufacturing (p. 94)
- joint venture (p. 94)
- foreign direct investment (FDI) (p. 95)
- multinationals (p. 95)
- mini-nationals (p. 95)
- globalization (p. 99)
- adaptation (p. 99)
- customization (p. 101)

Academic Vocabulary
- potential (p. 85)
- infrastructure (p. 85)
- proprietary (p. 94)
- corporate (p. 97)

Assess for Understanding

2. **Define** What is *economic interdependence?*
3. **Describe** How are governments involved in international trade?
4. **Explain** Why is the U.S. balance of trade skewed toward a trade deficit?
5. **Imagine** What are possible reasons for using each of the three trade restrictions?
6. **Discuss** What are the relative merits of three trade agreements and alliances?
7. **Compare and Contrast** How is a global environmental scan different from a SWOT analysis?
8. **Debate** What are the advantages and disadvantages of using globalization (mass marketing) versus customization (market segmentation) for a new food product and for newly designed golf balls? What is different in the way the products would be marketed?
9. **Discuss** Should organizations that promote free trade have environmental or social checks and balances? Why or why not?

 21st Century Skills

Teamwork Skills

10. International Trade Benefits Work in a group to prepare an oral presentation to explain international trade to a foreign language class in your school. Include an explanation and examples of why it is important, its benefits and disadvantages, and what government measures affect or regulate it. Also include what business ventures foster it and why learning a foreign language is beneficial for pursuing a career in the global marketplace. Present your findings in a written outline, using word processing software, and create an oral presentation, using presentation software. Cite your sources.

Technology Applications

11. Global Recession Research the global recession in 2008–2009 and how it affected business activities in one country. Consider how that country's balance of trade, foreign direct investment, and GDP were affected. Use word processing software, charts, and graphs to prepare a short report on your findings.

e-Marketing Skills

12. Global Scan Visit the Web site for the CIA's World Fact Book to conduct a global environmental scan for a country of your choice. Decide if it is a country where you could sell American-made products or if it is a country where you might want to have goods manufactured. Consider the following questions as you complete your research:

- Are any of your competitors in the market in this country?
- What are the risks of exporting as compared to foreign direct investment (FDI)?
- What will you need to do to distinguish your product from others in the country?
- What resources (human, capital, and natural) will you need?

Build Academic Skills

Social Studies

13. Embargo on Cuba The United States placed a trade embargo on Cuba in 1962. Research how that embargo has changed between 2000 and 2009. What U.S. companies benefited from those changes? If the embargo was lifted completely, what U.S. companies would find business opportunities in Cuba?

English Language Arts

14. Diversity and the Global Marketplace Prepare a brief presentation that addresses the impact and value of diversity in the marketplace, as well as how diversity affects marketing in a global marketplace. Include specific examples in your oral presentation.

Mathematics

15. If the exchange rate is 13 Mexican pesos for one U.S. dollar, how many pesos would you get for $5,000? Research prices for items such as food and lodging in Mexico. How many days could you afford to stay in Cancun? Use a spreadsheet program to present a report on the daily costs of your trip.

Math Concept **Choosing an operation** To solve this problem, multiply the U.S. dollar amount by the number of pesos it is worth.

For help, go to the **Math Skills Handbook** located at the back of this book.

Standardized Test Practice

Directions Read the following questions. On a separate piece of paper, write the best possible answer for each one.

1. Assume the exchange rate between the United States dollar and Euro is .77, which means that $1 is equal to .77 Euros. How much would $50 be worth in Euros?

   A. $27.00   **C.** $38.50
   B. $77.00   **D.** $88.50

2. **True or False** Adaptation and customization are examples of mass marketing on a global scale.

   T

   F

3. _____ is when a government establishes economic policies that restrict imports in order to protect domestic industries.

Test-Taking Tip

When working on a test, keep things moving along. Work on a problem until you get stuck. Think about it for a minute or two, and if nothing comes to mind, then drop it and go on to another problem.

DECA Connection Role Play

Intern
Advertising Agency

Situation Assume the role of an intern in a global advertising agency. A new client is an educational toy company that is considering marketing its goods abroad. This client has had great success with its products in the domestic market. However, this company is unsure whether its toys will be successful across the globe.

Since this company has not marketed its products internationally, its employees do not know about the concepts of licensing, contract manufacturing, franchising, joint venture, and foreign direct investment. You may not need to explain the differences between each of these concepts. However, you will need to make a recommendation to the company about how it should do business internationally.

Activity You are to prepare an outline of a presentation to your mentor (judge). Include the pros and cons of international trade and the challenges that companies face when marketing toys in a foreign country.

Evaluation You will be evaluated on how well you meet the following performance indicators:

- Explain the nature of global trade.
- Discuss the impact of cultural and social environments on global trade.
- Assess global trends and opportunities.
- Discuss the global environment in which businesses operate.
- Identify considerations in implementing international marketing strategies.

 connectED.mcgraw-hill.com

Download the Competitive Events Activity for more Role-Play practice.

A Marketing Plan
for a Recession-Proof Toy

What was your favorite childhood toy? Do you think it was recession-proof?

Scenario

You work for a toy manufacturer that sells toys in different countries. There is a global recession, which does not appear to be ending soon. Mattel® Inc. and Hasbro® Inc., large global toy manufacturers, have lowered their sales projections. Walmart® created its own doll line to sell for $5 and cut the prices of other toys. Toy departments at K-Mart® and Sears'® look for toys that will sell. Spin Master® makes popular Bakugan™ products, and another small toy manufacturer came out with a tiny robotic hamster that retails for $10.

The owner of your company has put together a committee of employees from the design, production, and marketing departments. Each member of the team is expected to come up with an idea for a new recession-proof toy and marketing plan for it.

The Skills You'll Use

Academic Skills Reading, writing, social studies, researching, and analyzing

Basic Skills Speaking, listening, thinking, and interpersonal

Technology Skills Word processing, presentation, spreadsheet, telecommunication, the Internet

Your Objective

Design a toy and create a marketing plan for it so that it can be successful in any economic environment.

STEP 1 Do Your Research

Conduct research to find out about toy companies that have created popular toys that have captured the imagination of the public. Also, conduct research about how economic factors have affected the toy industry. As you conduct your research, answer these questions:

- What political, economic, socio-cultural, and technological factors affected the toy industry during a recent recession?
- What marketing strategies were used by toy companies that did well during a recession?
- What toys appeal to children all over the world?
- What global issues have to be considered when designing a new toy?

Write a summary of your research.

STEP 2 Plan Your Project

Now that you have completed your research, you need to begin planning your project.

- Conduct a PEST analysis.
- Design a new toy by making a drawing or a model.
- Write a marketing plan for your new toy. Include the PEST analysis, objectives, and marketing strategies.
- Include suggestions for your plan's implementation, execution, and evaluation.
- Use your knowledge of economics, business cycles, and the global marketplace to make a plan for how to sell your ideas to the committee.

STEP 3 Connect with Your Community

- Share your design idea with trusted adults and children to gauge their interest in your toy.
- Ask children to identify the features they enjoy in the toys they have.
- Find similar information about consumers of toys in different countries.

STEP 4 Share What You Learn

Assume your class is the committee the owner established to come up with new toy ideas.

- Present your toy design and marketing ideas in an oral presentation. Be prepared to answer questions.
- Explain how toy companies can meet the needs of consumers during a recession.
- Provide rationale for your project with supporting research.
- Present your complete marketing plan in a written format using word processing software.
- Use software to create a slide presentation to accompany your oral report. Include one slide for each key topic in your marketing plan.

STEP 5 Evaluate Your Marketing and Academic Skills

Your project will be evaluated based on the following:

- Knowledge of global recessions and the toy industry
- Knowledge of economics, business cycles, and global marketing strategies
- Toy design and marketing plan
- Rationale for recommendation
- Organization and continuity of presentation
- Mechanics—presentation and neatness
- Speaking and listening skills

MARKETING CORE FUNCTIONS

 Market Planning

 Pricing

 Product/Service Management

 Promotion

Marketing Internship Project Checklist

Plan
✓ Conduct research on toys and recessions.
✓ Design a toy and marketing plan for it.
✓ Use the results of a PEST analysis to inform your marketing plan.

Write
✓ Describe what happens to the toy industry during a recession.
✓ Explain how the results of the PEST analysis will help the committee decide whether to develop your toy.

Present
✓ Present the new toy design and the rationale behind your marketing plan.
✓ Respond to questions posed by the audience.
✓ Consider the needs and experiences of the audience as you present research to your class.

 connectED.mcgraw-hill.com

Evaluate Download a rubric you can use to evaluate your final project.

my marketing portfolio

Internship Report When you have completed your Marketing Internship Project and oral presentation, put your written report and printouts of key slides from your oral presentation in your Marketing Portfolio.

Marketing Plan for a Recession Select a different market and a company of your choice in that market. For example, imagine that you work for a hotel chain that has locations around the world. A global recession is affecting your firm significantly. Conduct research and create a marketing plan for your hotel chain to weather this recession. How have hotels survived in other recessions? What marketing strategies do hotels use? How does your research support your proposed marketing plan? How will you use your knowledge of economics, business cycles, and global marketing strategies to create an effective plan? Prepare a written report and an oral presentation.

BUSINESS AND SOCIETY

Plan an Eco-Project

Essential Question How can companies operate successful businesses while meeting the needs of society?

Businesses not only provide goods and services, but they also have a role in local and global communities. Developing green marketing strategies has become one of the ways that socially responsible companies build consumer loyalty.

Project Goal

In the project at the end of this unit, you will develop an effective eco-project for a business.

Prepare for the Project

As you read this unit, use this checklist to prepare for the Marketing Internship Project at the end of this unit:

- Find some companies that promote eco-friendly initiatives on the Internet.
- Consider the different kinds of eco-friendly initiatives.
- Go to a local business that promotes positive environmental practices and observe its customers.

  **connectED.mcgraw-hill.com**

Project Activity
Complete a worksheet activity about social responsibility and green marketing strategies.

Marketing practitioners must recognize they serve enterprises but also act as stewards of society.

MARKETING CORE FUNCTIONS IN THIS UNIT

 Marketing Information Management

 Market Planning

Visual Literacy

Print and online advertisements are important marketing tools. This online ad promotes Aquafina®'s commitment to reduce its environmental impact in many ways.

How does this advertisement illustrate Aquafina's commitment to the environment?

SHOW WHAT YOU KNOW

the free enterprise system

Visual Literacy People who own small businesses like local shops are self-employed. If you have ever done things like yard work, babysitting, or pet sitting—and earned money doing those things, then you have been self-employed. You provided services for a client who paid you. *Do you want to be self-employed in the future? Why or why not?*

Discovery Project

Being Self-Employed

Essential Question
What are the advantages and disadvantages to being self-employed?

Project Goal

Interview someone who is self-employed. Self-employed individuals are entrepreneurs who engage in private enterprise because they own their businesses. The person may be self-employed as a plumber, an electrician, a doctor, an insurance broker, or an owner of an auto repair shop, an accounting firm, a flower shop, a bakery, or a candy store.

Ask Yourself...

- How will you find a self-employed person in your community?
- How should you approach the person to ask for an interview?
- What questions will give you helpful information during the interview?
- How will you present information you learned during the interview?

Analyze and Interpret Assess the opportunities and problems entrepreneurs have in a market-oriented economy.

 connectED.mcgraw-hill.com

Activity
Get a worksheet activity about self-employment.

Evaluate
Download a rubric you can use to evaluate your project.

DECA Connection

DECA Event Role Play

Concepts in this chapter are related to DECA competitive events that involve either an interview or role play.

Performance Indicators The performance indicators represent key skills and knowledge. Your key to success in DECA competitive events is relating them to the concepts in this chapter.

- Explain the concept of the free enterprise system.
- Explain the concept of competition.
- Explain the principles of supply and demand.
- Identify factors affecting a business's profit.
- Describe types of business activities.

DECA Prep

Role Play Practice role-playing with the DECA Connection competitive-event activity at the end of this chapter. More information about DECA events can be found on DECA's Web site.

READING GUIDE

Objectives

- **Explain** the characteristics of the free enterprise system.
- **Distinguish** between price and nonprice competition.
- **Explain** the theory of supply and demand.

The Main Idea

Countries in the global marketplace have market-oriented economic systems that feature the traits of the free enterprise system: competition, property ownership, risk, and the profit motive.

Vocabulary

Content Vocabulary
- private enterprise
- patent
- trademark
- copyright
- competition
- price competition
- nonprice competition
- monopoly
- business risk
- profit
- supply
- demand

Academic Vocabulary

You will find these words in your reading and on your tests. Make sure you know their meanings.
- purchase
- interact

Graphic Organizer

Draw or print this chart to take notes about the traits of the free enterprise system.

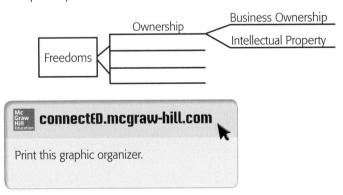

connectED.mcgraw-hill.com

Print this graphic organizer.

MARKETING CORE FUNCTION

Market Planning

Traits of Private Enterprise

BASIC PRINCIPLES

The founders of the United States defined freedom of choice as rights that are central to our society. Consumers have the freedom to **purchase** goods and services. They make these purchases with the income they earn. This income is earned from their wages and salaries at their jobs. If a consumer owns a business, income can also come from the profits of that business.

People can then invest their money in banks to earn interest or in businesses to earn dividends. All these freedoms are part of a market-oriented economic system. They are fundamental to the concept of private enterprise. **Private enterprise** is business ownership by ordinary people, not the government. It is the basis of a market-oriented economy. Private enterprise is also known as free enterprise.

The basic elements of the free enterprise system include the freedom to own property, the freedom to compete, the freedom to take risks, and the freedom to make a profit. People are encouraged to start and operate their own businesses as a part of the free enterprise system. These businesses are part of a competitive system that has no involvement from the government.

The marketplace determines prices through the interaction of supply and demand. If the supply of a product exceeds the demand, the price tends to drop. If demand is greater than supply, the price tends to go up. The government does not set prices or distribute goods and services.

The market-oriented economic system in the United States is modified because the government intervenes from time to time. It issues rules and regulations for businesses and also directly intervenes on a limited basis. It does this to protect citizens. For example, during the recession in 2008–2009, the United States government intervened in businesses such as banks and the auto industry. The government did this because it was determined that some business practices needed to be regulated.

 As You Read

Apply Consider the experiences of a self-employed person you know as you read about free enterprise.

You can opt to use your personal interest in something to open your own business. *How is this choice a defining part of free enterprise?*

Your Choice

You may or may not decide to invest your money in a company listed on the New York Stock Exchange. *What are the pros and cons of investing in company stocks?*

Being a Stockholder

OWNERSHIP

In the free enterprise system, people are free to own property, such as cars, computers, and homes. They can also own natural resources such as oil and land. You can buy anything you want as long as it is not prohibited by law. You can also do what you want with your property. You can give it away, lease it, sell it, or use it for yourself. If you engage in the free enterprise system, you try to make money from your property ownership.

" freedoms found in private enterprise make it enticing to be a business owner. "

BUSINESS OWNERSHIP

The free enterprise system encourages individuals to own businesses. In the United States, there are some restrictions on how and where those businesses may operate. Businesses may be restricted in where they can locate. These restrictions come in the form of zoning laws.

Most businesses are zoned so that they are far away from areas that are zoned for private housing. Manufacturers may be forced to comply with environmental and safety measures. They need to make products in a way that does not hurt the environment or endanger their employees.

There are many types of business. People who start and operate their own businesses are called entrepreneurs. Others support business by investing their money in parts or shares of a company. These shares of a business are called stocks and the investors are called stockholders. There are preferred stocks and common stocks. Common stockholders have voting rights so they can influence management policies. Preferred stockholders do not have voting rights. However, when a company earns money, they receive payments sooner than common stockholders. Company stocks are bought and sold daily. When a company is doing well, stock prices generally increase as more people want to buy that stock.

INTELLECTUAL PROPERTY RIGHTS

Intellectual property rights are protected. That means that a product or idea a person creates or invents is legally protected from being copied. Patents, trademarks, copyrights, and trade secrets are intellectual property rights.

If you get a **patent** on an invention, you alone own the rights to that item or idea. To ensure that protection, you would apply for a utility patent in the U.S. Patent and Trademark Office. If the patent is granted, you would have the exclusive rights to make, use, or sell that invention. The patent on your invention would protect it for up to 20 years. During this time, anyone who wanted to manufacture your product would have to pay you for its use through a licensing agreement.

A **trademark** is a word, name, symbol, sound, or color that identifies a good or service. It cannot be used by anyone but the owner. Unlike a patent, a trademark can be renewed forever, if it is being used by a business.

Trademarks A Chinese company owns the trademark "i-phone," so Apple cannot use "iPhone" to market that product in China.

A **copyright** involves anything that is authored by an individual, such as writings (books, magazine articles, etc.), music, and artwork. It gives the author the exclusive right to reproduce or sell the work. A copyright is usually valid for the life of the author plus 70 years.

A trade secret is information that a company keeps and protects for its use only. However, it is not patented. For example, Coca-Cola's® formula for Coke is a trade secret that is not protected by a patent, but the company guards the information.

When a company wants to use another's name, symbol, creative work, or product, it must get permission to do so and pay a fee for the use. A licensing agreement protects the originator's name and products. A T-shirt manufacturer might be granted a licensing agreement with the National Football League (NFL) so that it can produce T-shirts with NFL logos on them. The company will have to pay NFL Properties a fee for this permission. It will also have to agree to certain standards to protect the NFL's reputation. In addition, the NFL has control over all teams' logos and how the teams can use them.

COMPETITION

The free enterprise system encourages businesses to attract new customers and keep old ones. Other businesses try to take those same customers away. This struggle for customers is called **competition**.

Competition is an essential part of the free enterprise system. It is one of the ways the free enterprise system benefits consumers. Competition forces businesses to produce better-quality goods and services at reasonable prices.

MARKETING CASE STUDY

Instant Photo Nostalgia

The Polaroid® Company stopped production of its instant film on December 31, 2008, for its 60-year old Polaroid brand Instant cameras. Loyal users of the iconic camera were so upset they flocked to a Web site called SavePolaroid.com. Web site visitors could share their nostalgic stories. One of the Web site founders wrote, "Watching a Polaroid picture develop is like watching a memory form right before your eyes."

Polaroid Responds to Consumers

First, Polaroid introduced the Polaroid PoGo™ instant printer. The company then created the next-generation instant camera--the Point & Shoot digital camera. Camera users can select, crop, edit, and print the digital photos instantly. With the new technology, photos are completely devleoped when they leave the printer, just as they were in the original Polaroid cameras.

English Language Arts/Writing

Discuss What risk did Polaroid take when it stopped production of the film used in its traditional instant camera knowing it still had a strong following of consumers? Share your opinion with a partner and then discuss the topic as a class.

Businesses constantly look for ways to develop new products and improve old ones to attract new customers. Competition results in a wider selection of products from which to choose. The results of these efforts increase the nation's output of goods and services, as well as its standard of living.

There are two basic strategies that businesses use to compete: price competition and nonprice competition.

PRICE AND NONPRICE COMPETITION

Price competition focuses on the sale price of a product. The assumption is that, all other things being equal, consumers will buy the products that are lowest in price.

The marketing strategies used by Walmart® and Southwest Airlines® are examples of price competition. Both use their low prices as their competitive advantage. Companies that run sales and offer rebates are using price competition. A $5,000 cash-back offer by an auto manufacturer and a retailer's one-day sale that offers a 15 percent discount storewide are examples of price competition.

In **nonprice competition**, businesses choose to compete on the basis of factors that are not related to price. These factors include the quality of the products, service, financing, business location, and reputation. Some nonprice competitors also stress the qualifications or expertise of their personnel. Businesses that use nonprice competition may charge more for products than their competitors do.

Examples of nonprice competition in advertising programs stress a company's reliability, tradition, market knowledge, and special services. Free shipping and same-day delivery are examples of nonprice competition.

These examples of price and nonprice competition seem to suggest that businesses adopt one strategy or the other. In our value-oriented society, however, it is not uncommon for businesses to try to do both. As competition increases, you may see more price-oriented competitors offering services they have never offered in the past.

MONOPOLIES

When there is no competition and one firm controls the market for a given product, a monopoly exists. A **monopoly** is exclusive control over a product or the means of producing it.

Monopolies are not permitted in a market-oriented economic system because they prevent competition. A company can charge whatever it wants because there is no chance of price competition from another company. It can also control the quality of a product and who gets it. These nonprice factors cannot be challenged by other companies either. Without competition, there is nothing to stop a company from acting without regard to customers' wants and needs.

One of the most publicized monopoly cases in recent history involved Microsoft®, the computer software company. A federal judge declared Microsoft's Windows operating system a monopoly. Its technology dominance was said to have stifled innovation. The judge ruled that the situation was unfair to consumers and Microsoft's competitors. The ruling found that Windows' dominance was harmful to the free enterprise system.

The U.S. government has allowed a few monopolies to exist. These monopolies exist mainly in industries where it would be wasteful to have more than one firm. These regulated monopolies, however, are on the decline.

Utility companies, such as gas and electric companies, have been deregulated. This practice allows customers to choose their own electric and gas suppliers. The government still controls gas and electric companies' prices, but it imposes price restrictions that prevent the formerly regulated monopolies from charging excessive prices.

Along with the benefits that come from competition and private ownership of property, businesses also face risk. **Business risk** is the potential for loss or failure. As the potential for earnings gets greater, so does the risk. Putting money in the bank with guaranteed interest rates is less risky than investing in the stock market. Simply starting a company is a risk.

If you wanted to open your own business, you would probably put your savings into the enterprise. You make money if the business is successful; but if the business fails, you lose all your savings. One out of every three businesses in the United States fails after one year of operation.

Businesses also run the risk of being sued or having their name tarnished from bad publicity. This bad publicity may not even be accurate, but it can still be very damaging. Natural disasters could also ruin a business. While these events cannot be prevented, businesses must do everything they can to manage risks.

Many high-end car companies choose to compete based on factors other than price. Instead they stress their quality and reputation. *What are some other examples of businesses that use nonprice competition?*

Nonprice Competition

When an industry develops and profits are growing, more people enter that industry. This increases competition and the risk of failure for individual firms. When there are more companies in a market for the same product, they must compete for customers in the same market. Those companies that cannot compete effectively will face the possibility of failure.

You may have read of businesses closing operations in an effort to reduce losses and become more competitive. For example, Levi Strauss & Co® closed its manufacturing plants in North America and now contracts with foreign manufacturers to make its garments.

Risk is also involved in the development of new products. Product introductions are costly and risky. Up to 85 percent of new products fail in the first year. It is difficult to assess the need for a product that does not exist yet. Some products that failed quickly include Harley Davidson® perfume, Gerber® Singles for adults, and Bic® underwear produced by the disposable pen company.

Bankruptcy

This Company filed for bankruptcy and was forced to close its doors. A deep recession and stiff competition led to the company's demise. *How do you think this company's failure affected its employees, the communities where they were located, and its competitors?*

Profit is the money earned from conducting business after all costs and expenses have been paid. Profit is often misunderstood. Some people think the money a business earns from sales is its profit. That is not true. The range of profit for most businesses is one percent to five percent of sales. The remaining 95 to 99 percent goes to pay costs, expenses, and business taxes.

Profit is the motivation for taking the risk of starting a business. It is the reward for taking that risk. It is also the reward for satisfying the needs and wants of customers and consumers. Businesses may use their profits to pay owners or stockholders, or they may elect to reinvest those profits in their businesses.

Profits are good for our economy in many ways. The concept of profit is the driving force in a market-oriented economic system. It encourages people to develop new products and services in the hope of making a profit. Without profit, few new products would be introduced.

Profit remains high when sales are high and costs are kept low. This encourages companies to work in an efficient way that helps to conserve precious human and natural resources. Profits provide money for a company to keep its facilities and machinery up-to-date. Then the business can produce goods more efficiently.

ECONOMIC COST OF UNPROFITABLE FIRMS

An unprofitable business faces many problems. One of the first things businesses do when their profits decline is to lay off employees. Stockholders in unprofitable companies can lose money if the stock value falls below what they paid for it. As more investors sell their stock in the poorly performing company, the company has fewer resources with which to conduct business.

Government also suffers when business profits decline. Poorly performing businesses pay less money to the government in taxes. When businesses lay off workers, there is a rise in unemployment. This causes an increase in the cost of social services and puts more stress on such agencies.

WendellandCarolyn/Getty Images

ECONOMIC BENEFITS OF SUCCESSFUL FIRMS

Profitable businesses hire more people. Employees may have higher incomes, better benefits, and higher morale. Investors earn money from their investments, which they spend or reinvest. Vendors and suppliers make more money, too. As employment and profits climb, the government makes more money from taxation of individuals and businesses. Companies and individuals are also more likely to donate to charities when they are doing well.

Remember that profitable companies attract competition, which is beneficial to the consumer. To satisfy consumers' wants and needs, they try to offer new products, the lowest prices, the highest quality, and the best service.

When people earn higher incomes, they have more money to spend. There is increased demand not only for expensive products such as cars, homes, and luxury products, but also for services provided by a variety of businesses, from hair salons to travel agencies.

SUPPLY AND DEMAND

In a market-oriented economy, supply and demand determine the prices and quantities of goods and services produced. To understand how prices are determined, you have to understand how supply and demand interact. See **Figure 5.1** (p. 120).

Supply is the amount of goods producers are willing to make and sell. The law of supply is the economic rule that price and quantity supplied move in the same direction. This means that as prices rise for a good, the quantity supplied generally rises. As the price falls, the quantity supplied by sellers also falls. Thus, suppliers want to supply a larger quantity of goods at higher prices so their businesses can be more profitable.

Demand refers to consumer willingness and ability to buy products. The law of demand is the economic principle that price and demand move in opposite directions. As the price of a good increases, the quantity of the good demanded falls. As the price falls, demand for the good increases.

When supply and demand **interact** in the marketplace, conditions of surplus, shortage, or equilibrium are created. These conditions often determine whether prices will go down, up, or stay the same.

SURPLUSES

Surpluses of goods occur when supply exceeds demand. If the price of a product is too high or seems unreasonable to most customers in the marketplace, the customers may decide not to buy it. Their decisions will affect the market. Businesses lower prices to encourage people to buy more of the product. They may run sales or special promotions to entice customers to buy the product.

One of the best examples of surpluses can be found in the produce section of a supermarket. Peaches, apples, broccoli, bananas, and other produce may be priced very low one week due to supply. When a given crop is in season, there is often an excess supply. The result is that farmers lower their prices to sell large quantities. Supermarkets that buy large quantities of the crop at the low price do the same. The surplus of produce affects the price of produce for producers, sellers, and consumers.

You can see how a produce shortage affects produce prices. When there is a poor season for growing oranges, you will find that the price of oranges is higher. For produce, extreme weather conditions such as a drought, flood, or freezing weather can affect the supply. However, when the product in question is a necessity, customers will pay the price determined by the market.

SHORTAGES

When demand exceeds supply, shortages of products occur. When shortages occur, businesses can raise prices and still sell their merchandise. An oil shortage increases the price of gasoline, so consumers who want to drive their vehicles pay the higher price. In many cases it is against the law to increase the price of a product or service during a shortage if the shortage is caused by a natural disaster, like a hurricane.

FIGURE 5.1 | **The Supply and Demand Theory**

Prices, Supply, and Demand Supply and demand both interact to determine the price customers are willing to pay for the goods producers are willing to make. *What product that you recently purchased could be used as an example of supply and demand in action?*

DEMAND

Demand refers to consumer willingness and ability to buy products. According to the law of demand, if the price drops, demand for a product usually increases. This is reflected in the demand schedule. It provides the points to plot a demand curve.

SUPPLY

Supply is the amount of goods producers are willing to make and sell. The law of supply states that at a higher price, producers will offer a larger quantity of products for sale. At a lower price, they will offer fewer products. This is reflected in the supply schedule. It provides the points to plot a supply curve.

Demand Schedule for Athletic Shoes Sold at Retail	
Price per Pair	Number Demanded
$155	600
140	800
125	1,100
110	1,500
95	2,000
80	3,000
65	3,400
50	4,600
35	6,200

Supply Schedule for Athletic Shoes Sold at Retail	
Price per Pair	Number Supplied
$155	6,000
140	5,800
125	5,600
110	5,400
95	5,000
80	4,400
65	3,400
50	2,000
35	1,000

EQUILIBRIUM

Equilibrium exists when the amount of product supplied is equal to the amount of product demanded. On the graph, this is the point where the supply and demand curves meet. It is also the point where both producer and consumer are satisfied with the price. The equilibrium price, therefore, is the price at which customers are willing to buy and producers are willing to sell.

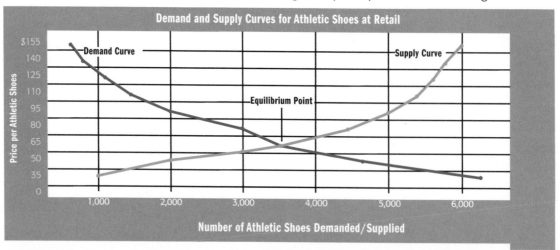

Demand and Supply Curves for Athletic Shoes at Retail

High prices increase the cost of doing business, which in turn affects profits. For example, in 2005 Hurricanes Katrina and Rita struck oil-producing states along the Gulf Coast of the United States. The damage to refineries and drilling rigs resulted in shortages of petroleum. These oil shortages caused increased fuel prices and affected all types of companies. For example, Clorox® faced higher costs, because the company uses an oil-based resin in many of its household cleaning products. Furniture and bedding companies were also affected, because petroleum is used to make a chemical component in the foam found in upholstery. The oil shortages affected carpet mills and plastics manufacturers in a similar way.

EQUILIBRIUM

When the amount of a product supplied is equal to the amount that is demanded, a state of equilibrium exists. When supply and demand are balanced, the result is that all parts of the economy benefit. Consumers are able to purchase goods and services at fair prices, which means that companies experience a steady and predictable flow of business. Consumers tend to buy the entire stock of any product that is available, which allows businesses to keep their shelves clear of excess merchandise. Equilibrium of supply and demand allows everyone's needs and wants to be satisfied in the most efficient manner possible.

 After You Read | **Section 5.1**

Review Key Concepts

1. **Explain** why intellectual property rights are important in a society that allows its citizens freedom of ownership.
2. **Describe** how a company's failure affects the government and consumers.
3. **Explain** how a company with a monopoly can use the law of supply to increase its profits.

Practice Academics

Social Studies

4. If the local car wash increased its price for its basic car wash from $5 to $15, what might happen to demand for that service? What should happen if the opposite occurred—if the price was reduced from $15 to $5? What other factors could influence consumer demand in these situations?

Mathematics

5. A paint manufacturer reported a profit of $328 million on sales of $8.2 billion for its fiscal first quarter. What percentage of sales was its profit?

Math Concept **Number and Operations: Percents** A percent is a ratio comparing numbers to 100. To convert percents to decimals, move the decimal point two places to the left.

Starting Hints Divide profits by total sales. Multiply that decimal number by 100 to convert it to a percent.

 connectED.mcgraw-hill.com

Check your answers.

For help, go to the Math Skills Handbook located at the back of this book.

READING GUIDE

Before You Read

Connect When have you taken advantage of an opportunity?

Objectives

- **Compare** for-profit and nonprofit organizations.
- **Distinguish** between public and private sectors.
- **List** the major types of businesses in the organizational market.
- **List** the major functions of business.

The Main Idea

The major functions of a business—production or procurement, marketing, management, and finance—are a basis for determining the strengths and weaknesses of a company as part of a SWOT analysis.

Vocabulary

Content Vocabulary
- domestic business
- global business
- for-profit business
- nonprofit organization
- public sector
- private sector
- industry
- derived demand
- wholesalers
- retailers
- production
- management
- finance
- accounting

Academic Vocabulary

You will find these words in your reading and on your tests. Make sure you know their meanings.
- trend
- generate

Graphic Organizer

Draw or print a chart like the one below to classify business functions.

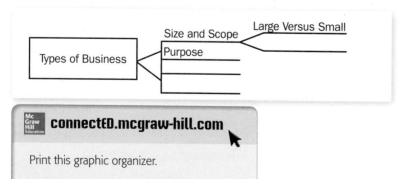

Mc Graw Hill Education connectED.mcgraw-hill.com

Print this graphic organizer.

MARKETING CORE FUNCTION

Market Planning

me. Section 5.2 | Business Opportunities

TYPES OF BUSINESS

In the free enterprise system, there are many opportunities to invest or work in many different types of businesses. In order to view those opportunities, it is a good idea to start by classifying businesses. To understand their differences, you will need to know the terminology associated with business classification. Keep in mind that a business may be classified in more than one category. A business can be categorized by its size and scope, by its purpose, and by its place within the industry.

As You Read

Classify Select a business in your community and categorize it by size, purpose, and place in the industry.

SIZE AND SCOPE

One of the easiest ways to describe a business is by its size. Is it large or small? The scope of a business refers to the extent of its business operation. Some businesses serve a small neighborhood, while others do business globally.

LARGE VERSUS SMALL BUSINESSES

A small business is one that is operated by only one or a few individuals. It generally has fewer than 100 employees. A large business is usually considered one that employs more than 1,000 people.

Nationwide, there are millions of small businesses. This category also contains many brick-and-mortar and Internet companies that often start off with small budgets and staffs. About 95 percent of all U.S. businesses are classified as small businesses. These types of businesses employ more than half of the private-sector (nongovernment) work force.

DOMESTIC VERSUS GLOBAL

A business that sells its products only in its own country is considered a **domestic business**. Because a domestic business limits its scope of operation to one country, its opportunities for growth are limited to customers within that country.

A **global business** sells its products in more than one country. The use of the Internet, along with faster transportation and financial transfers, makes it easier to do business globally. Products produced in one country are more easily sold around the world. The **trend** among large and small businesses is toward a more global market.

> **"You have many opportunities to invest and work in different types of businesses. "**

PURPOSE

A business exists to serve the needs of its customers in order to make a profit. The purpose of a business is to produce goods or provide a service, and profits are what is left over after all costs and expenses have been paid. However, there are other organizations that function like a business but have different purposes. To understand these differences in purpose, we need to distinguish between for-profit businesses and nonprofit organizations. We must also understand the similarities and differences between public and private enterprise. It is interesting to note that some private enterprises can be nonprofit, and some public enterprises aim to earn a profit.

FOR-PROFIT VERSUS NONPROFIT ORGANIZATIONS

A **for-profit business** seeks to make a profit from its operations. A **nonprofit organization** functions like a business but uses the money it makes to fund the cause identified in its charter. Nonprofit organizations **generate** revenue through gifts and donations. Some sell goods or services. This generates income. Nonprofit organizations usually do not have to pay taxes on their income, but they have expenses. They pay employees and rent for their office space. Other expenses may include supplies, printing, and postage for letters sent requesting donations. The American Red Cross, Girl and Boy Scouts of America®, DECA, and other nonprofit organizations try to generate more income than expenses, just like a for-profit business. However, unlike profit-oriented businesses, nonprofit organizations use that extra money for their cause. Although there are many unpaid volunteers, a staff of paid workers is often also needed to manage the operation of a nonprofit organization.

PUBLIC VERSUS PRIVATE

In addition to charities, other organizations operate like businesses, but are not intended to earn a profit. Most local, state, and federal government agencies and services fall into this category. Take schools and libraries for example.

Their main purpose is to provide service to the people in the country or community in which they operate. At the federal level, there are military agencies, like the Army and the Air Force; social agencies, like Social Security and Medicare; and regulatory agencies, like the Food and Drug Administration and the Environmental Protection Agency. Government-financed agencies like these are part of the **public sector**. Businesses not associated with government agencies are part of the **private sector**.

Public and Private The Public Company Accounting Oversight Board, created by the Sarbanes-Oxley Act of 2002, is considered a private organization that has some public functions.

Public-sector organizations purchase one-third of all goods and services sold in the United States each year. Think about all the products and supplies purchased in the operation of your public school system. Can you see why businesses seek out customers in the public sector?

American Red Cross

The American Red Cross is a nonprofit organization that has employees and volunteers. You will see its efforts at natural disasters, providing help to people in their time of need. *As a nonprofit organization, how does it get the funds it needs to pay its employees, run the organization, and provide that assistance?*

Hope.

When Heartbreak Turns to Hope, You're There.

Down the street, across the country, around the world—you help save the day. Every day.

When you give blood or provide a hot meal to a disaster victim, train in first aid or help a member of our military, you reach out your hand. It's at that moment—when heartbreak turns to hope—that you're there through the American Red Cross.

We need you now more than ever.
Support disaster relief today. Visit redcross.org.

American Red Cross

1-800-RED CROSS | redcross.org

INDUSTRY & MARKETS

Businesses are often classified according to the industry they represent, the products they sell, and the markets they target. The government provides a system for classifying types of business by industry and sector. Products and markets are classified according to intended use. All of these classifications are interrelated with relation to the customers served.

NAICS

According to the U.S. Department of Labor, an **industry** consists of a group of establishments primarily engaged in producing or handling the same product or group of products or in rendering the same services. For 60 years, the U.S. government used the Standard Industrial Classification (SIC) system to collect data on businesses and analyze the U.S. economy. However, rapid changes in services and technology made a new system necessary. The United States, Canada, and Mexico jointly developed the North American Industry Classification System (NAICS). In a nutshell, it states that "establishments that do similar things in similar ways are classified together." NAICS uses a six-digit coding system to classify all economic activity into 20 industry sectors. For example, the information sector includes the industries involved in communications, publishing, and motion picture and sound recording, as well as Internet companies. Some of the subcategories of the Internet industry are Web search portals, Internet publishing and broadcasting, electronic shopping, and electronic auctions. The information in the NAICS can be helpful to businesses looking for new marketing opportunities. It is also helpful to people who want to find employment or invest in those sectors.

CONSUMER, ORGANIZATIONAL, AND SERVICE MARKETS

As you read in Chapter 2, the consumer market consists of customers who buy goods for personal use. The organizational market consists of business customers who buy goods for use in their operations. The two are interrelated because of the economic concept of derived demand. **Derived demand** in the organizational market is based on, or derived from, the demand for consumer goods and services.

When consumers decide to buy more automobiles, dealers need more cars. This means auto manufacturers will need an increased supply of auto components, such as tires, radios, batteries, and electronic parts. Companies that make such parts experience an increased demand as a result of consumer decisions to buy more cars.

Lane Oatey/Blue Jean Images/Getty Images

Due to the relationship between consumer and organizational demand, organizational companies look for opportunities to increase their business by studying consumer trends. Businesses that are service-related function in both consumer and organizational markets.

Businesses that are involved in the organizational market include extractors, construction and manufacturing businesses, wholesalers, retailers, and service-related firms.

Extractors are businesses that take something from the earth or its water supply. They include agriculture, forestry, fishing, and mining businesses. The products they extract are sold primarily to other businesses.

Construction companies build structures such as houses, office buildings, and manufacturing plants. Manufacturing involves producing goods to sell to other manufacturers or to wholesalers and retailers.

Wholesalers obtain goods from manufacturers and resell them to organizational users, other wholesalers, and retailers. Wholesalers are also called distributors. **Retailers** buy goods from wholesalers or directly from manufacturers and resell them to the consumer. For the most part, retailers cater to the consumer market.

Service-related businesses are companies that provide intangible products to satisfy needs and wants of consumers and businesses. Consumer services include such things as dry cleaning, hair styling, entertainment (movies and theater), transportation, and insurance. It also includes personal needs, such as lawn-cutting, child care, and housekeeping.

Business services follow the same concept. That is why some firms specialize in accounting, marketing, management, insurance, shipping, and finance. There are also professional services—those provided by professionals such as doctors, dentists, and lawyers.

Internet-related services, such as Web portals, Web-casting, Web site design, and Web advertising have created opportunities that did not exist many years ago. For example, e-commerce (short for "electronic commerce") is the buying and selling of products through the use of electronic networks. Even traditional retailers adapt their marketing to e-commerce, resulting in the term *e-tailing*.

Reading Check

Compare What is the difference between retailers and wholesalers?

THE FUNCTIONS OF BUSINESS

Regardless of the type of business, there are four main functions involved in an organization's operation. They are production or procurement, marketing, management, and finance. The ways each business performs these activities may differ. However, all four are essential for running a business or organization. The success of business is dependent on how well these activities are coordinated, managed, and performed.

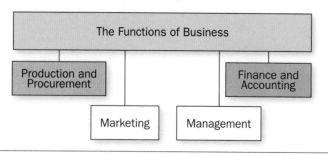

A company that has a great product but is poorly managed will not succeed. A company will also fail if it lacks the resources to pay for experienced personnel or to maintain inventory levels so products are available for sale. Poor financial record keeping can lead to poor management decisions, which may result in poor performance. If inaccurate accounting causes investors to believe that a company is more profitable than it really is, a corporation's reputation may be damaged. That in turn can lead to bad publicity and lower stock prices. Thus, the four business functions must be viewed in relation to one another. As you evaluate the strengths and weaknesses conducted during a SWOT analysis, review all four activities.

PRODUCTION AND PROCUREMENT

The process of creating, growing, manufacturing, or improving on goods and services is called **production**. A farmer grows wheat. Ford® Motor Company manufactures cars. Van conversion companies improve newly manufactured vans to make them more suitable for a driver who is disabled. Production, as a function of business, is found in industries. Such industries include farming, mining, forestry, manufacturing and service-related operations.

When evaluating this function of business in a SWOT analysis, look for innovation, speed to market, efficiency, and level of success with products. Company leaders focus on efficient production and consider many situations that may affect it, such as the law of diminishing returns. This law states that if one factor of production is increased while others remain the same, overall returns will decrease after a certain point. Companies that want to be leaders in an industry produce the most innovative products and do so before their competitors. Efficiency helps to keep prices down and sales up, which makes for a profitable company.

Hewlett-Packard® is one of the nation's largest patent holders. It has more than 15,000 patents in the United States and 37,000 worldwide. It adds about 1,500 new patents per year. Anything that is not patented is protected by trade secrets. As a result, it is an industry leader in information technology (IT).

PROCUREMENT

Procurement involves buying materials, products, and supplies needed to run a business. Manufacturing businesses need raw materials and parts to make the goods they sell. For example, clothing companies buy fabric, thread, buttons, and zippers. Procurement is sometimes referred to as sourcing because it involves researching suppliers, negotiating prices, and following through on purchases made. A SWOT analysis would involve evaluation of inventory management of the supplies needed to keep production at full capacity at all times. Buying the right quality materials at the right price would factor into that evaluation as well.

Retail and wholesale businesses buy ready-made products and resell them. A supermarket (retailer) buys cans of soup, fresh produce, frozen foods, dairy products, and the other non-food items for resale. Most of these products were purchased from manufacturers, while a few may have been purchased from wholesalers.

SWOT ANALYSIS, WHOLESALERS AND RETAILERS

In a SWOT analysis, you evaluate wholesalers and retailers on their merchandising ability. The five rights of merchandising are having the right goods, having them at the right time, having them in the right place, having them at the right price, and having them in the right quantity.

Predicting customer demand and product preferences is a difficult task, as is determining the price at which those products will sell.

MARKETING

All activities from the time a product leaves the producer or manufacturer until it reaches the final consumer are considered marketing activities.

All types of business, regardless of size, scope, intended purpose, and products sold use marketing activities in their operations. Manufacturers, service operations, wholesalers, and retailers buy goods for use in their operations and sell their finished products to customers.

All related marketing activities support the buying and selling functions. For example, research helps to determine what products to make or purchase, as well as how to price and promote them. Promotion educates customers about a company's products and is used to stimulate sales.

The Groupe Danone, a Paris food company has spent millions of dollars on research and development to find the right mix of ingredients for functional foods. Product development was based on science and clinical studies. Research results produced products like Danone's Activa and DanActive. Both are yogurts with special bacteria that have health benefits. These probiotic yogurts were marketed with higher prices than regular yogurts and succeeded in the marketplace.

In a SWOT analysis, you evaluate the four Ps of the marketing mix and how well they focus on the intended target market(s). They should also be reviewed in relation to the company's objectives and sales performance.

MANAGEMENT

Management is the process of achieving company goals by effective use of resources through planning, organizing, and controlling.

Management determines the corporate culture, ethics, and mission or vision for a firm. These include the way a company goes about doing business, values and principles that guide behavior, and a description of long-range goals.

Planning involves establishing company objectives and strategies to meet those objectives. The planning process involves setting goals and then determining the best way to meet them.

Organizing involves specific operations, such as scheduling employees, delegating responsibilities, and maintaining records.

Controlling has to do with overseeing and analyzing operating budgets to suggest the most cost-effective measures for a company to follow. Analysis of financial reports, such as cash-flow and profit and loss statements, is part of controlling.

A SWOT analysis evaluates the personnel who run a company. Important indicators are the levels of expertise of the CEO (or owner in a smaller operation) as well as the firm's key managers.

FINANCE AND ACCOUNTING

Finance is the function of business that involves money management. **Accounting** is the discipline that keeps track of a company's financial situation. If you want to analyze a company's finances, you would study its balance sheet, profit and loss statement, and cash-flow statement.

Buying Fresh Foods

Many food and drink companies emphasize the fresh or natural qualities of their products. *What business function do the products in this ad perform? What function of business is involved with supermarkets that purchase these products?*

BALANCE SHEET

A balance sheet reports a company's assets, liabilities, and owner's equity. Assets are things a company owns. Liabilities represent money owed by a business to its creditors.

If most of a company's assets have not been paid for yet, a company's financial situation is not positive. For example, if a company had assets of $100,000 and liabilities of $75,000, its owner's equity is only $25,000. In this case, creditors own more of the company than the owners.

PROFIT AND LOSS STATEMENTS

Profit and loss statements reflect the ongoing operations of a firm. They include income from sales revenue and investments, as well as costs and expenses of doing business.

A profitable company generates more income than it pays out for costs of goods and expenses to run the business. When a business suffers a loss, its costs and expenses exceed its revenue.

FINANCIAL STATEMENTS AND THE SWOT ANALYSIS

In a SWOT analysis, all three types of financial statements can provide important information regarding how well a business is doing financially.

A profitable business with high owner's equity allows a company to grow. It can invest in more research and development that can lead to new products and more efficient methods of producing them. A profitable business can also expand its operations by building new facilities or acquiring other businesses.

 After You Read | **Section 5.2**

Review Key Concepts

1. **Discuss** the significance of small businesses to the U.S. economy.
2. **Explain** why DECA is classified as a nonprofit organization.
3. **List** What information is reported in a company's balance sheet? In its profit and loss statement?

Practice Academics

Social Studies

4. Research a nonprofit organization to determine how it began and how it derives its income. What percentage of its donations is spent on its cause and what percentage is spent on administration? Share your findings in a written report and an oral presentation.

Mathematics

5. What is the owner's equity of a company that has assets of $750,000 and liabilities of $200,000?

   Math Concept **Theory Problem Solving: Using Formulas** The accounting equation defines a company's worth as its assets minus liabilities.

 connectED.mcgraw-hill.com

Check your answers.

For help, go to the Math Skills Handbook located at the back of this book.

The Free Enterprise System

The free enterprise system means companies have freedom to own, to compete, to profit, and to risk.

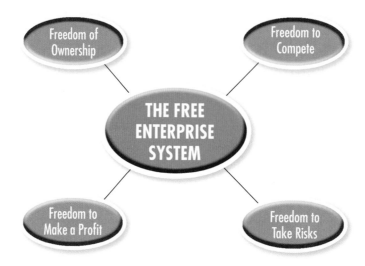

Businesses can be categorized by their size and scope as well as their purpose.

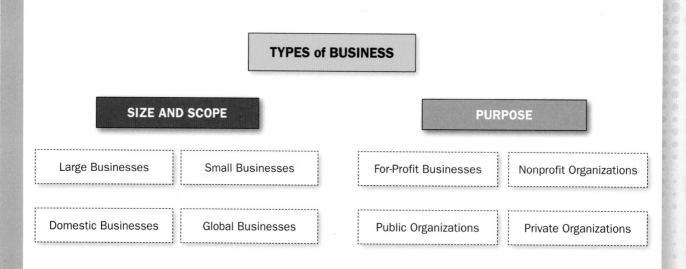

Review and Activities

Written Summary

- The free enterprise system involves freedom of ownership, freedom to compete, freedom to make a profit, and freedom to take risks.
- Price competition involves competing with a lower price. Nonprice competition involves special services and reputation.
- As prices increase, demand decreases.
- As prices increase, supply increases.
- The equilibrium point is where supply and demand curves meet.
- Unlike profit-oriented businesses, nonprofit organizations use the money they make (profit) to fund the causes identified in their charters.
- The public sector is all organizations funded by the government. The private sector is nongovernmental organizations.
- Extractors, construction companies, manufacturers, wholesalers, and retailers are in the industrial market.
- The major functions of business are production and procurement, marketing, management, and finance and accounting.

Review Content Vocabulary and Academic Vocabulary

1. Think of an example of each of these vocabulary terms in everyday life.

Content Vocabulary
- private enterprise (p. 113)
- patent (p. 114)
- trademark (p. 115)
- copyright (p. 115)
- competition (p. 115)
- price competition (p. 116)
- nonprice competition (p. 116)
- monopoly (p. 117)
- business risk (p. 117)
- profit (p. 118)

- supply (p. 119)
- demand (p. 119)
- domestic business (p. 123)
- global business (p. 123)
- for-profit business (p. 124)
- nonprofit organization (p. 124)
- public sector (p. 124)
- private sector (p. 124)
- industry (p. 125)
- derived demand (p. 125)
- wholesalers (p. 126)

- retailers (p. 126)
- production (p. 127)
- management (p. 128)
- finance (p. 128)
- accounting (p. 128)

Academic Vocabulary
- purchase (p. 113)
- interact (p. 119)
- trend (p. 123)
- generate (p. 124)

Assess for Understanding

2. **Identify** What are the characteristics of the free enterprise system?
3. **List** What are some examples of price and nonprice competition?
4. **Explain** What is the principle of supply and demand?
5. **Contrast** How are nonprofit and for-profit organizations different from each other?
6. **List** What businesses are in the organizational market?
7. **Identify** What are the four main functions of business?
8. **Identify** Are you employed in the public or private sector if you work for a company that does computer programming for a government agency? Explain.
9. **Infer** What can you say about a company that has strong production and procurement divisions but weak management and accounting practices?

Communication Skills

10. Learn about Business Interview five adults to learn about their jobs and the companies that employ them. Ask questions about their job responsibilities to determine in which main function of business they work. Identify whether the companies that employ them are domestic or global in scope and if they are in the private or public sector. Identify their NAICS classification. Prepare a table using a word processing program to report your findings in an organized manner. Share your findings with classmates in an oral presentation.

Financial Literacy Skills

11. How Much Profit? If your company has sales of $5,877,700, costs of $2,938,850, and expenses of $2,762,519, does it make a profit or suffer a loss? What is the dollar amount of the profit or loss? What percentage of sales does the profit or loss represent?

Everyday Ethics

12. Comparative Advertisements Advertisers that make direct comparisons with competitors may be misleading or using puffery. For example, a Subway ad compared its foot-long sandwich to a Big Mac and claimed its sandwich had "less fat." What it did not say in the ad is that the sandwich had "more sodium, carbohydrates, calories, and sugar than the Big Mac." The FTC ordered Subway to stop those misleading ads. An example of puffery might be a statement such as "America's favorite pasta" because "favorite" is a word that has no standard by which to be measured. Review an advertisement that makes a comparison with a competitor. Does the ad include any research to support its claims? Note whether the ad is misleading or uses puffery. Share your findings with classmates.

e-Marketing Skills

13. Patents on the Web Visit the Web site for the U.S. Patent Office to learn more about the different types of patents. Write a short report on them and note the difference in length of time each is granted.

Build Academic Skills

English Language Arts

14. Planning for Demand Write two paragraphs about how a business may or may not chose to use supply and demand theory when establishing prices for limited supplies that consumers need before or after a natural disaster, such as a flood, hurricane or tornado.

Social Studies

15. The International Economy and Business Research how companies responded to the global economic crisis in the late 2000s. Provide specific examples of bankrupt companies and marketing strategies of companies that remained in business. Share your findings with the class.

Mathematics

16. Profit from Sales Determine the profit a company makes with sales of $3,540,200, costs of $1,820,600, and expenses of $1,078,575. What percentage of sales does the profit represent? Round your answer to the tenth decimal place.

Math Concept **Number and Operations: Choosing an operation**
The profits of a company equal total sales minus any operating expenses.

For help, go to the **Math Skills Handbook** located at the back of this book.

Standardized Test Practice

Directions Read the following questions. On a separate sheet of paper write the best possible answer for each one.

1. What is the net worth of a company with assets of $12,555,000 and liabilities of $11,633,000?
   A. $9,200
   B. $922,000
   C. $9,265,631
   D. $24,188,000

2. **True or False?** A trademark protects a company's invention from being used by another company without permission.

   T

   F

3. If you want to analyze a company's finances, you would study its balance sheet, profit and loss statement, and _____ statement.

Test-Taking Tip

Taking tests can be stressful. Stay relaxed. If you begin to get nervous, take a few deep breaths slowly to relax yourself, and then get back to work.

DECA Connection Role Play

Company Owner Internet T-Shirt Company

Situation You are to assume the role of an owner of an Internet T-shirt company. You have been successful for the last two years with your T-shirt designs and marketing plan. At present your Internet sales have been approximately $1,000,000. Costs and expenses totaled 85 percent of sales, so you have made a profit before taxes. Your current net worth is around $400,000.

Now you want to open a brick and mortar retail T-shirt store. To do so, you need to convince investors that you understand the basics of the free enterprise system and the economics involved in business. You need a minimum of $200,000 to open the store. You are hoping to get ten investors to contribute $20,000 each.

Activity You are to meet with a potential investor (judge) who expects you to discuss and justify your business proposal.

Evaluation You will be evaluated on how well you meet the following performance indicators:

1. Explain the concept of the free enterprise system.
2. Explain the concept of competition.
3. Explain the principles of supply and demand.
4. Identify factors affecting a business's profit.
5. Describe types of business activities.

 connectED.mcgraw-hill.com

Download the Competitive Events Workbook for more Role-Play practice.

legal and ethical issues

SHOW WHAT YOU KNOW

Visual Literacy All types of businesses can demonstrate social responsibility in different ways. For example, helping to build homes for people in need can benefit an entire community. *How might a mobile restaurant benefit your community?*

Discovery Project

Social Responsibility Begins With You

Essential Question What are companies doing to support social causes and how can you help?

Project Goal

Work with a partner to research companies that support causes important to you and your friends and family. The causes can be related to charitable donations, safe driving, environmental efforts, or other socially responsible acts. Select at least two companies to present. Explain what they do to support their causes. Evaluate the effectiveness of their efforts in supporting that cause. Identify how you can support their efforts.

Ask Yourself...

- Which causes are most important to you and your partner?
- Which companies are involved with those causes?
- What should you include in your description of their efforts to support the cause?
- How will you evaluate the companies' social responsibility efforts?
- What can you do to support their efforts?
- How will you present the information you researched?

 Synthesize and Present Research Synthesize your research by describing how each company is socially responsible in your presentation.

---

 connectED.mcgraw-hill.com

Activity
Get a worksheet activity about social responsibility.

Evaluate
Download a rubric you can use to evaluate your project.

DECA. Connection

DECA Event Role Play

Concepts in this chapter are related to DECA competitive events that involve either an interview or role play.

Performance Indicators The performance indicators represent key skills and knowledge. Your key to success in DECA competitive events is relating them to the concepts in this chapter.

- Explain the nature of business ethics.
- Explain the role of business in society.
- Discuss the nature of law and sources of law in the United States.
- Describe legal issues affecting businesses.
- Describe the United States' judicial system.

DECA Prep

Role Play Practice role-playing with the DECA Connection competitive-event activity at the end of this chapter. More information about DECA events can be found on DECA's Web site.

READING GUIDE

Before You Read

Discuss What effect does the government have on your life?

Objectives

- **Explain** the role of government in the private enterprise system.
- **Identify** federal regulatory agencies and laws that protect consumers, workers, investors, and the environment.
- **Provide** examples of the impact of government on business.

The Main Idea

In the U.S. private enterprise system, the government plays a role in safeguarding its principles and the welfare of its citizens.

Vocabulary

Content Vocabulary
- Food and Drug Administration (FDA)
- Consumer Product Safety Commission (CPSC)
- Equal Employment Opportunity Commission (EEOC)
- Occupational Safety and Health Administration (OSHA)
- Securities and Exchange Commission (SEC)
- Environmental Protection Agency (EPA)
- Federal Trade Commission (FTC)

Academic Vocabulary

You will find these words in your reading and on your tests. Make sure you know their meanings.
- structure
- administration

Graphic Organizer

Draw or print this chart to take notes about the U.S. government and its role in the private enterprise system.

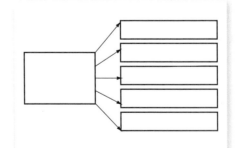

 connectED.mcgraw-hill.com

Print this graphic organizer.

MARKETING CORE FUNCTION

Market Planning

Government and Laws

Section 6.1

THE ROLES OF GOVERNMENT

Government actions have a great impact on business and its operations. Thus, it is important to understand how government functions and how it affects businesses. The stability of a government, the stability of its **structure**, and the stability of its legal system are always part of the analysis of any business (the environmental scan). The government plays the roles of provider of services, customer, regulator, enforcer of private (free) enterprise, and monitor of the economy. Government laws and regulations affect business.

As You Read

Predict How do you think the government affects business?

STRUCTURE OF THE UNITED STATES GOVERNMENT

The United States government has three branches. They are the executive, legislative, and judicial branches. The power to make changes that affect the country is split between the branches. This system of checks and balances prevents any one branch of government from becoming too powerful. Similar branches of government exist at the state and local levels. Business owners and trade groups must follow the actions and directives of all branches and levels of government, because they all affect business operations.

> ❝ **The stability of a government and its policies shape the political climate of a country.** ❞

EXECUTIVE BRANCH

The executive branch of the federal government includes the Office of the President; Executive Departments (Interior, Commerce, Defense), as well as independent agencies and corporations, boards, commissions, and committees; and quasi-official agencies. Each president's **administration** has different programs that impact business.

The U.S. Department of Agriculture (USDA) is an agency that is part of the executive branch. It provides the inspection, grading, and certification of beef, lamb, and pork, for example. The meat grades are used as a marketing tool by retailers and restaurants to distinguish the better cuts from less expensive ones. The USDA also provides a grading service for dairy products.

Where to Find Government Information

To find out about current legislation or information about government programs, you can go to the U.S. government Web site. There is even a special section for topics of interest to teens. *Why might you visit the government Web site?*

There's no place like USA.gov.

Have you ever wondered how the Wizard of Oz seemed to know everything? Well, the secret's out and it's USA.gov. You can find everything from student loans to government auctions and government benefits to, well, almost anything. So go to the official source of federal and state government information, USA.gov. It can make you as all-knowing as the Wizard of Oz.

USA.gov
1 (800) FED-INFO

A public service message from the U.S. General Services Administration

LEGISLATIVE BRANCH

The legislative branch of the U.S. government is the U.S. Congress. It is made up of the Senate and the House of Representatives. There are two senators for each state. The number of members of the House of Representatives depends on the population of each state. The members of Congress debate and vote on laws and regulations. Lobbyists try to influence the votes on bills that affect their interests. Lobbyists are not part of the legislative branch, however. They simply try to affect what laws are passed by Congress.

For example, some politicians, farm groups, and the Consumer Federation of America lobbied for mandatory country-of-origin labeling (COOL) on meat products. The mandatory labeling was part of the 2002 and 2008 farm bills. COOL became effective on March 16, 2009.

All types of meat, fish (shellfish and frozen), and fresh fruits and vegetables, as well as some nuts and ginseng must be labeled with their country of origin. Retailers that sell these food products must notify customers about the country of origin for all these products. The use of COOL is just one way the legislative branch affects how goods and services are bought and sold.

JUDICIAL BRANCH

The judicial branch of government interprets, applies, and administers the laws of the United States. The judicial system consists of a network of courts at all levels of government. When the legislative or executive branches enact laws or regulations that negatively affect businesses, those businesses may appeal to the judicial branch of government. Any court decision may create opportunities for some and threats to others. In 2004, four regional telephone companies (Verizon®, BellSouth®, Qwest® Communications, and SBC® Communications) appealed part of the Telecommunications Act of 1996. It required them to make their phone networks available to competitors at heavy discounts. Congress sided with the telephone companies. This provision was originally established to combat the near-monopoly of regional companies.

The Recording Industry Association of America (RIAA), a trade group, brought copyright infringement suits against more than 30,000 individuals for illegally downloading music. In 2006, FreePeers Inc.®, the company that distributes BearShare™ file-sharing software, paid a $30 million settlement to major music labels.

The USDA, a government agency founded in 1862 by President Abraham Lincoln, controls the safety and quality of meat, poultry, and egg products. *What do you think this USDA inspector is looking for when inspecting this food?*

food Safety

THE ROLES OF SERVICE PROVIDER AND CUSTOMER

The government spends a lot of money to carry out its responsibility to ensure the safety and general welfare of United States citizens. Close to one-third of the country's gross domestic product is due to government spending.

To keep the country safe, the Department of Homeland Security spends money on border protection, disaster recovery, and on other measures such as airport security. To improve the country's infrastructure, the federal, state, and local governments fund the construction of roads and bridges.

Businesses that provide products and services for any government installation, project, or institution must adhere to certain guidelines. Why? Because it is taxpayers' money that the government is spending.

Federal Agencies Regulate			
products	employees	environment	businesses

THE ROLE OF REGULATOR

In the United States, most laws are designed to protect the safety, health, and welfare of individuals. At the federal, state, and local levels, these laws are carried out by government agencies.

The government acts as a regulator to protect consumers, employees, investors, and the environment and this affects businesses. Note that businesses must comply or suffer the legal consequences.

PROTECTING CONSUMERS

At the state and local levels, government agencies are involved with consumer protection. People who perform certain services, such as hairstylists, manicurists, and electricians, must be licensed. Local zoning laws about where homes, businesses, and farms can be located protect real estate investments and quality of life for residents.

Health departments inspect restaurants and other food-handling businesses to protect consumers. If a business fails these inspections, it is cited and required to correct the problems identified. Failure to do so can result in closure of the business.

DIGITAL NATION

Can the Spam

Spam messages, or unsolicited bulk e-mail, are sent by the billions each day. The federal law known as the CAN-SPAM Act tries to cut down on the negative effects of spam by setting rules for all commercial e-mail. These rules include:

- The "from" line, including the e-mail address, must identify the business sending the message.
- The subject line must be true to the content of the message.
- Offers in the e-mail must be truthful.
- Every message must include the sender's physical mailing address.
- Every message must clearly specify how recipients can opt out of future messages.
- Requests to opt out must be honored within ten days.

CAN-SPAM does not require senders to have permission to send commercial e-mail. However, most companies protect their reputation by only sending e-mail to people who have specifically asked for it.

English Language Arts/Writing

Locate a commercial e-mail message sent to you or a family member. Identify whether all of the CAN-SPAM requirements are met. Discuss your findings and the ethics of spam with your class.

 connectED.mcgraw-hill.com

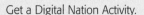

Get a Digital Nation Activity.

The Food and Drug Administration and the Consumer Product Safety Commission are two federal agencies that protect consumers. The **Food and Drug Administration (FDA)** regulates the labeling and safety of food, drugs, and cosmetics sold throughout the United States. It is responsible for the Nutrition Facts labels that are found on food packages. It monitors these labels to ensure that they are accurate.

The FDA approves new products and reviews products already on the market. For example, in 2004 the FDA banned an herbal stimulant *ephedra* because of health risks associated with products that contain that ingredient. In 2007, a new law required manufacturers to notify the FDA if there were any problems with dietary supplement pills. In 2009, the FDA found that some dietary supplement pills for weight loss contained hidden ingredients that could be harmful. One of the hidden ingredients was a pharmaceutical drug called *bumetanide*. Its inclusion in the weight-loss drug violated the law for supplements. The FDA issued alerts, and makers of those pills voluntarily recalled them.

In recent years, contaminated foods have also been addressed by the FDA. Food-borne illnesses come from tainted foods, such as peanut butter, cookie dough, and spinach and other produce. The risk of contamination causes the public to worry about unsafe foods (**Figure 6.1**). The government responds to those fears by passing legislation to give the FDA more oversight and power.

Regulations The FDA now requires food producers to notify them within 24 hours of potentially contaminated food products.

The **Consumer Product Safety Commission (CPSC)** is responsible for overseeing the safety of products such as toys, electronics, and household furniture. The CPSC is not responsible for oversight of food, drugs, cosmetics, medical devices, tobacco products, firearms and ammunition, motor vehicles, pesticides, aircraft, boats, and fixed-site amusement rides.

The CPSC was established under the Consumer Product Safety Act of 1972. That act gives the commission the authority to set standards for products that are considered hazardous. It also gives the commission the power to recall dangerous products. Product recalls are published at the CPSC Web site and communicated through radio and television announcements.

The Consumer Product Safety Commission covers many areas. It also enforces the Federal Hazardous Substances Act, the Flammable Fabrics Act, the Poison Prevention Packaging Act, and the Refrigerator Safety Act. The prime concern with these acts is the safety of children. It is a good idea for businesses to test products before marketing them to the public. Businesses should also keep up with new guidelines for labeling their products, especially regarding directions for safe use. An incident resulting from unsafe use can affect a company's reputation in the market. Businesses label their products with warnings and instructions so that consumers use them correctly.

PROTECTING WORKERS

The Equal Employment Opportunity Commission and the Occupational Safety and Health Administration are among the groups responsible for protecting employees at the federal level. Companies also must comply with minimum wage standards and other laws and regulations established by state and federal governments. One such regulation is the Family and Medical Leave Act. Other acts protect employees who report illegal practices by their employers. These laws protecting whistle-blowers are covered later in this section.

The **Equal Employment Opportunity Commission (EEOC)** is responsible for the fair and equitable treatment of employees with regard to hiring, firing, and promotions. Some of the laws it enforces are Title VII of the Civil Rights Act, the Equal Pay Act of 1963, the Age Discrimination in Employment Act of 1967 (ADEA), Sections 501 and 505 of the Rehabilitation Act of 1973, Titles I and V of the Americans with Disabilities Act of 1990 (ADA), and the Civil Rights Act of 1991. These laws prevent companies from discriminating against employees due to race, age, ability, gender, and other factors.

FIGURE 6.1 **The Government's Role in Protecting our Food**

Food-borne Illness The United States food industry is considered safe due to government regulations and cooperation from the food industry. However, food-borne illnesses can still occur. When contaminated food is not noticed, people get sick and can even die from tainted food. *Why might it be difficult for the government to ensure food safety?*

SPINACH OUTBREAK IN 2006 In 2006, fresh bagged spinach was contaminated with Escherichia coli (E.coli) bacteria. The spinach was traced to a farm in California, but the actual cause for the contamination could not be identified. The processing plant that sold the bagged spinach was not responsible for the contamination. Since that business sold the spinach to food stores and restaurants, the recall involved 26 states. E. coli outbreaks in the United States are most often found in leafy greens and other fresh produce.

PEANUT SALMONELLA OUTBREAK OF 2009 An extensive recall of tainted peanut-containing products in 2009 covered 46 states. It affected manufacturers of peanut-containing products who purchased an ingredient from the Peanut Company of America. The recall involved brownies, cakes, candy, cereal, cookies, donuts, ice cream, snack bars, and pet foods. All of these products were tainted with Salmonella bacteria. Interestingly, jars of peanut butter from major national brands were not recalled.

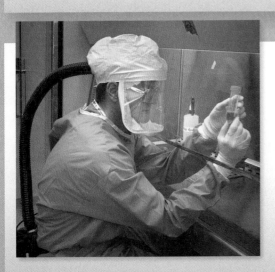

THE CDC The Center for Disease Control and Prevention (CDC), part of the U.S. Department of Health and Human Services, is involved in the investigation of food-borne illnesses. This agency works with the Food and Drug Administration (FDA) and state health agencies. The government's recall Web site explains how often food recalls are initiated by responsible companies. The Food Safety Enhancement Act of 2009 helps the FDA to prevent food-borne illness. It creates measures to ensure food safety in the United States.

Businesses must adhere to the health and safety policies established by the United States Department of Labor. The **Occupational Safety and Health Administration (OSHA)** sets guidelines for workplace safety and environmental concerns. It also enforces those regulations. For example, construction workers must wear hard hats for protection.

The Family and Medical Leave Act (FMLA) of 1993 requires employers that qualify to grant eligible employees up to a total of 12 work weeks of unpaid leave during any 12-month period. This leave is given for one or more of the following reasons: the birth and care of the newborn child of the employee; placement with the employee of a son or daughter for adoption or foster care; to care for an immediate family member (spouse, child, or parent) with a serious health condition; or to take medical leave when the employee has a serious health condition.

PROTECTING INVESTORS

The **Securities and Exchange Commission (SEC)** regulates the sale of securities (stocks and bonds). It is responsible for issuing licenses to brokerage firms and financial advisers. It also investigates any actions among corporations, such as mergers, that affect the value of stocks. This protects investors from deceptive practices. The SEC requires that all information about a corporation that is given to investors is truthful. This protects the investor and the corporation.

Companies whose shares are traded on the stock exchange must publish the company's annual report.

A company prospectus must also be provided. A prospectus is a document offered to potential investors when they are making a decision about whether to invest in a company. Corporations must prepare an annual report at least once a year to show its investors how the company has performed. On a more frequent basis, such corporations report their profits and stock dividends for publication in the media.

PROTECTING THE ENVIRONMENT

The **Environmental Protection Agency (EPA)** was established in 1970 to protect human health and our environment. Its responsibilities include monitoring and reducing air and water pollution. It oversees recycling and hazardous waste disposal.

For example, the 1970 Clean Air Act was amended in 1990 to make it more effective. In 2004, new rules to improve air quality were added. One of those rules involves stricter pollution controls on diesel engines used in industries such as construction, agriculture, and mining. Two other industries that will have similar emission standards are makers of diesel locomotives and marine diesel engines.

Environmental laws cover problems such as acid rain, asbestos, lead poisoning, mercury, mold, ozone depletion, pesticides, radon, and littering.

Construction workers and engineers visiting construction sites must wear hard hats for protection. *Why is worker safety important for companies?*

For example, new laws regarding distribution of advertising materials went into effect on April 1, 2001. A company can be fined if it distributes advertising materials inappropriately.

ENFORCER OF THE PRIVATE-ENTERPRISE SYSTEM

The **Federal Trade Commission (FTC)** has the responsibility of enforcing the principles of a private enterprise system and protecting consumers from unfair or deceptive business practices. As an independent agency, it reports to Congress on its actions. Its commissioners are nominated by the president and confirmed by the Senate. The FTC runs three bureaus: the Bureau of Consumer Protection; the Bureau of Competition; and the Bureau of Economics.

BUREAU OF CONSUMER PROTECTION

The Bureau of Consumer Protection is responsible for enforcing consumer protection laws and trade regulation rules. It investigates individual companies and industry-wide operations. In addition, it initiates lawsuits against companies that violate these laws and regulations. There are seven divisions with special responsibilities: privacy and identity, advertising, consumer/business education, enforcement, financial, marketing, and planning and information.

▶ The Privacy & Identity Protection Division oversees issues related to consumer privacy, credit reporting, identity theft, and information security. It enforces the related statutes and rules.

▶ The Advertising Division enforces truth-in-advertising laws. It makes sure that any claims a company makes in an advertisement can be fulfilled by the product or service.

▶ The Consumer and Business Education Division disseminates information and gives consumers tools to make informed decisions—and gives businesses tools needed to comply with the law.

▶ The Enforcement Division enforces laws involving the Internet; the Postal Service; textile, wool, fur, and care labeling; and energy use. For example, clothing labels must identify fabric content, country of origin, and care instructions.

▶ The Financial Practices Division covers the Truth-In-Lending Act, as well as leasing and privacy issues. It helps consumers make informed choices for credit cards or loans.

▶ The Marketing Practices Division is responsible for responding to fraudulent activities and scams. This division enforces the Telemarketing Sales Rule, the 900-Number Rule, the Funeral Rule, and the Magnuson-Moss Act.

▶ The Division of Planning and Information provides information and help for consumers who report identity theft and other fraud-related complaints.

Raisins: Good for Your Health

This ad provides information about the nutritional value of raisins. *What concerns might the FDA and FTC have about the content of advertisements for food?*

Sea Hunt

Whales were once valued mainly for meat, oil, and bone. Now they are a storehouse for the production of numerous household products. These include umbrella spokes, candles, animal feed, cosmetics, vitamin supplements, and perfume. In the late 19th and early 20th centuries, many whale species were pushed to the edge of extinction.

IWC In 1986, the International Whaling Commission regulated whaling more strictly. Many countries signed on. Norway objected. Today Norway hunts whales sustainably, but at a higher rate than other countries. Norwegian whalers believe they have the right to hunt this species. Anti-whaling groups believe that it is wrong to hunt whales. They ask, "Why not take part in a lucrative industry such as whale *watching*?"

English Language Arts/Writing

Compose Norway is not legally obligated to honor the whale ban. What do you think? Compose a letter to the Norwegian Prime Minister that expresses your position on the issue.

Here are some entry-level phrases that are used in conversations about marketing all over the world.

English	Norwegian
Hello	Hallo/Hei
Goodbye	Ha det bra
How are you?	Hvordan har du det? (Vŭr/done hăr doo dā)
Thank you	Mange takk (Mŭng/yā tŭck)
You're welcome	Vær så god (Vă-shî-goo)

BUREAU OF COMPETITION

The FTC's antitrust responsibilities involve prevention of anti-competitive mergers and business practices. Some of the acts that the bureau enforces include the following:

- ▶ The Federal Trade Commission Act prohibits unfair methods of competition.
- ▶ The Sherman Antitrust Act (1890) outlawed all contracts and agreements that would limit trade or competition in interstate commerce. It also prevents one company from undercharging for an item or service in order to put the competition out of business. This practice is known as *predatory pricing*.
- ▶ The Clayton Antitrust Act (1914) reduced loopholes in the Sherman Antitrust Act and covered mergers and acquisitions.
- ▶ The Hart-Scott-Rodino Amendment to the Clayton Act (1976) requires companies to notify antitrust agencies before planning a merger.
- ▶ The Robinson-Patman Act (1936) prohibits price discrimination, the practice of selling the same goods or services to different customers for different prices.

Distribution laws also fall under the FTC's jurisdiction. Several states have similar laws. The growth of the Internet and e-commerce makes these laws especially relevant. One example of distribution law is the sale of tobacco products to minors. It is illegal to sell tobacco products or distribute samples to underage customers. Retailers that do not comply with the law can be fined or arrested.

BUREAU OF ECONOMICS

The Bureau of Economics studies the impact of its actions on consumers and reports its findings to Congress, to the executive branch, and to the public. Its reports cover antitrust, consumer protection, and regulation. In certain instances, it may also provide information on pending bills' legislation.

MONITOR OF OUR ECONOMY

To ensure economic stability of the United States, the government monitors our economy and controls our monetary supply through the Federal Reserve System. This is our nation's central bank. When the Federal Reserve Board of Governors thinks that the economy is moving too fast or too slowly, it reacts to correct the problem. When prices are going up too fast, the board may increase interest rates to slow economic activity. Higher interest rates discourage borrowing money and expansion by businesses. The Federal Reserve Board of Governors might also lower interest rates during a slow economic period. This practice encourages people to invest or borrow money.

BUSINESS SUPPORTER

The Small Business Administration (SBA) is a United States government agency that provides support to small businesses. The role of the SBA is to encourage the free enterprise system by providing counseling and educational materials to prospective business owners. Additional support comes in the form of loan guarantees for some business owners who cannot get conventional loans. Since its founding in 1953, the SBA has provided billions of dollars in loans and guarantees to thousands of companies, making it the largest financial backer of business in the U.S.

INTERNATIONAL ISSUES

Governments in other countries may not provide the legal protection or infrastructure necessary to ensure that businesses operate in a safe and secure manner. Thus, it is important to analyze the U.S. government's role in promoting free enterprise and its ability to enforce those principles overseas. For example, lower labor costs have led many U.S. businesses to set up factories in China. However, limited intellectual property protection and a complicated legal system also make China a challenging place for companies to market and sell U.S. products.

 After You Read   Section 6.1

Review Key Concepts

1. **Identify** five roles the government plays in a private enterprise system.
2. **Compare and contrast** the roles of the three bureaus run by the Federal Trade Commission.
3. **Describe** how antitrust laws promote healthy competition in a private enterprise system.

Practice Academics

Social Studies

4. Research the Credit Card Accountability, Responsibility, and Disclosure (CARD) Act of 2009. Explain its main principles. Note the requirements necessary for young people who wish to carry their own credit cards. Include your opinion about the marketing and distribution of credit cards to teenagers and young adults. How would you have liked the law to read for teenagers? Defend your ideas objectively.

Mathematics

5. The Truth in Lending legislation requires banks and other lending institutions to clearly disclose their annual interest rates. If the monthly interest rate on an outstanding credit card is 2.5 percent, what is the annual interest rate?

Math Concept **Number and Operations: Percents** A percent is a ratio comparing numbers to 100. To convert percents to decimals, move the decimal point two places to the left.

Starting Hints To solve the problem, multiply the percent value of the monthly interest rate by 12, the number of months in a year.

 connectED.mcgraw-hill.com

Check your answers.

For help, go to the Math Skills Handbook located at the back of this book.

READING GUIDE

Before You Read

Judge Why do you think it is a good idea for companies to be socially responsible?

Objectives

- **Provide** examples of a business's social responsibilities.
- **Explain** the concept of business ethics.
- **Apply** guidelines for ethical behavior.

The Main Idea

Socially responsible and civic-minded businesses are concerned with their workers, customers, communities, and the environment. Business ethics are part of social responsibility and play a role in decisions made by businesses.

Vocabulary

Content Vocabulary

- flextime
- telecommuting
- Ad Council
- green marketing
- ethics
- Better Business Bureau
- price gouging
- whistle blowing

Academic Vocabulary

You will find these words in your reading and on your tests. Make sure you know their meanings.

- role
- policy

Graphic Organizer

Draw or print this outline to organize information on social responsibility, ethics in business, and the guidelines for ethical behavior. Link key concepts together for each topic.

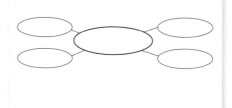

 connectED.mcgraw-hill.com

Print this graphic organizer.

MARKETING CORE FUNCTION

 Market Planning

Social Responsibilities and Ethics

BUSINESS AND SOCIAL RESPONSIBILITY

Corporate scandals and unethical behavior have a negative effect on consumer confidence and the image of a company. It is essential to see the **role** of business in society not only as provider of goods and services, but also as a participant in the society at large.

Anyone can choose to go into business in a private enterprise system, but everyone must abide by local, state, and federal laws that apply to businesses. Some of those laws encourage fair business practices. Others protect consumers, workers, investors, and the environment.

Apart from following the law, should businesses have any further social responsibility? Some business owners feel they should. They believe the business's role in society includes actions affecting its employees, its consumers, its communities, and the environment. These civic-minded businesses set themselves apart from others on the basis of management's vision of their role in the workplace, marketplace, community, and environment.

As You Read

Connect Think of two business practices that demonstrate social responsibility and ethics.

IN THE WORKPLACE

Many businesses recognize their employees' needs outside the workplace and try to accommodate these needs. In so doing, they create a friendly workplace environment. Some employee benefits offered by socially responsible companies include flextime, telecommuting, extended family leave, on-site child care, health care benefits, and time off with pay.

FLEXTIME

Flextime allows workers to choose their work hours. Possible arrangements include early start/early finish (7 A.M.–3 P.M.), late start/late finish (10 A.M.–6 P.M.), and even four-day workweeks (four 9- or 10-hour days, followed by a 3-day weekend).

> **❝ Social responsibility and ethics are part of business and marketing plans. ❞**

TELECOMMUTING

Telecommuting involves working at home, usually on a computer. Employees can send completed tasks by e-mail or mail-in disk. Telecommuting helps reduce office space requirements. Because these employees do not have to commute, this benefit is also good for the environment. It reduces gas consumption.

EXTENDED FAMILY LEAVE

Some companies offer employees family leave with pay in addition to the time required by the Family and Medical Leave Act. In some cases, the time off could be as long as one year. Such a **policy** allows companies to retain valued employees. These employees are encouraged to stay with a company that allows such flexibility.

ON-SITE CHILD CARE

On-site child care has grown in popularity with the increase in two-income families. Some employers have expanded it to include on-site schools and on-site clinics for children who are ill. Any form of the benefit tends to reduce employee absenteeism and employee turnover.

HEALTH CARE BENEFITS

With rising health care costs, health care insurance paid for by employers is a major employee benefit. Some health care benefits cover employees and their dependents, and may extend into retirement.

TIME OFF WITH PAY

Time off with pay includes vacations, sick days, and personal days. Paid vacations are generally part of an employee's contract. The time allotted for the paid vacation is generally based on the length of time an employee has been with the company.

IN THE MARKETPLACE

Consumers are the focus of companies that follow the marketing concept. These businesses are concerned about consumers' perceptions of a company and about issues that impact consumers.

PROVIDING INFORMATION

Socially responsible companies work with the government and consumer groups to provide important information to consumers. The National Consumers League and the FDA created a public education campaign about the safe and proper use of over-the-counter pain relievers.

The **Ad Council** is a nonprofit organization that helps produce public service advertising campaigns for government agencies and other qualifying groups.

EMPLOYING SELF-CENSORSHIP

The Federal Communications Commission (FCC) establishes standards for broadcasting. Beyond those regulations, network executives establish their own policies for self-regulation. Many channels have no-advocacy policies. Each station reviews commercials that might be considered controversial. If a commercial is not socially acceptable, is inaccurate, or poses a legal liability, station management may reject it.

RESPONDING TO CONSUMER CONCERNS

Socially responsible companies look for ways to respond to consumers' concerns. For example, a U.S. government report identified obesity as a major social problem. As a result, many companies sought solutions that promote good health.

IN THE COMMUNITY

United States companies provide community support in many ways. Multi-nationals consider how they affect the global community.

Many local businesses support community efforts. You may know of a local business that funds a Little League team or that sponsors a holiday food drive for the needy.

Many large companies support community causes as well. Ben & Jerry's®, the ice cream manufacturer, donates 7.5 percent of its pretax earnings to needy people and groups that strive for social change and environmental protection. Newman's Own® food company donates its profits and royalties after taxes to educational and charitable causes.

The United Nations World Business Council for Sustainable Development (WBCSD), a coalition of international companies, has a mission "to provide business leadership as a catalyst for change toward sustainable development, and to promote the role of eco-efficiency, innovation, and corporate social responsibility."

IN THE ENVIRONMENT

Socially responsible companies are concerned about our environment. They have programs that work toward saving Earth for future generations.

Alternatives to the traditional transportation fuels of gasoline and diesel fuel are being developed. Some fuels create less pollution than gasoline. These "clean fuels" can include alcohol, electricity, natural gas, and propane.

In **green marketing**, companies engage in the production and promotion of environmentally safe products. Such products may be labeled *ozone-safe*, *recyclable*, *environmentally friendly*, or *biodegradable*. Green marketing helps companies build consumer loyalty. Many consumers are willing to pay more for products that are environmentally friendly. Green products are not always more expensive.

Reading Check

Describe What are some benefits of responsible business practices?

Addressing the Issues

Many companies are developing marketing plans that include corporate social responsibility efforts on many fronts. *How do businesses and markets benefit from community-oriented market plans?*

BUSINESS ETHICS

A major aspect of social responsibility is business ethics. **Ethics** are guidelines for good behavior. Ethical behavior is based on knowing the difference between right and wrong—and doing what is right. Ethical behavior is truthful and fair. It takes into account the well-being of everyone. There is often a fine line between legal issues and ethical issues, especially when cultural differences are involved. Ethical businesses also follow the laws.

ETHICS AND CONSUMERISM

Consumerism involves the relationship of marketing to a company's customers. It is the societal effort to protect consumer rights by putting legal, moral, and economic pressure on business. Individual consumers, consumer groups, government, and socially responsible business leaders share this effort. The greatest growth in consumerism took place from the early 1960s until about 1980.

President John F. Kennedy's Consumer Bill of Rights states that consumers have four basic rights:

▶ To be informed and protected against fraud, deceit, and misleading statements, and to be educated in the wise use of financial resources
▶ To be protected from unsafe products
▶ To have a choice of goods and services
▶ To have a voice in product and marketing decisions made by government and business

ETHICS IN MARKETING

Consumerism and corporate scandals have caused businesses to address many ethical issues. Some issues involve marketing in general, as well as its specific functions and activities. Ethical principles are important in business. They reflect the management of the company and the trust between a company and its stakeholders.

SELF-REGULATION

Ethical companies are proactive. They join organizations that help to create an ethical business environment. One such organization is the **Better Business Bureau** (BBB). Established in 1912, the BBB is a nonprofit organization that promotes self-regulation among businesses. To be a member of the BBB, a business must "agree to

Everyone can appreciate technologies that go from gas-friendly to gas-free.

That's why Chevy™ offers eight 2007 models that get 30 MPG highway or better,* plus more vehicle choices today than any brand that run on cleaner-burning, mostly renewable E85 ethanol. It's also why, this fall, we'll offer both Malibu® Hybrid and Tahoe® Hybrid—America's first full-size hybrid SUV.** And why we've put tremendous design and engineering resources in place to make Concept Chevy Volt™† — our extended-range electric vehicle—a reality. Now that's technology everyone can appreciate. Do more. Use less. Find out how at chevy.com   AN AMERICAN REVOLUTION

FUEL EFFICIENCY   E85 ETHANOL   HYBRID   ELECTRIC   FUEL CELL

Socially Responsible Businesses

This advertisement shows how businesses can use their technology to save energy. *Why might all types of businesses be interested in using their resources responsibly?*

follow the highest principles of business ethics and voluntary self-regulation, and have a proven record of marketplace honesty and integrity." The BBB has a strict Code of Advertising as well.

Ethical companies subscribe to the American Marketing Association's (AMA) Code of Ethics. The Code addresses honesty and fairness as well as rights and duties in all areas of marketing and organizational relationships.

ETHICAL ISSUES RELATED TO MARKETING FUNCTIONS

There are ethical issues that involve marketing functions such as pricing, management of marketing information, and selling.

Price Gouging

Price gouging is pricing products unreasonably high when the need is great or when consumers do not have other choices.

In the pharmaceutical industry, patented prescription drugs are granted monopoly status for a period of time. The pricing of the drug during that time is an area of dispute. The companies argue that high prices are due to time and money spent on research and development. Many consumer groups think this is a case of price gouging. They say it is unfair for consumers to pay high prices for drugs they need to stay alive.

Some states have laws that govern price gouging during disasters, like hurricanes or tornadoes. Products in high demand, such as hotel rooms, bottled water, flashlights, food, and fuel, are often priced higher due to the unusual demand created by the catastrophe.

Marketing Information

Industries that maintain customer databases containing personal information have a responsibility to keep that information private. Banks, doctors, and marketing research companies must not share that information with anyone unless you give them permission to do so. Product research and marketing research must report findings honestly by disclosing all the facts involved in the research design and results.

MARKETING CASE STUDY

Tide's "Loads of Hope" campaign

Laundry detergent brand Tide® launched its "Loads of Hope" campaign, a cleverly named program that goes into areas struck by natural disasters and provides free laundry service to the victims. The program started after Hurricane Katrina, when the program's "CleanTruck" went into the hardest hit areas and did more than 20,000 loads of laundry for those who had been hurt by the storm.

Reaching out through social media

The Loads of Hope program also did an interesting experiment in March 2009. It wanted to find out how best to market through social media. Tide hosted a "Digital Night," 40 social media experts were challenged to sell as many t-shirts as possible through social media by the end of the night. When it was all over, the winning team sold $50,000 worth of t-shirts—and Tide matched that amount, giving the money to charity.

Math

If the second-place team on Digital Night sold 15 percent fewer shirts than the team that won, how much money did the second-place team earn?

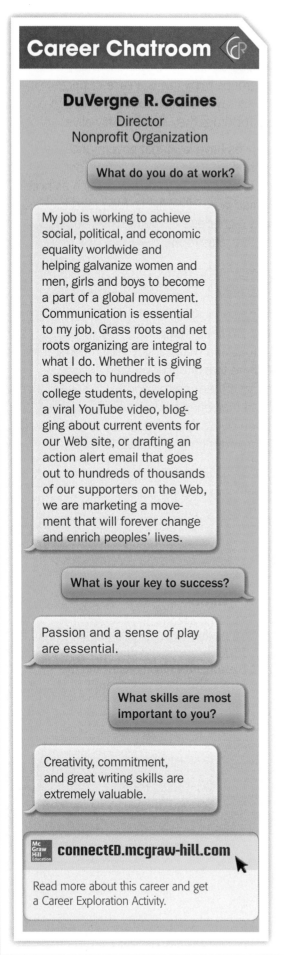
Selling Practices

Unethical selling practices involve bribes, kickbacks, favors, and high-pressure closing tactics. Cultural differences complicate this issue. In some Asian countries, businesspeople expect to receive a gift as part of a business relationship. The same gift in the United States might be considered a bribe.

Another issue involving bribes and kickbacks is defining what they are. Is taking a client out to dinner a bribe? Is giving a customer a free gift for buying a product a kickback? Some companies avoid these ethical issues by imposing strict rules against offering any type of gift to customers. Their buyers are also not allowed to accept gifts, no matter how inexpensive they are.

High-pressure selling tactics and failure to follow through on promises made to close a sale are other examples of unethical selling practices. A reason for this unethical behavior can be pressure to meet sales quotas set by management. Sales people feel pressure to sell, so they hound customers and make promises they cannot keep, just to make a sale.

MANAGERIAL AND PERSONNEL ISSUES

Management ultimately makes the decisions about major ethical issues that confront a business. From the top level to the supervisory level, managers must take responsibility for establishing ethical practices. They must become role models for ethical conduct within a firm. Employees follow management's expectations. Their decisions impact how customers view the company.

PROPER ACCOUNTING AND REPORTING

The Sarbanes-Oxley Act of 2002 was passed in response to the corporate scandals that involved misuse of company funds and unethical corporate governance. This legislation addresses accounting and proper reporting of a corporation's financial situation. Company executives and their consulting firms can be held accountable for misinformation.

WHISTLE-BLOWING

The Sarbanes-Oxley Act of 2002, as well as many other laws involving management and personnel issues, include whistle-blowing protection. **Whistle-blowing** is reporting an illegal action of one's employer. If you discovered that financial records were altered in order to cover up personal purchases made by the top executives, would you report it? If you did, you would be a "whistle-blower." If you were fired for whistle-blowing, you would have recourse under several federal laws governing whistle-blowing.

Making a decision to be a whistle-blower involves personal ethics. Employees who face such decisions find it easier to report offenses when a company has specific guidelines for making ethical decisions and a way to report these offenses.

GUIDELINES FOR ETHICAL BEHAVIOR

Companies with an interest in ethical business behavior develop guidelines to help employees make ethical decisions. People make the decisions, so business ethics are related to personal ethics. There are specific steps you can take and questions to ask to guide you through the process of making decisions involving ethical issues.

To make the right choices, employees should follow these steps:

1. Get the facts.
2. Identify all parties concerned.
3. Think of all your alternatives.
4. Evaluate your alternatives by asking yourself:
   - Is it in compliance with the law?
   - Does it go against company policy?
   - How does it affect everyone involved?
   - Is it right, fair, and honest?
   - Will it build good will for the company?
   - Am I comfortable with it?
   - How will it hold up to public scrutiny?

 After You Read | **Section 6.2**

Review Key Concepts

1. **Explain** Why are employee benefits that demonstrate social responsibility helpful for businesses and their employees?
2. **Describe** how businesses demonstrate social responsibility in the marketplace and in the community.
3. **Define** business ethics.

Practice Academics

Social Studies

4. Research the Privacy Act and identify who must comply with the law. Evaluate whether you must comply with it. If you do not have to comply with the law, think of instances when privacy is an ethical issue. Explain. Write a short report on your findings using a word-processing program.

Mathematics

5. Stealing by employees is a big problem in retail chain stores. One company solved the problem with an employee-education program. Inventory loss through theft declined steadily over the next six months. Management wants to present the results of the program at a board meeting. Identify the type of graph that would be most effective in showing this decline and explain why.

Math Concept **Data Analysis and Probability: Representing Data**
There are different types of charts and graphs to represent various mathematical relationships.

Starting Hints Think about the different types of charts and graphs management might use and the mathematical relationships each shows, such as pie charts, bar graphs, or line graphs. Choose the type that is useful for showing change over time.

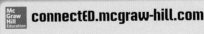 **connectED.mcgraw-hill.com**

Check your answers.

For help, go to the **Math Skills Handbook** located at the back of this book.

Legal and Ethical Issues

Socially responsible businesses address issues in the workplace, marketplace, community, and environment.

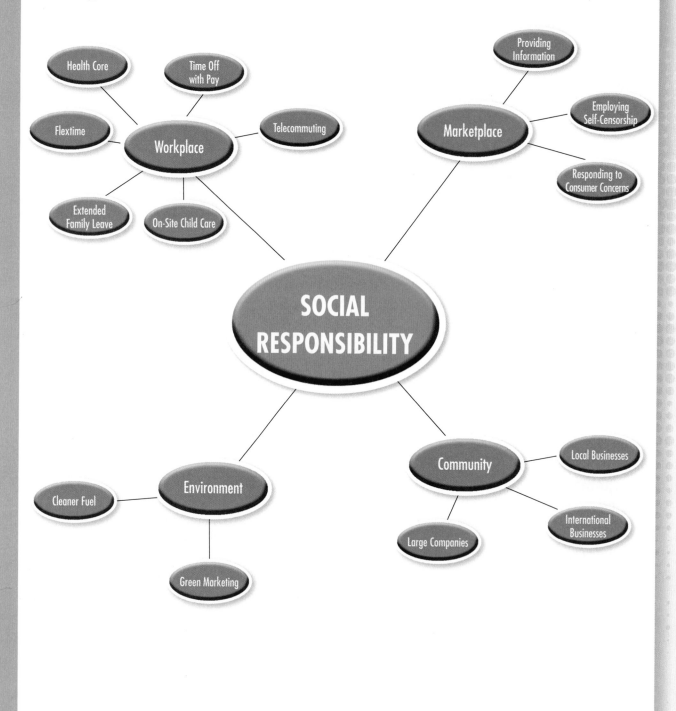

Review and Activities

Written Summary

- The government plays a critical role in enforcing private enterprise and providing for the health, safety, and welfare of its citizens.
- The Food and Drug Administration (FDA) and the Consumer Product Safety Commission (CPSC) are two federal agencies that protect consumers.
- The Equal Employment Opportunity Commission (EEOC) and the Occupational Safety and Health Administration (OSHA) protect employees.
- The Securities and Exchange Commission (SEC) protects investors and the Environmental Protection Agency (EPA) protects the environment.
- The Federal Trade Commission (FTC) promotes private enterprise and protects consumers from unfair or deceptive business practices.
- Socially responsible businesses have policies and programs that address issues in the workplace, marketplace, community, and environment.
- Business ethics are guidelines for good behavior.
- Some guidelines for ethical behavior include getting the facts, identifying all parties concerned, thinking of alternatives, and evaluating alternatives.

Review Content Vocabulary and Academic Vocabulary

1. Label each of these vocabulary terms as a noun, verb, or adjective.

Content Vocabulary

- Food and Drug Administration (FDA) (p. 140)
- Consumer Product Safety Commission (CPSC) (p. 140)
- Equal Employment Opportunity Commission (EEOC) (p. 140)
- Occupational Safety and Health Administration (OSHA) (p. 142)

- Securities and Exchange Commission (SEC) (p. 142)
- Environmental Protection Agency (EPA) (p. 142)
- Federal Trade Commission (FTC) (p. 143)
- flextime (p. 147)
- telecommuting (p. 147)
- Ad Council (p. 148)
- green marketing (p. 148)
- ethics (p. 150)

- Better Business Bureau (p. 150)
- price gouging (p. 151)
- whistle blowing (p. 152)

Academic Vocabulary

- structure (p. 137)
- administration (p. 137)
- role (p. 147)
- policy (p. 147)

Assess for Understanding

2. **Decide** How closely should the government monitor food production?
3. **Compare and Contrast** How do federal regulatory agencies protect consumers, workers, investors, and the environment?
4. **Discuss** Why is it important for the Federal Reserve to regulate and enforce private enterprise?
5. **Sequence** What is the chain of events that might result from a company's decision to offer its employees flextime and telecommuting?
6. **Connect** How is the use of price gouging connected to antitrust concerns?
7. **Describe** Why is it important for businesses to be proactive about ethical practices?
8. **Consider** Are you a whistle blower if you know your employer is doing something illegal or unethical? Explain your decision objectively.
9. **Imagine** What if one of the laws or ethical practices described in this chapter did not exist? How would this absence affect marketing?

21st  Century Skills

Teamwork Skills

10. **Carbon Footprint** Work in a group to research and report on a variety of socially responsible business efforts with regard to the environment. Look at carbon footprint efforts, green marketing, packaging, and other eco-friendly measures. Create an oral presentation using presentation software.

Financial Literacy Skills

11. **Minimum Payment** A credit card company offers an annual percentage rate of 21 percent. The balance on your credit card is $1,000, and the minimum payment due is $100. If you make the minimum payment, what will the balance on your credit card be the next month, assuming you did not make any new purchases?

e-Marketing Skills

12. **Research Skills** Imagine that you are the financial controller for a large business. You have recently reviewed your business' profits and you were happy to find more money than you expected. After consulting with the board of directors and your company's CEO, you have decided to donate the money to charity. Research a charity that you think your business should support.

   - Describe your business and its role in the market.
   - Identify the charity your business should support.
   - Justify your choice of charity.
   - Explain your business' marketing efforts required for the suggested charity.
   - Create an advertisement that shows the partnership between your business and the charity.

Build Academic Skills

Social Studies

13. **Government Bailout** In 2008 and 2009, the U.S. government took measures to shore up the financial sector and the auto industry. It bailed out both industries with taxpayers' money. Research the factors that led up to these extreme measures, note the companies involved, and any controversies that occurred. Discuss these bailouts with regard to the role of government in a private enterprise system. Present your findings in a written report.

Science

14. **Music and Technology** Research how recorded music was played from the 1950s to present day. Create a timeline to show the way music lovers enjoyed their favorite tunes during each decade. Discuss the role technology played in the transformation of music. What legal and ethical issues caused problems in that transformation? Report your findings in a written report and use presentation software to present your findings to the class.

Mathematics

15. **The Price of Recycling** If the local recycling plant pays $0.10 per pound for aluminum cans, how many pounds of cans would it take to get $25?

   Math Concept **Using Algebraic Symbols** Write an equation using an algebraic symbol for the unknown quantity before solving the problem.

   For help, go to the **Math Skills Handbook** located at the back of this book.

Standardized Test Practice

Directions Read the following questions. On a separate sheet of paper write the best possible answer for each one.

1. Which government agency is responsible for overseeing the safety of toys?
   A. Food & Drug Administration
   B. Federal Trade Commission
   C. Consumer Product and Safety Commission
   D. Occupational Safety and Health Administration

2. True or false? The Better Business Bureau is a government agency.
   T
   F

3. The Consumer Bill of Rights was established by _____.

Test-Taking Tip

Study for tests over a few days or weeks and continually review class material. Do not wait until the night before and then try to learn everything at once.

Juice Images/Alamy

DECA Connection Role Play

Manager
Auto Parts Store

Situation Assume the role of manager of a locally owned auto parts store. Earlier this week you learned that your business computer system was hacked, and some customer credit information was accessed. You have since installed a state-of-the-art safeguard system to better protect customer information. This system is designed to scramble customer information so that it is useless to thieves. The system also makes it much more difficult to hack your business computers.

You are notifying your customers that their credit card information may have been stolen. You are explaining the situation and how it is being handled to a part-time employee (judge). The employee (judge) asks why it is so important to notify all of the customers since there is a chance they will not be affected by the data theft.

Activity You are to explain to the employee (judge) that you have an ethical responsibility to protect customer information. You must further explain that customer trust is essential to operate a successful business, and that it is in your best interest to be honest with your customers about the situation.

Evaluation You will be evaluated on how well you meet the following performance indicators:

1. Explain the nature of business ethics.
2. Explain the role of business in society.
3. Discuss the nature of law and sources of law in the United States.
4. Describe legal issues affecting businesses.
5. Describe the United States' judicial system.

connectED.mcgraw-hill.com

Download the Competitive Events Workbook for more Role-Playing practice.

An Eco-Project
for a Sports Footwear Company

Businesses around the world are becoming environmentally aware and "going green." How can a company become eco-friendly?

Scenario

You work for a sports footwear company. Your new CEO came from a company that was involved with the World Business Council for Sustainable Development (WBCSD). Since membership in the WBCSD is by invitation only, companies that want to join must already be engaged in projects that help save the planet. Having a commitment to the environment is in line with the WBCSD's mission. A partnership with Live Earth is an example of an eco-friendly initiative.

Your CEO wants your company to develop an environmental program and also apply for membership in the WBCSD.

The Skills You'll Use

Academic Skills Reading, writing, social studies, researching, and analyzing

Basic Skills Speaking, listening, thinking, and interpersonal

Technology Skills Word processing, presentation, telecommunications, and the Internet

Your Objective

Your objective is to develop an effective eco-project (initiative) for your company, a global manufacturer of sports footwear.

STEP 1 Do Your Research

Go to the Internet or your school library. Find out about different companies involved in eco-friendly projects. Then devise an idea for your own project for your company. As you conduct your research, answer these questions:

- What costs are associated with your project?
- What are the political, economic, socio-cultural, and technological factors (PEST analysis) that may affect your project?
- Is your project both legal and ethical worldwide?
- What role does the U.S. government play in environmental protection?
- What are the basic qualifications for invitation to the WBCSD?

Write a summary of your research.

STEP 2 Plan Your Project

Now that you have completed your research, you need to begin planning your project.

- Conduct a PEST analysis.
- Write a marketing plan for your eco-friendly project, including the PEST analysis, objectives, and marketing strategies.
- Provide rationale for your project with supporting research.
- Include suggestions for your project's implementation, execution, and evaluation.
- Use your knowledge of the private enterprise system, the government's role, types of businesses, and the U.S. legal system to be sure your project is appropriate.

STEP 3   Connect with Your Community

- Observe green marketing initiatives by local businesses and global companies.

- Interview a small business owner who engages in eco-friendly business practices. Tell the business owner about your ideas for your project and ask for feedback.

- Test your ideas by conducting interviews with other trusted adults at home, at school, at work, or in your community. Ask for feedback.

- Revise your project plans as needed to incorporate any good feedback or constructive criticism.

STEP 4   Share What You Learn

Assume your class is a board of the company's top executives that will be in charge of implementing the environmental initiative.

- Present your findings in an oral presentation and be prepared to answer questions.

- Explain how companies can operate successful businesses while meeting the needs of society.

- Describe the requirements for invitation to the WBCSD.

- Use software to create a slide presentation to accompany your oral report. Include one slide for each topic in your marketing plan.

STEP 5   Evaluate Your Marketing and Academic Skills

Your project will be evaluated based on the following:

- Knowledge of current eco-projects in the real world of business

- Research to support your selection of eco-project features

- Creativity and interest in your eco-project

- Organization and continuity of presentation

- Mechanics—presentation and neatness

- Speaking and listening skills

MARKETING CORE FUNCTION

 Market Planning

Marketing Internship Project Checklist

Plan

✓ Research current eco-friendly trends in your company's market.

✓ Use the results of a PEST analysis to inform your market plan for the initiative.

✓ Consider how complex it will be to implement the initiative internally.

Write

✓ Describe current eco-projects in your company's industry.

✓ Explain how the results of the PEST analysis will help your company's leaders decide whether to commit to this initiative.

Present

✓ Present your marketing plan and justify its implementation.

✓ Respond to questions posed by the audience.

✓ Consider the needs and experiences of the audience as you communicate your research with your class.

 connectED.mcgraw-hill.com

Evaluate Download a rubric you can use to evaluate your final project.

---

my marketing portfolio

Internship Report Once you have completed your Marketing Internship Project and oral presentation, put your written report and a few printouts of key slides from your oral presentation in your Marketing Portfolio.

Research and Develop a Marketing Plan Do research and create a marketing plan for another socially conscious issue a company may support. Consider projects involving health-related issues, homelessness, disaster relief, or a local issue. Does your research provide the rationale to support the issue? How engaging and creative is your plan? Does it meet the criteria set forth in the objectives of the marketing plan? How will you implement and evaluate the plan? Prepare a written report and an oral presentation.

UNIT 4

SKILLS FOR MARKETING

Marketing Internship Project

Financial Literacy 101

Essential Question How do you teach financial literacy to the younger generation?

Today many people are not financially literate. The government and financial institutions recognize the need to teach financial literacy at a younger age so that future consumers can develop skills to avoid financial difficulties, such as excessive debt. The solution is to start teaching financial literacy to children, just as we teach reading and writing.

Project Goal

In the project at the end of this unit, you will design a Web site and interactive program to teach financial literacy to children and teens.

Prepare for the Project

As you read this unit, use this checklist to prepare for the Marketing Internship Project at the end of this unit:

- Conduct research on financial literacy programs and initiatives.
- Make a list of ideas for making the Web site interactive and fun.
- Visit a local bank, credit union, or other financial institution and find out what materials they use to educate their customers about financial literacy.

 connectED.mcgraw-hill.com

Project Activity
Complete a worksheet activity about financial literacy.

AMERICAN **MARKETING** ASSOCIATION

Today's consumers are completely wired; it is crucial to find new ways to reach people.

MARKETING CORE FUNCTIONS IN THIS UNIT

 Marketing Information Management

 Market Planning

The Hands on Banking® program makes it easy to learn about money

Hands on Banking

With the *Hands on Banking* program, you can learn how to manage money on your own and even have a little fun doing it. Available through Wells Fargo, it's got all the tools you need, from calculators to worksheets to guides on banking, budgeting, credit, and more.

Visit handsonbanking.org, elfuturoentusmanos.org, or stop by and talk with a banker.

Together we'll go far

wellsfargo.com

SHOW WHAT YOU KNOW

Visual Literacy
In this ad, Wells Fargo Bank® offers tools and resources to help its customers to develop financial management skills for business and life. *How does this advertisement communicate the benefits of developing financial literacy at a young age?*

basic math skills

Visual Literacy Marketers use basic math skills in every phase of marketing. Purchasing, advertising and promotion, distribution, pricing, selling, entrepreneurship, and finance all involve math. *How can math skills help you save money on the things you buy?*

Discovery Project

Using Basic Math Every Day

Essential Question How do marketers use basic math skills?

Project Goal

Assume that you are employed in a camera store that sells computers, printers, and software, as well as cameras and photographic accessories. Data shows that the profit margin on major categories of products and supplies sold for the past year was as follows: cameras at 25 percent, lenses at 27 percent, memory cards at 28 percent, batteries at 19 percent, printers at 26 percent, printer ink at 30 percent, and photo paper at 33 percent. Identify a trend or pattern in the data. Consider the different ways to display this data in a graph. Present information to your class that emphasizes the trend or pattern you identified.

Ask Yourself...

- How might this information affect the store's advertising program?
- How would the total sales in dollars in each category also affect advertising?
- What is the most effective way to present this data?
- What trends or patterns do you see in the data?

 Problem Solving What additional data would be helpful for making advertising decisions?

 connectED.mcgraw-hill.com

Activity
Get a worksheet activity about basic math skills.

Evaluate
Download a rubric you can use to evaluate your project.

DECA Connection

DECA Event Role Play

Concepts in this chapter are related to DECA competitive events that involve either an interview or role play.

Performance Indicators The performance indicators represent key skills and knowledge. Your key to success in DECA competitive events is relating them to the concepts in this chapter.

- Demonstrate problem-solving skills.
- Develop a personal budget.
- Set financial goals.
- Maintain financial records.
- Demonstrate responsible behavior.

DECA Prep

Role Play Practice role-playing with the DECA Connection competitive-event activity at the end of this chapter. More information on DECA events can be found on DECA's Web site.

READING GUIDE

Before You Read

Connect When do you use basic math skills in your everyday life?

Objectives

- **Express** numbers with letters, using commas and hyphens.
- **Explain** fractions.
- **Perform** basic math operations with decimal numbers and round answers.
- **Convert** fractions to decimal equivalents.

The Main Idea

Jobs in marketing and business require math skills.

Vocabulary

Content Vocabulary

- digits
- fractions
- numerator
- denominator
- mixed number
- decimal number

Academic Vocabulary

You will find these words in your reading and on your tests. Make sure you know their meanings.

- survey
- formula

Graphic Organizer

Draw or print this chart to write down examples of rounding from three decimal places to the nearest tenth, converting a fraction to a decimal, and calculating the area of a rectangular room.

Math Operations

Rounding from 3 Decimal Places to The Nearest 10th	Converting a Fraction to a Decimal	Calculating Area of a Rectangular Room

 connectED.mcgraw-hill.com

Print this graphic organizer.

MARKETING CORE FUNCTION

Pricing

Math Fundamentals

WRITING WHOLE NUMBERS

Our numbering system is composed of ten basic symbols called **digits**: 0, 1, 2, 3, 4, 5, 6, 7, 8, and 9. Each digit represents a number and can be combined to represent larger numbers, such as 25; 186; 5,749; and 46,732.

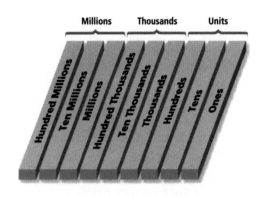

> **A company must know how many products are in its warehouse to do inventory.**

The numbers in the previous paragraph are all whole numbers because they can be written without fractions or decimals. Each digit in a whole number represents how many of something. The digit on the far right represents the number of ones. The next digit to the left represents the number of tens. So, in the number 25, there are five ones and two tens.

 As You Read

Analyze Consider the relationships of fractions, decimal numbers, and percentages to marketing.

Knowing the place name for each digit and for groups of digits is necessary for reading numbers and writing them in words. You use this skill, for example, when you write a check. The check format requires that amounts be written in both numbers and words. Follow these five steps when you read whole numbers or write them in words:

1. Separate the number into groups of three digits: units, thousands, and millions. Very large numbers may include groups of digits for billions, trillions, and even higher groups.

2. Separate the groups with commas.

   (Name of the three-digit group)   (Comma)

   36,750 ⟶ thirty-six thousand, seven hundred fifty

   (The name of this group is units, but it is not written.)

3. When writing the names of whole numbers, never use the word *and*.

   360 ⟶ three hundred sixty

   (No *and*)

4. Use hyphens in numbers less than 100 that are written as two words.

   29 ⟶ twenty-nine

   (Use a hyphen.)

5. When a three-digit group is made up of only zeros, do not write the name of the group.

   3,000,375 ⟶ three million, three hundred seventy-five

   (There are no thousands, no words are written.)

 Reading Check

Recall When will you need to write numbers in numbers and words?

FRACTIONS

The marketing research department of a soap company did a **survey**. They found that two thirds of the people who bought their new dish detergent thought it did a better job than the competition. This means that for every three people surveyed, two were pleased with the new product and one was not. Many jobs in business, especially in marketing, require a good understanding of fractions.

Fractions are numbers used to describe or compare parts of a whole. The top number, the **numerator**, represents the number of parts being considered. The bottom number, the **denominator**, represents how many parts in a whole. For example, the shaded area in the rectangle below is $\frac{3}{5}$ (three fifths) of the total rectangle.

Numerator, the number of parts being considered

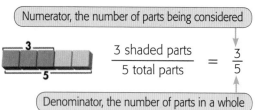

$$\frac{3 \text{ shaded parts}}{5 \text{ total parts}} = \frac{3}{5}$$

Denominator, the number of parts in a whole

In the example below, the number of circles is $\frac{2}{7}$ (two sevenths) of the total number of shapes.

$$\frac{2 \text{ circles}}{7 \text{ shapes}} = \frac{2}{7}$$

Here are more examples illustrating the same principle.

$$\frac{\text{Number of shaded parts}}{\text{Total number of parts}} = \frac{3}{8}$$

$$\frac{3 \text{ shaded parts}}{\text{Total number of parts}} = \frac{3}{3} = 1$$

One whole circle is shaded.

$$\frac{5 \text{ shaded triangles}}{4 \text{ triangles in a square}} = 5/4 \text{ of a square}$$

A fraction can describe a number greater than 1.

When the numerator is greater than the denominator, the fraction describes a number greater than one. It can be written as a **mixed number**, which is a whole number and a fraction.

$$\frac{6}{5} = 1\frac{1}{5}$$ ← Mixed number

Numerator is greater than denominator.

PRACTICE 1

What fraction of each shape is shaded?

1.   2.   3.

4.   5.

Answer each question with a fraction:

6. If you spend eight hours a day sleeping, what fraction of the day are you asleep?

7. You have saved $75 of the $250 you need to buy a new printer. What fraction of the money do you still need to save?

8. A class has 12 females and 18 males. What fraction of the class is female?

9. If one-third of your family's income is spent on housing, what fraction is left for other expenses?

10. Seventy-five cents represents what fraction of one dollar?

connectED.mcgraw-hill.com

Check answers to all practice sets.

✓ Reading Check

Recall What is the name for a fraction that has a greater numerator than its denominator?

DECIMAL NUMBERS

A **decimal number** is another way to write a fraction or mixed number whose denominator is a power of 10 (10, 100, 1000, etc.). The decimal number 5.3 means $5 + 0.3$ or $5 + \frac{3}{10}$ or $5\frac{3}{10}$. The decimal number 935.47 can be broken down as $900 + 30 + 5 + \frac{4}{10} + \frac{7}{100}$.

Knowing place names is necessary for reading decimals and writing them in words. Decimal place names apply to digits to the right of the decimal point.

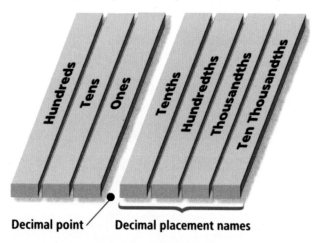

Decimal point / **Decimal placement names**

To read a decimal number or write it in words, follow these steps. Use 15.083 as an example.

1. Begin with the whole number to the left of the decimal point *(fifteen)*.

More and more people pay bills online or use electronic funds transfer, but writing checks is still an essential skill. On a check, the amount must be written in words and as a decimal number. *What other math skills are required to manage a checking account?*

Representing Numbers

2. Read or write *and* for the decimal point.
3. Read or write the number to the right of the decimal point as a whole number *(eighty-three)*.
4. Use the name of the decimal place of the final digit *(thousandths)*.

The result is *fifteen and eighty-three thousandths*.

You may also hear decimal numbers read using the whole number and the names of the digits in the decimal places. In this method, *point* stands for the decimal point. For example, 9.7 could also be read as *nine point seven;* 15.083 might be read as *fifteen point zero eight three*.

WRITING NUMBERS

Why is it important for you to know how to write decimals and fractions and to understand the relationship between the two?

The relationship between decimals and fractions is important for writing checks. After writing the amount as a decimal, you must write it again. This time it is in words for the dollars and a fraction for the cents. (See **Figure 7.1** on p. 168.)

PRACTICE 2

Write the decimals in words. Write the money amounts in words for dollars and fractions for cents. Write the words in decimals.

1. 7.8
2. 0.4
3. 33.67
4. 0.083
5. $87.40
6. $639.89
7. $132.07
8. Six thousand, one hundred sixty-four and eight tenths
9. Four hundred four and seven hundredths
10. Seven hundred twenty-one dollars and thirty-seven cents

 Reading Check

Apply What are two ways of reading *14.20?*

FIGURE 7.1 A Personal Check

Writing a Personal Check On a check, you must write the amount in decimals, in fractions, and in words. *Why do you think the amount must be written in words and numbers?*

June Jones
123 West St.
Silver Springs, CO 63312

47/1600   **0500**
Date ——— Decimal form

Pay to the
order of: **XYZ Company** $ **324.57**

Three hundred twenty-four and 57/100 Dollars

Cents written as a fraction

BANK ONE
Silver Springs, CO 633...
Dollars written in words

Memo ———   *June Jones*

•:055121000: 00123456700:•   **0500**

OPERATIONS WITH DECIMAL NUMBERS

To add or subtract decimal numbers, first list the numbers vertically. Keep the decimal points in line with each other. Then add or subtract as you would with whole numbers. Sometimes you may need to write zeros to fill a column.

1.45 + 3.4 = ?

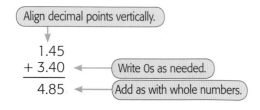

Align decimal points vertically.

```
  1.45
+ 3.40   ← Write 0s as needed.
  4.85   ← Add as with whole numbers.
```

13.4 – 7.56 = ?

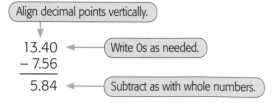

Align decimal points vertically.

```
 13.40   ← Write 0s as needed.
- 7.56
  5.84   ← Subtract as with whole numbers.
```

MULTIPLYING DECIMAL NUMBERS

The carpet store was having a sale on carpeting priced by the square yard. What is the area of carpeting for a room that is 9.6 yards long and 4.25 yards wide? To multiply decimal numbers, use the following two-step process.

1. Multiply the two numbers as if they were whole numbers. Ignore the decimal points for now.

2. Add the number of decimal places in the numbers being multiplied. Start from the right and count the same number of decimal places in the product and insert the decimal point.

9.6 × 4.25 = ?

```
    4.25   ← 4.25 has two decimal places.
  × 9.6    ← 9.6 has one decimal place.
   2550
   3825
  40.800
```

Place the decimal three places to the left.

Complete the following addition and subtraction problems with decimal numbers.

1. 6.3 + 9.4 =

2. 5.8 + 7 =

3. 8.6 + 6.04 =

4. 20.04 + 7.7 =

5. 0.08 + 4.075 =

6. 0.04 + 0.25 =

7. 3.71 + 0.6 + 1.89 + 11 =

8. 7.6 – 3.6 =

9. 54.9 – 27 =

10. $10 – $3.99 =

11. 7.5 – 2.11 + 26.045 =

12. 33.4 – 9.428 =

13. Maps To Go paid the following shipping charges in the first week of April: FedEx—$15.75, $32.00, $16.75; UPS—$23.69, $84.27, $47.88, $119.57, $63.74. What was their total shipping charge for that week?

14. Ruben was given a roll of paper 35 yards long. He was asked to make four banners for the upcoming student elections. Two banners need to be 13.75 yards in length, one banner is to be 7.5 yards, and the final banner is to be 2 yards in length. How much more paper will he need?

Since 40.800 = 40.8, the answer is 40.8 square yards.

$$\begin{array}{r} 0.25 \\ \times\ 0.3 \\ \hline 0.075 \end{array}$$

0.25 ← 0.25 has two decimal places.

× 0.3 ← 0.3 has one decimal place.

Add a 0 in the product in order to have three decimal places.

Multiply amounts of money as you would other decimal numbers. Remember to include the dollar sign in your answer.

$$\begin{array}{r} \$4.98 \\ \times\ \ \ 2 \\ \hline \$9.96 \end{array}$$

Write the dollar sign.

ROUNDING DECIMAL NUMBERS

Sometimes you may have to round a decimal number. This is especially common when multiplying with amounts of money, as when figuring tax amounts, discounts, and so on.

Use the following steps to round decimal amounts.

Round 16.842, 16.852, and 16.892 to the nearest tenth.

1. Find the decimal place you are rounding to.

16.842   16.852   16.892

Tenths place

2. Look at the digit to the right of that place.

16.842   16.852   16.892

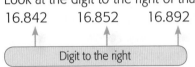

Digit to the right

3. If the digit to the right is less than 5, leave the first digit as is. If the digit is 5 or greater, round up.

16.842 rounds to 16.8

Less than 5

16.852 rounds to 16.9

5

16.892 rounds to 16.9

Greater than 5

When you are working with amounts of money, use the same steps to round your answer to the nearest cent (the nearest hundredth).

$$\begin{array}{r} \$2.87 \\ \times\ 0.045 \\ \hline 1435 \\ 1148\ \ \\ \hline \$.12915 \end{array}$$ rounds to $0.13

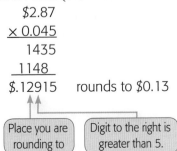

Place you are rounding to   Digit to the right is greater than 5.

PRACTICE 4

Complete the following multiplication problems with decimal numbers. Round any money amounts to the nearest cent.

1. 4.8
$\times 8$

2. 26.3
$\times 2.04$

3. 5.14
$\times .5$

4. 27.26
$\times 0.49$

5. 9.5
$\times .0001$

6. 3.87 × 10 =

7. 0.687 × 100 =

8. 12.345 × 1,000 =

9. Gasoline costs $3.52 per gallon when you pay with a credit card, but $3.47 when you pay with cash. How much do you save on a 12-gallon purchase if you pay with cash?

10. Every month you deposit $75 into a savings account for insurance costs. Your insurance expenses for this year were four equal payments of $219.50. How much remained in your savings account after the last payment?

11. Your phone company charges a $3.95 monthly long distance service fee plus $0.05 per minute for long distance phone calls. How much will you pay if you have 646 minutes of long distance calls for the month?

DIVIDING DECIMAL NUMBERS

Division of decimal numbers is similar to division of whole numbers. Follow the steps below to divide decimal numbers.

1. Set up the division problem as you would with whole numbers.

69.7 divided by 1.724 $= 1.724\,)\overline{69.7}$

2. Shift the decimal point in the divisor so that the divisor becomes a whole number. The divisor is the number you are dividing by. Then shift the decimal point in the dividend the same number of decimal places. The dividend is the number to be divided. Write zeros in the dividend, if necessary, in order to place the decimal point.

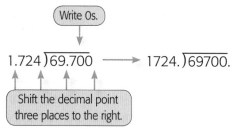

3. Place a decimal point in the answer space directly above its new position in the dividend. Then divide as with whole numbers.

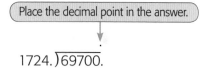

You may need to write extra zeros after the decimal point in order to complete the division.

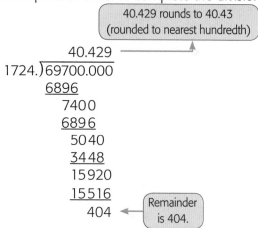

Some decimal answers will continue infinitely as you write zeros to the right of the decimal point. *Repeating decimals* will repeat a number or pattern of numbers.

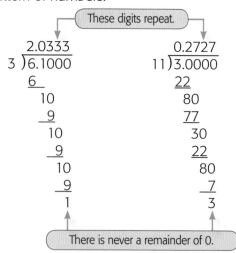

CONVERTING FRACTIONS TO DECIMALS

Decimals are easier than fractions to add, subtract, multiply, and divide. To convert any fraction to a decimal, simply divide the numerator by the denominator.

PRACTICE 5

Complete the following division problems. Round answers to the nearest thousandth.

1. $514 \div 15 =$
2. $38.6 \div 3.7 =$
3. $3.865 \div 8.25 =$
4. $7.8 \div 0.035 =$
5. $0.01 \div 2 =$
6. $4.002 \div 0.75 =$
7. If you are paid $11.02 per hour, how many hours must you work to pay for a computer that is priced at $495.90?
8. Compare the cost of Brand X and Brand Y laundry detergent. Which is the better buy? Brand X is $6.59 for 64 ounces. Brand Y is $10.79 for 96 ounces.

Numerator → $\frac{1}{4}$ ← Denominator $= 1 \div 4 = 4\overline{)1.00}$

$$\frac{1}{4} = 1 \div 4 = 4\overline{)1.00}$$
$$\begin{array}{r} 0.25 \\ 4\overline{)1.00} \\ \underline{8} \\ 20 \\ \underline{20} \\ 0 \end{array}$$

$$\frac{2}{3} = 2 \div 3 = 3\overline{)2.000}$$
$$\begin{array}{r} 0.666 \\ 3\overline{)2.000} \\ \underline{18} \\ 20 \\ \underline{18} \\ 20 \\ \underline{18} \\ 2 \end{array}$$

There is never a remainder of 0.

In its decimal form, $\frac{2}{3}$ is a repeating decimal. When working with repeating decimals, you may round to the nearest hundredth in most cases. Thus, $\frac{2}{3} = 0.67$.

✔ Reading Check

Apply Why are decimals more common than fractions when expressing values related to money?

MARKETING CASE STUDY

GEICO Campaign

The insurance company GEICO has always been known for humorous and innovative advertising campaigns. GEICO's ads often point out how consumers can save money easily. GEICO brought us ad campaigns that featured the GEICO gecko, as well as the cavemen who are offended when something is described as "so easy, even a caveman could do it." In a more recent ad campaign begun in 2009, GEICO featured the "Kash" character.

The character of Kash is a stack of money, with two eyes on top—literally the money you could be saving if you switched to GEICO. The stack of bills usually appears out of nowhere and surprises people. Many of GEICO's ads play slightly on the fear and uneasiness a customer might feel when spending too much money.

English Language Arts/Writing

The Kash ads work by implying to viewers that they are wasting their money. Consider the pros and cons of this direct approach. Write a brief response that establishes your opinion on this topic.

The GREEN Marketer

Web Searches That Give Back

What if you could help the environment just by doing a Web search? Search engines such as GoodSearch and EveryClick donate some of the money they collect from advertisers to the charity of your choice. Charity shopping portals such as iGive and WeCare partner with online merchants. These merchants donate a small amount of each purchase made through the portal to charity.

Little by Little A penny per search may not seem like a lot of money. However, the combination of these small contributions on a large scale results in a significant amount of money. Searchers who share their experience on the site with their friends increase the potential for more contributions to the charities. These word-of-mouth recommendations happen on a large scale on the Internet. This results in more traffic to the search engine and more contributions to the charities.

Mathematics

A charity search engine donates one penny to the Environmental Defense Fund for each search performed. Use the following search totals to determine how much money the charity earned in the past year: First Quarter: 123,987 searches; Second Quarter: 319,546 searches; Third Quarter: 250,983 searches; Fourth Quarter: 299,419 searches. Create a bar graph that displays these totals and the total amount earned by the charity.

 connectED.mcgraw-hill.com

Get an activity on green marketing.

CALCULATING SURFACE MEASUREMENTS

When planning to install new carpeting or to use space in an office, warehouse, or retail store, you will need to calculate the area of floor surface. The area of a surface is the number of squares of a certain measure that the surface covers.

If you measure the length and width in feet, the area will be expressed in square feet. If you measure in inches, the area will be expressed in square inches.

To compute the area of a rectangle or square, multiply the length of one side by the length of the side next to it. The shorter length is commonly called the width. The formula for the area of a rectangle is

$$A = l \times w$$

where A stands for area, l for length, and w stands for width.

The **formula** for the area of a square is really the same, but because there is no difference in the length and width, it may be written

$$A = s^2$$

where A stands for area and s stands for side.

Formulas in Business
Webcasters, agreeing to pay royalties for music streamed online, use formulas to calculate payments.

BUSINESS APPLICATIONS OF SURFACE MEASUREMENTS

Calculating surface is a business skill that retailers use to figure out the floor space they need or how this space can be rearranged. It is also necessary for anybody who sells, distributes, or manufactures products that need to have an exact area measurement. For example, how would you go about deciding how much fabric you would need to reupholster a sofa?

You would measure each area that needs to be covered. You would then have several geometric shapes with perimeter measurements. With that information, you could calculate the area measurement of each shape and add them to find the amount of fabric needed.

PRACTICE 6

The owner of a retail store wishes to replace the carpeting. The store measures 92 feet long and 50 feet wide. The new carpet is priced at $35 per square yard and sales tax is 8 percent. Calculate the surface area of the floor, and estimate the cost of material to replace the carpet, including sales tax. (Remember that there are nine square feet in one square yard.)

 After You Read **Section 7.1**

Review Key Concepts

1. **Write** the whole number 3,010,049 in words, using commas and hyphens correctly.
2. **Round** $6.875 to the nearest cent and to the nearest dollar.
3. **Convert** the fraction $\frac{1}{8}$ to its decimal equivalent.

Practice Academics

English Language Arts

4. Research careers that require good basic math skills, and write one or more paragraphs describing how math is used in these careers.

Mathematics

5. Explain why the decimal number 6.25 correctly represents $6.25 when talking about money, but does not correctly represent 6 hours and 25 minutes when talking about time.

Math Concept **Ways of Representing Numbers** The value of a digit in a number depends on the number system used and the value of the place in which it appears.

Starting Hints To solve this problem, think about the different number systems we use. For example, how many hundredths, tenths, ones, and tens are there in a decimal or money amount like 34.56 and $34.56? What does each digit mean in 3 hours and 4 minutes? Think about the place value of each digit in each number.

connectED.mcgraw-hill.com

Check your answers.

For help, go to the **Math Skills Handbook** located at the back of this book.

READING GUIDE

Before You Read

Connect When have you had to represent a math concept visually?

Objectives

- **Use** a calculator to solve math problems.
- **Convert** percentages to decimals and decimals to percentages.
- **Read** graphs used to present mathematical data.

The Main Idea

Calculators, computers, algebraic thinking, and statistics are all important tools for marketing professionals.

Vocabulary

Content Vocabulary

- RPN
- percentage
- bar graph
- line graph
- circle graph
- pie chart

Academic Vocabulary

You will find these words in your reading and on your tests. Make sure you know their meanings.

- estimate
- percent

Graphic Organizer

Draw or print this chart to write an example of calculating tax on a sale, estimating a gratuity, and illustrating or comparing data.

Calculation Examples

Calculating Tax on a Sale	Estimating for a Gratuity	A Simple Chart or Graph to Illustrate and Compare Data

 connectED.mcgraw-hill.com

Print this graphic organizer.

MARKETING CORE FUNCTION

Selling

 Interpreting Numbers

USING A CALCULATOR

Many people use calculators to pay bills, create budgets, and balance their checkbooks. There are two basic types of calculators. The most widely used type uses algebraic logic to enter numbers. This is the type of calculator used in the problems in this section.

The other type uses **RPN,** an entry method in which the operators follow the operands. Using RPN, you enter the first amount and press the enter key, then the second amount, and then the operation (added to, subtracted from, multiplied by, or divided into the first amount). If you have a calculator that uses RPN, read the instruction book that accompanies your calculator very carefully. You will get a very different answer if you enter numbers as if using algebraic logic.

> **“ Calculators simplify the computation that is common in both the business world and in people's personal lives. ”**

If you expect to be hired in sales or any other marketing job, you will almost certainly use a calculator. Besides simply knowing which buttons to press, you will be expected to work accurately. You will need to know how to work with fractions and amounts of money. You also need to have an understanding of how the calculator computes with multiple operations.

 As You Read

Connect When have you used a calculator to solve a problem?

ESTIMATE, THEN OPERATE

Many people follow the guess-and-check method. They **estimate** first, and then enter the problem in the calculator. Finally, they check the displayed answer against the estimate.

$$388 + 995 = ?$$

Estimate: $400 + 1,000 = 1,400$
Enter the problem:

 1,383

Displayed answer

Check: 1,383 is close to the estimate of 1,400.

$$480 \times 112 = ?$$

Estimate: $500 \times 100 = 50,000$
Enter the problem:

④ ⑧ ⓪ ⊗ ① ① ② ⊜ 53,760

Displayed answer

Check: 53,760 is close to the estimate of 50,000.

It is important to estimate your answers when you use a calculator. You may make errors when entering numbers or operations. It is a good idea to have an estimate of the answer in mind. For example, if you are expecting an answer of about 300, you will know something is wrong if the displayed answer on your calculator is 3,300.

You should check the display after you enter each number and operation. If you make an error, press the Clear Entry key ⓒⒺ to remove the last entry. Suppose you want to multiply 5.8 × 7.2, but you enter ⑤ · ⑧ ⊗ ⑦ ②. Press ⓒⒺ to delete the last two keystrokes. Then you can reenter the second number correctly. The first number will remain in the calculator. Press the Equals key ⊜ and the answer will be displayed: 41.76.

Jennifer Bachman

**Regional Corporate Relations Director
American Cancer Society**

What do you do at work?

My role with the American Cancer Society is to develop a strategic, mutually beneficial relationship with companies. This relationship includes engaging their employees in events and volunteer opportunities with the organization, increasing support of the Society's events, and building initiatives that help people stay well, get well, find cures, and fight back.

What is your key to success?

I believe a strong work ethic is an innate skill that will push an individual to go above and beyond his or her job duties, and see what is best for the greater good of a company. This is something I look for in new employees and something I am proud to possess.

What skills are most important to you?

The skills most important to my current role are relationship management and building hard-working, strong communication skills; aligning and matching company objectives; and trust and honesty.

 connectED.mcgraw-hill.com

Read more about this career and get a Career Exploration Activity.

HOW TO MAKE ENTRIES

You can ignore leading zeros (as in 0.6 or 0.375) and trailing zeros (as in 9.250 or 41.500).

Number	Keystrokes Entered	Display
0.785	⚬ ⑦ ⑧ ⑤	0.785
5.10	⑤ ⚬ ①	5.1

For mixed numbers or fractions, convert the fractions to decimal form first. To enter $5\frac{1}{4}$, first enter ① ÷ ④. Then add the whole number by entering + ⑤.

For money problems, include the dollar sign. You may also have to round the displayed answer to the nearest cent.

Display	Answer Written as Money Amount
5.25	$5.25
25.368216	$25.37 (Round to nearest cent)
76514.1	$76,514.10

You can perform a series of calculations on more than two numbers. When only addition and subtraction are involved, the calculator will perform these operations as they are entered.

⑧ ⚬ ⑥ + ① ① ⚬ ⑨ − ③ ⚬ ⑥ ② = 16.88

When only multiplication and division are involved, the calculator will perform these operations as they are entered.

⑦ ⑦ ⑤ ÷ ⑤ × ① ⚬ ⑨ ⑥ = 303.8

Calculations that involve addition or subtraction with multiplication or division are more complex. You will need to check how your calculator performs these operations. Most calculators will do the operations as they are entered.

$6 + 4 \times 6$ will be calculated as
$\boxed{6 + 4} \times 6 =$

$10 \quad \times 6 = 60$

$6 \times 4 + 6$ will be calculated as
$\boxed{6 \times 4} + 6 =$

$24 \quad + 6 = 30$

$4 \times 2 + 1 \div 3$ will be calculated as
$\boxed{4 \times 2} + 1 \div 3 =$

$\boxed{8 \quad + \quad 1}$

$9 \div 3 = 3$

TEN-KEY BY SIGHT OR TOUCH

Ten-key calculators have been popular for many years. They use algebraic entry. Most computer keyboards have a 10-key keypad along the right side of the board. (There are actually more than 10 keys; the 10-key name refers to the digits 0 through 9.) With practice, you can learn to operate a 10-key keypad by touch, just as you learned to type the alphabetic characters on a keyboard by touch. This allows very fast operation and is a valuable skill for online point-of-sale entries, accounting, using spreadsheet programs, and other computer-related applications.

While learning to use a 10-key keypad, keep your fingers close to the home row of keys.

On a 10-key keypad, these are the 4, 5, and 6 keys. Try to keep your arm, wrist, and hand in a straight line. Do not rest your wrist on your desk or the counter. Relax your fingers and press the keys lightly. Frequent, short periods of practice are most effective in developing speed with accuracy. Courses for developing skill on a 10-key keypad are available at many community colleges and on the Internet.

Reading Check

Recall Why should you estimate before you calculate?

To be sure that the amount they are charged for a multi-purchase sale is accurate, some people take a calculator when they go shopping. *What math skills are required to check the checker?*

Everyday Calculator Use

PERCENTAGES

Two **percent** of a company's revenue goes to pay for insurance. This means that $2 of every $100 that comes in goes to pay for insurance.

Percentage is a number expressed as parts per 100. Thus, a number expressed as a percentage represents the number of parts per 100.

To write a whole number or a decimal number as a percentage, multiply it by 100. A simple way to do this is to move the decimal point two places to the right.

> Move the decimal point two places to the right.

$0.70 = 0.7 \times 100 = 70\%$ or $0.70 = 70\%$

$0.05 = 0.05 \times 100 = 5\%$ or $0.05 = 5\%$

$2.5 = 2.5 \times 100 = 250\%$ or $2.50 = 250\%$

> Write 0s as needed.

You can use a calculator to do this operation.

⟨.⟩⟨7⟩⟨×⟩⟨1⟩⟨0⟩⟨0⟩⟨=⟩ $70 = 70\%$

⟨2⟩⟨.⟩⟨5⟩⟨×⟩⟨1⟩⟨0⟩⟨0⟩⟨=⟩ $250 = 250\%$

CONVERTING FRACTIONS TO PERCENTAGES

To write a fraction or mixed number as a percentage, first convert the fraction to decimal form. Do this by dividing the numerator by the denominator. If there is a whole number, add it to the converted fraction. Then multiply by 100. You can use a calculator to do this operation.

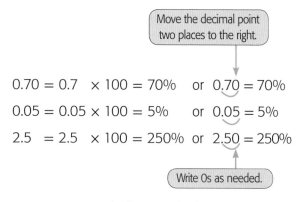

$\frac{1}{2} = $ ⟨1⟩⟨÷⟩⟨2⟩⟨×⟩⟨1⟩⟨0⟩⟨0⟩⟨=⟩ $50 = 50\%$

$\frac{3}{8} = $ ⟨3⟩⟨÷⟩⟨8⟩⟨×⟩⟨1⟩⟨0⟩⟨0⟩⟨=⟩
$37.5 = 37.5\%$

$4\frac{2}{5} = $ ⟨2⟩⟨÷⟩⟨5⟩⟨+⟩⟨4⟩⟨×⟩⟨1⟩⟨0⟩⟨0⟩⟨=⟩
$440 = 440\%$

CONVERTING PERCENTAGES TO DECIMALS

Sometimes it may be easier to complete a math problem by changing a percentage to a decimal. You can change a percentage to a decimal number by dividing by 100. A simple way to do this is to move the decimal point two places to the left.

> Move the decimal point two places to the left.

$24.8\% = 24.8 \div 100 = .248$
or $24.8\% = 0.248$

$0.5\% = 0.5 \div 100 = 0.005$
or $0.5\% = 0.005$

> Write 0s as needed.

You can use a calculator to do this operation.

$12.6\% = $ ⟨1⟩⟨2⟩⟨.⟩⟨6⟩⟨÷⟩⟨1⟩⟨0⟩⟨0⟩⟨=⟩ 0.126

$1.4\% = $ ⟨1⟩⟨.⟩⟨4⟩⟨÷⟩⟨1⟩⟨0⟩⟨0⟩⟨=⟩ 0.014

You can also convert a percentage with a fraction or mixed number to a decimal by using a calculator.

$7\frac{1}{4}\% = $ ⟨1⟩⟨÷⟩⟨4⟩⟨+⟩⟨7⟩⟨÷⟩⟨1⟩⟨0⟩⟨0⟩⟨=⟩
0.0725

PERCENTAGE PROBLEMS

Percentage problems are often encountered in marketing jobs. For example, you may be asked to figure a gratuity, a discount amount, or the amount of sales tax. You may have to figure the total selling price, including the tax. You may be asked to figure the percentage of commission on your total sales.

Most percentage problems will involve finding a percentage of a number. To do that, multiply the decimal equivalent of the percentage by the number.

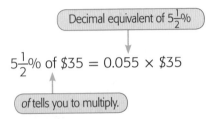

$$5\tfrac{1}{2}\% \text{ of } \$35 = 0.055 \times \$35$$

Follow these steps to solve percentage problems.

1. Estimate the answer.
2. Translate the problem into a math statement.
3. Do the calculations.
4. If necessary, round money amounts to the nearest cent.
5. Check your answer.

Three types of percentage problems are explained below. Solve the first problem by estimating the answers. Solve the other problems with a calculator.

1. Suppose you and three friends have enjoyed dinner at a restaurant. When the waiter brings the check, you decide to treat your friends and pay for dinner. To figure the gratuity (tip), you will not need to dig out a calculator because you know how to estimate. The total on the check is $98.58, including tax. You know that a 15 percent gratuity is usual, so you round the total to $100. You know that 10 percent of $100 is $10, and 15 percent is $1\tfrac{1}{2}$ times 10 percent. Your estimate for the gratuity is $15, and a good estimate is all that is needed. You leave $115.

2. Suppose you have sold a set of golf clubs listed at $395.99 to someone eligible for a 15% discount. How much in dollars and cents will you allow as a discount on the golf clubs?

- *First*: *Estimate the answer.* Round the list price to $400. Figure that 10% of $400 is $40. Since 15% is $1\tfrac{1}{2}$ times 10%, estimate the discount at about $60 ($1\tfrac{1}{2}$ times $40).
- *Second*: *Translate the problem into a math statement.*

  15% of $395.99 = 0.15 × $395.99
- *Third*: *Do the calculations.*

  0.15 × $395.99 = $59.3985
- *Fourth*: *Round the answer to the nearest cent, if necessary.* $59.3985 rounds to $59.40
- *Finally*: *Check the answer against your estimate.* The amount $59.40 is reasonably close to the estimate of $60. The discount is $59.40.

3. If sales tax is $6\tfrac{1}{2}\%$, how much tax should you collect on the sale of the golf clubs? Before you can figure the tax, you have to find out the net selling price.

   List price – discount = net price

   $395.99 – $59.40 = $336.59

   Now you can proceed, following the guidelines given above.

   - *Estimate*: Round $6\tfrac{1}{2}\%$ to 7% and $336.59 to $300. A 7% sales tax means that $7 tax is collected on every $100 in sales. So you can estimate the tax to be $21 (3 × $7).
   - *Translate*: $6\tfrac{1}{2}\%$ of $336.59 = 0.065 × $336.59
   - *Calculate*: 0.065 × $336.59 = $21.8784
   - *Round*: $21.8784 rounds to $21.88
   - *Check*: $21.88 is reasonably close to the estimate of $21. The sales tax to be collected is $21.88.

 Reading Check

Apply How would you use percentages to calculate the tip at a restaurant?

READING CHARTS AND GRAPHS

In marketing, people need to use numbers to describe market trends, growth of sales, and other data. Graphs present such information in a way that is easier to understand. It is easy to tell that one bar is longer than another or that a line is going up or down. It is harder to try to understand data by reading lists of multiple numbers. A graph shows the relationship between two or more kinds of data.

BAR GRAPHS

A **bar graph** is a drawing made up of parallel bars whose lengths correspond to what is being measured. The bar graph in **Figure 7.2** shows the percent of people who own cell phones by different age groups. The bottom of the graph lists the age groups. Each group is represented by a bar of a certain height. There is a vertical line along the left side of the graph. It shows the percentage of individuals in each age group who own cell phones. The bar graph provides a clear visual representation of this data.

To find out the percentage of 12- to 17-year-olds who own cell phones, draw an imaginary line across the top of the bar for that age group. Then note where that line intersects the left side of the graph. The result is 48 percent.

LINE GRAPHS

Another kind of graph you have probably seen is a line graph. A **line graph** is a line (or lines) that joins points representing changes in a quantity over a specific period of time. It is very useful for charting sales, prices, profits, output, and things that people expect to change over time. The information can help predict future trends so that businesses can make plans to prepare for them.

The line graph in **Figure 7.2** charts changes in cell phone subscribers and fixed line (land line) subscribers over a 12-year period. Along the bottom of the graph are the years. Along the left side are the percentages of cell phone and fixed line subscribers. As you can see by following the lines, cell phone use increased steadily during that time period. Fixed line use peaked in 2006 and has declined somewhat since then. This kind of information can help marketers determine how to market their products. It can also help stores decide how much merchandise to order for the following year.

FIGURE 7.2 | Bar Graph, Line Graph, and Pie Chart

How to Use Charts and Graphs Bar graphs, line graphs, and circle, or pie graphs are used to display different kinds of data. Here is how to choose the best type of graph to show your data. *How are graphs used?*

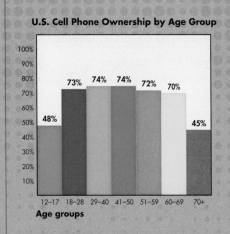

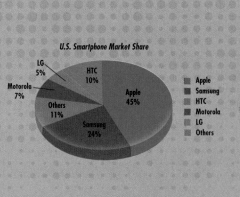

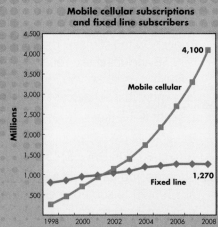

FIGURE 7.3 Main Reasons for Using the Web

Frequency Tables Display Counts Frequency tables are used to show counts for particular categories or intervals. This frequency table shows the number of Web-site uses, or hits, by purpose of visit. *What was the most frequent purpose for using the Web? How might marketers use this information?*

Purpose for Use	Count or Frequency of Uses	Percent of Responses
Education	2,020	16%
Shopping	1,725	13%
Entertainment	1,977	15%
Work	2,168	17%
Communication	1,165	9%
Personal information	2,421	19%
Time-wasting	1,219	9%
Other	286	2%
Total responses	**12,981**	**100%**

CIRCLE GRAPHS

A **circle graph** is a pie-shaped figure that shows the relative sizes of the parts of a whole. Pie graphs can show the costs of different aspects of manufacturing, a department's budget, or how income from sales is used by a company.

Circle graphs offer an easy way to understand how a whole relates to its parts. A circle graph is better known as a **pie chart**, because it looks like a pie that is cut into slices of relative sizes. Pie charts allow companies to see how successful they were compared to other companies. They can use this information to assess their place in the market.

The pie chart in **Figure 7.2** shows a percentage breakdown of smartphone sales among the manufacturers. Without reading the numbers, you can see which company has the largest share of the smartphone market.

FREQUENCY TABLES

A frequency table lists numbers, fractions, or percentages for different intervals. It can reveal information for things like consumer buying behavior. For example, the frequency table in **Figure 7.3** shows information about different uses of the Web.

PRACTICE 7 (PROJECT)

The information in the following frequency table is data from a survey by age group on the uses of the Web. Based on this information, create a bar graph for the age ranges of 11–20 and 21–25.

PRIMARY USE OF THE INTERNET
Percentage of Responses

	Ages 11–20	Ages 21–25
Education	17%	16%
Shopping	8%	12%
Entertainment	19%	17%
Work	8%	15%
Communication	12%	10%
Personal Information	16%	17%
Time-wasting	16%	11%
Other	4%	2%
Total responses	100%	100%

Reading Check

Apply When would you use a pie chart instead of a bar graph to display data?

ALGEBRAIC THINKING

Charts and graphs help organize information so we can analyze it and make decisions. But how do we analyze numbers to make sense of them? We use algebraic thinking to look for patterns and relationships. These patterns are called functions in mathematics. We also use symbols to represent variables, which are numbers we are not sure of or those that will change. For example, Asami, a marketing analyst, finds that 30 percent of those who buy a new car will purchase four new tires after two years. Asami's company needs to plan ahead. She wants to know how many tires this group will purchase three years from now.

Asami lets n stand for the number of new cars purchased next year, and t stand for the number of tires purchased in three years. Then, she writes an equation: $t = n \times 30\% \times 4$. So, if she estimates that 1 million new cars are sold next year, she knows that this group will purchase $1,000,000 \times 0.30 \times 4 = 1.2$ million tires in three years.

Reading Check

Recall What is a variable?

DESCRIPTIVE STATISTICS

Statistics are used to describe and summarize data. It makes the data more meaningful and easier to understand.

If you read the sports page of your local newspaper, you know something about statistics. Professional baseball, basketball, and football standings indicate the ranking of teams by games won and lost. They also show the percentage of wins for each team. Box scores for a baseball game include statistics on each team member's times at bat, hits, runs batted in, and runs scored.

Business Ethics and Math
Accountants must keep accurate records of their companies' finances and do so in a transparent way.

BUSINESS APPLICATIONS OF DESCRIPTIVE STATISTICS

In business, statistics are used in analyzing data. For example, Naoki is doing a study to track how many people use the Internet to make purchases.

He collects data on thousands of people and uses statistics to find the following measures:

- The distribution
- The central tendency
- The dispersion

The distribution is a summary of the frequency of values for a variable such as age. This may be presented in a frequency distribution table that lists the percentage of customers making Internet purchases by age group.

Customers by Age	Percentage
12–17	48%
18–28	73%
29–40	74%
41–50	74%
51–59	72%
60–69	70%
70 and up	45%

The central tendency of a distribution is an estimate of the center of the distribution. Here are the three main estimates of central tendency:

- Mean
- Median
- Mode

The mean, also known as the *average,* is the most common way of describing central tendency. The mean is computed by adding up all the values and dividing by the number of values. Thus, the average of the values 4, 8, 13, 28, 35, 44, and 56 is 188 divided by 7 = 26.86, rounded to 27.

The median is the exact middle of a set of values. The median in the set of values above is 28. Notice that it is very close to the mean of 27. If there are an even number of values, the median is the mean of the two middle values.

The mode is the most frequently occurring value. You would not look for a mode in a set of only seven values, but it can be useful when there is a large number of values.

For example, you take a final exam in your marketing class. When the exams are corrected and graded, the scores range from 65 to 95. No more than two students receive the same score, except that 5 students scored 81. Thus, 81 is the mode.

Dispersion is the spread of values around the central tendency. The simplest way to measure the dispersion is with the range. The range is the highest value minus the lowest value. With final exam scores between 65 and 95, the range is 30. This is how far the scores are dispersed from the center of the scores.

 After You Read | **Section 7.2**

Review Key Concepts

1. **Calculate** the decimal equivalent of $\frac{2}{3}$. Round to the nearest thousandth.
2. **Determine** the decimal equivalent of 25 percent. What is the percentage equivalent of 1?
3. **Explain** how graphs are helpful in representing numerical data. What are three common forms of graphic representation?

Practice Academics

Social Studies

4. Use the Internet to learn about and define the CPI (Consumer Price Index) and the inflation rate. Draw a line graph representing the inflation rate over a recent ten-year period.

Mathematics

5. Employees who work overtime are usually paid time-and-a-half. This term means they are paid one-and-a-half times as much per hour as usual. How do you write time-and-a-half as a percentage? If your regular pay rate is $18 per hour, how much is your hourly rate for overtime?

   Math Concept **Number and Operations: Representing Numbers**
   Fractions can be converted to decimal numbers or percents.

   Starting Hints To solve this problem, write the expression "time-and-a-half" as 1.5, the decimal number. Multiply the decimal 1.5 by 100 to convert it to a percentage. Multiply the regular pay rate by the percentage to determine the over-time pay rate.

    **connectED.mcgraw-hill.com**

   Check your answers.

For help, go to the Math Skills Handbook located at the back of this book.

Basic Math Skills

Basic math skills such as using whole numbers, decimals, and fractions have a variety of applications in business.

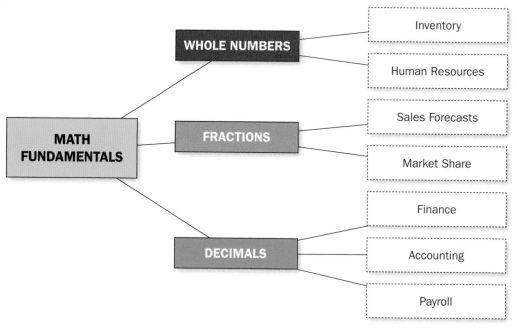

MATH FUNDAMENTALS

WHOLE NUMBERS
- Inventory
- Human Resources

FRACTIONS
- Sales Forecasts
- Market Share

DECIMALS
- Finance
- Accounting
- Payroll

Charts and graphs present data in a way that is easier to understand than series of numbers.

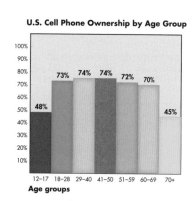

U.S. Cell Phone Ownership by Age Group

Age groups	Ownership
12–17	48%
18–28	73%
29–40	74%
41–50	74%
51–59	72%
60–69	70%
70+	45%

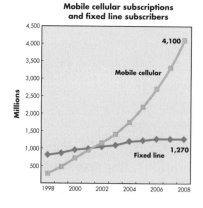

Mobile cellular subscriptions and fixed line subscribers

Mobile cellular — 4,100
Fixed line — 1,270

(Millions, 1998–2008)

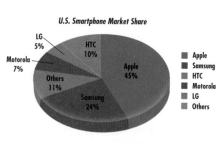

U.S. Smartphone Market Share
- Apple 45%
- Samsung 24%
- HTC 10%
- Motorola 7%
- LG 5%
- Others 11%

Review and Activities

Written Summary

- When reading numbers, writing numbers, and writing checks, it is necessary to know the placement name for each digit and for groups of digits.
- A fraction is a number used to describe a part of a whole amount.
- A decimal number is a fraction or mixed number whose denominator is a power of 10.
- Rounding decimal numbers is common when multiplying with amounts of money, as when figuring tax, discounts, and gratuities.
- To convert a fraction to a decimal, divide the numerator by the denominator.
- There are two basic types of calculators.
- The more commonly used type of calculator uses the algebraic entry system.
- The other type of calculator uses the reverse-entry system.
- Charts and graphs present data in a way that is easier to understand than a long series of numbers.
- Charts and graphs are used to describe market trends, growth of sales, and other data.

Review Content Vocabulary and Academic Vocabulary

1. Arrange the vocabulary terms below into groups of related words. Explain why you put the words together.

Content Vocabulary
- digits (p. 165)
- fractions (p. 166)
- numerator (p. 166)
- denominator (p. 166)
- mixed number (p. 166)
- decimal number (p. 167)
- RPN (p. 175)
- percentage (p. 178)
- bar graph (p. 180)
- line graph (p. 180)
- circle graph (p. 181)
- pie chart (p. 181)

Academic Vocabulary
- survey (p. 166)
- formula (p. 172)
- estimate (p. 175)
- percent (p. 178)

Assess for Understanding

2. **Justify** Why is it important to know how to use algebraic operations by hand when calculators are available?

3. **Compare** When would you use fractions to present information? When would you use decimals for the same purpose?

4. **Contrast** What are the rules for adding or subtracting decimal numbers and the rules when multiplying and dividing decimal numbers?

5. **Identify** When have you seen percentage used? How would the presentation of this information change if the percentage was converted to a decimal? A fraction?

6. **Discuss** Why is it important to estimate your answer when using a calculator?

7. **Connect** How are the uses of different types of graphs connected to different measures of central tendency?

8. **Contrast** What are the different uses for bar graphs, line graphs, and circle graphs in business?

9. **Imagine** How can you share information about a changing market share to an audience that has difficulty with fractions, percentages, and decimals?

21st Century Skills

Problem-Solving Skills

10. Calculating Estimates of Central Tendency
Suppose students in your class had the following scores on a final examination: 54, 56, 57, 59, 60, 62, 66, 69, 71, 73, 74, 76, 79, 82, 84, 85, 85, 85, 87, 89, 90, 91, 92, 93, and 94.

A. What is the mean?

B. What is the median?

C. What is the mode?

Financial Literacy Skills

11. Reaching a Savings Goal Suppose that you have a part-time job, and you have saved $200 toward your goal of buying a new computer priced at $2,500. How much more will you have to save? If you can save $75 each week, how long will it take to save enough to buy the computer?

Everyday Ethics

12. Hard Times and Hard Numbers During the summer, a well-known hotel offers luxury rooms at $150 a night. In order to offer such a low price, hotel executives have to lay off hundreds of housekeepers who make $15 an hour. Then they hire new temporary housekeepers who make $8 an hour. Representatives of the hotel say that bad economic times make it necessary to lose staff in order to save money and give customers fair prices. But only veteran housekeepers, the lowest-paid staffers, are laid off. Write a one-page response to this situation that discusses whether it is cost-effective or ethical to lay off the lowest-paid employees of a company.

e-Marketing Skills

13. Starting an Online Business Imagine that a wealthy relative has offered to provide you with start-up costs up to $50,000 to set up your own online business. Research the costs associated with starting the e-business of your choice. Prepare a pie chart showing how much money should be allocated for each type of cost.

Build Academic Skills

Social Studies

14. Economics The global economy has expanded trade between the United States and many countries in recent years. Locate information about the dollar value of goods imported and exported in a recent year. (Hint: If you are using the Internet, use key words such as *top ten U.S. export and import partners.*) Draw a bar graph depicting the dollar value of imports from the top six countries.

English Language Arts

15. Population Growth and Environmental Quality Some researchers state that human population growth is the greatest threat to the world's environment. Use the Internet to research U.S. and world population growth in recent years and forecasts for population growth in the future. Also, research the effects of population growth on availability of food and water, fisheries, and forests. Then prepare a line graph showing the relationship of population to these resources.

Mathematics

16. Using a Calculator Use a calculator to solve the following problem: Your local sales tax is 8.25 percent. What would be the tax on an item that sold for $35?

Math Concept Number and Operations: Rounding Numbers that end with the digits 5 through 9 are rounded up. Round down if the number ends with 4 or less.

For help, go to the **Math Skills Handbook** located at the back of this book.

Standardized Test Practice

Directions Read the following questions. On a separate piece of paper, write the best possible answer for each one.

1. What is the product of $259 × .0875 expressed in the correct form of measure?

   A. $22.66

   B. $22.67

   C. $26.66

   D. $26.67

2. True or false? When dividing decimal numbers, some answers will continue infinitely.

   T

   F

3. A _____ graph is a good choice for charting sales, prices, profits, and things that change over time.

Test-Taking Tip

Begin studying for a test a week or more before the test. Reviewing your textbook and notes for 20 or 30 minutes a day is far more effective than studying two or three hours on the night before a test.

DECA Connection Role Play

High School Marketing Student

Situation Assume the role of a high school marketing student. You have been hired for your first job. You are looking forward to working and earning money. You must develop a budget for yourself so that you can make wise use of your money. You will save a portion of your take-home pay from each paycheck. Part of your savings will be set aside for your future college expenses. Another part will be used to buy a laptop computer. You also have expenses that must be considered that include gas for your car, entertainment, clothing, and spending money.

You have been working on your personal budget. Make notes of realistic amounts for your planned savings and expenses. Use the amount of $160 as your weekly take-home pay to calculate the amounts you will budget for savings and the expenses listed above. Your best friend (judge) knows you are working on your personal budget. Your friend (judge) asks you why you are doing so much planning.

Activity You are to explain to your friend (judge) the importance of setting financial goals and managing your money in order to achieve them. You are to also explain the role a written budget plays in helping you achieve your goals. Use the figures you calculated for the budget items as examples.

Evaluation You will be evaluated on how well you meet the following performance indicators:

1. Demonstrate problem-solving skills.
2. Develop a personal budget.
3. Set financial goals.
4. Maintain financial records.
5. Demonstrate responsible behavior.

 connectED.mcgraw-hill.com

Download the Competitive Events Workbook for more Role-Play practice.

Blend Images - JGI/Jamie Grill/Getty Images

Chapter 8

Section 8.1
Defining
Communication

Section 8.2
Speech and Writing

communication skills

SHOW WHAT YOU KNOW

Visual Literacy Communicating clearly is necessary for success in school or in business. The ability to send a message that is easily understood is critical to all aspects of marketing. *Why do marketers need to have strong communication skills?*

Discovery Project

Business Communication

Essential Question What are four basic patterns that are effective for structuring a formal speech?

Project Goal

Your department head has asked you to prepare a written communication to a group of new employees. The purpose is to welcome them into the company, inform them about the company, and tell them what is expected of them on the job. Use your imagination, make up a company name, and prepare a rough draft.

Ask Yourself...

- What form of written communication will you use?
- Why will you use that form of communication?
- How will you plan to use language effectively?
- How will you address questions they might have?

 Organization and Communication How will you organize your thoughts to communicate effectively?

---

 connectED.mcgraw-hill.com

Activity
Get a worksheet activity about business communication.

Evaluate
Download a rubric you can use to evaluate your project.

DECA Connection

DECA Event Role Play

Concepts in this chapter are related to DECA competitive events that involve either an interview or role play.

Performance Indicators The performance indicators represent key skills and knowledge. Your key to success in DECA competitive events is relating them to the concepts in this chapter.

- Extract relevant information from written material.
- Prepare simple written reports.
- Organize information.
- Participate in a staff meeting.
- Make oral presentations.

DECA Prep

Role Play Practice role-playing with the DECA Connection competitive-event activity at the end of this chapter. More information on DECA events can be found on DECA's Web site.

READING GUIDE

Before You Read

Connect When have you had to be an effective communicator?

Objectives

- **Define** effective verbal and nonverbal communication.
- **Explain** the role of listening in communication.
- **Explain** why awareness of cultural differences is important.
- **Define** reading for meaning.

The Main Idea

Effective communication is a key component of marketing. It includes sending and receiving messages that are understood by sender and receiver. Improving listening and reading skills will lead to success.

Vocabulary

Content Vocabulary

- communication
- channels/media
- feedback
- barriers
- setting
- distractions
- emotional barriers
- jargon

Academic Vocabulary

You will find these words in your reading and on your tests. Make sure you know their meanings.

- process
- respond

Graphic Organizer

Draw or print this chart to take notes about the listening process.

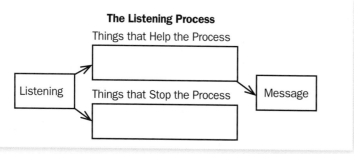

connectED.mcgraw-hill.com

Print this graphic organizer.

MARKETING CORE FUNCTIONS

- Marketing Information Management
- Selling

Defining Communication

THE COMMUNICATION PROCESS

Communication is the **process** of exchanging messages between a sender and a receiver. These messages contain information, ideas, or feelings. The skills used to send and receive these messages are called communication skills. They include listening, reading, speaking, and writing. These skills allow a speaker or writer to present a message clearly and concisely. This allows a listener or reader to understand it easily.

As You Read

Consider What are the differences between listening and reading and between speaking and writing?

CHANNELS OR MEDIA

Channels, or **media**, are the avenues through which messages are delivered. Examples include face-to-face conversations, telephone calls, text and instant messages, written memos, letters, reports, e-mail, and online chat and messaging through social networking sites. Channels differ in terms of how much content they can carry, the speed with which the message is delivered, cost of the message, and its quality. The choice of medium depends on the relative importance of these factors in the delivery of the message.

FEEDBACK

A receiver's response to a message is known as **feedback**. For example, if your boss asks you to post a report on the company Web site, you will probably ask some questions about what to include and when to post it. Feedback allows participants to clarify the message. It also ensures that all parties understand its meaning.

BARRIERS

Barriers are obstacles that interfere with the understanding of a message. They can be verbal barriers, such as vague or unclear language or a language or dialect that is unfamiliar to the receiver. For example, some people use the words *soda*, *pop*, *soda pop*, or even something else to describe the same drink. Marketers need to make sure the language they are using is appropriate for and understandable by their audiences. This applies to cross-cultural marketing as well. For example, the Spanish language has many dialects. People from different Spanish-speaking countries, such as Cuba, Mexico, Spain, and the Dominican Republic, often use different Spanish words to express the same concept. Businesses that try to target customers who are Hispanic must know about these cultural backgrounds.

> **Effective communication is vital in every aspect of business.**

SETTING

The **setting** is where communication takes place. It includes place, time, sights, and sounds. It can be a barrier to communication. A salesperson at an electronics store may find it difficult to explain the features of a video camera to a customer if the music department across the aisle has a stereo playing at full volume.

Reading Check

Recall What are the four elements of the communication process?

LISTENING

Listening for understanding is one of the most valuable communication skills. Listening is an active mental process. It involves recognizing, assimilating, assessing, and evaluating what is heard. (See **Figure 8.1** on page 195 for a list of barriers to listening.) Listening plays an important role when handling customer complaints, understanding feedback, recognizing clients' needs, and following directions.

Listening
Usually, taking notes while listening will help you remember details, but in brief conversations note taking can interfere with communication.

TECHNIQUES FOR EFFECTIVE LISTENING

Listening, like all skills, must be learned. Effective listening is comprised of eight core components—purpose, plan, feedback, common interest, evaluate, listen, conclusion, and note taking. Practicing the listening techniques in this section will help you to improve your listening skills and become a more effective listener.

IDENTIFY THE PURPOSE

Prepare to listen by learning and reviewing the purpose of the communication. Managers planning a group meeting send out an agenda in advance so everyone will know the meeting's purpose. When a customer sets up a meeting, understand the meeting's purpose to be prepared to **respond** to the customer's questions.

LOOK FOR A PLAN

When you listen to a structured speech, think about how the speaker has organized the presentation. Be alert at the beginning of the speech because the speaker may give an outline of the main ideas of the talk. If you see a structure or pattern, it will be easier to see how the different parts of the message fit together. Face-to-face conversations are often informal and unplanned, so just stay focused on the message instead of thinking about structure.

GIVE FEEDBACK

When you are speaking about business, listen carefully, and then give feedback to show whether you have understood the message. Without interrupting, you can nod your head, smile, or frown. Look for an opportunity to ask questions when the speaker pauses or completes his or her point. Think through what has been said.

Many cultures use different gestures to show respect or greeting. *What are some gestures that you use to demonstrate greeting or respect?*

Cultural Norms

Summarize your understanding of the message. Acknowledge your understanding respectfully or ask the speaker for clarification if you are uncertain.

When a speaker is giving instructions, it may be better to interrupt with questions than to wait for a pause. That way, a confusing point can be clarified and you can follow the remainder of the directions. However, before interrupting, be sure that the speaker is comfortable with this approach.

SEARCH FOR A COMMON INTEREST

Effective listening is easier when you are interested in the ideas being discussed. If you find the subject boring and are tempted to tune out, resist the temptation. Nodding and repeating key words will help you stay focused and let the speaker know that you are interested. Tuning out can become a bad habit and can cause you to miss important information.

EVALUATE THE MESSAGE

It is important to know how to respond appropriately to a message. You must evaluate it. For example, if a customer shares a personal point of view with you, even if you disagree, it would be inappropriate to make a sudden judgment. Doing so could be destructive to your relationship. Instead, try to see the message from the speaker's point of view. Listen carefully and try to understand the new information even if it conflicts with your view. Relax and do not become defensive. Recognize that the other person's experience may be unlike yours. Different experiences may cause differences in perception. Ask polite but probing questions to understand the message better. Try to identify any parts of the speaker's message with which you agree.

LISTEN FOR MORE THAN VERBAL CONTENT

Listen for more than just words in the speaker's message. What is communicated by the speaker's rate of speech, pitch, volume, and voice quality?

Awareness of cultural differences will help in the understanding of vocal cues. In the United States and other Western countries, including Canada, Australia, and Great Britain, speakers are expected to look at and speak directly to listeners. In many Asian countries, however, speakers show respect by averting their eyes, speaking in soft tones, and approaching their subject indirectly. A speaker in Canada who wants to say "No" will simply say "No." In Korea, a person who wants to communicate the same message may say, "That might be very difficult." Both statements mean "No," but the messages reflect cultural differences.

Understanding Mongolia

For thousands of years, the home of the Tsaatan has been the forested taiga of northern Mongolia. In one of the world's remotest regions, the Tsaatan still live and tend their herds like the "reindeer people" before them. Not much has changed—until recently.

Something New Taking their fate in their own hands, the Tsaatan have invited visitors to live alongside them and experience their daily life. Newcomers sleep in tepees, bake traditional bread, help with daily chores, listen to stories, or simply sit back and observe ancient ways. Communication is key. It is a good idea to bring an interpreter, but written etiquette guidelines offer suggestions.

English Language Arts/Writing
Communication is not always verbal. Use what you know about nonverbal communication to think of ways that the Tsaatan and the tourists might communicate.

Here are some entry-level phrases that are used in conversations about marketing all over the world.

English	Mongolian (Tuvan)
Hello	Экии (Ā/kee)
Goodbye	Байырлыг (Buy/yer/lĭg)
How are you?	Кандыг тур силер? (Kŏn/dyg tour see/lair)
Thank you	Улуу-биле четтирдим (oo/loo bĕ/lĕ chĕt/tur/dĭm)
You're welcome	Ажырбас (Ăzh/yr-băs)

LISTEN FOR A CONCLUSION

Listen carefully for the speaker's conclusion. You may want to take action based on it. Do not jump to your own conclusion before the speaker has finished presenting the facts that support his or her conclusion. Be prepared to check your understanding by asking well-thought-out questions. If the situation is a formal one, wait to ask questions at the right time. Intelligent questions indicate not only interest but also respect for the speaker's work.

TAKE NOTES

Try to identify a plan in the presentation of formal meetings. Then structure your notes according to the plan. Take notes on the main points presented at business meetings. Important points are often preceded by signal words such as *first, second, next, then, another, therefore,* and *thus.* If there is a summary at the end of the meeting, listen carefully and check your notes to make sure you understood the main ideas.

BARRIERS TO LISTENING FOR UNDERSTANDING

A barrier to receiving a message can be environmental, such as a plane flying overhead or a cell phone ringing loudly. It may involve attitudes and characteristics of the listener. Some common barriers include the following:

▶ **Distractions** Distractions are things that compete with the message for the listener's attention. These can include noises, conversations, and competing thoughts. One way to overcome distractions is to move away from them.

▶ **Emotional barriers** Emotional barriers are biases against the sender's opinions that prevent a listener from understanding. Poor listeners close their minds to things with which they disagree. Good listeners always listen with an open mind.

▶ **Planning a response** Planning a response occurs when the receiver of the message stops listening and begins to think about what to say next. A person cannot focus on the message and plan a response at the same time.

Listeners must avoid or overcome any barriers to concentrate on the message.

 Reading Check

Explain Why is listening a good communication skill?

FIGURE 8.1 | Barriers to Listening

Listen Carefully Barriers to listening interfere with communication. They prevent the listener from receiving and understanding the messages sent to them. *How can you be a good listener?*

DISTRACTIONS Distractions interfere with the ability to listen well. You may be distracted by thoughts about another subject. Focus your attention on the speaker's words.

EMOTIONAL BARRIERS When you have a negative emotional reaction to something someone says, it prevents you from concentrating on what is being said. To overcome this barrier, try to keep an open mind.

PLANNING A RESPONSE If you are trying to figure out what to say when another person is still speaking, you will not take in all that he or she is saying. To overcome this barrier, listen carefully until the other person has finished, and then respond.

READING

Reading, like listening, is an active mental process of receiving and understanding a message. Reading skills are essential for all jobs. In fact, they are usually needed to get a job in the first place. Applicants must read online job postings and help-wanted ads. In the workplace, reading skills are needed to interpret information in schedules, graphs, training manuals, letters, memos, e-mails, and reports.

KNOW THE PURPOSE OF YOUR READING

Many of the techniques for effective listening also apply to reading. For instance, it is helpful when reading to

▶ look for a plan

▶ search for an interest

▶ evaluate the message

A valuable technique for building good reading skills is to keep in mind the purpose for your reading. Good readers know *why* they are reading. When you read a novel, magazine, or newspaper, typically your purpose is reading for pleasure. You are hoping to simply enjoy what you are reading, so can read as fast or as slowly as you want.

When you read a job application form or a company memo, you have to read more carefully because you have a different purpose. This is information that is important to know in order to do your job well. Every word must be read carefully to ensure that you gain a complete understanding. You can accomplish this by using strategies that help you read for meaning.

Reading for Meaning
Focus
Summarize
Connect
Visualize
Build Vocabulary

READING FOR MEANING

Reading for meaning requires that a person read carefully. He or she must figure out the meaning of new words, search for answers, and analyze and evaluate information—often in a short period of time.

Most job-related reading assignments involve reading for meaning. For example, you may be required to search for sources online or read through a large report to find information about marketing trends. Another job-related reading task is checking facts.

There are five strategies that can improve the ability to read for meaning:

1. **Focus your mind.** The mind does not focus on a subject automatically. It must be trained. Monitoring your thoughts when you read can keep you focused. Think about how each paragraph relates to your purpose for reading.

2. **Summarize as you read.** As you finish each paragraph and section of the text, mentally review what you have just read and summarize it. If you do not understand the text, go over it again. If it is still unclear, jot down a question so that you can follow up on it later.

3. **Make connections.** Think about how the material relates to ideas or information with which you are familiar.

4. **Form mental pictures.** Try to form pictures of the people, places, things, and situations described. This can help you remember the material in a meaningful way.

5. **Build your vocabulary.** You may come across words that are unfamiliar when reading. Skipping over these words may cause you to miss key points in the message. Try to figure out the meaning by the way the word is used in the sentence. Use a dictionary and learn how to use the thesaurus and dictionary included in office computer software. Looking up words will improve your vocabulary and your understanding.

In job-related reading, you may come across **jargon**, a specialized vocabulary used by members of a particular group. Because these words or meanings are not commonly used, they are often not listed in standard dictionaries. If you do find a dictionary entry for a word that is often used as jargon, the definition given may not match the way it is used in a professional setting.

For example, when *market* is used by people who work in marketing, it is an example of jargon because it has a specific meaning for marketers. In the dictionary, *market* may be defined as "any place where business is conducted." To marketing professionals, however, *market* means "a group of people or organizations that share a need for a particular product and have the willingness and ability to pay for it."

Learning the jargon used in your field will make it easier for you to do job-related reading. You will be able to better understand information that relates to your profession. Asking questions about the way specific terms are used will help you familiarize yourself with words not found in the dictionary. Once you learn the jargon, you will be able to effectively communicate with others in your field.

You can expect to exchange job-related text messages and e-mails with co-workers, supervisors, customers, and suppliers. In addition to understanding the jargon used in your job, you will also need to learn the keyboard shortcuts and abbreviations specific to your company's business. You will find that these communication skills are vital to doing any job well.

 After You Read | **Section 8.1**

Review Key Concepts

1. **Explain** how feedback, barriers, and setting may affect communication.
2. **Identify** some strategies you can use to improve your listening skills.
3. **Discuss** how jargon can be a barrier to communication.

Practice Academics

English Language Arts

4. First, write an e-mail message to a friend asking when he or she can meet to discuss a class assignment. Second, write a short letter to your boss or your teacher asking when he or she can discuss a question about your job or your class assignment. Discuss with a partner how each of these pieces of writing is different.

Mathematics

5. Assume that the average person is awake for about 16 hours each day. If we spend 70 percent of our waking hours communicating, how many hours do we spend communicating in an average week?

Math Concept **Number and Operations: Representing Percents** A percent is a ratio comparing numbers to 100.

Starting Hints To solve this problem, convert the percent to a decimal by moving the decimal two places to the left. Multiply the average number of waking hours by the decimal equivalent of the percent to get the answer.

connectED.mcgraw-hill.com

Check your answers.

For help, go to the **Math Skills Handbook** located at the back of this book.

READING GUIDE

Share When have you had to change the way you spoke or wrote for different audiences?

Objectives

- **Explain** how to organize and present your ideas.
- **Demonstrate** professional telephone communication skills.
- **Explain** how to write effective business letters and persuasive messages.

The Main Idea

Speaking and writing are ways to send messages. Building professional speaking and writing skills will ensure that your messages are communicated successfully.

Vocabulary

Content Vocabulary
- persuade
- enumeration
- generalization

Academic Vocabulary

You will find these words in your reading and on your tests. Make sure you know their meanings.
- enhance
- sequence

Graphic Organizer

Draw or print this chart to write speaking tips in one circle and writing tips in the other. Write tips for both in the overlapping space.

Tips for Effective Communication

Effective Speaking — Speaking Writing — Effective Writing

 connectED.mcgraw-hill.com

Print this graphic organizer.

MARKETING CORE FUNCTIONS

Marketing Information Management

Promotion

Speech and Writing

SPEAKING

People use speech to answer the telephone, to ask questions, and to discuss plans at meetings. In marketing, speaking has applications in customer relations, presenting marketing plans, and television advertising. Speaking is an important part of most aspects of business and marketing, so it is important to know how to speak effectively.

As You Read

Consider How is talking with your friends different from presenting to your class?

SHOW RESPECT

In most business situations, the most important rule is to show courtesy and respect for others. Whether handling a customer complaint or addressing a coworker at a meeting, maintain a friendly tone and always use proper grammar and vocabulary.

KNOW THE PURPOSE

As with listening and reading, it is helpful when speaking to know your purpose. Most often, speaking is done to inform, persuade, or entertain.

▶ **Inform**—Conversations with customers and general business meetings are held to inform others—to pass on information. When speaking to inform, be clear and concise—get to the point.

▶ **Persuade**—Marketing involves sending messages that convince others to change how they think or what they do. To **persuade** someone is to convince that person to change an opinion in order to get him or her to do what you want. Before you prepare to speak, identify your listeners' needs. Then talk about how you, your company, or your product can meet those needs. Persuasive speaking is also important in conflict resolution, when there is a need to present a point of view or suggest a solution.

▶ **Entertain**—Sometimes the purpose of speaking is to entertain others. Salespeople frequently need to entertain clients or customers. It is not necessary to be a comedian to joke and tell stories. This kind of informal speaking helps create a comfortable atmosphere, build friendships, and improve customer relations.

USING YOUR VOICE AND NONVERBAL CUES

Good communicators use their voices effectively, changing their tone and pace to improve delivery. Some people, such as news or sports commentators, have a natural talent for delivery. With practice, you too can improve communication by better controlling your voice.

> **“ Speaking is an important part of most jobs. ”**

Nonverbal cues that can **enhance** presentation are body language and eye contact. When speaking, maintain eye contact with your listeners as much as possible.

SPEAKING FORMALLY

Effective speaking strategies are even more important in formal settings. Whether the speech is used to present a marketing plan to your marketing department or to give a speech to an audience of 500 people, the guidelines are the same. A good speech has a formal structure or organization. It begins with an opening statement that summarizes the topics to be covered. It ends with a concluding statement that reviews these topics. In between, four basic patterns can be used to structure the message. Visual aids often accompany the words spoken.

ENUMERATION

Enumeration is listing items in order. This strategy is often used when giving directions or explaining a process with steps. Use signal words, such as *first, second, third,* or *next,* to help the listener. These signal words show the relationship between what you have already said and what you will say next.

GENERALIZATION WITH EXAMPLES

Many speakers use generalizations to make a point. A **generalization** is a statement that is accepted as true by most people. Speakers support generalizations with evidence and examples. This creates confidence in the listener. For example, when you make a general statement, such as "Most people would rather have a smartphone than a plain cellular phone," you could support the claim with evidence. For example, "A Gallup poll on consumer preferences found that 75 percent of ordinary cell-phone users plan to replace their phones with a smartphone smartphone when they need a new phone."

Using evidence to support your generalizations also helps your listeners remember the main points. Signal words, such as *for instance* and *for example*, will help get your point across.

CAUSE AND EFFECT

When you present an issue in terms of cause and effect, you attempt to demonstrate that one event or situation is the cause of another. For example, you can show how implementing your marketing plan will allow the client to meet a sales goal. This pattern can be used effectively to persuade the listener. Use signal words or phrases, such as *therefore, consequently,* and *as a result* to help the listener understand the **sequence.**

COMPARE AND CONTRAST

Another pattern often used to persuade a listener is compare and contrast. In this pattern, new ideas are explained by showing how they are similar to or different from the ideas listeners already know. This approach is particularly useful when working in cross-cultural situations. Signal words or phrases such as *similarly, however, nevertheless,* and *on the other hand*, help to make the differences and similarities clear.

SPEAKING ON THE TELEPHONE

In most telephone conversations, your listener cannot see you. That means you cannot rely on facial expressions and body language to get your message across. The message is communicated only by voice, so a pleasant voice is very important.

Whether calling or answering, greet the other person in a cheerful but formal way. For example, you might say, "Customer Relations, this is Maria. How may I help you?" This greeting signals to the caller that he or she has reached the right number. Use a pleasant tone, enunciate clearly, and speak directly into the mouthpiece. Speak loudly enough for the other person to hear, but do not shout. Be courteous and respectful. Never interrupt when the other person is speaking. These guidelines are especially important when using a cellular phone, as sound quality often is not as clear as on land lines.

Speaking on the Phone
While video phones allow people to see each other as they speak, it is still important to be clear and direct while you speak on any kind of phone.

It is also necessary that you convey all the necessary information. It may be a good idea to write down key points before a phone call. Telephone customer service representatives and telemarketers use scripts.

Be prepared to take a message. Note the time of the call, the caller's name and message, and the return phone number. Repeat the telephone number to the caller to make sure it is correct. Most companies make use of voice mail so that callers may leave a message when the person is unavailable.

 Reading Check

Contrast How is enumeration different from generalization?

WRITING

Much business and marketing communication is in written form. A written message is necessary when there is a large volume of material and presenting it verbally would be impractical. Writing is also necessary when a permanent record of the communication is required. For instance, legal documents, manuals describing company policy, and letters confirming the terms of a deal are all written.

Writing takes more time and thought than a conversation. One advantage of writing a message rather than speaking it is that there is more time to organize the message. If your future is in marketing, you will need to develop effective business correspondence skills to write letters, e-mail, memos, and reports.

Each of these requires correct grammar, spelling, punctuation, and formatting. Marketing writing may also include print ads, scripts, and packaging.

BASIC CONSIDERATIONS IN WRITING

As with listening, reading, and speaking, it is important to know the reason for writing. The following are three basic considerations in writing:

1. **Know your audience.** Before you begin writing, think about who will receive your message. What do you know about them? Do they have the same experiences as you? Why will they read your message? What do they know about the subject? Answering these questions will help you to write a meaningful message.

MARKETING CASE STUDY

Gatorade® Simplifies with "G"

Few things are more iconic in the world of sports than Gatorade. Weary football players drink it from paper cups on the sidelines and excited players dump a cooler of it on their coach's head to celebrate victories. One of Gatorade's rebranding campaigns switched the focus to the amazing things athletes can do when they drink Gatorade. A part of that campaign involved simplifying the name down to simply "G."

A Call-to-Action

Gatorade flavors have traditionally had names like *Rain* or *X-Factor*, but under the rebranding, those names were switched to "calls-to-action." For instance, "Be Tough," "No Excuses" or "Bring It." Print ads show athletes in various poses, next to the letter G. On the bottles themselves, the name has also been simplified to the letter "G," alongside a redesigned lightning bolt logo.

English Language Arts/ Writing

Compose Gatorade conveys a message about its product by showing athletes in action next to the letter "G." Translate the impact of this image into words. Discuss whether it is more effective to describe the image or capture its message visually.

Many of today's marketing jobs require the ability to communicate well on the phone. *What are some advantages and disadvantages of telephone communication?*

2. **Know your purpose.** Why are you writing? Most of your marketing writing is done to inform, confirm, inquire, answer, or persuade. Marketing messages are often written to persuade. Some messages combine two or more purposes.

3. **Know your subject.** To write effective messages, you need in-depth knowledge and you must know how to relate what you know to what the customer wants to know. You may be well educated on certain subjects, but almost every new assignment will require further research.

DEVELOPING A WRITING STYLE

Writing style differs from industry to industry. The executives of a company generally establish the company's writing style. It usually includes guidelines on when to use formal and informal communication. As you read company letters, official e-mail, memos, and reports, you will gain a feel for how the firm wishes to present itself to clients.

In formal business writing, it is generally best to use a direct yet respectful conversational style. Whether writing to inquire, inform, or persuade, your writing should be crisp, clear, and easy to read. Be professional, but do not use big words to impress others. Use the grammar and spelling checkers on your word processing program to fix common errors. Always review your writing one final time to ensure that all errors are corrected.

If you sometimes overlook mistakes, ask a colleague to proofread your work.

Personalize your message by using the name of the person who will receive it. When writing to someone outside your company, be formal until you have developed a relationship in which it would be appropriate to be more informal and personal in your writing.

You may want to use jargon in your messages to people in your professional field. However, when writing to a mixed audience, it is best to avoid jargon. If jargon is necessary, clearly define any technical words.

USE LANGUAGE EFFECTIVELY

Pay attention to the words and phrases used by your clients, vendors, and associates. If they are different from the ones you generally use, translate your ideas and feelings into language that makes sense to them. Using the words and phrases familiar to your audience in your communications can be a powerful persuasive technique.

ORGANIZE YOUR THOUGHTS

Construct your persuasive message in three parts:

1. an opening paragraph
2. a persuasive body
3. a concluding paragraph

In the opening paragraph, grab your readers' attention. State clearly why you are writing and involve them in some way, perhaps addressing them using *you* if appropriate.

Begin each body paragraph with a topic sentence. Follow with three to five sentences in which you develop a single point. Use connectives, such as *therefore* and *so you see*. Ethical writing requires honesty, so be sure to acknowledge any significant point of view that may differ from your own. There is nothing wrong with presenting evidence showing that your view is more likely to result in the desired outcome. If you can, quote a recognized expert or survey to add support for your case. Try to create a vivid image to help your reader see your point of view.

Your concluding paragraph should be positive and interesting. It should strongly support the message outlined in your introduction. Restate the points made in the body. Cite the evidence in support of each point. Emphasize the overall reason your position, product, or service is worth considering. Finally, state exactly what action should be taken next to achieve the mutually acceptable outcome.

FORMS OF WRITTEN COMMUNICATION

Most business writing is in the form of letters, e-mail, memos, and reports. Each of these formats follows its own very specific rules of style.

LETTERS

Written communication with people outside the company is usually done with business letters or e-mail. Letters are the more formal of the two. They are used for purposes such as official announcements, thank yous, and confirmations of business transactions. In direct-mail marketing, targeted letters are often written addressing the needs or interests of specific groups.

E-MAIL

E-mail is the method of choice for fast, informal communication with those inside and outside the company. Marketers often use e-mail for informal contacts between the firm and the client. E-mail has the advantage of speed over other forms of written communication. With e-mail, files can be attached to, or sent along with, the message.

While e-mail norms differ between companies, a typical interoffice e-mail contains the following:

▶ An informative subject title

▶ A traditional (not personal) greeting

▶ A concise, clearly stated body

▶ A statement regarding the type of response needed

▶ A formal closing and signature (For the signature, type your name, company, address, phone and fax number, and e-mail address.)

Although e-mail has a reputation for speed and informality, it is important to remember that, like all written communication, it leaves a permanent record. Business e-mails are official documents. They are the property of the company or firm.

Many companies have strict e-mail policies. The following rules are found in most e-mail policies:

▶ Save only essential e-mail.

▶ Do not forward e-mail without the sender's express permission.

▶ Seek permission, and then use extreme care when forwarding confidential e-mails.

▶ Use only copyrighted materials that you have permission, or have paid, to use.

▶ Do not use company computers for personal e-mail except as specifically allowed.

When writing business e-mail, follow the guidelines for business writing described above. Compose your messages carefully, and use conventional business language and style. One difference is that e-mail messages tend to be shorter and more concise than letters.

MEMOS

In most businesses, e-mail, instant messaging, and even texting have, to a considerable extent, replaced the use of memos. A memorandum, or memo, is a written message to someone in the company. It is usually brief and covers only one subject. Most memos are written in a simple format that has a standard set of headings. The standard headings include the sender's and receiver's names, the date, the subject, and a message in paragraph form. Correct grammar, spelling, and punctuation are as important in a memo as in letters and reports.

BUSINESS REPORTS

Business reports usually cover lengthy topics, such as yearly sales, survey results, or problems that need attention. Some, called "in-house reports," are meant to be read only by company employees. Others, such as reports to stockholders, are written for a wider audience and are more formal. An in-house report can be written by a company department to let management know the results of a project, or a report might move from one department to another. For example, the sales department may produce a report to tell the design department how customers like a product. Several people may give input to produce the report, but one person is usually responsible for writing the final document.

Many of the techniques used in preparing a speech are also appropriate in preparing a report. Enumeration, generalization with example, cause and effect, and compare and contrast are patterns of organization that work well for reports. A simple report can be brief, perhaps as short as one page. Complex reports include more data and may use a variety of charts and graphs.

COMPANY PUBLICATIONS

Many companies produce internal publications for their employees, such as newsletters or employee handbooks of policies and procedures. These are often available online at password-protected pages on the company Web site. (Publishing them online saves money and conserves paper.) Some companies produce external publications, such as promotional brochures about the company or its products. A communications department writes internal publications, while a marketing department writes external publications.

MEETINGS AND PARLIAMENTARY PROCEDURE

Parliamentary procedure is a structure for holding group meetings and making decisions. DECA, for example, uses this structure for its meetings. Parliamentary procedure favors the opinion of the majority of a group, but the viewpoint of the minority is not overlooked. Parliamentary procedure has a very specific structure.

A QUORUM

A quorum is a proportion of the membership required to conduct official business. It may be a set number of members, such as 20. A quorum may also be a certain percentage of the membership, such as 51 percent.

ORDER OF BUSINESS

The meeting follows a standard order of business, which is called an agenda. The standard format for a meeting is as follows

1. **Call to order** This statement alerts all members that the meeting is beginning and that they should be quiet.

2. **Minutes of the meeting** The secretary reads the minutes, which are a written record that outlines the decisions made at the last meeting.

3. **Treasurer's report** The treasurer reports the money received since the last meeting, the money spent, and the current balance.

4. **Committee reports** Each committee presents a report to let the entire membership know what has been done and what else is left to do.

5. **Old business** Any issues that were discussed but were not decided on become old business.

6. **New business** New ideas are brought up at the end of the meeting.

7. **Adjournment** This is the official end of the meeting. The secretary records the time of adjournment in the minutes.

THE MOTION

After being allowed to speak by the chairperson, a member makes a motion, or proposal. Another member must second the motion. After discussion, a vote is taken on the motion.

 After You Read | **Section 8.2**

Review Key Concepts

1. **Describe** how each of the most common purposes for speaking might be used in a business situation.

2. **Explain** the nature of effective verbal communication and why written messages have some advantages over spoken messages.

3. **Explain** the importance of using correct grammar, spelling, punctuation, and formatting when writing effective business correspondence.

Practice Academics

English Language Arts

4. Imagine you need to share your company's new waste management policies with your employees. Write a memo about the policies and summarize it orally to a partner. Have your partner read your memo and discuss how reading and listening to the memo was different.

Mathematics

5. Communication on the Internet travels at the speed of light—186,000 miles per second. How long would it take an e-mail to travel 5,000 miles? Round your answer to the nearest one-thousandth of a second.

Math Concept **Measurement: Process** Apply appropriate techniques, tools, and formulas to determine measurements.

Starting Hints To solve this problem, divide the distance 5,000 miles by the travel speed of communication on the Internet, 186,000 miles per second, to determine the amount of time it takes for that e-mail to travel.

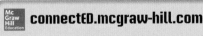 **connectED.mcgraw-hill.com**

Check your answers.

For help, go to the **Math Skills Handbook** located at the back of this book.

Communication Skills

The communication process includes channels, barriers, feedback, and setting.

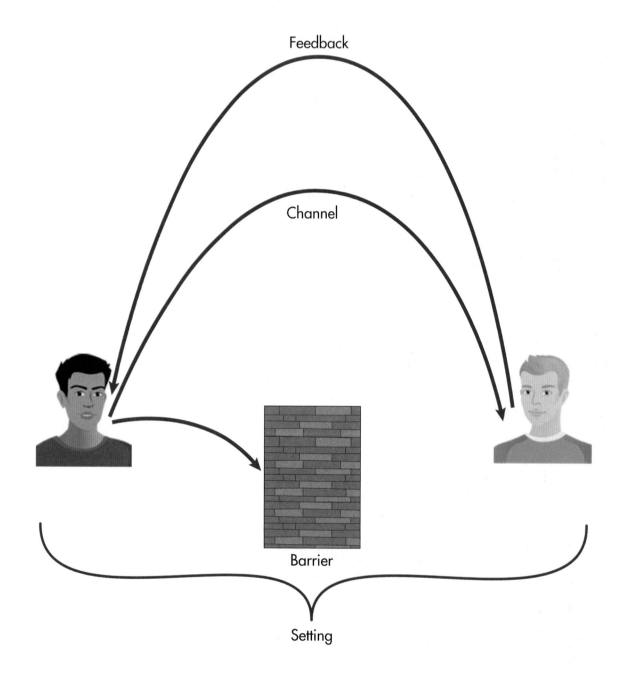

Review and Activities

Written Summary

- Communication is effective when the speaker or writer presents the message clearly and concisely so that the listener or reader can understand it easily.

- Listening is especially important when communicating with customers' complaints and needs.

- The global economy has brought new pressures on companies to communicate with customers and vendors around the world.

- Overcoming cultural barriers to listening with understanding is now more important than ever.

- As the volume of information to be absorbed increases, reading for meaning—the ability to differentiate what is important from what is not—is becoming an important business skill.

- Most business and marketing jobs require the ability to communicate a message clearly, concisely, and courteously by speaking and writing.

- It is especially important to communicate effectively on the telephone because the listener cannot see you.

- The patterns used to organize a formal speech also apply to writing.

- Persuasion is used to convince others of the value or importance of an idea or thing.

- The simplest and often most effective way to persuade others is to learn their needs and propose a way to fulfill them.

Review Content Vocabulary and Academic Vocabulary

1. Write each of the vocabulary terms below on an index card, and the definitions on separate index cards. Work in pairs or small groups to match each term to its definition.

Content Vocabulary
- communication (p. 191)
- channels/media (p. 191)
- feedback (p. 191)
- barriers (p. 191)
- setting (p. 191)
- distractions (p. 194)
- emotional barriers (p. 194)
- jargon (p. 197)
- persuade (p. 199)
- enumeration (p. 200)
- generalization (p. 200)

Academic Vocabulary
- process (p. 191)
- respond (p. 192)
- enhance (p. 199)
- sequence (p. 200)

Assess for Understanding

2. **Discuss** Why is it important to have awareness of cultural differences when doing business?

3. **Suggest** What are some ways to break down one of the barriers to effective listening?

4. **Weigh** What are the pros and cons of using the telephone for business communication?

5. **Compare and Contrast** What is similar and different about the way a business writes a memo with the way you write an essay for school?

6. **Evaluate** What writing style did you use in an assignment you completed for another class?

7. **Imagine** When might jargon confuse an audience? How can this problem be overcome?

8. **Revise** How can you improve a previous assignment to include persuasion, enumeration, or generalization?

9. **Discuss** Are you more comfortable with written or oral communication?

 21st Century Skills

Communication Skills

10. Preparing a Formal Speech You have been asked to speak at a state marketing conference on the topic *New Technology for Marketing*. Research current products that would interest people in the marketing field. Prepare an outline of your speech and indicate how you might use enumeration, generalization with examples, cause and effect, or compare and contrast patterns in your presentation.

Financial Literacy Skills

11. Budgeting Your paycheck does not seem to last until the next payday even now. You do not know where all the money goes. A budget will help you get more for your money. The first step is to keep a list of every dollar you spend in the next two weeks. Record how you spent this money and identify how you can save more.

e-Marketing Skills

12. Designing a Web Page Partner with a classmate to design an order form that customers can use to order merchandise from a company that sells casual clothing. Each partner should contribute ideas. Include all of the information that you would need from a customer to fill an order. Use the following questions to help you design your Web page:

- What types of casual clothing does your store sell?
- How will customers know whether the clothes fit them if they cannot try them on first?
- Can the order form be printed out, written on, and sent through the mail, or does it need to be completed entirely online? How does your choice of approach meet your customers' needs?
- What happens if an item is out of stock?
- How can customers contact the company with questions about their order?

Build Academic Skills

Social Studies

13. Culture Research differences in how people from cultures outside of the United States communicate when speaking. Consider such differences in how those from other cultures greet one another, and whether and how they shake hands, make eye contact, or gesture. Write a half-page report about your findings.

English Language Arts

14. Writing Imagine that you are composing a press release for your business. Write three versions of the press release. In one, write the press release so that an elementary school student can understand it. In another, write the press release so that your peers can understand it. In the final paper, write the press release so that your market share can understand it. Compare the writing styles in each press release and discuss the effectiveness and appropriateness of each.

Mathematics

15. Find Total Cost You have been asked to make arrangements for an off-site meeting for your company. A local hotel charges $250 to rent a conference room for a half day and $400 for a full day. The hotel charges $18 per person for each lunch served and $35 per person for each dinner served. How much will it cost to rent the conference room for two and one-half days and to provide lunch and dinner for 16 people for two days?

Math Concept Problem Solving: Multi-Step Problems When a word problem involves multiple steps and is confusing, outline the information you know before you solve.

For help, go to the **Math Skills Handbook** located at the back of this book.

Standardized Test Practice

Directions Read the following questions. On a separate piece of paper, write the best possible answer for each one.

1. When listening, you will learn more if you pay close attention to the speaker's
   A. rate of speech
   B. pitch
   C. volume
   D. all of the above

2. True or false? Planning a response is a very common block to listening.
   T
   F

3. Nonverbal cues that can enhance your presentation are body language and _____ _____.

Test-Taking Tip

Arrive early and do not talk to other students just before you enter the room to avoid being distracted.

DECA Connection Role Play

Employee
Fast-Food Restaurant

Situation Assume the role of experienced employee of a franchise fast-food hamburger restaurant. The restaurant's corporate office has decided to begin offering healthier menu options that will be available in one month. The healthier menu options will include three new entrée salads. The new salads include tossed salad greens with tomato and cucumber slices, Caesar salad, and Greek salad with green pepper and cucumber slices. All salads will cost $4.99. Grilled chicken is available as an optional topping for an additional $1.99. Salad dressings include the choice of vinaigrette, low-fat Thousand Island, Caesar dressing, and low-fat Caesar dressing.

Your manager (judge) has given you a written description of the new menu items. The manager (judge) has also asked you to prepare a description of the new salad items and the reasons they are being added to the menu. You will make your presentation to the staff at the next staff meeting.

Activity You are to prepare an outline of the information you will present at the staff meeting. Be prepared to answer staff questions. You are to review your presentation with your manager (judge) before the staff meeting.

Evaluation You will be evaluated on how well you meet the following performance indicators:

1. Extract relevant information from written material.
2. Prepare simple written reports.
3. Organize information.
4. Participate in a staff meeting.
5. Make oral presentations.

 connectED.mcgraw-hill.com

Download the Competitive Events Workbook for more Role-Play practice.

Chapter 9

Section 9.1
Computer Applications

Section 9.2
Technology and
Marketing

technology for marketing

Visual Literacy Advances in technology have brought about the most productive period in United States and world history. Fast and powerful computer applications make it easy to do business and communicate with people all over the world. *What opportunities and challenges does fast-paced global communication present?*

Discovery Project

Software Applications

Essential Question	How has computer technology increased productivity?

Project Goal

Assume that you are an employee at a popular bicycle shop that sells products and does repairs. Because of your background in technology, your boss has asked you to make recommendations for upgrading software applications for the store. Presently, the only software used by the store includes two older programs for word processing and billing. Use your imagination regarding what would benefit the store. Research types of software programs on the Internet. Then recommend which types of programs should be considered as well as one or two brand names of programs.

Ask Yourself...

- What key words will you use to initiate your research?
- How will you determine the needs of the store that can by solved with new software?
- How could discussing the software needs and possible products with another employee help you with your project?

 Problem Solving What criteria will you use when selecting software products to recommend?

 connectED.mcgraw-hill.com

Activity
Get a worksheet activity about marketing technology.

Evaluate
Download a rubric you can use to evaluate your project.

DECA Connection

DECA Event Role Play

Concepts in this chapter are related to DECA competitive events that involve either an interview or role play.

Performance Indicator The performance indicators represent key skills and knowledge. Your key to success in DECA competitive events is relating them to the concepts in this chapter.

- Describe the use of technology in operations.
- Explain the impact of technology on retailing
- Explain the use of technology in customer relationship management.
- Describe the scope of the Internet.
- Demonstrate Web-search skills.

DECA Prep

Role Play Practice role-playing with the DECA Connection competitive-event activity at the end of this chapter. More information on DECA events can be found on DECA's Web site.

READING GUIDE

 Before You Read

Connect How do you use computers to help with routine tasks?

Objectives

- **Identify** nine types of computer applications.
- **Explain** how computer applications are used in business and marketing.

The Main Idea

Careers in marketing require an understanding and skillful use of computers and several types of software.

Vocabulary

Content Vocabulary

- word-processing programs
- database programs
- accounting programs
- spreadsheet programs
- desktop publishing programs
- graphics and design programs
- presentation software
- home page
- hypertext markup language (HTML)
- communications programs
- Wi-Fi

Academic Vocabulary

You will find these words in your reading and on your tests. Make sure you know their meanings.

- analyze
- edit

Type of Software	Uses
Word-Processing	
Database	
Accounting	
Spreadsheet	
Desktop Publishing	
Graphics and Design	
Presentation	
Web page Editor	
Communications	

Graphic Organizer

Draw or print this chart to note the nine types of software discussed in this section.

 connectED.mcgraw-hill.com

Print this graphic organizer.

MARKETING CORE FUNCTIONS

 Marketing Information Management

 Promotion

Computer Applications

TYPES OF APPLICATIONS

For personal use, daily planners and calendar applications manage time. Financial software manages money. Some applications serve as address books, while others help manage photos. For business use, virtually all businesses use computer applications. Medical offices use programs to schedule patients and track billing. Hotels use applications to manage room assignments and generate bills. Software is constantly being written, tested, and marketed to meet business needs.

As You Read

Predict What computer applications do you think marketers use?

WORD-PROCESSING PROGRAMS

Word-processing programs are applications that create text documents that may contain a few graphics. The benefits of a word-processing program include being able to determine the format of a document and see on screen exactly how the document will look when printed out. This is called "WYSIWYG," which stands for "What You See Is What You Get." Word-processing programs help develop more effective business correspondence by correcting and editing mistakes in spelling, grammar, punctuation, and formatting.

These programs also provide accurate word counts and add design elements, among many other features. The most common word-processing program is Microsoft Word®. There are many others, even free word-processing programs that you can find by searching the Internet. Businesses use word-processing programs to do the following:

- Write letters and memos.
- Produce research papers and reports.
- Develop business and marketing plans.
- Write contracts.
- Take notes and record meeting minutes.
- Create announcements.
- Create product manuals.

> **"There is a computer application for just about every purpose imaginable."**

DATABASE PROGRAMS

Database programs are applications that store and organize information. Database programs allow users to sort, find, filter, and organize information. A database can hold information about a company's products, orders, shipments, and customers. The power of a database is its ability to link that information together. Common database software includes Filemaker Pro®, Microsoft Access®, and 4D®. Database programs are available online, too, and some are free. Marketers use database programs to help with the following business needs:

- Maintain customer lists for automated mass mailings.
- Keep information about guests and vendors for parties and events.
- Catalog furniture and assets for insurance records.
- Manage time and track billable hours.
- Catalog personnel records.
- Scan the Internet to find suppliers and customers.
- Track the searches and purchases of clients visiting Web sites.

Suppose you are using a database of your company's mailing list. That mailing list contains the names and addresses of more than 3,000 customers. With one keystroke, the database can alphabetize the list by last name, group the addresses by ZIP code, or display only those customers who use post office boxes. Including purchase histories in the database allows you to quickly pull up a list of all customers who made purchases during a certain month or who purchased a certain dollar amount of merchandise.

Open-Source Applications
Some software developers create programs that are free for anyone to use and develop.

ACCOUNTING PROGRAMS

The purpose of accounting is to collect and present financial data. **Accounting programs** can store and retrieve financial records and process all business transactions automatically. They can also provide an immediate and accurate picture of a company's financial status at any time. Accounting software is available for small businesses, large businesses, and every size of business in between. The most popular accounting program for small and medium-sized businesses is Intuit QuickBooks®.

Most large companies use an integrated computer system known as *Enterprise Resource Planning* (ERP). Before ERP, such functions as human resources, customer relations, supply chain management, manufacturing functions, and warehouse management each had a separate accounting program. ERP integrates data and processes of all functions of a business into a single database.

Accounting software is available for specific industries, such as manufacturing, shipping, medicine, law, and many others. Some businesses have their own custom accounting software written to their specifications.

SPREADSHEET PROGRAMS

Spreadsheet programs can organize, calculate, and **analyze** numerical data. With spreadsheets, you can perform financial and scientific calculations, organize numeric information, illustrate data with charts and graphs, and create professional-looking reports. Spreadsheets graphically display the relationship of data in the form of charts and graphs. It is often easier for people to understand charts than raw data. Microsoft Excel® is the most popular spreadsheet program. Businesspeople use spreadsheets to perform the following tasks:

- Develop a budget.
- Analyze financial performance.
- Track loans or mortgages.
- Track stock and bond performance.
- Schedule projects.
- Manage business assets.
- Produce profit and loss statements.
- Calculate and produce a payroll.
- Track client/customer responses.
- Build relationship marketing.
- Track sales and service.

With a spreadsheet program, you can perform financial calculations, illustrate data with charts and graphs, and create professional-looking reports and presentations. *How might you use spreadsheet programs for school purposes?*

Using a Spreadsheet Program

A spreadsheet consists of a grid of rows and columns. Users enter data and formulas into cells on the grid. The program performs calculations with speed and accuracy not possible by hand or with a calculator. When you change one piece of information, the spreadsheet automatically updates all related numbers. For example, you can see how adjusting the price of a product would affect sales, taxes, and the overall budget.

DESKTOP PUBLISHING PROGRAMS

Part word processor and part graphics application, **desktop publishing programs** enable users to **edit** and manipulate both text and graphics in one document. Desktop publishing software can produce documents that are creative, attractive, professional, and easy to read. The two most popular commercial programs are Adobe InDesign® and QuarkXPress®. Marketers use desktop publishing in the following ways:

- Create layouts for newsletters, books, brochures, and advertisements.
- Create professional-looking forms, such as invoices and project planning sheets.
- Create product manuals.

GRAPHICS AND DESIGN PROGRAMS

Graphics and design programs are software applications for creating and modifying images. Designers can create graphic elements themselves with the drawing tools provided by the software. Or, they can use photos and ready-made artwork, such as Clip art. These images are usually grouped together in categories like business, food, sports, people, places, animals, cartoons, and holidays. There are dozens of graphics programs, with some of the most common being Adobe Photoshop®, Adobe Illustrator®, CorelDRAW®, and Flash®. Marketers and businesses can use graphics programs to do the following:

- Design marketing promotion materials.
- Create logos and letterheads.
- Illustrate floor plans and furniture arrangements.

- Create professional-looking illustrations and photographic prints.
- Create images for presentations or for Web pages and Internet ads.

PRESENTATION SOFTWARE

Presentation software produces slide shows or multimedia presentations. This software helps users organize ideas and concepts to be presented in a meeting. Businesses and marketers can use presentation software to help with these tasks:

- Prepare verbal and visual information for meetings.
- Present and discuss ideas interactively via the Internet with clients in other cities or countries.
- Create slide shows using pictures or Web pages.
- Add voice narration to accompany visual material.

Presentation software can incorporate a series of slides, film clips, and streaming video. Presentations can include text, bulleted lists, graphs, photographs, and screen shots. It can even include interactive problem and decision situations. Voice narration can create a feeling of a live meeting even if participants are not together.

Software Programs

Many popular software programs are excellent for doing business tasks, but some are not. Research different products before you go shopping for a program. *What are some advantages and disadvantages of buying and downloading software online?*

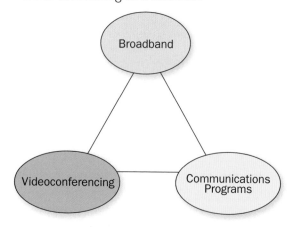

With a desktop publishing program, you can produce documents that are creative, attractive, professional, and easy to read. *What are some of the benefits of creating documents that are attractive and easy to read?*

Desktop Publishing

As global interaction in the business world increases, programs like this simplify communication and cut down on travel time. Some examples of presentation software programs are Microsoft PowerPoint® and Apple Keynote®.

WEB-PAGE EDITORS

The Internet has become an integral part of our world. Many businesses use their Web sites to promote their companies and products and to stay connected to their customers.

Web sites feature a **home page**, which is the entry point for a Web site. It gives general information to introduce the company, person, or product. The home page has links to other pages containing additional information, such as product details and contact information. The home page can also link to an online store or other interactive resources.

Creating a Web page used to require writing very specific, detailed, and complicated code, called **hypertext markup language (HTML)**.

Today Web-editing programs enable people to create Web pages as if they were using a word processor or a desktop publishing program. Some of the most popular of these applications are Macromedia® Dreamweaver® and Microsoft FrontPage®.

COMMUNICATIONS PROGRAMS

Communications programs enable users to communicate with other users through their computers. The key to using any communication software is connecting to a network.

Broadband

Videoconferencing

Communications Programs

Presentation software has become an indispensable tool in many business meetings. *What are some ways you might use presentation software in your school or personal activities?*

Show and Tell

BROADBAND AND WIRELESS (G3) TECHNOLOGY

Broadband technology allows information to move through cable TV or special DSL phone lines. It transmits large amounts of data at very high speeds. Broadband allows audio chat or video conferencing to take place in real time (without delay) and complex Web pages to load in seconds.

Wireless routers provide Internet connectivity without a physical connection. This technology, called **Wi-Fi** (*wireless fidelity*), creates a wireless Internet connection with radio frequencies.

Third and fourth generation (3G and 4G) technology uses mobile phones to transmit data wirelessly. With a connector plugged into a USB port, a computer can connect to the Web from any location where there is cell-phone coverage.

This popular technology will continue to grow as the technology moves into more countries and becomes cheaper to use.

VIDEOCONFERENCING

Videoconferencing has many advantages. Its greatest professional advantage is that it can reduce the need for expensive business travel. Travel time and expenses can be dramatically reduced by holding videoconferences rather than meeting in person.

COMMUNICATIONS PROGRAMS

Communications programs include e-mail software such as Microsoft Outlook® and Apple Mail®; instant-messaging software such as AOL Instant Messenger®; and videoconferencing software such as Apple iChat® and Skype®.

 After You Read   **Section 9.1**

Review Key Concepts

1. **Describe** how you would use graphics and design programs and presentation software to create information to share with customers.
2. **Suggest** reasons for the popularity of database programs in business settings.
3. **Explain** what might happen to a business that does not use computer applications effectively.

Practice Academics

English Language Arts

4. Research the latest technological products that would appeal to people between 17 and 22. Suggest how marketers might sell these products.

Mathematics

5. The cable company charges a $49.95 one-time connection fee, which includes the price of hardware. The cost of service is $45.95 per month. The phone company charges $79.95 for the connection fee and hardware, plus $29.95 per month. What is the difference in the cost of the two plans for a 12-month period?

Math Concept **Multi-Step Problems** Solving some problems requires more than one operation used in a logical order.

Starting Hints Multiply the monthly fee of each plan by 12 to find the annual fee for each plan. Add the connection and hardware charge to each plan to determine the total cost for the service.

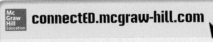

connectED.mcgraw-hill.com

Check your answers.

For help, go to the **Math Skills Handbook** located at the back of this book.

READING GUIDE

 Before You Read

Connect What everyday activities would you do differently if you could not use the Internet or computers?

Objectives

- **Describe** the computer software programs that are influencing and reshaping marketing.
- **Explain** how the Internet and the World Wide Web can increase business productivity.

The Main Idea

The Internet and technological innovations are providing businesses with new marketing opportunities to offer better service to customers.

Vocabulary

Content Vocabulary
- Enterprise Resource Planning (ERP)
- World Wide Web
- Internet
- hypertext transfer protocol (HTTP)
- uniform resource locator (URL)
- firewall
- site map

Academic Vocabulary

You will find these words in your reading and on your tests. Make sure you know their meanings.
- consists
- link

Graphic Organizer

Draw or print this chart to write in the five types of specialized computer technology that marketers use.

 **connectED.mcgraw-hill.com**

Print this graphic organizer.

MARKETING CORE FUNCTIONS

 Marketing Information Management

 Promotion

m.e. Section 9.2 Technology and Marketing

TECHNOLOGY FOR MARKETING

Today marketing software includes point-of-sale systems, interactive touch-screen computers, interactive TV, just-in-time schedulers, customer relationship management, and enterprise resource planning systems.

As You Read

Connect What are some ways you have used technology to make purchases?

POINT-OF-SALE SYSTEMS

A common use of computers in retailing is the point-of-sale (POS) system. This system **consists** of cash registers and peripherals, such as scanners, touch screens, handheld checkout devices, printers, and electronic kiosks. Scanners feed information directly from merchandise tags or labels into a computer to update inventory. See Chapter 16 for more information on POS systems.

> **Computer and software applications are shaping the way marketers conduct business.**

INTEGRATED MARKETING SOFTWARE

For a company to be truly successful, it must be tuned in to its customers needs and wants. Managing the relationships the company has with its customers is at the core of a business strategy called customer relationship management (CRM). This strategy now employs technology to gather and analyze customer information, including viewing customers' sales histories, and customizing promotions for particular groups of customers that a company wants to target.

New CRM applications are Internet-enabled, fully integrated Web-service applications. A customer can place an order online. The customer can also check the progress of the order either on the Web or by telephone. A company, in turn, can track all of that information in order to better serve its customers.

In addition to tracking the business the customer is doing with the company, it can suggest other products the customer may want to purchase. Through "cookies" stored in the customer's computer, it can generate ads for other Web sites targeting the customer's interests. CRM can also track the customer's satisfaction level at each step in the sales process.

Point-of-sale systems (POS) serve the same purpose as cash registers, but they also scan bar codes, update inventory, and track information that can be helpful in store management. *What stores do you shop in where POS systems are used? What stores do you shop where a POS system is not used?*

Point-of-Sale Checkout

The GREEN Marketer

E-Mail Marketing: Saving Trees

E-mail is a cheaper, faster, and more environmentally friendly way to reach customers than traditional print mail. It is quick to produce and send. It does not require paper, ink, or fuel for transportation.

Offering customers the option to switch from print to e-mail for statements, bills, and other communications helps companies save money and create an environmentally aware image.

Mining Data

For marketers, e-mail is also a rich source of market information. By studying what links customers click in e-mail, marketers can discover what they are interested in and what kinds of offers motivate them to buy. Marketers can use this information to create new advertisements or products that will interest their customers.

Social Studies

Imagine Brainstorm a few ideas for technology such as email that can be used to replace print or personal communication. Describe how these changes would affect the use of resources by people around the world.

---

 connectED.mcgraw-hill.com

Get an activity on green marketing.

ENTERPRISE RESOURCE PLANNING (ERP)

Enterprise resource planning (ERP) software is used to integrate all parts of a company's business management, including planning, manufacturing, sales, marketing, invoicing, payroll, inventory control, order tracking, customer service, finance, and human resources. Both CRM and ERP applications can help generate marketing reports and solve marketing problems.

INTERACTIVE TOUCH-SCREEN COMPUTERS

A touch screen is a computer display screen that responds to human touch. This allows the user to interact with the computer by touching words or pictures on the screen. (See **Figure 9.1**.) Tablets, such as Apple's iPad, and many smartphones, such as Apple's iPhone®, use touchscreen technology.

Interactive computers are on shelves in retail stores and in stand-alone kiosks at malls and airports. Computer-assisted transactions are well suited for products, goods, and services that are fairly standard and receptive to programmable decision making. Costly or complex products need a degree of personal contact that is not possible without a salesperson.

INTERACTIVE TELEVISION

Interactive TV systems use satellite technology and computer hardware and software to make the TV function like a computer. Advertisers like the idea of interactive television because consumers can instantly get more information about products through their TVs. Some shopping channels offer the ability to buy merchandise using the TV's remote control.

THE CLICKSTREAM

Interactive TV also benefits marketers because of the click stream. Every click of the remote control goes into a database for later analysis. From this data, an idea of individual viewers and what motivates them emerges. Programmers can use this data to monitor viewers' reactions to content and then use that information in the future. Over time marketers can develop psychological profiles of individual viewers that provide an enormous amount of information.

✓ Reading Check

Analyze When are computer-assisted transactions and programmable decision making not suitable for customers?

FIGURE 9.1 | Marketing with Interactive Technology

Conversing with a Computer Interactive technology provides a way to have a conversation with a computer. It is changing the way products and services are marketed. It has also made sales and ordering more streamlined and efficient. Let's look at some ways interactive technology is used in marketing. *Why is it important for marketers to know how to use interactive technology?*

TOUCH-SCREEN COMPUTERS, COMPUTERIZED SALESPEOPLE Touch-screen computers allow customers to locate product information without the help of salespeople. The computers can check inventory and prices, suggest other merchandise a customer might like, and even connect to a wedding gift registry created in another state.

INTERACTIVE TV With interactive TV, viewers can vote for their favorite TV character, access information related to a program, download reality show contestant biographies, or **link** to an online store. Sports fans can use interactive TV to get up-to-the-minute results for their favorite teams or athletes.

E-COMMERCE E-commerce allows customers to view products, compare prices, and order—all at the click of a mouse. They can compare prices and styles at hundreds of online stores in a matter of minutes without leaving home. Information supplied when placing orders is captured in a database and used by a marketer to generate future sales.

THE WORLD WIDE WEB

Although the terms are often used synonymously, the **World Wide Web** and the **Internet** are actually two different things. The Web is a part of the Internet and is a collection of interlinked electronic documents. These pages are viewed with a browser. A browser is any piece of software that tells the computer what Web content to display. Web pages contain links that prompt the browser to load a new page.

Researcher Tim Berners Lee invented the technology behind the Web. He developed the **hypertext transfer protocol (HTTP)** that links documents together. He also developed the **uniform resource locator (URL)**, which is the protocol used to identify and locate Web pages on the Internet. It is also known as a *Web address*.

Today there are billions of pages on the Web. Hundreds of thousands of new Web pages are added every week. Because the World Wide Web does not have a system for locating or categorizing content, companies have developed an assortment of Web directories and search engines to help users find what they want.

The Internet

The World Wide Web

SEARCH ENGINES

Two of the most popular search engines are Google® and Yahoo!®. Google is by far the largest with a database of more than a trillion URLs. Many of the most useful and common Web pages are known to all search engines, but there are also many sites and pages identified only by one or two search engines. Always check other search engines to find sites missed by Google and Yahoo!.

Search engines try to return results that relate well to your search terms. But they are also designed to make money for the company. To do that, search engines will place paid advertisers near or high up in the search results listings. Ads may also appear alongside your search results.

ELECTRONIC MAIL

E-mail represents another revolutionary change prompted by the development of the Internet. E-mail is popular because it is delivered immediately. Also, the sender and receiver do not have to be available at the same time.

For example, an appliance store employee can e-mail an order for new merchandise to a shipper in a different time zone. The shipper can acknowledge the order when the employee arrives at work, and the merchandise can be prepared for shipment almost immediately.

One annoying aspect of using e-mail is the high number of messages from sources unknown to you. These messages are known as *spam*. All e-mail programs have filters that sort out spam, usually placing it in a separate folder, such as "junk mail." The CAN-SPAM law, passed by Congress in 2003, bans certain spamming techniques and requires senders to include a valid address. Although the law has made it easier to install filters to block spam, unwanted e-mail is still a problem.

Protecting Digital Data
Cyberattacks on 27 South Korean commercial and government Web sites in September 2009 temporarily jammed over half of them.

Another misuse of e-mail is phishing, which is an attempt to get you to share personal information. This is more of a problem on personal computers used at home than at the workplace.

An example is an e-mail that appears to be from your bank. It includes your bank's logo, name, and address—everything that makes it look like an official request from your bank for information. You should not provide information to such requests as they are attempts to gain information that could be used to commit fraud. Banks do not request information in this way.

INTRANETS AND EXTRANETS

An intranet is a private, secure network, usually within a company or organization that contains proprietary company data and can be accessed only by internal users. Some businesses have developed networks for their customers, employees, partners, and suppliers. These networks, called extranets, enable customers to access data stored on an internal server. A firewall protects the security of sensitive information. A **firewall** is a hardware and software checkpoint for all requests for inputs of data, incoming and outgoing. The firewall reviews the message to make sure that the data content is safe and acceptable for others to view.

WEB-SITE DEVELOPMENT

A business develops a Web site as a convenient and far-reaching way to inform customers, potential employees, business partners, and even investors about the company and the products it offers. A Web site can also enable the business to sell its products, to provide related resources, and to handle services and inquiries after the sale.

Any Web site's domain name comes from the Internet Corporation for Assigned Names and Numbers (ICANN). The domain name is the part of a URL that identifies a server or service provider. Top-level domains are three-letter extensions, which follow the dot in a Web address. Examples of top-level generic domains include *.com* and *.biz* for businesses and *.org* for nonprofit organizations.

Companies should plan to incur several costs to develop Web sites, including domain name registration, development and maintenance of the Web site, and subscription to a server (if one is not available in-house).

Most business Web sites have similar components that include the following: a branding logo, content, a shopping cart for electronic purchases, a secured payment system for purchases, and general policies related to privacy, shipping, returns, and sales taxes. Other features may include video, podcasts, contact information, user-generated product reviews, as well as customer-service live chat capability for customers.

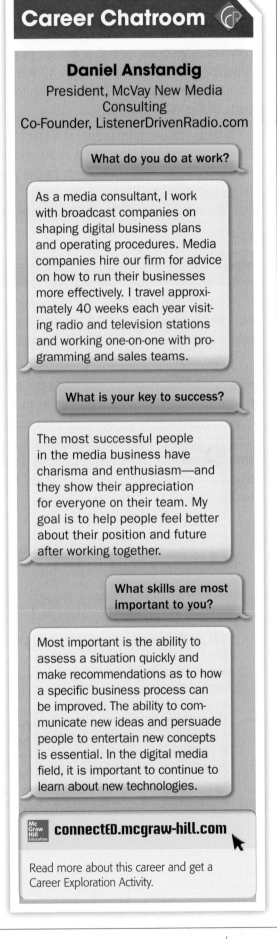

Career Chatroom

Daniel Anstandig
President, McVay New Media Consulting
Co-Founder, ListenerDrivenRadio.com

What do you do at work?

As a media consultant, I work with broadcast companies on shaping digital business plans and operating procedures. Media companies hire our firm for advice on how to run their businesses more effectively. I travel approximately 40 weeks each year visiting radio and television stations and working one-on-one with programming and sales teams.

What is your key to success?

The most successful people in the media business have charisma and enthusiasm—and they show their appreciation for everyone on their team. My goal is to help people feel better about their position and future after working together.

What skills are most important to you?

Most important is the ability to assess a situation quickly and make recommendations as to how a specific business process can be improved. The ability to communicate new ideas and persuade people to entertain new concepts is essential. In the digital media field, it is important to continue to learn about new technologies.

connectED.mcgraw-hill.com

Read more about this career and get a Career Exploration Activity.

When developing a Web site, the designer and make a site map. A **site map** outlines what can be found on each page within the Web site. This concept in Web-site design is known as *global navigation*. The site map guides a viewer to the desired information and provides links to different parts of the Web site.

A Web-site designer prepares a layout grid for every page within a Web site. Layout grids identify all the Web-page elements, such as the title of the page, the branding logo, the placement of banner ads, the content, related links, and a navigation bar for movement within the site.

E-COMMERCE

E-commerce is the process of conducting business transactions on the Internet. E-commerce sales figures have risen dramatically over the years.

As e-commerce grows, it is redefining the relationship between the seller and the buyer. E-commerce can exist B2B (business to business) or B2C (business to consumer). Web markets differ from traditional markets in that they are always open for business—24 hours a day, seven days a week. Also, they are not affected by costly middlemen and distribution channels.

Suppliers all over the globe can compete if they can deliver the quality, price, quantity, and service demanded by the customer and are deemed trustworthy financially and ethically.

PROTECTING DIGITAL DATA

Digital data is not always safe. Sometimes a hard disk crashes and the data stored on it cannot be retrieved. Sometimes files are accidentally deleted, or files become corrupted and cannot be read. Optical disks and USB flash drives provide for convenient, portable backup of files. Portable external hard drives can be stored off-site and are easy to retrieve and access.

Computer files are vulnerable to viruses, worms, spyware, and malware. Viruses and worms can destroy your data. Spyware and malware can track all your online activity and collect personal information or force you to visit certain sites. To protect your data, you should back up your files regularly, use reputable anti-virus and anti-spyware software, and install a computer firewall.

Reading Check

Recall What is the difference between an intranet and an extranet?

MARKETING CASE STUDY

The Orbitz Hovercraft

The online travel-booking site Orbitz has some stiff competition, so it added a feature that automatically issues refunds to travelers if the price of a flight or hotel room goes down after they buy their tickets. To publicize the new feature, Orbitz built a quirky ad campaign around a man in a hovercraft who delivers the rebate checks.

Delivering the Benefit

In one ad, a man is watering his lawn when the hovercraft lands. When he asks the pilot why he did not just mail him the check, he replies, "Sir ... we have a hovercraft!" Another ad sees the check delivered to golfers on a golf course. Both ads used quirky, dry humor to catch the attention of viewers.

Science

Discuss Think of the technology required to make this program possible. Share with a partner how Orbitz might keep track of the various prices involved to make the refund system work.

ONLINE LEARNING

Many courses of study are available online. In fact, you have many courses from which to choose. Many colleges and universities now offer courses online that can lead to a two-year (AA) degree, a four-year degree (BA), and even a post-graduate degree, such as a master's degree (MA). Many working adults enroll in courses to advance their careers and they complete their studies at home.

There are hundreds of course offerings listed on various Web sites. Some of these offerings include marketing-related classes in the following seven areas:

- Marketing
- Business Administration
- Financial Planning
- Small Business and Entrepreneurship
- Graphic Design and Multimedia
- Accounting
- Web Design and Animation

Private schools, colleges, and universities throughout the United States are adding more online courses every year. The costs for online courses are generally less than for attending classes in person.

 After You Read   **Section 9.2**

Review Key Concepts

1. **Describe** how specialized computer systems are used for marketing.
2. **Distinguish** between uses of the Internet and uses of the World Wide Web for business.
3. **Explain** why it is important for businesses to protect their data.

Practice Academics

English Language Arts

4. Write an e-mail message to a vendor asking for specifications of a new printer that your company plans to market. Use your own knowledge of printers to help construct your message.

Mathematics

5. The following ratio shows the total Internet sales for one particular shoe company as compared to the total Internet shoe sales for the industry: $364,840/$2,168,760. What percent of the total Internet shoe sales does this particular company have? Round your answer to the nearest whole percent.

Math Concept **Ways of Representing Numbers** A ratio compares two numbers. Ratios can be expressed as fractions. When the comparison is a part of a whole, the numerator of the fraction usually represents the part, and the denominator represents the whole.

Starting Hints To solve this problem, divide the numerator by the denominator of the ratio to get a decimal. Multiply the decimal by 100 to get the percent. Round your answer to the nearest whole percent.

  connectED.mcgraw-hill.com

Check your answers.

For help, go to the Math Skills Handbook located at the back of this book.

Technology for Marketing

Business needs are fulfilled by computer software applications for communications, accounting and record keeping, publishing, design, and presentation.

COMPUTER APPLICATIONS

Business Needs	Communications	Accounting and Record Keeping	Publishing	Design	Presentation
How They Are Met	• Word Processing Programs • Email and IM Programs	• Database Programs • Accounting Programs • Spreadsheet Programs	• Desktop Publishing Programs • Web-page Editing Programs	• Graphics and Design Programs • Web-page Editing Programs	• Presentation Software • Web-page Editing Programs

The World Wide Web is used in many ways in the workplace. Businesses search for information on the Internet, send and receive emails, develop and design Web sites, buy and sell products, and protect their private information from harm.

Search Engines

Electronic Mail

Web-Site Development

The World Wide Web in the Workplace

E-Commerce

Protecting Digital Data

Review and Activities

Written Summary

- Computer software applications satisfy business needs for communication, word processing, accounting and record keeping, publishing, and graphic design.
- Broadband and wireless technology, videoconferencing, and communication programs help businesses stay in touch with each other.
- Computer technologies developed especially for marketing fulfill needs in the areas of point-of-sale systems, integrated marketing programs, interactive touch-screen computers, interactive TV, and the Internet.
- The World Wide Web is one part of the Internet.
- Business done on the Internet is called e-commerce.
- Companies need to be careful to protect their digital data on the Internet.

Review Content Vocabulary and Academic Vocabulary

1. Arrange the vocabulary terms below into groups of related words. Explain why you put the words together.

Content Vocabulary
- word-processing programs (p. 213)
- database programs (p. 213)
- accounting programs (p. 214)
- spreadsheet programs (p. 214)
- desktop publishing programs (p. 215)
- graphics and design programs (p. 215)
- presentation software (p. 215)
- home page (p. 216)
- hypertext markup language (HTML) (p. 216)
- communications programs (p. 216)
- Wi-Fi (p. 217)
- enterprise resource planning (ERP) (p. 220)
- World Wide Web (p. 222)
- Internet (p. 222)
- hypertext transfer protocol (HTTP) (p. 222)
- uniform resource locator (URL) (p. 222)
- firewall (p. 223)
- site map (p. 224)

Academic Vocabulary
- analyze (p. 214)
- edit (p. 215)
- consists (p. 219)
- link (p. 221)

Assess for Understanding

2. **Describe** What are some ways marketers use spreadsheet programs?
3. **Explain** How are graphics and design programs used in marketing?
4. **Determine** Which type of program would you use to share information with a group of people who are far from you? What are the benefits to this approach?
5. **Discuss** What opportunities and difficulties are presented by the use of interactive technology for marketing?
6. **Create** How would you use the Internet to market a local company?
7. **Judge** What are the benefits and risks associated with e-commerce?
8. **Connect** How does the use of the Internet for marketing purposes relate to segmented marketing?
9. **Distinguish** What is the difference between a firewall and antivirus software?

21st Century Skills

Social Responsibility Skills

10. Recycling Technology In the past, many people tossed their old computers, monitors, and printers, in the garbage. Today people are more socially responsible. Make a list of the places that will accept these articles for recycling. Share your class's list with the school so that any old computers and peripherals are reused or recycled.

Financial Literacy Skills

11. Take-Home Pay You started a new job recently, and today you received your first paycheck. It was quite a bit less than you expected. When you were hired, you were told that you would earn $12 an hour. Over the first two weeks, you worked 30 hours, so you thought you would be paid $360. You asked your boss about it, and she simply said the difference was taken out for deductions. What does that mean? What deductions can legally be taken out of your paycheck? How are these deductions used?

Everyday Ethics

12. Green Eggs with SPAM You visit a new Mom & Pop café that holds weekly drawings for free treats and prizes. It requires signing up with your email address. The café promises not to share your information with any outside parties, but you start receiving a lot of spam after signing up. Even if a company promises not to sell your email address, it is possible for spammers to access the company's computers if they are not secure. Discuss with your class whether it is ethical for the restaurant to keep running this promotion.

e-Marketing Skills

13. Touchscreen Technology Research touchscreen technology. Find out what products are available and the differences between them. Answer the following questions:

Is this technology feasible for a medium-sized hardware store with 30 employees?

What is the range of costs for a single touchscreen checkout system?

How does this technology prevent theft?

Build Academic Skills

Science

14. Technology Use the Internet to research the technical qualities and specifications of a computer peripheral product, such as a printer or scanner,
and provide your recommendation of the best product for the cost.

English Language Arts

15. Research and Reporting Most businesses use computers built on the PC platform, but Macintosh (Apple) computers have made gains in the U.S. market. Research these two platforms for ease of use, reliability, customer service, available software, and expected cost over five years. Read articles on the Internet and in computer magazines. Write a recommendation for which computer system you think a local business should use.

Mathematics

16. Faster than Fast A millisecond (ms) is a unit of time used to describe how long it takes a computer to complete an operation. 1 second = 1,000 ms. If a computer can execute 35 operations per millisecond, how many operations can it complete in one minute? (60 seconds per minute)

Math Concept) Measurement Measure objects and apply units, systems, and processes of measurement.

For help, go to the **Math Skills Handbook** located at the back of this book.

Standardized Test Practice

Directions Read the following questions. On a separate piece of paper, write the best possible answer for each one.

1. When you want to store a lot of information, you would probably choose the following type of program:
   A. word-processing
   B. accounting
   C. database
   D. none of the above

2. True or false? Spam can be an annoying aspect of using e-mail.
   T
   F

3. A good method of backing up computer files is to use an external _____ _____.

Test-Taking Tip

If there is time, quickly read through the test for an overview before you begin.

DECA Connection Role Play

Partner Bookstore

Situation Assume the role of new partner in a family-owned bookstore. You recently purchased a share in a bookstore that has been owned by a relative (judge). The store specializes in the mystery genre and locating signed books and first editions. The bookstore has been in operation for over 50 years and has been successful in the past. In recent years sales have declined, but the store has remained open because of loyal customers and the services it provides.

Before you purchased the partnership, you studied the operation and noted changes that would need to be made to improve the store's competitive position, attract new customers, and provide better overall customer service. You also secured agreement from the other owner to institute those changes. The most important change you plan to make is to add up-to-date technologies in the store.

Activity You are to make an outline of the technology additions you are planning, the uses of each, and how each will benefit the store's operation. You will then explain the information from your outline to your partner (judge).

Evaluation You will be evaluated on how well you meet the following performance indicators:

1. Describe the use of technology in operations.
2. Explain the impact of technology on retailing.
3. Explain the use of technology in customer relationship management.
4. Describe the scope of the Internet.
5. Demonstrate Web-search skills.

 connectED.mcgraw-hill.com

Download the Competitive Events Workbook for more Role-Play practice.

interpersonal skills

SHOW WHAT YOU KNOW

Visual Literacy Good interpersonal skills help establish relationships with coworkers and clients. They enable people to work effectively with those of different cultural, religious, and socioeconomic backgrounds. *If you were asked to travel to another country, how would you prepare to interact with its people?*

Discovery Project

Interpersonal Relationships

Essential Question Why are ethics, managing conflict, and teamwork important parts of interpersonal relationships?

Project Goal

You will soon be given responsibility for handling customer complaints. Your boss has asked you to develop a procedure to follow when dealing with customer complaints. Research ideas to include in your plan. You may want to search for how to handle customer complaints. Then prepare a one- or two-page plan outlining a step-by-step procedure for handling customer complaints.

Ask Yourself...

- What kinds of complaints do your customers usually have?
- What would likely be a good first step in handling a complaint?
- Would location make a difference in how effective you might be in handling a complaint?

 Analysis What criteria will you use to guide your selection of items to include in your procedure document?

 connectED.mcgraw-hill.com

Activity
Get a worksheet activity about interpersonal relationships.

Evaluate
Download a rubric you can use to evaluate your project.

DECA Connection

DECA Event Role Play

Concepts in this chapter are related to DECA competitive events that involve either an interview or role play.

Performance Indicators The performance indicators represent key skills and knowledge. Your key to success in DECA competitive events is relating them to the concepts in this chapter.

- Foster positive working relationships
- Explain the use of feedback for personal growth.
- Demonstrate ethical work habits.
- Identify desirable personality traits important to business.
- Describe the nature of emotional intelligence.

DECA Prep

Role Play Practice role-playing with the DECA Connection competitive-event activity at the end of this chapter. More information on DECA can be found on DECA's Web site.

READING GUIDE

Before You Read

Connect Describe how your interpersonal skills have helped you form relationships.

Objectives

- **Identify** the personal traits necessary for ethical action in the workplace.
- **List** important interpersonal skills.
- **Perform** effectively in diverse environments.
- **Manage** conflicts by using appropriate negotiation skills.

The Main Idea

Self-development and interpersonal skills are essential to handling work situations effectively among diverse people.

Vocabulary

Content Vocabulary
- self-esteem
- initiative
- time management
- assertiveness
- flexibility
- ethics
- equity
- negotiation
- empathy

Academic Vocabulary

You will find these words in your reading and on your tests. Make sure you know their meanings.
- perceive
- demonstrate

Graphic Organizer

Draw or print this chart to list personality traits and interpersonal skills.

Personality Traits

Friendliness courtesy tact					

  connectED.mcgraw-hill.com

Print this graphic organizer.

MARKETING CORE FUNCTION

 Selling

Personal Interactions

BUILDING GOOD RELATIONSHIPS

A positive self-image, an understanding of the rules of acceptable behavior, and an awareness of different cultural, religious, and socioeconomic backgrounds are some of the factors involved in building good relationships.

As You Read

Predict How does acceptable behavior relate to awareness of different cultural backgrounds?

SELF-ESTEEM AND SELF-AWARENESS

Self-awareness is how you **perceive** yourself. **Self-esteem** is how you perceive your worth or value as a person. It is one of the basic building blocks of successfully interacting with others. Having an awareness of your self-esteem is important because it allows you to believe in yourself and improves your attitude at work.

How do you **demonstrate** self-esteem in the workplace? When you value yourself and know how you would like to be treated, it allows you to treat others the same way—with respect, friendliness, and patience. You need to do more than just talk about the way you would like to be treated.

Another way you show self-esteem is in your work habits and grooming. Dressing appropriately and behaving in a confident yet courteous way shows that you respect yourself and your work. Arriving at work on time shows that you value yourself as a professional.

Setting goals for your career and personal development is an aspect of self-awareness and self-esteem. You cannot get anywhere if you do not know where you are headed. Share these goals with your manager so he or she can assist you in your career development.

POSITIVE ATTITUDE

Your attitude is your mental outlook, which shapes the way you view people and situations. People with a positive attitude welcome a difficult assignment as a challenge. They look for something positive even when they experience setbacks. They also accept constructive criticism as a way to improve. Their attitude is a model for other workers. It can inspire them to do the best work they can do.

> **"Successfully interacting with others and developing good human relations depends on many factors."**

INITIATIVE AND RESPONSIBILITY

Initiative means taking action and doing what needs to be done without being asked. If you come up with a new idea, initiative allows you to act on it. Demonstrating initiative shows that you are interested and enthusiastic.

Accepting responsibility means that you are willing to be held accountable for your actions. After taking the initiative to begin a job, you must accept responsibility for completing it. Employers and customers value responsible employees because they fulfill their promises and do what is expected of them. An employee who takes initiative and is responsible is reliable. Employers. coworkers, and customers know they can depend on someone who can be counted on to take action and follow through.

SELF-CONTROL

People who exercise self-control take careful, measured steps and do not act on impulse or emotion. Self-control in the workplace allows you to stop and analyze a situation before reacting to it emotionally.

This skill is very important when handling conflict. Self-control and orderly behavior inspire confidence in customers and in coworkers. People who cannot control themselves tend to be perceived as overly emotional, irresponsible, inattentive, and uninterested in the customer. They may not be taken seriously.

CREATIVITY

Creativity is the ability to use the imagination to invent. Creativity is used in marketing to think of new products and to develop new ways to present products. It also allows you to find new ways of doing your job. Creativity can help you analyze problems from a new and fresh perspective.

TIME MANAGEMENT

Time management means budgeting your time to accomplish tasks on a certain schedule. Time-management principles involve establishing goals, setting deadlines, allocating enough time for each task, tackling the most difficult task first, and being realistic. In order to be effective in your work, you must be able to use time wisely. Managing time well is an example of responsible behavior. To manage your time, follow these guidelines:

1. Make a list of the tasks you need to complete.
2. Determine which task is most important considering your time frame.
3. Continue to rank the tasks.
4. Create a schedule based on your list.

When you are working on one task, do not let yourself worry about another one. You may, however, be able to work on more than one task at a time. Managing multiple tasks at once is called multitasking.

Creativity enables you to find new ways of doing things. It is a valuable trait to have in many different kinds of work. *What applications does creativity have in marketing?*

Creative Solutions

STRESS MANAGEMENT

Stress is a reaction to outside pressure. It can have mental or physical effects. An example of mental stress might be your reaction if your manager asked you to prepare an extensive research report on competing products by 9:00 A.M. the next day when you already had plans to study for an upcoming exam all evening.

Stress can also have physical effects. It can energize, motivate, and excite us. The negative aspects of stress, though, are often harmful. Stress-related anxiety can trigger various physical reactions, collectively called the "fight-or-flight" mechanism. This can result in an increased heart rate and an aroused mental state. Reactions like this can become dangerous when they occur too often.

Research suggests that a hormone released by bodies under stress suppresses the immune system and can lead to long-term health problems. Highly stressed people catch colds and flu more often than those who can handle or relieve their stress. Learning to manage stress is a valuable workplace skill.

STRESS RELIEF

Researchers who have studied stress agree that three main elements help prevent stress: regular exercise, a balanced diet, and enough sleep. They also suggest engaging in recreation, making reasonable compromises, and accepting what you cannot change. At work, taking a minute to breathe deeply and consciously relax is a good stress reducer. Maintaining a sense of humor when things get tense also helps. When you are dealing with stress away from work, try getting a massage or watching a television program or movie. Getting involved in activities you enjoy, such as sports, reading, or listening to music, is a good way to relieve stress. Helping someone in need can help relieve stress by putting things in perspective.

ASSERTIVENESS

Assertiveness is standing up for what you believe. People will respect you if you can be assertive without being pushy or aggressive. Show confidence and speak with authority. For example, suppose you are working with a client who ridicules your opinion. In a very professional and respectful way, you should reassert your contribution. Be sure to point out its strengths in a clear and precise manner. Offer support for any claim that you make. Valid evidence will put you in a strong position to influence others. Assertiveness is a skill that takes time to learn. Confidence in being assertive comes with experience and practice.

WORLD MARKET
TURKEY ☪

Skilled Bargaining

Tourists visiting Istanbul will want to shop the old-fashioned way—in Turkey's famous Grand Bazaar. The bazaar's 58 covered streets and the blend of sounds, sights, and smells invite a buying frenzy.

Goods include copper vessels, gold jewelry, hand-worked carpets, glazed pottery and tiles, and colorful spices heaped in trays.

Game Play Haggling gets the best price, and locals don't hesitate to offer advice. First, keep a poker face and never show too much interest in something you want. Let the shopkeeper quote the first price, then make a counter offer that's 25 to 50 percent less. When a total has been reached, a verbal contract—and a sale—have been made. Finally, smile.

Social Studies
Imagine Think of a product that people in the United States routinely haggle over and compare these products to those haggled over in a marketplace in Turkey.

Here are some entry-level phrases that are used in conversations about marketing all over the world.

English	Turkish
Hello	merhaba
Goodbye	güle
Yes/No	evet/hayir
Thank you	tesekkür ederim
You're welcome	buyrun

FLEXIBILITY

Flexibility allows you to adapt to changing circumstances. A flexible person can learn from others, accept criticism, and grow. To develop flexibility, listen with an open mind. Be willing to try new approaches.

As you will see in the next section, flexibility will help you be a productive team member. Businesses value employees with this trait because flexibility enables a business to move forward and adapt to changing markets.

Reading Check

Analyze Why is awareness of your self-esteem important in the workplace?

ETHICS IN THE 21ST-CENTURY WORKPLACE

Ethics are the basic values and moral principles that guide the behavior of individuals and groups. In most cultures, ethical behavior includes honesty, integrity, and a sense of fair play. Ethical behavior also means treating all people with respect. People who practice ethical behavior usually gain the trust of coworkers and clients.

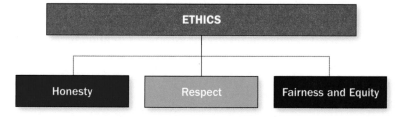

HONESTY

Honesty in the workplace is an important part of ethical behavior. It includes telling the truth, maintaining confidentiality, and not spreading gossip. Respect for company property and making an effort to prevent theft are other aspects of workplace honesty.

Honesty is the basis for trust, which is essential to a good business relationship. People who are honest display strong personal integrity. Integrity is the quality of always behaving according to the moral principles that you believe in, so that people respect and trust you.

RESPECT

The number-one rule when speaking to business clients or customers is to show respect. That applies to interactions with coworkers as well. You demonstrate respect by listening with an open mind to the other person's point of view, then addressing any differences of opinion with courtesy and tact. This is especially important if there is a disagreement or conflict, for instance, when handling a customer complaint. While it may not always be easy to be courteous and pleasant, practice showing respect to others. They will admire your character and look forward to interacting with you in the future.

FAIRNESS AND EQUITY

People expect to be treated the way others are treated. **Equity** means that everyone has equal rights and opportunities. Never give special privileges to an employee for reasons that are unrelated to his or her work performance.

Sometimes a business establishes standards to maintain fairness. Equality is also protected through both federal and state laws. Such standards and laws can prevent discrimination in procedures such as hiring and firing. For example, employment laws forbid discrimination due to gender, age, religion, or national origin. Federal laws include the Americans with Disabilities Act of 1990, which protects qualified individuals with disabilities from discrimination. If an employee believes that he or she has been the victim of discrimination, the employee can file a complaint with the United States Equal Employment Opportunity Commission (EEOC).

AVOIDING STEREOTYPES

It is very important to become aware of any prejudices we may have and to eliminate them. Take some time to reflect on your own interests, experiences, and background. A person's interests often reflect his or her values. Our experiences shape how we think and view the world. You can understand other people better by making an effort to learn about their interests and experiences. By adopting this perspective, you will find it much easier to understand others, and they will be much more likely to understand you. Mutual understanding is a major factor in good communication. Positive workplace relationships and success in marketing are based on mutual understanding and respect.

Reading Check

Interpret Why is it important to be ethical in the workplace?

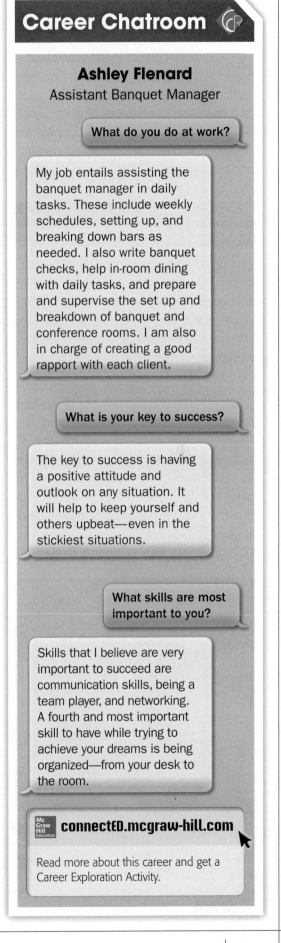

MANAGING CONFLICT

Like stress, conflict in the workplace can be productive or counterproductive. Counterproductive conflict can cause lost time and resources as well as a decrease in efficiency. Productive conflict can energize a person, group, or organization. However, successfully managing conflict requires understanding, skill, knowledge, and experience.

CONFLICT AND NEGOTIATION

Companies can help prevent conflict by creating an atmosphere in which all employees are accepted despite their differences in beliefs, values, backgrounds, or experiences. However, no company can completely prevent conflict in the workplace. When conflicts arise, they must be negotiated.

Negotiation is the process of working with the parties in conflict to find a resolution. Negotiating requires a willingness to work together. The key to any successful negotiation is clear communication. As you learned in Chapter 8, there are four basic skills involved in the communication process: listening, reading, speaking, and writing. Negotiation involves two of these communication skills: listening and speaking.

SPEAKING

The first step in negotiation is defining as clearly as possible the problem as each person sees it. Facts and feelings must be presented from each individual's perspective. This usually goes more smoothly when "I statements" are used. For example, avoid the aggressive tone in "You make me mad when you. . . ." Instead, say, "I become upset when you. . . ." Instead of saying "Your description of the problem is confusing," say, "I am confused about what the problem is."

Avoid placing blame because it puts people on the defensive. Participants should take some time to plan ahead what they will say. If possible, set a time and place to meet that is convenient for everyone involved. A quiet, neutral place with limited distractions is ideal.

LISTENING

Listening is an active process in which all of your attention is focused on the speaker. Encourage the speaker to share his or her feelings and thoughts. Maintaining eye contact with the speaker shows that you are interested and want to understand what is being said. Planning a response before the speaker's point is made is a distraction that can cause misunderstandings.

When negotiating conflict resolution, all parties must be willing to work together to find a fair solution. *How are compromise and communication used in negotiation?*

Negotiating Conflicts

Try to empathize, or show empathy, with the person who is speaking. **Empathy** is an understanding of a person's situation or frame of mind. Remember that people of different ages, genders, cultures, and abilities may have had experiences that are unfamiliar to you. Do not make the mistake of assuming that certain viewpoints and behaviors are universal. There are many people in the world with ideas that are very different from yours.

Six simple techniques for negotiating conflict resolution can be helpful:

1. Show respect.
2. Recognize and define the problem.
3. Seek a variety of solutions.
4. Collaborate.
5. Be reliable.
6. Preserve the relationship.

The problem is solved only when both sides reach a common understanding and agreement about what actions are to be taken. Never assume you understand the other person without asking some verification questions. For example, you might ask, "Is this what you meant by. . . ?" or "Did I understand correctly when. . . ?" These types of questions make sure that everyone understands everyone else's point of view. This level of understanding is essential for conflict management.

After You Read | Section 10.1

Review Key Concepts

1. **Compare and contrast** assertiveness and flexibility as positive character traits.
2. **Describe** four ways to apply ethical behavior in the workplace.
3. **Connect** the use of good communication skills to the process of negotiation.

Practice Academics

English Language Arts

4. Suppose that you recently started a new part-time job and found it difficult to get all of your school homework done after work and still get a good night's sleep. You feel exhausted and find it hard to concentrate on school or work. You wonder whether you can manage your time better. List the tasks that you need to complete and rank them in order of importance. Prepare a daily schedule of activities and note whether you will be able to multitask.

Mathematics

5. Assume that your company's current health insurance plan costs $658 per month per employee. There are 114 employees. Another health insurance company would charge 6 percent less. What would be the total savings per year?

   Math Concept **Algebra: Using Symbols** You can represent and analyze mathematical situations and structures using algebraic symbols.

   Starting Hints To solve this problem, let s stand for the total savings over 12 months. Write and solve an equation using the information from the problem: $s = \$658 \times 0.06 \times 114 \times 12$

 connectED.mcgraw-hill.com

Check your answers.

For help, go to the Math Skills Handbook located at the back of this book.

READING GUIDE

Before You Read

Connect When have you benefited from working on a team rather than by yourself?

Objectives

- **Discuss** how to receive and handle customer complaints.
- **Identify** skills needed to be a good team member and provide leadership.
- **List** six aspects of successful teamwork.

The Main Idea

Team member skills will help your team achieve its goals.

Vocabulary

Content Vocabulary
- teamwork
- cross-training
- consensus
- agreement

Academic Vocabulary

You will find these words in your reading and on your tests. Make sure you know their meanings.
- achieve
- conflict

Graphic Organizer

Draw or print this chart to list six aspects of successful teamwork.

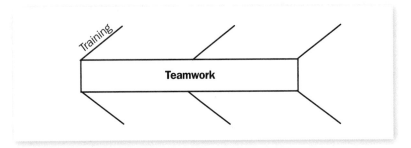

 **connectED.mcgraw-hill.com**

Print this graphic organizer.

MARKETING CORE FUNCTION

Promotion

INTERPERSONAL SKILLS IN MARKETING

As an employee, you should be familiar with your company's basic procedures in responding to customers. Know when to refer the customer to a manager or when a question involves information that your department does not have.

As You Read

Connect Consider the skills you have and need to be a good team member.

ADDRESSING CUSTOMERS' CONCERNS

To respond promptly and intelligently to customer concerns, you need to be familiar with company procedures. These procedures can be part of a company manual. They may also be shared with you in a presentation after you are hired. You should know how to handle the following situations:

▶ **Requests and questions**–You will need to learn the proper procedures for handling customer requests and questions. You will also need to know what you should say to customers if you cannot answer their questions yourself.

▶ **Directions**–You will need to be able to give clear and concise directions to your store or office. Local customers may be able to use informal directions, such as "our store is three blocks past the public garden on the right." Out-of-town customers will need more specific directions.

▶ **Management's role**–You will need to know under what circumstances a manager should be called to talk to a customer.

▶ **Business policies**–You will need to be able to explain business policies to customers. These may include return or exchange procedures and the company policy on checks or credit cards.

ADDRESSING CUSTOMERS' COMPLAINTS

Most customers never let the company or store know they have a complaint. Only 4 to 8 percent of customers who have a concern or complaint share their problem with the company. If a customer brings you a concern, it is important to deal with it and attempt to rectify the problem right away. Moreover, you have an opportunity to learn something that may help you improve the service you provide. You may also be able to prevent damage to the company and stop the problem from recurring.

Complaints cover a range of issues. Some are genuine errors on the part of the company, such as a faulty product or a bad service experience. Others stem from misunderstandings, such as poorly written directions on a product's package. The customer may even suggest how the company can improve its service.

> **"** Good working relationships between employees and customers or clients depend on the interpersonal skills of employees. **"**

Since so few customers share their complaints, it is important to take these customers seriously. If you solve a problem for one customer, there is a chance that you have solved the same problem for many other customers who did not speak up. Seeking customer satisfaction always benefits a company in the long run.

Your company should develop a procedure to follow when dealing with customer complaints. Here are some guidelines for this procedure:

▶ **Listen.** First, listen completely and openly to the customer's complaint so that you are sure you understand it.

▶ **Take the customer aside.** If the customer is talking loudly, try to take him or her aside—if possible, into a separate room. A sales counter or desk can seem like a barrier. Standing side by side in a quiet place may ease the tension.

▶ **Repeat.** When appropriate, repeat the facts of the complaint to show the customer that you understand the details of the situation from his or her perspective. If you can explain what caused the problem for the customer, state your explanation clearly. Do not place blame on anyone.

▶ **Get help.** If you feel you need assistance from a coworker or a supervisor, let the customer know this and seek assistance promptly. Any time a customer is behaving aggressively, get help immediately.

▶ **Establish a plan.** Try to reach an agreement with the customer about the next course of action. Suggest action that is consistent with the company's policy. Then be absolutely certain to follow through on the action agreed upon.

✓ **Reading Check**

Explain Why is it important for all marketing employees to know how to address customer concerns?

MARKETING CASE STUDY

MLB's "Beyond Baseball" Campaign

Baseball is a popular sport in the United States, but it is also a major cultural force that goes beyond the game itself. The marketers at Major League Baseball (MLB) realized this and channeled that spirit into a new ad campaign called "This is Beyond Baseball," which included a 30-minute TV special and a series of 20 commercials.

Fan Feedback

While traditional sports marketing involves focusing on the players, the new MLB campaign focuses on the fans. In one commercial, "Beyond Optimism," a series of fans of various teams expresses how confident they are that their team is going to make it all the way to the post-season. The tone of the commercial emphasizes that each spring is a "fresh start," and a new baseball season is lifted up as a positive event for fans.

English Language Arts

Ask Discuss with a partner whether it is more effective for MLB to focus on the fans rather than the players in this series of advertisements. Have each partner take a different side of the discussion and then share with the class.

TEAMWORK

A team is a group of people who work together to achieve a common goal. **Teamwork** is work done by a group of people to achieve a common goal.

Teamwork is becoming increasingly important in the business world. According to football coach Vince Lombardi, "Individual commitment to a group effort—that is what makes a team work, a company work, a society work, a civilization work." This commitment includes many behaviors and attitudes. It is important for team members to keep these behaviors and attitudes in mind. The following descriptions are six important aspects of teamwork. (See **Figure 10.1** on page 244.)

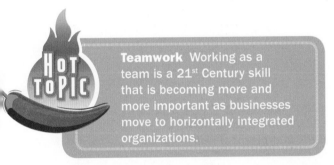

HOT TOPIC

Teamwork Working as a team is a 21st Century skill that is becoming more and more important as businesses move to horizontally integrated organizations.

TRAINING

To be an effective team member, you must have training for all the tasks you will perform. You have probably heard of cross-training in sports. **Cross-training** means preparing to do many different activities.

On the job, people are cross-trained for many tasks on a team. This gives the team flexibility and diverse strengths. Every worker has different abilities. A company's workers can train each other to turn weaker skills into strengths. Work becomes more enjoyable when you know you will not be doing the same activity every day.

TEAM PLANNING

Before you start working on a project, make a plan as a team. Team planning involves setting goals, assigning roles, making agreements, sharing responsibility, and giving feedback. These practices will allow all members of the team to work together effectively.

TEAM GOALS

Team members must be involved in defining a goal in order to feel committed to it. This results in greater company loyalty and stronger team spirit. If team members know that their input is valued and considered, they will work harder to meet a goal.

Members should reach a consensus about goals. A **consensus** is a decision about which all members of a team approve. Therefore, all team members must be allowed to state their opinions. The final agreement may require team members to make a compromise. Being flexible as an individual helps you learn to compromise as a team member. It is likely that every individual on a team will have to compromise at some point. It is important for a team to keep this shared compromise in mind.

ASSIGNING ROLES

Team projects often work more smoothly if the team appoints a leader who coordinates tasks. Each person on the team needs to know which part of the process he or she is responsible for each day. Members are usually assigned tasks based on their skills and experience. These role assignments can change as the project evolves. This possibility of change is one reason cross-training is so valuable. It makes it easier for team members to change roles if necessary.

AGREEMENTS

An **agreement** is a specific commitment that each member makes to the group. When team members make agreements, the team becomes stronger and more cohesive. A team's agreements must be consistent with its goals.

It is important that each team member feel connected to the company's goals as well as to the team's goals. This connection is known as team loyalty. Team loyalty and positive peer pressure help to encourage people to keep their agreements. Members of the team will be more likely to make agreements if there is a high level of team loyalty.

SHARED RESPONSIBILITY AND SHARED LEADERSHIP

Shared responsibility means that each member must feel responsible for the whole team's efforts. If there is a problem during a project, all team members need to assess how they may be able to solve it. A team member who says the phrase, "that's not my job" is not being a responsible team member. Team leaders must work to develop each team member's sense of ownership.

Shared leadership allows all team members to perform some management functions. There will be times when team members have to respond to issues quickly. They may not have time to discuss the issue with the team leader, or the team leader may not be available.

Team members need to feel confident to take care of issues independently if it is necessary to do so.

FEEDBACK

When giving feedback, make sure you are respectful. If you are overly critical, the feedback will not serve its purpose. Instead, it will alienate the team member being evaluated. Feedback is most effective when it identifies a behavior or attitude that can be changed. It also helps to give an example or model of this behavior or attitude.

Reading Check

Recall How is cross-training essential to teamwork?

FIGURE 10.1 | Teamwork

Succeed Together As many businesses move away from a top-down management style toward a team approach, it is important for employees to understand how a team works and what is expected of individual members. *What are some of the interpersonal skills that you need to be a valuable team member?*

Training Each member of a team needs to keep up with the team. This means having the necessary skills to do your job and staying current with the best practices in your field.

Team Planning Teams are usually assigned projects. Planning how to carry out those projects is the team's responsibility. Teams often include individuals with different strengths. For example, an advertising team may include an illustrator, a copywriter, a production coordinator, and a marketing specialist.

Team Goals The team sets goals. For an advertising team, that might mean completing a new ad or an entire advertising campaign by a certain date. Team goals must be aligned with the goals of the company.

Delegation/Agreements Members of the team are assigned different tasks, depending on their skills. Each team member agrees to complete the assigned task. On an advertising team, the graphic artist lays out graphics on a computer, the copywriter develops slogans and copy, and the production coordinator works with outside vendors.

Shared Responsibility/Leadership Everyone on the team shares responsibility for achieving the team's goal. Members of the team usually select a manager, or owner, to keep track of schedules and handle any difficulties that arise.

LEADERSHIP SKILLS

One definition of leadership is helping members of a group **achieve** their goals. Leaders need self-confidence and a willingness to take the initiative to solve new or unusual problems. Leaders need problem-solving, social judgment, and communication skills to define the problem, gather information, analyze the problem, and generate plans for a solution. Good leaders understand people and social systems and are able to motivate others to work together. **Conflict** resolution helps members of a group work together. A team can only be as successful as its members. For a team to be successful, it is important that each member is willing and able to work to achieve the team's goals.

BEING A VALUABLE TEAM MEMBER

What makes a person a good team member?

- Make the team's goals your top priority.
- Listen actively and offer suggestions.
- Build positive group dynamics with team members.
- Communicate with team members.
- Follow up on assignments.
- Work to resolve conflicts among team members.
- Respect the members of your team.
- Try to inspire others to get involved.
- Think creatively and present your ideas with enthusiasm.

 After You Read | **Section 10.2**

Review Key Concepts

1. **Define** teamwork and explain how it applies to the business world.
2. **List** the personal strengths and interpersonal skills required of a good leader.
3. **Identify** personal traits and interpersonal skills that make a person a good team member.

Practice Academics

English Language Arts

4. Conduct research to identify a current example of teamwork in the workplace. Share this information with your class and discuss how it might apply to the classroom.

Mathematics

5. A marketing company currently orders 370 boxes of pens each year at $4.50 per box. A new office supply company offers a deal for you to switch to their company. The new supply company will give you 15 free boxes of pens if your company orders pens from them. If you order from the new supply company, how much money will your company save?

Math Concept **Problem Solving** Monitor and reflect on the process of mathematical problem solving.

Starting Hints The problem tells you how many boxes of pens are ordered each year, how many boxes of pens the new supply company will give you for free, and the cost of one box of pens. Calculate the cost savings by multiplying the cost per box by the number of boxes your company will be given for free.

 **connectED.mcgraw-hill.com**

Check your answers.

For help, go to the Math Skills Handbook located at the back of this book.

Interpersonal Skills

Good interpersonal skills build effective working relationships with coworkers and clients.

Understanding the team goals, the roles assigned to individual team members, and shared responsibilities will help make you a valuable team member.

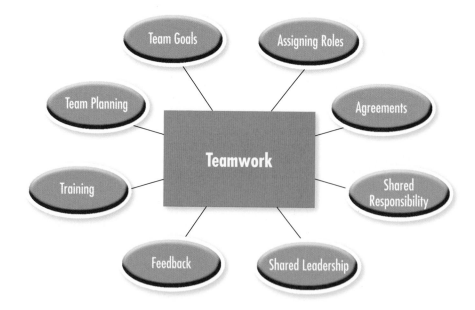

Review and Activities

Written Summary

- Good interpersonal skills are necessary for building effective working relationships with coworkers and clients.
- Personality traits such as assertiveness and creativity can help people work effectively with others.
- Ethical behavior in today's workplace involves demonstrating respect for people of diverse backgrounds.
- Conflict negotiation requires good communication skills.
- Teamwork means a group of people work together toward a goal.
- Understanding the team goals, the roles assigned to individual team members, and shared responsibilities will help make you a valuable team member.

Review Content Vocabulary and Academic Vocabulary

1. Write a memo introducing yourself to the class. Use each of the following vocabulary terms in your memo.

Content Vocabulary
- self-esteem (p. 233)
- initiative (p. 233)
- time management (p. 234)
- assertiveness (p. 235)
- flexibility (p. 236)
- ethics (p. 236)
- equity (p. 237)
- negotiation (p. 238)
- empathy (p. 239)
- teamwork (p. 243)
- cross-training (p. 243)
- consensus (p. 243)
- agreement (p. 243)

Academic Vocabulary
- perceive (p. 233)
- demonstrate (p. 233)
- achieve (p. 245)
- conflict (p. 245)

Assess for Understanding

2. **Explain** Which personality traits might help you become a better friend and coworker?
3. **Explain** Why is initiative important in good working relationships?
4. **Describe** How can asking about others' interests and experiences help to prevent bias?
5. **Identify** What is the one thing that a team must do before it can begin its work?
6. **Discuss** How can sharing responsibility and leadership be helpful in achieving team goals?
7. **List** What are the five conventions that can help teams overcome obstacles?
8. **Describe** What are the characteristics of a team that works well in business? Why?
9. **Create** What are some positive teamworking behaviors you practice?

21st Century Skills

Problem-Solving Skills

10. Managing Conflict Think of a conflict that you have observed in the past (but do not use names) or create a story about a conflict. Then prepare instructions for the most effective steps to take in managing this conflict.

Financial Literacy Skills

11. Managing Credit You have decided that you need a new computer to help get your homework done. The total cost is $840. You decide to charge it on a credit card. The interest rate is 18 percent, so the minimum monthly payment the first month is $33.60. If you only pay the minimum each month, about how long will it take to pay for the computer?

e-Marketing Skills

12. Re-Selling on the Web You have heard about people who buy and sell products via online auction sites on the Web. So you and a friend are exploring the idea as a way of earning some money. What research and planning will you do to determine whether this is an idea worth pursuing? Here are some questions to consider:

- How will you keep track of money?
- How will you ship products?
- Who will pay for shipping?
- What products will you sell?
- How can you be sure your products will sell?
- Where will you find products to sell?

Build Academic Skills

Social Studies

13. Interactions Among People, Groups, and Institutions Talk with four people you know from different places or in different ways. Ask them about their interests (hobbies or what they like to do in their spare time). After you have spoken with each person, identify the role each plays in society and in their work or school group.

English Language Arts

14. Reading and Writing Conduct research on one of the following topics related to interpersonal skills: 1) ethics in the workplace, 2) managing conflict, or 3) teamwork on the job. Write a half-page summary about what you learned from your reading.

Mathematics

15. Discounted Pricing Math is a basic skill for team members. Your boss asks you to determine how much will be discounted from the price of a computer that has a list price of $1,499 and a discount of 15 percent. What answer would you give her?

Math Concept **Problem Solving: Process** You can solve this problem by figuring the dollar amount of the discount and then subtracting it from the total. Or you can subtract the discounted percentage from 100 and multiply that percent by the total.

For help, go to the **Math Skills Handbook** located at the back of this book.

Standardized Test Practice

Directions Read the following questions. On a separate piece of paper, write the best possible answer for each one.

1. When addressing customer complaints, a good procedure would include:
   A. listening
   B. taking the customer to a quiet location
   C. repeating facts the customer states
   D. all of the above

2. True or false? Self-awareness is how you perceive yourself.
   T
   F

3. Conflict resolution helps members of a group work _____.

Test-Taking Tip

Look through the test and answer the easy questions first. Then you will know about how much time to allow for the more difficult questions.

DECA Connection

Manager
Travel Agency

Situation Assume the role of manager of a travel agency. The travel agency specializes in putting together custom tour packages for travel groups. Your upcoming 14-day tour of China has been very popular. The tour package includes airfare from your location, transfers, hotel accommodations, and admission to scheduled tourist destinations. The tour is expensive and each reservation requires a $1,500 non-refundable deposit. The tour is completely sold out with several customers on a waiting list for any cancellations. The China tour is scheduled to depart in six weeks.

One of your regular customers has booked two reservations for the China tour. The customer has come to the agency to tell the booking agent (judge) that he/she must cancel both of the tour reservations because of a family illness. The customer has also requested a refund on the deposit. The agent (judge) has followed company policy and explained that the deposit is non-refundable. The customer is upset and promising to find another travel agency. The agent (judge) has asked to discuss the situation with you and would like for you to consider making an exception and refund the customer's deposit.

Activity You are to decide whether or not to refund the customer's deposit and explain the reasons for your decision to the travel agent (judge).

Evaluation You will be evaluated on how well you meet the following performance indicators:

1. Foster positive working relationships.
2. Explain the use of feedback for personal growth.
3. Demonstrate ethical work habits.
4. Identify desirable personality traits important to business.
5. Describe the nature of emotional intelligence.

 connectED.mcgraw-hill.com

Download the Competitive Events Workbook for more Role-Play practice.

Peter ten Broecke/Getty Images

management skills

SHOW WHAT YOU KNOW

Visual Literacy Each company brings people together to perform different jobs, but everyone works toward the common goal of business success. Managers plan, organize, and control human resources, technology, and materials. *What are some skills that a manager would need to have?*

Discovery Project

Management Styles

Essential Question What are several different management styles, and why are they effective?

Project Goal

Work with a partner to research and make a list of various management styles and associated skills. Identify three different types of small businesses in your area. Find out the names and contact information of a manager at each business. Interview the manager at each business, asking which management style best describes the way he or she interacts with employees. Write a report describing each management style. Include descriptions of each small business and its product.

Ask Yourself...

- How will you find businesses and managers in your community?
- What questions will you ask the managers?
- How will you describe your findings in your report?
- How will you present your report?

 Synthesize and Present Research Synthesize your research and findings by writing a report that distinguishes between the management styles.

 connectED.mcgraw-hill.com

Activity
Get a worksheet activity about management styles.

Evaluate
Download a rubric you can use to evaluate your project.

DECA. Connection

DECA Event Role Play

Concepts in this chapter are related to DECA competitive events that involve either an interview or role play.

Performance Indicators The performance indicators represent key skills and knowledge. Your key to success in DECA competitive events is relating them to concepts in this chapter.

- Explain the concept of management.
- Explain the role of ethics in human resources management.
- Demonstrate responsible behavior.
- Explain the nature of staff communication.
- Make oral presentations.

DECA Prep

Role Play Practice role-playing with the DECA Connection competitive-event activity at the end of this chapter. More information on DECA events can be found on DECA's Web site.

READING GUIDE

Before You Read

Connect When do you have to manage your time or your resources?

Objectives

- **Explain** how horizontally organized companies differ from vertically organized companies.
- **Name** the three levels of management in a vertically organized company.
- **Explain** how a self-management team functions.

The Main Idea

Two types of management structures are vertical and horizontal or a combination of both.

Vocabulary

Content Vocabulary
- management
- vertical organization
- top management
- middle management
- supervisory-level management
- horizontal organization
- empowerment

Academic Vocabulary
You will find these words in your reading and on your tests. Make sure you know their meanings.
- resource
- individual

Graphic Organizer

Draw or print this chart to take notes on the types of business organization.

Print this graphic organizer.

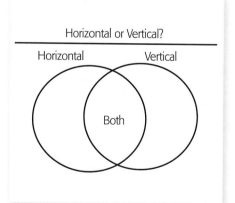

Horizontal or Vertical?

Horizontal   Vertical

Both

MARKETING CORE FUNCTION

 Marketing Information Management

Management Structures

LEADERSHIP IN THE 21ST CENTURY

New leaders come from diverse backgrounds. Global competition is creating companies and managers who are united by common goals and ideals. Business leaders in the United States and around the world expect many changes in the coming years as a result of globalization.

As You Read

Predict What is the difference between vertical and horizontal organization?

TYPES OF MANAGEMENT STRUCTURE

Management is the business function of planning, organizing, and controlling all available resources to achieve company goals. To facilitate effective management, businesses are most often organized either vertically or horizontally.

VERTICAL ORGANIZATION

For a long time, the role of management was to keep an eye on workers. In large, traditional companies, managers reported to higher levels of management. Managers were responsible for the proper operation of a particular department. Though updated and more worker friendly than in the past, the traditional vertical organization remains today. A **vertical organization** is a hierarchical, up-and-down organizational structure in which the tasks and responsibilities of each level are clearly defined.

Management Levels

In the vertically organized company, there are three basic levels of management: top management, middle management, and supervisory-level management.

Those who make decisions that affect the whole company are **top management**. CEO (chief executive officer), president, COO (chief operating officer), CFO (chief financial officer), and vice president are some of the top-management titles. They manage people and the structure of the company. The functions of top (or executive) management include setting a direction for the company as a whole, identifying **resources** and methods for meeting goals, and controlling the systems and structures of the company.

> " **Managers** utilize human resources, technology, and material resources. "

Employees at the **middle management** level implement the decisions of top management. Middle management plans how the departments under them can work to reach top management's goals. They are supervised by the organization's top management. However, middle management's role involves implementation more than it does supervision. They monitor the effectiveness of the plans they implement.

In **supervisory-level management**, managers supervise the employees who actually carry out the tasks determined by middle and top management. Supervisors assign duties, monitor day-to-day activities in their department, and evaluate the work of production or service employees. Supervisors also set priorities for their departments, work to keep within budgets, and monitor their teams' workflow. The performance of their departments is supervised by middle management.

Free Thinking

Brainstorming is an important activity for most self-managing teams. *What else do self-managing teams do?*

Teamwork

This group of people is designing a new building together. *In a horizontal organization, who is the manager?*

HORIZONTAL ORGANIZATION

Many companies have downsized in order to increase their efficiency and productivity. These companies needed more than staff cuts to become more efficient. The answer was a new type of management structure. In **horizontal organization**, top management shares decision making with self-managing teams of workers who set their own goals and make their own decisions.

Self-Managing Teams

At the heart of horizontal organization is a restructuring of the traditional management hierarchy. Levels of management are eliminated, and the number of supervisors is reduced. This is known as flattening the organization. Instead of reporting up a chain of command, employees are organized into teams that manage themselves. This also addresses the needs of individual personalities and places employees where they are most productive.

Self-managing teams in a horizontal organization gather information, analyze it, and take collective action. They are responsible for making decisions, completing tasks, and coordinating their activities with other groups in the company.

Encouraging team members to contribute to and take responsibility for the management process is known as **empowerment**. Empowerment reinforces team spirit, contributes to company loyalty, and usually increases productivity and profits.

Organization by Process

A second characteristic of horizontal companies is organization by process. Self-managing teams are organized around particular processes, such as developing new products or providing customer support. Teams made up of people with different specializations replace functional divisions, such as the finance department or engineering department.

In a horizontally organized company, for example, a product development team may include a variety of specialties. Some employees may research market trends, others may be experts in technology, and some may focus on budgeting and finance, but they all work together to create new products.

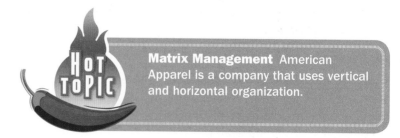

Hot Topic

Matrix Management American Apparel is a company that uses vertical and horizontal organization.

Customer Orientation

The third characteristic of horizontal organization concerns the team's focus. In vertical organizations, workers tend to look to management for direction. In horizontal companies, workers focus on the customer.

For example, you can buy Starbucks coffee beans in Starbucks coffee shops, or you can buy them in grocery stores and supermarkets. Different marketing teams within Starbucks focus on each different type of customer. One team is concerned with the wants and needs of the **individual** who buys beans in the Starbucks store. Another is concerned with the needs of the supermarket.

By focusing on these different customers, instead of on a product or process, managers have direct access to customer feedback. The ideal result is to have satisfied customers, high productivity, large profits, and contented investors.

Matrix Management

Matrix management is a cross between vertical and horizontal types of management, with features borrowed from both types. Individual employees are responsible to a supervisor in their department (vertical) and to their team (horizontal). A matrix organization facilitates placement of employees where they are needed most.

 After You Read   **Section 11.1**

Review Key Concepts

1. **Explain** the difference between a vertical and a horizontal company.
2. **List** two advantages of horizontal organization.
3. **Identify** three levels of management in a vertical organization.

Practice Academics

English Language Arts

4. Research how people organize a company for either vertical management or horizontal management. Then write a half-page report on your findings

Mathematics

5. Your company produces and markets kitchen appliances. Sales last year totaled $3,685,250. The company goal is to increase sales by 10 percent this year. Your division's goal is to achieve 40 percent of total sales. What is the dollar value of your division's goal?

> **Math Concept** **Number and Operations: Multiplying by a Percent Greater than 100** Percents greater than 100 represent values greater than one. A percent greater than 100 can be converted to a decimal number greater than one.

Starting Hints To solve this problem, multiply last year's sales by the decimal equivalent of 110 percent to determine the dollar amount of the total sales goal. Multiply the total sales by the decimal equivalent of 40 percent to determine your division goal.

 connectED.mcgraw-hill.com

Check your answers.

For help, go to the Math Skills Handbook located at the back of this book.

READING GUIDE

Before You Read

Connect Why do you think it might be important for managers to have good interpersonal skills?

Objectives

- **Name** three functions of management.
- **Describe** the management techniques used by effective managers.
- **Explain** how to manage employees properly.

The Main Idea

Understanding basic management functions is essential to success in the field of marketing.

Vocabulary

Content Vocabulary
- planning
- organizing
- controlling
- mission statement
- remedial action
- exit interview

Academic Vocabulary

You will find these words in your reading and on your tests. Make sure you know their meanings.
- identify
- require

Graphic Organizer

Draw or print this chart to write in management functions and techniques.

connectED.mcgraw-hill.com

Print this graphic organizer.

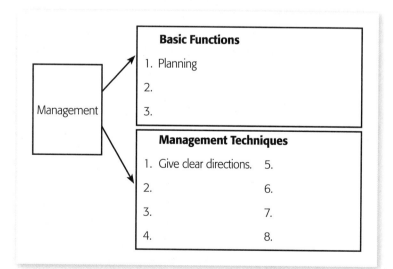

Basic Functions

1. Planning

2.

3.

Management

Management Techniques

1. Give clear directions.   5.

2.   6.

3.   7.

4.   8.

MARKETING CORE FUNCTION

Marketing Information Management

m.e. Management Functions

WHAT MANAGERS DO

Management decisions affect all employees. This means that communicating and motivating people are two of the most important management skills.

As You Read

Consider When have you seen or heard about these management styles in action?

BASIC MANAGEMENT FUNCTIONS

Whether a company is organized vertically or horizontally, the management functions remain the same. All managers perform certain basic functions of planning, organizing, and controlling, as outlined in **Figure 11.1** on page 258.

Planning involves setting goals and determining how to reach them. **Organizing** includes establishing a time frame in which to achieve the goal, assigning employees to the project, and determining a method for approaching the work. **Controlling** is the process of setting standards and evaluating performance.

All three of these management functions involve making decisions. Following a formal decision-making process can be helpful when making complicated decisions.

The decision-making process usually includes these steps:

1. Define the problem.
2. **Identify** the options available.
3. Gather information and determine the consequences of each option.
4. Choose the best option.
5. Take action.
6. Evaluate the results.

PLANNING

Good management planning is realistic, comprehensive, and flexible. It includes plans for the short- and long-range uses of people, technology, and material resources.

> **"Managers make decisions in addition to supervising and directing the actions of others."**

To be effective, a management plan should be a written statement that identifies resources that can be used to meet a given goal. The plan should be clear and direct. When completed, the plan should be distributed to and discussed with everyone who is involved.

ORGANIZING

Organizing is a coordinated effort to reach a company's planning goals. It involves assigning responsibility, establishing working relationships, hiring staff to carry out the work, and directing the work of employees. Some companies set up staffing as a separate function. Staffing involves recruiting, hiring, training, and evaluating workers.

CONTROLLING

Controlling is the process of comparing a plan with actual performance. It involves three activities: setting standards, evaluating performance according to those standards, and solving problems in the evaluation. Some companies designate *directing* as a separate function. The purpose of directing is to influence the behavior of employees so that they are effective in helping the company achieve its goals.

Before setting standards, many companies compose a **mission statement**, which is a description of the ultimate goals of a company. A mission statement summarizes why a company exists. It identifies goods or services offered and the target market.

After a company establishes goals in a mission statement, it adopts standards that are consistent with the goals. Here are some examples of standards:

▶ Financial standards—profit, cash flow, sales

▶ Employee standards—productivity, professional conduct, dress

▶ Customer satisfaction standards—sales returns, customer complaints, repeat business, referrals

▶ Quality control standards—production line checks for defects in materials or workmanship, repair requests, recalls

▶ Environmental standards—policies and practices that conserve resources and avoid damaging or polluting the natural environment

Managers use standards to evaluate both company and individual performance. When performance does not meet established standards, managers must identify and solve the problem.

EFFECTIVE MANAGEMENT TECHNIQUES

Whether you become a supervisor in a traditionally organized vertical company or a member of a self-managing team, you will need to develop management skills. The most effective management techniques are usually a matter of common sense.

GIVE CLEAR DIRECTIONS

Directing others **requires** good communication skills. Good communication is necessary at every level of management. Even the best employees will not be productive if they do not know what they are expected to do. A supervisor should give all the direction required for each job and encourage employees to ask questions about instructions if they are not clear.

FIGURE 11.1 | Management Functions

Three Basic Functions Managers plan, organize, and control. Here are the management functions required of the manager, or owner, of a marketing team developing an ad campaign for a new car. In this case, the company structure is horizontal. *What skills are necessary to be a manager?*

Planning In this stage, the team develops a plan covering the entire life of the ad campaign, from market research to tracking the campaign's effectiveness. The manager of the team must be sure that the team's plans and goals are aligned with the company's plans.

Organizing When the plan is set, the manager organizes its execution. With input from other members of the team, the manager delegates responsibilities, determines schedules, coordinates work, and keeps everyone on track to meet team goals.

Controlling When the project is complete, the manager should determine its effectiveness. If it was not successful, the manager must find out what went wrong.

BE CONSISTENT

If you have decided that a job must be completed in a certain way, make sure that all employees follow this standard. Do not make exceptions unless there is a good reason to do so.

TREAT EMPLOYEES FAIRLY

Set reasonable standards of performance and apply those standards to everyone. However, you should always consider the employees' points of view when making decisions. Listen to suggestions from your employees, and consider acting on them. Take time to explain your reasoning if you believe an employee is wrong. Employees will be more productive when treated fairly.

BE FIRM WHEN NECESSARY

Each situation requiring disciplinary action is different. A friendly suggestion may be all that is needed to get most employees on the right track. With others, you may have to be direct and firm. Give appropriate directions and be certain the employee understands your expectations.

Sometimes employee problems are caused by the inappropriate behavior of one employee toward another. In this case, have a discussion with the employees to solve the problem. Listen to what both parties have to say and be reasonable but firm.

SET A GOOD EXAMPLE

Set a good example in everything you do on the job. Doing this one simple thing will make your supervisory job much easier.

DELEGATE RESPONSIBILITY

Some supervisors and middle managers do too much work themselves. If a manager is taking work home almost every night, it usually means resources are not being managed well. The manager may not be delegating enough tasks to capable employees with lighter workloads who are willing to do more.

Organize your work responsibilities and then decide which ones you can delegate to others. Decide which employee can best handle each task. Take time to teach employees how to do new tasks. Monitor and evaluate the tasks that have been delegated. This will allow you more time to concentrate on the most important tasks.

HOT TOPIC

Responsibility Being too remote and working in isolation are common leadership blind spots that can impair an organization.

MARKETING CASE STUDY

FedEx: "We Understand"

Recessions take a serious toll on businesses everywhere. FedEx adapted its marketing strategy to address uncertainty that many companies feel during an economic downturn. In early 2009, it launched the "We Understand" campaign. This campaign reminded people "that FedEx understands . . . and offers solutions for . . . the various needs of our customers."

Emotional and Financial Appeal

The campaign used emotional appeal to show people how FedEx products and services help them do better business and survive tough economic times. Ads from the campaign also used humor to attempt to cut through pessimism. The campaign also demonstrated that FedEx services are less expensive than competitors' services.

English Language Arts

Research Research what type of management structure FedEx uses. Write a paragraph about how FedEx management might train employees to implement a campaign like "We Understand."

FOSTER TEAMWORK

As mentioned earlier, teamwork is especially important in horizontally organized companies. As a manager or group owner, you can foster teamwork in a number of ways. Encourage team members to step outside their areas of specialization and learn about other aspects of the process for which they are responsible. Try to promote honest discussion before decisions are made. Listen respectfully to the comments and opinions of other team members, and encourage others in the group to do likewise. Respond to the comments and concerns of team members to develop a feeling of trust. Treat all team members equally. A team will not succeed if some members are treated unfairly.

BE ETHICAL

Ethical behavior involves understanding how your actions affect others and striving to make honest and just decisions. Management is responsible for promoting ethical behavior by example.

MANAGEMENT STYLES

Management style is the overall type of leadership used by a manager. The two basic management styles are *authoritarian* and *democratic*. All other styles are variations of one of these or a combination of both. An authoritarian manager makes all the decisions. Communication is mostly from top down. A democratic manager allows employees to take part in decision-making. Communication flows in both directions.

Variations of the two basic management styles include *participatory* and *teamwork*. In a participatory team, directions are given by management, but employees may complete a task without close supervision. In the *teamwork* variation, management allows employee teams to decide how best to complete a project.

Still other variations of management style used in some companies are *discussion management* and *delegating style*. In discussion management, managers meet frequently with employees about how tasks should be accomplished. In the delegating style, managers assign tasks to employees who they believe can complete them.

Different workplaces and situations call for different management styles. Diverse personalities, too, can make one management style more effective than another. Most managers strike a balance somewhere between authoritarian and democratic styles, and then adjust their style according to company objectives and the situation.

EMPLOYEE MOTIVATION

Motivating employees is a key skill for any manager. The more people feel that they are appreciated, the harder they work. Managers should provide frequent feedback to employees and formally evaluate them each year. Identifying long-term goals and rewarding employees who help meet them are important ways to motivate those whom you manage.

REWARDS

It is important to reward smart work, not busy work. A person who looks busy may not necessarily be getting the work done. To get results, reward results.

Identify those workers who value not only speed but quality. Ask them to suggest ways to improve job performance.

Enthusiastic long-term employees are the key to success in most companies. Reward loyalty by investing in continuing education for employees and promoting from within. Also, praise employees for their good ideas and successes. Employees who feel appreciated for their hard work are likely to continue to feel motivated to do a good job.

ENCOURAGE CREATIVITY

A reasonable amount of conformity is necessary in every company in order to maintain standards, but do not let conformity stifle creativity. Encourage employees to be creative, and remind them that they will not be penalized for mistakes. Sometimes, it is necessary to take risks when being creative.

Reading Check

Recall What are the basic management styles and variations?

HUMAN RESOURCES

Without effective managers, team members, and employees, the best technology and material resources would be of little value to a business. Most companies have a human resources (HR) department that handles recruitment, hiring and firing, training, and other employee matters. Employee records are maintained in a file within the human resources office. These include records of an employee's hiring, participation in training programs, performance evaluations, disciplinary action, and awards.

RECRUITING

Recruiting is the process of electing employees from a pool of applicants. Employees can be recruited from a number of different sources. Some include current employees, walk-in applicants, media advertising, state employment services, public and private employment agencies, schools, and the Internet.

CURRENT EMPLOYEES

Job openings should be posted where all employees can see them. The notice should include the job title and duties, qualifications, contact name, and sometimes the salary. Current employees are a good source for referrals.

WALK-INS

Some applicants walk into the human resources office and ask to be considered for a job. Some companies accept electronic "walk-ins" on their Web sites and at their hiring kiosks. Walk-ins usually complete an application form and may be given information on jobs that might soon become available. They might take the company's employment tests.

MEDIA ADVERTISING

Most companies use media advertising in newspapers and on the Internet to recruit applicants. Advertisements that do not disclose the name of the company are usually not very effective. The nature of the job and required qualifications should be clearly indicated in an advertisement.

Advertising on online job boards can be expensive. Social networking Web sites are increasingly used to locate potential employees and often cost nothing to use.

STATE EMPLOYMENT SERVICES

State employment offices provide screening and testing of prospective applicants. State offices and private employment agencies try to match listings of applicants with job openings. State or public agency services are free, but private agencies charge a fee when an applicant is hired.

SCHOOLS

High schools can be a good source for jobs that do not require specialized skills. Vocational and technical schools are sources for applicants who have learned a variety of specialized skills. Colleges are the source for applicants with higher-level skills.

DISCRIMINATION AND THE LAW

Laws against discrimination govern employers and recruitment agencies. These laws apply before an employee is hired. It is important to avoid discriminatory remarks and actions in all recruiting efforts. Federal law prohibits employers from discriminating on the basis of race, color, religion, gender, national origin, age, sexual orientation, or disability. The U.S. Equal Employment Opportunity Commission enforces and regulates these laws.

HIRING NEW EMPLOYEES

For the employer, the purpose of the interview is to determine whether an individual has the skills and abilities to perform well on the job.

Before managers interview job applicants, they must follow all the laws that govern the hiring process. They should be aware of which kinds of questions are illegal or unacceptable.

It is a good idea to conduct at least two interviews with applicants who seem well qualified. It is also a good idea to have at least two people interview final applicants. Ask only questions that are job related. If you are interviewing more than one applicant for the same job, ask each one exactly the same questions in exactly the same order. You need to allow the applicant to ask questions, too. It is the interviewer's responsibility to explain such things as wages and benefits.

Before hiring an applicant, most employers do some pre-employment testing. It may include an aptitude test to predict how well an applicant can perform certain tasks. Some companies give personality tests. Many companies ask prospective employees to be tested for illegal drugs.

ORIENTATION AND TRAINING PROGRAMS

Orienting new employees includes more than simply training them for their positions. It is important to make new employees feel valued and welcome and to familiarize them with the working environment. Orientation may take as little as a couple of hours or as long as a few days.

Only 32 percent of Americans with disabilities aged 18 to 64 are working, but two-thirds of those who are unemployed would rather be working. *Which commission prohibits discrimination on the basis of a disability?*

Ability, Not Disability

For the company, the purpose of a job interview is to determine whether an applicant can perform well on the job. *As a manager, how would you prepare to interview several applicants for the same job?*

The Interview

Orientation commonly includes the following:

▶ Tour of the company facilities and introductions to coworkers

▶ Description of the company's history, mission, and values

▶ Training on use and routine maintenance of equipment, such as point-of-sale systems, product scanners, computers, and printers

▶ Information on locations of facilities

▶ Information about payroll, benefits, and various company policies

All new employees need on-the-job training. As a supervisor, you may train new employees yourself or delegate this task to an experienced employee. Make sure that all job duties are explained and that new employees understand how to complete them.

SCHEDULING EMPLOYEES

Employee scheduling is the process of determining which employees should work at what times. Very small companies can handle the scheduling of employees quite simply without any special computer program. Today, though, most companies use some type of computer scheduling.

HANDLING COMPLAINTS AND GRIEVANCES

Employee complaints or grievances should be taken just as seriously as customer complaints. Most employee complaints fall into one of three categories: other employees, the quality of the company's product or service, or their own work situation.

Complaints about other employees should be handled with care and discretion. Conflicts in the workplace can damage morale and productivity. Some employees care about the quality of the company's products and bring problems to the attention of management. The employee who has complained should be kept informed at every step.

When a complaint involves the employee's work situation, gather the facts, report the findings to the employee who has complained, and make your decision. Then clearly explain to the employee the reasons and nature of your decision.

In most business situations, a grievance is considered more serious than a complaint. Agreements between management and labor unions almost always include a procedure for processing a complaint against the company.

Flash Shelton
Owner/President
Just Fix It, Inc.

What do you do at work?

We do home repair and remodel work for residential and commercial properties. Besides managing the business, meeting with customers, and following up on jobs, I am always thinking of ways to bring in new customers and keep the ones I *have* happy. To market the business, we use ads in phonebooks and on the Internet. Our Web site and involvement with community events are good sources of advertising, too.

What is your key to success?

Being successful requires knowledge, skills in management, networking, communication and marketing, customer service, reliability, trustworthiness, and a great imagination.

What skills are most important to you?

Overall knowledge of the job and good management skills are essential. You need drive and determination. Customer service and people skills are key. Another important skill is the ability to hire good help. Finally, take pride in what you do—it's not *just* a job.

 connectED.mcgraw-hill.com

Read more about this career and complete a Career Exploration Activity.

ASSESSING EMPLOYEE PERFORMANCE

Assessment enables a manager to develop better workers and a more efficient and profitable company. In many companies, newly hired employees are placed on probation for a period of three to six months. Near the end of the probationary period, the employee is evaluated. If performance is satisfactory, the employee's status is changed to permanent. Usually, all employees are evaluated yearly. In many companies, the employee completes a self-evaluation form, and the supervisor completes the same form on the employee. Then a meeting is scheduled so that the supervisor and the employee can compare and discuss any differences in opinion.

REMEDIAL ACTION

It is the supervisor's responsibility to discuss substandard performance with the employee. Sometimes, remedial action is necessary. **Remedial action** is a means of encouraging appropriate workplace behavior in order to improve employee performance. Two approaches to remedial action are preventive discipline and corrective discipline.

PREVENTIVE DISCIPLINE

Preventive discipline focuses on managing employees in a way that prevents behavior that might require directly disciplining an employee. Its purpose is to encourage employees to follow the rules. Preventive discipline techniques might include involving employees in setting standards, encouraging employees to meet standards, and communicating standards clearly. It is also helpful to implement methods for controlling absences and to implement training programs in self-discipline and the recognition and prevention of workplace harassment.

CORRECTIVE DISCIPLINE

In some cases, corrective discipline is necessary. This usually begins with a verbal warning and an explanation of what will be required. Next is a written warning to the employee with a copy for the employee's personnel file. If the problem is not resolved, the third action is suspension from work without pay. The suspension usually lasts from one to five days and comes with a warning that if the problem is not corrected, the employee may be fired.

Corrective counseling is sometimes effective. This involves a discussion between the employee and a human resources counselor about the problem and what must be done to correct it.

DISMISSING EMPLOYEES

Most companies have to face the task of firing an employee for poor performance or bad behavior. Before this decision is made, certain procedures must be followed. A supervisor or manager must give the employee verbal and written warnings. This informs the employee that his or her performance or behavior is not acceptable. These warnings should be included on the employee's performance assessment form in the personnel file. The employee may be placed on probation and given time to change. When a decision is made to dismiss a worker, a letter of dismissal should be written, along with separate checks for final salary and severance pay.

THE EXIT INTERVIEW

When an employee leaves the company, an **exit interview** is arranged that will allow the employee and manager to get feedback. Exit interviews are often conducted with human resources rather than with the employee's supervisor. An employee always has the right not to participate in an exit interview.

An employee who is leaving voluntarily may have feedback on work conditions. If the employee is being dismissed, the reason should be discussed in the exit interview. Usually, an employee will be given advance notice of termination. As a manager, you must decide whether to have the employee continue working or leave immediately.

 After You Read | **Section 11.2**

Review Key Concepts

1. **List** the three functions of management.
2. **Explain** the meaning of delegating responsibility.
3. **Discuss** the purpose of assessing employee performance.

Practice Academics

English Language Arts

4. As manager of your department, you have noticed that one of your employees has been complaining quite a bit. Complaints range from the lack of recent wage increases to dissatisfaction with the work situation to gripes about another employee whistling on the job. Discuss with a partner how you might address the situation or the employee.

Mathematics

5. Grocery store clerks are negotiating with their company management for a 6.5-percent increase in their hourly wage. The average hourly wage of a clerk is $14.75. The company has 35 clerks who each work a 40-hour week, 50 weeks per year. The clerks receive a two-week paid vacation each year. What would the pay raise cost per year?

Math Concept **Number and Operations: Computation** Fluent computation requires a logical sequence of steps.

Starting Hints To solve this problem, multiply the hourly wage by the decimal equivalent of 6.5 percent to find the increase in wages the employees want. Multiply the number of employees by the number of hours worked each week, 40, to determine the total number of hours worked by all the employees.

connectED.mcgraw-hill.com

Check your answers.

For help, go to the **Math Skills Handbook** located at the back of this book.

Management Skills

Vertically organized companies have top management, middle management, and supervisory-level management. Horizontal companies have top and middle management and self-managed teams.

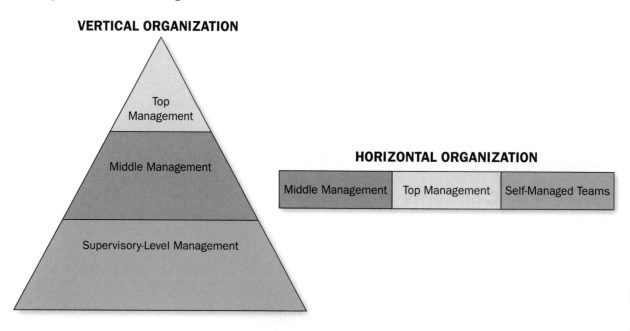

VERTICAL ORGANIZATION

Top Management

Middle Management

Supervisory-Level Management

HORIZONTAL ORGANIZATION

Middle Management	Top Management	Self-Managed Teams

Management functions are planning, organizing, and controlling. Effective management techniques include properly training employees, letting them know what is expected, and treating them fairly.

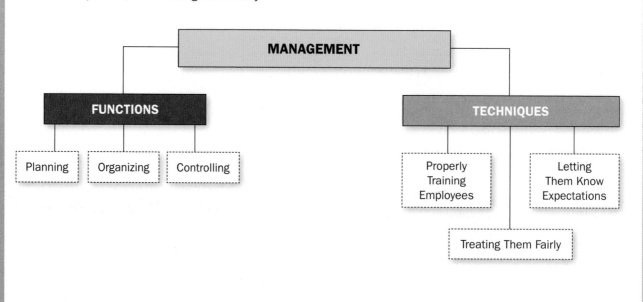

MANAGEMENT

FUNCTIONS

Planning | Organizing | Controlling

TECHNIQUES

Properly Training Employees | Letting Them Know Expectations

Treating Them Fairly

Review and Activities

Written Summary

- The global marketplace will influence the kind of leadership companies will need in the future.
- Businesses are organized in one of two ways: vertically or horizontally.
- Traditional, vertically organized companies have three levels of management: top management, middle management, and supervisory-level management.
- Horizontal companies have top and middle management. Horizontally organized companies have self-managed teams that set their own goals and make their own decisions.
- Basic management functions are planning, organizing, and controlling.
- Effective management techniques involve properly training employees, letting them know what is expected of them, and treating them fairly.
- In case of poor performance or unacceptable behavior, the employee should receive warnings, which should be included in the employee's personnel file. A letter of dismissal should be given to the employee at dismissal time, along with the final salary amount due.

Review Content Vocabulary and Academic Vocabulary

1. Create multiple-choice test questions for each content and academic vocabulary term.

Content Vocabulary
- management (p. 253)
- vertical organization (p. 253)
- top management (p. 253)
- middle management (p. 253)
- supervisory-level management (p. 253)
- horizontal organization (p. 254)
- empowerment (p. 254)
- planning (p. 257)
- organizing (p. 257)
- controlling (p. 257)
- mission statement (p. 258)
- remedial action (p. 264)
- exit interview (p. 265)

Academic Vocabulary
- resource (p. 253)
- individual (p. 255)
- identify (p. 257)
- require (p. 258)

Assess for Understanding

2. **Contrast** What is the difference between horizontally organized and vertically organized companies?
3. **Identify** What are three levels of management?
4. **Describe** How does a self-managed team function?
5. **Consider** How do the three functions of management affect employees?
6. **Imagine** What are the benefits of the six management techniques used by effective managers?
7. **Create** What would you include in an orientation program for your school?
8. **Consider** How can a company benefit from empowerment?
9. **Compose** How would you notify an employee that he or she needs remedial action? Write your response.

21st  Century Skills

Leadership Skills

10. Management and Motivation A week ago you were promoted to a supervisory level in charge of 20 employees that manufacture electric motors. On the first day you noticed that there were problems, but you decided to observe for a few days as you plan what action to take. Some workers are sloppy in their work, some seem unsure about how to perform certain tasks, and there is general disharmony in the group. What are some actions that you will take to improve production, behavior, and harmony? Share suggestions with a partner.

Financial Literacy Skills

11. Sales Projections Your company produces and markets electronic equipment. Sales last year totaled $2,776,540. The company goal is to increase sales by 5 percent this year. Your division goal is to achieve 20 percent of total sales. What is the dollar value of your division goal?

Everyday Ethics

12. Taking Charge You are a cashier at a clothing store. Your manager tells you she must go out of town for the weekend, and that you will be in charge of the store while she is away, but you will not receive extra pay. She says if anyone asks to speak to a manager to say you are the manager. Is it ethical to tell customers that you are the manager, even if you are a substitute manager? Discuss what you would do in this situation and why.

e-Marketing Skills

13. Feasibility Study You are the manager of a small computer and electronics store. The owner has asked that you research the feasibility of setting up an online business that would be operated from your store. Research this topic and write your recommendations.

Build Academic Skills

Social Studies

14. Business Locations An automobile company is considering opening a new assembly plant in your state. The plant would add about 10,000 new jobs and require workers of all education and training levels. What part of the state would you suggest and why? Share a list of reasons for your selection.

English Language Arts

15. Workplace Environment Select a clothing store that carries clothing you like. Research and write about ethical policies the company follows in terms of working conditions for employees.

Mathematics

16. Plan Office Space Calculate the square feet of space required to organize an office area to accommodate six employees. Each cubicle will be 25 square feet. Plan for three cubicles on each side of the office (for a total of six cubicles) and a 4-foot wide hallway down the middle of the office.

Math Concept **Geometry: Calculating Area** The formula for area is length times width. Area is always measured in square units, such as square feet.

For help, go to the **Math Skills Handbook** located at the back of this book.

Standardized Test Practice

Directions Read the following questions. On a separate piece of paper, write the best possible answer for each one.

1. Self-managed teams are part of which type of organization?
   A. traditional
   B. vertical
   C. horizontal
   D. none of the above

2. Since 2009, it has been illegal to fire employees.
   T
   F

3. When an employee leaves a company, the human resources department will usually arrange a(n) _____.

Test-Taking Tip
If time allows, review both questions and answers so you can avoid misreading a question.

DECA Connection Role Play

Manager Bicycle Store

Situation Assume the role of newly hired manager of a bicycle store. The store sells and services a wide range of bicycles for individuals who enjoy cycling as a hobby. The store also sells a comprehensive selection of cycling accessories that include bike helmets, gloves, water bottles, and clothing. Eight sales associates who are all experienced cyclists staff the store. The staff is knowledgeable about the bicycles and accessories the store sells.

Store sales are acceptable, but not great, and staff morale is low. The shop's owner (judge) has hired you to improve sales and staff morale. You have had a discussion with each of the sales associates to get to know each of them and to try to discover the reasons for the low morale. You have learned that many of the sales associates feel that the previous manager did not appreciate their efforts and that their ideas regarding the shop were not taken seriously. You have determined that improving staff morale will help motivate the staff and lead to improved store sales.

Activity You are to outline some ways to improve staff morale. Once you have outlined your ideas you are to present them to the shop's owner (judge) before presenting them at this week's staff meeting.

Evaluation You will be evaluated on how well you meet the following performance indicators:

1. Explain the concept of management.
2. Explain the role of ethics in human resources management.
3. Demonstrate responsible behavior.
4. Explain the nature of staff communication.
5. Make oral presentations.

  connectED.mcgraw-hill.com

Download the Competitive Events Workbook for more Role-Play practice.

Financial Literacy 101
to Teach Money Smarts

How much money do you have in your savings account, and what do you plan to do with it?

Scenario

Research indicates that close to 50 percent of high-school-aged teens are not financially literate. In the future, pensions are not going to be available to the younger generation as they may be replaced with 401(k) accounts. Stories abound about college students who charge so much money to credit cards that they get themselves in debt that lasts long after graduation.

As part of a statewide initiative, the local chamber of commerce has commissioned your company to create a Web site with an interactive program to make learning financial literacy fun and effective for young children and teens.

The Skills You'll Use

Academic Skills Reading, writing, social studies, researching, and analyzing

Basic Skills Speaking, listening, thinking, and interpersonal

Technology Skills Word processing, presentation, spreadsheet, telecommunication, and the Internet

Your Objective

Design a fun-filled, interesting, and interactive "Financial Literacy 101" Web site that teaches children and teens about financial literacy.

STEP 1 Do Your Research

Conduct research to identify financial literacy programs that currently exist online. For example, search for national campaigns designed to help teens. Also search for credit unions and banks that sponsor financial literacy programs. As you conduct your research, answer these questions:

- What is the definition of financial literacy?
- What topics are included in financial literacy programs?
- How do financial literacy programs target young people?
- Which parts of the financial literacy programs will young people find interesting?

Write a summary of your research.

STEP 2 Plan Your Project

Now that you have completed your research, you need to begin planning your project.

- Conduct a survey of your peers to evaluate their financial literacy.
- Determine topics to be included in the financial literacy Web site.
- Design storyboards for a Web site that invites young people to learn about how to handle their own finances now and in the future.
- Plan interactive aspects of the Web site so that it is fun and interesting and young people will want to use it.
- Think about indicators that you can use to measure whether your program is effective.
- Use your knowledge of mathematics, communication skills, technology, and interpersonal skills to design an effective financial literacy program.

STEP 3 Connect with Your Community

- Gather published financial literacy materials from local banks and other financial institutions.
- Interview one or more trusted adults at home, at school, at work, or in your community about financial literacy. Consider talking to a business teacher at your school or ask a politician what financial literacy initiatives are being considered by the government.
- Takes notes during your interviews, and transcribe your notes after the interviews.

STEP 4 Share What You Learn

Assume your class is a committee from the Chamber of Commerce that will be in charge of approving the content of the financial literacy program.

- Present your project plan in an oral presentation. Be prepared to answer questions.
- Define financial literacy and explain its importance.
- Explain how to teach financial literacy skills to the younger generation.
- Present your Web-site design storyboards.
- Provide rationale for your ideas and your Web-site design.
- Use software to create a slide presentation to accompany your oral report.

STEP 5 Evaluate Your Marketing and Academic Skills

Your project will be evaluated based on the following:

- Knowledge of financial literacy and currently available programs
- Web-site design and interactive program for financial literacy
- Research to support your selection of topics and program features
- Organization and continuity of presentation
- Mechanics—presentation and neatness
- Speaking and listening skills

MARKETING CORE FUNCTIONS

Marketing Information Management

Market Planning

Marketing Internship Project Checklist

Plan

✓ Research financial literacy and explain its importance.

✓ Research currently available financial literacy programs.

✓ Design plans for an interactive Web site that teaches financial literacy.

Write

✓ Write a summary of your research.

✓ Explain why an interactive Web site about financial literacy is important.

Present

✓ Present research that supports the topics included in a financial literacy program.

✓ Present the design for your Web site.

✓ Suggest evaluation tools to measure the effectiveness of the program.

 connectED.mcgraw-hill.com

Evaluate Download a rubric you can use to evaluate your final project.

my marketing portfolio

Internship Report Once you have completed your Marketing Internship Project and oral presentation, put your written report and a few printouts of key slides from your oral presentation in your Marketing Portfolio.

Teen Driving Safety Program According to the National Highway Traffic Safety Administration, in a recent year, 35 percent of teen fatalities were due to motor vehicle accidents. Allstate Insurance Company cites additional facts: "Nearly 5,000 young people die in car crashes every year. Another 300,000 teens are injured in car crashes each year." Your firm wants to lower those statistics. What kind of interactive Web site can you design to help in that endeavor? What topics should be included and how can they be demonstrated? Prepare a written report and an oral presentation.

selling overview

SHOW WHAT YOU KNOW

Visual Literacy Many different types of businesses employ salespeople, so there are many different kinds of sales careers. *Does a career in sales appeal to you? What kind of businesses might you be interested in working for as a salesperson?*

Discovery Project

Is a Career in Selling for You?

Essential Question What aspects of selling interest you?

Project Goal

Research some sales career options in all types of business enterprises (e.g., Internet, retail, manufacturing, and service industries). Investigate the employment requirements, pay scales, and benefits for entry level as well as the executive-management level. Research the advantages and disadvantages of a selling career. Which aspects of a selling career interest you, and which aspects do not appeal to you? Write a report that summarizes your research and your evaluation of selling as a career.

Ask Yourself...

- Where will you find employment requirements, pay scales, and benefits for different sales employment levels?
- What are the advantages and disadvantages of a selling career?
- What aspects of a selling career interest you?
- How will you present your findings?

 Synthesize and Present Research Synthesize your research by writing a report that summarizes your research and your evaluation of selling as a career.

 connectED.mcgraw-hill.com

Activity
Get a worksheet activity about sales careers.

Evaluate
Download a rubric you can use to evaluate your project.

DECA Connection

DECA Event Role Play

Concepts in this chapter are related to DECA competitive events that involve either an interview or role play.

Performance Indicators The performance indicators represent key skills and knowledge. Your key to success in DECA competitive events is relating them to concepts in this chapter.

- Explain the nature and scope of the selling function.
- Explain the selling process.
- Explain business ethics in selling.
- Describe the use of technology in the selling function.
- Explain the nature of sales management.

DECA Prep

Role Play Practice role-playing with the DECA Connection competitive-event activity at the end of this chapter. More information on DECA events can be found on DECA's Web site.

READING GUIDE

Before You Read

Reflect When have you had to convince someone to do something?

Objectives

- **Explain** the purpose and goal of the selling function.
- **Discuss** how selling is related to the marketing concept.
- **Describe** Customer Relationship Management.
- **Analyze** sales trends and technology.
- **Summarize** sales management responsibilities.
- **Explain** legal and ethical sales issues.

The Main Idea

The marketing concept comes alive in the sales function with the help of emerging trends and technology. Customer Relationship Management (CRM) and sales management efforts help to achieve the purpose and goal of selling.

Vocabulary

Content Vocabulary

- customer relationship management (CRM)
- call report
- sales quota

Academic Vocabulary

You will find these words in your reading and on your tests. Make sure you know their meanings.

- solidify
- interface

Graphic Organizer

Draw or print this diagram to write details on Selling and the Marketing Concept, and Sales Management.

Selling and the Marketing Concept

Purpose and Goal

Sales Trends and Technology

MARKETING CORE FUNCTION

Selling

McGraw Hill Education connectED.mcgraw-hill.com

Print this graphic organizer.

Sales Management

Legal and Ethical Issues

The Sales Function

SELLING AND THE MARKETING CONCEPT

Selling is an important marketing function. Why? Because selling generates the revenue that a business needs to operate. Successful companies have loyal customers. Loyal customers provide steady revenue for a company. They may recommend the company to others. This personal recommendation helps businesses grow. It is the sales division in a company that performs most of the tasks to find new customers, make sales, and keep current customers satisfied.

As You Read

Connect How do companies try to make you a loyal customer?

PURPOSE AND GOAL

The purpose of selling is to help customers make satisfying buying decisions, with the goal of creating ongoing, profitable relationships with them. As such, it is the essence of the marketing concept—businesses satisfying customers' needs and wants while making a profit. To make a profit, business must generate sales. Businesses' revenues are based on sales. This revenue is critical to keeping a company in business.

The marketing concept has created a customer-centered focus that companies have embraced. Departments coordinate their functions to help the sales function succeed. The marketing, customer service, and technology departments all work together to support sales efforts. Their respective activities ensure customer satisfaction.

For example, a potential customer may visit a company's Web site and request product information. That request may be directed to the customer service department for a response, with a copy to the sales department for follow-up.

With the information obtained from the customer service staff, the sales staff is better prepared to satisfy the customer's request.

> " **No company can stay in business if its products do not sell.** "

SALES TRENDS AND TECHNOLOGY

Marketers know that identifying the needs of customers and satisfying them can be profitable. However, only recently have firms made a dedicated effort to use **customer relationship management (CRM)**. This system involves finding customers and keeping them satisfied.

CRM has flourished due to new computer technology. Businesses have a tremendous amount of information about their customers at their finger tips. Company Web sites and e-mails have helped businesses communicate with customers on a frequent basis. Computer software has revolutionized the sales function. Let's look at some of the emerging trends and technologies that affect marketing and specifically help CRM.

WEB SITES AND SOCIAL MEDIA

Many companies have their own Web sites that provide product information. Some are designed for online purchases, while others tell visitors where a product may be purchased. To connect with the visitors who are customers or potential customers, companies often provide relevant educational information about topics of interest to visitors to the site. Some include fun, interactive games.

These encourage customers to return to the site frequently. All effective Web-site designs include the principles of selling that you will learn in this unit. For customers who need personal assistance, a Web site may offer contact information to speak with a salesperson.

Many businesses participate in social media sites, such as Facebook and Twitter. Both of these sites help companies stay in touch with their customers by receiving and sending business communications. Company Web sites and social media outlets allow companies to be accessible to potential customers nationally and globally.

E-MAIL

Another technology that helps in sending and receiving business communication is e-mail. E-mails are an efficient way to prepare written communication. E-mails can be used to thank customers for their orders and to address customer service issues. Businesses and customers can track orders and delivery status quickly and easily via e-mail. Thus, communication between companies and their customers can be quick and efficient, which helps to **solidify** relationships even after a sale is made.

Through extensive databases that keep track of customer purchases, companies are able to send targeted e-mails to their customers. The targeted e-mails update customers regarding new promotions and new products that fit their needs based on their past purchases. This information technology tool helps marketing efforts to create sales. There are a variety of software programs and companies that offer this service to businesses.

CUSTOMER LOYALTY PROGRAMS

To keep customers loyal, some companies offer special rewards programs to their regular customers. Airlines offer frequent flier programs. Pharmacies give their loyal customers discounts based on their level of purchases each month. Credit card companies, like American Express® and Capital One®, offer points based on purchases that can be redeemed for goods and services. E-mailed questionnaires with prize entries or advance notice of special sales are other methods marketers have developed to create and reinforce loyalty. Manufacturers offer special pricing programs and other incentives to customers who generate a certain amount of sales volume.

Company Web Sites

Companies have several ways of selling their products to consumers. In this ad for Lucky Brand® Jeans, readers are provided the Web site address for this brand where they can shop online or find a store that carries this brand. *Why would a company sell its products online and also in retail stores?*

COMPUTER SOFTWARE

Computer software for the sales function is available for all types of businesses. Some companies purchase software that can be customized for their business. Others may subscribe to CRM services offered by Web-based companies. For example, Oracle® CRM OnDemand and salesforce.com host customer relationship management services. Other software companies specialize in a variety of sales-related areas, such as sales automation, sales territory management, sales forecasting, and management of compensation and incentive programs.

MOBILE DEVICES

Salespeople today are very connected. They can send and receive business communications while away from the office. Their mobile devices or laptops can be programmed to **interface** with their company's computer system. While visiting with a customer, a sales representative can check on the customer's past purchases, product availability, price changes, and more.

PARTNERSHIPS

Some companies become partners in an effort to solve a customer's problem. Oracle and IBM® were partners in an effort to design an Oracle CRM system for Konica Minolta® Business Solutions U.S.A. The result was improved collaboration with the direct sales force. Sales lead generation and follow-up were made easier and more efficient.

To successfully maintain sales accounts, company sales representatives must stay in contact with customers. Sales representatives act as partners or consultants for their customers. For example, a manufacturer of artificial knees or hips may have a sales representative present in the operating room during a medical procedure in case a question or problem comes up. In addition to developing expertise about the products, a sales representative for a medical supply company also goes through extensive medical training. This traning allows a sales representative to answer any questions the customer may have about a product's specifications and how it can be used.

By examining successful partnerships in business and elsewhere, marketers have discovered that enduring relationships are built on trust and commitment, and require a lot of time and effort to maintain.

Reading Check

Define What is customer relationship management?

Promoting Loyalty

CVS/pharmacy has a special program called "ExtraCare® ," the largest retail rewards program in the U.S. ExtraCare offers automatic savings, personalized coupons, and other incentives to customers who opt-in. *Why do you think companies use loyalty programs?*

SALES MANAGEMENT

Sales management establishes the guidelines and policies for the sales team. Sales managers plan, organize, and control the sales function. They establish the structure of the sales organization. During planning, sales managers prepare and monitor sales budgets, establish realistic sales forecasts and quotas for certain divisions, and supervise individual sales personnel.

It is the job of sales management to hire and train members of a company's sales staff and assign them to specific territories. The managers analyze sales reports, hold sales meetings, and design compensation plans and incentive programs to motivate the sales staff. The sales staff's performance and ethical and legal conduct is monitored by sales managers. Sales managers also meet with management of other divisions to collaborate and develop new sales opportunities. Input from sales about what customers want can help in the development of new products.

COMPANY POLICIES

Company policies and goals must be communicated to the sales staff by sales management. For example, a company may have a goal of increasing market share by 10 percent in the coming year. To do so, the company needs to sell more of its products. That goal must be communicated to the sales staff. To reach that goal, an atmosphere of teamwork and integrity among workers would be necessary. Other company policies are created to ensure that personnel are performing their tasks effectively. For example, sales personnel may be required to complete call reports each time they visit a customer. A **call report** is a written report that documents a sales representative's visit with a customer. It includes customer information for the company database, the purpose and outcome of the visit, as well as any follow-up that is necessary.

MARKETING CASE STUDY

Adidas's Sales Automation

To prepare for a meeting with a customer, the Adidas® sales force usually checks inventory. But frustration would set in when some products were no longer available after a sale was made. A sales representative would have to call the customer to revise the order. Or, worse, phone customer service while on a sales call, interrupting the selling process. So, Adidas gave laptops to its sales staff so they could interface with the company's computer system to check real-time inventory.

Improving the Process

To improve on this solution, Adidas turned to AT&T™ and Atlas2Go, an automated sales-force application. The software program can run on a wireless BlackBerry® device. With this system, sales representatives check inventory on the spot while taking a customer's order. This improvement reduced frustration, errors, and the need to change orders. Another unforeseen benefit was the ability to spot product trends quickly.

Social Studies

Analyze Discuss how supply and demand resulted in sales representatives having immediate access to a company's inventory during the sales process.

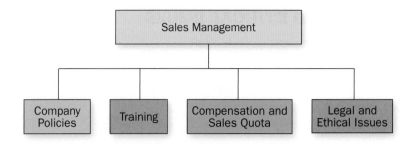

```
                    ┌─────────────────────┐
                    │  Sales Management   │
                    └──────────┬──────────┘
         ┌─────────────┬───────┴───────┬──────────────┐
 ┌───────┴──────┐ ┌────┴─────┐ ┌───────┴────────┐ ┌───┴──────────┐
 │   Company    │ │ Training │ │ Compensation   │ │  Legal and   │
 │   Policies   │ │          │ │ and Sales Quota│ │ Ethical Issues│
 └──────────────┘ └──────────┘ └────────────────┘ └──────────────┘
```

TRAINING

A four-step process is often used by sales managers who are ultimately responsible for training new sales personnel. The four steps are explanation, demonstration, trial, and critique. The person conducting the training first explains and then demonstrates a sales technique. In the next step, the new sales associate performs the newly learned task or demonstrates product knowledge in a role-playing format. The final step involves constructive criticism by the trainer. This sales training program works well for all steps in the sales process. It reinforces sales techniques and emphasizes the marketing concept with new and veteran sales associates.

COMPENSATION AND SALES QUOTAS

Salespeople are compensated by straight commission, straight salary, or salary plus commission. Some field sales staff also receive benefits, such as a company car and expense account. Company policies govern what is covered under the expense account.

Commission salespeople get paid only when they sell something. Salaried salespeople get paid a set amount, regardless of how much they sell. Salary plus commission salespeople generally have a set salary, and their commission rate is lower than the rate received by salespeople who are paid only commission.

Regardless of the method of compensation, sales managers often establish sales quotas. A **sales quota** is a dollar or unit sales goal set for the sales staff to achieve in a specified period of time. Sales managers make sales forecasts based on sales reports to predict what sales can be expected in the future. Managers must regularly monitor sales reports to see if quotas are being met. Some companies offer incentives to salespeople to encourage them to meet—and even exceed—their quotas. Incentives could include recognition, a gift, and/or a monetary bonus.

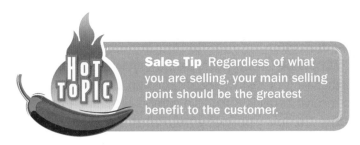

Career Chatroom

Lori Blinder
Beauty and Fashion Director
Fitness® Magazine

What do you do at work?

My responsibility is to grow revenue. I sell programs including digital, retail, event sponsorships, and print. I work to increase *Fitness'* visibility and awareness with the client and agency side of the beauty and fashion community, and create opportunities to open doors. I attend industry events and work to create partnerships that leverage beauty advertising.

What is your key to success?

I come to work everyday with a positive attitude. I love what I do and feel that my passion and integrity are keys to developing trust among my clients and my coworkers.

What skills are most important to you?

It is important to multi-task, have an entrepreneurial spirit, and manage your time. You also need to be aggressive and persistent without being overbearing and annoying. Listen to your clients and understand their goals. Finally, deal with whatever challenges come your way *and* keep a smile on your face.

 connectED.mcgraw-hill.com

Read more about this career and get a Career Exploration Activity.

LEGAL AND ETHICAL ISSUES

Ethical businesses work hard to acquire and keep new customers. Since salespeople have direct contact with customers, they represent their company and its reputation. Ethical businesses do not permit their salespeople to engage in sales techniques that may cause legal problems or damage the business's reputation.

SALES PRESSURE

Commission sales and sales quotas can create pressure on the sales staff to produce sales. If not taught properly in selling ethics and legal issues, sales associates may engage in hard-sell tactics. They may also lie to prospective customers. For example, it is both illegal and ethically wrong for a salesperson to promise, say, a two-week delivery of an order, just to make the sale, knowing that it will actually take four weeks for delivery. When the merchandise does not arrive on time, the buyer may not accept the order. In this case, the salesperson could have arranged a partial shipment to be delivered in two weeks, with the remainder being shipped later. That solution would have benefited both the customer and the company.

Sales Tip Regardless of what you are selling, your main selling point should be the greatest benefit to the customer.

Commission salespeople often have to meet quotas in order to get paid. *How do you think quotas might put pressure on salespeople?*

Sales Quotas

SALES CONTRACTS

It is important to remember that a sales order or purchase order is a legal agreement. It is a contract between the buyer and seller that is signed by both parties. It contains all the elements of a legal contract: an offer, an acceptance, consideration (price and terms), competent parties (buyer and seller), legal form, and legal subject matter.

A sales contract specifies what product or service is being offered, how much, and at what price. When the buyer signs the contract, it becomes a binding agreement to purchase the product or service at the price shown on the contract. The contract typically also contains language that spells out any guarantee or warranty that goes with the purchase.

SALES REGULATIONS

In certain selling situations, such as real estate, the buyer is given a set period of time, perhaps 24 to 48 hours, in which the agreement can be canceled without penalty.

Another aspect of a sales contract is full disclosure of the facts. In a contract providing services, all services and materials that will be used should be clearly identified. Pricing information must be accurate and based on services actually performed. In real estate dealings, full disclosure of all potentially negative factors (e.g., mold, termites, radon) must be disclosed by the seller.

Sales regulations protect the buyer against fraudulent or unethical selling practices. They give the buyer confidence that the item being purchased matches the seller's description.

 After You Read | **Section 12.1**

Review Key Concepts

1. **Explain** the purpose and goal of selling.
2. **Discuss** which trends and technologies help businesses with customer relationship management.
3. **Explain** the role that sales management plays in the sales process.

Practice Academics

Social Studies

4. Why must salespeople follow ethical sales practices and know about sales contracts? What are the ramifications if they do not?

Mathematics

5. Assume a salesperson has earned $35,000 as a base salary, plus 5 percent commission on sales of $800,000. Determine the salesperson's income for the year.

Math Concept **Ways of Representing Numbers** An increase in a number can be represented by a percent greater than 100.

Starting Hints Convert the 5 percent to a decimal. Multiple sales by .05 (5 percent) to determine the salesperson's commission for the year. Add the commission to the base salary to determine the salesperson's yearly income.

 connectED.mcgraw-hill.com

Check your answers.

For help, go to the **Math Skills Handbook** located at the back of this book.

READING GUIDE

Before You Read

Connect What type of product would you enjoy selling? Why?

Objectives

- **Define** personal selling.
- **Identify** sales positions.
- **List** the steps in the sales process.
- **Analyze** how customers make buying decisions.
- **Evaluate** selling as a career option.

The Main Idea

An understanding of the purpose of selling and the different levels of customer decision making can help salespeople determine how they will perform the steps of a sale.

Vocabulary

Content Vocabulary
- personal selling
- organizational selling
- cold call
- telemarketing
- extensive decision making
- limited decision making
- routine decision making

Academic Vocabulary
You will find these words in your reading and on your tests. Make sure you know their meanings.
- pre-sold
- perquisite

Graphic Organizer

Draw or print this chart to make three lists that include sales positions, the seven steps of a sale, and the three levels of consumer decision making.

Sales Positions	Steps of a Sale	Customer Decision Making
Retail businesses	A - Approach	Extensive
	N - Needs determined	L
	P -	R
	O -	
	C -	
	S & R -	

 connectED.mcgraw-hill.com

Print this graphic organizer.

MARKETING CORE FUNCTION

Selling

Sales Careers

PERSONAL SELLING

Personal selling is any form of direct contact between a salesperson and a customer. The key factor that sets it apart from other forms of promotion is the two-way communication between the seller and the buyer. Sales positions may have different titles, such as sales representative or account executive. Look in the "Help Wanted" or "Jobs" section of a print or online newspaper under "Sales Positions" to see the various names associated with a sales career. Regardless of the sales title, salespeople follow certain steps in the sales process. These steps are based on how customers make their buying decisions.

As You Read

Connect How might your need for sales assistance change for different products?

TYPES OF SALES POSITIONS

Salespeople work in retail businesses, industrial businesses, service businesses, telemarketing firms, nonprofit organizations, and Internet companies. As you read about these business categories, analyze the respective sales positions in order to see which ones interest you.

RETAIL BUSINESSES

Retail selling is unique because customers come to the store. Non-personal selling techniques, such Internet Web sites, advertising, and displays, help to create store traffic. Retail customers are **pre-sold** due to these promotional efforts. The salesperson's job involves simply offering customer service. When retail customers are not pre-sold, they require a salesperson's assistance to help them make a buying decision.

> " **Personal selling involves two-way communication between the buyer and seller.** "

INDUSTRIAL AND SERVICE BUSINESSES

Manufacturers, wholesalers, and many service businesses (banks, advertising agencies, insurance companies, consulting firms) are involved with organizational sales.

Organizational selling involves sales exchanges that occur between two or more companies or business groups. The sales process may take place in the seller's showroom or company headquarters (inside sales) or at a customer's place of business (field or outside sales).

When the sales exchange occurs at a customer's place of business, it is up to the salesperson to make contact with the customer. Sales representatives will call to make an appointment prior to a visit. In other cases, sales representatives may make a **cold call**, which means they will visit without an appointment.

TELEMARKETING AND NONPROFIT

Telemarketing is telephone solicitation to make a sale. Consumer goods and services that are commonly sold over the telephone include magazine or newspaper subscriptions and long-distance telephone services. Service contracts for newly purchased appliances, televisions, and computers are also sold over the telephone. Products that are purchased on a regular basis by businesses, such as cleaning supplies or office supplies like computer or copy paper, may be sold through telemarketing. Also, many nonprofit organizations use telemarketing to solicit donations.

In 2003, U.S. Congress passed legislation making it more difficult for telemarketers to operate. The law prohibits telemarketers from calling any phone number that has been registered with the national Do Not Call Registry, established by the Federal Communications Commission. This law significantly reduces the number of people telemarketers may legally contact.

INTERNET WEB SITES AND SALES

Many Internet Web sites have supporting sales staff to handle customers who call to place an order. The sales support staff must know sales techniques to help callers make a buying decision.

Companies that have a presence on the Internet (e.g., Google, Yahoo!, Bing, and Amazon) sell advertising space to generate revenue. They have sales employees who solicit that business.

STEPS OF A SALE

The sales process involves solving your customer's problems with your product. Salespeople play a vital role in this process. They gather information about customers, advise them about which products would best suit their needs, and then lead them to a decision to buy.

Depending on the customer's decision-making process, salespeople may or may not go through all the seven steps of a sale (see **Figure 12.1**).

1. **Approach the customer**—greeting the customer face-to-face
2. **Determine needs**—learning what the customer is looking for in order to decide what products to show and which product features to present first in the next step of the sale
3. **Present the product**—educating the customer about the product's features and benefits, as well as its advantages over the competition
4. **Overcome objections**—learning why the customer is reluctant to buy, providing information to remove that uncertainty and helping the customer to make a satisfying buying decision
5. **Close the sale**—getting the customer's positive agreement to buy
6. **Perform suggestion selling**—suggesting additional merchandise or services that will save your customer money or help your customer better enjoy the original purchase
7. **Build relationships**—following up by creating a means of maintaining contact with the customer after the sale is completed

Telemarketing is a type of sales position that uses telephone solicitation to sell products or services. *How do you think the Do Not Call Registry has changed the use of telemarketing?*

The other chapters in this unit discuss in more detail various selling principles and techniques for each step in the sales process.

CUSTOMER DECISION MAKING

Some customers need no help from salespeople, and others require significant time and effort. There are three distinct types of decision making—extensive, limited, and routine. How a person makes a decision is affected by the following factors:

▶ Previous experience with the product and company

▶ How often the product is purchased

▶ The amount of information necessary to make a wise buying decision

▶ The importance of the purchase to the customer

▶ The perceived risk involved in the purchase (such as, uncertainty about how the product will work)

▶ The time available to make the decision

EXTENSIVE DECISION MAKING

Extensive decision making is used when there has been little or no previous experience with an item. This category includes goods and services that have a high degree of perceived risk, are very expensive, or have high value to the customer. For a business, products in this category include expensive manufacturing machinery or land for a new building site. At the individual level, a consumer who is buying a first car or home will use extensive decision making.

LIMITED DECISION MAKING

Limited decision making is used when a person buys goods and services that he or she has purchased before but not regularly. There is a moderate degree of perceived risk involved, and the person often needs some information before buying the product.

FIGURE 12.1 **The Steps of a Sale**

Remembering the Steps A mnemonic device, such as ANPOCS, can help you remember the steps of a sale. *How do the final two steps add value to a sale that has been closed?*

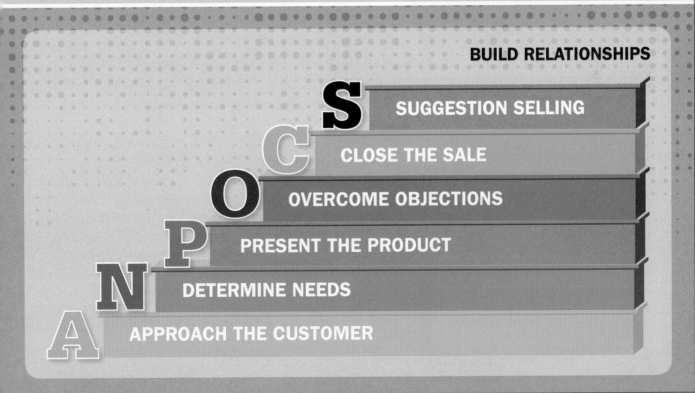

BUILD RELATIONSHIPS

S SUGGESTION SELLING

C CLOSE THE SALE

O OVERCOME OBJECTIONS

P PRESENT THE PRODUCT

N DETERMINE NEEDS

A APPROACH THE CUSTOMER

Selling Rio

The city of Rio de Janeiro is known for the samba, Carnival, beaches, and Corcovado Mountain. The XXXI Olympics was added to that list when the International Olympic Committee (IOC) voted to hold the 2016 Summer Olympics there. Besides "unrivaled natural beauty," the IOC was impressed by public support, financial guarantees, the chance to bring social improvement, and a large under-18 population.

Persistence Rewarded Rio bid on the 1936, 2004, and 2012 Games, but never made the cut. That is, until it became the first South American city to be awarded the event. It is dubbed "Live your passion." An estimated $14.4 billion pays for 34 venues with 12,500 athletes from 205 countries.

English Language Arts

Create Use the steps of selling to write a brief proposal to "sell" Rio to the IOC.

Here are some entry-level phrases that are used in conversations about marketing all over the world.

English	Brazilian Portuguese
Hello/Hi	Alo/Oi
Goodbye	Tchau
Yes/No	Sim/Não
Please	Por favor
Thank you	Obrigado/Obrigada
You're welcome	De nada

Consumer goods and services in this category might include a second car, certain types of clothing, furniture, and household appliances. Goods and services that a firm might buy using limited decision making include computer programs and office equipment. Fashion retailers who buy products for resale may look for new suppliers when fashion trends change.

ROUTINE DECISION MAKING

Routine decision making is used when a person needs little information about a product that he or she is buying. This is generally attributed to a high degree of prior experience with it or a low perceived risk. The perceived risk may be low because the item is inexpensive, the product is bought frequently, or satisfaction with the product is high. Some consumer goods and services in this category include grocery items, newspapers, and certain brand-name clothing and cosmetics. Customers who have developed brand loyalty for a product will use routine decision making. Expensive items, such as cars, may be purchased routinely if the customer has strong brand loyalty to one car manufacturer. This is the same for electronic or computer products.

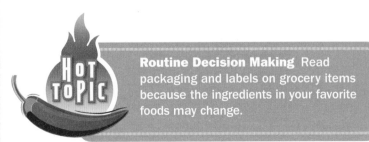

Routine Decision Making Read packaging and labels on grocery items because the ingredients in your favorite foods may change.

Businesses that simply reorder goods and services without much thought are using routine decision making. Retailers and wholesalers might purchase staple items for resale (goods that must always be kept in stock).

Products that businesses buy routinely for use in their operations include raw materials, office supplies, and maintenance services. Many offices may have a standing order with an office supply company for computer paper, pens, and folders. They know how much they use each month and assume that those quantities will remain constant. These items will continue to be routine purchases until there is a problem with the product or with the supplier. When this happens, the business would use limited decision making to change suppliers or products.

 Reading Check

Recall What are the three types of customer decision making?

A CAREER IN SALES

There is a sales career opportunity in almost every area of interest you may have. For example, if you have an interest in science, there are sales opportunities in pharmaceutical, medical, and chemical companies.

SALES CAREER BENEFITS

Successful salespeople may move up into a sales management position because their success is noticeable. Some salespeople are given car allowances and expense accounts, which are considered **perquisites** (perks) of the job. Other financial benefits are commission on your sales, sales contests with prizes for the top sellers, and bonuses for superior sales achievements.

CHARACTERISTICS OF SUCCESSFUL SALESPEOPLE

The characteristics of effective salespeople are honesty, good interpersonal skills, and problem-solving ability. Salespeople must be honest if they want to keep their customers for years to come. Repeat sales are necessary for success in sales.

Being comfortable speaking with customers and clients makes the selling job much easier. Communication and interpersonal skills can be developed by practicing them. Problem-solving is essential to sales because you need to assess a customer's situation in order to recommend the correct product or solution to a problem.

 After You Read   **Section 12.2**

Review Key Concepts

1. **Explain** how personal selling differs from other forms of promotion.
2. **Identify** the type of sales position in which a salesperson would visit a customer's place of business.
3. **Discuss** the reasons why there are so many sales career opportunities in different types of businesses.

Practice Academic Skills

English Language Arts

4. Write two paragraphs discussing the factors that might influence the level of customer decision making in the purchase of a bicycle by an avid rider.

Mathematics

5. If a telemarketing company has a million names in its database and 27 percent of them just registered with the national Do Not Call Registry, how many active customers will the sales staff still be able to call?

   Math Concept **Ways of Representing Numbers** A decrease in a number can be represented by a percent less than 100.

   Starting Hints Think of the reduced database as 73 percent (100%–27%) of its current database. Convert 73 percent to a decimal by moving the decimal point two places to the left. Multiply that decimal number by the current number of names in the current database.

 **connectED.mcgraw-hill.com**

Check your answers.

For help, go to the **Math Skills Handbook** located at the back of this book.

Selling Overview

The sales process involves specific steps. Throughout the process salespeople build relationships with customers.

Approach the Customer	Determine Needs	Present the Product	Overcome Objections	Close the Sale	Suggestion Selling

The three main characteristics of effective salespeople are honesty, good communication skills, and problem-solving ability.

MAIN CHARACTERISTICS OF EFFECTIVE SALESPEOPLE

HONESTY

GOOD COMMUNICATION SKILLS

PROBLEM-SOLVING ABILITY

Review and Activities

Written Summary

- The purpose of selling is to help customers make satisfying buying decisions, with the goal of creating ongoing, profitable relationships.
- Customer relationship management (CRM), a system that involves finding customers and keeping them satisfied.
- Company Web sites, social media, e-mails, and computer software have revolutionized CRM.
- Sales managers plan, organize, and control the sales function and establish the structure of the sales organization.
- Three forms of customer decision making are extensive, limited, and routine.
- The seven steps of a sale include: approach the customer, determine needs, present the product, overcome objections, close the sale, perform suggestion selling, and build relationships as follow up.
- Salespeople work in retail, industrial, service, telemarketing, and Internet businesses, as well as nonprofit organizations.

Review Content Vocabulary and Academic Vocabulary

1. Create a fill-in-the-blank sentence for each of these vocabulary terms. The sentence should contain enough information to help determine the missing word.

Content Vocabulary
- customer relationship management (CRM) (p. 277)
- call report (p. 280)
- sales quota (p. 281)
- personal selling (p. 285)
- organizational selling (p. 285)
- cold call (p. 285)
- telemarketing (p. 286)
- extensive decision making (p. 287)
- limited decision making (p. 287)
- routine decision making (p. 288)

Academic Vocabulary
- solidify (p. 278)
- interface (p. 279)
- pre-sold (p. 285)
- perquisites (p. 289)

Assess for Understanding

2. **Compare** What is the relationship between selling and the marketing concept?
3. **Identify** How are e-mails, customer loyalty programs, or the use of mobile devices used to ensure customer satisfaction?
4. **Contrast** How is retail selling different from organizational selling?
5. **Determine** What are some products you purchase that involve routine decision making?
6. **Consider** What aspects of a career in selling appeal to you and which ones do not?
7. **Role Play** How should a sales manager deal with a high-performing sales representative that closes a lot of sales using high-pressure tactics?
8. **Demonstrate** Why is honesty a characteristic of an effective seller?
9. **Apply** How can CRM computer software help companies with the sales function?
10. **Judge** Which of the seven steps of a sale may not be involved if customers use routine decision making, and which ones may not be involved when using limited decision making?

21st  Century Skills

Teamwork Skills

11. Everyday Ethics Why do you think salespeople are sometimes depicted in movies as dishonest? With a partner, research sales ethics in business magazines, on the Web or through interviews with salespeople. Make a list of the characteristics of ethical salespeople. Use that list to prepare a simple "Code of Sales Ethics." Present your code to the class.

Financial Literacy Skills

12. Compensation Options Which sales compensation offer do you prefer? You can opt to get paid either a yearly salary of $50,000 *or* an 8-percent commission on all sales you close. The sales territory you would be assigned has historically generated $800,000 in sales. If sales remain the same, what would you earn in commission? What would your commission be if sales were to drop by 15 percent next year in your territory because of a weak economy? Choose one of the compensation options and explain why you selected that plan.

e-Marketing Skills

13. Online Sales Find a consumer products company that has a Web site where it sells its products online. Find another company that has a Web site that directs customers to retail stores to buy its products. How are the Web-site designs different? Why do you think some companies sell online while others do not? In your opinion, which type of company Web site is more effective and why? Suggest changes that could make the other more effective. Here are some factors to consider:

- How profitable is the company?
- What shipping options does the company offer?
- Where is the company located? (Even online companies have physical locations.)
- How are the sales teams different for each company?

Build Academic Skills

Social Studies

14. Self-Analysis List and analyze your personal interests and abilities to see if they match the characteristics of effective salespeople. How could you test your sales ability?

Science

15. Technology for Selling Sales managers use technology on a regular basis to monitor sales results. Research online computer software programs available to sales managers to help them with their work. Look for emerging technologies in marketing. Start with companies that offer CRM programs, as well as sales territory analysis, sales forecasting, and any other technological tools that would benefit them or their sales staff. Write a short report on your findings.

Mathematics

16. Sales Costs What percentage of sales revenue goes to the cost of sales for the XYZ company? XYZ offers salary plus commission and bonuses for sales personnel who reach their sales quotas. It has eight salespeople, each earning a base salary of $45,000 plus a 2-percent commission on sales. Sales were $3 million, and bonuses totaled $30,000 for the year.

Math Concept **Problem Solving** First, determine total sales costs for the XYZ company. Add the cost of sales bonuses to the cost of the base salaries of the sales personnel and their respective commission to get total sales costs.

For help, go to the **Math Skills Handbook** located at the back of this book.

Standardized Test Practice

Directions Read the following questions. On a separate piece of paper, write the best possible answer for each one.

1. What is 6 percent of $675,000?
   - **A.** $64,500
   - **B.** $48,000
   - **C.** $40,500
   - **D.** $45,000

2. Personal selling involves two-way communication between a buyer and seller.

   T

   F

3. The purpose of selling is to help customers make satisfying buying decisions with the goal of creating _____, _____ relationships with them.

Test-Taking Tip

Taking tests can be stressful. If you begin to get nervous, take a few deep breaths slowly and relax.

DECA Connection Role Play

Sales Representative
Apparel Manufacturer

Situation To earn a $100 bonus at the end of each month as a sales representative, your sales must exceed $310,000. Only goods that are actually shipped count toward the sales quota. To date, your sales are $283,780.

You just met with one of your steady customers who placed a $50,000 order with the stipulation that delivery of the goods must be in two months from today's date. Company policy requires that you must get permission from your sales manager to extend the date of shipping. If you do not get permission for the extension, the goods will be shipped immediately, which is company policy. If you do get the extension, you will not reach your sales quota for the month. You need the bonus to pay bills. This sales order will also help your manager reach the sales goals set by upper-level management.

What will you do? The customer is waiting to hear back from you regarding the delivery extension before finalizing the order. You must meet with your sales manager (judge) to explain your customer's request for the delivery extension.

Activity Make a decision on how you think the order should be processed. Prepare notes on what you will say to your sales manager. You will then use your notes when you actually meet with your customer (judge).

Evaluation You will be evaluated on how well you meet these performance indicators:

1. Explain the nature and scope of the selling function.
2. Explain the selling process.
3. Explain business ethics in selling.
4. Describe the use of technology in the selling function.
5. Explain the nature of sales management.

 connectED.mcgraw-hill.com

Download the Competitive Events Workbook for more Role-Play Practice.

beginning the sales process

SHOW WHAT YOU KNOW

Visual Literacy Getting the inventory organized and coordinated with any special promotions is part of a retail salesperson's job. *How do these merchandising tasks help salespeople prepare for the sales process?*

Discovery Project

SWOT Analysis for an Athletic Shoe

 Essential Question Why is product information and knowledge of the competition so important in preparing for selling?

Project Goal

Select an athletic shoe to research. Learn everything you can about the shoe. How is it constructed? What materials are used in its construction? Is there a patent on its design? What is its retail price? What special features would appeal to prospective customers? Research a competing athletic shoe to see if the shoe you selected has an advantage over its competition.

Ask Yourself...

- How will you find information about athletic shoes?
- How will you select the specific athletic shoe to research?
- How will you find a competing athletic shoe?
- How will you present your findings?

 Synthesize and Present Research Synthesize your research on a competing athletic shoe and present your findings on whether the shoe you selected has an advantage over its competition.

 **connectED.mcgraw-hill.com**

Activity
Get a worksheet activity about conducting a SWOT analysis.

Evaluate
Download a rubric you can use to evaluate your project.

DECA Connection

DECA Event Role Play

Concepts in this chapter are related to DECA competitive events that involve either an interview or role play.

Indicators The performance indicators represent key skills and knowledge. Your key to success in DECA competitive events is relating them to concepts in this chapter.

- Acquire product information for use in selling.
- Analyze product information to identify product and features.
- Establish relationship with client/customer.
- Prepare for the sales presentation.
- Analyze customer needs.

DECA Prep

Role Play Practice role-playing with the DECA Connection competitive-event activity at the end of this chapter. More information on DECA events can be found on DECA's Web site.

READING GUIDE

Before You Read

Consider Do you think everyone who buys an item has the same reasons for buying it? Why or why not?

Objectives

- **Explain** how salespeople get ready to sell.
- **List** sources of product information.
- **Explain** feature-benefit selling and how it creates selling points.
- **Identify** consumer buying motives.
- **List** prospecting methods and explain how prospects are qualified.

The Main Idea

Getting ready to sell involves preliminary activities that help salespeople with the sales process, such as learning about the product, industry, and customer, to develop effective selling points.

Vocabulary

Content Vocabulary
- merchandising
- feature-benefit selling
- product features
- physical features
- extended product features
- customer benefits
- selling points
- buying motives
- rational motives
- emotional motives
- patronage motives
- prospecting
- prospect
- referrals
- endless-chain method
- cold canvassing

Academic Vocabulary
- shadowing
- longevity

Graphic Organizer

Draw or print this outline of the preliminary activities associated with the sales process.

Print this graphic organizer.

I. Getting ready to sell	II. Feature-Benefit Selling	III. Prospecting
A. Product Knowledge 1. 2. 3. B. C.	A. Product Features 1. 2. 3. B. C. D. E. Customer Buying Motives 1. 2. 3. 4.	A. Prospecting Techniques 1. 2. 3. B.

MARKETING CORE FUNCTION

Selling

Preliminary Activities

GETTING READY TO SELL

To be successful in sales, salespeople do their homework. They gather information about their products, industry trends, and competition. In retail situations, salespeople also perform tasks involved with merchandising.

As You Read

Connect Analyze your backpack or a piece of clothing you are wearing. Find information on or in the product that might be useful in developing a selling point for it.

PRODUCT KNOWLEDGE

Salespeople must know their products so they can match them to customers' needs and wants. Product knowledge is essential when educating consumers and demonstrating a product. It is easy to gain product knowledge if you know where to locate product information. Sources of product information include experience with the product, published materials, Web sites, and formal training.

EXPERIENCE

Using a product is the best source of direct experience. Some businesses offer discounts to their salespeople to encourage them to use their merchandise. You can also get experience with a product by studying display models or visiting a manufacturing facility to see how it is made. Friends, relatives, coworkers, and customers can tell you about their experience with a product too.

PUBLISHED MATERIALS AND WEB SITES

Product information is found on Web sites and in published materials such as, labels, user manuals, manufacturer warranties and guarantees, catalogs, and promotional materials.

Manufacturers and suppliers provide additional information and training materials in many cases. Web sites of manufacturers, retailers, and wholesalers provide an opportunity to view and study products.

> **" Work associated with selling begins before a salesperson speaks with a client or a customer. "**

TRAINING

Formal training may be the best way to educate salespeople on certain products. Most industrial salespeople receive product knowledge through training sessions. Some salespeople spend months attending classes and **shadowing** experienced salespeople before selling on their own.

In retail settings, training is likely to be less structured. Information might be shared informally to the sales staff as new merchandise is received or selected for promotion. Some of the training materials may be provided by the supplier.

INDUSTRY TRENDS AND COMPETITION

Salespeople read periodicals to keep up with competitors and trends. Salespeople in the apparel industry read *Women's Wear Daily*, while those in the food industry read *Supermarket News*. All industries have trade publications related to their industry.

Standard & Poor's is a company that offers a trade reports by industry. It is available in college and public libraries and online.

A Source of Product Information

Hang tags, packaging, and labels provide a wealth of information about the special features of a product and how they function. *Why do manufacturers include so much information on hang tags and product packaging?*

- Technically advanced yarns draw moisture away from the body

- Keeps you cool and dry

- Breathable

- Pre-washed

- SPF 40 protection

Perspiration escapes

G-FRESH

Effective and knowledgeable salespeople research their competition to be prepared when customers ask them to compare their product with a competitor's. A visit to a competitor's Web site can provide a wealth of information about its products and policies. If a company does not have a Web site, salespeople can try to secure a competitor's catalog and price list. They also might purchase a competitor's product and examine it. It is a good idea to prepare a SWOT analysis (strengths, weaknesses, opportunities, threats) when you gather information on competitors to see how their products compare to your products.

MERCHANDISING

Merchandising involves coordination of sales and promotional plans with buying and pricing. You are already familiar with merchandising seen in fast-food establishments with special sales promotions. These restaurants give away small toys related to a current movie or popular character with the purchase of a child's meal. Signs and a display of the toys are visible in the fast-food restaurant. All order takers are familiar with the promotion. The same effort is made in all retail operations and other businesses that run promotions.

The right place, time, price, and quantity are considered when displaying products. These factors are essential to effective merchandising.

Products being promoted are generally moved to a location in the retail store that is visible. When running a sale or promotion, retailers must be sure that they have a sufficient quantity of products available. They will need to arrange to restock products frequently. If supplies run out during a promotion, not only will sales will be lost, but customers will be unhappy.

Signs explaining the promotion should be visible throughout the store. Window and interior displays should be updated as part of visual-merchandising activities. Price tags should be updated and computer systems adjusted with the new promotional pricing. To ensure maximum return, store managers work closely with the sales staff to organize and coordinate these tasks in a timely manner. Getting all of these preparations done on time will allow sales personnel to spend time with customers.

 Reading Check

Contrast How is training different in industrial selling and retail selling?

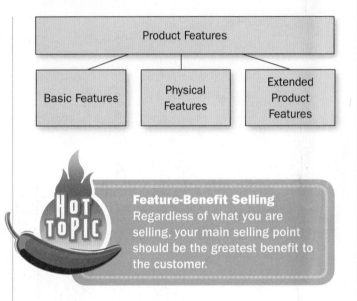

Salespeople must learn all they can about trends, competition, and changes occurring in their field. *What do you observe about people on the street and at your school that would help you sell a new fashion trend?*

Industry Trends

FEATURE-BENEFIT SELLING

Matching the characteristics of a product to a customer's needs and wants is a concept called **feature-benefit selling**. This concept is the basis for developing the selling points used in the sales presentation. Why? Because many people believe that customers do not buy products; rather, they buy what the products will do for them. Consumers purchase leather shoes for their appearance, easy care, comfort, and **longevity.** They purchase computers for increased productivity. People buy insurance for emotional and financial security.

Salespeople work on constructing selling points for their product by using the feature-benefit selling concept. All the information researched on their product, industry trends, and competition is used to develop the selling points. An understanding of the customer's buying motives helps to establish the right priority for the selling points to include in the sales presentation. Let's take a closer look at how feature-benefit selling creates effective selling points and advantages over the competition.

PRODUCT FEATURES

The first step in preparing selling points is to study a company's products and sales policies. They are the foundation for building effective selling points. **Product features** are basic, physical, or extended attributes of the product or purchase.

```
                    Product Features
                          |
        ┌─────────────────┼─────────────────┐
   Basic Features      Physical         Extended
                       Features          Product
                                        Features
```

HOT TOPIC

Feature-Benefit Selling
Regardless of what you are selling, your main selling point should be the greatest benefit to the customer.

BASIC FEATURE

The most basic feature of a product is its intended use. A person buys an automobile for transportation and buys a watch to tell time. Basic product features are apparent and, therefore, generally accepted without question. So, salespeople do not have to spend time explaining basic product features unless the product is new and unusual. For example, an inventor of a new product would have to explain how to use the invention. The very first automobile was in this category. New technologies today fit in this category as well. When a product is new, explaining why customers would need such a product requires educating them about its intended use.

Identifying Product Features and Benefits

The information in this product insert visually identifies the product features and some of their corresponding benefits for FL-AIR 4 suitcases. *What are two extended product features that you would need to know in order to sell this product effectively?*

PHYSICAL FEATURES

Physical features of a product are tangible attributes that help explain how a product is constructed. For a jacket, its physical attributes are the fabrics used for the outer shell and insulation, as well as the type of collar, pockets, closure (buttons, snaps, or zipper), and sleeve design. How the seams are finished off and the garment's sizes are also physical attributes.

EXTENDED PRODUCT FEATURES

Extended product features are intangible attributes related to the sale of a product that customers find important. For example, customers might consider the reputation of a company or brand name of a product to be an extended feature. This may be true because there is reduced risk in doing business with a well-established company and brand. Significant company policies include warranties, guarantees, extended service contracts, financing, and customer service availability. Promotional support provided by a supplier to help sell a product is an extended feature found in organization sales situations. The price of a product is an extended product feature, which may be one of its most important features.

CUSTOMER BENEFITS

Customer benefits are the advantages or personal satisfaction a customer will get from a good or service. It is a salesperson's job to analyze product features from the customer's point of view. The first step in this analysis is to view the product feature in terms of how it functions. For example, air pockets in the heel of a running shoe (product feature) cushion the impact on pavement (function). Translating that information into a personal consumer benefit requires knowing what the customer values. In the case of the running shoe, the air pockets (feature), which cushions the impact on pavement (function), give the wearer more comfort when running or walking and help to protect the foot from injury (benefits).

SELLING POINTS

A **selling point** is created by noting the function of a product feature and explaining how it benefits a customer. Selling points are the result of the product analysis used in feature-benefit selling. If you review a well-designed catalog or Web site, you will see selling points in print. When communicating with customers in person, selling points form the foundation for the sales presentation. It is a good idea to practice writing selling points as *selling sentences*.

The GREEN Marketer

Understanding the Green Consumer

Green consumers are not all the same. With a variety of demographics, they represent all age brackets, income levels, and ethnic backgrounds. They are motivated to make purchases according to different wants and needs. Some are concerned about health; others about the environment, fair trade, or their kids' well-being; and still others about saving energy to save money.

Shades of Green Green consumers also come in different shades, from "deep greens," consumers who always put the environment first, to "light greens," who pick green options only when they are convenient and budget-friendly. Marketers must be aware of these shades of green and all of the ones in between if they want to be successful.

English Language Arts
Create Browse a supermarket for a food or cleaning product that is environmentally friendly. Write 50 words for an in-store display that will appeal to as many green consumer needs and segments as possible.

 connectED.mcgraw-hill.com

Get an activity on green marketing.

Here are a few examples of effective selling points that may be used in retail and organizational sales situations.

▶ **Retail sales situation**
- Customer: man or woman looking for jeans
- Product: a pair of jeans
- Selling point: The soft cotton denim fabric has 1 percent spandex (feature), which allows the jeans to stretch (function) and makes them comfortable to wear (benefits).

▶ **Organizational sales situation**
- Customer: operations manager for an ice cream manufacturer
- Product: insulated jacket
- Selling point: The insulation in this garment (feature) is effective in cold temperatures (function), so it will protect your workers and allow them to perform at maximum efficiency while working in the freezer (benefits).

ADVANTAGES

In feature-benefit selling, salespeople also must consider their competition. Let's say your competitor uses inferior fabrics. Your garment uses better fabric. The advantage in this case can be used as a major benefit. Your higher-quality garment will last longer than your competitor's product. All advantages over your competition become selling points for your product.

CUSTOMER BUYING MOTIVES

To determine effective customer benefits for product features, it is a good idea to learn what motivates customers to buy. **Buying motives** are reasons a customer buys a product. As such, they influence buying behavior and buying decisions. Understanding customer motivation is not an easy task. Customers are not always aware of their inner motivations. Even when they are, they may not communicate them to you. As you gain experience in sales, you will get a better feel for reading customers' motives, which can be classified as rational, emotional, or patronage. To make the salesperson's task even more difficult, these motives may be combined or different for the same product. The difficulty depends on the customer and the sales situation.

RATIONAL MOTIVES

Rational motives are conscious, logical reasons for a purchase. Rational motives include product dependability, time or monetary savings, product quality, and good customer service. Customers are often interested in products because of rational motives. For example, customers may say they are looking for a dependable automobile with a history of excellent customer service.

EMOTIONAL MOTIVES

Emotional motives are feelings experienced by a customer through association with a product. Emotional motives are feelings such as social approval, fear, power, love, and prestige. Social approval may be one of the reasons that customers buy certain brands of cars, clothing, or accessories. Customers are generally reluctant to share their emotional motives for making a purchase. You may have to tactfully incorporate emotional motives into a sales presentation. Life insurance is a product that evokes emotions.

PATRONAGE MOTIVES

Patronage motives are reasons for remaining a loyal customer of a company. Currently satisfied customers possess patronage motives. Trust and confidence have been established through past experiences. Patronage motives make it easy to sell a company's products.

MULTIPLE MOTIVES

Most buying decisions involve a combination of motives. For example, people buy car tires for dependability (rational motive) and fear because they care about the safety of loved ones (emotional motive). Two customers could have different motivations for buying the same product. One person may buy shoes for comfort (rational motive), while another may buy the same shoes to make a fashion statement (emotional motive).

Reading Check

Recall What are three ways by which product features can be identified?

PROSPECTING

Looking for new customers is called **prospecting**. A **prospect**, or a sales lead, is a potential customer.

A potential customer may be a business or an individual. For example, a manufacturer of golf accessories would consider a newly opened retail golf shop as a prospect or sales lead. The person responsible for doing the buying for that store's golf accessories would also be considered a prospect or lead.

Prospecting is especially important in organizational selling situations. Service-related businesses and retailers search for new business opportunities by prospecting too. Any salesperson or business that wants to expand a customer base might use some of the following prospecting techniques.

PROSPECTING TECHNIQUES

There are several techniques and practices employed by salespeople and businesses to generate sales leads. They include customer referrals, cold canvassing, and employer-generated leads.

CUSTOMER REFERRALS

Satisfied customers are excellent sources for finding new customers. Sales representatives ask their customers for **referrals**—the names of other people who might buy the product. Referrals open the market to potential customers whom a salesperson might not have reached without a recommendation. When salespeople ask previous customers for names of potential customers, they are using the **endless chain method**. The endless chain method helps companies construct and maintain a list of prospects. Some companies offer discounts or gifts to customers who give referrals.

MARKETING CASE STUDY

Olympus: Selling Medical Technology

Olympus is known for making digital cameras for consumers. It also produces medical cameras for doctors that integrate high-definition television (HDTV) signals for improved image quality. The tiny camera at the end of a flexible scope can move around in the body, allowing a doctor to see from many angles. This device assists surgeons performing "laparoendoscopic single-site surgery," a less risky operation using a very small incision to remove a damaged organ or a tumor.

Competing Advantages

Olympus was first to introduce HDTV in its "videoscopes." Another competitor is Stryker, a company that also sells artificial hips and knees. HDTV medical cameras cost more than non-HDTV cameras. Competitors selling non-HDTV cameras can use price as a selling point. In addition, hospitals must upgrade their monitors and other devices to accommodate HDTV technology, which can be costly.

English Language Arts

Research Conduct research on competing medical video cameras. Write a selling point for an Olympus HDTV medical camera, noting the feature, function, and benefit.

COLD CANVASSING

Cold canvassing is a process of locating as many potential customers as possible without checking leads beforehand. Cold canvassing is also sometimes called "blind prospecting" because it is a hit-and-miss method. One example is a real estate agent going door-to-door in a neighborhood, asking people if they would like to sell their homes. Another example of cold canvassing is a stockbroker selecting names from a telephone book at random and calling them. Insurance salespeople look through newspapers for birth announcements, while caterers and florists may check out engagement announcements. Use of trade directories, such as the *Thomas Register of American Manufacturers*, can be useful for organizational sales representatives. In addition, commercial lists of prospects can be purchased and used for cold canvassing. An Internet search engine can provide a huge selection of sales-lead companies that specialize in different industries.

EMPLOYER SALES LEADS

Some firms employ entire telemarketing teams to generate leads for their sales staffs. They also attend trade shows, where they display products for review by buyers in the industry. Interested buyers provide information for follow-up. Leads are categorized by territory and passed along to the sales staff. In some cases, customer service representatives may qualify, or evaluate, the leads for the professional sales staff. They do this by calling the prospects to see if they meet certain qualifications. Leads can be generated and qualified by using the Internet and the Web site of a prospective corporate customer.

QUALIFYING PROSPECTS

Once sales leads are generated, they need to be qualified before any sales effort is made. There are three important questions to ask in order to properly evaluate a sales lead. The following questions will help determine whether a prospect meets the qualifications for a sales call:

▶ Does the prospective customer (an individual, company, or organization) need the product or service?

▶ If the prospect is a company or an organization, who is authorized to make a purchase? Does the salesperson have an appointment with a person who has that authority?

▶ Does the prospective customer have the financial resources to pay for the product or service?

Salespeople can use the process of cold canvassing get help generating leads by going door-to-door. *What other prospecting techniques might a real-estate agent use to generate leads?*

finding New Customers

ANSWERS TO QUESTIONS

To find answers to these "three basic questions to evaluate a sales lead, " company customer-service representatives or salespeople have to make inquiries and do some background research. In some cases, a simple phone call may be all that is necessary to determine whether a lead needs a particular product.

For example, a manufacturer of work uniforms specializes in clothing designed to be worn by workers who spend time in cold environments. The apparel company's salespeople may ask leads whether they have any employees who work outdoors in the winter. They may also ask leads whether they employ people who work in refrigerated warehouses or freezer boxes. If the answer to these questions is "no," the lead should be considered a dead end. If a lead answers "yes," then it might be a potential customer.

The next questions might be: "How many employees work in those cold environments?" and "Who in the company is responsible for purchasing employees' work clothing?" The answers to these questions can reveal how much apparel the prospect might need and give the salesperson the name of a person to contact.

Additional research is necessary to determine whether the potential customer has the ability to pay its bills. Sales representatives can read the company's annual reports or subscribe to the database listings of a firm like Dun & Bradstreet®, which monitors businesses' financial situations. If a company has a need for the product and has a good credit rating, it would be a qualified prospect.

The research done during prospecting can become the basis of a strong sales presentation when meeting a qualified prospect face-to-face.

 After You Read **Section 13.1**

Review Key Concepts

1. **List** three things that salespeople do to get ready to sell.
2. **Explain** how a customer might use a combination of rational, emotional, and patronage buying motives when purchasing a hybrid automobile.
3. **Identify** three prospecting techniques.

Practice Academics

English Language Arts

4. Write a selling sentence for a smartphone feature by incorporating and identifying in parentheses the feature, function, and consumer benefit.

Mathematics

5. You own a men's clothing store. A sign in your store advertises three shirts for $30.39. Not counting sales tax on clothing, how much would you charge a customer who needs only two shirts?

   Math Concept **Estimation** Estimating before you begin calculating can help you make sure you have calculated properly.

   Starting Hints To solve this problem, divide the sale price of three shirts by three to determine how much each shirt costs. Multiply the cost of one shirt by two to determine the price of two shirts.

connectED.mcgraw-hill.com

Check your answers.

For help, go to the **Math Skills Handbook** located at the back of this book.

READING GUIDE

Before You Read

Predict Why is asking a customer "May I help you?" not an effective way to begin a sale in a retail environment?

Objectives

- **Demonstrate** how to properly approach a customer to open a sale.
- **Differentiate** between organizational and retail sales approaches.
- **List** three retail approach methods.
- **Discuss** when and how to determine customer needs.

The Main Idea

The actual sales presentation begins when you approach customers to open the sale and determine their needs.

Vocabulary

Content Vocabulary

- greeting approach
- service approach
- merchandise approach
- nonverbal communication
- open-ended question

Academic Vocabulary

You will find these words in your reading and on your tests. Make sure you know their meanings.

- rapport
- astute

Graphic Organizer

Draw or print this outline of this section's content.

I. The approach	II. Determining needs
A. Approach in organizational selling	A.
1.	B.
2.	1.
a.	2.
b.	3.
B. Approach in retail selling	
1.	
2.	
a.	
b.	
c.	

 connectED.mcgraw-hill.com

Print this graphic organizer.

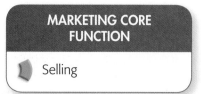

MARKETING CORE FUNCTION

Selling

Section 13.2 First Steps of a Sale

THE APPROACH

The approach, also known as the *sales opening,* is the first face-to-face contact with the customer. Salespeople can make or break a sale during their first few minutes with a customer. They must learn how to properly approach a customer to open a sale. The approach sets the mood for the other steps of the sale. Its purpose is to establish **rapport** (a positive relationship) with the customer whether for organizational or retail selling.

In order to achieve an effective sales opening, salespeople must remember to do the following:

▶ Treat customers as individuals. Never stereotype a person because of age, sex, race, religion, appearance, or any other characteristic.

▶ Be aware of the customer's personality and buying style. Some customers like to do business quickly. Others prefer a methodical pace.

▶ Show interest in the customer by maintaining good eye contact and showing friendliness.

▶ Learn and use the customer's name to personalize the sale when possible.

▶ Grab the customer's attention. Incorporate a theme in the approach that is related to the presentation and the customer's buying motives.

▶ Recognize that sales approaches differ in organization selling and retail selling situations.

As You Read

Predict How does the approach differ depending on the sales situation?

ORGANIZATIONAL SELLING

In organizational selling, salespeople usually make an appointment prior to making a sales call. This ensures that their customers have time to meet with them. Some may not call in advance.

When they arrive without notice, they are "cold calling." The likelihood of being seen by the customer diminishes. When cold calling, it is a wise practice to ask customers if it is a good time to see them. This courtesy is appreciated by busy businesspeople.

> ❝ **You can make or break a sale during the approach.** ❞

ARRIVE EARLY

Field sales representatives should always arrive early for a sales call. This allows the salesperson to gather his or her thoughts. It also shows professionalism and courtesy because it ensures the salesperson will not be late for the sales call. In some cases, it allows the salesperson to observe the customer's place of business. Here are a few examples of how to make use of observations.

▶ If your customer is a retail store buyer, you can spend time walking through the store to see which competing brands are carried. You can also observe customers in the store to see if they appear to be part of your product's target market.

▶ If you sit in the waiting room for a purchasing agent in a manufacturing facility, you can read all the plaques on the walls and any industry or company literature on display. These items may be helpful in your approach as well as other steps of the sale.

▶ In the customer's office, you may observe something that will help you establish rapport. It might be a college plaque, a sports trophy, a painting, or something else that uncovers your customer's interests. For example, if the customer keeps golf clubs in his or her office, making small talk about this interest during the initial approach can help the salesperson to establish rapport with the customer.

Some observant business people say they can tell if they are going to do business with people just by a handshake. *Why are first impressions so important in sales?*

Etiquette Is Important

GREET AND ENGAGE CUSTOMER

The first step in the initial approach involves proper business etiquette. The salesperson greets the customer by name and introduces him- or herself and the company with a firm handshake and a smile. After the proper greeting and introductions, the next statement or question should engage the customer.

Engaging a Current Customer

When meeting with customers you visit frequently, you can be more personal. Comments on recent events in the customer's industry or personal recollections about the customer's family, interests, or hobbies can create a smooth meeting. This technique puts the customer at ease and helps open lines of communication.

Learning what is appropriate to say regarding personal matters is critical. When personal conversation is not appropriate, you can still engage in small talk to establish a relationship with the customer.

Engaging a New Customer

As noted, any common interest shared between the salesperson and the customer may also be used to engage the customer. That common interest might range from a personal connection (e.g. graduated from the same college) to sports-related passions (e.g. participant or fan).

You can also use information gathered during prospecting to create an opening statement. It is best to pick a theme that is related to the presentation and the customer's buying motives. For example, "When I spoke with you last week, you indicated an interest in looking at new golf accessories to enhance your current assortment." You can also use current topics in the industry with a new customer. For example, "According to *Supermarket News*, food stores that are going green are attracting new customers. My company has the products that will help you take advantage of that growing trend." Topics that are always of interest to organizational customers include reducing costs, increasing productivity, improving profits, and generating more business.

RETAIL SELLING

In most retail selling situations, the salespeople do not know customers prior to meeting them. The exception occurs when retail salespeople have steady customers whom they know well. In both cases, timing and type of approach are important.

TIMING THE RETAIL APPROACH

Timing the approach depends on the types of customers and on the products being sold. When customers are in an obvious hurry, you should approach them quickly. When customers seem undecided, it is best to let them look around before making the approach. Many customers prefer to shop around before buying. They appreciate salespeople who show interest while allowing them to make their own decisions. These casual lookers will seek help when they need it.

RETAIL APPROACH METHODS

There are three methods to use for the initial retail approach: greeting, service, and merchandise or theme. You must evaluate the selling situation and the type of customer to determine which method is best. In some cases, you may use one, two, or all three approaches as part of your sales opening.

Greeting Approach

With the **greeting approach**, the salesperson welcomes the customer to the store. This lets the customer know that the salesperson is available for questions or assistance. This can be simple.

For example, simply greet a customer with "Good morning." If a frequent customer arrives, using the customer's name in the approach makes the customer feel important.

When you greet the customer, it is important to use a rising tone in your voice. Regardless of whether the customer responds in a friendly manner, it is extremely important for the salesperson to smile and continue to be friendly.

After greeting the customer, pause for a few seconds. Out of courtesy, most customers will respond. If they need help, they will tell you how you can assist them. If they are just looking, they will let you know. The greeting approach establishes a positive atmosphere and opens the lines of communication. It can also be incorporated easily into the other two retail approach methods.

Service Approach

With the **service approach**, salespeople ask customers if they need assistance. One way to use this method is to ask, "How may I help you?" An open-ended question such as this one offers the customer a greater opportunity to respond with more than "yes" or "no." The wrong way to use the service approach is to ask, "May I help you?" This question is ineffective because customers will often say, "No, thank you, I am just looking." That customer response ends communication between the customer and salesperson.

Merchandise or Theme Approach

With the **merchandise approach**, or theme approach, the salesperson makes a comment or asks questions about a product in which the customer shows an interest. You may say something about the product's features and benefits or typical customer buying motives. It should give the customer some information that is not immediately apparent to the eye.

Focus the conversation on the customer's interest. With a jacket, you might say, "That children's jacket comes in several other colors." If you have no indication of the exact interest, you can talk about the item's popularity, its unusual features, or its special values. You can also ask a question, such as "Is that the size you need?" or "Were you looking for a comfortable children's jacket?" This themed approach is effective in retail sales because it focuses attention on the product and the sales presentation. It increases customer interest and could encourage a purchase. In addition, customers may not see the desired style, size, or color on the selling floor. The merchandise approach lets the customer know what is available.

Reading Check

Recall What are three methods of retail approaches?

In retail stores, salespeople must judge when to approach customers and which retail sales method is most appropriate to use. *How would you know when you should approach a customer in a retail shoe store?*

The Right Approach

When you begin determining needs, first ask general questions about the intended use of the product and any previous experience with it. Build your questions around words like *who, what, when, where, how,* and *why*. You might ask the following questions of a prospective customer who wants to purchase a copier:

▶ What type of copier are you presently using?

▶ Why is that copier not meeting your needs?

▶ How many copies will you be making every week or month?

▶ Do you need a copier to also serve as a printer?

How to Refine Questions

Once you have an idea about the customer's general needs, then you can ask more specific questions relating to the product. These might include inquiries about size, color, and any special features desired. In the case of the copier, you might ask questions about the need to enlarge or reduce the size of the original and whether the customer needs to collate or staple copies. Does the customer want to make color copies or will a copier that makes only black-and-white copies be sufficient? Does the customer plan to use the copier at home or for business purposes? You may need to find out how soon the product is needed, what kind of space it will be housed in, and whether the customer might need to have the copier delivered. The more you know about a customer's problems and needs, the better. This knowledge helps in the process of coming up with solutions to customers' problems and needs.

Questioning is a very important skill and must be done carefully. Always be sure to keep in mind that customers may be very protective of their privacy. Privacy concerns may include cost and price. For example, customers can get upset when asked, "How much money do you want to spend?" A customer may not want to share details about his or her budget or financial situation. Whenever possible, it is better to ask how a customer intends to use a product and to discuss any past experience that person might have had with something similar. Those kinds of details keep the focus on the customer, the product, and how best the salesperson can help. That information should be enough to help most customers select a product that not only suits their specific needs but also fits within their personal price range.

Reading Check

Predict How do you think salespeople determine their customers' needs?

Business relies on documents. Documents rely on TASKalfa.

Productivity is: TASKalfa

Document imaging is essential to business productivity. For every company. For every individual. The TASKalfa Color MFP Series delivers fully-networked document imaging capabilities that are efficient, affordable, and flexible. High-speed scanning from the optional dual scan document processor. Advanced paper handling, including heavy paper stock for professional-quality document output. A simple-to-navigate user-friendly touch screen control panel. And a wide array of advanced finishing options. All backed by Kyocera's award-winning ultra-reliability. Making sure everyone in your company is as productive as possible. That's TASKalfa's #1 Priority. To find out more, visit www.kyoceramita.com.

People Friendly.

KYOCERA

© KYOCERA MITA CORPORATION. KYOCERA MITA AMERICA, INC. 2009 Kyocera Corporation, "People Friendly", the Kyocera "smile", "TASKalfa" and the Kyocera and "TASKalfa" logos are trademarks of Kyocera.

Determining Needs

Printers come in many sizes. Depending on a business' needs, there is a printer to fit those needs. *How do questions you would ask a customer who uses printers at home differ from the questions you would ask a customer who uses printers for business?*

Question Do's and Don'ts

Here are some other "do's and don'ts" guidelines for questioning customers:

1. Do ask open-ended questions that encourage customers to do the talking. **Open-ended questions** are those that require more than a "yes" or "no" answer.

   For example, you could ask, "What do you dislike about the copier you're presently using?" The answer to such a question will provide valuable information about a customer's needs.

2. Do ask clarifying questions to make sure you understand customers' needs.

   To do this, use opening lines such as: "Let me see whether I understand what you want," or, "Am I correct in assuming that you're looking for a product that can . . .?"

3. Don't ask too many questions in a row. This will make customers feel as if they are being cross-examined.

   Give the customer plenty time to answer any questions you might have, and be sure to listen carefully and respond thoughtfully. A good salesperson learns how to develop a professional yet conversational manner.

4. Don't ask questions that might embarrass customers or put them on the defensive.

   For example, when selling skis, it is often necessary to determine the customer's weight, but a customer may feel uncomfortable giving this information. In such a situation, you might have the various weight classes listed. Then you can simply ask which is the customer's category. In this way, you avoid having to ask the person, "How much do you weigh?"

 After You Read Section 13.2

Review Key Concepts

1. **Discuss** the importance of knowing how to ask the right questions.
2. **List** three retail approach methods.
3. **Identify** when salespeople should determine customers' needs.

Practice Academics

English Language Arts

4. Work with a partner to prepare and perform a skit that demonstrates how to properly approach and determine the needs of a customer in the market for a pair of running shoes.

Mathematics

5. Based on your analysis of the customer's needs, a premium of $1,800 per year is required for long-term health care insurance for your client. You want to offer a quarterly payment schedule. There is a surcharge of $30 per quarter for this service. What are the quarterly payments?

   Math Concept **Using Symbols** You can use algebraic symbols to represent unknown quantities and write equations to solve problems.

   Starting Hints To solve this problem, let q represent the quarterly payment. Use it to write an equation to fit the situation described in the word problem. The equation should show that q equals the yearly premium divided by four to determine the quarterly premium, plus the $30 surcharge.

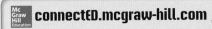 **connectED.mcgraw-hill.com**

Check your answers.

For help, go to the Math Skills Handbook located at the back of this book.

Beginning the Sales Process

Finding new customers can be achieved through three prospecting methods: customer referrals, cold canvassing, and employer sales leads.

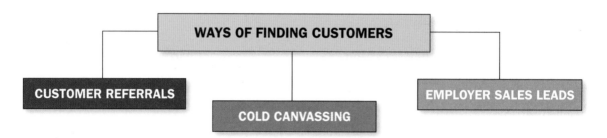

The approach in organizational selling is different from that in retail selling.

ORGANIZATIONAL SELLING	RETAIL SELLING
Arrive Early	Timing the Approach
Greet and Engage Customer	Method of Approach

Review and Activities

Written Summary

- To prepare for a sale, salespeople study products, industry trends, and competition.
- Matching the characteristics of a product to a customer's needs and wants is feature-benefit selling. Customers may have rational and emotional motives for buying.
- A prospect or lead is a potential customer.
- The approach step of the sales process can make or break the sale.
- The three purposes of the approach are to begin a conversation, build a relationship, and focus on the product.
- The three retail sales approaches are service, greeting, and merchandise.
- Determining needs is a step in the sales process that should begin as soon as possible and continue throughout the process.
- Three methods to determine needs are observing, listening, and asking questions.

Review Content Vocabulary and Academic Vocabulary

1. Write each of the vocabulary terms below on an index card, and the definitions on separate index cards. Work in pairs or small groups to match each term to its definition.

Content Vocabulary
- merchandising (p. 298)
- feature-benefit selling (p. 299)
- product features (p. 299)
- physical features (p. 301)
- extended product features (p. 301)
- customer benefits (p. 301)
- selling points (p. 301)
- buying motives (p. 302)
- rational motives (p. 302)

- emotional motives (p. 302)
- patronage motives (p. 302)
- prospecting (p. 303)
- prospect (p. 303)
- referrals (p. 303)
- endless-chain method (p. 303)
- cold canvassing (p. 304)
- greeting approach (p. 308)
- service approach (p. 309)
- merchandise approach (p. 309)

- nonverbal communication (p. 310)
- open-ended question (p. 313)

Academic Vocabulary
- shadowing (p. 297)
- longevity (p. 299)
- rapport (p. 307)
- astute (p. 310)

Assess for Understanding

2. **Identify** What are the sources of product information?
3. **Explain** How does feature-benefit selling create selling points?
4. **Describe** Why are customers' buying motives sometimes difficult to determine?
5. **Evaluate** What would you do with a customer who has been loyal in the past but now has new needs?
6. **Role-Play** What would you say in your approach to a customer who is standing in front of a specific television set? Explain why you elected to use that retail approach method.
7. **Generate** What types of questions would you ask to determine a customer's needs?
8. **Communicate** How can you use nonverbal communication to express an idea to someone? Demonstrate by doing.
9. **Role-Play** What would you say to clarify a customer's needs if that customer told you she was looking for an athletic shoe that did not look like an athletic shoe?

21st  Century Skills

Communication Skills

10. Writing to Sell Write a sales letter to prospective customers. The purpose of the letter is to get them to make an appointment to see you in person so you can discuss your party planning services. Include a minimum of three selling points in your letter. Be sure to add a means of contacting you to follow up.

Financial Literacy Skills

11. Assessing the Cost You have decided to buy a list of sales leads for your small business. You buy a list of sales leads for $2,500. Of the 500 sales leads in that list, only 65 percent of them had the correct addresses, and only 20 percent of those leads became qualified prospects. What is the cost per qualified prospect?

Everyday Ethics

12. Selling Credit Credit card companies catch consumers' attention by promising low fixed-interest rates. However, rates can go up again for a variety of reasons. Although Congress has stepped in to help regulate credit card practices, interest rates have increased for many people. Explain whether you think it is ethical to offer a certain credit rate to "sell" customers, and then later raise it, even if a customer has complied with all terms in good faith.

e-Marketing Skills

13. Determining Needs Online Evaluate the Web site of a company that sells computers. Try to determine how the Web-site design is set up to determine customers' needs. What options are presented on the opening page? What is the next option presented to the online customer? What principles of questioning to determine needs did you observe in the design and content of that Web site?

Build Academic Skills

English Language Arts

14. Selling Points Choose a consumer product you might sell. Study all related product information, industry trends, and competition. Prepare five selling points for that item to demonstrate your knowledge of feature-benefit selling and customer buying motives.

Science

15. Scientific Inquiry Write ten questions in the proper sequence for a product of your choice. Then answer those questions two different ways to demonstrate how two customers looking at the same product might have different needs.

Mathematics

16. Managing Travel Time You are stuck in traffic, and you are going to be late for your first meeting with a potential customer. You are traveling at 15 miles an hour and have 7 miles to go. If it is 8:30 a.m., at what time can you expect to arrive if you keep traveling at that speed?

Math Concept **Using Formulas** Rate (r), time (t), and distance (d) are related according to the formula $rt = d$. If you know two of the quantities, you can find the third using this formula.

For help, go to the **Math Skills Handbook** located at the back of this book.

Standardized Test Practice

Directions Read the following questions. On a separate sheet of paper write the best possible answer for each one.

1. A promotional flyer states, "Buy one purse and get a second one (of the same value or less) for half price." What is the cost for two purses priced at $21.99 and $25.99?

   A. $34.99

   B. $35.99

   C. $36.99

   D. $37.99

2. The endless chain method of prospecting involves customer referrals.

   T

   F

3. When you explain the function and customer benefit of a product feature, you are creating a _____ _____ for the product.

Test-Taking Tip

After you begin taking a math test, jot down important equations or formulas on scrap paper. This will help you to remember them as you take the test.

DECA. Connection Role Play

Salesperson
Shoe Store

Situation You are a sales trainee (participant) in a retail store that sells footwear. New stock has just arrived. As you look through the material sent by the manufacturer that is in the shoe box, you find the following information: padded collar and tongue, leather upper, patented heel design, heel cushioning, arch support, comfort support system, and lightweight sole has millions of air bubbles. This walking shoe comes in both men's and women's styles and regular, narrow, and wide widths. It is available in black, brown, and beige. As part of your sales training, you are expected to prepare selling points for this new shoe, and practice the sales opening and determining needs steps of the sales process.

Activity In ten minutes the store manager (judge) will test your product knowledge about this new walking shoe to see if you can identify the product's features and benefits. Then you will be asked to practice the sales opening and determining needs steps of the sales process. You are to assume that a customer has stopped to look at the display of these new walking shoes.

Evaluation You will be evaluated on how well you meet these performance indicators:

1. Acquire product information for use in selling.

2. Analyze product information to identify product and features.

3. Establish relationship with client/customer.

4. Prepare for the sales presentation.

5. Analyze customer needs.

 connectED.mcgraw-hill.com

Download the Competitive Events Workbook for more Role-Play practice.

presenting the product

MINCHAT

SHOW WHAT YOU KNOW

Visual Literacy Some products are sold to customers for personal use, while others are sold for business use. For product presentation to be effective, you must know the customer's intended use for the product. *How might you decide which product features to communicate during product presentation?*

Discovery Project

Selling Back-to-School Products

Essential Question How do you present and sell electronic products for back-to-school customers?

Project Goal

Assume that you work in a store that sells electronics. You must train other sales associates on effective product presentations for the back-to-school market. Anticipate questions or concerns that the sales associates should expect from back-to-school customers. Create a training session for these associates to use.

Ask Yourself...

- Which products should be included in the sales training?
- What questions and concerns are often asked by customers who purchase these products?
- How will you prepare for the training session?
- What product presentation skills will you demonstrate in your training?

 Synthesize and Present Develop a training session for sales associates on the presentation of electronic products for the back-to-school market.

 connectED.mcgraw-hill.com

Activity
Get a worksheet activity about product presentation.

Evaluate
Download a rubric you can use to evaluate your project.

DECA Connection

DECA Event Role Play

Concepts in this chapter are related to DECA competitive events that involve either an interview or role play.

Performance Indicators The performance indicators represent key skills and knowledge. Your key to success in DECA competitive events is relating them to concepts in this chapter.

- Demonstrate product knowledge.
- Convert customer/client objections into selling points.
- Recommend specific products.
- Demonstrate initiative.
- Provide legitimate responses to inquiries.

DECA Prep

Role Play Practice role-playing with the DECA Connection competitive-event activity at the end of this chapter. More information on DECA events can be found on DECA's Web site.

READING GUIDE

Before You Read

Connect When have you had to effectively present something to an audience?

Objectives

- **Describe** the goal of the product presentation.
- **Explain** how products are selected for the presentation.
- **Explain** what to say during the product presentation.
- **List** techniques that help create effective product presentations.

The Main Idea

The product presentation step of the sales process allows a salesperson to share product knowledge with customers. Customers' needs and wants should be matched with product features and benefits.

Vocabulary

Content Vocabulary
- layman's terms

Academic Vocabulary

You will find these words in your reading and on your tests. Make sure you know their meanings.
- collate
- swatches

Graphic Organizer

Draw or print this chart to take notes about how to create an effective product presentation.

connectED.mcgraw-hill.com

Print this graphic organizer.

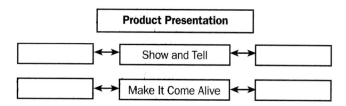

MARKETING CORE FUNCTION

Selling

Product Presentation

ORGANIZING THE PRODUCT PRESENTATION

When you do a puzzle, you analyze the various parts by shape and size. You might select the straight-edged pieces to use for the frame. When you sell, you analyze your customer's needs and buying motives. Then you use that information to begin framing your product presentation. The goal of the product presentation is to effectively present the features and benefits of a product that best match your customer's needs and buying motives.

As You Read

Consider How can you hold a customer's interest throughout the sales process?

SHOW AND TELL

Your first decision in the product presentation step of the sale is what product or products to show your customer. Then you must think about what you are going to say and how you are going to say it. This is the step of the sale in which you have the opportunity to share your expertise with the customer. You have put a lot of preparation into learning about the product you sell and how to communicate its selling points. This preparation will assist you now. Remember, you are the expert, and you have the solutions to your customer's problems and needs.

WHICH PRODUCTS DO YOU SHOW?

After you have learned the customer's intended use of a product, you should be able to select a few samples that match those needs. You may select technically advanced cameras for customers who want a camera for professional use. Novice customers might want fully automatic cameras.

When your product selection is not exactly accurate, ask questions to get the feedback you need to select a different model or style. Determining customer's needs occurs throughout the sales process.

> 66 **Selling is, in many ways, like putting together a jigsaw puzzle.** 99

WHAT PRICE RANGE SHOULD YOU OFFER?

Sometimes you will not know the customer's price range. Your knowledge of the intended use may be insufficient to determine a price range. In these cases, begin by showing a moderately priced product. You can move up or down in price once you begin to get the customer's feedback.

If you are offering consulting services or a quote on a major project, such as a kitchen renovation, you may need to get some idea of the customer's budget. In that case, you can provide the customer with a price range. For example, "Our fees range from $100 for our basic service up to $500 for our premium services." This technique will help you discover your customer's price range without asking "How much did you want to spend?"

It is not a good idea to introduce price early in the product presentation unless it is a major selling point. This is because you need time to show your clients or customers how valuable your product is to them. You know that if a product is something that you would really need and want, price becomes less of a factor in a purchase decision.

HOW MANY PRODUCTS SHOULD YOU SHOW?

To avoid overwhelming your customer, show no more than three products at a time. It is difficult for most people to remember all the features of more than three items during a presentation. When a customer wants to see more than three, put away the displayed products in which the customer shows no interest.

Show and Tell Provide useful information to the customer, and teach him or her to use the product, thereby enhancing its value.

WHAT DO YOU SAY?

In this step of the sales process, present the product's selling points. Educate customers by explaining how the product's features relate to their respective needs. Use highly descriptive adjectives and active verbs when describing product features. Avoid generalized descriptions, such as *nice*, *pretty*, and *fine*.

Avoid using slang and terms that have double meanings. For example, when selling an expensive suit to a corporate executive, you should not say something like, "You look cool in that suit." In such a situation, it would be more appropriate to point out the fine fabric used in the suit or the quality of the tailoring.

When selling industrial products, you can use the appropriate jargon to communicate with industrial buyers at their level of expertise. As you may recall from Chapter 8, jargon is specialized vocabulary used by members of a particular group. If you know the meanings of the terms used by your customers, you will be able to address their needs more professionally and effectively.

When selling products to retail customers, you should use layman's terms. **Layman's terms** are words the average customer can understand. If you are selling electronics, instead of talking about motherboards and processors, you could say, "This computer is fast and reliable."

 Reading Check

Identify What is the goal of product presentation?

In some businesses, salespeople rely on showroom displays for their product presentations. Displays help show off a product in a setting or in use. *What businesses rely on displays to showcase their product? How do salespeople use those displays for their product presentations?*

Displays

©Steve Hix/Somos Images/Corbis

PLAN THE PRESENTATION

Planning is necessary for an effective product presentation. Consider how you will present the product to the customer and how you will demonstrate its selling points. What sales aids will add to your presentation? Finally, how will you involve the customer?

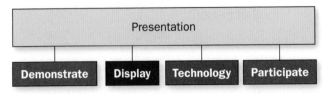

PRESENTING AND DEMONSTRATING THE PRODUCT

The way you physically present a product to the customer presents an image of its quality. Handle it with respect and use hand gestures to show the significance of certain features. For example, when presenting an expensive ring or watch to a customer, you might place it on a velvet pad rather than directly on a glass display counter.

Demonstrating the product in use helps to build customer confidence. This is especially true if you are selling an item that requires manipulation or operation, such as a camera, computer, or smartphone. To demonstrate the features of a copier, you might show how it can enlarge or reduce a document as well as **collate** and staple multiple copies. The capabilities of computer software products can be easily demonstrated directly on a computer.

USING DISPLAYS AND SALES AIDS

In retail selling situations, product displays can help in the product presentation. Mannequins give salespeople the opportunity to show how a complete outfit might look on the customer. When selling china, silverware, and glasses, a complete table-setting display gives customers an idea of how those products would look in their own homes. Manufacturers also display their products in their own showrooms to make it easier for their salespeople to sell.

When it is impractical to display or demonstrate the actual product or when you want to emphasize certain selling points, you can use sales aids in your presentations. Sales aids may include samples, fabric **swatches**, reprints of magazine and newspaper articles, audiovisual aids, and scaled models.

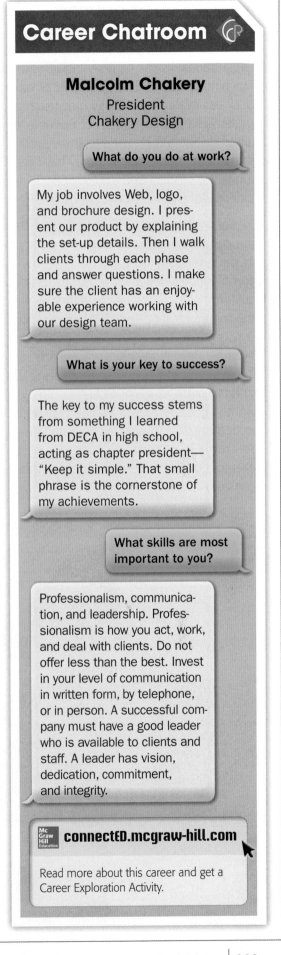

Career Chatroom

Malcolm Chakery
President
Chakery Design

What do you do at work?

My job involves Web, logo, and brochure design. I present our product by explaining the set-up details. Then I walk clients through each phase and answer questions. I make sure the client has an enjoyable experience working with our design team.

What is your key to success?

The key to my success stems from something I learned from DECA in high school, acting as chapter president—"Keep it simple." That small phrase is the cornerstone of my achievements.

What skills are most important to you?

Professionalism, communication, and leadership. Professionalism is how you act, work, and deal with clients. Do not offer less than the best. Invest in your level of communication in written form, by telephone, or in person. A successful company must have a good leader who is available to clients and staff. A leader has vision, dedication, commitment, and integrity.

connectED.mcgraw-hill.com

Read more about this career and get a Career Exploration Activity.

Photographs, drawings, graphs, charts, specification sheets, customer testimonials, and warranty information can also be used as sales aids. Organizational sales representatives who sell machinery, industrial components, or other business-related technology may use high-tech, multimedia presentations. For example, computer-aided design can be used to show products in three-dimensional views. It may have the ability to rotate the product and highlight special features. Videos can show a product in use.

For a riding lawnmower, you could show the customer articles in magazines that rate its performance. You could also use any complimentary letters or testimonials from satisfied customers as a sales aid, or share the warranty the manufacturer offers. These sales tactics help consumers build confidence in the company because they show that the company stands behind its products. If you were selling this product to retailers for resale purposes, you may even want to use samples of the lawnmower's blade to demonstrate its effectiveness and durability. You might also show a video to demonstrate its ease of operation, safety features, and high-quality construction.

Be creative when determining which sales aids will help you in your particular product presentation. Manufacturers of industrial ovens might show a video of how quickly and efficiently the oven performs. Insurance salespeople might use graphs and charts to show how dividends will accumulate or to compare the benefits of one policy to another. They might even use a computer to personalize the presentation of that information for each customer and show different policy plans for that person.

INVOLVING THE CUSTOMER

It is best to get the customer physically involved with the product as soon as possible in the sales presentation. Appeal to the customers' five senses. You could have your customers hold and swing golf clubs, and try on and walk around in a pair of shoes. Allow customers to feel the ease of using a computer keyboard or mouse and listen to the sound quality and see the vivid colors on a television. Customers will want to test-drive an automobile or taste and smell food products. Some cosmetic companies offer free makeovers so a customer can see how the products enhance their appearance.

Allowing customers to try a product or service lets them participate in the sale. *Why is it so important to get a product into the customer's hands or involve the customer in some other way during the sales presentation?*

Try It Out

You can also involve your customer verbally during the sales presentation by confirming selling points. Ask a question that is guaranteed to produce a positive response. You might say, "This jacket is wind and water resistant. Don't you think that feature will come in handy on an outdoor trip?" Pause for the customer's answer. If you get the customer's agreement on several selling points, you know you are on the right track with the selected product.

HOLDING THE CUSTOMER'S ATTENTION

When you involve a customer in the sale, you help him or her make intelligent buying decisions. You also help yourself because the customer is generally more attentive when doing more than just listening to what you say.

If you are losing your customer's attention, ask a simple question. Regaining your customer's attention is essential if you are to continue with the sales presentation. The key is keeping the customer involved.

After You Read | **Section 14.1**

Review Key Concepts

1. **Explain** how to identify which priced product you should show when you cannot determine a customer's intended price range.
2. **Explain** how you might involve the customer in a product presentation about a high-tech product.
3. **Describe** how to involve a customer in the product presentation when selling fresh bread and pastries to a restaurant.

Practice Academics
English Language Arts

4. Write a detailed plan that covers the product presentation for a product of your choice. For at least one product feature, include what you will say, how you will demonstrate that feature, what sales aids you will use, how you will use them, and how you will involve your customer.

Mathematics

5. You work in a fabric store. A customer wants to buy 15 feet of wool fabric. If the price per yard is $16.50, how much do you charge?

> **Math Concept** **Measurement** Measure objects and apply units, systems, and processes of measurement.

Starting Hints To solve this problem, divide 15 by 3 to convert the amount of feet into the amount of yards. Multiply $16.50 by the number of yards the customer wants to determine the total price.

connectED.mcgraw-hill.com

Check your answers.

For help, go to the Math Skills Handbook located at the back of this book.

READING GUIDE

Before You Read

Connect When have you had to respond to an objection?

Objectives

- **Distinguish** objections from excuses.
- **Explain** why you should welcome objections in the sales process.
- **Explain** the five buying decisions on which common objections are based.
- **Demonstrate** the general four-step method for handling customer objections.
- **List** seven methods of answering objections and identify when each should be used.

The Main Idea

Objections are helpful in the sales process because they provide an opportunity to further determine customers' needs and problems. Objections are easily managed when you know the basis for them.

Vocabulary

Content Vocabulary
- objections
- excuses
- objection analysis sheet
- substitution method
- boomerang method
- superior-point method
- third-party method

Academic Vocabulary

You will find these words in your reading and on your tests. Make sure you know their meanings.
- paraphrase
- compensate

Graphic Organizer

Draw or print this chart to take notes about ways to handle objections.

Mc Graw Hill Education **connectED.mcgraw-hill.com**

Print this graphic organizer.

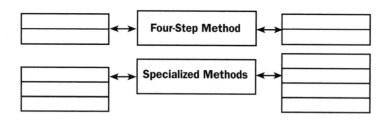

MARKETING CORE FUNCTIONS

Selling

 Objections

UNDERSTANDING OBJECTIONS

Objections are concerns, hesitations, doubts, complaints, or other reasons a customer has for not making a purchase. Objections should be seen as positive. They give feedback and an opportunity to present more information to the customer.

Anticipate and plan potential answers to objections. This will help you feel more confident in your responses to customers. Then select the most appropriate method for handling those objections to promote success.

> **" Objections should be welcomed in sales. "**

Objections can be presented as questions or statements. An example of a question would be: "Do you carry any other brands?" A statement would be: "These shoes don't fit me." For questions, simply answer the question posed. For statements, you may need more selling expertise.

Excuses are reasons given when a customer has no intention of buying. In retail sales situations, the most common excuse is: "I am just looking." When you are faced with that statement, be polite and courteous. Encourage customers to look around and ask you any questions they may have.

In organizational sales situations, clients may simply refuse to see the salesperson. In that case, it is best to leave a business card and ask to see the person at a more convenient time.

It can be difficult to distinguish between objections and excuses. A statement or question that seems to be an excuse may be an objection. For example, "I didn't plan to buy today" may really mean "I don't like the styles you have available." When you suspect that may be the case, ask additional questions to get to the real reason for the disinterest in your product or products.

As You Read

Predict What are methods salespeople use to handle objections?

Objections should be welcomed. However, some objections may be excuses instead. *How can a salesperson determine if a customer is giving an objection or an excuse?*

Digital Vision/SuperStock

PLAN FOR OBJECTIONS

Objections can occur at any time during the sales process and should be answered promptly. A customer who must wait to hear responses to questions or concerns will become preoccupied with the objection. When that happens, you may lose the customer's attention and confidence.

Objections can guide you in the sales process by helping you redefine the customer's needs and determine when the customer wants more information. A customer may say, "This item is very expensive." What the person may really mean is: "Tell me why this product costs so much." This objection not only lets you know why the customer is reluctant to buy, but also gives you an opportunity to bring out additional selling points.

So, you should welcome objections. They are not necessarily the sign of a lost sale. Research shows a positive relationship between customer objections and a successful sales outcome.

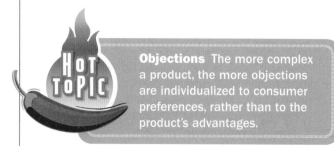

Objections The more complex a product, the more objections are individualized to consumer preferences, rather than to the product's advantages.

You can prepare yourself for most objections that might occur in a sales situation by completing an **objection analysis sheet**, a document that lists common objections and possible responses to them. The actual objections may be slightly different from those you anticipated. However, thinking of responses can give you an idea of how to handle other objections.

You can incorporate anticipated objections into your product presentation so they do not become objections. You must be cautious about this, however. You do not want to include so many objections in your product presentation that you introduce doubt, especially if none existed before. Saying "I guess you're worried about the safety of this snowmobile," may introduce a fear that was not a previous concern.

A better way to handle the same situation would be to emphasize the safety features of the vehicle. You might say, "The suspension on this snowmobile is specially designed to keep it stable. It's very safe to operate."

COMMON OBJECTIONS

When you list general customer objections, you will see that they fall into certain categories. Most objections are based on five key decisions the customer must make before buying—decisions about need, product, source, price, and time. This is true for both retail and organizational sales situations. The actual objections will vary because of the difference in purchase motivation. Retail customers generally are making a purchase for personal use. Business-to-business customers are buying for a company's operation. Wholesalers and retailers are buying for resale purposes.

The following are examples of customer objections. They provide a starting point for the creation of an objection analysis sheet.

NEED

Objections related to need usually occur when the customer does not have an immediate need for the item. They may happen when the customer wants the item but does not truly need it. A supermarket owner may say, "I just don't have enough shelf space for another cereal brand." A comment, such as "I like these sandals, but I really don't need another pair," is an objection based on a conflict between a need and a want.

PRODUCT

Objections based on the product are more common. They include concerns about things such as ease of use, quality, color, size, or style. "I don't buy 100-percent cotton shirts because they have to be ironed" is a product objection.

SOURCE

Objections based on source often occur due to negative past experiences with the firm or brand.

A customer might say, "The last time I placed an order with your company, I received it two weeks after the promised date."

PRICE

Objections based on price are more common with high-quality, expensive merchandise. You might hear statements such as "That's more than I wanted to spend."

TIME

Objections based on time reveal a hesitation to buy immediately. These objections are sometimes excuses. Customers usually have a real reason for not wanting to make a purchase on the spot. A customer might say, "I think I'll wait until July to buy those sandals when you have your summer sale."

You will probably hear many different kinds of objections once you begin selling. You should note them for future reference.

FOUR-STEP METHOD FOR HANDLING OBJECTIONS

Successful salespeople have learned to use a very basic strategy when answering all objections or complaints. It consists of four basic steps: listen, acknowledge, restate, and answer.

LISTEN CAREFULLY

Remember to be attentive, maintain eye contact, and let the customer talk. Also watch for nonverbal cues in order to interpret the true meaning of what is being said.

ACKNOWLEDGE THE OBJECTIONS

Acknowledging objections demonstrates that you understand and care about the customer's concerns. Show empathy for the customer's problem. Some common statements used to acknowledge objections include the following: "I can see your point" or "Other customers have asked us the same question."

MARKETING CASE STUDY

IBM's Presentation Centers

IBM® has designed "client centers" around the world to impress customers with technology and consulting services. Customers are brought to the facilities for sales presentations. The entire experience is planned, from when they are picked up at the airport to the actual product presentations. This approach ensures that all clients are treated in a professional manner with customer satisfaction as the focal point. What to say and when to say it is mapped out for the sales staff. The timing of product demonstrations and sales pitches is based on IBM's research.

Hands-On Presentation

At IBM's Industry Solution Lab, future technology is displayed alongside current technology. Clients can also interact with technology for different industries. This hands-on experience makes a day-long sales meeting engaging and more meaningful than just watching PowerPoint® presentations.

English Language Arts

Evaluate Do you think salespeople can handle customer objections effectively in these sales presentations? Discuss with your class.

These acknowledgments make customers feel that their objections are understandable, valid, and worthy of further discussion. This does not mean that you agree with the customers, but it acknowledges the objection. Disagreeing with customers, or saying, "You're wrong," will put customers on the defensive, and you might lose the sale.

RESTATE THE OBJECTIONS

To be sure you understand a customer's objection, restate it in one of the following ways:

"I can understand your concerns. You feel that. . . . Am I correct?"

"In other words, you feel that. . . ."

"Let me see if I understand. You want to know more about. . . ."

Do not repeat the customer's concerns word for word. Instead, **paraphrase** the objections. A customer might say, "The style is nice, but I don't like the color." You could paraphrase the objection by asking, "Would you be interested in the jacket if we could find your size in another color?"

ANSWER THE OBJECTIONS

Answer each objection tactfully. Never answer with an air of superiority or suggest that the person's concern is unimportant.

Think of yourself as a consultant, using the objections to further define or redefine the customer's needs. In some cases, you will have to get to the bottom of the specific objection before answering it completely. For example, before answering the price objection, revisit the features on the more expensive model. Then see if the customer's needs can be met with a less expensive model.

SPECIALIZED METHODS OF ANSWERING OBJECTIONS

There are seven specialized methods for answering objections: substitution, boomerang, question, superior point, denial, demonstration, and third party.

Listening carefully is the best way to understand objections. Being attentive and making eye contact shows that you are listening. *How would you show a customer that you understand his or her objection?*

Listening to Objections

Purestock/SuperStock

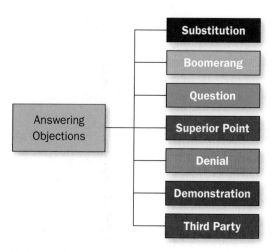

SUBSTITUTION

Sometimes a customer is looking for a specific brand or model of a product that you do not carry. Or maybe the customer does not like the product you show. In any of those cases, you may want to use the **substitution method**, which involves recommending a different product that would still satisfy the customer's needs. Assume a customer says, "I don't like the way this dress looks on me." In this case, you may want to suggest a different style that is more becoming on your customer.

BOOMERANG

An objection can be returned to the customer in the same way that a boomerang returns to the thrower. The **boomerang method** brings the objection back to the customer as a selling point. Here is an example:

Customer: This ski jacket is so lightweight. It can't possibly keep me warm.

Salesperson: The jacket is so light because of an insulation material called Thinsulate. The manufacturer guarantees that Thinsulate will keep you warmer than other fiberfill insulation, without the bulk and extra weight.

When using the boomerang method, you must be careful not to sound as if you are trying to outwit the customer. Use a friendly, helpful tone to explain how the objection is really a selling point.

QUESTION

The question method is a technique in which you question the customer to learn more about his or her objections. To uncover their real objection, you can simply ask, "Why do you feel that way?" Their answer may unearth a lot of information that will reveal the real reason for the objection. A customer may say, "I don't like receiving my e-mails on a mobile phone."

MEXICO

The Silver Belt

As a global leader in silver production, Mexico is known for its "Silver Belt." this is an area rich with silver deposits. The country also boasts the city of Taxco. Nestled in the hills near Mexico City, Taxco has been called "The Silver Capital of the World."

Past to Present The Spaniards opened Taxco's first silver mine in the early 16th century. It was not until 1929 that American William Spratling helped put the city on the map. He trained apprentices to design and work silver into jewelry and other wares.

Now hundreds of silversmiths showcase creations on Taxco's streets. Travelers come to buy reasonably priced bracelets, earrings, necklaces, rings, and dinnerware.

Social Studies

Research The number "925" is stamped on quality silver. Research and explain the number's history and meaning as part of a sales presentation for a silver product.

Here are some entry-level phrases that are used in conversations about marketing all over the world.

English	Spanish
Hello	Hola
Goodbye	Adiós
How are you?	Cómo es usted?
Thank you	Gracias
You're welcome	De nada

When you ask why they feel that way, you may learn that the customer is annoyed that mobile phones beep frequently. Additional questions could be used to re-define the customer's needs in this case. A selling point can be explained regarding the cell phone's ability to mute sounds.

SUPERIOR POINT

The **superior-point method** is a technique that permits the salesperson to acknowledge objections as valid, yet still offset or **compensate** them with other features and benefits. This method is often used when price is an objection. In that case, you must show the value-added aspects of doing business with your company. Some value-added topics that can be used in organizational sales situations include research and development that goes into products, the ongoing support the company will provide, the certainty of on-time delivery, the company's history and reputation, and its market knowledge. Here is an example:

Customer: Your prices are higher than the prices of your competitors.

Salesperson: That's true. Our prices are slightly higher, but with good reason. We use better quality wool in our garments that will last five to ten years longer than the wool in our competitors' garments. Plus, we guarantee the quality for life. You can return the product if you ever have a problem with it, and we'll repair it free of charge.

DENIAL

The denial method is when the customer's objection is based on misinformation. It is best to provide proof and accurate information in answer to objections. This method is also used when the objection is in the form of a question or inquiry. When using the denial method, you must back up your reply with proof and accurate facts. Consider an example:

Customer: Will this shirt shrink?

Salesperson: No, it won't shrink because the fabric is made of 50-percent cotton and 50-percent polyester. The polyester will prevent shrinkage.

DEMONSTRATION

The demonstration exemplifies the adage, "Seeing is believing." Here is an example:

Customer: I can't believe that jacket can fold up into itself to become a zippered pouch.

Salesperson: I'm glad you brought that up. Let me demonstrate how easy it is to stuff this jacket into the pocket pouch and then zip it up.

The demonstration method can be quite convincing and should be used when appropriate. Conduct only demonstrations you have tested, and make sure they work before using them on a customer in a sales situation.

THIRD PARTY

The **third-party method** involves using a previous customer or another neutral person who can give a testimonial about the product.

Customer: I can't see how this machine can save me $1,000 in operating costs the first year.

Salesperson: Frank Smith, one of my customers, questioned the same point when he bought his machine a year ago. He now praises its efficiency and says that his costs have gone down by $1,200. Here's a letter I recently received from him.

In any given sales situation, it is unlikely that you will use all seven methods of answering objections. You will create effective combinations over time that will work best for you.

 After You Read | **Section 14.2**

Review Key Concepts

1. **Explain** the difference between excuses and objections.
2. **List** what you can do to prepare for objections.
3. **Describe** the four-step method for handling objections.

Practice Academics

English Language Arts

4. Prepare an objection analysis sheet for a child's bicycle with training wheels and a basket. Include at least five different objections and responses to depict different specialized methods for handling objections. Use a word-processing program to prepare your written document.

Mathematics

5. An outdoor clothing retailer can buy rain-resistant coats that last for eight years at a cost of $25 per coat. The other option is buying coats that last for two years at a cost of $10 per coat. If the retailer wants to order 40 coats, which option offers the biggest savings?

   Math Concept **Problem Solving** Solve problems that arise in mathematics and other contexts.

   Starting Hints To solve this problem, multiply $10 by 40, and then $25 by 40, to determine the total cost of the jackets. Divide each total by the number of years the jackets are good for to determine the cost per year. Compare the two amounts to determine which one is a bigger savings.

 **connectED.mcgraw-hill.com**

Check your answers.

For help, go to the Math Skills Handbook located at the back of this book.

Presenting the Product

Objections are based on five buying decisions: need, product, source, price, and time.

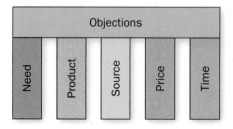

The four-step method for handling customer objections is listen, acknowledge, restate, and answer.

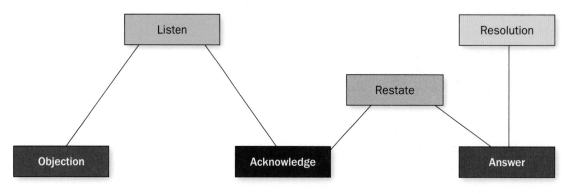

The goal of the product presentation is to present the product's selling points that relate to the customer's needs and wants.

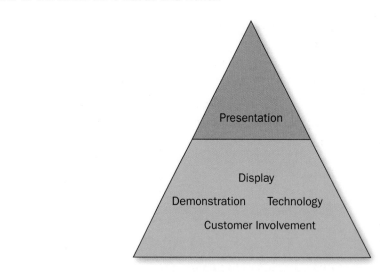

Review and Activities

Written Summary

- The goal of product presentation is to match a customer's needs and wants to a product's features and benefits.
- When selecting products to show, consider customer needs and price range, and limit selection to three items.
- To make your product presentation lively and effective, handle the product with respect, demonstrate product features, involve the customer, and use sales aids.
- Objections are reasons for not buying or doubts that occur during a sales presentation.
- Objections can help clarify a customer's needs and provide an opportunity to introduce additional selling points.
- Objections are based on five buying decisions: need, product, source, price, and time.
- Four steps for handling customer objections are listen, acknowledge, restate, and answer.
- Seven specific methods for handling objections include substitution, boomerang, question, superior point, denial, demonstration, and third party.

Review Content Vocabulary and Academic Vocabulary

1. Think of an example of each of these vocabulary terms in everyday life.

Content Vocabulary
- layman's terms (p. 322)
- objections (p. 327)
- excuses (p. 327)
- objection analysis sheet (p. 328)
- substitution method (p. 331)
- boomerang method (p. 331)
- superior-point method (p. 332)
- third-party method (p. 333)

Academic Vocabulary
- collate (p. 323)
- swatches (p. 323)
- paraphrase (p. 330)
- compensate (p. 332)

Assess for Understanding

2. **Identify** What is the goal of the product presentation step in the sales process?
3. **Explain** What techniques help create an effective product presentation?
4. **Rephrase** How can you explain the features of a high-tech product such as a digital camera to someone who has never used one before?
5. **Discuss** How do objections help in the sales process?
6. **Create** What objections would you have to purchasing a new pair of shoes right now?
7. **Role-Play** Use the boomerang or superior point method to respond to a customer's objection for a product of your choice.
8. **Evaluate** How can you help an employee who does not always explain a product's features in layman's terms?
9. **Contrast** What makes objections different from excuses?

21st Century Skills

Teamwork Skills

10. Business-to-Business Work with a team to prepare a product presentation for a business-to-business product. It can be sold for resale purposes or used in the operation of a business. Consider products such as retail apparel, machine parts for manufacturing, or business consulting services. Share your product presentation with the class.

Financial Literacy Skills

11. Return on Investment In order to sell products that are purchased for resale, you must show customers their projected return on investment (ROI). The ROI is based on the difference in *percentage* between the price you charge resellers and the price they charge their customers. Calculate the ROI for the following products. Assume the products were sold using the Manufacturer's Suggested Retail Price (MSRP).

Product	Quantity	Unit Price	MSRP	ROI
Video Games	3,000	$6.65	$14.99	____
CDs	1,000	$4.75	$ 9.99	____

e-Marketing Skills

12. Product Demo Services Research companies on the Internet that provide product demonstration services to businesses. What services and technologies would help a company sell its products in the following situations? Take the position of a sales representative in each situation. Write a proposal to your manager that includes which services and technologies you will need. Be sure to explain how these resources will support your ability to sell well.

a. A frozen food company will be exhibiting at a trade show and wants potential customers to taste its new products.

b. A firm wants to show its products in three dimensions to illustrate specific product features.

c. A manufacturer wants to digitally demonstrate its machinery in use to potential customers.

Build Academic Skills

Social Studies

13. Handling Objections How can you use the methods for handling objections for situations you may encounter in your personal life? Provide an example.

Science

14. Make a Chart You work as a sales associate for a global electronics retailer. Select two competing products to compare regarding their features and prices. Make a chart that shows this comparison for use in the product-presentation step of the sales process. Share your chart with classmates and be prepared to answer their questions and handle objections from them.

Mathematics

15. Calculate the Customer Price Your customer wants to buy 20 square yards of carpet for one room of a house that measures 5 yards by 4 yards, and 12 square yards of carpet for another room that measures 3 yards by 4 yards. The price per square foot of carpet is $8.25. How much would you charge the customer?

Math Concept **Converting Units** 1 yard is equal to 3 feet. Divide the number of feet to determine the number of yards, and then multiply the number of yards to convert to feet.

For help, go to the **Math Skills Handbook** located at the back of this book.

Standardized Test Practice

Directions Read the following questions. On a separate sheet of paper write the best possible answer for each one.

1. Which of the following statements should not be used in the product presentation of a formal overcoat?

   A. This jacket is made of a special fabric that repels water.

   B. The fabrics used in this jacket make it machine washable.

   C. You look totally awesome in that jacket.

   D. The specially designed sleeves in this jacket give you full range of motion.

2. It is a good idea to have customers handle a product and respond to questions in order to involve customers in the product presentation step of the sales process.

   T

   F

3. In the _____ method for answering objections, the objection is converted into a selling point.

Test-Taking Tip

If you are reading too much into a question, skip it and try to answer it later with fresh eyes.

DECA Connection Role Play

Manager
Gourmet Produce Department

Situation You are the manager of the produce department in your local grocery store. In the next month, your department will begin to carry a limited number of exotic tropical fruit varieties. The new fruit varieties are ones that have not been carried by food stores in your area. Your gourmet store is able to stock these tropical fruits because the produce buyer has made an exclusive arrangement with a group of fruit growers on several Caribbean islands. Some of the tropical fruits that the store will have in stock include carambola, guava, and passion fruit. These new tropical fruit varieties will be carried as introductory items and in small quantities.

You have determined that proper presentation of the tropical fruit varieties will help to familiarize customers with the new varieties and help to sell them better, thereby making the introduction a success. Your idea for introducing the new produce items is to have a produce department employee demonstrate the handling of each variety, offer tasting samples of each, and have recipes available that feature each of the new produce items.

Activity You are planning to approach the store manager (judge) to describe your idea for introducing the new tropical fruit varieties and seek approval for implementing your ideas. You are to include in your discussion the fact that your ideas include the three basic methods of proper product presentation.

Evaluation You will be evaluated on how well you meet the following performance indicators:

1. Demonstrate product knowledge.
2. Convert customer/client objections into selling points.
3. Recommend specific products.
4. Demonstrate initiative.
5. Provide legitimate responses to inquiries.

 connectED.mcgraw-hill.com

Download the Competitive Events Workbook for more Role-Play practice.

closing the sale

Don Mason/Blend Images LLC

SHOW WHAT YOU KNOW

Visual Literacy The sale is closed when your customer makes a commitment to buy. An effective salesperson also masters techniques and skills to ensure that the customer will be satisfied with the purchase. *Why is customer satisfaction so important in the sales process?*

Discovery Project

Closing the Sale and Customer Satisfaction

Essential Question How do you close a sale and make a steady customer?

Project Goal

Working with two partners, assume you are a salesperson in the home furnishings department of a retail store. For the next sales meeting, you have been asked to conduct a role play. It will demonstrate how to sell to customers who want to renovate or redecorate their homes. The role play focuses on do-it-yourself projects. Your goal is to sell the products that customers need to complete their projects. You must also explain a strategy to use to make them loyal customers. You are expected to emphasize closing the sale, customer satisfaction strategies, and follow-up.

Ask Yourself...

- What questions does someone who is renovating their home ask?
- Which sales techniques will you include in your role plays?
- How can you monitor the customer's satisfaction?
- How will you present the role plays?

 Role Play Present your role play about selling to customers who want to renovate or redecorate their homes. Emphasize closing the sale, customer satisfaction strategies, and follow-up.

 connectED.mcgraw-hill.com

Activity
Get a worksheet activity about closing the sale.

Evaluate
Download a rubric you can use to evaluate your project.

DECA Connection

DECA Event Role Play

Concepts in this chapter are related to DECA competitive events that involve either an interview or role play.

Performance Indicators The performance indicators represent key skills and knowledge. Your key to success in DECA competitive events is relating them to concepts in this chapter.

- Close the sale.
- Demonstrate suggestion selling.
- Explain the role of customer service as a component of selling relationships.
- Explain key factors in building a clientele.
- Plan follow-up strategies for use in selling.

DECA Prep

Role Play Practice role-playing with the DECA Connection competitive-event activity at the end of this chapter. More information on DECA events can be found on DECA's Web site.

READING GUIDE

Before You Read

Reflect What questions do you ask of salespeople when you are shopping?

Objectives

- **Identify** customer buying signals.
- **List** a few tips for closing a sale.
- **Decide** on appropriate specialized methods for closing a sale.

The Main Idea

At a certain point in the sales process, your customer will be ready to make a purchase. In this section, you will learn how to close a sale.

Vocabulary

Content Vocabulary
- closing the sale
- buying signals
- trial close
- which close
- standing-room-only close
- direct close
- service close

Academic Vocabulary

You will find these words in your reading and on your tests. Make sure you know their meanings.
- commit
- perseverance

Graphic Organizer

Draw or print this chart to identify information you need to know in order to close a sale.

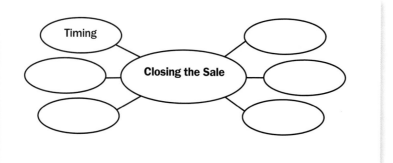

 connectED.mcgraw-hill.com

Print this graphic organizer.

MARKETING CORE FUNCTION

Selling

How to Close a Sale

CLOSING CONCEPTS AND TECHNIQUES

Closing the sale is obtaining positive agreement from the customer to buy. All your efforts up to this step of the sale have involved helping your customers make buying decisions.

To close a sale, salespeople need to recognize when a customer is ready to buy. Sometimes it is so natural that the customer closes the sale for you. In many situations, however, the customer waits for the salesperson to close the sale.

As You Read

Predict What can salespeople do to make closing the sale more effective?

TIMING THE CLOSE

Some customers are ready to buy sooner than other customers; therefore, you must be flexible. You might show a customer a product and almost immediately detect an opportunity to close the sale. Other times, you may spend an hour with customers and still find that they are having difficulty making a decision.

You should never feel pressured to complete an entire sales presentation just because you planned it that way. The key to closing sales is customer readiness.

BUYING SIGNALS

When attempting to close a sale, look for **buying signals**, the things customers say or do to indicate a readiness to buy. These signals may be nonverbal and include facial expressions and body language. You know customers are ready to buy when they say, "This is exactly what I was looking for." Other comments that may be clues about their readiness include: "Do you have these same shoes in black?" "When would I be able to get delivery?" When a customer has mentally decided on the purchase, it is time to close the sale.

> 66 **Closing the sale is based on customer readiness to buy.** 99

Determining when a customer is ready to buy is sometimes difficult for a novice salesperson. *Looking at this photo, what customer cues might suggest that it is time to close the sale?*

Customer Readiness

Purestock/SuperStock

TRIAL CLOSE

You may attempt a trial close to test the readiness of a customer and your interpretation of a positive buying signal. A **trial close** is an initial effort to close a sale.

Trial closes are beneficial for two reasons. For one, if the trial close does not work, you will still learn from the attempt. Customers will most likely tell you why they are not ready to **commit** to buying. On the other hand, if the trial close does work, you will reach your goal of closing the sale. In both cases, you are in an excellent position to continue with the sales process.

TIPS FOR CLOSING THE SALE

Professional salespeople recognize closing opportunities, help customers make a decision, and create an ownership mentality for the customer. They rely on proven and tested techniques. They often use the techniques discussed in the following pages. You will find it easier to attempt trial closes and close more sales if you use these techniques. As you learn to be a salesperson, you will want to avoid saying or doing a few things when closing a sale.

RECOGNIZE CLOSING OPPORTUNITIES

Having a major obstacle removed usually makes a customer receptive to buying the product or service. You can also use effective product presentations to close the sale. Dramatic product presentations often prove important selling points and excite the customer about owning the product. Take advantage of high customer interest at these times and attempt to close.

HELP CUSTOMERS MAKE A DECISION

When a customer is having difficulty making a buying decision, stop showing additional merchandise. You should also narrow the selection of items by removing those products that are no longer of interest to the customer. You can do this by asking, "Which of these items do you like the least?" Once you reduce the selection to two items, you can help a customer decide by summarizing the major features and benefits of each product. You can also explain any advantages or disadvantages of each item being considered. Both methods help you to focus the decision making on important considerations.

Close the sale by capitalizing on customer interest and excitement with a product. *Why are effective product demonstrations so helpful in closing the sale?*

Exciting Product Demonstrations Close the Sale

Juice Images/Glow Image

CREATE AN OWNERSHIP MENTALITY

Use words that indicate ownership, such as *you* and *your*. When presenting selling points, you might say, "You will appreciate these waterproof hiking shoes on your next hiking trip when it starts to rain." Using *you* and *your* when explaining selling points helps customers visualize themselves owning those products. Your selling points become more personal and therefore more effective in helping customers develop an ownership mentality.

AVOID THREATENING WORDS

When possible avoid words, like *now* and *today* because they have the connotation of having to act immediately. Customers may feel too much pressure in making a buying decision and may change their mind altogether. This approach may accidentally trigger an objection related to time that the customer did not have before.

GET MINOR AGREEMENTS

Solicit minor agreements on selling points that you know your customer has observed or experienced. For example, "Those newly designed golf shoes are comfortable, aren't they?"

When you get positive reactions from your customer throughout the sales process, that same positive frame of mind will help create a natural closing.

PACE YOUR CLOSING

If you think the customer is ready to make a buying decision, stop talking about the product. At that point, close the sale. Continuing to talk about a product after a customer's readiness is apparent may annoy that customer. It may even cause you to lose the sale.

On the other hand, do not rush a customer into making a buying decision. Be patient, courteous, polite, and helpful, and always remember that your primary interest is customer satisfaction.

SPECIALIZED METHODS FOR CLOSING THE SALE

Attempt to close the sale as soon as you recognize a buying signal. Your method for doing this depends on the selling situation. Certain selling situations warrant the use of specialized methods, including the which close, standing-room-only close, direct close, and service close methods.

When customers are overwhelmed with too many options, it is difficult for them to make a buying decision. *If a customer has five pairs of shoes to try on and wants to see more shoes, what should the salesperson do?*

Too Many Options Doom a Sale

The GREEN Marketer

TerraCycle™ Grows Greener

TerraCycle, Inc., is one of a number of eco-friendly companies in today's marketplace. Its products, packaging, and product use are all eco-friendly. For TerraCycle's all-natural plant food, the company uses organic waste to feed worms. Then the worms' waste is processed and used to make an all-natural plant food that is packaged in recycled soda bottles. To acquire these bottles, TerraCycle relies on fund-raising efforts by schools and nonprofit organizations.

Good Results TerraCycle Plant Food is exceptional in that it outperforms synthetic plant food products in many ways and is safe to use. The product is sold in retail stores, such as Walmart®, Home Depot®, Whole Foods,® Ace Hardware®, Do It Best®, and True Value®, with a 100-percent satisfaction guarantee.

Science
Create You work in a store that sells TerraCycle Plant Food. Think of a scientific product demonstration or display that would help close the sale for this eco-friendly product.

 connectED.mcgraw-hill.com

Get an activity on green marketing.

WHICH CLOSE

The **which close** is a closing method that encourages a customer to make a decision between two items. If you follow the tips for closing a sale, you will remove unwanted items to bring the selection down to two. Compare the selling points of each item, and then ask the customer, "Which one do you prefer?" This method makes it easier for a customer because only one simple decision must be made.

STANDING-ROOM-ONLY CLOSE

The **standing-room-only close** is a method used when a product is in short supply or when the price will be going up in the near future. This close should be used only when the situation honestly calls for it because it may be perceived as a high-pressure tactic. In many situations, a salesperson can honestly say, "I'm sorry, but I can't promise that I'll be able to make you this same offer later."

The standing-room only approach is often used in selling high-demand real estate. Customers must often be prompted to act on a hot property that will be off the market quickly. They also may be prompted to act if an item is advertised at a low price and there is a limited supply at that price. For example, "The item you like is part of a special promotion. It is the last one we have in your size."

Again, keep in mind that this approach can turn off a customer if he or she feels that you are pressuring them into a sale. Always be tactful and courteous to the customer in these situations.

DIRECT CLOSE

The **direct close** is a method in which you ask for the sale. You would use the direct close method when the buying signal is very strong. Here is one example of dialogue to use when using a direct close approach to a sales situation: "Can I assume that we're ready to talk about the details of your order?" "It appears you like everything I have shown you. Now we just need to discuss the quantity you will need."

You can use a statement like the one above and replace "quantity" with other specifics of the order, such as delivery, shipping terms, or special instructions. Positive statements by the customer to direct close approaches let you know that the customer is ready to buy. You can continue closing the order by addressing the specifics of the order.

In a retail situation, you might simply ask a question regarding payment, such as: "How would you like to pay for this purchase—cash, check, or credit card?"

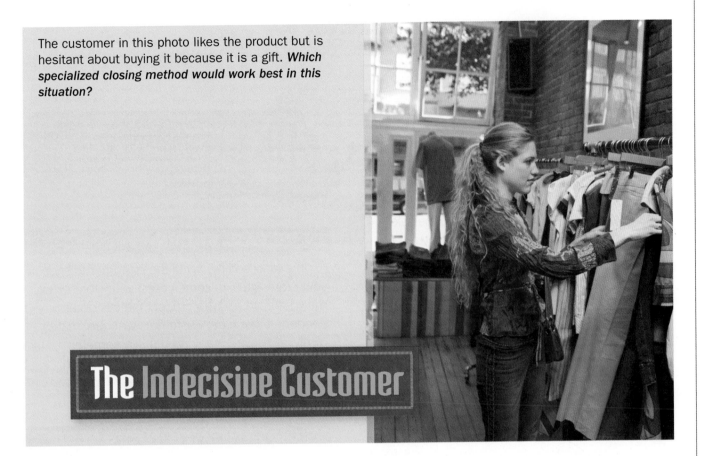

The customer in this photo likes the product but is hesitant about buying it because it is a gift. *Which specialized closing method would work best in this situation?*

The Indecisive Customer

SERVICE CLOSE

Sometimes you may run into obstacles or instances that require special services to close the sale. The **service close** is a method in which you explain services that overcome obstacles or problems. Such services include gift wrapping, a return policy, special sales arrangements, warranties and guarantees, and bonuses or premiums. You might want to explain the store's return policy when a customer hesitates but seems to be willing to make the purchase anyway. This is an especially good idea when a customer is purchasing the item as a gift for someone else.

Special sales arrangements are used to close the sale when the customer needs help paying for the item or order.

The Service Close in Business-to-Business Situations

In an organizational selling situation, the sales representative would talk about the terms of the sale, discussing points such as when payment is expected. For example, payment could be due 30 or 60 days after the date of the invoice.

Customers may also need information about credit terms to help them decide to buy. In other cases, customers may need a sample to try out before purchasing large quantities. Sometimes offering a sampling program is beneficial if it is a new purchase or the buyer is changing vendors. The buyer needs proof that your product is a better substitute for the one currently being used.

The Service Close in Retail

In a retail selling situation, the use of credit and checks as well as special buying plans, such as layaway, can be suggested. When a customer questions the quality of the merchandise, perhaps you can explain that a warranty, or guarantee, is offered on the product. When your business offers the same quality merchandise at the same price as your competitors' price, your service may be the only factor that affects the buying decision.

Reading Check

Analyze Why is it important for salespeople to help customers make decisions?

FAILURE TO CLOSE THE SALE

Do not assume that every sales presentation should end in a sale. Even the best salespeople can sell to only a fraction of their prospects.

You should also not take a failure to close the sale personally. The customer had reasons for not buying your product at that time. It is possible that your product did not meet your customer's needs. In that case, you would not have closed the sale anyway. In other cases, the customers may not need your product at that time but may in the future.

How do you handle a failed closing and what can you learn from it? Let's take a look at what you can do in a retail sales situation and in an organizational sales situation. Also, let's see how feedback can help you and your company.

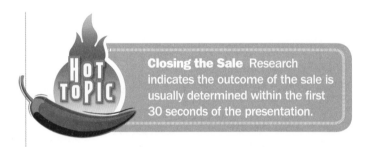

Closing the Sale Research indicates the outcome of the sale is usually determined within the first 30 seconds of the presentation.

IN RETAIL SALES

In a retail setting, invite the customer to shop in your store again. In some cases, your store simply may not have had the product the customer needed at that time. Customers who are treated nicely, even when they do not buy something, remember that experience and will return on another occasion. Thus, you will have a second chance to satisfy their needs and wants.

IN ORGANIZATIONAL SALES

Not all sales calls require a closing. Business-to-business salespeople may negotiate on large accounts for months before closing the sale. So, the first few sales calls may be building blocks upon which you develop a relationship and learn more about your customers' needs and wants. During that process, you become a partner and consultant in solving your customers' problems and satisfying their needs.

In organizational selling situations, it is not uncommon for buyers to be convinced by a sales presentation but not yet ready to buy. In such a situation, it is extremely important that the salesperson leave an opening for a return sales call. However, if you clearly sense an impending turndown, it is better to make a graceful exit and leave the possibility for a future sales call. In both cases, leave a business card with those prospects. Research suggests that **perseverance** is the way to succeed. So, remember every sales contact has the potential to become a successful sale in the future.

In some business-to-business selling situations, the buyer may have some feelings of guilt. These feelings could be due to their rejection of your sales proposition in favor of a competitor's.

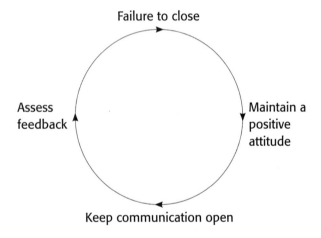

Failure to close

Maintain a positive attitude

Keep communication open

Assess feedback

MAINTAIN A POSITIVE ATTITUDE

The attitude of the salesperson who has not made the sale should be no different than the attitude of the successful salesperson. It is very important for the salesperson to smile and be friendly after failing to make a sale. Customers appreciate a sincere salesperson who has their best interest in mind.

You will have many more opportunities for success, particularly if you treat your customers with courtesy and respect. Be positive and leave the door open for future opportunities.

This is especially true when you and the buyer have established a good relationship. In such a case, the buyer may respond to an appeal for consideration in the next order.

If you have established excellent rapport with the buyer, you may be able to ask him or her what factors led to the decision to buy from another source. An appeal for constructive criticism may work for you if you have earned the buyer's respect from past interactions.

FEEDBACK

Experienced salespeople capitalize on defeat and come away from an unsuccessful selling experience with something to show for it. A customer who does not make a purchase is still a prospect for future business. Be alert to what purchases today's non-buyer may make in the future.

It is important to get feedback on why a customer did not buy. Try to learn what factor or factors influenced that decision. You may learn that the factors were out of the buyer's control.

For example, a new company policy or budgetary constraints may be the reason for not buying. Or you may learn that the buyer is purchasing a competitor's product because of its lower price.

Any feedback you receive can help you and your company in the future. For example, information obtained may help your company decide on future products, pricing, and marketing policies. Your company may learn a customer's opinion about what it needs to do to outsell competitors in the marketplace. The call report you complete will have all those details in it for management to review and act upon.

One popular misconception about selling is that salespeople are born, not made. It is true that effective salespeople possess certain behavioral characteristics. These characteristics include confidence, problem-solving abilities, honesty, and a sincere desire to be helpful.

However, success in selling is the result of training, apprenticeship, and experience. Learning one's products and how to handle various situations comes with experience and hard work.

 After You Read | **Section 15.1**

Review Key Concepts

1. **Contrast** getting minor agreements with pacing your closing.
2. **Describe** what you would say when closing the sale to create an ownership mentality.
3. **Identify** the specialized method you would use to close the sale in this situation: A customer is interested in an item but wants to wait to purchase it when it goes on sale.

Practice Academics

English Language Arts

4. Write a dialogue between two people closing a sale in either a retail or an organizational setting.

Mathematics

5. To close the sale, you offer layaway as an option, which requires a 20-percent deposit. What would the required deposit be on a $1,099 television?

Starting Hints To solve this problem, convert 20 percent to a decimal by moving the decimal point two places to the left. Multiply $1,099 by the decimal number to determine the amount of the deposit.

 connectED.mcgraw-hill.com

Print this graphic organizer.

For help, go to the Math Skills Handbook located at the back of this book.

READING GUIDE

Connect When have you been contacted by a company after making a purchase?

Objectives

- **Explain** the benefits of suggestion selling.
- **List** the rules for effective suggestion selling.
- **Demonstrate** appropriate specialized suggestion selling methods.
- **Discuss** strategies for maintaining and building a clientele.
- **Explain** the importance of after-sale activities and customer service.
- **Discuss** what salespeople can do to plan for future sales.

The Main Idea

After you close the sale, there are many things you can do to enhance customer satisfaction. Creating a positive relationship with customers will ensure future business.

Vocabulary

Content Vocabulary
- suggestion selling

Academic Vocabulary
You will find these words in your reading and on your tests. Make sure you know their meanings.
- appreciated
- volume

 MARKETING CORE FUNCTION

Selling

Graphic Organizer

Draw or print this chart to summarize key points for suggestion selling and for building a clientele.

 connectED.mcgraw-hill.com

Print this graphic organizer.

Suggestion Selling
Benefits
Rules
Methods

Section 15.2

Customer Satisfaction

SUGGESTION SELLING

Maintaining and building a clientele is crucial for future sales. The actual sale is just the beginning of a relationship with the customer. To keep customers, it is important to make a good impression, get to know your customers, and provide excellent customer service. One significant part of this process is suggestion selling.

Suggestion selling is selling additional goods or services to the customer. It involves selling other items to customers that will ultimately save time and money or make the original purchase more **appreciated**. It is important to the sales process because it helps to improve customer satisfaction, and it increases sales for the business.

Consider the customer who buys an electronic toy for a child, takes it home, and only then realizes that batteries are needed for it to function. That means another trip to the store before the child can play with the toy. The salesperson might have had a sure sale with a suggestion to buy batteries.

As You Read

Predict What makes some companies better than others in creating loyal customers?

BENEFITS OF SUGGESTION SELLING

Suggestion selling benefits the salesperson, the customer, and the company. You benefit because customers will want to do business with you again, so your sales will increase. Since salespeople are often evaluated according to their sales figures, you will be viewed as an effective salesperson. Your customers benefit because they are pleased with their purchase. The company benefits because the time and cost involved in suggestion selling is less than the cost of making the original sale.

Selling is a process of persuasion, so the principles of persuasion apply to it. A counter clerk at McDonald's will ask you whether you would like a drink, French fries, or a hot apple pie with your meal. The clerk is using a suggestion selling approach.

> **" The actual sale is the beginning of a relationship with a customer. "**

Consider the two purchases in the following chart. The second purchase includes an extra item suggested by the salesperson. Note that the extra time spent on suggestion selling significantly increased the firm's net profits. Expenses rose, but not in proportion to the sales **volume**. There are two reasons for this. First, less time and effort are needed for suggestion selling compared to the initial sale. Second, certain business expenses (such as utilities and rent) remain the same despite the extra sales activity.

Purchase 1		Purchase 2	
Pants	$75	Pants	$75
		Shirt	$35
Total	$75	Total	$110
Cost of goods	−$37	Cost of goods	−$55
Gross Profit	$38	Gross Profit	$55
Expenses	−$12	Expenses	−$15
Net profit	$26	Net profit	$40

RULES FOR SUGGESTION SELLING

Here are five basic rules for suggestion selling:

1. **Use suggestion selling after the customer has made a commitment to buy but before payment is made or the order written.** Introducing additional merchandise before the sale has been closed can create pressure for the customer. The only exception to this rule involves products whose accessories are a major benefit. If you are showing a retailer a new type of video game system, you may need to tell the retailer about the exciting new video games that will be sold in conjunction with that new system.

2. **Make your recommendation from the customer's point of view and give at least one reason for your suggestion.** You might say, "For your child to enjoy this toy immediately, you'll need two AAA batteries."

3. **Make the suggestion definite.** In most cases, general questions invite a negative response. Do not ask, "Will that be all?" Instead say, "This oil is recommended by the manufacturer for this engine."

4. **Show the item you are suggesting.** Merely talking about it is not enough. In many cases, the item will sell itself if you let the customer see and handle it. You may place a matching purse next to the shoes the customer has just decided to buy, adding some commentary. You might say, "This purse matches your shoes perfectly, doesn't it?"

5. **Make the suggestion positive.** You could say, "Let me show you the matching top for those slacks. It will complete the outfit beautifully." You would certainly never say, "You wouldn't want to look at scarves for your new coat, would you?" Such a negative statement shows a lack of enthusiasm or a lack of confidence on the part of the salesperson.

SUGGESTION SELLING METHODS

Suggestion selling methods are: offering related merchandise, recommending larger quantities, and calling attention to special sales opportunities. **Figure 15.1** shows examples of different ways to use suggestion selling.

OFFERING RELATED MERCHANDISE

Suggesting related merchandise, also known as *cross-selling*, increases the use or enjoyment of the customer's original purchase. Cross-selling is probably the easiest suggestion selling method. The related merchandise can be a good or service. For example, accessory items can be sold with the original purchase—perhaps a tie to match a new suit or a service contract for a new appliance.

RECOMMENDING LARGER QUANTITIES

Suggesting a larger quantity is often referred to as *up-selling*. This method works in retail settings when selling inexpensive items or when savings in money or time and convenience are involved. You may tell a customer who wants to buy one pair of socks, "One pair costs $4, but you can buy three pairs for $10.

In organizational sales situations, the salesperson may suggest a larger quantity so that the customer can take advantage of lower prices or special considerations like free shipping.

CALLING ATTENTION TO SPECIAL SALES OPPORTUNITIES

Salespeople are obligated to communicate special sales opportunities to their customers.

In retail sales, routinely inform your customer of the arrival of new merchandise. You could comment on a special sale by explaining, "We're having a one-day sale on all items in this department. You might want to look around before I process your purchase."

In organizational sales situations, sales representatives show new items to their customers after they have completed the sale of merchandise requested. Thus, the salesperson has an opportunity to establish a rapport with the customer before introducing new merchandise.

Reading Check

Identify Describe a scenario in which you would use up-selling.

FIGURE 15.1 | Suggestion Selling

Suggestion-selling involves selling other items to customers that will ultimately save time and money or make the original purchase more enjoyable. Let's see how suggestion selling methods might be used by a sales representative that sells goods and services for pets.

UP-SELLING A salesperson who sold dogsled harnesses may suggest larger quantities to make a customer eligible for special discounts.

CROSS-SELLING The salesperson should suggest related items of merchandise, such as pet treats to reward good dogs.

SPECIAL SALES OPPORTUNITIES When a company runs a special promotion on products unrelated to the original purchase, or wants to introduce a new product or service, like pet photography, it is up to the sales representative to share that information with the customer. These might be suggested after making the original sale.

Ingram Publishing; Ariel Skelley/Blend Images LLC; Ingram Publishing

MAINTAINING AND BUILDING A CLIENTELE

Making a sale is the first step in maintaining and building a clientele. Maintaining a clientele is necessary for repeat sales, which are necessary for businesses to be successful. Also, satisfied customers often help generate new customers by telling others about their positive experiences. It also costs more to find new customers than it costs to keep current customers satisfied. Positive customer- or client-relations require a lot of attention after the sale. After-sale activities by the sales and customer service staff, as well as planning for future sales, are key factors in building a clientele.

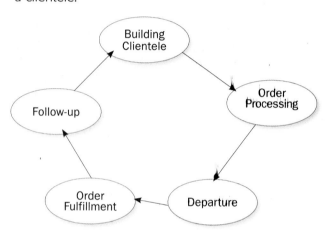

AFTER-SALES ACTIVITIES

The time you spend with your customer after a sale is just as important, if not more important, than the time you spent making the sale. After-sale activities include order processing, departure, order fulfillment, and follow-up. All these activities need to be handled in such a way that the customer wants to do business with you again. Satisfied customers become steady customers, which is a goal in selling: to generate repeat business.

ORDER PROCESSING

In retail selling, bag the merchandise with care. Products such as glassware may require individual wrapping before bagging. Expensive clothing may be left on hangers and enclosed in special bags made for that purpose. Work quickly to bag your customer's merchandise and complete the payment process.

In business-to-business sales, complete the paperwork quickly and accurately. Review the order with your customer and leave the customer with a copy of it along with your business card.

Cross-Selling

Selling related merchandise is an easy method of suggestion selling. *What is the key to suggesting related merchandise, as clearly identified in this L.L. Bean catalog page?*

Great alone, better together

DEPARTURE

Before customers depart or before you leave your clients' offices, reassure your clientele of their wise buying choices. If an item needs special care or specific instructions, take the time to educate your customer about it. You may want to remind the customer, for example, that to get the best results from a Teflon-coated frying pan, it should be preheated. When selling new automobiles, this would be a good time to show your customers how to work some of the electronic devices, such as the GPS system. This extra time spent with customers helps ensure customer satisfaction.

Always thank your customers. Even when a customer does not buy, express your gratitude for the time and attention given to you. Invite customers back to the store, or ask for permission to call again in the near future.

ORDER FULFILLMENT

In organizational selling situations, order fulfillment is based on the purchase order or sales order. If a purchase order involves special instructions, salespeople need to communicate those special instructions to other company employees. This helps to ensure that everything is done to the customer's precise specifications.

For example, salespeople may alert the shipping department when part of an order is to be shipped to different locations or at different times. Salespeople may speak directly with the manufacturing manager regarding specifications for embroidery of a customer's name on employee uniforms. The salesperson's attention to these details can avoid potential problems with the current sale and future sales.

In a retail store, order fulfillment is a simple process of the customer paying for merchandise and carrying it away.

In telemarketing or online sales, order fulfillment gets more complicated. It includes taking the order, financial processing (such as credit card information), picking the right product, packing it well, and shipping it according to the customer's preference. In some companies, fulfillment also includes customer service, technical support, managing inventory, and handling returns and refunds. Success often depends as much on appropriate fulfillment strategies as it does on having the right product at the right price. Some of the most successful online retailers have established their own fulfillment centers to ensure prompt delivery. Amazon.com, BarnesandNoble.com, and Dell® Computer all have their own fulfillment centers. Another approach is to outsource fulfillment to a third party.

MARKETING CASE STUDY

Selling Fitness at Equinox

Equinox Fitness is an upscale fitness club with locations in several U.S. cities. Its original system of developing and following up on leads was paper-based. Frustration with the outdated sales system created a high turnover of sales staff. It was clear that selling fitness memberships had to move into the computer age.

Microsoft Solution

Equinox had a lot of information about its customers, so it knew its target market. But it needed a boost, provided by the Microsoft Gold Certified Partner, Customer Effective. This system improved the process of member applications, while gathering data for sales presentations. Equinox also created its own Equinox Selling Process (ESP), a sales training tool for staff at its clubs. ESP provides sales techniques and support to help the sales staff close membership sales.

English Language Arts

Evaluate Discuss with a partner the risks and benefits involved in making a system-wide change to an established selling process. What are the advantages of using modern technology if the trade-off is having to retrain the entire sales force?

This allows a company to concentrate its efforts on marketing the products. The goal in all forms of order fulfillment is to make the customer happy.

FOLLOW-UP

The follow-up includes making arrangements to follow through on all promises made during the sales process. It also includes checking on your customer's satisfaction with his or her purchase. Here are a few follow-up ideas:

▶ Call the shipping department to confirm a special delivery date.

▶ Check to make sure that delivery occurs as promised.

▶ Call the customer and explain any delay.

▶ Phone customers a week or two after the purchase to see if they are happy with the selection.

▶ Send a thank-you note with your business card attached.

CUSTOMER SERVICE

The role of customer service cannot be emphasized enough as a part of developing selling relationships. Salespeople do their job generating new customers. Customer service is needed to keep those customers happy. Businesses recognize the importance of customer service.

Employees provide excellent customer service to maintain their clientele. Customer service has many dimensions. It includes offering a variety of special services and handling customer complaints.

OFFERING SPECIAL SERVICES

Many customer services are designed to keep customers loyal by providing ongoing communication with them and help after the sale. Some of these special services include e-mail and social media interaction, online support, special retail and vendor services, and customer training.

E-Mail and Social Media

Businesses have recognized the benefits of keeping communication lines open with customers on an ongoing basis. Some use e-mail to provide customers with information regarding new products and special promotions on a regular basis. Businesses are legally required to get permission to send customers email. Customers must "opt-in" and agree to receive the emails. A business must also give customers the opportunity to "opt-out" if they no longer want to get emails from the company.

Social media opportunities include weblogs (blogs), Facebook®, Twitter®, and other Internet platforms that permit businesses to create a dialogue with customers on a frequent basis.

Proper handling of after-sale activities helps to ensure customer satisfaction with the entire shopping experience. *What else should the salesperson do before the customer departs?*

After-Sale Activities

The goal of customer service, whether handled by a customer service department or by the salesperson, is customer satisfaction and retention. **Why is customer service an important part of sales?**

Customer Satisfaction

Company CEOs may blog about new products and services. Facebook and Twitter allow companies to interact with customers. Businesses on Facebook may create games or other special activities to engage customers. Customers' comments recorded on Facebook and Twitter often get responses from the company. This ongoing dialogue between the customer and the company provides customers with a personal response. It also helps companies address unforeseen problems they may not have discovered otherwise.

Online Customer Support

Many retailers and manufacturers offer answers to frequently asked questions (FAQs) on their respective Web sites. Their Web sites may also provide a link to a customer service center. This link allows customers to ask questions and receive replies via e-mail or a phone call from a customer service representative. This online customer support is extremely useful with products that require installation or manipulation.

Special Retail Services

Many retailers offer a bridal and/or baby registry. Engaged couples and expecting parents select items they like, and that list is made available to anyone who wants to buy them gifts. In some auto dealerships, specific customer service representatives are assigned to each customer to handle appointments and questions with auto problems and regular servicing. Merchandise returns and customer inquiries are often handled by a special customer service department.

Special Vendor Services

Large retailers may require vendors to provide additional services as part of their sales agreement. Some of those services may include keeping track of retail inventory, providing merchandising services, restocking promotional materials, and designing packages to meet their shelf-space requirements. A retailer that is very important to a vendor may employ its own staff whose sole responsibility is servicing that one big account.

Customer Training

When a product is purchased by a company that requires instruction before using it, hands-on training may be provided to customers. Apple®, Inc., offers everyone who purchases an Apple computer one year of free training.

More advanced instruction may be offered to companies when a new computer software program is installed. Key employees may attend classes provided by the vendor. Instead of formal classes at the company's headquarters, the training may be held in the customer's place of business or at a convenient location for the customer.

Manufacturers that sell products for resale may provide training materials to retailers' and wholesalers' sales staff. Computer-aided instruction, videos, training manuals, and other items may be used to educate the retail sales staff about a product's features and benefits. The manufacturer's sales representative may also provide personal instruction about how to handle customer questions and possible objections.

Nadja Specht
Chief Marketer
Nuvota, LLC

What do you do at work?

I teach small business owners marketing fundamentals, using plain language, through marketing workshops, coaching, and consulting. This allows those who are unfamiliar with new terms and technology to understand how they can use today's marketing tools to attract customers. I want clients to get the marketing knowledge they need to make decisions independently so they can sell their products effectively.

What is your key to success?

It helps to have a great education, the right professional experiences, and to learn from mistakes. Beyond that, the key is to follow my instincts, believe in myself, and have endurance.

What skills are most important to you?

Analytical thinking: being detail-oriented and comfortable with number crunching. Conceptual thinking: not getting overwhelmed by details and unknowns, but creating a high-level conceptual framework. Emotional intelligence: being able to listen and adapt to clients' different personalities and needs to deliver quality service.

 connectED.mcgraw-hill.com

Read more about this career and get a Career Exploration Activity.

HANDLING CUSTOMER COMPLAINTS

A manufacturer often has customer service representatives that handle telephone and e-mail customer complaints. Many companies also provide 800 numbers so customers can easily contact them with questions or complaints.

In business-to-business sales, customer complaints should be relayed to the sales representatives responsible for those customers. In some cases, the personal attention of the sales representative is required to ensure complete customer satisfaction and to maintain good relations with the customer.

How these complaints are handled is crucial to maintaining clientele. Customers expect immediate action when they file complaints. Positive customer-client relations require compassionate and understanding customer service personnel and sales associates who are problem solvers. The main goal is customer satisfaction.

In some cases, going the extra mile may be needed to keep a customer. For example, if a customer complains that a product is defective, you may have to replace it or offer a full refund. If the wrong product was delivered, you may have to use an overnight delivery service to get the product to the customer in time. In essence, you need to do whatever is necessary (within reason) to solve the problem and make the customer happy.

PLANNING FUTURE SALES

Successful salespeople strive to develop relationships with their customers and work to improve their sales techniques. Getting to know a customer personally is helpful when making future sales calls. To become an effective salesperson, self-evaluation is imperative.

KEEPING A CLIENT FILE

You can use the time immediately after the sale to plan for your next encounter with the customer. Take notes on your conversation with the customer. Keep this in a file for future reference. In retail sales, note a customer's preference in color, style, and size, as well as the person's address and telephone number. In business-to-business selling, record personal information on the buyer's marital status, children, and hobbies to assist with future sales visits. Record changes in buying patterns that may lead to future sales. Note any future service dates for appliances or cars so that you can send a reminder when the time comes. Be sure to inform your company of any changes you uncover, such as changes in personnel responsible for buying, as well as address or telephone changes, so that company files can stay up to date.

EVALUATE YOUR SALES EFFORTS

Even if your company has a formal method of reviewing your efforts, you should conduct your own evaluation. In your evaluation, consider the following:

▶ What were the strong points of your sales presentation?

▶ How could you have improved your performance?

▶ What would you do differently next time?

▶ What can you do now to solidify your relationship with your customer if you made the sale?

Asking yourself these questions can help you improve your selling skills as well as your business skills in general. They will enable you to look forward to your next sales opportunity. That kind of attitude will help you become more effective with each sales contact. It will also help you become more successful in building a strong relationship with your customers.

Some businesses send questionnaires or call customers to check on how well they were treated by the sales and service staff. The results of these surveys are passed on to salespeople so they can improve their sales techniques.

 After You Read | **Section 15.2**

Review Key Concepts

1. **Explain** how suggestion selling benefits the salesperson, company, and customer.
2. **Name** three related items that could be used for suggestion selling after a customer's decision to buy a tent for camping purposes.
3. **Discuss** what a salesperson should do as a follow-up to a sale.

Academic Skills

English Language Arts

4. Assume you are training a new salesperson. Prepare a written plan that covers suggestion selling, after-sale activities, and planning for future sales. Use a product of your choice to provide examples of related merchandise to suggest and examples of how to build a relationship with customers after the sale.

Mathematics

5. You sold a $460 item via the Internet to a European customer, a Japanese customer, and a customer in New Zealand. Use the chart below to calculate the total amount due for the product with duties and customs for each of the three customers.

	Europe	Japan	New Zealand
Duties & Customs	20%	9%	50%

Math Concept **Ways of Representing Numbers** A percentage can be represented by a number that is less than one.

Starting Hints To solve this problem, convert each of the percents to a decimal by moving the decimal point two places to the left, or divide them by 100. Multiply $460 by each of the decimals to determine the duties and customs charges for each country. Add the duties and custom charges of each country to $460 to determine the total cost for each customer.

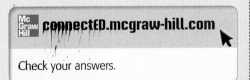

connectED.mcgraw-hill.com

Check your answers.

For help, go to the **Math Skills Handbook** located at the back of this book.

Closing the Sale

Four specialized methods for closing a sale are: which close, standing-room-only close (SRO), direct close, and service close.

Suggestion selling is important because it helps generate more sales revenue for a company and helps to create more satisfied customers.

Review and Activities

Written Summary

- Customer buying signals help a salesperson determine a customer's readiness to buy.
- Close the sale as soon as the customer is ready to buy.
- Use success in answering objections or presenting a product as an opportunity to close.
- Help customers make a decision and create an ownership mentality.
- Four specialized methods for closing a sale include: the direct close, the which close, the standing-room-only close, and the service close.
- Suggestion selling helps generate sales revenue and create satisfied customers.
- Three specialized suggestion-selling methods include the following: offering related merchandise, or cross-selling; selling larger quantities, or up-selling; and calling attention to special sales opportunities.
- After-sales activities are important for maintaining and building a clientele. They include order processing, departure, order fulfillment, follow-up, customer service, keeping client files, and evaluating sales efforts.

Review Content Vocabulary and Academic Vocabulary

1. Use each of these vocabulary words in a written sentence.

Content Vocabulary
- closing the sale (p. 341)
- buying signals (p. 341)
- trial close (p. 342)
- which close (p. 344)
- standing-room-only close (p. 344)
- direct close (p. 344)
- service close (p. 345)
- suggestion selling (p. 349)

Academic Vocabulary
- commit (p. 342)
- perseverance (p. 346)
- appreciated (p. 349)
- volume (p. 349)

Assess for Understanding

2. **Identify** What are customer buying signals?
3. **Justify** Which specialized closing method(s) would you use when a customer does not have enough cash to make the purchase today?
4. **Discuss** Why is suggestion selling an important part of the sales process?
5. **Explain** Why is using suggestion selling before closing the sale a problem?
6. **Write** What would you include in a follow-up letter to a new customer?
7. **Discuss** How can effective customer service influence the retention of clientele?
8. **Define** What are the definitions of the terms *direct close* and *service close*?
9. **Plan** How would you maintain and build clientele for a company that has a few electricians who are hired for jobs with contractors and many more electricians who handle maintenance and repairs for businesses and residences?

21st Century Skills

Communications Skills

10. Role Play With another student playing the role of a customer, perform a role play in which you demonstrate how you would sell a product of your choice to an individual customer. Be sure to close the sale and conduct suggestion selling as part of the role play presentation. Finalize the sale by taking payment and packaging the product.

Financial Literacy Skills

11. What's Your Commission? You take an order from an organizational customer that includes the following items: 35 boots @ $49.50 each, 70 gloves @ $8.50 each, and 25 jackets @ $65 each. This order qualifies for a 5-percent discount. Determine your 8-percent commission on this sale. Try using a spreadsheet program to display your calculations.

Everyday Ethics

12. House Accounts A salesperson closes the sale on one of the biggest accounts she has ever landed. It has potential to grow bigger. The vice president of sales congratulates her and then proceeds to explain a company policy regarding *house accounts:* All large accounts are reclassified as house accounts and are serviced by the vice president. This policy ensures continuity and provides large accounts with special attention. The sales rep would earn commission on the initial sale, but not on future sales for this account. Do you think this selling policy is ethical? Why or why not?

e-Marketing Skills

13. Online Suggestion Selling Visit two online companies that sell snowboards and find products that can be used for suggestion selling. Share your opinion on how effective these companies are at suggestion selling. What improvements to the Web site would you suggest to increase sales of additional merchandise?

Build Academic Skills

Social Studies

14. Economics In a recessionary period, what can companies do to help salespeople close more sales? Research the most recent recession and provide examples of what two companies have done to help close sales.

Science

15. Applied Technology Research at least two different online sales companies to identify and evaluate the strategies used to close a sale and provide online customer support. How do these practices differ between consumer and organizational customers?

Mathematics

16. Managing Time Sara is a sales associate for a telecommunications company. She attends an average of 21 client meetings each month. Her manager has recently asked sales associates to increase the number of client meetings they have each month by 30 percent. How many meetings will Sara then have?

> **Math Concept** **Relationships Among Numbers: Percents** To determine the percent of a number, for example 25 percent of 50, multiply the number (50) by the decimal equivalent of the given percent (0.25). If a value is increased by a certain percent, add the two values together.

For help, go to the **Math Skills Handbook** located at the back of this book.

Standardized Test Practice

Directions Read the following questions. On a separate piece of paper, write the best possible answer for each one.

1. Which of the following sales tactics is not considered effective suggestion selling?

    A. Up selling—suggesting a larger quantity to save money or time

    B. Cross selling—suggesting related merchandise

    C. Special sales—suggesting products on sale or new items

    D. Down selling—suggesting products the customer does not need

2. It is a good idea to use words like "I" and "me" when you are trying to create an ownership mentality for your customers.

    T

    F

3. A _____ close is the initial effort to close a sale.

Test-Taking Tip

Budget your time, making sure you have enough time to answer all the questions on a test.

DECA Connection Role Play

Assistant Manager Men's Clothing Store

Situation You are the assistant manager of an independent, upscale men's clothing store. Store sales have been declining. Top management believes that the decline in sales is because the sales associates are not well trained in closing the sale, suggesting related items, or developing an on-going relationship with customers.

Activity You are to prepare a training plan for the sales staff that demonstrates how to close the sale, how to suggest additional merchandise, and what can be done as a follow-up to keep customers loyal. The store's regional manager (judge) wants to see your plan before you present it at the next staff meeting.

Evaluation You will be evaluated on how well you meet the following performance indicators:

- Close the sale.
- Demonstrate suggestion selling.
- Explain the role of customer service as a component of selling relationships.
- Explain key factors in building a clientele.
- Plan follow-up strategies for use in selling.

connectED.mcgraw-hill.com

Download the Competitive Events Workbook for more Role-Play Practice.

Chapter 16

Section 16.1
Sales Transactions

Section 16.2
Cash Registers

Section 16.3
Purchasing, Invoicing,
and Shipping

using math in sales

Visual Literacy In most stores a computer called a Point of Sale (POS) terminal functions as an electronic cash register. This allows the business to keep track of sales, inventory, and new merchandise. *How many stores where you shop do not use electronic cash registers?*

Discovery Project

Survey of Math for Sales

Essential Question Why are math skills important in sales?

Project Goal

Conduct research or make observations regarding the importance of math in sales. Identify at least four instances of the use of math in sales. Share this information with your class in a role play or presentation.

Ask Yourself...

- What math skills have you used when you are buying products?
- What are some of the specific uses of math that you might likely need in sales?
- Do you have a good basic background in the math skills that you would need?
- What math skills will you need to brush up on to be efficient in sales?

 Role Play Create a brief skit or presentation that demonstrates the uses of math in sales.

---

 connectED.mcgraw-hill.com

Activity
Get a worksheet activity about using math in sales.

Evaluate
Download a rubric you can use to evaluate your project.

DECA Connection

DECA Event Role Play

Concepts in this chapter are related to DECA competitive events that involve either an interview or role play.

Performance Indicators The performance indicators represent key skills and knowledge. Your key to success in DECA competitive events is relating them to concepts in this chapter.

- Describe the use of technology in operations.
- Calculate miscellaneous charges.
- Select the best shipping method.
- Demonstrate systematic behavior.
- Organize information.

DECA Prep

Role Play Practice role-playing with the DECA Connection competitive-event activity at the end of this chapter. More information on DECA events can be found on DECA's Web site.

READING GUIDE

Before You Read

Predict What kinds of math does a salesperson use to finish a transaction?

Objectives

- **List** all types of retail sales transactions.
- **Process** purchases, returns, and exchanges.
- **Generate** and process sales documentation.
- **Calculate** sales tax, discounts, and shipping charges.

The Main Idea

There are many ways to complete a purchase transaction. Basic math skills are essential in all sales transactions.

Vocabulary

Content Vocabulary
- sales check
- layaway
- on-approval sale
- cash-on-delivery (COD) sale
- sales tax
- allowance

Academic Vocabulary
You will find these words in your reading and on your tests. Make sure you know their meanings.
- transfer
- area

Graphic Organizer

Draw or print this chart to list six types of retail sales transactions.

Types of Retail Sales Transactions		
1. Cash or Check	2.	3.
4.	5.	6.

 connectED.mcgraw-hill.com

Print this graphic organizer.

MARKETING CORE FUNCTION

Selling

Sales Transactions

TYPES OF RETAIL SALES

Most retail sales will use cash, debit, or credit card sales for consumer goods. However, you may deal with layaway (or will-call) sales, on-approval sales, and cash-on-delivery (COD) sales. You will also handle returns, exchanges, allowances, sales tax, and shipping charges.

As You Read

Connect List the differences in handling various methods of payment.

CASH OR CHECK SALES

A cash sale is a transaction in which the customer pays with cash or a check. When the customer uses cash, you record the transaction on the register, give the customer change and a receipt, and wrap the item. When a customer writes a check, you may need to verify his or her identity by requesting a driver's license or another form of identification. You will have to learn the policy of your employer about accepting checks.

SALES CHECKS

A **sales check** is a written record of a sales transaction. It includes such information as the date of the transaction, the items purchased, the purchase prices, sales tax, and the total amount due. It is valuable to a customer as a receipt.

A complete sales check shows the customer's name, address, and phone number. It may have the time of the sale and the name of the salesperson. Handwritten sales checks are less common than printed ones. Some businesses still use them. The transaction is recorded in a sales-check book that has at least two copies of each form. One copy is given to the customer. One is kept by the business as a record of the sale.

MATH SKILLS FOR HANDWRITTEN SALES CHECKS

Math is necessary when preparing handwritten sales checks. The five steps of this process are shown in **Figure 16.1** on page 366. Occasionally, you will not be given a unit price, and you will need to calculate it on your own. This occurs when items are sold in multiple quantities, such as three reams of paper for $18. To find the selling price of one item in an instance like this, you divide the total price by the number of items: One ream of paper in this example would be $6 ($18 ÷ 3).

When the result of the division is uneven, any fraction of a cent is rounded up and charged to the customer. The price of one ream of paper when three reams are $16.99 is calculated as follows: $16.99 ÷ 3 = $5.6633 or $5.67.

> **" As a salesperson or cashier, you will handle several types of sales transactions. "**

DEBIT CARD SALES

Businesses that have an encrypted, or coded, personal identification number (PIN) pad can ask customers whether they would like to pay with debit or credit. Customers who choose "debit," key in their private PIN. The terminal then dials out and checks to see whether there are enough funds in the customer's account to pay for the sale. If so, the funds are transferred to the merchant's account. The customer does not need to sign a sales draft.

FIGURE 16.1 Sales Check—Multiple Purchases

Adding Complexity The basic sales check becomes more complicated when the customer buys several items or several units of one item. *How can you be sure that the final sales check is accurate?*

Step 1—Multiply unit price times quantity for each item and extend the amounts to the last column. Remember that the last two digits on the right are cents. Place a decimal point to their left, or enter them to the right of the vertical line dividing the last column into two unequal parts.

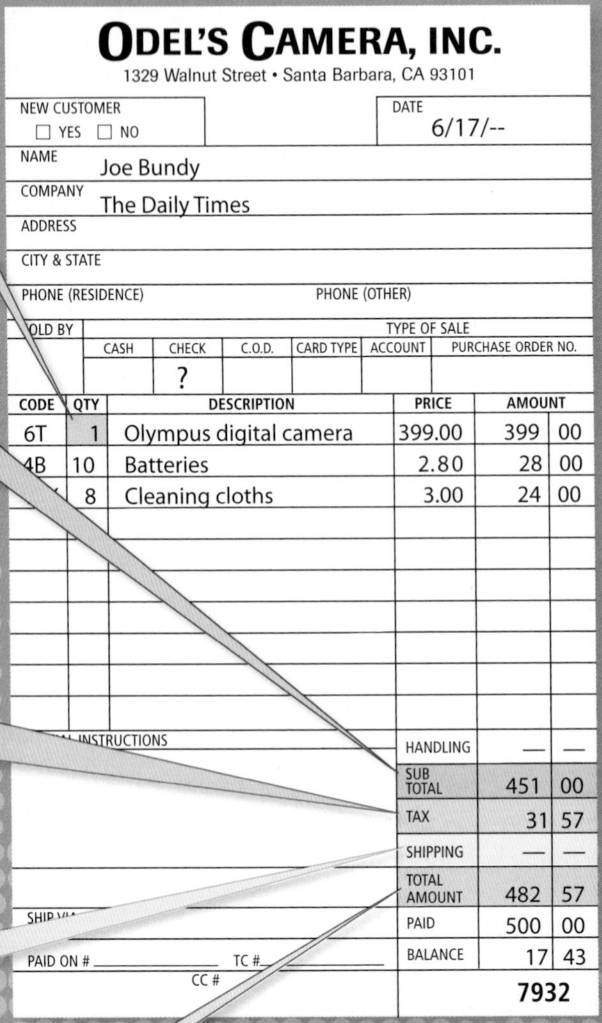

Step 2—Add item amounts to arrive at the merchandise subtotal. Enter this figure on the appropriate line.

Step 3—Calculate sales tax or look it up in a tax table. The buyer must pay sales tax on all retail sales totals. It is a percentage of the merchandise subtotal. In most states, food and prescription medicine are exempt from sales tax, as are shipping charges.

Step 4—Calculate shipping charges. You need to decide if you will use U.S. mail or a specific express mail carrier.

Step 5—Add subtotal, tax, and shipping to get the purchase total. This is the amount the customer will pay.

ODEL'S CAMERA, INC.
1329 Walnut Street • Santa Barbara, CA 93101

NEW CUSTOMER ☐ YES ☐ NO

DATE 6/17/--

NAME Joe Bundy

COMPANY The Daily Times

ADDRESS

CITY & STATE

PHONE (RESIDENCE)   PHONE (OTHER)

SOLD BY

TYPE OF SALE

	CASH	CHECK	C.O.D.	CARD TYPE	ACCOUNT	PURCHASE ORDER NO.
		?				

CODE	QTY	DESCRIPTION	PRICE	AMOUNT	
6T	1	Olympus digital camera	399.00	399	00
4B	10	Batteries	2.80	28	00
	8	Cleaning cloths	3.00	24	00

SPECIAL INSTRUCTIONS

HANDLING	—	—
SUB TOTAL	451	00
TAX	31	57
SHIPPING	—	—
TOTAL AMOUNT	482	57
PAID	500	00
BALANCE	17	43

SHIP VIA

PAID ON # _____ TC # _____

CC # _____

7932

ADVANTAGES OF DEBIT CARD PAYMENTS

The bank that issues the debit card charges the merchant a flat rate per sale, such as $0.59 per sale, regardless of the amount of the sale. Debit cards are a convenience to many customers who prefer not to use a credit card. It also benefits those who do not carry either a checkbook or large amounts of cash or who cannot get approval for a credit card. Most merchants prefer payment by debit card to payment by check because they have access to the money much sooner. There is also no risk of delays in payment due to insufficient funds. The cost to the merchant is less than when the customer pays with a credit card.

CREDIT CARD SALES

Statistics show that by accepting credit cards, businesses can increase sales by as much as 40 percent. Primarily because of this potential for increased sales, most businesses today accept one or more of the major credit cards. These cards are Visa®, MasterCard®, American Express®, and Discover®.

CREDIT CARD PAYMENT ON THE INTERNET

Credit cards are also the most frequently used method of payment for Internet purchases. For safety reasons, the payment data (card number, expiration date, security code, cardholder's identity) sent via the Internet are encrypted. This makes it more difficult for unauthorized individuals to gain access to a customer's card numbers. Many Internet sites also allow the consumer to make purchases with a gift certificate that has a security code the customer must enter.

CREDIT CARD PAYMENT COSTS TO THE MERCHANT

If a company accepts credit cards, it pays a fee to the bank or agency that handles the billing and recordkeeping for each card transaction processed. This fee is a percentage of credit sales based on a sliding scale, which means that it varies according to the size of the store account and how the charges are processed.

Suppose one store had Visa sales of $100,000 in one month and another store had Visa sales of only $2,000 in that same month. The company with the sales of $100,000 would pay a smaller percentage for handling.

DIGITAL NATION

Making Online Purchases Safe

Identity theft and credit card theft are concerns for many online shoppers. In fact, a recent study showed that almost half of all shoppers have abandoned an online order because they were worried that an online retail Web site might not be secure. This represents billions of dollars in lost sales.

Encryption and Secure Connections Reputable online businesses transmit customers' personal and financial information using encryption, or data scrambling. Only authorized users who have the correct "key" can unscramble the data. Data security "trustmarks," such as those from TRUSTe and VeriSign, demonstrate that an online store is secure against data theft. Secure e-commerce sites also use an "HTTP secure" connection. A Web page with a secure connection for purchases has the letters "https" at the beginning of its Web address.

English Language Arts

Evaluate Visit an e-commerce Web site. What information does the company offer about its security practices? Place an item in the shopping cart and look for trustmarks on the checkout page. Does the site seem secure? Discuss your findings with the class.

 connectED.mcgraw-hill.com

Get a Digital Nation Activity.

HOW ARE CREDIT CARD PAYMENTS PROCESSED?

For many businesses, the amount of each credit card sale is electronically deposited in the business's bank account as the sale is made. A credit card sales check, or receipt, is issued by the cash register. The credit card company deducts its service charges from the store's bank account.

PRACTICE 1: CREDIT CARD FEES

Calculate the impact credit card fees would have on the business described below.

1. At Carol's Pearls and Stones, Visa sales are usually between $13,000 and $15,000 per month. The Visa handling charge is a sliding scale. For $10,000 to $14,999, it charges 3 percent of sales; for $15,000 to $19,999, 2.5 percent; and for $20,000 to $29,999, 2 percent. That means that for a purchase of $22,000, Visa collects a fee of 3 percent on the first $14,999, a fee of 2.5 percent on the next $5,000, and a fee of 2 percent on the remaining $2,001. Visa collects a total of $614.97.

   a. Carol had $15,500 in Visa sales in one month. How much more did she earn than if sales had been $14,300?

   b. How much would Carol have earned in that month if her shop had made $21,000 in Visa sales?

2. Carol has decided to accept the Diners Club card at her shop. The handling charges are 1 percent higher than those for Visa at each sales level. If Carol had $19,000 in Diners Club sales, how much more would she pay in handling fees than she would have for the same amount in Visa sales?

3. Carol had $13,600 in cash sales, $14,800 in Diners Club sales, and $15,200 in Visa sales one month. What were her net sales after handling charges?

---

 connectED.mcgraw-hill.com

Check your answers to all Practice sets.

The store normally has access to the customers' payment funds the next day. However, some businesses opt to have credit card fees deducted monthly.

Today businesses rarely take manual credit card slips to the bank. Most businesses process manual credit card sales over the phone, using an automated system provided by their bank. This can also be done by keying in the credit card and sales information directly into their credit card terminal.

GETTING CREDIT AUTHORIZATION

While credit cards are a convenient alternative to more traditional forms of payment, some fraud is always possible. Many retail businesses set a floor limit, a maximum amount a customer is allowed to charge to a credit card. This practice protects them against losses due to the use of stolen or fake credit cards. Illicit charges are disputed by the true cardholder and the credit card company. The store is liable for only the amount of the floor limit.

Fraud Users of stolen credit cards test the card by making small purchases, a practice that can alert the company that the card may have been stolen.

Most modern cash registers include an integrated credit authorizer. An electronic credit authorizer can also be a device that reads data encoded on credit cards. The sales clerk inputs the amount of the sale into the device. The data is then transmitted to a computer, which returns an approval or disapproval in less than a minute.

RECORDING CREDIT OR DEBIT CARD SALES

As a salesperson in retail business, you will probably process many credit card sales. If the transaction is manual, you write the information on the sales check by hand or use a mechanical imprinter to **transfer** the customer's name and account number to the sales slip. You give one copy to the customer and keep one for the seller.

Another copy goes to the bank or credit card agency. Electronic recording of credit card sales is so common that it has almost completely replaced manually prepared sales checks.

LAYAWAY SALES

Removing merchandise from stock and keeping it in a separate storage **area** until the customer pays for it is called **layaway**, or will-call. The customer makes a deposit on the merchandise and agrees to pay for the purchase within a certain time period. The customer receives the merchandise when the bill is fully paid. If it is not paid for within the time period, the goods are returned to stock. The deposit is not refunded.

ON-APPROVAL SALES

An **on-approval sale** is an agreement that allows a customer to take merchandise (usually clothing) home for further consideration. Some department and specialty stores extend this special privilege to their regular customers.

If the goods are not returned within an agreed-upon time, the sale is final. The customer must then send a check or return to the store to pay for the merchandise. Credit card information may be taken from the customer so that the sale can be processed if the customer decides to keep the item. This is a safe way for retailers to handle on-approval sales because there is much less risk involved.

CASH-ON-DELIVERY SALES

A **cash-on-delivery (COD) sale** is a sales transaction that occurs when a customer pays for merchandise at the time of delivery. Because the customer must be present to receive the merchandise being delivered, COD sales are not as efficient as other types of sales transactions.

Reading Check

Summarize What are the different types of retail sales transactions?

FIGURE 16.2 **Refund Slip**

Refund Policy Most businesses give customers refunds or exchanges under certain circumstances. *Why do stores often insist that customers have a sales receipt before giving a refund?*

BFF Fashions		REFUND SLIP		
STORE NO.	DATE	ITEM RETURNED	AMOUNT	
	2---	SKIRT	45	00
NAME Stacy McClintock				
ADDRESS 777 Seaview Lane				
CITY & STATE Marblehead, MA 01945				
TELEPHONE NO. 781-882-0252		TAX	3	15
CUSTOMER'S SIGNATURE *Stacy McClintock*		TOTAL AMOUNT	48	15
EMPLOYEE NO. 6P	AUTHORIZED BY *G. Smith*	REASON FOR RETURN Wrong color		
		No refunds after 30 days; No refunds without receipt.		

READING GUIDE

Before You Read

Connect When have you ordered something by mail? What types of forms are involved?

Objectives

- **Prepare** purchase orders and invoices.
- **Explain** shipping terms.

The Main Idea

Writing a purchase order, creating an invoice, and figuring shipping are part of the sales process, especially in business-to-business sales.

Vocabulary

Content Vocabulary
- purchase order (PO)
- invoice
- terms for delivery
- free-on-board (FOB)

Academic Vocabulary
You will find these words in your reading and on your tests. Make sure you know their meanings.
- overseas
- tradition

Graphic Organizer

Draw or print this chart to list the six types of information needed to complete a purchase order or invoice.

Information Needed	
Purchase Order	Invoice
1. Item number	

 connectED.mcgraw-hill.com

Print this graphic organizer.

Section 16.3 | Purchasing, Invoicing, and Shipping

PURCHASE ORDERS

A **purchase order (PO)** is a legal contract between the buyer and the supplier. This document lists the quantity, price, and description of the products ordered, along with the terms of payment and delivery. In **Figure 16.3**, notice the information routinely included in a purchase order:

- ▶ **Item number** The vendor's catalog designation for the merchandise ordered

- ▶ **Quantity** The number of units ordered

- ▶ **Description** What is being ordered

- ▶ **Unit** How the item is packaged and priced (individually, by the dozen, or by the team)

As You Read

Contrast List the differences between purchase orders and invoices.

- ▶ **Unit cost** The price per unit

- ▶ **Total** The extension, or the result of multiplying the number of units by the cost per unit

Note that if you order several items on the same PO, the total of all extensions is entered at the bottom of the total column. This amount is used to compute sales tax, if any.

> **" When a business purchases something from another business, the first step is to prepare a purchase order. "**

FIGURE 16.3 | **Purchase Order**

A Legal Document A purchase order is a legal contract between a buyer and a seller.
How would you determine the extension cost of an item from the unit cost?

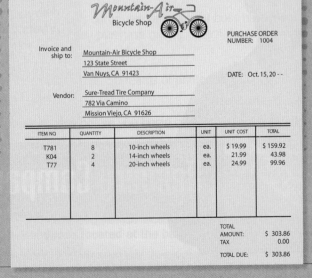

 21st Century Skills

Communication Skills

10. Convincing the Boss You are the buyer in a women's specialty clothing shop. Almost every day someone comes into the shop and asks for a particular brand of shoe. Your manager has not carried that brand of shoe because he does not like doing business with the company. You have calculated how much money the store is losing by not carrying the shoes. Write an e-mail to your manager that explains how much more income the store would gain if it carried the shoes.

Financial Literacy Skills

11. Business Loan You are planning to open a bicycle shop. You will need a loan for $15,000 to get started. A bank will loan you the money at 6 percent, with payments for 5 years of $289.99 per month. A credit union will loan you the money at 5.5 percent, with payments for 5 years of $286.52 per month. What will be the total cost over 5 years for each loan?

e-Marketing Skills

12. Customer Satisfaction Your company is considering expanding its e-marketing division. Your boss has asked you to research how satisfied customers are with their online buying experience. Use your own online buying experiences and ask others for ideas, and then prepare a questionnaire to be circulated to learn the level of satisfaction with purchasing goods online. Here are some ideas to consider:

- How will you measure customer satisfaction?
- What technological resources does your company have?
- When will the questionnaire be shared with customers?
- How will the questionnaire's results be shared with customers?

Build Academic Skills

Social Studies

13. Digital Archives Use the Internet to research the history of digital-scanning technology and its use. Use presentation software to create a report on your findings.

English Language Arts

14. Forms of Payment Most retail stores accept cash, checks, debit cards, and credit cards. In the stores where you shop, ask if all these forms of payment are accepted and which is the most popular and least popular with customers. Then write a half-page (or more) report summarizing your findings.

Mathematics

15. Calculating Total Cost You prepare a purchase order for the following items: 214 T-shirts at $14.85 each, 68 shirts at $19.99 each, 95 jackets at $20.80 each, and 45 jackets at $23.40 each. What is the total cost of the merchandise if no sales tax is added?

Math Concept **Multi-Step Problems** Outline the information you know before you solve this word problem. List the information you know and decide how to use it to solve the problem.

> For help, go to the **Math Skills Handbook** located at the back of this book.

Standardized Test Practice

Directions Read the following questions. On a separate piece of paper, write the best possible answer for each one.

1. Which of the following is NOT a type of retail sales transaction?
   A. Cash
   B. Debit card
   C. Credit card
   D. UPC

2. An RFID tag makes it possible to read all the items in a cart simultaneously while they are all still in the cart.
   T
   F

3. Currency and checks collected in sales transactions are deposited in the _____.

Test-Taking Tip

When studying for a test from a textbook, re-read the chapter summaries. They do a good job of summarizing important points.

DECA. Connection Role Play

Accountant
Wholesale Gift Warehouse

Situation You work as an accountant in the accounting department of a wholesale business that sells gift items to retail businesses. You have been working at this job for two months. During this time you have been diligent about learning all that you can about your new position and performing your job duties to the best of your abilities.

Your supervisor (judge) has noticed your hard work and conscientious approach to your job. Your supervisor (judge) is considering assigning you some more advanced duties. Before doing so, your supervisor (judge) wants to be certain that you understand purchase orders and invoices, their purposes, their similarities, their differences, and how extensions and other charges are calculated. Therefore, your supervisor (judge) has asked you to discuss that information in a meeting that will take place later today.

Activity You are to prepare any notes that you will need for the meeting to discuss purchase orders and invoices. Once you have completed your preparation, you will meet with your supervisor (judge).

Evaluation You will be evaluated on how well you meet the following performance indicators:

1. Describe the use of technology in operations.
2. Calculate miscellaneous charges.
3. Select the best shipping method.
4. Demonstrate systematic behavior.
5. Organize information.

 connectED.mcgraw-hill.com

Download the Competitive Events Workbook for more Role-Play practice.

A Sales Plan
for a Sports Product

Selling is easy when you believe in your product. Sports products have a track record of success.

Scenario

The sports world has inspired products of all types for fans, from sports clothing and bobblehead dolls to wall graphics of popular athletes and sports teams. For example, Fathead® vinyl wall graphics cost between $19.99 and $99.99 and are sold via a Web site and through retailers, such as Target®. The price of these graphics depends on size and the popularity of the athlete.

Your company has decided to market its own line of vinyl wall graphics. The products are made of high-quality vinyl and adhesive for the same price as Fathead. Your company has its own Web site and is opening kiosks in shopping malls. For products to sell in kiosks, your sales staff must be well trained.

The Skills You'll Use

Academic Skills Reading, writing, social studies, researching, and analyzing

Basic Skills Speaking, listening, thinking, and interpersonal

Technology Skills Word processing, presentation, spreadsheet, telecommunication, and the Internet

Your Objective

To create a training plan for new sales employees that will be selling your company's reusable wall graphics in a shopping mall kiosk.

STEP 1 Do Your Research

Go to the Internet to conduct research about reusable vinyl wall graphics. For example, visit Fathead's Web site and other wall-graphic sites to see the variety of wall graphics sold and their major selling points. As you conduct your research, answer these questions:

- How and where are removable vinyl wall graphics used?
- What are the features and benefits of vinyl wall graphics?
- Who are the prospective customers for wall graphics?
- How are wall graphics currently marketed?

Write a summary of your research.

STEP 2 Plan Your Project

Now that you have completed your research, you need to begin planning your project.

- Create a table of information comparing your products' selling points with the selling points of your competition.
- Write a sample script to demonstrate how to approach a customer, to determine the customer's needs, and to respond when confronted with customer objections.
- Develop an exciting product presentation that covers the major selling points, involves customers, and makes use of sales aids.
- Provide possible scenarios for closing the sale and suggestion selling.

STEP 3 Connect with Your Community

- Interview one or more trusted adults at home, at school, at work, or in your community to see if they own wall graphics. Find out what they like and dislike about them.
- Look for examples of wall graphics on autos, in school, and other public places.
- Visit a retail store that carries wall graphics to see how they are priced and merchandised.

STEP 4 Share What You Learn

Assume your class is a committee comprised of the vice president of sales and experienced sales representatives who must approve your sales training program.

- Present your sales training plan in an oral presentation. Be prepared to answer questions.
- Present your plan in a written report.
- Use software to create a slide presentation to accompany your oral report. Include one slide for each key topic found in the written report.

STEP 5 Evaluate Your Marketing and Academic Skills

Your project will be evaluated based on the following:

- Knowledge of the sales process and effective selling techniques
- Knowledge of reusable wall graphic products
- Completeness of the sales training plan, including an evaluation rubric
- Organization and continuity of presentation
- Mechanics—presentation and neatness
- Speaking and listening skills

Marketing Internship Project Checklist

Plan

✓ Conduct research on reusable wall graphic companies and how they are marketed.

✓ Design an effective sales training program for new sales associates.

Write

✓ Summarize your research.

✓ Write a report detailing your sales plan.

✓ Write a sample script to demonstrate how to approach a customer, to determine the customer's needs, and to respond when confronted with customer objections.

Present

✓ Present your sales training plan.

✓ Present sample dialogue for each step of the sale.

✓ Present suggested sales aids for use in the kiosks.

 connectED.mcgraw-hill.com

Evaluate Download a rubric you can use to evaluate your final project.

my marketing portfolio

Internship Report Once you have completed your Marketing Internship Project and oral presentation, put your written report and a few printouts of key slides from your oral presentation in your Marketing Portfolio.

Selling Wall Graphics in the Organizational Market Your employer sells removable vinyl wall coverings to businesses for window and point-of-purchase displays. They come in widths of 30, 48, 60, and 75 inches and lengths of 75, 150, and 300 inches in a variety of textures. They are flame and smoke certified. Prepare a written and oral sales plan for an upcoming trade show where you will work at your company's exhibit. What will you say and do during the sales process? What sales aids will be needed? How will you evaluate your efforts?

MARKETING CORE FUNCTION

 Selling

PROMOTION

Marketing Internship Project

A Promotional Campaign

Essential Question How do you create an effective promotional campaign to reach a target market?

Before a company can design a promotional campaign, it must first clearly identify its target market—the potential customers for a product. The promotional mix depends on the customer profile for the product. Once the target market is identified and profiled, you can design the theme and select the correct media to reach that group.

Project Goal

In the project at the end of this unit, you will design a promotional campaign, complete with the theme and promotional mix.

Prepare for the Project

As you read this unit, use this checklist to prepare for the Marketing Internship Project at the end of this unit:

- Notice how hybrid automobiles are promoted.
- Consider media to use as part of a promotional mix for a hybrid car.

 connectED.mcgraw-hill.com

Project Activity
Complete a worksheet activity about creating an effective promotional campaign.

AMERICAN MARKETING ASSOCIATION

Clearly define your brand and make sure consumers get the message.

MARKETING CORE FUNCTIONS IN THIS UNIT

Market Planning

Promotion

FAIR TRADE COCOA

The richest, tastiest ice cream in the world uses the fairest ingredients—like cocoa harvested from Fair Trade farms in the Dominican Republic. Fair Trade ensures farmers a fair wage and benefits their families, their communities and the environment. It's another way that Ben & Jerry's works to make the best possible ice cream in the best way possible. Go to benjerry.com to learn more about responsible sourcing.

It's what's inside that counts.

SHOW WHAT YOU KNOW

Visual Literacy

Companies are increasingly calling attention to their focus on social and "green" issues as a way to promote their products or brands. *How does Ben & Jerry's® emphasis on using Fair Trade ingredients give customers a positive impression of its ice cream?*

promotional concepts and strategies

SHOW WHAT YOU KNOW

Visual Literacy Businesses promote themselves to create a favorable image, attract customers, build product awareness, and create sales. Promotion includes advertising, direct marketing, personal selling, public relations, and sales promotions. *What unique promotional activities have you observed recently?*

Discovery Project

Promoting Products

Essential Question What makes a promotion successful?

Project Goal

Imagine you work for a marketing agency that represents a sports beverage company. You have been assigned to develop a promotional plan to attract young people (ages 16–25) to the product. Create a promotional mix by using advertising, direct marketing, sales promotions, and public relations activities. Your plan should include specific examples of how each type of promotion will be used to reach your target market.

Ask Yourself...

- How will you identify the specific product to promote to teens and young adults?
- How will you use advertising, direct marketing, sales promotion, and public relations activities to promote the product?
- How will you organize your promotional plan?
- How will you present your promotional plan?

 Organize and Present Organize your information into a promotional plan for the product, and use presentation software to present your plan.

 connectED.mcgraw-hill.com

Activity
Get a worksheet activity about promoting products.

Evaluate
Download a rubric you can use to evaluate your project.

DECA. Connection

DECA Event Role Play

Concepts in this chapter are related to DECA competitive events that involve either an interview or role play.

Performance Indicators The performance indicators represent key skills and knowledge. Your key to success in DECA competitive events is relating them to concepts in this chapter.

- Explain the role of promotion as a marketing function.
- Plan displays and themes with management.
- Create displays.
- Create promotional signs.
- Coordinate activities in the promotional mix.

DECA Prep

Role Play Practice role-playing with the DECA Connection competitive-event activity at the end of this chapter. More information on DECA events can be found on DECA's Web site.

READING GUIDE

Before You Read

Imagine What might happen if businesses did not promote their products?

The Main Idea

The combination of personal selling, advertising, direct marketing, sales promotion, and public relations makes up the promotional mix.

Objectives

- **Explain** the role of promotion in business and marketing.
- **Identify** types of promotion.
- **Distinguish** between public relations and publicity.
- **Explain** elements of a news release.
- **Describe** the concept of the promotional mix.

Vocabulary

Content Vocabulary
- promotion
- product promotion
- institutional promotion
- promotional mix
- advertising
- direct marketing
- social media
- sales promotion
- public relations
- news release
- publicity
- push policy
- pull policy

Academic Vocabulary

You will find these words in your reading and on your tests. Make sure you know their meanings.
- via
- target

Graphic Organizer

Draw or print this chart and write examples for each different type of promotion.

connectED.mcgraw-hill.com

Print this graphic organizer.

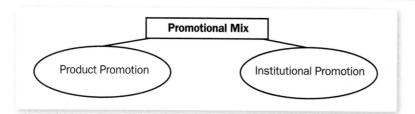

Promotional Mix

Product Promotion   Institutional Promotion

MARKETING CORE FUNCTION

Promotion

The Promotional Mix

PROMOTION IN MARKETING

Promotion is one of the four Ps of the Marketing Mix (Product, Place, Price, & Promotion). As such it is any activity that helps in the exposure or sale of a product. Promotion is persuasive communication. Companies use promotional techniques to enhance their public image and reputation, and to persuade people to value their products. Nonprofit and charitable organizations rely on promotional activities to educate the public about an issue or cause. They also use it to advocate for changing laws or policies. The goals of promotional activities are summarized by the phrase for the acronym AIDA—first attract Attention, then build Interest and Desire, and finally ask for Action.

As You Read

Contrast Distinguish between the different types of promotion.

Product promotion is a promotional method used by businesses to convince prospects to select their goods or services instead of a competitor's brands. Promotional activities explain the major features and benefits of the product, identify where it is sold, advertise sales, answer customer questions, and introduce new offerings. Product promotion also helps businesses foster good relations with existing customers. These positive relations enhance customer loyalty.

> **Companies use promotion to build awareness and inform people about their products.**

Institutional promotion is a promotional method used to create a favorable image for a business, help it advocate for change, or take a stand on trade or community issues. As part of institutional promotional efforts businesses maintain Web sites to provide news, product and general information, and to answer questions. Institutional promotions do not directly sell a product. However, these activities do build goodwill to enhance a company's reputation and foster a favorable image for the company. This image may also help sales efforts.

Reading Check

Recall What are two types of promotion?

Promoting a Business

Institutional promotion is an important type of promotion. *How does endorsement by a research company benefit a business?*

TYPES OF PROMOTION IN THE PROMOTIONAL MIX

The **promotional mix** is the cost-effective combination of personal selling, advertising, direct marketing, sales promotion, and public relations strategies used to reach company goals. Each of the five basic categories in the promotional mix plays a vital role in promoting businesses and their products.

Through advertising, direct marketing, sales promotion, and public relations, companies communicate with customers in many ways other than direct contact. Personal selling, on the other hand, requires direct personal contact with the customer.

PERSONAL SELLING

Personal selling requires sales representatives to generate and maintain direct contact with prospects and customers. Direct contact like this can take the form of personal meetings, in-home demonstrations, e-mail and telephone correspondence.

Personal selling is one of the most expensive forms of promotion. Typically, personal selling takes place after other promotional activities have been tried.

ADVERTISING

Advertising is a form of nonpersonal promotion in which companies pay to promote ideas, goods, or services. These promotions are presented through a variety of media outlets.

Advertising can be found everywhere, on billboards, business cards, brochures, Internet, magazines, newspapers, phone directories, grocery store receipts, radio, television, sports arenas, cars and buses, restaurant menus, and Web sites. With advertising, a company engages in a one-way communication to the customer and prospective customer.

DIRECT MARKETING

Direct marketing is a type of promotion that companies use to address individuals directly and not through a third party medium (such as television, radio, or the Internet). One traditional form of direct marketing is direct mail, which is sent **via** standard mail to a home or business. Another form is telemarketing in which customers are called on the phone and asked directly for goods or services.

Direct marketing is a special type of advertising. *How does direct marketing differ from advertising?*

Targeting Your Customers

Promotions are also done through e-marketing to reach consumers who use the Internet to shop and research information. E-marketing is any promotion that is delivered via the Internet. It includes search engine marketing (paid search), Web site optimization, e-mail marketing, mobile phone applications (apps), and the use of social media.

Social media is electronic media that allows people with similar interests to participate in a social network. Social networks, such as Facebook®, LinkedIn®, YouTube®, and Twitter®, help businesses reach prospective customers.

The goals of direct marketing are to generate sales or leads for sales representatives to pursue. Direct marketing gives recipients an incentive to respond by visiting a store or Web site, calling a toll-free number, returning a form, or sending an e-mail. Targeted customers receive special offers or incentives, such as money-off coupons, limited-time sales, special merchandise offers, loyalty points for future purchases, and free delivery.

Both print and electronic direct marketing allow a business to engage in one-way communication with its customers about product announcements, special promotions, bulletins, customer inquiries, and order confirmations. However, as a result of consumer complaints about unwanted electronic direct mailings, Congress passed the CAN-SPAM Act of 2003. This act requires senders of unsolicited commercial e-mail to give recipients a way to opt out of e-mails. It also prohibits the use of deceptive subject lines and headers. In addition, it requires businesses to provide valid return addresses on their e-mails.

The Federal Trade Commission banned many pre-recorded, automated telemarketing solicitations, or "robocalls," in 2009. However, certain automated calls from charitable organizations, politicians, and healthcare providers are permitted. Telephone calls made by humans for selling products and services are also allowed unless the phone number is listed on the National Do Not Call Registry.

SALES PROMOTION

According to the American Marketing Association (AMA), **sales promotion** represents all marketing activities—other than personal selling, advertising, and public relations—that are directed at business or retail customers to boost sales. Sales promotions include coupons, money-off promotions, competitions, product samples, and point-of-purchase displays. The objectives of sales promotions are to increase sales, inform potential customers about new products, and create a positive business or corporate image.

HOT TOPIC

Electronic Appeal
An e-mail message costs about $7 per response versus $48 for traditional direct mail.

PUBLIC RELATIONS

Public relations (PR) activities help an organization to influence a target audience. Public relations campaigns try to influence general opinion and create a favorable public image for a person, organization, or a company, its products, or its policies. An example is a campaign to encourage business to sponsor the Children's Miracle Network, a national network of children's hospitals. Sponsors are featured in publications, print ads, mentioned during radio fund-raisers, and also help distribute paper miracle balloons for customer donations at local outlets. Public relations staff try to cultivate a positive image with reporters who may cover a specific industry.

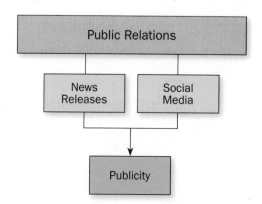

FIGURE 17.1 News Release

Step-by-Step Directions News releases sent through postal mail to the media should be double-spaced and typed on letterhead stationery. Margins should be about one-and-one-half inches to allow the editor to make notes. Always submit copy that is clean, legible, and free of spelling errors. News releases published on a Web site are limited by the design of the Web page, but must also identify the company and follow the rules listed below. *What kind of news goes in a news release?*

BOARDING SUPPLIES GO ONLINE WITH BIG AIR

1 The first paragraph should answer the Who, What, When, Where, and Why questions.

Dateline: July 15. . . Miami Beach, FL
Contact Name: Keith Ramos
Contact Phone: 1-555-309-5800
Web Site: http://www.x-boards.com

MIAMI BEACH, FL-July 15-Boarding supplies and accessories are now just a click away at X-Boards.com. No more driving to the nearest city to find name-brand apparel, gear, helmets, pads, shoes, board-building supplies, *and* boards for surf, street, and snow.

2 The story with important facts should be developed within the next few paragraphs.

Ladies and dudes who love surfing, kite-boarding, skateboarding, and snowboarding can search hundreds of products throughout the awesome mega-selection at X-Boards.com, and have supplies and accessories delivered directly to their home.

With 18 years' experience as a retailer in the board business and 3 years as an online source of board sporting news, the owners of X-Boards.com are very concerned about safety as well as style and quality. Bringing boarders the best quality products is the number one goal at X-Boards.com.

"I'm X-tremely pleased with your pricing, selection, and your speed of service!" says customer Andy Hagan.

3 When first identifying people, include the full name and title or position of the person. Avoid using Mr., Ms., Mr., Dr., etc. After the complete name is cited, use the person's last name thereafter.

Surfers, skateboarders, and snowboarders will enjoy browsing the best buys, closeouts, discounts, and new products sections on the Web site.

Also, our customer service team is knowledgeable, helpful, and available from 9 A.M. to 9 P.M., Monday through Saturday, providing the best possible service to each customer. Free shipping is available for many products.

4 More information that is slightly less important can follow.

To learn more about X-Boards.com, please visit our Web site at this address:
http://www.x-boards.com

For an interview or further information, please contact Keith Ramos at 1-555-309-5800.

###

5 The entire news release should be brief—just one page. Do not number the page. At the bottom of the page, type "###"to signify the end of the news release.

6 Always include the name, and phone number of the contact person sending out the news release.

WRITING NEWS RELEASES

Although there are many media tools, one of the most important ones is the news release. A **news release** is an announcement sent to the appropriate media outlets (see **Figure 17.1**).

The release announces newsworthy developments about a company's goods or services, distribution channels, facilities and operations, partners, revenues and earnings, employees, and events.

As you can see from the figure, there are many parts of the news release that do not change. It is important for companies to format their news releases correctly. This format makes it easier for the audience to find and use information.

USING SOCIAL MEDIA

Businesses also use social media to interact with customers and get feedback on the company, its products, and services. People communicate and maintain a degree of personal control through the Internet, cell phones, and input devices. Social networks provide businesses with a way to obtain opinions and speak directly with potential and existing customers. The potential to reach prospective customers is tremendous. For example, Facebook allows businesses and organizations to create unique profiles, sign up fans, send messages, and create status reports. Businesses can reach more than 890 million users on Facebook each day.

PUBLICITY

Through news releases and social media, businesses gain publicity. **Publicity** involves bringing news or newsworthy information about an organization to the public's attention. This process is known as *placement*.

In addition its use by businesses, publicity can also make the public aware of certain people, specific products or services, efforts by nonprofit or government agencies, and arts and entertainment opportunities. A public rally for a political issue or candidate is aimed at raising publicity among voters at election time. When a recording artist is interviewed on the radio, that singer or band is trying to publicize their music.

A publicity campaign can be launched to achieve various goals. The main function of publicity is to develop a positive perception or awareness of the organization and its products in the marketplace. The right kind of publicity can create and maintain a company's positive image. However, negative publicity can devastate it. People like to do business with respectable companies. Companies engage in such image-building activities as sponsoring cultural events, awarding scholarships, and donating money, land, or equipment for public use.

Unlike advertising, the placement of publicity is free. For example, a one-minute story on the evening news about a company costs nothing. However, a few seconds of advertising time on the same broadcast can cost thousands of dollars.

Cost is not the only advantage of publicity. Newspapers, television and radio news programs, and customer-generated responses through social media are usually viewed as more objective than advertisers. People are more likely to pay attention to and believe news stories and customer feedback than advertisements. Publicity might appear as a media story or as part of a larger story or report. These formats make the information appear more credible to many people.

The disadvantage of publicity is that its content, unlike paid advertising, is not controlled by the business that issues it. The media select the context and story angle and decide when and how to present the content.

Short-post forums on Twitter, YouTube videos, and customer-generated online opinions on social networking sites can quickly spread negative or unverified stories. This kind of negative publicity is likely to get as much attention as positive stories about company products or community contributions. Businesses work to generate positive publicity and avoid negative publicity through effective public relations.

Reading Check

Recall What are the major types of promotion in the promotional mix?

FIGURE 17.2 Developing a Promotional Mix

Strategies to Reach the Goal The promotional activities that marketers choose for promoting a particular product form the promotional mix. *How do the elements in a promotional mix work together?*

Step 1 Identify the Target Market

A business must identify its targeted customers to design the best message and the best way to reach them.

Step 2 Establish Objectives

A promotional mix must have objectives to accomplish, such as to create brand awareness, introduce a new product, build an image, or generate more sales.

Step 3 Design Promotional Message

Appropriate images or words should be selected to communicate with the target market. The selected message will largely dictate the format used, such as graphics, sound, electronic or print messages, or personal sales presentations.

Step 4 Select Promotional Activities

The type of promotional method(s) used must be based upon stated objectives, the desired message, and prioritized by available resources.

Step 5 Allocate Budget Amounts

A promotion budget should be based upon the "ideal" promotional mix and can include all promotional methods or a selected number based upon available resources.

Step 6 Measure Results

Promotional methods and the results achieved must be continually evaluated. The results will determine whether the planned activities should continue or be revised to meet objectives.

THE CONCEPT OF PROMOTIONAL MIX

Most businesses use more than one type of promotion to achieve their promotional goals. They use a cost-effective mix of promotional strategies that include advertising, selling, sales promotion, direct marketing, and public relations strategies. This mix assures them that their product will be widely recognized.

Once a product is recognized, it is easier to sell. These sales generate revenue for the company. It uses this revenue to offset the cost of using the promotional strategies. Companies learn which strategies are most effective in their promotional mix through this process.

How do companies develop a promotional mix? A business establishes a promotional mix by following a process that begins with identifying the **target** market. This process continues through a series of steps and ends with the company measuring the results of the mix. **Figure 17.2** shows the process in developing a promotional mix. It is represented as a cycle because a promotional mix must be on-going and continuous. The strategies in the mix are designed to complement one another. Information that is learned in one cycle of the mix is applied to the next cycle.

MARKETING CASE STUDY

Ladies and Gentlemen . . . The Beatles: Rock Band!

The popular music video game Rock Band® got a high-profile reintroduction with "The Beatles: Rock Band." In this game, players take on the roles of the Fab Four. It was not only the first Beatles game, it was also the first time the band's music became available in digital format. This allowed for some special advertising opportunities.

From Liverpool to You

Ads for the game utilized artful images from the game itself. The game features colorful animations of the band and how the musicians changed over time. A commercial also showed everyday people inserted into iconic parts of Beatles imagery. One ad showed people walking across Abbey Road. The promotion also referenced the new Beatles boxed CD sets, which were released at the same time as the game.

English Language Arts

Collaborate With a partner, create a basic promotional mix for this product, incorporating creative, nontraditional ideas. Present your ideas to the class using presentation software or poster boards.

For example, the process starts with a target market. Imagine that you work for a company that designs, manufacturers, and sells hiking equipment. It has national name brand recognition. Your company plans to introduce a totally new and improved lightweight backpack. Since your objectives are to introduce a new product, build awareness and create sales, your message must reach hikers and outdoor enthusiasts about the benefits of buying your new product. Your promotional mix must include methods for meeting all of these goals.

The marketing department selects the best promotional activity to reach the target market. It then develops a budget for advertising, direct marketing, and sales promotional activities. The selected promotional activities must complement one another, and they must be able to reach the potential market. They must also be realistic in terms of the budget for the promotion.

Advertising and direct marketing create awareness of a business's product. At the same time, public relations helps cultivate a favorable image and brand recognition. Sales promotional activities stimulate sales, reinforce advertising, and support selling efforts. Finally, personal selling builds on all of these previous efforts by completing the sale. Your company's budget will give you an idea of how to fund each of these areas of promotion.

Elements of the promotional mix must be coordinated. For example, national advertising should be reinforced by local promotional efforts. Many consumer product manufacturers give or sell retailers decorations or in-store displays to reinforce a national campaign. The national and local efforts need to be communicated to the store personnel. Being made aware of any coupons, rebates, contests, and featured promotional items allows staff to encourage customer participation.

When promoted products are not available as advertised or the selling staff is uninformed about a promotion, sales are lost and customers are dissatisfied. If these employees are informed of such promotions, they will be able to more effectively engage their customers. This engagement leads to more sales and more revenue.

The total promotional mix and each strategy in the mix must be measured on how well they met the objectives. The results determine whether promotional strategies are revised, improved, or discontinued.

PROMOTIONAL BUDGET

In large companies, the marketing department has many roles. It determines the promotional mix, establishes the budget, allocates resources, coordinates the campaign, supervises any outside resources, and measures the results.

It is important to consider all aspects of the promotional mix when developing the promotional budget. Determining the ideal budget is difficult. Often, a promotional budget is based on a percentage of sales. Other times, it is based on an estimate of what competitors spend on advertising, direct marketing, and sales promotion. There is no precise way to measure exact results of spending promotional dollars. This lack of precision makes it difficult to determine the ideal amount for the promotional budget. Its overall success is usually based upon whether the total effort led to increased sales.

It is vital for companies to study the effects of their promotional mix. It is like an experiment. They need to isolate a variable and monitor its effects. After the promotion is done, the company can assess the impact of the promotion and make a plan for the next time around.

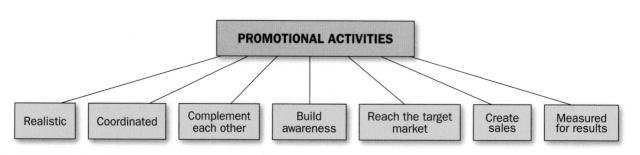

THE PUSH-PULL CONCEPT

Manufacturers often develop a promotional mix for each segment of the distribution channel. To promote a product to large retailers that sell its products, a manufacturer might want to use a mix of advertising, personal selling, and trade discounts. This type of promotion, known as the **push policy**, is used with partners in the distribution channel. The manufacturer pushes the product through the distribution channel to the retailer. The main purpose of the promotion is to convince a retailer to stock the products being promoted.

This strategy is especially useful at trade shows and exhibitions, where cross-promoting is possible. It is a helpful strategy for manufacturers whose products do not have strong brand identity.

The same manufacturer might use a different promotional mix of local and national advertising, in-store displays, sales promotion, and public relations to reach consumers. The **pull policy** directs promotional activities toward consumers. The idea is to entice (or pull) the consumer into the store (or Web site) to buy the product. A typical pull marketing strategy would be to offer "half-off" deals or clearance sales.

This pull policy of promotion is designed to create consumer interest and demand. Consumer demand pulls the product through the distribution channel by encouraging wholesalers and retailers to carry a product. As mentioned, this strategy relies heavily on consumer advertising, premiums, samples, in-store displays, and demonstrations.

 After You Read Section 17.1

Review Key Concepts

1. **Explain** why promotion is an important marketing function.
2. **Identify** when to use product and institutional promotion.
3. **Contrast** the push and pull policies in promotional mixes.

Practice Academics

Social Studies

4. Customer-driven responses on Web sites, such as Facebook® and Twitter®, have changed the way businesses promote goods and services. Investigate the concept of social media and its effect on business. Write a paragraph on how business responds to customer-driven comments.

Mathematics

5. An outdoor apparel company has established a promotional budget of $1,000 to be spent in the following manner: $300 for a print advertisement in an outdoor magazine; $450 for an online advertisement campaign; $150 for premiums (decal stickers imprinted with the company name); $100 donation to a local outdoor program for children to build public relations. What percentage of the total budget is spent on each promotional category?

Math Concept **Number and Operations** Estimate before computing your answer to be sure your calculations are accurate.

Starting Hints To solve this problem, divide each dollar amount spent by the total dollar amount of the promotional budget, $1,000, to get a decimal. Multiply the decimal by 100 to determine what percent of the budget each category requires.

 **connectED.mcgraw-hill.com**

Check your answers.

For help, go to the **Math Skills Handbook** located at the back of this book.

READING GUIDE

Before You Read

Connect What promotional tie-ins or loyalty programs have you participated in?

Objectives

- **Define** sales promotion.
- **Explain** the use of promotional tie-ins, trade sales promotions, and loyalty marketing programs.

The Main Idea

Sales promotion includes different techniques to increase sales and inform customers about a company's products.

Vocabulary

Content Vocabulary

- sales promotions
- trade promotions
- consumer promotions
- coupons
- premiums
- incentives
- promotional tie-ins
- loyalty marketing programs
- kiosks

Academic Vocabulary

You will find these words in your reading and on your tests. Make sure you know their meanings.

- distribution
- register

Graphic Organizer

Draw or print this chart to list examples for different types of sales promotions.

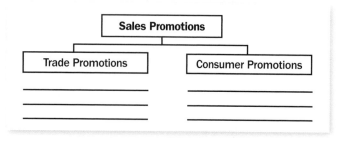

connectED.mcgraw-hill.com

Print this graphic organizer.

MARKETING CORE FUNCTION

Promotion

m.e. Types of Promotion

SALES PROMOTION

Sales promotions are incentives that encourage customers to buy products or services. Sales promotions build brand awareness, encourage customers to try a new product, increase purchases by current customers, or reward customer loyalty. Sales promotions are usually supported by advertising activities that include trade promotions and consumer promotions.

As You Read

Consider How might you promote a product that you like?

TRADE PROMOTIONS

Trade promotions are sales promotion activities designed to get support for a product from manufacturers, wholesalers, and retailers. More money is actually spent on promoting to businesses than to consumers. Major trade promotions include promotional allowances, cooperative advertising, slotting allowances, sales force promotions, and trade shows and conventions. Good business ethics require that trade promotional payments and awards be offered in a uniform manner. It also requires that terms be clearly spelled out and that no one is penalized for not achieving the goals. These requirements ensure that trade promotions are conducted fairly.

Trade Promotions	
Allowances	Quotas
Advertising	Trade Shows

PROMOTIONAL ALLOWANCES

Promotional allowances represent cash payments or discounts given by manufacturers to wholesalers or retailers for performing activities to encourage sales. For example, promotional allowances are sometimes used to encourage wholesalers or retailers to stock a large quantity of a product. The cash payment or price discount gives wholesalers and retailers an incentive to sell, so they are more likely to promote the product.

> **"** **Sales promotions may be either business-to-business (B2B) or business-to-consumer (B2C) activities.** **"**

COOPERATIVE ADVERTISING

A manufacturer supports the retailer by helping to pay for the cost of advertising its product locally. This practice is known as *cooperative advertising*.

SLOTTING ALLOWANCES

A slotting allowance is a cash premium paid by a manufacturer to a retailer to help the retailer cover the costs of placing the manufacturer's product on the shelves. Slotting allowances can range from a few thousand dollars to several million dollars per product. In addition to buying space in the store, slotting allowances also pay for a retailer's discount specials on a product, charges for store shelves, penalties for poor sales, store advertising, and display costs.

SALES FORCE PROMOTIONS

Sales force promotions are awards given to dealers and employees who successfully meet or exceed a sales quota. Such quotas can apply to a specific period of time, such as a month, one day, or a year, or for a product or line of products.

Sales force promotions vary, but they may include cash bonuses or prizes such as merchandise or travel awards.

TRADE SHOWS AND CONVENTIONS

Trade shows and conventions showcase a particular line of products. One of the largest trade shows is the annual Consumer Electronics Show in Las Vegas, which attracts more than 190,000 manufacturers, retailers, product engineers, and developers. Many participating companies invest millions of dollars in their display booths. Trade shows provide businesses with opportunities to introduce new products, encourage increased sales of existing products, meet customers and partners in the **distribution** chain, and gain continued company and product support.

 Reading Check

Analyze Why are trade promotions effective?

CONSUMER PROMOTIONS

Consumer promotions are sales strategies that encourage customers and prospects to buy a product or service. Consumer promotions support advertising, personal selling, and public relations efforts. Major consumer sales promotion devices include coupons, premiums, deals, incentives, product samples, sponsorships, promotional tie-ins, product placement, loyalty marketing programs, and point-of-purchase displays.

COUPONS

Coupons are certificates that entitle customers to cash discounts on goods or services. Manufacturers use coupons to introduce new products, to enhance the sales of existing products, and to encourage retailers to stock and display both. Coupons are placed on or inside product packages, in newspapers, and magazines.

Increasingly, companies use strategies to drive consumers to download and print online coupons. For example, a food manufacturer runs a summer online coupon program in partnership with supermarkets. Printed or online coupons are available for a limited time, and their value expires after a certain date.

Stores that accept coupons send them to the manufacturers' headquarters or to a clearinghouse to be sorted and passed along to redemption centers. The centers, in turn, reimburse the stores for the face value of each coupon plus a handling charge of about eight cents per coupon. The centers then bill the manufacturers.

Coupons Starting in 2008, Groupon offered deal-of-the-day coupons for certain stores if enough customers in one city signed up to use them.

PREMIUMS

Premiums or giveaways are low-cost items given to consumers at a discount or for free. They are designed to increase sales by building product loyalty and attracting new customers. They can also persuade nonusers to switch brands.

The fundamental concept behind premium marketing is that people will be more motivated to buy a product when they are offered an added-value gift in exchange. Three types of popular consumer premiums are factory packs, traffic builders, and coupon plans.

Factory packs, or in-packs, are free gifts placed in product packages or as a container premium. This form of premium is especially popular with cereal manufacturers. Toy companies can cross-market or cross-sell their products with cereal companies. Children who eat the cereal and play with the toys will have a positive impression of both companies.

Traffic builders are low-cost premiums, such as pens, key chains, pocket calendars, and coffee mugs. They are given away to consumers for visiting a new store or attending a special event.

Each time a customer uses the premium, he or she is reminded of the company and the experience. This practice can foster positive feelings for the company. Some of these premiums also feature contact information for the company so it is easier for the customer to get in touch.

Trade promotion is an important type of promotion. *How do trade shows and conventions help businesses promote their products?*

Coupon plans are ongoing programs offering a variety of premiums in exchange for labels or coupons obtained from a product. A customer might send a manufacturer three soup-can labels in exchange for a recipe book. This exchange tells the company not only that their customers want recipes but also which products they purchase. If a soup company never received labels in the mail for one of its products, it would know not to market these products in association with this promotion.

One drawback to using premiums is that customers may think they are disposable. It is important for a company to not flood customers with too many premiums. This practice increases the chances that the premiums will be discarded.

DEALS

Deals or price packs offer short-term price reductions that are marked directly on the label or package, such as a retailer selling T-shirts for $10.50 each for one or $6 each for two or more. A deal might also "bundle" two-related products together, such as a free wing chair with a purchase of a discounted sofa.

INCENTIVES

Incentives are generally higher-priced products, awards, or gift cards that are earned and given away through contests, sweepstakes, special offers, and rebates. Businesses use incentives to promote many products because they create customer excitement and increase sales.

Contests are games or activities that require the participant to demonstrate a skill. Contest winners win such prizes as scholarships, vacations, and money. Many companies, such as McDonald's®, Kellogg's®, Kraft® Foods, and General Mills® have product promotions in the form of Internet games. Incentives are often offered to collect points in exchange for other games or gifts.

Sweepstakes are games of chance. (By law in most states, no purchase is necessary in order to enter a contest or sweepstakes.)

Special offers and rebates are discounts offered by businesses to customers who purchase an item during a given time period. Manufacturers and retail stores frequently use special offers and rebates to encourage customers to buy their products. Increasingly, a traditional marketer will offer an incentive for consumers to go online and **register** to make a purchase or receive a discount from a marketer.

Product samples are especially important when promoting new products. *Can you think of some products that make good product samples?*

Product Samples

PRODUCT SAMPLES

Another form of consumer sales promotion is the product sample. A product sample is a free trial size of a product sent through the mail, distributed door-to-door, or given away at retail stores and trade shows. Detergents, toothpastes, shampoos, deodorants, and colognes are frequently promoted this way. Samples are especially important in promoting new products. Drug manufacturers frequently give samples to doctors and dentists so their patients can try new products.

SPONSORSHIP

Sponsors often negotiate the right to use their logos and names on retail products to enhance their corporate image. The sponsoring company pays a fee for rights to promote itself, its products or services at an event (such as a concert), with a group (such as a NASCAR® car racing team), with a person (such as a well-known basketball player), or at a physical site (such as a stadium).

Obtaining naming rights at a particular location is a high-profile promotional effort. A title sponsor is an organization that pays to have its name incorporated into the name of the sponsored location, such as The Home Depot® Center or a U.S. Olympic Training site on the publicly owned campus of California State University. Sponsorship deals must be able to withstand public and media scrutiny. The effectiveness of the particular sponsorship is measured by the response of those who actually view the title or logo.

PROMOTIONAL TIE-INS, CROSS-PROMOTION, CROSS-SELLING

Promotional tie-ins, also known as *cross-promotion* and *cross-selling* campaigns, are activities that involve sales promotions between one or more retailers or manufacturers.

Partners combine their advertising and sales promotional activities to conduct a promotion that will create additional sales for each partner. Promotional tie-ins can be complex and involve several companies. For example, Jack in the Box® teamed with Dr. Pepper® on a promotional tie-in directed at video gamers. Customers who bought combo meals received game pieces on drinks for prizes including GameStop® gift cards, Xbox 360® consoles, and several game rooms equipped with home theaters and recliners.

Another good example of promotional tie-ins can be found in breakfast cereals and at fast-food restaurants. When a blockbuster animated feature is about to hit theaters, a movie studio often cross-promotes the film by offering ticket discounts in cereal boxes or toys with kids' meals.

The GREEN Marketer

Green Premiums

At many eco-friendly companies, promotional premiums have been dropped in favor of clever, environmentally friendly alternatives.

Popular eco-premiums range from organic-cotton tote bags and recycled-paper notepads to biodegradable golf tees and mouse pads that are crafted from old tires. Some companies even donate to a choice of charities instead of offering flashy and expensive premiums to high-profile clients. Green premiums both promote a company and give it a positive image.

Mathematics

Calculate Assume the cost of a traditional premium is $0.75 per premium and the cost of an eco-friendly premium is $1.10 per premium. Calculate the difference in price for 12,000 units of each premium as a dollar amount and as a percentage. Which option would you choose to promote your company?

 connectED.mcgraw-hill.com

Get an activity on green marketing.

PRODUCT PLACEMENT

Product placement is a consumer promotion that involves the verbal mention or appearance of a brand-name product in a television series, movie, or sporting event. It can even happen in a commercial for another product. For example, on the *American Idol* television series, the Ford Focus® was shown and the Sprint Nextel® phone was used as a prop. Product placement has increased on television shows because technology allows viewers to fast forward through paid commercials. One example of product placement in a movie took place in the Tom Hanks' movie *Cast Away* where FedEx® packaging and a Wilson® soccer ball were prominently featured. Both companies received international exposure.

LOYALTY MARKETING PROGRAMS

Loyalty marketing programs, also known as *frequent buyer, reward,* or *frequent shopper programs,* reward customers by offering incentives for repeat purchases.

The airline industry instituted one of the first such promotions, the frequent flyer program. These programs reward customers with free air travel once they have accumulated a designated amount of travel miles. Hotel industry chains, such as Hilton®, Hyatt®, and Marriott®, have adopted frequent guest programs in which consumers can earn free lodging by spending a designated dollar amount on lodging.

Customer loyalty means that customers are so satisfied with a brand or retailer that they continue to buy that brand or patronize that business even when they have others from which to choose. Most loyalty marketing programs do not cost anything for participation. However, large warehouse chains, such as Costco®, BJ's®, and Sam's Club®, require a membership fee for their loyalty cards that entitle the customer to large discounts.

Large and small businesses in many industries have adopted loyalty marketing programs. Hallmark®, a greeting card and gift chain, has *Crown Rewards*®. Customers can earn points for dollars spent and trade them for certificates on future purchases. Many local restaurants use simple loyalty cards that entitle frequent users to a free meal after a set number of purchases.

Grocery chains have also implemented loyalty programs. Customers who sign up for a frequent shopper card can accumulate points for every purchase. These points can then be applied to discounts on future shopping trips, or for stores that have gas stations, savings on fuel purchases.

Kiosks allow customers to obtain product information. *How do kiosks help businesses interact with customers?*

Interacting with Customers

ONLINE LOYALTY MARKETING PROGRAMS

Online versions of loyalty programs have also become popular. The Internet search engine Yahoo! awards points to users who buy from certain retailers or visit certain Web sites. Yahoo! also negotiated with the airline industry to allow consumers to convert their points into frequent flyer miles. This arrangement benefits both Yahoo! and the airlines.

Companies can also use email to notify loyal customers of exclusive sales. They may also be directed to special online-only discounts or given a chance to try new products first.

POINT-OF-PURCHASE DISPLAYS

Point-of-purchase displays are displays designed primarily by manufacturers to hold and display their products. They are usually placed in high-traffic areas and promote impulse purchases. By exposing potential customers firsthand to a company's products, point-of-purchase displays stimulate sales and serve as in-store advertising.

Kiosks are point-of-purchase displays that are stand-alone structures. Web-based or display-screen kiosks disseminate information to customers. Store kiosks offer new ways to interact with the sales staff, provide opportunities for cross-selling, and improve customer service.

 After You Read | **Section 17.2**

Review Key Concepts

1. **Contrast** trade promotions and consumer sales promotions.
2. **Contrast** contests, sweepstakes, special offers, and rebates.
3. **Explain** why a business would want product placement in entertainment media.

Practice Academics

English Language Arts

4. Conduct research to identify advantages and disadvantages for companies that seek naming rights for publicly financed or owned buildings such as stadiums, hospitals, or schools. Identify and label the advantages and disadvantages in a two-column table and share this information with your class.

Mathematics

5. Promotional discounts are given to stores by manufacturers to place their products in preferred locations in the store and to display their products in store windows. A ski manufacturer sells a local ski shop 35 pairs of their new skis for $7,000, which is a discount of $2,625. What is the percentage of the discount given to the store? (Round your answer to the nearest whole percent.)

Math Concept **Number and Operations** A decimal can be multiplied by 100 to be represented by a percentage.

Starting Hints To solve this problem, subtract the discount amount from the purchase amount of each item to determine the net cost. For each item, divide the discount dollar amount by the purchase amount to get a decimal. Multiply each decimal by 100 to get the percent discount.

 connectED.mcgraw-hill.com

Check your answers.

For help, go to the **Math Skills Handbook** located at the back of this book.

Promotional Concepts and Strategies

A business develops a promotional mix by following a step-by-step process, from identifying the target market through to measuring the results.

There are many ways for businesses to promote their goods and services to consumers.

Review and Activities

Written Summary

- Promotion is any form of communication a business uses to inform, persuade, or remind people about its products and its image.
- A promotional mix is the cost effective combination and use of five strategies, advertising, selling, sales promotion, direct marketing, and public relations, to reach objectives.
- Public relations create a positive image about a business, its products, or its policies.
- Publicity tries to place positive information about a business in the media. It is not advertising because it is free.
- Sales promotion is a short-term incentive given to encourage consumers to buy a product or service.
- Sales promotions can be classified either as trade promotions or consumer sales promotions.

Review Content Vocabulary and Academic Vocabulary

1. Create a fill-in-the-blank sentence for each of these vocabulary terms. The sentence should contain enough information to help determine the missing word.

Content Vocabulary
- promotion (p. 395)
- product promotion (p. 395)
- institutional promotion (p. 395)
- promotional mix (p. 396)
- advertising (p. 396)
- direct marketing (p. 396)
- social media (p. 397)
- sales promotion (p. 397)
- public relations (p. 397)
- news release (p. 399)
- publicity (p. 399)
- push policy (p. 403)
- pull policy (p. 403)
- sales promotions (p. 405)
- trade promotions (p. 405)
- consumer promotions (p. 406)
- coupons (p. 406)
- premiums (p. 407)
- incentives (p. 408)
- promotional tie-ins (p. 409)
- loyalty marketing programs (p. 410)
- kiosks (p. 411)

Academic Vocabulary
- via (p. 396)
- target (p. 401)
- distribution (p. 406)
- register (p. 408)

Assess for Understanding

2. **Explain** What is the purpose of promotion in marketing?
3. **Imagine** How might aggressive direct marketing affect public relations?
4. **Contrast** What is the difference between public relations and publicity?
5. **Draft** What new product will your company's press release introduce?
6. **Compare** What is similar about trade promotions and consumer promotions?
7. **Apply** When developing a promotional mix, at what stage will you consider push and pull policies?
8. **Consider** Why are sales promotions generally limited-time opportunities?
9. **Discuss** What are the purposes of promotional tie-ins, trade show promotions, and loyalty marketing programs?

21st Century Skills

Social Responsibility Skills

10. Targeting Kids? Many manufacturers of consumer products and large restaurant chains offer Internet games or "advergames." These advergames for children can be fun and enjoyable, though they do promote a company's products to kids. Discuss the possible objections parents or caregivers might have to these games.

Financial Literacy Skills

11. Coupon Promotions Online coupons are a popular type of sales promotion. A food manufacturer has introduced a new pecan-and-almond nut-cluster snack. You obtain a manufacturer's online coupon for $1 off the snack that retails for $7.99. The store also has a sale and the snack is being offered at $6.49 for a limited time. What percentage discount would you receive if you used the coupon during the sale?

Everyday Ethics

12. Name Game David met Goliath in a Malaysian court case, McCurry v. McDonald's. Located in Kuala Lumpur, McCurry was a small local restaurant serving traditional Indian dishes. McDonald's believed that using the prefix "Mc" was too similar to its name. But after eight years of legal affairs, Malaysia's highest court ended the case in favor of McCurry. The publicity was great promotion for McCurry and many could not understand why McDonald's filed suit. What do you think?

e-Marketing Skills

13. Online Entrepreneurship Imagine that you are a store manager of a retail store. The owner has asked you to provide a rationale for starting an online store. Gather this information for the owner:
- Projections for growth of online shopping.
- Reasons for the growth of online shopping.
- Ways your store can achieve growth in online shopping.

Build Academic Skills

English Language Arts

14. Member Benefits Loyalty marketing programs, also known as *frequent shopper, frequent buyer, rewards,* or *incentive programs*, are offered by companies in many different industries. Identify a few companies that offer loyalty marketing programs. Analyze the name of each program and suggest reasons the company may have chosen that particular name.

Social Studies

15. Promoting Ideals Companies assist with activities that benefit the civic, social, and cultural life of a community. Examples include partnerships with nonprofit organizations, such as Habitat for Humanity®, or sponsorships of events like the Special Olympics®. Research corporate Web sites, annual reports, magazines, or library resources to identify a company that uses institutional promotion. Present your findings to the class orally by describing the company and its sponsored activities that are examples of institutional promotion.

Mathematics

16. Promotional Spending A large amount of money is spent on promotional activities in the United States every year. The average budget breaks down as follows: 50 percent for advertising, 30 percent for sales promotion, and 20 percent for trade promotion. Use these percentages to calculate the amount a company will spend on each type of promotion if its overall budget is $400,000.

Math Concept **Problem Solving: Computing Percentages** When determining what percentage the dollar amount is of another dollar amount, start by dividing the smaller amount by the larger amount.

For help, go to the **Math Skills Handbook** located at the back of this book.

Standardized Test Practice

Directions Read the following questions. On a separate piece of paper, write the best possible answer for each one.

1. Which of the following is a form of nonpersonal promotion in which companies pay to promote ideas, goods, or services in a variety of media outlets?
   A. Advertising
   B. Public Relations
   C. Personal Selling
   D. Sales Promotions

2. Direct marketing is a type of advertising that sends a promotional message to a mass audience.
   T
   F

3. Incentives to encourage customers to buy products or services are known as _____.

Test-Taking Tip

Though your first answers may often be correct, do not be afraid to change an answer if, after you think about it, you believe it is incorrect.

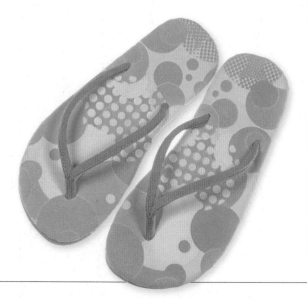

DECA Connection Role Play

Promotions Manager Beach Resort

Situation You work as promotions manager of a small beachside resort on a Caribbean island. The resort has been in business for more than 30 years. The owners and management have maintained the buildings and grounds in a state of near perfection. All of the guest rooms have been recently refurbished. The resort also offers guests many amenities, including an indoor pool, outdoor salt-water pool, spa, gourmet restaurant, casual restaurant, tennis courts, access to golf, and many others.

The resort has enjoyed near capacity bookings during the winter months. The winter months are the resort's prime season. It is very important that the resort have as many bookings as possible during these months. Most of your customers during the winter months are from northern areas and fly down to your island to stay for a week or longer.

During the past few years, your winter season bookings have consistently fallen short of expectations. The management team has noted a correlation between the decrease in bookings and warmer than usual winters in the northern areas where your customers reside. The resort's general manager (judge) feels that now is the time to promote the resort to help increase prime season bookings. The general manager (judge) has asked you to recommend some promotional ideas to help achieve this goal.

Activity You are to outline your promotional ideas, and then make recommendations to the resort general manager (judge) that will help increase prime-season bookings.

Evaluation You will be evaluated on how well you meet the following performance indicators:
1. Explain the role of promotion as a marketing function.
2. Plan displays and themes with management.
3. Create displays.
4. Create promotional signs.
5. Coordinate activities in the promotional mix.

 connectED.mcgraw-hill.com

Download the Competitive Events Workbook for more Role-Play practice.

visual merchandising and display

Visual Literacy Visual merchandising is often the first contact the customer has with a business. Window and interior displays promote an image for a business and its merchandise. *Why do you think visual merchandising and display are an important part of promotion?*

Discovery Project

The Right Presentation

Essential Question How do stores use their space to project an image and to present their products?

Project Goal

Work with a partner to visit a store where you and your friends shop. Create a visual merchandising and display report for the store by observing the store and interviewing a store supervisor. Develop a written report by describing the four elements of visual merchandising: storefront, (types of signs, marquee, entrances, and window displays), store layout (layout of selling space, location of storage space, location and use of personnel space, description of services in customer space), store interior (graphics, signage, color, sound, lighting, fixtures), and interior displays (types of interior displays).

Ask Yourself…

- What store will you identify to investigate in your community?
- How will you arrange transportation and schedule the necessary time for the visit?
- What staff member will you interview to obtain information?
- How will you organize your written report?

 Synthesize and Present Research Synthesize your research and present your design ideas, using the four elements of visual design for attracting teen shoppers.

 connectED.mcgraw-hill.com

Activity
Get a worksheet activity about visual merchandising.

Evaluate
Download a rubric you can use to evaluate your project.

DECA Connection

DECA Event Role Play

Concepts in this chapter are related to DECA competitive events that involve either an interview or role play.

Performance Indicators The performance indicators represent key skills and knowledge. Your key to success in DECA competitive events is relating them to concepts in this chapter.

- Explain the use of visual merchandising in retailing.
- Create displays.
- Create promotional signs.
- Plan visual merchandising activities.
- Plan/schedule displays/themes with management.

DECA Prep

Role Play Practice role-playing with the DECA Connection competitive-event activity at the end of this chapter. More information on DECA events can be found on DECA's Web site.

READING GUIDE

Before You Read

Connect What memorable visual displays have you seen at stores?

Objectives

- **Explain** the concept and purpose of visual merchandising.
- **Identify** the elements of visual merchandising.
- **Describe** types of display arrangements.
- **Understand** the role of visual merchandisers on the marketing team.

The Main Idea

Visual merchandising and displays are important promotional strategies to sell products and services, attract potential customers, and create a desired business image.

Vocabulary

Content Vocabulary
- visual merchandising
- display
- storefront
- marquee
- store layout
- fixtures
- point-of-purchase displays (POPs)
- interactive kiosk

Academic Vocabulary

You will find these words in your reading and on your tests. Make sure you know their meanings.

- project
- concept

Graphic Organizer

Draw or print a scorecard like the one below to list the key features of each visual merchandising element.

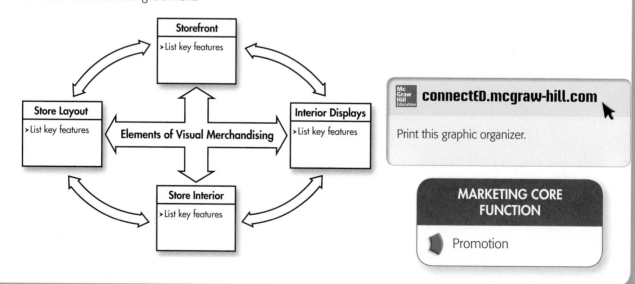

connectED.mcgraw-hill.com

Print this graphic organizer.

MARKETING CORE FUNCTION

Promotion

VISUAL MERCHANDISING AND DISPLAY

Visual merchandising coordinates all of the physical elements in a place of business to **project** an image to customers. Visual merchandising attracts customers, creates a desired business image, and promotes interest in products or services.

The term *visual merchandising* is sometimes used interchangeably with the term *display*, but they are not the same. Display is a much narrower **concept** and makes up only one element of visual merchandising. **Display** refers to the visual and artistic aspects of presenting a product or service to a target group of customers to encourage a purchase. Visual merchandising, by contrast, includes the visual and artistic aspects of the entire business environment. Keep this distinction in mind when you read about these concepts.

As You Read

List Think of a product you recently purchased at a store and list the visual merchandising elements that were used to attract buyers.

Successful businesses create distinct, clear, and consistent images for their customers. A good image sets a business apart from its competition. This image is made up of a unique blend of store characteristics, location, products, prices, advertising, public relations, and personal selling.

An image can include the design and layout of the store, its logo and signage, the unique lines of merchandise the store carries, the design of the store's Web site, a distinct promotional or ad campaign, and a targeted base of shoppers. A store's image should highlight what sets it apart from the competition. A good image will attract positive attention and loyal customers.

This chapter primarily focuses on visual merchandising in retail stores. However, manufacturers and wholesalers also use visual merchandising to sell their products. Visual merchandising is used extensively in manufacturers' showrooms and at trade shows and other conventions.

> " **The appearance of buildings and store interiors are promotional strategies to sell products and services.** "

THE ROLE OF VISUAL MERCHANDISERS

Visual merchandisers are responsible for the total merchandise or service presentation that helps to build the overall business or brand image. They design, create, and maintain the design elements of the building and displays. As active members of the marketing team, they promote a business's image and sales of its products or services.

As with all aspects of marketing, the goal of visual merchandisers is to attract customers to a store or business and keep them coming back. A visual merchandiser creates a selling space that is inviting and engaging and which allows customers to enjoy their shopping experience.

Reading Check

Explain Why is a display considered part of visual merchandising?

ELEMENTS OF VISUAL MERCHANDISING

The goal of visual merchandising is to create a positive shopping experience that will compel customers to return. Merchandisers consider four elements as key to achieving this goal: storefront, store layout, store interior, and interior displays. These elements lead customers into a store and keep them there once they have entered.

STOREFRONT

The exterior of a business is known as the *storefront*. The **storefront** includes a store's sign or logo, marquee, outdoor lighting, banners, planters, awnings, windows, and the exterior design, ambiance, landscaping, and lighting of the building. Consider The Home Depot® stores, for example. They are typically large buildings with bold graphics, bright orange signs, a convenient location near a highway, and a large, well-lit parking lot that provides easy access for customers. Unique storefronts build brand identity and help a company distinguish itself from its competitors and surrounding stores.

SIGNS

Outdoor signs are designed to attract attention, advertise a business, and project brand identity. The design of the sign should be original and easily recognizable. The name, letters, logo, materials, and colors used help create the store's desired image. An upscale clothing store might use an elegant script font in signage. A toy store, such as Toys 'R' Us®, uses bright primary colors to emphasize a youthful and playful image in its logo.

MARQUEE

A **marquee** is a canopy that extends over a store's entrance. Marquees are built over theater entrances, where names of the latest plays or movies are displayed. Marquees also can show the store's name, key products, hours of operation, phone number, and URL (web address). A company can exploit this highly visible space for advertising.

ENTRANCES

Entrances are usually designed with customer convenience and store security in mind. Smaller stores normally have only one entrance, while larger stores have several. The average midsize business needs at least two entrances. One is on the street for pedestrians and another is next to the parking lot for patrons who drive.

Types of entrances include revolving, push-pull, electronic, and climate-controlled entrances. Climate-controlled entrances are often found in indoor shopping malls. Each of these entrances projects a certain image. Electronically controlled sliding doors suggest a practical, self-service business. Push-pull doors with fancy metal or wooden push plates or bars suggest a full-service establishment.

Businesses use exterior design features such as signs, logos, marquees, lighting, and various landscaping features. *Why do you think large retail chains develop standardized storefronts?*

Storefront Design

Effective window displays get shoppers' attention. *Why are display windows useful for visual merchandising?*

Attracting Attention

WINDOW DISPLAYS

Display windows are especially useful for visual merchandising. Window displays attract prospects, create excitement for the products on display, and initiate the selling process. Customers who window shop are often drawn into stores by their window displays.

STORE LAYOUT

Store layout refers to ways that stores use floor space to facilitate and promote sales and serve customers. A typical store layout divides a store into four distinct spaces:

▶ **Selling space** is used for interior displays, wall and floor merchandise, product demonstrations, self-service and informational kiosks, sales transactions, and aisles for customer traffic flow.

▶ **Storage space** is for items that are kept in inventory or stockrooms. Customers do not see these items unless they ask to see an alternate version of a product that is in the selling space.

▶ **Personnel space** is allocated to store employees for office space, lockers, lunch breaks, and restrooms. These areas are marked with signs so that customers will not enter.

▶ **Customer space** is designed for the comfort and convenience of the customer and may include sandwich, soda, and coffee shops, in-store restaurants, seating, lounges, and recreation areas for children.

Store-layout planners and visual merchandisers decide how much selling space to allow for the entire floor space of the store. These planners also determine the type of interior and window displays to use for products and related items. They design specific customer traffic patterns to encourage browsing and impulse shopping.

STORE INTERIOR

Once the general placement of merchandise has been determined, store personnel can develop the visual merchandising approaches for the building's interior. Mannequins, decorations, comfortable seating, and innovative props are all valuable tools for creating a memorable shopping experience. The selection of floor and wall coverings, lighting, colors, store fixtures, interior signage, and graphics powerfully impact the customers' shopping experience and their image of the store.

Many quick-serve restaurant chains design and include recreational areas as part of their store layout. *What are the benefits for restaurants that create this type of customer space?*

The Importance of Customer Space

Businesses also use earth-friendly systems and fixtures to appeal to socially conscious consumers and to save on operating costs. "Green" awareness is the focus on reducing environmental damage by reducing energy costs, recycling scarce resources, and adopting practices to protect and improve the Earth's environment. For example, retail chains and quick-service eateries nationwide have installed tables and chairs made from recycled materials. Newly built Kohl's® department stores use recycled materials and have onsite recycling and water-saving fixtures with its Green Scene initiative.

Green Stores Buildings can be LEED certified, which means they are Leaders in Energy and Environmental Design.

GRAPHICS, SIGNAGE, COLOR, AND SOUND

Interior graphics and signage help promote a particular product brand and a specific line of products. They also provide directions to various departments or assist with a special promotional campaign, such as a demonstration, special sale, or a holiday promotion.

Interior graphics and signage are important in today's self-service environment. Box stores, mega-stores, and super centers, such as Costco® and Sam's Club®, develop giant signs, graphics, and banners to assist customers. Overhead digital signage, including in-house TV networks, is also found in many grocery stores and larger stores. Digital signage communicates product promotions and periodic public service announcements.

Point-of-purchase graphics are interior features that can decorate walls, windows, shelves, ceilings, and floors to reinforce product and store image. These interior features can also display merchandise.

MARKETING CASE STUDY

5 Gum: Interactive Display

To promote the launch of its 5® Gum brand in France, Wrigley® created a colorful "augmented reality" application that invites users to create their own custom music and video mixes. The 5 Mixer allows users to scratch like a DJ by manipulating printed symbols in front of a Webcam. Different onscreen markers represent different flavors of the gum.

Digital Display
This high-tech, cutting-edge campaign plays heavily on the "cool factor" associated with music-mixing and real-time interaction with a Web site. Anybody with an inkjet printer and a Webcam can take part. People can make music with no experience or special equipment. This audio-visual interactive display extends the 5 brand to entirely new audiences.

English Language Arts
Analyze How can engaging the customer's artistic creativity create a positive association with the brand being marketed? How might Wrigley® visually modify this audio-visual campaign for different countries? Discuss your responses with a partner.

For example, clothing can be displayed high on the walls, and sports equipment can be suspended from ceilings. This technique has the advantages of saving space and attracting customers with unique and higher-than-eye-level views.

Different colors and color schemes appeal to different types of customers. Specialty stores catering to teens might favor bright colors and lighting. Stores catering to adults might choose subdued colors and soft lighting to create a more subtle effect.

Background music and sound in stores can set a particular mood, encourage customers to shop, and be used to announce special product offerings. Sound can also reinforce a particular brand, business image, or target a particular customer.

LIGHTING

Lighting draws attention to store areas and specific products. Large warehouse stores often choose fluorescent or high-intensity discharge lighting. High-end, prestige retailers might install expensive chandeliers. Some specialty stores use newer lighting technologies, such as light-emitting diodes (LED) and compact fluorescent lighting (CFL). Stores might also choose certain lighting options for environmental reasons as well. For example, Starbucks® stores use LED lighting, which lowers operating costs and reduces energy consumption.

FIXTURES

The principal installations in a store are the fixtures. Fixtures are permanent or movable store furnishings that hold and display merchandise. Basic types of fixtures include display cases, tables, counters, floor and wall shelving units, racks, bins, stands, and even seating areas. Fixtures are strategically placed to maximize sales. For example, brightly colored front counters attract impulse purchases of competitively priced items, such as candy and magazines.

A business cultivating an upscale image might enhance its fixtures by painting them or covering them with textured materials (e.g., carpeting, fabric, cork, or reed). A business catering to discount buyers uses basic and unadorned shelf fixtures. The width of a store's aisles is related to its fixtures. The width of aisles and positioning of the fixtures and displays influence traffic patterns and buying behavior.

Many clothing stores have added comfortable seating areas near fitting rooms for people who might be waiting on a friend or family member who is trying on clothing. These seating areas give the store more of an upscale atmosphere.

WORLD MARKET

ITALY

Italian Taste

The icy treat known as *gelato*, Italian for *frozen*, has been the favorite of Italians since the 16th century. Created for nobility, the recipe reached the Italian citizens and was handed down through generations. Enjoyed worldwide today, gelato is a symbol of Italian pride.

World of Variety The best gelato depends on "honest" ingredients: milk, sugar, pure flavorings, seasonal fruit, and nuts. The result is creamier than ice cream with half the fat. Gelato is typically displayed in rows of eye-popping colors with mouth-watering flavors, from almond to *zabaione* (custard).

English Language Arts

Create You are opening a gelato shop. Sketch a layout of the store and display of the products, including the color scheme. Explain the reasons behind your designs.

Here are some entry-level phrases that are used in conversations about marketing all over the world.

English	Italian
Hello	Salve
Goodbye	Arrivederci
How are you?	Come stai?
Thank you	Grazie
You're welcome	Prego

connectED.mcgraw-hill.com

Get an activity on global marketing.

INTERIOR DISPLAYS

Interior displays show merchandise, provide customers with information, encourage customers to shop, reinforce advertisements, and promote a store's image. About one out of every four sales is generated by an interior display. There are five types of interior displays: architectural displays, closed displays, open displays, point-of-purchase displays, and store decorations.

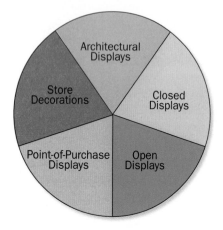

ARCHITECTURAL DISPLAYS

Architectural displays are model rooms that show customers how merchandise can be arranged in their homes. Examples include kitchens, bedrooms, and living rooms. This displays take up a considerable amount of room, so not all stores are able to use these kinds of displays.

CLOSED DISPLAYS

Closed displays allow customers to see but not handle merchandise without assistance from a salesperson. Closed displays are used for valuable items, such as jewelry, electronic devices, and other high-value items where theft, security, or breakage is a concern.

OPEN DISPLAYS

Open displays allow customers to handle and examine the merchandise without the help of a salesperson. Shelves, counters, and tables for food and hardware items can function as open displays. Open displays are an efficient way to sell products, so they have an important place in today's self-service selling environment.

POINT-OF-PURCHASE DISPLAYS

Point-of-purchase displays (POPs) are stand-alone structures that serve as consumer sales promotion devices. Most POPs are manufactured units with bold graphics and signage. They hold, display, and dispense products or provide information. Point-of-purchase displays encourage immediate purchases.

POPs that display products can be temporary, semi-permanent, and permanent. Temporary units are used for a short period of time and are normally not restocked after the featured merchandise is sold. An example is Hickory Farms® sausage and cheese kiosks for the winter holiday season. Semi-permanent units are used for themed promotions and are restocked for up to a year. Permanent units are designed for repeat usage over time. Vending machines for candy, beverages, snack items, and Automatic Teller Machines (ATMs) are examples of permanent point-of-purchase units.

POPs also provide services, directions to locate products, and offer tips on product usage. Examples include computer touch screens for digital-photo processing stands and gift registries. Blood-pressure testing stations, menu-planning units, and cosmetic stations to match a customer's preferences, coloring, and skin type are all POPs.

Point-of-purchase displays are designed to promote impulse purchases. *Why are they more effective at supporting new products than more established products?*

Unplanned Purchases

Interactive Kiosks

Interactive kiosks are interactive point-of-purchase displays that are free-standing, full-service retail locations. They are actually computer terminals that provide information access via electronic methods. Kiosks are placed in a variety of locations such as stores, businesses, shopping malls, and airports. They can be operated year-round or on a seasonal basis. They play a growing role in point-of-sale and self-serve merchandising. Interactive Web-based kiosks have pedestal-mounted, high-tech screens. Immediate product availability, online ordering capabilities for out-of-stock or larger items, and more reliable technology have led to increased popularity. Examples include interactive kiosks for DVD rentals, music, video games, postal services, digital photographs, airline tickets, and concert and theater tickets.

STORE DECORATIONS

Store decorations are displays that may coincide with seasons or holidays. Bold and colorful banners, signs, and props create the appropriate atmosphere to encourage related holiday purchases.

Items such as clothing are difficult to showcase in a closed display. The cosmetic department uses many types of displays. Items such as brushes and accessories may be part of an open display. Other items could be contained in a closed display to prevent customers from sampling them inappropriately. Point-of-purchase displays may serve as product or service information sources. In the case of interactive Web-based kiosks, they dispense products. Interior displays complement one another and create a positive, interactive buying experience.

 After You Read | **Section 18.1**

Review Key Concepts

1. **Differentiate** between visual merchandising and a display.
2. **Elaborate** on how the four elements of visual merchandising are related.
3. **Identify** five types of displays and how they are used.

Practice Academics

Social Studies

4. Some stores build new buildings or redesign existing ones to receive Leadership in Energy and Environmental Design (LEED) certification from the U.S. Green Building Council. Conduct research to find out the requirements to receive certification. Write a paragraph on the certification process and levels of certification.

Mathematics

5. A strip mall in Dallas has store spaces in several different sizes. There are eight 300-square-foot stores, one 800-square-foot store, and one 900-square-foot store. Two of the 300-square-foot stores are vacant. The others are occupied. What is the ratio of vacant space to occupied space? What percent of the space is occupied?

Math Concept **Ratios** A ratio compares two related numbers. Ratios are often expressed as fractions.

Starting Hints Compute the total space of the strip mall. Compute the amount of vacant space and compare the two totals.

 connectED.mcgraw-hill.com

Check your answers.

For help, go to the **Math Skills Handbook** located at the back of this book.

READING GUIDE

Before You Read

Predict What personal traits and technical skills do you need to design an effective store display?

Objectives

- **List** the five steps in creating a display.
- **Explain** how artistic elements function in display design.
- **Describe** the importance of display maintenance.

The Main Idea

Visual merchandisers must know the rules of artistic design to create displays that enhance sales, attract customers, and sustain customer loyalty.

Vocabulary

Content Vocabulary
- props
- color wheel
- complementary colors
- adjacent colors
- triadic colors
- focal point
- proportion
- formal balance
- informal balance

Academic Vocabulary
You will find these words in your reading and on your tests. Make sure you know their meanings.
- equip
- principles

Graphic Organizer

Draw or print this process chart to list in order the steps to create a display.

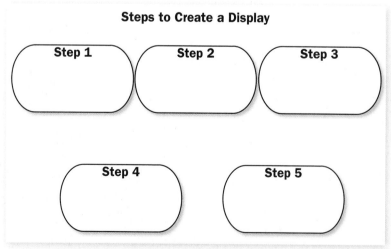

Steps to Create a Display

Step 1   Step 2   Step 3

Step 4   Step 5

connectED.mcgraw-hill.com

Print this graphic organizer.

MARKETING CORE FUNCTION

Promotion

DISPLAY DESIGN AND PREPARATION

Visual merchandisers help companies to attract customers and sell products. They have a limited amount of time to do this. Having a limited time frame to attract customers means that a business must plan its displays carefully. They must be targeted so that they appeal to customers.

Displays must be sensitive to individual perceptions, appeal to targeted customers, and support the overall business image. Failing to support the image of the business can be a huge problem. Consider a traditional clothing store. If it started using abstract displays of trendy merchandise, it might gain new customers. However, it would run the risk of losing loyal customers who preferred its old design choices.

When planning and preparing displays, retailers and merchandisers must be sensitive to cultural and ethnic diversity. Many companies employ marketing specialists in cross-cultural and ethnic design to adapt displays to a target market. All display design and selection involves five steps.

 As You Read

Consider What design skills do you have that would help you create a display?

STEP 1: SELECT MERCHANDISE FOR DISPLAY

The merchandise selected will determine the theme and all other supporting elements of the display. Display merchandise must also be visually appealing as well as contemporary to attract customers. New, popular, and best-selling products are often selected for display. The merchandise on display must also be appropriate for the season, its target audience, and for the store's geographic location.

STEP 2: SELECT THE TYPE OF DISPLAY

The merchandise selected for display determines the type of display to use and **equip**. There are four basic kinds of displays: displays that feature just one product; displays that feature similar products; displays that feature related products; and displays that feature an assortment or cross-mix of products.

A *one-item display* is best for a single-item product promotion of advertised specials or a newly developed product. An example might be an Apple® iPod set on a show box with a promotional logo. One-item displays are usually created for a single product promotion or an advertised special.

> **" In the retail environment, a display has about four to six seconds to attract a customer's attention, create a desire, and sell the product. "**

Similar-product displays show one kind of product but feature several brands, sizes, or models. An example would be a display of digital cameras by different manufacturers. This type of display allows customers to compare products.

A *related-product display* features products that are meant to be used together. An apparel store's related-product display might feature casual-wear. Shirts, pants, sweaters, and shoes would all be included. These displays are designed to entice customers to buy more than one item.

Assortment or cross-mix displays feature a collection of different or unrelated product lines placed on counters in the main aisles of a store. They are typically used by supermarkets, discount stores, and large mass-merchandising stores. This type of display has a special appeal to bargain hunters.

Props, or properties, are objects that hold the merchandise on display or support the display setting. Props are not for sale and are classified as decorative or functional. *Decorative props* include floor coverings and wall treatments, while *functional props* include items that hold the merchandise, such as shelves or hangers.

STEP 3: CHOOSE A SETTING

Displays can be presented in different settings. The setting depends on the image the business wants to project. The three types of settings are realistic, semi-realistic, and abstract.

A realistic setting depicts a room, area, or recognizable locale. The scene could be a restaurant, a park, or a party. Functional props, such as tables, chairs, plants, risers, books, dishes, and mannequins, provide the details.

A semi-realistic setting suggests a room or locale but leaves the details to the viewer's imagination. Decorative props, such as, a cardboard sun, a beach towel, a surfing poster, and a small sprinkling of sand would be enough to create the rest of the beach scene in the customer's mind. Businesses use semi-realistic settings when either space or budgets do not permit realistic settings.

An abstract setting does not imitate or even try to imitate reality. It focuses on form and color rather than on reproducing actual objects. Wide bands of torn colored paper placed as an accent behind or around merchandise can create an attractive abstract visual image that has little or nothing to do with reality.

Abstract settings do not require large amounts of storage space for props. Remember that stores may have props for a variety of seasonal promotions. These props can occupy a lot of space in the store's storage space. Also, abstract settings often use inexpensive everyday objects. Display specialists often use materials such as cardboard, paper, string, yarn, ribbon, and paint to create abstract settings.

The merchandise on display must be appropriate for the target market. *What are the four basic types of displays?*

Display Design

STEP 4: MANIPULATE THE ARTISTIC ELEMENTS

The artistic elements of a display include line, color, shape, direction, texture, proportion, balance, motion, and lighting. These **principles** of display influence your perception without you knowing it.

Line	Color	Shape
Direction	Texture	Proportion
Balance	Motion	Lighting

LINE

Lines within displays can direct the viewer's attention. Various types of lines create different impressions. Straight lines suggest stiffness and control, while curving lines suggest freedom and movement. Diagonal lines give the impression of action. Vertical lines project height and dignity. Horizontal lines convey confidence.

COLOR

Color selection is a critical step in developing displays. Colors are important because they can emotionally engage a customer to make a purchase decision. The colors selected for a display should contrast with those on the walls, floors, and fixtures around them. For example, a store decorated in pastels should feature displays that use darker, stronger colors.

FIGURE 18.1 The Color Wheel

Color Matters The color wheel is structured to show both similarities and differences in color. Effective displays use colors that draw customers' attention but do not compete with the product. *How would you use this wheel to create complementary color harmony?*

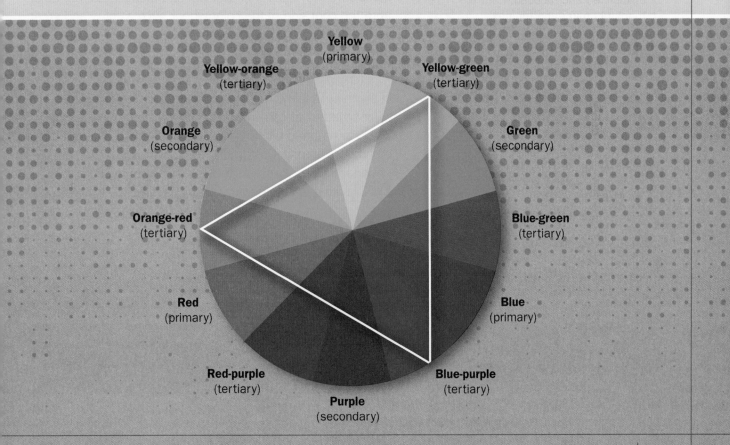

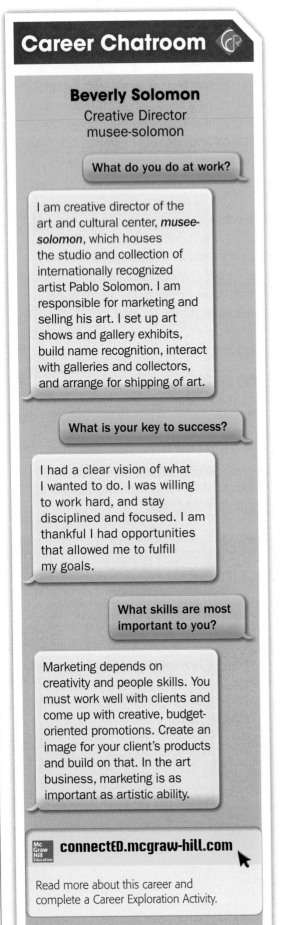
The standard **color wheel**, shown in **Figure 18.1** on page 431, illustrates the relationships among colors. **Complementary colors** are opposite each other on the color wheel and create high contrast. Red and green, blue and orange, and yellow and purple are examples of pairs of complementary colors.

Adjacent colors, also called "analogous colors," are located next to each other on the color wheel and share the same undertones. Successive adjacent colors (such as yellow-orange, yellow, and yellow-green) form families, or groups of colors, that blend well with each other.

Triadic colors involve three colors equally spaced on the color wheel, such as red, yellow, and blue. Triadic color harmony, as shown by the triangle on the color wheel in **Figure 18.1** on page 429, creates vivid and contrasting colors. Triadic color schemes can be achieved by rotating the triangle within the color wheel.

Color and color groups create specific moods and feelings, such as calmness or excitement. Colors from the warm side of the color wheel, such as red and yellow, convey a festive mood that works well with lower-priced merchandise. These colors must be used cautiously. Their contrast is so great that it can detract from the merchandise and even irritate customers. This problem can usually be avoided by varying the shades of the colors somewhat to lessen their contrast. It is important to make sure they keep their warmth and friendliness too. Colors from the cool side of the color wheel, such as blue and green, represent calm and refinement. They are often associated with higher-priced merchandise.

Customers' expectations about color are also important in planning displays. Customers have come to expect certain color schemes at certain times of the year. Earth tones are more common in fall, while bright colors and pastels are common in spring. Customers' reactions to colors are also important. Red evokes excitement, so it should not be used in a display that is designed to convey calmness.

SHAPE

Shape refers to the physical appearance, or outline, of a display. Shape is determined by the props, fixtures, and merchandise used in the display. Display units might resemble squares, cubes, circles, and triangles. Displays that have little or no distinct shape, known as *mass displays*, are also an option. Dollar stores, discounters, and supermarkets often use mass displays to display large quantities and to indicate low price.

DIRECTION

A good display directs the viewer's eye to the merchandise, moving a viewer's attention seamlessly from one part of the display to another. This smooth visual flow is called "direction." Effective displays create direction by using techniques such as color, repetition, and lighting patterns. These displays also create direction by arranging merchandise in a pattern that guides a customer's eye.

Effective displays should also have a **focal point**, an area in the display that attracts attention first, above all else. A good method of creating an effective focal point is to build the display elements in a triangular shape. The focal point is created by placing the strongest shape at the top, or apex, of the imaginary triangle in the display. A viewer's eyes will naturally travel to the strongest shape within a display. This arrangement helps keep the eyes moving up and over the merchandise. Displays that lack a focal point are said to be unfocused. Typically, an unfocused display contains too many items, too many shapes, or too many props outside the imaginary triangle.

TEXTURE

Texture is the look of the surfaces in a display. It can be smooth or rough. The contrast between the textures used in a display creates visual interest. Products that are smooth, such as flatware, should be placed against backgrounds or props that are rough. This contrast allows the products to "pop," or stand out from the backgrounds where they are placed.

PROPORTION

Proportion refers to the relationship between and among objects in a display. The merchandise should always be the primary focus of a display. Props, graphics, and signs should be in proportion to the merchandise. They should not dominate the display.

BALANCE

Display designers also pay attention to balance when creating displays. They place large items with large items and small items with small items to create **formal balance** in a display. When a large item is on one side of a display, an equally large item should be on the other side for balance. The opposite effect can also be appealing to customers. To create **informal balance**, designers place several small items with one large item within the display. An example of an informal display would be an adult mannequin placed next to several shallow baskets of flowers that are elevated on a prop to the mannequin's height.

MOTION

Motion is playing an increasingly important role in display design. Animation can be achieved through the use of motorized fixtures, mannequins, and props. Mechanical mannequins have been used for years in holiday displays. Motion should be used sparingly to accentuate merchandise, not overpower it.

LIGHTING

Proper lighting is critical to attractive displays. Spotlights, floodlights, and rotating, colored, or flashing lights can highlight individual items. Lighting can help make merchandise appear more attractive. It is recommended that display lighting be two to five times stronger than a store's general lighting. Colored lighting in displays can create dramatic effects. Lighting used with reflective items, such as crystal, jewelry, and fine china, needs careful attention. The lighting in a fine housewares department would be much different than the lighting in a teen clothing department.

The lighting in the dressing rooms is not part of a display, but it should be considered. Dressing-room lighting that is glaring and unflattering will negatively affect a consumer's buying decisions. This is true even if the merchandise was lit appropriately in the display on the sales floor.

STEP 5: EVALUATE THE COMPLETED DISPLAY

Do the displays enhance the store's image, appeal to customers, and promote the product in the best possible way? Was a theme creatively applied? Were the color and signage appropriate? Was the result pleasing? These are just some of the questions that visual merchandisers consider when evaluating the effectiveness of displays.

Reading Check

Recall List in order the five steps used to create a display.

Displays have a limited time frame to attract customers. *Do you think that this store's window display would catch the attention of the customers it is targeting? Why?*

Display Design

DISPLAY MAINTENANCE

Once a display has been constructed, it needs to be maintained and eventually dismantled. Individual businesses have different policies regarding the duration of displays or how long they stay up. Some businesses, such as electronics stores, change out certain displays once a week to accommodate newly released items. Most businesses check their displays daily for damage, displacements, or missing items caused by customer handling and purchases. Folded and stacked clothing items in a display should be organized and restocked frequently. One of the first steps in dismantling a display is to organize, label, and pack or reshelve stock.

Proper display maintenance can keep the merchandise fresh and attractive to customers. Poor maintenance can create a negative image not only of the merchandise but also of the store. Display fixtures and props should be cleaned and merchandise dusted on a regular basis. Customers are not likely to be enthusiastic about purchasing items that are displayed on dusty or dirty fixtures. A customer may also ignore or pass by a display that is poorly stocked or appears disorganized. A final step in dismantling a display is to repair, replace, or discard damaged display materials. Any new stock that had been on display must also be returned to its proper place in the store.

 After You Read   **Section 18.2**

Review Key Concepts

1. **Explain** why the first step in display preparation is so important.
2. **Differentiate** between decorative and functional props.
3. **Describe** how formal balance and informal balance are achieved in a display.

Practice Academics

English Language Arts

4. Compose a letter to a local business. In your letter, describe how the store's display is effective or how it could be improved. Provide suggestions and examples.

Social Studies

5. Visit a boutique store to observe point-of-purchase displays (POPs). Ask permission to sketch a display on a poster board. Ask the store owner why and how product display choices were made. Annotate your sketch with the comments and answers.

 connectED.mcgraw-hill.com

Check your answers.

Visual Merchandising and Display

Elements of visual merchandising that create a positive customer experience are storefront, store layout, store interior, and interior displays.

Prescribed steps and principles for artistic design help create effective displays that attract customers and keep them coming back.

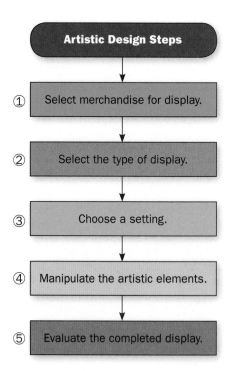

Artistic Design Steps

① Select merchandise for display.

② Select the type of display.

③ Choose a setting.

④ Manipulate the artistic elements.

⑤ Evaluate the completed display.

Review and Activities

Written Summary

- Visual merchandising is an important part of a business's total promotional mix.
- Visual merchandising must be coordinated with advertising, direct marketing, personal selling, and sales promotion efforts.
- Visual merchandising and in-store displays help to sell products, build brand image, and create store image.
- The four elements of visual merchandising that create a positive customer experience are storefront, store layout, store interior, and interior displays.
- Types of interior displays include architectural displays, store decorations, open displays, closed displays, and point-of-purchase displays.
- Businesses create effective displays by using prescribed steps and principles for artistic design to attract customers for new and repeat business.

Review Content Vocabulary and Academic Vocabulary

1. Write each of the vocabulary terms below on an index card, and the definitions on separate index cards. Work in pairs or small groups to match each term to its definition.

Content Vocabulary
- visual merchandising (p. 419)
- display (p. 419)
- storefront (p. 420)
- marquee (p. 420)
- store layout (p. 421)
- fixtures (p. 423)
- point-of-purchase displays (POPs) (p. 424)
- interactive kiosk (p. 425)
- props (p. 428)
- color wheel (p. 430)
- complementary colors (p. 430)
- adjacent colors (p. 430)
- triadic colors (p. 430)
- focal point (p. 431)
- proportion (p. 431)
- formal balance (p. 431)
- informal balance (p. 431)

Academic Vocabulary
- project (p. 419)
- concept (p. 419)
- equip (p. 427)
- principle (p. 429)

Assess for Understanding

2. **Describe** What is the concept and purpose of visual merchandising?
3. **Identify** What are the types of display arrangements?
4. **Summarize** What role do visual merchandisers play on the marketing team?
5. **Create** How will you follow the five steps in creating an effective display for a business?
6. **Elaborate** How do artistic elements function in designing displays?
7. **Compose** How should employees dismantle a display once it is done being used? Write a step-by-step guide.
8. **Role Play** What design elements will you and a business partner consider as you plan a display in your store?
9. **Evaluate** How could an environmentally friendly approach benefit your store?

21st  Century Skills

Problem-Solving Skills

10. Window Display Work with a classmate to select a product or product category that interests the team. Use a poster board to sketch a potential window display for the selected item(s). You must identify the product or product category, type of setting for the product, functional and decorative props, and appropriate signage to use with your display.

Financial Literacy Skills

11. Display Tool Box You have been asked to order and assemble a display with the following items from a local store: scissors and stapler $15.15; a glue gun $9.95; a tape measure $5.49; razor blades and utility knife $5.49, paper towels and window spray $3.49; small tools (hammer, screwdriver and pliers) $15.65; and a notebook and a pad of paper, $2.95. Assume a sales tax of 6 percent. What will be the total cost of these items for your employer?

e-Marketing Skills

12. Interactive Kiosks Imagine that you work with digital signage for a large visual merchandising firm that wants to introduce digital signage to large-volume grocery stores. You have been asked to explain the idea to the management team of the grocery stores. Write a paragraph answering these questions:

- How is digital signage used in product promotion?
- What are the advantages of digital signage for this type of environment?
- What are the disadvantages of digital signage for this type of environment?
- Which local stores use digital signage?
- How can you learn from these stores' use of digital signage?

Build Academic Skills

Social Studies

13. Institutional Displays Work with a partner to design and create an institutional display for a local charity, volunteer, or non-profit agency. The team must identify and research the organization, its goals and objectives, and suggest ideas for a possible interior display. When finished, present a summary of your research and how the display might appear to the class.

Science

14. Science and Technology Retailers desire lighting that highlights merchandise but also reduces energy and replacement costs. Conduct research on the technology of compact fluorescent lights (CFL) or light-emitting diodes (LED) lighting and the potential applications for visual merchandising and display. Recommend a way to incorporate these lighting systems into a local store.

Mathematics

15. Calculate Budgeted Expenses Charlie owns a company that makes all-natural soap. Last year he spent 2 percent of the company's profits ($84,300) to get good placement on the shelves of grocery stores. This year he will only be able to spend $1,000 on the placement in grocery stores. What is the percent decrease? (Round your answer to the nearest whole percent.)

Math Concept **Mixed Numbers** When determining the value of a certain percent of the whole, convert the percent to a decimal by dividing it by 100, or move the decimal point two places to the left.

For help, go to the **Math Skills Handbook** located at the back of this book.

Standardized Test Practice

Directions Read the following questions. On a separate piece of paper, write the best possible answer for each one.

1. Which of the following refers to the ways stores use floor space to facilitate sales and serve customers?
   A. Interior displays
   B. Storefront
   C. Store interior
   D. Store layout

2. Point-of-purchase displays are a consumer sales promotion device.
   T
   F

3. Colors found opposite each other on the color wheel are called _____ colors.

Test-Taking Tip

When taking a test, keep moving along. Think about a problem for a minute or two, and if no answer comes to mind, then go on to the next problem. Come back to the other one later.

DECA Connection Role Play

Assistant Manager Clothing Store

Situation You are the assistant manager of a locally owned clothing store that sells merchandise targeted to teens and young adults. The store is located in a family friendly suburban area situated in a strip shopping center three miles from a large high school. Other businesses in the center include a music store, fast-food restaurant, grocery store, and drug store. Your store's merchandise consists mostly of casual clothing, some dressier items, and accessory items.

It is now mid-summer, approaching the back-to-school shopping season. The first shipment of back-to-school clothing is due to arrive soon. The store manager (judge) has decided it is time to plan storewide back-to-school visual merchandising. The store manager (judge) has asked for your help and ideas with the planning of the back-to-school visual merchandising. You will meet with the store manager (judge) later today to discuss your ideas. This meeting will focus on planning store signage and merchandise displays.

Activity You are to make notes about your ideas for the back-to-school store signage and merchandise displays. You will then meet with the store manager (judge) to present your ideas for the back-to-school store signage and merchandise displays.

Evaluation You will be evaluated on how well you meet the following performance indicators:

1. Explain the use of visual merchandising in retailing.
2. Create displays
3. Create promotional signs.
4. Plan visual merchandising activities.
5. Plan/schedule displays/themes with management.

 connectED.mcgraw-hill.com

Download the Competitive Events Workbook for more Role-Play practice.

advertising

SHOW WHAT YOU KNOW

Visual Literacy There are many types of advertising to match the needs and budgets of large and small businesses. Advertising media comes in many forms and is shown in many places. *How do you think a business decides what to spend and where to advertise its goods and services?*

Discovery Project

The Advertising Plan

Essential Question How does a business create an advertising plan?

Project Goal

Work with a classmate to select a good or service to promote. Develop a one-year advertising plan and a written report that includes a description of your target audience, the media that will be used for advertising, the costs of each advertising medium, and an estimated budget for each month and a whole year. Your advertising plan must be appropriate for your geographical location and reflect the types of media available with realistic costs.

Ask Yourself...

- What is your good or service and your target audience?
- What media will you select to use in your advertising plan?
- How will you determine media costs and a budget for the advertising plan?
- How will you organize the advertising plan and written report?

 Organize and Interpret What types of advertising will be the most effective in reaching your target audience?

 connectED.mcgraw-hill.com

Activity
Get a worksheet activity about advertising.

Evaluate
Download a rubric you can use to evaluate your project.

DECA Connection

DECA Event Role Play

Concepts in this chapter are related to DECA competitive events that involve a comprehensive test and either an interview or role play.

Performance Indicators The performance indicators represent key skills and knowledge. Your key to success in DECA competitive events is relating them to concepts in this chapter.

- Explain types of advertising media.
- Analyze a sales promotional plan.
- Develop an advertising campaign.
- Calculate media costs.
- Prepare a promotional budget.

DECA Prep

Role Play Practice role-playing with the DECA Connection competitive-event activity at the end of this chapter. More information on DECA events can be found on DECA's Web site.

READING GUIDE

Before You Read

Connect What effective advertisements have you seen recently?

Objectives

- **Explain** the concept and purpose of advertising in the promotional mix.
- **Identify** the different types of advertising media.
- **Discuss** the planning and selection of media.

The Main Idea

Advertising is an important element of promotion. Businesses advertise to promote their ideas, goods, and services.

Vocabulary

Content Vocabulary
- advertising
- promotional advertising
- institutional advertising
- media
- print media
- transit advertising
- broadcast media
- Internet advertising
- podcast
- blogs
- specialty media
- media planning

Academic Vocabulary

You will find these words in your reading and on your tests. Make sure you know their meanings.
- region
- networks

Graphic Organizer

Draw or print this chart to organize your notes about the types of media used for advertising.

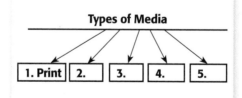

Types of Media

| 1. Print | 2. | 3. | 4. | 5. |

 connectED.mcgraw-hill.com

Print this graphic organizer.

MARKETING CORE FUNCTION

Promotion

Advertising Media

ADVERTISING AND ITS PURPOSE

Advertising is nonpersonal promotion which promotes ideas, goods, or services by using a variety of media. The average city dweller is exposed to more than 3,000 advertising messages every day. Advertisers control the message, where it will be seen or heard, and how often it will be repeated.

Depending on its purpose, marketers can use advertising to introduce a new business or change a company image. Advertising can also promote a new product or an existing one, encourage the use of a particular service, or encourage business-to-business transactions.

As You Read

Classify How would you classify the advertisements you have seen in the past week?

PROMOTIONAL AND INSTITUTIONAL ADVERTISING

There are two main types of advertising: promotional and institutional. **Promotional advertising** is advertising designed to increase sales. The targets of promotional advertising can be either consumers or business-to-business customers. Sometimes promotional advertising encourages potential customers to ask for information, call for appointments, participate on the Internet, or enter a retail store.

Promotional advertising generates leads or develops prospects that can lead to a purchase and increased sales for a business. Promotional advertising is an effective way to support direct selling, visual merchandising and display, and other sales promotion activities.

Institutional advertising is advertising designed to create a favorable image for a company and foster goodwill in the marketplace. Companies often perform public service advertising and underwrite the cost of ads to help community and nonprofit groups promote their services or projects. Institutional advertising does not directly increase sales. However, by connecting its name to a worthy cause, a company creates a good impression with potential customers.

> **"** Advertising is everywhere—television, radio, magazines, stores, Internet, billboards, schools, sports arenas, and even on highway road signs. **"**

MASS ADVERTISING

Mass advertising enables companies to reach large numbers of people with their messages. Certain media, such as television and radio, lend themselves to mass advertising. Thanks to today's sophisticated technology, advertisers can also carefully target their messages to select audiences. This is known as targeted advertising. Advertising demonstrates the features and benefits of a good or service. As a result, advertising encourages business customers and general consumers to buy products.

Reading Check

Contrast How are promotional advertising and institutional advertising different?

TYPES OF MEDIA

Media are the agencies, means, or instruments used to convey advertising messages to the public. The four general categories of advertising media are print, broadcast, Internet, and specialty. The advertising message and the target audience determine the type of media that is used.

TYPE	EXAMPLE
Print	Newspaper
Broadcast	Television
Internet	Opt-in e-mail
Specialty	Giveaways

PRINT MEDIA

Print media includes advertising in newspapers, magazines, direct mail, signs, and billboards. This is one of the oldest and most effective types of advertising.

NEWSPAPER ADVERTISING

Newspapers continue to be an important advertising outlet for many consumer-oriented products and services. It is estimated that about 43 million households in the United States subscribe to a newspaper, a number that has declined over 20 years. Advertisers want their ads to be seen, so high numbers of readers are very important. Newspapers offer a variety of advertising options, including the ad size, its location, and the frequency of ad insertions. This flexibility enables companies to select the options that best suit their budgets and advertising goals.

MARKETING CASE STUDY

Under Armour Shoes!

Under Armour® is known for manufacturing clothing and accessories for athletes. However, the company needed a marketing campaign to announce the launch of its new footwear line. The company developed the "Athletes Run" campaign, which featured appearances from a number of world-class athletes. The campaign focused on the concept that "all runners are athletes and all athletes run."

Celebrating Training

The ads aired on TV networks watched by athletes. They spotlighted the effort and dedication that goes into becoming great at a sport. The spots included professional athletes such as Brandon Jacobs, formerly of the New York Giants, retired soccer star Heather Mitts, Jeff Samardzija of the Chicago White Sox, Olympic volleyball player Nicole Branagh, and others.

English Language Arts/Writing

In addition to magazine and TV ads aimed at athletes, what are some other media this brand might use for advertisements? Create a brief ad for the new footwear line and explain how the company will use it.

Direct-mail advertisers have a wide choice of printed advertisement formats—letters, catalogs, and postcards—limited only by postal regulations. Direct mail also includes electronic advertising campaigns. This flexibility enables direct mailers to test various creative approaches and obtain valuable results for perfecting future campaigns.

Disadvantages

There are disadvantages to direct mail. It yields a low level of response in relation to the number of items sent. An average return or redemption rate of 1 to 3 percent for printed direct mail is typical. Poorly planned and executed direct-mail campaigns yield less than a one-half percent response.

Direct mail also has an image problem. Many people think of printed or electronic direct-mail advertising as junk mail. The cost of printed direct mailing can be high because it includes producing and printing each piece of the mailing, collating it, buying mailing lists, and paying for postage to send it.

DIRECTORY ADVERTISING

The best example of a directory that accepts advertising is the telephone directory. In the *White Pages*, businesses and residents receive a free alphabetical listing of their phone numbers and addresses.

In the *Yellow Pages*, businesses pay for an alphabetical listing and, if desired, a display ad. The listings and ads appear under general category headings. Switchboard® is an online Internet-based version of the *Yellow Pages*. Consumers can find a business and maps with directions. The digital version provides advertising opportunities using interactive display ads. Advertisers can adjust their information, offers, or messages. In contrast, printed versions must remain the same until a directory is reprinted and distributed.

Directory advertising has some unique advantages. It is relatively inexpensive and can be used to target all demographic groups. For example, 99 percent of adults in the United States are familiar with the *Yellow Pages*. Printed directories are usually kept for at least a year or until another one is provided.

OUTDOOR ADVERTISING

Local, regional, and national businesses use outdoor signs for advertising. There are two types of outdoor signs: non-standardized and standardized. Nonstandardized outdoor signs are used by companies at their places of business or in other locations throughout the community. An example is a sign displaying a company's logo at the entrance to its office building.

Standardized outdoor signs, or billboards, are purchased from advertising companies. Billboards have standard sizes that are designed to be viewed from more than 50 feet away. Digital technologies have been integrated into some billboards, so that they appear as flat-screen televisions with impressive images. Billboard displays can use lights, moving parts, attachments and Bluetooth® technologies to attract attention. These types of billboards are common in densely populated metropolitan areas.

Billboards are classified by size. Called "bulletins," the largest of this type of billboard is 14 feet by 48 feet. Smaller versions are called "posters." Posters are outdoor panels and come in various sizes. They are changed three to four times each year. Bulletins are advertising signs placed along major highways that are changed every six months to a year.

Advantages and Disadvantages

Outdoor advertising is highly visible and relatively inexpensive. It provides a 24-hour a-day, 7-days-a-week message, and can be located to reach a specific geographical area. Drawbacks of outdoor advertising include limited viewing time and increasing government regulations. Outdoor advertising is usually restricted to highways, secondary roads, and areas zoned for commercial and industrial uses.

TRANSIT ADVERTISING

Transit advertising is advertisement seen on public transportation. It includes printed posters inside buses, taxis, and trains, as well as ads on public benches, bus-stop shelters, kiosks, and newsstands. Station advertising is seen near or in subways and in airline, bus, ferry, and railroad terminals.

Almost everyone is familiar with the advertising on public transportation, such as advertising on buses, and in subway stations and cars. *What are some advantages of transit advertising?*

Transit Advertising

Transit advertising reaches a wide and sometimes captive audience. This type of advertising is economical and has a defined market of people who are traveling.

BROADCAST MEDIA

Broadcast media encompass radio and television. By age 66, the average person spends nearly ten years watching 2 million television commercials and almost six years listening to the radio. You can see why advertising through broadcast media is popular. Most of the 1,700 commercial television stations are affiliated with one of the major **networks**—ABC, CBS, NBC, or Fox. In addition, there are about 6,100 local cable systems. Network and cable television has mass appeal and is found in nearly all American households.

TELEVISION ADVERTISING

Most television advertisements are 30- or 60-second spots. An exception is the infomercial, which is a 30- or 60-minute advertisement. Infomercials promote products, such as cookware, exercise equipment, and appliances, using a talk-show type setting. Viewers can order the advertised merchandise by calling a phone number, visiting a Web site, or writing to an address.

Network television is the ultimate mass-advertising medium for many businesses because it combines all these elements—sight, sound, action, and color—to produce a compelling advertising message. As a result, television is a very effective medium for demonstrating a product's features and benefits. Cable television allows advertisers to target their advertising messages to audiences with a specific interest, such as history, music, sports, or travel.

Businesses can use local television advertising to market their products or services to a specific geographic area. Local companies can also place commercials inside network programming delivered by cable providers. "Smart" television systems allow viewers to push a button during a commercial to request more information. Use of this technology has become increasingly popular among political candidates at election time.

Hot Topic

Television Habits On average, households with annual income under $30,000 watch 5 hours and 20 minutes per day, while those with income over $100,000 watch 3 hours and 40 minutes per day.

There are some disadvantages to television advertising. It has the highest production costs of any type of media and a high cost for the TV time purchased. Production costs for a network TV commercial average more than $400,000. Prime-time and special-event costs are high. A 30-second ad for the Super Bowl costs about $4.5 million.

Smaller companies cannot usually afford network-television advertising, or they must buy time in less desirable time slots. Another disadvantage is that many viewers change stations, leave the room, or use devices that allow them to view commercial-free programming.

RADIO ADVERTISING

Radio is a medium that can be heard just about anywhere. It is also a timely medium. Radio advertisers can update or change their advertising messages daily or hourly. Radio has the immediacy of newspapers without the high production costs of television. More than 14,000 AM and FM radio stations reach 96 percent of all people age 12 and over in a given week. With the growth of Internet radio stations, one-third of Americans listen to streaming stations. This ability to reach a wide audience makes radio an extremely efficient and cost-effective advertising medium.

Radio advertisers can carefully target their audiences when they select the station on which to broadcast their ads. Most radio station programming already targets a specific segment of the radio listening market.

Radio advertisements are presented in 10-, 20-, 30-, or 60-second time periods. These messages are effective in encouraging people to buy because an announcer or actors—along with background music, jingles, slogans, and sound effects—can add excitement, drama, or humor.

However, goods or services can only be described, not seen. Advertisers cannot rely on visual involvement to hold a listener's attention. That is why a catchy jingle is important. Radio advertisements also have a short life span.

INTERNET ADVERTISING

Internet advertising is a form of advertising that uses either e-mail or the World Wide Web. It is still a modest part of overall advertising spending, but it is growing steadily. As print ads declined with newspaper subscriptions, online ads have grown. Examples include opt-in e-mail ads, banner ads, pop-up ads, search engine ads, and rich-media video ads. These ads are increasingly combined

Billboard Advertising

Large billboards can use spectacular displays with lights, attachments, and moving parts to attract attention. *What are the benefits of outdoor advertising?*

with animation, video, and sound with interactive features to deliver more exciting advertising messages. Another area of Internet advertising is social marketing. This involves customer-generated feedback generated when a company invites consumers to submit comments and advertising ideas about the company's products.

OPT-IN E-MAIL ADS

Electronic direct-mail advertising is sent via e-mail. Today most advertising of this type is sent to prequalified groups of people. This is known as opt-in e-mail because recipients requested it or authorized it. Many of these e-mails provide links so that the recipient can click through to a company's Web site. This enables most companies to track exactly how many people visit their site by clicking on the link in the e-mail. It is also cost-effective and easy to update with personalized messages for each recipient.

BANNER AND SEARCH ENGINE ADS

Most online advertising appears as banner or display ads. Banner ads come in various shapes and sizes, but usually as a rectangle seen at the top, bottom, or side of a Web page.

Some advertisers use pop-up banner ads, which are TV-like spots that pop up between Web pages. They can also be inserted in audio or video streams, either live or on-demand. A viewer clicks on the ad to get to the advertiser's Web site—or to close the ad window to resume Internet use.

Search engine ads appear while using a search engine, such as on Google®, Bing®, or MSN Search®. These ads are short text lines that appear and direct the user to an advertiser's Web site. Advertisers can buy search terms that appear if a term is mentioned in the search results.

Online advertisers have found that bold colors, top-of-page placement, animation, calls to action, and limited frequency of exposures all help increase the number of visitors to Web sites.

But even using these techniques, online advertisers report response rates as low as 0.3 percent. In other words, for every 1,000 banner ads, only three in 1,000 users click on the online ad to visit the advertiser's Web site.

RICH-MEDIA AND VIDEO ADS

Rich-media banner ads combine animation, video, and sound with interactive features. Podcasting began as a way to listen to music from an electronic MP3 file in a digital music player, such as an iPod® device. A **podcast** can now be any brief digital broadcast that includes audio, images, and video delivered separately or in combination. Podcast ads provide additional opportunities for Internet advertisers.

Rich-media banner and video ads provide instant, detailed feedback about how much time viewers spend watching or listening to the ads. Rich-media and video ads entice viewers to make an online purchase or to submit their demographic data in real time. These ads generate better brand recognition and higher sales than do static online ads.

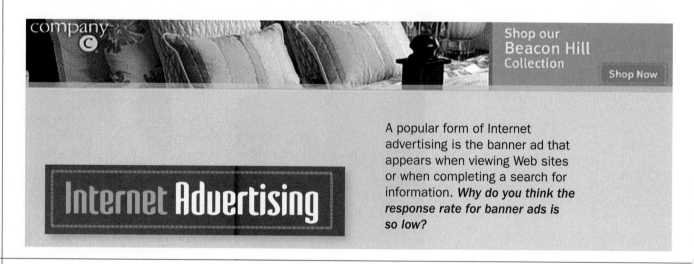

A popular form of Internet advertising is the banner ad that appears when viewing Web sites or when completing a search for information. *Why do you think the response rate for banner ads is so low?*

SOCIAL-MEDIA ADVERTISING

Large companies use social media to get across their advertising messages. These companies invite consumers to interact with their products, often through personal blogs. **Blogs** are personal Web sites where individuals share thoughts, pictures, and comments with visitors.

Sometimes companies encourage ideas and opinions for advertising messages, read product blogs, generate or share videos about their product, or establish business pages on social media networks. Companies use social networks in the belief that people trust the opinions of their friends and peers. Product endorsement through social networks boosts image and sales.

Examples of social-media advertising include the National Football League asking fans to submit Super Bowl ad ideas; Johnson & Johnson® using a YouTube® channel linked to the Olympics; and Coca-Cola®, Starbucks® or Pizza Hut® having business pages on Facebook®. Social media, such as Twitter®, and Facebook, allow companies opportunities to interact with their target audience. Companies can also learn about their target audience through platforms like Geofeedia, which monitors and analyzes real-time, location-based social media activity from anywhere.

These interactions allow companies to develop advertising messages, create customer profiles, develop sales leads, provide special offers, and maintain customer feedback. This informs them of the image and performance of their products.

SPECIALTY MEDIA

Specialty media, also known as *giveaways* or *advertising specialties*, are relatively inexpensive useful products that are imprinted with the company's name, message, or logo.

To be successful as advertising tools, specialty items must be practical, used frequently, and displayed in locations with high visibility. Common items that fit this description are appointment books, calendars, magnets, pens, pencils, shirts, caps, and bags. Specialty items carry the identity of the business sponsoring them and an advertising message.

Disadvantages include limited distribution of items and advertising to people who would never consider buying the product or patronizing the business.

Companies often have business pages on popular social-networking Web sites. *What are the advantages for businesses to participate in social-network marketing?*

OTHER ADVERTISING MEDIA

Businesses are constantly creating innovative and unusual means of transmitting their messages to potential customers. Examples include:

▶ Ad-supported TV screens at airports, gas stations, health clubs, and subways

▶ Digital billboards at sports arenas

▶ On-screen movie theater ads

▶ Messages on diaper-changing stations, trash cans, bathroom stalls, elevators, and even hot-air balloons.

IN-STORE ADVERTISING

Increasingly, retailers are using in-store advertising techniques. These include:

▶ Ceiling and floor graphics

▶ Electronic shelf ads

▶ Supermarket-cart displays

▶ Instant-coupon machines

These techniques—as well as kiosks, sound systems, and closed-circuit television networks—advertise products within stores.

NEW MEDIA

New media advertising is interactive and Internet-driven. It uses new electronic media devices, such as Web-enabled small-screen iPods®, cell phones, laptops, and video games to reach an increasingly mobile population. Advertisers go to those places on the Internet where they can find their target customers: websites, blogs (Web logs), vlogs (video logs), visual and audio newscasts, RSS news feeds, and social networking sites (Facebook®, Twitter®).

Improved ways to access the Internet continue to provide marketers with creative advertising opportunities to market their goods and services. This includes Third-Generation (3G) and Fourth-Generation (4G) and Fifth-Generation (5G) wireless networks, Voice-Over-Internet Protocol (VOIP) telephony, Home Networking, and Wi-Fi.

 Reading Check

Identify What are five types of media used for advertising?

MEDIA PLANNING AND SELECTION

Media planning is the process of selecting the appropriate advertising media and deciding the time or space in which ads should appear to accomplish a marketing objective. To select and compare different types of media, companies use media-planning software, media-cost data, and audience information. The choice of a particular advertising medium ultimately depends on the product to be advertised and the demographics and lifestyles of the target audience. The size of the advertising budget and the types of media available in the geographical area are also factors.

To establish the media plan and select the right medium to use, advertisers must ask and answer three basic questions:

1. Can the medium present the product and the appropriate business image?

2. Can the desired customers be targeted with the medium?

3. Will the medium get the desired response rate?

The media plan provides the opportunity to present a compelling message and project the desired business image to the target market.

 After You Read   **Section 19.1**

Review Key Concepts

1. **Determine** which form of advertising would most likely be used by a small company with a limited budget.
2. **Identify** potential drawbacks with using the two types of broadcast media.
3. **Connect** the practice of media planning to the concept of market segmentation.

Practice Academics

Science

4. Scientists are researching how the brain responds to the effects of colors, logos, product features, smell, touch, music, and jingles used in advertising messages. Conduct research on the science of neuromarketing. Choose an advertisement and identify how one of its features is related to neuromarketing.

Mathematics

5. Assume that total Internet advertising revenue by format was $16.9 billion for one year. What advertising revenue amounts were generated in each format category, if search-engine ads represented 40 percent, display ads 22 percent, rich media and videos 7 percent, and e-mail 2 percent?

   Math Concept **Computation** Determining a value's percent of the whole is a matter of division.

   Starting Hints To solve this problem, divide the amount spent for each medium by the total amount spent on advertising to get a decimal number. Then multiply the decimal point and determine the percent.

 connectED.mcgraw-hill.com

Check your answers.

For help, go to the **Math Skills Handbook** located at the back of this book.

READING GUIDE

Before You Read

Predict What financial and design factors do advertisers have to consider?

Objectives

- **Identify** media measurement techniques.
- **Explain** techniques used to evaluate media.
- **Summarize** how media costs are determined.
- **Explain** promotional budget methods.

The Main Idea

Businesses need to reach as many targeted customers as possible. It is important to calculate costs and measure media effectiveness to reach a potential audience.

Vocabulary

Content Vocabulary

- audience
- frequency
- impression
- cost per thousand (CPM)

Academic Vocabulary

You will find these words in your reading and on your tests. Make sure you know their meanings.

- crucial
- objective

Graphic Organizer

Draw or print this chart to take notes about media measurement and rates.

MEDIA RATES	
Newspaper How Are Rates Determined?	**Magazine** How Are Rates Determined?
_____ _____ _____ _____	_____ _____ _____ _____
Internet How Are Rates Determined?	**Radio & Television** How Are Rates Determined?
_____ _____ _____ _____	_____ _____ _____ _____

 connectED.mcgraw-hill.com

Print this graphic organizer.

MARKETING CORE FUNCTION

 Promotion

Section 19.2

Media Rates

MEDIA MEASUREMENT

Media planners must consider the correct medium to use for advertising, its costs, and how to measure overall advertising effectiveness. To understand media measurement, you need to become familiar with several key terms.

The number of homes or people exposed to an ad is called the **audience**. The audience for print media is the total number of readers per issue.

Readership in print media is measured by surveys or estimated by circulation. The audience figure is normally higher than its circulation because more than one person can read a single issue of a printed newspaper or magazine.

From an advertiser's point of view, the audience figure better reflects the actual number of people exposed to an ad. **Frequency** is the number of times an audience sees or hears an advertisement.

> **" Everyone knows that it pays to advertise, but the questions are "How well?" and "Was it worth the cost?" "**

A single exposure to an advertising message is an **impression**. Online media measurement is measured through surveys and computer software tracking systems to calculate the number of people who view a particular ad.

When advertisers buy time on television or radio or space in print or online, they typically hope for the largest audience, greatest frequency, and most impressions possible. This helps ensure that their products or services are exposed to as many potential customers as possible.

Television media measurement is based upon data collected by ACNielsen Media Research® for a sample of TV viewers in more than 200 TV markets. This data is gathered through the use of either diaries filled out by sample households or set-top meters attached to televisions or cable or satellite boxes. The most important measurement of viewing behavior occurs during what are called "sweeps months" four times a year—in February, May, July, and November.

The Arbitron Company® similarly measures radio advertising in more than 272 markets. To determine radio listenership, Arbitron has sample households fill out diaries describing what stations they listened to and when they tuned in. Arbitron also collects data on listening behavior by means of cell-phone-sized Portable People Meters. The meter records data whenever the person wearing it is exposed to encoded signals from radio stations, regardless of their location.

Cost per thousand (CPM) is the media-measurement cost of exposing 1,000 readers or viewers to an advertising impression. (The "M" in CPM stands for *mille*, which is the Latin word for 1,000.) Cost per thousand is the comparison tool used to determine the effectiveness of different types of broadcast, print, and digital media.

It is important to know whether you are spending your advertising dollars effectively. Knowing the potential audience, how frequently your advertisement will be seen, and its CPM can tell you whether the rates charged by various media are right for your advertising budget.

 As You Read

Predict How do businesses measure the effectiveness of their advertising media?

MEDIA RATES

To reach customers, advertisers use a set format that is defined in terms of time (e.g., 30-second TV commercial) or space (e.g., half-page newspaper ad). Media costs vary greatly, not just by type of media but also by geographical location and audience. For example, a quarter-page newspaper ad in a large city daily newspaper costs four to eight times more than the same-sized ad costs in a small-town weekly. It is virtually impossible to quote exact rates for each type of media advertising.

Businesses research rates for specific newspapers and magazines by visiting individual Web sites or by looking up rates in various publications from the Standard Rate and Data Service®.

Another important service for both advertisers and print media is provided by the Audit Bureau of Circulations® (ABC). Print media publishers subscribe to the ABC to verify their circulation figures. A circulation audit is **crucial** to publishers because it enables them to verify circulation numbers to advertisers. Circulation figures are important selling points when publications want to attract and retain their advertisers.

NEWSPAPER RATES

Newspaper advertising rates are divided into two categories depending on whether the ad is a classified ad or a display ad.

Classified ads are grouped, or classified, into specific categories, such as help wanted, real estate, personals, or auto sales. They are effective for selling everything from services to houses to job openings. People or businesses that buy classified ads usually pay by the word or line of type.

Display ads enable the advertiser to depict the product or service being advertised. Advertisers use a mix of art or photographs, headlines, copy, and a signature or logo of the product or business. Display ads are generally larger than classified ads. Their cost is based upon the amount of space used and the ad's position in the newspaper.

Newspapers quote display advertising rates by the column inch. A column inch is an area that is one-column wide by one-inch deep. If a newspaper quotes a column-inch rate, you simply multiply the number of columns by the number of inches to determine the total number of column inches. Then multiply the total column inches by the rate. For example, if the rate for a column inch is $17, then a single ad (called an "insertion") that measures three columns by four inches long will cost $204.

$$\$17 \times 3 \text{ columns} \times 4 \text{ inches} = \$204$$

Newspaper Advertising Rates

- Factors that Affect Rates
- Comparing Rates

FACTORS THAT AFFECT RATES

The open rate, or noncontract rate, represents the basic charge for a minimum amount of advertising space. The open rate, referred to as the noncontract rate, is used for infrequent advertisers. It is the highest rate charged for a display ad.

Advertising rates also vary depending on when an advertisement will appear in a paper. A newspaper may charge a Monday-through-Thursday rate of $29 per column inch, a Friday rate of $30, a Saturday rate of $32, and a Sunday rate of $35 per column inch.

The location of an ad is another factor. Display ads are usually sold at run-of-paper rates. Run-of-paper allows the newspaper to choose where to run an ad in the paper. For a higher rate, advertisers can run ads in guaranteed or preferred locations, such as the back cover. The use of color also affects the advertising rate. Color ads are sold at a higher price than black-and-white ads. The frequency of advertising lowers the amount charged. Businesses that advertise in the newspaper may contract to guarantee the newspaper that they will use a certain amount of space for a specified time period. They are granted contract rates, which are discounted from the open rate.

Contracts can be written in a number of ways. A yearly frequency contract guarantees that an advertiser will use a minimum number of column inches each week for 52 weeks. A bulk-space contract guarantees that a minimum number of inches will be used when the advertiser chooses within a 12-month period.

COMPARING RATES

The cost per thousand (CPM) measurement is useful in comparing the cost of advertising to reach 1,000 readers in one newspaper with the cost of advertising to reach 1,000 readers in another newspaper. The comparison is made by using the following formula:

Cost of the Ad × 1,000/Circulation = CPM

Suppose the cost of an ad in the *Times* is $500, and the paper has a circulation of 500,000. Its CPM would be calculated as follows:

$500 × 1,000/500,000 = $500,000/500,000 = $1 per 1,000 readers

Suppose the cost of an ad in the *Tribune*, a competing paper, is $600, and the paper has a circulation of 300,000. Its CPM would be calculated as follows:

$600 × 1,000/300,000 = $600,000/300,000 = $2 per 1,000 readers

All other things being equal, an advertiser would probably choose the *Times* over the *Tribune*. Of course, all other things might not be equal. The *Tribune's* circulation could include more of the advertiser's target market, or the paper could offer a special ad placement. CPM is a convenient measure that enables advertisers to compare costs.

MAGAZINE RATES

Magazine rates are based on circulation, the type of readership, and production techniques. To calculate the actual cost of magazine advertising, you need to become familiar with terms found on magazine advertising rate cards. These terms include bleed, black-and-white rates, color rates, full-color, premium position, and discounts. (See **Figure 19.1**, page 457.)

Bleed means that half- or full-page ads are printed to the very edge of the page, leaving no white border. Magazines generally charge between 15 to 20 percent extra for bleeds.

The lowest rates that magazines offer for display ads are black-and-white rates for black-and-white advertisements. Color rates are offered for color ads. Each time a magazine adds color to an ad, the rates increase. Four-color advertisements, also called full-color are the most expensive to buy.

Premium position refers to ad placement. Ads placed in premium spot, such as on the back cover or the inside of the first page, cost more.

Magazines quote display advertising rates by the color type and position of the advertisement. *Why would a full-page, black and white ad cost more than a half-page full-color ad?*

Magazine Rates

RATE DISCOUNTS

Frequency discounts are offered to advertisers who run the same ad several times during the year. The magazine may publish an entire schedule of rates for the number of times during the year that an advertiser contracts to advertise. The rate per issue decreases as the frequency increases.

Another discount is a commission—a percentage of sales given by the magazine to the advertising agency for placing the ad for the advertiser. A typical commission is 15 percent.

Take a look at the rate card. You would calculate the cost of a full-page, four-color advertisement with bleed as follows:

$23,300	1 page, four-color rate
× .15	
$ 3,495	extra cost for bleed

$23,300	1 page, four-color rate
+ 3,495	
$26,795	for 1 page, four-color, with bleed

An ad agency placed the ad and it took the commission and the cash discount. The total cost of the above ad to the agency would be as follows:

$26,795.00	1 page, four-color, with bleed
× .15	ad agency's commission
$ 4,019.25	

$ 26,795.00	1 page, four-color, with bleed
− 4,019.25	agency's commission
$ 22,775.75	net cost of ad to agency after commission

× .02	cash discount percentage if paid within 10 days of invoice

$ 455.52	cash discount

$22,775.75	net cost of ad to agency after commission
− 455.52	cash discount
$22,320.23	net cost to advertising agency for one full-page, four-color ad with bleed after cash discount and agency commission

As with newspapers, the CPM is used to compare the cost of advertising in several magazines. If a magazine has a circulation of 2 million and charges $35,000 for a full-page, black-and-white ad, the CPM would be $17.50.

$$\$35,000 \times 1,000/2,000,000 = \$17.50$$

INTERNET RATES

Internet advertising rates are based on the type of display format desired. Options include banner ads (mini, mid-page, vertical, horizontal, floating, expandable), rich-media ads, pop-up and pop-under ads. Online ad rates are set on a CPM rate based on page views. Web analytic services can monitor this.

Additional online advertising options include paid listings at portal sites, sponsorship of Web sites, and newsletters sold on a flat-fee basis. Per-click rates are often used in search engine and opt-in e-mail advertisements.

Pay-for-sale advertising is another online option. It is used when e-marketers sign up other businesses to share a link or display ads. These businesses often sell related products. Commissions are paid to the other businesses as a percentage of sales only when sales are made through the affiliated link.

A Premium Location

This ad appeared in a premium position of a consumer magazine—on the back cover. *Why are higher rates charged for premium advertisements?*

FIGURE 19.1 Magazine Rate Card

Ad rates are based on color. *Based on this magazine rate card, what is the cost of a half-page, four-color ad paid in ten days from the issuance of the invoice?*

General Rates

RATE BASE: Rates based on a yearly average of 1,100,000 net paid A B C
A member of the Audit Bureau of Circulation

SPACE UNITS	BLACK & WHITE	BLACK & ONE COLOR	FOUR COLOR
1 page	$16,000	$19,630	$23,300
2 columns	11,620	14,560	18,170
½ page	10,130	13,550	17,200
1 column	5,920	9,530	12,180
½ column	3,020		

Covers

Second Cover	$25,520
Third Cover	23,300
Fourth Cover	27,020

BLEED CHARGE: 15%
AGENCY COMMISSION: 15%
CASH DISCOUNT: 2% 10 days, net 30 days

Bleed accepted in color, black & white, and on covers, at an additional charge of 15%. No charge for gutter bleed in double-page spread.

Premium Positions: A 10% premium applies to advertising units positioned on pages 1, 2, and 3. A surcharge of 5% applies to bleed units in premium positions.

Rate Change Announcements will be made at least two months in advance of the black & white closing date for the issue affected. Orders for issues thereafter at rates then prevailing.

ISSUANCE AND CLOSING DATES

A. On sale date approximately the 15th of month preceding date of issue.

B. Black & white, black & one color, and four-color closing date, 20th of the 3rd month preceding date of issue. Example: Forms for August issue close May 20th.

C. **Orders for cover pages noncancellable. Orders for all inside advertising units are noncancellable 15 days prior to their respective closing dates.** Supplied inserts are noncancellable the 1st of the 4th month preceding month of issue. Options on cover positions must be exercised at least 30 days prior to four-color closing date. If order is not received by such date, cover option automatically lapses.

RADIO RATES

When purchasing radio time, a business needs to decide what kind of radio advertising to use. There are three options: network radio advertising, national spot-radio advertising, and local radio advertising. It is important to know the difference between spot-radio and spot commercials. Spot radio refers to the geographical area an advertiser wants to reach with its advertising. Spot commercials are advertising messages of one minute or less that can be carried on network radio or spot radio.

Businesses with a national customer base usually choose network radio advertising or national spot-radio advertising. Network radio advertising is broadcast from a network studio to all affiliated radio stations throughout the country. Network radio advertising allows advertisers to broadcast ads, special programs, and radio talk shows simultaneously to several markets.

The following radio airtimes are listed from most expensive to least expensive:

▶ Class AA: Morning drive time: 6 A.M. to 10 A.M.
▶ Class A: Evening drive time: 4 P.M. to 7 P.M.
▶ Class B: Home worker time: 10 A.M. to 4 P.M.
▶ Class C: Evening time: 7 P.M. to midnight
▶ Class D: Nighttime: midnight to 6 A.M.

Rates are higher during early morning and late afternoon listening times, also called "drive times." Radio stations also offer less costly, run-of-schedule (ROS) airtimes. ROS airtime allows a radio station to decide when to run the ad. Week-day and weekend rates, weekly package plans, and discounts differ from station to station.

TELEVISION RATES

Advertising rates for television also vary with time of day. It is more expensive, for example, to advertise during the prime time hours of 7 P.M. to 10 P.M. than during other hours. The rates charged for other time slots, such as day (9 A.M. to 4 P.M.), late fringe (10:35 P.M. to 1:00 A.M.), or overnight (1 A.M. to 5 A.M.) are lower due to smaller numbers of viewers. Advertisers try to play their messages during the time slots that enable them to reach the most customers.

Reading Check

Infer Why is it virtually impossible to compare advertising rates from different media?

It is more expensive to advertise during prime time than during other hours of the day. *Why do advertisers want to broadcast television ads during prime time?*

Television Advertising

PROMOTIONAL BUDGET

The promotional budget considers not only the cost for developing and placing or airing advertising, but also the cost of staffing the department or advertising campaign. The advertiser must consider short- and long-term benefits of the effort. There are four common promotional budgeting methods:

1. **Percentage of Sales** In this method, the budget is based on a percentage of past or anticipated sales. For example, the current budget for advertising might be 5 percent of last year's sales, or 5 percent of projected sales for the coming season. In either case, the advertising budget is tied to figures that could be too high or too low for the current market condition.

2. **All You Can Afford** With this method, the business first pays all expenses, then applies the remainder of funds to promotional activities.

This method is often used for only a short time. It is popular in small businesses. The **objective** is to build sales and reputation quickly.

3. **Following the Competition** With this method, an advertiser matches its competitor's promotional expenditures or prepares a budget based on the competitor's market share. A drawback is that it is based on only the competitor's objectives.

4. **Objective and Task** With this method, the company determines goals, identifies the steps to meet goals, and determines the cost for promotional activities to meet the goals. This is the most effective method because it focuses on the company's goals and how it will reach them.

 After You Read | **Section 19.2**

Review Key Concepts

1. **Contrast** possible ad rates for a small weekly newspaper with a large daily newspaper.
2. **Explain** how CPM determines the rates television and radio stations charge for advertising.
3. **Suggest** a reason that following the competition is not the best model for creating a promotional budget.

Practice Academics

English Language Arts

4. In the percentage-of-sales method, a business builds the advertising budget on a percentage of past or anticipated sales. Think of reasons this approach may not work in a slow economy. Create a brief dialogue between two or more members of a company who are discussing the use of this method in a slow economy.

Mathematics

5. What is CPM for a magazine that has a circulation of 1.7 million and charges $35,000 for a full-page, black-and-white advertisement?

   Math Concept **Operations** The CPM is the cost per thousand, and is used to determine the cost of advertising per 1,000 people in an audience.

   Starting Hints To solve this problem, multiply the cost of the ad by 1,000.
   Divide the number obtained from multiplying the cost by 1,000 by the total audience to determine the CPM.

 connectED.mcgraw-hill.com

Check your answers.

For help, go to the **Math Skills Handbook** located at the back of this book.

Advertising

Advertising presents a message to buy a product or to accept an idea. Businesses select the best advertising medium for their target market. After media is selected, a business prepares a media plan. Media planners calculate the costs and measure advertising effectiveness. Once a business selects its promotional methods and goals, a promotional budget is developed.

Review and Activities

Written Summary

- The main purpose of advertising is to present a message that encourages the customer to buy a product or service or to accept an idea.
- Businesses must choose the most appropriate advertising media for their target market. Advertising media include print, broadcast, Internet, and specialty.
- Businesses prepare media plans that explain how they will implement their advertisements.
- Choosing the correct medium to use from all the available types of media is a very complex effort.
- Media planners must concern themselves not only with the correct medium to use and its costs but also with how to measure overall advertising effectiveness.
- Once a company decides on its promotional methods and goals, it must create a promotional budget.

Review Content Vocabulary and Academic Vocabulary

1. Write true-or-false statements using each vocabulary word. Ask a partner to determine whether each statement is true or false and explain why.

   ### Content Vocabulary
   - advertising (p. 441)
   - promotional advertising (p. 441)
   - institutional advertising (p. 441)
   - media (p. 442)
   - print media (p. 442)
   - transit advertising (p. 445)
   - broadcast media (p. 446)
   - Internet advertising (p. 447)
   - podcast (p. 448)
   - blogs (p. 449)
   - specialty media (p. 449)
   - media planning (p. 451)
   - audience (p. 453)
   - frequency (p. 453)
   - impression (p. 453)
   - cost per thousand (CPM) (p. 453)

   ### Academic Vocabulary
   - region (p. 443)
   - networks (p. 446)
   - crucial (p. 454)
   - objective (p. 459)

Assess for Understanding

2. **Describe** What is the concept and purpose of advertising in the promotional mix?
3. **List** What are the different types of advertising media?
4. **Summarize** What is the process used in planning and selecting media?
5. **Compute** What is the cost of a two-column, four-color, full bleed advertisement (based on the rates in Figure 19.1)?
6. **Distinguish** What is the difference between frequency and impression?
7. **Role Play** How can you convince your manager to use a different type of advertising for a new product?
8. **Assess** What is the best promotional budget method to use during the current economic climate?
9. **Suggest** What are some reasons businesses are shifting advertising dollars from print and TV to the Web?

21st  Century Skills

Communication Skills

10. Interview Contact and schedule an interview with the owner or manager of a local business. Identify the types of advertising used by the business. You must develop an introduction to use before the interview, an interview script, a one-page summary of the answers, and a thank-you letter after the interview.

Financial Literacy Skills

11. Click-Through Internet advertising rates are based on the type of display format the customer wants. Ads rates are normally based upon the number of viewer click-throughs per thousand. Calculate the number of impressions for each of these ads:

Type of Ad	Click-Through Rate	Number of Impressions/thousand
Expandable banner	0.3 percent	
Floating Ad	5.0 percent	
Floating expandable	1.4 percent	
Push-down banner	0.3 percent	

Everyday Ethics

12. Texting and Driving Mobile technology may be lethal—at least on the road. A nationwide study reports that nearly 6,000 people were victims of drivers who were distracted by using cell phones and other similar devices. The U.S. Transportation Secretary said it is "an epidemic, and it seems to be getting worse each year." Make a list of three basic rules for drivers who have these devices. Write a public service announcement (PSA) for radio, highlighting your rules.

e-Marketing Skills

13. Social Networking Imagine that you work for a company that is considering purchasing a business page on a social-networking Web site. Conduct research on the concept of social networking and personal blogs. You have been asked to summarize your findings. Include the following in your report:

- List the benefits of having a business page on a social network Web site.

- Identify some disadvantages of social networks and personal blogs.

Build Academic Skills

English Language Arts

14. Communication Skills Some television content is developed for babies and toddlers. Parents may be tempted to use TV viewing as an electronic babysitter, as there are so many children's TV shows, DVDs, and videos available. Conduct research on responsible ways to handle television viewing. Create a public service announcement that gives parents tips for how to watch TV with young children.

Science

15. Science and Technology Some people believe that Internet advertising and online shopping has advantages for protecting the environment. Develop a one-page outline with broad topic headings, such as "Energy," "Resources," and "Social Benefits." List some possible ways to save valuable resources or recycle them as a result of using Internet advertising versus print advertising.

Mathematics

16. CPM Calculations Calculate the CPM for an ad that costs $12,000 in a magazine that has a circulation of 8,500,000 people. (Round your answer to the nearest cent.)

Math Concept **Computation** Computing the CPM for ads in certain publications involves multiplication and division.

For help, go to the **Math Skills Handbook** located at the back of this book.

Standardized Test Practice

Directions Read the following questions. On a separate sheet of paper, write the best possible answer for each one.

1. Which of the following is a type of media that includes advertising in newspapers, magazines, and direct mail?
   A. Broadcast media
   B. Online media
   C. Print media
   D. Specialty media

2. The number of homes or people exposed to an advertising message is called the "frequency."
   T
   F

3. The media cost of exposing 1,000 readers or viewers to an advertising impression is known as the _____.

Test-Taking Tip

Concentration can reduce anxiety when you are taking a test. Pay close attention to one question at a time.

DECA. Connection Role Play

Owner
Paint and Wallpaper Store

Situation Your store will open for business in one month. It is located in the downtown area of a mid-sized town. The population of your trade area is a mix of young professionals without children and families with young children.

Your store will stock paints manufactured by a national company that is known for its high quality and wide variety of colors. Your stock will also include wallpaper produced by high-quality manufacturers who make both traditional and contemporary wallpaper designs. You will also sell all the accessories and tools necessary for both professionals and amateurs to complete their projects.

You want your store to have a successful start. You know that you must let potential customers know about your store and the merchandise you sell. You are thinking about launching a small advertising campaign to introduce your store. Your promotional budget is limited. You must plan carefully and get the most from your advertising dollars. You are planning to meet with a friend (judge) who has much experience in advertising to ask for guidance and advice.

Activity Make notes about your ideas for a small advertising campaign to introduce the store. List the objectives of the campaign and several types of advertising media you are considering. You will discuss your ideas with your friend (judge).

Evaluation You will be evaluated on how well you meet the following performance indicators:

1. Explain types of advertising media.
2. Analyze a sales promotional plan.
3. Develop an advertising campaign.
4. Calculate media costs.
5. Prepare a promotional budget.

 connectED.mcgraw-hill.com

Download the Competitive Events Workbook for more Role-Play practice.

print advertisements

Visual Literacy Print advertisements have the ability to attract attention and help sell goods and services. Writing style, design, and the images in ads depend on the product and where the print ad appears. *Think of a print ad you have seen recently. What makes it effective?*

Discovery Project

The Print Advertisement

Essential Question What key components make a print advertisement effective?

Project Goal

You and a classmate are employed at a sporting goods store. You and your partner must design a print advertisement for a product offered by the store. Your ad must include a headline, advertising copy, an illustration, and a signature. Develop your print advertisement and prepare a brief class presentation explaining the reasons for its design and why you believe the ad is effective.

Ask Yourself...

- What is your product and its target market?
- What will your headline and advertising copy say?
- What will your illustration and signature look like?
- How will you design the advertisement and organize your presentation?

 Analyze What type of print advertisement will best attract your target audience?

---

 connectED.mcgraw-hill.com

Activity
Get a worksheet activity about designing print ads.

Evaluate
Download a rubric you can use to evaluate your project.

DECA Connection

DECA Event Role Play

Concepts in this chapter are related to DECA competitive events that involve either an interview or role play.

Performance Indicators The performance indicators represent key skills and knowledge. Your key to success in DECA competitive events is relating them to concepts in this chapter.

- Explain the components of advertisements.
- Explain the importance of coordinating elements in advertisements.
- Explain the nature of effective written communication.
- Edit and revise written work consistent with professional standards.
- Orient new employees.

DECA Prep

Role Play Practice role-playing with the DECA Connection competitive-event activity at the end of this chapter. More information on DECA events can be found on DECA's Web site.

READING GUIDE

Analyze Compare print ads from a recent newspaper or magazine. What are key elements they share?

Objectives

- **Discuss** how advertising campaigns are developed.
- **Explain** the role of an advertising agency.
- **Identify** the main components of print advertisements.

The Main Idea

Successful advertising campaigns include essential elements to help sell goods and services.

Vocabulary

Content Vocabulary

- advertising campaign
- advertising agencies
- logotype
- headline
- copy
- illustration
- clip art
- signature
- slogan

Academic Vocabulary

You will find these words in your reading and on your tests. Make sure you know their meanings.

- experts
- statistics

Graphic Organizer

Draw or print this chart to organize your notes about the components of a print ad.

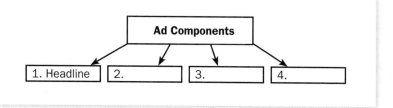

```
        ┌─────────────────────┐
        │   Ad Components      │
        └─────────────────────┘
     ↓        ↓        ↓        ↓
┌───────────┐┌──────┐┌──────┐┌──────┐
│1. Headline││2.    ││3.    ││4.    │
└───────────┘└──────┘└──────┘└──────┘
```

connectED.mcgraw-hill.com

Print this graphic organizer.

MARKETING CORE FUNCTION

Promotion

Elements of Advertising

Section 20.1

THE ADVERTISING CAMPAIGN

To advertise a product or service, a company must plan an advertising campaign. An **advertising campaign** is a group of advertisements (print and digital), commercials, and related promotional materials and activities that are designed as part of a coordinated advertising plan to meet the specific goals of a company.

An advertising campaign involves the creation and coordination of a series of advertisements placed in various types of media. Broadcast, print, Internet, outdoor, and specialty advertisements are organized around a particular theme. The theme of an advertising campaign is the central message that a company hopes to communicate to potential customers. The theme can be used to promote a specific product or service or a mix of the company's various products and services.

> " To advertise a product or service, a company **must** plan an advertising campaign. "

The size and the financial resources of a business determine whether an advertising campaign is developed by an in-house advertising department, a few designated individuals, or an advertising agency. Advertising agencies from outside the company can be full-service or limited-service. These distinctions indicate the agency's level of involvement in the creation and production of the advertisement. Regardless of how it is developed, an advertising campaign should be part of a promotional effort that includes personal selling, public relations, and sales promotion.

Planning an integrated advertising campaign involves a series of steps:

1. **Identify the target audience** Advertisers analyze the market for a product or service and determine which potential customers should receive messages.

2. **Determine objectives** An advertiser identifies the objectives, such as increasing brand awareness or sales, changing customer attitudes, or increasing knowledge about the product.

3. **Establish the budget** Advertisers decide what to spend on advertising over a set period of time. It is important to make sure that advertising dollars are spent as effectively as possible.

4. **Develop the message** Advertisers develop the overall theme and messages based on the features, benefits, and uses of a particular product or service. The message can also be used to highlight a company's unique mix of products and services.

5. **Select the media** The target audience and available funds determine the best media to use, such as TV, radio, Internet, or print. Selections are based upon which media will have the best chance to reach the target audience and stay within the budget.

6. **Evaluate the campaign** Advertisers use market research to see if the campaign met its objectives and if the advertising messages were well received. Metrics, such as improvement in sales, increases in sales leads, and response rates for direct mail may be used to determine if a print advertising campaign was successful.

 As You Read

Reflect What elements of graphic design have you noticed in ads?

ADVERTISING AGENCIES

Advertising agencies are independent businesses that specialize in developing ad campaigns and crafting the ads for clients. Depending on the scope and size of the advertising campaign and the needs of the business, agencies can serve as a full-service agency or a limited-service agency. There are also new models that advertising agencies can follow.

Types of Advertising Agencies

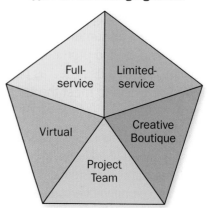

Full-service agencies plan an entire advertising campaign by setting objectives, developing advertising messages and strategies, and completing media plans. They also select media and coordinate related activities such as sales promotion and public relations.

Larger businesses often select a full-service agency to be the agency of record to handle all aspects of the campaign. The agency of record does all the necessary research, media selection, copy development, and artwork. Advertising agencies employ specialists, such as copywriters, graphic artists, media **experts**, marketing researchers, and legal advisers to help with the development and execution of campaigns.

Limited-service agencies specialize in one aspect of the campaign, such as creative services, media planning, or media buying for an advertising campaign. Larger companies are increasingly selecting specialists, such as those who concentrate only on Internet advertising, to develop different aspects of an advertising campaign. Global consumer brands also make use of specialty agencies to develop or tailor campaigns to specific countries, ethnic groups, or other target markets.

Technology and e-commerce opportunities have led many businesses to employ in-house staff for some advertising functions, such as Web-site development and maintenance. Some companies assist in-house resources with the work of freelance professionals or limited-service agencies.

NEW MODELS FOR ADVERTISING AGENCIES

Some new models for advertising agencies include several business formats. They are creative boutiques, project team agencies, and virtual agencies.

A creative boutique is a specialized service agency that helps businesses with creative production. In a creative boutique, the advertiser develops the message and copy but outsources the design and production of the advertisement. This type of organization enables the advertiser to create ads more quickly than a traditional agency could.

Agencies that are organized around a project team provide research, copywriting, creative execution, and media placement without the overhead of a larger agency. Teams can come together to do one project, and then move on to the next when the ad campaign is complete.

In a virtual agency, one individual coordinates the work of a network of experienced freelancers. A freelancer is a self-employed person who sells work or services by the hour, day, or job, rather than working on a regular salary basis for one employer. One of the benefits of this type of agency is that the agency has lower overhead expenses, which means lower costs for the client.

Reading Check

Recall What are the types of advertising agencies?

DEVELOPING PRINT ADVERTISEMENTS

Although they are only one part of an advertising campaign, print advertisements are very important to most campaigns. Print advertisements have four key elements: headline, copy, illustrations, and signature (see **Figure 20.1** on page 470).

Some advertisements also include a company's slogan, logo, and, if required, product disclosures. A **logotype** or logo is a graphic symbol for a company, brand, or organization. It can be used separately or in combination with a signature.

Ads that must include mandatory disclosures, terms, and conditions may display them on the bottom of a print advertisement. For example, a car or truck ad that advertises better gas mileage must disclose the Environmental Protection Agency's (EPA) estimated mileage at the bottom of the ad.

FIGURE 20.1 | Elements of a Print Advertisement

Keys to Ad Success A print advertisement usually contains four elements: headline, copy, illustration, and a signature. Some advertisements also include the company's slogan and product disclosures. *How do the elements of an ad work together?*

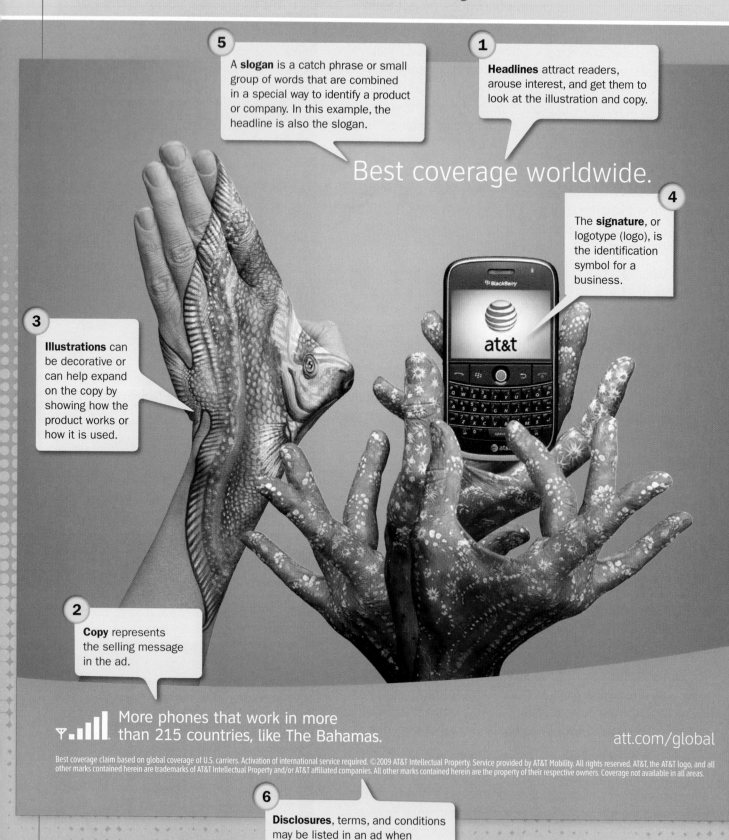

5 A **slogan** is a catch phrase or small group of words that are combined in a special way to identify a product or company. In this example, the headline is also the slogan.

1 **Headlines** attract readers, arouse interest, and get them to look at the illustration and copy.

4 The **signature**, or logotype (logo), is the identification symbol for a business.

3 **Illustrations** can be decorative or can help expand on the copy by showing how the product works or how it is used.

2 **Copy** represents the selling message in the ad.

Best coverage worldwide.

More phones that work in more than 215 countries, like The Bahamas.

att.com/global

Best coverage claim based on global coverage of U.S. carriers. Activation of international service required. ©2009 AT&T Intellectual Property. Service provided by AT&T Mobility. All rights reserved. AT&T, the AT&T logo, and all other marks contained herein are trademarks of AT&T Intellectual Property and/or AT&T affiliated companies. All other marks contained herein are the property of their respective owners. Coverage not available in all areas.

6 **Disclosures**, terms, and conditions may be listed in an ad when discussing product features.

Each key element enhances the overall theme and promotes the product. The four fundamental elements of a print advertisement are applicable for ads in other media, too. As you read this section, think of ways these concepts would apply to preparing television, radio, and Internet ads.

HEADLINE

The **headline** is the phrase or sentence that captures the readers' attention, generates interest, and entices them to read the rest of the ad. Headlines quickly grab attention to a product. Headlines are responsible for the overall effectiveness of most advertising campaigns. Many experts believe that every print ad, including brochures, flyers, newspaper ads, and magazine ads, needs a headline. A headline leads readers into the ad's illustration. It makes them want to read the copy to learn more about the product's benefits.

PURPOSE OF HEADLINES

Headlines must be attention-getters or the ad may not be read. More than 80 percent of the people who look at an advertisement just read the headline. Research shows that words such as *free*, *new*, *now*, and *your* attract attention.

Effective headlines target an audience. They have advertising appeal and provide reasons for purchasing a good or service. The motivation for purchasing helps to identify potential customers. Headlines appeal to people by using a variety of motivators, such as profit, love, fear, fun, and vanity. Effective headlines allow the advertised product to project an image for the potential customer.

A headline provides a benefit for the reader. It promises something that matches a need or want. Benefits might include more miles per gallon, better service, or fewer cavities.

Headlines lead to the copy and illustration. Headlines are often written so that readers grasp the entire point of the ad simply by viewing the headline, seeing the illustration, and reading a few words of copy. Other times, headlines have a sub-headline to either clarify or expand on the main idea expressed in the headline.

Sub-headlines are usually found in smaller type close to the headline. Powerful headlines draw potential customers into reading the copy.

WRITING EFFECTIVE HEADLINES

Before writing a headline, a copywriter must know the needs of the target market. These needs might relate to price, delivery, performance, reliability, service, or quality. The headline must identify a benefit of the product.

Effective headlines stress these benefits by making a promise, asking a question, posing a challenge, or using a testimonial. Key words are often used in headlines to link the benefits in a personal way to the reader. Research has found that the words used most frequently in successful headlines include *you*, *your*, *how*, and *new*.

Most headlines are brief and usually consist of five to fifteen words. Studies show that people have difficulty processing more than seven words at one time. One effective and short headline is for Sure® deodorant: "Works all day. Just like you." It is possible to create longer headlines that are effective if they are striking or touch on specific emotions. A headline used by DeBeers® diamonds reads: "When She Describes This Anniversary To Her Friends, She'll Start With 'Once Upon A Time.'"

Catchy Headlines

An effective headline grabs attention in print advertisements. *Explain why headlines are so important in a print ad.*

Good Copy Is Simple and Direct

Each element of an ad enhances the overall theme and promotes the product. *How are these three Western Union ads similar to each other?*

In a recent study, creative directors from several major advertising agencies analyzed award-winning print advertisements to determine what their headlines had in common. They discovered that 32 percent of the headlines used familiar sayings—with a twist. For example, "When it rains, it pours®" (Morton® salt). About 23 percent of the headlines made use of opposites, for example, "Eats Gravel. Sips Fuel" (Chevy Silverado truck).

COPY

The **copy** is the selling message of a written advertisement. The headline of your copy should identify a need for the customer. The copy then should detail how the product meets the customer's needs. As with headlines, copy should be based on market research and the business objectives for the advertising campaign. For example, the objectives may be to introduce a new product, build an image, attract new customers, answer inquiries, or generate sales to existing customers.

Here are some tips to write compelling, effective copy:

1. Your copy should be conversational and written in a very personal, friendly style. Keep your copy personal by using familiar language and casual phrases and terms.

2. Good copy is simple and direct. Copy can vary from a few words to several paragraphs. Copy does not need to be extensive to get a message across. It shows how using a product can help a customer or solve a problem.

3. Copy should appeal to the senses. Through the words, the customer should be able to see, hear, touch, taste, or even smell a product. This can be done through using descriptive adjectives and action words.

4. Your copy should have news value by providing specific information. It should tell the *who, what, when, where, why,* and *how* of your product. Remember that facts about your product are more powerful than claims. Use case histories, examples, **statistics**, performance figures, dates, and quotes from experts whenever possible.

5. Your copy should generate interest, encourage awareness, and create desire. Key words used in the copy, such as *easy, guaranteed, hurry, now, price,* and *save* establish an immediate connection with a reader. Customers also enjoy being on the cutting edge when using innovative products, and words such as *new, improved,* and *introducing* give that impression.

6. Advertising copy should provide a personal call to action now or in the near future. It should always be written in the second person and in the active rather than the passive voice. For example, you would write, "This item will help you," rather than the more passive phrase, "You will be helped by this item." Words such as *last chance, limited supply,* or *special bonus offer* help create a sense of urgency and need for immediate action.

A call for action tells the reader to buy your product, visit your store or Web site, or contact the business or organization. Asking for immediate action is especially important to local advertisers. For example, most print ads in local newspapers seek immediate action for sale items or special events. On the other hand, most national advertisers are not looking for immediate action, but seek action in the near future. They desire to keep the product name in front of the public by building brand awareness for new prospects and brand loyalty for current customers.

Good copywriters write in short sentences, sentence fragments, or bulleted lists, if there is a lot of information. Try to avoid the use of commas. Long sentences and too many commas distract readers. White space in the copy breaks up the text and creates an illusion of shorter sentences and fewer words. Print ads with less copy and more white space have higher recall rates.

ILLUSTRATION

The **illustration** is the photograph, drawing, or other graphic elements that is used in an advertisement. An illustration should be clear enough to attract, hold attention, and even encourage action. It also integrates the headline and copy. The illustration and the headline motivate the consumer to read at least the first sentence of the copy.

The illustration and its graphic elements send a message that is hard to communicate with words alone. For example, illustrations show the product, how it works, and its safety features. Illustrations should also project the desired image or benefit such as convenience, entertainment, or status.

Sometimes consumers need to see the product in use. For example, models might wear featured clothing items. Businesses also need to choose images that will not become outdated too soon. Illustrations should be selected and evaluated periodically to match and convey the desired business image.

Photographs are effective in advertisements when a sense of reality is necessary. It is important for consumers to see how some products look or how they are used. Consumer products such as cars, computers, cosmetics, electronic equipment, furniture, sporting equipment, and vacation resorts are often depicted in photographs.

Drawings can show a part of a product that the reader would not normally see. Cut-away drawings and illustrations of products and equipment help reveal important features not visible in a photograph. They also help the reader understand how a product is made and works.

Illustrations should be balanced with other ad components and take up about one-third of an entire ad's space. Headlines should also use one-third of the ad's space, with the remaining one-third used for copy and the signature.

Businesses often use clip art in their print ads. **Clip art** includes inexpensive or free images, stock drawings, and photographs. Suppliers, manufacturers, or trade associations can provide clip art for print ads. When clip art is not appropriate, professionals may be hired to photograph or illustrate situations or products.

SIGNATURE

Print ads are not complete without the name of the advertiser, or sponsor. The **signature** (name of the advertiser) or logotype (logo) is the distinctive identification symbol for a business. The signature usually appears at the bottom of an ad. A well-designed signature gets instant recognition for a business. No advertisement is complete without it.

In national ads, the signature is the name of the firm. It may also include the corporate symbol and slogan. The signature in local advertisements usually includes the business's name, address, telephone number, business hours, map and directions, or slogan. Many advertisers also include their Web-site address for contact information.

Go Big.
I always push myself as far as I can go. But at the end of the day, I come back to milk. The protein helps build muscle and the unique mix of nutrients helps me refuel. So eat right, train hard and drink lowfat milk. Gotta roll.

body milk
www.bodybymilk.com

got milk?

Got Milk?

The use of celebrities or athletes is an effective way to attract viewers to read the copy. *Who do you think the target market might be for this ad?*

SLOGAN

A **slogan** is a catchy phrase or words that identify a product or company. These advertising slogans have the power to attract attention and arouse interest for the company or its product. To support a firm's signature, many businesses create and use slogans that will help their customers identify the firm and its image.

Here are some literary devices that copywriters use when developing slogans for advertising campaigns:

▶ **Alliteration** This device uses repeating initial consonant sounds: "Welcome to the World Wide Wow" (AOL).

▶ **Paradox** This is a statement that is a seeming contradiction that could be true: "The taste you love to hate" (Listerine® mouthwash).

▶ **Rhyme** Slogans might use rhyming words or phrases: "Give a hoot, don't pollute" (United States Forest Service).

▶ **Pun** This technique is a humorous use of a word that suggests two or more of its meanings or the meaning of another word similar in sound: "Time to Re-Tire" (Fisk Tires).

▶ **Play on words** This device cleverly uses words to mean something else: "Let your fingers do the walking" (*Yellow Pages*®).

 After You Read | **Section 20.1**

Review Key Concepts

1. **Explain** why a headline is an important part of a print ad.
2. **Describe** what illustrations should show about a product.
3. **Generate** a slogan for a product you use and explain the literary device you used.

Practice Academics

English Language Arts

4. Review the latest issues of consumer or trade magazines for ad slogans that use different copy writing techniques (alliteration, paradox, rhyme, pun, or play on words). Identify the advertised product, its sponsor, and the technique used for each ad slogan. Share your favorite ad with the class and explain why you enjoy it.

Mathematics

5. Your company plans to run an ad in a newspaper. What is the cost per thousand (CPM) of a print ad that costs $125 in a newspaper with a community circulation of 6,000?

   Math Concept **Computation** Determining the cost per thousand (CPM) of ads is a matter of multiplying the cost by 1,000, and then dividing by the number of people that will view it.

   Starting Hint To solve this problem, multiply $125 by 1,000, and then divide by the audience size.

 connectED.mcgraw-hill.com

Check your answers.

For help, go to the **Math Skills Handbook** located at the back of this book.

READING GUIDE

Before You Read

Predict How might the use of color in a print ad affect a viewer's reaction?

Objectives

- **Explain** the principles of preparing an ad layout.
- **List** advantages and disadvantages of using color in advertising.
- **Describe** how typefaces and sizes add variety and emphasis to print advertisements.

The Main Idea

Advertisers must understand effective design principles when developing ad layouts in order to quickly attract the attention of a targeted audience.

Vocabulary

Content Vocabulary
- ad layout
- advertising proof

Academic Vocabulary
You will find these words in your reading and on your tests. Make sure you know their meanings.
- technique
- emphasis

Graphic Organizer

Draw or print this chart for taking notes on the principles of ad design.

> **Tips for Developing Effective Ad Layouts**
>
> 1. Leave white (unused) space. _____
> 2. _____
> 3. _____
> 4. _____

 connectED.mcgraw-hill.com

Print this graphic organizer.

MARKETING CORE FUNCTION

 Promotion

Advertising Layout

PRINT ADVERTISING LAYOUTS

An **ad layout** is a sketch that shows the general arrangement and appearance of a finished ad. It clearly indicates the position of the headline, illustration, copy, and signature.

There are different sources for ad layout services, including newspaper salespeople, magazine representatives, and advertising agency personnel including art directors, copy editors, or account executives. In addition, desktop publishing programs are useful for smaller businesses.

You do not need to be an artist to develop an ad layout. You submit a rough draft of an idea, and the vendor creates a final ad based upon your information. You do need to make sure, however, that all the information is correct.

As You Read

Evaluate How do businesses assess the effectiveness of their advertisements?

COMPONENTS OF EFFECTIVE AD LAYOUTS

Ad layouts should be prepared in the same size as the final advertisement. Newspapers and magazines offer certain rates on pre-calculated ad sizes. Typical ad sizes are: $\frac{1}{16}$ page, $\frac{1}{8}$ page. $\frac{1}{4}$ page, $\frac{1}{2}$ page, and full page.

The illustrations should be large enough to show the product in use and grab attention through size, humor, or dramatic content. Print ads that feature large visuals (60 to 70 percent of the total ad) are the best attention-getters. The image projected in the layout should be appropriate for the target audience.

> **"** Visual elements like color, different typefaces, and font sizes bring print advertisements to life. **"**

NO ONE GROWS KETCHUP LIKE HEINZ.

That's because every red, ripe tomato in every bottle is grown only from Heinz seeds. It's what helps us deliver the uniquely thick, rich flavor that America loves.

HEINZ. GROWN, NOT MADE.™

Learn more at www.heinzketchup.com.

Focal Point

A single visual is a basic advertising layout design. *How does this ad design create a memorable image for the viewer?*

The ad should make generous use of white or unused space for a clean look. A proper balance of white space and color highlights the image or drawing that you want the consumer to notice. White space also helps to make copy legible and creates an "eye flow" for the ad. The typeface, style of printing type, and size should be easy to read and appropriate for the target audience.

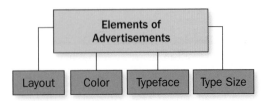

Elements of Advertisements
- Layout
- Color
- Typeface
- Type Size

TYPES OF ADVERTISING LAYOUTS

There are several popular types of ad layouts that designers use in print advertisements. The best ads contain a focal point and lines of force that guide the reader to the copy through photographs and illustrations.

The single-visual layout design is a **technique** that uses a single illustration as a focal point with a very short headline and little copy. It is a simple, basic design but creates a powerful image.

The top-heavy layout places the illustration in the upper half to upper two-thirds of the space or on the left side of the layout. In this layout a strong headline is placed before or after the illustration, and the copy follows.

The illustrated layout uses photos or other images to show how a product can be used—or to illustrate additional technical concepts. An illustrated layout often gets attention by its dramatic presentation, the kinds of illustrations, or by using humor.

The Ogilvy layout, named after advertising expert David Ogilvy, arranges each ad element into a specific order. The elements are presented from top to bottom, in the order most people view them. Research shows that most people view ads in the following order: illustration, photo caption, headline, copy, and signature.

The Z layout is organized with the most important items an advertiser wants viewers to see (often the headline) placed on the top of the Z. Since a reader's eye will normally follow the path of the Z, the illustrations and copy are on the line going down. The signature and "call to action" are at the bottom of the Z in the lower right corner.

MARKETING CASE STUDY

AT & T Hands On

AT&T's popular "Hands" ads highlighted the company's international presence in the wireless communication industry. In these creative print ads, hands were painted and posed in unusual ways to hint at the many parts of the world where customers can use AT&T's wireless service. (See Figure 20.1 on page 470.)

Worth a Thousand Words

The images use visual clues to represent different global regions. In one picture, a left hand is shaped and colored like an angel fish, while several right hands depict an orange reef with an AT&T phone sitting on top. Another ad shows two hands painted as elephants, holding a phone between them. Unique in the world of print ads, the AT&T "Hands" ads rely on the relationship between illustration and copy.

English Language Arts

Create Think of a product that you use often. Design a print ad that incorporates the use of the product. Be sure to combine the elements of illustration and copy in your design.

COLOR IN PRINT ADVERTISEMENTS

A color ad is usually more realistic and visually appealing than a black-and-white advertisement. In fact, research proves that color newspaper ads can increase the readership of ad copy by as much as 80 percent over black-and-white ads. In addition, studies have also shown that full-color ads are often more cost effective than two-color ads (usually black and another color) because of their increased response rates.

Although color commands the viewer's attention by adding excitement and realism, each added color raises the cost of the advertisement. Adding another color can increase costs by as much as 35 percent. When businesses use color in advertisements, the added cost must be continually measured against the desired results.

Advertisers must consider the appropriate colors for the product and target market. For example, red is used for passion, excitement, and power. It is often used in automobile and food advertising. Also, when developing ads for global markets or ethnic groups in the United States, advertisers must be sensitive to the different meanings that color conveys to people of various cultures and countries.

TYPEFACES FOR PRINT ADVERTISEMENTS

Many typefaces and type sizes are effective for use in print advertisements. Advertisers make sure to select styles and type sizes that are distinctive, yet appropriate for the business and specific target audience.

The look and appearance (design) of the type is called the "typeface." A complete set of letters in a specific size and typeface is called a "font." The appearance of the typeface affects the entire character of an advertisement.

An advertiser would choose a large, bold typeface in a headline when the goal is to convey the message forcefully. A smaller, lighter typeface might be selected when the words in a headline are to be conveyed more gently or subtly. In general, print advertisers should use one typeface for headlines and prices, and another typeface for copy.

A Different League

This ad demonstrates several components of an effective advertising layout. *What principles of advertising layout are represented in this ad?*

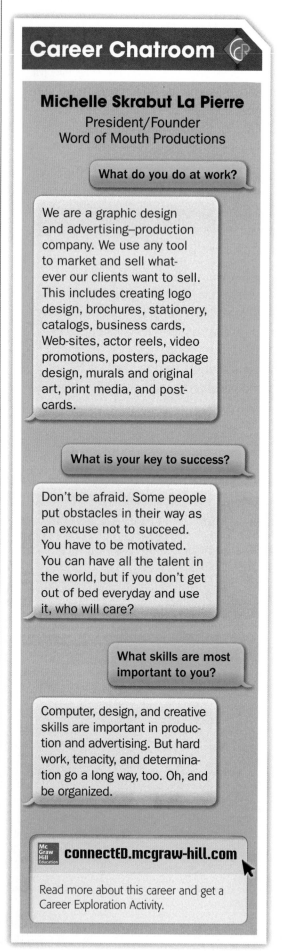
TYPE SIZES FOR PRINT ADS

Type size is measured in points. There are 12 points to one pica, and 6 picas to 1 inch. So a point is about $\frac{1}{72}$ of an inch. Word-processing program allows you to select type size.

One way to classify typefaces is serif or sans serif. A serif typeface has short crosslines at the upper and lower ends of the letters. Times Roman and Palatino are two commonly used serif fonts. Here are examples of these fonts in 10-point and 24-point type. Can you see the crosslines at the top and bottom of the letters T and P?

Times Roman, 10-point

Times Roman, 24-point

Palatino, 10-point

Palatino, 24-point

A sans serif font is one that is *sans* (French for "without") any crosslines. These fonts are popular because their simple design makes them very easy to read. Some common sans serif fonts are Arial, Helvetica, and Futura. Here are examples:

Arial, 10-point

Helvetica, 16-point
Futura, 24-point

The preferences and characteristics of the target market will dictate the choice of the type size. A study found that one-third of readers over 65 do not read ads because the type is too small. This means that a 14-point font would be a better choice than a 10-point font for ads designed to reach readers over 65. Many companies use serif typefaces and 12-point font sizes in most ad copy. Type that is too small or difficult to read will lower the readership of an ad.

You can add variety and **emphasis** by using different sizes of typefaces, italics, boldface, and combinations of capital and lowercase letters. The message remains the same, but capitalizing different words may change the effect on the viewer.

Focal Point Research indicates that using a serif font stresses the horizontal direction, helping people to read more easily.

CHECKING ADVERTISING PROOFS

When designers create advertisements, an advertising proof is developed. The **advertising proof** is a presentation of an ad that shows exactly how it will appear in print. Most proofs are developed and delivered in a digital format, which saves time and money.

The advertising proof is sent to the advertiser for review and approval. Before giving final approval, the advertiser makes an evaluation based on the following criteria:

▶ The ad should be bold enough to stand out on a page, even if it is placed next to other ads.

▶ The overall layout should look clean and uncluttered and should guide the reader through the copy.

▶ The typefaces and type sizes should be easy to read and help to emphasize the message.

▶ The signature should be apparent and distinctive.

▶ The intended message and image projected must be appropriate for the target audience.

In addition, it is important to make sure that all prices printed in an ad are accurate and that all brand names and company names are spelled correctly. Any errors found in the proof must be marked and returned for correction before the ad is finally published.

 After You Read | **Section 20.2**

Review Key Concepts

1. **Explain** how to create a focal point and eye movement using a Z ad layout.
2. **Describe** how to select the size and type of a typeface.
3. **List** three things that you should look for in an advertising proof.

Practice Academics

English Language Arts

4. Conduct research on popular advertising campaigns from the past. Select one of these advertising campaigns and write a one-page newspaper editorial in reaction to it. Be sure to mention the company, name of the campaign, and the year or years that the campaign ran.

Mathematics

5. You must create a Web banner advertisement for a new hybrid automobile. If the Web banner advertisement has a click-through rate of one percent and is sent to 55,000 people, how many people will visit the banner Web site?

Math Concept **Computation** It is necessary to convert percents to their decimal equivalent before using them in computations.

Starting Hints Divide one percent by 100 to get a decimal. Multiply the decimal by the number of people who received the ad to determine the number of visitors.

 connectED.mcgraw-hill.com

Check your answers.

For help, go to the Math Skills Handbook located at the back of this book.

Print Advertisements

Print advertisements usually contain four key elements.

HEADLINE	**ILLUSTRATION**
COPY	**SIGNATURE**

Businesses need to follow ad layout principles when developing print advertisements.

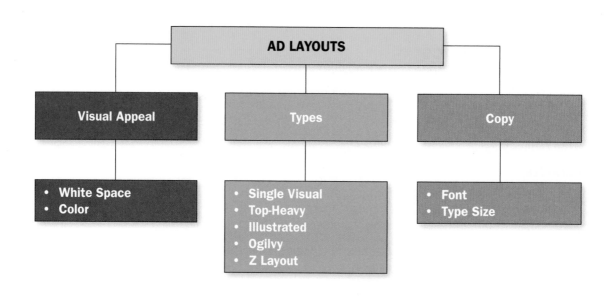

AD LAYOUTS

Visual Appeal
- White Space
- Color

Types
- Single Visual
- Top-Heavy
- Illustrated
- Ogilvy
- Z Layout

Copy
- Font
- Type Size

Review and Activities

Written Summary

- Print advertisements usually contain four key elements: headline, copy, illustrations, and signature.
- Some advertisements also include the company's slogan, which is often presented with or near the signature.
- Each of the four key elements enhances the overall theme of a product promotion.
- The four fundamental elements of a print advertisement are applicable to ads in other media.
- An advertising campaign coordinates a series of ads around a theme.
- Ad agencies specialize in developing ad campaigns and crafting ads for clients.
- Businesses need to follow ad layout principles when developing print advertisements.
- Companies can turn to a variety of sources for help in developing their ad layouts.
- The sources can include full-service, limited-service, creative boutique, project team, and virtual agencies.

Review Content Vocabulary and Academic Vocabulary

1. Classify these terms into different categories and explain why you placed the words together.

   Content Vocabulary
   - advertising campaign (p. 467)
   - advertising agencies (p. 468)
   - logotype (p. 469)
   - headline (p. 471)
   - copy (p. 473)
   - illustration (p. 473)
   - clip art (p. 474)
   - signature (p. 474)
   - slogan (p. 475)
   - ad layout (p. 477)
   - advertising proof (p. 481)

   Academic Vocabulary
   - experts (p. 468)
   - statistics (p. 473)
   - technique (p. 478)
   - emphasis (p. 480)

Assess for Understanding

2. **Describe** How are advertising campaigns developed?
3. **Identify** What are the different types of advertising agencies?
4. **Contrast** How is a logo different from a signature?
5. **Invent** What advertising copy would you create for a new athletic shoe?
6. **Infer** Why would an S-shaped layout not be useful for an ad?
7. **Role Play** What are some possible areas of concern when using color in print ads?
8. **Justify** What style of type (size and font) would you use to advertise grape juice to retired married couples?
9. **Analyze** Why do local supermarkets, banks, pharmacies, and department stores frequently use print advertising?

21st Century Skills

Critical Thinking Skills

10. Ads and the Law One of the most successful print advertising campaigns is the "Got Milk?" campaign. These ads are developed on behalf of America's Milk Processors Board and are paid for by individual dairy producers. Producers are charged a per-head fee on cattle to pay for the campaign. That means dairy producers were charged more if they had more cattle. Discuss whether this payment method is fair.

Financial Literacy Skills

11. The Cost of Advertising A small, independently owned business has hired a full-service advertising agency to develop an advertising campaign. The advertising agency will charge $3,500 a month to run the campaign. If the campaign runs for a year, what will be the yearly contracted amount? What will it cost the business each quarter?

e-Marketing Skills

12. Online Advertising Imagine that you work for a local travel agency. You are considering placing Internet display ads on several travel Web sites. Your manager agrees about the need for advertising but is not convinced that the Internet is the best medium. Use what you know about advertising to convince your manager to follow through with this ad campaign.

- Identify the strengths of Internet advertisements.
- Explain the features of Internet ads that cannot be replicated in print.
- Find examples of Internet ads for an agency that will develop the ad.
- Present the examples of Internet ads to your manager for feedback.

Build Academic Skills

English Language Arts

13. Advertising Layout Skills There are several popular types of ad layouts that designers use in print advertisements. Review newspapers and magazines to research and find print advertisements. Select a print ad for each layout design. Organize your materials and give a presentation on how each ad represents a different layout design.

Science

14. Science, Technology, and Ads Marketers use scientific data to design advertising campaigns. Examples include personal data mining; analyzing keywords and phrases from Internet searches; calculating direct-mail response rates; and researching purchase behavior. Identify the use of a scientific principle or technological innovation that has application for print advertising. Share an ad that features this principle or feature.

Mathematics

15. Calculate Advertising Credit Your home store has an arrangement with a manufacturer of patio furniture. The store receives a 4-percent advertising credit on total yearly sales. What is your advertising credit on sales totaling $68,000?

Math Concept **Computation** A percent discount is usually calculated as an amount off an original price, not an amount off an already discounted price. To figure the amount of a discount, convert fractions and percents to decimals, and multiply.

For help, go to the **Math Skills Handbook** located at the back of this book.

Standardized Test Practice

Directions Read the following questions. On a separate sheet of paper, write the best possible answer for each one.

1. Which of the following provides the selling message in a print advertisement?

   A. Copy

   B. Headline

   C. Illustration

   D. Signature

2. Clip art in a print ad can include images, stock drawings, and photographs.

   T

   F

3. The sketch that shows the general arrangement and appearance of a finished ad is known as the _____.

Test-Taking Tip

Look for key words in test directions, such as *choose*, *describe*, *explain*, *compare*, *identify*, *similar*, *except*, and *not*.

DECA Connection Role Play

Manager
Small Hotel

Situation Your hotel is located in the historic district of a popular tourist destination. It has 30 guest rooms in a building and has been in operation for 145 years. The hotel has recently been renovated and redecorated. Bookings run at near capacity during the spring and fall months. Bookings during the summer and winter months are not as good. They reach about 70 percent of capacity. You advertise in upscale lifestyle magazines and in magazines that appeal to the traveling public.

You recently hired a new employee (judge) for your assistant manager position. You plan to train the new employee (judge) in all aspects of the hotel operation. You have assigned the new employee (judge) the task of creating a magazine advertisement that announces the hotel's redecoration. Before the new employee (judge) begins working on the advertisement, you are to meet with the employee (judge) to explain print advertisements and their components.

Activity You are to explain to the new employee (judge) each of the components of print advertisements and the importance of coordinating those elements. You are also to explain the importance of ensuring that the copy is correct and that the advertisement meets the standards of your hotel.

Evaluation You will be evaluated on how well you meet the following performance indicators:

1. Explain the components of advertisements.
2. Explain the importance of coordinating elements in advertisements.
3. Explain the nature of effective written communication.
4. Edit and revise written work consistent with professional standards.
5. Orient new employees.

  connectED.mcgraw-hill.com

Role Plays Download the Competitive Events Workbook for more Role-Play practice.

Promotional Campaign
for a Hybrid Automobile

What kind of promotional campaign would be most effective to reach the target market for a hybrid automobile?

Scenario

Your advertising agency has an automobile company as a potential client. It is coming out with a new hybrid automobile that will be in direct competition with the Toyota® Prius and other hybrid automobiles in that price range, such as the Ford® Fusion Hybrid and Honda® Civic Hybrid. The promotional campaign must be exciting, creative, and engaging.

You must decide how the advertising dollars should be spent. Which media should make up the promotional mix? Who makes up the target market? The theme for the promotional campaign must speak to that target market.

The Skills You'll Use

Academic Skills Reading, writing, social studies, researching, and analyzing

Basic Skills Speaking, listening, thinking, and interpersonal

Technology Skills Word processing, spreadsheet, presentation, telecommunications, and the Internet

Your Objective

Your objective is to design an effective promotional campaign to introduce your client's new hybrid automobile to the target market.

STEP 1 Do Your Research

Conduct research to find out about hybrid automobiles and people who buy them. How do hybrid cars function? What are the features and benefits of owning one? Study the promotional efforts of hybrid automobile manufacturers. What models are in the price range of your major competitor? As you conduct your research, answer these questions:

- What are the major hybrid automobiles in the same price range?
- What political, economic, socio-cultural, and technological factors may shed light on how the creative promotional campaign should be designed?
- Who is the target market for a hybrid automobile?
- What media and messages are competitors using to sell their hybrid automobiles?

Write a summary of your research.

STEP 2 Plan Your Project

Now that you have completed your research, you need to begin planning your project.

- Create a name for the new hybrid automobile and draft a theme that will be used for all promotional materials.
- Conduct a PEST analysis.
- Create a profile of a potential hybrid automobile customer.
- List and design materials that will be part of your promotional mix.
- Prepare a calendar of events to indicate when each phase of the promotional campaign should take place.
- Write a press release for the introduction of the new hybrid.
- Provide rationale for your plan with supporting research and a budget for your client's approval.
- Present your ideas in a written report.

STEP 3 Connect with Your Community

- Interview a trusted adult in your community who drives a hybrid car. Find out what he or she likes and dislikes about hybrid cars.
- Interview a retail car sales associate to learn the features and benefits of hybrid automobiles.
- Take notes during the interviews, and transcribe your notes after the interviews.

STEP 4 Share What You Learn

Assume your class is your client's marketing department staff that will decide if your advertising agency will get the job.

- Present your findings in an oral presentation. Be prepared to answer questions.
- Use software to create a slide presentation to complement your oral report. Include one slide in your presentation for each topic in your written report.
- Present samples of the promotional mix.

STEP 5 Evaluate Your Marketing and Academic Skills

Your project will be evaluated based on the following:

- The promotional campaign's theme and how it relates to the suggested target market
- The customer profile, calendar of events, press release, and promotional budget
- The coordination among the many facets of the promotional plan
- Creativity in the sample materials that are part of the promotional mix
- Research data to support the rationale for your plan
- Organization and continuity of presentation
- Mechanics—presentation and neatness
- Speaking and listening skills

MARKETING CORE FUNCTIONS

 Promotion

 Market Planning

Marketing Internship Project Checklist

Plan

✓ Conduct research on companies that make and sell hybrid automobiles.

✓ Design a comprehensive promotional campaign for a new hybrid automobile.

Write

✓ Explain how results of the PEST analysis will help you design an effective promotional campaign.

✓ Describe your ideas for your promotional campaign in a written report.

✓ Write a press release for the introduction of the new hybrid automobile.

Present

✓ Present research supporting your rationale for the theme and budget of the promotional campaign.

✓ Present your promotional campaign.

✓ Present samples of the promotional mix (e.g., magazine ad, television commercial, Web site, and/or social media connection).

 connectED.mcgraw-hill.com

Evaluate Download a rubric you can use to evaluate your final project.

my marketing portfolio

Internship Report Once you have completed your Marketing Internship Project and oral presentation, put your written report and a few printouts of key slides from your oral presentation in your Marketing Portfolio.

Research and Design a Promotional Campaign Do research and create the promotional mix for a product of your choice. Consider a smartphone, surfboard, jeans, sports apparel or equipment, or a food product. Does your research data support the rationale for the theme of the promotional campaign? Are your sample promotional materials creative and directed to a specific target market? Are your budget and calendar of events realistic? Is the campaign coordinated? Prepare a written report and an oral presentation.

DISTRIBUTION

Marketing Internship Project

A Distribution Plan

Essential Question What channel or channels of distribution will help grow a small business?

If you sell in the consumer or organizational market, you may find more than one channel of distribution to help grow your business. When you use several channels of distribution, you must be careful not to compete with your customers. If your business grows as a result of your business expansion in different markets, how do you handle the increased demand? What changes must be made in inventory management and shipping?

Project Goal

In the project at the end of this unit, you will develop new channels of distribution and corresponding logistics (inventory management and shipping) for a growing business.

Prepare for the Project

As you read this unit, use this checklist to prepare for the Marketing Internship Project at the end of this unit:

- Think about possible channels of distribution for art objects.
- Consider how inventory management and shipping requirements might change as a business grows.
- Speak with small business owners to learn how they handle logistics for their products.

 connectED.mcgraw-hill.com

Project Activity
Complete a worksheet activity about distribution planning.

 AMERICAN MARKETING ASSOCIATION

Distribution is where you'll find the action.

MARKETING CORE FUNCTIONS IN THIS UNIT

Channel Management

Market Planning

Your favorite authors. *Fast.*

Same Day Delivery in Manhattan.

—— *Free shipping* on orders of $25 or more.* ——

Over 1 million books, CDs, and DVDs in stock and ready for Same Day Delivery. Order by 11am, get it by 7pm.

www.bn.com

25A

SHOW WHAT YOU KNOW

Visual Literacy
Barnes & Noble® stores in New York City advertised an extra service to their customers: same-day delivery. *How does this advertisement illustrate the importance of thinking about distribution?*

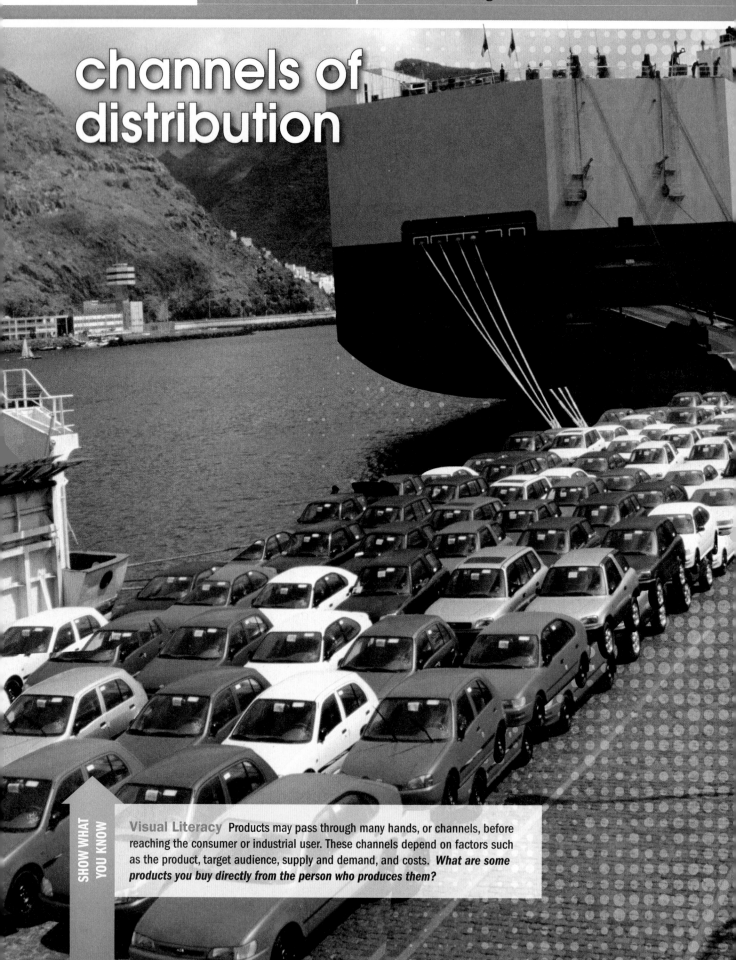

channels of
distribution

Visual Literacy Products may pass through many hands, or channels, before reaching the consumer or industrial user. These channels depend on factors such as the product, target audience, supply and demand, and costs. *What are some products you buy directly from the person who produces them?*

Discovery Project

From Producer to Final User

Essential Question How is a product moved from the manufacturer to the customer?

Project Goal

Select a product and describe how and by whom that product is transported from the manufacturer to the customer. You might select a type of produce, a computer, a digital SLR camera, a smartphone, a car, or any other product. Then visualize the path that product will take to reach the end user. (Hint: See **Figures 21.1** and **21.2** on pages 496–497.) Conduct additional research as necessary. Write a detailed report of how the product moves from manufacturer to the consumer.

Ask Yourself...

- What key words will you use to initiate your research?
- Would the channels of distribution for this product be different than for other products?
- Who would determine the channels of distribution for this product?

 Analyze What are some criteria that would determine the channels used to distribute a product?

 connectED.mcgraw-hill.com

Activity
Get a worksheet activity about channels of distribution.

Evaluate
Download a rubric you can use to evaluate your project.

DECA Connection

DECA Event Role Play

Concepts in this chapter are related to DECA competitive events that involve either an interview or role play.

Performance Indicators The performance indicators represent key skills and knowledge. Your key to success in DECA competitive events is relating them to concepts in this chapter.

- Explain the nature of channels of distribution.
- Explain the nature of channel-member relationships.
- Explain the nature and scope of channel management.
- Explain legal considerations in channel management.
- Explain ethical considerations in channel management.

DECA Prep

Role Play Practice role-playing with the DECA Connection competitive-event activity at the end of this chapter. More information about DECA events can be found on DECA's Web site.

FIGURE 21.1 **Distribution Channels—Consumer Products**

Products are distributed to consumers through five channels. In the past, most consumer goods were not distributed using direct distribution (Channel A) because consumers were accustomed to shopping in retail stores. E-commerce is changing that for many products. *Which channel is used most often for items that go out of date quickly or need servicing?*

CHANNEL A

Manufacturer/Producer Directly to Consumer

There are six ways in which direct distribution is used for consumer goods.

1. Selling products at the production site.
2. Having a sales force call on consumers.
3. Using catalogs or ads to generate sales.
4. Using telemarketing.
5. Using the Internet to make online sales.
6. Using TV infomercials.

CHANNEL B

Manufacturer/Producer to Retailer to Consumer

This is the most commonly used channel for merchandise that dates quickly or needs servicing.

CHANNEL C

Manufacturer/Producer to Wholesaler to Retailer to Consumer

This method is used for goods that are always carried in stock and whose styles do not change frequently.

CHANNEL D

Manufacturer/Producer to Agents to Wholesaler to Retailer to Consumer

This is the channel for manufacturers who wish to concentrate on production and leave sales and distribution to others.

CHANNEL E

Manufacturer/Producer to Agents to Retailer to Consumer

This is the channel chosen by manufacturers who do not want to handle their own sales to retailers. The agent simply brings the buyer and seller together.

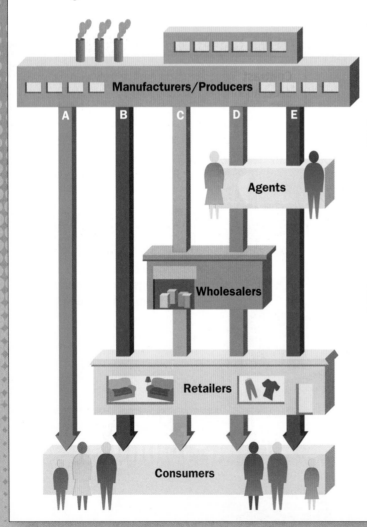

FIGURE 21.2 **Distribution Channels—Industrial Products**

Industrial buyers have different needs than those of retail buyers, so they use different channels of distribution. The least common channel in the consumer market—direct distribution (Channel A)—is the most common in the industrial market. *Which channel is most often used to distribute major equipment used in manufacturing?*

CHANNEL A

Manufacturer/Producer Directly to Industrial Users

This is the most common method of distribution for major equipment used in manufacturing and other businesses. The manufacturer's sales force calls on the industrial user to sell goods or services.

CHANNEL C

Manufacturer/Producer to Agents to Industrial Distributors to Industrial Users

Small manufacturers who do not have the time or money to invest in a direct sales force may prefer this channel.

CHANNEL B

Manufacturer/Producer to Industrial Distributors to Industrial Users

This channel is used most often for small standardized parts and operational supplies needed to run a business.

CHANNEL D

Manufacturer/Producer to Agents to Industrial Users

This is another channel used when a manufacturer does not want to hire its own sales force. The agent represents the manufacturer for sale of the goods but does not take possession or title.

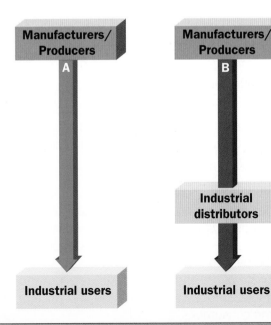
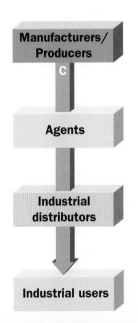

EXAMPLES OF CHANNELS OF DISTRIBUTION

Different channels of distribution are generally used to reach the customer in the consumer and industrial markets.

When selling to the industrial market, a manufacturer would sell paper napkins to industrial distributors who, in turn, would sell the napkins to restaurants.

When selling to the consumer market, the company would sell napkins to a wholesaler or use food brokers to sell to retailers, such as grocery stores or party supply shops.

Not every option works best for every product or company. Despite the potential for success, a product can fail with the wrong channel of distribution.

DISTRIBUTION CHANNELS FOR CONSUMER PRODUCTS AND SERVICES

Few consumer products are marketed using direct distribution (Channel A) because most consumers have become accustomed to shopping in retail stores. The most common indirect channel in the consumer market is Producer to Retailer to Consumer (Channel B).

MANUFACTURER/PRODUCER DIRECTLY TO CONSUMER (CHANNEL A)

Direct distribution can be used in six different ways to deliver products to consumers:

1. Selling products at the production site. Examples include factory outlets or farmers' roadside stands.
2. Having a sales force call on consumers at home. Examples include Avon® and Tupperware®.
3. Using catalogs or ads to generate sales.
4. Calling consumers on the telephone (telemarketing). (The National Do Not Call registry sets limits on this method.)
5. Using the Internet to make online sales.
6. Using TV infomercials.

   In this channel, there are no middlemen. That means the prices a customer pays can be low. Retailers do not have to pay rent for a store that houses the goods, agents do not have to be paid commission, and wholesalers do not have to negotiate prices and shipping with retailers and agents. All of these processes increase the final price of the product for the consumer.

MANUFACTURER/PRODUCER TO RETAILER TO CONSUMER (CHANNEL B)

This channel is used most often for products that become out of date quickly or need regular servicing. Clothing and automobiles are sold this way. Chain stores and online retailers use this channel. Retailers do not have to involve agents or wholesalers to acquire their products. The distribution of a product from the manufacturer or producer to the retailer is quick and efficient. The short length of this channel makes it easy for consumers to stay up to date with a company's products at a relatively low price.

Channel A Dell Computers uses channel partnership because it sells via the Internet, so it needs assistance from shippers like FedEx and UPS.

MANUFACTURER/PRODUCER TO WHOLESALER TO RETAILER TO CONSUMER (CHANNEL C)

This method of distribution is most often used for staple goods, which are items that are always carried in stock and whose styles do not change frequently. The manufacturer sells to the wholesaler, who then handles the sales, warehousing, and distribution of the goods to retailers. Consumer goods sold this way include supermarket items, flowers, candy, and stationery supplies.

MANUFACTURER/PRODUCER TO AGENTS TO WHOLESALER TO RETAILER TO CONSUMER (CHANNEL D)

Manufacturers who prefer to concentrate on production and leave sales and distribution to others use this channel. The agent sells to wholesalers who are involved in storage, sale, and transportation to retailers. The retailer then sells to consumers.

MARKETING CASE STUDY

DirecTV's NFL Sunday Ticket

Football fans are a passionate bunch. Few things are more important to them than their favorite games. Sunday is the big day for professional football. Highlighting fans' football fever, DirecTV® created a TV commercial with a comedian as the "NFL Sunday Ticket" self-help counselor. Celebrities like LL Cool J, Eli Manning, and Peyton Manning also appeared in the ads. DirecTV promoted its product as the ultimate way to deliver the games to viewers.

Delivering More Action

With so many games on any given Sunday, football fans are used to doing a lot of channel flipping. The DirecTV spots advertise the Sunday Ticket service as a way for viewers to watch up to eight games simultaneously on a single television. All games are in high-definition, and DirecTV can deliver them to many brands of cell phones.

Mathematics

Compute Analyze this information: Suppose there are 32 teams in the NFL. There are 16 games in the regular season. There are 17 weeks of games. Each team has a bye week during which they do not play a game. How many teams have a bye week each week?

MANUFACTURER/PRODUCER TO AGENTS TO RETAILER TO CONSUMER (CHANNEL E)

Manufacturers who do not want to handle their sales to retailers use this channel. The agent brings the buyer and seller together. Expensive cookware, meat, cosmetics, and many supermarket items are sold this way. It may be more cost-effective for the company to use agents to sell its products. This choice allows the company's manufacturers to spend time and money creating the best products possible.

DISTRIBUTION CHANNELS FOR INDUSTRIAL PRODUCTS AND SERVICES

Industrial users shop differently and have different needs than consumers, so they use different channels of distribution. The least-used channel in the consumer market—direct distribution (Channel A)—is the most used channel in the industrial market. Often, a business or industry's needs are defined by the products or services it provides. These groups do not have to shop around for different products like consumers do. They already know which products they need.

MANUFACTURER/PRODUCER DIRECTLY TO INDUSTRIAL USERS (CHANNEL A)

This method of distribution is most often used for major equipment used in manufacturing and other businesses. The manufacturer's sales force calls on the industrial user to sell goods or services. For example, a Xerox® sales representative sells copier machines directly to manufacturers and commercial businesses.

MANUFACTURER/PRODUCER TO INDUSTRIAL DISTRIBUTORS TO INDUSTRIAL USERS (CHANNEL B)

This channel is used most often for small standardized parts and operational supplies needed to run a business. Industrial wholesalers (distributors) take ownership of the products, stock them, and sell them as needed to industrial users. A restaurant-supply wholesaler buys pots, pans, utensils, serving pieces, and paper products from various manufacturers to sell to restaurant owners. The industrial user is able to choose from a variety of small standardized products for its business. It would cost a lot of time and money for an industrial user to shop at many different manufacturers or producers.

There are five channels of distribution to transfer goods from producer to consumer. *Which channel was most likely used to transfer the goods like the high-end cosmetics in this photo?*

Distribution Channels

MANUFACTURER/PRODUCER TO AGENTS TO INDUSTRIAL DISTRIBUTORS TO INDUSTRIAL USERS (CHANNEL C)

Small manufacturers may prefer to use the services of an agent, who represents the manufacturer for sale of the goods. The agent coordinates a large supply of the product. The agent does not take possession or title of the goods, but sells the goods to the industrial wholesaler. The wholesaler in turn stores, resells, and ships them to the industrial user. Agents can work for several producers at one time.

MANUFACTURER/PRODUCER TO AGENTS TO INDUSTRIAL USERS (CHANNEL D)

Some manufacturers cannot afford a sales force, and other manufacturers simply do not want to manage a sales force. These manufacturers use agents to sell their products to industrial users, but they cut out the distributor and ship their merchandise directly to the industrial users. This method keeps distribution costs low. Many types of industrial products are distributed in this manner, including construction equipment, farm products, and dry goods.

 After You Read   **Section 21.1**

Review Key Concepts

1. **Identify** the term that describes the path a product takes from producer to final user.
2. **Explain** the function of intermediaries.
3. **Name** the two distribution channels.

Practice Academics

English Language Arts

4. A new sporting goods apparel company plans to sell its products through catalogs and online. As the new marketing manager, you purchased a large list of prospective customers. You want to send catalogs only to people who have an interest in your company's products. Write a catchy, persuasive letter to be e-mailed to prospective customers interested in receiving your catalog.

Mathematics

5. A manufacturer makes an item that costs $12.50 to produce. The markup when sold to the distributor is 20 percent. What is the cost to the distributor? When the distributor sells this item to the retailer, the markup is 40 percent. How much will the retailer pay?

   Math Concept **Computation** When figuring a cost after a markup, multiply the original cost by one plus the decimal equivalent of the percent of the markup.

   Starting Hints To solve the problem, convert the percents to a decimal for each markup. Multiply the production cost by one plus the decimal equivalent of the distribution markup, or 1.2, to determine the cost to the distributor. Multiply the cost to the distributor by one plus the retail markup, or 1.4, to determine the cost to the retailer.

 connectED.mcgraw-hill.com

Check your answers.

For help, go to the **Math Skills Handbook** located at the back of this book.

READING GUIDE

Connect How might a marketing plan include distribution?

Objectives

- **Explain** distribution planning.
- **Name and describe** the three levels of distribution intensity.
- **Explain** the effect of the Internet on distribution planning.
- **Describe** the challenges of international distribution planning.

The Main Idea

You must know how distribution decisions affect an entire company and how decisions affect international markets and e-marketplaces.

Vocabulary

Content Vocabulary
- exclusive distribution
- integrated distribution
- selective distribution
- intensive distribution
- e-marketplace

Academic Vocabulary

You will find these words in your reading and on your tests. Make sure you know their meanings.
- control
- maintain

Graphic Organizer

Draw or print this chart to note the main components of distribution planning.

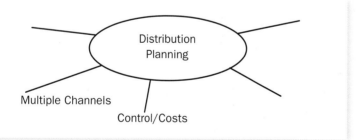

 connectED.mcgraw-hill.com

Print this graphic organizer.

MARKETING CORE FUNCTION

 Channel Management

Distribution Planning

UNDERSTANDING DISTRIBUTION PLANNING

Distribution planning involves decisions about a product's physical movement and transfer of ownership from producer to consumer. This chapter focuses on transfer of ownership issues. Distribution decisions affect a firm's marketing program. Some of the major considerations are the use of multiple channels, **control** versus costs, intensity of distribution desired, and involvement in e-commerce.

As You Read

Analyze How does the Internet facilitate channels of distribution?

MULTIPLE CHANNELS

A producer uses multiple channels when its product fits the needs of both industrial and consumer markets. For example, a snack food company sells its pretzels, drinks, and cookies to supermarkets, movie theaters, stadiums, and other sports arenas. It also sells to schools, colleges, and hospitals. Each new market poses questions regarding the exact channel of distribution needed to reach it.

CONTROL VERSUS COSTS

All manufacturers and producers must weigh the control they want to have over the distribution of their products versus their costs and profitability. Many businesses have sales representatives who work directly for the company, but there are costs to maintain a sales force. A company can also use a network of independent agents and distributors, but that might result in less control over where its products and services are sold and for how much.

WHO DOES THE SELLING?

A manufacturer must decide how much control it wants over its sales function. It can use its own sales force, or it may decide to hire agents to do the selling.

A direct sales force is costly. In-house sales representatives are on the company payroll, receive employee benefits, and are reimbursed for expenses. The manufacturer, though, has complete control over them. It can establish sales quotas and easily monitor each sales representative's performance.

> " **Distribution planning involves decisions about a product's physical movement and transfer of ownership from producer to consumer.** "

With an agent, a manufacturer loses some of its control over how sales are made. This is because agents work independently, running their own businesses. The agent's interests may not always be exactly the same as those of the manufacturer.

However, the relative cost of using agents can be lower than hiring an in-house sales staff. No employee benefits or expenses must be paid because agents are independent businesspeople. Another benefit is that agents are typically paid a set percentage based on what they sell. This ensures that the cost of selling a product or service is always the same in relation to sales generated.

DISTRIBUTION INTENSITY

Distribution intensity depends on how widely a product will be distributed. There are three levels of distribution intensity: exclusive, selective, and intensive.

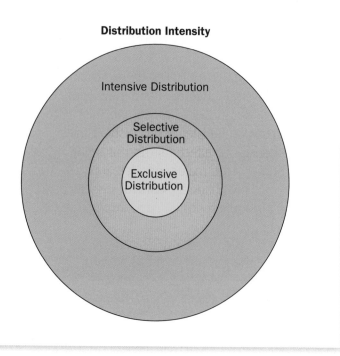

Distribution Intensity

Intensive Distribution

Selective Distribution

Exclusive Distribution

EXCLUSIVE DISTRIBUTION

Exclusive distribution involves distribution of a product in protected territories in a given geographic area. Dealers are assured that they are the only ones within a certain geographic radius that have the right to sell the manufacturer's or wholesaler's products. Prestige, image, channel control, and a high profit margin for both the manufacturer and intermediaries are among the reasons that companies choose this distribution strategy.

The exclusive distribution method also encourages distributors to advertise the products they sell and to provide any customer service that might be necessary after the sale. Franchised operations use exclusive distribution planning. An example of this kind of franchised operation is a distributor that supplies a specific name-brand item to all the stores in a particular region.

In addition, wholesalers may sponsor voluntary groups in which a retailer agrees to buy and **maintain** a minimum inventory of the wholesaler's products. One example of a voluntary group sponsored by a wholesaler is the National Auto Parts Association (NAPA). Retailers affiliated with NAPA buy most of their stock directly from NAPA and participate in its promotions.

Some manufacturers own and run their own retail operations. This variation on exclusive distribution is **integrated distribution**. The manufacturer acts as wholesaler and retailer for its own products. For example, Gap® Inc. sells its clothing in company-owned retail stores.

SELECTIVE DISTRIBUTION

Selective distribution means that a limited number of outlets in a given geographic area sell a manufacturer's product. The goal is to select channel members that can maintain the image of the product. These channel members are also good credit risks, aggressive marketers, and good inventory planners.

Intermediaries are selected for their ability to cater to the final users that the manufacturer wants to attract. For example, designers Armani and Vera Wang sell their clothing only through stores that appeal to the affluent customers who buy their merchandise. They do not sell goods in a chain store or a variety store.

INTENSIVE DISTRIBUTION

Intensive distribution involves the use of all suitable outlets to sell a product. The objective is complete market coverage, and the ultimate goal is to sell to as many customers as possible, in all the various locations they shop. A good example of this is motor oil. Motor oil is marketed in quick-lube shops, farm stores, auto-parts retailers, supermarkets, drugstores, hardware stores, warehouse clubs, and other mass merchandisers to reach the maximum number of customers.

Distribution Intensity To select a distribution channel, identify competitors' channels, assess strengths and weaknesses, analyze costs, and decide per your overall plan.

E-COMMERCE

E-commerce actually means "electronic commerce." E-commerce is the process in which products are sold to customers and industrial buyers over electronic systems such as the Internet. You already learned that e-tailing is retail selling via the Internet. This online shopping outlet is called the **e-marketplace**. The amount of business that is now conducted electronically has grown immensely in recent years with widespread Internet usage and the popularity of Web sites that have become online marketplaces.

Travel industry researchers estimate that almost 60 percent of all travel bookings were made online in 2012. Consumers have also become accustomed to buying books, toys, and other goods on the Internet. This trend has led to the term "Black Monday," which refers to the first Monday after the start of the holiday shopping season. This Monday after Thanksgiving is the day on which consumer Web site traffic in the United States is traditionally the busiest of the year.

E-marketplaces for business-to-business (B2B) operations provide one-stop shopping and substantial savings for industrial buyers. Online catalogs of products supplied by different companies make it easier for corporate buyers to compare prices and get the best deal.

E-marketplaces provide smaller businesses with the exposure that they could not get elsewhere. Small businesses can also use social networking sites such as Twitter® and Facebook® to share information about their products. These sites allow consumers to see what is available for sale at a company's store. The company can reach consumers directly through the use of the Internet.

In each of the past five years, a greater proportion of B2B trade has taken place via the Internet. For example, many companies with locations in different parts of the country find it more efficient to use dedicated Web sites for restocking and tracking of their office supply needs. This trend is expected to continue in the future.

 Reading Check

Identify What are the three levels of distribution intensity?

Channels of Distribution

Manufacturers or producers may choose one or more paths (channels) to distribute products to the final user.

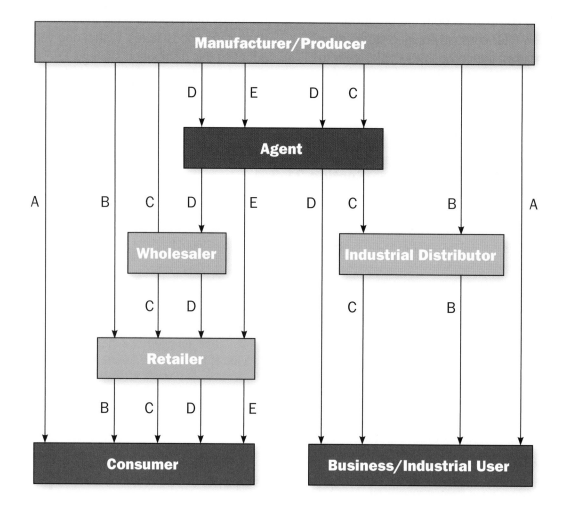

Review and Activities

Written Summary

- Manufacturers or producers may choose one or more paths (channels) to distribute products to the final user.

- The channels used to distribute consumer products usually differ from those used to distribute to the industrial market.

- Manufacturers or producers may use multiple channels of distribution to reach different markets. Product distribution in foreign markets often requires special planning.

- Distribution intensity may be exclusive, selective, or intensive.

Review Content Vocabulary and Academic Vocabulary

1. Explain how each term relates to the subject of the chapter or the unit.

Content Vocabulary
- channel of distribution (p. 493)
- intermediaries (p. 493)
- wholesalers (p. 493)
- rack jobbers (p. 493)
- drop shippers (p. 494)
- retailers (p. 494)
- brick-and-mortar retailers (p. 494)
- e-tailing (p. 494)
- agents (p. 495)
- direct distribution (p. 495)
- indirect distribution (p. 495)
- exclusive distribution (p. 504)
- integrated distribution (p. 505)
- selective distribution (p. 505)
- intensive distribution (p. 505)
- e-marketplace (p. 505)

Academic Vocabulary
- commission (p. 493)
- automatic (p. 494)
- control (p. 503)
- maintain (p. 504)

Assess for Understanding

2. Explain What is the place decision?

3. Name What is another term for intermediaries?

4. Identify What are two types of intermediaries?

5. List What are four non-store retailing methods?

6. Distinguish What are the most common methods of distribution for consumer products and for industrial products?

7. Generate What are some questions to consider in establishing a distribution plan?

8. Contrast When would it be beneficial to use exclusive distribution rather than intensive distribution?

9. Describe What is the difference between the cost of having a direct sales force and the cost of using independent sales agents?

21st Century Skills

Communication

10. Distribution in Other Cultures Identify a company. Explain how it might want to distribute its products in another country. Select the country and explain why you chose the distribution channel.

Financial Literacy Skills

11. Distribution Planning It costs you $4.95 to make a graphic t-shirt. You are considering selling the shirts to wholesalers and retail stores. A wholesaler will buy 500 shirts for $3595. Retail stores will buy 100 shirts for $645. What will your profit be per shirt from each distribution channel?

Everyday Ethics

12. Power Source More than half the electricity generated in the United States comes from coal. It is extracted through traditional mining and by mountaintop removal, a process that blasts away the tops of mountains to reach the underlying veins of this fossil fuel. However, mountaintop removal damages the environment in ways that cannot be undone. Discuss whether it is ethical to blast away mountaintops to make the production and distribution of coal easier.

e-Marketing Skills

13. E-Commerce and Distribution Conduct research on the effect of e-commerce on the channels of distribution used for consumer and industrial products. Write a report summarizing current information about types of products sold and dollar sales figures for those products.

Build Academic Skills

Science

14. The Impact of Technology The process of distributing products uses a wide range of technologies. From the vehicles used to transport goods to the Internet and e-commerce, there are many ways to reduce costs and modify product distribution. What are some technologies or gadgets you use that may be helpful to distributors? Share your ideas with your class.

Social Studies

15. Planning for Global Distribution You have just been hired as a marketing consultant for an automobile accessories manufacturing company that wishes to expand its business worldwide. Your job is to develop a plan for sales and distribution of their products in the global market. Research the steps that must be taken to begin selling the company's products in European, Asian, and South American countries. Describe what considerations should be given to differences in culture. Write a two-page report on your findings.

Mathematics

16. Calculate Savings The price of a best-selling DVD is $19.00 at a local store. You can purchase the same DVD through an e-tailer for $10.20 plus 20 percent for shipping charges. How much will you save by purchasing the DVD through the e-tailer?

Math Concept **Computations** Calculating the amount saved by purchasing one product instead of another involves comparison.

For help, go to the **Math Skills Handbook** located at the back of this book.

Standardized Test Practice

Directions Read the following questions. On a separate piece of paper, write the best possible answer for each one.

1. In distributing products from the producer to the consumer, which of the following could be a channel member?
   A. Wholesaler
   B. Retailer
   C. Agent
   D. All of the above

2. True or false? Direct distribution occurs when goods are sold by the producer directly to the consumer.

   T

   F

3. The businesses that move products from the manufacturer to the final user are called _____.

Test-Taking Tip

In a true or false test, every part of a true statement must be true. If any part of the statement is false, the answer has to be false.

DECA Connection Role Play

Owner
Wholesale Kitchen Appliance Company

Situation Your company sells the finest kitchen appliances available. You have agreements with all of the appliance manufacturers whose appliances your company offers for sale that you have selective distribution of their appliances.

Earlier this week you finalized an agreement to become the exclusive distributor for the most sought-after brand of European kitchen appliances. The European brand represents a significant financial investment for your company. You feel that the investment is worthwhile because of the quality of the appliances and the prestige of distributing these appliances. Your exclusive distribution rights mean that your company will be the only one in this country to sell the European brand.

You are very happy about selling the European appliance line and the potential it offers your company. You have called a special staff meeting to announce that your company is the country's exclusive distributor of the European appliance line.

Activity You are to explain to your employees (judge) the significance of your company being the exclusive distributor of the European appliances line. You must also explain exclusive distribution and how it differs from the selective distribution of your other appliance lines.

Evaluation You will be evaluated on how well you meet the following performance indicators:

1. Explain the nature of channels of distribution.
2. Explain the nature of channel-member relationships.
3. Explain the nature and scope of channel management.
4. Explain legal considerations in channel management.
5. Explain ethical considerations in channel management.

connectED.mcgraw-hill.com

Download the Competitive Events Workbook for more Role-Play Practice.

physical distribution

SHOW WHAT YOU KNOW

Visual Literacy Produce like the fruit in this photo are often transported great distances before they are purchased by consumers or businesses. The ability to transport products quickly and efficiently helps the growth of our economy. *What factors might affect transportation costs?*

Discovery Project

Transportation Systems

Essential Question What factors must companies consider when transporting goods?

Project Goal

Assume that you are employed by a furniture manufacturer that sells its products nationwide. You have been asked to evaluate your current truck transportation system. The company is deciding between a common carrier, its own fleet, or a combination of both to transport its products. You have been asked to prepare a written report that identifies the pros and cons for each transportation option.

Ask Yourself...

- Why are trucks used for the distribution of your product?
- What are the advantages for using a common carrier, your own fleet, or both?
- What are the disadvantages for using a common carrier, your own fleet, or both?
- How will you organize your written report?

 Organize and Interpret Summarize your research by explaining which form of transportation is the best for your company and why.

 connectED.mcgraw-hill.com

Activity
Get a worksheet activity about distributing products.

Evaluate
Download a rubric you can use to evaluate your project.

DECA Connection

DECA Event Role Play

Concepts in this chapter are related to DECA competitive events that involve either an interview or role play.

Performance Indicators The performance indicators represent key skills and knowledge. Your key to success in DECA competitive events is relating them to concepts in this chapter.

- Select the best shipping method.
- Explain the role of distribution centers.
- Explain the storage process in warehouse operations.
- Explain distribution issues and trends.
- Discuss shipping methods used with food products.

DECA Prep

Role Play Practice role-playing with the DECA Connection competitive-event activity at the end of this chapter. More information about DECA events can be found on DECA's Web site.

READING GUIDE

Before You Read

Connect What channels of transportation are used to deliver your favorite products to you?

Objectives

- **Describe** the nature and scope of physical distribution.
- **Identify** transportation systems and services that move products from manufacturers to consumers.
- **Name** the different kinds of transportation service companies.

The Main Idea

Success in today's business environment requires companies to deliver products efficiently and effectively to their customers around the world.

Vocabulary

Content Vocabulary

- physical distribution
- transportation
- common carriers
- contract carriers
- private carriers
- exempt carriers
- ton-mile
- carload
- freight forwarders

Academic Vocabulary

You will find these words in your reading and on your tests. Make sure you know their meanings.

- regulate
- options

Graphic Organizer

Draw or print this chart to list the advantages and disadvantages of each type of transportation system.

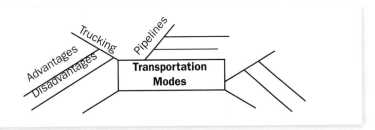

connectED.mcgraw-hill.com

Print this graphic organizer.

MARKETING CORE FUNCTION

Channel Management

Transportation

THE NATURE AND SCOPE OF PHYSICAL DISTRIBUTION

Physical distribution comprises activities for delivering the right amount of product to the right place at the right time. Physical distribution is a key link between a business and its customers. Physical distribution ensures that products reach final customers by using a network of distributors, warehouses, and retailers. Customer satisfaction depends upon the success of this process.

> **" After a company chooses its channels of distribution, it decides how to move its products through those channels. "**

The global market is a competitive, rapidly changing place. Business owners and managers have many ways to help assure continued success in the global and domestic markets. They can store goods in convenient locations. They can also create fast, reliable means of getting the goods to customers.

Physical distribution is also known as logistics. It involves order processing, transportation, storage, stock handling, as well as inventory control of materials and products. The purchase of a product initiates the movement of products through a physical distribution system. Marketing experts believe that between 20–25 percent of the value of a product includes physical distribution costs. Physical distribution is the third-largest expense for most businesses. This expense is surpassed only by the costs of material and labor.

Physical distribution can be viewed as a system of links for the efficient movement of products from warehouse to retailer to customer. The links include customer service, transportation, storage, order processing, inventory, and packaging. When setting their distribution goals, business owners need to ask themselves questions about these links. What level of customer service should be provided? How will the products be shipped? Where will the goods be located? How many warehouses should be used? How should orders be handled? How much inventory should be kept at each location? What kinds of protective packaging and handling are required?

Each link in the system affects the other links. For example, a business that provides customized personal computers may transport finished products by air rather than by truck. Faster delivery times may allow lower inventory costs, which would make up for the higher cost of air transport.

Businesses need to make the physical distribution system as efficient and cost effective as possible. At the same time, physical distribution needs to be coordinated with other business functions, such as purchasing, finance, production, packaging, and promotion. Suppose a business has planned to launch promotional ads for a new product available on a certain date. If the distribution system is unreliable, the product may not arrive at stores in time. This error will cost the business customers and cause the business to lose credibility.

 As You Read

Predict Consider the effects of changing the transportation system a business always uses.

TYPES OF TRANSPORTATION SYSTEMS

Transportation is the marketing function of moving a product from the place where it is made to the place where it is sold. It is estimated that up to 8 percent of a company's sales revenue is spent on transportation.

There are three factors that affect transportation costs. First is the distance between the source and the destination. Second is the means of transportation. Third is the size and quantity of the product to be shipped.

Since transportation costs are a significant part of each sale, manufacturers, wholesalers, and retailers look for the most cost-effective delivery methods. An efficient distribution system moves products with minimal handling to minimize costs and maximize customer satisfaction.

Decisions made about transportation are closely related to several other distribution issues. Access to appropriate transportation plays a part in choosing a location for a business or facility.

The means of transportation, such as air, water, or land, may determine the form of packing materials used. The means of transportation may also affect the size and frequency of shipments. Transportation costs may be reduced by sending larger shipments less frequently. However, it is also necessary to consider the costs of maintaining extra inventory. The connection among these decisions means that careful planning and scheduling can help save on transportation costs.

There are five major transportation systems, or modes, used move products: trucks, railroads, waterways, pipelines, and air carriers.

In many cases, there are several sources and many destinations for the same product. This adds a significant level of complexity to the challenge of minimizing transportation costs. The percentage of freight carried by each transportation mode is shown in **Figure 22.1**.

FIGURE 22.1 **Transportation Systems**

This pie chart shows the percentage of freight shipped by each type of single-mode transportation in the United States. *Why do you think the percentage of freight carried by trucks is so large?*

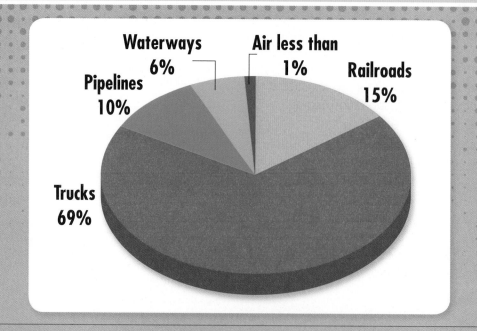

Waterways 6%
Pipelines 10%
Air less than 1%
Railroads 15%
Trucks 69%

TRUCKING

Trucks, or motor carriers, are the most frequently used transportation mode. Trucks are readily available and ideally suited for transporting goods over short distances. They carry higher-valued products that are expensive for a business to keep in inventory. They also carry products with a limited shelf life, such as produce, meat, and dairy products. Lightweight shipments transported over moderate distances are generally handled by trucks. Nearly 80 percent of those shipments weigh less than 1,000 pounds each. Businesses use trucks for virtually all intracity (within a city) shipping and for 26 percent of the intercity (between cities) freight traffic in the United States.

State and federal transportation agencies **regulate** motor carriers used for interstate (between states) commerce. They regulate the number of hours motor carrier operators can drive without stopping and the length of rest periods. State transportation agencies regulate fuel taxes, safety issues, and rates charged for intrastate (within a state) trucking.

TYPES OF CARRIERS

Businesses that use trucks to move their products have several different **options**. They can use for-hire carriers, private carriers, or a combination of both. For-hire carriers include common carriers and contract carriers.

Common carriers are trucking companies that provide transportation services to any business in their operating area for a fee. Common carriers must treat all customers equally. Less-than-truckload carriers provide shipments in which freight from multiple shippers are consolidated into a single truckload. Carriers can change their rates or geographical areas, as long as they do not charge rates that are different from their published rates. More than one-third of all motor freight is handled by common carriers.

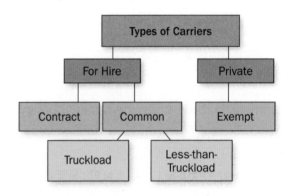

The physical movement of products involves transportation. It is estimated that up to 8 percent of a company's sales revenue is spent on transportation. *Why is an effective transportation system important for a company?*

Transportation function

Contract carriers are for-hire trucking companies that provide equipment and drivers for specific routes, according to agreements between the carrier and the shipper. A contract carrier can provide services on a one-time basis or on a continuing basis.

Contract carriers negotiate fee agreements with each customer and usually transport goods for more than one business. Contract carriers can legally charge different rates to each business. However, they must file their contracts with the appropriate state or federal regulatory agency.

When using for-hire carriers, a business does not need to invest in transportation equipment. However, for-hire carriers offer less flexibility for rush deliveries, direct shipments, and special pick-ups or handling.

PRIVATE CARRIERS

Private carriers are trucking companies that transport goods for an individual business. A company can own or lease transportation equipment. In many cases, the carrier's primary business is not transportation. For example, a grocery store chain may own and operate a private fleet to deliver produce and goods to its stores. Significant capital investment is needed to own a private fleet.

Cost is a major factor in selecting transportation. Starting a private-carrier operation requires a large investment in equipment and facilities. Private carriers allow a business to have control over equipment, maintenance, availability, routes, delivery times, and handling procedures. A business can also quickly change schedules, routes, and delivery times to meet customers' needs.

Many businesses use a combination of private and for-hire carriers. They may use their own trucks for local deliveries and common or contract carriers for shipments beyond their local service areas.

Exempt carriers are trucking companies that are free (exempt) from direct regulation of rates and operating procedures. This exemption allows their rates to be lower than those of common carriers.

MARKETING CASE STUDY

UPS Races with NASCAR

Most of the advertising done by international delivery service UPS® is serious and businesslike. It communicates the benefits of using "Brown" and how it can help companies succeed. One ad campaign, though, took a more light-hearted tone. It put a NASCAR® driver to the test against UPS drivers.

Taking Brown for a Spin

In the four-part series of ads, a well-known race car driver is challenged by UPS drivers to "race the truck." Eventually, the race car driver ends up driving the brown truck on a NASCAR track. The series not only promoted the UPS service and told the story of how fast it is, but it also tied in with the UPS sponsorship of the NASCAR racer.

English Language Arts

Investigate Identify three other brands that are sponsors of NASCAR vehicles. Discuss possible values these sponsorships have for each company.

Local transportation firms may also receive exempt status if they make short-distance deliveries within specified trading areas in cities. In most cases, exempt carriers transport agricultural products.

ADVANTAGES AND DISADVANTAGES OF TRUCK TRANSPORTATION

Trucks are a convenient form of transportation. They can pick up products from a manufacturer, wholesaler, or retailer and deliver them door-to-door to just about any location. Trucks can make rapid deliveries, which reduces the need for businesses to carry large inventories between shipments.

Some disadvantages of trucks are that they cost more to operate than rail and water carriers. Trucks are susceptible to delays due to traffic jams, road conditions, and severe weather. Trucks are also subject to size and weight restrictions, which can vary from state to state, making interstate travel difficult in some situations.

RAILROADS

Railroads are another major form of transportation in the United States. Trains transport nearly 15 percent of the total ton-miles of freight shipped in the United States. A **ton-mile** is the movement of one ton (2,000 pounds) of freight one mile. Rail transportation is typically used for long-distance shipping. It is less expensive than air transportation. The delivery speed of rail transportation is comparable to the delivery speed of trucks over long distances. Rail transportation is faster than marine waterway transportation. Deregulation and the introduction of larger-capacity freight cars have created opportunities in areas previously dominated by motor carriers.

Trains are excellent for moving heavy and bulky freight, such as coal, steel, lumber, and grain. Specialized rail cars also haul certain products over long distances. For example, refrigerated cars keep perishable products such as milk, fruit, and vegetables from spoiling. Tankers haul combustible or hazardous materials, such as chemicals. Rail cars with ramps can transport automobiles.

PRICING AND DELIVERY SERVICES

Shippers pay lower rail transportation rates if they fill an entire boxcar. A **carload** is the minimum number of pounds of freight needed to fill a boxcar. Carload weights are established for different classifications of goods. Once a shipment reaches the minimum weight, the shipper pays the lower rate, regardless of the physical size of the shipment.

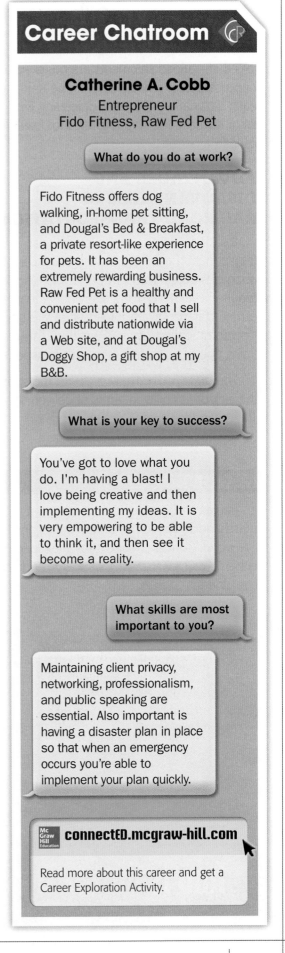

Career Chatroom

Catherine A. Cobb
Entrepreneur
Fido Fitness, Raw Fed Pet

What do you do at work?

Fido Fitness offers dog walking, in-home pet sitting, and Dougal's Bed & Breakfast, a private resort-like experience for pets. It has been an extremely rewarding business. Raw Fed Pet is a healthy and convenient pet food that I sell and distribute nationwide via a Web site, and at Dougal's Doggy Shop, a gift shop at my B&B.

What is your key to success?

You've got to love what you do. I'm having a blast! I love being creative and then implementing my ideas. It is very empowering to be able to think it, and then see it become a reality.

What skills are most important to you?

Maintaining client privacy, networking, professionalism, and public speaking are essential. Also important is having a disaster plan in place so that when an emergency occurs you're able to implement your plan quickly.

connectED.mcgraw-hill.com

Read more about this career and get a Career Exploration Activity.

The term *less-than-carload* refers to a freight shipment that falls short of the minimum weight requirements to fill a boxcar. Rates charged for less-than-carload shipments are more expensive, because partial carloads have to be unloaded at each destination. The extra unloading time and labor increase the shipping rates for less-than-carload amounts.

ADVANTAGES AND DISADVANTAGES OF RAILROAD TRANSPORTATION

Railroads are one of the lowest-cost transportation modes, because trains carry large quantities at relatively low per-unit costs. Trains require 50 to 70 percent less energy than a motor carrier to transport freight, and they are seldom slowed or stopped by bad weather. This makes trains one of the safest modes of transportation.

The biggest disadvantage of rail transport is the lack of flexibility in terms of delivery locations. Trains can pick up and deliver goods only at designated stations along rail lines.

MARINE SHIPPING

Barges and container ships transport merchandise within the United States and around the world. Container ships carry their loads in either 20- or 40-foot-long standardized truck-size containers.

WATERWAYS

Inland shipping is shipping from one port to another on connecting rivers and lakes. The St. Lawrence Seaway, the Great Lakes, and the Mississippi and Ohio Rivers are all inland shipping routes.

Intracoastal shipping is the shipping of goods on inland and coastal waterways between ports along the same coast. For example, shipments can be sent from Virginia to North Carolina through the Dismal Swamp Canal.

International waterways are the oceans, seas, and rivers that connect continents and countries. Almost all overseas nonperishable freight, such as heavy equipment, steel, ore, forest products, grain, and petroleum is transported by container ships and barges because of the low cost.

ADVANTAGES AND DISADVANTAGES OF MARINE SHIPPING

The biggest advantage of marine transportation is the low cost. However, they are also the slowest form of transportation.

Marine shipping has other disadvantages. Buyers that are located far from the port city must have products off-loaded from container ships onto railroad cars or motor carriers to reach their destination. This added cost of distribution reduces some of the cost advantages of marine shipping.

Intermodal transportation combines two or more modes of transportation to get products to the customer. *Why might a company use both marine and road shipping methods?*

Two Is Better Than One

Marine shipping is affected by bad weather and seasonal conditions. Great Lakes shipping, for example, is closed for two to three months in the winter.

INTERMODAL TRANSPORTATION

Intermodal transportation combines two or more transportation modes to maximize the advantages of each. Piggyback service involves carrying loaded truck trailers over land on railroad flatcars. Trucks then take the trailers to their final destinations. Fishyback service involves shipping loaded truck trailers over water on ships and barges. Piggyback and fishyback services combine all the advantages of truck transportation with the lower costs of rail and marine transportation.

PIPELINES

Pipelines are usually owned by the company using them, and in these instances, they are considered private carriers.

There are more than 2.6 million of pipelines within the United States.

Pipelines are most frequently used to transport oil and natural gas. They move crude oil from oil fields to refineries, where it is processed. The refined products, such as gasoline, are then trucked to retail outlets such as your local gasoline station.

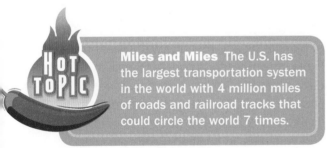

Miles and Miles The U.S. has the largest transportation system in the world with 4 million miles of roads and railroad tracks that could circle the world 7 times.

ADVANTAGES AND DISADVANTAGES OF PIPELINES

The construction of pipelines requires a high initial investment, but operational costs are relatively small. Pipeline transportation has the best safety record among all major transportation systems. Products carried through pipelines move slowly but continuously and suffer minimal product damage or theft. These products are not subject to delivery delays due to bad weather. The risk of a pipeline leak is low, but when a leak does occur, the damage to the environment can be extensive.

AIR CARGO SERVICES

Currently, air cargo services are less than 1 percent of the total ton-miles of freight shipped. High-value, low-weight, time-critical items, such as overnight mail, are often shipped by air. Certain high-value products, such as emergency parts, instruments, and medicines, may also be shipped by air. Air cargo has space and weight restraints, so most products that are transported in smaller containers are well suited for this form of shipment.

Specialized firms offer ground support to businesses that use air cargo services. These firms collect shipments from businesses and deliver them to the air terminal where they are loaded onto commercial airliners or specialized air cargo planes.

The Federal Aviation Administration (FAA) regulates air transportation, but airlines and air transport companies set their own rates. Air cargo service carriers offer such things as wide-bodied jets that can ship more goods and specialized packaging designed to help prevent damage.

ADVANTAGES AND DISADVANTAGES OF AIR TRANSPORTATION

The greatest advantage for air transportation is its speed. A fast delivery time allows businesses to satisfy customers who need something quickly. It also reduces inventory expenses and storage costs.

The greatest disadvantage of air transportation is its cost. It is by far the most expensive form of distribution. Air cargo rates are at least twice as costly as truck rates. Other disadvantages of air cargo services include mechanical breakdowns and delays in delivery caused by bad weather. Although it is a rare occurrence, airlines can be disrupted by terrorism or suspected terrorism.

 Reading Check

Recall What are the five transportation systems used to move products?

TRANSPORTATION SERVICE COMPANIES

Transportation service companies handle small- and medium-size packages. Some examples of these companies are the U.S. Postal Service®, express delivery services, bus package carriers, and freight forwarders.

U.S. POSTAL SERVICE

More than two centuries have passed since Benjamin Franklin was appointed the first Postmaster General in 1775. Today, the U.S. Postal Service is a primary source for shipping small packages by parcel post or first-class mail. Parcel post is used for shipping packages weighing up to 70 pounds and no larger than 130 inches in combined length and girth. With nearly 212,000 vehicles, The U.S. Postal Service boasts the largest civilian ground fleet in the world. The U.S. Postal Service also ships via international and domestic express mail, and they offer special services for commercial customers. If a package is sent cash on delivery (COD), the recipient must pay to receive the package.

For an extra fee, parcel post can be insured against loss or damage. Parcel post can also be express-mailed at higher rates to guarantee next-day delivery. The U. S. Postal Service has a Click-N-Ship® online service that prints shipping labels and accepts payment for packages shipped to domestic and international locations.

EXPRESS DELIVERY SERVICES

Express delivery services specialize in delivering small, lightweight packages, envelopes, and high-priority mail usually weighing less than 150 pounds. Express delivery companies, such as FedEx®, DHL®, and the United Parcel Service®, offer door-to-door pick-up, delivery, and COD services. Shipments can be made nationally or internationally by airplane, truck, bus, or train. Rates are based on speed of delivery, size and weight of package, distance to be sent, and type of service to be used. Regular service usually takes from two to three days; more expensive next-day service is also available.

During the last 40 years, express carriers have become important players in physical distribution. Their role is likely to become even more important as technology continues to make an impact on global economy and the world market place. FedEx began operations in 1971. After decades of purchasing and merging with other businesses, FedEx now transports over 10.5 million shipments daily. It has the world's largest civil fleet of 654 aircraft, 300,000 employees, and more than 1,900 service centers serving 220 countries and territories. In addition, FedEx provides integrated logistics and technology solutions, and international logistics and trade information technology.

DHL, a pioneering express delivery carrier, started shipping from San Francisco to Honolulu in 1969. It was the first carrier to introduce express international shipping via airplane to Eastern Europe in 1983 and to China in 1986. DHL is the largest company specializing in international express shipping. It sends packages to approximately 120,000 destinations in more than 220 countries.

Some people prefer to print their own shipping labels. The U.S. Postal Service makes it possible for customers to pay for and print shipping labels online. *How does this service help customers with their shipping needs?*

A New Approach

BUS PACKAGE CARRIERS

Bus package carriers provide same-day or next-day package delivery service to businesses in cities and towns along their scheduled routes. For example, Greyhound's PackageXpress®, delivers packages weighing less than 100 pounds and smaller than 30″ × 47″ × 82″ in size.

The cost of bus package transportation services depends on the weight of the package, the distance it will travel, and service level. Daily buses run to larger cities, such as Boston, Chicago, New York and San Francisco. This provides opportunities for some businesses to move their products quickly and at reasonable rates.

FREIGHT FORWARDERS

Freight forwarders are private companies that combine less-than-carload or less-than-truckload shipments from several businesses and deliver them to their destinations. They gather small shipments into larger lots, and then hire a carrier to move them, usually at reduced rates. By combining shipments, freight forwarders often obtain truckload or carload rates and can lower transportation costs for shippers. Freight forwarders also provide logistical services that help businesses select the best transportation methods and routes.

 After You Read | **Section 22.1**

Review Key Concepts

1. **Explain** why transportation is related to customer service.
2. **Differentiate** between common, contract, and private carriers.
3. **List** the benefits of intermodal transportation.

Practice Academics

English Language Arts

4. The Transportation Security Administration (TSA) was established to protect the nation's transportation systems. Select one type of system (truck, rail, air, marine, or pipeline) to research. Identify TSA security regulations for the selected system. Discuss how they balance safety with freedom of movement for people and commerce.

Mathematics

5. An auto parts manufacturing company sold $964,000 in auto parts to a car manufacturing company last year. This year the same car company's order was 14 percent less than last year's order. How much money will the auto parts company lose this year in the order from the car company? How much money did the auto parts company make from the car company?

   Math Concept **Computation** Determining losses is a matter of subtracting the smaller amount from the larger amount.

   Starting Hints To solve this problem, multiply the decimal form of the percent by the amount of the order last year. Subtract the dollar amount for the 14 percent from the order amount from last year.

    connectED.mcgraw-hill.com

   Check your answers.

For help, go to the **Math Skills Handbook** located at the back of this book.

READING GUIDE

Before You Read

Connect How might the law of supply and demand relate to inventory storage?

Objectives

- **Explain** the concept and function of inventory storage.
- **Identify** the types of warehouses.
- **Discuss** distribution planning for international markets.

The Main Idea

Inventory storage allows a business to keep its products in a safe location until they are needed or ready to be sold.

Vocabulary

Content Vocabulary

- storage
- private warehouse
- public warehouse
- distribution center
- bonded warehouse

Academic Vocabulary

You will find these words in your reading and on your tests. Make sure you know their meanings.

- ensures
- restrict

Graphic Organizer

Draw this chart to take notes about different types of warehouses.

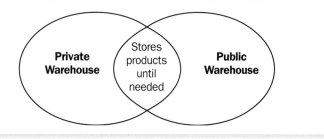

 connectED.mcgraw-hill.com

Print this graphic organizer.

MARKETING CORE FUNCTION

 Channel Management

Inventory Storage

THE STORAGE OF GOODS

Storage is part of a marketing function and refers to the holding of goods until they are sold. The amount of goods stored is called an "inventory." The storage function facilitates the movement of products through the distribution channel as products are sold.

There are many reasons why storing goods is an essential activity for most businesses. First of all, products are stored until orders are received from customers. Products might also need to be stored because production has exceeded consumption, or demand decreases.

> **Products are produced in large quantities, but they must be stored until they are sold.**

Sometimes, agricultural commodities such as corn, wheat, and soybeans may only be available during certain seasons. Commodity storage makes these products available year-round and **ensures** that their price remains relatively stable.

Some purchasers buy in quantity to get discounts on their purchases, and then store the items until they are needed. Finally, products are stored at convenient locations to provide faster delivery to customers.

Storing products adds time and place utility to them. Products must be available for customers when and where they want them. The costs involved in storing products include space, equipment, and personnel. Storage also means spending money (or capital) on inventory rather than investing it in another activity that could provide a larger return.

Businesses balance product storage costs against the possibility of not having products available for customers when they want to buy them. Most products are stored in warehouses, or facilities, in which goods are received, identified, sorted, stored, and dispatched for shipment.

Internet-based stores do not require physical retail space, but still require warehouses to store goods. This kind of warehouse fills orders directly from customers.

As You Read

Connect What products that you use do not need to be stored?

PRIVATE WAREHOUSES

A **private warehouse** is a storage facility designed to meet the specific needs of its owner. Any producer, wholesaler, or retailer has the option of owning a private warehouse.

A private warehouse is valuable for companies that move a large volume of products. Specialized conditions, such as a temperature-controlled environment, may be built into the facility. Private warehouses often house other parts of the business operation, such as offices.

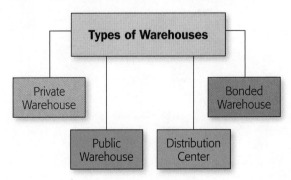

A disadvantage is that private warehouses are costly to build and maintain. In a recent survey, large retailers reported spending 51 percent of their total physical distribution costs on warehouse expenses. Transportation costs accounted for the remaining 49 percent. Private warehouses should be considered only when a significant amount of merchandise needs to be stored. Doing so makes the total operating costs of private warehouses lower than the operating costs of public warehouses.

Hot Topic

Economic Impact Industry and household spending on transportation accounts for nearly 10 percent of the U.S. gross domestic product.

PUBLIC WAREHOUSES

A **public warehouse** is a storage and handling facility offered to any individual or company that will pay for its use. Public warehouses rent storage space. They may also provide additional services to businesses, such as shipment consolidation, receiving, unloading, inspecting, reshipping, order filling, and truck terminal operation services.

Public warehouses are helpful to businesses that have low- to medium-volume storage needs or seasonal production.

There are five types of public warehouses:

1. **Bulk storage warehouses** keep products only in bulk form, such as chemical and oil.

2. **Cold storage warehouses** handle perishables, such as fruits, vegetables, and frozen products.

3. **Commodity warehouses** store agricultural products, such as, tobacco, cotton, or grain.

4. **General merchandise warehouses** handle products that do not require specialized handling.

5. **Household goods warehouses** store personal property storage, household articles, and furniture.

DISTRIBUTION CENTERS

A **distribution center** is a warehouse designed to speed delivery of goods and to minimize storage costs. The main focus in a distribution center is on sorting and moving products, not on storing them. Distribution centers are planned around markets rather than transportation requirements. They can cut costs by reducing the number of warehouses and eliminating excessive inventory.

Storage activity facilitates the movement of products through the distribution channel. *What is the purpose of storage?*

The Importance of Storage

Some businesses, such as paint companies Sherwin-Williams and Benjamin Moore, use their distribution centers to physically change the product for the final customer. Their distribution centers perform additional functions such as mixing ingredients, labeling, and repackaging for shipments to retailers.

Every distribution center has its own methods and systems of operation. A typical center may employ an unloader, a receiver, a hauler, a put-away driver, a replenishment driver, an order filler, and a loader.

- The unloader unloads trucks and breaks down pallets.
- The receiver inventories and tags unloaded pallets using a mobile cart computer unit and printer.
- A hauler transports received pallets, with equipment, from the receiving dock to the storage racks.
- A put-away driver loads the product into racks with a forklift.
- The replenishment driver pulls a product from the racks, with a forklift, and prepares it for the order filler.
- The order filler locates the ordered product and moves it to a designated location.
- The loader wraps the pallets and loads the trucks.
- The cycle begins again with the unloader.

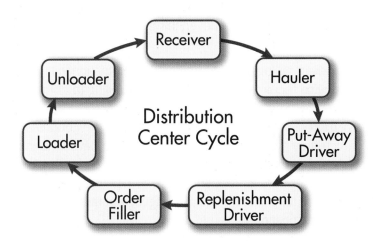

Distribution Center Cycle

The name by which the distribution center is known is based on the purpose of the operation. A retail distribution center distributes goods to retail stores. An order fulfillment center distributes goods directly to consumers.

Distribution centers also consolidate large orders from many sources and redistribute them as separate orders for individual accounts or stores in a chain. Merchandise stays a short time in a distribution center.

Transporting Beauty

The saying, "A woman's hair is her crowning glory," has been around since ancient times. In India, human hair ranks as the "crowning" export. The country's hair care business took off in the 1960s and now makes more than $2 billion annually.

Before reaching the market, human hair is collected by the ton from barber shops, villages, and temples. Then it is sorted, washed, dried, and bundled into varying lengths. The 6- to 45-inch tresses are then shipped to Asia, Europe, and North America.

Faith to Fashion Many celebrities seek this natural hair. One source is found at Hindu temples where women shave their heads as an act of sacrifice, known as *tonsuring*. They believe that losing their hair "unloads" their pride to God. What do they think of these women in other countries wearing the hair as extensions and wigs? "I think it's wonderful. Why not? I have no need for it," says one devotee.

Social Studies
In India, some cut their hair to overcome pride. Westerners do the opposite. Discuss how each of these practices relates to its culture.

Here are some entry-level phrases that are used in conversations about marketing all over the world.

English	Hindi
Hello/Goodbye	Namaste
Yes/No	Ji ha/Ji nahi
Please	Kripaya
Thank you	Dhanyavad
You're welcome	Koi bat nahi

BONDED WAREHOUSES

Bonded warehouses are public or private warehouses that store products that require payment of a federal tax. Imported or domestic products cannot be removed until the required tax is paid. Although they are charged storage fees, businesses can save on taxes by taking goods out of storage only when needed.

 Reading Check

Recall What are some types of storage facilities available to businesses?

DISTRIBUTION PLANNING FOR INTERNATIONAL MARKETS

Distribution is of critical importance in global marketing. The U.S. Department of Commerce estimates that for every $1 billion worth of U.S. products sold abroad, 5,000 jobs are supported at home. Exports support one-sixth of the total manufacturing and agricultural output of the United States. In other words, 16 percent of everything made or grown in the U.S. is shipped to other countries.

However, selling to customers in the international marketplace requires more planning than selling to domestic customers. Businesses that sell internationally must follow U.S. export laws as well as the import laws of the countries to which they are selling. Some countries also have laws that **restrict** how products may be transported to and within those countries. Businesses frequently have to deal with conflicting bureaucratic regulations, multiple language barriers, and complex negotiations.

Extensive distribution planning is needed in a global marketplace. Consider the example of high-tech, complex products. The parts used to manufacture items such as automobiles, computers, wireless phones, and jet airliners are made in several countries. The parts are then shipped to other countries for final assembly, and the finished product is shipped to still more destinations. All these stages of production require that a manufacturer plan effectively. A company needs to make sure not only that the process is efficient and cost-effective but also that it follows the various rules and regulations of all the countries involved.

In order to deliver their goods successfully, businesses must understand other countries' physical transportation systems. In the U.S. or Europe, it might take only a day or two for an shipment to get from the manufacturing plant to the store by rail or truck.

In some less-developed nations, however, the air-cargo or rail systems may not be reliable enough to assure delivery of goods in a timely and efficient manner. Other countries may not have the networks of roads and highways needed to support dependable truck deliveries. In some parts of the world, for example, many consumer goods are still transported to market by bicycle or cart.

It is also important to understand how retail institutions in other countries differ from American retail institutions. Consider all the different kinds of food that are available in grocery stores near you. Many of the items we take for granted, such as milk, cheese, eggs, and frozen foods, may be hard to find in stores in less-developed countries.

In some parts of the world, electricity is still unreliable, even in the bigger cities. As a result, retailers in remote locations are left with little or no capacity to refrigerate or freeze items that can easily spoil. This lack of storage facilities means that supermarkets, which are so common in the U.S., are rare in developing countries.

 After You Read | **Section 22.2**

Review Key Concepts

1. **Explain** the four reasons why merchandise is stored.
2. **List** three services that might be offered at a public warehouse.
3. **Describe** a bonded warehouse.

Practice Academics

English Language Arts

4. Conduct research on the latest issues impacting the transportation industry. Use information from the American Trucking Association (ATA), the Association of American Railroads (AAR), the United States Department of Transportation, or other transportation news sources. Summarize these issues in a one-page report.

Mathematics

5. The Cost per Order is one measure of warehouse productivity. The Cost per Order is represented by the ratio Total Warehouse Cost to the Total Orders Shipped. What is the Cost per Order for a company that has a total warehouse cost of $850,000 and shipped a total of 95,000 orders in a one-year period?

Math Concept **Operations** When a problem asks for the price "per" item, more often than not, the operation you want to use is division.

Starting Hint To solve this problem, divide the total cost of the items by the total number of items.

Check your answers.

For help, go to the **Math Skills Handbook** located at the back of this book.

Physical Distribution

Physical distribution or logistics involves transportation, storage, order processing, stock handling, and inventory control.

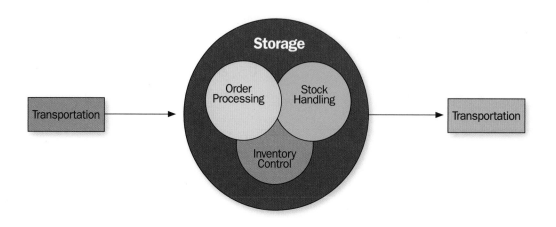

The different kinds of transportation systems include trucking, railroads, marine shipping, pipelines, and air cargo services.

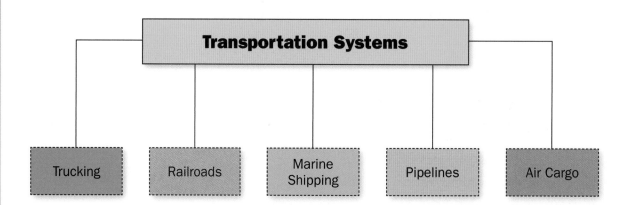

Review and Activities

Written Summary

- Physical distribution links a business and its customers.
- Physical distribution comprises all the activities that help to ensure that the right amount of product is delivered to the right place at the right time
- Physical distribution is also known as logistics.
- It involves transporting, storing, order processing, stock handling, and inventory control of materials and products.
- The different kinds of transportation include marine, air, pipeline, and land transportation, which includes both trucking and railroads.
- Storage is the marketing function of holding goods until they are sold.
- Storing goods is an essential activity for most businesses.
- Products are stored in warehouses or distribution centers until orders are received from customers.
- Globalization is increasing the importance of international distribution.

Review Content Vocabulary and Academic Vocabulary

1. Use each of these vocabulary terms in a written sentence.

Content Vocabulary
- physical distribution (p. 515)
- transportation (p. 516)
- common carriers (p. 517)
- contract carriers (p. 518)
- private carriers (p. 518)
- exempt carriers (p. 518)
- ton-mile (p. 519)
- carload (p. 519)
- freight forwarders (p. 523)
- storage (p. 525)
- private warehouse (p. 525)
- public warehouse (p. 526)
- distribution center (p. 526)
- bonded warehouse (p. 528)

Academic Vocabulary
- regulate (p. 517)
- options (p. 517)
- ensures (p. 525)
- restrict (p. 528)

Assess for Understanding

2. **Summarize** What is the nature and scope of physical distribution?
3. **Name** What are the transportation systems and services used to move products from manufacturers to consumers?
4. **List** What are the different kinds of transportation service companies?
5. **Justify** Why is inventory storage important in marketing?
6. **Distinguish** What are the different types of warehouses?
7. **Contrast** What makes a distribution center different from other types of warehouses?
8. **Role-Play** What factors will you discuss with your manager when considering whether to expand distribution to countries abroad?
9. **Create** What would a map of a transportation system look like for an orange that is sold at your local grocery store?

 21st Century Skills

Everyday Ethics

10. **Damaged Merchandise** You work in a distribution center. A carton containing several items has been damaged during an incoming shipment. As you fill out a damaged merchandise form, a coworker suggests that you take some of the items, since they may not be missed. How do you think management would view this suggestion? How do you view it? Discuss with a partner.

Financial Literacy Skills

11. **U-Pick-Up** You can have camping equipment shipped directly to your home for $12.75 or have it delivered to an outdoor store that is 45 miles from your house. Your truck gets 18 miles/gal, and gas costs $2.75/gallon. Calculate what it would cost for you to drive to pick up your item. Would you save more if you picked it up yourself or paid for the shipping costs?

e-Marketing Skills

12. **Research Rates** Imagine that you are employed in a manufacturing firm that ships small electric motors weighing 25 pounds to locations in the United States. Investigate how much it would cost to send one package from your location to Chicago, Illinois. The shipment must arrive within five days either by the U.S. Postal Service or an express delivery service such as FedEx or United Parcel Service.

- List the steps that you must take to send the package through the Postal Service.
- List the steps that you must take to send the package through an express delivery service.
- What were the lowest costs for each?
- What additional services were available for you to purchase?

Build Academic Skills

English Language Arts

13. **Trucking Regulations** Conduct research about the advantages and disadvantages of federal regulation of the trucking industry. Write a 100-word paper summarizing your findings.

Science

14. **Wireless Technology** Radio frequency identification, satellite communications, and cellular networks are used for physical distribution systems and inventory storage. Describe how one of these forms of technology is used in the delivery of products or inventory storage. Present a short description of how this technology is used in shipping to your class.

Mathematics

15. **Calculate Savings** A large manufacturer can save 25 percent by using a distribution service instead of a private warehouse. The cost of the distribution service would total $55,450. How much money will the manufacturer save by using the distribution service?

   Math Concept **Computation** Calculating the amount saved by using one service instead of another is a matter of comparing the numbers.

For help, go to the **Math Skills Handbook** located at the back of this book.

Standardized Test Practice

Directions Read the following questions. On a separate piece of paper, write the best possible answer for each one.

1. Which of the following single modes of transportation moves the largest percentage of freight in ton miles?

   A. Air

   B. Pipelines

   C. Railroads

   D. Trucks

2. Physical distribution is the marketing function of moving a product from the place where it is made to the place where it will be sold.

   T

   F

3. The activity that refers to the holding of goods until they are sold is known as _____.

Test-Taking Tip

When studying for a test, write important ideas, definitions, and formulas on flash cards.

DECA. Connection Role Play

Shipping/Receiving Manager Online Gourmet Food Retailer

Situation The best-selling products for your company are cheeses and spices. Small producers that have limited production capabilities make the cheeses. The cheeses are all produced from certified organic ingredients. Cheese is considered a perishable product; therefore, it requires special handling for storage and shipping.

The spices you sell include both well-known and rare varieties. All of the spices are of the highest quality and arrive fresh from their producers in sealed glass jars. Spices are not as perishable as the cheeses you sell, but they do need to be shipped to your customers while they are very fresh. For that reason, you stock only limited quantities of each variety.

Your customers understand that they may have to wait a couple of days for their spice orders. Customers feel that the quality and freshness are worth the brief delay. You are in the process of training a new employee (judge) in your department.

Activity You are to explain to the new employee (judge) the importance of proper storage of each of the gourmet food items. You are to also explain the equally important factor of selecting the best shipping method for each item.

Evaluation You will be evaluated on how well you meet the following performance indicators:

1. Select the best shipping method.
2. Explain the role of distribution centers.
3. Explain the storage process in warehouse operations.
4. Explain distribution issues and trends.
5. Discuss shipping methods used with food products.

 connectED.mcgraw-hill.com

Download the Competitive Events Workbook for more Role-Play Practice.

purchasing

SHOW WHAT YOU KNOW

Visual Literacy Buyers in the clothing industry view designs prior to purchasing new collections. They must budget and plan seasonal purchases. New designs are presented at trade shows and in private business settings. *What might be some sources for information about suppliers of products, materials, and services?*

Discovery Project

From Producer to Final User

Essential Question How does a buyer at a retail store plan purchases for upcoming resale?

Project Goal

You and a partner are buyers for a retail store or chain of stores. Select a product or group of products for resale at the store. With your partner, learn all you can about how to plan a purchasing program for the coming months or season. Conduct research and also interview at least three store buyers or managers. Share your purchasing plan with the class.

Ask Yourself...

- What will you investigate in your research?
- What questions will you ask buyers and managers during your interviews?
- What information is contained in a purchasing plan?

 Solve Problems What are some criteria you would use for selecting goods for purchase?

---

 connectED.mcgraw-hill.com

Activity
Get a worksheet activity about planning purchases.

Evaluate
Download a rubric you can use to evaluate your project.

DECA Connection

DECA Event Role Play

Concepts in this chapter are related to DECA competitive events that involve either an interview or role play.

Performance Indicators The performance indicators represent key skills and knowledge. Your key to success in DECA competitive events is relating them to concepts in this chapter.

- Explain the nature and scope of purchasing.
- Place order/reorders.
- Persuade others.
- Select vendors.
- Evaluate vendor performance.

DECA Prep

Role Play Practice role-playing with the DECA Connection competitive-event activity at the end of this chapter. More information on DECA events can be found on DECA's Web site.

READING GUIDE

Before You Read

Connect What happens when you cannot find a product you need at a store because it is sold out?

Objectives

- **Define** the terms used to describe organizational buyers.
- **Explain** how planning purchases differs between an industrial market and a resellers' market.
- **Describe** the six-month merchandising plan and explain its calculations.
- **Explain** the concept of chain-store buying.

The Main Idea

Purchasing for a business is important, because the costs of running a business are affected by the buyer and by the services needed to run the business.

Vocabulary

Content Vocabulary
- organizational buyers
- wholesale and retail buyers
- six-month merchandise plan
- open-to-buy (OTB)
- centralized buying
- decentralized buying

Academic Vocabulary
You will find these words in your reading and on your tests. Make sure you know their meanings.
- predicts
- technical

Graphic Organizer

Draw or print this chart to write two or three sentences describing these markets: industrial, resellers, government, and institutional.

Market	Notes
Industrial	
Resellers	
Government	
Institutional	

 connectED.mcgraw-hill.com

Print this graphic organizer.

MARKETING CORE FUNCTION

 Channel Management

The Role of the Buyer

PLANNING PURCHASES

Organizational buyers purchase goods for business purposes, usually in much larger quantities than purchased by the average consumer. They must have knowledge about the products they buy and understand the operations of their firm. Knowledge of the manufacturing and service operations is especially important.

As You Read

Compare Identify the similarities and differences of the four markets.

INDUSTRIAL MARKETS

In manufacturing and service businesses, the people responsible for purchasing may be known as *purchasing managers*, *industrial buyers*, or *procurement managers*.

Although their specific job titles may vary, all of these individuals share the same function in common—to purchase goods and services for use by the business.

In manufacturing businesses, planning purchases often requires industrial buyers to be directly involved with production planning.

Consider the following case of a purchasing manager for a manufacturer that makes specialty clothing designed for outdoor activities. This example will help give you an idea of the various duites and responsibilities involved in planning purchases for a business.

Initially, the purchasing manager reviews the company's master production schedule for details of production needed to meet sales requirements. Let's say that the marketing department **predicts** that the company will be able to sell 500 of the manufacturer's Style Number 1900 jackets in the coming season.

The purchasing manager must know exactly how much fabric, insulation, and thread and how many zippers it will take to produce a single Style Number 1900 jacket. This list is called a "bill of materials." The total of all the materials necessary to make one jacket can then be multiplied by 500. The resulting figure will show exactly what needs to be purchased in order to produce the number of jackets that will meet the sales goal.

> **" Having a handle on business trends that affect a buyer's industry is important, especially when buying for resale purposes. "**

In order to determine when to buy the items needed, the purchasing manager would be responsible for materials requirement planning (MRP). MRP includes a **technical** analysis of when to make the purchases so they are available when needed, according to the production schedule. The purchasing manager must therefore know the capacity of the manufacturing facility. The individual must make sure the company has enough room to house all the supplies and raw materials and the inventory of finished goods.

Timelines and delivery of all supplies must be followed and checked on a regular basis to maintain the master production schedule. This ensures that everything is as it should be for manufacturing to progress at an appropriate rate.

RESELLERS' MARKETS

The resellers' market is found in wholesaling and retailing operations where the person responsible for purchasing is simply called a "buyer." **Wholesale and retail buyers** purchase goods for resale. They forecast customers' needs and buy the necessary products. All buyers must plan far in advance of the selling season to know how much of each item to purchase.

Buy to Sell Buyers decide which goods are best, choose suppliers, negotiate prices, and award contracts ensuring the product's timely receipt.

SIX-MONTH MERCHANDISE PLAN

Buyers plan their purchases by preparing a **six-month merchandise plan**, which is the budget that estimates planned purchases for a six-month period. (See **Figure 23.1** on page 540 for a nearly completed merchandise plan.)

The first figure calculated on a merchandise plan is the planned sales figure. In most cases, buyers determine this figure by using the previous year's monthly sales figures. Then they adjust them to reflect the firm's current-year sales goal.

Suppose sales for a particular month last year totaled $100,000, and this year's goal is to increase sales by 10 percent. This year's planned sales for the month would be calculated as follows:

Desired increase: $100,000 \times .10 = $10,000

Planned sales: $100,000 + $10,000 = $110,000

You could also reach the same result in a single step:

$$100,000 \times 1.10 = $110,000$$

Purchasing and inventory control go hand in hand. Buyers need to know what sells and what does not. Companies need to figure out their projected sales to order the correct quantities of merchandise. *What can happen if a this dress shop runs out of a popular dress just before prom season?*

Buy to Sell

The company goal for the current year is derived from a study of last year's sales, current market and economic conditions, and an analysis of the competition. Projection of accurate planned sales figures is important because all other figures on the merchandise plan are computed on the basis of this figure.

Buyers must ensure that there is enough stock to accommodate the planned sales volume. This is also known as *beginning-of-the-month* (*BOM*) *inventory*. To project this figure, a buyer checks the previous year's records for how much stock was needed in relation to monthly sales. Sales were $40,000 in a given month, and the BOM stock value for that month was $120,000. Therefore, the stock-to-sales ratio is 3 to 1. The buyer can apply that same ratio to the planned figure for another month if both economic and market conditions are similar.

Here is how the BOM figure on the merchandise plan is calculated. Suppose the stock-to-sales ratio is 2:1 (usually reported as 2). This means that to accommodate a given sales volume, twice that amount of stock must be kept on hand.

In other words, BOM inventory should be twice the amount of anticipated sales. If sales are $5,000, then the BOM would be $10,000.

The end-of-the-month (EOM) stock figure is closely related to the BOM stock figure. The BOM stock figure for any given month is the EOM stock figure for the previous month.

Planned retail reductions take into account reductions in the selling price, shortages of merchandise caused by clerical errors, employee theft, and customer shoplifting. Such reductions in earnings and merchandise shortages ultimately affect the amount of money that must be planned for purchases.

Planned retail reductions can be calculated in two different ways. One is to calculate reductions as a percentage of planned sales. Suppose planned reductions have historically been 10 percent of planned sales. If planned sales for the month are $25,000, planned reductions for that month would be calculated as follows:

$$\$25,000 \times .10 = \$2,500$$

MARKETING CASE STUDY

Frito-Lay Buys Local

FritoLay ™
Good fun!

When you buy a bag of chips and crunch into them, you are eating a product that started out as a potato in the ground— from California, Texas, or other states. That was the idea behind Frito-Lay's "Local" campaign, which speaks to the trend of buying products obtained from local suppliers.

Meet the Suppliers

"While Lay's Potato Chips have been one of the most popular snacks since they were introduced, what people might not realize is how many communities across the country play a role in the creation of America's favorite potato chip," said a Frito-Lay vice president. The company purchases potatoes from 80 different farms in 27 states. Some of the actual farmers appeared in Lay's TV ads, which emphasized the notion that the company is "closer to home than people might expect."

English Language Arts/Writing

Discuss You are the buyer for a competing potato chip manufacturer and have decided to buy potatoes from local growers. What type of purchase is buying potatoes for potato chips? What information would you need before you could plan your purchase?

FIGURE 23.1 Six-Month Merchandise Plan

This nearly completed model merchandise plan is based on the following assumptions: Sales are expected to increase by 10 percent over last year; last year's stock-to-sales ratios should be used to complete this year's BOM stock figures; this year's planned reductions should be 5 percent lower than last year's; and the planned BOM for August is $264,000. *What are the planned purchase figures for May through July?*

Spring Season 20___   Department ___Toys___
                                                      No. ___6124___

		February	March	April	May	June	July	Total
Sales	Last year	82,000	96,000	90,000	100,000	94,000	80,000	
	Plan	90,200	105,600	99,000	110,000	103,400	88,000	
	Actual							
Retail Stock BOM	Last year	328,000	336,000	297,000	360,000	291,400	224,000	
	Plan	360,800	369,600	326,700	396,000	320,540	246,400	
	Actual							
Retail Reductions	Last year	12,300	14,400	13,500	15,000	14,100	12,000	
	Plan	11,685	13,680	12,825	14,250	13,395	11,400	
	Actual							
Purchases	Last year	N/A	N/A	N/A	N/A	N/A	N/A	
	Plan	110,685	76,380	181,125				
	Actual							

Some companies set goals of reducing planned reductions from the previous year. Assume that a firm's goal is to reduce this year's planned reductions by 5 percent from last year's figure. Last year's reductions totaled $700; therefore this year's planned reductions would be figured this way:

Desired decrease: $700 × .05 = $35

Planned reductions: $700 – $35 = $665

This result could also be reached in a single step: $700 × .95 = $665

The planned purchase entry shows the retail-dollar purchase figures that a firm needs to achieve its sales and inventory projections for each month. Planned sales, BOM stock, and reductions are all necessary for determining planned purchases (P). That includes planned sales (PS), planned EOM/BOM stock, and planned reductions (R).

The formula for planned purchases is:

$$(PS + EOM\ stock + R) - BOM\ stock = P$$

Assume that planned sales are $10,000, planned EOM stock is $25,000, planned reductions are $500, and BOM stock is $20,000. Using the formula, planned purchases would be calculated this way:

$$(\$10,000 + \$25,000 + \$500) - \$20,000 =$$

$$\$35,500 - \$20,000 = \$15,500$$

OPEN-TO-BUY

During the buying season, a buyer may want to know the **open-to-buy (OTB)**, which is the amount of money a retailer has left for buying goods after considering all purchases received, on order, and in transit.

OTB is calculated this way:

P − (goods received + goods ordered) = OTB

Assume that merchandise received against the planned purchase figure just calculated is $6,500 so far, and merchandise on order against it is $2,000. The present OTB would be as follows:

$15,500 − ($6,500 + $2,000) = OTB

$15,500 − $8,500 = $7,000

This $7,000 figure represents the retail value of the goods that the buyer may purchase at the time. However, the problem is not solved here.

There is a way to determine the actual money the buyer has to spend. You must calculate the markup percentage used by the buyer and deduct that figure from the retail value. Assume that the markup percentage is 45 percent, based on the retail value of the merchandise.

Here is the formula for determining the OTB at cost:

100% − markup % =

% attributed to cost of the item

% attributed to cost × retail value =

OTB at cost

100% − 45% markup = 55% (cost)

55% (cost) × $7,000 (retail) =

$3,850 OTB at cost

Therefore, in the end, the buyer has $3,850 to spend with all other costs considered. You can see how this extra step makes a big difference in the final amount.

Reading Check

Identify What is the six-month merchandise plan?

Buyers need to understand their customers and the products they sell in order to make purchasing decisions. *How can the knowledge of a company's customers and products improve a buyer's purchasing power?*

Purchasing Power

PLANNING PURCHASES FOR A CHAIN-STORE OPERATION

The buying process for all branches in a chain store operation is usually done in a central location, such as company headquarters. This process is called **centralized buying**. Buyers will purchase all the items for a department or part of a department. There may be three buyers for women's shoes—one for casual shoes, another for traditional shoes, and still another for better shoes. To coordinate the efforts of those three buyers, there would be a merchandise or division manager. This person would oversee all shoe buyers, which may include those for men's, children's, and women's shoes.

Chain stores use centralized buying to create a unified image for the chain. Another benefit of centralized buying is quantity discounts. Stores can negotiate with vendors because of the large volume of goods that they purchase at one time.

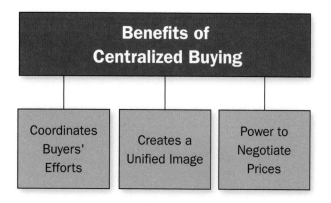

DECENTRALIZED BUYING

Sometimes chain stores want to have special goods in their stores that are not available elsewhere in the chain. In these cases, local store managers or their designated buyers are authorized to make special purchases for their individual stores. This is **decentralized buying**. Decentralization occurs when authority for retail decisions is made at lower levels in the organization.

Retailers constantly make trade-offs between efficiency and sales potential. Centralized buying is more efficient and decentralized buying has more sales potential. This potential is due to the decisions that tailor merchandise to local markets.

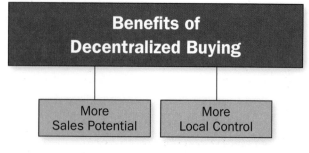

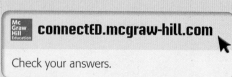

GOVERNMENT MARKETS

There are also buyers for government markets. Federal, state, and local agencies are the government units responsible for purchasing goods and services for their specific markets. There are more than 89,000 government units in the United States. These include the departments of sanitation, public libraries, and local school boards.

Government markets make up one of the largest single markets for retail goods and services in the world. In the United States, the federal government is a huge consumer of goods, ranging from food for school lunches to military equipment. No one federal agency is responsible for all government buying.

INSTITUTIONAL MARKETS

One final segment of the market includes institutions and nonprofit organizations that do not compete in the business world in the same way retailers and wholesalers do. These institutions include hospitals, museums, libraries, prisons, schools, colleges, places of worship, civic clubs, and various foundations that do not work solely for profit.

Many institutions and nonprofit organizations have unique buying needs. Some of these organizations may purchase goods and services for use in the production of their own goods or services.

 After You Read | **Section 23.1**

Review Key Concepts

1. **List** three job titles that can be used to describe people responsible for purchasing in manufacturing and service businesses.
2. **Explain** how a bill of materials is used in planning purchases.
3. **Identify** two benefits of centralized buying.

Practice Academics

English Language Arts

4. Work with a partner to create a role-play about purchasing for business. Consider presenting topics such as employee theft, customer shoplifting, disagreements about EOM/BOM totals, or whether to use centralized or decentralized buying. Submit a script for your role-play.

Mathematics

5. An office supply company has planned purchases in the amount of $23,000. If the company has goods received in the amount of $7,500 and goods ordered in the amount of $12,000, what is the open-to-buy (OTB) for the company?

Math Concept **Algebra** The open-to-buy (OTB) is the amount of money left for buying goods after all purchases received and on order have been considered.

Starting Hints To solve this problem, find the sum of the goods received and goods ordered. Subtract the sum you found from the planned purchase amount for the company.

 connectED.mcgraw-hill.com

Check your answers.

For help, go to the **Math Skills Handbook** located at the back of this book.

READING GUIDE

Before You Read

Connect How do you decide where to buy products that are offered at different stores?

Objectives

- **List** the three types of purchase situations.
- **Explain** the criteria for selecting suppliers.
- **Name** the factors involved in negotiating terms of a sale.
- **Describe** the various Internet purchasing methods.

The Main Idea

The details of the purchasing process help describe the buyer's job responsibilities.

Vocabulary

Content Vocabulary
- want slips
- consignment buying
- memorandum buying
- reverse auction

Academic Vocabulary

You will find these words in your reading and on your tests. Make sure you know their meanings.
- evaluates
- journals

Graphic Organizer

Draw or print this chart to write in three types of purchase situations and four criteria for selecting suppliers.

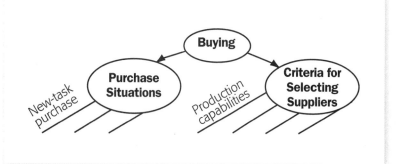

connectED.mcgraw-hill.com

Print this graphic organizer.

MARKETING CORE FUNCTION

Channel Management

The Purchasing Process

UNDERSTANDING THE PROCESS

The ways that buyers select suppliers, how the terms are negotiated, and how the Internet is used are all factors that affect the entire buying or purchasing process. In addition, there are many types of purchase situations.

As You Read

Compare Consider the differences between the types of purchase situations.

TYPES OF PURCHASE SITUATIONS

How difficult is the task of a purchasing manager or a buyer? The answer depends on which type of purchase situation is considered. Let's review the three types of purchase situations: new task purchase, modified rebuy, and straight rebuy.

NEW-TASK PURCHASE

In a new-task purchase situation, a purchase is made for the first time. It can be triggered by a formerly unrecognized need, a new manufacturing process, or organizational change. This can be the most complicated buying situation, because it involves a first-time purchase. In a retail or wholesale operation, salespeople prepare **want slips**, which are customer requests for items not carried in the store. The buyer **evaluates** want slips to determine if the requests warrant the purchase of new merchandise.

> **The level of difficulty for a buyer varies depending on the type of purchasing situation.**

MODIFIED REBUY

In a modified-rebuy situation, the buyer has had experience buying the good or service, but some aspect of the purchase changes. Perhaps the buyer is purchasing from a new vendor because the previous vendor went out of business or increased prices significantly. Other reasons for investigating new vendors may come from an analysis of the competition through comparison shopping. Buyers may also analyze current trade information found in trade publications or trade shows.

Finally, retail buyers may hire the services of a resident buying office. Resident buying offices are retailers' representatives in a geographic area where many suppliers of a given product are located. New York City's garment district, for example, is a central market for clothing. Resident buying offices send information to retail buyers on a regular basis. They inform buyers about new merchandise offerings, closeouts, or fashion trends.

STRAIGHT REBUY

In a straight-rebuy situation, the buyer routinely orders the goods and services purchased from the same vendor(s) as in the past. Staple goods such as office supplies fall into the straight-rebuy category for wholesale and retail buyers. The purchase of certain manufacturing supplies may be considered a straight rebuy.

SELECTING SUPPLIERS

The criteria for selecting suppliers fall into a few key categories. They include production capabilities, past experiences, product quality, special buying arrangements, special services, and negotiated terms such as pricing.

PRODUCTION CAPABILITIES

When dealing with a source for the first time, buyers may request specific information about the source's production capabilities. They may even visit a facility in person to see it in operation. Buyers may ask for business references to determine the source's reputation in the industry. These factors would be extremely important when selecting suppliers and transportation businesses as partners in a just-in-time production arrangement.

Issues of production capabilities for some companies go beyond the actual physical plant and focus on ethical and social issues. Companies may require a review of facilities to ensure that they are not operating sweatshops. Sweatshops are factories characterized by poor working conditions and negligent treatment of employees. Being associated with a sweatshop can be very damaging to a company's reputation.

Some companies also try to determine whether suppliers are following green environmental practices. The popularity of green marketing has led more companies to take environmental concerns very seriously.

PAST EXPERIENCES

Many buyers maintain resource files and **journals** that document past experiences with vendors. All basic information, such as products carried, prices, delivery and dating terms, and the names of sales representatives, is recorded. Buyers also note evaluations of products, delivery performance, and customer service.

A major factor in selecting a supplier is the quality of goods it offers. Retail buyers keep accurate records of customer returns and the reasons for the returns. Returns relating to the quality of the goods may cause buyers to stop doing business with the supplier. It is important to clearly define standards of quality for products that buyers will purchase from suppliers. Standards should be explained to suppliers so they understand the criteria by which product quality is measured.

SPECIAL BUYING ARRANGEMENTS

Most suppliers may have specific policies regarding merchandise returns and sales arrangements. Two special types of sales and return policies are consignment buying and memorandum buying.

Clothes you buy in the United States are often manufactured abroad. Hong Kong is a central market for the garment industry. *Look at the tags on a few items of clothing (at home or at a store). List the countries where the clothes were made.*

Country of Origin

In **consignment buying**, goods are paid for only after the final customer purchases them. The supplier owns the goods until the wholesaler or retailer sells them. Many suppliers offer consignment buying as an incentive when introducing a new line of goods. However, a problem can arise with consignment buying when merchandise is stolen or damaged, raising the question of who must pay.

Memorandum buying occurs when the supplier agrees to take back any unsold goods by a certain pre-established date. The buyer pays for all the goods purchased but is later reimbursed for all the goods returned under the terms of the agreement. This buying arrangement allows for returns.

SPECIAL SERVICES

Businesses today demand more services from their suppliers. Almost all retailers demand that manufacturers place universal product codes (UPCs) on goods. Having the codes on all products saves the retailer time because individual items do not have to be marked with a price. The codes also allow retailers to track inventory easily as each sale is immediately recorded electronically in a central database.

HOT TOPIC

See the Latest To get the most from trade shows sponsored by vendors and industry associations, a buyer should have an action plan.

NEGOTIATED TERMS

Buyers must negotiate prices, dating terms, delivery arrangements, and discounts. Discounts are any reductions from the quoted price. Such reductions are generally granted for the buyer's performance of certain functions. These are discussed in Chapter 26.

Dating terms include when a bill must be paid and the discount permitted for paying early. There are several dating variations for specific situations. A company may allow the dating terms to take effect later than the invoice date. This is known as advance dating. It is sometimes offered to businesses as an incentive to buy before the buying season.

 Reading Check

List What are the criteria for selecting a supplier?

The GREEN Marketer

Walmart Checks Green Credentials

How can companies be sure that products and supplies they buy are made without harm to workers or the environment? In 2009, Walmart® introduced an original solution with its "Sustainability Index." Walmart asked suppliers how their actions affect the environment and local communities. Suppliers were given a survey. It assessed energy and climate, material efficiency, natural resources, and people and community.

Supplier Comparison The company prints this supplier information on product labels. This allows customers to compare the environmental impact of different items. In the long-term, there will be a global database with this type of information from all types of companies. This database will have information that will help consumers.

Mathematics
Calculate A study shows that consumers are willing to pay up to 15 percent more for green products. If a bottle of Clorox® Green Works cleaner costs $3.49, and a bottle of standard Clorox cleaner costs $2.99, will the green cleaner sell well?

 connectED.mcgraw-hill.com

Get an activity on green marketing.

An invoice may be dated January 15 and include the following advance dating terms: 2/10, net 30, as of March 1.

In other situations, additional days may be granted for the discount (called "extra dating"). This special dating may be used to encourage a buyer to purchase new merchandise. In still another situation, the terms begin when the buyer's firm receives the goods, which is ROG dating (receipt of goods).

INTERNET PURCHASING

Business-to-business (B2B) e-commerce has revolutionized the purchasing function for businesses in the industrial and reseller markets. The volume of B2B transactions is much higher than all other types of online transactions combined. The main reason for this is that a lot more steps are involved in the manufacture of a product than in the sale to a customer. For example, a computer maker uses parts from several different suppliers, all of which require separate B2B transactions. However, only one transaction is needed to complete a sale to the customer. As a result, organizational buyers account for 80 percent of the total dollar value of all transactions conducted online.

The trend toward increased use of online buying is expected to continue. This is partly because organizational buyers have come to depend heavily on timely information from suppliers. Supplier information can be easily and quickly communicated via the Internet. Another advantage of online purchasing is that it dramatically reduces marketing costs for many types of goods and services.

B2B e-commerce transactions cover all aspects of a company's purchasing needs, from office supplies such as paper and staples to raw materials needed for manufacturing. Electronic procurement software and the Internet together make the process more efficient. Before e-commerce became possible, a company may have employed a large purchasing department to order supplies and other materials in person, over the phone, or through the mail. They would have to personally track and account for many individual purchases, which can result in errors and delays. Web-based systems make procurement simpler and more cost-effective.

Most companies have their own Web sites from which other companies may make purchases directly. Growing in popularity, however, are electronic exchanges where registered users can buy and sell their goods online. Most of these exchanges are in specific industries, such as Converge IT Product Procurement, an open market for electronic components, computer products, and networking equipment.

Another Internet purchasing trend involves online auction companies. An auction usually involves a seller setting an asking price and buyers trying to outbid each other. In other cases, a reverse auction takes place. In a **reverse auction**, companies post what they want to buy, and suppliers bid for the contract.

Purchasing online through third parties has both advantages and disadvantages. The biggest advantage is lower prices. However, as with most businesses on the Internet, privacy is a problem. Some companies fear that competitors will know how much was paid for materials and supplies.

In order to address privacy concerns, some companies, like Intel and General Electric®, began operating reverse auctions. GE expanded its trading process network (TPN) to serve other companies, and later sold the division to a private buyer, GXS, which services 70 percent of Fortune 500 companies.

Another problem with the online purchasing process, especially in a reverse auction, is that unknown companies could artificially deflate prices by bidding low prices. Such a practice would benefit buyers but cause bad relationships with suppliers.

 After You Read   Section 23.2

Review Key Concepts

1. **List** three ways a buyer can acquire information for a modified rebuy.
2. **Explain** the difference between consignment buying and memorandum buying.
3. **Identify** one advantage and one disadvantage of purchasing online.

Practice Academics

English Language Arts

4. You have been the buyer for a medium-sized department store for several years and were recently promoted to assistant manager. A salesperson who has assisted you in buying some product lines has been promoted to your old position. However, she is unsure about different types of purchases. Prepare a clear description of a new-task purchase, a modified rebuy, and a straight rebuy for your co-worker.

Mathematics

5. Vendor A sells 144 (1 gross) coffee bowls at $685.50 with free shipping. Dating terms are 2/10, net 30. Vendor A is offering a 2 percent discount on the cost of one gross. Vendor B's offer is $5.25 per bowl for one gross, with shipping charges of $25, and payment is COD. Which vendor is offering the better deal?

    Math Concept **Operations** Knowing which operations to use, and when to use them, is critical in problem solving.

    Starting Hints To solve this problem, determine the discount applied to Vendor A by multiplying the total cost of the bowls by .02 to determine the discount. Subtract the value of the discount from the total cost to determine Vendor A's price. Multiply Vendor B's price by 144 to determine the cost for a gross of their bowls, and add the cost of shipping to determine the total price.

 connectED.mcgraw-hill.com

Check your answers.

For help, go to the Math Skills Handbook located at the back of this book.

Purchasing

The three types of purchase situations are new-task purchase, modified rebuy, and straight rebuy.

Purchase Situations

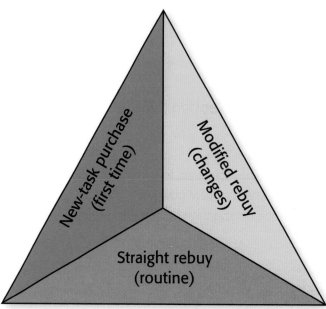

New-task purchase (first time)

Modified rebuy (changes)

Straight rebuy (routine)

Primary criteria for selecting suppliers are production capabilities, past experience, special buying arrangements, and special services.

Criteria for Selecting Suppliers

Production Capabilities	Past Experience
Special Buying Arrangements	Special Services

Written Summary

- Organizational buyers in industrial and resellers' (wholesale and retail) markets purchase goods in much greater quantities than the average consumer.

- Buyers for government markets make purchases of goods and services for one of the largest single markets in the world.

- The three types of purchase situations are new-task purchase, modified rebuy, and straight rebuy.

- The primary criteria for selecting suppliers are production capabilities, past experience, special buying arrangements (such as consignment buying and memorandum buying), and special services.

- The Internet has revolutionized purchasing in the industrial and resellers' markets.

- Online buying is expected to grow in the coming years.

Review Content Vocabulary and Academic Vocabulary

1. Use each of these vocabulary terms in a written sentence.

Content Vocabulary
- organizational buyers (p. 537)
- wholesale and retail buyers (p. 538)
- six-month merchandise plan (p. 538)
- open-to-buy (OTB) (p. 540)
- centralized buying (p. 542)
- decentralized buying (p. 542)
- want slips (p. 545)
- consignment buying (p. 547)
- memorandum buying (p. 547)
- reverse auction (p. 549)

Academic Vocabulary
- predicts (p. 537)
- technical (p. 537)
- evaluates (p. 545)
- journals (p. 546)

Assess for Understanding

2. List What are three titles for manufacturing or service business buyers?

3. Identify What type of planning is used to guide purchasing by organizational buyers and by resellers?

4. Explain What is a six-month merchandise plan?

5. Justify Why should chain stores use centralized buying?

6. Contrast What are the differences between the three types of purchasing situations?

7. Create What is a list of criteria you might use to evaluate suppliers?

8. Decide As the owner of an independent music store, will you use consignment buying or memorandum buying? Why?

9. Consider How would selling be different if the Internet could not be used?

21st Century Skills

People Skills

10. **Supervisor as Teacher** You are the supervisor of cashiers in a retail store. Today you observed one of the cashiers making mistakes keying in SKU codes when an item will not scan. When you asked her if she was having trouble keying in the codes, she said she was not having any trouble: "The customers like me to check them out fast, so if I make a mistake keying in all those numbers, I don't worry about it." Create a role-play script in which you explain the importance of correct SKU entry to this employee.

Financial Literacy Skills

11. **Discounts and Profits** You purchase computer components for resale at a trade discount of 40 percent. If you buy a monitor with a retail price of $450, what is your discount? What is your net cost? When you resell the monitor for $450, what will be your gross profit?

Everyday Ethics

12. **Green Initiatives** The European Union banned retailers from purchasing any more standard bulbs, so stores have hoarded them in stock. The fluorescent bulbs are more expensive. However, they use 80 percent less energy and last eight to ten years. Not everyone agrees with the EU's choice to ban the bulbs. Discuss with your class whether green initiatives should be mandatory.

e-Marketing Skills

13. **Researching Web Sites** Choose a product that you find interesting and might want to market in the future. Search out pages from at least six Web sites that look most interesting. Evaluate the pages, then describe what you believe are the best aspects of all of the sites you have reviewed.

Build Academic Skills

English Language Arts

14. **Observing and Reporting** You are a salesperson in a specialty clothing store. Over the past month, about ten people have asked about a line of clothing that your store does not carry. You have filled out several want slips and left them with the buyer. However, this new line has not been added to the store's stock. You feel sure that adding these items would increase sales. Write an e-mail message to the buyer stating why you believe adding these items would increase sales.

Science

15. **Technology** Investigate the ways in which technology is improving the coordination of products in supply chains. You may wish to research the use of Global Positioning Systems, Portable Digital Assistants, or tracking devices as they relate to supply chains. Share with your class one innovation you find interesting.

Mathematics

16. **Calculate a Sales Total** You prepare a purchase order for the following: 130 pants at $14.15 each, 58 pants at $16.99 each, 74 pants at $21.30 each, and 45 pants at $23.80 each. What is the total cost of the merchandise?

> **Math Concept** **Multi-Step Problems** When a word problem involves multiple steps, it is helpful to outline the information you know before you solve.

For help, go to the **Math Skills Handbook** located at the back of this book.

Standardized Test Practice

Directions Read the following questions. On a separate piece of paper, write the best possible answer for each one.

1. Planned retail reductions take into account:
   - **A.** Reductions in the selling price
   - **B.** Shortages of merchandise caused by clerical mistakes
   - **C.** Employee theft
   - **D.** Customer shoplifting
   - **E.** All of the above

2. A want slip must be completed before purchasing goods in a straight-buy situation.

   T

   F

3. The beginning-of-the-month and end-of-the-month inventories are indicated by the abbreviations _____ and _____.

Test-Taking Tip

If each item on a test is worth the same number of points, skip questions that are confusing, and then come back to them after you have answered all the rest of the questions.

DECA. Connection Role Play

Buyer
Coat & Jacket Department

Situation You are a buyer for a local department store. While at market recently, you viewed a new line of jackets manufactured by a vendor that your store has not used before. The sample jackets are of high quality and excellent construction. The styling of the jackets reflects the latest in teen fashion trends. Everything about the jacket line makes you want to purchase them for your store. The jackets show every sign of becoming best sellers.

Store buying policy is that all new vendors must be reviewed before orders can be placed with them, and that the merchandise manager (judge) must approve all orders before ordering from a new vendor. You have informally asked other buyers about the vendor's reputation and determined that other buyers view the vendor as reliable, that samples reflect the actual quality of items, and that the vendor ships as promised.

You want to add these jackets to your fall merchandise purchases. You would like to purchase a limited quantity of several styles from the jacket line. Before doing so you must discuss the purchase with your merchandise manager (judge) to win approval for the purchase.

Activity You are to discuss this situation with your merchandise manager (judge) and persuade the merchandise manager that the jackets will be a wise and profitable purchase for your department and store.

Evaluation You will be evaluated on how well you meet the following performance indicators:

1. Explain the nature and scope of purchasing.
2. Place order/reorders.
3. Persuade others.
4. Select vendors.
5. Evaluate vendor performance.

 connectED.mcgraw-hill.com

Role Plays Download the Competitive Events Workbook for more Role-Play practice.

stock handling and inventory control

Visual Literacy Proper procedures for stock handling allow businesses to move products to customers in a timely and efficient manner. The receiving process is an important part of inventory management and control. *How does the effective handling of stock relate to customer service?*

Discovery Project

Technology for Stock and Inventory

Essential Question How can technology improve stock and inventory procedures?

Project Goal

You are employed as a supply chain executive for a large retail chain that sells musical instruments. You have been asked to research a technology or technological process that could improve stock handling and inventory control for your firm. You will give an oral presentation about the technology to senior management for possible implementation.

Ask Yourself...

- How does technology affect stock handling and inventory control?
- What are the advantages of using a selected technology or process?
- What are the disadvantages of using a selected technology or process?
- How will you organize your oral report?

Solve Problems Describe how stock handling procedures and inventory management are related.

 connectED.mcgraw-hill.com

Activity
Get a worksheet activity about stock and inventory.

Evaluate
Download a rubric you can use to evaluate your project.

DECA Connection

DECA Event Role Play

Concepts in this chapter are related to DECA competitive events that involve either an interview or role play.

Performance Indicators The performance indicators represent key skills and knowledge. Your key to success in DECA Competitive events is relating them to concepts in this chapter.

- Explain stock handling techniques used in receiving deliveries.
- Describe inventory control systems.
- Maintain inventory control systems.
- Motivate team members.
- Foster positive working relationships.

DECA Prep

Role Play Practice role-playing with the DECA Connection competitive-event activity at the end of this chapter. More information on DECA events can be found on DECA's Web site.

READING GUIDE

Before You Read

Reflect What do stores do to prepare their merchandise for sale?

Objectives

- **Describe** the receiving process.
- **Explain** stock handling techniques used in receiving deliveries.

The Main Idea

All businesses must have a stock handling process in place to receive deliveries of materials or products. This process affects maintenance of inventory levels.

Vocabulary

Content Vocabulary

- receiving record
- blind check method
- direct check method
- spot check method
- quality check method
- source marking
- preretailing marking method

Academic Vocabulary

You will find these words in your reading and on your tests. Make sure you know their meanings.

- routing
- errors

Graphic Organizer

Draw or print this chart to identify key steps in the stock handling process.

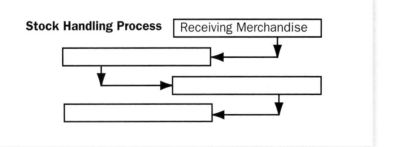

Stock Handling Process | Receiving Merchandise

 connectED.mcgraw-hill.com

Print this graphic organizer.

Stock Handling

STOCK HANDLING

Manufacturing companies depend on suppliers to deliver parts or raw materials used in making finished products accurately and on time. When these parts or materials are delivered to the warehouse, plant, or store, they must be received into stock. Information about them must be recorded and tracked. For example, a door-handle manufacturer has a contract with an automobile assembly plant to supply door handles for pickup trucks. The manufacturer delivers door handles almost every day to keep pace with production at the assembly plant.

As You Read

Sequence What happens after a business receives the products it orders?

The parts or raw materials used in making finished products must be tracked just as retailers track the merchandise they receive. The steps in the stock handling process include receiving goods; checking them; marking them with information, if necessary; and delivering them to a place where they will be used, stored, or displayed for sale. The receiving clerk checks in the door handles at the truck assembly plant. He or she must make sure that the correct part has been delivered in the right quantity. This clerk must also be sure that the door handles get to the assembly line in time to be installed on the truck doors. The receiving clerk also records that information about the parts in the system. This ensures that inventory levels are correct and that the accounts payable department knows to pay the invoice from the door-handle manufacturer.

Incoming raw materials, parts, or merchandise are received, inspected, and recorded. *Why is receiving stock or merchandise an important step in the stock handling process?*

Receiving Merchandise

Mike King
Manager
Used Car Dealer

What do you do at work?

My job involves wholesaling, buying, and reconditioning pre-owned vehicles to sell on our lot and to other dealers. I attend auctions about three times a week and work two shifts on the floor. It is important for our dealership to keep at least 70 units on the lot at all times because our sales quota is to flip 50 cars a month. At auctions, I am looking to stock our inventory with vehicles that I think our customers will want.

What is your key to success?

Motivation is key for me. Being in commission sales, I have to keep my motivation up and stay positive.

What skills are most important to you?

Networking is number one. If you can't network, you will not make it in this business. Product and market knowledge is very important too—know pricing and what you'll be able to sell a car for either at wholesale or retail.

 connectED.mcgraw-hill.com

Read more about this career and get a Career Exploration Activity.

RECEIVING MERCHANDISE

Stock or merchandise ordered by a business is received and checked. The store manager or owner should be aware of the shipping date and can prepare for receipt of the merchandise. In retail settings, the items are often marked with a selling price before they are transferred to the sales area. In larger businesses, several people might perform this function. In smaller businesses, a salesperson, manager, or even the owner may do this job. Retail chain stores often schedule weekly deliveries of ordered inventory to arrive at each store on a predetermined day of the week. Knowing when the merchandise will arrive can help in scheduling extra staff.

> " **Whether a business receives raw materials, parts, or merchandise for resale, it needs a process to handle the items.** "

FACILITIES

The location of the storage area for received products depends on the type and size of the business. Smaller businesses may use a backroom or may even place items in store aisles when they are received. Most businesses, however, reserve a specific area for receiving activities. These activities may include unpacking, pricing, assembly, and disposal of shipping materials.

Large businesses and chain stores sometimes have separate warehouses or distribution centers where merchandise is received and stored. Then it is taken to the department or branch store that needs it. Facilities such as these have large bays with loading docks that open at the height of the truck bed for easy unloading. Loading docks usually have covered or enclosed platforms to protect merchandise from weather damage.

RECEIVING RECORDS

A **receiving record** is information recorded by businesses about the goods they receive. The information can be recorded either manually or electronically. Hand-held laser scanners and imagers can capture signatures, take images, and read product codes. Mobile computers can capture images to document shipment damage and signatures to reduce shrinkage, or the loss of goods, at the receiving dock.

Transferred merchandise is accompanied by a form describing the items, style numbers, colors, sizes, cost, and retail prices. Duplicate copies of the transfer forms are retained as a record of merchandise on hand.

Stock transfers between departments can occur when merchandise is carried by more than one department. Stock transfers may also occur when the demand for merchandise in one department creates a need for additional merchandise. Stock transfers can also occur when the merchandise is used for sales promotions, such as displays, advertising illustrations, or fashion shows, and also when the merchandise is used for installation or repairs in various departments.

Stock transfers between stores occur to meet unexpected demand or to fill requests by customers. A customer may find the perfect dress but may find that the branch of the store is sold out of the size needed. Some stores will call another branch to find out if it has the item in stock and have it sent over, or the customer may choose to pick it up at the other store.

Finally, stock transfers from a store to a distribution outlet can occur when off-season and nonsalable merchandise is moved to surplus or discount stores. A store may choose to transfer all of its winter clothing to an outlet store if the stock does not sell out during after-season sales.

 After You Read | **Section 24.1**

Review Key Concepts

1. **Explain** why a receiving record is important.
2. **List** the four methods used for checking merchandise.
3. **Explain** how UPC codes assist in marking merchandise.

Practice Academics

English Language Arts

4. Research the history and development of Electronic Product Codes (EPCs) or Radio Frequency Identification (RFID) tags. Write a one-page paper on the current status of electronic product codes in warehouses, distribution centers, physical distribution systems, or retail store settings.

Mathematics

5. A gift store calculated the cost of price marking its merchandise to be $43,000 a year in employee time. The store estimates that it can save 25 percent of this cost by switching to source marking for most of its merchandise. What is the amount of the savings?

Math Concept **Computation** When the amount saved is given as a percent, the first step is to convert the percent to a decimal. Multiplying this decimal by the total cost will give the amount saved.

Starting Hints To solve this problem, convert the percent to a decimal by moving the decimal point two places to the left. Multiply the decimal equivalent of the percent by the total cost of price marking in employee time to determine the amount that can be saved.

 connectED.mcgraw-hill.com

Check your answers.

For help, go to the Math Skills Handbook located at the back of this book.

READING GUIDE

Before You Read

Connect Think about a time you went to a store, and an item you wanted was not available. How did you react?

Objectives

- **Describe** the process for providing effective inventory management.
- **Explain** the types of inventory control systems.
- **Relate** customer service to distribution.
- **Analyze** sales information to determine inventory turnover.
- **Discuss** technology and inventory management.

The Main Idea

Inventory owned by a business represents a capital investment until the products are sold. Effective inventory management and accurate inventory systems increase profits.

Vocabulary

Content Vocabulary

- inventory
- inventory management
- just-in-time (JIT) inventory system
- perpetual inventory system
- physical inventory system
- cycle counts
- stockkeeping unit (SKU)
- dollar control
- unit control
- inventory turnover

- basic stock list
- model stock list
- never-out list
- real-time inventory systems

Academic Vocabulary

You will find these words in your reading and on your tests. Make sure you know their meanings.

- complex
- authorized

Graphic Organizer

Draw or print this chart to take notes on inventory systems.

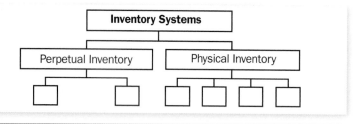

 connectED.mcgraw-hill.com

Print this graphic organizer.

MARKETING CORE FUNCTION

 Channel Management

 Inventory Control

INVENTORY MANAGEMENT

One of the major expenses of running a business is the purchasing of merchandise, or the items bought for reselling to customers. The amount of merchandise on hand at any particular time is known as inventory. The inventory managed by a business depends on the type of business. The business may be a producer (such as a farming enterprise), a manufacturer (such as an automobile company), a wholesaler, or a retailer. Based on the type of business, **inventory** can include raw materials, parts purchased from suppliers, manufactured sub-assemblies, work-in-process, packaging materials, or finished goods. Wholesalers' and retailers' inventories include all merchandise available for resale.

 As You Read

Understand Why must businesses maintain proper inventories?

Inventory management is the process of buying and storing materials and products while controlling costs for ordering, shipping, handling, and storage. Inventory management is usually the responsibility of the supply chain manager. This person's job is to maintain just the right level of inventory to meet the supply-and-demand needs of a business. Having the wrong merchandise in stock, holding too many slow-selling items, or not storing enough fast-selling items are challenges faced by the supply chain manager every day.

Unnecessarily high inventories can create many problems for a business. In addition to using up storage space, personnel costs increase for security and warehouse staff, as do inventory insurance premiums, which may lead to increased interest expenses. Businesses can lose money, and profits may decrease.

> **"Products are purchased in large quantities to lower costs and ensure availability, but they must be stored until they are sold. "**

DISTRIBUTION, INVENTORY MANAGEMENT, AND CUSTOMER SERVICE

The most important goal of any business is to meet the needs of its customers. Businesses must manage inventory so that customers have the merchandise they want when they want it. Having too little inventory results in lost sales and dissatisfied customers. Every business must carry the desired products in sufficient quantities. Every business must provide quality customer service if the overall business is to be successful.

JUST-IN-TIME INVENTORY

A **just-in-time (JIT) inventory system** controls the flow of parts and materials into assembly and manufacturing plants. A JIT inventory system coordinates demand and supply so that suppliers deliver parts and raw materials just before they are needed for use. This system allows plants to keep only small stocks on hand to avoid tying up money and inventory space.

Electronic data interchanges (EDI) tell suppliers and transportation companies which items are needed and when to deliver them to meet production needs. Suppliers deliver parts on a schedule so they arrive just in time for use in the production process. A late shipment can bring an entire manufacturing operation to a standstill.

QUICK RESPONSE DELIVERY

Quick response delivery (QRD) systems apply just-in-time principles to retailers. Sometimes retailers allow manufacturers or vendors to manage their inventory by sharing point-of-sale information. QRD programs shorten the time between when a product is made, distributed, and sold by letting the suppliers stock and reorder merchandise. Quick response programs assure that merchandise is restocked to correct levels at precisely the time when the additional stock is needed. This helps retail businesses avoid out-of-stock situations and reduce inventory holding costs.

CHALLENGES OF INVENTORY MANAGEMENT

Inventory management is **complex** because a business has to correctly anticipate demand for its products. At the same time, a business has to keep overall inventory investment as low as possible.

Retail businesses are expected to do the following:

▶ Maintain the right quantities of merchandise without running out of stock.

▶ Keep a wide product assortment (with low investment) without compromising customer needs and wants.

▶ Purchase merchandise at large volumes to gain the lowest prices while not buying more than it will sell.

▶ Pay attention to what customers are buying and what they are not buying.

▶ Keep a current inventory on hand.

Good inventory management balances the costs of maintaining a large inventory with the benefits of maintaining a large inventory. The costs of inventory include not only the cost of the items in stock but also the costs of storage, insurance, and taxes. Inventory ties up working capital, which is money that could be used for other purposes. It is not effective for a company to maintain large inventory holdings if money could be spent more effectively to benefit the business somewhere else. Effective inventory management helps increase working capital and allows a business to pay for other business expenses.

 Reading Check

Contrast How is just-in-time inventory different from quick response delivery?

Depending on the type of business, inventory can represent raw materials, parts, work-in-progress, sub-assemblies, and finished goods. *Why is inventory control so important?*

INVENTORY SYSTEMS

Two methods of tracking inventory are the perpetual inventory system and the physical inventory system.

PERPETUAL INVENTORY SYSTEM

A **perpetual inventory system** tracks the number of items in inventory on a constant basis. The system tracks all new items purchased and returned, as well as sales of current stock. An up-to-date count of inventory is maintained for purchases and returns of merchandise, sales and sales returns, sales allowances, and transfers to other stores and departments. Reordering and restocking items whenever quantities become low can help avoid loss of sales. This system tracks sales and other transactions as they occur.

MANUAL SYSTEMS

In a manual system, employees gather paper records of sales and enter that information into the inventory system. These records can include receiving department records, sales checks, price tickets, cash register receipts, stock transfer requests, and other documents used for coding and tabulation.

Employees use computer-generated merchandise tags are used to record information about the vendor, date of receipt, department, product classification, price, color, size, and style.

The merchandise tags from items sold are sent in batches to a company-owned tabulating facility or to an independent computer service organization. Here, the coded information is analyzed through the use of computer software.

COMPUTER-BASED SYSTEMS

Computer-based systems for controlling inventory are increasingly popular, even among smaller businesses. They are also faster and more accurate than manual systems. Employees at a point-of-sale terminal use hand-held laser guns, stationary lasers, light pens, or slot scanners. These feed sales transaction data directly from Universal Product Codes (UPCs), sales checks, or merchandise tags into a computer. Businesses then print the information for review and action.

Electronic Data Interchange (EDI) involves computer-to-computer information exchanges and relays of sales information directly to a supplier. The supplier uses the sales transaction data to ship additional items automatically.

WMS The use of headsets allows employees to keep both of their hands free for other warehouse tasks.

PHYSICAL INVENTORY SYSTEM

Under a physical inventory system, information about stock levels is not continually maintained. A **physical inventory system** is an inventory system in which stock is visually inspected or actually counted to determine the quantity on hand.

Inventory data can be captured in many ways, from high-tech methods to manual counts. Some of the most popular methods for larger retailers are scanned bar codes and keypad entry onto hand-held devices.

For most businesses, the process of identifying and counting all items is time consuming. Therefore, inventory is usually counted when the quantity of merchandise is at its lowest point.

Even if a perpetual inventory system is used, physical inventories are still conducted periodically or on a regular annual basis. A physical inventory allows a business to calculate its income tax, determine the correct value of its ending inventory, identify any stock shortages, and plan future purchases. There are several methods used.

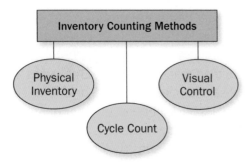

INVENTORY COUNTING METHODS

To count inventory, businesses often use a combination of methods. A business can have its regular employees count the inventory, or the process can be conducted by an outside inventory service company. Major national retailers typically have thousands of items stocked in many different locations around the country. These large chains of stores tend to use outside companies, such as Washington Inventory Services, RGIS, or smaller regional or local firms. After the counting is completed, the total value of the inventory is then determined. This value is reported on the business's financial statements.

PHYSICAL INVENTORY METHOD

The most popular method of inventory management is to physically count the inventory. Most businesses do this once a year. Others do this on a semiannual, quarterly, or more frequent basis. Inventory clerks usually work in pairs. One counts merchandise, while the other one records the count. Physical inventories are usually wall-to-wall store inventories, which often require that the business close temporarily to conduct the inventory.

CYCLE COUNT METHOD

Many businesses use cycle counts either in combination with an annual physical inventory or alone to track inventory. **Cycle counts** involve a portion of the inventory being counted each day by stockkeeping units so that the entire inventory is accounted for on a regular basis. With this method, the entire inventory is never counted at one time.

A **stockkeeping unit (SKU)** is coded information for a specific product used for inventory control. Each product has a unique series of numbers and letters embedded in the code. For example 59G10-1 may be a code for specific shirt. The 59 may represent the brand, the "G" is the color green, the "10" is the size, and the "1" is the season. Businesses develop their own codes based on the information they need for inventory control purposes.

A variation of the cycle method is used by manufacturers' representatives when they visit a business on a regular basis, take the stock count, and write a new order. Unwanted merchandise is removed from stock and returned to the manufacturer through a predetermined, **authorized** procedure.

VISUAL CONTROL METHOD

Visual control is a method used to monitor physical inventory levels. Smaller businesses place stock cards on pegboards with stock number information and descriptions for each item displayed. The stock cards specify the number of each item to be kept in stock. This method can be inaccurate because it does not account for misplaced merchandise. The amount to reorder is the difference between the number on hand and the specified number to be stocked. The number to stock may be an estimate of sales for a typical period of time.

TRENDS IN INVENTORY METHODS

As businesses become increasingly competitive, more efficient and effective inventory management methods will be developed. This will surely include recording inventories by using SKU or UPC codes, greater use of technology in taking inventories, increased use and frequency of cycle counts by SKU, increased use of Internet technologies to link with vendors, and increased vendor participation.

Most businesses use both systems. The perpetual system gives an up-to-date inventory record throughout the year. The physical system gives an accurate count that can be compared to the perpetual records to identify any errors or problems.

The perpetual inventory records help the business track sales and manage its merchandise. After a physical inventory is taken, the ending inventory amount becomes the beginning inventory for the year that follows. Purchases by the business during the year are added to this amount, while sales are subtracted. Ending inventory is calculated in the example that follows:

Number of Items for 1/1/20_ _ to 6/30/20_ _	
Beginning inventory, 1/1/20_ _	1,000
Net purchases (purchases less purchases and allowances returned)	+ 300
Merchandise available for sale	1,300
Less net sales (sales less returns and allowances)	− 1,050
Ending inventory, 6/30/20_ _	250

Sometimes, the ending inventory shown in the perpetual inventory system does not match the physical count of inventory. When the physical count shows less merchandise than is supposed to be in inventory, a stock shortage or shrinkage has occurred. Theft, receiving errors, incorrect counting, and selling errors can cause shortages for a business.

In the example, the ending inventory figure of 250 items is the perpetual inventory. It is possible that this is not the most accurate count. If the physical inventory system showed ending inventory of 225, a stock shortage of 25 would have occurred. It is not until the physical inventory is taken that the company really knows if its ending inventory records are correct. The perpetual inventory can be used as an estimation.

✓ Reading Check

Recall What are two main inventory systems?

WORLD MARKET
BAHAMAS

Resort Inventory

One definition of "luxury" is indulgence in comforts and pleasures beyond those necessary for a reasonable standard of living. Nygård Cay in the Bahamas, is much more. Described as "a wonderland of excess," the 4.2-acre luxury resort rents for about $42,000 a day.

Inventory for Paradise What you get includes Mayan stone architecture, a 32,000-square-foot grand hall with a 100,000-pound glass ceiling, ten bedrooms, two pools, many Jacuzzis, and a 24-seat movie theater that can screen one to three movies. But there is more—waterslides, a water trampoline, a human aquarium, game courts, an 82-foot yacht and a 48-foot fishing vessel, themed cabanas, a chauffeured Hummer, and a staff of 20. Mother Nature, however, provides the best the luxury retreat offers: exotic birds and plants, the electric blue seas and white sands of the Caribbean, and daily temperatures averaging a balmy 77° F.

English Language Arts
Catalog Write a paragraph describing your ideal vacation, including the product amenities that a hotel might stock, and the stock lists it would use.

Here are some entry-level phrases that are used in conversations about marketing all over the world.

English	Bahamian Creole
Hello	Hello dere
Goodbye	Bye-Bye
How are you?	How ya doin'?
Thank you	Tanks
You're welcome	Ya're wery velcome

STOCK CONTROL

Stock control involves monitoring stock levels and investments in stock so that a business runs efficiently. Monitoring systems include dollar versus unit control methods, inventory turnover calculations, and three stock lists.

DOLLAR VERSUS UNIT CONTROL

Inventory management involves both dollar control and unit control of merchandise held in inventory. **Dollar control** represents the planning and monitoring of the total inventory investment made by a business during a stated period of time. A business's dollar control of inventory involves information about the amount of purchases, sales, dollar value of beginning and ending inventory, and stock shortages. This information helps a business determine the cost of goods sold and the amount of gross profit or loss during a given period of time. By subtracting operating expenses from the gross profit, the business can determine its net profit or loss.

Unit control is a stock control method that measures the amounts of merchandise a business handles during a stated period of time. Unit control allows a business to adjust inventory to sales. Unit control lets the business determine how to spend money available under a planned budget. In a unit control inventory system, merchandise is tracked by stockkeeping unit. Tracking the SKUs gives valuable sales information on those items that are successful and those that are not selling. A business can use this information to make better merchandising decisions. Sales promotions can be run to sell slow-moving items or to spotlight popular ones.

Unit-control records also allow purchasing personnel to see what brands, sizes, colors, and price ranges are popular. By keeping track of this information, buyers can understand customer preferences and order accordingly. Finally, unit-control records specify when items need to be ordered. When a minimum stock amount is reached, an order is placed for more stock. This system ensures that adequate assortments are available and helps avoid out-of-stock situations.

MARKETING CASE STUDY

Fiesta Movement

The Ford® Motor Company's Fiesta subcompact car was first produced in 1976. Although it was produced by a United States automaker, it was very popular in Europe. In fact, it has only been available in the United States as an import since the 1980s. That situation changed in 2010. Ford decided to start selling the Fiesta to U.S. consumers.

New Marketing Mix

Ford introduced the Fiesta to U.S. consumers through social media. Rather than simply using a blog post, tweet, or Facebook® status update, the company did something different. It started a movement. The Fiesta Movement involved 100 people in the United States who used social media in a variety of ways. They were given Fiestas 18 months before the car was available to the general public. They blogged, tweeted, and posted pictures of the car on social networks. This resulted in a 38% increase in brand awareness without any money spent on advertising.

English Language Arts

Evaluate Ford changed the way it interacted with its customers during the Fiesta Movement. It allowed its customers to communicate and spread influence on its behalf. Discuss the risks and benefits of Ford's use of social media.

INVENTORY TURNOVER

The most effective way to measure how well inventory is being managed is to look at inventory turnover. **Inventory turnover** is the number of times the average inventory has been sold and replaced in a given period of time. The higher the inventory-turnover rate, the more times the goods were sold and replaced. For example, imagine that you own a swimsuit shop that regularly orders 100 swimsuits per order. The stock sells out quickly during July but more slowly in August. Your inventory turnover rate is higher in July.

In retailing and wholesaling operations, the key is moving inventory so there is cash available to buy more fast-selling merchandise. High turnover rates mean that merchandise is selling quickly. That means higher profit for the business because its money is not tied up in inventory.

Inventory turnover is also a good measure of success for businesses to use in evaluating suppliers and products from year to year. Businesses use industry inventory-turnover rates to compare a particular business with the operations of similar businesses.

Inventory-turnover rates by industry are available from trade associations and commercial publishers. One such publisher is Dun & Bradstreet, which publishes Industry Norms and Key Business Ratios. Inventory-turnover rates can be calculated in dollars (retail or cost) or in units.

CALCULATING TURNOVER RATES

Turnover rates are a measure of how well a business is managing its assets and inventory. Retailers that want to learn the rate at retail compute their inventory turnover rate as follows:

$$\frac{\text{Net sales (in retail dollars)}}{\text{Average inventory on hand (in retail dollars)}}$$

When net sales during a period are $49,500 and average inventory is $8,250, the inventory turnover is 6:

$$\frac{\$49,500}{\$8,250} = 6$$

To determine the average inventory, use inventory amounts for each of the months included in the time period being considered. Total these, as shown in the second column below, and then calculate the average.

Month	Inventory	Net Sales
January	$50,000	$10,000
February	55,000	15,000
March	68,000	20,000
April	64,000	19,000
May	63,000	21,000
June	60,000	20,000
Totals	**$360,000**	**$105,000**

To get the average inventory for the six-month period, divide by the number of months:

$$6 = \frac{\$360,000}{\$60,000}$$

Finally, to calculate inventory turnover, divide total net sales (see the third column above) by average inventory:

$$\frac{\$105,000}{\$60,000} = 1.75$$

This figure means that the average inventory was sold and replaced 1.75 times during the six-month period.

Inventory-turnover rates can also be calculated at cost and unit levels. When only cost information about inventory is available, inventory turnover can be calculated with this formula:

$$\frac{\text{Cost of goods sold}}{\text{Average inventory (at cost) on hand for a given time period}}$$

When a business wants to look at the number of items carried in relation to the number of items sold, it calculates its stock-turnover rates in units with this formula:

$$\frac{\text{Number of SKUs sold}}{\text{Average SKUs on hand (for a given time period)}}$$

STOCK LISTS

There are three plans used to monitor different types of goods—staple items, fashionable items, and very popular items. They are the basic stock list, model stock list, and never-out list.

A **basic stock list** is used for those staple items that should always be in stock. This list specifies products that a store should always carry based upon the type of business. A basic stock list in a men's clothing store would include items such as T-shirts, underwear, and dress socks. The basic stock list at a card store would include birthday cards, blank cards, thank you cards, and cards for special occasions, such as weddings and anniversaries.

A basic stock list specifies the minimum amount of merchandise that should be on hand for particular products. It is based on expected sales for a given period. It shows the quantity of items that should be reordered, as well as the colors, styles, and sizes that should be carried.

Retailers assign each product a code for ease in recording when the products are purchased and sold.

A **model stock list** is used for fashionable merchandise. Fashion items change relatively rapidly; therefore, these lists are less specific than basic stock lists. The information contained in model stock lists identifies goods by general classes (blouses, skirts, dresses, slacks) and style categories (short sleeve, long sleeve), sizes, materials, colors, and price lines. Style numbers are not included because each manufacturer's style numbers change each year. Although model stock lists identify how many of each type of item should be purchased, the buyer must actually select specific models at the market. A **never-out list** is used for best-selling products that make up a large percentage of sales volume. Items are added to or taken off the list as their popularity increases or declines.

Reading Check

Recall What are the three types of stock lists?

New electronic processes and systems can assist with inventory management and improve customer service. *How can electronic systems such as Quick Response Delivery lead to better customer service?*

Using Technology

THE IMPACT OF TECHNOLOGY

Sophisticated information-gathering hardware and software has been developed to track items from the purchase order to the final customer sale. **Real-time inventory systems** use Internet technology that connects applications, data, and users in real time. This technology allows a company to constantly track every product it sells. Each product is tracked from when it is manufactured, to when it arrives in the warehouse, to when the customer orders it online, to when it arrives at the buyer's door. These systems and technologies include:

▶ Standardized shipping container marking (SCM) as a way to identify case and case contents.

▶ Radio frequency identification (RFID) to allow retailers to track and authenticate pallets, cartons, and products without relying on barcodes.

▶ Warehouse Management Systems (WMS) utilizing radio frequency (RF) terminals, pick-to-light terminals (PTL), and voice-directed small computers with headsets to locate stored items quicker and to improve accuracy.

▶ Universal Product Codes (UPCs) with standard product identifier barcode symbols to capture SKU-level information at the point of sale.

▶ Quick Response Delivery (QRD) computer systems to replenish inventory based upon consumer demand and point-of-sale information.

▶ Electronic Data Interchange (EDI) transactions to exchange standard business transactions or information by electronic computer-to-computer transfers, requiring little or no human intervention.

 After You Read | **Section 24.2**

Review Key Concepts

1. **Describe** the difference between a perpetual and a physical inventory.
2. **List** the three different inventory counting methods.
3. **Explain** how to calculate stock turnover rates.

Practice Academics

English Language Arts

4. Investigate smart cards or radio frequency identification (RFID) tags and write a one-page report on the current usage of RFID technology in retail stores.

Mathematics

5. Calculate the inventory turnover for a company that has annual net sales totaling $240,000 and an average inventory on hand of $160,000 throughout the year. What does your answer represent?

Math Concept **Problem Solving** The inventory-turnover rate is a measure of how often the average inventory is sold and replaced during a given time period. Dividing the net sales by the cost of the average inventory on hand yields the inventory-turnover rate.

Starting Hint To solve this problem, divide the total net sales by the average inventory on hand to determine the turnover rate.

 connectED.mcgraw-hill.com

Check your answers.

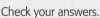 For help, go to the **Math Skills Handbook** located at the back of this book.

Stock Handling and Inventory Control

The stock handling process includes receiving, checking, marking, and delivering goods. Methods of checking merchandise include blind check, direct check, spot check, and quality check.

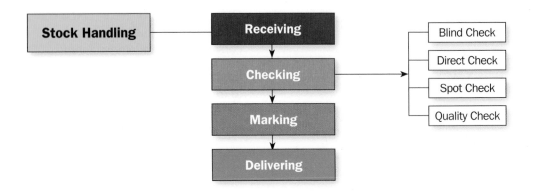

Inventory management is the process of buying and storing materials and products for sale while controlling costs for ordering, shipping, handling, and storage. Inventory systems include perpetual inventory systems and physical inventory systems.

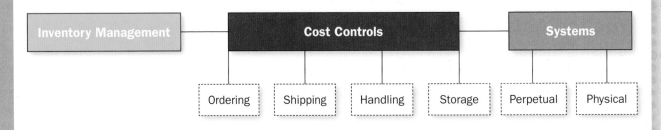

Review and Activities

Written Summary

- The steps in the stock handling process include receiving goods, checking them, marking the goods with information if necessary, and delivering them to their selling or storing location.
- Methods of checking merchandise include the blind-check method, the direct-check method, the spot-check method, and the quality-check method.
- Inventory management is the process of buying and storing products for sale while controlling costs for ordering, shipping, handling, and storage.
- Inventory systems include perpetual inventory systems and physical inventory systems.
- Technology is changing the way inventory is controlled.
- Retailers use standards like UPCs, EDI, and SCM.
- Real-time inventory systems track all stages from manufacture to delivery.

Review Content Vocabulary and Academic Vocabulary

1. Create multiple-choice test questions for each content and academic vocabulary term.

Content Vocabulary
- receiving record (p. 558)
- blind check method (p. 559)
- direct check method (p. 560)
- spot check method (p. 560)
- quality check method (p. 560)
- source marking (p. 561)
- preretailing marking method (p. 562)
- inventory (p. 565)
- inventory management (p. 565)
- just-in-time (JIT) inventory system (p. 565)
- perpetual inventory system (p. 567)
- physical inventory system (p. 568)
- cycle counts (p. 568)
- stockkeeping unit (SKU) (p. 568)
- dollar control (p. 570)
- unit control (p. 570)
- inventory turnover (p. 571)
- basic stock list (p. 572)
- model stock list (p. 572)
- never-out list (p. 572)
- real-time inventory systems (p. 573)

Academic Vocabulary
- routing (p. 559)
- errors (p. 560)
- complex (p. 566)
- authorized (p. 568)

Assess for Understanding

2. **Explain** What is the receiving process?
3. **Describe** Which stock handling techniques are used in receiving deliveries?
4. **Summarize** What is the process for providing effective inventory management?
5. **Justify** Why use a blind check the first time you receive an order from a supplier?
6. **Connect** How is customer service related to distribution?
7. **Analyze** What is the inventory turnover for a company that has annual net sales totaling $75,000 and an average inventory on hand of $40,000 throughout the year?
8. **Role Play** How would you introduce a new employee to the different types of checks?
9. **Imagine** What possible future trends might develop in inventory management?

21st Century Skills

Communication Skills

10. Explaining Damages You are a receiver in a warehouse. You know that a coworker has been damaging incoming merchandise through deliberate and careless behavior. However, your manager suspects that you are at fault and has approached you about these events. How would you handle this situation? Role play the situation with a partner.

Financial Literacy Skills

11. Calculating Unit-Turnover Rates You manage a ski shop at a resort and have been asked to compare your store's average turnover rate in units to a competitor's rate for a six-month period. For the time period, your store sold 50 pairs of skis, while your competitor sold 100 pairs of the same ski. Using the following chart, determine which store has a better turnover rate for this item.

	Your Store (SKU on hand)	Your Competitor
Oct	40	125
Nov	30	75
Dec	20	50
Jan	15	50
Feb	10	35
March	5	25

e-Marketing Skills

12. Smartphones Imagine that you work for a technology firm that manufactures smartphones with digital-camera and Web-browser features. Investigate the process of using your smartphone to launch 2-D barcodes to cosmetic retailers. Keeping the retailers' needs in mind, consider the following questions:

- What advantages do 2-D barcodes offer relative to 12-digit barcodes?
- What steps must you take to sell the concept?
- What benefits might 2-D barcodes have?
- What technological improvements must your smartphones have to read 2-D barcodes?

Build Academic Skills

Science

13. Interactive Barcodes Two-dimensional (2-D) barcodes are similar to UPC codes, but are interactive and can store additional information, such as a Web site or an e-mail address. Conduct research to learn how this emerging technology might be used to benefit businesses. Describe in writing how 2-D bar codes could improve one aspect of a local business.

English Language Arts

14. Quick Response Delivery Systems Many retailers are letting their suppliers manage their inventory by sharing point-of-sale information through electronic data exchanges. Conduct research on quick response systems and vendor managed inventory. Discuss the benefits and risks of this approach.

Mathematics

15. Inventory Turnover For a six-month period, a company had an inventory-turnover rate of 4, and the cost of the average inventory on hand was $14,725. What were the net sales for this company during this six-month period?

Math Concept **Analyzation** The inventory-turnover rate is a measure of how often the average inventory is sold and replaced during a given time period.

For help, go to the **Math Skills Handbook** located at the back of this book.

Standardized Test Practice

Directions Read the following questions. On a separate sheet of paper, write the best possible answer for each one.

1. Which of the following methods of checking inventory includes inspecting workmanship and the general characteristics of the received merchandise?

   A. Blind check method

   B. Direct check method

   C. Quality check method

   D. Spot check method

2. A perpetual inventory system tracks the number of items in inventory on a constant basis.

   T

   F

3. The number of times the average inventory has been sold and replaced in a given period of time is called _____.

Test-Taking Tip

At the beginning of a test, review it quickly to see what kinds of questions are on the test to help plan your time. You may find multiple choice, matching, true or false, short answer, extended response, and essay questions.

DECA. Connection Role Play

New Manager Small Hotel

Situation The housekeeping staff have mentioned that several key supplies for the guest rooms, public spaces, and meeting rooms have run very low before being reordered. These supplies are necessary for the smooth running of the hotel and for guest convenience. When reorders are placed for those supplies, they must be delivered by rush delivery. This increases shipping costs, which increases the cost of supplies to the hotel.

Just yesterday you observed two boxes in a corner of the hotel's receiving dock. As you investigated the contents of the boxes, you found that one box contained a reorder of guest room bars of soap, and the other contained a reorder of hotel logo note pads. You have had complaints from customers attending meetings at the hotel that packages are not ready for them when they arrive.

You have researched the problem and determined that the cause of the problem is poor inventory control of hotel supplies and inefficient procedures for receiving deliveries.

Activity You are to meet with the hotel's operations manager (judge) to discuss the situation. You will discuss the need for proper inventory control, the types of inventory control systems suitable for the hotel, and the maintenance of the inventory control system. You will also review procedures for receiving packages.

Evaluation You will be evaluated on how well you meet the following performance indicators:

1. Explain stock-handling techniques used in receiving deliveries.
2. Describe inventory control systems.
3. Maintain inventory control systems.
4. Motivate team members.
5. Foster positive working relationships.

 connectED.mcgraw-hill.com

Download the Competitive Events Workbook for more Role-Play practice.

A Distribution Plan
for a Growing Business

An artist who makes and ships small art objects has simple distribution needs. How might this entrepreneur manage an expanding business and distribution?

Scenario

For several years an artist who designs small sculptures has been selling art items at local arts and crafts fairs as well as through mail order. The orders are easily packaged and shipped via the U.S. Postal Service. However, after visiting a trade show, this artist was commissioned to mass-produce replicas of one sculpture for a retail chain store with locations throughout the United States. This expansion requires mass production using a new inventory management system and a review of current shipping methods.

The artist has hired your firm to handle the details. Your firm has contracted with a manufacturer to make the replicas but now sees an opportunity to sell replicas of the artist's other designs through new channels of distribution.

The Skills You'll Use

Academic Skills Reading, writing, social studies, researching, and analyzing

Basic Skills Speaking, listening, thinking, and interpersonal

Technology Skills Word processing, spreadsheet, presentation, telecommunications, and the Internet

Your Objective

Your objective is to prepare a plan to help grow this artist's business by developing new channels of distribution and planning the logistics required to expand this business.

STEP 1 Do Your Research

Conduct research to identify competitors in the market and find out what channels of distribution they use to sell their products. As you conduct your research, answer these questions:

- Who makes up the target markets for the company's products?
- What channels of distribution will reach those target markets?
- How will the products be stored, inventoried, and shipped?
- Does the company have other companies that handle the logistics (inventory management and shipping)?
- Does the company use the U.S. Postal Service for shipping?

Write a summary of your research.

STEP 2 Plan Your Project

Now that you have completed your research, you need to begin planning your project.

- Research different channels of distribution that could be used to sell the artist's work.
- Select one or two target markets.
- Decide on the channels of distribution that would be used to reach those target markets.
- Create a diagram or flowchart to illustrate the channels of distribution you select.
- Develop a written plan for warehousing, distribution, and shipping to those target markets.

STEP 3 | Connect with Your Community

- Visit a local art gallery or curio shop and ask the business owner or manager how distribution and shipping are handled.
- Take notes during your interview, and transcribe the notes after your interview.

STEP 4 | Share What You Learn

Assume your class is your company's sales staff that will be responsible for presenting this plan to the artist for approval.

- Present your findings in an oral presentation. Be prepared to answer questions.
- Display and explain the diagram or flowchart illustrating suggested channels of distribution.
- Use software to create a slide presentation to accompany your oral presentation. Include one slide for each topic in your written plan.

STEP 5 | Evaluate Your Marketing and Academic Skills

Your project will be evaluated based on the following:

- Knowledge of the market
- Understanding of various channels of distribution that can be used to sell products
- Suggestions for handling the logistics for the expanded business
- Research data to support the rationale for your plan
- Organization and continuity of presentation
- Mechanics—presentation and neatness
- Speaking and listening skills

MARKETING CORE FUNCTIONS

 Channel Management

Market Planning

Marketing Internship Project Checklist

Plan
✓ Conduct research on companies that sell products similar to the artists's creations.
✓ Design a plan to grow the artist's business through new channels of distribution.

Write
✓ Write a summary of your research.
✓ Transcribe your interview notes.
✓ Write a plan that includes your reccommendations for warehousing, distribution, and shipping.
✓ Design a visual to illustrate the channels of distribution.

Present
✓ Present research that supports your rationale for new channels of distribution for specific target markets.
✓ Present your logistics plan for warehousing, distribution, and shipping.

 connectED.mcgraw-hill.com

Evaluate Download a rubric you can use to evaluate your final project.

my marketing portfolio

Internship Report Once you have completed your Marketing Internship Project and oral presentation, put your written report and a few printouts of key slides from your oral presentation in your Marketing Portfolio.

Research and Design a Distribution Plan Research and create a distribution plan for a bakery that makes breads and desserts. It has purchased a facility to make these items in large quantities. What are the potential target markets? What channels of distribution are needed? Who are the competitors in the new channels of distribution? What logistical plan do you have for inventory management of baking supplies and finished products? What shipping methods do you recommend? Will you hire a logistics company or handle everything yourself? Prepare a written report and an oral presentation.

PRICING

Marketing Internship Project

A Pricing Plan

Essential Question How does a business price a new product line?

In order to price products, marketers study their competition, costs, and what the consumer is willing to pay. Since many factors can influence what consumers are willing to pay, marketers conduct a PEST analysis and a SWOT analysis. Once a company analyzes that information, it will have a handle on what the customer is willing to pay. Then it can work backward to determine what the product should cost to produce, market, and still make a profit.

Project Goal

In the project at the end of this unit, you will design a pricing plan for a new line of greeting cards with an American heritage theme.

Prepare for the Project

As you read this unit, use this checklist to prepare for the Marketing Internship Project at the end of this unit:

- Learn about American heritage observances.
- Take notice of the prices of greeting cards.
- Observe pricing strategies used to introduce new product lines.
- Visit a store that carries greeting cards and observe its customers.

 connectED.mcgraw-hill.com

Project Activity
Complete a worksheet activity about pricing.

In a recession economy, consumers tend to be more sensitive about price.

MARKETING CORE FUNCTIONS IN THIS UNIT

 Market Planning

 Pricing

Visual Literacy

Many consumer Web sites allow shoppers to view and compare products and prices from various companies and then buy directly from the site. *How could a partnership with an online price comparison site allow a merchant to market its products more effectively?*

price planning

SHOW WHAT YOU KNOW

Visual Literacy Furniture retailers target different age groups of males, females, and families because their needs and budgets differ. Furniture products for young families are different than furniture products for older men and women. *How might the retail outlet where a product is sold affect the product's suggested retail price?*

Discovery Project

Analysis of Pricing Products

Essential Question What factors go into pricing grooming products for teenagers?

Project Goal

Work with a partner to analyze the prices of grooming and beauty products for a specific target market. Compare competing companies that sell similar products for that target market. The products may be cosmetics, grooming aids, or skin care for males or females. Check them out online and in different types of retail outlets (pharmacies, supermarkets, department stores). Analyze the prices and explain the goals and factors that must have been considered when pricing these products.

Ask Yourself...

- How will you select a specific target market?
- How will you decide on which product lines to research?
- How will you analyze the goals and factors that go into pricing products?
- How will you organize and present your report?

 Analyze and Interpret Provide research to back up your analysis of goals and factors that go into pricing beauty and grooming products.

 connectED.mcgraw-hill.com

Activity
Get a worksheet activity about pricing products.

Evaluate
Download a rubric you can use to evaluate your project.

DECA Connection

DECA Event Role Play

Concepts in this chapter are related to DECA competitive events that involve either an interview or role play.

Performance Indicators The performance indicators represent key skills and knowledge. Your key to success in DECA Competitive events is relating them to concepts in this chapter.

- Explain factors affecting pricing decisions.
- Select an approach for setting a base price (cost, demand, competition).
- Set prices.
- Explain the nature of overhead/operating costs.
- Maintain collaborative partnerships with colleagues.

DECA Prep

Role Play Practice role-playing with the DECA Connection competitive-event activity at the end of this chapter. More information on DECA events can be found on DECA's Web site.

READING GUIDE

Before You Read

Predict How do you think the other Ps of the marketing mix will affect pricing?

Objectives

- **Recognize** the different forms of pricing.
- **Explain** the importance of pricing.
- **List** the goals of pricing.
- **Differentiate** between market share and market position.

The Main Idea

Price is one of the Ps of the marketing mix. As such, many factors must be considered when pricing a product.

Vocabulary

Content Vocabulary
- price
- return on investment (ROI)
- market share
- market position

Academic Vocabulary

You will find these words in your reading and on your tests. Make sure you know their meanings.
- labor
- strategies

Graphic Organizer

Draw or print this chart to take notes about the scope, significance, and major goals of pricing.

Scope and Significance	Goals

connectED.mcgraw-hill.com

Print this graphic organizer.

MARKETING CORE FUNCTION

Pricing

Price Planning Issues

WHAT IS PRICE?

Price is the value in money (or its equivalent) placed on a good or service. It is usually expressed in monetary terms, such as $40 for a sweater. Price may also be expressed in nonmonetary terms, such as free goods or services in exchange for the purchase of a product. As the payment given in exchange for transfer of ownership, price forms the essential basis of commercial transactions.

The oldest form of pricing is the barter system. Bartering involves the exchange of a good or service for another product. It does not involve the use of money. You may remember offering your friend a bag of chips for his cheese and crackers when you were in elementary school. That was bartering. Today's methods are more sophisticated, but the principle is the same. For example, a business might exchange some of its products for advertising space in a magazine or newspaper. Some companies will also exchange advertising spots on their Web pages as a form of bartering, or an equal trade.

As You Read

Analyze What role does price play in marketing planning?

RELATIONSHIP OF PRODUCT VALUE

The value that a customer places on an item or service can make the difference between spending $25,000 or $80,000 on a new automobile, or $20 or $150 on a concert ticket. Value is a matter of anticipated satisfaction. If consumers believe they will gain a great deal of satisfaction from a product, they will place a high value on it. They will also be willing to pay a high price.

A seller must be able to gauge where a product will rank in the customer's estimation. Sellers try to decide whether it will be valued much, valued little, or valued somewhere in between. This information can then be considered in the pricing decision. The seller's objective is to set a price high enough for the company to make a profit but not so high that it exceeds the value potential customers place on the product.

Cost and Price An item's cost may have little to do with its price if price depends on what the market will pay.

VARIOUS FORMS OF PRICE

Price is involved in every marketing exchange. The fee you pay a dentist to clean your teeth, the amount you pay for a new pair of shoes, and minor charges such as bridge tolls and bus fares are all prices. Rent is the monthly price of an apartment. Interest is the price of a loan. Dues are the price of membership. Tuition is the price you pay for an education. Wages, salaries, commissions, and bonuses are the various prices that businesses pay workers for their **labor**. Price comes in many forms and goes by many names.

> **" Pricing helps define a company's image and reflects what customers expect to pay. "**

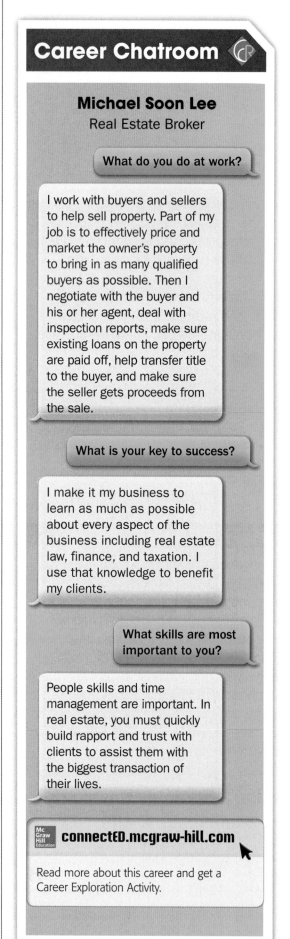
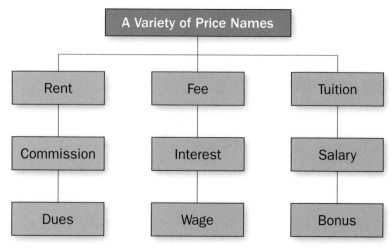

A Variety of Price Names

- Rent
  - Commission
    - Dues
- Fee
  - Interest
    - Wage
- Tuition
  - Salary
    - Bonus

IMPORTANCE OF PRICE

Price is an important factor in the success or failure of a business. Setting a price may seem like a simple task, but there is much more involved than just adding a few dollars to the wholesale cost. A well-planned pricing strategy should result in fair and appropriate prices. Appropriate pricing helps establish and maintain a firm's image, competitive edge, and profits.

Many customers use price to make judgments about products and the companies that make them. A higher price may mean better quality from an upscale store or company to some customers. To other customers, a lower price means more value for their money.

Advertising **strategies** are closely aligned to a company's image. Walmart's® low-price policy is the main focus of its advertising strategy. Some retailers stress that they offer the lowest prices in town. Others promise that they will beat any other store's prices. In such cases, price plays an important role in establishing the edge a firm enjoys over its competition.

Finally, price helps determine profits. Marketers know that sales revenue is equal to price times the quantity sold. In theory, sales revenue can be increased either by selling more items or by increasing the price per item. However, the number of items sold may not increase or they may even remain stable if prices are raised. **Figure 25.1** shows what may happen.

It is also important to remember that an increase in price can increase profits only if costs and expenses can be maintained. You will explore this factor in Section 25.2.

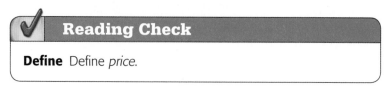

Reading Check

Define Define *price.*

FIGURE 25.1 **Projected Effects of Different Prices on Sales**

An increase in the price of an item may not produce an increase in sales revenue.
Explain why an increase in price does not always mean an increase in revenue.

Price per Item ·	Quantity Sold ·	Sales Revenue
$50	200	$10,000
$45	250	$11,250
$40	280	$11,200
$35	325	$11,375
$30	400	$12,000
$25	500	$12,500

GOALS OF PRICING

Marketers are concerned with earning a profit, or return on investment, as their primary goal of doing business. There are times when other pricing goals become important. Gaining market share and meeting the competition are the other main goals of doing business.

Goals of Pricing

Gaining Market Share

Earning a Profit

Meeting the Competition

EARNING A PROFIT

Return on investment (ROI) is a calculation that is used to determine the relative profitability of a product. The formula used for calculating the rate of return on investment is as follows:

Rate of Return = Profit/Investment

Profit is another word for *return*, which explains the expression return on investment. Assume your company sells watches to retailers for $9 each. Your cost to make and market the watches is $7.50 per unit. Remember that profit is money earned by a business minus costs and expenses, so that your profit on each watch is $1.50:

$$\$9.00 - \$7.50 = \$1.50$$

Your rate of return is 20 percent:

$$\$1.50/\$7.50 = .20$$

A company may price its products to achieve a certain return on investment. Let's say that you run a watch company. Your company wants to achieve a return on investment of at least 25 percent on a new model. To determine the price at which the new watch would have to sell, you would begin by working backward. Start with a target price, which is the price at which you want to sell the watch. Then determine how your company can get costs down so the price will bring your target return.

Take into consideration the suggested retail price you think consumers are willing to pay for the watch. Target pricing will then take on another dimension. Chapter 26 discusses more about target pricing for the customer.

GAINING MARKET SHARE

A business may forgo immediate profits for long-term gains in some other area. One goal, for example, might be to take business away from competitors. The business is trying to increase its market share in this case. For example, in 2009 Walmart sold over 100 toys for $10 each in an effort to garner market share from its major competitor Toys "R" Us® during the holiday season. **Market share** is a firm's percentage of the total sales volume generated by all competitors in a given market.

Businesses constantly study their market share to see how well they are doing with a given product in relation to their competitors. Visualize the total market as a pie. Each pie slice represents each competitor's share of that market. The biggest slice of the pie represents the firm that has the largest percentage of the total sales volume.

MARKET POSITION

Marketers are also interested in their market position. **Market position** is the relative standing a competitor has in a given market in comparison to its other competitors.

To monitor market position, a firm must keep track of the changing size of the market and the growth of its competitors. Competitors are ranked according to their total sales volume. Thus, the company or brand with the highest sales volume would be ranked number one. Enterprise has grown from number three and is now ranked number one in auto rentals. See **Figure 25.2**.

IMPROVING MARKET SHARE AND MARKET POSITION

Pricing is one means of improving market share and market position. Other means of accomplishing the same goals may involve increased advertising expenditures, changes in product design, and new distribution outlets. For example, during the holiday season, Toys "R" Us opened mall-based kiosks in order to increase its share of the toy market.

FIGURE 25.2 **Car Rental Market Share**

The graph shows that Enterprise group has the largest share of market in car rentals. Thus is it is ranked number one in that category. *What is the market position of all the car rental competitors shown in the chart?*

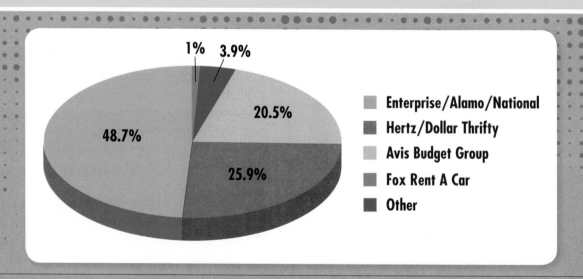

- Enterprise/Alamo/National
- Hertz/Dollar Thrifty
- Avis Budget Group
- Fox Rent A Car
- Other

MEETING THE COMPETITION

Some companies simply aim to meet the prices of their competition. They either follow the industry leader or calculate the average price, and then position their product close to that figure. Airline pricing appears to follow this pattern. Most airlines charge around the same price for the service provided.

How else do you compete when you do not want to rely on price alone? You compete on the basis of other factors in the marketing mix.

These nonprice competing factors might include quality or uniqueness of product, convenience of business location or hours, and level of service. For example, TD Bank is open seven days a week and offers hours from 8:30 A.M. until 8:00 P.M. during weekdays. Automobile manufacturers compete with warranties and maintenance agreements, some offering coverage for five or ten years, or 50,000 or 100,000 miles, respectively. A computer store may offer free installation of software and training to teach you how to use your new software.

 After You Read | **Section 25.1**

Review Key Concepts

1. **Explain** the relationship between product value and price in a consumer's mind.
2. **Explain** why a higher price does not always bring in higher sales revenue.
3. **Identify** other ways, besides price, that marketers have to accomplish the goal for improving market share.

Practice Academics

Social Studies

4. What problems might a company face when trying to compete with price in a different country? Create a list of possible issues and compare it with a partner. Discuss why your lists are similar or different.

Mathematics

5. A skincare company has developed a new line of lotion. Each bottle of lotion costs $10.00 to make and market, and it is sold for $28.50. What is the rate of return on investment?

Math Concept **Rate of Return** The rate of return measures the profitability of a product. The return on an investment is calculated by dividing the profits by the cost of the investment.

Starting Hints To solve this problem, subtract the cost of making the lotion from the selling price to determine profit. Divide the profit by the cost of making the lotion to get the rate of return in decimal form. Multiply the decimal rate of return by 100 to convert it to a percent.

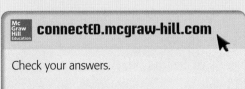
connectED.mcgraw-hill.com

Check your answers.

For help, go to the **Math Skills Handbook** located at the back of this book.

READING GUIDE

Before You Read

Predict What are some factors that might influence prices?

Objectives

- **List** the four market factors that affect price planning.
- **Analyze** demand elasticity and supply-and-demand theory.
- **Explain** how government regulations affect price planning.

The Main Idea

Pricing requires the examination of many factors. Skipping even one aspect of the pricing process could cost a business millions of dollars in lost sales, fines, and/or lawsuits.

Vocabulary

Content Vocabulary
- break-even point
- demand elasticity
- law of diminishing marginal utility
- price fixing
- price discrimination
- unit pricing
- loss leader

Academic Vocabulary
You will find these words in your reading and on your tests. Make sure you know their meanings.
- constant
- equate

Graphic Organizer

Draw or print this chart to note factors that affect price and legal and ethical considerations in pricing.

Factors that Affect Price	Legal & Ethical Considerations
Costs and Expenses	Price Fixing

 connectED.mcgraw-hill.com

Print this graphic organizer.

MARKETING CORE FUNCTION

Pricing

Section 25.2 — Price Planning Factors

MARKET FACTORS AFFECTING PRICES

How do businesses make pricing decisions? The answer is not simple. **Constant** changes in the marketplace force businesses to review pricing decisions frequently. There are four key market factors that must be considered when reviewing and establishing prices. They are costs and expenses, supply and demand, consumer perceptions, and competition.

Most price planning begins with an analysis of costs and expenses. Many of these are related to current market conditions. For example, the cost of raw materials may increase a manufacturer's costs to make an item.

As You Read

Connect Relate the goals of pricing to the factors involved in making a pricing decision.

COSTS AND EXPENSES

Today's economic environment is competitive and becoming more globalized. To compete, businesses must constantly monitor, analyze, and project prices and sales in the light of costs and expenses. They do this because sales, costs, and expenses combine to determine a firm's profit. Many factors have to be considered when raising or lowering prices. This is true even if the impulse to increase or decrease is a direct and seemingly logical reaction to events in the marketplace.

RESPONSES TO INCREASING COSTS AND EXPENSES

When oil prices go up, you will often see an increase in rates charged by airlines, shipping companies, and gas stations. How else could businesses maintain their profit margins? Let's look at other options.

Some businesses have found that price is so important in the marketing strategy of a product that they hesitate to make any price changes. They will reduce the size of an item before they will change its price. A candy manufacturer might reduce a candy bar from 4 to 3.5 ounces instead of increasing its price.

> **" Pricing decisions involve extensive analysis of many factors. "**

Another option manufacturers have for keeping prices to a minimum is to drop features that their customers do not value. Some airlines have stopped serving meals and offer only beverages. Eliminating a small portion of its service helps a company stay competitive.

Some manufacturers respond to higher costs and expenses by adding more features or upgrading the materials in order to justify a higher price. For example, the Ford® Motor Company designed more comfortable supercabs on some of its trucks and charged more for those models.

RESPONSES TO LOWER COSTS AND EXPENSES

Prices may occasionally drop because of decreased costs and expenses. Aggressive firms are constantly looking for ways to increase efficiency and decrease costs. Improved technology and less expensive materials may help create better-quality products at lower costs. For example, the prices of personal computers and high-definition televisions have fallen because of improved technology.

The GREEN Marketer

Eco-Luxury at a Premium Price

Upscale green consumers are willing to pay more for eco-friendly goods so they can enjoy the good life and remain supportive of environmental initiatives. "Eco-luxury" products come in all types: ecologically managed spa vacations, organic French linen sheets, hybrid cars from Lexus® and Mercedes® , and more.

A Growing Market With pricey products like these, companies are tapping into the luxury market. They also attract earth-conscious consumers looking for a sustainable splurge. Customers may be willing to spend more money on these products because of their environmental friendliness.

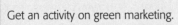

Mathematics
Calculate A Lexus LS Hybrid gets 20 miles per gallon (mpg), and a Lexus LS gets 16 mpg. If the Lexus LS hybrid costs $106,000 and the LS costs $73,000, how much will the buyer pay for each gallon of gas saved in 4 years (10,000 miles/yr)?

 connectED.mcgraw-hill.com

Get an activity on green marketing.

BREAK-EVEN POINT

Manufacturers are always concerned with making a profit. They are especially concerned when marketing a new product and when trying to establish a new price. In these circumstances, manufacturers carefully analyze their costs and expenses in relation to unit and dollar sales. To do this, they calculate their break-even point.

The **break-even point** is the point at which sales revenue equals the costs and expenses of making and distributing a product. After this point is reached, businesses begin to make a profit on the product.

Suppose a toy manufacturer plans to make 100,000 dolls that will be sold at $6 each to retailers and wholesalers. The cost of making and marketing the dolls is $4.50 per unit, or $450,000 for the 100,000 dolls. How many dolls must the toy manufacturer sell to cover its costs and expenses? To calculate the break-even point, divide the total amount of costs and expenses by the selling price:

$$\$450,000 \div \$6 = 75,000$$

SUPPLY AND DEMAND

Demand tends to go up when price goes down, and down when price goes up. This statement is accurate as a general rule. However, demand for some products does not respond to changes in price. The degree to which demand for a product is affected by its price is called **demand elasticity**. Products have either elastic demand or inelastic demand. Chapter 5 examined supply-and-demand theory in detail.

ELASTIC DEMAND

Elastic demand refers to situations in which a change in price creates a change in demand. Changes in the price of steak can serve as an example. If the price of steak were $8 per pound, few people would buy steak. If the price were to drop to $5, $3, and finally $2 per pound, however, demand would increase at each price level.

LAW OF DIMINISHING MARGINAL UTILITY

These increases would not continue indefinitely, however. At some point, they would be limited by another economic law. The **law of diminishing marginal utility**, which states that consumers will buy only so much of a given product, even though the price is low. Let's say that detergent went on sale, and you bought five bottles of it. Three weeks later a new sale is announced for the same detergent, but you already have enough to last for months. You do not need to take advantage of the new sale.

INELASTIC DEMAND

Inelastic demand refers to situations in which a change in price has very little effect on demand for a product. If milk prices were to increase, parents with young children may still pay the higher price. During the holiday season, you may see parents willing to pay a higher price for a popular toy than they would normally pay. Since there is no substitute for that toy, it is an example of inelastic demand.

FACTORS INFLUENCING DEMAND ELASTICITY

Five factors determine whether demand is elastic or inelastic. They are brand loyalty, price relative to income, availability of substitutes, luxury versus necessity, and urgency of purchase. See **Figure 25.3** on page 594 for details.

CONSUMER PERCEPTIONS

Consumer perceptions about the relationship between price and quality or other values also play a role in price planning. Some consumers **equate** quality with price. They believe a high price reflects high quality. A high price may also suggest status, prestige, and exclusiveness. Sometimes a higher-priced item may be the better choice. However, consumers should be aware that many businesses sell identical items for significantly different prices.

Some businesses create the perception that a particular product is worth more than others by limiting the supply of the item in the market. They do this by coming out with a limited edition of a certain model and charging a higher price. Why? The reasoning is that the value of the item will increase as a result of its exclusiveness.

Personalized service can add to a consumer's perceptions about price. Many consumers are willing to pay more for items purchased from certain businesses because of the service those businesses might offer.

Businesses can charge slightly higher prices because consumers are willing to pay for the added service. Five-star restaurants offer fancy place settings, well-designed interiors, and an attentive wait staff to make your dining experience more elegant.

COMPETITION

Price must be evaluated in relation to the target market, as one of the four Ps of the marketing mix. A company can use a lower price when its target market is price conscious, such as senior citizens on fixed incomes. When its target market is not price conscious, a company can resort to various forms of nonprice competition.

Nonprice competition minimizes price as a reason for purchasing. It creates a distinctive product through product availability and customer service. The more unusual a product is perceived to be by consumers, the greater the marketer's freedom to set prices above those of competitors.

Setting the Price Along with figuring your costs, know your market's limits, your competitors' pricing, and your goals.

Marketers change prices to reflect consumer demand, cost, or competition. When products are very similar, price often becomes the sole basis on which customers make their decisions. Shoppers are more likely to buy less expensive brands if they see no difference between products. Competitors watch each other closely. When one company changes its prices, other companies usually react.

When competitors engage in a battle to attract customers by lowering prices, a price war results. Price wars are good for consumers, who can take advantage of lower prices. However, the lower prices reduce profit margins and can lead to business failure. For example, Amazon®, Walmart®, and Target® tried to outdo each other by reducing the price on selected popular books to below $9. None of these companies made money on those books, and their price war hurt the publishing industry, as well as retail book stores.

 Reading Check

Explain When might demand for a product go up?

UNFAIR TRADE PRACTICES

Unfair Trade Practices Law, also known as *Minimum Price Law*, prevents large companies with market power from selling products at very low prices. If they did this, it would drive out competition. In general, the federal law prohibits pricing that has a predatory intent or that harms competition or consumers.

Many states have enacted "sales below cost" or "unfair sales" statutes that may prohibit certain below-cost pricing, even though they would be permitted under federal law. The state laws were enacted to prevent retailers from selling goods below cost plus a percentage for expenses and profit. Some states have passed such laws that cover all products, while others have included only specific products, such as gas, milk, or insurance.

In states where minimum price laws are not in effect, an item priced at or below cost to draw customers into a store is called a **loss leader**. This means the business takes a loss on the item to lead customers into the store. Retailers use popular, well-advertised products as loss leaders. Their hope is that customers will buy other items at regular prices while shopping.

PRICE ADVERTISING

The Federal Trade Commission (FTC) has developed strict guidelines for advertising prices. For exmaple, the FTC's price advertising guidelines forbid a company from advertising a price reduction unless the original price was offered to the public on a regular basis for a reasonable and recent period of time. Another rule says that a company may not claim that its prices are lower than its competitors' prices without proof based on a significant number of items.

Also, a premarked or list price cannot be used as the reference point for a new sale price unless the item has actually been presented for sale at that price.

Bait-and-switch advertising, in which a business advertises a low price for an item that it ultimately has no intention of selling, is not just unethical, it is illegal. For example, when a customer comes in and asks for the advertised item, salespeople switch the customer to a higher-priced item by saying that the advertised product is out of stock or of poor quality.

MARKETING CASE STUDY

Shoppers' Response to Higher Prices

Food shoppers reacted poorly to a $0.25 increase in ConAgra Foods' Banquet® Meals. The increase in price was due to increased costs on food products in that product line. Banquet frozen meals sold for $1.00 in food stores before the price increase. When the price went up to $1.25, sales of Banquet frozen meals dropped significantly.

ConAgra Foods' Response

ConAgra Foods decided to take measures to get the suggested retail price of Banquet meals back to the original $1.00 price point. It removed foods that were costly, such as barbecued chicken, and replaced brownies with mashed potatoes. It also created new entrees with meat patties, beans, and rice. Portions were reduced to cut costs too.

Social Studies

ConAgra Foods' Banquet Meals were priced too highly for their market. However, their price increase may have been successful if it was smaller. Consider the effects of changing the price to $1.10. Discuss with a partner whether you think customers would still have purchased the meals.

PRICING ETHICS

Most ethical pricing considerations arise when interpreting pricing laws. Some businesses, such as computer chip makers and pharmaceutical companies, spend a lot of money for research and development of new products. Once the product is actually created, its manufacturing cost may be relatively small. When you compare the selling price of a computer chip to the cost of manufacturing it, the price may seem unusually high. However, if the costs of developing the chip are also taken into account, the selling price may seem to be more reasonable.

Price gouging is when a price is set higher than normal for a product or service that is suddenly in high demand. Gouging is unethical and against the law in many states, especially when it happens during a state of emergency as a result of a natural disaster or labor strike.

In the wake of a natural disaster, essentials such as food, water, ice, power generators, lanterns, lumber, and hotel rooms may be in very short supply. Charging excessive prices for these necessities following a disaster is always unethical and usually illegal. For example, raising the price of a hotel room from $100 to $500 following a hurricane would be price gouging.

 After You Read   **Section 25.2**

Review Key Concepts

1. **Identify** four pricing options a business might consider in response to increased costs and expenses.
2. **List** five factors that affect demand elasticity.
3. **Name** the government agency that regulates price advertising.

Practice Academics

Social Studies

4. Identify the federal laws involved in the following situations: (a) price fixing; (b) price discrimination; and (c) resale price maintenance.

Mathematics

5. You work for a company that makes and sells watches. Calculate the break-even point for a watch that costs $14 to make and market, and that will be sold for $40. The total quantity that will be sold at that price is 100,000 watches.

   Math Concept **Computing the Break-Even Point** The break-even point is the point at which revenue equals the costs of production and distribution. To determine the break-even point, first compute the total production and distribution costs for all products. Dividing the total cost of production by the selling price will yield the number of products that must be sold to break even.

   Starting Hints To solve this problem, multiply $14, the cost to make one watch, by the total number of watches produced to determine the total cost of production. Divide total production costs by selling price, $40, to get break-even point.

 connectED.mcgraw-hill.com

Check your answers.

For help, go to the **Math Skills Handbook** located at the back of this book.

Price Planning

Goals of pricing may be earning profit, gaining market share, and/or meeting competition. Four factors affect pricing: costs and expenses, supply and demand, consumer perceptions, and competition.

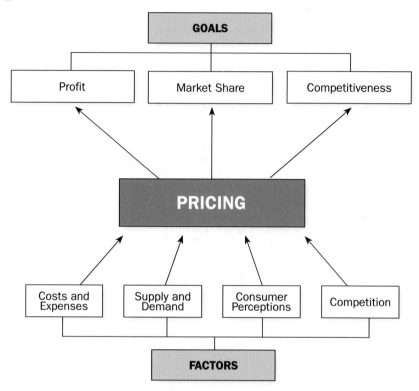

Government regulations control price fixing, price discrimination, resale price maintenance, minimum price, unit pricing, and price advertising.

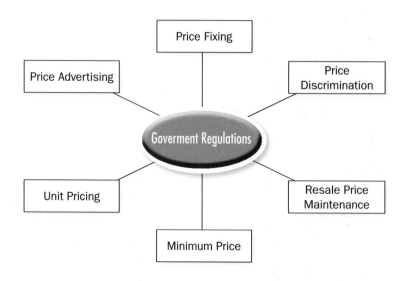

Review and Activities

Written Summary

- Forms of pricing may include fees, fares, tuition, rent, wages, and commissions.
- Pricing is a key factor in the success or failure of a product or service and a business.
- The goals of pricing are earning profit, gaining market share, and meeting competition.
- Four factors that affect pricing are costs and expenses, supply and demand, consumer perceptions, and competition.
- The law of supply and demand means demand goes up when price goes down, and demand goes down when price goes up.
- Demand elasticity is the degree to which price affects demand.
- Government regulations control price fixing, price discrimination, resale price maintenance, minimum price, unit pricing, and price advertising.

Review Content Vocabulary and Academic Vocabulary

1. Write true-or-false statements using each vocabulary word. Ask a partner to determine whether each statement is true or false and explain why.

Content Vocabulary
- price (p. 585)
- return on investment (ROI) (p. 587)
- market share (p. 588)
- market position (p. 588)
- break-even point (p. 592)
- demand elasticity (p. 592)
- law of diminishing marginal utility (p. 592)
- price fixing (p. 595)
- price discrimination (p. 595)
- unit pricing (p. 595)
- loss leader (p. 596)

Academic Vocabulary
- labor (p. 585)
- strategies (p. 586)
- constant (p. 591)
- equate (p. 593)

Assess for Understanding

2. **List** What are the different forms of price?
3. **Explain** Why is pricing important?
4. **Identify** What are the main goals of pricing?
5. **Differentiate** What is the difference between market share and market position?
6. **Give** What are some examples of the four factors that affect price?
7. **Discuss** What role does the government play in regulating the pricing process?
8. **Role Play** What might a manufacturer and a customer discuss about the pricing of a newly developed product?
9. **Analyze** Which demand elasticity factors come into play when a company decides to increase the price of a luxury automobile, if its research indicates that 80 percent of its customers have purchased this same vehicle for the last ten years?

Century Skills

Ethical Skills

10. Price Wars Research historical examples and current examples of price wars. Consider the effect of price wars on consumers, the companies involved, and the industry. What ethical dilemmas are involved for companies that consider engaging in price wars?

Financial Literacy Skills

11. Home Business Profits Assume that you make and sell jewelry that you create from your own designs. You operate the business from your home, so you currently do not have to pay rent or utilities on office space. It costs you $8.00 for materials, and you sell the jewelry for $20. If you make 100 jewelry items, when do you break even? Of what significance is the break-even point to making a profit?

Everyday Ethics

12. Used Car Trends Car shoppers who want to save money might ask, "What about a used car?" Buyers, however, could find themselves stuck with many car problems if they do not do their homework. A mechanic should evaluate the car, and a background report should be done. Read the contract before signing. Remember, "The big print typically gives, the little print typically takes away." Discuss whether it is ethical for used car salespeople to put constrictive terms and conditions into the fine print at the end of a contract.

e-Marketing Skills

13. Online Pricing Online merchants constantly study their competitors' prices. Assume you work for an online merchant that sells computers. Research the prices of three comparable computers. Write a report on your price analysis and recommendations for pricing those items on your company Web site.

Build Academic Skills

Social Studies

14. Economics Printers are priced quite reasonably in relation to the cost of making and marketing them. Research how companies that make printers cover their costs and remain profitable. Consider the accessories that a printer needs in the course of its daily use. Select a model of printer and estimate how much it would cost over the course of a year.

Science

15. Scientific Inquiry Research natural disasters such as major hurricanes. What products were in demand before and after the disaster? How did companies that sell those products price them? Create a graph that shows the supply and demand curves for such products before and after a disaster.

Mathematics

16. Return on Investment A toy company has launched a new product that has a manufacturing cost of $5.75 and a marketing cost of $3.00. The toy is being sold for $14.50. What is the return on investment (ROI) for the product?
(Round your answer to the nearest whole percent.)

Math Concept **Computation** The ROI is calculated by dividing the profits by the cost of investment.

For help, go to the **Math Skills Handbook** located at the back of this book.

Standardized Test Practice

Directions Read the following questions. On a separate sheet of paper write the best possible answer for each one.

1. A firm's percentage of the total sales volume generated by all competitors in a given market is
   A. market position.
   B. market share.
   C. its breakeven point.
   D. market demand.

2. When a product is a necessity, demand tends to be elastic.
   T
   F

3. A calculation that is used to determine the relative profitability of a product is called _____.

Test-Taking Tip

If you want to use a calculator at a testing site, make sure it is authorized. Also, make sure other electronic devices, such as phones and pagers, are turned off.

DECA. Connection Role Play

Owner
Cleaning Service

Situation Your company specializes in cleaning for businesses. You and your business partner (judge) have been in business for five years. You employ 15 employees. You train each cleaning employee to clean the business thoroughly and to treat the customer's property with care and respect. You provide all of the equipment and supplies for normal cleaning tasks.

Most of your customers use your service daily. Because of the number of cleaners you employ and the time involved at each business, you are unable to accept new customers except when an existing customer leaves your service. Because of the quality and care your service offers, you are able to charge top-dollar prices.

You have been considering expanding your business. A custom homebuilder has approached you. The builder would like to explore the possibility of having your service clean the completed homes. You and your partner (judge) have many things to consider before accepting or declining the builder's offer. One of the factors you must carefully consider is the pricing of your company services for the proposed cleanings.

Activity You are to discuss with your partner (judge) some of the factors in terms of cost, demand, and competition that must be considered before pricing the proposed cleanings.

Evaluation You will be evaluated on how well you meet the following performance indicators:

1. Explain factors affecting pricing decisions.
2. Select an approach for setting a base price (cost, demand, competition).
3. Set prices.
4. Explain the nature of overhead/operating costs.
5. Maintain collaborative partnerships with colleagues.

 **connectED.mcgraw-hill.com**

Download the Competitive Events Workbook for more Role-Play practice.

pricing strategies

Visual Literacy The retail market for fashion accessories is extremely competitive. The pricing model depends not only on the cost, but on what consumers are willing to pay to be in style. *What pricing strategies would you use when deciding on the price of a popular fashion accessory?*

Discovery Project

Pricing Electronics

Essential Question How do you set the price for a new electronic product?

Project Goal

Work with a partner to decide on a price for a new electronic game console that is breaking into the lucrative gaming market. Major players in this market are Xbox and Playstation. Assume the new game console is similar to these. Go online or in person to a store that sells electronic games consoles to see how they are priced. Identify the product's life cycle. Determine the pricing strategies used to market electronic games. Also consider marketing the new electronic product in another country with an emerging market for these games. Summarize your findings in a report.

Ask Yourself...

- How will you find businesses that sell electronic game consoles?
- How will you conduct research on their pricing strategies?
- How will you decide on the price for a new product?
- How will you organize and present your report?

 Synthesize and Present Research Synthesize your research by summarizing your findings and providing the rationale for your suggested retail price of a new electronic game console.

---

 connectED.mcgraw-hill.com

Activity
Get a worksheet activity about pricing.

Evaluate
Download a rubric you can use to evaluate your project.

DECA Connection

DECA Event Role Play

Concepts in this chapter are related to DECA competitive events that involve either an interview or role play.

Performance Indicators The performance indicators represent key skills and knowledge. Your key to success in DECA competitive events is relating them to concepts in this chapter.

- Select an approach for setting a base price (cost, demand, competition).
- Describe pricing strategies.
- Set prices.
- Organize information.
- Adjust prices to maximize profitability.

DECA Prep

Role Play Practice role-playing with the DECA Connection competitive-event activity at the end of this chapter. More information on DECA events can be found on DECA's Web site.

READING GUIDE

Before You Read

Predict Why do you think there is variation in the prices of products?

Objectives

- **Name** three pricing policies used to establish a base price.
- **Explain** two polar pricing policies for introducing a new product.
- **Explain** the relationship between pricing and the product life cycle.

The Main Idea

It is important to establish a base price from which price adjustments can be made. Various situations and company policies can affect the pricing of a product.

Vocabulary

Content Vocabulary
- markup
- one-price policy
- flexible-price policy
- skimming pricing
- penetration pricing

Academic Vocabulary

You will find these words in your reading and on your tests. Make sure you know their meanings.
- relation
- allocated

Graphic Organizer

Draw or print this chart to take notes about the pricing policies that can affect the base price of a product.

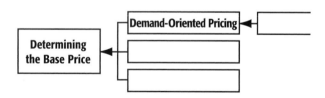

```
                    ┌──────────────────────────┐   ◄──┌────────┐
                    │ Demand-Oriented Pricing  │      │        │
┌──────────────┐ ◄─┤                          │      └────────┘
│ Determining  │    ├──────────────────────────┐
│ the Base Price│◄──┤                          │
└──────────────┘    └──────────────────────────┘
                    ┌──────────────────────────┐
                    │                          │
                    └──────────────────────────┘
```

 connectED.mcgraw-hill.com

Print this graphic organizer.

MARKETING CORE FUNCTIONS

Pricing

Market Planning

Basic Pricing Policies

BASIC PRICING CONCEPTS

Demand, competition, and cost all influence pricing policies and are important in establishing a base price for a product. Each factor is the basis for the three strategies used for setting base prices: demand-oriented pricing, competition-oriented pricing, and cost-oriented pricing.

As You Read

Analyze Consider policies and situations that marketers use to establish the base price for new and old products.

DEMAND-ORIENTED PRICING

Marketers who use demand-oriented pricing attempt to determine what consumers are willing to pay for specific goods and services. The key to this method of pricing is the consumer's perceived value of the item. The price must be in line with this perception, or the item will be priced too high or too low for the target market. Inappropriate pricing could cause the product to fail.

Demand-oriented pricing relies on the basic premises of supply-and-demand theory and on demand elasticity factors. The higher the demand, the more a business can charge for a good or service. This is true even though the good or service and its cost do not change.

COMPETITION-ORIENTED PRICING

Marketers may elect to take one of three actions after learning the competitors' prices: price above the competition, price below the competition, or price in line with the competition (going-rate pricing). In this pricing method, there is no **relation** between cost and price or between demand and price.

Competitive-bid pricing, one type of competition-oriented pricing strategy, determines the price for a product based on bids submitted by competitors to a company or government agency. In such cases, some companies will try to enter the lowest bid in order to obtain the contract.

> ❝ **A major factor in determining the profitability of any product is establishing a base price.** ❞

COST-ORIENTED PRICING

In cost-oriented pricing, marketers first calculate the costs of acquiring or making a product and their expenses of doing business. Then they add their projected profit margin to these figures to arrive at a price. Resellers use different terminology than used by manufacturers and service businesses in the process.

RESELLERS

Resellers calculate prices using the concept of markup. **Markup**, generally expressed as a percentage, is the difference between an item's cost and sale price. For example, if an item costs $10 and the percentage of markup on cost is 40 percent, the retail price would be $14 ($10 × .40 = $4; $10 + $4 = $14).

Markup pricing is used primarily by wholesalers and retailers, who are involved in acquiring goods for resale. The markup on products must be high enough to cover the expenses of running the business and must include the intended profit. However, retailers must make sure the intended profit does not exceed a reasonable price.

MANUFACTURERS AND SERVICE BUSINESSES

Manufacturers and service businesses use a more sophisticated pricing method than markup pricing. They do this because all fixed and variable expenses are calculated separately. Fixed expenses are those expenses that do not change based on production. Fixed expenses include things such as rent, interest on loans, executives' salaries, advertising, and insurance. Variable expenses are associated with the production of the good or service. These include costs related to labor and supplies. When a manufacturer is running at full capacity, the percentage of fixed expenses **allocated** to each product becomes smaller. This permits the manufacturer to charge a lower unit price for goods. **Figure 26.1** shows how a manufacturer may determine the price for a jacket.

Manufacturers also consider the prices they will charge resellers (wholesalers and retailers) for their products to set a base price. This can be done in two ways. You can work backward from the final retail price to find the price for the wholesalers.

Or, you can do this in reverse, by working forward from costs and expenses to the final retail price. These two methods are illustrated in **Figure 26.1.**

The second table of information in Figure 26.1 lists the steps in working backward. The suggested retail price is established first on the basis of consumer demand and competition. Next, the markups desired by the wholesalers and retailers are deducted sequentially from the suggested retail price. Finally, the base price that the manufacturer will charge the wholesaler is determined. Note that the price to the wholesaler must be high enough to cover the manufacturer's costs, any expenses, and the intended profit.

Figure 26.1 also shows the steps for working forward from the manufacturer's cost. Expenses and intended profit must be considered, and then the wholesaler's and retailer's markups are added to the manufacturer's price to arrive at the base selling price. Competition and consumer demand may be left out of the pricing decision if the price is set at this point.

Pricing Food Products

This ConAgra Foods® ad suggests that its products' prices will help generate sales volume for a retailer. *Which method of calculating a price to charge retailers did this manufacturer most likely use? Explain.*

Pricing a Jacket Manufacturers take cost of materials, labor, expenses, and intended profit into consideration when determining the unit price for an item. When calculating the wholesale price, the manufacturer subtracts all the markups for channel members. When calculating the retail price, the manufacturer calculates all of its costs, then calculates resellers' markups to determine the price that retailers will charge their customers.

UNIT PRICE FOR A JACKET

Materials *(fabric, insulation, thread, zipper, pockets)*	$12.00
Labor *(piecework)*	$2.00
Fixed expenses *(overhead)*	$.75
Intended profit margin	$4.25
Price to business customer	$19.00

CALCULATING THE WHOLESALE PRICE

Manufacturer's suggested retail price *(MSRP)*	$100
Retailer's markup *(40% of retail price)*	− $40
Wholesaler's price to retailer *(subtract retailer's markup from MSRP)*	= $60
Wholesaler's markup *(20% of wholesale price)*	− $12
Manufacturer's price to wholesaler * *(subtract wholesaler's markup from wholesaler's price)*	= $48
* This amount must cover costs, expenses, and profit for the manufacturer.	

CALCULATING THE RETAIL PRICE

Cost of producing the item	$40
Manufacturer's expenses and intended profit *(20% of cost)*	+ $8
Manufacturer's price to wholesaler *(Cost plus expenses and intended profit margin)*	= $48
Wholesaler's markup *(25% of price wholesaler paid for item)*	+ $12
Wholesaler's price to retailer *(Manufacturer's price to wholesaler + markup)*	= $60
Retailer's markup *(66.67% based on price paid to wholesaler)*	+ $40
Retailer's base price to consumer	= $100

ESTABLISHING THE BASE PRICE

To establish the base price or price range for a good or service, three different pricing approaches are useful.

Cost-oriented pricing helps marketers determine the price floor for a product. This is the lowest price at which it can be offered and still be profitable.

Demand-oriented pricing determines a price range for the product that is defined by the price floor and the ceiling price. This is the highest amount consumers would pay.

Competition-oriented pricing may be used to ensure that the final price is in line with the company's pricing policies. For example, a retail store may set a policy to always offer prices that are lower than its competitors' prices. Combining pricing considerations offers a good range within which a company can establish its base price. If a company decides to go with the competition-oriented pricing strategy, it still knows how much it can lower its prices if necessary. It can lower its prices based on the cost-oriented pricing figures.

 Reading Check

Recall Identify three types of pricing.

PRICING POLICIES AND PRODUCT LIFE CYCLE

A basic pricing decision every business must make is to choose between a one-price policy and a flexible-price policy. A business also needs to consider how a new product will be introduced. That choice will determine the pricing decisions that follow throughout the product's life cycle.

ONE-PRICE VERSUS FLEXIBLE-PRICE POLICY

A **one-price policy** is one in which all customers are charged the same prices. Prices are quoted to customers using signs and price tags. Deviations from a one-price policy are not allowed. Most retail stores employ a one-price policy. A one-price policy offers consistency and reliability. It also allows retailers to estimate sales and profits because they know the set price.

A **flexible-price policy** is one in which customers pay different prices for the same type or amount of merchandise.

This kind of policy permits customers to bargain for merchandise. This means the customer can negotiate a price rather than pay a fixed price established by the seller. Most retail stores avoid using flexible pricing because it can cause legal problems, and it may keep some customers away.

A flexible-price strategy is common for goods such as used cars, artwork, antiques, furniture, and selected jewelry. One disadvantage of a flexible-price policy is that it does not offer consistent profits. It can be difficult to estimate sales revenue because of the flexible nature of the price. However, with computer technology and huge databases, such estimations may become more feasible.

PRODUCT LIFE CYCLE

Products move through four stages: introduction, growth, maturity, and decline. Pricing plays an important role in this sequence.

NEW PRODUCT INTRODUCTION

A business may price a new product above, in line with, or below its competitors' prices.

This choice depends on the philosophy of the business and on market conditions. When a going-rate strategy is not used to introduce a new product, two methods may be used: skimming pricing or penetration pricing.

Method 1 Skimming pricing is a pricing policy that sets a very high price for a new product. This kind of policy can be used any time demand is greater than supply. Such a policy is designed to capitalize on the high demand for a product during its introductory period.

Businesses that use this method recognize that the price will have to be lowered once the market for the product shifts to more price-conscious customers. While the product is hot, the business will enjoy a high profit margin. Another advantage of skimming pricing is that the price may be lowered without insulting the target market. One disadvantage of skimming pricing is that the high initial price generally attracts competition. Also, if the initial price is far above what consumers pay, sales will be lost and profits diminished.

Pricing Electronics

Computers, cameras, and other electronic items quickly go out of date as new technology emerges and becomes more common. *How does this rapid product life cycle affect pricing?*

Method 2 Penetration pricing is the opposite of skimming pricing: The price for a new product is set very low. The purpose of penetration pricing is to encourage as many people as possible to buy the product, and thus penetrate the market. This type of pricing is most effective in the sale of price-sensitive products (items with elastic demand). SONY® used a penetration-pricing strategy when it introduced its first PlayStation® game console.

To penetrate the market quickly with penetration pricing, mass production, distribution, and promotion must be incorporated into the marketing strategy. The product should take hold in a short period of time. This allows the marketer to save money on fixed expenses (through mass production) and to increase the profit margin (through volume sales).

The biggest advantage of penetration pricing is its ability to capture a large number of customers in a relatively short period of time. This blocks competition from other companies.

If the product is not in high demand, however, the lower price will cause the marketer to suffer a bigger loss than it would have if a higher initial price had been set.

Price Policy Points Price carefully. With underpricing, your market thinks the product is not very good. With overpricing, the competition is boosted.

PRICING DURING THE PRODUCT STAGES

Pricing during subsequent periods in a product's life cycle is determined by which pricing method was originally used—skimming or penetration. Sales increase rapidly during the penetration stage, and total costs per unit decrease because the volume absorbs fixed costs. The main goal of marketers is to keep products in this stage as long as possible.

Sales of products introduced with skimming pricing must be monitored. Once sales begin to level off, the price should be lowered for the price-conscious target market.

Very little price change will be made in the growth stage for products introduced with penetration pricing. When demand decreases and sales begin to level off, competition is generally very keen. Marketers look for new market segments to hold the prices for their products. They may look for other distribution outlets or suggest additional uses for a product.

The marketer's goal during the maturity stage is to stretch the life of a product. Some companies do this by reducing their prices. Others revise products by adding new features or improvements. Companies may also look for new target markets. Another option is to seek new markets in other nations in the global marketplace. Products that have been sold in the United States for many years may be in the introductory or growth stage in other places. By using such techniques, marketers can significantly extend a product's life cycle. The maturity stage may last a long time. When efforts are not successful, however, a product moves into decline.

Sales decrease and profit margins are reduced in the decline stage. Like the maturity stage, the decline stage can last for a long time. Companies are forced to reduce the price to generate sales. To maintain profitability, marketers reduce manufacturing costs or cut back on advertising and promotional activities. Once a product is no longer profitable, it is phased out. However, discontinuing a product does not necessarily mean a company no longer earns revenue from the product. Some discontinued products, especially those used in business and industrial settings, may continue to earn money through support services such as selling supplies and service and repair contracts.

 After You Read | **Section 26.1**

Review Key Concepts

1. **Name** the types of businesses that use markup to determine prices.
2. **Explain** why manufacturers consider the final consumer with a suggested retail price when calculating the price to charge wholesalers.
3. **List** the advantages of using a one-price policy.

Practice Academics

English Language Arts

4. Write a paragraph to reflect your opinion of flexible pricing policies from a customer's point of view.

Mathematics

5. Apply the "pricing backward from retail price" approach to calculate the manufacturer's price to a wholesaler for a product that has a suggested retail price of $300. Assume that the retailer's markup on the retail price is 40 percent, and the wholesaler's markup is 20 percent.

   Math Concept **Backward Pricing** To determine the manufacturer's price, work backward from the retail price. Subtract the retailer's and wholesaler's markup from the manufacturer's suggested retail price.

   Starting Hints To solve this problem, multiply the retail price by the decimal equivalent of 40 percent to determine the retailer's markup. Subtract the value of the retailer's markup from the retail price. This will give the wholesaler's price. Multiply the wholesaler's price by the decimal equivalent of the wholesaler's markup, 20 percent, and subtract this amount from the wholesaler's price to determine the manufacturer's price.

 connectED.mcgraw-hill.com

Check your answers.

For help, go to the **Math Skills Handbook** located at the back of this book.

READING GUIDE

Before You Read

Predict Why do you think prices change over time?

Objectives

- **Describe** pricing strategies that adjust the base price.
- **List** the steps involved in determining a price.
- **Explain** the use of technology in the pricing function.

The Main Idea

Price adjustments allow businesses to stay competitive. The right pricing strategy can help increase sales and profitability.

Vocabulary

Content Vocabulary

- product mix pricing strategies
- price lining
- bundle pricing
- geographical pricing
- segmented pricing strategy
- psychological pricing
- prestige pricing
- everyday low prices (EDLP)
- promotional pricing

Academic Vocabulary

You will find these words in your reading and on your tests. Make sure you know their meanings.

- ultimate
- vehicles

Graphic Organizer

Draw or print this chart to identify strategies for adjusting prices and steps in setting prices.

Price Adjustment Strategies	Six Steps in Determining Price
1. Product mix strategies	1.
a. Price lining	2.
b.	3.
c.	4.
d.	5.
e.	6.

connectED.mcgraw-hill.com

Print this graphic organizer.

MARKETING CORE FUNCTIONS

Pricing

Market Planning

Pricing Process Strategies

ADJUSTING THE BASE PRICE

To adjust base prices, marketers use the following pricing strategies: product mix, geographical, international, segmented, psychological, promotional pricing, discounts and/or allowances. Businesses can remain competitive by using these strategies in the appropriate situations.

As You Read

Connect Note pricing strategy examples from your own observations as a consumer.

PRODUCT MIX STRATEGIES

Product mix pricing strategies involve adjusting prices to maximize the profitability for a group of products rather than for just one item. One product may have a small profit margin, while another may be high to balance the effect of the lower-priced one. These strategies include price lining, optional product pricing, captive product pricing, by-product pricing, and bundle pricing.

PRICE LINING

Price lining is a pricing technique that sets a limited number of prices for specific groups or lines of merchandise. A store might price all its blouses at $25, $35, and $50. Marketers must be careful to make the price differences great enough to represent low, middle, and high-quality items. Price lines of $25, $26, $27, and $28, for example, would confuse customers because they would have difficulty figuring out their basis.

An advantage of price lining is that the target market is fully aware of the price range of products in a given store. In addition, price lining makes merchandising and selling easier for salespeople who can readily draw comparisons between floor and ceiling prices.

OPTIONAL PRODUCT

Optional product pricing involves setting prices for accessories or options sold with the main product. One example is options for cars. All options need to be priced so that a final price for the main product can be established.

> **" Marketers can use specific pricing strategies to fit different economic and market conditions. "**

CAPTIVE PRODUCT

Captive product pricing sets the price for one product low but makes up for it by pricing the supplies needed to use that product high. Ink-jet printers are low in price, but the ink cartridges required for the printers have high markups.

BY-PRODUCT

By-product pricing helps businesses get rid of excess materials used in making a product by using low prices. Wood chips that are residual by-products from making furniture may be sold at a very low price to other manufacturing companies that use wood chips in making their products.

BUNDLE PRICING

With **bundle pricing**, a company offers several complementary, or corresponding, products in a package that is sold at a single price. The one price for all the complementary products that go with the main item is lower than if a customer purchased each item separately. An example of bundle pricing is when computer companies include software in the sale price of a computer.

Bundling helps businesses sell items (parts of the package) that they may not have sold otherwise. As such, bundling increases a company's sales and revenue.

GEOGRAPHICAL PRICING

Geographical pricing refers to price adjustments required because of different shipping agreements. The FOB (Free On Board) origin or point-of-production shipping arrangement would not require a price adjustment because the customer pays the shipping charges. With FOB destination pricing, the seller pays for the shipping and assumes responsibility for the shipment until it reaches the buyer. When determining the price to charge a buyer, shipping charges must be included in the calculations and the adjustment to the base price.

INTERNATIONAL PRICING

When doing business internationally, marketers need to set prices that take into consideration costs, consumers, competition, laws, regulations, economic conditions, and the monetary exchange rate. Costs may include shipping, tariffs, or other charges. Consumers' income levels, perceptions, and lifestyles determine adjustments to the price.

The country's distribution system is another factor because in some countries, several resellers may be involved to get the products to the final consumers.

SEGMENTED PRICING STRATEGIES

A **segmented pricing strategy** uses two or more different prices for a product, though there is no difference in the item's cost. This strategy helps businesses optimize profits and compete effectively. Four factors can help marketers use segmented pricing strategies:

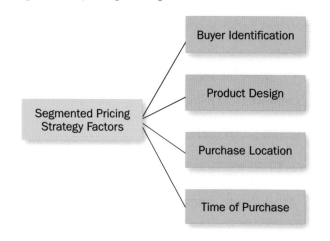

MARKETING CASE STUDY

Caribou Coffee at Home

When budgets tighten and people can't afford specially made coffee, they tend to make coffee at home, rather than buying it at a coffee house. The Caribou Coffee™ Company sells its classic coffee blends at Caribou Coffee locations and supermarkets across the country as well as online. This allows their customers to enjoy their quality coffee at a lower cost.

Segmented Pricing

A 12-ounce bag of Caribou Blend coffee costs $9.99 ($0.83 per ounce) in the supermarket. However, a 1-pound bag of the same coffee can cost $10.99 ($0.69 per ounce) online. Buying coffee in a local supermarket is faster than waiting for an online purchase to arrive, so the cost is slightly higher. Caribou Blend coffee may also cost more in a supermarket located in Los Angeles than in a supermarket located in Cleveland. The difference in price is due to the purchase location.

English Language Arts

Location and Pricing What are some of the reasons purchase location might affect the price of a product? Identify another marketing campaign that relies on segmented pricing.

BUYER IDENTIFICATION

Recognizing a buyer's sensitivity to price (demand elasticity) is one way to identify a customer segment. For example, to attract customers on fixed incomes, some businesses offer senior citizen and student discounts. Airlines offer different classes of travel—first class and coach. First-class travelers pay a significantly higher price to get to the same destination. Another segment may be based on purchases. Companies may offer incentives to loyal customers to encourage them to do more business with them. Some supermarkets and pharmacies have customer loyalty programs whereby loyal customers pay less on selected merchandise.

PRODUCT DESIGN

Manufacturers may also create different prices for different product styles that do not reflect the cost of making the item. Instead, the demand for a given style is the cause of the difference in price. For example, a red-colored washer and dryer may be priced higher than a white set.

PURCHASE LOCATION

Purchase location involves pricing according to where a product is sold and the location of the good or service. Tickets for Broadway shows in New York City will be priced higher than those for the same show when it goes on the road.

TIME OF PURCHASE

Some types of businesses experience highs and lows in sales activity. During peak times, they are able to charge more because of increased demand. Telephone companies often charge more for long-distance calls made during business hours, a peak time.

PSYCHOLOGICAL PRICING STRATEGIES

Psychological pricing strategies are pricing techniques that help create an illusion for customers. They are often based on a buyer's motivation for making a purchase and purchasing habits. For price-conscious customers, five cents could make a difference in the price they are willing to pay. Among common psychological pricing techniques are odd-even pricing, prestige pricing, multiple-unit pricing, and everyday low prices (EDLPs).

ODD-EVEN PRICING

A technique that involves setting price figures that end in either odd or even numbers is known as *odd-even pricing*. This strategy is based on the psychological principle that odd numbers ($0.79, $9.95, $699, $1.99) convey a bargain image.

Even numbers ($10, $50, $100) convey a quality image. Marketers use the odd-even technique to project an image. Some companies use even numbers as part of promotional campaigns. For example, Subway's® $5 foot-long sandwich became the focus of an advertising campaign. McDonald's® and Burger King® offered $1 meal promotions, which convey a value-pricing strategy.

PRESTIGE PRICING

Prestige pricing sets higher-than-average prices to suggest status and high quality to the consumer. Many customers assume that higher prices mean better quality. Rolls-Royce® automobiles, Waterford® crystal, and Rolex® watches are all prestige-priced products.

MULTIPLE-UNIT PRICING

Some businesses have found that pricing items in multiples, such as three for $1.00, is better than selling the same items at $.34 each. Multiple-unit pricing suggests a bargain and helps to increase sales volume.

EVERYDAY LOW PRICES

Everyday low prices (EDLP) are low prices set on a consistent basis with no intention of raising them or offering discounts in the future. Everyday low prices are not as deeply discounted as promotional prices, which creates sales stability. Other benefits include reduced promotional expenses and reduced losses due to discounting.

A Winning Psychology
Walmart, the world's largest retailer, took EDLP to countries like Germany and Korea where the concept was new.

PROMOTIONAL PRICING

Promotional pricing is generally used in conjunction with sales promotions wherein prices are reduced for a short period of time. Common types of promotional pricing are loss leader pricing (discussed in Chapter 25), special-event pricing, and rebates and coupons.

LOSS LEADER PRICING

Loss leader pricing is used to increase store traffic by offering very popular items of merchandise for sale at below-cost prices. The theory behind this practice is that customers will be attracted by the low price. Once in the store, they will buy regularly priced merchandise in addition to the loss leader item.

SPECIAL-EVENT PRICING

In special-event pricing, items are reduced in price for a short period of time, based on a specific event. For example, stores may promote back-to-school, Presidents' Day, or anniversary sales. Manufacturers offer special promotions to wholesalers and retailers willing to advertise or promote a manufacturer's products.

REBATES AND COUPONS

Rebates are partial refunds provided by the manufacturer to consumers. To receive the rebate, a customer buys the product, and then sends in a rebate form along with the product's proof of purchase and a store receipt. Manufacturers offer rebates to wholesalers and retailers for purchasing certain quantities of goods before the manufacturer runs a special product promotion. Coupons allow customers to take reductions at the time of purchase. Coupons may be found in newspapers, advertisements, product packages, and even on sales receipts printed by retailers, such as supermarkets.

DISCOUNTS AND ALLOWANCES

Discount pricing involves the seller offering reductions from the usual price. Such reductions are generally granted in exchange for the buyer performing certain actions. These include cash discounts, quantity discounts, trade discounts, seasonal discounts, and special allowances.

CASH DISCOUNTS

Cash discounts are offered to buyers to encourage them to pay their bills quickly. Terms are generally written on the invoice. For example, 2/10, net 30 means that a 2 percent discount is granted if the bill is paid in ten days.

QUANTITY DISCOUNTS

Quantity discounts are offered to buyers for placing large orders. Sellers benefit from large orders through the lower selling costs involved in one transaction, as opposed to several small transactions. Quantity discounts also offer buyers an incentive to purchase more merchandise than they originally intended to purchase.

Two types of quantity discounts are noncumulative and cumulative. Noncumulative quantity discounts are offered on one order, while cumulative quantity discounts are offered on all orders over a specified period of time.

Cumulative discounts may be granted for purchases made over six months. For example, all purchases for that period are used to determine the quantity discount offered. In other cases, buyers may be required to sign a contract that guarantees a certain level of business. Advertisers who agree to use a specified number of column inches in their newspaper ads might be charged cheaper contract rates. Generally, the more you advertise, the less you pay per column inch.

TRADE DISCOUNTS

Trade discounts are not really discounts at all but, rather, the way manufacturers quote prices to wholesalers and retailers. Many manufacturers establish suggested retail prices, or list prices, for their items. They grant discounts from the list price to members of the channel of distribution. A manufacturer might grant wholesalers a 40 percent discount from the list price and retailers a 30 percent discount.

The manufacturer might also quote the discounts in series, such as 25 percent and 10 percent for retailers and wholesalers, respectively. Series, or chain, discounts are calculated in sequence, with discounts taken on the declining balance as shown below. The example is based on a list price of $50.

Retailer's discount

$50 × .25 = $12.50

Cost to retailer

$50 − $12.50 = $37.50

Wholesaler's discount

$37.50 × .10 = $3.75

Cost to wholesaler

$37.50 − $3.75 = $33.75

In series discounts, note that the wholesaler's discount is based on the retailer's discount, not the original list price.

SEASONAL DISCOUNTS

Seasonal discounts are offered to buyers willing to buy at a time outside the customary buying season. Manufacturers offer discounts to obtain orders for seasonal merchandise early so that production facilities and labor can be used throughout the year.

Other businesses use seasonal discounts to cut anticipated costs. For example, many retailers drastically reduce prices on swimsuits after the summer season. A good time to buy a winter coat is in the spring, when retailers sell them at a discount. Such retailers prefer to sell this merchandise at a lower markup than pay the costs of warehousing it until the following year. A variation on this device is used by vacation resorts. They offer vacationers lower rates to encourage use of resort facilities during the off season. For example, a ski resort may offer attractive rates during the summer months.

ALLOWANCES

Trade-in allowances go directly to the buyer. Customers are offered a price reduction if they sell back an old model of the product they are purchasing. Consumers are generally offered trade-in allowances when purchasing new cars or major appliances. Companies usually get such allowances when purchasing machinery or equipment. Occasionally, real estate transactions may use a trade-in allowance approach. Buyers may offer a house or other piece of property as partial payment for a different property.

 Reading Check

Analyze Would a higher price benefit a high-end product?

THE PRICING PROCESS AND RELATED TECHNOLOGY

As one of the four Ps of the marketing mix, pricing is the most flexible because ongoing pricing strategies and prices can be changed quickly.

DETERMINING PRICES

Six steps are used to determine prices: establish pricing objectives, determine costs, estimate demand, study the competition, decide on a pricing strategy, and set prices.

STEP 1: ESTABLISH PRICING OBJECTIVES

Pricing objectives must conform to the company's overall goals: making profit, improving market share, and meeting the competition. Pricing objectives should be specific, time sensitive, realistic, and measurable. Increasing sales of a given product is not a good pricing objective. Increasing unit or dollar sales by 20 percent in one year compared with the previous year is better because it is time-sensitive (one year), specific, and measurable (20 percent increase). At the end of one year, a company can evaluate and make revisions if the pricing objective was not met.

STEP 2: DETERMINE COSTS

For wholesalers and retailers, money owed to vendors plus freight charges equals the cost of an item. Service providers must consider the cost of supplies plus the cost of performing the service. The cost of materials and labor used in a manufactured product make up the item's cost. A business must keep accurate records and understand that changes in costs and in economic conditions may affect its **ultimate** pricing decision.

STEP 3: ESTIMATE DEMAND

Marketers study the size of the market to determine the total number of possible customers for a given product. From their basic research, marketers estimate the percentage of potential customers who might buy that new product. Much of this analysis is based on supply-and-demand theory and exceptions due to demand elasticity.

STEP 4: STUDY THE COMPETITION

You need to investigate what prices your competitors are charging for similar goods and services. Businesses subscribe to services that provide competitive information on a daily basis. In today's computer age, it is easy to go online to check out competitors' prices.

STEP 5: DECIDE ON A PRICING STRATEGY

You need to revisit the pricing objectives and decide on a pricing strategy or strategies that will help you accomplish your objectives. Everything you learned in this section will help you in this endeavor. However, you must remember that as economic and market conditions change, strategies may require changes too.

STEP 6: SET PRICES

Setting the published price that you see on price tickets, Web sites, price sheets, catalogs, and promotional materials is the final step. It is important that all the above steps are carefully considered. Customers' reactions to price changes must be considered before marketers decide if and when to change their published prices.

PRICING TECHNOLOGY

Technology applications for pricing are evident in the data that are now made available to marketers when making pricing decisions. They are also evident in the tools and **vehicles** for providing price information to customers.

SMART PRICING

Smart pricing allows marketers to make intelligent pricing decisions based on enormous amounts of data. Web-based pricing technology crunches this data into timely, usable information. Software that combines sales data with inventory data results in pricing recommendations, which the pricing team can accept, revise, or reject. Previous sales data are compared with current sales data.

This comes from from the store's point-of-sale system. They are also compared with its merchandising system, which includes all items' inventory levels. All these data help to set prices for new merchandise, and when to take markdowns, if any, on current merchandise in stock. This system gives this company the ability to adjust prices according to changing market conditions.

COMMUNICATING PRICES TO CUSTOMERS

Electronic gadgets provide customers with real-time pricing information. Retailers that invest in electronic shelves and digital price labels can change prices quickly and easily. They also can alert in-store shoppers to deals based on customers' buying habits.

Kiosks in retail stores allow customers to scan a product to determine its price. In supermarket chains, customers scan their own merchandise and pay for the products without the assistance of a clerk. With these new technological advances, older price-marking techniques, such as printed price tags, are quickly becoming a thing of the past in certain industries.

RFID TECHNOLOGY

Advanced technology that may revolutionize pricing and inventory control is called "radio frequency identification," or RFID. RFID is wireless technology that involves tiny chips embedded in products. A chip has an antenna, a battery, and a memory chip filled with a description of the item for sale.

 After You Read   **Section 26.2**

Review Key Concepts

1. **Identify** the key factor in deciding price lines.
2. **Explain** why bundling discourages comparison shopping.
3. **Compare** everyday low pricing with promotional pricing.

Practice Academics

Social Studies

4. Describe the factors that would come into play when setting the price for a cell phone if you were selling it in Brazil or Egypt. Identify and explain an approach you would use for pricing.

Mathematics

5. Determine the price a wholesaler would pay for an item with a list price of $80 if the wholesaler receives a discount of 15 percent.

Math Concept **Discounts** Discounts are usually presented as a percent off of the manufacturer's price. To determine the value of a discount, convert the percent to a decimal and multiply it by the regular price. To determine the price after a discount, simply subtract this value from the regular price.

Starting Hints To solve this problem, convert the percent discount to a decimal by moving the decimal place two places to the left. Multiply the decimal by $80 to determine the value of the discount. Subtract the wholesale discount amount from $80 to determine the respective price after the discount.

 connectED.mcgraw-hill.com

Check your answers.

For help, go to the Math Skills Handbook located at the back of this book.

Pricing Strategies

The three types of pricing are demand-based, cost-based, and competition-based. All can be used to establish the base price.

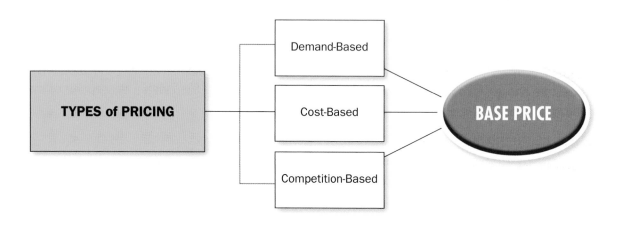

Adjustments to the base price can be made using these strategies: product mix, geographical, international, segmented, psychological, promotional, and discounted.

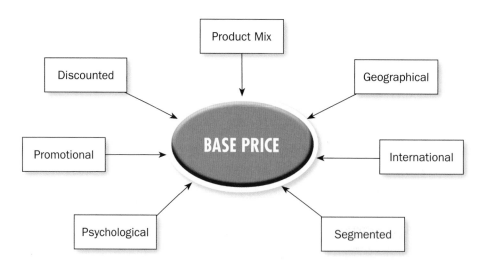

Review and Activities

Written Summary

- Establishing a base price for a product can be accomplished by combining cost-oriented, demand-oriented, and competition-oriented policies, and considering resellers' needs.
- Businesses must decide whether to use a one-price policy or a flexible price policy.
- The product life cycle should be considered in the pricing process. Two polar pricing strategies for the introduction of a product are skimming pricing and penetration pricing.
- Once a base price is established, price adjustments are made using pricing strategies: product mix pricing, geographical pricing, international pricing, segmented pricing, psychological pricing, promotional pricing, and discounts and allowances.
- Six steps to determine prices are establishing pricing objectives, determining costs, estimating demand, studying competition, deciding on a strategy, and setting actual price.
- Pricing technology has revolutionized the way businesses make pricing decisions.

Review Content Vocabulary and Academic Vocabulary

1. Create multiple-choice test questions for each content and academic vocabulary term.

Content Vocabulary
- markup (p. 605)
- one-price policy (p. 608)
- flexible-price policy (p. 608)
- skimming pricing (p. 609)
- penetration pricing (p. 610)
- product mix pricing strategies (p. 613)
- price lining (p. 613)
- bundle pricing (p. 613)
- geographical pricing (p. 614)
- segmented pricing strategy (p. 614)
- psychological pricing (p. 615)
- prestige pricing (p. 616)
- everyday low prices (EDLP) (p. 616)
- promotional pricing (p. 616)

Academic Vocabulary
- relation (p. 605)
- allocated (p. 606)
- ultimate (p. 618)
- vehicles (p. 618)

Assess for Understanding

2. Identify What are three ways to find a base price?

3. Explain Why does pricing change during a product's life cycle?

4. Contrast What is the major difference in the two polar pricing strategies for introducing a new product?

5. Suggest How can the six types of pricing strategies be used to adjust the base price?

6. Sequence What are six steps in the pricing process?

7. Imagine What kinds of new technology are used in pricing?

8. Define What is the definition of the term *psychological pricing*?

9. Calculate Forty percent of your customers place large orders during a 3-month period, while the remaining customers place smaller orders over a 12-month period. Which will you offer all your customers: cumulative or noncumulative quantity discounts? Why?

21st  Century Skills

Problem-Solving Skills

10. **Selling Toys** Use the steps in determining price to set a price for a children's toy that you think will be popular during the holiday season. The economy is in a recession, so the pricing objective is to sell this toy at a reasonable price. The cost to manufacture the toy is $2.15. Remember the manufacturer needs to cover its expenses and make a profit (20%) on this item and so do the wholesalers (25% markup) and retailers (66.7% markup). Show your calculations and how you used the six steps in determining the final price to the customer.

Financial Literacy Skills

11. **How Much to Charge?** You have determined that consumers are willing to pay only $25 for a widget. If wholesaler's markup is 20 percent and retailer's markup is 40 percent, what price should you charge wholesalers for a widget? What does that price have to cover?

e-Marketing Skills

12. **Pricing Technology** Research smart pricing technology. Cite where and how it is used, and especially look at how it may be used with online ads found on search engines. You may want to consider the questions below as you conduct your research. Prepare a written report on your findings.

    - How are customers affected by this technology?
    - How are businesses affected by this technology?
    - What are some advantages and disadvantages of the smart pricing technologies you found in your research?
    - How might businesses use their pricing strategies as an advertising strategy?
    - How do smart pricing techniques fit into a rapidly expanding global economy?

Build Academic Skills

Social Studies

13. **Economics** For a fund raising project, you ordered 50 items at $5, 25 items at $8 and 25 items $10. You are not sure all these items will sell well. Explain the markup, selling price, and pricing strategy you suggest to make at a minimum profit of $700.

Science

14. **Scientific Inquiry** Conduct research on the price 20 teens are willing to pay for a concert ticket for three different popular groups. Analyze your findings to determine the ceiling and floor prices. Report your findings in a chart and note the price you would recommend for each group's next tour.

Mathematics

15. **Calculate Incentive Discounts** Promotional discounts are given to stores by manufacturers to place products in preferred locations or to pay for ads, displays, or in-store demonstrations. What is the percent discount to stock an item that has a purchase amount of $10,800 and a discount amount of $600? (Round your answer to the nearest whole percent.)

    Math Concept **Percent Discount** When a discount is given in a dollar amount, it can be converted to a percent by dividing the dollar value of the discount by the purchase amount and then multiplying by 100.

    For help, go to the **Math Skills Handbook** located at the back of this book.

Standardized Test Practice

Directions Read the following questions. On a separate sheet of paper, write the best possible answer for each one.

1. If you want to capture a large number of customers in a relatively short period of time when introducing a new product, you would use

   A. cost-oriented pricing

   B. flexible pricing

   C. skimming pricing

   D. penetration pricing

2. An effective price-lining policy for jackets would be $50, $52, and $55.

   T

   F

3. _____ are partial refunds provided by the manufacturer to consumers.

Test-Taking Tip

Just before taking a test, avoid talking to other students. Text anxiety can be contagious.

DECA Connection Role Play

Consultant
New Business Owners

Situation You are consulting for a company that offers advice and assistance to prospective new business owners. Your current client (judge) is planning to open a business that will provide various errand services to customers in the community. Some of the services the client (judge) plans to provide include collecting mail and packages while customers are away, dog walking, grocery shopping, picking-up dry cleaning, and other related errands. Your research of the planned target market indicates that the residents are primarily working couples that do not have a lot of free time.

The client (judge) has limited business experience and is eager for the business to succeed. Your client (judge) is uncertain about the pricing of the services of the new business and has questions about pricing strategies and determining prices for the services. You are meeting with your client (judge) later today to discuss pricing for the services of the proposed business.

Activity You are to discuss with your client (judge) the steps in determining prices for the proposed services and some pricing strategies appropriate for the new business.

Evaluation You will be evaluated on how well you meet the following performance indicators:

1. Select an approach for setting a base price (cost, demand, competition).

2. Describe pricing strategies.

3. Set prices.

4. Organize information.

5. Adjust prices to maximize profitability.

 connectED.mcgraw-hill.com

Download the Competitive Events workbook for more Role-Play practice.

pricing math

SHOW WHAT YOU KNOW

Visual Literacy Supermarkets and department stores typically carry many different brands and varieties of products at a wide range of prices. *Why do you think these retailers frequently mark down items or put them on sale?*

Discovery Project

Pricing Markups and Discounts

Essential Question How do retailers calculate original markups, knowing that prices will be reduced later in the season?

Project Goal

Work with a partner to analyze a retailer's original prices and subsequent discounts on ten items. Assume the retailer purchased 200 of each of those ten items. In scenario #1, 75 percent of those items sold at the original price and the remainder sold at the reduced price. In Scenario #2, assume the opposite was true. So, 25 percent sold at the original price and 75 percent sold at the reduced price. Determine the difference in sales revenue. If the cost of each item was 50 percent of the original retail price, what was the original dollar markup? (original price − cost = dollar markup). Once the discount was taken, what was the dollar markup on each item (reduced price − cost = dollar markup)?

Ask Yourself...

- How will you find stores that are discounting their goods?
- How will you decide on which goods to use for this project?
- What computer software program could help you do the calculations for this assignment?
- How will you analyze and report your findings?

 Synthesize and Present Research Synthesize your research by analyzing the two scenarios and showing the dollar effect each has on the retailer. Discuss what your analysis says about setting original prices when you know the prices will be reduced later in the season.

 connectED.mcgraw-hill.com

Activity
Get a worksheet activity about markups and discounts.

Evaluate
Download a rubric you can use to evaluate your project.

DECA Connection

DECA Event Role Play

Concepts in this chapter are related to DECA competitive events that involve either an interview or role play.

Performance Indicators The performance indicators represent key skills and knowledge. Your key to success in DECA competitive events is relating them to concepts in this chapter.

- Identify factors affecting a business's profit.
- Determine cost of product (breakeven, ROI, markup).
- Demonstrate responsible behavior.
- Adjust prices to maximize profitability.
- Describe the nature of profit and loss statements.

DECA Prep

Role Play Practice role-playing with the DECA Connection competitive-event activity at the end of this chapter. More information on DECA events can be found on DECA's Web site.

READING GUIDE

 Before You Read

Connect Why is setting a price an important part of the marketing mix?

Objectives

- **Explain** how a company's profit is related to markup.
- **Use** the basic formula for calculating a retail price.
- **Calculate** dollar and percentage markup based on cost or retail.
- **Calculate** markdowns in dollars and percentages.
- **Calculate** maintained markup in dollars and percentages.

The Main Idea

Pricing and profit have a direct relationship to each other. Retailers use different formulas for calculating prices, markups, and markdowns.

Vocabulary

Content Vocabulary
- gross profit
- maintained markup

Academic Vocabulary

You will find these words in your reading and on your tests. Make sure you know their meanings.
- convert
- visual

Graphic Organizer

Draw or print this chart to insert the formula for calculating a retail price in the middle circle. Use outer circles to note other formulas.

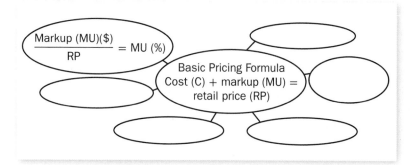

connectED.mcgraw-hill.com

Print this graphic organizer.

Calculating Prices

PROFIT AND MARKUP

A businessperson says, "We made a profit of $50 from buying the radio for $100 and selling it for $150." The businessperson is only partially correct. The difference between the retail price of $150 (which is equal to 100 percent) and the $100 cost ($66\frac{2}{3}$ percent) is the markup, or margin, of $50 ($33\frac{1}{3}$ percent), not the profit.

As You Read

Analyze How do you think profit relates to markup on prices?

Profit is the amount left over from revenue after the costs of the merchandise and expenses have been paid. The markup (margin) on an item, however, is the same as gross profit. **Gross profit** is the difference between sales revenue and the cost of goods sold. Expenses must still be deducted in order to get net (actual) profit. Therefore, a business must have a markup that is high enough to cover expenses and provide the profit needed to be successful when deciding on a price.

Let's compare profit with retail markup by using the above figures and sales of 300 radios. Look at **Figure 27.1** on page 628 for this comparison. On an income statement, sales revenue would be $45,000 (100 percent), less cost of goods sold of $30,000 ($66\frac{2}{3}$ percent), which would equal gross profit of $15,000 ($33\frac{1}{3}$ percent). If expenses were $9,000 (20 percent), the gross profit ($33\frac{1}{3}$ percent) would be enough to cover expenses and earn a net profit before taxes of $6,000 or $13\frac{1}{3}$ percent ($6,000 divided by $45,000; or $33\frac{1}{3}$ percent − 20 percent).

BASIC MARKUP CALCULATIONS

Retailers and wholesalers use the same formulas to calculate markup. We will use only retail prices here to make these formulas easier to understand. Note, however, that wholesale prices can be substituted in any of the markup formulas.

> **" Retail price and markup correlate with a business's income statement. "**

The most basic pricing formula is the one for calculating retail price. It states in mathematical terms the relationship that has been discussed in the last two chapters. Retail price is a combination of cost and markup. Knowing these two figures will enable you to calculate retail price. Here's how:

Cost (C) + markup (MU) = retail price (RP)

For example,

$14 (C) + $6 (MU) = $20 (RP)

Two other formulas can be derived from this basic formula—cost and markup.

Retail price (RP) − markup (MU) = cost (C)

$20 (RP) − $6 (MU) = $14 (C)

Retail price (RP) − cost (C) = markup (MU)

$20 (RP) − $14 (C) = $6 (MU)

You will rely on these three formulas throughout this chapter. The formulas and their terms will be cited in abbreviated form (for example, C + MU = RP).

FIGURE 27.1 **How an Income Statement Relates to Markup**

Income Statement and Retail Pricing When retailers and wholesalers set the prices on their goods, they consider the effect the prices will have on their bottom line—profit. Markup on all products must ultimately cover their costs and expenses. Let's look at how retail pricing and markup correlate with an income statement. *What part of the income statement relates to markup?*

Sales Revenue of $30,000 represents 100 percent of the money a firm has to run its business.

Cost of Goods Sold is the cost to purchase or make items for sale. In this example, the cost of goods sold is 47.5 percent of the money the firm generated from sales revenue. ($14,250 divided by $30,000 = .475 or 47.5%)

Gross Profit or Gross Margin is the difference between sales revenue and cost of goods sold: $30,000 − $14,250 = $15,750. The gross profit high enough to cover expenses and leave money left over for profit. In this case, it represents 52.5 percent of total sales revenue ($14,250 divided by $30,000 = .525 = 52.5%). Note that the gross profit and markup percentages are the same.

Income Statement		
Sales Revenue 500 items @ $60/item	$30,000	100%
Cost of Goods Sold 500 items @ $28.50/item	$14,250	47.5%
Gross Profit	$15,750	52.5%
Less Expenses	$11,250	37.5%
Net Profit (before taxes)	$ 4,500	15.0%

Net Profit (before taxes) is the amount left over from revenue after the cost of the merchandise sold and expenses are paid. Net profit before taxes is 15 percent of total sales revenue ($4,500 divided by $30,000 = .15 = 15%).

Retail Pricing	
$60 RP	100%
$28.50 C	47.5%
$31.50 MU	52.5%

Expenses include salaries, rent, utilities, and other costs of running a business. In this case, expenses represented 37.5 percent of sales revenue ($11,250 divided by $30,000 = .375 or 37.5%).

Retail Pricing Chart Note that the markup of $31.50 × 500 = $15,750, which is the same as the gross profit on the Income Statement.

PRACTICE 1

Use the retail price formula and its variations to do the following problems.

1. A jacket costs $50, and the markup is $49.99. What is its retail price?

2. A pen has a retail price of $2.49, and its markup is $0.83. What is its cost?

connectED.mcgraw-hill.com

Find answers to all Practice activities.

PERCENTAGE MARKUP

In the Practice examples, markup was expressed as a dollar amount. In most business situations, however, the markup figure is generally expressed as a percentage. We will distinguish between these two forms of markup (dollar and percentage) throughout the rest of the chapter. In calculations, dollar markup will be represented with the abbreviation MU($) and percentage markup with the abbreviation MU(%).

Expressing markup in either dollar or percentage form is not the only choice that wholesalers and retailers have in making markup calculations. They may also decide to compute their markup on either cost or retail price if they choose to use the percentage form.

Most choose to base the markup on retail price for three reasons. First, the markup on the retail price sounds like a smaller amount. This sounds better to customers who know the markup percentage and makes the price seem reasonable.

Second, future markdowns and discounts are calculated on a retail basis. Third, profits are generally calculated on sales revenue. It makes sense to base markup on retail prices when comparing and analyzing data that play a role in a firm's profits.

Any person working in business or retail will find the skill of being able to calculate percentage markup very valuable. Here are the steps for calculating the percentage markup on retail. They will be easier to follow if we use an example. Assume that you want to calculate the percentage markup on a pair of brass bookends that Chris's Specialty Store stocks for $49.50 (cost) and sells for $82.50 (retail price).

STEP 1   Determine the dollar markup.

$$RP - C = MU(\$)$$
$$\$82.50 - \$49.50 = \$33.00$$

The GREEN Marketer

Saving Green by Buying Green

Do companies that make sustainable products have to charge higher prices? Not necessarily. Peet's® Coffee charges the same price for its Fair Trade Blend as it does for its Peet's signature blend. The Fair Trade Blend allows for a living wage for Costa Rican farmers. Sneakers from Simple® Shoes and jeans from Levi's® Eco line are also sustainable products. They are made with organic cotton, yet they cost the same as conventional styles.

Profit Trade-Off Many businesses accept a lower profit margin on their green products. These products may have a higher wholesale cost. However, this higher cost is offset by the chance to win over "green" consumers. This strategy pays off with an expanded customer base.

Mathematics

Compute If the ingredients for a bag of Newman's Own ® Organics cookies cost $0.89 with Fair Trade cocoa, and $0.81 with conventional cocoa, what is the cost difference for 12,000 bags? If wholesale markup is 35 percent, what would Newman's Own charge retailers for a bag of Fair Trade cocoa cookies?

connectED.mcgraw-hill.com

Get an activity on green marketing.

STEP 2 To change the dollar markup to the percentage markup, divide it by the retail price. The result will be a decimal.
MU($) ÷ RP = MU(%) on retail
$33.00 divided by $82.50 = .4

STEP 3 Change the decimal to a percentage by shifting the decimal point two places to the right. This figure is the percentage markup on retail.
.40 = 40%

Retailers may find the percentage markup on cost to be helpful. The calculation is the same, except for Step 2. Using the same facts from above, you calculate the percentage markup on cost as follows:

STEP 1 Determine the dollar markup.
RP − C = MU($)
$82.50 − $49.50 = $33.00

STEP 2 To change the dollar markup to the percentage markup, divide by cost.
MU($) ÷ C = MU(%) on cost
$33.00 divided by $49.50 = .6667

STEP 3 Change the decimal to a percentage. This figure is the percentage markup on cost. .6667 = 66.67%

PRACTICE 2

Calculate markup percentages; round your answers to the tenths place.

1. The retail price of an alarm clock is $39.99, and its cost to the retailer is $20. (A) What is the markup percentage based on its cost? (B) Based on its retail price?

2. A pair of slippers costs a retailer $7.50, and its markup is $5.49. (A) What is the markup percentage based on its cost? (B) Based on its retail price?

3. A camera's retail price is $249.99, and its markup is $112.50. (A) What is the markup percentage based on its cost? (B) Based on its retail price?

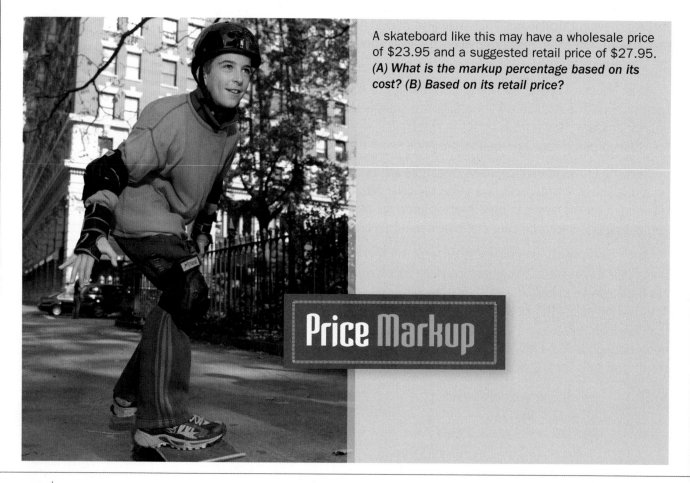

A skateboard like this may have a wholesale price of $23.95 and a suggested retail price of $27.95. *(A) What is the markup percentage based on its cost? (B) Based on its retail price?*

Price Markup

FIGURE 27.2 | Markup Equivalents

Markup Equivalents Table This sample markup equivalents table allows users to convert markups on retail to markups on cost and vice versa.
A 20-percent markup on retail is equal to what markup percent based on cost?

Markup on Retail	Markup on Cost	Markup on Retail	Markup on Cost
4.8%	5.0%	25.0%	33.3%
5.0	5.3	26.0	35.0
6.0	6.4	27.0	37.0
7.0	7.5	27.3	37.5
8.0	8.7	28.0	39.0
9.0	10.0	28.5	40.0
10.0	11.1	29.0	40.9
10.7	12.0	30.0	42.9
11.0	12.4	31.0	45.0
11.1	12.5	32.0	47.1
12.0	13.6	33.3	50.0
12.5	14.3	34.0	51.5
13.0	15.0	35.0	53.9
14.0	16.3	35.5	55.0
15.0	17.7	36.0	56.3
16.0	19.1	37.0	58.8
16.7	20.0	37.5	60.0
17.0	20.5	38.0	61.3
17.5	21.2	39.0	64.0
18.0	22.0	39.5	65.5
18.5	22.7	40.0	66.7
19.0	23.5	41.0	70.0
20.0	25.0	42.0	72.4
21.0	26.6	42.8	75.0
22.0	28.2	44.4	80.0
22.5	29.0	46.1	85.0
23.0	29.9	47.5	90.0
23.1	30.0	48.7	95.0
24.0	31.6	50.0	100.0

STEP 3 Calculate the dollar markup.
RP − C = MU($)
$11.25 − $6.75 = $4.50

STEP 4 Check your work by multiplying the retail price you calculated in Step 2 by the percentage markup on retail price given originally. The answer will match the dollar markup you calculated in Step 3, if your retail price is correct.
RP × MU(%) = MU($)
$11.25 × .40 = $4.50

You can use a **visual** device called the "retail box" (see **Figure 27.3** on page 633) to help you remember this sequence of calculations. This retail box organizes your information and makes it simple to check your work.

> **PRACTICE 4**
>
> Calculate retail price and markup in these two problems by using the retail method. Then double-check your answers to see if your retail price is correct.
>
> **1.** (A) Find the retail price and (B) dollar markup for a box of cereal that costs $3.41 and has a 5 percent markup on retail. (C) Double-check your answer.
>
> **2.** A golf bag costs the retailer $75.60 and has a 60 percent markup on retail. Calculate this golf bag's (A) retail price and (B) dollar markup. (C) Double-check your answer.

Reading Check

Recall Explain the cost method of pricing.

CALCULATIONS FOR LOWERING PRICES

When a business lowers its prices, new sale prices and new markups must be calculated. Let's look at the steps used in calculating markdowns (lowered prices), maintained markups, and the actual sale prices derived from these calculations. Businesses also need to figure out how to price merchandise left in stock, and how to minimize the effects of theft and employee errors.

MARKDOWNS

To reduce the quantity of goods in stock, businesses will sometimes mark down merchandise by a certain percentage (MD[%]). They advertise the markdown percentages, such as 20 to 40 percent off.

LOWERING PRICES

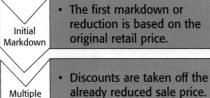

- **Initial Markdown** — The first markdown or reduction is based on the original retail price.
- **Multiple Markdown** — Discounts are taken off the already reduced sale price.

CALCULATING MARKDOWN PERCENTAGES

To calculate a percentage markdown, the dollar markdown is divided by the original price. For example, assume an item had an original price of $25 and a sale price of $19.99. A retailer can advertise the $19.99 sale price as 20 percent off. Here are the calculations: $25 (original price) − $19.99 (sale price) = $5 (markdown); $5 (markdown) divided by $25 (original price) = .2 = 20 percent.

INITIAL MARKDOWN

The first markdown or reduction is based on the original retail price. For example, a music store sells CDs for $16. The store wants to mark down the CDs by 25 percent to make room for new products. An easy way to arrive at the sale price for the CDs is to consider what percentage of the original price will equal the sale price. The procedure requires two steps, but the percentage calculation is so easy that you can probably do it in your head and save some time. Here are the steps involved:

STEP 1 Determine what percentage of the original price will equal the sale price. This is simply a matter of subtracting the markdown percentage from 100 percent.

RP(%) − MD(%) = SP(%)

100% − 25% = 75%

STEP 2 To find the sale price, multiply the retail price by the decimal equivalent of the percentage calculated in Step 1.

RP × SP(%) = SP

$16 × .75 = $12

MULTIPLE MARKDOWNS

When multiple markdowns are considered due to special sales promotions, you take the discounts off the already reduced sale price. For example, assume an item that had an original price of $60 was marked down 20 percent. Customers were offered an additional 15 percent discount off the reduced price. The price customers would pay for that item would be $40.80.

To arrive at $40.80, calculate the first sale price ($60 × .80 = $48), and then calculate the next markdown based on the already reduced price to get the final sale price the customer would pay ($48 sale price × .85 = $40.80).

MAINTAINED MARKUP

When a retailer marks down goods, the markup and markup percentage change. The difference between an item's final sale price and its cost is called the **maintained markup**.

Initial markups need to be higher than maintained markups if a retailer is to meet revenue and profit goals. The initial markup for an item must reflect the fact that during a selling season there will be shrinkage, breakage, employee discounts, and end-of-season markdowns.

On Black Friday retailers offer "early bird specials" in conjunction with other promotions to entice shoppers to shop in the morning. *With large discounts, a consumer may pay only $25 for a sweater that originally sold for $79. How can a retailer offer such big discounts and remain in business?*

Big Cheese Photo/SuperStock

A maintained markup represents the weighted average markup for an item. This is calculated as:

(Total actual revenues received − the cost of goods sold) divided by total actual revenues received.

Price Appeal Prestige pricing is a case of a markup that suggests a high level of quality or status for a product.

Businesses must plan ahead for markdowns. Careful planning helps businesses to remain profitable and competitive in the marketplace. Reductions in the original retail price include employee discounts, shrinkage, damaged goods allowances, and special sales events. For businesses to enjoy the profit margin needed to be successful, they must take these factors into account.

The concept of maintained markup becomes extremely important in planning the original price of the item and all future markdowns.

Let's consider an example. Assume that a video game that cost Zap Electronics $25 to manufacture and originally sold for $50 is marked down 20 percent. The maintained markup (expressed in both dollars and as a percentage) is calculated as follows:

STEP 1 Calculate the new sale price.
100% − 20% = 80%
$50 × .80 = $40

STEP 2 To determine the maintained markup in dollars (MM$), subtract the cost from the sale price.
SP − C = MM($)
$40 − $25 = $15

STEP 3 To determine the maintained markup percentage, divide the maintained markup in dollars by the sale price. *Note*: Round percents to the tenths place.
MM($) ÷ SP = MM(%)
$15 ÷ $40 = .3750
.375 = 37.5%

PRACTICE 6

Now try the same type of computation on your own.

A piece of luggage that costs the retailer $65 to stock sells for $139.99 (retail price). The retailer wants to mark down the luggage by 25 percent. (A) Determine the sale price and (B) maintained markup in dollars, and then (C) calculate the maintained markup percentage. Round the markup percentage to the tenths place.

Anti-theft devices such as security cameras help prevent stock shortages. *What other measures can be taken to reduce a shortage in stock?*

Stock Shortage Prevention

MERCHANDISE REMAINING IN STOCK

Consider a store that sells sweaters, coats, and gloves. When spring arrives, the retailer may be left with unsold merchandise. How does the store determine prices for items returned to inventory? The main consideration is the value of the merchandise. For example, if the store's cost to purchase a sweater from the manufacturer is $40, a 25 percent markup would result in a selling price of $50. This is a simple process if the cost to the store for sweaters is consistent. However, other factors can complicate pricing for inventory remaining in stock. If the cost of sweaters varies, a price planner must consider how much of each type of sweater has been purchased at each cost level. The store then applies the retail method of inventory planning, which takes into account the average cost to the store of all merchandise.

PLANNING FOR STOCK SHORTAGES

When a retailer purchases merchandise from a supplier or manufacturer and various factors prevent the store from recording a sale, profits are negatively affected. Issues such as theft, shoplifting, damaged merchandise, errors in inventory tracking, and mistakes at the checkout counter cost retailers millions of dollars a year in lost sales revenue.

As a result, all businesses take steps to try to limit the problem. You may have noticed anti-theft devices in stores. These can take the form of electronic tags and detectors, special mirrors, and security cameras. Stores should be sure that employees have up-to-date training on stocking and point-of-sale systems. Retailers should also track the rate of "inventory shrinkage" and use this data to help set prices. Stores may choose to mark up merchandise by a greater percentage to account for a high rate of shrinkage.

 After You Read | **Section 27.1**

Review Key Concepts

1. **Discuss** why retailers prefer to use markup percent based on the retail price instead of the markup percent on cost.
2. **Identify** when the markup equivalents chart is used to calculate retail prices.
3. **Explain** when the initial markup is the same as the maintained markup.

Practice Academics

English Language Arts

4. **Explain** the relationship between retail pricing and an income statement. Provide an example.

Mathematics

5. You own a kitchen supply store. What is the retail price of an item that costs the business $45 and has a markup of $25?

> **Math Concept** **Backward Pricing** Markups can be represented as a percent or a dollar value. If the markup is in the form of a percentage, multiplication is used. When it is represented as a dollar amount, simple addition can be used.
>
> **Starting Hint** To solve this problem, add the amount of the markup to the cost to determine the retail price.

 connectED.mcgraw-hill.com

Check your answers.

For help, go to the Math Skills Handbook located at the back of this book.

READING GUIDE

Before You Read

Connect What was the last discounted item you purchased?

Objectives

- **Utilize** a general procedure for figuring discounts and net prices.
- **Calculate** discounts in dollars and percentages.
- **Calculate** net amount.

The Main Idea

Discounts affect the final price a customer will pay. It is essential to learn how to calculate discounts and the net price payable.

Vocabulary

Content Vocabulary
- employee discounts

Academic Vocabulary

You will find these words in your reading and on your tests. Make sure you know their meanings.
- series
- minimum

Graphic Organizer

Draw or print this chart to record procedures for calculating discounts and the net amount payable. Also note examples of discounts offered by employers and vendors.

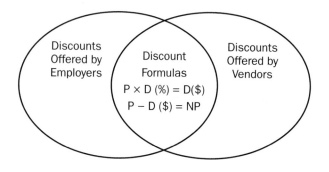

Discounts Offered by Employers

Discount Formulas
$P \times D \, (\%) = D(\$)$
$P - D \, (\$) = NP$

Discounts Offered by Vendors

 connectED.mcgraw-hill.com

Print this graphic organizer.

MARKETING CORE FUNCTION

Pricing

DISCOUNTS

Recall that a discount is a reduction in the price of goods and services sold to customers. You already know markdowns are essentially discounts offered to retail customers. Retailers also offer discounts to their employees as a job benefit. Manufacturers and other vendors offer discounts to their customers to encourage prompt payment and stimulate business. Below is a review of how discounts are calculated.

> **" Discounts and allowances are price adjustments given to employees for purchases and also offered by vendors to their customers. "**

When you want to calculate the discount in dollars and the net price, follow the steps below.

STEP 1 Multiply the price (P) by the discount percentage [D(%)] to get the dollar amount of the discount [D($)].
$$P \times D(\%) = D(\$)$$

STEP 2 Subtract the discount from the price to get the net price (NP), or the amount that the customer will actually pay.
$$P - D(\$) = NP$$
Here is an example: A business is offering a 35 percent discount on an item that sells for $150.
$$\$150 \times .35 = \$52.50$$
$$\$150 - 52.50 = \$97.50$$

When you simply want to know the net amount due, multiply the price by the net price's percentage equivalent, as follows:

STEP 1 Subtract the discount percent from 100 percent. This figure represents the net price's percentage equivalent (NPPE).
$$100\% - D(\%) = NPPE$$
$$100\% - 35\% = 65\%$$

STEP 2 Then multiply the original price by that net price's equivalent percentage to get the net price.
$$P \times NPPE = NP$$
$$\$150 \times .65 = \$97.50$$

As You Read

Compare How do you decide between using net amounts and calculating discounts?

EMPLOYEE DISCOUNTS

Discounts offered by employers to their workers are **employee discounts**. Employee discounts encourage employees to buy and use their company's products. In so doing, businesses hope employees will project confidence in and enthusiasm for those products. This is especially important for the sales staff and customer service representatives, so they can speak about the products from firsthand experience. Employee discounts can range from 10 percent to 30 percent for entry-level employees and as high as 50 percent or more for top-level executives. Some companies even offer discounts to family members of their employees.

Pricing Math

The cost method of pricing and the retail method of pricing are used to calculate markups.

Cost Method of Pricing — Markup Equivalents Table Converts Markups on Retail to Markups on Cost and Vice Versa — Retail Method of Pricing

A variety of discounts are offered to vendors as well as employees.

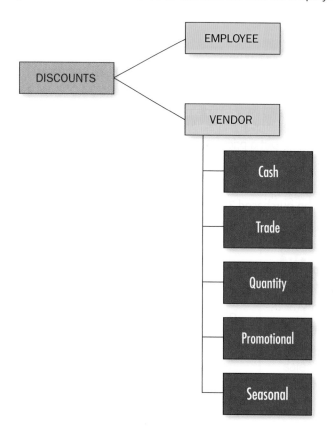

DISCOUNTS
- EMPLOYEE
- VENDOR
  - Cash
  - Trade
  - Quantity
  - Promotional
  - Seasonal

Review and Activities

Written Summary

- Gross profit on an income statement is the same as gross margin or markup in pricing.
- The basic formula for markup is Cost + Markup = Retail Price.
- To calculate a markdown, multiply the markdown percent by the retail price. To arrive at the sale price, subtract the dollar markdown from the original retail price.
- Maintained markup is the difference between sale price and cost.
- One procedure for calculating discounts is to multiply the price by the discount percentage, and then subtract that amount from the original price to find the net price.
- Cash discounts are offered to customers with dating terms such as 2/10, net 30. The 2 represents the discount percentage.
- Quantity discounts may be quoted on a quantity price list that provides unit prices for specific quantities purchased.

Review Content Vocabulary and Academic Vocabulary

1. Write true-or-false statements using each vocabulary word. Ask a partner to determine whether each statement is true or false and explain why.

   Content Vocabulary
   - gross profit (p. 627)
   - maintained markup (p. 635)
   - employee discounts (p. 639)

   Academic Vocabulary
   - convert (p. 633)
   - visual (p. 634)
   - series (p. 641)
   - minimum (p. 641)

Assess for Understanding

2. **Connect** How does profit relate to markup?
3. **Identify** What is the formula that calculates retail price?
4. **Explain** How are dollar and percentage markups calculated?
5. **Process** How do you calculate the discount and net price for a $45 item with a 15 percent discount, and also calculate just the net price?
6. **Calculate** A company is granted a $150 promotional discount for including a product in its flyer. What is the percentage of the discount of a $5,000 invoice?
7. **Identify** Which two groups get trade discounts off the manufacturer's list price?
8. **Define** What is *gross profit*?
9. **Compute** You buy a case of 48 headphones for $240 and sell all of them for $10 each. What is the markup percentage based on retail? What is the percentage of total sales revenue that is the gross profit?

21st Century Skills

Communication Skills

10. Borrowing a Discount You work at a clothing store that offers a 15-percent employee discount. One of the items you and your five friends need for your Halloween costumes is sold at your store. Your friends want you to buy that item in their respective sizes with your employee discount. However, your store policy does not allow this. How would you explain this to your friends?

Financial Literacy Skills

11. Actual Cost Determine the cost for each of the following items. Use the markup equivalents chart to convert the markup on cost to the markup on retail in order to do your calculations.

Item	Markup on Cost	Suggested Retail Price	Cost
Model #510	50%	$15.00	?
Model #512	25%	$72.50	?
Model #514	100%	$99.99	?

Everyday Ethics

12. Special Discounts Many supermarkets offer special discounts on selected items to customers who have frequent-shopper cards. Due to privacy concerns, some customers do not want their purchases traced through such a program. However, they do not want to pay higher prices. One customer with a card pays $2.25 for the loaf of bread, but a customer without the card pays $3.59. What advantage does the card-carrying customer have by percentage? Discuss whether this price advantage is fair.

e-Marketing Skills

13. Budgeting Small Favors Conduct research online to find a favor (small gift) for a charity golf tournament. All 100 participants will receive this favor, and you would like it to be imprinted with the name of the charity. Your budget is $750, but if you spend less, more money goes to the charity. Be sure to include shipping charges and taxes in your calculations, as well as imprint charges. Present three favors, along with your calculations in a chart, and your recommendation in an oral report.

Build Academic Skills

English Language Arts

14. Language Arts Prepare a written advertisement for a special sale on boots and include the total discount savings in dollars and percentage. The original retail price of the boots was $250. The first markdown taken two weeks ago was a 10-percent markdown. Now the store is offering a 20-percent markdown off the already reduced price. Show your calculations in the advertisement.

Science

15. Scientific Inquiry Conduct research to analyze price discounting strategies used by supermarkets and other food stores located geographically close to one another. Are they discounting the same or different products? How much of a discount are they offering? Report your findings and analysis in a written report.

Mathematics

16. Calculate Percentage Markup A card store buys boxes of candy for $5.50 and puts a $4.49 markup on each box. (A) What is the percentage markup on the cost? (B) What is the percentage markup on retail?

> **Math Concept** **Computation** When a markup is given as a dollar amount, dividing the markup value by the cost gives the percentage markup in decimal form.

For help, go to the **Math Skills Handbook** located at the back of this book.

Standardized Test Practice

Directions Read the following questions. On a separate sheet of paper, write the best possible answer for each one.

1. What is the maintained markup percentage for an item that cost a retailer $37 with an original retail price of $85 that was later marked down 15 percent?

   A. 48.0%

   B. 48.8%

   C. 56.5%

   D. 72.3%

2. The markup percentage equivalent for a 100-percent markup on cost is a 50-percent markup retail.

   T

   F

3. The difference between sales revenue and the cost of goods sold is _____.

Test-Taking Tip

When studying in small groups, make sure your study group includes only students who are serious about studying. Some should be at your level of ability or better.

DECA Connection Role Play

Owner
Specialty Shop

Situation Your store sells leather briefcases, purses, and small leather goods. You sell only high-quality items made by established vendors. Your business is successful. You are not content to allow the shop to rest on its reputation.

Always seeking opportunities to add items related to your basic stock items, you recently met a local artist who hand-paints original designs on silk scarves. The artist is seeking a retail outlet to sell the scarves. The artist works with rectangular and square-shaped scarves. The artist will sell the rectangles to your shop for $30.00 each and the squares for $45.00 each. You view this as a great opportunity for your business since the artist is willing to sell to your shop exclusively.

You have decided that you will be able to attain a higher markup on the scarves than on your basic stock items. Your normal markup on basic stock items is 40%. Because of the exclusive nature of the scarves, you feel that you can easily set the retail prices at $70.00 for the rectangles and $90.00 for the squares. Your assistant manager (judge) has asked to explain why you plan to use a higher markup on these items.

Activity You are to explain to the assistant manager (judge) how the additional markup on the scarves can benefit the store's overall profitability and help cover overhead and operating costs.

Evaluation You will be evaluated on how well you meet the following performance indicators:

1. Identify factors affecting a business's profit.

2. Determine cost of product (breakeven, ROI, markup).

3. Demonstrate responsible behavior.

4. Adjust prices to maximize profitability.

5. Describe the nature of profit and loss statements.

 connectED.mcgraw-hill.com

Download the Competitive Events Workbook for more Role-Play practice.

A Pricing Plan
for New Greeting Cards

Greeting cards for Americans can be multicultural, celebrating diverse heritages. How would you design and price a new line of American heritage cards?

Scenario

Your company specializes in greeting cards and related specialties. Its Web site has an e-greeting card capability. Also, retail stores that carry your cards are listed online. The company is considering a new line of paper greeting cards that celebrate American heritages.

The suggested retail price for this new line of cards is between $.99 and $5.99. The retailer's markup will be between 40 and 50 percent of the suggested retail price. The cost of printing the cards depends on the size and quality of paper used. Overhead and marketing expenses also affect pricing. Your company wants a gross profit of 40 percent for e-greeting cards and paper greeting cards sold to retailers. You need to calculate the minimum and maximum costs per card to achieve the gross profit goal for your pricing plan.

The Skills You'll Use

Academic Skills Reading, writing, social studies, researching, and analyzing

Basic Skills Speaking, listening, thinking, and interpersonal

Technology Skills Word processing, spreadsheet, presentation, telecommunications, and the Internet

Your Objective

Your objective is to design and price a potentially profitable new line of greeting cards that feature monthly American heritage observances.

STEP 1 Do Your Research

Conduct research to find out the months during which various American heritages are observed or celebrated. Identify competing greeting card companies, as well as retailers and Internet companies that sell greeting cards. As you conduct your research, answer these questions:

- What are the competitors' retail prices for paper and e-greeting cards?
- Which American heritages do the competitors' cards celebrate?
- What are the political, economic, socio-cultural, and technological factors that could impact the designs, pricing, and marketing of American heritage-themed greeting cards?
- What do the product costs have to be in order to price the new line competitively?

Write a summary of your research.

STEP 2 Plan Your Project

Now that you have completed your research, you need to begin planning your project.

- Conduct a PEST analysis.
- Conduct a SWOT analysis to identify the strengths, weaknesses, opportunities, and threats involved with this new greeting card line.
- Design sample greeting cards that feature various American heritages.
- Write a pricing plan for the new line of greeting cards by using your knowledge of pricing strategies and profit margins to decide how the greeting cards should be priced.
- Write a rationale for your plan with supporting research and suggestions for marketing the new product line.

STEP 3 Connect with Your Community

- Interview the owner or manager of a store that carries greeting cards to see where your new product line might fit in the store's merchandising scheme.
- Take notes during your interview, and transcribe your notes after your interview.
- Test your sample greeting card designs and suggested retail prices on ten people to see how receptive they are to your ideas.

STEP 4 Share What You Learn

Assume your class is the product manager and staff that will decide if your plan has the potential to be implemented by the company.

- Present your findings in an oral presentation. Be prepared to answer questions.
- Use software to create a slide presentation to accompany your oral presentation. Include one slide for each topic in your pricing plan and written rationale.
- Share your greeting card designs.

STEP 5 Evaluate Your Marketing and Academic Skills

Your project will be evaluated based on the following:

- Your product designs with regard to cultural diversity within the United States
- Your pricing plan's potential for being profitable
- Accurate calculations to determine the cost necessary to achieve suggested retail prices
- Research data to support the rationale for your plan
- Organization and continuity of presentation
- Mechanics—presentation and neatness
- Speaking and listening skills

MARKETING CORE FUNCTIONS

 Market Planning

Pricing

Marketing Internship Project Checklist

Plan

✓ Conduct research on companies that make and sell greeting cards in retail stores and on the Internet.

✓ Conceive a pricing plan for a new line of greeting cards that you design for a specific target market.

Write

✓ Write a pricing plan for the new line of greeting cards, using your knowledge of pricing strategies and profit margins.

✓ Explain how the results of the PEST analysis help you decide on prices.

✓ Explain supporting research and suggestions for marketing the new product line.

Present

✓ Present research that supports your rationale for pricing strategies and product designs.

✓ Present your pricing plan.

✓ Display samples of your greeting card designs.

  connectED.mcgraw-hill.com

Evaluate Download a rubric you can use to evaluate your final project.

my marketing portfolio

Internship Report Once you have completed your Marketing Internship Project and oral presentation, put your written report and a few printouts of key slides from your oral presentation in your Marketing Portfolio.

Research and Develop a Pricing Plan Research and create a complementary product line with an American heritage theme for kites, flags, figurines, coffee mugs, T-shirts, or other products that target a specific ethnic group. Does your research data support the rationale for the product line and suggested pricing plan? Is your pricing plan calculated correctly and does it achieve a satisfactory profit margin? Are your product designs culturally appropriate for the target market? Prepare a written report and an oral presentation.

MARKETING INFORMATION MANAGEMENT

Marketing Internship Project

A Marketing Research Study

Essential Question How can marketing research help improve a company's products for its target market?

In order to develop successful products and avoid costly marketing mistakes, companies rely on accurate marketing information gathered from primary and secondary sources. Marketing research studies analyze results by demographic factors such as income, age, and ethnicity.

Project Goal

In the project at the end of this unit, you will develop an effective marketing research study for a mobile phone company.

Prepare for the Project

As you read this unit, use this checklist to prepare for the Marketing Internship Project at the end of this unit:

- Consider the various mobile phone companies and the products they offer.
- Make a list of mobile phone features.
- Visit mobile phone retailers to observe merchandising and promotional strategies.

 **connectED.mcgraw-hill.com**

Project Activity
Complete a worksheet activity about conducting a marketing research study.

AMERICAN MARKETING ASSOCIATION

Marketing research links the consumer, customer, and public to the marketer through information.

MARKETING CORE FUNCTIONS IN THIS UNIT

 Marketing Information Management

Market Planning

What do I need to know today?

There are moments in life

when sound bites just won't do.

Moments when you want to know,

really know.

And for that you need to go

beneath the headlines

and beyond the chatter.

That's where we live.

Where tireless research reveals not just facts,

but opportunities.

Where you're exposed to perspectives

that enable you to make the right choices

for your family,

your career,

your life.

To live every day

informed,

prepared,

inspired.

THE WALL STREET JOURNAL.
live in the know

SHOW WHAT YOU KNOW

Visual Literacy

The Wall Street Journal publishes business, economic, and financial news along with information about technology, personal finance, and consumer trends. *How could you use information from a news provider to help inform a marketing research project?*

Chapter 28

Section 28.1
Marketing Information

Section 28.2
Issues in Marketing
Research

marketing research

SHOW WHAT YOU KNOW

Visual Literacy Marketing research is the process of obtaining information needed to make effective marketing decisions. Marketers use this information to create business plans, solve problems, and make decisions about products. *What kinds of business decisions do you think marketers make as a result of conducting marketing research?*

Discovery Project

The Purpose of Marketing Research

Essential Question How can research be used to gain data about marketing opportunities?

Project Goal

You and a classmate are employed to perform marketing research for a new electronic product that your team identifies. Your team has been asked to conduct a research project to gain information about the potential market for the product. You have been asked to provide a written report to management about the target market for the product. You will also report on some marketing information systems and methods used in marketing research.

Ask Yourself...

- What is your product, who uses your product, and what competitive products currently exist?
- Where will your potential customers purchase the product?
- What types of media (print, broadcast, electronic) do your potential customers use?
- How will you organize your written report?

 Synthesize and Present Research Synthesize your research by reporting about the target market for the product and some marketing information systems and methods used in marketing research.

 connectED.mcgraw-hill.com

Activity
Get a worksheet activity about marketing research.

Evaluate
Download a rubric you can use to evaluate your project.

DECA Connection

DECA Event Role Play

Concepts in this chapter are related to DECA competitive events that involve either an interview or role play.

Performance Indicators The performance indicators represent key skills and knowledge. Your key to success in DECA competitive events is relating them to concepts in this chapter.

- Explain the nature of marketing research.
- Explain the nature of marketing research problems/issues.
- Assess information needs.
- Explain the nature of marketing research in a marketing information management system.
- Prepare simple written reports.

DECA Prep

Role Play Practice role-playing with the DECA Connection competitive-event activity at the end of this chapter. More information on DECA events can be found on DECA's Web site.

READING GUIDE

 Before You Read

Connect Why do you think some businesses fail while others succeed in the marketplace?

Objectives

- **Describe** the purpose of marketing research.
- **Explain** the characteristics and purposes of a marketing information system.
- **Identify** procedures for gathering information using technology.

The Main Idea

Marketing research provides information to create a business plan, solve problems, and make decisions about products.

Vocabulary

Content Vocabulary
- marketing research
- marketing information system
- database marketing
- database

Academic Vocabulary

You will find these words in your reading and on your tests. Make sure you know their meanings.
- obtained
- overall

Graphic Organizer

Draw or print this chart for taking notes about the main concepts of marketing research.

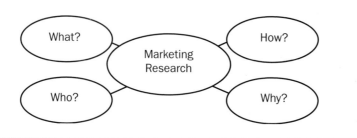

connectED.mcgraw-hill.com

Print this graphic organizer.

MARKETING CORE FUNCTION

Marketing Information Management

Marketing Information

DEFINING MARKETING RESEARCH

A major health and beauty manufacturer marketed its brand of toothpaste in overseas markets. The brand was advertised in Southeast Asia by saying that "it whitens teeth." However, sales were disappointingly low. What went wrong?

Even though the product had a global focus, it did not have global appeal, at least not in Southeast Asia. Careful marketing research would have revealed that, as a cultural tradition, much of the local population chews betel nuts, which blacken teeth. Few Southeast Asians purchased the product.

> **Success in business relies on effective marketing research.**

Marketing research involves the process and methods used to gather information, analyze it, and report findings related to marketing goods and services. Businesses use marketing research to identify marketing opportunities, solve marketing problems, implement marketing plans, and monitor marketing performance.

Marketing research can apply to any aspect of marketing. Coca-Cola®, a food-and-beverage manufacturer, might research the potential sales and market for a new product line of fruit drinks. Wells Fargo®, a bank, might conduct customer satisfaction research on the quality of its mortgage lending service.

Market research and marketing research are often confused. *Market* research is a narrow concept that deals specifically with the gathering of information about a market's size and trends. *Marketing* research is a broader concept that includes a wider range of activities. While it may involve market research, marketing research is a more general, systematic process that can be applied to a variety of marketing issues. Marketing research includes areas such as research into new products, and new methods of distribution, such as through the Internet.

The main purpose of marketing research is to obtain information. Researchers need to know about the preferences, opinions, habits, trends, and plans of current and potential customers. This information helps marketers in many ways. Before developing a product, marketers conduct research to determine the product that customers want. The research minimizes potential losses when introducing the new product. Consumers accept only one out of every ten new products introduced into the marketplace. So, it is important to gain information about consumer likes and dislikes.

Marketing research is used by companies to do the following:

► Determine consumers' attitudes and preferences.
► Test product features.
► Determine market size and growth potential.
► Learn about competitive products.
► Determine buying cycles.
► Understand how the company is perceived by the public.

As You Read

Analyze Compare and contrast the terms *market research* and *marketing research*.

WHY IS MARKETING RESEARCH IMPORTANT?

Businesses that do not pay attention to different markets and to what consumers are buying and why are likely to make costly mistakes. Because of the high failure rate of new products, marketing research can make or break a business plan.

The information **obtained** from research helps businesses increase sales and profits. Research answers questions about what products to produce, at what price to sell the products, who will buy the products, and how to promote the products.

Research also helps businesses solve marketing problems and gauge the potential of new product ideas. For example, Stouffer's® spent almost 13 years doing marketing research and development before starting its Lean Cuisine™ product line. Stouffer's studied consumers' interest in health and dieting. They conducted consumer panels to find out what dieters liked and disliked about diet meals. Using the information, the company developed its product, tested its package design, and held pilot sales of the product in several large cities before national distribution. The product was a tremendous success, with more than $125 million in sales after the first year of national distribution.

Research also helps a company keep track of what is happening with its current markets. Through research, a company can determine its major competitors, what its competitors are offering, which products consumers prefer, and if customers are satisfied with those products.

DETERMINING THE VALUE OF INFORMATION

Information can be useful, but what determines its real value to a business? The value of information is generally determined by the following:

▶ A company's ability and willingness to act on the information.

▶ The accuracy of the information.

▶ The level of uncertainty that would exist without the information.

▶ The amount of variation in the possible results.

▶ The level of risk consumers are willing to take on a new product or service.

▶ The reaction of competitors to any decision improved by the information.

▶ The cost of the information in terms of time and money.

WHO USES MARKETING RESEARCH?

Small businesses usually do not have separate research specialists or departments. There, marketing research is done informally by the owners, managers, and employees. A small business would likely find large-scale marketing research too costly. Instead they may depend on friends, family, or their customers to point out what is working and what is not. However, small businesses have access to the ever-growing amount of information available on the Internet.

If it is in their budget, some businesses may hire outside service providers who specialize in marketing research. Sometimes actual costs and findings are shared by a number of companies in large syndicated research studies. Larger companies often have in-house research departments and marketing personnel to plan and conduct marketing research. There are more than 2,000 research companies in the U.S. Full-service companies design and conduct surveys, tabulate and analyze data, and prepare reports.

Interviewing-services companies collect data through interviews. Some interviewing companies specialize in multilingual survey services.

An initial search online will reveal a seemingly endless variety of research collection tactics. For example, a restaurant may offer a free appetizer to customers who complete a telephone or online survey about their dining experience. You may have noticed an increasing number of pop-up surveys on the Web sites you visit.

Trade associations representing various manufacturers, wholesalers, and retailers conduct marketing research. For example, industry trade associations, such as the National Retail Federation, collect industry data to help their members understand the markets for their products. Nonprofit organizations, such as hospitals, conduct patient satisfaction surveys to improve on programs and services. State and federal government agencies conduct research to gather information on a variety of issues and concerns.

The National Retail Federation conducts an annual *Holiday Consumer Intentions and Actions* survey. *Why do national associations conduct marketing research surveys?*

The Most Popular Toys

MARKETING INFORMATION SYSTEMS

The data collected in marketing research must be sorted and stored so that the results can be put to good use. Many businesses have sophisticated marketing information systems. These systems are used to organize, collect, and store marketing research data for future decisions. A **marketing information system** is a set of procedures and methods that regularly generates, stores, analyzes, and distributes information for making marketing and other business decisions. Timely marketing information provides a basis for decisions about product development or improvement, pricing, packaging, distribution, media selection, and promotion.

Most marketing information systems rely heavily on data about current customers, **overall** product sales reports, and inventory levels. Marketers use marketing information systems to design advertising campaigns, develop promotional plans, and sell directly to customers. (See **Figure 28.1**.) Data that should be part of a marketing information system include the following:

▶ Customer profile data, such as the results of previous marketing studies regarding buying behavior, shopping patterns, customer demographics, and lifestyles research.

▶ Company records, such as sales results, expenses, supplier data, and production schedules.

▶ Competitors' records, such as their prices, products, and market share.

▶ Government data, such as price trends, new regulations and laws, and economic projections.

▶ Marketing research reports that are produced and sold by research firm.

DATABASE MARKETING

Information technologies have made the collection and analysis of data for decision making much easier. **Database marketing**, or customer relationship management (CRM), is a process of designing, creating, and managing customer lists. These customer lists contain information about individuals' characteristics and transactions with a business.

Customer lists are developed from customer touch points, such as face-to-face sales, direct-mail responses, telephone or e-mail purchases, service requests, or Web-site visits. Marketing lists can also be obtained through third-party companies that specialize in selling databases of names and addresses to specific markets. Once a customer list is developed, marketers can use it for locating, selecting, and targeting customers with special programs and services.

CONSUMER DATABASES

Information about consumers and their buying habits are stored in computer databases. A **database** is simply a collection of related information about a specific topic. Typical sources from which the information is obtained are charity donation forms, application forms for any free product or contest, product warranty cards, subscription forms, and credit application forms.

REI®, an outdoor recreational products retailer, has a database of people to whom it sends its catalogs. American Express® maintains a database of its card members and their addresses. This database also includes what they buy, where they buy it, where they dine out, and how much money they spend. The company uses the information to send their card members special, customized offers on products, hotels, restaurants, and travel.

 Reading Check

Recall What are some marketing information systems?

FIGURE 28.1 | Obtaining Market Research Data

Public and private organizations provide valuable information for exploring the market potential for products and services. *Why is the data on this metropolitan statistical area (MSA) found in this chart, for example, important for marketing information systems?*

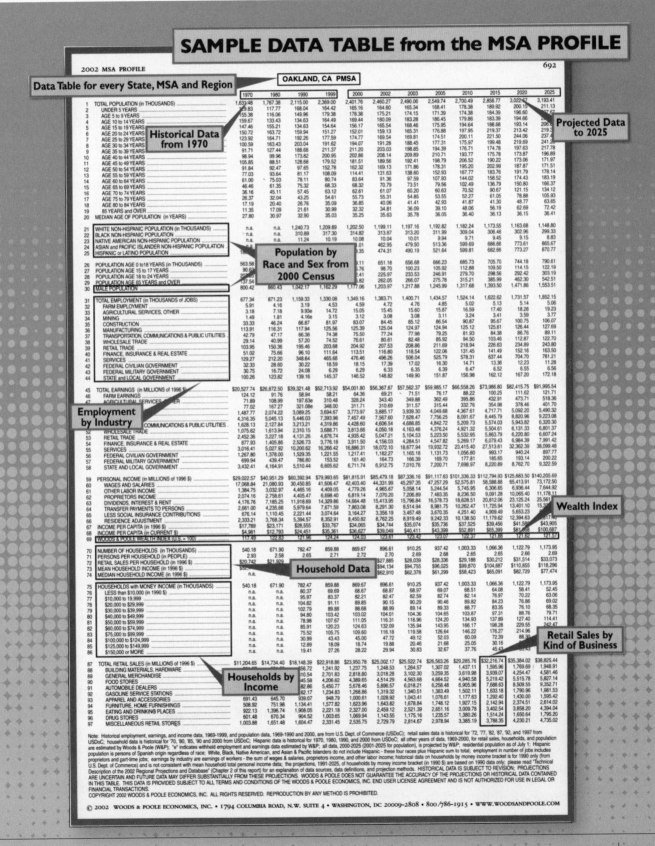

SAMPLE DATA TABLE from the MSA PROFILE

Note: Historical employment, earnings, and income data, 1969-1999, and population data, 1969-1990 and 2000, are from U.S. Dept. of Commerce (USDoC); retail sales data is historical for '72, '77, '82, '87, '92, and 1997 from USDoC; household data is historical for '70, '80, '85, '90 and 2000 from USDoC; Hispanic data is historical for 1970, 1980, 1990, and 2000 from USDoC; all other years of data, 1969-2000, for retail sales, households, and population are estimated by Woods & Poole (W&P); "e" indicates withheld employment and earnings data estimated by W&P; all data, 2001-2025 (2001-2025 for population), is projected by W&P; residential population as of July 1; Hispanic population is persons of Spanish origin regardless of race; White, Black, Native American, and Asian & Pacific Islanders do not include Hispanic; four races plus Hispanic sum to total; and Hispanic in number of jobs includes proprietors and part-time jobs; earnings by industry are measure of workers - the sum of wages & salaries, proprietors and other labor income; historical data on households by money income bracket is for 1990 only (from U.S. Dept. of Commerce) and is not consistent with mean household total personal income data; the projections, 1991-2025, of households by money income bracket (in 1990 $) are based on 1990 data only; please read "Technical Description of the 2002 Regional Projections and Database" (Chapter 2 of this report) for an explanation of data sources, data definitions, and projection methods. HISTORICAL DATA IS SUBJECT TO REVISION; PROJECTIONS ARE UNCERTAIN AND FUTURE DATA MAY DIFFER SUBSTANTIALLY FROM THESE PROJECTIONS. WOODS & POOLE DOES NOT GUARANTEE THE ACCURACY OF THE PROJECTIONS OR HISTORICAL DATA CONTAINED IN THIS TABLE. THIS DATA IS PROVIDED SUBJECT TO ALL TERMS AND CONDITIONS OF THE WOODS & POOLE ECONOMICS, INC. END USER LICENSE AGREEMENT AND IS NOT AUTHORIZED FOR USE IN LEGAL OR FINANCIAL TRANSACTIONS.
COPYRIGHT 2002 WOODS & POOLE ECONOMICS, INC. ALL RIGHTS RESERVED. REPRODUCTION BY ANY METHOD IS PROHIBITED.

© 2002 WOODS & POOLE ECONOMICS, INC. • 1794 COLUMBIA ROAD, N.W. SUITE 4 • WASHINGTON, DC 20009-2808 • 800/786-1915 • WWW.WOODSANDPOOLE.COM

Chapter 28 · Marketing Research | **659**

USING TECHNOLOGY TO GATHER INFORMATION

Specialized equipment, loyalty programs, and computer software are increasingly used to gather database information. Barcode scanners at point-of-sale terminals provide information on sold merchandise and existing inventory levels.

CUSTOMER LOYALTY PROGRAMS

Many businesses create special loyalty programs to assist in data collection by providing "valued customer cards" to customers.

A loyalty program offers discounts and other rewards to encourage customers to shop at a particular retailer. This concept benefits both the retailer and the customer. Customers who participate in loyalty programs can save money, and as a result, they are likely to return to the same retailer. Examples include Staples® *Teacher* and Ace® *Hardware Reward* programs. Customers who choose to enroll in such programs fill out an application that generally requires a minimal amount of identifying or demographic data, such as their name and address. In return, the customer is given a loyalty program card.

The cards are visually similar to credit or debit cards. Loyalty cards may also be called rewards cards, points cards, advantage cards, or club cards. Cards usually have a barcode or magnetic stripe for easy scanning. Small key ring cards are often used for convenience and easy access. Cardholders are typically entitled to either a discount on the current purchase, or an allowance of points that can be used for future purchases. The business in turn collects data on household demographics, lifestyles, and purchase behavior.

Loyalty The first loyalty card program was started by the Safeway® supermarket chain in 1998 to track customer purchase behavior.

COMPUTER SOFTWARE

Existing company software can track activity online and combine that information with existing customer databases.

COOKIES

Online retailers may automatically upload small data files called "cookies" to customers' computers. Cookies keep track of how often and how much time a person spends at a Web site or views an ad. Businesses use this type of data to target an audience with ads for products. The ads can then appear at certain times and in specific geographical locations.

DATA-MINING SOFWARE

Data-mining software can be purchased from specialized companies to analyze existing and external business databases. For example, sales of a product during a particular period can be compared with sales when the product is moved or displayed in a different store location. Data-mining software also collects information from other customer databases to match and identify patterns that help businesses promote their products or advertise them in more timely or effective ways.

CONSUMER PRIVACY

Privacy is a central element of the Federal Trade Commission's (FTC) consumer protection mission. In recent years, advances in computer technology have changed the way information is collected. Technology has helped make it possible for detailed information about people to be compiled and shared with greater ease and cost effectiveness than ever before. This provides benefits for society as a whole and for individual consumers as well. For example, it is easier for law enforcement to track down criminals and for banks to prevent fraud. Consumers can learn about new products and services, which allows them to make better-informed purchasing decisions.

As personal information has become more accessible, it is important that everyone—companies, associations, government agencies, and consumers—take precautions to protect against the misuse of personal information and the risks of hacking. Another part of the FTC's mission is to educate consumers and businesses about the importance of personal information privacy, including the security of personal information. Under the FTC Act, the Commission guards against unfairness and deception by enforcing companies' privacy promises about how they collect, use, and secure consumers' personal information.

Many companies that collect information about their customers sell the information to others. New homeowners may find their mailboxes are loaded with offers from landscapers and furniture stores.

This is likely because the mortgage companies sold the homeowners' information to local businesses that specialize in home and garden services. This exchange of information among businesses has led to complaints of invasion of privacy.

Other businesses offer clients the choice of being added to mailing lists. Some businesses, such as Yahoo!®, go a step further and have strict bans on selling data from customer registration lists. The government, however, has regulations regarding protecting the privacy of consumers. For example, banks and hospitals offer detailed privacy statements that ensure the protection of clients' personal information. Marketers often defend the need to gather information about customers and their buying habits by stating that this data helps improve customer service.

 After You Read   **Section 28.1**

Review Key Concepts

1. **Explain** why marketing research is important.
2. **Identify** what organizations conduct marketing research.
3. **Describe** a customer database.

Practice Academics

Social Studies

4. Conduct research to acquire information about the concept of database marketing. Write a one-page paper on how database marketing improves customer relationships.

Mathematics

5. You work for a medical supplies company that spends $38,000 annually for researching new product ideas. $5,700 of that money was spent researching a new tool for surgery. What percentage of the overall research dollars does this represent?

Math Concept **Number and Operations: Percents** A percent is a ratio that compares values to 100. A percent can also be thought of as a part of a whole. When figuring what percentage a value is of another value, divide the part by the whole. This gives the decimal equivalent of the percent.

Starting Hints To solve this problem, divide $5,700 by the total amount spent on researching new product ideas to get the decimal equivalent of the percent. Multiply the decimal by 100 to get the percent it represents.

 connectED.mcgraw-hill.com

Check your answers.

For help, go to the **Math Skills Handbook** located at the back of this book.

READING GUIDE

Before You Read

Predict What would happen if marketing research was not used in product development?

Objectives

- **Identify** the methods of conducting marketing research.
- **Discuss** trends and limitations in marketing research.

The Main Idea

Different types of marketing research improve a business's ability to solve problems and successfully market products and services.

Vocabulary

Content Vocabulary
- quantitative research
- qualitative research
- attitude research
- market intelligence
- media research
- product research

Academic Vocabulary
You will find these words in your reading and on your tests. Make sure you know their meanings.
- anticipate
- associated

Graphic Organizer

Draw or print this chart to note the differences between quantitative research and qualitative research.

Quantitative Research
1.
2.

Quantitative and Qualitative Research

Qualitative Research
1. Attitude Research
2.

 connectED.mcgraw-hill.com

Print this graphic organizer.

MARKETING CORE FUNCTION

 Marketing Information Management

Issues in Marketing Research

TYPES OF MARKETING RESEARCH

Marketing research is usually divided into two broad types of research: quantitative and qualitative. **Quantitative research** answers questions that begin with "how many" or "how much." To help you remember, think of the word "quantity," which is an amount or a number of something. Quantitative research usually gathers information from large samples of people. Quantitative research uses surveys or questionnaires to obtain numbers and responses of people to certain activities. The surveys can be answered independently or by an interviewer. They can be answered either in writing or orally.

Qualitative research focuses on smaller numbers of people (usually fewer than 100) and tries to answer questions that begin with "why" or "how." Qualitative research relies heavily on in-depth, one-on-one interviews, small group settings, and observations. Rather than prepared survey questions constructed ahead of time, this research uses focused discussions about a topic. Qualitative research is not limited to products. It is also conducted to answer questions about attitudes and behaviors, market segments, advertising media, brands, prices, employees, and every other aspect of marketing.

Most marketing research combines quantitative and qualitative methods. Sometimes many companies or organizations share actual costs and findings to perform marketing research in large syndicated research studies.

As You Read

Identify What types of marketing research do successful businesses use?

ATTITUDE RESEARCH

Attitude research, also known as *opinion research*, is designed to obtain information on how people feel about certain products, services, companies, or ideas. Attitude research is used in marketing to ascertain opinions among consumers and the public in general. It is also used within organizations when employee attitude surveys are conducted. Satisfaction studies conducted by mail surveys or telephone interviews are the most common ways to get at individuals' opinions. Customers are usually asked to rate "how satisfied" they are with a good or service they purchased or used.

> **The type of research that businesses conduct depends on the problem that they are trying to solve.**

Opinion polls are another example of attitude research. An opinion poll is a survey of public opinion from a particular population sample. Carefully designed questions are asked of the sample group, then the answers are compiled to represent the opinions of a population. Gallup Consulting® conducts opinion polls on politics, elections, business and the economy, social issues, and public policy. Based on random samples of the population, opinion poll results can be generalized for the entire population. A business considering a major expansion might be interested in the attitude of the general population toward the economy.

MARKET INTELLIGENCE

Market intelligence, also known as *market research*, is concerned with the size and location of a market, the competition, and segmentation within the market for a particular product. Businesses use existing market data and new research to assemble a profile of present and potential customers, competitors, and the overall industry. Market intelligence helps define potential target markets for a particular good or service and helps identify how to reach potential customers.

A company's current sales and projected sales data are part of market intelligence. Sales data help businesses project the potential sales for a product and **anticipate** problems related to future sales. Sales trends for various products may also be compared to determine whether a product's sales are increasing or declining.

SALES FORECASTING

Business owners need to make predictions in order to plan investments, launch new products, and decide when to stop producing products. For most businesses, sales forecasting is crucial.

Sales forecasting is an attempt to estimate the future sales of an existing product. A company calculates a total estimate of the market for a product, analyzes its own sales and the sales of its competitors, and then estimates its individual share of the market. The share that is assigned to a particular company is called its "market share," or sales penetration of the market.

Based on these research findings, a business can then take steps to try to increase its market share. Businesses can increase their sales penetration by making changes in the product, its pricing, promotion efforts, or distribution strategy.

Estimation of market share and research into market segmentation are used for new products in both consumer and industrial markets. The goal of market share and segmentation studies is to investigate potential markets and define the specific characteristics of the target market.

Businesses often use software to assist with sales and market forecasting. These computer programs are able to analyze current market data and then use this information to predict future sales.

Syndicated Research Firms

There are more than 2,000 research companies in the United States, categorized as either interviewing services or full-service companies. *Based upon content in this ad, what kind of market research services are offered by Zoomerang™?*

Meet Nick. Zoomerang Sample Member Nº 2,487,103. He's a dad. An anthropologist. A poker player. And a sucker for coming-of-age movies. He's ready to tell you all about that—and more than 500 other aspects of his life, opinions, preferences, and tastes.

He's one of more than 2.5 million people who make up Zoomerang Sample—the fastest, smartest way to reach your target consumers with pinpoint accuracy. Whether you're doing an online survey or an online focus group, with Zoomerang Sample you'll stay in touch with the evolving tastes and preferences of your target market. So you can draw sharper insights and make more informed decisions. Just ask Nick.

1 (888) 760-3182 or visit us at www.zoomerang.com

 zoomerang

Get Your FREE Sample Info Kit 1(888) 760-3182

Zoomerang and Zoomerang Sample are part of MarketTools, Inc. Zoomerang Sample is sourced from MarketTools' ZoomPanel of more than 2.5 million participants.

ECONOMIC FORECASTING

Economic forecasting is an attempt to predict the future economic conditions of a city, a region, a country, or other part of the world. This kind of research requires extensive knowledge of economic statistics and trend indicators.

Several federal agencies collect information on key economic indicators. Economic indicators are used in the analysis of past and current economic performance to help predict future performance. These indicators include new building construction, industrial production, the stock market, inflation and interest rates, money supply, and consumer and producer price indexes.

Most businesses rely on government data to predict economic conditions, and then they adjust their business activities depending on the economic outlook. Businesses use this information to help plan for long-range expansion. This research helps to determine whether to cut costs when unfavorable economic conditions are predicted. These conditions may include higher interest rates or raw materials costs.

Private companies, such as Woods and Poole Economics®, specialize in long-term economic and demographic projections. The database contains projections through the year 2040 for every state, region, county, and metropolitan statistical area (MSA). This information helps marketing researchers analyze the makeup of the population. To do this, they collect information about age, race, gender, employment by industry, personal and household income, and retail sales by type of business.

MEDIA RESEARCH

Media research, also known as *advertising research*, focuses on issues of media effectiveness, selection, frequency, and ratings. Businesses conduct research to determine which media are most effective for getting an advertising message to a particular market.

Media research is used to measure brand awareness, advertisement recall, brand image, effectiveness of advertising copy, and audience size. These studies are used to measure attitudes and opinions toward a brand and its image.

They also measure how well individual ads are remembered, and whether print, broadcast, or Internet advertising increased product sales.

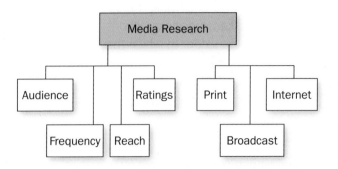

MEDIA ADVERTISING MEASURES

Important statistics for media measurement include *audience*, *frequency*, *reach*, and *ratings*. Audience is the number of homes or people exposed to a particular advertising medium. Frequency is the number of times a viewer in the audience sees or hears an ad. Reach is the percentage of the target audience that will see or hear an ad at least once. Ratings are the total number of audience impressions delivered over a set period of time.

To obtain these important media advertising measures, businesses request information from the print, broadcast, and electronic media of interest to them. In most cases, the information received would include a rate card. The rate card lists the advertising costs, its circulation or viewership figures, deadline dates, and other requirements for submission of an advertisement. Other information might involve the age, income, interests, hobbies, occupations, and attitudes of readers, subscribers, or viewers. Another way to measure advertising research on the various media is to subscribe to *Standard Rate and Data Service*® (SRDS), which publishes media rates and data for the advertising industry.

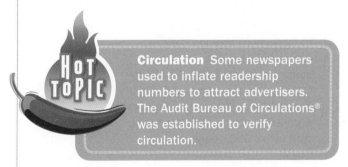

Circulation Some newspapers used to inflate readership numbers to attract advertisers. The Audit Bureau of Circulations® was established to verify circulation.

RESEARCHING PRINT MEDIA

Marketing researchers can use different techniques to discover people's reactions to an advertisement. To determine the ad's effectiveness, readers are asked specific questions. They may be asked about the extent to which they noticed the ad, remembered it, and **associated** it with the advertised brand. The ad is also measured on its ability to change the consumer's beliefs, attitudes, or intended behavior.

Using consumer panels is another technique for measuring print advertising effectiveness. Consumer panels, also called "focus groups," are groups of people who are questioned periodically to provide information on research issues. A consumer panel can be comprised of a cross-section of people or individuals who share common characteristics, such as senior citizens, single parents, college-educated adults, or teenagers. Oral, written, or observed behavioral responses are recorded to indicate panel members' reactions to an advertisement.

Readership in print media is measured by surveys or estimated by circulation. Established in 1914, the Audit Bureau of Circulations® is a nonprofit organization of advertisers, advertising agencies, newspaper, and magazine publishers. It provides audits on average circulation, average print, and online readership circulation, total combined audiences, and total Web-site users for newspapers and magazines.

Mediamark Research and Intelligence® (MRI) and the Simmons Market Research Bureau® are syndicated research companies. They provide audience and media data. MRI's *Survey of the American Consumer*™ is a source of audience data for the U.S. consumer magazine industry. Simmons provides *Shopper Behavior Graphics*™, which provides data for retail mailing lists and computer software for media behavior. These companies conduct reading studies to see if participants can recall a magazine logotype, have read the magazine, and can remember where they read it during a recent period.

MARKETING CASE STUDY

Giant Eagle's Fuelperks

The grocery store chain Giant Eagle® recently started selling more than food and pharmacy items. They now have GetGo® fuel stations at or near many of their locations. Giant Eagle offers fuel discounts to customers through their fuelperks! program. Customers scan their Giant Eagle Advantage Card® when they shop at Giant Eagle. With fuelperks! customers earn 10 cents per gallon off fuel with every $50 spent at Giant Eagle.

For five years

Giant Eagle offered its customers another discount called foodperks!® Customers who used the foodperks! program saved money on their purchases in the grocery store.

Giant Eagle is able to track and monitor its customers' purchases and offer discounts and coupons when they complete a transaction.

Math

Calculate You recently signed up for a rewards card and began earning gas discounts at your market. You spent $263.82 on groceries in the past month. Regular unleaded gas is sold at $2.89 per gallon at your local gas station. How much will you pay per gallon if you use your discount?

RESEARCHING BROADCAST MEDIA

Most broadcast ad testing research is done on television commercials. Testing research can use quantitative or qualitative research techniques, such as personal interviews, theater tests, in-home testing, or focus groups, to get reaction to planned TV advertisements.

Nielsen Media Research, Inc.®, provides audience measurement information for the television industry. Nielsen estimates the audience by measuring a national sample of the viewing habits of 26,000 people in 10,000 homes. Nielsen's measurement information is recorded by "people meters" on TV sets, set tuning meters, and diaries that monitor viewing.

Nielsen counts the number of viewers in meter-equipped households to get the number of households using TV, the share of the audience that is tuned to a particular station, and the rating, or percentage of viewers, for a particular television program. With time-shifted viewing, Nielsen also measures on demand and streaming programs on remote devices. Broadcast, cable, and satellite networks, distributors, and advertisers use the data to decide on which programs they advertise.

The Arbitron Ratings Company® assembles important data on radio advertising. Arbitron produces radio audience measurements and sells software that analyzes advertising expenditure data. Arbitron surveys radio listeners to obtain the size and audience in 294 local markets serving more than 4,600 radio stations. It also has developed a "portable people meter" to compile audio broadcasts from a variety of broadcast media. The information provides audience listening data to a station and identifies tuned-in programs.

RESEARCHING INTERNET MEDIA

The effectiveness of Internet advertising is often measured with tracking studies. Tracking studies can be either Web-centric or user-centric. The Web-centric method logs the total number of people who have visited a Web site or views an online ad. The *interaction*, *click-through*, and *dwell rates* for particular ads are stored on the Internet provider's network. Advertisers can then decide on the Web site or online advertising that was most effective.

The user-centric method focuses on demographic and lifestyle profiling. It often involves metering software placed in ads that track computer usage and Web-site visits. User-centric surveys and tracking software identify the types of people visiting a Web site to get audience and lifestyle profiles. Advertisers then target audiences by Web-surfing behavior.

WEB ANALYTICS

There are many services, such as WebTrends, Adobe Analytics, and Google Analytics, that can analyze Web activity and do tracking studies. They create detailed statistics about traffic and sales for businesses and organizations. Google Analytics is the most widely used service on over half of the top Web sites.

Google Analytics tracks visitors from all referrers, or sources, such as search engines like Bing, Yahoo, or Google, and social networks like Facebook. Reports show the number of direct visits to the particular Web site and from referred sites. Importantly for marketers, Web analytic services can track and analyze display advertising, pay-per-click networks, and e-mail marketing. An analysis shows how well a Web page is performing, where visitors come from, how long they view a page, and from what geographical location. It can also segment visitors by various demographic characteristics.

Some of Google Analytics' features include AdWords, search engine optimization, and e-commerce reporting. Adwords' paid service posts a few lines of advertising copy above, below, or beside a list of search results on Google. An image can also accompany the short ad copy. *Remarketing* is also used in connection with AdWords, allowing a business's ad to display on other Web sites once an individual has visited the business's Web site. Search engine optimization identifies the most effective key words to use on a Web site so that visitors will find it when doing a search. E-commerce reporting tracks sales activity and performance, showing transactions, and revenue.

However, many people have ad filtering programs on their computers, such as Adblock, which prevents traffic and users from being tracked. In addition, any individual can block or delete tracking cookies, which are tiny pieces of data uploaded to your computer when you visit a Web site. Nevertheless, Web analytics provides technological tools for marketers to more effectively design and manage online marketing campaigns.

PRODUCT RESEARCH

Product research centers on evaluating product design, package design, product usage, and consumer acceptance of new and existing products. Many new products and their packages are designed, tested, changed, and introduced each year. Product research is also conducted to collect information about competing products.

NEW PRODUCT RESEARCH

Concept testing is typically used in the early stages of product development. Concept testing attempts to get information on the product, pricing, advertising, and product positioning before product introduction. Concept testing, product positioning, and pricing studies are frequently done with focus groups or in-depth interviews to get initial consumer reaction to a description of a product, rather than to particular product.

Early product development also focuses on brand research. Brand research uses word and personality association techniques to develop brand names. Branding research attempts to develop product names that will closely relate to consumers' feelings and attitudes about the product. After a new product has been developed, other marketing research methods are used.

Product placement tests are a way of measuring new product acceptance. One type of product placement test has consumers try a product and give their opinions as to quality and performance. Product testers are asked questions about specific aspects of the product. A tester of body lotion may be asked about the lotion's texture, scent, consistency, oiliness, and absorption into the skin. Another method of product placement is to place products on retail shelves to observe the rate of customer sales.

Choice studies or blind tests are sometimes used for new products. A choice study or blind test allows a product or package to be evaluated without the aid of brand names. The products are packaged generically and identified by letter or number. Consumer panels (focus groups) or individuals give feedback on new products.

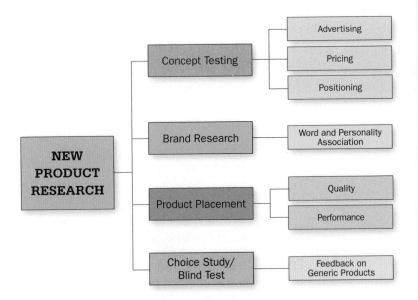

EXISTING PRODUCT RESEARCH

Customer satisfaction questionnaires and interviews are used to gather information about existing goods and services for both the industrial and consumer markets. Industrial satisfaction surveys focus on products utilized by business and manufacturing firms. Customer satisfaction surveys provide a rich data source for businesses interested in customer attitudes toward existing retail products and services.

A consumer who makes a major purchase may be contacted by a firm that specializes in customer satisfaction studies. A leading company in this field is J.D. Power and Associates, which is well-known for its ratings on vehicle quality, reliability, and dependability. If you buy a new car, you may get a follow-up phone call, e-mail, or letter from J.D. Power asking about your buying experience and your impressions of the quality of your vehicle. The company compiles research gained from thousands of these customer surveys into data showing which automakers offer the most reliable and dependable models. Information like this can help guide consumers in their buying decisions. It can also assist automakers in determining what factors are most important to their customers.

Reading Check

List What areas does media research study?

Brave New Robots

For decades inventors have been dreaming up mechanical gizmos to perform the tedious tasks of daily life. The dream became a reality with robotics. In fact, the robotics industry may eventually rival the automobile and computer industries.

Dream Machines Hoping to create a billion-dollar industry, South Korea has ambitious plans for two robot theme parks and a variety of "service robots" to work in housekeeping, school teaching, firefighting, and elderly care fields. The Korea Advancement Institute of Science and Technology partnered with a U.S. robotics company to produce a robot called "Einstein HUBO" (humanoid robot). Designed with Einstein's face, it moves, talks, recognizes facial expressions, and even "flashes a dashing smile."

Here are some entry-level phrases that are used in conversations about marketing all over the world.

English	Korean
Hello	Anyonghashimnika
Bye	Anyonghekashipsheo
Yes/No	Nay/Anyo
Please	Butakhamnida
Thank you	Kamsahamnida
You're welcome	Chunmaneyo

English Language Arts

Write Korea hopes to develop a "wearable robot." Conduct research on this product. Write ten questions for a focus group testing this new product.

TRENDS IN MARKETING RESEARCH

The nature and scope of marketing research is rapidly changing to keep pace with a changing marketplace. The trend toward a global marketplace means increased international competition for U.S. companies, which must improve or change products frequently to hold on to their customers.

In this environment product quality and customer satisfaction are the keys to business success. To maintain customer satisfaction, companies need to understand their customers' needs. They also need information that tells them how well they are meeting those needs. Research that measures these qualities has become the fastest growing form of marketing research.

Another important trend is the use of both internal and external information in managing a business. Total quality management (TQM) programs place a premium on gathering and using database research in improving business operations.

MARKETING RESEARCH IN A GLOBAL MARKETPLACE

A company doing business internationally must consider different countries' cultures that could affect a product's success. This factor requires research to determine the cultural preferences and traditions of the parts of the world in which they want to market their products.

GLOBAL STRATEGIES

Different strategies are used based on the part of the world in which the company is marketing. A fast food company like McDonald's® focuses on marketing popular domestic items with a twist that appeal to the diners in the international location. For example, the menu at a McDonald's in India might feature a Maharaja Mac®, which is a Big Mac® made of lamb or chicken meat because most Hindu people do not eat beef.

GOING GLOBAL WITH THE 4 P'S

The four Ps of marketing—product, price, placement, and promotion—are all affected as a company transitions into the global marketplace.

▶ **Product** A global company is one that can create a single product and only have to alter certain elements for different markets. For example, Coca-Cola® uses the same bottle shape for all markets, but they change the bottle size and the language on the packaging.

▶ **Price** Price will always vary from market to market. Price is affected by the costs of local product development, ingredients, and delivery.

▶ **Placement** Placement decisions must take into account the product's position in the marketplace. For example, a high-end product would not be distributed at a "dollar store" in the U.S. Conversely, a product promoted as a low-cost option in France would not be sold in an expensive boutique.

▶ **Promotion** Promotion, especially advertising, is generally the largest expense in a global company's marketing budget. If the goal of a global company is to send the same message worldwide, then delivering that message in a relevant, engaging, and cost-effective way is the challenge.

LIMITATIONS OF MARKETING RESEARCH

Few companies can conduct as much marketing research as they would like to conduct. The amount of information that can be gathered is limited by the amount of money and time a company can afford to spend on the equipment and number of personnel needed to conduct the research.

Marketing managers make multiple and overlapping strategic decisions in the process of identifying and satisfying customer needs. They make decisions about potential opportunities, target market selection, market segmentation, planning and implementing marketing programs, marketing performance, and control.

Marketing research information also has its limitations. The decisions are complicated by interactions between the controllable marketing variables of product, pricing, promotion, and distribution.

Marketing managers must also factor into this mix the consumers themselves. Customers in a test-market situation may say they like a particular product, and they may indicate that they would strongly consider buying it, but there is no guarantee they will actually purchase the product when it goes on the market.

In addition, fast-changing markets may not allow time for research. There is a time lag between identifying the need for a product, collecting the marketing research, and presenting the findings so the business can decide whether to produce the product. Business conditions, customer buying habits, and customer preferences can change.

Despite these limitations, marketing research provides valuable information. Businesses will continue to rely on marketing research to obtain the best possible information about customers and the marketplace.

 After You Read | **Section 28.2**

Review Key Concepts

1. **Differentiate** between attitude and market intelligence research.
2. **Explain** the purpose of media research.
3. **Explain** the purpose of product research.

Practice Academics

English Language Arts

4. Perform library or online research to investigate a country of your choice and develop a two-page paper on its location, demographics, traditions, lifestyles, and culture. Include recommendations for conducting market research in your selected country.

Mathematics

5. You plan to purchase a health club targeted to professionals aged 22 to 55 in your town. Research shows that 3,250 households in your target market spend $900 a year on fitness activities. There is one other health club that serves 30 percent of your target market. What would be your annual sales forecast for the center?

Math Concept **Problem Solving: Multi-Step Problems** When solving problems that require multiple steps, list the information given and the information for which you will be solving. This will clarify the relationship between the two.

Starting Hints To solve this problem, determine the percent of households you hope to service by subtracting 30 percent from the total market of 100 percent. Multiply the decimal equivalent of this percent by the total number of households to determine the number of households in the target market. Multiply the number of households in the target market by the amount they spend on fitness activities each year to determine the annual sales forecast.

 connectED.mcgraw-hill.com

Check your answers.

For help, go to the Math Skills Handbook located at the back of this book.

Marketing Research

Marketing information is used to identify marketing opportunities, solve marketing problems, implement marketing plans, and monitor marketing performance.

Marketing research methods include attitude research, market intelligence, media research, and product research.

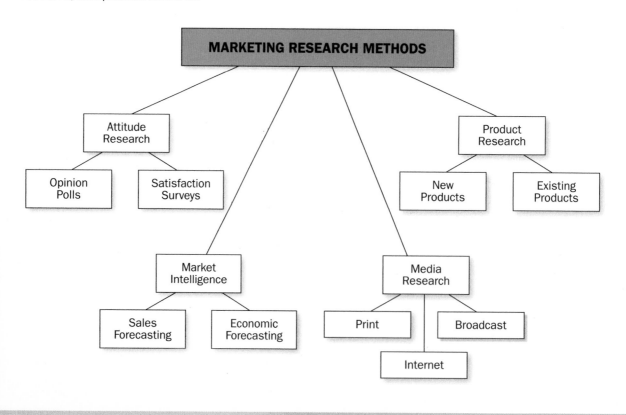

Review and Activities

Written Summary

- Marketing research involves the marketing function that links the consumer, customer, and public to the marketer through information.
- Marketing information is used to identify marketing opportunities, solve marketing problems, implement marketing plans, and monitor marketing performance.
- A marketing information system is a set of procedures and methods that regularly generates, stores, analyzes, and distributes marketing information for use in making marketing decisions.
- Marketing research is usually divided into two broad types of research: quantitative and qualitative.
- Marketing research involves the process and methods used to gather information, analyze it, and report findings related to marketing goods and services.
- The nature and scope of marketing research are rapidly changing to keep pace with a changing marketplace.
- Marketing research information provides much information but does have limitations.

Review Content Vocabulary and Academic Vocabulary

1. Write your own definition for each content and academic vocabulary term.

Content Vocabulary

- marketing research (p. 655)
- marketing information system (p. 658)
- database marketing (p. 658)
- database (p. 658)
- quantitative research (p. 663)
- qualitative research (p. 663)
- attitude research (p. 663)
- market intelligence (p. 664)
- media research (p. 665)
- product research (p. 668)

Academic Vocabulary

- obtained (p. 656)
- overall (p. 658)
- anticipate (p. 664)
- associated (p. 666)

Assess for Understanding

2. **Identify** What is the purpose of marketing research?
3. **Characterize** What are the characteristics and purposes of a marketing information system?
4. **Sequence** What are the procedures for gathering information using technology?
5. **Contrast** How does quantitative research differ from qualitative research?
6. **Explain** What are the methods of conducting marketing research?
7. **Suggest** What is one trend affecting marketing research?
8. **Define** How do you define the term *market intelligence*?
9. **Create** How might one limitation of marketing research affect a business? (Identify the limitation.)

21st  Century Skills

Teamwork Skills

10. Honest Answers? You have a part-time job in the marketing research department of a large corporation. You and three coworkers are gathering information through mailed surveys. Your supervisor wants each of you to complete at least 30 surveys a day, which can be difficult. One coworker adds responses to some incomplete surveys that have missing responses in order to reach the quota of 30 surveys. What should you do? Discuss with a partner.

Financial Literacy Skills

11. Calculating Household Market Research You work for a full-service marketing research firm. You have been asked to calculate the total amount spent on market research. If $753 is spent on each of 2,400 households, what is the total amount?

e-Marketing Skills

12. Mobile Phone Research Imagine that you are employed in an interviewing-services research firm that collects data through the Internet, by telephone, by mail, and by in-person interviews. You are assigned to investigate the use of mobile phones for collecting interview data for clients. Investigate the process and benefits of using mobile phones for data collection.

- List the steps that you must take to sell the concept to your clients.
- What potential benefits might data collection by mobile phone give clients?
- What are some methods you could use to collect data on mobile phones?
- How can customers' information be studied and analyzed on a large scale?

Build Academic Skills

Social Studies

13. Data-Mining Technologies Perform library and online research using at least three different sources of information on data-mining technologies and software applications. Compare and contrast the views of marketing professionals with privacy advocates on the benefits and disadvantages of data mining. Identify the sources used and outline the benefits and disadvantages in a one-page outline.

English Language Arts

14. Nature and Scope of Marketing Research Review a current or online article from *The Wall Street Journal, Inc., BusinessWeek, Forbes, Money, Advertising Age, Brandweek*, or your local newspaper. Find one current marketing research activity and write a one-page report on the nature and scope of the activity.

Mathematics

15. Calculating Costs for Direct Mail Your company plans to send a marketing questionnaire to 40 percent of the names on a mailing list of 20,000 people. The mailing list was purchased from another company for $0.20 per name. Each questionnaire costs $0.10 to print; mailing costs are $0.55 each; and the cost of writing the questionnaire, analyzing the information, and preparing the report is $15,000. What is the total cost?

Math Concept **Multi-Step Problems** When solving problems that require multiple steps, make a list of the information given in the problem and information for which you are solving. This will clarify the relationship between the two.

For help, go to the **Math Skills Handbook** located at the back of this book.

Standardized Test Practice

Directions Read the following questions. On a separate piece of paper, write the best possible answer for each one.

1. Which of the following types of marketing research includes information about sales and economic forecasting?
   A. Attitude and opinion research
   B. Market intelligence
   C. Media research
   D. Product research

2. The amount of research information collected is limited by time, money, and personnel.
   T
   F

3. What type of research answers the questions of "how many" and "how much"?

Test-Taking Tip

To cope with the stress of taking a test, view the test as an opportunity to show how much you have studied and to receive a reward for the work you have done.

DECA Connection Role Play

Business Information Manager Catalog/Online Gifts Company

Situation You work for a well-established gift items business. The company has been in business for more than 40 years. During the early years, business was conducted exclusively through a mail-order catalog. Then the Internet led the business to add a Web site and online catalog for customer orders.

Business is good, but the rising costs of paper, printing, and postage are causing management to make a careful assessment of the print catalog that is mailed to customers six times a year. The big questions are the following: Should the company stop production of the print catalog and do business from only the Web-site catalog? Or should the company publish the print catalog less frequently? Or should the company continue to publish the catalog as it is now?

The company president (judge) has asked you to assess the situation and make recommendations about the print catalog. Before you can make any recommendations about this issue you must have additional information. You know that your company will need to conduct some marketing research in order to make an informed decision about the print catalog. You feel that this important decision warrants the hiring of a marketing research firm.

Activity You are to list several points that need to be addressed and note how marketing research can help provide the information your company needs. You will then present your ideas and information to the company president (judge).

Evaluation You will be evaluated on how well you meet the following performance indicators:

1. Explain the nature of marketing research.
2. Explain the nature of marketing research problems/ issues.
3. Assess information needs.
4. Explain the nature of marketing research in a marketing information management system.
5. Prepare simple written reports.

 connectED.mcgraw-hill.com

Download the Competitive Events Workbook for more Role-Play practice.

conducting marketing research

SHOW WHAT YOU KNOW

Visual Literacy The personal interview is one method of collecting data for market research. *What do you think might be the advantages and disadvantages to this method of data collection?*

Discovery Project

The Marketing Survey

Essential Question How can marketing surveys obtain important data for identifying customer's needs and wants?

Project Goal

You and a classmate have been hired to conduct marketing research for a vacation home manufacturer. Your team has been asked to develop a ten-question survey to gather information to identify people who currently own a home in your area, their willingness to purchase a vacation home, and their basic demographics. You have been asked to design a survey that addresses this information for the company.

Ask Yourself...

- What questions will your team ask on the survey?
- How will you determine home ownership and vacation home interest?
- What types of demographic questions will you ask?
- How will you organize your survey instrument?

 Synthesize and Present Research Synthesize your research by designing a ten-question survey that identifies people who currently own a home in your area and their willingness to purchase a vacation home.

 connectED.mcgraw-hill.com

Activity
Get a worksheet activity about marketing surveys.

Evaluate
Download a rubric you can use to evaluate your project.

DECA Connection

DECA Event Role Play

Concepts in this chapter are related to DECA competitive events that involve either an interview or role play.

Performance Indicators The performance indicators represent key skills and knowledge. Your key to success in DECA competitive events is relating them to concepts in this chapter.

- Describe methods to design research studies.
- Describe options businesses use to obtain marketing-research data (e.g., primary and secondary research).
- Discuss the nature of sampling plans (i.e., who, how many, how chosen).
- Evaluate questionnaire design (e.g., types of questions, question wording, routing, sequencing, length, layout).
- Explain the use of descriptive statistics in marketing decision making.

DECA Prep

Role Play Practice role-playing with the DECA Connection competitive-event activity at the end of this chapter. More information on DECA events can be found on DECA's Web site.

READING GUIDE

Before You Read

Reflect What research do you do when you are planning to buy a new product?

Objectives

- **Explain** the steps in designing and conducting marketing research.
- **Compare** primary and secondary data.
- **Collect** and interpret marketing information.
- **Identify** the elements in a marketing research report.

The Main Idea

Marketing research provides insight for developing strategies that will increase sales and profits.

Vocabulary

Content Vocabulary
- problem definition
- primary data
- secondary data
- survey method
- sample
- observation method
- point-of-sale research
- experimental method
- data analysis

Academic Vocabulary

You will find these words in your reading and on your tests. Make sure you know their meanings.
- determine
- specific

Graphic Organizer

Draw or print this chart to record the steps for conducting marketing research.

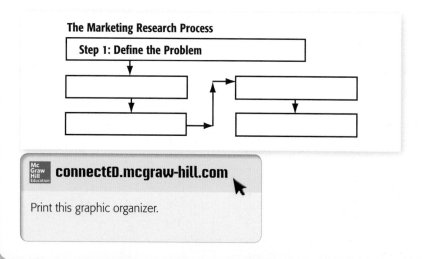

The Marketing Research Process

Step 1: Define the Problem

connectED.mcgraw-hill.com

Print this graphic organizer.

MARKETING CORE FUNCTION

Marketing Information Management

THE MARKETING RESEARCH PROCESS

The five steps for conducting marketing research are defining the problem, obtaining data, analyzing the data, recommending solutions, and applying the results. Each step is performed in this order to arrive at solutions to a problem or research issue. **Figure 29.1** on page 680 provides more details about each step in the research process.

As You Read

Predict What would happen if one of the steps of research were omitted?

STEP 1: DEFINING THE PROBLEM

The most difficult step in the marketing research process is defining the problem. **Problem definition** occurs when a business clearly identifies a problem and what is needed to solve it. The business identifies a research question and the information that is necessary to answer it.

For example, a convention and resort center wants to know whether its staff, services, and facilities are meeting the needs of its guests. The business needs this information so that it can continually improve its services as a resort and convention destination.

> **❝ Conducting marketing research improves decision making and creates opportunities. ❞**

With the problem defined, the researcher can create objectives for the study that will help answer the research problem. Objectives might include determining customer satisfaction in the following categories: reservation procedures, accommodations, guest services, and meeting and recreational facilities.

The actual questions that will be included in the research instrument are formulated by first considering the objectives. You will learn more about writing questions later in this chapter. For now, you should know that objectives and questions must correlate with one another. Here are two examples:

▶ **Objective:** Determine the level of guest satisfaction with the resort and convention center's facilities.
Question: On a scale of 1 to 5, with 1 being very poor and 5 being excellent, how would you rate the quality of the meeting facilities? (Please offer a rating for each of the facilities you used.)

▶ **Objective:** Determine levels of satisfaction with the resort and convention staff services.
Question: On a five-point scale, with 1 being very unsatisfied to 5 being very satisfied, how would you rate the staff's courtesy? How would you rate the staff's friendliness?

These questions are necessary so that guests' ratings of the center's facilities and staff services can be analyzed separately. If each question was not included in the research instrument, each of the objectives could not be accomplished.

Every business faces limits in the form of time and financial resources. Therefore, all companies need to obtain the information necessary to solve the problems they identify and make the marketing decisions that are most important.

FIGURE 29.1 The Marketing Research Process

Five Research Steps Marketing research helps businesses find solutions to problems. There are five steps in the marketing research process. It begins with defining the problem or research issue. It ends with applying the results of the research. Following the steps in sequence is important because each step depends on the steps that come before it. *What can researchers do after the data are analyzed?*

1 Defining the Problem

The problem or research issue is identified and goals are set to solve the problem.

2 Obtaining Data

Researchers obtain data from primary and secondary sources.

3 Analyzing Data

Researchers compile, analyze, and interpret the data.

4 Recommending Solutions

Researchers come up with potential solutions to the problem and present them in a report.

5 Applying the Results

The research results are put into action.

STEP 2: OBTAINING DATA

The second step in the marketing research process is obtaining data. During this second step, data are collected and examined in terms of the problem or problems being studied. The word *data* means facts. There are two types of data used in marketing research: primary and secondary. **Primary data** are data obtained for the first time and used specifically for the particular problem or issue under study. **Secondary data** have already been collected for some purpose other than the current study. Secondary data are less expensive to collect than primary data. Therefore, it is most cost effective for a company to first decide what secondary data it can use.

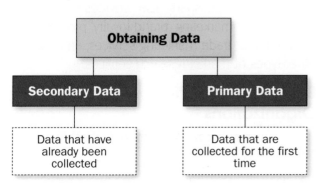

SOURCES OF SECONDARY DATA

Secondary data are obtained from both internal sources (inside the company) and external sources (outside the company). An excellent source of internal secondary data is the marketing information system of a business. A marketing information system is an internal way to collect data used to measure monthly sales, **determine** the geographic distribution of customers, track customer buying patterns, and identify popular items on the market. Secondary data are usually collected from a number of sources.

Internet Sources

The Internet has increased the availability of secondary data from a variety of sources. Some secondary information is available for free through a company's home page. A company's description of its products, services offered, locations, sales revenue, number of employees, product specifications, and pricing is often available. However, Web site information is used primarily for promotional purposes. So, any information obtained from Web sites should be verified through other, more objective sources.

MARKETING CASE STUDY

Palm Prē with the "Flow"

Smartphone maker Palm, Inc.® , needed to make a splash in the competitive smartphone market with its new Prē phone, which takes aim at the best-selling iPhone® and Blackberry® devices. So, it created a quiet, subtle ad campaign around a woman who tells viewers of the phone's benefits. One commercial in particular, though, went beyond subtle understatement.

Going with the Flow

In the "Flow" spot, a woman sits on a stone in the middle of a beautiful green field. She is surrounded by hundreds of people in orange suits doing choreographed movements. The screen switches to aerial views, revealing patterns and wave-like movements the dancers are creating, as the woman asks, "Isn't it beautiful when life simply flows together?"

English Language Arts

Analyze Define the problem that marketers might have identified as step two of the marketing research process for the Palm Prē product. List methods of obtaining marketing research data that Palm most likely used to find out which features shoppers want in a new smartphone. In what ways do you think Palm's commercial reflects marketing research for the product and its potential customer base?

Digital dossiers, which provide company profiles on public corporations, income statements, and balance sheets, are available online for a fee. Business clearinghouses, such as Hoover's™ Online, Dow Jones Factiva®, Standard and Poor's NetAdvantage®, LexisNexis®, and Mergent Online™, are a few examples.

U.S. and State Government Sources

State departments of commerce and small business development centers can provide useful information. Data collected by U.S. government agencies can be accessed on the Internet for free or for a small fee. Such data may include population demographics, specific markets, industries, products, economic news, export information, and legislative trends. The Small Business Administration, U.S. Department of Commerce, U.S. Census Bureau, U.S. Securities and Exchange Commission, and the Bureau of Labor Statistics can also provide secondary data.

The *United States Census* and the *Statistical Abstract of the United States* contain hundreds of tables, graphs, and charts that can be useful when analyzing information. These publications feature data such as income, personal expenditures, age, and family size, in areas as small in size as ZIP code areas.

Specialized Research Companies

An active and growing number of specialized research companies, or syndicated services, also offer secondary data for business needs in print and electronic formats. Specialized companies sell demographic data, five-year forecasts, consumer purchase information, business data, census information, and consumer classification reports to businesses.

An example is Mediamark Research and Intelligence (MRI), which provides comprehensive demographic, lifestyle, product usage, and exposure data to all forms of advertising media. MRI is the nation's leading producer of multimedia audience research for advertisers, agencies, and magazines. The company also provides research for consumer marketing, brand loyalty, promotional opportunities, trade marketing services, and many other types of market research services.

Business Publications and Trade Organizations

Business publications, such as *Forbes*, *Business Week*, the *Wall Street Journal*, and *Marketing Management Journal*, are also good sources of secondary data. National and statewide trade associations often publish secondary data in articles, reports, and books.

Important information can be obtained from a variety of secondary data sources like this Web site. *What benefits and risks are involved in the use of secondary data?*

Examples of trade associations that provide marketing research include the Advertising Research Foundation, American Association for Public Opinion Research, American Marketing Association, Council of American Survey Research Organizations, and the Marketing Research Association. Check the *Small Business Sourcebook* or the *Encyclopedia of Business Information Sources* for major books, trade journals, and organizations in **specific** business categories.

Advantages of Secondary Data

The greatest advantage of secondary data is that it can be obtained easily. Secondary data are on the Internet, and often available free of charge. The data are also in corporate, public, and college libraries. The data are also available for purchase from syndicated services. The U.S. Census Bureau can provide nationwide data that would cost any firm a great deal of time and money to research on its own.

Disadvantages of Secondary Data

There are two major disadvantages associated with secondary data. First, the existing data may not be suitable or specific for the problem under study. For example, little or no secondary data exist for new or innovative products.

The other disadvantage is that secondary data may sometimes be inaccurate. Federal census data are collected every ten years. As a result, projections based on the most the recent census may not be correct for the current year. Despite these limitations, a business should first investigate free or low-cost secondary data to solve a marketing problem.

SOURCES OF PRIMARY DATA

When marketing researchers cannot find information they need from secondary data, they collect primary data. Primary research data can be obtained through company research projects or specialized research organizations (see **Figure 29.2**). Large companies often have their own marketing research staff to conduct primary research. However, both large and small companies use research organizations. National research organizations contract with businesses and organizations to provide attitude and opinion, market, media, and product research services. The Nielsen Company®, Kantar Group®, Arbitron Inc.®, J.D. Power and Associates®, and Opinion Research Corporation® are some of the leading research organizations in the U.S. Primary data are collected using three methods: the survey method, the observation method, and the experimental method.

FIGURE 29.2 Primary Data Collection Methods

Collecting Primary Data This chart shows the most common methods used to collect primary data by market research firms. *Why do you think Internet surveys have replaced the telephone as the most popular method of data collection?*

Method of Survey Data Collection
Internet
Telephone (landline + cell)
Mail
In-Person
Mall Intercept
Hybrid (combines two or more methods)

The Survey Method

The **survey method** is a research technique in which information is gathered from people through the use of surveys or questionnaires. The surveys can be answered independently or by an interviewer, either in writing or orally. It is the most frequently used way of collecting primary data.

When designing a survey, marketers determine the number of people to include in a survey. Researchers can survey the entire target population if it is small. This is called a "census." However, researchers usually cannot survey the entire target population because it is too large, and time and money are limited. Instead, researchers use a sample of the target population to get results.

A **sample** is a part of the target population that represents the entire population. The size of the sample depends on the amount of money the company has to spend and the degree of accuracy that is needed. Generally, the larger the sample, the more accurate are the results.

After determining the size of the population to survey, a marketer must decide what type of survey to conduct. Surveys can be conducted in person, by phone (using personal calls and prerecorded messages), by mail (regular and email), or by using the Internet. When the marketer decides exactly how to conduct the survey, he or she then writes the questions according to the type of survey that will be used.

Census The *Census of 1790* was the first known survey in the United States. Marketing research for consumers was initiated in 1923 by Arthur Nielson.

Internet, Mail, and Telephone Surveys

Internet surveys are now the primary way of collecting primary data. Internet-based research allows for real-time data collection, multiple-choice questions, and open-ended, text-based answers. They are also less intrusive than phone calls.

E-mail surveys are surveys sent to a sample of people who are on a list of electronic-mail addresses. Respondents reply through e-mail. A *Web survey* is a survey uploaded to a Web site. People are asked to participate by visiting the designated Web site to answer questions online.

Data collection with e-mail and Web surveys is quick, since responses are automatically tabulated when they are completed. Disadvantages include having e-mail addresses and lists that are not accurate. Also, some people dislike receiving uninvited e-mail surveys, or lack computer proficiency or access to the Web. These disadvantages contribute to low response rates.

A standard *mail survey* is efficient and relatively inexpensive. Respondents are generally honest in their responses. Respondents are not interrupted with a phone call or e-mail message, and they can complete the survey at their leisure.

The *telephone survey* is a quick way to reach a potentially large audience (96 percent of households have phones). The use of mobile and smartphones for survey research is increasingly being used. However, the telephone method is somewhat limited by *Do Not Call* registry rules.

To increase response rates, some companies combine techniques, such as mail, Internet, and telephone invitations to take part in surveys.

The Interview Method

The personal interview involves questioning people face-to-face for a period of 10 to 30 minutes. Interviews can be conducted in individual homes and offices. But to reduce costs, researchers usually conduct interviews at central locations. Because centralized personal interviews first began in shopping malls, they are called "mall intercept interviews." A major advantage of interviews is that it is easier to get people to respond to personal interviews than to Internet, telephone, or mail surveys.

Another form of personal interview is the focus group interview. A focus group interview involves 8 to 12 people who are brought together to evaluate advertising, a particular product, package design, or a specific marketing strategy under the direction of a skilled moderator.

The moderator must direct the discussion to accomplish the objectives of the study. Focus group facilities usually include conference and observation rooms with audio and video equipment.

The Observation Method

The **observation method** is a research technique in which the actions of people are watched and recorded either by cameras or by observers. Properly performed and recorded observations supply better results than those obtained with survey techniques.

Mystery shopping is a form of observation that views interactions between customers and employees. A mystery shopper is a researcher who poses as a customer and goes into a business to observe employees and operations. A restaurant, for example, might want to observe the wait staff in their approach, sales presentation, product knowledge, and suggestion selling techniques.

Observation research is faster than conducting personal interviews, plus people are unaware that they are being observed, so they are acting as they normally would. This type of research is also cost effective.

Point-of-sale research is a powerful form of research that combines natural observation with personal interviews to explain buying behavior.

Point-of-sale researchers observe shoppers to decide which ones to choose as research subjects. Participants can be chosen based upon variables, such as time of day (morning, afternoon, or evening) or the product that was purchased.

After observation, researchers approach the selected shoppers and ask them questions. Shoppers can easily remember the reason why they purchased a product because they have just made the decision to buy. Researchers might also gain additional input from other family members or shopping companions.

The Experimental Method

The **experimental method** is a research technique in which a researcher observes the results of changing one or more marketing variables while keeping all the other variables constant under controlled conditions. The experimental approach can be used to test new package designs, media usage, and new promotions.

For example, a manufacturer may want to compare two different colors for its new laundry detergent packaging. One group of consumers is shown the proposed package color. The other group is shown the same product with different package colors. Each group's responses are measured and recorded. Because only the package colors have been changed, the different responses are attributed to the color.

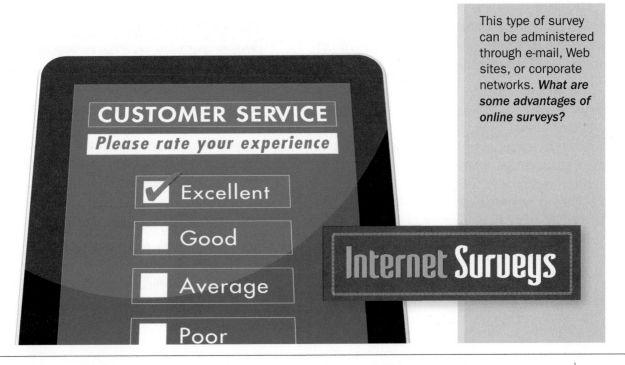

This type of survey can be administered through e-mail, Web sites, or corporate networks. *What are some advantages of online surveys?*

Experimental research can provide useful information. However, it is used less frequently than other methods. It is used less often because people usually respond differently in actual buying situations.

Impact of Technology

Computer technologies have had a tremendous impact on marketing research. Quantitative and qualitative survey research can be done on the Internet through e-mail and Web surveys, computer-aided Web interviewing, and focus group sessions. Audio-visual effects, graphics, company logos, and brands can be included in Internet surveys.

Computer-assisted, telephone-dialing surveys allow a prerecorded voice to qualify a respondent, and then to ask a series of survey questions. Automated dialers can be used to increase the number of telephone survey responses by placing multiple calls and automatically rejecting those with busy signals, answering machines, and voicemail.

Fax broadcasting allows businesses to send questionnaires to a select group of fax numbers. Interactive voice response is similar to voicemail as callers are greeted by a recorded voice that leads them through a series of questions. Responders use the telephone keypad to provide their answers.

STEP 3: ANALYZING THE DATA

The third step in the marketing research process is data analysis. **Data analysis** is the process of compiling, analyzing, and interpreting the results of primary and secondary data collection.

A-P Super Service, Inc., created a customer survey about the quality and efficiency of the auto mechanics' repair service. A-P Super Service received 120 completed surveys. Answers were organized so that the percentage of men and women responding to each question was clearly shown. Data were cross-tabulated to determine such things as how men and women differ in their perceptions of the service. The answers to a question about the quality of service might be presented as shown in the following table. The number of respondents is given in parentheses after the question.

Question: How would you rate the quality of service provided by A-P Super Service, Inc.? (N = 120)

Rating	Men	Women
Excellent	30%	60%
Good	15%	10%
Average	20%	20%
Fair	20%	5%
Poor	15%	5%

As you can see, female customers of A-P Super Service, Inc., have a more favorable impression of the quality of service than the male customers have. This information shows the owner that the shop's image among its male customers needs to be improved.

DATA MINING

Data mining is a computer process that uses statistical methods to extract new information from large amounts of data. A database may contain subtle relationships or patterns that only a mathematical search process can identify. Competitive, demographic, site, and location data obtained through data mining assists in forecasting and predicting sales opportunities.

Data mining also allows researchers to generate lists of potential survey respondents and to design surveys for primary data collection. Marketing information data is stored, sorted, and used to improve new and existing products and services.

STEP 4: RECOMMENDING SOLUTIONS TO THE PROBLEM

Conclusions drawn from research are usually presented in an organized and detailed written report. Recommendations must be clear and well supported by the research data. A typical research report includes the following elements:

- ▶ Title page
- ▶ Acknowledgments of people who assisted in the research effort
- ▶ Table of contents
- ▶ List of tables, figures, charts, and graphs

- Introduction (includes the problem under study, its importance, definitions, limitations of the study, and basic assumptions)
- Review of the research information (including the results of any secondary data reviewed for the research effort)
- Procedures used (research technique or techniques used to obtain primary data)
- Findings
- Recommendations
- Summary and conclusions
- Appendixes
- Bibliography

In evaluating any research, managers may find that the study was inconclusive and that additional research is needed. They may also conclude that the research suggests specific changes or new courses of action.

After the research has been completed and any actions are taken, a business should carefully monitor the results of those changes. A business needs to know whether the specific actions taken are successful. The research effort can be considered a success if the resulting decisions lead to higher profits in the form of increased sales, greater efficiency, or reduced expenses.

 After You Read | **Section 29.1**

Review Key Concepts

1. **Name** four sources of secondary data information for research studies.
2. **Identify** the three methods used to collect primary data.
3. **Explain** the difference between survey research and observation research.

Practice Academics

Science

4. Locate the U.S. Census Bureau's Web site and the *County Business Patterns Economic Profile* for your county. Identify the number of employees in your county and the annual payroll for your county. Find the total estimated employment by size of business and industry that employs the most people. Make a pie or bar graph of the data that you find.

Mathematics

5. New research shows that 75 percent of an ice cream shop's customers live within one mile of the store, another 15 percent live within two miles of the store, and the remaining 10 percent live within five miles of the store. If the total number of customers is 6,820 at the ice cream shop, how many customers live within one mile of the store?

   Math Concept **Number and Operations: Percents** A percent is a ratio that compares values to 100. A percentage can also be thought of as a part of a whole.

   Starting Hints Convert the percent representing customers who live within one mile of the store to a decimal by moving the decimal point two places to the left. Multiply the decimal by the total number of customers to get the number of customers who live within one mile of the store.

 connectED.mcgraw-hill.com

Check your answers.

For help, go to the Math Skills Handbook located at the back of this book.

READING GUIDE

Before You Read

Predict Why is the survey method an important way to collect information?

Objectives

- **Design** a marketing research survey.
- **Administer** a marketing research survey.

The Main Idea

Marketing researchers must construct survey instruments that will provide valid and reliable information needed to make good business decisions.

Vocabulary

Content Vocabulary
- validity
- reliability
- forced-choice questions
- open-ended questions

Academic Vocabulary

You will find these words in your reading and on your tests. Make sure you know their meanings.
- mutually
- accurate

Graphic Organizer

Draw or print this chart to outline this section by listing headings, subheadings, and key concepts.

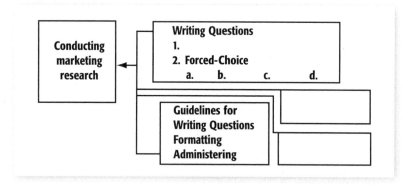

connectED.mcgraw-hill.com

Print this graphic organizer.

MARKETING CORE FUNCTION

Marketing Information Management

The Marketing Survey

CONSTRUCTING THE QUESTIONNAIRE

A questionnaire is a set of questions used to generate data in order to answer the research problem and accomplish the objectives of the study. Questionnaires should provide data that have validity.

A questionnaire has **validity** when the survey questions measure what was intended to be measured. For example, a researcher designs a questionnaire to measure customer satisfaction with a hotel's lodging services. Questionnaires that are poorly written or that do not address lodging services will not have validity.

As You Read

Compare What are the similarities between written survey instruments and scripted interviews?

Research questionnaires should also have reliability. **Reliability** exists when a research technique produces nearly identical results in repeated trials. Reliability requires that the questions ask for the same type of information from all the respondents.

Questions should be clear and easily understood so that all participants understand the question in the same way. Asking a question in a restaurant survey such as "Was your food hot?" would not yield a reliable answer. "Hot" could be interpreted as either the level of spiciness or the temperature of the food.

A valid and reliable questionnaire must be well written, correctly formatted, and properly administered. A questionnaire directed at hotel guests may not be appropriate for the purchaser of a new vehicle. It is also important to ask questions only of customers who have actually used the product or service in question.

> **" A well-constructed survey motivates people to complete questions and provide accurate information. "**

TYPES OF QUESTIONS

Survey questions can be either open-ended or forced-choice. **Forced-choice questions** ask respondents to choose answers from possibilities given on a questionnaire. Forced-choice questions are the simplest questions to write and also the easiest to tabulate. They can be two-choice, multiple-choice, or rating-scale questions. A two-choice question might ask respondents to provide a simple yes-or-no answer or to choose between one of two given answers. A multiple-choice question presents a short list of answers from which to choose. A rating-scale question asks for a ranking, such as "between 1 and 5." Respondents may also be asked to rank a list of specific activities or task in order of preference.

Open-ended questions ask respondents to construct their own response to a question. "What changes or additions to your hotel room would you recommend?" is an example of an open-ended question.

Some surveys have a space for general comments or suggestions. This type of open-ended question allows respondents to give opinions in their own words. Open-ended questions generate a wide variety of responses that are sometimes difficult to categorize and tabulate. As a result, most researchers prefer forced-choice questions.

YES/NO QUESTIONS

Two-choice questions give the respondent only two options, usually yes or no. Yes-or-no questions should be used only when asking for a response on one issue. You could use a yes-or-no question to ask questions like these:

"Did you have a problem during your stay?"

☐ **YES**   ☐ **NO**

"If **YES**, did you report it to the staff?

☐ **YES**   ☐ **NO**

You would not ask: "Did you have a problem and did you report it?" The customer may have different answers for the two issues that the question addresses.

Having a question that asks about more than one issue decreases validity and reliability. Yes-or-no questions are most often used as filter questions. Filter questions help to guide respondents to answer only those questions that apply. In cases in which there is a range of choices and yes-or-no questions are not appropriate, you would use multiple-choice questions or rating-scale questions for your survey.

MULTIPLE-CHOICE QUESTIONS

Multiple-choice questions give the respondent several choices. When constructing multiple-choice questions, it is important to make the options **mutually** exclusive and comprehensive enough to include every possible response.

In order to be sure that all options are covered, many surveys have a space for the option "other." For example, a car rental company might ask its customers the following question:

When you have a choice of the car rental companies listed below, which do you prefer? (check one)

☐ Avis   ☐ Hertz

☐ Budget   ☐ Other _____

☐ Enterprise

Offering the choice of "other" increases the reliability of a questionnaire. If "other" was not an option, respondents who use an unlisted car rental service might not give an answer at all, or they might choose an inaccurate answer from the list based on their limited choices. Either of these actions by respondents would result in misleading survey results.

RATING-SCALE QUESTIONS

Other forced-choice questions may ask respondents to rate a product or service based upon a scale. A variety of customer conditions, perceptions, and situations can be measured using rating scales.

Some of the most common rating scales measure levels of agreement, beliefs, frequency, importance, quality, satisfaction, and use. Examples of wording include a satisfaction scale that ranges from *completely satisfied* to *completely dissatisfied*, a quality scale that ranges from *excellent* to *poor*, or an amount-of-use scale that ranges from *never use* to *frequently use*.

Some questionnaires ask respondents to rate a product or service based on a percentage scale, on which 100 would be a perfect score. Others ask for ratings based on a numerical scale. Many consumer Web sites ask users to give products they purchase ratings of between 1 and 5 stars.

Research indicates that questionnaires which use five-point and seven-point rating scales result in the most reliability and validity. The following is an example of a five-point rating questionnaire used to rate the quality of front desk staff.

How would you rate the quality of service provided by the hotel's front desk?

	Excellent	Very Good	Good	Fair	Poor
Courtesy	5 ☐	4 ☐	3 ☐	2 ☐	1 ☐
Speed at check-in	5 ☐	4 ☐	3 ☐	2 ☐	1 ☐
Check-out process	5 ☐	4 ☐	3 ☐	2 ☐	1 ☐
Accuracy of bill	5 ☐	4 ☐	3 ☐	2 ☐	1 ☐

RATING SCALE STATEMENTS

In some surveys respondents answer statements rather than questions. They respond to belief or behavior statements to describe their attitudes, opinions, or preferences. A seven-point rating scale for a level of agreement rating scale might include *completely agree* (CA), *somewhat agree* (SA), *agree* (A) *neither agree nor disagree* (N), *disagree* (D) *somewhat disagree* (SD), and *completely disagree* (SD).

Below are examples of statements that might be used to measure attitudes and opinions in a health-care questionnaire. The respondents relate their personal experiences to the statements when responding.

As you can see, if someone had to answer yes or no to these questions, the researcher might not get an **accurate** picture. That is why it is often easier to use descriptive statements for research on attitudes and opinions.

Indicate your level of agreement with the following statements:

Completely Agree	Somewhat Agree	Agree	Neither Agree Nor Disagree	Disagree	Somewhat Disagree	Completely Disagree

"I am extremely health conscious."

| CA ☐ | SA ☐ | A ☐ | N ☐ | D ☐ | SD ☐ | CD ☐ |

"I do not like vegetables."

| CA ☐ | SA ☐ | A ☐ | N ☐ | D ☐ | SD ☐ | CD ☐ |

"Eating low-cholesterol foods is important to me."

| CA ☐ | SA ☐ | A ☐ | N ☐ | D ☐ | SD ☐ | CD ☐ |

"The cafeteria should serve heart-healthy foods."

| CA ☐ | SA ☐ | A ☐ | N ☐ | D ☐ | SD ☐ | CD ☐ |

Lost Respondents

This graph shows the number of people who do not complete a survey based upon the number of survey questions. *Based upon the data provided in this graph, what implications about survey research rates can you draw?*

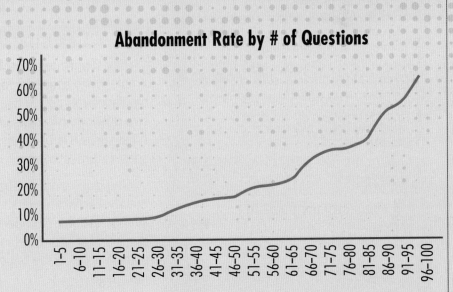

Abandonment Rate by # of Questions

The GREEN Marketer

Convincing the Green Consumer

Consumers' spending does not always match their attitudes. Many Americans say they value environmentalism, yet relatively few buy green products.

Market research shows that consumers are more likely to switch to green items, however, if they are told about their specific benefits.

Package Benefits Seventh Generation®, for example, states on its packaging that if every family replaced just one roll of nonrecycled toilet paper with a recycled roll, we could save 448,000 trees every year.

English Language Arts

Create You have agreed to write a level-of-agreement survey for Ranch Market to assess consumers' environmental attitudes. First, write three statements to assess beliefs or opinions. Next write three statements that assess whether consumers would buy green products at the market.

 connectED.mcgraw-hill.com

Get an activity on green marketing.

BASIC GUIDELINES FOR WRITING QUESTIONS

Each question should be written clearly and as briefly as possible. Use the same rating scales for all similar questions. It is important not to ask leading questions, which suggest a correct answer. An example of a leading question is: "Do you prefer X or the more reasonably priced Z?" The phrase "more reasonably priced" could influence the respondents to answer Z.

You should avoid any bias, which is a systematic error introduced by encouraging one outcome or answer over the others. It is also important to avoid questions that might cause a respondent to guess at the meaning of your question. The following is an example of a question that might cause a respondent to guess:

How many students in your high school drink coffee on a daily basis?

☐ Less than 10

☐ 10–49

☐ 50–99

☐ 100–149

☐ 150–199

☐ over 200

Without asking every student in school, the respondent cannot answer the question without guessing.

When a survey questionnaire is finished, it is a good idea to pretest the wording of the questions. This pretest allows for correction of any misleading questions, directions, or problems on the questionnaire.

FORMATTING

Questionnaires must have good visual appearance and ample white space for respondents. Different colors and typefaces can add to the design appeal, but use no more than two different ink colors and typefaces. The preferred color for most surveys is black on light paper and an easy-to-read font, such as Times Roman.

The questionnaire should be short enough to be answered quickly. Distinct headings should be placed on all individual survey sections. Numbers should be placed on all individual questions. If your questionnaire requires more than one page, place a note on the bottom of each page to continue to the next page.

It is good practice to vary the format between the questions and the options. For example, you might set the questions in sentence format and options to questions or statements capitalized or set in boldface type. Another format would be to set the questions in sentence format and boldface type with options in sentence format. Questions and multiple-choice answer selections should be short. Instructions and other text used in the survey should use common language so they will be understood by respondents. Varying the format is also a good way to keep the survey interesting for the respondents.

You should place boxes □, circles ○, or brackets [ ] next to your possible options. These symbols tell the respondents where they should place their answers.

CONTENT FORMATTING

Directions for completing written surveys must be clear for each section or group of questions. All of the questions need to be numbered. Questions generally follow a sequence starting with screening questions, and then leading to more specific questions.

Screening questions are asked at the beginning of the survey. For example, if an interviewer wanted to study the views of young adults, he or she might ask, "Are you between the ages of 18 and 29?" If the respondent answers yes, the interviewer administers the survey. If the answer is no, then the person would not be included in the study. Such information is placed at the beginning of a questionnaire only to "screen" or qualify a respondent. General and specific questions about the business are asked next.

Demographic questions are used to identify such traits as gender, age, ethnic background, income, and education. Demographic questions can help a business to determine, for example, that most of its customers live in the Northeast, are between the ages of 30 and 55, and have incomes between $45,000 and $65,000. Demographic profiles are typically grouped together at the end of a questionnaire. This is because respondents are more likely to answer personal questions after completing the other questions.

Lastly, many surveys provide an open-end section for comments and suggestions. Companies frequently ask permission to follow-up and provide a contact point, if respondents desire additional information.

Reading Check

Recall What are three types of questions used on surveys?

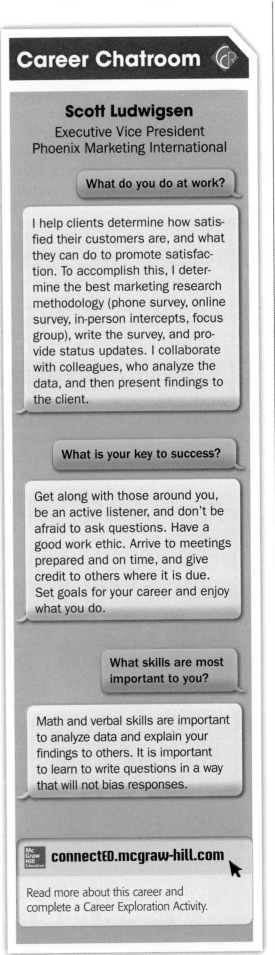

Career Chatroom

Scott Ludwigsen
Executive Vice President
Phoenix Marketing International

What do you do at work?

I help clients determine how satisfied their customers are, and what they can do to promote satisfaction. To accomplish this, I determine the best marketing research methodology (phone survey, online survey, in-person intercepts, focus group), write the survey, and provide status updates. I collaborate with colleagues, who analyze the data, and then present findings to the client.

What is your key to success?

Get along with those around you, be an active listener, and don't be afraid to ask questions. Have a good work ethic. Arrive to meetings prepared and on time, and give credit to others where it is due. Set goals for your career and enjoy what you do.

What skills are most important to you?

Math and verbal skills are important to analyze data and explain your findings to others. It is important to learn to write questions in a way that will not bias responses.

connectED.mcgraw-hill.com

Read more about this career and complete a Career Exploration Activity.

ADMINISTERING QUESTIONNAIRES

The response rate for most surveys is only ten percent or less, so proper administration can improve response rates. All surveys should have deadlines for completion. All surveys should also include clear and concise instructions on how to complete the questionnaire. These must be very easy to understand, so use short sentences and basic vocabulary.

Types of Surveys	
Mailed Surveys	E-mail Surveys
In-Person Surveys	Web Surveys

MAILED SURVEYS

A mailed questionnaire should be sent first-class with a hand-signed cover letter, and it should be personalized if the potential respondent is known. First impressions are important, so make the envelope stand out. Envelopes with bulk mail permits or generic labels are perceived as unimportant. This will generally produce a lower response rate.

This expensive marketing research technique is used when expert opinions are needed or to get very detailed information from customers. *What are some of the expenses involved with personal or in-depth interviews?*

Personal Interviews

Include a well-written cover letter. The respondent's next impression comes from the cover letter. The cover letter provides your best opportunity to convince the respondent to complete the survey. The cover letter or introductory remarks should explain the purpose of the survey. It also should clearly state the deadline for returning the questionnaire. A postage-paid return envelope should be included with the questionnaire for the respondent's convenience. However, you should also print the return address on the questionnaire itself because questionnaires are easily separated from the reply envelopes.

E-MAIL AND WEB SURVEYS

As with traditional mailed surveys, e-mail and Web surveys should be brief. E-mail and Web surveys should limit the number of screens that respondents have to scroll through to answer questions or statements.

Graphics and images can enhance the appearance of a Web survey. However, too many graphics or excessive use of animation can be distracting. Annoyed respondents are not likely to complete the survey. Internet surveys should allow respondents to stop and complete the survey at a later time.

IN-PERSON SURVEYS

Questionnaires that are not mailed should have a brief explanation of the survey's purpose placed on the questionnaire itself. A plan should be established for selecting participants in an unbiased way. Whether done in the respondent's home, over the phone, or in a mall, it is important that the interviewer be skilled and discreet. The interviewer should have the ability to answer questions from the respondents. The interviewer should recognize when it may be appropriate to ask more complex or sensitive questions.

Personal interviews can provide very detailed information, but they require special training to conduct effectively, can be time-consuming, and might be difficult to analyze and interpret.

Personal interviews can be useful when you need to collect detailed information from a relatively small group of people. Interviews can be used to explore issues and options to a greater extent than written surveys. In a personal interview, reactions to visual materials, such as ads or actual product samples, can be collected.

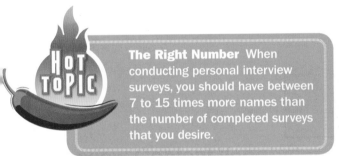

The Right Number When conducting personal interview surveys, you should have between 7 to 15 times more names than the number of completed surveys that you desire.

INCENTIVES

Many marketing researchers offer incentives and set deadlines for completing surveys to increase response rates. For example, to get a quicker response, a company may enter the first 100 respondents into a drawing for a cash prize; or each participant may receive a gift card or a discount on the company's product. Other incentives might include token gifts such as notepads, pens, refrigerator magnets, mini calendars, key rings, participation in a raffle or lottery, or a donation to a charity in the respondent's name. Studies have shown that incentives do work to increase response rates, so it may be a wise investment for companies to consider.

 After You Read | **Section 29.2**

Review Key Concepts

1. **Explain** the difference between validity and reliability.
2. **Discuss** important considerations for constructing options for multiple-choice questions.
3. **Explain** why it is important that surveys have a strong visual appearance.

Practice Academics

English Language Arts

4. Perform library or online research on a recent opinion poll or survey of a local, state, or national issue. Write a one-page summary, noting when the poll was conducted, the issue that was researched, and the findings.

Mathematics

5. A gift store conducts a study to estimate yearly sales. Use the following data to estimate yearly sales for the gift store: 700 people pass the store each day, 5 percent enter the store and spend an average of $23, and the store is open 356 days during the year.

Math Concept **Problem Solving: Multi-Step Problems** When solving problems that require multiple steps, list the information given in the problem as well as the particular points that need to be resolved.

Starting Hints Determine the number of people that enter the store by multiplying the decimal equivalent of 5 percent by the total number of people that pass the store each day. Multiply the number of people that enter the store each day by the average amount of money spent by each person to determine the average sales each day.

 connectED.mcgraw-hill.com

Check your answers.

For help, go to the **Math Skills Handbook** located at the back of this book.

Research Study
on Mobile Phones

Companies look to consumers for feedback on new products. How can marketing research help in that endeavor?

Scenario

Your marketing research company has been hired to study a specific target market for mobile phones—teenagers. The client's objective for doing the study is to develop products specifically designed for the teenage market.

You need to find out how teens use their cell phones, what features are most important to them, how best to promote a new phone, and who pays for the phones. The results of the study will be used to design a new cell phone and a marketing plan for it.

The Skills You'll Use

Academic Skills Reading, writing, social studies, researching, and analyzing

Basic Skills Speaking, listening, thinking, and interpersonal

Technology Skills Word processing, presentation, spreadsheet, telecommunication, and the Internet

Your Objective

Your objective is to develop an effective marketing research study on teenaged cell phone users for your client, a mobile phone company.

STEP 1 Do Your Research

Conduct research on cell phones. Find out about all the features, prices, and promotional materials used by mobile phone companies to target teens. Also, look for issues related to cell phones and teenagers. As you conduct your research, answer these questions:

- Which mobile phone companies specifically target teens and how do they do so?
- What main features are found on the majority of cell phones?
- What are the current prices for mobile phones?
- What are the current issues (in the media) regarding teens and cell phone usage?

Write a summary of your research.

STEP 2 Plan Your Project

Now that you have completed your research, you need to begin planning your project.

- Define the research issue (problem) and objectives for the marketing research study.
- Conduct secondary research on cell phones and teens.
- Review marketing research methods to decide which one will work best.
- Develop questions for use in the marketing research study.
- Conduct primary research.
- Write a report that summarizes your research, defines the research issue, details the study's objectives, includes the questions asked in the study, reports the results of the study, analyzes the data generated by the study, and makes recommendations for marketing strategies.

STEP 3 Connect with Your Community

- Interview one or more trusted adults at home, at school, at work or in your community. Find out what issues concern them regarding teen cell phone usage.

- Take notes during your interviews and transcribe your notes after your interviews.

- Visit a store that sells mobile phones to review the products and promotional materials used to target teens.

- Observe people using their cell phones to see how, when, and where they use them.

STEP 4 Share What You Learn

Assume your class is the client's staff who will apply the results of your study.

- Present your results in an oral presentation. Be prepared to answer questions.

- Present your written report, complete with recommendations and suggested marketing strategies.

- Use software to create a slide presentation to accompany your oral presentation. Include one slide for each topic in your written report.

STEP 5 Evaluate Your Marketing and Academic Skills

Your project will be evaluated based on the following:

- The marketing research study's design (problem and methodology)
- Secondary and primary research findings
- Analysis of findings and recommendations for the client
- Samples of suggested ideas
- Organization and continuity of presentation
- Mechanics—presentation and neatness
- Speaking and listening skills

MARKETING CORE FUNCTIONS

 Marketing Information Management

 Market Planning

Marketing Internship Project Checklist

Plan

✓ Conduct secondary research on how teens use mobile phones, parents' concerns, and marketing strategies used to target teens.

✓ Conduct a marketing research study on teens and cell phones.

Write

✓ Create a written report, complete with recommendations and suggested marketing strategies.

✓ Explain the findings and analysis of the data.

Present

✓ Present a marketing research problem and methodology used to conduct the study.

✓ Present findings and recommendations.

✓ Display ideas for implementing the recommendations.

 connectED.mcgraw-hill.com

Evaluate Download a rubric you can use to evaluate your final project.

my marketing portfolio

Internship Report Once you have completed your Marketing Internship Project and oral presentation, put your written report and a few printouts of key slides from your oral presentation in your Marketing Portfolio.

Marketing Research Study for a New Client Conduct a marketing research study for a new client of your choice. Consider companies that target teens or choose a different target market. Your new client could be a retail store that wants to change its product offerings or a video game company that wants consumer input for designing new games. Define the problem, obtain the data, analyze the data, report your findings, make recommendations, and include samples of your suggestions.

PRODUCT AND SERVICE MANAGEMENT

Marketing Internship Project

A Product Design and Marketing Plan

Essential Question How can a company conceive and market an exciting new product?

Developing and marketing new products can be a challenge. How does a company go about accomplishing this? Pet product manufacturers all want to please the millions of dedicated pet owners who cherish their pets. Offering new products that will excite pet owners is essential to success in the growing pet industry.

Project Goal

In the project at the end of this unit, you will develop an exciting new pet product and marketing plan for a client.

Prepare for the Project

As you read this unit, use this checklist to prepare for the Marketing Internship Project at the end of this unit:

- Go online to find current news about the pet industry.
- Consider the different kinds of pets and pet products.
- Visit a local retailer that sells pet products to observe their pricing, merchandising, and promotional strategies.

 connectED.mcgraw-hill.com

Project Activity
Complete a worksheet activity about product planning.

AMERICAN MARKETING ASSOCIATION

Some products and services are all the better thanks to a differentiating ingredient.

MARKETING CORE FUNCTIONS IN THIS UNIT

 Market Planning

Product/Service Management

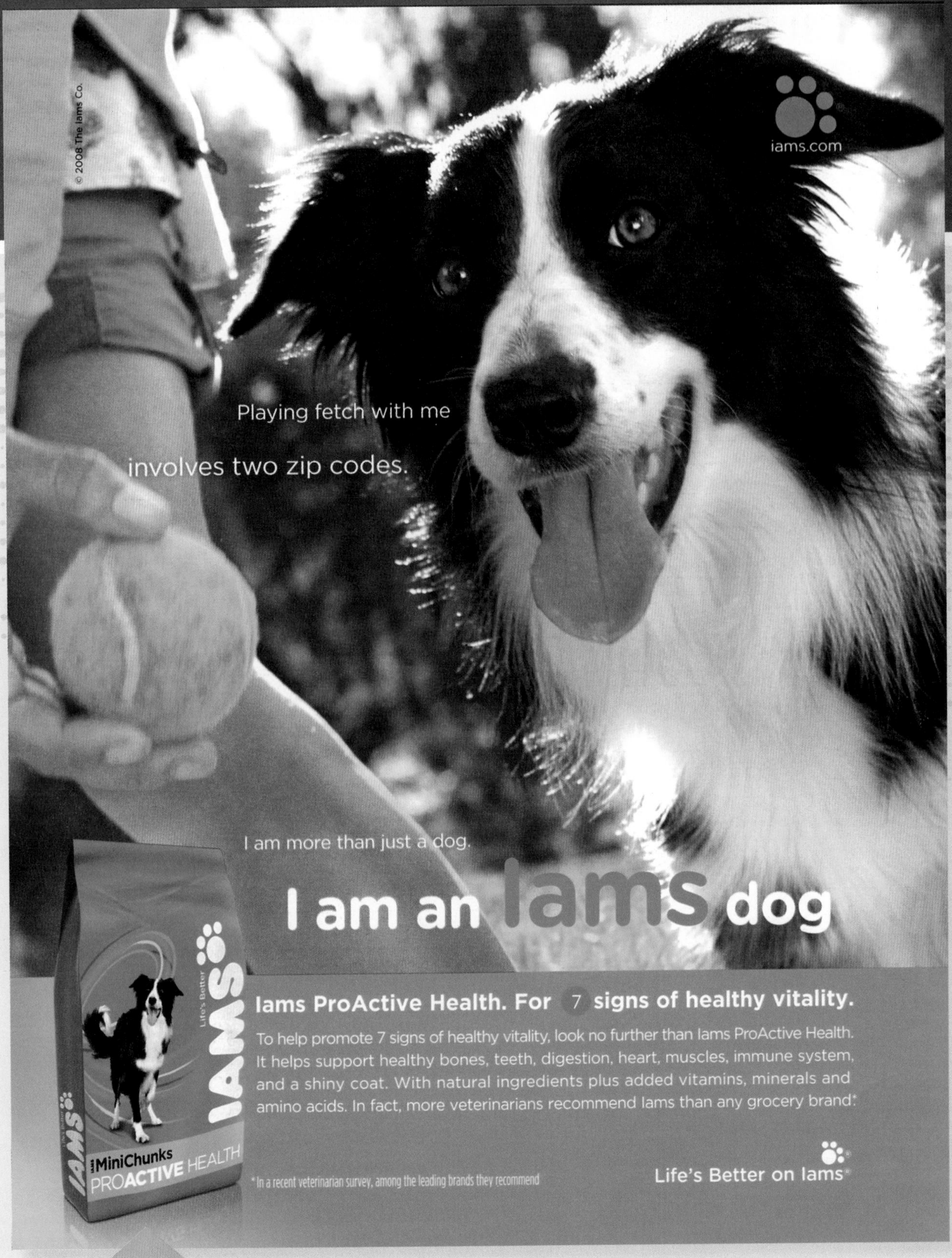

© 2008 The Iams Co.
iams.com
Playing fetch with me
involves two zip codes.
I am more than just a dog.
I am an Iams dog
Iams ProActive Health. For 7 signs of healthy vitality.
To help promote 7 signs of healthy vitality, look no further than Iams ProActive Health. It helps support healthy bones, teeth, digestion, heart, muscles, immune system, and a shiny coat. With natural ingredients plus added vitamins, minerals and amino acids. In fact, more veterinarians recommend Iams than any grocery brand.*
*In a recent veterinarian survey, among the leading brands they recommend
Life's Better on Iams®
IAMS
Life's Better
MiniChunks
PROACTIVE HEALTH

SHOW WHAT YOU KNOW

Visual Literacy
Pet owners are important to manufacturers of pet products. Even in a recession, pet owners spend money on their pets. ***What does this advertisement tell you about the products and services that Iams offers to pets and their owners?***

product planning

SHOW WHAT YOU KNOW

Visual Literacy Businesses plan, position, test, and manage the new and existing goods and services they create. The product planning process also includes determining the right product mix and product mix strategies. *What do you think is necessary to make a new product successful?*

Discovery Project

New Product Plan

Essential Question How do businesses develop a new product and position it for sale?

Project Goal

Assume that you and a classmate are employed in research and product development for a large consumer products manufacturer. Your team has developed a new consumer product. Management has asked your team to design a plan to identify, place, and sell the new product.

Ask Yourself…

- What is your product and its target market?
- How will you define your product by price and quality?
- What are your product's features and benefits?
- How will your product be viewed by competitors?

 Synthesize and Present Research Synthesize your research by designing a product plan that identifies, places, and sells the new product.

 connectED.mcgraw-hill.com

Activity
Get a worksheet activity about product planning.

Evaluate
Download a rubric you can use to evaluate your project.

DECA Connection

DECA Event Role Play

Concepts in this chapter are related to DECA competitive events that involve either an interview or role play.

Performance Indicators The performance indicators represent key skills and knowledge. Your key to success in DECA competitive events is relating them to concepts in this chapter.

- Explain the nature and scope of the product/service management function.
- Identify the impact of product life cycles on marketing decisions.
- Explain the concept of product mix.
- Demonstrate adaptability.
- Make oral presentations.

DECA Prep

Role Play Practice role-playing with the DECA Connection competitive-event activity at the end of this chapter. More information on DECA events can be found on DECA's Web site.

READING GUIDE

Before You Read

Predict Think of a new product you or a friend recently purchased. Do you think it will become successful? Why or why not?

Objectives

- **Describe** the steps in product planning.
- **Explain** how to develop, maintain, and improve a product mix.

The Main Idea

Product planning allows a business to plan marketing programs that increase sales through making products that customers want.

Vocabulary

Content Vocabulary
- product planning
- product mix
- product line
- product item
- product width
- product depth
- prototype
- product modification

Academic Vocabulary

You will find these words in your reading and on your tests. Make sure you know their meanings.

- unique
- comparable

Graphic Organizer

Draw or print this chart to write in the seven key steps in product development.

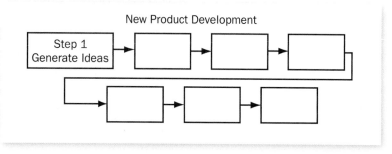

New Product Development

Step 1
Generate Ideas

 connectED.mcgraw-hill.com

Print this graphic organizer.

MARKETING CORE FUNCTION

Product and Service Management

PRODUCT PLANNING

A product can be a tangible item (Apple iPad™), a service (Twitter® micro-blogging service), an idea (a plan for a public relations campaign), an abstract belief (obtain a good education), or a combination of all of these concepts. A product includes its physical features, the seller's reputation, the seller's services, and the way the product is viewed by people.

Product planning involves making decisions about the features and services of a product or idea that will help sell that product. These decisions relate to product features, such as packaging, labeling, and branding. They also relate to services, such as product warranties, that are necessary to support the product.

Product planning allows a business to coordinate existing products and features offered to customers. It also allows them to add new products and delete products that no longer appeal to customers. Product planning requires creativity as well as the ability to interpret current customer needs and forecast new trends.

 As You Read

Analyze What marketing activities must occur prior to launching a new product?

PRODUCT MIX

The **product mix** includes all the different products that a company makes or sells. A large manufacturer may have a variety of products in different categories. For example, Kraft Foods© has hundreds of products in the areas of snacks, beverages, cheese, groceries, and convenience meals. Kraft's major brands include Kraft®, Maxwell House®, Nabisco®, Oscar Mayer®, Oreo®, and Philadelphia® products.

Retailers frequently sell more than one product brand. Doing so helps prevent companies from depending on just one product. It also helps companies keep up with the ever-changing marketplace and with diverse customers. For example, a large appliance store might sell LG®, Panasonic®, Sharp®, Sony®, and Toshiba® television sets. Retail stores must plan their product mix carefully because most cannot carry all the product brands that may be available.

> **" A product is anything a person receives in an exchange. "**

Stores need to offer a good selection, but adding more product brands may not result in increased sales. In fact, adding too many brands may result in fewer sales. The added brands may not be as popular as those already in stock.

VARIATIONS IN PRODUCT MIXES

Have you ever heard of *Grand' Mère*® or *Trakinas*®? Both are brands that Kraft sells outside the United States. *Grand' Mère* is a popular coffee in France. *Trakinas* is a cookie sold in Argentina, Brazil, and China. Kraft has a diverse international market. So, Kraft carries product mixes for different cultures and customer needs around the world.

Even similar types of businesses in the domestic market offer different product mixes. The Gap® and Men's Wearhouse® are both apparel stores, yet they offer different product mixes. The Men's Wearhouse focuses on a mix of classic attire for business. The Gap carries a product mix of more casual, trendsetting clothing.

All the different products and brands that a company makes is its product mix. *How does a product line differ from a product item?*

Product Mix

The type and number of products to be carried must be based on the objectives of the business, the image the business wants to project, and the market it is trying to reach. This makes product mixes **unique** to each business.

PRODUCT ITEMS AND LINES

A **product line** is a group of closely related products manufactured or sold by a business. Examples include all the car models produced by the Lincoln® division of the Ford Motor Company® or all the cereals produced by Kellogg's®.

A **product item** is a specific model, brand, or size of a product within a product line. Typically, retailers carry several product items for each product line they sell. A Harley-Davidson® motorcycle dealer might carry several Softail® models, such as the Fat Boy®, Softail Deluxe®, or Heritage Softail® Classic.

PRODUCT WIDTH AND PRODUCT DEPTH

The width and depth of a company's product offerings define a product mix. **Product width** refers to the number of different product lines a business manufactures or sells. A retailer that sells three brands of jeans—Lee®, Levi's® and Wrangler®—has a product width of three.

Product depth refers to the number of items offered within each product line. The product depth is the number of sizes, price ranges, colors, fabric type, and styles for each brand of jeans.

Product mix strategies vary with the type of business. Red Lobster® restaurants specialize in seafood dinners. They have considerable product depth within a narrow product line (seafood entrées). Other restaurants may offer broader menus that include steak, chicken, pork, and pasta dinners, as well as seafood. Their product mix may have greater width but less depth than Red Lobster's product mix.

Both manufacturers and retailers must decide on the width and depth of their product mix. To determine its product mix, a business needs to identify its target market, its competitors, and the image it wants to project. After a target market and an image are identified, a business must determine which product lines and items to manufacture or sell. Businesses must also periodically review whether its existing product lines need to be expanded, modified, decreased, or eliminated.

Reading Check

Contrast What is the difference between product planning and product mix?

PRODUCT MIX STRATEGIES

A product mix strategy is a plan for determining which products a business will manufacture or stock. Businesses can use different product mix strategies depending on their resources and objectives. Some businesses develop completely new products to add to their existing product lines. Others expand or modify their current product lines. Sometimes businesses drop existing products to allow for new product offerings.

To make these decisions, a business must take an objective look at sales as well as other factors such as current trends. A product that has experienced success in the past may not continue to thrive if it fails to respond to changing consumer wants and needs.

DEVELOPING NEW PRODUCTS

New product development is an important business strategy for large consumer product manufacturers. The W.E. Kellogg Institute for Food and Nutrition Research has 400,000 square feet devoted to global product development. The Institute has office space, innovation labs, research facilities, an experimental production area, and a pilot plant for its cereal and snack lines.

Successful new products can add substantially to a company's overall sales and boost its market share. (See **Figure 30.1** on page 710.) Often a slight variation of the original or existing product can lead to increased sales.

Procter & Gamble® (P&G) is the number one U.S. manufacturer of personal care and household products. It devotes roughly 15 percent of its research and development budget to developing new products. Innovative P&G products that have created new consumer-goods categories include Febreze® Air Fresheners, the Swiffer® dry-mop system, and the Olay® anti-aging cosmetic line.

According to one study, new products (those less than five years old) account for about 35 percent of total sales for major consumer and industrial goods companies. New products can help a company's image by building the company's reputation among customers as an innovator and leader. In addition, a new product may increase markups and profits to sellers. This is because prices on new products tend to be 10 to 15 percent higher than that of some older, **comparable** products.

DIGITAL NATION

The Wisdom of Crowds

"Crowdsourcing" is a popular new approach to product development that uses social media to gather ideas from customers. To encourage customers to comment, companies set up blogs, Facebook® pages, Twitter® feeds, online polls, and even dedicated Web sites. Many companies ask for feedback about a specific idea or part of the business.

Free Ideas Pour In

Coffee chain Starbucks® created Mystarbucksidea.com, where tens of thousands of customers posted and voted on ideas for new drinks, food, and merchandise. They also vented frustrations and shared solutions to problems. Some customers even posted money-saving ideas, such as saving paper by turning off automatic receipt printing. The site also included a blog on which Starbucks explained how it implemented customers' ideas.

English Language Arts

Create Imagine that 22,000 people vote for a drink recipe submitted to a coffee company's Web site. What should the company do to test the idea? Write a paragraph with your ideas.

 connectED.mcgraw-hill.com

Get a Digital Nation Worksheet Activity.

FIGURE 30.1 Top Innovations of the Decade

New Ideas These ten innovations have significantly changed the world of marketing. *Why are new and innovative products and ideas so important?*

Top Marketing and Tech Innovations of the Decade
Ad Networks and Exchanges
Broadband Penetration
Digital Video Recorders (DVRS)
Flash (web-based technology)
Global Positioning Systems (GPS)
iPhones
Open Application Programming Interface Systems (APIS)
Search Marketing
Social Networks
Twitter® (micro-blogging service)

Source: Advertising Age, December 14, 2009

New product development generally involves seven key steps (see **Figure 30.2**):

1. Generating ideas
2. Screening ideas
3. Developing a business proposal
4. Developing the product
5. Testing the product with consumers
6. Introducing the product (commercialization)
7. Evaluating customer acceptance

GENERATING IDEAS

Creativity is essential for new product development. New product ideas come from a variety of sources, including customers, competitors, channel members, and company employees. Current and existing customers are frequently involved in focus groups and consumer panels. These groups are created to generate new product ideas in as many categories as possible.

Many companies that manufacture consumer packaged goods use a task force approach to new product development. With this approach, employees from departments such as marketing, sales, manufacturing, finance, and research and development, take a new concept from the idea stage through the seven steps of product development.

Companies that manufacture and sell industrial products may establish venture teams that are independent of any particular department. Venture teams normally develop new products that are not part of the company's existing business.

Best Buy®, a consumer electronics firm, involves employees working in idea incubators. Idea incubator teams often include salespeople, computer programmers, and engineers who brainstorm ideas. Team members work and live together in housing complexes for several weeks and exit with ideas for new products, services, and processes.

Microsoft® has developed product ideas using Windows Live® with actual users. The company maps user activities, tests new ideas, and runs statistical tests with controlled scientific experiments on new product ideas.

SCREENING IDEAS

During the screening process, ideas for products are evaluated. This process is done early on, before significant resources like time and money are used up. New product ideas are matched against the company's overall strategy, which defines customers, target markets, competitors, and existing competitive strengths.

FIGURE 30.2 The Steps in New Product Development

From Ideas to New Products There are several key steps for new product development. *How does an idea lead to a new product or service?*

Steps 1 and 2

GENERATING AND SCREENING IDEAS

Generating ideas involves tracking cultural trends and observing customer behaviors. Screening ideas for new products includes eliminating possibilities until one or two ideas are selected for development.

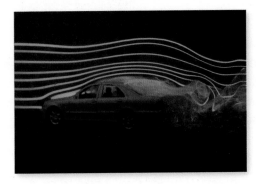

Steps 3, 4, 5

WRITING A BUSINESS PROPOSAL/ DEVELOPING THE PRODUCT/ TESTING THE PRODUCT

A business proposal evaluates the proposed product in terms of size of market, potential sales, costs, profit potential, technology, the competition, and the level of risk involved. During the development and testing stage, a prototype is made and tested.

Step 6

INTRODUCING THE PRODUCT

If customer response is favorable, the product is introduced into the marketplace.

Step 7

EVALUATING CUSTOMER ACCEPTANCE

After the product has been introduced, marketers track customer acceptance.

Marketing in Russia

A country with eleven time zones, Russia is a huge, sparsely populated nation with wide variations in demographic, psychographic, and geographic factors. This makes marketing products in Russia particularly challenging. It is difficult if not impossible to create one message that can reach all Russian people.

Translating Messages The Russian lanuage has many suffixes, prefixes, and idiomatic flourishes. This makes it not only a very colorful language but also a language that is difficult to precisely translate American marketing copy into. To counter this, marketers from other nations must customize their messages carefully.

Social Studies

Research and Create Find out different customs and symbols in Russia. Use your research to develop some ideas about how you might market a product or service there.

Here are some entry-level phrases that are used in conversations about marketing all over the world.

English	Russian	
Hello	Privyet	Привет
Goodbye	Da zvidanja	до свидания
Yes/No	Da/Nyet	Да/Нет
Please	Pazjalste	Пожалуйста
Thank you	Spasiba	Спасибо
You're welcome	Ne za chto	Не за что

During the screening process, marketers evaluate new ideas for potential conflicts with existing products. What would a manufacturer of digital thermometers do if a new way to measure body temperature were invented? Suppose the invention was a disposable plastic strip that turned colors depending on body heat. Would the new product be in conflict with the existing product such as a digital thermometer?

A screening might involve concept testing with consumers. Consumers would identify qualities they like and dislike about the new concept, and whether they would buy such a product. If the company planned to market the new product globally, opinions from proposed foreign markets should be obtained.

The purpose of the screening stage is to find the products that deserve further study. A large number of products are rejected in the screening stage, making it an important early step.

DEVELOPING A BUSINESS PROPOSAL

Marketers evaluate a product idea that makes it through the screening process in terms of its profit potential. A business proposal is developed to evaluate the new product. Marketers must consider the size of the market, potential sales, costs, profit potential, technological trends, overall competitive environment, and level of risk.

During this stage, the company must also consider production requirements. How long will it take to create and introduce the new product? Can it be produced efficiently and at a competitive price? The business must plan a program to study the realities of making and marketing the new product.

DEVELOPING THE PRODUCT

During product development, the new product idea takes on a physical shape, and marketers develop a marketing strategy. The company makes plans relating to production, packaging, labeling, branding, promotion, and distribution.

During this phase of product development, technical evaluations are made to see whether the company can produce the new product and whether it is practical to do so. The Ben & Jerry's® ice cream company had difficulties when it first developed Cherry Garcia ice cream. The original idea was to add whole chocolate-coated cherries to the ice cream. But the whole cherries were too large to go through the production machinery, which caused the chocolate to break off the cherries. After numerous tests, the company finally added the cherries and the chocolate separately.

In addition to detecting difficulties with product production, a business must conduct tests on products to see how they will hold up during normal and not-so-normal use by the consumer.

A new product may be tested for durability in the lab. Testers use machines and experiments that will reproduce the actions or motions that the product will undergo during use. Technical problems should be detected at this stage so that they can be corrected before full-scale production begins.

Millions of dollars can be spent on this stage of product development for testing, prototypes, and research. A **prototype** is a model of the new product. Usually only a few models are made at first, as the business tests the idea and makes changes to improve the final product. A concept car is an example of a prototype.

New Product Launches
Every year more than 70,000 new consumer products are introduced in North America.

The government requires extensive scientific testing in various stages for some products, such as prescription drugs and genetically engineered food products. These tests end with testing on human beings to determine side effects and problems with a product's safety. Getting final approval from the government for use by the general public can take years.

TESTING THE PRODUCT WITH CONSUMERS

New products are usually test-marketed in certain geographic areas to see whether consumers will accept them. Larger companies establish research and development departments that work with marketing staff, marketing research staff, and outside research companies to develop and test new products.

For example, PepsiCo® developed a low-calorie soft drink for the European market. Because international customers typically do not like diet beverages, the company spent more than two years testing the drink with different flavors. Finally, one flavor combination met the company's goal of having at least 40 percent of potential consumers choose Pepsi Max® over a competitor's product.

Not every new product must be test-marketed. A focus-group evaluation during development can provide additional input into final product design, revealing potential problems before production.

In some cases, the costs of test marketing, focus-groups, or direct-marketing tests may be too high. Marketers may skip the testing of other products because they do not yet have a product to be evaluated. Sometimes a company delays test marketing to keep information away from competitors. Such information might help competitors get a similar product on the market.

INTRODUCING THE PRODUCT

This stage is also called "commercialization." Introducing a new product can be expensive. For example, to convince adults to use Crest Whitening Expressions® toothpaste in cinnamon, citrus, and herbal mint flavors, Procter & Gamble spent about $80 million on a marketing campaign.

New products must be advertised to introduce their benefits to consumers. A new or revised distribution network may be needed. The company may need to develop training programs for its sales force.

To pay these costs, the company must get its new products into the market as quickly as possible. The first company to introduce a new product has an advantage in acquiring customers and in building brand loyalty.

EVALUATING CUSTOMER ACCEPTANCE

The purpose of this step is to evaluate customer acceptance of the product and the marketing strategies used to introduce the product. Scanning equipment and computer systems can be used to compile large amounts of sales and market data on existing and new products. From this information, customized reports can be prepared. These reports help answer key questions such as:

▶ How often do customers buy the new product?
▶ When did customers last buy the new product?
▶ Where are the best customers for our new product?
▶ What new products are customers buying?

DEVELOPING EXISTING PRODUCTS

Companies constantly review their product mix to see if they can further expand their product lines or modify existing products. They do this to build on an already established image, to appeal to new markets, and to increase sales and profits.

One disadvantage of adding new product versions and products to a company's product mix is cost. The additions increase inventory, promotion, storage, and distribution costs. New products also may take sales away from existing products. A brand or corporate name is usually placed on the new product. If the product is unpopular, poorly made, or harmful, all products with the corporate name may suffer. However, the disadvantages usually do not keep a company from improving its existing products.

LINE EXTENSIONS

Companies can expand product offerings by adding new product lines, items, or services, which may or may not be related to current products. Consider the varieties of Tylenol®. Some varieties include Tylenol Flu, Tylenol Cold, Tylenol PM, and Tylenol Allergy Sinus. These products also come in a variety of forms, such as tablets, caplets, and gel caps. Each of these products is a line extension of the original Tylenol headache pain product.

A line extension is intended to be a different product that appeals to somewhat different needs of consumers. In essence, the company wants to provide a wider range of choices to increase product depth within a line. Line extensions are easy to market because customers are already familiar with the original product on which the extension is based.

PRODUCT MODIFICATIONS

A **product modification** is an alteration in a company's existing product. Modified products may be offered in new and different varieties, formulations, colors, styles, features, or sizes. Product modifications are a relatively quick and easy way to add new products to a company's product line. When modifying a product, the old product may be phased out. Packaging can also be modified to appeal to consumers and attract them to the new product.

DELETING A PRODUCT OR PRODUCT LINE

Sometimes companies decide that they will no longer produce or sell a particular product or even a whole product line. There can be many reasons for this move.

Obsolescence	Replacement with New Products
Loss of Appeal	Lack of Profit
Changes in Company Objectives	Conflict with Other Products in a Line

OBSOLESCENCE

Changes in technology have caused many products to be discontinued over time. An obsolete item is something that is no longer useful. For example, some analysts say telephone land lines are on their way to obsolescence. Music listening devices have evolved from 45 RPM records and $33\frac{1}{3}$ RPM albums, eight-track tapes, cassette tapes, and CDs to MP3 players and computer downloads.

LOSS OF APPEAL

As consumer tastes change, companies drop products that no longer appeal to old tastes and interests. For example, new video games with better visual effects and improved interactive features replace earlier versions to spark continued customer interest and appeal. Older products or versions may have some lasting loyalties that generate revenue, but the manufacturers must decide whether these benefits are worth the expense of keeping the item in their product mixes.

CHANGES IN COMPANY OBJECTIVES

Sometimes a product or entire product mix does not match a company's current objectives. After operating in Japan for 30 years, the Wendy's® hamburger chain closed its 70 restaurants there. While still looking at international expansion, the company focused on Yoshinoya® and other restaurants. The company closed its outlets and discontinued its product in this market to meet new company objectives.

LACK OF PROFIT

Product developers may drop products when sales reach such a low level that the return on sales does not meet company objectives.

CONFLICT WITH OTHER PRODUCTS IN THE LINE

Sometimes products take business away from other products in the same product line. Increased sales of one product can cause decreased sales of another product in that line.

REPLACEMENT WITH NEW PRODUCTS

To encourage retailers to cover costs of putting a new product onto limited shelf space, manufacturers pay slotting fees or allowances. A slotting fee is a cash premium a manufacturer pays to a retailer for the costs involved with placing a new product on its shelves.

Slotting fees may pay for a retailer's discounted specials on a new product, store shelf space, penalties for poor sales, advertising, and display costs. Slotting fees for consumer products range from a few thousand dollars to more than $100,000 per product.

According to a Federal Trade Commission study, a nationwide product launch might cost more than $2 million in slotting fees alone. Slotting fees help the retailer balance the costs associated with accepting a new product. A retailer must mark down eliminated products and pay for software, labor, and materials to change price labels and enter a new product into the inventory.

 After You Read   **Section 30.1**

Review Key Concepts

1. **Differentiate** between product depth and product width.
2. **Name** the types of criteria used to screen new product ideas.
3. **List** four reasons for expanding a product line.

Practice Academics

English Language Arts

4. Perform online or library research to obtain information about slotting fees. Write a one- or two-page paper on the advantages and disadvantages of slotting fees from a manufacturer's and a retailer's perspective.

Mathematics

5. A towel manufacturing company had total sales of $34,250 in 2009. In 2010, the company's total sales were $42,780. What is the percentage increase in sales from 2009 to 2010?

Math Concept **Percent Increase** A percent is a ratio that compares values to 100. Percents represent parts of a whole. When determining the percentage of an increase in values, such as sales, first determine the nominal increase by subtracting. Convert that to a decimal number by division.

Starting Hints To solve this problem, subtract the total sales in 2009 from the total sales in 2010. Divide the difference by the total sales in 2009 to determine the decimal equivalent of the percentage increase.

 connectED.mcgraw-hill.com

Check your answers.

For help, go to the **Math Skills Handbook** located at the back of this book.

READING GUIDE

Before You Read

Predict How might marketing strategies differ for new products and existing products?

Objectives

- **Identify** the four stages of the production life cycle.
- **Describe** product positioning techniques.

The Main Idea

Products go through different stages of growth and decline. Various marketing strategies help sustain product sales over time.

Vocabulary

Content Vocabulary
- product life cycle
- product positioning
- category management
- planograms

Academic Vocabulary

You will find these words in your reading and on your tests. Make sure you know their meanings.
- awareness
- guarantee

Graphic Organizer

Draw or print this chart to record each stage in the product life cycle and to list sales characteristics and marketing strategies for each stage.

Stages in the Product Life Cycle

Stages	Sales Characteristics	Marketing Strategies
Introduction		

 connectED.mcgraw-hill.com

Print this graphic organizer.

MARKETING CORE FUNCTION

 Product/Service Management

Sustaining Product Sales

THE PRODUCT LIFE CYCLE

The **product life cycle** represents the stages that a product goes through during its life. There are four basic stages of the product life cycle: introduction, growth, maturity, and decline (see **Figure 30.3** on page 718). The product life cycle has an impact on the marketing strategy and the product mix. The length of a product life cycle varies with the product. For example, products purchased for events, such as decorations and gift wrap, have very short life cycles. Appliances, automobiles, and some consumer food and household products have much longer life cycles. At each stage in the product life cycle, marketers must adjust their product mix and their marketing strategies to ensure continued sales.

As You Read

Connect Think of a product you recently purchased. Why did you select that product instead of another similar product?

MANAGING IN THE INTRODUCTION STAGE

When the product is introduced to the market, a company focuses its efforts on promotion and production. The major goal is to draw the customer's attention to the new product. The company works to build its sales by increasing product **awareness** and develop a market for the product. Special promotions get the customer to try the new product. There may also be increased costs due to new packaging and distribution expenses. This is also the time when intellectual property protection such as patents and trademarks are obtained. Because of these activities, the costs of introducing a product are high. Therefore, introduction is usually the least profitable stage of the life cycle.

MANAGING IN THE GROWTH STAGE

In the growth stage, the company seeks to build brand preference and increase market share. During the growth phase of the product life cycle, the product is enjoying success. This is demonstrated through increasing sales and profits. Much of the target market knows about and buys the product. Advertising now focuses on consumer satisfaction, rather than on the benefits of new products.

> **A product has a life cycle with several stages: introduction, growth, maturity, and decline.**

By this time, the competition is aware of the success of the product. The competition is also likely to offer new products in order to compete. To keep its product sales growing, the company may enter into price competition or introduce new models. The company may also decide to modify the existing product to offer more benefits than the competition offers.

MANAGING IN THE MATURITY STAGE

A product reaches the maturity stage when its sales decrease or slow down. The product has more competition now, or most of the target market consumers already own the product. Advertising continues to reinforce the product brand, but the promotional costs are lower than in the introduction stage.

During this stage, a company spends more of its marketing dollars fighting off the competition, which now has similar products. Because of competing brands, the product loses market share and has lower profits.

Slotting fees may rise during this stage as the company seeks to maintain its market share. At this stage, the company has to decide whether it can continue to improve the product to maintain market share and extend the life of the product.

MANAGING IN THE DECLINE STAGE

During the decline stage, sales fall. Profits reach the point where they are smaller than the expenses. Management needs to decide how long it will continue to support the product.

In the decline stage, advertising and promotional costs are reduced to maximize profits on declining sales. If the company believes that the product has reached the end of its life cycle, the company deletes the product entirely from its product mix.

Besides dropping the product, the company can use other product mix strategies to try to gain further sales from a declining product. These strategies include selling or licensing the product, recommitting to the product line, discounting the product, regionalizing the product, and updating or altering the product.

> Sell or License the Product
>
> Recommit to the Product Line
>
> Discount the Product
>
> Regionalize the Product
>
> Update or Alter the Product

SELL OR LICENSE THE PRODUCT

Many companies sell or license their poorly performing products to risk-taking companies. Risk-taking companies try to revitalize the product by changing the product's image or introducing it to a new market. By rejuvenating products, companies may regain lost market share and generate more profit.

FIGURE 30.3 | Understanding the Product Life Cycle

Product Stages The life cycle of a product can be divided into four stages: introduction, growth, maturity, and decline. *Why are sales relatively slow during the maturity stage?*

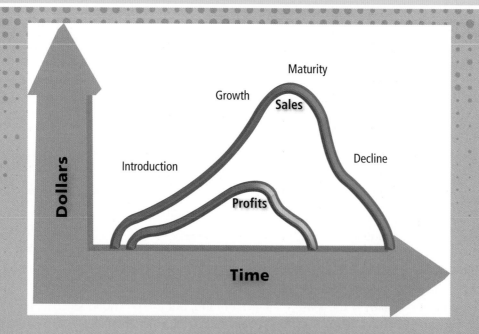

RECOMMIT TO THE PRODUCT LINE

Some companies decide that a declining product has other possible uses that can help improve sales. Knox® lost sales as people spent less time making fancy gelatin desserts. The company found a new use for the product that appealed to a different market. By adding Knox gelatin to JELL-O® mixes, it allowed consumers to make hand-held desserts. The new JELL-O Jigglers® desserts are especially popular with children. This new use for the product helped Knox improve its sales.

Even with recommitment and advertising of new product uses, there is no **guarantee** that a product will continue to have enough sales. Eventually, a company may need to discontinue the product.

DISCOUNT THE PRODUCT

Many declining product lines can be saved from deletion by discounting them to compete with cheaper store brands or private brands. Companies that discount declining products often advertise with phrases such as "compare and save" to stimulate sales.

REGIONALIZE THE PRODUCT

Sometimes companies decide to sell declining products only in the geographical areas where there is strong customer loyalty. By marketing its product only in those areas, the company avoids the cost of national advertising and distribution.

UPDATE OR ALTER THE PRODUCT

Certain products can be altered or modernized to avoid deletion. Some products can be redesigned, packaged differently, or reformulated. An example of an updated product is baking soda.

Baking soda, as its name suggests, was traditionally used for baking cakes. As this purpose declined, product developers and marketers found new ways to use baking soda: an odor-removing agent (e.g., cat litter) and cleanser (e.g., toothpaste and household cleaners). Tide® laundry detergent—originally available only in powder form in a box—was reformulated in liquid form and repackaged in a plastic bottle. The liquid product appealed to new and existing customers alike. By modernizing and altering product lines, the company expanded into a new area and avoided a product deletion of an existing product.

Companies spend large amounts of money to develop and promote consumer and industrial products. As a result, they are reluctant to delete products without trying one of the above strategies. When products must be dropped, a company needs to plan the move carefully to avoid disappointing customers and damaging the company's image.

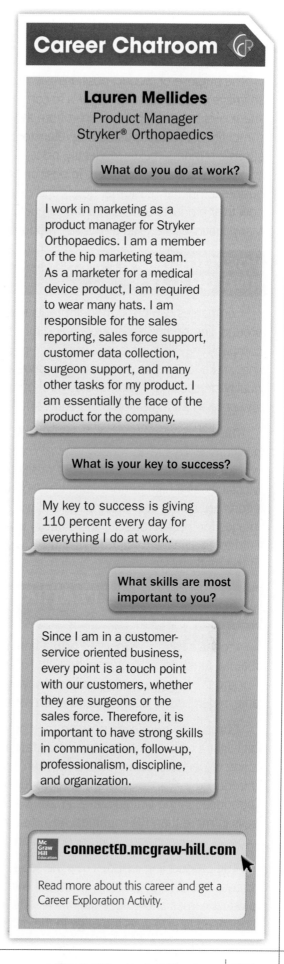

Career Chatroom

Lauren Mellides
Product Manager
Stryker® Orthopaedics

What do you do at work?

I work in marketing as a product manager for Stryker Orthopaedics. I am a member of the hip marketing team. As a marketer for a medical device product, I am required to wear many hats. I am responsible for the sales reporting, sales force support, customer data collection, surgeon support, and many other tasks for my product. I am essentially the face of the product for the company.

What is your key to success?

My key to success is giving 110 percent every day for everything I do at work.

What skills are most important to you?

Since I am in a customer-service oriented business, every point is a touch point with our customers, whether they are surgeons or the sales force. Therefore, it is important to have strong skills in communication, follow-up, professionalism, discipline, and organization.

connectED.mcgraw-hill.com

Read more about this career and get a Career Exploration Activity.

PRODUCT POSITIONING

The purpose of product positioning is to create an image of a product that appeals to consumers. The goal is to set the product apart from the competition. **Product positioning** refers to the efforts a business makes to identify, place, and sell its products in the marketplace. To position products, businesses identify customer needs and determine how their products compare to the competition. Many strategies are used to position products.

POSITIONING BY PRICE AND QUALITY

Companies can position their products in a product line on the basis of price and quality. A company may offer an economy line, a mid-priced line, and a luxury line. Positioning by price and quality stresses high price as a symbol of quality or low price as an indication of a good value.

The Ford Motor Company® deliberately positions its Focus® as an economical compact car while still emphasizing quality. Ford positions its Mustang® as a high-performance car. Promotional efforts are aimed at creating price and quality images for these products. This strategy enables Ford to give each of its products a unique position in the marketplace.

POSITIONING BY FEATURES AND BENEFITS

Products can be associated with a general feature, attribute, or customer benefit. For example, Rockport® shoes are positioned as always comfortable, regardless of active, casual, or dress use.

Companies frequently position their products to highlight a unique or perceived characteristic. Axe®, a line of personal care products for men, was first introduced in France in 1983. The product was introduced in the United States in 2003 and now sells in more than 60 countries. Advertising for the product is adventurous and unconventional.

The product line includes cologne sticks, body sprays, and shower gels. It is promoted with bold product names and unique fragrances. Axe is positioned to give guys the edge in the dating game. These product features and its perceived unique characteristic have made it one of the world's most popular male grooming brands.

POSITIONING IN RELATION TO THE COMPETITION

Some businesses position their products to compete directly with the products of other companies. Positioning in relation to the competition is a common strategy when a firm is trying to establish an advantage over another firm. It is not always a good idea to compete head-to-head with the industry leader. It might be better to compete as the underdog. Southwest Airlines® does a good job of doing that by telling potential customers that the airline is the low-fare alternative to other larger airlines.

New Product Failures Every year between 60 and 80 percent of new grocery store products fail.

POSITIONING IN RELATION TO OTHER PRODUCTS IN A LINE

Individual products may be positioned in relation to other products in the same line. Starting with the original iPod® fit-in-your-pocket music player, Apple has introduced other handheld players that not only store songs and playlists, but also have added features. The iPod nano® plays music and shoots video. The iPod touch® is a music player and a pocket computer with a 4-inch screen for playing games, viewing movies, and more. Each product has unique features and benefits, but each appeals to the different needs of customers.

 Reading Check

Contrast How is positioning a product in relation to competition different from positioning it in relation to other products in a line?

CATEGORY MANAGEMENT

Many manufacturers and retailers are adopting a process for marketing and selling their products known as *category management*. **Category management** is a process that involves managing product categories as individual business units. A category may include a group of product lines with the same target market and distribution channels. The process is designed to put manufacturers and retailers in touch with customer needs.

The category manager is responsible for all the brands for one generic product category, such as foods, beverages, or health and beauty products. The category manager is responsible for the profits or losses of the product mix and product lines in the category. The position evolved out of the position of product manager. A product manager handles a particular product and has more direct interaction with the company's sales force. A category manager is responsible for a generic category and has more interaction with other managers from finance, production, and research and development.

The manufacturer can customize a product mix within a category according to customer preference on a store-by-store basis. Using scanned data on product sales and other market data, manufacturers assist retailers with their product mix. In examining product mix, a manufacturer determines which of its products a particular retailer does not carry. It also identifies products that would have strong sales potential for both the retailer and the manufacturer. This analysis helps the manufacturer recommend an optimum product mix by projecting sales volume and profits for a retailer. The manufacturer then suggests adding or deleting certain items to its product mix. If the category manager feels that one product is decreasing sales of other products in the same category, this one product may be discontinued.

Another way manufacturers can help retailers is through **planograms**. A planogram is a computer-developed diagram that shows retailers how and where products within a category should be displayed on a shelf at individual stores. A planogram is shown in **Figure 30.4** (page 722).

MARKETING CASE STUDY

Style Meets Sound

Roxy® is a brand of Quiksilver®, Inc., a sports/casual lifestyle company that produces and distributes a mix of apparel, footwear, and other products for the youth market and board culture. The Roxy brand targets active, fashion-conscious young women. While exploring new product concepts, Roxy decided to partner with sound specialist JBL®, Inc., to create a new market category of portable audio products.

Uniquely Positioned

As Roxy's director of entertainment and sports marketing observes, music is a huge part of everyday living for most young people, and "Listening to music with great sound technology makes all the difference." So, the two companies developed a unique collection of stylish and colorful headphones—some with velvet earpieces—that also deliver high-quality sound. With this positioning strategy, Roxy and JBL plan to deliver more chic tech to the market.

English Language Arts

Collaborate Work with a partner to think of a new sports or music-related product. Write a summary of how you would *position* this product in the market for success.

FIGURE 30.4 | Planograms

Display Locations These diagrams show how and where products within a category should be displayed on shelves and on end racks at stores. *Why are planograms useful to retailers?*

Aisle 3

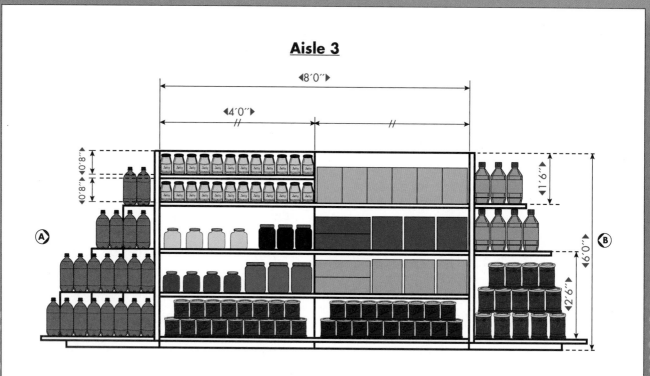

A: End Rack

B: End Rack

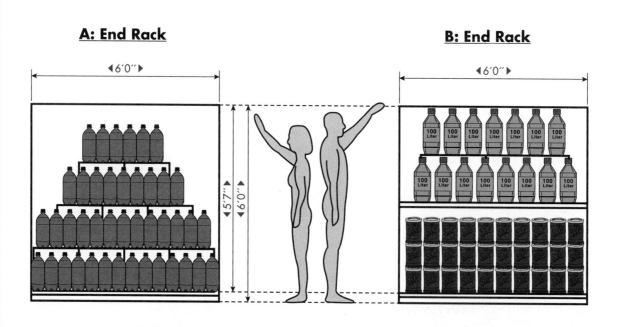

A planogram such as the examples in **Figure 30.4** (page 722) helps maximize a product's potential. Placement can also be used to highlight related products. Manufacturers can customize planograms for specific types of stores. Each store can stock more products that appeal to customers in its trading area and fewer products that have limited appeal.

The next time you visit a supermarket, walk down an aisle and notice the way products are placed on the shelves. The store's planogram will indicate that items such as baking supplies be stocked together. Sugar, flour, cooking oil, and baking powder will be grouped vertically, with like items positioned side-by-side. Name-brand products are typically placed at eye level for maximum exposure. Lower-priced generics are often displayed on bottom shelves.

Different planograms may be used to position products at a clothing store. A planogram at a clothing retailer may focus more on display design and layout. Designer apparel and other featured product lines are placed so as to attract the store's targeted customer base.

After You Read | Section 30.2

Review Key Concepts

1. **Define** the concept of product positioning.
2. **Identify** the strategies a business might use during a product's growth stage.
3. **Identify** the strategies a business might use during a product's decline stage.

Practice Academics

English Language Arts

4. Perform library or online research on the history of a popular consumer product. Write a one-page report identifying the product, its manufacturer, when it was introduced, where it is currently sold, its features, and benefits.

Mathematics

5. An electronics company has two products that are declining. One of these products should be deleted. Product A costs $45 per unit to produce and sells for $90. The storage, distribution, and promotion costs average $2.30 per unit. Last year, 22,500 units were sold. Product B costs $36 to produce and sells for $74. Its storage, distribution, and promotion costs average $4.50 per unit. Last year 51,000 units were sold. Which product is less profitable and should be deleted?

Math Concept **Computing Profit** When solving problems that involve calculating the profit, make a list of all the costs involved. Subtracting the total costs of the product from the total sales equals the profit of the product.

Starting Hints To solve this problem, determine the dollar amount in sales by multiplying the retail price by the number of products sold for both products. Determine the total cost of each product by adding the production and distribution costs per item and multiplying by the total number of products sold. Then subtract the total costs from the total sales.

 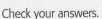 **connectED.mcgraw-hill.com**

Check your answers.

For help, go to the **Math Skills Handbook** located at the back of this book.

Product Planning

Product planning identifies features needed to sell products, services, or ideas. Businesses use different product mix strategies depending on resources and objectives.

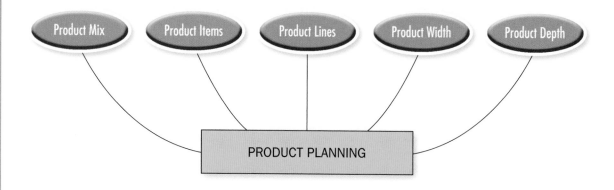

Product Mix · Product Items · Product Lines · Product Width · Product Depth

PRODUCT PLANNING

Product positioning involves considering the product's price and quality, its features and benefits, its relation to the competition, and its relation to other products in the product line.

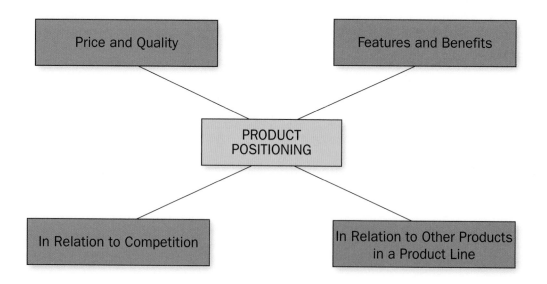

Price and Quality

Features and Benefits

PRODUCT POSITIONING

In Relation to Competition

In Relation to Other Products in a Product Line

Review and Activities

Written Summary

- Product planning involves deciding what features are needed to sell a business's products, services, or ideas.
- A product mix strategy is the plan for how the business decides which products it will make or stock.
- Businesses can use different product mix strategies depending on their resources and their objectives.
- A product life cycle represents the stages that a product goes through during its life: introduction, growth, maturity, and decline.
- The goal of product positioning is to set the product apart from the competition.
- Category management is a process that involves managing product categories as individual business units.

Review Content Vocabulary and Academic Vocabulary

1. Write true-or-false statements using each vocabulary word. Ask a partner to determine whether each statement is true or false and explain why.

Content Vocabulary
- product planning (p. 707)
- product mix (p. 707)
- product line (p. 708)
- product item (p. 708)
- product width (p. 708)
- product depth (p. 708)
- prototype (p. 713)
- product modification (p. 714)
- product life cycle (p. 717)
- product positioning (p. 720)
- category management (p. 721)
- planograms (p. 721)

Academic Vocabulary
- unique (p. 708)
- comparable (p. 709)
- awareness (p. 717)
- guarantee (p. 719)

Assess for Understanding

2. **Define** What is the product planning process?
3. **Sequence** What are the steps in product development?
4. **Infer** How would you describe product mix?
5. **Process** How do marketers develop, maintain, and improve product mix?
6. **Suggest** What would you recommend for an established company that has a staple product that is in the decline stage?
7. **Contrast** What are the different product positioning techniques?
8. **Role-Play** As a merchandiser, how can you explain the use of *planograms* to a retailer?
9. **Justify** How does category management help manufacturers and retailers?

21st  Century Skills

Communication Skills

10. **Customer Complaints** You are the store manager for a grocery store that has recently changed merchandise locations. You are confronted by a frustrated customer who cannot find a desired product and complains that the new layout is not logical. What can you do to assist the customer and to encourage continued shopping?

Financial Literacy Skills

11. **Calculating Gross Profit** What is the gross profit from 420 products that cost $1.30 to produce and sell for $2.00? What is the gross profit? What is the difference in percent between these totals?

e-Marketing Skills

12. **Product Line Extensions** Imagine that you are employed in research and development for a large food manufacturer. The firm uses online research to review product lines of major food manufacturers for possible product ideas. You have been assigned to review one of the following Web sites (Campbell's®, J.M. Smucker®, Hershey® Foods, Kellogg's®, H.J. Heinz®, General Mills®, Kraft®, Del Monte®, or Stouffer®) and identify five products and the product line extensions for each product.

- Who is the manufacturer and what five products were reviewed?
- List the product line extension for each of the five products.

Build Academic Skills

English Language Arts

13. **Technology in Automobiles** Conduct research on an existing or planned technology that is developed for automobiles today. Identify the name of your source(s) and prepare a written report of 150–200 words about how the technology has impacted driving, vehicular safety, or the environment.

Science

14. **Virtual Product Development** New high-tech products are being developed by coordinating software with electrical and mechanical design disciplines. Perform library or online research about virtual product development. Identify the name of the article, its source, and explain how scientists and engineers can speed delivery of new products to market. Write a one-page summary describing your research.

Mathematics

15. **Slotting Fees** Retailers sometimes charge manufacturers slotting fees for helping to introduce merchandise. Assume that a small retail chain charges $2,000 per store for a new brand of sandwich bread, while a mass market merchandiser charges $10,000 per store for the same product. To how many stores could you sell your brand of sandwich bread if your company has a slotting allowance budget of $60,000 and must include at least two mass market stores?

Math Concept **Calculating Fees** Calculating fees is done by multiplying the dollar amount of fees by the number of stores that will be charged a fee.

For help, go to the **Math Skills Handbook** located at the back of this book.

Standardized Test Practice

Directions Read the following questions. On a separate piece of paper, write the best possible answer for each one.

1. During which phase of the product life cycle would improving the product be a good strategy?

    A. Introduction Stage

    B. Growth Stage

    C. Maturity Stage

    D. Decline Stage

2. Product depth refers to the number of different product lines a business manufactures or sells.

    T

    F

3. All the different products that a company makes or sells are called _____.

Test-Taking Tip

Read and consider all of the answer choices before you choose the best response to the question. Examine each answer choice and think about how each differs from the others.

DECA Connection Role Play

Manager
Supermarket

Situation You are a manager of a large supermarket that is part of a regional chain. Your chain of supermarkets has been in business for many years. The supermarkets have a reputation for providing excellent customer service and extensive product width and depth. Prices at the stores are known to be somewhat higher than at similar supermarkets and higher than at discount supermarkets. Your customers know that they will find the exact item they want at your store.

Within the last year, a chain of upscale supermarkets has opened stores in your region. The chain sells many of the same products as your chain in their modern, clean, well-lit, and appealing stores. The competing chain does things differently from yours. Their product prices are significantly lower, and their product width and depth are much narrower than your chain's. Since the opening of your competitor's stores, sales at stores in your chain have declined notably.

In order to meet the competition's pricing, management of your chain has decided to narrow the product depth of many of the product lines you carry. This means that some product sizes will no longer be stocked in your stores. Your chain will carry only the best-selling sizes in most of your product lines.

Activity You are to discuss the product changes at this week's staff (judge) meeting. Your explanation should address the product changes, the reason for them, and a way to explain the changes to customers.

Evaluation You will be evaluated on how well you meet the following performance indicators:

1. Explain the nature and scope of the product/service management function.

2. Identify the impact of product life cycles on marketing decisions.

3. Explain the concept of product mix.

4. Demonstrate adaptability.

5. Make oral presentations.

 connectED.mcgraw-hill.com

Download the Competitive Events Workbook for more Role-Play practice.

branding, packaging, and labeling

Visual Literacy Branding, packaging, and labeling create perceived product differences or emphasize real differences. Packages and labels provide information to consumers and have distinctive lettering and designs. *Why do you think it might be important for a product to have a specific brand, package, and label?*

Discovery Project

Brand Personality

Essential Question How do brands and branding elements create a distinct image and personality for a product?

Project Goal

Assume that you work for a company that helps clients develop product brands and branding strategies. You have been asked by a client to research and analyze the brand personality for an existing consumer product. You are to prepare a written report on the brand personality for the product.

Ask Yourself...

- What is your product brand?
- How will you describe your brand's benefits, features, and symbols for the product?
- How does the brand represent your company? How does the brand make you or customers feel when using its product?
- How will you organize your report and summarize the brand's personality?

 Synthesize and Present Synthesize and analyze your research by preparing a written report on the brand personality for the product.

connectED.mcgraw-hill.com

Activity
Get a worksheet activity about branding strategies.

Evaluate
Download a rubric you can use to evaluate your project.

DECA Connection

DECA Event Role Play

Concepts in this chapter are related to DECA competitive events that involve either an interview or role play.

Performance Indicators The performance indicators represent key skills and knowledge. Your key to success in DECA competitive events is relating them to concepts in this chapter.

- Explain the nature of corporate branding.
- Describe factors used by businesses to position corporate brands.
- Explain the nature of product/service branding.
- Develop strategies to position a product/business.
- Describe the nature of product bundling.

DECA Prep

Role Play Practice role-playing with the DECA Connection competitive-event activity at the end of this chapter. More information on DECA events can be found on DECA's Web site.

READING GUIDE

Before You Read

Connect What influences your decision to purchase a product?

Objectives

- **Discuss** the nature, scope, and importance of branding in product planning.
- **Identify** the various branding elements.
- **List** three different types of brands.
- **Explain** how branding strategies are used to meet sales and company goals.

The Main Idea

A company name and its products should project a positive image. An important part of product and service management is to select, promote, and protect the company image and personality of its brands.

Vocabulary

Content Vocabulary
- brand
- brand name
- trade name
- brand mark
- trade character
- trademark
- national brands
- private distributor brands
- generic brands
- brand extension
- brand licensing
- mixed brand
- co-branding

Academic Vocabulary

You will find these words in your reading and on your tests. Make sure you know their meanings.
- component
- distinctive

Graphic Organizer

Draw or print this chart to take notes on the branding process.

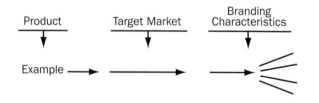

 connectED.mcgraw-hill.com

Print this graphic organizer.

MARKETING CORE FUNCTION

 Product/Service Management

BRANDING

Branding is an important **component** of the product planning process. A **brand** is a name, term, design, symbol, or combination of these elements that identifies a business, product, or service, and sets it apart from its competitors.

Developing a brand strategy can be one of the most challenging steps in the process. However, it is a crucial step when creating a company identity. A brand consistently and repeatedly tells customers and prospective customers why they should buy the company's products or services.

A brand can be used to identify one product, a family of related products, or all products of a company. Brands suggest a product's benefits, features, or qualities. For example, a company may want to develop a brand that suggests quality and reliability. Another company may want to develop a brand that suggests fun and excitement.

When a company defines its brand strategy and uses it in every interaction with its market, the company strengthens its message and its relationships. Brands are important assets and powerful tools for marketing and selling products.

As You Read

Analyze Why are brands so important to the success of a business?

ELEMENTS OF BRANDING

Brands are developed to target customers' needs and preferences. The target audience should feel that a brand is created just for them. Branding elements include brand names, trade names, brand marks, trade characters, and trademarks. These elements often combine to form a firm's corporate symbol or name.

Successful brands have tremendous value and frequently become global brands. Global brands appeal to consumers across cultural or political boundaries. For example, Coca-Cola® is an effective global brand. The brand projects an image of consistent quality, but it adapts its beverages to consumer needs within individual countries.

BRAND NAME

A **brand name**, or product brand, is a word, group of words, letters, or numbers that represent a product or service. An effective brand name should be easily pronounced, **distinctive**, and recognizable. Brand names are heavily marketed and are important company assets. Examples of brand names include Ford Focus®, Pepsi®, Barbie®, and Big Mac®. (See **Figure 31.1** on page 734.)

> **❝ Branding gives a company and its products distinct personalities. ❞**

TRADE NAME

A **trade name**, or corporate brand, identifies and promotes a company or a division of a particular corporation. The trade name is the legal name of the business. Trade names reflect the quality, value, and reliability of the organization. Trade names are used for investors, media, governmental purposes, and to support a company's product brands. Procter & Gamble®, IBM®, Disney®, Kellogg's®, Nike,® and Google® are trade names, or corporate brands. Trade names are legally protected and rarely change. If a trade name does change, it most often occurs because of a corporate merger or an acquisition.

BRAND MARK, TRADE CHARACTER, AND TRADEMARK

A **brand mark** incorporates a unique symbol, coloring, lettering, or design element. A brand mark is visually recognizable. Examples of brand marks are the Apple® Computer's apple or McDonald's® golden arches. A **trade character** is a specific type of brand mark, one with human form or characteristics. Some examples of trade characters include Betty Crocker's Jolly Green Giant®, Keebler Elves®, and the Pillsbury Doughboy®.

A **trademark** is a brand name, brand mark, trade name, trade character, or a combination of these elements that is registered with the federal government and has legal protection. Trademarks are used to prevent other companies from using a similar element that might be confused with the trademarked one. The U.S. Patent and Trademark Office grants trademark rights. Disputes regarding trademarks are settled in federal courts.

Trademarks are followed by a registered trademark symbol (®). Examples include Kellogg's Rice Krispies® cereal, and the Visa® credit card. Unregistered trademarks are followed by another symbol (™) and have limited protections. When elements of branding are registered as trademarks, they cannot be used or misused by other companies.

IMPORTANCE OF BRANDS IN PRODUCT PLANNING

Branding establishes an image for a product or company and projects that image to its customers and the marketplace. Companies should put careful consideration into developing their brand name and brand image. The use of brands is important in product planning for several reasons:

▶ **To build product recognition and customer loyalty**—It is important that customers easily recognize a company's branded products when they make repeat purchases.

▶ **To ensure quality and consistency**—Through branding, companies communicate to customers consistent quality and performance, purchase after purchase. Branding suggests consistency. For example, nine out of ten people will pay 25 percent more to buy GE's Soft White® light bulbs rather than another brand. The GE Soft White brand is perceived to be of higher quality and a better value than lower-priced competitors.

Trade Characters

Trade characters like the Michelin® man help build successful brands for their product categories. *Why might companies use trade characters when advertising their brands?*

- **To capitalize on brand exposure**—Branding helps companies extend their products or services into new target markets. It also helps introduce new product lines or categories. When Burger King® announced the BK Veggie™ burger, the company wanted to target new customers. Customers and prospects are more willing to try new products that carry a familiar brand name.

- **To change company or product image**—With careful planning, companies can also adjust or reposition a corporate or product brand's image to expand sales. For example, Aol.® changed its logotype AOL to Aol., and its brand symbol from a triangle to various backgrounds. The company used the new brand mark and the redesigned backgrounds of a fish, skateboarder, monster, and other objects to update, change, and re-energize the image for one of the first Internet service providers. The new brand mark and its different backgrounds project a new company image about the breadth of its services.

GENERATING BRAND NAMES

An estimated 75 percent of all companies introduce a new product name every year. The U.S. Patent and Trademark Office receives more than 400,000 trademark applications per year. It is understandable why some companies find it increasingly difficult to secure desirable corporate or product names.

Some companies use computer software programs that specialize in generating brand names. These programs will check to see if a name is already owned and trademarked by another company. Other companies hire branding agencies, naming consultants, or public relations firms to generate and check the availability of brand names.

Branding is so important to product planning that more than 60 percent of all companies conduct market research to test new brand names before they are released. After a name has been generated and researched, companies will then conduct brand-loyalty research to gauge the brand's effectiveness.

Once established, brand names are carefully protected. New brand names may be created when a business adds new product lines, seeks a new domestic or international market, or attempts to update its existing brand image. Brand names can also change as a result of trademark lawsuits and court decisions.

TYPES OF BRANDS

Manufacturers, wholesalers, and retailers brand their

products. As a result, there are three classifications of brands. There is one for each type of company that brands its products: national brands (manufacturers), private distributor brands (wholesalers and retailers), and generic brands.

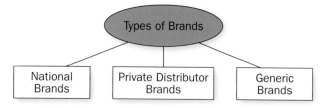

```
                    ┌─────────────────┐
                    │ Types of Brands │
                    └─────────────────┘
           ┌──────────────┼──────────────┐
  ┌─────────────┐  ┌───────────────────┐  ┌─────────┐
  │  National   │  │ Private Distributor│  │ Generic │
  │   Brands    │  │      Brands        │  │ Brands  │
  └─────────────┘  └───────────────────┘  └─────────┘
```

NATIONAL BRANDS

National brands, also known as *producer brands*, are owned and initiated by national manufacturers or by companies that provide services. Some national brands for goods include Hershey Foods®, Colgate-Palmolive®, Whirlpool®, Sunoco®, and Ford®. Some service companies that generate national brands are Delta Airlines®, Hilton Hotels®, Avis® rent-a car, Wells Fargo® banking services, and AFLAC® insurance.

THE IMPORTANCE OF NATIONAL BRANDS

National brands generate the majority of sales for most consumer product categories.

Approximately 65 percent of all appliances, 78 percent of all food products, 80 percent of all gasoline, and 100 percent of all cars are national brands

Branding Style The Helvetica font was created more than 50 years ago by the Haas type foundry in Switzerland and is used for most corporate brand names and logos.

Electronic technologies have created a new category of national brand—the Internet brand. There are Internet brands for both consumer goods and services. Internet consumer product brands include Amazon® and eBay®. Internet service brands include Google®, Bing®, and MSN® search engines, and social media brands such as Facebook®, Twitter®, YouTube®, and LinkedIn®.

National brands are also associated with an image. They appeal to consumers who believe that

FIGURE 31.1 Top Global Brands

Global Recognition Some brands that are recognized around the world are a company's most valuable asset. *What is the brand value of the top five global brands?*

Rank	Name of Brand	Brand Value ($ millions)	Country of Ownership
1	Apple	118,863	USA
2	Google	107,479	USA
3	Coca-Cola	81,563	USA
4	IBM	72,244	USA
5	Microsoft	61,154	USA
6	GE	45,480	USA
7	Samsung	45,462	South Korea
8	Toyota	42,392	Japan
9	McDonalds	42,254	USA
10	Mercedes-Benz	34,338	Germany

Source: Interbrand Study Best Global Brands 2014

a national brand will have consistent standards of quality, dependability, performance, and reliability.

PRIVATE DISTRIBUTOR BRANDS

Private distributor brands, known as *private brands*, *store brands*, *dealer brands*, or *private labels*, are developed and owned by wholesalers and retailers. The manufacturer's name may not appear on the product.

Private distributor brands include Radio Shack® electronic items, Nordstrom's Caslon® women's apparel, and Walmart's Great Value® food and general merchandise product brands. Private distributor brands appeal to customers who want the quality and performance of national brands at a lower price. Some private brands, such as Sears' Craftsman® tools, have become so popular and respected that they rival national brands in sales and customer recognition.

Many large supermarket and retail chains have private distributor brands. In the United States, more than 800 categories of private label goods exist in clothing, food products, paper products, medications, vitamins, and pet foods.

THE INCREASING POPULARITY OF PRIVATE BRANDS

Private distributor brands are increasing their global market share in most product categories. Private brands represent 45 percent of the market in Switzerland, 28 percent in Great Britain, 19 percent in Canada, and 16 percent in the U.S.

Private brands are popular with retailers because they usually carry higher gross margins. For example, 7 Eleven® sells 180 private label items priced up to 20 percent lower than national brands. Thus, they are more profitable than national brands. Also, because private brands are not sold at competitors' stores, they help cultivate customer loyalty.

GENERIC BRANDS

Generic brands are products that do not carry a company identity. The packaging for generic products simply describes the item, such as "pancake mix" or "paper towels." Generic brands are generally sold in supermarkets and discount stores. These unbranded products are often priced 30 to 50 percent lower than manufacturer brands and 10 to 15 percent lower than private distributor brands. Companies that manufacture and sell generic brands do not heavily advertise or promote these products and, therefore, can pass on savings to customers.

Generic products include more than 300 product categories, including vitamins, auto parts, food staples, and pharmaceuticals. Generic products are offered in more than 250 retail chains in the United States, and more than 75 percent of all U.S. supermarkets carry generic items.

 Reading Check

Explain What is the difference between a brand mark and a trademark?

BRANDING STRATEGIES

Companies develop and rely on a variety of branding strategies to meet sales and company objectives. Some of these strategies include brand extensions, brand licensing, mixed branding, and co-branding. Effective use of different brand strategies can increase sales of branded products and maximize company profits.

BRAND EXTENSION

Brand extension is a branding strategy that uses an existing brand name to promote a new or improved product in a company's product line. For example, Ocean Spray® extended its cranberry juice drink product line by adding flavors, including Cran®Apple, Cran®Cherry, and Cran®Grape fruit blends. Launching new products is costly, and the failure rate for new products is high. Sometimes companies can reduce this risk by using an already established brand name.

A risk that companies face when they employ a brand extension strategy is overextending a product line and diluting or weakening the brand.

When does brand dilution occur? If a brand includes too many products, the original brand and other selections in the product line may lose recognition and appeal with customers.

BRAND LICENSING

Brand licensing is a legal authorization by a brand owner to allow another company (the licensee) to use its brand, brand mark, or trade character for a fee. The agreement explains all the terms and conditions under which the brand may be used.

Companies license their brands to increase revenue sources, enhance company image, and sell more of their core products. For example, the National Football League® (NFL) has a licensing arrangement with EA SPORTS®. EA SPORTS uses NFL team names, logos, and individual players in their video games to try to attract customers. Licensed products must always support the brand strategy and image of the company—in this case, the NFL grants the license to use its name.

MARKETING CASE STUDY

EA's Branding Savvy

Electronic Arts' (EA) is one of the world's leading electronic-games companies. Its branding strategies have long included brand licensing and co-branding. They are essential components of its marketing plan and concept development process. Forging partnerships with sports organizations as well as consumer products, such as Dr. Pepper® , EA has depended on such strategic alliances to reach fans.

Virtual Competition

The company's popular game brand EA SPORTS™ was one of the first to tap into the lucrative gaming software and online gaming markets. EA developed cool action-game franchises, such as NBA Live, NASCAR Thunder™, and SSX for snowboarding. Partnering with Major League Gaming, the largest professional video game league in the world, EA can provide online tournament functionality for many of its sports titles. As EA's president says, EA is ushering in "a new era of video game competition."

English Language Arts

Create Think of a theme for a new electronic-game series. Write a one-page description of the game concept and include your ideas for co-branding or licensing for this new product.

MIXED BRANDS

Some manufacturers and retailers use a mixed brand strategy to sell products. A **mixed brand** strategy offers a combination of manufacturer, private distributor, and generic brands to consumers.

A manufacturer of a national brand agrees to make a product for sale under another company's brand. For example, Michelin® manufactures its own brand of tires as well as tires for sale at Sears under the Sears brand name. A mixed-brand strategy enables a business to maintain brand loyalty through its national brand and reach several different target markets through private brands. This strategy increases its overall product mix. It can maximize its profits by selling a private brand product without damaging the reputation and the sales of its national brand product.

CO-BRANDING

A **co-branding** strategy combines one or more brands in the manufacture of a product or in the delivery of a service. For example, Smucker's® sugar-free preserves are made with Splenda®. This strategy enables companies to capitalize on the popularity of other companies' goods and services to reach new customers and ideally increase sales for both companies' brands.

To ensure that all partners benefit from co-branding, it is essential that potential partners are compatible. The partners do not need to be the same size or have comparable reputations. Co-branding can work with one or several partners. Co-branding can also work when two or more retailers share the same location. For example, Starbucks Coffee® has an agreement with Barnes & Noble® to establish coffee shops inside their bookstores.

 After You Read   **Section 31.1**

Review Key Concepts

1. **Explain** the difference between a brand name and a trade name.
2. **Describe** brand extension and brand licensing.
3. **Define** mixed branding and co-branding.

Practice Academics

English Language Arts

4. Conduct research to obtain information about why multinational companies, such as Kellogg's®, Procter & Gamble®, and others, often use different brand names for the same product sold in various countries. Prepare a one-page written report on your findings.

Mathematics

5. Compare the brand values of two paper-products companies. Company A has a brand value of $1.95 billion and Company B has a brand value of $1.3 billion. How many times greater is the brand value of A than B?

   Math Concept **Division** When determining how many times greater a value is compared to another value, the operation to use is division.

   Starting Hints To solve this problem, divide Company A's brand value of $1.95 billion by Company B's brand value to determine the answer.

 connectED.mcgraw-hill.com

Check your answers.

For help, go to the Math Skills Handbook located at the back of this book.

READING GUIDE

Before You Read

Predict What would happen if consumer products were not packaged and labeled?

Objectives

- **Explain** the functions of product packaging.
- **Identify** the functions of labels.

The Main Idea

Packaging and labels put a "face" on a product. Effective packaging and labeling help sell a product.

Vocabulary

Content Vocabulary

- package
- mixed bundling
- price bundling
- blisterpacks
- aseptic packaging
- cause packaging
- label
- brand label
- descriptive label
- grade label

Academic Vocabulary

You will find these words in your reading and on your tests. Make sure you know their meanings.

- integral
- periods

Graphic Organizer

Draw or print this chart to take notes about the functions of packaging.

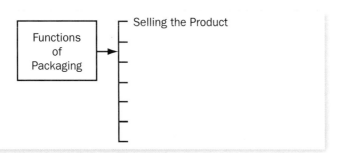

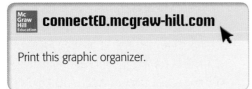

connectED.mcgraw-hill.com

Print this graphic organizer.

MARKETING CORE FUNCTION

Product/Service Management

Packaging and Labeling

PACKAGING

A **package** is the physical container or wrapping for a product. A package represents the size, shape, and final appearance of a product at the time of sale. A product's package is an **integral** part of product planning. It is estimated that 10 percent of a product's retail price is spent on the actual package, its design, and development.

As You Read

Connect Consider how product packaging and labeling help you as a consumer.

FUNCTIONS OF PACKAGING

Aside from holding products, packaging fulfills several functions. Those functions include selling the product, communicating product identity, providing information, meeting customer needs, protecting consumers, protecting the product, and theft reduction.

SELLING THE PRODUCT

Customer reaction to a product's package and its brand name is an important factor in its success or failure in the marketplace. Attractive, colorful, and visually appealing packages have promotional value and can carry important messages about the product's performance, features, and benefits. A well-designed package is a powerful point-of-purchase selling device. In today's self-service environments, an attractive package can make a product stand out from its competition.

Sometimes marketers package, or bundle, two or more different goods or services in one package. This is known as **mixed bundling**. For example, airlines often bundle airfare, lodging, and car rental packages together for vacationers.

> **Innovative product packages and clear labels can lead to double-digit sales growth.**

Price bundling occurs when two or more similar products are placed on sale for one package price. Price and mixed bundling provide cheaper prices for the goods and services than if they were purchased separately.

A container's design can minimize sales lost to competitors' products. It can even create new sales opportunities. Pump soap containers were designed to be neater, cleaner, and easier to use than bar soaps. These new containers have not replaced bar soaps. Instead, they provide a choice for customers. Pump-type dispensers created new sales and started an entire new line of soap products.

COMMUNICATING PRODUCT IDENTITY

Packages can promote an image such as prestige, convenience, or status. How does packaging communicate with consumers? The design, color, words, and labels on the package all talk to the consumer.

Color is one of the main design elements for packages because it can attract attention and project an image. For example, research indicates that red packaging communicates vitality, sensibility, and dependability. Yellow makes packages look larger and conveys the image of sun, warmth, happiness, and newness. Blue packaging conveys an image of cleanliness, and feelings of knowledge, confidence, and credibility. Green projects a natural and healthy image. White packaging implies freshness, while black implies status, quality, and richness.

PROVIDING INFORMATION

A package provides useful information for the customer. Many package labels give directions for using a product, the contents, product guarantees, nutritional information, instructions for care, and warnings about potential hazards.

MEETING CUSTOMER NEEDS

When designing packages, product planners analyze customer lifestyles and create packaging for customer convenience, functionality, and family size. To improve convenience, Nabisco® created its patented resealable opening for its Chips Ahoy!® cookies. Customer demands for a better way to use all of the contents led to the Heinz Ketchup® upside-down bottle.

Product packages also come in various sizes for different market segments. Family packs meet the needs of larger families, while smaller packages are made for individuals. Some examples include multipacks of beverages such as soda and juice, bulk sizes of paper packages, single-serving cans of soup, and family meals at fast-food outlets.

PROTECTING CONSUMERS

A package can also improve product safety. For example, many products that were formerly packaged in glass now come in plastic containers.

To avoid misuse or product tampering, over-the-counter medications and cosmetics are sold in tamper-resistant containers. Airtight containers are used to protect against spoilage of perishable food, such as dairy, fruit, meat, and vegetable products.

Many products are packaged in childproof containers that feature sealed lids that are more difficult to open. This reduces the chances of accidental spills and poisonings. Product planners must consider these factors, or companies risk of losing business and harming their brand images.

PROTECTING THE PRODUCT

A package must protect a product during shipping, storage, and display. The package design should also prevent or discourage tampering, prevent shoplifting, and protect against breakage. **Blisterpacks** are packages with preformed plastic molds surrounding individual items arranged on a backing. "Packing peanuts" are a loose-fill packaging and cushioning material used to prevent damage to products during shipping. Packing peanuts may be reused or recycled.

Sending the Message

The design, color, words, and labels on a package all help to communicate product identity to consumers. *What kind of identity and image is projected by this product's package?*

START GETTING **FIVE** SERVINGS OF VEGETABLES EVERY DAY.

WE'VE GOT YOUR FIRST **THREE** RIGHT HERE.

COULD'VE HAD A V8

Stores must strike a balance between product protection and consumer frustration with packages that are difficult to open. Because of governmental concerns about consumer injuries when trying to open clamshell-type packages, Best Buy®, Amazon®, and other leading retailers are working on simpler, easier-to-open package designs.

THEFT REDUCTION

Packaging may also help reduce theft. Some packages, for example, are intentionally made larger than the product. Consider software packages, where the packaging is much larger than the discs inside. This larger packaging makes it more difficult for a thief to steal it . Electronic anti-theft devices are often attached to packages.

CONTEMPORARY PACKAGING ISSUES

Product packaging offers companies unique opportunities to incorporate the latest technologies and address lifestyle changes, as well as environmental, social, and political concerns.

ASEPTIC PACKAGING

Aseptic packaging uses technology that keeps foods fresh without refrigeration for long **periods**.

The process involves separately sterilizing the package and the food product, and then filling and sealing the package in a sterile environment. Examples of aseptic packaging include paperboard boxes for juices, puddings, syrups, flavored milks, and liquid eggs. Aseptic packages are convenient because they can be stored unopened or can be refrigerated in the package.

ENVIRONMENTAL PACKAGING

Companies are developing packages that respond to consumer demand for environmentally sensitive designs. Public opinion surveys show that most Americans support less wasteful packaging and better recycling efforts. For example, several local and state governments have proposed fees on disposable plastic bags that are used to carry purchases.

In response to consumer concerns, companies are promoting reusable shopping bags and making more space-saving packages. Such packages may be biodegradable, reusable, recyclable, and safer for the environment.

Helping the Environment

This advertisement promotes how this company uses solar energy and how it will help make a greener planet. *How could a manufacturer benefit from focusing its marketing messages on environmental concerns?*

We're living up to our name.

SunChips® snacks are now made with the help of solar energy in California.

As of April 22nd, one of our plants is using solar energy to help make SunChips® snacks. Not just because it's in our name, but because it's part of our vision for a healthy planet. It's a small step, but a step in the right direction.

live brightly
www.sunchips.com

Actual solar collectors at our SunChips® plant in Modesto California.

Coca-Cola® introduced a new plastic bottle in 2010 that is partially made from sugarcane and molasses. The PlantBottle™ is recyclable and uses a renewable resource—plants. It is made with 30-percent plant material and reduces carbon emissions by up to 25 percent, compared with petroleum-based PET plastic bottles.

Many companies that manufacture spray products, such as hair products and air fresheners, have switched from using aerosol cans to pump dispensers. These containers do not release ozone-destroying chlorofluorocarbons, or CFCs, into the atmosphere.

CAUSE PACKAGING

Some companies are also using their packages to promote social and political causes. This practice is known as **cause packaging**. The issues promoted on the packages may be totally unrelated to the products inside.

Ben & Jerry's ice cream cartons promote saving the rain forests and express opposition to the use of bovine growth hormone to stimulate milk production in cows. Another example is the internationally recognized symbol of breast cancer awareness—a pink ribbon. Because the symbolic pink ribbon is in the public domain, it has been seen on a wide variety of products, from body wash to portable DVD players to cookie cutters.

Printing messages on packages encourages consumers to participate in or think about issues. In many ways, cause packaging is also a company's effort to differentiate its products from those of its competitors.

Reading Check

Explain What is the difference between mixed bundling and price bundling?

LABELING

A **label** is an information tag, wrapper, seal, or imprinted message that is attached to a product or its package. The main function of a label is to inform customers about a product's contents and give directions for use. Labels also protect businesses from legal liability if a consumer is injured during the use of its product. Fear of litigation (law suits), consumer pressure, government regulation, and concern for consumer safety are all factors that have compelled manufacturers to place more detailed information on labels. There are three kinds of labels: brand, descriptive, and grade.

Three Kinds of Labels

| Brand Label |
| Descriptive Label |
| Grade Label |

The **brand label** gives the brand name, trademark, or logo. For example, some bananas are stickered with the Chiquita® brand label. Although this is an acceptable form of labeling, it supplies insufficient product information. The U.S. government may approve laser-etched labels. This technology, already used in many countries, allows companies to place produce look-up codes

(PLUs), brand names, logos, and country-of-origin information on fruits and vegetables. The process is designed to help track and trace produce-borne illnesses.

A **descriptive label** gives information about the product's use, construction, care, performance, and other features. For example, food labels include product illustrations, weight statements, dating and storage information, ingredients, product guarantees, and the manufacturer's name and address. Product illustrations must represent what is in the package. Weight statements give the net weight of the entire product minus the package or liquid in which it is packed.

Date and storage information is necessary for food items. Date information includes the "packed on" date (date food was packed), the "sell by" date (last date product should be sold), the "best if used by" date (last date for use for top quality), and the expiration date (date after which the product should not be used). Storage information tells how the product should be stored to have the least waste and best quality. Descriptive labels do not necessarily always contain all the information that consumers need when making a buying decision.

Nonfood labels usually provide consumers with instructions for the proper use and care of products. They also give manufacturers a convenient place to communicate warranty information and product use warnings. Notices of electrical hazard, flammability, and poisonous ingredients are required on the labels of certain categories of products. Labels might also contain symbols that give basic instructions on how to wash, cook, or care for the product.

Labels also include the manufacturer's name and address, so consumers can write for more information or to register a complaint. Many labels also include the company's Web address, encouraging consumers to visit for more information. Some labels include a customer-service phone number that consumers can use for questions or problems.

A **grade label** states the quality of the product. For example, eggs are grade-labeled AA, A, and B; corn and wheat are grade-labeled 1 and 2; and canned fruit is often grade-labeled A, B, or C. Beef is graded as prime, choice, or select.

LABELING LAWS

Labeling laws have been enacted to prevent manufacturers from misleading consumers with deceptive or incomplete packaging labels.

Many package labels must now meet local, state, and federal standards. Federal laws require that the name and address of the manufacturer, packer, or distributor, and the quantity of contents appear on labels.

The Fair Packaging and Labeling Act (FPLA) of 1966 established mandatory labeling requirements and authorized the U.S. Food and Drug Administration (FDA) and the Federal Trade Commission (FTC) to establish packaging regulations. A 1992 amendment to the FPLA called for packages of selected products to include metric measurements. The amendment, which went into effect in 1994, requires that product weight be listed in American and metric weights and measures.

In today's global marketplace, companies must also consider the labeling laws of other countries. Some countries require bilingual labels. Others require that every ingredient in a product be listed on the label.

Meeting Customer Needs

Packaging designers look at how customers interact and use products. *Why is it necessary to study customer lifestyles?*

The GREEN Marketer

Green Yogurt

A new breed of businesspeople is combining profit with progress. Take Gary Hirshberg, who transformed Stonyfield Farm from a tiny farming school in New Hampshire into the leading organic yogurt brand in the United States.

The company buys milk from family farms, donates 10 percent of profits to environmental groups, and offsets its CO_2 emissions—all while still making a profit.

Eco-Packaging Before many others did it, this company evaluated its own carbon footprint. As part of its mission, Stonyfield set up a sustainable packaging team to create the most environmentally sustainable product packaging possible. Their goal is to achieve 100 percent sustainable packaging. Packaging has been reduced by about 1 million pounds per year.

Science

Ask Find out the meaning of the term *carbon footprint* and how packaging impacts it. Do research to find three products with "green" packaging and explain what qualifies their packaging as sustainable.

---

connectED.mcgraw-hill.com

Get an activity on green marketing.

THE FDA

The federal Nutrition Labeling and Education Act of 1990 protects consumers from deceptive labeling. This act, administered by the FDA, requires that labels give nutritional information on how a food fits into an overall daily diet. Labels must clearly state the amount of calories, fat, carbohydrates, sodium, cholesterol, and protein in each serving. Labels must also state the percentage of a daily intake of 2,000 calories. The act also regulates health claims in that it allows the use of only certain descriptive words on labels. These words include *light* and *lite*, *free* (as in *fat free*, *salt free*, *cholesterol free*), *low*, *reduced*, and *good source of*.

The FDA also requires that U.S. manufacturers of certain products place health warnings on their packages. Beginning in 1989, all alcoholic beverage labels had to carry the following statements: "According to the Surgeon General, women should not drink alcoholic beverages during pregnancy because of the risk of birth defects. Consumption of alcoholic beverages impairs the ability to drive a car or operate machinery and may cause health problems." Similar warnings of health risks are required on cigarette package labels.

In 2009, the FDA issued regulations regarding the labeling of products made with genetically engineered animals. Companies are not required to label food products containing genetically modified organisms. Such labeling is voluntary.

THE FEDERAL TRADE COMMISSION

The Federal Trade Commission is responsible for regulating labeling and monitoring advertising that is false or misleading.

The Care Labeling Rule of 1972 requires that care labels be placed in textile clothing. This rule ensures that specific information about the care of garments be detailed on labels, including information related to washing, drying, and ironing.

The FTC released guidelines in 1992 for companies to follow when making environmental claims on labels. Previously, many environmental terms had definitions that were not clear. When using the term *recycled* to describe the content of its products, a company must demonstrate proof of the claim. It must prove that it has retrieved or recovered a certain amount of scraps or materials from the waste stream.

The term *recyclable* can be used only if the product or package can be reused as raw material for a new product or package. The terms *ozone safe* and *ozone friendly* can be used only if the products do not contain any ozone-depleting chemicals. The terms *degradable*, *biodegradable*, and *photodegradable* can be used only if the product will decompose into elements found in nature within a short time after disposal.

U.S. DEPARTMENT OF AGRICULTURE

Increasing sales of organic foods led the U.S. Department of Agriculture (USDA) to issue legal standards, certification requirements, and penalties for misuse of organic labels. The Organic Foods Production (OFPA) Act of 1990, as amended, requires labeling based on the percentage of organic ingredients in a product.

Organic foods are produced without hormones, antibiotics, herbicides, insecticides, chemicals, genetic modification, or germ-killing radiation. The required product labeling and ingredients differ for foods marketed as *100 percent organic, organic* or *made with organic ingredients*. The USDA Organic label requires both products and producers to be certified.

The Country of Origin Labeling (COOL) Act of 2002 is also administered by the USDA and requires that a country-of-origin label be placed on all fruits, vegetables, peanuts, meats, and fish.

The Food Allergen Labeling and Consumer Protection Act (FALCPA) of 2004 applies to consumer packaged foods regulated by the FDA. The FDA does not regulate meat, poultry, and egg products. This is the job of the Food Safety and Inspection Service (FSIS). The FSIS has established policies for processors to voluntarily add FSIS-approved allergen statements to the labeling of meat, poultry, and egg products. This can help allergen-sensitive individuals to make informed food choices for all foods, including those not regulated by the FDA.

 After You Read Section 31.2

Review Key Concepts

1. **Differentiate** between a label and a brand label.
2. **Identify** the types of information found on a food label.
3. **Name** three federal agencies that regulate packaging and labeling.

Practice Academics

English Language Arts

4. Perform library or online research on one of the federal labeling laws as explained in this chapter. Write a one-page report on the purpose of the law, its provisions, and penalties for violating the law.

Mathematics

5. The newest law firm in town paid a total of $33,860 to a marketing firm for the research and development of the firm's corporate trade name and trademark. From this budget, a Web-site developer was paid $9,475 for her creative work on the project. Her salary was what percentage of the entire amount?

   Math Concept **Division** When solving problems that involve percents, it is usually a matter of dividing one value by another.

   Starting Hints To solve this problem, divide the salary of the Web-site developer by the total amount paid to the marketing firm to determine what percent the developer's salary was of the total.

 connectED.mcgraw-hill.com

Check your answers.

For help, go to the **Math Skills Handbook** located at the back of this book.

Branding, Packaging, and Labeling

A brand is a name, term, design, or symbol that identifies a product or service. Brands may include a trade name, brand name, brand mark, trade character, and trademark.

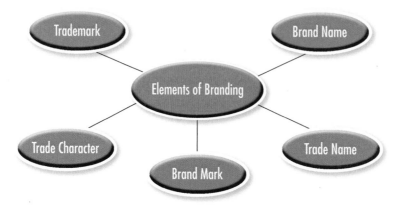

Brand extensions, brand licensing, mixed brand, and co-branding strategies increase sales.

BRANDING STRATEGIES	
BRAND EXTENSION	MIXED BRANDS
BRAND LICENSING	CO-BRANDING

Packaging helps companies sell a product, communicate its identity, provide information about the product, meet customer needs, protect customers, protect the product, and prevent theft.

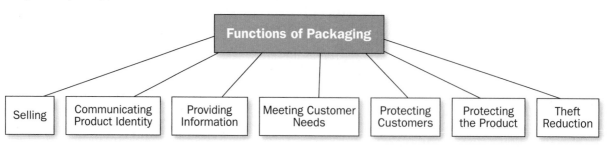

Review and Activities

Written Summary

- A brand is a name, term, design, or symbol (or combination of these elements) that identifies a product or service.
- Brands can include a trade name, brand name, brand mark, trade character, and trademark.
- Branding strategies include brand extensions, brand licensing, mixed branding, and co-branding.
- Effective use of brand strategies can increase sales of branded products and maximize company revenues.
- The functions of packaging include promoting and selling the product, defining product identity, providing information, expressing benefits and features to customers, ensuring safe use, and protecting the product.
- The main function of a label is to inform customers about a product's contents and give directions for use.
- Labels also protect businesses from legal liability that may occur if a consumer misuses the product.

Review Content Vocabulary and Academic Vocabulary

1. Label each of these content and vocabulary terms as a noun, verb, or adjective.

Content Vocabulary
- brand (p. 731)
- brand name (p. 731)
- trade name (p. 731)
- brand mark (p. 732)
- trade character (p. 732)
- trademark (p. 732)
- national brands (p. 734)
- private distributor brands (p. 735)
- generic brands (p. 735)
- brand extension (p. 736)
- brand licensing (p. 736)
- mixed brand (p. 737)
- co-branding (p. 737)
- package (p. 739)
- mixed bundling (p. 739)
- price bundling (p. 739)
- blisterpacks (p. 740)
- aseptic packaging (p. 741)
- cause packaging (p. 742)
- label (p. 742)
- brand label (p. 742)
- descriptive label (p. 742)
- grade label (p. 743)

Academic Vocabulary
- component (p. 731)
- distinctive (p. 731)
- integral (p. 739)
- periods (p. 741)

Assess for Understanding

2. **Explain** What are the nature, scope, and importance of branding in product planning?
3. **Contrast** What are the differences between the various branding elements?
4. **Identify** What are three different types of brands?
5. **Apply** How are branding strategies used to meet sales and company goals?
6. **Demonstrate** What are the functions of product packaging?
7. **Justify** What are the functions of labels?
8. **Define** What are the definitions of the terms *descriptive label* and *grade label*?
9. **Consider** Why is packaging important to product planning?

 21st Century Skills

Teamwork Skills

10. Products and Brand Extensions You and a classmate work for a consumer products manufacturer. You have been asked by management to identify the products offered in a competitor's branded product line. Use the Internet and corporate Web sites to find out the brand extensions within the brand line. With your partner, prepare a written report about the products, the number of brand extensions, and various features of the products.

Financial Literacy Skills

11. Calculating Barcode Costs A global company wants to design a barcode that is fun and memorable as part of a new package. If design costs for an exclusive barcode total $4,000, what percentage does this represent for a package that costs $50,000 to develop?

Everyday Ethics

12. Truth in Labeling The FDA has developed guidelines for *voluntary* labeling on genetically modified products. Do you believe it is the obligation of a grocery store to label its fruits and vegetables as genetically engineered or otherwise? Write a two-paragraph statement expressing your opinion.

e-Marketing Skills

13. Guide to Environmental Labels You are a product planner for a large food manufacturer. You are to go to the Consumer Reports® Greener Choices™ Web site to get an expert opinion on eco-labels for the food category. Select one product from the food category. Identify one eco-label for a specific product and the certifying agency or organization. List five other products that may also carry this eco-label. What product did you investigate in the food category?

Build Academic Skills

English Language Arts

14. Brand Licensing Use publications, such as *Brandweek, AdWeek, BusinessWeek,* and entertainment and sports publications, or online research to investigate brand licensing arrangements in the sports or entertainment fields. Identify the name of your source(s) and prepare a one-page report that summarizes the arrangement, the parties and companies involved, and length of the licensing agreement.

Science

15. Environmental Packaging Marketers are increasingly using packaging materials that are reusable, recyclable, and safer for the environment. Perform library or online research about the science and technologies used to recycle one selected item (paper, cardboard, glass, plastic, wood or another packaging material of your choice) used in product packaging. Identify the name of the article, its publisher, the packaging material investigated, and explain the recycling process for it. Write a one-page summary describing the process.

Mathematics

16. Private Distributor Brands Some larger U.S. stores have created private distributor brands for their stores. This allows them to sell goods at a lower retail price. At one such store, its private distributor brand accounts for 60 percent of total annual sales. If the total annual sales were $86,450,735, what were the sales for the private distributor brand?

Math Concept **Calculating Percent** Calculate percent by multiplying the total sales dollar amount by the decimal form of the percent given.

For help, go to the **Math Skills Handbook** located at the back of this book.

Standardized Test Practice

Directions Read the following questions. On a separate piece of paper, write the best possible answer for each one.

1. Which of the following is a name, term, design, symbol, or combination of these elements that defines a product and distinguishes it from its competitors?
   A. Brand
   B. Brand mark
   C. Trademark
   D. Trade character

2. Generic brands carry company identity on the package.
   T
   F

3. An information tag, wrapper, seal, or imprinted message attached to a product is known as a(n) _____.

Test-Taking Tip
Have a nutritious meal and avoid junk food before taking a test. Studies show that you need good nutrition to concentrate and perform at your best.

DECA Connection Role Play

Representative Business Advice Company

Situation You represent a company that specializes in advising businesses about overcoming their business challenges. Your current client (judge) is the sales manager for a local office supply chain. The chain sells all of the major national brand products.

The chain recently began selling a limited range of products produced for the company and sold with the company name on the packages. Some of the products include office paper, pens, markers, pencils, paper clips, staplers and staples, and other small office products. The store brand products are of excellent quality, made from recycled materials where possible, and sell for less than the national brands.

However, the store products are not selling very well. The sales manager (judge) has asked you study the situation and make recommendations. Your study has shown that the products, while having the store name, have few identifying factors on the packaging and no coordination of the packaging of various products. You think the office supply chain needs to establish a company brand identity that can be extended to the packaging of the store brand products.

Activity You are to meet with the sales manager (judge) to explain your findings and recommend that the office supply chain establish a company brand. You are to also explain branding and its importance to the business and sales of the store brand products.

Evaluation You will be evaluated on how well you meet the following performance indicators:

1. Explain the nature of corporate branding.
2. Describe factors used by businesses to position corporate brands.
3. Explain the nature of product/service branding.
4. Develop strategies to position a product/business.
5. Describe the nature of product bundling.

  connectED.mcgraw-hill.com

Download the Competitive Events Workbook for more Role-Play practice.

extended product features

Visual Literacy Product and service warranties protect consumers from faulty or defective products after a sale. The use of credit allows a customer to purchase a product with a promise to pay later. *How do warranties and the use of credit affect consumer rights and responsibilities?*

SHOW WHAT
YOU KNOW

LIMITED WARRANTY

A **limited warranty** is a written guarantee that may exclude certain parts of the product from coverage or require the customer to bear some of the expense for repairs resulting from defects. For example, a limited warranty could specify that the manufacturer will pay for replacement parts but charge the customer for labor or shipping.

IMPLIED WARRANTIES

Most major consumer purchases are covered by written manufacturer warranties after a purchase for a certain period of time (usually 90 days up to one year). When there are no written warranties, implied warranty laws apply. An **implied warranty** is one that takes effect automatically by state law whenever a purchase is made. There are two types of implied warranties: a warranty of merchantability and a warranty of fitness for a particular purpose.

WARRANTY OF MERCHANTABILITY

A **warranty of merchantability** is the seller's promise that the product sold is fit for its intended purpose. Some examples of sellers' promises are a gasoline-powered lawnmower that will cut the grass and an electric table saw that will cut wood.

WARRANTY OF FITNESS

A **warranty of fitness for a particular purpose** is used when the seller advises a customer that a product is suitable for a particular use, and the customer acts on that advice. A customer, for example, might buy a small truck based on a salesperson's recommendation that it will pull a trailer of a certain weight. The dealership must take back the truck and refund the buyer's money if it turns out that the truck cannot tow the anticipated load.

WARRANTY DISCLAIMERS

Warranties often have disclaimers. A **disclaimer** is a statement that contains exceptions to and exclusions from a warranty.

Businesses use disclaimers to limit damages that can be recovered by a customer. A common type of disclaimer limits recovery to a refund of the purchase price. It can specifically exclude any other costs paid, by the owner as a result of product failure. Another common disclaimer waives customers' rights under implied-warranty laws.

Extended Warranties

Extended warranties are beneficial to businesses and consumers. *List several consumer benefits of extended service warranties.*

Extending your warranty now – while you can save 20% – ensures you won't miss even one day of these terrific benefits.

Up to three full years of freedom from costly repair bills.

Whether you choose a one-, two- or three-year Service Contract, we'll pay all costs for covered repairs needed to keep your product operating at its best. So you'll get the most from your major appliance with the least risk to your budget.

A brand new product if we can't fix yours.

It's true! Our new replacement coverage entitles you to a brand new major appliance with the latest features if yours can't be fixed, or if it's more efficient to replace it. What's more, your new Frigidaire product will come with a brand new manufacturer's warranty.

Fast, convenient, in-home service with a toll-free call.

Your Frigidaire Service Contract ensures you'll never have to search through the Yellow Pages for a qualified repair person. Whether your product needs minor adjustments or major repairs, reliable in-home service is one free and easy phone call away.

Top-quality service from Frigidaire factory-trained experts.

You wouldn't want "just anyone" to service your valuable Frigidaire product. That's why we use the most trustworthy professionals in the industry, and train them on Frigidaire models just like yours. So you can rely on our specialists to do the job fast – and do the job right.

Quick access to the correct replacement parts.

With a Frigidaire Service Contract, you won't have to worry about inferior replacement parts or unnecessary waits for a particular component. We maintain a large supply of top-quality parts to ensure your product will be running like new again in no time.

Eligibility to renew your coverage.

If you sign up today for your Frigidaire Service Contract, you can look forward to continuing your manufacturer's protection for the life of your product. Unlike companies who only stand behind products when they're new, we go the distance with you. So don't miss out.

Receive the best possible protection for the best possible price. Mail us your Service Contract Notice today.

EXTENDED WARRANTIES

Extended warranties or service contracts provide repairs or preventive maintenance for a specified length of time beyond a product's normal warranty period. Customers pay extra for this contract at the time of purchase or shortly afterward. Costs range from a few dollars on a low-cost item to hundreds or even thousands of dollars on a higher-priced item, such as a car. There is often a deductible amount, which the customer pays before work is performed.

Extended warranties are beneficial to both businesses and customers. Businesses benefit by receiving additional money (and more profit, if the product performs as expected) on the original sale of a product. Customers benefit from the assurance of long-term satisfaction with their purchase.

There are also disadvantages to service contracts. Some repairs are covered under the standard manufacturer's warranty, so the customer pays for something that is already available. It is also not unusual for customers to forget that they purchased a service contract if service is needed.

Extended Service Contracts An estimated 12 to 20 percent of people who buy extra repair or service contracts never use them.

OTHER EXTENDED PRODUCT FEATURES

Product planners may also create extended product features to boost customer satisfaction. These features include delivery, installation, billing, service after the sale, directions for use, technical assistance, and training.

Businesses gain feedback by conducting customer-service and satisfaction surveys. After an initial purchase, customers are frequently asked to submit product registration cards. This is a way to gain customer data and ideas for product and service improvements. If privacy is a concern, read the fine print. In many cases, only minimal information, if any, is required to qualify for warranties.

 Reading Check

Recall How do warranties affect product planning?

CONSUMER LAWS AND AGENCIES

Businesspeople need a working knowledge of relevant federal, state, and local laws. Manufacturers must be sure that their products meet all legal requirements. Products must be safe, **adequately** labeled, and properly advertised. If they are not, the manufacturer could face fines or product recalls.

Larger companies often employ consumer affairs or legislative specialists to advise management about legal requirements. Smaller companies may join trade associations to stay informed about existing and pending laws that affect their products.

FEDERAL STATUTES

Some products are regulated by more than one agency. Making sure products meet all federal product safety standards is an important function of product planning. For example, cars and trucks have their emission standards set by the Environmental Protection Agency (EPA). Their price stickers are regulated by the Federal Trade Commission (FTC). Any potentially dangerous design flaws are investigated by the National Highway Traffic Safety Administration.

MAGNUSON-MOSS CONSUMER PRODUCT WARRANTY ACT

Many of the warranty features have their origins in a federal statute—the Magnuson-Moss Consumer Product Warranty Act of 1975. This statute governs written warranties for all consumer products costing $15 or more. It sets minimum standards for such warranties, rules for making them available before a product is sold, and provisions for lawsuits against manufacturers if a warranty is not fulfilled. The FTC enforces this act.

CONSUMER PRODUCT SAFETY ACT

Other federal statutes help to protect consumers by requiring companies to manufacture and sell safe products. The Consumer Product Safety Act of 1972, for example, established the Consumer Product Safety Commission (CPSC).

This agency monitors the safety of more than 15,000 nonfood items, including toys; household, outdoor, sports, recreation, and specialty products; and appliances. The agency issues standards for the construction, testing, packaging, and performance of these products. When the CPSC finds any product defective or dangerous, it can:

▶ Issue a product safety alert.
▶ Require warning labels on the product.
▶ Recall the product and order repairs.
▶ Withdraw the product or prohibit its sale.

Since its inception, the CPSC has recalled more than 5,000 products. CPSC studies have found that less than 5 percent of recalled toys, 60 percent of child safety seats, and 90 percent of major appliances are returned for repairs and replacement. Notices for unsafe products are communicated through the media and placed in all U.S. Postal Service offices.

CONSUMER PRODUCT SAFETY IMPROVEMENT ACT

High lead-content paint used in children's toys imported into the United States and other product safety issues led to the passage of the Consumer Product Safety Improvement Act of 2008. This law requires third-party testing of children's products (used by children 12 years of age or younger) including toys, cribs, small parts, baby bouncers, walkers, and strollers.

FOOD, DRUG, AND COSMETIC ACT

The Food, Drug, and Cosmetic Act of 1938 is a federal statute designed to ensure that products are "safe." Safe, in this case, means pure, wholesome, and effective. This law covers features such as informative labels and truthful advertising. The Food and Drug Administration is responsible for the safety of drugs, medical devices, foods, and some food supplements. It also enforces the act. The agency regulates the advertising and sale of imported and exported items. These items include foods, drugs, cosmetics, medical devices, animal drugs, animal feed, and products that emit radiation.

STATE STATUTES

The most common form of state consumer protection regulation affects service businesses. Most states require certain individuals to meet training requirements. For example, many health-care professionals must be licensed or state certified before legally practicing in those professions. The process usually involves testing and payment of a fee.

LEMON LAWS

Nearly all states have lemon laws to protect customers. Lemon laws are statutes designed to protect consumers from poorly built cars. Under most lemon laws, a car is a lemon if it is out of service at least 30 days during the first year of ownership, or if four attempts have been made to fix the same problem. Lemon owners are entitled to a refund or a comparable replacement car.

Many states have incorporated arbitration programs into their lemon laws. In arbitration, an impartial third party decides if the vehicle is a lemon and the amount of the refund. In most cases, the arbitrator's ruling is not binding on the parties. The owner can sue the carmaker if he or she is not satisfied with the outcome. The benefit of arbitration is that it saves all parties the delays and costs often associated with a lawsuit.

Reading Check

Define What is the Consumer Product Safety Act?

CONSUMER RIGHTS AND RESPONSIBILITIES

Consumers can take several steps when they have not been adequately protected by a warranty:

▶ Contact the business via phone, letter, or e-mail.

▶ Contact the local, state, or federal offices that can assist with consumer complaints.

▶ Take legal action if all else fails.

Consumers can sue manufacturers or retailers on at least three grounds: breach of federal law (written warranty), breach of state law (implied warranty), and negligence. *Negligence* means failure to take proper or reasonable care. When a company does not fulfill its warranty or shows carelessness, consumers have the right to go to court.

Courts have held manufacturers, retailers, and food suppliers liable for defects in products or when injury or illness is caused by use of the product. Class action suits are lawsuits filed by more than one party. It is estimated that Bridgestone/Firestone® spent more than $1.5 billion in product recalls and legal fees on cases related to SUV rollover accidents.

Products should be tested thoroughly. Manufacturers should pay attention to product and package design and provide warnings on the package and labels about any potential hazards. When a manufacturer suspects a problem with a product, it may be more cost effective to recall that product than to risk liability and a damaged reputation.

Private distributors can limit their liability by questioning manufacturers before accepting a product for sale. They should obtain the manufacturer's test data and determine the company's ability to stand behind the product before it is put on store shelves.

Businesses should encourage their customers to be responsible consumers and remind them of their duty to be informed. Customers are responsible for reading and following the safety directions provided with products. This is especially important with items for children, such as car seats, cribs, and toys.

 After You Read | **Section 32.1**

Review Key Concepts

1. **Explain** the difference between an express warranty and an implied warranty.
2. **Explain** the difference between a full warranty and a limited warranty.
3. **Describe** a warranty disclaimer.

Practice Academics

English Language Arts

4. Select a household item such as an appliance, electronic device, or other item that comes with a warranty. Write a one-page paper that identifies the product, type of warranty (full or limited), the terms of the warranty, and whether or not the warranty is appropriate for this type of product.

Mathematics

5. You work for a telecommunications company that has an annual marketing budget of $3,560,700. The company spent a total of $1,250,420 on print ads that include a written warranty for service. What percentage of the total marketing budget was spent on the ads? (Round your answer to the nearest whole percent.)

Math Concept **Percents** A percent problem compares a part to a whole. Percent can be determined by using division.

Starting Hints To solve this problem, divide the amount spent on print ads, $1,250,420, by the total amount of money in the marketing budget. This gives you the equivalent decimal value. Multiply the decimal value by 100 to get the percent.

 connectED.mcgraw-hill.com

Check your answers.

For help, go to the Math Skills Handbook located at the back of this book.

READING GUIDE

Before You Read

Predict What might happen if consumers could not use credit cards to pay for purchases?

Objectives

- **Describe** the importance of credit.
- **Explain** various sources of consumer credit.
- **Identify** the types of credit accounts extended to consumers.
- **Discuss** how businesses use trade credit.

The Main Idea

Extending credit to customers and accepting credit cards for purchases are important to product planning. Using credit wisely can benefit a business and its customers.

Vocabulary

Content Vocabulary
- credit
- 30-day accounts
- installment accounts
- revolving accounts
- budget accounts

Academic Vocabulary

You will find these words in your reading and on your tests. Make sure you know their meanings.
- exceeded
- enable

Graphic Organizer

Draw or print this chart to take notes about the features of credit.

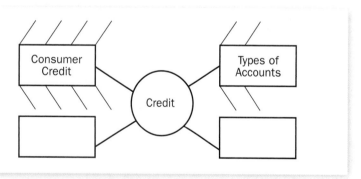

 connectED.mcgraw-hill.com

Print this graphic organizer.

MARKETING CORE FUNCTION

Product/Service Management

m.e. Section 32.2 | Credit

CREDIT AND ITS IMPORTANCE

Credit is essentially loaned money, providing the opportunity for businesses or individuals to obtain products or money in exchange for a promise to pay later. Credit allows most consumers to make major purchases, such as homes, automobiles, appliances, furniture, and recreational vehicles.

Consumers also use credit to make less costly purchases, such as meals, clothing, groceries, and movies. Credit cards are convenient, easy to use, and more secure than carrying cash. However, if credit cards are not managed carefully, it can be easy for consumers to lose track of spending.

The use of credit is essential to the United States and global economies. Federal Reserve Board and U.S. Census data indicate that the average American adult carries more than $3,752 in revolving debt (mainly credit cards), and average household debt exceeds $7,394.

As You Read

Connect What are the advantages and disadvantages of using credit for purchases?

THE ROLE OF CREDIT

Businesses and consumers alike use credit to purchase goods and services. Credit is also used between manufacturers, wholesalers, and retailers to buy materials, equipment, supplies, and services for their businesses or to sell to other businesses.

Millions of people and thousands of businesses would not be able to buy necessary goods and services without credit. By extending credit to its customers, a business provides an incentive to purchase and enhances its sales and profits.

CONSUMER CREDIT

Companies that offer credit, such as banks, retail stores, and oil companies, typically issue credit cards. Federal Reserve surveys indicate that about 75 percent of U.S. households have at least one credit card. However, the average cardholder has about 3.5 credit cards.

> **Does a credit card offering $10,000 of credit sound better than one offering $10,000 of debt?**

Customers fill out credit applications to provide information about their sources of income and credit history. If they meet the company's lending requirements, they receive a credit card and agree to a credit contract that establishes the rules governing the use of the card. These rules include interest rates on outstanding balances. Consumers should read the fine print carefully. Frequently, the card issuers include disclaimers that allow them to change the terms at any time.

Credit cards are issued with credit limits based on customers' ability to pay, their payment histories, and credit score (see **Figure 32.1** on page 762). A credit limit is a preapproved dollar amount. Customers can accumulate balances up to that amount. Credit limits can range from as little as $500 for first-time cardholders to thousands of dollars.

Purchases made by credit cards go through a computerized preapproval process prior to the purchase. This assures the store or company that a customer has not **exceeded** his or her credit limit.

FIGURE 32.1 | Credit Scores

Calculating Your Score A credit score is a number usually between 350 (poor) and 850 (excellent). The number represents the risk in lending money and is used to determine credit limits offered to consumers. *Why are the five categories represented in the chart important factors in determining a credit score?*

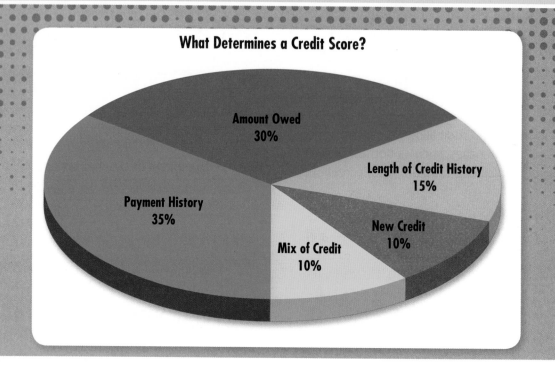

What Determines a Credit Score?

- Amount Owed 30%
- Length of Credit History 15%
- Payment History 35%
- Mix of Credit 10%
- New Credit 10%

BANK CREDIT CARDS

Banks or their subsidiaries issue bank credit cards. Visa® and MasterCard® sponsor bank credit cards, but these companies do not issue them directly. Banks that issue credit cards set their own fees and interest rates. Examples of such banks are Chase® and Bank of America®.

An annual fee is a flat yearly charge similar to a membership fee. Annual fees vary from card to card, so it is important to comparison shop when deciding on a credit card. Interest rates are tied to other lending rates such as the prime rate or the Treasury bill rate. These are called "variable-rate plans." Other plans, which are not specifically tied to changes in other rates, are called "fixed-rate plans."

Retailers who belong to a bank credit card system either electronically process credit card sales or mail the credit card forms to the bank for payment. First, the bank deducts a service fee from the sale amount. Then it remits the balance to the retailer.

STORE AND GASOLINE CREDIT CARDS

Some businesses are large enough to offer their own credit cards, known as *proprietary* or *house* cards. Examples of national chains that issue credit cards are JC Penney®, Nordstrom®, and Target®.

Examples of gasoline cards are Shell® and Sunoco Rewards® cards. They offer cash rebates on gas purchases at affiliated stations and allow customers to track gasoline purchases separately.

Usually, proprietary cards do not have an annual fee, but they do have high interest rates. A business prefers customers to use proprietary cards because it receives income from finance charges, usually generated from the interest charged. Finance charges on unpaid credit card balances are very expensive. Depending on an applicant's credit history, annual percentage rates (APRs) can range from 13.99 percent to 22.99 percent or more on purchases. Cash advance rates can be as high as 24.99 percent.

TRAVEL AND ENTERTAINMENT CARDS

Travel and entertainment cards, such as American Express®, are issued to pay for airline, hotel, and other business-related expenses. These types of cards are often accepted for other types of goods and services. They have annual fees and service charges, and often require that transaction balances be paid in full each month. Travel and entertainment credit card companies charge retailers higher service fees than credit card companies do for processing the payment. Some businesses choose not to pay these fees, so these cards are not universally accepted.

REWARD CARDS

Reward cards are credit cards that offer some type of reward or incentive to consumers who use them. Rebates, awards, or points are offered when credit purchases are made. These cards are often co-branded and offer rewards in cash, airline miles, hotel discounts, or special offers.

Some reward cards offer special services. For example, the Visa® Signature card shown in the ad below offers benefits such as concierge services and other special offers. Card members can use the Visa Signature concierge service to make travel arrangements, buy event tickets, make restaurant reservations, and arrange for business services.

Individuals who plan to carry balances on a reward credit card should search for a card with the lowest interest rate. Consumers who pay the balance every month may find that reward cards offer the best deal.

AFFINITY CARDS

Affinity cards are credit cards issued by banks to show a consumer's loyalty to a team, school, charity, business, or other organization. The organization solicits its members or customers. The card issuer returns a percentage (usually less than one percent) of the interest to the organization and gives reward points or miles to the customer.

DEBIT CARDS

A debit card is like a mobile automated teller machine (ATM). Consumers authorize the seller to withdraw funds directly from their bank accounts at the time of sale. About 25 percent of all consumer transactions are made with debit cards.

Signature debit cards require a signature on the receipt when you make a purchase. The purchase is processed through a card-processing network like Visa or MasterCard, and money is deducted from the user's account in a couple of days.

Credit Card Rewards

This ad describes the benefits Visa Signature card members can get when staying at certain hotels. *What target markets might be particularly interested in the spcial features of this particular credit card?*

PIN type debit cards are scanned electronically at the point of sale. Such transactions require the customer to enter a PIN number. With PIN debit cards the money is deducted from the bank account immediately. Some cards work both ways.

SPECIAL CUSTOMER CARDS

While neither a credit nor a debit card, these special customer cards **enable** customers to receive reward points or a percentage of money back in rewards on purchases made at sponsoring stores. Examples of these cards include Best Buy's Reward Zone® program and the Winn-Dixie® Customer Reward Card. Customers can use the reward points stored on the card for cash discounts, coupons, and prizes on future purchases at the sponsoring store.

SECURED AND UNSECURED LOANS

Loans are also a form of credit. Consumers and businesses can obtain secured loans and unsecured loans to use for the purchase of goods and services.

In secured loans, something of value, such as real estate or property, motor vehicles, machinery, or merchandise, is pledged as *collateral.* Collateral is security used to protect the interests of the lender. The collateral helps to ensure that a loan will be repaid. If the loan is not repaid by the borrower, the lender keeps the pledged collateral items to cover the debt.

Consumers and businesses can also obtain unsecured loans, which represent a written promise to repay a loan. Unsecured loans do not require collateral to protect the interests of the lender. Instead, unsecured loans rely on the excellent credit reputation of the borrower who pledges in writing to repay the loan. In either case, a credit contract is signed to detail payment terms and penalties for not meeting those terms.

TYPES OF CREDIT ACCOUNTS

Four major consumer credit plans are in use today: regular or 30-day accounts, installment accounts, revolving accounts, and budget accounts. The dollar amount a customer pays to use credit is called the "finance charge." A finance charge may include interest costs and other charges associated with transactions.

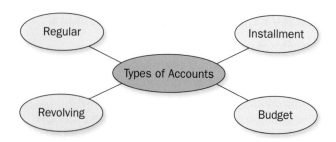

REGULAR

Regular charge accounts, or **30-day accounts**, enable customers to charge purchases during a month and pay the balance in full within 30 days after they are billed. There is no finance charge for this type of plan as long as the bill is paid on time.

INSTALLMENT ACCOUNTS

Installment accounts, or time-payment plans, allow for payment over a period of time. Installment accounts are normally used for large purchases, such as a college education, appliances, cars, furniture, and vacation travel. Installment accounts offer a certain interest rate over a set period of time. Installment accounts sometimes require a down payment and a separate contract for each purchase.

REVOLVING ACCOUNTS

Revolving accounts are charge accounts offered by a retailer that sets the credit limit and payment terms. The minimum payment is usually a certain percentage on the balance owed or a minimum dollar amount, such as $15. The customer can choose to pay more than the minimum payment to reduce the balance owed. An interest charge is added to the unpaid balance for the billing period.

Customers can make purchases up to the credit limit when using a revolving account. Under most credit card arrangements, regular accounts become revolving accounts if the full amount is not paid for the billing period. Most billing cycles are 25-day periods.

BUDGET ACCOUNTS

Budget accounts allow account holders to pay for purchases over a specific period of time without incurring a finance charge. The most common interest-free time period is 90 days, but can be a year or longer. Some retailers who handle expensive products, such as furniture and appliances, offer budget accounts. Budget accounts do not require the customer to pay any interest charges if the amount owed is paid within the interest-free time period. Finance charges are applied if the amount is not paid within the specified time period. Offering budget accounts is a way that a company can stay competitive.

BUSINESS CREDIT

Banks were once the primary source of money to help businesses support their operations. However, banks are now likely to lend only to well-established companies. A business can apply for a line of credit from a bank. This type of loan allows a company to borrow up to a certain amount of money from the bank and pay it back regularly over time. A business may be able to borrow using its assets as security or collateral. If the company does not pay back the loan, the bank can then take away those assets.

Another way that businesses can borrow is more similar to the way consumer credit works. Business credit, or trade credit, involves companies extending loans to other companies. It is a source of short-term financing provided by a company within the same industry. If a company needs certain goods or services, a supplier agrees to deliver them and to allow the company to pay within a certain amount of time.

Imagine you have a business that makes and sells custom team logo apparel to various schools in your area. You need a supply of t-shirts, sweatshirts, hats, and jackets in various colors along with ink and fabric to create the logos. A supplier agrees to let you purchase the materials you need as long as you pay within 90 days after delivery. This arrangement gives you time and money to create, manufacture, and market your products and pay your bill to the supplier out of your sales revenue.

Business or trade credit is similar to consumer credit in that businesses extend loans for goods and services. A supplier sells raw materials, equipment, and inventory to a business that agrees to pay with credit. Unlike consumer credit, trade credit does not involve the use of a credit card. Letters of credit and credit memorandums or drafts are used in trade credit arrangements. The parties involved agree to payment terms.

Reading Check

Analyze What is the difference between consumer and business credit?

LEGISLATION AFFECTING CREDIT

Federal laws, rules, and regulations are designed to protect consumers, their credit standing, and their rights when using credit. Government regulations require businesses to inform consumers about the use of credit. Businesses must also establish procedures for notification, billing, and debt-collection activities.

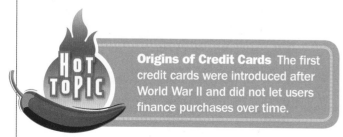

Origins of Credit Cards The first credit cards were introduced after World War II and did not let users finance purchases over time.

The Truth in Lending Act of 1968 requires that lenders disclose information about annual percentage rates, the name of the company extending credit, the amount financed, the total purchase price minus any down payments and taxes, the actual finance charge in dollars, a payment schedule, and late payment penalties.

The Fair Credit Reporting Act of 1971 requires that a lender report the name and address of the credit bureau used when a consumer is denied credit. The act gives consumers the opportunity to check their credit histories for errors that prevent them from obtaining credit.

The Fair Credit Billing Act of 1974 requires lenders to correct billing errors within 90 days of a consumer complaint, limits cardholder liability, and dictates that consumers be given a statement of their credit rights.

The Equal Credit Opportunity Acts of 1975 and 1976 set guidelines for the review of applications for credit. These acts also prohibit discrimination based on age, gender, race, religion, or marital status.

The Fair Debt Collection Practices Act of 1978 establishes required conduct for debt collectors and prevents harassing or abusing customers to collect debts.

MARKETING CASE STUDY

Rewarding Credit

Consumers wanting to avoid credit-card expenses may choose to cut back on charging purchases. However, because rewards credit cards offer incentives, or rewards, many cardholders are inclined to continue using them. Rewards include cash-back rebates, gas rebates, airline tickets, or even gift cards and specialty items.

Reward or Penalty?

The typical rewards card comes with higher interest rates. But the wise consumer will pay off a balance in full before the next bill, so no interest accrues. Also, restrictions usually apply to redeeming rewards. However, newer cards, such as the Capital One® Venture card, streamlined the terms so that redemption is easier. With no limits on when, where, or how to earn miles, no blackout dates, and a simple points formula, the company hopes customers take advantage of the rewards perks.

Mathematics

Compute You earn two mileage points per dollar on purchases charged to your rewards card. You just charged $1,565 for computer equipment. How many miles did you earn?

The Fair Credit and Charge Card Disclosure Act of 1988 requires credit card issuers to provide information about the costs of credit and charge accounts. This information helps consumers better understand the terms of their credit cards. It is also aimed at preventing card issuers from surprising consumers with hidden fees and other charges.

The Fair and Accurate Credit Transactions Act of 2003 requires businesses to verify identities and addresses before opening accounts to fight identity theft. Consumers can correct errors more easily in their credit files, opt-out of sharing their information for marketing purposes, and are entitled to a free credit report once a year.

The Credit Card Accountability, Responsibility and Disclosure (CARD) Act of 2009 makes significant changes in how consumers access and use their credit cards. It establishes how interest is charged and how interest rates change. It also limits credit card fees and requires a 45-day notice of increases in rates, fees, and finance charges.

The CARD Act requires a creditor to send a bill to a card holder at least three weeks before payment is due on an account. Bills must include details about the length of time needed to pay off the balance. In addition, anyone under the age of 21 must obtain a co-signer or provide proof that the applicant can make payments.

 After You Read   **Section 32.2**

Review Key Concepts

1. **Explain** why credit is an important extended product feature.
2. **Discuss** the difference between a credit card and a debit card.
3. **Explain** how travel and entertainment charge cards differ from bank, store, and gasoline credit cards.

Practice Academics

English Language Arts

4. Perform library or online research on how to use credit responsibly. Write a one-page report on how consumers can maintain the best possible credit scores.

Mathematics

5. Your local grocery store offers "store dollars" for every $100 spent in the store. For every $100 you spend at the grocery store, you earn 5 store dollars. If the average person spends $400 at the grocery store each month, how many months would it take to earn 60 store dollars?

   Math Concept **Multi-Step Problems** When solving problems that require multiple steps, make a list of the information given in the problem, as well as the information for which you will be solving. This will make the relationships between what you are looking for and what is given clear.

   Starting Hints To solve this problem, divide the average monthly amount spent at the store by $100. Multiply this number by the amount earned in store dollars per $100 spent at the store. This is the number of store dollars earned per month. Divide 60 store dollars by the number of store dollars earned each month to find out how many months it will take.

 connectED.mcgraw-hill.com

Check your answers.

For help, go to the Math Skills Handbook located at the back of this book.

21st Century Skills

Problem-Solving Skills

10. Conduct a search of available credit cards. Choose a type of card (balance transfer, low-interest, cash-back, reward, frequent flyer, pre-paid, or secured credit) to investigate. Review a total of three different cards offered for the card type you selected and recommend the best choice. Identify the type of card, three cards of that type, your choice of card, and your rationale for choosing the card. Provide a one-page outline of the results and your recommendation.

Financial Literacy Skills

11. Calculating Payments Assume that a consumer has a credit card balance and wants to pay only a minimum monthly payment. What is the monthly minimum payment for a balance of $2354.00 with a 17.99 percent annual interest rate?

e-Marketing Skills

12. Product Safety Imagine you are employed in product planning for a large children's toy manufacturer. Go to the Consumer Product Safety Commission Web site to investigate a toy product that was recently recalled. Select one children's toy product and find out its manufacturer, the date and reasons for the recall, and available remedies for consumers who have purchased the product. Summarize your findings in a one-page written report that includes this information:

- Name of the product
- Date of recall
- Manufacturer
- Reasons for the recall
- Available remedies for purchasers

Build Academic Skills

English Language Arts

13. Extended Product Warranties Conduct research on the advantages and disadvantages of extended product warranties or service contracts. Identify the name of your source(s). Prepare a one-page report that summarizes the advantages and disadvantages of extended product warranties.

Social Studies

14. Better Business Bureaus Better Business Bureaus are organizations that seek to resolve problems that arise from purchases made by businesses and consumers. Perform library or online research on a Better Business Bureau located within your state. Identify its name, location, goals, and services provided to consumers. Summarize your findings in a one-page written report.

Mathematics

15. Consolidating Debt A household has $14,000 in credit card debt and pays 3 percent per month interest on all credit card payments. The family gets an offer for a new credit card. It promises no minimum payment for three months on all balance transfers, and then a 5-percent interest rate thereafter. Assuming that the household pays only the interest each month on a $14,000 balance, under which scenario will the customer spend less money over a year?

Math Concept Interest Rates Credit card interest rates are based on a percentage of the credit card's monthly balance. When figuring the total amount of interest paid each year, it is important to understand that the interest rate might not be applicable for the entire year.

For help, go to the Math Skills Handbook located at the back of this book.

Standardized Test Practice

Directions Read the following questions. On a separate piece of paper, write the best possible answer for each one.

1. Which of the following warranties guarantees that if a product is found defective within the warranty period, it will be repaired or replaced at no cost to the purchaser?
   - **A.** Full warranty
   - **B.** Implied warranty
   - **C.** Limited warranty
   - **D.** Warranty of merchantability

2. Credit allows businesses or individuals to obtain products or money in exchange for a promise to pay later.

   T

   F

3. A credit card issued by banks to demonstrate a consumer's loyalty to a team, university, charity, business, or other organization is known as a(n) _____ card.

Test-Taking Tip

Before the test, study over a few days or weeks, continually reviewing class material. Do not wait until the night before and try to learn everything at once.

DECA Connection Role Play

Credit Evaluator
Automobile Dealership

Situation You work for a business that sells new and used automobiles. The business is large and well-established, having been in business for more than 20 years. Your job is to work with the company sales associates to establish the credit worthiness of customers applying for company credit to purchase automobiles. Most customers use some type of credit to make automobile purchases. Many customers arrange financing for their purchases through their banks or credit unions. Many other customers decide to finance their purchases through your company. Before extending credit to a customer, it is important to determine whether the customer is a credit risk. Management has recently hired a new sales associate (judge). It is your job to explain the role of credit in your business to the new sales associate (judge).

Activity You are to meet with the new sales associate (judge) to explain the role credit plays in your business and its importance to both your business and your customers. You are also to explain the importance of establishing the creditworthiness of customers and the legal considerations for granting credit.

Evaluation You will be evaluated on how well you meet the following performance indicators:

- Discuss the nature of environmental law.
- Explain the nature of agency relationships.
- Discuss legal issues affecting businesses.
- Identify legal considerations for granting credit.
- Determine creditworthiness of customers/clients.

 connectED.mcgraw-hill.com

Download the Competitive Events Workbook for more Role-Play practice.

Create a Design
for a New Pet Product

Pet product companies embrace pet owners' desire to create a great life for their pets. What new products would you create to appeal to both pets and pet owners?

Scenario

The pet industry is growing every year. U.S. pet owners spend more than $56 billion on their pets annually. Pet food sales account for $22 billion, while the rest of the sales are for pet clothing, accessories, toys, medicine, grooming, and pet services. Research indicates that pet owners "humanize" pets, which means they are treated like family members. This booming industry includes pet hotels and spas, magazines for pet owners, Animal Planet® on television, and even Web sites for sharing photos and videos of pets via a social network.

A pet product company wants your marketing firm to capitalize on the booming pet economy by creating an exciting new product and a marketing plan to launch it.

The Skills You'll Use

Academic Skills Reading, writing, social studies, and research

Basic Skills Speaking, listening, thinking, and interpersonal

Technology Skills Word processing, presentation software, spreadsheet, telecommunication, and the Internet

Your Objective

Your objective is to conceive a new or improved pet product for your client and prepare a marketing plan.

STEP 1 Do Your Research

- Research all aspects of the pet industry, looking for trends in pet food, medicine, services, clothing, toys, and accessories.
- Research current political, economic, socio-cultural, and technological factors that may affect the pet industry.
- Study current advertisements and packaging of pet products.
- Visit online sites that have a pet theme.
- Visit Web sites for pet food manufacturers (e.g., Nestle's Ralston Purina®) pet stores (e.g., PetSmart®), pet sections of supermarkets, and pet e-tailers (e.g., Petco®).
- Find independent social media sites for pet owners.
- Research potential competitors and pricing of competitive products.

Write a summary of your research.

STEP 2 Plan Your Project

Now that you have completed your research, you need to begin planning your project.

- Develop your new product concept by following the steps for product development.
- Develop a marketing plan that includes the following: objectives, situation analysis (environmental scan and SWOT analysis) to support your new product concept, identification of the target market, marketing mix details (product, place, price, and promotion), as well as your ideas for implementation, evaluation, and control.
- Design product packaging and promotional materials.

STEP 3 Connect with Your Community

- Interview one or more trusted adults who are pet owners to identify any unmet needs and to get ideas about the best way to communicate with them about a new product (e.g., social media, magazines, television). Describe your product idea to these pet owners and ask for feedback.

- Interview pet store owners or managers to find out which products sell the most and how to get shelf space for a new pet product. Describe your product idea and ask for feedback.

STEP 4 Share What You Learn

Assume your class is the client's executives—the decision makers.

- Present your research findings and ideas in an oral presentation. Be prepared to answer questions.

- Describe your new product idea and your marketing plan and display your packaging and promotional materials.

- Use software to create a slide presentation to accompany your oral presentation. Include one slide for each topic in your marketing plan.

STEP 5 Evaluate Your Marketing and Academic Skills

Your project will be evaluated based on the following:

- Knowledge of the pet market
- Comprehensive PEST and SWOT analyses
- Proper use of marketing terminology
- Product feasibility and rationale for it
- Organization and continuity of presentation
- Mechanics—presentation and neatness
- Speaking and listening skills

MARKETING CORE FUNCTIONS

 Product/Service Management

Market Planning

Marketing Internship Project Checklist

Plan

✓ Research the current pet market and successful pet products.

✓ Brainstorm ideas to capitalize on current trends in the pet market.

Write

✓ Describe your research findings and create a marketing plan outline with all essential components in a written report.

✓ Explain how the results of the PEST and SWOT analyses helped you conceive the new product and develop the marketing plan.

Present

✓ Present your idea for a new pet product with rationale supported by your research.

✓ Present your marketing plan with a specific target market, price, place, and promotion ideas for the product.

✓ Display sample packaging for your product and promotional materials.

---

 connectED.mcgraw-hill.com

Evaluate Download a rubric you can use to evaluate your final project.

---

my marketing portfolio

Internship Report When you have completed your Marketing Internship Project and oral presentation, put your written report and a few printouts of key slides from your oral presentation in your marketing portfolio.

Design a New Product in a Different Industry Design a new product based on a trend in a consumer or an organizational market. Conduct an environmental scan (PEST analysis) to support your idea. Then conduct a SWOT analysis for the company that will make the product. To test your product concept, conduct marketing research. Prepare a marketing plan, complete with your target market and your ideas for the marketing mix (product, place, price, and promotion). Prepare a written report and an oral presentation.

ENTREPRENEURSHIP AND FINANCE

Marketing Internship Project

A Business Plan

Essential Question How would you go about starting a new business?

To start a new business, you must do a lot of research. You need to find a niche—a need or want that is not being fulfilled. For an online business, you need to do more research on how to build a Web site and keep it going. The steps for starting an online business are the same as for starting a brick-and-mortar business. However, there are a few additional concerns with an online business, such as consumer privacy and other legal issues involving e-commerce.

Project Goal

In the project at the end of this unit, you will transform an idea into a business plan for a new online business.

Prepare for the Project

As you read this unit, use this checklist to prepare for the Marketing Internship Project at the end of this unit:

- Fnd out about government regulations covering e-commerce.
- Brainstorm ideas for an online business.
- Ask friends and family members what online businesses they use and why.

 connectED.mcgraw-hill.com

Project Activity
Complete a worksheet activity about conducting a marketing research study.

The average American spends at least six hours per week online.

MARKETING CORE FUNCTIONS IN THIS UNIT

- Marketing Information Management
- Market Planning

HOW TO SPOT
A WEB SITE
YOU CAN TRUST.

It's industry-leading encryption, so you can submit information online without fear of it being stolen. It's one-click authentication, so you can be sure a site is legitimate and not a fraud scheme. And it's always anchored with the Check—the most recognized and trusted brand on the Internet. Learn more at TrustTheCheck.com.

SHOW WHAT YOU KNOW

Visual Literacy
This ad promotes a company that shows Internet users that a Web site has been verified as authentic and trustworthy. *How does this advertisement communicate the importance of online business to potential entrepreneurs?*

entrepreneurial concepts

Visual Literacy Do you like to plan your own day and make your own decisions? If so, you might like to own your own company and be the boss. You might even have an interest in a subject that you could use to start the business. *What are some questions you would need to answer before deciding to start up your own business?*

Discovery Project

Planning a Start-Up Business

Essential Question Where can you find answers to questions you might have about starting your own business?

Project Goal

Work with a partner as you begin planning how to start a business. Choose a business. Begin with your own list of the questions that you think will need to be answered as you develop your plan. Then use the Internet to do your research. Use key words such as *how to start a business*, *starting a small business*, and *becoming an entrepreneur*. Next contact several local business owners and request interviews with them about how to start a business. Write a report describing what you have learned about starting up your own business.

Ask Yourself...

- What questions will you ask business owners during your interviews?
- What do small business owners need to know when they are starting a business?
- What are some of the steps you could take to increase the likelihood that your business would succeed?
- How will you describe your findings?

 Synthesize and Present Research Synthesize your research by writing a report describing what you have learned about starting up your own business.

 connectED.mcgraw-hill.com

Activity
Get a worksheet activity about entrepreneurship.

Evaluate
Download a rubric you can use to evaluate your project.

DECA Connection

DECA Event Role Play

Concepts in this chapter are related to DECA competitive events that involve either an interview or role play.

Performance Indicators The performance indicators represent key skills and knowledge. Your key to success in DECA competitive events is relating them to concepts in this chapter.

- Explain the types of business ownership.
- Describe legal issues affecting businesses.
- Explain the organizational design of businesses.
- Explain how organizations adapt to today's markets.
- Demonstrate responsible behavior.

DECA Prep

Role Play Practice role-playing with the DECA Connection competitive-event activity at the end of this chapter. More information on DECA events can be found on DECA's Web site.

READING GUIDE

Before You Read

Connect Think of some successful entrepreneurs. What are possible reasons for their success?

Objectives

- **Define** entrepreneurship.
- **Describe** the advantages of entrepreneurship.
- **Explain** the risks of entrepreneurship.
- **List** the characteristics and skills of entrepreneurs.
- **Understand** the importance of small business in various economies.

The Main Idea

Entrepreneurship has many advantages, including personal freedom and financial reward. It also has disadvantages, such as accepting risk.

Vocabulary

Content Vocabulary
- entrepreneurship
- entrepreneurs

Academic Vocabulary

You will find these words in your reading and on your tests. Make sure you know their meanings.
- indication
- domestic

Graphic Organizer

Draw or print this chart to list the characteristics of entrepreneurship.

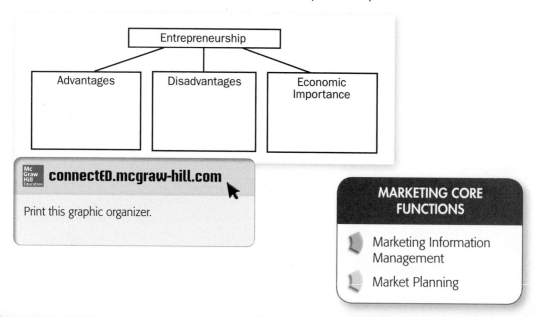

connectED.mcgraw-hill.com

Print this graphic organizer.

MARKETING CORE FUNCTIONS

Marketing Information Management

Market Planning

 (within header graphic) **Section 33.1** | Entrepreneurship

WHAT IS ENTREPRENEURSHIP?

Entrepreneurship is the process of starting and operating your own business. **Entrepreneurs** are people who create, launch, organize, and manage a new business and take the risk of business ownership. You are an entrepreneur if you have provided babysitting services or cut someone's lawn for pay. Entrepreneurs often have an idea, or business concept, that drives their business. An entrepreneur combines this vision with the means to manufacture the product (or provide the service) and market it. The contributions entrepreneurs make to the economy both within and outside the United States can be remarkable.

As You Read

Connect Compare the characteristics of an entrepreneur to your own personality. Would you make a good entrepreneur?

The results of entrepreneurship can change our lives in other ways, too. Consider these examples:

▶ Henry Ford introduced the mass production of vehicles by making them affordable to average people. His entrepreneurship revolutionized transportation and transformed lifestyles.

▶ William Hewlett and David Packard started a small business in Packard's garage near Stanford University in California. They invented the floppy memory disk and the first pocket calculator. Their business grew into the giant Hewlett-Packard Corporation. Hewlett-Packard produces a vast array of computer products, including laser printers. These products changed the speed with which people process information.

These entrepreneurs became famous and wealthy as a result of starting and growing their businesses. However, it is important to recognize that not all entrepreneurs achieve such success.

Some entrepreneurs start companies simply because they want to be their own bosses and make their own business decisions.

> **❝ Entrepreneurs make major contributions to our economy by providing jobs for their employees. ❞**

ADVANTAGES OF ENTREPRENEURSHIP

The advantages of entrepreneurship can include personal freedom, personal satisfaction, increased self-esteem, and increased income. Entrepreneurs set their own work schedules and make their own decisions. They are able to try out their own new ideas, direct their energies into business activities, and take control of their businesses and their work settings.

Many business owners are willing to put in the extra effort to make their businesses succeed because of financial rewards. With success often comes money, and this potential motivates many entrepreneurs.

DISADVANTAGES OF ENTREPRENEURSHIP

Being an entrepreneur has disadvantages, too. These include a high level of stress, possible setbacks, the risk of failure, potential loss of income, long and irregular hours and the need to handle multiple tasks.

Selling Eco-Fashion

Everything old is new again, at least in the world of eco-fashion. Turning yesterday's trash into today's ready-to-wear is the trend. Environmental entrepreneurs are developing businesses with earth-friendly names, such as "Save the Planet" and "Greenloop." They build their marketing plans around green products. They attract customers who want to do good as well as look good in clothes made from recycled wares and natural fibers.

Raw Material Worn tires and old denim take shape as ultra-cool sneakers. Fabric made from wood, bamboo, or corn turns into high-end haute couture. Reclaimed Coke® cans add sparkle when recycled as sequins. For the conscientious shopper, dressing "green" means wearing conviction with style.

English Language Arts
Create Think of an object at home that could be recycled as a product for a new business venture. Describe in writing the new product and business, along with the pros and cons of starting the new business.

 connectED.mcgraw-hill.com

Get an activity on green marketing.

Most new businesses have a restricted cash flow because of start-up costs. As a result, an entrepreneur may not meet his or her personal financial needs during the first year of operation, or even longer. Increased income comes only when the business succeeds.

Entrepreneurs are not 40-hours-per-week people. To succeed, they must meet the needs of the marketplace. This often means long and irregular hours.

Running a business requires doing many tedious, time-consuming tasks. To save money, new business owners may do many of these jobs themselves. Among the tasks they may perform is time-consuming paperwork. This paperwork includes tending to accounts payable, accounts receivable, payroll, and government forms.

THE RISKS OF ENTREPRENEURSHIP

Starting a new business requires a major commitment of time, money, and effort. A new business owner must be a risk taker. It is often necessary to quit a job, work long hours, invest savings, and borrow money—all with no guarantee that the new business will succeed. The amount of money you would need to start a new business depends on many factors, such as the type of business and the location. There are many stories about people starting a business on a shoestring (very little money). However, most small business owners underestimate how much capital they will need to start a new business and make it successful.

If you plan to start a business, it is always better to save up the money you will need to get started or borrow as little as possible. More than half of all new businesses fail within two to three years. Therefore, careful planning is essential to help you avoid facing a huge debt.

ENTREPRENEURSHIP AS A CAREER CHOICE

Being an entrepreneur can be exciting and greatly rewarding, but it is not for everyone. Those who succeed have certain skills and personal characteristics that enable them to meet the challenges of business ownership.

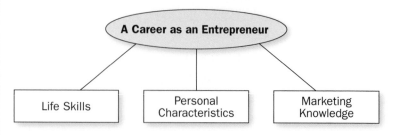

First, entrepreneurs must have the skills necessary to run their business. Beyond specific skills, most successful entrepreneurs share a number of characteristics:

Characteristics of Successful Entrepreneurs

- ▶ Determination
- ▶ Self-motivation, self-discipline, and self-confidence
- ▶ Strong organizational skills
- ▶ Leadership ability
- ▶ Creativity
- ▶ Willingness to work hard
- ▶ Spirit of adventure
- ▶ Good social skills

DO YOU HAVE WHAT IT TAKES?

You can answer this question by doing a self-evaluation—an assessment of your personal qualities, abilities, interests, and skills. The self-evaluation in **Figure 33.1** on page 782 was developed by the Small Business Administration (SBA). Think about each queston and write your honest answers on paper. Answering "yes" to most or all of these questions suggests that you may have the right characteristics for success.

Before you start a business, ask family members, friends, and other businesspeople that are in the same or a similar business about their experiences. Do research on the type of business you want to start. All this information should give you a good **indication** of whether you are ready to join the millions of small-business owners in the United States.

MARKETING AND ENTREPRENEURSHIP

Entrepreneurs may have the business and technical skills they need to produce and provide a quality product or service. However, they may overlook the importance of marketing. Entrepreneurs who possess a good understanding of marketing have an advantage over those who do not.

Here are some helpful resources. The American Marketing Association has a special interest group devoted to helping entrepreneurs develop marketing skills—the Marketing and Entrepreneur Special Interest Group. The National Federation of Independent Businesses (NFIB) has the "Business Toolkit," an award-winning online library of management information.

Reading Check

Summarize What are some risks of being an entrepreneur?

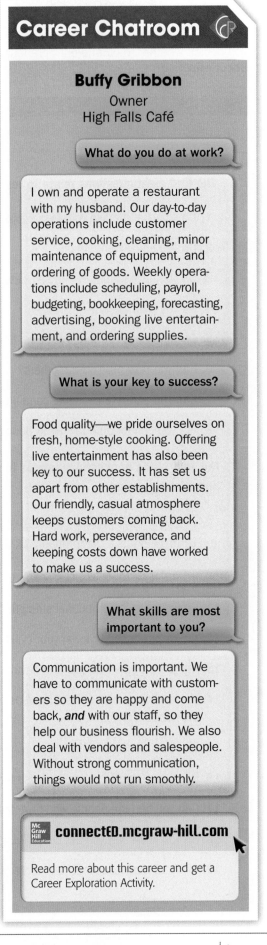

Career Chatroom

Buffy Gribbon
Owner
High Falls Café

What do you do at work?

I own and operate a restaurant with my husband. Our day-to-day operations include customer service, cooking, cleaning, minor maintenance of equipment, and ordering of goods. Weekly operations include scheduling, payroll, budgeting, bookkeeping, forecasting, advertising, booking live entertainment, and ordering supplies.

What is your key to success?

Food quality—we pride ourselves on fresh, home-style cooking. Offering live entertainment has also been key to our success. It has set us apart from other establishments. Our friendly, casual atmosphere keeps customers coming back. Hard work, perseverance, and keeping costs down have worked to make us a success.

What skills are most important to you?

Communication is important. We have to communicate with customers so they are happy and come back, *and* with our staff, so they help our business flourish. We also deal with vendors and salespeople. Without strong communication, things would not run smoothly.

connectED.mcgraw-hill.com

Read more about this career and get a Career Exploration Activity.

FIGURE 33.1 | Self-Evaluation

Know Yourself A clear understanding of your strengths and skills will help you decide whether to pursue entrepreneurship. *What do your answers say about you?*

The first eight questions relate to your personality characteristics. YES NO

1. Do you like to make your own decisions?

2. Do you enjoy competition?

3. Do you have willpower and self-determination?

4. Do you plan ahead?

5. Do you like to get things done on time?

6. Can you take advice from others?

7. Can you adapt to changing conditions?

8. Are you comfortable talking to people you do not know or have just met?

The next series of questions relates to your physical, emotional, and financial well-being.

9. Do you understand that owning your own business may entail working 12 to 16 hours a day, probably six days a week and maybe on holidays?

10. Do you have the physical stamina to handle a business?

11. Do you have the emotional strength to withstand the strain?

12. Are you prepared to lower your living standard for several months or years?

13. Are you prepared to lose your savings?

14. Do you know which skills and areas of expertise are critical to the success of your business?

15. Do you have these skills?

16. Does your idea for a business use these skills?

17. Can you find the people who have the expertise you lack?

18. Do you know why you are considering this business?

19. Will your business meet your career aspirations?

TRENDS IN ENTREPRENEURSHIP

Entrepreneurs and small-to-medium businesses play a key role in the **domestic** economy and the global economy. They generate growth at a much faster rate than other larger and more established businesses. Consider these statistics:

▶ Eighty percent of the new jobs created annually come from businesses that are less than five years old.

▶ Ninety percent of all U.S. businesses have fewer than 20 employees.

▶ Firms with fewer than 500 employees were responsible for 50 percent of the gross domestic product (GDP).

▶ About one in ten adults in the United States are planning to start a new business.

▶ As many as 25 percent of all U.S. workers are self-employed.

Several trends in the marketplace have fostered the growth of entrepreneurship. These trends include the availability of technology, increased global communication, the rise of the Internet and e-commerce, and an increasingly diversified society and market. The U.S. Small Business Administration (SBA) provides loans to help small businesses in the competitive global economy. The SBA Web site provides business owners with helpful information. This includes access to government services, help with regulations, and applications for help, money, and training. The SBA is also providing more opportunities to work with government buyers and ways to compete in international markets.

 After You Read   **Section 33.1**

Review Key Concepts

1. **Compare** being an entrepreneur with being an employee.
2. **List** the personal characteristics required of an entrepreneur that describe you.
3. **Explain** how small businesses contribute to the U.S. economy.

Practice Academics

Social Studies

4. You have decided to become an entrepreneur. You want to investigate types of business that are socially responsible, environmentally sensitive, personally interesting, and financially rewarding. Research at least three types of business that you believe would meet these criteria. Read business magazines, research online, and interview business owners. Write a report explaining why one of these types of business would be satisfying to you.

Mathematics

5. You live in a city known for entrepreneurship. The city had 1,600 new business start-ups in one year. How many new start-ups is this per week?

Math Concept **Measuring Time** Determining the frequency of events over a certain time period is usually accomplished with division.

Starting Hints Divide the total number of start-ups by 52, the number of weeks in a year, to determine how many businesses start up each week.

 connectED.mcgraw-hill.com

Check your answers.

For help, go to the **Math Skills Handbook** located at the back of this book.

READING GUIDE

Before You Read

Connect What steps might you take before opening a business of your choice?

Objectives

- **Identify** the forms of business ownership.
- **Name** the legal steps to take in establishing a business.

The Main Idea

Going into business involves deciding how to enter a business, determining its organizational form, and following the steps to make it legal.

Vocabulary

Content Vocabulary

- franchise
- sole proprietorship
- unlimited liability
- partnership
- general partnership
- limited partnership
- limited liability
- corporation
- stockholders
- foreign corporation
- limited liability company (LLC)
- Doing Business As (DBA)
- Articles of Incorporation

Academic Vocabulary

You will find these words in your reading and on your tests. Make sure you know their meanings.

- community
- vary

Graphic Organizer

Draw or print this chart to write down the steps to establish a new business.

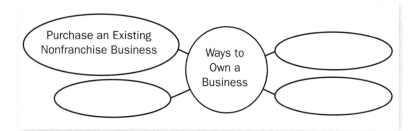

 connectED.mcgraw-hill.com

Print this graphic organizer.

Section 33.2 | Business Ownership

BUSINESS OWNERSHIP OPPORTUNITIES

You may become an entrepreneur if you (1) purchase an existing nonfranchise business, (2) take over the family business, (3) start a new business, or (4) purchase a franchise business.

As You Read

Connect Compare the pros and cons of the four forms of business organization.

PURCHASE AN EXISTING NONFRANCHISE BUSINESS

When an entrepreneur buys an existing nonfranchise business, there is usually little or no help from the previous owner. The buyer must investigate why the business was sold. Business records, the condition of the property, and inventory must be closely examined. The reputation of the business in the **community** must be considered. In some cases, the new owner may contract the services of the previous owner to assist with management during a transition period.

TAKE OVER A FAMILY BUSINESS

Similar considerations for purchasing an existing business apply to taking over a family business. Will the fact that the previous owner is a family member help or hurt the new owner? The new owner must explore potential conflicts with family members. Succession planning (transition to the next generation), managing growth, and family relations may be challenging when taking over and running a family business.

❝ There are four ways to start a business. ❞

START A NEW BUSINESS

Starting a new business gives an entrepreneur great freedom of choice. The new business owner can start the business of his or her choice and plan it from the ground up. He or she can decide where it is located, what it sells, and how it is organized. There are no old debts to settle and no bad reputation to overcome. On the other hand, it is up to the new owner to establish the business's reputation and build a customer base.

PURCHASE A FRANCHISE

A **franchise** is a legal agreement to sell a parent company's product or services in a designated geographic area. McDonald's Corporation and Taco Bell® are examples of companies that sell franchises. They are franchisors. The franchisee (the person buying the business) has to invest money to buy the franchise. The franchisee also pays an annual fee and a share of the profits. In exchange, the franchisor provides a well-known name, a business plan, advertising, and the proven methods and products of the parent company.

In franchise businesses, new business owners have a lot of help. The business planning is done by the franchisor. Planning includes management training, merchandising, and day-to-day operations.

A disadvantage of franchising is the initial cost. A large amount of capital is needed to purchase most franchises. The franchisee must also pay high initial fees to begin operations. Many franchisors are very strict about how the franchise is run.

Reading Check

Contrast How are nonfranchise and franchise businesses similar? How are they different?

There are many different forms of business and various ways of organizing a company. This Web site presents a company that helps new owners through the incorporation process. *Why might an entrepreneur need assistance with setting up a business?*

FORMS OF BUSINESS ORGANIZATION

The choice of which legal organization or structure a new business should have is a critical decision. It may make the difference between the success or failure of the business. The form determines how fast business decisions are implemented and how well the business competes in the marketplace. There are four possible forms of business organization (see **Figure 33.2** on page 788): sole proprietorship, partnership, corporation, and limited liability company (LLC).

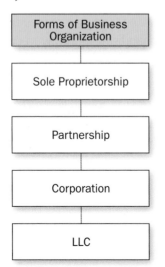

The choice depends on the financial and tax situation of the owner, the type of business, the number of employees who will be hired, and the level of risk involved in the new business. As a business grows, these factors may change and may require reorganization. A business could start out as a sole proprietorship, grow into a partnership, and ultimately become a corporation.

SOLE PROPRIETORSHIP

A **sole proprietorship** is a business that is owned and operated by one person. This is the most common form of business ownership. Approximately 70 percent of all U.S. businesses are sole proprietorships. Sole proprietors usually have a special skill by which they can earn a living. For example, plumbers, contractors, and many entrepreneurs who start Web-site businesses are often sole proprietors. The sole proprietor must provide the money and management skill to run the business. In return for all this responsibility, the sole proprietor is entitled to all the profits.

Advantages A sole proprietorship is relatively easy to start. The sole proprietor provides the money to start the business. For instance, a plumber buys tools and a truck, leases work space and buys office supplies, and spends money to advertise the business. A sole proprietorship is generally taxed less than other forms of business, and there is greater freedom from government regulation. Because the owner is usually the only investor in the business, that person is entitled to all the profits. A sole proprietorship also gives the owner great control over the business.

Disdvantages The primary disadvantage of a sole proprietorship is financial. The owner is responsible for all business debts and any legal judgments against the company. If the business does not do well, its debts may exceed its assets. If that happens, creditors can claim the owner's personal assets, such as a home, cars, and savings. The owner of a sole proprietorship has **unlimited liability**, which means that the owner's financial liability is not limited to investments in the business. It extends to include whether the owner can personally make payments on any debts owed by the business.

THE PARTNERSHIP

A **partnership** is a legal agreement between two or more people to be jointly responsible for the success or failure of a business. Partnerships represent about 10 percent of U.S. businesses. Common partnerships in your community may include real estate agencies, law offices, and medical offices.

A partnership is formed by a partnership agreement, usually prepared by an attorney, which specifies the responsibilities of each partner. Partners share the profits if the business is a success and the losses if it fails. Profits are usually divided according to the amount of time and money each partner invests. There are two kinds of partnerships: general and limited.

GENERAL PARTNERSHIP

In a **general partnership**, each partner shares in the profits and losses. As in the sole proprietorship, partners have shared unlimited liability for the company's debts. Also, each partner's share of the business profits is taxed as personal income.

MARKETING CASE STUDY

Flat-Rate Shipping from the U.S. Postal Service

One of the frustrations of online shopping, for both buyers and sellers, is the sometimes-complex nature of figuring out shipping costs.

A recent ad campaign by the United States Postal Service® put the focus on its flat-rate shipping service. The campaign focused on how it could benefit businesses by making everything simpler.

Keeping It Simple

In one ad, a postal carrier visits two partners who own a hobby shop. Their new toy robot kit is a huge hit, but they are struggling with shipping. The carrier shows them a flat-rate box, which is the perfect size for the robot, and which will cost them the same amount of postage no matter where they send it. The carrier tells them that with the U.S. Postal Service, shipping is simple: 'With a flat-rate box from the Postal Service – if it fits, it ships!'

English Language Arts

Analyze Discuss the advantages and disadvantages of a flat-rate shipping method for entrepreneurs, especially for planning a partnership business.

FIGURE 33.2 | Business Organization

The Four Forms of Business Ownership The legal organization of a business is a key decision for an entrepreneur. It determines how fast business decisions can be made, how well the business will compete in the marketplace, and how quickly it can raise money. *Which form of business ownership is easiest to establish?*

SOLE PROPRIETORSHIP

A sole proprietorship gives an entrepreneur the greatest control over business decisions and all the profits. It also exposes the owner to greater risks.

PARTNERSHIP

Partners share decision-making responsibility as well as the business's profits and losses. In a limited partnership, a limited partner is responsible for losses only to the level of his or her investment in the business. The general partner is fully responsible for losses.

CORPORATION

Corporations are owned by stockholders, who may range in number from one to millions. Each stockholder owns a portion of the business and is responsible for losses only to the level of his or her investment. In a corporation, the owners may not be involved in the day-to-day decision making for the business. With this type of organization, the benefits and risks are shared among the stockholders. Corporations can raise money relatively easily, but the decision-making process can be slow.

LIMITED LIABILITY COMPANY

The limited liability company (LLC) is a combination of a partnership and a corporation. Its owners (members) have only limited liability, and it has tax benefits not available to a corporation.

LIMITED PARTNERSHIP

In a **limited partnership**, each limited partner is liable for any debts only up to the amount of his or her investment in the company. Every limited partnership, however, must have at least one general partner who has unlimited liability. In exchange for limited liability, the limited partners have no voice in the management of the partnership. **Limited liability** means that the personal assets of the owners cannot be taken if a company does not meet its financial obligations or if it gets into legal trouble. The withdrawal of a limited partner does not dissolve the partnership.

Advantages A partnership combines the skills of the owners. It may make more capital available, allowing easier operation and expansion. Each partner has a voice in the management of the business. A partnership is taxed solely on the profits of the business and regulated less heavily than a corporation.

Disdvantages The owners may not always agree on business decisions, yet the actions of one partner are legally binding on the other partners. This means that all partners must assume their share of the business debt. They must also be responsible for the shares of any partners who cannot pay. Finally, the business is dissolved if one partner dies. It can be reorganized as a new partnership, but the process is time consuming and costly.

THE CORPORATION

A **corporation** is a legal entity created by either a state or a federal statute, authorizing individuals to operate an enterprise. In other words, a corporation is a business that is owned by several people but is considered to be just one person or entity under the law. A corporation has several unique features:

- ▶ **Legal permission to operate** To operate a business as a corporation, the owners must file an application with state officials for permission. Once the application is approved, this document becomes the corporation's charter.

- ▶ **Separate legal entity** A corporation is a separate legal entity that is created by law. A corporation can borrow money, sign contracts, buy or sell property, and sue and be sued in court.

- ▶ **Stockholders** Stockholders are the owners of a corporation and have limited liability. The ownership of a corporation is divided into shares of stock. The corporation can raise money by selling stocks.

- ▶ **Board of Directors** Stockholders own the corporation, but often they do not manage it. Instead, the stockholders elect a board of directors that is responsible for major decisions that affect the company.

Corporations also offer owners limited liability. Unlike a partnership, a corporation is not affected by the death, incapacity, or bankruptcy of an officer or a shareholder.

TYPES OF CORPORATIONS

The two main types of corporations are private and public corporations. A public corporation is a business entity created by the federal, state, or local government. This group can include incorporated cities as well as school, transit, and sanitation districts.

A private corporation is formed by private persons. It includes closely held corporations or "close corporations." This category also includes publicly held corporations. These are sometimes called "public corporations" even though they are subject to different rules than the public corporations described above.

A closely held corporation is owned by a few persons or a family. Shares or stocks of a closely held corporation are not sold to the public. On the other hand, a publicly held corporation is one whose stock (shares) is owned by a large group of people. Selling stock helps a corporation raise capital. In the United States, stocks or shares of a publicly held corporation are usually sold on the New York Stock Exchange (NYSE), Euronext™, the American Stock Exchange (AMEX®), or the National Association of Securities Dealers Automated Quotations (NASDAQ®) system.

If a corporation succeeds, the value of the stock rises, and stockholders benefit. Stockholders own their shares with limited liability. For example, if a stockholder purchases $1,000 worth of Dell Computers stock and the company fails, the investor would lose the investment amount but would not be responsible for the company's debt.

FORMING A CORPORATION

Forming a corporation is a complicated process. An entrepreneur must determine the company's internal corporate structure. This is defined by its bylaws, and the processes for selecting a board of directors and electing officers. The officers handle the day-to-day operations. In small corporations, members of the board of directors are usually elected as the officers of the corporation.

An entrepreneur must also choose the state in which to incorporate (establish) the company. For small companies, it is generally best to do this in the state where the company will do business. A **foreign corporation** is one that is incorporated under the laws of a state that differs from the one in which it does business. *Foreign* in this context means another state, not another country. Foreign corporations must register with each state in which they intend to do business.

Advantages Each owner has limited liability. It is easier to raise capital with corporations than with other forms of business. Capital is often needed for expansion. Owners can easily enter or exit the business simply by buying or selling stock. Management is shared. Each area of the business is handled by someone with expertise in that area.

Disadvantages The process of formation can be complex, and the accounting and record keeping can be complicated. Government regulation is increased. There are taxable corporate profits, which means shareholders are taxed on dividends they earn and on profits made from the sale of a stock.

LIMITED LIABILITY COMPANY

The **limited liability company (LLC)** is a relatively new form of business organization that is a hybrid of a partnership and a corporation. LLCs are now allowed in all 50 states. The LLC is sometimes incorrectly called a "limited liability corporation," instead of company. The federal government does not recognize an LLC as a classification for federal tax purposes. Thus, an LLC must file a corporation, partnership, or sole proprietorship tax return. Its owners, or members, are protected from personal liability. All profits and losses pass directly to the owners without taxation of the entity itself.

Reading Check

Summarize What are the forms of business organization?

LEGAL STEPS TO ESTABLISHING A BUSINESS

Before an entrepreneur can officially open the doors of a new business, he or she must take specific steps to legally establish and protect the business. These steps **vary** depending on whether the business will be a sole proprietorship, partnership, a corporation, or a limited liability company.

New business owners may wish to consult an accountant, attorney, or other business advisor to determine the best organization for a new business. When a corporation is formed, the laws of many states require that an attorney be hired. An attorney can guide the entrepreneur through the complicated process of incorporation. The entrepreneur must check the laws of the state in which she or he is incorporating.

To form a sole proprietorship or partnership, a business owner must file for a DBA at the local county clerk's office. A **DBA (Doing Business As)** is the registration by which the county government officially recognizes that a new proprietorship or partnership exists.

A DBA also protects the name of the business for a certain number of years. This name protection applies only to the county where the business is registered. There is usually a filing fee for registration.

To form a corporation, an entrepreneur must file Articles of Incorporation with the Corporation and Securities Bureau in the state's Department of Commerce. **Articles of Incorporation** identify the name and address of a new corporation, its purpose, and the names of the initial directors.

They also include the amount of stock that will be issued to each director. There is a filing fee, but the business becomes protected. No other business may register under that business's name. The forms, applications, and information on filing fees can be obtained from the state's Department of Commerce.

An LLC is established by filing Articles of Organization with the state. This document describes the LLC and lists the names of its members and initial managers. Many states also require LLCs to have an operating agreement. For the company to have the tax advantage of an LLC, this document must show that the company is distinct from a corporation.

Depending on the type of business and where it is located, a new owner may have to obtain one or more licenses in order to operate.

Licenses establish minimum standards of education and training for people who practice in a particular profession. They also regulate where businesses can locate, and they protect neighborhoods and the environment.

Individual states license many businesses and occupations, such as doctors, accountants, cosmetologists, barbers, marriage counselors, and pharmacists. Licensing is done to protect the public from unqualified people practicing in a business. Licensing also helps maintain the health and welfare of the citizens.

In addition to state licenses, the community may require special local licenses or permits to comply with zoning ordinances, building codes, and safety standards.

 After You Read **Section 33.2**

Review Key Concepts

1. **Name** the four ways to become a business owner.
2. **List** the four legal forms of business organization and note which is the most common.
3. **Name** an advantage of a limited liability company.

Practice Academics

Social Studies

4. The U.S. government protects copyrights, trademarks, and patents for new businesses. Research these terms on the Internet and write a description of the type of protection provided for each.

Mathematics

5. A friend who just opened a new business works 12 hours a day, 5 days a week, 50 weeks a year. How many hours does this person work annually?
To how many 40-hour workweeks is this equivalent?

Math Concept **Solving Time Problems** When solving problems that ask for values associated with time periods, know the equivalent measurements. For example, there are 24 hours in a day, 7 days in a week, and 52 weeks in a year.

Starting Hints Multiply the number of hours worked each day by the number of days worked each week, and then the number of weeks worked each year to determine the total number of hours worked in a year. Divide the total hours worked in a year by 40 to determine the number of 40-hour workweeks.

 connectED.mcgraw-hill.com

Check your answers.

For help, go to the Math Skills Handbook located at the back of this book.

Entrepreneurial Concepts

There are many factors to consider when starting a business. It is necessary to weigh the advantages and disadvantages of owning the business.

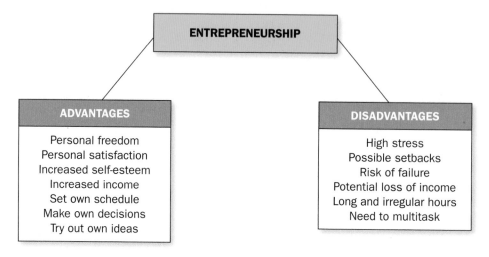

ENTREPRENEURSHIP

ADVANTAGES

Personal freedom
Personal satisfaction
Increased self-esteem
Increased income
Set own schedule
Make own decisions
Try out own ideas

DISADVANTAGES

High stress
Possible setbacks
Risk of failure
Potential loss of income
Long and irregular hours
Need to multitask

Individuals have to take three steps to start a business. The business can take four forms and be one of four types.

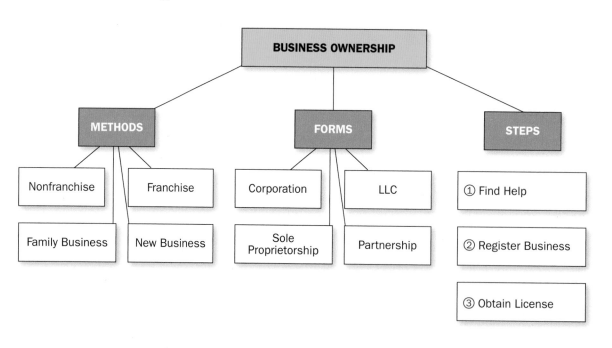

BUSINESS OWNERSHIP

METHODS

Nonfranchise
Franchise
Family Business
New Business

FORMS

Corporation
LLC
Sole Proprietorship
Partnership

STEPS

① Find Help
② Register Business
③ Obtain License

Review and Activities

Written Summary

- Being an entrepreneur involves risk taking but can bring personal and financial rewards.
- Advantages of entrepreneurship include being your own boss and earning a good income if the business succeeds.
- Entrepreneurs can try out their own ideas, set their own work schedules, and make their own business decisions.
- Disadvantages of entrepreneurship include the risk of failure, long working hours, and the potential loss of income.
- Entrepreneurship is important to the U.S. economy. It creates jobs, which provide income to individuals and communities.
- The four ways to become a business owner are (1) purchase an existing business, (2) take over the family business, (3) start a new business, and (4) purchase a franchise business.
- The four forms of business organization are (1) sole proprietorship, (2) partnership, (3) corporation, and (4) limited liability company.

Review Content Vocabulary and Academic Vocabulary

1. Create multiple-choice test questions for each content and academic vocabulary term.

Content Vocabulary
- entrepreneurship (p. 779)
- entrepreneurs (p. 779)
- franchise (p. 785)
- sole proprietorship (p. 786)
- unlimited liability (p. 787)
- partnership (p. 787)
- general partnership (p. 787)
- limited partnership (p. 789)
- limited liability (p. 789)
- corporation (p. 789)
- stockholders (p. 789)
- foreign corporation (p. 790)
- limited liability company (LLC) (p. 790)
- Doing Business As (DBA) (p. 790)
- Articles of Incorporation (p. 790)

Academic Vocabulary
- indication (p. 781)
- domestic (p. 783)
- community (p. 785)
- vary (p. 790)

Assess for Understanding

2. **Identify** What is an entrepreneur?
3. **Consider** What are the risks of entrepreneurship?
4. **Offer** What are the advantages of entrepreneurship?
5. **Delineate** What are the characteristics and skills needed to be a successful business owner?
6. **Infer** Why are small businesses important to the U.S. economy?
7. **Sequence** How do entrepreneurs become business owners?
8. **Define** What is a DBA?
9. **Decide** What are some advantages and disadvantages of a franchise business?

21st  Century Skills

Social Responsibility Skills

10. Social Responsibility You have decided to become an entrepreneur. You know that you will have to learn a great deal to run a business. However, you have also become very interested in social responsibility and environmental concerns. Conduct research on what businesses are doing to preserve the environment and be more socially responsible. Write a description of how you would plan your own business, addressing these concerns.

Financial Literacy Skills

11. Expenses You and a friend are considering a business picking up and delivering clothing for a local cleaning service. Your major expense would be for the purchase of a used van. Suppose that you have located a suitable van at a local dealer priced at $6,000. If you can pay 20 percent down, find out the interest rate a local bank or credit union would charge for a loan. How much would the monthly payments be and for how many months?

Everyday Ethics

12. Finding a Need In 1981, an attorney established a company called CMG Worldwide after he realized that many deceased celebrities had no one to safeguard their interests. CMG negotiates the use of clients' names and images in a variety of commercial contracts, from TV ads to posters and T-shirts. Elvis Presley, CMG's first client, brings in more than $50 million each year. Other CMG clients include Babe Ruth, Ella Fitzgerald, Duke Ellington, Mark Twain, and Marilyn Monroe. Even if a client's estate or family approved, should a deceased celebrity represent a product he or she would not have liked when alive? Express your opinion in a brief paragraph.

e-Marketing Skills

13. e-Marketing Problems Investigate the difficulties faced by new online businesses. Research on the Internet, using key words such as *e-marketing problems* and *online marketing problems*. List the problems, starting with what you believe would be the most difficult, ending the list with the easiest problem to solve.

Build Academic Skills

Social Studies

14. Matching Interests Interview an entrepreneur who owns and operates a retail business that you think might be interesting. Ask questions about what the owner likes and dislikes about owning a business. Ask how he or she got started in business and what knowledge, skills, and personal qualities are important for success. As you listen, you may think of and ask other questions. Prepare a written summary of your interview.

English Language Arts

15. Business Organization Conduct Internet research to learn how to form either a partnership or a corporation. You can find information by searching with key words such as *forming a partnership*, and *forming a corporation*. Write a one- or two-page report on your findings.

Mathematics

16. Calculate Profit A clothing company had a sales revenue of $4,000,000 last year. Its profit was $2,500,000. Of that profit, 20 percent was allocated for new equipment. How much is left after the purchase of the new equipment?

Math Concept **Solving Multi-Step Problems** When solving problems that require multiple steps, make a list of the information given in the problem, as well as the information for which you will be solving. This will make clear the relationships between what you are looking for and what is given.

For help, go to the **Math Skills Handbook** located at the back of this book.

Standardized Test Practice

Directions Read the following questions. On a separate piece of paper, write the best possible answer for each one.

1. A corporation is owned by the
   A. members
   B. board of directors
   C. stockholders
   D. partners

2. A limited liability company (LLC) is a cross between a partnership and a corporation.
   T
   F

3. The most common form of business ownership is a _____.

Test-Taking Tip

If you do not know the answer on multiple-choice and true/false questions, always guess if there is no penalty for wrong answers, but never guess if there is a penalty.

DECA Connection Role Play

Consultant
Start-Up Company

Situation You are a consultant for a business that advises potential entrepreneurs about realizing their dream of owning their own business. Today you are going to meet with a new client (judge). The new client (judge) is a jewelry designer who works with sterling silver and semi-precious stones. The jewelry designer (judge) has been making jewelry as a hobby for the past three years. The jewelry designer (judge) has sold his/her jewelry to family, friends, and at craft fairs. The jewelry designer's (judge's) reputation for beautiful and unique designs has spread throughout your community.

Customer demand for the jewelry has increased to the point where the designer (judge) feels that the time has come to open his/her own shop. The jewelry designer (judge) has found a perfect location for a shop. The building has space for a workroom and a showroom/sales area. The building is located in an area that is adjacent to the shops of other artists.

The reasonable rent has convinced the designer (judge) that the time is right to open the business. The jewelry designer (judge) has little business experience and has many questions for you. Today's meeting will focus on some basics of business ownership.

Activity You are to discuss with the jewelry designer (judge) the types of business ownership and organizational design for the proposed business, as well as some of the legal issues that affect businesses.

Evaluation You will be evaluated on how well you meet the following performance indicators:

1. Explain the types of business ownership.
2. Describe legal issues affecting businesses.
3. Explain the organizational design of businesses.
4. Explain how organizations adapt to today's markets.
5. Demonstrate responsible behavior.

  connectED.mcgraw-hill.com

Download the Competitive Events Workbook for more Role-Play practice.

risk management

SHOW WHAT YOU KNOW

Visual Literacy Risk is part of doing business. Managing risk is part of the planning process for every business. Risk management strives to prevent risks that can be avoided. It also aims to minimize the risks that are beyond the control of a business. *What kinds of risks might be avoided and minimized for a business?*

Discovery Project

Retail Risks

Essential Question How does a business manage its risks?

Project Goal

You and a classmate work for a company that helps clients develop risk management plans for retailers. The client has asked you to plan an internal theft and shoplifting prevention plan. Research some strategies that stores use to prevent internal theft and shoplifting. You are to prepare a written report on the specific measures that your team would recommend for handling retail theft.

Ask Yourself...

- How will you find out about other stores' policies and strategies?
- What general policies and procedures regarding retail theft would you recommend?
- What specific measures would you recommend to handle internal theft?
- What specific measures would you recommend to handle shoplifting?
- How will you organize your report and summarize your recommendations?

 Synthesize and Present Research Synthesize your research by preparing a written report on the specific measures that your team would recommend for handling retail theft.

 connectED.mcgraw-hill.com

Activity
Get a worksheet activity about risk management.

Evaluate
Download a rubric that you can use to evaluate your project.

DECA Connection

DECA Event Role Play

Concepts in this chapter are related to DECA competitive events that involve either an interview or role play.

Performance Indicators The performance indicators represent key skills and knowledge. Your key to success in DECA competitive events is relating them to concepts in this chapter.

- Determine the factors affecting business risk.
- Follow established security procedures/policies.
- Identify the key loss prevention methods retailers use to reduce shrinkage.
- Describe the concept of insurance.
- Explain the nature of risk management.

DECA Prep

Role Play Practice role-playing with the DECA Connection competitive-event activity at the end of this chapter. More information on DECA events can be found on DECA's Web site.

READING GUIDE

Before You Read

Predict What are some possible risks for businesses?

Objectives

- **Explain** the nature and scope of risk management.
- **Identify** the various types of business risks.

The Main Idea

Risk is part of doing business. Businesses manage risks to benefit public interest, safety, and the environment and to comply with existing laws.

Vocabulary

Content Vocabulary
- business risk
- risk management
- economic risks
- natural risks
- human risks

Academic Vocabulary

You will find these words in your reading and on your tests. Make sure you know their meanings.
- stress
- internal

Graphic Organizer

Draw or print this chart to identify business risks and provide examples of those risks.

connectED.mcgraw-hill.com

Print this graphic organizer.

MARKETING CORE FUNCTION

 Product/Service Management

Business Risk Management

WHAT IS RISK MANAGEMENT?

The primary goal of every business is to make a profit. However, there is no guarantee that this will happen. A business may experience a lower return on investment than was expected. The business may experience a loss after all the expenses have been paid. The possibility of financial loss is what is known as *business risk*. A **business risk** is a situation that can lead to financial gain, loss, or failure. A business cannot eliminate all risk, but marketers can use their planning skills to reduce and manage their risks.

According to the American Risk and Insurance Association, **risk management** is the systematic process of managing an organization's risks to achieve objectives in a manner consistent with public interest, human safety, environmental needs, and the law. Risks are managed by using the best available marketing information, analyzing opportunities, and making wise decisions.

As You Read

Analyze Is it possible for a business to eliminate business risks?

TYPES OF BUSINESS RISKS

Risks to businesses come in many forms. Economic, natural, and human risks are among the types of risks that a business may experience.

ECONOMIC RISKS

Economic risks are risks that result from changes in overall business conditions. These changes can include the level or type of competition, changing consumer lifestyles, population changes, limited usefulness or style of some products, product obsolescence, government regulation, inflation, or recession.

Failure to keep up with competition may lead to lost sales and economic risk. Foreign competition is also a threat. Products can often be produced and sold for less than similar domestic products.

> **" Risk management is an around-the-clock, every day-of-the-year concern for businesses. "**

Consumer lifestyles and population changes are other economic risks facing modern businesses if they fail to adapt goods or services to meet customers' changing interests and needs.

The limited usefulness or style of some products is another potential economic risk. Prices are frequently reduced on products to sell them at the end of the season. Every price reduction reduces both revenue and profits.

Some products inevitably become obsolete or outdated. Known as *product obsolescence*, this type of economic risk frequently concerns businesses that depend on the latest trends to market goods and services. Obsolescence occurs because new products are constantly being developed, and new trends are being started. When a new product is hipper, faster, more convenient, or more efficient than its earlier versions, the older product becomes obsolete.

Changes in the general business environment caused by inflation or recession can also present economic risks for retail businesses. For example, businesses in a geographic area experiencing high unemployment will suffer because consumers will likely cut back on purchases.

Government Regulations

Government laws and regulations can also result in economic risks. Laws that require businesses to pay for such things as special licenses or permits, street and sewer improvements, special assessments for environmental clean-ups, parking, and general upkeep may contribute to reduced profits.

Another risk is product recall. A product recall is a request to return to the maker a part of a product or an entire product. This usually occurs when safety is in question. A recall is an effort to limit liability and to avoid or curb negative publicity.

Product recalls, or even the threat of recalls, by government agencies can affect sales and profits. Companies experience additional expenses because product recalls require notification to all owners through paid media outlets, customer mailings, and provisions for free repair and replacement parts.

In addition to expensive repairs and replacements, companies with recalled products that caused injuries or deaths face high legal costs and injury claim settlements. These companies may also suffer from damaged reputations, which can be costly to rebuild.

NATURAL RISKS

Natural risks are risks that are caused by natural occurrences. They can result in loss or damage of property and may cause a business to shut down for a period of time. Common natural risks include catastrophes such as floods, tornadoes, hurricanes, fires, lightning, droughts, and earthquakes.

Some risks that are caused by people are also natural risks: Power outages, civil unrest, oil spills, arson, terrorism, and even war are classified as natural risks. Businesses can insure against unexpected losses from some natural risks, but not all. For example, a typical business insurance policy may not cover damage caused by acts of war or riots; special insurance may be required to cover regional threats such as earthquakes or floods.

Weather is an example of a natural risk. Some businesses and products depend on predictable weather for success. Ski resorts depend on normal snowfall levels to operate ski lifts, sell lodging and ski packages, and fill restaurants. A mild winter season or below-normal snowfall represents lost revenues and a natural risk for ski resorts.

Ski resorts depend on normal snowfall levels to stay in business. For this type of business a lack of snow is a natural risk. *What other types of risks can you identify in this picture?*

Natural Risks

Protecting business property against the risk of loss by fire is a direct way to manage risk. Installing smoke detectors, portable fire extinguishers, and automatic sprinklers, for example, can help to protect staff, property, and revenue.

HUMAN RISKS

Human risks are risks caused by employee dishonesty, errors, mistakes, and omissions as well as the unpredictability of customers or the workplace itself. Human risks range from internal risks and customer theft to employee- and customer-related injuries.

HUMAN RISKS	
Theft	Environment
Employees	Computers

Internal and Customer Theft

A National Retail Security Survey of 106 retail chains found that overall theft in the United States was estimated at over $36 billion a year. Total theft represented 1.51 percent of retail sales and continues to grow every year. Employee theft represents the largest share of retailer unexplained losses.

The most common employee theft includes not processing transactions or not scanning items for people at cash registers. Other types of employee theft include making false merchandise returns, gift card fraud, embezzlement, and stealing merchandise.

Customer theft is a loss caused by shoplifting, fraudulent activities, or nonpayment. The National Retail Federation has estimated that shoplifting alone adds 3 to 5 percent to the cost of each product just to cover losses. This loss is passed on to all of us in the form of higher prices to cover inventory shortages, pay for security personnel, and install theft-prevention systems. Additional examples of customer dishonesty include the nonpayment of accounts, and paying for goods and services with fraudulent checks, credit cards, or gift cards.

Employee Risks

Employees represent another human risk for business by engaging in fraudulent or improper business practices. For example, members of management at the energy trading giant Enron Corporation and its accounting firm, Arthur Andersen LLP, used questionable accounting techniques that inflated profits and hid losses. These fraudulent practices resulted in the company declaring bankruptcy, which became one of the largest bankruptcies in U.S. history. Thousands of Enron

employees lost their jobs, and many people lost savings they had invested in Enron stock. In addition, Arthur Andersen LLP, previously one of the top five accounting firms in the United States, lost its auditing license and sold its assets to competitors.

Skills and Working Environment

In a restaurant, failing to properly cook or handle food can lead to customers becoming ill or hospitalized. To reduce risks of this type, many companies have created safety programs that **stress** the importance of proper food handling.

Customer or employee accidents are potential human risks. Commercial airlines, for example, prepare crews for mechanical-related emergencies but also for human risks. A passenger might fall in the aisle, break an arm, and sue the airline. Retail businesses take precautions to keep customers safe when rain, ice, or liquid cleaners create slippery floors. An employee might be injured on the job by faulty machinery or improperly built structures. Employee illnesses could also be caused by toxic fumes or other environmental hazards.

Another potential risk faced by employers is the threat of sexual harassment, stalking, or physical violence. Violent crime in the workplace accounts for 15 percent of the violent acts experienced by U.S. residents age 12 or older. Trade associations, such as the Food Marketing Institute®, provide materials to help businesses assess policies and practices dealing with workplace violence.

Handling Risks Risk management started with insurance protection against natural disasters. Now it includes electronic security, information technology, legal compliance, strategic planning, workplace threats, and worker safety.

Computer-Related Crime

"Cybercrime" has emerged as a significant new risk for businesses. Employees who use their company's network to visit untrusted Web sites can mistakenly download "malware," or malicious computer software. Malware programs, including "worms" and "viruses," can be disastrous to information and communication systems and **internal** computer networks. Computer worms and viruses are often spread through unwanted or "spam" e-mail. Some spam is harmless, but e-mail attacks containing malicious links have been known to infect millions of computers and disable entire networks.

Individuals may also illegally penetrate, or "hack," the security of computer systems to gain access or information for mischievous or criminal purposes. Hacking may include industrial espionage, such as stealing proprietary company information, client lists, or bank accounts.

Computer crime is committed by many kinds of people, from current or past employees to professional gangs of cyber-thieves. Protecting a business from computer crime requires a secure computer network that utilizes passwords, encoded firewall programs, and virus detectors. It requires being vigilant about scanning for operational or human security risks that affect technology. It is also important to stay current on security alerts released by software publishers.

In order to avoid becoming the victims of cybercrime, businesses must install reputable and up-to-date antivirus software on their computer systems. Employers need to train staff on privacy policies and the proper handling of confidential information related to voicemail, e-mail, and Internet use. Companies also need their employees to be on the lookout for potential issues such as "phishing." A common scam involves official-looking requests for information that are actually fraudulent. A business should always verify that such requests are legitimate before giving out account numbers. All these steps are necessary to help minimize the risk of computer intrusion, customer identity theft, and information theft.

 After You Read | **Section 34.1**

Review Key Concepts

1. **Explain** why changing lifestyles pose an economic risk for a business.
2. **List** three examples of natural risks.
3. **Identify** the causes of human risks for a business.

Practice Academics

English Language Arts

4. Conduct research on a major natural disaster that occurred within the last decade. Write a one-page paper that identifies the natural disaster, its location, and the physical and human costs involved with the disaster. Identify any administration, legal, or environmental changes (e.g., better emergency preparedness, improved building or zoning changes, etc.) made by local, state, and national officials to assist with the future natural disasters.

Mathematics

5. In the clothing industry, it is estimated that 3 to 5 percent is added to the price of a product to cover shoplifting losses. Calculate the price of a $149.99 cell phone without the 3-percent "hidden tax" due to shoplifting losses.

Math Concept **Reducing Values Using Percents** Reducing values by a given percent requires multiplication to determine the value of the percent and subtraction to determine the price after the reduction.

Starting Hints To solve this problem, multiply the selling price by .03, the percent of hidden tax, to determine the dollar value of the tax. Subtract the dollar value of the hidden tax from the selling price to determine the price without the hidden tax.

 connectED.mcgraw-hill.com

Check your answers.

For help, go to the Math Skills Handbook located at the back of this book.

READING GUIDE

Before You Read

Predict What are some of the methods businesses use to handle risks?

Objectives

- **Explain** effective security and safety precautions, policies, and procedures.
- **Describe** the various ways businesses can manage risk.
- **Explain** the concept of insurance.

The Main Idea

Businesses use various strategies to help prevent, avoid, and protect against accidents, injuries, fires, thefts, defective products, and environmental and other disasters.

Vocabulary

Content Vocabulary
- insurance policy
- extended coverage
- fidelity bonds
- performance bonds

Academic Vocabulary
You will find these words in your reading and on your tests. Make sure you know their meanings.
- undergo
- devices

Graphic Organizer

Draw this chart and fill in the boxes with different methods of handling risk.

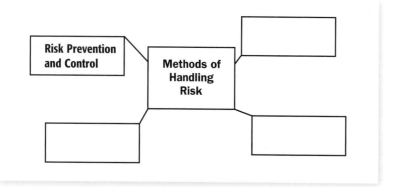

connectED.mcgraw-hill.com

Print this graphic organizer.

MARKETING CORE FUNCTION

 Product/Service Management

Handling Business Risks

WAYS OF HANDLING BUSINESS RISKS

There are four basic ways that businesses can handle risks: risk prevention and control, risk transfer, risk retention, and risk avoidance. An effective risk prevention program for a business should use a combination of all these methods.

RISK PREVENTION AND CONTROL

Business risks can be handled through prevention and control. Many common types of risks can be controlled and minimized by screening and training employees, providing safe working conditions and sufficient safety instruction, preventing external theft, and by deterring employee theft.

As You Read

Identify Consider some ways a business might manage or protect itself from risks.

SCREENING AND TRAINING EMPLOYEES

The best way to prevent the human risk of employee carelessness and incompetence is through effective employee screening, orientation, and training. Background screening on all job applications, checking references, requiring driver licenses, and verifying citizenship are often used to assist in new employee selection. Many employers also use pre-employment tests for basic and technical skills to find the right people. Larger companies and some smaller ones now require prospective employees to **undergo** testing for illegal drugs before being hired. Substance abuse can lead to increased human risk by causing employees to be careless and more likely to ignore or forget safety rules.

> **"Risk managers must develop effective programs and techniques for a variety of risks."**

When employees begin a new job, orientation, training, and instruction is normally provided. The training may be brief verbal instruction or extensive training that lasts several weeks or months. Workers should be trained in the policies, procedures, and processes dealing with human risks. This can minimize the risk of lost sales through human errors, mistakes, or omissions.

PROVIDING SAFE CONDITIONS AND SAFETY INSTRUCTION

According to the most recent U.S. Bureau of Labor Statistics, there were over 4,628 workplace deaths in the United States due to unintentional injuries. The rate of fatal injuries for U.S. workers was 3.4 fatalities for 100,000 workers.

Nonfatal workplace injuries and illnesses involved 3.8 million workers. Over half of these injuries required days away from work, job transfers, or job restrictions.

Based on these numbers alone, it is clear that safety and health information must be provided to all employees. When all employees receive safety instruction and have safe working conditions, the potential for on-the-job accidents is greatly reduced.

To manage such risks, businesses should design all employee work zones and customer selling areas for efficient foot traffic and storage. They can also provide training on proper ways to safely lift, store, and deliver merchandise.

Many companies address workplace health and safety by developing programs that includes these strategies:

- ▶ Creating committees to check for hazards
- ▶ Correcting hazards before accidents occur
- ▶ Complying with all state and federal health and safety regulations
- ▶ Investigating and recording all workplace incidents and accidents
- ▶ Providing protective clothing and equipment
- ▶ Placing first-aid kits near workstations
- ▶ Posting directions to nearby health-care facilities
- ▶ Offering employee classes in first aid and CPR
- ▶ Tracking workdays missed due to accidents or injuries
- ▶ Scheduling regular safety meetings and trainings
- ▶ Distributing written safety and health plans
- ▶ Offering incentives for improved safety records
- ▶ Addressing workplace threats such as sexual harassment or violence
- ▶ Communicating business standards and policies

CONTROLLING EMPLOYEE THEFT

One of the most costly forms of human risk is theft by employees and customers. Employee theft represents the greatest part of all unexplained business losses due to theft. The most recent National Retail Security Survey estimated that internal theft from retail stores costs Americans more than $18.1 billion each year.

Most employee theft occurs at the point-of-sale (POS) terminal, or cash register. To protect against employee theft, many businesses have installed POS terminals that generate reports that monitor cash discrepancies, cash register transactions, employees' discounts, gift-card purchases, refunds by employees, merchandise returns, sales reports, and void transfers. By analyzing these data, businesses can improve the chances of catching dishonest employees.

Closed-circuit television systems also lower the risk of employee theft. These systems include hidden cameras operated and observed by security personnel in a control room and backed up with recording equipment.

MARKETING CASE STUDY

Insuring Sports and Events

Most companies must sign up for standard liability coverage to do business as usual. This is especially important if they have employees and deal with the public. However, some businesses and organizations cannot be covered by standard policies. Instead, they are insured by companies that specialize in niche markets like sports and events.

Risky Business

For protection that goes beyond kneepads and helmets, insurance companies such as Sportsinsurance.com or Nationwide® provide liability coverage for all kinds of sports. These sports include football, soccer, baseball, basketball, extreme sports, and more. Owners and organizers need insurance for themselves, their teams and leagues, their athletes, their employees, and even their volunteers at events, sports camps, and tournaments. With so much money invested in sports activities, insurance is a safe bet in case bad weather, accidents, and injuries put employees on the "DL" (disabled list).

English Language Arts

Compose Conduct research to find out whether your school needs insurance for hosting a sports event, such as a championship football game. What kind of coverage must the school have?

PREVENTING SHOPLIFTING

Shoplifting is external theft that involves stealing merchandise from a business. It is estimated that shoplifting causes one-third of lost inventory.

To deter shoplifting, businesses can educate employees about shoplifting prevention guidelines. Adequately lighting store layouts, storing expensive items in locked display cases, or tagging products with electronic anti-theft **devices** can reduce shoplifting. Many stores use digital video cameras, electronic gates, and wall or ceiling mirrors to cut down on the risk of theft.

Many states have passed strict laws regarding shoplifting. However, apprehending shoplifters is a significant risk. Businesses can be sued for allegations of false arrest, false imprisonment, malicious prosecution, excessive use of force, or physical assault. To limit their liability, retailers must educate themselves and their employees about acceptable shoplifter detention policies.

REDUCING WORKPLACE THREATS

Violent crime in the workplace is real. It is estimated that more than 2 million personal thefts and more than 200,000 car thefts occur annually at work. Employees also experience incidents of sexual harassment and stalking while working.

Robbery is stealing of money or merchandise by violence or threat. Many police departments provide instruction on how to prevent and handle armed robberies. Businesses can lower their workplace threat risks and protect their employees by taking the following steps:

▶ Developing and communicating workplace violence policies

▶ Training employees on how to handle incidents

▶ Increasing lighting in and outside

▶ Limiting the amount of money kept on hand

▶ Handling bank deposits discreetly

▶ Installing cameras

▶ Hiring security guards and extra employees to assure double coverage

▶ Installing bulletproof glass in cashier cubicles

▶ Opening back doors only for freight or trash

▶ Installing switches for remotely locking doors

▶ Making sure doors are locked and alarms are set

RISK TRANSFER

Some business risks can be handled by transferring the risk of loss to another business or party. Risk transfer methods include purchasing insurance, promoting product and service warranties, and transferring risk through business ownership.

PURCHASING INSURANCE

A business can insure property and people against potential loss by purchasing insurance policies. An **insurance policy** is a contract between a business and an insurance company to cover a specific business risk. A business can buy an insurance package that combines two or more types of insurable risks of loss.

Closed-circuit television systems can help to deter both employee and customer theft. *What other systems do retailers use to help prevent theft?*

Insurance companies estimate the probability of loss due to natural risks, such as fire, lightning, and wind damage, and human risks, such as theft and vandalism. The insurance company then looks at the business's location, past experience, limits, and type of business to determine an insurance rate.

A business located in a neighborhood with a higher crime rate is charged higher rates for insurance coverage. This business has a higher likelihood of making a claim against the insurance company for losses.

PROPERTY INSURANCE

One of the most common forms of business insurance is property insurance. Property insurance covers the loss of or damage to buildings, equipment, machinery, merchandise, furniture, and fixtures. Coverage can be purchased for up to the full replacement value of the building or inventory, or for a portion of the replacement value.

Property insurance policies can be purchased with optional extended coverage endorsements. An **extended coverage** endorsement provides protection against types of loss that may not be covered under a basic property insurance policy.

Extended coverage may include off-premise property, rental cars, valuable papers and records, fire department service charges, water leakage, sewer back-ups, and personal property of others, including theft. Property insurance typically includes the following features:

- ▶ **Replacement Cost Coverage** This reimburses the business owner for the replacement cost of buildings and other personal property. A co-insurance penalty may apply if the insured business purchases less coverage than the reconstruction value of property. This means, for example, that the insurance company might pay 80 percent of the covered items, and the insured pays the balance.

- ▶ **Automatic Increase Protection** This policy feature adjusts the coverage to compensate for inflation on both the building and its contents.

- ▶ **Business Interruption** This feature compensates a business for loss of income during the time after a catastrophe when repairs are being made to a building. This coverage will also reimburse other expenses that continue during the repair period, such as interest on loans, taxes, rent, advertising, and salaries.

LIABILITY INSURANCE

Business liability insurance protects a business against damages for which it may be held legally liable, such as an injury to a customer or damage to property of others.

Transferring Risk

Insurance policies are a way of transferring risk from the business owner to an insurance company. How much you pay for such insurance depends on how high the risk of loss appears to the insurer. *How can an insurer help a business determine its insurance needs?*

Primary business liability insurance is usually provided for claims up to $1 million. This type of insurance may be extended to cover business premises, company operations, customer medical expenses, and product and advertising liability claims.

Product liability insurance protects against business losses resulting from personal injury or property damage caused by products manufactured or sold by a business. Many businesses purchase product liability insurance to protect against potential customer claims. They may choose to do so even though private laboratories and government agencies may have tested the products extensively.

Fidelity bonds provide insurance that protects a business from employee dishonesty. Businesses usually require employees who handle money, such as bank tellers and cashiers, to be bonded. If a bonded employee steals money or merchandise, the bonding company pays the loss. Individuals who are to be bonded are subject to background checks before a bond is issued.

The bankruptcy or insolvency of a contractor during a construction contract will likely cause a project to be delayed. This will lead to additional expenses for another contractor to finish the work. Therefore, it is not uncommon to require contractors to provide insurance. **Performance bonds**, also called surety bonds, provide financial protection for losses that might occur when a construction project is not finished due to a contractor's impaired financial condition.

Owners or managers of a business may purchase life insurance. A sole proprietor (individual business owner) is usually required to have life insurance in order to borrow money. The policy will guarantee that there will be money to pay off the sole proprietor's debts and obligations if he or she dies. Life insurance for a business partner can provide the money needed for other partners to continue the business. This occurs when the insured partner dies if the other partners are named as beneficiaries and receive proceeds from the policy.

Credit insurance protects a business from losses on credit extended to customers. Credit life insurance pays off the balance due for loans granted by banks, credit unions, and other financial institutions if the borrower dies.

Workers' compensation insurance covers employees who suffer job-related injuries and illness. This insurance covers medical care, a portion of lost wages, and permanent disability. It also protects employers from lawsuits that may be filed by an employee injured on the job.

All states have specific workers' compensation insurance coverage. These requirements are based on the number of employees and prescribed time periods.

PROMOTING PRODUCT AND SERVICE WARRANTIES

Warranties are promises made by a manufacturer or distributor with respect to the duration of performance and quality of a product. Businesses can transfer risks by informing customers about existing manufacturer warranties for defective products and required repairs. They can also offer extended product and service warranties that lengthen the warranty period through third-party service and repair providers.

TRANSFERRING RISKS THROUGH BUSINESS OWNERSHIP

The type of business ownership determines the amount of risk that is managed. In a sole proprietorship, the individual owner assumes all risks. Partnerships enable the partners to share in the business risks. Corporations allow the stockholders, as owners, to share the business risks. The corporate form of ownership offers the most protection from losses.

Reading Check

List What are the ways for businesses to transfer risk?

RISK RETENTION

In some cases, it is impossible for businesses to prevent or transfer certain types of risks. Therefore, they retain or assume financial responsibility for the consequences of loss. This process is called "risk retention." A business has to assume the loss—or retain the risk—if customer trends change and merchandise remains unsold. Most retailers assume the loss of a certain percentage of goods due to damage or theft.

It is possible to underestimate the risk, such as when merchandise is purchased in anticipation of high demand, but weather, fashion trends, or customers' purchasing habits change. A business may attempt to generate a profit by taking a risk, such as purchasing land for future development or sale through subdivision.

RISK AVOIDANCE

Certain risks can be avoided by anticipating the risks and rewards in advance. Risk avoidance means that a business refuses to engage in a particular activity, such as producing or selling a certain product or offering a particular service.

Avoidance may seem like a good strategy to avoid all risks. However, avoiding risks also means missing out on the potential gain that accepting or retaining the risk may have offered.

Market research can lead businesses to conclude that the investment risk in some goods or services is not worth the potential gain. All business decisions should be made with the consideration of both potential benefits and potential risks. Avoiding unacceptable business risks should be a key consideration in any marketing decision.

 After You Read   **Section 34.2**

Review Key Concepts

1. **Identify** the strategies used for risk prevention and control.
2. **Explain** the purpose of an insurance policy.
3. **List** three different ways that a business can transfer risks.

Practice Academics

English Language Arts

4. Conduct research on retailer theft. Write a one-page report on how businesses are attempting to stop employee or customer theft. Your report must identify the source and date of your information, the type of theft you investigated, and methods businesses use to control it.

Mathematics

5. Your local grocery store chain reported a total of $845,855 lost as a result of theft from stores in one year. Of this amount, 58 percent is assumed to be internal theft. How much money is assumed lost due to internal theft?

   Math Concept **Calculating Percents** Calculating the value a percent represents is a matter of converting the percent to a decimal and multiplying.

   Starting Hints Convert the percent to a decimal by moving the decimal point two places to the left. Multiply the decimal by $845,855 to determine the dollar amount that was lost due to internal theft.

    connectED.mcgraw-hill.com

   Check your answers.

For help, go to the Math Skills Handbook located at the back of this book.

Risk Management

Business risks fall into three categories: economic, natural, and human.

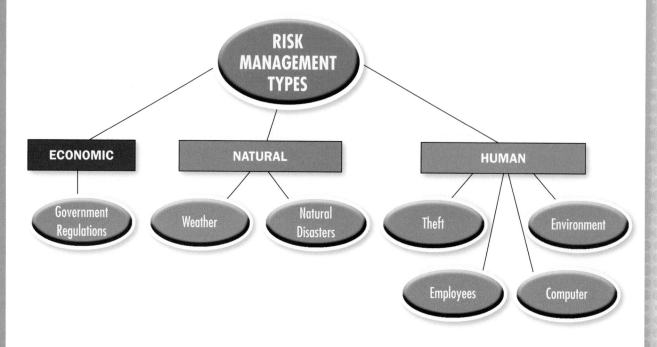

There are four strategies businesses use to manage risk: prevention and control, transfer, retention, and avoidance.

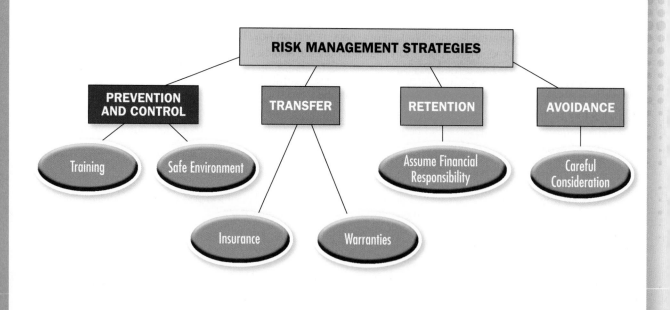

Review and Activities

Written Summary

- Business risks can lead to financial gain, loss, or failure.
- Risk management is the process of managing risk in an ethical way.
- Business risks fall into three categories: economic, natural, and human.
- Businesses manage risks of financial loss through loss prevention and control, transfer, retention, and avoidance.
- Safe working conditions, external and internal theft control, insurance, warranties, and ownership changes are risk management techniques.

Review Content Vocabulary and Academic Vocabulary

1. Write true-or-false statements using each vocabulary word. Ask a partner to determine whether each statement is true or false and explain why.

   Content Vocabulary
   - business risk (p. 799)
   - risk management (p. 799)
   - economic risks (p. 799)
   - natural risks (p. 800)
   - human risks (p. 801)
   - insurance policy (p. 807)
   - extended coverage (p. 808)
   - fidelity bonds (p. 810)
   - performance bonds (p. 810)

   Academic Vocabulary
   - stress (p. 802)
   - internal (p. 802)
   - undergo (p. 805)
   - devices (p. 807)

Assess for Understanding

2. **Explain** What are the nature and scope of risk management?
3. **Identify** What are the various types of business risks?
4. **Describe** How do safety procedures and policies help a business reduce risk?
5. **Consider** Which security policies and procedures would you use as a business owner?
6. **Suggest** How can businesses manage risks?
7. **Define** What is the concept of insurance?
8. **Justify** Why do businesses need risk management?
9. **Role Play** How can you convince a customer to use product and service warranties for a product that is advertised for its quality of construction and durability?

 Century Skills

Social Responsibility

10. Healthful Habits Conduct research on the importance of hygiene in food-service establishments. Identify the kinds of risks faced by employees and customers. Provide a one-page memo to staff explaining the importance of personal hygiene. Include recommendations for good practice in the workplace to protect coworkers and the general public.

Financial Literacy Skills

11. Calculating Theft Costs Assume that you would like to purchase a smartphone that retails for $259. It was estimated in 2009 that about 1.51 percent of retail sales was lost to overall theft. What would your product cost, if 1.51 percent were not added to its price due to theft? How much would you save?

e-Marketing Skills

12. Workplace Threats Imagine that you work for a risk management firm. You have been asked by a client to design a workplace safety plan for a quick-serve restaurant that employs late-night and early-morning employees. Perform Internet research on workplace security and make five recommendations regarding worker safety and operational safety. Outline your recommendations in a one-page written report.

- What specific recommendations will you make for worker safety?
- What specific recommendations will you make for operational safety?
- How will you implement these recommendations?

Build Academic Skills

English Language Arts

13. Extended Product Warranties Conduct research on the advantages and disadvantages of extended product warranties. Identify the name of your source(s) and prepare a one-page report that summarizes the advantages and disadvantages of extended product warranties.

Science

14. Business and the Environment The U.S. Environmental Protection Agency (EPA) plays a significant role in preventing, correcting, and eliminating potential environmental risks. Conduct research using the EPA's Web site. Describe a recent action or situation involving a business and actions taken by the agency to protect the public interest. Identify the business name, location, situation, and actions planned or taken to protect consumers. Summarize your findings in a one-page written report.

Mathematics

15. Calculate Losses from Theft Calculate the amount of net sales lost to an electronics store with annual sales of $8,359,000 and a shoplifting rate of 3.2 percent.

Math Concept Calculating Losses Solutions to problems that ask values of losses are most often given as a percent. Convert the percent to a decimal number and multiply to find the dollar value.

For help, go to the **Math Skills Handbook** located at the back of this book.

Standardized Test Practice

Directions Read the following questions. On a separate piece of paper, write the best possible answer for each one.

1. A business that provides safe working conditions and safety instruction is handling risks by which of the following methods?

   A. Risk avoidance

   B. Risk prevention

   C. Risk retention

   D. Risk transfer

2. Customer dishonesty is an example of a natural risk.

   T

   F

3. The possibility of financial loss is what is known is known as a(n) _____.

Test-Taking Tip

When answering multiple-choice questions, ask yourself if each option is true or false. This may help you find the best answer if you are not sure.

DECA. Connection Role Play

Employee
Dry Cleaners

Situation Assume the role of an experienced employee of a dry cleaning establishment. The store has been in business for 40 years. It has an outstanding reputation. The store also handles specialty cleaning of leather items, quilts, and bridal gowns. You are training a new counter person (judge). You mention that the owners carry insurance on the building and equipment, and on the items they clean. The new employee (judge) wants to know why the business carries so much insurance when it has a good reputation.

Activity You are to explain to the new employee (judge) why the dry cleaner carries insurance and some of the risks that can be protected against by purchasing insurance.

Evaluation You will be evaluated on how well you meet the following performance indicators:

1. Determine the factors affecting business risk.
2. Follow established security procedures/policies.
3. Identify the key loss prevention methods retailers use to reduce shrinkage.
4. Describe the concept of insurance.
5. Explain the nature of risk management.

---

connectED.mcgraw-hill.com

Download the Competitive Events Workbook for more Role-Play practice.

Chapter 35

Section 35.1
The Business Plan

Section 35.2
Marketing and Financial
Plans

developing a business plan

Visual Literacy A business plan includes a plan for making a new business succeed. It includes a philosophy and mission statement, describes an organizational scheme, identifies various marketing strategies, and provides a detailed financial plan. *Why must entrepreneurs research all available sources of funding and opportunities to raise capital?*

Discovery Project

Start-Up Planning

Essential Question How does an entrepreneur develop a business plan?

Project Goal

You and a classmate are partners in a proposed new product or service business. The first step in developing a business plan is to describe the type of business and complete a team self-analysis. The team must also develop and agree on an organization and marketing plan for the business. Your team must prepare a written report that describes the business, its organization, and marketing plans.

Ask Yourself...

- How will your team describe the product/service and analyze the team's special skills?
- How will your team organize the new business?
- What pricing policies and promotional strategies will your team use?
- How will your team organize the written plan for these three sections of a business plan?

 Synthesize and Present Synthesize your research by describing in a report the important elements in your business plan including the description and analysis, organization, and marketing plans.

 connectED.mcgraw-hill.com

Activity
Get a worksheet activity about business plans.

Evaluate
Download a rubric that you can use to evaluate your project.

DECA Connection

DECA Event Role Play

Concepts in this chapter are related to DECA competitive events that involve either an interview or role play.

Performance Indicators The performance indicators represent key skills and knowledge. Your key to success in DECA competitive events is relating them to concepts in this chapter.

- Assess personal interests and skills needed for success in business.
- Identify a company's unique selling proposition.
- Conduct an environmental scan to obtain business information.
- Conduct market analysis.
- Describe factors that affect the business environment.

DECA Prep

Role Play Practice role-playing with the DECA Connection competitive-event activity at the end of this chapter. More information on DECA events can be found on DECA's Web site.

FIGURE 35.1 **Outline for a Business Plan**

The Business Plan A business plan is a written plan prepared for a new business. *What is the purpose of the plan for a potential investor or lender?*

BUSINESS PLAN OUTLINE

1

Section 1 describes the general concept of the proposed business, outlines the entrepreneur's special skills, and analyzes the potential market.

I. Description and analysis
   A. Type of business
   B. Business philosophy
   C. Product and service plan
   D. Self-analysis
     1. Education and training
     2. Strengths and weaknesses
     3. Plan for personal development
   E. Trading area analysis
     1. Geographic, demographic, and economic data
     2. Competitive analysis
   F. Market segment analysis
     1. Target market
     2. Customer buying behavior
   G. Operational plan

2

Section 2 discusses how the business will be organized, describes the product or service to be offered, and details the marketing plan.

II. Organizational plan
   A. Proposed organization
     1. Type of ownership
     2. Steps in establishing business
     3. Personnel needs
   B. Proposed good/service
     1. Manufacturing plans and inventory policies
     2. Suppliers

3

Section 3 describes the way the business will price, promote, and distribute its products and services.

III. Marketing plan
   A. Pricing policies
   B. Promotional activities

4

Section 4 identifies the sources of capital and projects income and expenses.

IV. Financial plan
   A. Sources of capital
     1. Personal sources
     2. External sources
   B. Projected income and expenses
     1. Personal financial statement
     2. Projected start-up costs
     3. Projected personal needs
     4. Projected business income
     5. Projected business expenses
     6. Projected income statement(s)
     7. Projected balance sheet
     8. Projected cash flow

Industry trade and professional associations can also be rich **sources** of data. Entrepreneurs can obtain research results and data from local chambers of commerce, local and county government offices, and state economic development agencies and boards. The U.S. Small Business Administration and its resource partner, the Senior Corps of Retired Executives (SCORE®), can refer you to potential sources of information and classes for aspiring entrepreneurs. Many community colleges and universities also have small business development centers or agencies. These places provide information, referrals, and resources to develop a winning business plan.

TYPE OF BUSINESS

A business plan begins with a description of the type of business you have or plan to start. In part of the plan, you will present marketing research data and review significant trends that will influence the success of your proposed business. You should also provide an explanation of how a current or changing situation has created an opportunity for your business to fulfill consumer demand.

BUSINESS PHILOSOPHY

In the company description, you state your business philosophy. A **business philosophy** contains beliefs on how a business should be run. It also demonstrates an understanding of the business's role in the marketplace. The business philosophy reveals your attitude toward your customers, employees, and competitors. A business philosophy should also include a mission statement and a vision statement. A mission statement expresses the specific aspirations of the company. A vision statement states the scope and purpose of the company.

PRODUCT AND SERVICE PLAN

After identifying a business philosophy, you describe the product and/or service that will be offered. You will explain the potential consumer benefits and why your product or service will be successful. Include as many facts, trends, and statistics as you can, and be thorough in your research and documentation. Unsupported data, speculation, and personal assumptions will not convince investors and lenders to lend you money.

This small business owner has a business plan that describes and analyzes every aspect of his business. *Why is a business plan important for a small business owner?*

Small Business Owner

SELF-ANALYSIS

The next part of the business plan includes a self-analysis—a description of your personal education and professional training, an appraisal of your strengths and weaknesses, and any plans you have for continued personal and professional development.

EDUCATION AND TRAINING

Indicate any education and training that has prepared you to operate the new business you are planning. For example, if you are planning to open a tax preparation business, you should highlight your bachelor's degree in accounting along with your state-issued license to work as a Certified Public Accountant. If you have worked for another company that prepares tax returns, you should also be sure to highlight that experience.

Your education and work experience show potential lenders that you understand the industry you hope to enter. They demonstrate your interest in your chosen field and your commitment to succeeding in it. They also show that you have the skills required to run a successful business.

SPECIAL STRENGTHS

Many businesses require the owner or operator to have a special license. For example, the owner of an adult foster care center, an automotive repair shop, or a styling salon is required to possess a special occupational license. Special certification is also required for operators of child day care, construction, and electrical businesses.

In this part of the business plan, you should highlight all the professional licenses, certifications, skills, and strengths that you have obtained. You should also explain how they will be useful in starting up and operating the proposed business.

You should also clearly describe any personal traits and work habits that you believe will help you manage the business. Examples of leadership activities, personal initiatives, and willingness to work hard add strength to your business plan. Be sure to mention any involvement in professional organizations that might reflect well on your ability to successfully operate your own business. Also note your involvement in any relevant volunteer activities that can help demonstrate your sense of commitment and responsibility.

MARKETING CASE STUDY

The kgb Plan: Got Questions?

If you are having trouble remembering the name of that actor in the TV show you watched as a kid, you might try a Google search or another online service, such the kgb (Knowledge Generation Bureau). Send a text message and get an answer on your cell phone. Unlike free search engines, however, "kgb agents" respond for 99 cents per question.

Targeting Texters

This service has been in the directory assistance business since 1992.

Because customer behavior changed, they changed. They decided to expand its business plan to keep up with the changes in customer activities: People don't call for information anymore, they text. The CEO explains the kgb philosophy: "We wanted to rebrand the kgb—we're democratizing information." And as part of its marketing plan, a series of TV commercials depict people in humorous situations desperately in need of an answer.

English Language Arts

Collaborate With a partner, write a hypothetical Description and Analysis for the first section of this company's business plan. Refer to **Figure 35.1** and conduct Internet research as needed.

PLAN FOR PERSONAL DEVELOPMENT

You should also describe how you will acquire the needed skills that you might currently lack or need to improve. Needed skills can be gained through additional training or membership in trade associations. Skills may also be acquired by hiring or partnering with other professionals to assist you in managing the business. Plans for continuing personal development show your intent to improve on your existing skills and abilities as a business owner.

Self-Employment You are not alone, if you want to start a business. On average, 543,000 individuals per month create new businesses.

TRADING AREA ANALYSIS

The trading area analysis part of the plan defines your trading area. A **trading area** is the geographical area from which a business draws its customers. Before going into business, you must analyze the trading area to become familiar with geographic, demographic, and economic data, and with the competition.

It is very important that you do this research and analysis before choosing where you will conduct business. Your location is likely to become a long-term financial commitment that will be difficult to change if it does not work out.

Information about the population in your trading area is available from your local chamber of commerce or state department of commerce. You can also consult the most recent local U.S. Census data in your library or on the Internet.

GEOGRAPHIC, DEMOGRAPHIC, AND ECONOMIC DATA

Geographic data include population distribution figures, or how many people live in a certain area. Demographics are identifiable and measurable population statistics, such as age, gender, marital status, and race/ethnicity. Knowing the demographics of a trading area helps to identify market trends that have a direct impact on a business.

Prevailing economic conditions are crucial factors affecting any business. National and state economic conditions affect businesses by increasing or decreasing the demand or need for products or services.

The GREEN Marketer

Green Building = Smart Business

Having an eco-friendly location can help a business's image and its bottom line. In fact, many new companies plan for "green" building sites in their business plans, flying their "green" colors to draw customers.

Good Habits Businesses can dramatically reduce costs by increasing building insulation, planting native plants for shade and beauty, using solar panels, and opening blinds to increase available sunlight. Employees can get involved, too, by recycling waste and shutting off computers and task lights at the end of each workday.

Science
Create Imagine that you are planning to open a restaurant in your town. Describe the area and the type of building you have chosen, and explain your choice. Brainstorm ten ways to "green" your operation.

connectED.mcgraw-hill.com

Get an activity on green marketing.

Economic factors include business growth projections, trends in employment, interest rates, economic statistics, stock market forecasts, and governmental regulations. Tax increases or decreases levied by the local, state, and federal governments affect consumer buying power.

It is important to include and analyze the disposable income potential of consumers in your trading area. Disposable income is the personal income remaining from wages after all taxes are taken out. Disposable income is also called "buying income."

A special measurement called a "buying power index" (BPI) has been developed to help new business owners determine the buying power for a given target market. The BPI index factors total population, total income, and total retail sales figures. These figures are used to determine an overall indicator of an area's sales potential. A market can be a state, region, county, or metropolitan statistical area (MSA). These factors are then expressed as a percentage of total potential U.S. sales. You can find more information on buying power indexes in *Demographics USA*, which is published annually by Trade Dimensions International.

An excellent source of information on local economic conditions is your local bank. Bank officials often have business projections for major geographical areas and for most types of businesses located in their immediate area.

In addition, the Small Business Administration (SBA) has provided funding for over 1,000 small business development centers (SBDCs) housed in leading universities, colleges, and economic development agencies. Millions of rural and urban entrepreneurs have received no-cost consulting services and low-cost training from SBDCs. Other good sources of information are business publications available at public libraries, colleges, and universities, or on the Internet.

COMPETITIVE ANALYSIS

As a new business owner, you must analyze your competition. List all the competitors in your trading area: their products, prices, locations, quality of products, strengths, and weaknesses. Try to estimate your competitors' sales volume.

It is also helpful to identify how competitors promote and sell their products. These factors can help demonstrate how a business will be different and better than the competition.

Information about competitors can be found through annual reports and business publications, such as those published by Dun & Bradstreet®, and from the Internet, local chambers of commerce, trade associations, and the *Yellow Pages*.

MARKET SEGMENT ANALYSIS

A business plan contains a market segment analysis: a description of your target market and the buying behavior of your potential customers.

TARGET MARKET

A target market is a group of people identified as those most likely to become customers. They are the people that you want to reach with your business. A target market is identified by common geographic characteristics such as region, county size, size of city, density of population, and climate of the area. Target markets can also be categorized by demographic characteristics such as age, gender, marital status, family size, income, occupation, education, religion, culture, or ethnic background.

Target Market Characteristics

Geographic Characteristics	Demographic Characteristics	
• Region	• Age	• Occupation
• County Size	• Gender	• Education
• City Size	• Marital Status	• Religion
• Population Density	• Family Size	• Culture
• Climate	• Income	• Ethnicity

Businesses carefully identify target markets so they can meet the needs and wants of different individuals for their goods and services. Your task as an entrepreneur is to decide which market to target and how to do it. The challenging part here is how to reach your target market. You have many options available to you in terms of advertising and promotion.

CUSTOMER BUYING BEHAVIOR

After you have identified the target market, explain how the buying behavior of potential customers will be a good match for your products and services. **Buying behavior** is the process that individuals use to decide what they will buy, where they will buy it, and from whom they will buy it.

OPERATIONAL PLAN

The operational plan explains where a business is located—at home or in a bought or leased facility away from home. This section also describes competing and complementary businesses, hours of operation, visibility, customer safety and accessibility, and how zoning regulations will be met for the business.

Operational Plan

Operational Plan	
Location	Visibility
Other Businesses	Customer Safety
Hours	Zoning

LOCATION OF THE BUSINESS

The location of your business is largely determined by the products and services that you plan to provide and your personal preferences.

Is it important for you to be in close proximity to family members and friends? Do you want to locate in your community or away from where you currently live?

Other intangible issues such as atmosphere of the community, character of the neighborhood, commuting and travel distance, working hours, and other preferences enter into any location decision.

Entrepreneurs who offer contracted services, such as computer, child care, housekeeping, technical, or online services, can locate their business in an existing residence. Home-based businesses have distinct cost advantages for any entrepreneur. But many new businesses need to consider other location options away from a home or residence.

If another business location is needed, should you buy, lease, or build a facility? The advantages of leasing often outweigh the other options for most new businesses. With leasing, you avoid a large initial cash outlay. Another benefit is that your risk is reduced by the shorter time commitment. Also, your lease expenses are tax deductible. The process of buying or building is more complex and almost always requires major financing.

Regardless of whether you buy, lease, or build, you need to compare certain terms of each method of financing for your place of business.

Some businesses seek out the perfect location to attract customers. *Why would a business want to be located in a beautiful neighborhood?*

The Importance of Location

Those terms include monthly rent, utilities, other required payments, and the length of commitment.

For risk management purposes, you must investigate insurance policies. You must be sure that appropriate coverage is provided by you or the owner. An attorney should review any lease or contract before you sign it. An attorney can also help you to fully understand your obligations. He or she can negotiate the best possible terms before finalizing the lease agreement.

COMPETING AND COMPLEMENTARY BUSINESSES

There are many things to consider when selecting a location. Before you decide on location, consider the number and size of potential competitors in the area. If your business is similar in size and merchandise to your competitors, you may want to locate near them. Nearness to competitors can encourage comparison shopping and generate customer traffic. For example, restaurants and auto dealers are often located in close proximity to each other to attract targeted customers.

On the other hand, a larger business that offers more variety than the competition should be able to generate its own customers and, therefore, can be situated away from the competition. A complementary business is one that helps generate store traffic. A shoe store located next to a clothing store is an example of a complementary business.

HOURS OF OPERATION

The nature of your business will determine your location. This will help you decide whether you locate the business in your home, a freestanding location, mall, or neighborhood shopping center. That location, in turn, will determine your hours of operation and the number of customers who will see and patronize your business.

If you are a home-based or a free-standing business, you can determine your own hours of operation based on the needs of your customers. A business in a shopping mall or center needs to adhere to regular hours dictated by the mall or shopping center management.

Online businesses normally have extended hours of operation. For many businesses, the hours of operation can differentiate a business from the competition.

VISIBILITY

Restaurants, convenience stores, gas stations, and other businesses that rely on high visibility or prime locations may spend the extra money to locate in a high-traffic location. Such a high-traffic site may not be a priority for other businesses, and location savings might be better used for advertising, promotion, and other expenses.

CUSTOMER SAFETY

Customer safety is essential for all businesses. Customers should never have to think about whether they will have a safe experience while making a purchase or while waiting for a service to be performed.

Businesses need to protect themselves from potential lawsuits by making sure that customers are kept safe during business transactions. Therefore, a business plan should also include customer safety considerations.

Research the community's crime rate. You do not want to open your business where customers feel uncomfortable or are hesitant to visit. You can obtain crime rate information from the local police department, or you can conduct a city-specific search online.

Find out whether the fire department is a volunteer or municipal fire department. Then contact the fire department to inquire about safety codes that apply to your business. Use this research to help determine the location of your business.

CUSTOMER ACCESSIBILITY

Make sure your customers can get to your location easily. Identify the highways, streets, and public transportation options that are available to arrive at your site.

▶ Will traffic routes or congestion be an obstacle?

▶ Is there sufficient free parking or paid parking for a reasonable fee?

▶ Are the entrances, facilities, and parking accessible to customers with physical limitations?

ZONING AND OTHER REGULATIONS

After considering personal preferences, ownership options, hours of operation, visibility, customer safety and accessibility, you are ready to select a specific site location. You need to learn about any local ordinances or laws that may affect your business.

Research and learn about any restrictions that might prevent you from locating your business in a particular area. Zoning regulations vary among states and regions, and may change over time. Plans to build or renovate an office or building will require appropriate building permits. Operating a regulated business, such as a service station, requires local zoning approvals as well as state or federal licenses or permits.

 After You Read | **Section 35.1**

Review Key Concepts

1. **List** the four major parts of a business plan.
2. **Explain** why aspiring entrepreneurs should conduct a self-analysis as part of a business plan.
3. **Discuss** why knowledge about disposable income of potential customers is an important part of a business plan.

Practice Academics

English Language Arts

4. Conduct research on geographic, demographic, and economic data for a geographical area (village, city, county, region, or state) by reading city, county, or state government, local chamber of commerce, regional economic development agency, or U.S. Census publications. Write a one-page report that identifies geographic data on your selected community, demographic data such as age, gender, population, racial/ethnic, and educational statistics; and economic data such as income, major industries, labor force participation rates, levels of employment, labor force participation rates, and major industries.

Mathematics

5. Compute the buying power index for town B, given the following formula and information.
Buying Power Index = .5 × Area's Percentage for U.S. Effective Buying Power
+ .3 × Area's Percentage of U.S. Retail Sales
+ .2 × Area's Percentage of U.S. Population
Town B Percentage of U.S. Effective Buying Power = .025
Town B Percentage of U.S. Retail Sales = .005
Town B Percentage of U.S. Population = .006

Math Concept **Buying Power Index Formula** The buying power index formula involves a number of different variables. To solve for the buying power index, substitute the known value for the variables and multiply.

Starting Hints To solve this problem, write out the buying power index formula. Insert the given percentages for town B in the formula, and multiply to determine the buying power index.

 connectED.mcgraw-hill.com

Check your answers.

For help, go to the Math Skills Handbook located at the back of this book.

READING GUIDE

Before You Read

Predict What do lenders want to see in the organizational, marketing, and financial sections of a business plan?

Objectives

- **Explain** a business's organizational plan.
- **Construct** a marketing plan.
- **Describe** financing sources for businesses.
- **Identify** the financial elements of a business plan.

The Main Idea

The organizational plan explains to investors how a business will function. The marketing plan explains how it will market its products. The financial plan projects its future profitability.

Vocabulary

Content Vocabulary
- job descriptions
- organization chart
- equity capital
- debt capital
- collateral
- credit union

Academic Vocabulary

You will find these words in your reading and on your tests. Make sure you know their meanings.
- authority
- funding

Graphic Organizer

Draw or print this chart to describe the three business plan components explained in this section.

connectED.mcgraw-hill.com

Print this graphic organizer.

MARKETING CORE FUNCTION

Market Planning

Marketing and Financial Plans

ORGANIZATIONAL, MARKETING, AND FINANCIAL PLANS

A business plan explains to a potential lender or investor how you will organize, market, and finance a new business. The organizational plan describes your current and anticipated staffing needs. It describes how you will manufacture or purchase the goods you plan to sell. An organizational plan also includes a description of the products you plan to make or the services you will offer. It also lists potential suppliers and inventory policies.

The marketing plan details your proposed pricing policies and promotional activities. Your financial plan indicates sources of capital and projects the future profitability of the business.

As You Read

Analyze What marketing activities would you include in a business plan for a new business?

ORGANIZATIONAL PLAN

The organizational section of your business plan is a blueprint for the structure of your proposed business. You must construct a clear, solid foundation around which to build your business.

PROPOSED ORGANIZATION

There are three main types of business ownership structures: sole proprietorships, partnerships, and corporations. In this part of the plan, you identify which type you have chosen and explain why. The form of business ownership will have an impact on the rest of the business plan.

ESTABLISHING YOUR BUSINESS

Next you outline the steps to establish your business. The specific steps taken will depend on the type of business ownership you select.

> **" A business plan is a guide for organizing, marketing, and financing a business. "**

PERSONNEL NEEDS

Potential investors and lenders need to know that you can identify essential jobs for the business so that it will operate efficiently and successfully. List staffing needs in the business plan and identify the people who will perform those jobs.

Many new businesses begin as one-person operations. It is not unusual for an entrepreneur to handle all business functions from advertising and promotion to management to financial oversight. The selected organizational structure must be able to allow for more employees and more specialization of duties as the business grows.

JOB DESCRIPTIONS

Job descriptions are written statements listing the requirements of a particular job and the skills needed to fulfill those requirements. Each job description includes the purpose, qualifications and skills, duties, equipment, and expected working conditions. Detailed job descriptions help employees know exactly what is expected of them. Job descriptions also help measure their performance against those expectations.

PERSONAL SAVINGS

The most common method of financing a business is personal savings. Although you may not prefer this option, you probably cannot avoid investing part of your savings. Starting any new business involves risk. Your prospective investors and lenders will expect you to share in that risk.

PARTNERS

A partnership is another way to raise capital for your business. Partners may contribute their own money or have access to other sources. As with equity investors, you may have to share control of the business if you accept partners.

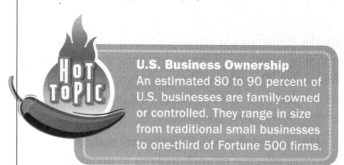

U.S. Business Ownership
An estimated 80 to 90 percent of U.S. businesses are family-owned or controlled. They range in size from traditional small businesses to one-third of Fortune 500 firms.

SHAREHOLDERS

Forming a corporation is another method of raising capital. You need to incorporate and obtain a charter to operate as a corporation. You sell stock to shareholders as a way of raising capital.

A corporation can raise large amounts of money, because shareholders have the opportunity to share in the growth and profits of a successful business. However, they lose only their original investment if the business is unsuccessful. Shareholders influence general corporate policy decisions. However, as long as you hold a majority of the shares, you control the corporation's daily activities.

DEBT CAPITAL

Debt capital is a term used to describe borrowed funds that must be repaid. Some debt capital sources are banks, credit unions, the Small Business Administration, friends, relatives, suppliers, and previous business owners.

Business Partners

Business partners work together to create a business plan. *What other plans do business partners need to make for a new business?*

Debt capital can work to your advantage when you finance a new business. Borrowing money and repaying it on a timely basis builds a good credit rating. In turn, a good credit rating makes it easier to borrow additional money. Although interest must be paid with the loan, that interest becomes a tax-deductible business expense.

Also, by financing with debt capital, you do not share control of the business with lenders. Since they are simply a source of financing for your company, your lenders do not have any input on the way you run the business.

There is a major disadvantage to using debt capital, however. If you are not able to pay back your debt, you could be forced into bankruptcy. That does not necessarily mean the business must close, but creditors might take control of the company away from the owner.

BANKS

Commercial banks are a common source of business financing. Although banks may be hesitant to lend money to start-up companies, they routinely lend to businesses that are established and which have a proven record of success. Banks know their local areas and economies well and offer a number of different loans and services with competitive and government-regulated terms.

Approximately 12 percent of businesses use commercial bank loans to finance their companies. Bank loans guaranteed by the government make up make up another 1 percent of start-up financing.

To evaluate the credit worthiness of a business owner, banks rely on criteria known as the six Cs of credit: character, capability, capital, collateral, coverage, and conditions.

FIGURE 35.2 Sources of Funding

Financing a Business There are several methods and sources for financing new businesses. The most common source is personal/family savings. *Why do you think personal or family savings is a major way of financing a new business?*

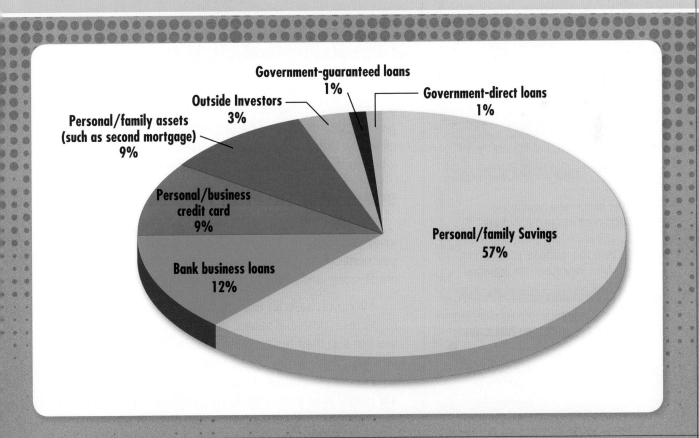

Government-guaranteed loans 1%
Government-direct loans 1%
Outside Investors 3%
Personal/family assets (such as second mortgage) 9%
Personal/business credit card 9%
Bank business loans 12%
Personal/family Savings 57%

Dale Little

President, Business Management
Strategist
Dale Little

What do you do at work?

My company specializes in business direction, budget reviews, analysis and revisions, marketing strategies, employee retention programs, customer/client base building, and customer/client service. Basically, I guide business owners and managers in the development, implementation, and review of their business plans. My work sessions are in the form of one-on-one meetings, group meetings, and seminars.

What is your key to success?

Tenacity and perseverance are the basis for any successful business venture. When these virtues are combined with the belief that every day is a success, regardless of unexpected dips and turns, your business will invariably be a success.

What skills are most important to you?

The key skills for a business management strategist include communication, organization, and being able to pay close attention to detail. Also important are grammar and writing skills.

 connectED.mcgraw-hill.com

Read more about this career and get a Career Exploration Activity.

- ▶ **Character and Capability** A résumé of your previous training and related work experience, including professional and personal references, will answer questions about your character and capability. Your personal credit history will also be reviewed to see if you regularly pay your bills on time.

- ▶ **Capital** How much of your own money, or capital, is to be invested in your new business? Banks, like other potential investors, will want to know how much capital you are willing to invest into your new venture.

- ▶ **Collateral** What assets (anything of value that you own) can be used as collateral for a loan? **Collateral** is something of value that you pledge as payment for a loan in case of default. Lenders usually require that the value of the collateral be greater than the amount of the loan. Examples of collateral include bonds, equipment, real estate, stocks, and vehicles. Some businesses may use accounts receivable, which is the sum of money owed to a business by its customers, as collateral. Banks want to know that your loan will be repaid, even if your business fails.

- ▶ **Coverage and Conditions** Banks will want to know the amount of insurance coverage that you carry. Also, what are the general circumstances of your business? How will the money help you grow your business, strengthen your market position, and make more money? This is outlined in the description and analysis section of your business plan.

CREDIT UNIONS

A **credit union** is a cooperative association formed by groups of employees for the benefit of its members. Compared to commercial banks, credit unions often charge lower interest rates on loans. To borrow money from a credit union, however, you must be a member. Credit unions often accept memberships for family members. Check with your parents, guardians, and credit union staff to determine your eligibility. Credit unions also use the six Cs of credit to decide whether they will accept your loan application.

SUPPLIER AND PREVIOUS OWNERS

Suppliers often provide low-cost loans for purchasing inventory, furniture, fixtures, and equipment on a delayed payment basis. This method of raising capital can improve your credit rating and stretch available cash.

If you purchase an existing business, consider the previous owner as a potential source of capital. Many sole proprietors want to see their businesses continue after they retire. Previous owners may provide you with a loan and a favorable repayment plan to get started. The rates on this type of loan are often lower than rates from a bank or credit union.

FINANCIAL STATEMENTS

After you have identified a potential source or sources of capital, the last part of your business plan requires development of projected income and expenses. This part of the business plan normally includes the following financial statements:

- ▶ Personal financial statement
- ▶ Projected start-up costs
- ▶ Projected personnel needs
- ▶ Projected business income
- ▶ Projected business expenses
- ▶ Projected income statement(s)
- ▶ Projected balance sheet
- ▶ Projected cash flow

Your financial statements display your personal financial records along with the projected income and expenses of your proposed business. A list of projected start-up costs shows how much money is needed to get your business going. A balance sheet can help you show how you plan to manage your company's finances. Estimates of projected income and cash flow are also especially important because they show your ability to pay back a loan or offer a return on investments.

Realistic projections of income and expenses in financial statements help to convince investors to loan you money for your new business. It can be challenging to obtain the money to start up a new company, but a solid business plan and detailed projections can overcome those challenges.

 After You Read   **Section 35.2**

Review Key Concepts

1. **Identify** the three main types of ownership.
2. **Explain** why personnel needs are identified in a business plan.
3. **Name** the six Cs of credit.

Practice Academics

English Language Arts

4. Perform library or online research on a favorite product. Find out the company that makes it and what types of activities are included in the company's marketing plan for that product. Write a one-page summary describing the marketing plan. Also make recommendations for a revised marketing plan.

Mathematics

5. A relative decides to loan you $16,000 with a simple interest rate of 5.5 percent, payable one year after the start of your new Internet business. How much will you owe at the end of the year?

Math Concept **Interest Rates** Interest is paid when money is loaned. Interest rates are expressed as percents of the money that was borrowed.

Starting Hints Convert the percent to a decimal by moving the decimal point two places to the left. Multiply the dollar amount that was borrowed by the decimal equivalent of the percent plus one to determine the total amount owed after one year.

 connectED.mcgraw-hill.com

Check your answers.

For help, go to the **Math Skills Handbook** located at the back of this book.

Developing a Business Plan

The Description and Analysis part of a business plan includes these sections: explaining the type of business, describing its philosophy, creating a product and service plan, completing a self-analysis, analyzing the trading area, analyzing the market segment, and developing an operational plan.

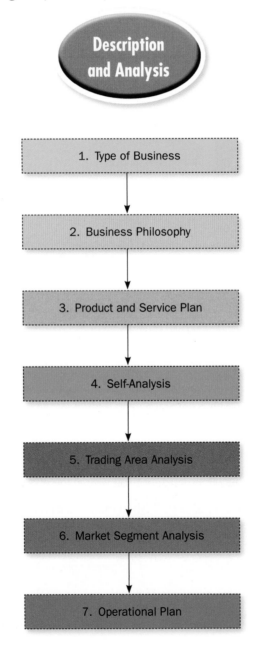

Description and Analysis

1. Type of Business

2. Business Philosophy

3. Product and Service Plan

4. Self-Analysis

5. Trading Area Analysis

6. Market Segment Analysis

7. Operational Plan

Review and Activities

Written Summary

- A business plan includes these sections: a description and analysis of the proposed business, an organizational plan, a marketing plan, and a financial plan.

- The description and analysis should include the following: type of business, business philosophy, product or service, self-analysis, trading area analysis, and market segment analysis.

- The organizational plan and marketing plan outline how the business will be organized and how it will be promoted.

- Most entrepreneurs need to borrow money to start a business. Investors and lenders want to see financial information about a business before they commit to making an investment.

- The financial plan includes sources of capital for the business and projections of income and expenses.

Review Content Vocabulary and Academic Vocabulary

1. Write true-or-false statements using each vocabulary word. Ask a partner to determine whether each statement is true or false and explain why.

   Content Vocabulary
   - business plan (p. 819)
   - business philosophy (p. 821)
   - trading area (p. 823)
   - buying behavior (p. 825)
   - job descriptions (p. 829)
   - organization chart (p. 830)
   - equity capital (p. 831)
   - debt capital (p. 832)
   - collateral (p. 834)
   - credit union (p. 834)

   Academic Vocabulary
   - expand (p. 819)
   - sources (p. 821)
   - authority (p. 830)
   - funding (p. 831)

Assess for Understanding

2. **Identify** What is the purpose and importance of a business plan?

3. **Consider** What are external planning considerations for developing a business plan?

4. **Evaluate** What are important factors for developing a business's organizational plan?

5. **List** What are important factors to include when developing a marketing plan?

6. **Suggest** What are some financing sources for businesses?

7. **Judge** How do the financial elements of a business plan set the stage for its future success?

8. **Discuss** Why is it important to have a business philosophy?

9. **Role Play** Your friend is starting a new business and believes that personal selling is the best way to promote the business. He thinks little effort needs to be spent on other promotional methods. What is his belief in personal selling, and how can you tell him what you think of this approach to promotional activities?

21st Century Skills

Social Responsibility Skills

10. Labor laws dealing with child labor, equal opportunity employment, health and safety, payment of wages, unemployment, and workers' disability insurance have been passed to protect employees. Conduct research dealing with a specific labor law in your state. Identify the labor law that you researched and prepare a one-page report on the purpose of the law and what protections are provided for employees.

Financial Literacy Skills

11. Calculating Employee Wages Assume that you had an employee that was paid $10.80 an hour during the week and time and one-half time on Sunday. If the employee worked four hours on Wednesday, three and a half hours on Thursday, six hours on Saturday, and four hours on Sunday, what was the total gross wages before any deductions?

Everyday Ethics

12. A Medical Business "You're sick, we're quick," says a slogan announcing a newer healthcare business, the Minute Clinic. Staffed by either a nurse practitioner or physician's assistant, the clinics are located in drugstores and shopping centers. They treat walk-ins with routine problems for minimal cost. The clinics have begun to attract public attention. Some critics, however, call this type of medical care "inappropriate." Write a paragraph explaining what the clinic's business philosophy might be, and express your opinion about the clinic's pros and cons.

e-Marketing Skills

13. Small Business Resources You are an intern for a small business development center at a community college. Your supervisor asked you to prepare a list of five Internet resources for small business owners in the areas of promotion and financing. You are to identify the URLs for each Internet resource and provide a brief summary of the resource materials.

Build Academic Skills

English Language Arts

14. The Need for Occupational Licensing Small business owner/operators and their employees often need to be licensed before they can open or work in a regulated industry. Perform library or online research on occupational licensing or licensure. Identify the reasons that governmental agencies require special licenses. Summarize your findings in a one-page written report.

English Language Arts

15. Business Structure Perform online or library research on multi-level marketing and how some companies use it. Write a two-paragraph description of this type of marketing structure for a company that could be used in a business plan.

Mathematics

16. Calculate Buying Power Index Determine the buying power indexes for Johnstown and Milton. Which location is more favorable for a new business?

Buying Power Index = .5 × Area's Percentage for U.S. Effective Buying Power

+ .3 × Area's Percentage of U.S. Retail Sales

+ .2 × Area's Percentage of U.S. Population

Johnstown Percentage of:
- U.S. Effective Buying Power = .0251
- U.S. Retail Sales = .0183
- U.S. Population = .025

Milton Percentage of:
- U.S. Effective Buying Power = .0181
- U.S. Retail Sales = .018
- U.S. Population = .0154

Math Concept **Representation** The buying power index is determined by multiplying a given constant by several variables, usually given as percents.

> For help, go to the **Math Skills Handbook** located at the back of this book.

Standardized Test Practice

Directions Read the following questions. On a separate piece of paper, write the best possible answer for each one.

1. Which part of a business plan contains information about the trading area and target market?

   A. Description and analysis

   B. Financial plan

   C. Marketing plan

   D. Organizational plan

2. A market segment analysis describes your trading area.

   T

   F

3. Something of value pledged as payment for a loan in case of default is _____.

Test-Taking Tip

Study for tests over a few days or weeks and continually review class material. Do not wait until the night before or try to learn everything at once.

DECA Connection Role Play

Loan Officer
Bank

Situation You are the loan officer for a bank. Your community has many aspiring new business owners. Many prospective business owners are unsure about the steps to take to give their new businesses the best chance of succeeding.

The community merchants and your bank have formed a business development committee. You are the bank's representative on the committee. The goal of the committee is to offer advice and answer questions for prospective entrepreneurs. Committee members offer advice on an individual basis and also give talks to groups of interested individuals.

Since you work for the bank, you have been designated as the provider of information about business plans, their importance, and use in helping a new business succeed. You are preparing to meet with an aspiring business owner (judge). The prospective new business owner (judge) would like to own a business, but is unsure about which type of business. The prospective new business owner (judge) has work experience, but is still in the thinking stages of planning for a new business and has many questions about preparing a business plan.

Activity You are to discuss business plans in general with the prospective new business owner (judge). Then you are to discuss the new business owner's (judge's) interests, skills, and the types of businesses being considered.

Evaluation You will be evaluated on how well you meet the following performance indicators:

1. Assess personal interests and skills needed for success in business.

2. Identify a company's unique selling proposition.

3. Conduct an environmental scan to obtain business information.

4. Conduct market analysis.

5. Describe factors that affect the business environment.

 connectED.mcgraw-hill.com

Download the Competitive Events Workbook for more Role-Play practice.

financing the business

Visual Literacy Start-up money is needed to make a good idea grow into a prosperous business. Most entrepreneurs must borrow the money or capital from commercial banks, credit unions, investors, and other lenders. *What do you think must be done to convince a lender to provide funding for a new business?*

Discovery Project

Preparing Financial Documents

Essential Question
How does an entrepreneur develop the necessary financial documents for a business plan?

Project Goal

You and a classmate are partners in a proposed new product or service business. Your team must choose the new business, and then research and prepare a written report that includes a personal financial statement, estimates the start-up costs, develops an income statement, balance sheet, and a cash flow statement for that business.

Ask Yourself...

- How will your team decide upon the type of new business you will develop?
- How will your team develop a personal financial statement and estimate start-up costs?
- How will your team complete the income statement for the business?
- How will your team complete a balance sheet and a cash flow statement?
- How will your team organize the financial section of a business plan?

Synthesize Research and Present Synthesize your research by describing and preparing important financial documents required in business plans when financing a new business.

 connectED.mcgraw-hill.com

Activity
Get a worksheet activity about financial documents.

Evaluate
Download a rubric that you can use to evaluate your project.

DECA Connection

DECA Event Role Play

Concepts in this chapter are related to DECA competitive events that involve either an interview or role play.

Performance Indicators The performance indicators represent key skills and knowledge. Your key to success in DECA competitive events is relating them to concepts in this chapter.

- Explain the role of finance in business.
- Set financial goals.
- Describe the nature of cash flow statements.
- Explain the nature of balance sheets.
- Describe the nature of income statements.

DECA Prep

Role Play Practice role-playing with the DECA Connection competitive-event activity at the end of this chapter. More information on DECA events can be found on DECA's Web site.

READING GUIDE

Before You Read

Predict What might happen if an entrepreneur did not include financial documents in a business plan?

Objectives

- **Explain** the purpose of financial documents.
- **Develop** a personal financial statement.
- **Determine** start-up costs for a business.

The Main Idea

A key reason for writing a business plan is to obtain financing to start a new business. It is important to prepare and include financial documents in a business plan.

Vocabulary

Content Vocabulary

- personal financial statement
- asset
- liability
- net worth
- start-up costs

Academic Vocabulary

You will find these words in your reading and on your tests. Make sure you know their meanings.

- assessing
- purpose

Graphic Organizer

Draw or print this chart to outline steps to prepare the financial section of a business plan.

Organized Financing

1. Prepare financial documents. _____
2. _____
3. _____

 Mc Graw Hill Education **connectED.mcgraw-hill.com**

Print this graphic organizer.

MARKETING CORE FUNCTIONS

Marketing Information Management

Market Planning

Financial Analysis

THE FINANCIAL PART OF A BUSINESS PLAN

Financial information is a major component of a business plan. In a business plan, you need to include financial documents that describe your personal finances as well as the financial needs of the business. By preparing financial statements, you determine the amount of money needed to operate the business as well as the amount that needs to be borrowed, if any.

As You Read

Analyze Assume that you are completing a business plan. Why do you think that it is necessary to include personal and start-up financial statements in the plan?

When you borrow money, the lender will want proof that you are able to repay the loan. The lender examines your credit history, collateral, and the prospects for business success. The financial documents included in your business plan show that you are able to pay off the loan.

There are five important financial documents normally included in a business plan:

▶ the personal financial statement
▶ start-up cost estimate
▶ income statement
▶ balance sheet
▶ cash flow statement

In this section, you learn about developing a personal financial statement and estimating start-up costs.

> " A business plan **helps obtain financing to** start a new business. "

THE PERSONAL FINANCIAL STATEMENT

A **personal financial statement** is a summary of your current personal financial condition. It is an important document to include in a business plan. You will need it when applying for additional money or capital to finance a new business. The personal financial statement gives a snapshot of your net worth at a particular point in time by looking at your assets and liabilities.

An **asset** is anything of monetary value that a person owns, such as cash, checking and savings accounts, real estate, or stocks. A **liability** is a debt that you owe to others, such as a car payment, credit card debt, rental payments, or taxes. A personal financial statement shows potential lenders that you have some money at risk as well as in your proposed business.

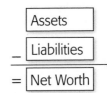

ASSETS

The first step in developing a personal financial statement is to identify assets. Be realistic about the current value of your assets. For example, if you have a car worth $11,700, do not round it up to $12,000.

Be sure to list all your cash assets (checking and savings accounts), any investments (bonds, insurance policies, mutual funds, and stocks), and personal assets (cars, clothing, furniture, and residence, if owned). Estimate the present value of each item. A lender will look for assets that could be sold to pay off the business loan if a new business fails. Provide a total value for each asset and a grand total for all assets.

This sample worksheet can be used to show an entrepreneur's personal net worth. *Why is the personal financial statement an important part of a business plan?*

Personal Financial Statement
Name: _____ Date: _____

Assets
Cash $_____
Savings Account $_____
Checking Account
Savings Bonds $_____
Stocks   and Bonds $_____
Mutual Funds $_____
Cash Value of Life Insurance $_____
Vehicles (owned not financed) $_____
Real Estate $_____
Retirement Accounts (401K or IRAs) $_____
Other Assets $_____
Total Assets $_____

Liabilities
Accounts Payable (i.e. credit cards) $_____
Contracts Payable (i.e. car loans) $_____
Notes Payable   (i.e. student loans) $_____
Taxes Payable $_____
Real Estate/Mortgage Loans $_____
Other Liabilities $_____
Total Liabilities $_____

Total Assets $_____
Less Total Liabilities $_____

Net Worth $_____

financial Statement

LIABILITIES

Next list your monthly liabilities or debt. These include payments for automobile loans, credit card accounts, mortgage loans, and rental payments. Calculate a total for each type of liability and a grand total for all of your liabilities.

NET WORTH

Next calculate your personal net worth. Your **net worth** is the difference between assets and liabilities. To find a business's net worth, subtract its debts from its assets. For corporations, net worth is called "stockholders' equity." For partnerships and sole proprietorships, it is called "owner's equity."

Your personal financial statement is one way to determine if you and your business are good credit risks. A lender will want a personal credit report to determine how well you have paid past debts.

A lender will also need a copy of your personal tax returns for the past three to five years. Past tax returns show how you earned money in the past.

You may plan to continue working at another job. If so, the lender will be interested in whether the income can cover your personal expenses until your new business becomes profitable.

> **PRACTICE 1: DEVELOP A PERSONAL FINANCIAL STATEMENT**
>
> 1. You have assets of $15,000 (car), $5,000 (savings), $1,000 (cash value of life insurance), $1,700 (cash), and personal property worth $2,500. What are your total assets?
> 2. You have liabilities of $10,000 (car loan), $5,000 (student loan), and $1,500 (credit card balances). What are your total liabilities?
> 3. What is your net worth?
>
>  **connectED.mcgraw-hill.com**
>
> Check your answers to all Practice sets.

ESTIMATING START-UP COSTS

How do you estimate how much capital is needed to start a business? **Start-up costs** are projections of how much money a new business owner needs for the business's first year of operation. Then, for that first year of operation, your income goal should be to reach a break-even point. The break-even point is reached when enough money is received to pay all operating expenses, including your salary, and to pay debt obligations.

The Small Business Administration (SBA) provides forms and worksheets to help new business owners. A worksheet like the one shown in **Figure 36.1** on page 846 can help determine start-up costs for a new business. A start-up cost estimate can also be used to project on-going operating costs after the business gets off the ground.

By **assessing** start-up costs before getting involved in a new business, you are protecting yourself and helping to ensure the viability of the proposed business. Start-up costs vary, depending on the type of business.

PRACTICE 2: DETERMINE START-UP COSTS

Your business has one-time costs of $25,000 and average monthly costs of $3,600. What are your total costs for the first quarter of operation? Using the same average monthly costs, what are your total costs for the year?

The amount of start-up money needed varies, but it is based on factors such as:

► **The nature of the proposed business** Manufacturing, wholesale, and retail businesses all have different needs and requirements.

► **The size of the business** Smaller businesses usually do not require as much money to start as larger ones.

► **The amount and kind of inventory needed** For example, it is much more costly to purchase inventory for a large supermarket than for a neighborhood convenience store.

► **The estimated time between starting the business and earning income** For example, a home-based accountant may start earning income within weeks, but a large accounting firm may not see a profit for many months or longer.

MARKETING CASE STUDY

Good Samaritans + Smartphones

A vision of Web developer Jason Kiesel, CitySourced started up from a meager investment of $100,000, small change in the world of new high-tech businesses. Recognized as a finalist at TechCrunch50, the CitySourced smartphone application was designed to improve communities.

Neighborhood Watch 2.0
As a "real-time civic engagement tool," the app allows citizens to identify urban blight, such as graffiti, trash, potholes, broken streetlights, stray shopping carts, and more. With a photo function, you take a picture of the problem and send it off with data to City Hall where participating governments process the report for resolution. Launched in large cities in California and other states, CitySourced's time- and money-saving concept is a civic-minded innovation.

Mathematics
Create and Calculate Think of a business you could launch that would require minimal start-up costs. Describe and name your business. Make a list of the equipment and supplies you might need to start, and then calculate that total cost.

FIGURE 36.1 Start-Up Costs Worksheet

Estimating Start-Up Costs The SBA has developed a worksheet for estimating start-up costs and operating expenses for new businesses. *Why is a start-up worksheet helpful to an entrepreneur?*

ESTIMATED MONTHLY EXPENSES	Your estimate of monthly expenses based on sales of $_____ per year	Your estimate of how much cash you need to start your business (See column 3)	What to put in column 2. (These figures are typical for one kind of business. You will have to decide how many months to allow for your business.)
Item	Column 1	Column 2	Column 3
Salary of owner	$	$	2 times column 1
All other salaries and wages			3 times column 1
Rent			3 times column 1
Advertising			3 times column 1
Delivery expenses			3 times column 1
Supplies			3 times column 1
Telephone and Internet			3 times column 1
Other utilities			3 times column 1
Insurance			Payment required by insurance company
Taxes, including Social Security			4 times column 1
Interest			3 times column 1
Maintenance			3 times column 1
Legal and other professional fees			3 times column 1
Miscellaneous			3 times column 1
STARTING COSTS YOU ONLY HAVE TO PAY ONCE			Leave column 2 blank
Fixtures and equipment			See separate worksheet
Decorating and remodeling			Talk it over with a contractor
Installation of fixtures and equipment			Talk to suppliers from whom you buy these
Starting inventory			Supplies will probably help you estimate this
Deposits with public utilities			Find out from utility companies
Legal and other professional fees			Lawyer, accountant, and so on
Licenses and permits			Find out from city offices what you need
Advertising and promotion			Estimate what you'll use for opening
Accounts receivable			What you need to buy more stock until credit customers pay
Cash			For unexpected expenses or losses, special purchases, etc.
Other			Make a separate list and enter total
TOTAL ESTIMATED CASH YOU NEED TO START	$	$	Add up all the numbers in column 2

▶ **The operating expenses** Operating costs must be paid before any income is received from sales.

▶ **Start-up expenses** Some are one-time costs while others are continuing costs that occur on an ongoing basis after the initial business start-up.

▶ **One-time costs** These are expenses that will not be repeated after you open the business. Examples include licenses, permits, telephone installation deposits, and charges for installation of equipment, fixtures, and machinery.

▶ **Continuing costs** These are expenses you will pay throughout the life of the business. Examples of continuing costs are payroll, monthly rent, advertising, supplies, insurance, repairs, maintenance, and taxes. Most businesses are not profitable immediately, so include at least three months of continuing costs when estimating the amount of cash you will need to get started.

Venture Capitalists Angel investors are wealthy individuals who provide venture capital, from a few thousand dollars to millions, for an ownership share in a new business.

Information is available from several reliable sources to help plan financial needs. (See **Figure 36.2**.) The Small Business Administration (SBA) provides information to people who want to start a new business. The SBA offers a wide variety of loan programs. These programs help small businesses borrow money from traditional lenders at reasonable interest rates. The National Federation of Independent Business (NFIB) has a section on its Web site devoted to helping entrepreneurs develop a budget specific to the needs of new small business owners. Similarly, the U.S. Chamber of Commerce Small Business Nation Web site features a Start Up Toolkit for new business owners.

You can also get estimates of start-up costs from people who are already in a similar business or from a trade association. State and local government agencies, such as a state department of commerce and local chamber of commerce, are valuable sources of cost information.

Reading Check

Understand How do start-up costs differ from personal costs?

FIGURE 36.2 | Financing Sources

Finding Funding There are many different sources for funding new businesses.
What is the difference between a primary and a secondary source of funding?

Primary Sources		Secondary Sources	
Long-term financing	*Short-term financing*	*Long-term financing*	*Short-term financing*
• Personal financing • Family and friends • Private investors • Equity financing • Leasing • Credit unions • SBA LowDoc	• Personal financing • Family and friends • Credit cards • Credit unions • Trade credit • Banks • SBA Microloans • SBA LowDoc	• Business alliances • SBA regular 7(a) program • Venture capital • SBICs • State and local public financing • Franchising • Asset-based financing	• SBA CAPLines • Consumer finance companies • Commercial finance companies • State and local public financing

FIGURE 36.3 **Personal Living Expenses**

Your Expenses This sample worksheet can be used to calculate your monthly living expenses. *Why do experts suggest that an entrepreneur have enough capital to pay for up to six months of living expenses?*

Personal Living Budget Worksheet

Regular Monthly Expenses (Fixed)

Rent or mortgage (include taxes, if required)	$_____
Home Equity Loan	$_____
Vehicles (include insurance)	$_____
Life Insurance	$_____
Medical Insurance	$_____
Other Insurance (premiums)	$_____
Other monthly payments (appliance and personal loans)	$_____
Subtotal	$_____

Utility Expenses (Variable)

Gas and Electricity	$_____
Telephone/Internet	$_____
Water and Sewer	$_____
Other expenses (garbage, landscaping, repairs)	$_____
Subtotal	$_____

Personal Expenses (Varies)

Clothing	$_____
Credit Card(s)	$_____
Doctors/Dentists	$_____
Education Expenses	$_____
Entertainment/Recreation	$_____
Food (at home)	$_____
Food (restaurants)	$_____
Gifts/Contributions	$_____
Prescriptions	$_____
Spending Money	$_____
Travel (gas, parking)	$_____

Budget Summary

Regular Monthly Expenses	$_____
Utility Expenses	$_____
Personal Expenses	$_____
Monthly Total	$_____

PERSONAL LIVING COSTS

Unless you are starting a new business while still working at another job, you will need money to live on during the start-up phase. Your personal living costs are expenses that are necessary for you to live. You need to project your monthly living expenses and household cash needs for at least the first year of business. (See **Figure 36.3**.) When starting a new business, you may be able to meet your personal expenses by working at another job or by relying on income from parents or a spouse.

If you choose not to work outside your business or seek any other income, you must have enough cash on hand to pay your personal expenses. Some experts suggest you have enough start-up capital to pay for up to six months of living expenses.

To get through the start-up period, set aside a fund for living expenses in a an account from which you can withdraw money without penalty. The amount should cover your general living expenses. Do not use the money for any other **purpose**.

 After You Read   **Section 36.1**

Review Key Concepts

1. **Define** asset, liability, and net worth.
2. **Explain** why it is important to assess start-up costs before starting a new business.
3. **Discuss** why knowledge about your own living expenses is important to your business plan.

Practice Academics

English Language Arts

4. Conduct research to obtain two different worksheets detailing initial cash requirements needed to start a business. Write a one-page report that compares and contrasts the similarities and differences between the two sample worksheets that you found.

Mathematics

5. Determine the total start-up costs for an online business by using the following data:
   - Initial expenses: legal: $1,500; office supplies: $400; office equipment: $3,500; design: $550; brochures: $650; Web site: $1,000; other: $700.
   - Money needed for reserve for a total of six months: monthly payroll: $8,000; monthly rent: $1,200; and monthly expenses: $750.
   - Start-up inventory: $4,000.
   What are the total start-up costs for a six-month period?

   Math Concept **Problem Solving: Start-Up Costs** Start-up costs include several different values. When determining start-up costs, make a list of all the things that are included.

   Starting Hints Total the amounts for initial expenses, the money needed for reserve, and the value of the start-up inventory. Add each of the values together to determine the total start-up cost.

 connectED.mcgraw-hill.com

Check your answers.

For help, go to the Math Skills Handbook located at the back of this book.

READING GUIDE

Objectives

- **Estimate** business income and expenses.
- **Prepare** an income statement.
- **Create** a balance sheet.
- **Interpret** a cash flow statement.

The Main Idea

The financial section of a business plan includes a projected income statement, balance sheet, and cash flow information. Financial institutions and investors want to know how a business will use their money and how it will be repaid.

Vocabulary

Content Vocabulary

- income statement
- gross sales
- net sales
- net income
- interest
- principal
- balance sheet
- cash flow statement

Academic Vocabulary

You will find these words in your reading and on your tests. Make sure you know their meanings.

- significant
- ratio

Graphic Organizer

Draw or print this outline to list key financial documents.

Financial Documents

1. Prepare an income statement. _____
2. _____
3. _____

 connectED.mcgraw-hill.com

Print this graphic organizer.

 MARKETING CORE FUNCTIONS

 Marketing Information Management

Market Planning

Financial Statements

ESTIMATING BUSINESS INCOME AND EXPENSES

After identifying personal living expenses and start-up costs, you are ready to complete other needed financial documents. The next step in the business plan is estimating income and the expenses for operating the business.

Many small businesses fail because they do not generate enough revenue to pay their costs and expenses. Estimating business income and expenses is a key part of your business plan. Lenders want to see financial estimates to decide whether to lend you money.

If you are buying an existing business, you will have previous operating results to use as a guide. You should be able to show lenders that the business has a proven track record and that it will continue to be successful under your ownership.

If you are starting a new business, you will need to estimate your potential revenue and the expenses of operating the business. You will need to take into account not only how much money you expect to bring in, but also how much it will cost to run the new company.

PREPARING AN INCOME STATEMENT

The financial document used to calculate revenue, costs, and expenses is the income statement. The **income statement** is a summary of income and expenses during a specific period such as a month, a quarter, or a year. This statement is often called a "profit-and-loss statement."

The income statement for an existing business shows the previous year's income, costs, and expenses. The income statement for a new or planned business estimates earnings and expenses for the first few months (or the first year) of operation. **Figure 36.4** on page 853 shows a sample projected quarterly income statement. Refer to this figure as you read about the parts of the income statement.

- -

❝ **lenders want** financial
documents that are
logical and realistic. ❞

- -

Income statements have several major parts: total and net sales, cost of goods sold, gross profit, expenses of operating the business, net income from operations, other income or expenses, net profit before income taxes, and net profit after income taxes. Each item on the income statement is added to or subtracted from total sales to find the amount of net profit or loss.

Total Sales
— Returns and Allowances
Net Sales
— Cost of Goods Sold
Gross Profit
— Operating Expenses
Net Income from Operations
— Other Expenses (Interest)
Net Profit (Loss) Before Taxes
— Taxes
Net Profit (Loss) After Taxes

Now we will see how to determine the different amounts for each part of the income statement.

Career Chatroom

Henry R. Keizer

U.S. Vice Chair/Global Head, Audit
KPMG International

What do you do at work?

As an auditor, I work with 55,000 partners and professionals at the accounting, tax, and advisory firm KPMG. Every day is different. I spend time meeting with clients, working with the firm's leaders to ensure consistency in KPMG International's firms in 144 countries, helping design new technologies that improve the way we work.

What is your key to success?

"Doing the right thing in the right way," describes the values by which I have lived throughout my career. It's amazing what you can accomplish when you stay focused on doing what's right.

What skills are most important to you?

Technical acumen, sound judgment, and interpersonal skills. An auditor needs to have a strong technical understanding to perform responsibilities. It is critical to understand the facts of a situation and draw the right conclusion. Having upfront, collaborative conversations with clients and conveying critical messages to teammates are important skills.

 connectED.mcgraw-hill.com

Read more about this career and complete a Career Exploration Activity.

ESTIMATING TOTAL SALES

The income generated by a business depends on the yearly volume of sales. Most new businesses grow slowly in the beginning. Therefore, be conservative in estimating your first-year sales.

Suppose you are starting a new T-shirt printing business. You have a contract for 2,000 shirts, which you will sell at $8 each wholesale. Your estimated total sales will be $16,000. If you think you could produce and sell ten times that number during your first year, you would estimate your total sales at $160,000.

It is important to calculate and verify a reasonable estimated sales volume. Compare it with projected industry figures for your business size and location. Trade associations, bankers, and industry publications can help you make sales and income estimates.

The accuracy of your sales estimates will also depend on the quality of your market analysis. Losses rather than profits are common during the first year of business. In your business plan, you will need to show how you will cover any losses by investing more capital or reducing your operating expenses.

CALCULATING NET SALES

The total of all sales for a given period of time is called **gross sales**. Your gross sales will simply be the total of all cash sales if your company sells only on a cash basis. Your company may accept credit cards, sell gift certificates, or offer merchandise on account. All of these different types of sales transactions must be totaled to arrive at gross sales.

Most businesses have some customer returns and allowances (credit granted to customers for damaged or defective goods kept by the customer). Therefore, the gross sales figure does not reflect the actual income from sales. The total of all sales returns, discounts, and allowances is subtracted from gross sales to get net sales. The **net sales** is the amount left after gross sales have been adjusted for returns and allowances. Look at **Figure 36.4** to find the net sales for each month.

COST OF GOODS SOLD

The total amount spent to produce or to purchase the goods that are sold is called the "cost of goods sold." Stock on hand is counted and calculated to determine beginning and ending inventory amounts. To calculate cost of goods sold, add goods purchased during the period to the beginning inventory value. Then subtract the amount of the ending inventory.

FIGURE 36.4 **Projected Quarterly Income Statement**

Financial Statement An income statement summarizes a business's income and expenses for a specific period of time. It gives a snapshot of the business's health and shows profits or losses. *Without a history how might a new business gather the information needed to project income and expenses?*

	Month 1	Month 2	Month 3	TOTAL
Sales	30,900	34,000	36,400	101,300
Less Returns & Allowances	900	1,000	1,400	3,300
NET SALES	30,000	33,000	35,000	98,000
Cost of Goods Sold	19,500	21,000	22,750	63,250
GROSS PROFIT	10,500	12,000	12,250	34,750
Operating Expenses				
Variable Expenses				
Advertising	300	350	350	1,000
Automobile	450	400	525	1,375
Dues and Subscriptions	15	20	18	53
Legal and Accounting	300	400	350	1,050
Miscellaneous Expenses	360	480	420	1,260
Office Supplies	120	160	140	420
Security	300	400	350	1,050
Telephone	90	120	105	315
Utilities	90	120	105	315
Total Variable Expenses	2,025	2,450	2,363	6,838
Fixed Expenses				
Depreciation	180	180	180	540
Insurance	300	300	300	900
Rent	800	800	800	2,400
Salaries and Payroll Taxes	5,600	5,600	5,600	16,800
Total Fixed Expenses	6,880	6,880	6,880	20,640
TOTAL EXPENSES	8,905	9,330	9,243	27,478
NET INCOME FROM OPERATIONS	1,595	2,670	3,007	7,272
Other Income	0	0	0	0
Other Expenses (Interest)	300	300	300	900
NET PROFIT (LOSS) BEFORE TAXES	1,295	2,370	2,707	6,372
Taxes	325	590	680	1,595
NET PROFIT (LOSS) AFTER TAXES	970	1,780	2,027	4,777

Net Sales is determined by subtracting returns and allowances from total sales.

Gross Profit is the difference between net sales and the cost of goods sold.

Operating Expenses are the costs of operating a business. They are divided into variable and fixed expenses.

Total Expenses is determined by adding the total variable expenses to the total fixed expenses.

Net Income From Operations is found by subtracting total expenses from gross profit.

Net Profit Before Taxes is calculated by adding other income to net income from operations, then subtracting interest expense.

Net Profit After Taxes is found by subtracting taxes from net profit before taxes. This amount represents the actual profit after income taxes are paid from operating the business for a certain period of time.

Beginning Inventory
+ Net Purchases, or Production Costs
Subtotal
− Ending Inventory
Cost of Goods Sold

Most service businesses do not provide goods to their customers. Therefore, they do not have to determine the cost of goods sold. Their gross profit is the same as net sales. Other businesses that produce or purchase products to sell must calculate the cost of goods sold.

DETERMINING GROSS PROFIT

Gross profit or gross margin on sales is the difference between the net sales and the cost of goods sold. The formula for calculating gross profit is:

Net Sales
− Cost of Goods Sold
Gross Profit

Once you know the cost of goods sold, calculate your gross profit by subtracting the cost of goods sold from net sales.

DETERMINING BUSINESS EXPENSES

The next major part of the income statement is the operating expenses. Operating expenses are the costs of operating the business, including variable and fixed expenses.

CALCULATING VARIABLE EXPENSES

Variable expenses change from one month to the next and fluctuate depending upon the sales volume of the business. Variable expenses include advertising, office supplies, and utilities. Variable expenses are often calculated as a percentage of some baseline amount. Advertising expenses, for example, may average 5 percent of total sales.

CALCULATING FIXED EXPENSES

Fixed expenses are costs that remain the same for a period of time. These types of expenses stay fixed for months, regardless of sales volume. Depreciation, insurance, rent, salaries, and payroll taxes are examples of fixed expenses.

Depreciation is a complicated fixed expense. Depreciation represents the amount by which an asset's value has fallen because of age, wear, or deterioration in a given period of time. IRS laws and rules govern the time period over which assets can be depreciated. An accountant can also determine the asset depreciation schedule and amounts to use for listing assets on income tax returns.

Projecting other fixed expenses usually is easier because you simply add all of your fixed costs, such as rent or insurance.

CALCULATING PAYROLL EXPENSES

To calculate payroll expenses, you must first estimate the number of employees you need to operate your business. Then research typical salaries in your area for the work the employees will perform. You can get help with salary information by consulting your state employment security agency (SESA) office. You can also review the help-wanted ads online and in the newspaper for similar jobs. You can also use the minimum wage as a starting point and decide how much more to pay for more skilled workers. A skilled worker should have a higher salary than an unskilled worker.

Payroll records are important to your employees and to your company. They are also used to prepare income tax returns. Your banker, an accountant, or a computer software publisher can set up a system to calculate, record, and issue payroll checks.

Your payroll records may be part of a cash disbursements journal where you keep records of all cash payments. You may prefer to keep payroll records in a separate payroll journal. Use a separate record for each employee. Each record will show one employee's pay period, hours worked, earnings, deductions, and net pay.

The amount earned by an employee is that person's gross pay. Net pay is what the employee receives after deductions for taxes, insurance, and voluntary deductions. Nancy Baker earns $11 an hour and worked 40 hours during the week; therefore, her gross pay is $440 ($11 × 40 hours).

Nancy's deductions total $125.66, so you would calculate her net pay by subtracting the deductions from her gross pay:

$440 − $125.66 = $314.34 (net pay)

Tax tables are available for calculating the amount to be deducted from each employee's pay for local, state, and federal income tax. The percentage of gross pay to be deducted for FICA (Social Security and Medicare taxes) changes frequently. Get the latest information from your local Social Security office.

Example: Find the net pay for Rosarita Ramirez, who worked a total of 44 hours during a week at $13 per hour. She is paid time-and-a-half for overtime (hours beyond 40 hours in a week). Her deductions totaled $105.25 for the week.

STEP 1   **Calculate the gross pay.**

$520.00 ($13 × 40 hours)
+   78.00 ($13 × 4 hours × 1.5)
$598.00 (gross pay)

STEP 2   **Subtract deductions.**

$598.00 (gross pay)
−   105.25 (total deductions)
$492.75 (net pay)

In estimating your total payroll expenses, you need to use current tax rates for local, state, and federal income taxes. Remember that, as the employer, you will also pay FICA and unemployment payroll taxes on your employees' earnings. You need to include those tax amounts in your total payroll expense estimate.

CALCULATING TOTAL EXPENSES

Once you have calculated all your operating (variable and fixed) expenses, you are ready to total your expenses. To calculate total expenses, add the variable expenses to the fixed expenses.

Total Variable Expenses
+ Total Fixed Expenses
Total Expenses

NET INCOME FROM OPERATIONS

After calculating your total expenses, the next step is to calculate net income from business operations. **Net income** is the amount left after the total expenses are subtracted from gross profit. The formula for calculating net income from operations is:

Gross Profit on Sales
− Total Expenses
Net Income from Operations

Suppose you own the "I Can Do That" Home Remodeling Company, which had gross profit on sales of $153,156 during the year. Your total operating expenses for the year were $88,991, so your net income from operations was:

$153,156 − $88,991 = $64,165

During the first year of operation, a business may have a net loss from operations. A net loss results when total expenses are larger than the gross profit on sales. The financial plan should address how the business intends to pay its debts in the short term.

CALCULATING OTHER INCOME

In the Net Income From Operations section, list money earned from sources other than sales. You may earn dividends on stocks or interest on accounts. **Interest** is the money paid for the use of money borrowed or invested. It is likely that you will use some of this money during the year. Therefore, you need to calculate interest only on the amount that is actually on deposit. Because of the time value of money, the money you have now is worth more than the same amount in the future. This is due to the interest it can earn. Unless the interest income that you expect to earn is **significant**, you may want to list this amount as zero in your business plan.

CALCULATING OTHER EXPENSES

The amount you borrow to start your business is called the **principal**. Interest is expressed as a percentage of the principal and is called the "rate of interest." For example, if you borrow $100 at 6 percent, the principal is $100 and the rate of interest is 6 percent. To find the amount of interest for one year, multiply the principal (p) times the rate of interest (r) times the length of time (t):

$$i = prt$$
$$(\$100 \times .06 \times 1 = \$6)$$

You would pay $6 in interest in the previous example.

The units in the rate of interest and time must agree. That is, if the rate of interest is expressed in years, then the time must be expressed in years as well. Both may be expressed in months. Check this before you do your math so that your answers will be correct. If the rate is given without reference to a time period, you can assume that it is for one year.

Suppose you are quoted a yearly rate and need to convert it to a monthly rate. There are 12 months in a year, so you would divide the yearly rate by 12 to get the monthly rate. When you are quoted a monthly rate and want to convert it to a yearly rate, multiply the monthly rate by 12.

Once you decide how much money you will need to borrow and how long it will take you to repay the loan, you can calculate your total annual (or monthly) interest. This amount is listed on the financial statement as Other Expenses (Interest).

NET PROFIT OR LOSS BEFORE TAXES

Net profit or net loss before taxes is calculated by adding other income to net income from operations, and then subtracting other expenses from the total.

Net Income from Operations
+ Other Income
_____
Subtotal
− Other Expenses
_____
Net Profit (or Loss) Before Taxes

PRACTICE 3: COMPLETE AN INCOME STATEMENT

Using the income statement shown below, answer the following questions:

1. How much did Mountain Air Bikes pay for the bikes it sold?
2. How much was the gross profit for the year?
3. How much were total operating expenses?
4. Which operating expense was the most costly?
5. How much net income was earned during the year?

Mountain Air Bikes
Income Statement for the Year Ended
December 31, 2---

Net Sales	$ 202,736
Cost of Goods Sold	$ 124,375
Gross Profit	$?
Operating Expenses	
Salaries	$ 28,022
Rent	$ 14,211
Utilities	$ 5,214
Advertising	$ 3,422
Total Operating Expenses	$?
Net Income From Operations	$?

NET PROFIT OR LOSS AFTER TAXES

Net profit (or loss) after taxes is the amount of money left over after federal, state, and local taxes are subtracted. You may be familiar with the more common term for this concept: the "bottom line." A traditional income statement shows all revenues and expenses over a specified time period with the result on the bottom line of the report. This amount represents the actual profit from operating the business for a certain period of time. The revenues are sometimes called the "top line" figures.

The projected income statement should be done on a monthly basis for new businesses. After the first year, projected income statements can be prepared on a quarterly basis.

The steps that follow are a summary of how to prepare a monthly projected income statement.

STEP 1 Estimate total sales.

STEP 2 Subtract sales discounts, returns, and allowances from total sales to calculate net sales.

STEP 3 List the estimated cost of goods sold.

STEP 4 Subtract the cost of goods sold from net sales to find gross profit on sales.

STEP 5 List each monthly operating expense, categorizing each as a variable or fixed expense.

STEP 6 Total the monthly operating expenses.

STEP 7 Subtract total operating expenses from gross profit on sales to find net income from operations. Put parentheses around any projected losses; for example, a projected loss of $1,000 would be identified as ($1,000).

STEP 8 Add other income such as interest on bank deposits and subtract other expenses, such as interest expense, from net income from operations. The result is net profit (or loss) before income taxes.

STEP 9 Estimate total taxes on the net income and subtract that amount from net profit. The result is net profit (or loss) after taxes.

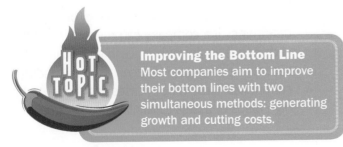

Improving the Bottom Line
Most companies aim to improve their bottom lines with two simultaneous methods: generating growth and cutting costs.

WORLD MARKET
ISRAEL

The Price of History

Antiquity is Israel's stock-in-trade. This small country has some of the world's largest archaeology sites, including Masada.

Situated on a plateau in the Judean Desert, Masada (Hebrew for "fortress") was built as a summer palace by King Herod more than 2,000 years ago. Masada is best known for the occupation from 66 A.D. to 73 A.D. by Jewish rebels who sought refuge from the Roman Empire. Archaeologists recovered coins, food, cloth, ceramic vessels, baskets, papyrus scrolls, and skeletal remains that revealed its history.

Financing the Dig Excavations depend on funding often from grants, loans, and charity. Today's major archaeological projects require professional staff, cutting-edge technology, and equipment. Funding these million-dollar ventures is a challenge, especially in tough economic times.

Social Studies
Interpret "That the future may learn from the past." Write a paragraph about what you think this means and how it could be used in a pitch for funding an excavation.

Here are some entry-level phrases that are used in conversations about marketing all over the world.

English	Hebrew
Hello/Goodbye	Shalom
Yes/No	Ken/Lo
Please	Bbevakasha
Thank you	Todah
You're welcome	Ein be'ad ma

THE BALANCE SHEET

A **balance sheet** is a summary of a business's assets, liabilities, and owner's equity.

ASSETS

Assets are anything of monetary value that you own. They are classified as current or fixed.

► Current assets are cash and anything of value that can be converted into cash in a year. Examples of current assets are cash in the bank, accounts receivable (money owed to you by your customers), and inventory.

► Fixed assets are used over a period of years to operate your business. Fixed assets cannot normally be changed into cash within a year. Examples of fixed assets include land, buildings, equipment, furniture, and fixtures. The assets of the business are needed to operate the business. When borrowing money to start a business, assets are also often used as collateral for the loan.

LIABILITIES

Liabilities are listed in another section of the balance sheet. Liabilities are the amounts that the business owes—for example, money owed for merchandise purchased. Liabilities are classified as either current or long-term.

► Current liabilities are the debts the business must pay during the upcoming business year. Examples of current liabilities are accounts payable (money owed to suppliers), notes payable (money owed to a bank), taxes payable, and money owed to employees for salaries.

► Long-term liabilities are debts that are due after 12 months. Some examples are mortgages and long-term loans.

EQUITY

Equity, or net worth, is the third section of the balance sheet. When you start a new business, you will likely invest personal savings in the business. The amount of the savings is your equity, or ownership interest, in the business. The money invested will be used to buy assets and to operate the business.

The assets owned by the business and the debts the business owes affect your equity. Remember, net worth is the difference between the assets of a business and its liabilities: Assets − Liabilities = Net Worth (Equity).

ANALYSIS OF FINANCIAL STATEMENTS

Lenders use **ratio** analysis to determine how a business is performing compared to other businesses in the industry. Ratios indicate whether a business has too much debt, is carrying too much inventory, or is not making enough gross profit. Information on the balance sheet and the income statement may be used to calculate these ratios. Lenders use ratio analysis to determine whether a business would be a good investment risk and whether its revenues could repay a loan.

Figures on the balance sheet show you the amount of your ownership interest (owner's or stockholders' equity) and the financial strength of a business on a given date. The data on the income statement shows how well the business is operating over a period of time. You may need information from both statements to calculate ratios.

A number of sources and directories exist to help you determine the common business ratios for your type of business. These include *Financial Studies of Small Business* published by the Financial Research Associates, *Industry Norms and Key Business Ratios* by Dun & Bradstreet, and *Almanac of Business and Industrial Financial Ratios* by Leo Troy.

LIQUIDITY RATIOS

Liquidity ratios analyze the ability of a firm to meet its current debts. One liquidity ratio is *current ratio*. Its formula is: current assets divided by current liabilities. The *acid test ratio*, or quick ratio, determines if a company can meet its short-term cash needs. Its formula is: cash plus marketable securities plus accounts receivables divided by current liabilities. In both cases, it is better to have high ratios of assets to liabilities.

ACTIVITY RATIOS

Activity ratios determine how quickly assets can be turned into cash. One such ratio is the *accounts receivable turnover*. This indicates the number of days it takes to collect the money owed by customers. To calculate this ratio, divide net sales by average trade receivables. In this case, it is better to have a lower ratio.

The *stock turnover ratio* measures how many days it takes to turn over (sell) the inventory. Too much inventory ties up cash that can be used to grow the business. The basic formula for this ratio is: cost of goods sold divided by average inventory.

PROFITABILITY RATIOS

Profitability ratios measure how well the company has operated during the past year. One ratio is *profit margin on sales*, which shows the rate of profit in percentages. This information is found on the income statement. Its formula is: net income divided by net sales. Another profitability ratio is the *rate of return on assets*, which shows how well you are doing when compared to other companies. The formula for this ratio is: net income divided by average total assets.

Reading Check

Explain Why do lenders use ratio analysis?

PRACTICE 4: COMPLETE A BALANCE SHEET

Using the balance sheet shown below, answer the following questions:

1. How much are the total assets for Mountain Air Bikes?
2. How much are the total liabilities?
3. What is Mountain Air's net worth?

Mountain Air Bikes
Balance Sheet December 31, 2---

Current Assets	
Cash	$ 10,000
Accounts Receivable	15,000
Inventory	68,000
Fixed Assets	
Building	120,000
Equipment	80,000
Vehicles	30,000
Total Assets	$?
Current Liabilities	
Notes Payable	$ 3,000
Accounts Payable	12,000
Salaries Payable	5,000
Taxes Payable	1,000
Long-Term Liabilities	
Notes Payable	90,000
Total Liabilities	$?
Net Worth	$?

CASH FLOW STATEMENT

A **cash flow statement** is a monthly plan that tracks when cash is expected to come into the business and when cash is expected to be paid out. A cash flow statement helps you determine whether you will have enough money to pay your bills on time. Businesses need cash to pay bills and their employees, and to use for unexpected expenses. The cash flow statement itemizes how much cash you started with, what your projected cash expenditures are, and how and when you plan to receive cash. It also shows when you will need to find additional funds and when you will have cash remaining. Most lenders will require you to estimate the business's cash flow for the first year of operation.

CASH PAYMENTS

When operating a business, one of your largest payments of cash will be for merchandise. You will most likely have to pay for part of the merchandise in cash and part of it on credit.

When estimating sales for the income statement, you include both cash and credit sales. In contrast, the cash flow statement shows only the amount you expect to receive in cash (for cash sales and payments for credit sales) during the month.

You may receive payment for most of your credit sales 30 days after the sales. You will also need to calculate your monthly costs for operating the business.

PREPARING A CASH FLOW STATEMENT

Use the following steps to prepare a cash flow statement:

STEP 1 Add the total cash on hand (in bank accounts) and money received from any loans to find your total start-up money.

STEP 2 Subtract the start-up costs to determine the amount of cash left for operation.

STEP 3 Enter the estimated cash you expect to receive from cash sales and credit sales for each month during the first year. Enter income amounts from business investments or additional loans.

STEP 4 Add all sources of cash receipts to find the total cash income for the month.

STEP 5 List the cost of goods you will buy for your inventory. Separate purchases for which you will pay cash and purchases you will make on credit, which you will pay for the next month.

For example, on the cash flow statement, the payment for goods bought on credit in Month 1 were purchased prior to the opening of the business. Add the cash and credit purchases to find the total cost of inventory purchases.

STEP 6 List the expenses you expect to pay during the month. These amounts are the same as those listed on the income statement, except for the depreciation expense.

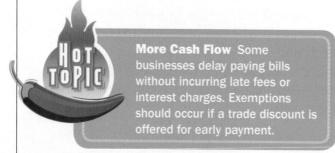

More Cash Flow Some businesses delay paying bills without incurring late fees or interest charges. Exemptions should occur if a trade discount is offered for early payment.

Depreciation is a means of spreading the cost of an asset over a period of years. The amount of depreciation is not an actual payment made by the business, so it is not listed on the cash flow statement.

STEP 7 Total all expenses for the month.

STEP 8 List amounts that will be paid out for capital expenditures. A capital expenditure is money paid for an asset used to operate the business. The purchase of a delivery truck would be a capital expenditure.

STEP 9 List any other payments that will be made, such as repayment of the principal and interest for the loan.

STEP 10 Add all the cash expenditures (cost of inventory purchased, expenses, capital expenditures, and other payments).

Subtract the total cash payments from the total cash received during the month to determine net cash flow.

The amount of any cash payments that are higher than cash receipts should be placed in parentheses to show a loss.

STEP 11 Add the beginning cash balance from the start-up column to the net cash flow for the month.

The result is the cash surplus for the month. When the costs of operating the business are higher than income added to the beginning of the cash balance, the business will have a deficit instead of a surplus.

In that case, the business will need additional cash for its operations. This amount is listed on the Cash Needs line.

The income statement does not take into account how long it may take a business to collect the cash from sales made on credit.

Reading Check

Recall What is the purpose of a cash flow statement?

LOANS

What can you do if your cash flow statement indicates you will need additional money during the year? You should be able to borrow money if your business has potential and your balance sheet shows enough assets to serve as collateral.

A loan can help you keep the business going during the start-up period and during slow sales months. When your cash flow projections indicate that you need to borrow money to meet monthly expenses, you will want to include monthly payments on the loan as a part of your cash needs for the rest of the year.

After You Read   Section 36.2

Review Key Concepts

1. **List** the major categories that are calculated on an income statement.
2. **Identify** the formula for determining gross profit.
3. **Explain** the purpose of a balance sheet.

Practice Academics

English Language Arts

4. Conduct research on the functions of money as well as the concept and importance of effective cash flow management. Write a one-page summary of your research and discuss how a business can improve its cash flow.

Mathematics

5. The Renford Furniture Company has total first-quarter sales of $425,000. Goods returned by customers amounted to $9,200. The cost of goods sold to customers was $187,000. The company's total fixed and variable expenses were $78,300. Calculate the following amounts: net sales, gross profit, and net income from operations.

   Math Concept **Number and Operations: Multi-Step Problems** With multi-step problems, make a list of all the things you are looking for. Also, include how the values are related to one another when making the list.

   Starting Hints To solve this problem, subtract the value of the items returned from the total sales to calculate the net sales. Subtract the cost of goods sold and goods returned from the net sales to determine the gross profits. Subtract the value of fixed costs and variable expenses from the gross profit to calculate the net income from operations.

 connectED.mcgraw-hill.com

Check your answers.

For help, go to the **Math Skills Handbook** located at the back of this book.

Financing the Business

Personal financial statements, start-up costs estimates, income statements, balance sheets, and cash flow statements are essential financial documents that are used in running a business.

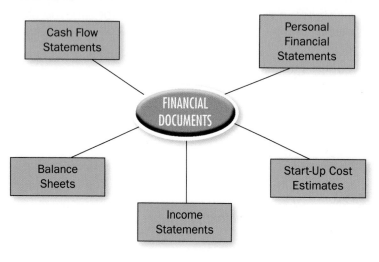

Liquidity ratios, activity ratios, and profitability ratios tell lenders about a business's debt, inventory, and profit.

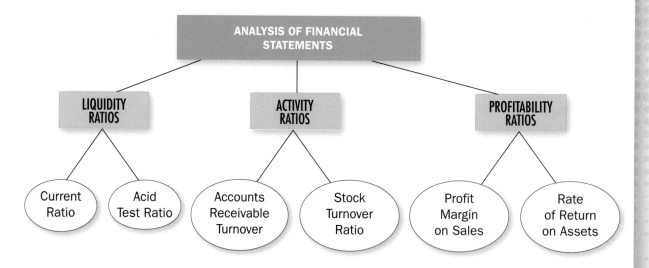

Review and Activities

Written Summary

- Five important financial documents are the personal financial statement, the start-up cost estimate, the income statement, the balance sheet, and the cash flow statement.
- The personal financial statement is a summary of your current personal financial condition.
- Start-up costs are a projection of how much initial money you will need for your first and continuing years of operation.
- You also need to estimate your personal living expenses.
- The next step is to estimate the money you expect to earn and to spend operating your business.
- The income statement is the financial document used to calculate a business's revenue, costs, and expenses.
- A balance sheet is a summary of a business's assets, liabilities, and owner's equity.
- A cash flow statement is a monthly plan that indicates when you anticipate cash coming into the business and when you expect to pay out cash.
- A cash flow statement shows whether you will have enough money to pay your bills.

Review Content Vocabulary and Academic Vocabulary

1. Arrange the vocabulary terms below into groups of related words. Explain why you put the words together.

Content Vocabulary
- personal financial statement (p. 843)
- asset (p. 843)
- liability (p. 843)
- net worth (p. 844)
- start-up costs (p. 845)
- income statement (p. 851)
- gross sales (p. 852)
- net sales (p. 852)
- net income (p. 855)
- interest (p. 856)
- principal (p. 856)
- balance sheet (p. 858)
- cash flow statement (p. 859)

Academic Vocabulary
- assessing (p. 845)
- purpose (p. 849)
- significant (p. 856)
- ratio (p. 858)

Assess for Understanding

2. **Discuss** What is the purpose of preparing financial documents?
3. **Explain** What is a personal financial statement?
4. **Determine** How do you determine start-up costs for a business?
5. **Estimate** How do you estimate business income and expenses?
6. **Develop** How do you create an income statement?
7. **Create** How do you create a balance sheet?
8. **Define** What is the definition of the term *net income*?
9. **Analyze** Your friend is starting a new business and believes that a cash flow statement is the same as an income statement. How do you analyze the difference and explain a cash flow statement?

Chapter 36 Review and Activities

Problem-Solving Skills

10. Building a Business Start-up costs are an important consideration when starting a new business. A close friend is starting a new landscaping business around an inland lake used by summer vacationers. He believes that he will not need extra capital for personal living expenses, since the business will generate immediate revenue to cover all living and business expenses. What problems can you foresee and what advice would you give to your friend?

Financial Literacy Skills

11. Monthly Living Costs Assume that you share an apartment with a roommate, dividing all rent, utility, and food expenses equally. Personal expenses are paid separately. For the past month, you and your roommate had the following expenses: apartment rent $650; utilities $60; and food expenses $170. Your own personal expenses totaled $245. What are your total living expenses for the month?

e-Marketing Skills

12. Franchising Opportunities Imagine that you are an aspiring entrepreneur investigating franchise business opportunities. Find the Web site for the International Franchise Association and browse its pages. Write a one-page summary that describes one specific franchising opportunity you found, including the kind of franchise (goods or services business), its potential for growth, and capital requirements for potential franchise owners.

- What franchise business opportunity did you investigate?
- What additional resources are available on the Web site that would be useful to an aspiring entrepreneur?
- What is the growth potential for the business?
- What are the capital requirements for franchise owners?

Build Academic Skills

English Language Arts

13. Education for Entrepreneurs The level of education attained by U.S. entrepreneurs can make a difference when starting a business. Perform library or online research on levels of education possessed by entrepreneurs. Identify any relationships that may or may not exist between a person's level of schooling and willingness to start a new business. Summarize your findings in a one-page written report.

English Language Arts

14. Investigating Start-Up Costs Conduct research on the start-up costs required for a specific type of business. Research people in business, suppliers, trade associations, Service Corps of Retired Executives (SCORE), the Small Business Administration, chambers of commerce, start-up guides, and business publications. Identify multiple resources and prepare a one-page report on the projected start-up costs for the selected business.

Mathematics

15. Planning Monthly Expenses Suppose that you are renting an apartment and earn a yearly salary of $43,200. Financial planning experts suggest that you spend no more than 30 percent of your monthly income on either rent or a mortgage. What is the most that you should spend on rent?

Math Concept **Problem Solving: Budgeting Rent** Calculate 30 percent of your monthly income to determine the maximum amount of rent you should pay.

For help, go to the **Math Skills Handbook** located at the back of this book.

Standardized Test Practice

Directions Read the following questions. On a separate piece of paper, write the best possible answer for each one.

1. Which of the following is a summary of income and expenses during a specific period, such as a month, quarter or year?
   A. Balance Sheet
   B. Cash Flow Statement
   C. Income Statement
   D. Personal Financial Statement

2. Net income is the amount left after total expenses are subtracted from gross profit.

   T

   F

3. The money that is paid for the use of money borrowed or invested is known as _____.

Test-Taking Tip

If you have time at the end of a test, check your answers and solutions. Make sure you answered each part of every question and that your answers all seem reasonable.

DECA Connection Role Play

Certified Public Accountant, Owner Accounting Firm

Situation You are the owner of a new business. As a Certified Public Accountant, you have worked for a general accounting firm for the past three years. You used that time to gain experience and to save money to open your business. Your business specialty is preparing financial documents for small businesses. You perform complete bookkeeping functions for your clients, prepare selected financial statements, and offer advice and guidance about the preparation and uses of business financial statements.

This afternoon you are going to meet with the new owner (judge) of a lawn and garden supply store. The new owner (judge) has recently purchased the business from the longtime previous owner. The new owner (judge) worked at the business for two years before deciding to make the purchase. For the past three years, the business has made little profit. The new owner (judge) realizes that it is necessary to make changes in the business's operation. The new owner (judge) has hired you to prepare several financial statements relating to the business. You have prepared a cash flow statement, balance sheet, and an income statement.

Activity You are to explain to the new owner (judge) about the information contained in each statement. You are to also explain how to use that information as a tool to guide the business to greater profitability.

Evaluation You will be evaluated on how well you meet the following performance indicators:

1. Explain the role of finance in business.
2. Set financial goals.
3. Describe the nature of cash flow statements.
4. Explain the nature of balance sheets.
5. Describe the nature of income statements.

connectED.mcgraw-hill.com

Download the Competitive Events Workbook for more Role-Play practice.

A Business Plan
for a New Online Business

Entrepreneurs continue to start up new online businesses. How can you make your dream to become an entrepreneur come true?

Scenario

Each year, more and more entrepreneurs are starting up online e-tail businesses instead of brick-and-mortar retail businesses. Bank loan departments receive applications from these entrepreneurs every week.

As an employee working in a bank's loan department, you have reviewed many loan requests for small businesses. Your supervisor asked you to prepare a sample business plan for an online business to use as a guideline for reviewing loans. In so doing, you realized you had a dream of your own—to be an entrepreneur. Growing up in a digital world, you find an online business appealing, especially for your first venture.

The Skills You'll Use

Academic Skills Reading, writing, social studies, researching, and analyzing

Basic Skills Speaking, listening, thinking, and interpersonal

Technology Skills Word processing, presentation, spreadsheet, telecommunication, and the Internet

Your Objective

Your objective is to transform an idea into a business plan for a new online business.

STEP 1 Do Your Research

Conduct research to find out about online businesses. How are they the same as brick-and-mortar businesses and how are they different? For example, how are sales taxes and consumer privacy handled? Spend time researching your interests and current trends to come up with a viable online business idea. As you conduct your research, answer these questions:

- What type of online business has the potential for success?
- What costs are involved in starting an online business?
- What political, economic, socio-cultural, and technological factors (PEST) could affect your online business?
- What are the strengths, weaknesses, opportunities and threats of your proposed online business? (SWOT analysis)

Write a summary of your reseach.

STEP 2 Plan Your Project

Now that you have completed your research, you need to begin planning your project.

- Choose an online business and provide rationale for it.
- Conduct a PEST and a SWOT analysis.
- Decide on the organization and vendors needed.
- Develop a marketing plan for the business.
- Determine the capital needed.
- Prepare proposed financial statements.
- Write a business plan that includes all of this information .

STEP 3 Connect with Your Community

- Visit online businesses on the Internet to see how they are set up.
- Visit government Web sites to learn about government rules and regulations for online businesses.
- Interview trusted adults who might be potential customers of your proposed business to see if your product or service is something they would buy online.
- Take notes during your interviews and transcribe your notes after the interviews.

STEP 4 Share What You Learn

Assume your class is a committee in a bank that decides on small business loans.

- Present your business plan in an oral presentation. Be prepared to answer questions.
- Use presentation software to create a slide presentation to accompany your oral presentation. Include one slide for each topic in your business plan.

STEP 5 Evaluate Your Marketing and Academic Skills

Your project will be evaluated based on the following:

- The business selected as well as the rationale and organization for it
- Your proposed marketing plan
- The capital needed and proposed financial statements
- Organization and continuity of your presentation
- Mechanics—presentation and neatness
- Speaking and listening skills

MARKETING CORE FUNCTIONS

 Marketing Information Management

Market Planning

Marketing Internship Project Checklist

Plan

✓ Conduct research on online businesses—products sold, government rules, and special considerations, such as payment options and consumer privacy issues.

✓ Conduct PEST and SWOT analyses.

Write

✓ Write a comprehensive business plan and marketing plan for your online business.

✓ Prepare proposed financial statements.

✓ Explain how the results of the PEST and SWOT analyses help you conceive the new product and develop the marketing plan.

Present

✓ Present research to support the rationale for your online business.

✓ Present your marketing plan for the proposed business.

✓ Present your financial plan for the proposed business.

 connectED.mcgraw-hill.com

Evaluate Download a rubric you can use to evaluate your final project.

my marketing portfolio

Internship Report Once you have completed your Marketing Internship Project and oral presentation, put your written report and a few printouts of key slides from your oral presentation in your Marketing Portfolio.

Create a Virtual Business With a virtual online business, you do not have to purchase supplies. Some virtual businesses exist as games on Facebook or on their own Web sites. Think of an appealing game in which players can buy virtual products. How can you inspire players to return your Web site? What business plan do you need? How do you develop marketing and financial plans? What competition will you have? What political, environmental, socio-cultural, and technological factors should you consider? What is your SWOT analysis? Prepare a written report and an oral presentation.

DEVELOPMENT

Marketing Internship Project

A Digital Résumé and Portfolio

Essential Question How do you create an effective digital résumé and portfolio for an internship position?

Before you can create a digital résumé and portfolio, you must take an inventory of yourself. What do you have to offer a prospective employer? What education and activities provide a snapshot of who you are? What accomplishments would you want to share with an employer to sell yourself?

Project Goal

In the project at the end of this unit, you will prepare a digital résumé and portfolio of your work to apply for a marketing internship program at a new soccer stadium.

Prepare for the Project

As you read this unit, use this checklist to prepare for the Marketing Internship Project at the end of this unit:

- Read some marketing internship job descriptions online or in print.
- Consider what you think should be included in your résumé and portfolios.

 connectED.mcgraw-hill.com

Project Activity
Complete a worksheet activity about resume.

Marketing professionals' sense of personal satisfaction . . . aligns directly with level of achievement and tenure in the profession.

MARKETING CORE FUNCTIONS IN THIS UNIT

 Product/Service Management

 Selling

RHYTHM IMPAIRED

Bob's victories at the office are legendary. Too bad his "victory dance" isn't a little less legendary.

DRINKS

**INNOVATE.
THINK BEYOND THE LABEL.**

Just because someone moves a little differently doesn't mean they can't help move your business forward. The same goes for people with disabilities.

*Innovate your thinking.
Download the "5 Myths & Real Facts" tip sheet now.*

**THINK
BEYOND
THE LABEL**.com

SHOW WHAT YOU KNOW

Visual Literacy
The group spearheading this campaign is a nonprofit organization that advocates on behalf of people with disabilities. The goal is to raise awareness that hiring people with disabilities makes good business sense. *How does this advertisement make a unique case in favor of embracing diversity in the workplace?*

identifying career opportunities

HOW WHAT YOU KNOW

Visual Literacy Increase your chances for a satisfying, successful working career by planning each step along the path to your career goal. *What are some of the steps that you might take to reach a career goal?*

Discovery Project

Begin a Personal Career Profile

Essential Question
How would your personal information help you choose and prepare for a career?

Project Goal

Begin writing personal information that will help you choose and prepare for a career. List some of your values (things that are important to you) and your interests. Describe your personality. Define your preferences for working with other people, data (information), and things. Describe your skills and aptitudes (activities that are easy for you to learn). Finally, estimate how much education and training (in years) you are willing to complete in order to reach your career goal. (Look at **Figure 37.1** on page 878 to help you complete your own Personal Career Profile.)

Ask Yourself...

- How will you understand and describe your values and interests?
- How will you describe honestly your own personality?
- How will you know your preferences for working with people, data, and things?
- How will you identify your skills and aptitudes?
- How much time are you willing to devote to additional education and training?

 Synthesize and Present Research Synthesize your research and self-analysis by beginning your own Personal Career Profile.

 connectED.mcgraw-hill.com

Activity
Get a worksheet activity about keeping customers.

Evaluate
Download a rubric that you can use to evaluate your project.

DECA Connection

DECA Event Role Play

Concepts in this chapter are related to DECA competitive events that involve either an interview or role play.

Performance Indicators The performance indicators represent key skills and knowledge. Your key to success in DECA competitive events is relating them to concepts in this chapter.

- Identify sources of career information.
- Assess personal strengths and weaknesses.
- Describe techniques for obtaining work experience.
- Explain possible advancement patterns for jobs.
- Utilize resources that can contribute to professional development.

DECA Prep

Role Play Practice role-playing with the DECA Connection competitive-event activity at the end of this chapter. More information on DECA events can be found on DECA's Web site.

READING GUIDE

Before You Read

Connect Are you interested in careers that your family or neighbors have? Why or why not?

Objectives

- **Assess** your goals, values, interests, skills, and aptitudes.
- **Appraise** your personality.
- **Complete** a career assessment.
- **Locate** career research resources.
- **Develop** a plan to reach your career goals.

The Main Idea

The first step in finding a suitable career is learning to know yourself. Assess your attributes and match them to a career that is right for you. Then compare your needs to career opportunities you have researched.

Vocabulary

Content Vocabulary
- lifestyle
- values
- aptitude
- *Occupational Outlook Handbook (OOH)*
- career outlook
- O*NET
- internship
- planning goals
- specific goal
- realistic goal

Academic Vocabulary

You will find these words in your reading and on your tests. Make sure you know their meanings.
- publication
- challenges

Graphic Organizer

Draw or print this chart to note key aspects of the six steps in the self-assessment process.

The Self-Assessment Process	
What do I do well?	

  connectED.mcgraw-hill.com

Print this graphic organizer.

MARKETING CORE FUNCTIONS

 Product/Service Management

 Selling

Define Goals

CHOOSING A CAREER

A career often includes a series of increasingly responsible jobs in one field or in related fields. Choosing a career requires careful thought and preparation. This six-step process can help guide you in making important career decisions:

1. Define your personal (lifestyle) goals.
2. Conduct a self-assessment.
3. Identify possible career choices and gather information on each choice.
4. Evaluate your choices.
5. Make your decision.
6. Plan how you will reach your goal.

As You Read

Compare Which of the six self-assessment areas will have the greatest impact on your career choice?

DEFINE YOUR PERSONAL GOALS

The first step in choosing a career requires that you do some reflecting. You need to think about what kind of life you think you would like to have. The type of life you would like to live is your personal **lifestyle**. What type of lifestyle do you want? How do you want to spend your time, energy, and money? The answers to these questions will help you set personal goals. Reaching these goals can help make possible the life you want to have in the future.

> **Your career is** the work you will do to earn a living over a period of years.

Your career choice will affect your lifestyle. Some careers will fit your personal goals better than others. If spending time with family is important to you, then you probably will not want a career that requires a lot of travel or weekend work. Religious observations may require that you not work certain days or times. Knowing your personal goals will help you find a career that adds to your lifestyle.

As a student, your life revolves around school, friends, and family. As an adult, your lifestyle will be influenced by these factors:

▶ Where you live (city, suburbs, or rural area)
▶ Type of housing in which you live
▶ Cultural environment in which you live, including the shopping and leisure activities you enjoy
▶ Your mode of transportation
▶ Relationships with your family and friends
▶ Work you do to earn a living

Your career is the key to your lifestyle because it will provide the funds needed to support your lifestyle. Before you can determine whether a career will be a good match with your personal goals, you need to identify and assess your goals.

CONDUCT A SELF-ASSESSMENT

Be prepared to record your findings in a notebook. Label the notebook "Self-Assessment File." Summarize your various assessments in paragraph form or, where appropriate, by using a rating scale.

YOUR VALUES

Values are beliefs that guide the way we live. Just as people have different abilities and personalities, they also have different values. Defining your system of values is essential in choosing a career.

The GREEN Marketer

Does Your Job Match Your Values?

Socially responsible companies strive to care for the earth, workers, and customers. Before applying for a job, careful job seekers research a company, including its green credentials.

Get the Answers Find the answers to these questions when you research a prospective company: Does the employer strive to reduce pollution and waste? Does the company support community organizations? Do managers communicate openly with workers? Knowing the answers can help you find the company that will be the best fit for you.

Social Studies

Evaluate Brainstorm ten values that are important to you in your career. For each value, write one question that you might research or ask in a job interview to see if the company is the right match for you.

 connectED.mcgraw-hill.com

Get an activity on green marketing.

Identify your values by focusing on the beliefs and actions that are important to you. If you are willing to work very hard to succeed, then you value achievement. Another possible value is the opportunity to express yourself.

YOUR INTERESTS

Most people spend 30 to 40 years working. It makes sense to choose work that interests you. Defining your interests, can help you gain a clearer picture of a career that will be fulfilling. To start evaluating your interests, write down what you like to do, such as leisure, school, social, and athletic activities.

You can also take a career interest survey. From a long list of activities, rate how much you like doing each of them. There are no right or wrong answers. Your score can help you find potential career matches. Go online to find a survey, or ask your school counselor or marketing teacher for information.

YOUR SKILLS AND APTITUDES

To be successful in any career, you need specific skills and aptitudes. An **aptitude** may be an ability or natural talent, or it may be the potential to learn a certain skill. Pursuing a career without the aptitude for the required skills may be a struggle and lead to disappointment. Once you know what skills are required to perform a job, you can determine if you have the aptitude to acquire those skills. For example, do you find it easy to sell goods to raise funds for your DECA chapter or another group? Are you good at organizing committees and inspiring others? Is math easy for you? Have you won prizes for your creativity? List your skills and aptitudes in your self-assessment file. Update your list as you develop new skills.

YOUR PERSONALITY

Your personality is the combination of all of the unique qualities that make you who you are. Understanding your personality characteristics can help you determine the types of work situations that will suit you best. Personality tests, available online and through your guidance counselor, can help you identify your personality type. For example, do you find stress to be an enjoyable challenge, or do you avoid it? Remember that there is no right or wrong kind of personality, just different kinds of people.

YOUR WORK ENVIRONMENT PREFERENCES

Your work environment refers to where you work. Work environment includes the physical location and its working conditions. Sights, sounds, and smells are all part of the working conditions.

You do not have to know all your preferences about working conditions now, but you should start thinking about them. For example, do you prefer to work indoors or outdoors? Do you like silence, or would you prefer some background noise?

Reflect You *do* things (communicate, plan, build), *know* things (graphic design, calculus, languages), and have *positive traits* (persistence, flexibility, tact).

YOUR RELATIONSHIP PREFERENCES

All jobs require working with information and ideas, people, or objects (things) individually or in combination. Any career you choose will likely involve an overlap of these categories. It is important to think about which interests you most. Do you like working with others or alone? Are you comfortable handling interpersonal conflicts at work? The answers to these questions can help you understand your relationship preferences.

IDENTIFY CAREER CHOICES AND GATHER INFORMATION

To research careers, you will need to gather information from a variety of sources. You will find current information at libraries or on the Internet. You can also learn a great deal through informational interviews, professional and trade organizations, and actual work experience.

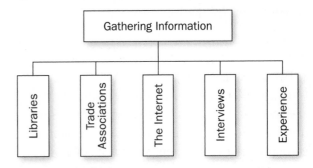

Gathering Information
- Libraries
- Trade Associations
- The Internet
- Interviews
- Experience

LIBRARIES

The *Occupational Outlook Handbook (OOH)* is available online and in libraries. The **Occupational Outlook Handbook (OOH)** describes what workers do on the job, working conditions, the training and education required, earnings, and expected job prospects in a wide range of occupations. The U.S. Department of Labor publishes an updated edition of the *OOH* every two years. The *OOH Quarterly* is published four times each year.

Living in the city can be exciting yet demanding. A rural setting offers a quieter, more relaxed lifestyle. *In which setting would you feel most comfortable, urban or rural?*

City or Country?

These **publications** provide valuable information on the number and types of jobs available in any field. This is known as the **career outlook**.

PROFESSIONAL AND TRADE ASSOCIATIONS

Professional and trade associations serve individuals and businesses with common interests. These are excellent sources for current information about careers in many professions.

Association members work in or are associated with the same industry. Some associations serve individuals in particular careers, such as the American Marketing Association or the Direct Marketing Association. These associations promote pooling of resources, technology cooperation, and common standards. Information is distributed in newsletters, journals, and reports and online.

THE INTERNET

O*NET, the Occupational Information Network, is the primary source for occupational information in the United States. The O*NET database includes information on skills, abilities, knowledge, work activities, and interests associated with occupations. The O*NET site provides information on how to use the O*NET database.

You can also find a wealth of resources for research from America's Career InfoNet Web site. The College Board also has a section on its Web site devoted to helping you research careers.

INFORMATIONAL INTERVIEWS

You may want to set up an informational interview with a professional who works in a field that interests you. You can learn about the demands, opportunities, and day-to-day realities of a career from an experienced person. Those who have met the **challenges** of a career are usually happy to talk about it.

Ask your teacher, counselor, family, and friends if they know people in the community who enjoy talking with young people about their work. You may also want to contact the public affairs or public relations officer at a professional association. Ask about career nights or other opportunities where you can speak with people who are currently working in the field.

Before any interview, prepare a list of questions that you want to ask. Here are some suggestions:

▶ How do you spend most of your time on the job?

▶ Which work activities do you like most?

▶ What skills will I need to do this type of work?

▶ What skills will I need to advance?

▶ What education and training will I need?

▶ Can I complete some of the training on the job?

▶ How much time do you spend working with ideas and information? With people? With objects?

▶ Will there be an increase in job opportunities in this field over the next several years?

▶ What impact will automation and new technology have on job opportunities in the next few years?

ON-THE-JOB EXPERIENCE

Many students work part-time after school, on weekends, or during the summer. An entry-level position in a field that interests you will offer you great experience. On-the-job experience offers many benefits that allow you to:

▶ Try out some of the work activities in your career field and decide how much you like doing them.

▶ Experience the work environment.

▶ Develop work habits that will help you succeed in your career.

▶ Broaden your understanding of the world of work and smooth the transition from school to work.

▶ Make career contacts who can serve as mentors or assist you when you are searching for a job.

▶ Build up your résumé, which will grow as you gain more working experience.

You may also explore an internship program. An **internship** offers students direct work experience and exposure to various aspects of a career, either with or without pay. Professional association and government Web sites usually have links to internship possibilities.

The value of an internship is in the experience and the contacts that you make. Employers seriously consider internship experience when reviewing candidates. It demonstrates high interest and a willingness to put in time to gain valuable experience. It gives you a definite competitive edge over applicants who do not have internship experience.

EVALUATE YOUR CHOICES

Once you identify one or more interesting careers, you can compare and contrast a potential career with your self-assessment. This evaluation can help determine whether a career that seems interesting is a good match.

Organize your task before you begin. Gather all your self-assessment notes and research on various careers. Create a personal career profile. Use an evaluation format that allows you to compare your self-assessment side-by-side with a particular career assessment (see **Figure 37.1** on page 878).

On the left side of the profile, write down all the information about yourself. Then make a copy of this form for each of your researched career choices. Using these copies, refer to your notes to fill in the career information on the right side of the profile form. Reread all the information.

It may also help to get some feedback on the information you have compiled. Share your profile with a friend, family member, teacher, or someone else you trust. Ask that person whether your self-assessment is accurate and whether the careers you have researched seem right for you.

The following questions will guide you as you evaluate your choices.

▶ Do the work values in this field match my personal values?
▶ If I am successful in this career, will I be able to achieve my personal lifestyle goals?
▶ Do the responsibilities match my skills and aptitudes?
▶ How well is this career suited to my personality?
▶ Does the work environment suit my work environment preferences?
▶ Does the career offer the kinds of work relationships I am seeking?

You may notice that many of these questions are similar to those you might ask during an informational interview with someone who works in a particular field. You may possess skills and aptitudes suited to many different careers, but an honest self-evaluation will help you determine which career is most suitable for you.

Reading Check

Summarize What are some helpful sources of information about careers?

An interview with a prospective employer offers you an opportunity to collect information about a job or career. *What other opportunities does the interview offer the interviewer and the interviewee? Do you think an interview is a good resource for gathering information about a career of interest to you? Why or why not?*

Interview for Success

FIGURE 37.1 **Personal Career Profile**

Is It a Match? A personal career profile helps you compare your self-assessment with a particular career. *Based on this career profile, how does Joan Smith's personal information match the information about a teaching career? Rank each category from 1 to 5, with 5 being the best match.*

Name __Joan Smith__

Date __September 4, 20--__

Personal Information	Career Information	Match (1–5, with 5 being the best match)
Your Values: The value scales I took showed that I like to help other people (humanitarianism). I like to be a leader. Doing creative things is fun, too.	**Values:** As a teacher I would have a chance to help others—that's what it's all about. Teachers certainly have plenty of opportunities to be leaders, too. Teachers also need to be creative!	
Your Interests: My hobby interests have always been photography, reading, and theater. My career interest survey showed that I might like a career in leading/influencing, selling, the arts, or maybe a humanitarian career.	**Career Duties and Responsibilities:** As a teacher, I would present information, and direct student discussions and activities in class. I would help each student individually, too. (Maybe I could teach marketing or general business.) A teacher's working conditions would be good in most schools. (Summers off!)	
Your Personality: I like people, and I have a good attitude toward learning. I have an open mind. I'm enthusiastic, too. However, I don't have the energy and drive that some people have. I don't know if I could work night after night.	**Type of Personality Needed:** A teacher must like kids, even when they aren't very likeable. I would have to prepare my lessons every day—couldn't just forget about them. Teachers need to be organized, too.	
Data-People-Things Preferences: I think I like working with people most of all. I wouldn't want to be stuck in an office all day with only "data" to talk to. I also wouldn't like working only with things. Some data would be all right, though.	**Data-People-Things Relationships:** Teachers work mostly with people—their students, the principal, parents. They work with data (information), too, though. I don't think they work much with things.	
Skills and Aptitudes: I may have some natural teaching skills—the kids at the YMCA always come to me for help. I helped several kids in Miss Moore's class. Business classes are easy for me.	**Skills and Aptitudes Needed:** Being able to present information so students can understand it is a very important skill. Of course, you must know your subject. An appetite for learning new approaches to teaching is important, too.	
Education/Training Acceptable: I sure never thought I would go to college—I never even liked doing the homework in high school. However, here I am a senior with no real prospects of a good job. Maybe college is the answer.	**Education/Training Required:** Four years of college (it sounds like forever, but I guess it does go fast) are required before you can begin teaching in most states. Some states require course work beyond that.	

DEVELOPING AN ACTION PLAN

A plan does not guarantee success, but it can help you to achieve success. A plan helps you remember what needs to be done and when. A plan also helps you prioritize, or put tasks in order. A plan outlines the steps that you need to follow to reach your ultimate goal.

In order to begin developing a plan, you must first complete a self-evaluation to determine your strengths, weaknesses, interests, skills, aptitudes, values, lifestyle goals, and work environment preferences. Then you will research possible career paths, identify possible career choices, gather information, and evaluate each of your choices.

Once you have completed your self-evaluation and researched your potential career options, you will have laid the groundwork to move forward. You will then be ready to make a career decision, develop your career action plan, and begin to act on your plan.

FORMULATE PLANNING GOALS

The small steps you take to get from where you are now to where you want to be in the future are called **planning goals**. They allow you to take charge of your life by helping you make decisions. Planning goals give your life a sense of direction and move you steadily toward your ultimate career goal. Every time you reach a goal, you gain confidence to move on to the next one.

A plan gives you a feeling of accomplishment. As you complete each part of your plan, you can cross it off, apply what you've learned, and move forward to the next step. Any progress you make toward your ultimate goal can also be rewarding in itself. With each step, you develop a better understanding of who you are and what you are best suited to do.

MARKETING CASE STUDY

Selling Digital Cameras

CASIO.®

Casio's *Exilim* camera line was first launched in 2002. Since then, all Exilim cameras have been thinner and smaller than most others on the market. Some are very small, about the size of a credit card, while others are larger digital devices for professional use. This strategy has helped Casio cameras win the J.D. Power customer satisfaction award.

Who Will Buy Them?

To sell these digital cameras, the marketers at Casio target different consumers. To do this, they highlight the features of each type of camera based on who is likely to use it. The high-end EX-F1 model is marketed to professional photographers. The middle-of-the-road Zoom models are targeted for the majority of consumers.

English Language Arts

Research Write a paragraph about how you would gather information about becoming a marketing manager for a digital camera company.

BE SPECIFIC

Make your planning goals as specific as possible. A **specific goal** is stated in exact terms and includes some details.

"I want to be successful," is not specific. "I want to complete my class in marketing this semester and earn at least a 'B'" is specific. This type of specific planning goal moves you forward toward your ultimate goal. When you are specific about your goals, you are more likely to formulate a plan to reach those goals.

BE REALISTIC

Planning goals must also be realistic. A **realistic goal** is one that you have a reasonable chance of achieving.

Think about all of the different skills and aptitudes that you possess. They will guide you in identifying both your ultimate career goal and your planning goals. Careful self-assessment can help you to focus on being realistic.

WORK BACKWARD

When you set your planning goals, you should work backward:

▶ Begin with your ultimate career goal.
▶ Decide what objectives you must accomplish along the way to achieve your ultimate goal.
▶ Determine the necessary medium- term goals.
▶ Determine the necessary short- term goals.

For example, suppose your ultimate career goal is to become a sustainable-design architect. A long-term goal may be to work for a top "green" architectural firm. In order to earn the credentials you will need to get such an opportunity, you might want to set a medium-term goal of earning your college degree in architecture. Another medium-term goal might be to start earning credentials. For example, you could set a goal to pass the U.S. Green Building Council's performance-based rating system to gain Leadership in Energy and Environmental Design (LEED) accreditation.

In order to prepare for your medium-term goals, you could set a short-term goal of working for a sustainable-housing construction company. This could start out as an unpaid internship designed to gain experience. Then, after you have gained experience as an intern, your next goal could be to get hired for a paid position with the company. Another short-term goal may be to investigate the type of specialized training you will need. There are many ways to do this. For example, you could subscribe to architectural trade publications and listservs or keep up-to-date by reading books and blogs about sustainable building.

Having a progressive series of goals allows you to test your ultimate career goal and make corrections or adjustments along the way. As you make progress toward your career goal, your experiences may reinforce your career decision or lead you to change your career goal. You may even discover another career that you find more interesting.

Think back to the example of wanting a career in "green" architecture. Based on your hands-on work experience in at the sustainable-housing construction company, for instance, you may discover that you would prefer a career working as a sustainable-design contractor rather than becoming an sustainable-design architect. Having a progressive series of goals allows you to adjust your path and your ultimate career goal at any point along the way.

PROFESSIONAL DEVELOPMENT

Whatever your career choice, you will need a plan of action to reach your goal. Your plan must include the concepts and strategies needed for personal and professional growth. Professional development is the process of obtaining the skills, qualifications, and experiences to continue to make progress in your chosen career.

Choosing education is much like choosing a career. Follow the complete decision-making process to select the best school and program for you. Your school counselor, library, and Web sites will have useful information.

Professionals must upgrade their existing skills and acquire new ones. Changes brought about by technology and global competition make lifelong learning key to any successful career.

If you are planning for education and training beyond high school, consider the following questions:

▶ What is my ultimate career goal?
▶ What courses can I take now that will help me to reach that career goal?
▶ What futher education and training are required?
▶ How much of this education and training must I complete before I enter this career?
▶ Where can I get this education and training?
▶ How much will this education and training cost, and how will I get the money?
▶ How much education and training can I get on the job?

OUTLINING YOUR PLAN

After you have answered these questions, begin writing your personal plan of action. Write down all of your goals, the dates that you plan to begin and reach each goal. Identify the skills you will need to improve progression in your career. Outline both the work experience goals and the educational goals you will need to achieve to meet your ultimate career goal. Be realistic about the timing of each step of your plan. Know that you will likely revise it as your situation changes and evolves. This will help keep you on track toward your ultimate career goal—the one that turns your dream lifestyle into reality.

 After You Read | **Section 37.1**

Review Key Concepts

1. **Name** the first two steps in choosing a career.
2. **List** three considerations that will help you formulate your planning goals.
3. **Identify** six areas to explore when conducting a self-assessment.

Practice Academics

English Language Arts

4. Use the Internet, your school career center, or a local library or bookstore to select two books on choosing a career. Look through each book and read the chapters dealing with self-assessment. Then make a chart comparing information from each book about self-assessment.

Mathematics

5. Assume that you will work for 46 years before you retire. You invest $8,000 in a retirement fund at the end of your first year. It compounds at an 8 percent annual rate of return for the next 45 years. How much will be in the account when you retire? Use the following equation to find the amount that will be in the account: Original Investment Amount ($8,000) × (1.08)^{45} where (1.08)^{45} is 31.9204494.

Math Concept **Compound Interest** Compound interest is interest paid on the principal and subsequently, on the principal plus the accumulated interest.

Starting Hint To solve this problem, multiply the initial amount invested by 31.9204494, the value of the compound interest over 45 years.

 connectED.mcgraw-hill.com

Check your answers.

For help, go to the Math Skills Handbook located at the back of this book.

READING GUIDE

 Before You Read

Connect What do you already know about careers in marketing?

Objectives

- **Explain** the importance of marketing careers to the U.S. economy.

The Main Idea

When considering a marketing career, learn about the requirements, opportunities, rewards, and trends. The more information you have, the easier it will be to make a career.

Vocabulary

Content Vocabulary
- occupational area

Academic Vocabulary

You will find these words in your reading and on your tests. Make sure you know their meanings.
- subordinate
- monitored

Graphic Organizer

Draw or print this chart to write down questions about a marketing career..

Questions About a Marketing Career

1. _____
2. Are there many jobs available? _____
3. _____

 connectED.mcgraw-hill.com

Print this graphic organizer.

MARKETING CORE FUNCTIONS

 Product/Service Management

 Selling

Careers in Marketing

IS A MARKETING CAREER FOR YOU?

The skills and knowledge you gain from studying marketing can also help you in school and on the job. These skills include writing, researching, communication, and analytical skills, among others.

As You Read

Identify What are three pros and three cons of a career in marketing?

AN OVERVIEW OF MARKETING CAREERS

Marketing provides perhaps the greatest diversity of opportunities of any career field—from purchasing merchandise, to selling, to designing ads, to steering the company as president. More than 30 million Americans earn a living in marketing. Job growth in marketing careers is expected to exceed 12 percent for the next ten years. Careers in marketing include an array of activities required to develop, promote, and distribute goods and services to consumers. When considered in this broad sense, marketing activities account for about one in every three American jobs.

BENEFITS OF A MARKETING CAREER

The most obvious benefit of a career in marketing is the opportunity to make an above-average income. Even for an entry-level or **subordinate** position, potential earnings are excellent. Due to the high visibility of many marketing positions, there are usually more opportunities to advance than in almost any other area of business. People who work in marketing frequently present and shape their ideas in meetings with company managers and executives.

> **"As you study marketing, you have the opportunity to evaluate marketing as a potential career."**

People who work in sales get constant feedback in the form of sales figures that are reviewed by management. People who work in advertising may develop ad campaigns that are acclaimed by professional associations. Promotions tend to come faster in marketing than in many other careers. However, a career in marketing can be stressful. There are pressures to succeed, and the results of one's efforts are highly visible.

EMPLOYMENT TRENDS IN MARKETING

The U.S. Bureau of Labor Statistics (BLS) projects that employment in marketing and sales will continue at a high level. The rapid growth of e-commerce provides many opportunities. However, Department of Labor projections indicate that competition for managerial jobs in marketing-related fields will be keen in most industries.

The rise in the number of single-person households, changes in recreational activities, and the increase in foreign competition are all **monitored** through market research and marketing information systems. To track these developing trends, companies are expanding their marketing programs and staffs.

Reading Check

Connect How many Americans earn a living in careers in marketing?

Career Chatroom

Acacia May

Senior Producer, Experiential

What do you do at work?

I plan and produce integrated marketing events. My clients have included a media production company and a PR firm. My job can involve finding locations, preparing invitations, creating guest lists, and designing tables. Some events are part of larger events, such as the Sundance Film Festival, awards shows, and conventions. I've also worked at full-service agencies where I collaborated with different departments that handle press, events, and even "celebrity wrangling," which means arranging for celebrities to attend events.

What is your key to success?

I try to be true to myself, and I enjoy this work. In this field, the possibility for promotion is good if you work hard, gain different experiences, and learn quickly.

What skills are most important to you?

I think being outgoing and having good people skills are important. This business involves a lot of networking. Also, clients want creative and innovative ideas. You need intelligence, organization skills, and self-motivation.

 connectED.mcgraw-hill.com

Read more about this career and get a Career Exploration Activity.

JOB LEVELS IN MARKETING

Many jobs exist within each of the occupational areas, or career applications, of marketing. Jobs in each marketing area can be categorized according to five skill levels.

Entry-Level Jobs
Career-Sustaining Jobs
Specialist Employees
Supervisors
Managers, CEOs, and Owners

▶ **Entry level jobs** usually require no prior experience and involve limited decision-making skills.

▶ **Career-sustaining jobs** require a higher level of skill and more decision making than entry-level jobs.

▶ **Marketing specialist employees** must show leadership ability and make many decisions on a daily basis. Being a marketing specialist is usually a long-term career goal.

▶ **Marketing supervisors** must have good management skills, the ability to make many decisions on a daily basis, and excellent marketing skills. This is the highest career level to which many people aspire. The prestige and income are generally quite high, and there is less risk involved than at the top management level.

▶ **Managers and CEOs/owners** are at the top level. People at this level are capable of running an entire company or a significant part of it. They must be highly skilled in a number of areas. They are responsible for the final success of the enterprise.

Room for More Worldwide estimates indicate that more than 30 percent of workers work in some aspect of marketing.

✓ **Reading Check**

Compare Which marketing job level would you prefer?

OCCUPATIONAL AREAS

An **occupational area** is a category of jobs that involve similar interests and skills. Focusing on one or two areas makes it much easier to find information about the career area that most interests you. Here are some career areas within the field of marketing:

- Advertising
- Customer Service
- E-Commerce
- Entrepreneur
- Fashion Merchandising
- Financial Services
- Food Marketing
- Importing/Exporting

- International Marketing
- Marketing Research
- Pharmaceutical/Medical Marketing
- Product Management
- Professional Sales
- Public Relations
- Real Estate
- Restaurant Management
- Retail Management
- Sales Management
- Service Marketing
- Sports Marketing
- Travel/Tourism/Hospitality Marketing

 After You Read **Section 37.2**

Review Key Concepts

1. **Name** three benefits of a career in marketing.
2. **Identify** and rank the ten major areas that you should consider when investigating careers. (Rank 1 as your highest priority and 10 your lowest priority.)
3. **List** five resources for researching careers.

Practice Academics

Social Studies

4. Select one of the following agencies to research: Federal Communications Commission, Federal Reserve board, Federal Trade Commission, Food and Drug Administration, or Internal Revenue Service. Write a one-page report on the agency and what it does. Explain how the agency impacts economic, market, and employment trends.

Mathematics

5. You receive an offer for a job in marketing that pays $42,500, plus the eligibility for a 12-percent bonus annually. Calculate the total annual salary assuming you are also paid a 12-percent bonus.

   Math Concept **Percent Problems** To calculate a 12-percent bonus, multiply the decimal form of the percent by the salary. Then add this amount to the annual salary to find the salary plus the bonus amount.

   Starting Hints Multiply the annual amount of pay for the job, $42,500, by 12 percent to determine the bonus amount. Add the amount of the bonus to the annual pay to calculate the total annual salary.

 connectED.mcgraw-hill.com

Check your answers.

For help, go to the Math Skills Handbook located at the back of this book.

Identifying Career Opportunities

Good career choices are based on a comprehensive self-assessment of values, interests, skills, aptitudes, personality, and personal lifestyle preferences.

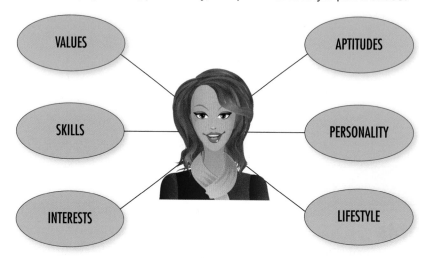

Your plan of action to reach your career goal requires setting specific and realistic short-, medium-, and long-range planning goals.

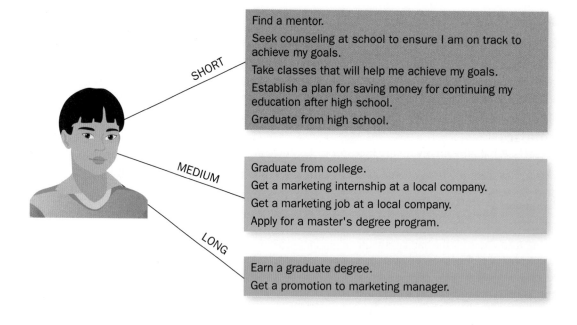

SHORT
Find a mentor.
Seek counseling at school to ensure I am on track to achieve my goals.
Take classes that will help me achieve my goals.
Establish a plan for saving money for continuing my education after high school.
Graduate from high school.

MEDIUM
Graduate from college.
Get a marketing internship at a local company.
Get a marketing job at a local company.
Apply for a master's degree program.

LONG
Earn a graduate degree.
Get a promotion to marketing manager.

Review and Activities

Written Summary

- Career choices are based on a comprehensive self-assessment of values, interests, skills, aptitudes, personality, and personal lifestyle preferences.
- Career planning includes looking at work values, lifestyle fit, and the education and training required. It also includes learning about the duties and skills required, and looking at helpful personality traits, work environment, and work relationships.
- A plan of action to reach a career goal requires setting specific and realistic short-, medium-, and long-range planning goals.
- Consider the benefits, employment trends, occupational areas, and job levels in marketing.

Review Content Vocabulary and Academic Vocabulary

1. Write each of the vocabulary terms below on an index card, and the definitions on separate index cards. Work in pairs or small groups to match each term to its definition.

Content Vocabulary
- lifestyle (p. 873)
- values (p. 873)
- aptitude (p. 874)
- *Occupational Outlook Handbook (OOH)* (p. 875)
- career outlook (p. 876)

- O*NET (p. 876)
- internship (p. 876)
- planning goals (p. 879)
- specific goal (p. 880)
- realistic goal (p. 880)
- occupational area (p. 885)

Academic Vocabulary
- publication (p. 876)
- challenges (p. 876)
- subordinate (p. 883)
- monitored (p. 883)

Assess for Understanding

2. **Contrast** What are values, lifestyle goals, interests, and aptitudes?
3. **Reflect** Why is it important to assess values, lifestyle goals, interests, and aptitudes when choosing a career?
4. **Identify** What are two methods for appraising your personality?
5. **Explain** What is a work environment?
6. **Consider** What areas should be investigated when completing a career assessment?
7. **Search** What are two online and two library career research resources?
8. **Role Play** How can you explain to a peer the purpose a personal career profile serves?
9. **Imagine** What is the most obvious benefit of a career in marketing?

21st  Century Skills

Communication Skills

10. Requesting an Informational Interview Write a script for what you would say in a telephone call requesting an informational interview. What impression would you want to make? Describe the tone of voice and manner of speaking you would use to make that impression.

Financial Literacy Skills

11. Calculating Payroll Taxes You are an assistant marketing manager for Big 12 Sporting Goods. Your gross monthly income is $4,900. Use the Internet to locate (1) the IRS monthly payroll tax table, (2) the payroll tax for your state, (3) the Social Security tax rate, and (4) the Medicare tax rate. What will be the amount of the payroll check you will receive each month? If you owned your own business and paid yourself a salary, how much more would be deducted from a $4,900 gross salary?

Everyday Ethics

12. Real World or Not? Are you interested in a career in television—with real people? Although reality shows have been around for decades in various forms, they usually refer to a particular type of program produced since 2000. Programming usually involves a competition between "real" people that awards career opportunities, a monetary payoff, or both to the winners. Reality shows have become a mainstay in American culture, as this headline notes, "History Channel stays the reality course." The channel's scheduled programs include a number of educational reality shows. Critics say reality TV brings out the worst in its participants. Create an idea or theme for a reality show that you think would bring out the best.

e-Marketing Skills

13. Defining e-Marketing Skills Use the Internet to locate blogs, Web sites, and articles that discuss e-marketing skills. Then write a half-page report in which you discuss the most important e-marketing skills and how you may go about developing these skills.

Build Academic Skills

English Language Arts

14. Personal Career Profile Research a career of your choice using the Internet. Then prepare a *Personal Career Profile* that compares all of the qualities you included in your self-assessment with the career you researched. (See **Figure 37.1** for an example.)

Social Studies

15. Develop a Plan of Action Follow the suggestions discussed in this chapter as you write a personal *Plan of Action* that will help you achieve your planning goals in the next several years. Remember to be as specific as possible.

Mathematics

16. Distinguishing Wages If the average national wage for an employee with a bachelor's degree is $52,000, while the average wage for an employee with a master's degree is $67,000, how much more does the person with the master's degree earn? (Provide your answer in dollars and in percentage.)

Math Concept **Determining Differences** Determining the difference between two numbers is a matter of subtracting the smaller amount from the larger amount.

For help, go to the **Math Skills Handbook** located at the back of this book.

Standardized Test Practice

Directions Read the following questions. On a separate piece of paper, write the best possible answer for each one.

1. O*NET is:
   A. a TV network.
   B. a program for searching the Internet.
   C. the Occupational Information Network.
   D. a Web site that displays NFL football scores.

2. Self-employed persons that operate their own small businesses must pay higher Social Security and Medicare taxes than employees of a company.

   T

   F

3. The _____ _____ _____, published by the U.S. Department of Labor, describes what workers do on the job, working conditions, the training and education needed, earnings, and expected job prospects in a wide range of occupations.

Test-Taking Tip

Even though your first choice is often correct, do not be afraid to change an answer if, after you think about it, it seems wrong to you.

DECA Connection Role Play

Employee
Career Guidance Company

Situation Your company specializes in offering advice and assistance to individuals who are entering the workforce for the first time or are seeking to change career fields. Some of the services your company offers include résumé review, advice about gaining relevant work experience, and exploration of career paths for job advancement.

At this point in time, the economy of your area is weak. There have been layoffs at many businesses throughout the area, and most others are not hiring new employees. Unemployment is high, and there are few jobs available. For each career position available, there are at least five applicants. Some of those applicants have several years of experience. The job market is particularly difficult for individuals entering the workforce for the first time.

Your current client (judge) is young and has limited work experience. The client (judge) is uncertain about the type of job he/she is seeking. The client (judge) is also interested in a job that will offer a career path and is seeking advice about creating a standout resume.

Activity You are to meet with the client (judge) and explain some sources of career information, ways to gain work experience, and advancement patterns along career paths.

Evaluation You will be evaluated on how well you meet the following performance indicators:

1. Identify sources of career information.
2. Assess personal strengths and weaknesses.
3. Describe techniques for obtaining work experience.
4. Explain possible advancement patterns for jobs.
5. Utilize resources that can contribute to professional development.

 connectED.mcgraw-hill.com

Download the Competitive Events Workbook for more Role-Play practice.

finding and applying for a job

Visual Literacy Finding job leads, attending job fairs, going through the application process, and getting interviews is a job in itself. These activities require more time than you might expect. *What might be some good sources for finding job leads?*

Discovery Project

Begin Your Career Portfolio

Essential Question What is a career portfolio and how can it help develop a career and life plan?

Project Goal

A career portfolio is an organized scrapbook of information about you and your best work, presented in an attractive and professional way. A good career portfolio is an essential tool for college and employment interviews. This project is just the beginning. At the end of this chapter, you will further develop your career portfolio. Go online to research ways to format and organize your portfolio and get ideas to get you started. You may find some sample career portfolios that can be helpful, too. After your research, begin to develop an outline of what will become your own career portfolio.

Ask Yourself...

- How will you format your career portfolio?
- How will you organize it?
- What should be included?
- Where will you find the information to be included?

 Synthesize and Present Research Synthesize your research by creating a format for a career portfolio, and begin to develop an outline of what will become your career portfolio.

 connectED.mcgraw-hill.com

Activity
Get a worksheet activity about preparing a career portfolio.

Evaluate
Download a rubric that you can use to evaluate your project.

DECA Connection

DECA Event Role Play

Concepts in this chapter are related to DECA competitive events that involve either an interview or role play.

Performance Indicators The performance indicators represent key skills and knowledge. Your key to success in DECA competitive events is relating them to concepts in this chapter.

- Utilize job search strategies.
- Complete a job application.
- Interview for a job.
- Prepare a résumé.
- Write a letter of application.

DECA Prep

Role Play Practice role-playing with the DECA Connection competitive-event activity at the end of this chapter. More information on DECA events can be found on DECA's Web site.

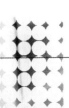

READING GUIDE

 Before You Read

Connect Find out how family members and friends found their jobs, and the job-hunting techniques they used.

Objectives

- **Identify** a variety of sources for job leads.
- **Describe** the best ways to develop job leads.

The Main Idea

It is important to know how to locate job leads. This will help you find a job in your chosen career.

Vocabulary

Content Vocabulary
- job lead
- networking
- public employment agencies
- private employment agencies
- staffing/temporary agencies

Academic Vocabulary

You will find these words in your reading and on your tests. Make sure you know their meanings.
- contacting
- pursuing

Graphic Organizer

Draw or print this chart to write in six types of sources for job leads.

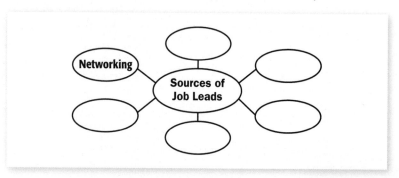

 **connectED.mcgraw-hill.com**

Print this graphic organizer.

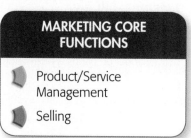

MARKETING CORE FUNCTIONS

- Product/Service Management
- Selling

Finding a Job

FINDING JOB OPENINGS

How do you uncover job opportunities? The best way to start is by **contacting** all of the sources available to you that might produce a job lead. A **job lead** is information about a job opening, perhaps providing some indication about the type of work and who to contact. You need to follow up on minor leads and research information about a company. Finding the right job requires getting leads and following up on them.

As You Read

Connect Think about which sources for job leads would be most productive for you.

NETWORKING

Often the best sources for job leads are people you know. Consider family, friends, and schoolmates and their families. You may also want to contact former employers, coaches, and teachers or professors. Local business owners and professionals can also be good sources. You might talk to members of a religious or community group to which you belong, and even acquaintances. All of these people form your network.

Networking is the art of building alliances. Finding contacts among people in your network is the most effective way to find a job. Most businesses welcome applications from friends of employees because they trust their employees' opinions. Make a list of all your contacts, including addresses, phone numbers, and e-mail addresses. Keep this list current, and add to it as your career and education progress.

Let your contacts know you are seeking employment and the type of work for which you are suited. Explain what you have to offer, and the types of companies or careers that interest you.

> **" Developing effective job-search and interview skills will help you make the most of your time and effort when job hunting. "**

Politely ask your contacts if they would be comfortable letting you know if they hear of any openings. They may not immediately know of the perfect job for you, but they can keep you in mind and even ask their friends and coworkers about openings. Networking is a mutual exchange, so be prepared to help them in return. Always let them know when you have responded to one of their leads and thank them for helping you.

Social networks on the Internet like Facebook®, and LinkedIn®, a professional network, are other options when searching for job leads.

SCHOOL COUNSELOR

When you are building your network, include your school guidance counselor. Local businesses frequently call school counselors for names of qualified students for part-time or temporary jobs.

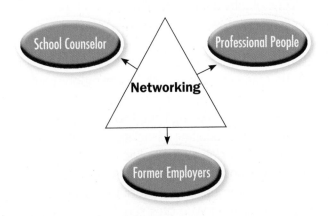

PROFESSIONALS YOU KNOW

You probably have occasional contact with professional people in your personal life—doctors, teachers, dentists, or lawyers. If you have good relationships with these people, they will probably be happy to help you in your job search. Since they are part of your network, you can ask them about people to contact, job prospects, or advice about the career you are **pursuing**.

FORMER EMPLOYERS

Whether you worked full-time, part-time, or in a temporary position, former employers may be good sources of job leads. They will likely help you find a job if they were pleased with your work.

Why Network? CareerXRoad's "Annual Sources of Hire Survey" reports that referrals, especially from employees, made up 27.3 percent of all new hires.

COOPERATIVE EDUCATION AND WORK EXPERIENCE PROGRAMS

Cooperative education teachers have contacts in the business community because they place and supervise students in part-time jobs. Students enrolled in cooperative work experience programs receive course credit and are sometimes paid as well.

SEARCHING THE INTERNET

Employers use the Internet extensively, and millions of jobs are posted at any given time. In addition to searching company Web sites for openings, search for opportunities on Indeed.com, Careerbuilder.com, HotJobs, and Monster.com. For jobs in marketing, also check MarketingJobs.com. There are also many professional associations that serve the marketing field. Those include the American Marketing Association, the Direct Marketing Association, the Public Relations Society of America, and the International Association of Business Communicators. Check the listings on their local chapter Web sites, too.

On employment Web sites, search for listings that are no more than a month old. Many job search engines and Web sites enable you to search by location, job type, industry, date of posting, and even salary. Some enable you to sign up for an e-mail alert to notify you when positions are posted. Check to see if there is a charge for this service. It is a great way to learn about opportunities as soon as they become available.

NEWSPAPERS AND MAGAZINES

For many years, the "Help Wanted" section of local newspapers was perhaps the best place to find job openings. While many employers have moved their job listings to their own Web sites or other online job-listing sites, do not overlook your local newspaper. These Help Wanted sections also provide information about the local job market. You will learn the qualifications required for different types of jobs. You may find information about salaries and benefits as well.

Follow up immediately on every ad that might lead to the job you want. Be aware, however, if an ad requires you to pay money or enroll in a course; it may be a disguised attempt to sell something rather than a genuine job offer.

In business newspapers and magazines, look for ads or articles about local and regional companies that are expanding, opening a new office, entering a new market, or introducing a new product. These companies are likely to be hiring. Many professionals depend on their association's magazine to alert them to job openings. Look online or in libraries for such publications.

EMPLOYMENT AGENCIES

Employment and temporary staffing agencies match workers with jobs. Most cities have several types of employment agencies. **Public employment agencies** are supported by state or federal taxes and offer free services to both job applicants and employers. **Private employment agencies** and **staffing/temporary agencies**, which are not supported by taxes, must earn a profit to stay in business. They charge a fee for their services, which is paid by either the job applicant or the employer.

Public employment agencies are identified by the names of the states in which they are located. The Texas Employment Commission and the California Employment Development Department are examples. In some cities, the state employment service is the only one available. When you fill out an application form at the public employment agency near you, you will be interviewed to determine your qualifications and interests. The agency will call you if it finds a job that is a good match. You will be told about the company and the duties of the job, and then referred for an interview if you are interested.

Many times, private employment agencies have job leads that are not listed with public agencies. Remember, however, that private agencies charge a fee if they succeed in placing you in a job. Make sure you know who is expected to pay the fee—it might be you. This would be stated in a contract you would be asked to sign. The employer will sometimes pay the fee for matching workers with higher-level jobs. The employee usually pays the placement fee for an entry-level job. The fee is usually a percentage of the salary for the first several months or even the first full year of employment.

MARKETING CASE STUDY

Monster Motivates

monster
Your calling is calling™

For one ad campaign, the online job search site Monster.com took an emotional and an inspirational approach to marketing its services. The company built a campaign called "Monster Works for Me," which included TV, radio, print, and Internet ads. Online ads in the campaign were scattered across a wide array of sites, including eBay, ESPN, MSN, and Hoovers.

Reaching the Job Seeker

One commercial featured the voices of various workers, explaining why they work: "I work for the future," "I work to create style," "I work because I care," "I work for my family." The spots portrayed a job as more than just a way to make money, but also a way to express passion—stressing that Monster.com is a better way for people to find the job that is right for them.

English Language Arts

Create Think of a marketing job that you might pursue as a "passion." Find listings for similar jobs online. Then write a complete listing for the job you would like to have.

Teaching Abroad

If you are interested in teaching English in another country, you may be in luck. The market for American teachers outside the United States is on the rise. This job offers a way to earn a living while experiencing a different culture.

A World Away Saudi Arabia is a Middle Eastern country seeking teachers for all grade levels. This energy superpower and largely Muslim nation needs English to compete and communicate. Though the country pays high salaries, it presents challenges for some women. One American was not permitted to drive or ride a bike. She was also required

to wear an *abaya*, a loose head-to-toe robe, when outside school. Nonetheless, when asked if she would do it again, she answered, "Yes! In an instant!"

Social Studies

Research Select a country where you might like to teach and outline its eligibility requirements and cultural characteristics that might differ from those of your culture.

Here are some entry-level phrases that are used in conversations about marketing all over the world.

English	Arabic
Hello	Salam
Goodbye	Maasalamah
Yes/No	Naam/la
Thank you	Shukran
You're welcome	Aafwan

Staffing services or temporary help agencies will test you, interview you, and match you with jobs that last from one day to several months. You will be assigned to a company, but the staffing service is your employer. Do your best work because temporary assignments can sometimes lead to permanent positions for the right candidate.

COMPANY PERSONNEL OFFICES

In large companies, the personnel office (often known as *Human Resources*, or HR) handles employment matters, including the hiring of new workers. If you have a networking contact within a large company whom you can ask about job openings, that is an advantage. If not, visit the organization's Web site and click on the "Jobs," "Careers," or "Join Us" links to see what positions are available. While you are visiting the company's Web site, try to find the name of the head of the department in which you are interested in working. Many sites include the names of key employees and their contact information. However, though some companies welcome phone inquiries about job openings, most do not. Be sure to ask a contact if a phone call or drop-in visit to inquire about openings is acceptable. A few large companies and most government agencies, such as the United States Postal Service, may post job openings on public bulletin boards.

If you call for an appointment, it is usually best not to discuss the job on the telephone. You will probably get more consideration by inquiring about the job after you arrive in person. If you are not sure about the best contact strategy, place a quick call to the personnel or human resources department to inquire what the company prefers. You will be better prepared if you have conducted your research about the organization. If the company sells consumer products, familiarize yourself with its products by studying the products and those of its competitors in stores or by reviewing them on their Web sites.

As you research the company, make a note of key words used in the ad. You will learn later how these terms can be helpful in preparing your job application.

The goal is to be fully prepared—as if you are going to an actual interview—whenever you contact a company in any manner. Bring your résumé even if you expect just to fill out an application.

 Reading Check

Explain What is networking?

FOLLOWING UP YOUR JOB LEADS

A letter of inquiry and a polished résumé will be beneficial when you contact the company by regular mail or via e-mail.

In most situations, you can learn about job openings on a company's Web site, through networking contacts, and via direct contact. If these actions do not yield the information you need about potential job openings, you can write a letter of inquiry.

A letter of inquiry, sometimes called a "broadcast letter" or a "marketing letter," describes your skills and defines your job goal.

Letters of inquiry sent to targeted companies can help you learn about unadvertised employment opportunities.

Before writing a letter of inquiry, you should have conducted your research about the company and found the name and contact details of the person to whom you should address your correspondence. Now you are ready to write a letter of inquiry. Be sure to include your résumé with your letter of inquiry as well as all of your contact information.

 After You Read   **Section 38.1**

Review Key Concepts

1. **Define** the term *job lead*.
2. **Discuss** the most effective way to find a job.
3. **Identify** nine possible sources of job leads.

Practice Academics

Social Studies

4. Many employers state in their ads that they are equal opportunity employers. Research the various equal opportunity federal employment laws. Write a summary of the kinds of discrimination that are prohibited by these laws.

Mathematics

5. You work for an employer that encourages workers to ride the train to work by providing train passes at the reduced rate of $16 per week. If you drive to work, your travel costs per week include $10.25 for gas, $25 for parking, and $20 for toll fares. Assuming you work 48 weeks per year, how much will you save if you ride the train?

Math Concept **Problem Solving: Multi-Step Problems** When solving problems that require multiple steps, make a list of the information given in the problem, as well as the information you will be solving. This will make the relationships between what you are looking for and what is given clear.

Starting Hints Add the cost of gas, parking, and toll fares to determine the weekly amount spent on the commute. Multiply the weekly cost of the commute by 48 to determine the amount spent in a year. Multiply the cost of a weekly train pass by 48 to determine what it would cost to ride the train to work.

 connectED.mcgraw-hill.com

Check your answers.

> For help, go to the **Math Skills Handbook** located at the back of this book.

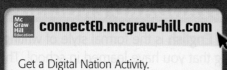
Therefore, everything you write and say to a prospective employer should be in standard English. Standard English employs correct grammar, spelling, pronunciation, and usage. The repeated use of interjections, such as "you know" or "like," is not advisable. Nonstandard pronunciations are also undesirable.

Employers will have several opportunities to evaluate your communication skills. Your letter of application or résumé will indicate your writing skills. Finally, when you are interviewed, the employer will evaluate your verbal communication skills. He or she will also take note of your ability to listen and interact in a businesslike manner.

FILLING OUT APPLICATION FORMS

Most application forms are short (from one to four pages) and ask similar questions. More and more companies and organizations are asking applicants to complete online forms. Companies usually design their own application forms, so you may find differences among various applications.

The application form provides information about your qualifications so company personnel can determine whether to interview you. The first rule of filling out an application form is to complete the form neatly and spell all words correctly. Whenever possible, ask a family member or trusted friend to check your application for errors or omissions. If you complete the form at the place of employment, use a pen with blue or black ink. Do not use colored inks.

Answer every question that applies to you. Write "N/A" for those questions that are not applicable. This shows that you did not overlook the item.

Use your full name, not a nickname, on the form. On most applications, your first name, middle initial, and last name are requested. Provide your complete address, including your ZIP code.

List a specific job title if asked about your job preference. Do not write "anything" as an answer. Employers expect you to know what type of work you can and want to do.

Most application forms include a section on education. Write the names of all the schools you have attended and the dates of attendance. There will also be a section on previous work experience. As a student, you may not have had much work experience. However, you can include short-term or unpaid jobs. Fill out this section in reverse chronological order. Begin with your current or most recent job and end with your first job.

Be prepared to list several **references**. Your references are people who know your work habits and personal traits well and will recommend you for the job. Make sure you ask permission of your references before listing them on an application form. Try to use professional references, such as your teachers, friends established in business, or former employers. Do not list classmates, relatives, or personal friends. Sign your name using your first name, middle initial, and last name. Your signature should be written, never typed or printed.

WRITING COVER LETTERS

A **cover letter** is a letter written by a job applicant to introduce the applicant to an employer and, hopefully, convince the employer to read the résumé. The cover letter should describe why the applicant is the best person to fill a specific job opening. Writing a cover letter is like writing a sales pitch about yourself. Your goal is to **convince** an employer that you are the best person to fill a specific job opening. Your cover letter should reflect your understanding of the company and how you may be able to meet its needs. Cover letters can be submitted via mail, e-mail, or fax. They usually accompany a résumé. A cover letter should be personalized for each position and addressed to an individual. Tell why you are interested in the position and describe your special qualifications for it.

Write a first draft to get down most of the main points. Next, revise your letter until you are pleased with the end result. Ask a teacher, parent or guardian, or friend in business to read and critique your letter. Then put the final touches on it and print out a copy.

Describe how you learned about the job opening in the first paragraph. The second paragraph should contain a description of how your education and experience qualify you for the job. Emphasize facts that make you especially well qualified for the job. Do not repeat the information in the résumé; instead, describe how that experience or education qualifies you for this position. If you have a lot to say about both your education and job experience, use a separate paragraph for each. Mention classes you have taken that are related to the job.

Finally, in your last paragraph, ask for an interview at the employer's convenience. State when you will be available, and provide your telephone number and e-mail address. If your e-mail address is unusual or quirky, create one with a mature name to use for your job search.

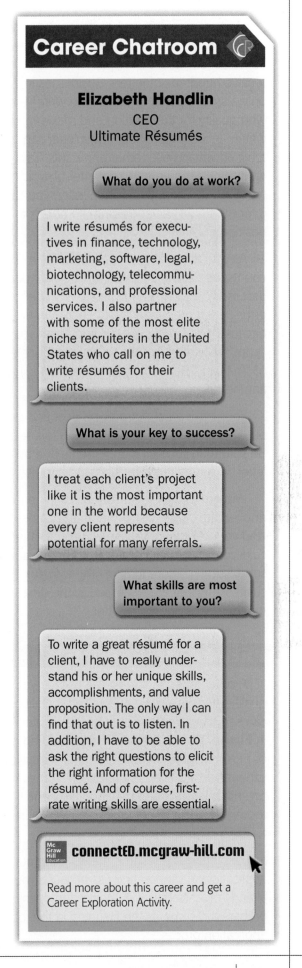

Career Chatroom

Elizabeth Handlin
CEO
Ultimate Résumés

What do you do at work?

I write résumés for executives in finance, technology, marketing, software, legal, biotechnology, telecommunications, and professional services. I also partner with some of the most elite niche recruiters in the United States who call on me to write résumés for their clients.

What is your key to success?

I treat each client's project like it is the most important one in the world because every client represents potential for many referrals.

What skills are most important to you?

To write a great résumé for a client, I have to really understand his or her unique skills, accomplishments, and value proposition. The only way I can find that out is to listen. In addition, I have to be able to ask the right questions to elicit the right information for the résumé. And of course, first-rate writing skills are essential.

connectED.mcgraw-hill.com

Read more about this career and get a Career Exploration Activity.

Many companies receive dozens of cover letters with résumés every week. Businesses that advertise jobs in the newspaper or online may receive hundreds of letters. Businesses interview only a small portion of those who write—those who qualify for the position and make an effective written presentation. Your cover letter can give you a big advantage over other applicants. Take the time to develop an effective letter of which you are really proud. Once you write a letter, you can adapt it for other jobs, personalizing the details to each position.

As with any sales pitch, a good first impression counts. Use the spell-check function of your word processing program to eliminate any spelling errors. Then proofread it with your own eyes because a computer will not know that you meant "from" instead of "form," or "manager" instead of "manger." Before you send your letter, have another person review it for accuracy.

Your letter must not only be neat and clear but also follow the rules outlined in this section. Be sure to include all the elements of a business letter, including the salutation and a formal closing.

Print your cover letter with black ink on white or off-white paper. Use paper that matches the kind you use for your résumé. Keep in mind that colored paper does not fax well. For electronic submission, be sure to apply the formatting suggestions that are discussed in the next section for your *electronic* cover letter.

PREPARING RÉSUMÉS

A cover letter and a résumé convey your qualifications in writing and sell your abilities. You can see an example of a traditional printed résumé in **Figure 38.1**. A **résumé** is a brief summary of personal information, education, skills, work experience, activities, and interests. A résumé organizes job-related facts about you and saves the employer time before and during an interview.

When you send an employer a résumé, include a cover letter. The résumé makes filling out job applications a simpler process because you have already organized all the information. Many people prepare a résumé as the first step in the job application process.

Even if you are not hired, many employers will keep your résumé on file for a certain period of time. If they have an opening for which you qualify in the future, they might call you.

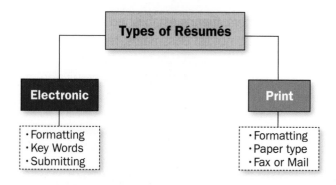

ELECTRONIC RÉSUMÉS

If you are applying for a position online, you may be required to submit an electronic résumé. Compose your electronic résumé using a word processing program.

ELECTRONIC FORMATTING ISSUES

The format of your electronic résumé should be text only. Save your résumé as a text-only file; this is the easiest way to **transmit** and read electronic files. Avoid bold type, italics, and underlining, which do not transmit well and make your résumé difficult to read. Stick to a commonly used traditional font, such as Times New Roman. Keep the font size between 12 and 14 points. Do not use tabs; use the space bar instead.

USING KEY WORDS

Companies that accept résumés electronically often search for job qualifications by looking for key words. It is very likely that a computer program, not a person, will first scan your résumé. The computer scans, or searches, for key words and phrases, and the résumé is summarized and ranked among other qualified candidates.

Because of this, it is important to use key words to describe what you can do. What are key words? Key words consist primarily of nouns. They are usually divided into three categories: job title, industry, and personal traits. You will have a list of key words or phrases from the initial research you did about the company, the industry, and the job.

FIGURE 38.1 Résumé

What Information Should You Include? Your résumé should show off your education, skills, and experience in the best way possible, using one page or a maximum of two pages. *What are some tips for writing a résumé?*

1

Objective Your objective statement should indicate the type of job you want. Change this item if you use the same résumé to apply for a different job.

2

Identification Include your name, address, telephone number, and e-mail address. Do not include your date of birth or your Social Security number.

Frank Johnson
1235 East Tenth Avenue
Ventura, CA 93003
(805) 555-6264
frankjohnson@yourname.com

Objective:
A marketing analyst position that would complement my academic and work experience.

3

Experience List experience related to the specific job for which you are applying, including volunteer work.

Experience:
9/04-present Assistant Marketing Analyst
Ventura Volvo
6580 Leland Street
Ventura, CA 93003

Used computer to estimate sales by model and make recommendations for inventory. Accessed databases using computer terminal to study inventory in relation to buying estimates. Studied historical applications, including media ads, price and color changes, and impact of season.

9/03-9/04 Marketing Assistant
KVEN Radio
Ventura, CA 93003

Assisted Communications Manager in publishing articles and ads, sales presentations, vendor contracts, and trade shows. Contacted vendors for advertising needs (charts, overheads, banners).

4

Education List schools attended from high school on, dates of attendance, and diplomas or degrees earned. Emphasize the courses that are related to the job you are applying for.

Education:
2002-2004 Ventura College. AA in Marketing. Dean's Honor Roll two semesters.

Courses included:
Marketing I and II
Marketing Information Systems
Advertising
Economics I and II
Computer Science

1999-2002 Ventura High School, Graduated in upper 10 percent of class. Served as Vice President of DECA two years.

5

Activities and Awards List school clubs or sports awards, and any recognition you received at work, school, or extracurricular settings.

Personal:
Hobbies include writing computer programs, tennis, and photography.

6

References Include up to three references on a short résumé. Or, indicate that they are available. Always ask people ahead of time if they are willing to be listed as references for you.

References:
Available upon request.

The information you gained from the Internet, publications, or networking will help you figure out which key words to use.

It is important to include industry-specific jargon, as many employers will search by industry language. Be sure to spell out all acronyms. For example, mention your membership in the American Marketing Association, not just AMA. You might not be considered for a job for which you are qualified if key words do not appear on your résumé.

Confidentiality is an issue when you post your résumé on the Internet. Remember that once posted on a career Web site, your résumé is a public document that is out of your control. You will need to provide information so that a potential employer can contact you. Usually, you have the option of limiting your personal information by including only an e-mail address or post office box. Since most employers prefer to contact applicants by telephone or e-mail, make sure your voice mail greeting is professional and brief. Check your messages and e-mails daily so you can respond promptly. Before e-mailing your résumé to employers, e-mail a copy to yourself so that you can review the message.

HOW TO SUBMIT YOUR RÉSUMÉ

When you have completed your cover letter and résumé, you can submit them as part of an e-mail. You can "cut and paste" the résumé into the body of an e-mail message rather than including it as an attached file. An attached file can be difficult to read unless it is created in a word processing program designated by the employer. Also, some employers may be hesitant to open file attachments because of the risk of computer viruses. Some companies will specify what type of electronic form they prefer; read online submission directions carefully to avoid having your résumé rejected.

TRADITIONAL PRINT RÉSUMÉS

In addition to your electronic résumé, prepare a print résumé. You can use it for positions that require a cover letter and résumé to be mailed or faxed. It is also a good idea to keep printed versions of your documents in case your computer files are ever erased or corrupted. If you print your own résumé, use black ink on white or off-white paper. Ideally, the paper should match the kind you use for your cover letter. Some applicants use local printing companies to print their résumés. If you have your résumé printed in this manner, inquire about prices and ask to look at samples of actual résumés. Shop around. Some printing companies offer package deals that include matching paper for your cover letters as well as envelopes.

PRINT FORMATTING ISSUES

As you can see in **Figure 38.1** on p. 903, the format of a résumé helps organize the material and enables the reader to find the information easily. You can review additional styles and formatting options for printed résumés. Look at the many résumé sample books that can be found in your library or bookstore. Many online job search sites also feature samples and free advice about preparing résumés and cover letters. Enter "résumé samples" on your favorite search engine to find many sites where you can view résumés. Many of these Web sites are free, but some do charge for samples. Some students hire writers to help them develop their résumés. You can find these experts in traditional or online *Yellow Pages*. Online résumé writing services can also be a resource. Prices, quality, and turnaround times vary; again, shop around.

PREPARING FOR AN INTERVIEW

What happens during an interview is usually what determines an employer's choice of one applicant over another applicant. It is critical to prepare yourself carefully for your interview. Your plan should include three steps: preparing for the interview, conducting yourself properly during the interview, and following up after the interview.

The employer's first impression of you will have a significant impact on his or her hiring decision. Appropriate dress and grooming, body language that shows confidence, and use of standard English all combine to make a good first impression.

DRESS AND GROOMING

More recently employers in many offices and stores have adopted a dress code known as *business casual.* This does not mean, however, that you should dress casually for an interview. It is better to take extra time and effort to make a good impression by dressing in a more formal way.

Your clothes should be neat, clean, and wrinkle-free for every interview. In some cases, appropriate interview dress depends on the job. In sales, for example, people dress formally and conservatively to make a good impression on customers.

Regardless of its style, your hair should be clean and neat. The interviewer will be observing you to see how well you will fit in, so a moderate hairstyle is prudent.

Employers will notice hands—be sure they are clean and your nails are neatly trimmed. Nail polish, if worn, should be clear or a pale, subtle color. Extravagant jewelry can be distracting. Too much makeup can also distract the interviewer. Avoid wearing perfume or cologne as well. Strong scents can be overwhelming and distracting, and some people are allergic to them.

THINGS TO KNOW

When you get a call from a company for an interview appointment, write down the date and time and the name of the interviewer. Check the spelling and make sure you can pronounce the interviewer's name correctly. Ask the receptionist for the pronunciation if it is unfamiliar to you.

Preparation is essential to a good interview. Research the types of questions you expect to be asked, and have a friend, family member, or teacher role-play the interview with you. Practicing your answers and then reviewing how you did is a good way to become more comfortable.

Before you get to your actual interview, take time to carefully review your résumé. Be ready to answer any questions about your education, work experience, and other qualifications.

The research you have conducted about a company will again come in handy in an interview situation. Your knowledge of the business will help you make a better impression. You will be able to speak intelligently about the company's products and operations. It will show that you are interested in the firm.

There are a few common sense basics to remember when interviewing for a job: Look at the interviewer, pay attention, do not hesitate to ask questions, and answer questions as precisely as you can. *Why is it a good idea to prepare a few questions before the interview?*

The Interview

The following questions are often asked of job applicants during interviews. Write the answers to these questions, and then practice answering them. Ask a family member, teacher, or friend to help you by asking the questions and giving you feedback on your anwers.

- ▶ Why do you want to work for this company?
- ▶ Do you want permanent or temporary work?
- ▶ Why do you think you can do this job?
- ▶ What jobs have you had? Why did you leave?
- ▶ What classes did you like best in school?
- ▶ In what school activities have you participated?
- ▶ What do you want to be doing in five years?
- ▶ Do you prefer working alone or with others?
- ▶ What are your main strengths and weaknesses?
- ▶ What salary do you expect?
- ▶ What grades have you received in school?
- ▶ How do you feel about working overtime?
- ▶ How many days were you absent from school last year?
- ▶ Why should I hire you?
- ▶ When can you begin work?

Under federal law, employers cannot make employment decisions on the basis of race or ethnicity, gender, religion, marital status, age, country of origin, sexual orientation, or physical and/or mental status. A job interviewer should not ask questions about these topics.

The law requires employers to give every job applicant the same consideration. This concept is known as equal opportunity. Questions asked during a job interview should address only the factors that relate to the ability of an applicant to carry out the work required.

The interviewer may unknowingly ask you an unlawful question, or that person may ask you a lawful question using the wrong words. In an interview setting, it is often best to give an answer based on the *intent* of the question.

For example, you may be asked whether you are a United States citizen. It is not legal to ask that question. However, it *is* legal to ask whether you are authorized to work in the United States. In such a case, it is usually best to respond to the question as if it had been worded properly.

Federal law makes it illegal to discriminate in hiring decisions based on a disability, unless it would cause the employer significant hardship. *What qualities do many disabled people have that would make them good employees?*

Ability

If asked unlawful questions, you have three choices, with the last choice being the most sensible:

1. You can answer truthfully if you feel your answer will not harm you.

2. You can say the question is inappropriate because of laws against discrimination in hiring (though this may prevent you from getting the job).

3. You can sidestep the question and base your answer on the requirements of the job and your ability to perform it.

APPROPRIATE CONDUCT DURING AN INTERVIEW

Always go alone to a job interview. If someone must accompany you on the day of the interview, ask that person to wait for you outside in a public location. Plan to arrive for your interview five to ten minutes early. Always allow some extra time in case you run into delays. Do not be too early, though. Waiting outside the interviewer's door for half an hour is not comfortable for you or the employer.

Turn off your cell phone before you enter the building where the interview will take place. A ringing cell phone during the interview will likely disqualify you. If your watch beeps, do not wear it.

Before you meet the interviewer, you may meet a receptionist, administrative assistant, or other employee. Be courteous and polite to anyone you meet. These people might be your future co-workers.

If you have not already completed an application form, you may be asked to do so before or after the interview. Be prepared by bringing a good pen or two with black or blue ink. You may also need to supply your Social Security number and your references. Bring along several copies of your résumé to the interview to leave with your interviewer(s). Your résumé will also help you to fill out an application form. A zippered folder is handy for carrying pens, copies of your résumé, and your list of references.

Remain standing until you are asked to sit down. Sit up straight, leaning forward slightly toward the interviewer to show interest. Relax and focus on your purpose to make the best impression.

Place your purse or briefcase on the floor by your chair. Never put anything on the interviewer's desk, even if there is room. This may appear disrespectful or too casual.

It is normal to feel a little nervous at the beginning of an interview. You will relax as the interview progresses. Keep your hands in your lap, and try to keep them still. Never place your hands on the interviewer's desk. Look the interviewer in the eye most of the time and listen to him or her carefully. Be careful not to interrupt when the interviewer is speaking. Be confident, smile, and be yourself. The employer has taken the time to interview you because he or she has confidence that you are a qualified candidate.

WHAT TO SAY IN AN INTERVIEW

Most interviewers begin by asking specific questions. Answer each question honestly. If you do not know the answer to a particular question, say so. The interviewer will probably be able to tell if you try to fake an answer. Keep your answers short and to the point.

Two particular questions often cause problems for young job applicants. These questions are: "What type of work would you like to do?" and "What compensation (wage or salary) do you expect?" You can answer the first question by giving the name of the specific job you want. The question about expected employment compensation is a little more difficult if you do not have a specific wage or salary in mind. The best approach is to do your research before the interview to find out the wages usually pay for the type of work for which you are applying. Once you have this information, you can answer with a range of pay suitable for the job.

Wages and benefits are usually discussed toward the end of an interview. If your interviewer does not mention pay, wait until the interview is almost over. Then ask how much the job pays. If you know that there will be a second interview before the job is offered, you may wait until then to ask about salary. You may also want to ask about benefits if you are applying for a full-time permanent job. Benefits may include paid vacation time, sick days, holidays, and insurance coverage.

The interviewer will expect you to ask some questions. This shows the interviewer that you have done your research and are interested in learning more. Job applicants often ask questions like those listed below:

- ► Why is the position vacant?
- ► What are the typical responsibilities for this position?
- ► Would I work individually or with a team?
- ► With what other areas of the company would I interact on a regular basis?
- ► What type of training or orientation would I receive?
- ► What are some of the issues the new hire will need to address immediately?
- ► Please tell me about the department in which I would work.
- ► What is the typical career path for someone starting in this position? What are the opportunities for advancement and what skills would be required?
- ► Will I have regular evaluations or reviews?
- ► What is the company's structure?
- ► To whom would I report?
- ► Will I need to take any tests as part of the interview process?
- ► What is the dress code?
- ► What are the hours of work?
- ► Would I be expected to work on weekends?
- ► Does the position require any travel?
- ► Is overtime common on this job?
- ► What benefits do you offer?
- ► When will you make your hiring decision?

CLOSING THE INTERVIEW

At the close of the interview, one of several things can happen. You may be offered the job, or you may be told that you will not be hired. More likely, however, you will be told that a decision will be made later. You may be asked to a second interview with someone else in the company, such as a department head. This usually means you have made a good impression in your first interview, and your chances of being offered the job are good.

If you are interested in the position, let the interviewer know. You can ask if another

interview is required. Be a good salesperson and say something like, "I am very impressed with what I've seen and heard here today, and I am confident that I could do an excellent job in the position you've described to me. When might you be in a position to make an offer?" If an offer is extended, accept it only if you are ready. If you are sure that you want it, accept it on the spot. If you want some time to think it over, be courteous and tactful in asking for that time. It is not unreasonable to want to think about this decision before making a commitment. Set a date when you can answer (usually 24 to 48 hours).

You will be able to sense when the interview is almost over. Then you should stand, smile, and thank your interviewer for his or her time and consideration. Shake hands and go. Be sure to thank the receptionist or administrative assistant on your way out.

FOLLOWING UP AFTER AN INTERVIEW

A thank-you letter or e-mail is an appropriate way to follow up most interviews. Thank the employer and reaffirm your interest in the job.

Include any information that you may have forgotten to mention during the interview that will help qualify you for the position. Your letter may be either handwritten or typed, but it must be neat.

Many employers check references and call your school for a recommendation. This may take several days. Unless you were told not to call, it is all right to telephone the employer five or six days after the interview. Ask to speak with the person who interviewed you. Then give your name and ask if he or she has made a decision on the job. This will let the employer know that you are still interested.

If you are not selected for the job, try not to be discouraged. Do not take it personally. Learn from the experience. You will be better prepared next time.

 Reading Check

Recall What is usually the best way to handle interview questions unrelated to your ability to carry out the work required?

AFTER YOU ARE HIRED

After you begin a new job, there are several steps you can take to enhance your career growth and future job searches:

▶ Thank all those who interviewed you.

▶ Analyze employer expectations in the business environment.

▶ Identify skills needed to enhance career progression.

▶ List accomplishments and awards received individually or as part of a team.

▶ If applicable, keep samples of your work (but get written permission from your employer first).

▶ Save copies of reviews and evaluations.

▶ Take advantage of any opportunity to learn new skills or receive training.

▶ Build your networking contacts.

▶ Volunteer for committee responsibilities unrelated to your job which may help you stand out in the company and may uncover your next career step.

▶ Be a team player and work to the best of your ability.

 After You Read | **Section 38.2**

Review Key Concepts

1. **List** the basic categories of information to include in a résumé.
2. **Name** three steps to achieve a successful interview.
3. **Describe** how to learn about a company in order to prepare for an interview.

Practice Academics Skills

English Language Arts

4. Find three job leads, including at least one in marketing. Prepare a résumé for one of these jobs. Use the format of the résumé in Figure 38.1, but include information only about yourself.

Mathematics

5. You want to determine the take-home pay for a new job offer. The job pays $18 per hour for 40 hours, plus an additional 5 hours per week at time-and-a-half. You will work 50 weeks per year. If the combined withholding of taxes on your pay is 28 percent, what will your total annual net pay be?

Math Concept **Problem Solving: Multi-Step Problems** When solving problems that require multiple steps, make a list of information given in the problem, as well as information you will be solving. This will make the relationships between what you are looking for and what is given clear.

Starting Hints To solve this problem, multiply the base pay by 1.5 to determine the value of time-and-a-half. Multiply the value of time-and-a-half by 5 and add it to $18 times 40 to determine the weekly salary. Multiply the weekly salary by 50 to determine the annual salary. Multiply the yearly salary by 0.72 to calculate the value after taxes.

 connectED.mcgraw-hill.com

Check your answers.

For help, go to the **Math Skills Handbook** located at the back of this book.

Finding and Applying for a Job

Job leads are found through networking contacts, the Internet, professional people, former employers, employment agencies, and temporary staffing agencies.

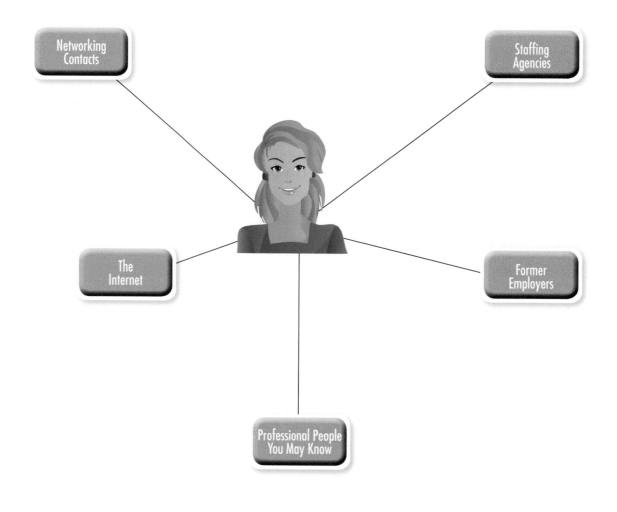

Review and Activities

Written Summary

- You can find job leads through many sources, and you should make use of most of them.
- Among the best sources are networking contacts, the Internet, professional people, former employers, and employment and temporary staffing agencies.
- You may apply for a job by filling out an application form or by submitting a résumé with a cover letter.
- The decision to hire is almost always made during or following the interview.
- For each job interview, conduct yourself properly during the interview, and follow up after each interview.

Review Content Vocabulary and Academic Vocabulary

1. Create a fill-in-the-blank sentence for each of these vocabulary terms. The sentence should contain enough information to help determine the missing word.

   Content Vocabulary
   - job lead (p. 893)
   - networking (p. 893)
   - public employment agencies (p. 894)
   - private employment agencies (p. 894)
   - staffing/temporary agencies (p. 894)
   - standard English (p. 899)
   - references (p. 901)
   - cover letter (p. 901)
   - résumé (p. 902)

   Academic Vocabulary
   - contacting (p. 893)
   - pursuing (p. 894)
   - convince (p. 901)
   - transmit (p. 902)

Assess for Understanding

2. **Contrast** What are two methods of contacting job leads and one advantage for each method?
3. **Describe** How do you network?
4. **Justify** Why is it important to include a cover letter with your résumé?
5. **Delineate** What information does a résumé contain?
6. **Role Play** How can you make a good first impression at a job interview?
7. **Create** What are some rules of conduct to follow during the interview?
8. **Sequence** What are appropriate ways to follow up after an interview?
9. **Share** What are the three criteria for a hiring decision?

21st  Century Skills

People Skills

10. **The Interview** Prepare a study sheet listing questions that you may be asked during an interview and the answers that you would give. Also, list questions that you would plan to ask an interviewer.

Financial Literacy Skills

11. **Salary Options** Following an interview for a job in sales, you are offered the job and told that you may have your choice of two methods of calculating your pay. Either you will be paid a straight salary of $800 per week or a base salary of $500 per week, plus commissions of 12 percent of sales. In your last job, you sold $4,000 a week. Assuming you will continue to sell at least that amount, which salary option should you take? What is the difference between the two?

e-Marketing Skills

12. **Marketing Yourself** You know that the process of applying for a employment is a job in itself. You have to convince an employer that you can perform the duties and carry out the responsibilities in a way that satisfies the company and helps make the company profitable. You do this by writing a convincing résumé and accompanying cover letter. You continue marketing yourself by performing well during your interviews. Write a one-page report describing how you will go about marketing yourself to an employer.

- What research will you perform before drafting your résumé and cover letter?
- How will you prepare ahead of time for your interview?
- What skills and character traits will you highlight in your documents and during the interview?
- What steps will you take after the interview to ensure that you leave a good impression?

Build Academic Skills

English Language Arts

13. **Following Up an Interview** You have just been interviewed for a job that you believe you would enjoy and that you think you could do very well. Write a thank-you letter to the interviewer. Remember to keep your letter brief and to the point.

Social Studies

14. **Gender Equity** Use the Internet to research gender pay equity in the United States. Write a one-page report on the history of this issue and current developments.

Mathematics

15. **Average Rate of Pay** You work full time for a local department store as a manager. For three days a week, you work a standard nine-to-five shift. For two days a week, you work a split shift. Your pay is $20 per hour. However, on the two days you work a split shift, you receive an 8-percent pay differential, which makes your pay $21.60 per hour for those two 8-hour days. What is your average rate of pay for the 40-hour week?

Math Concept **Number and Operations: Averages** You can determine an average by adding all the values and dividing by the number of values added. When calculating average pay, be sure to calculate the correct totals before dividing.

For help, go to the **Math Skills Handbook** located at the back of this book.

Standardized Test Practice

Directions Read the following questions. On a separate piece of paper, write the best possible answer for each one.

1. Employers most often make hiring decisions based on:

   A. how well you can do the job.

   B. how willing you are to do the job.

   C. how well you fit in.

   D. all of the above.

2. Key words are an important part of preparing electronic résumés.

   T

   F

3. The decision of whether to hire a job applicant is often made during the _____.

Test-Taking Tip

Start early. Make sure that you have sufficient time to study so that you are well prepared for the test.

DECA Connection Role Play

Marketing Student High School Class

Situation As part of your marketing class, you are able to earn an extra unit of credit if you find and secure a part-time job related to the field of marketing. Your teacher has provided information about the types of jobs that are acceptable in order to earn the extra credit. You have never applied for a job before now. The only job you have had is babysitting for neighbors. You know that there are several things you need to consider before you apply for a job and several things you can do to enhance your chances of being hired. A family friend (judge) works in the human resources department of a local business. Your friend (judge) has agreed to assist you in your job search, and to help you prepare to apply for your first job. Your friend (judge) has suggested that you meet this afternoon to discuss your job preparation efforts.

Activity You are to discuss with your friend (judge) your preparations for your search for your first job. Be sure to mention your résumé preparation and job application letter. You are also to discuss your preparations for using job-search strategies, completing job applications, and preparation for the interview process.

Evaluation You will be evaluated on how well you meet the following performance indicators:

1. Utilize job search strategies.
2. Complete a job application.
3. Interview for a job.
4. Prepare a résumé.
5. Write a letter of application.

 connectED.mcgraw-hill.com

Download the Competitive Events Workbook for more Role-Play practice.

SuperStock RF / SuperStock

A Digital Résumé
for a Marketing Internship

How would you prepare a digital résumé and portfolio for a marketing internship position?

Scenario

A new professional sports stadium will be opening in your community. There are several internships available in advertising, marketing, sales, and public relations. The job description for this stadium's internship program states that applicants must be able to prioritize assignments, attend to details, and handle several tasks at one time. Other qualities required are excellent interpersonal and communications skills. The intern must demonstrate professionalism, courtesy, and high motivation to learn. Interns may be asked to work on projects such as event planning, community relations, as well as conduct surveys and help with pre-game and post-game activities.

The Skills You'll Use

Academic Skills Reading, writing, social studies, researching, and analyzing

Basic Skills Speaking, listening, thinking, and interpersonal

Technology Skills Word processing, spreadsheet, presentation, telecommunications, and the Internet

Your Objective

Your objective is to prepare a digital résumé and portfolio to apply for a marketing internship program at a new soccer stadium.

STEP 1 Do Your Research

Conduct research to find job descriptions and requirements for marketing internship programs. Identify the key words that you should include in your digital résumé. Search for specific sports-team job opportunities to further refine the key words for your résumé. As you conduct your research, answer these questions:

- What key words and other information should you include in your résumé?
- What digital media have other applicants used to apply for marketing positions?
- What digital medium should you use to prepare your résumé and portfolio?

Write a summary of your research.

STEP 2 Plan Your Project

Now that you have completed your research, you need to begin planning your project.

- Research required skills and job description characteristics for a marketing internship position.
- Assess your skills, knowledge, and personal characteristics for inclusion in your résumé.
- Decide on the digital medium to use to prepare your résumé and present your portfolio of marketing projects.
- Use what you learn to prepare your résumé and digital portfolio.

STEP 3 Connect with Your Community

- Interview a human resources manager to find out what should be included in a résumé so that it stands out from others in the pool of applicants.
- Interview a marketing manager of a local business to determine which aspects of marketing appeal to you.
- Take notes during your interviews and transcribe your notes after your interviews.

STEP 4 Share What You Learn

Assume that your class is the human resources staff for the new professional sports team's stadium. The staff is responsible for selecting the marketing interns for in-person interviews.

- Present your résumé and digital portfolio in an oral presentation. Be prepared to answer questions
- Present a hard copy of your résumé and portfolio for further evaluation.

STEP 5 Evaluate Your Marketing and Academic Skills

Your project will be evaluated based on the following:

- Your résumé and portfolio for a marketing internship program
- Your understanding of the online job application process
- Selection and use of digital media for your résumé and portfolio
- Research on marketing internship requirements
- Organization and continuity of presentation
- Mechanics—presentation and neatness
- Speaking and listening skills.

Marketing Internship Project Checklist

Plan
- ✓ Conduct research on marketing internship programs.
- ✓ Design your own résumé and portfolio in a digital medium.

Write
- ✓ Explain the job descriptions and requirements for marketing internship programs you find.
- ✓ Write your résumé and create your portfolio.

Present
- ✓ Present your résumé and portfolio.
- ✓ Explain why you selected the digital media you used in your portfolio.

 connectED.mcgraw-hill.com

Evaluate Download a rubric you can use to evaluate your final project.

my marketing portfolio

Internship Report Once you have completed your Marketing Internship Project and oral presentation, put your written report and a few printouts of key slides from your oral presentation in your Marketing Portfolio.

Résumé and Portfolio Do research on a career of your choice. Learn the job requirements and necessary skills. Build a résumé and a portfolio for an internship for that career. Find out which related companies are hiring interns. Apply for an internship with one of the companies. What kind of résumé will you prepare? What key words will you include in your résumé? How will you present your résumé—in hard copy or digitally? What will you include in your portfolio? How will you prepare your portfolio for that position? Submit a hard copy of your résumé and portfolio. Decide what you will do after submitting your résumé and portfolio to follow up.

MARKETING CORE FUNCTIONS

 Product/Service Management

 Selling

Making Career Choices

A career differs from a job in that it is a series of progressively more responsible jobs in one field or a related field. You will need to learn some special skills to choose a career and to help you in your job search. Choosing a career and identifying career opportunities require careful thought and preparation. To aid you in making important career choices, follow these steps:

Steps to Making a Career Decision

1. Conduct a self-assessment to determine your:
   • values
   • lifestyle goals
   • interests
   • skills and aptitudes
   • personality
   • work environment preferences
   • relationship preferences

2. Identify possible career choices based on your self-assessment.

3. Gather information on each choice, including future trends.

4. Evaluate your choices based on your self-assessment.

5. Make your decision.

After you make your decision, plan how you will reach your goal. It is best to have short-term, medium-term, and long-term goals. In making your choices, explore the future opportunities in this field or fields over the next several years. What impact will new technology and automation have on job opportunities in the next few years? Remember, if you plan, you make your own career opportunities.

Personal Career Portfolio

You will want to create and maintain a personal career portfolio. In it you will keep all the documents you create and receive in your job search:

• Contact list
• Résumé
• Letters of recommendation
• Employer evaluations
• Awards
• Evidence of participation in school, community, and volunteer activities
• Notes about your job search
• Notes made after your interviews

Career Research Resources

In order to gather information on various career opportunities, there are a variety of sources to research:

• **Libraries.** Your school or public library offers good career information resources. Here you will find books, magazines, pamphlets, films, videos, and special reference materials on careers. In particular, the U.S. Department of Labor publishes three reference books that are helpful: the *Dictionary of ccupational Titles (DOT),* which describes about 20,000 jobs and their relationships with data, people, and things; the *Occupational Outlook Handbook (OOH),* with information on more than 200 occupations; and the *Guide for Occupational Exploration (GOE),* a reference that organizes the world of work into 12 interest areas that are subdivided into work groups and subgroups.

- **The Internet.** The Internet is becoming a primary source of research on any topic. It is especially helpful in researching careers.
- **Career Consultations.** Career consultation, an informational interview with a professional who works in a career that interests you, provides an opportunity to learn about the day-to-day realities of a career.
- **On-the-Job Experience.** On-the-job experience can be valuable in learning firsthand about a job or career. You can find out if your school has a work-experience program, or look into a company or organization's internship opportunities. Interning gives you direct work experience and often allows you to make valuable contacts for future full-time employment.

The Job Search

To aid you in your actual job search, there are various sources to explore. You should contact and research all the sources that might produce a job lead, or information about a job. Keep a contact list as you proceed with your search. Some of these resources include:

- **Networking with family, friends, and acquaintances.** This means contacting people you know personally, including school counselors, former employers, and professional people.
- **Cooperative education and work-experience programs.** Many schools have such programs in which students work part-time on a job related to one of their classes. Many also offer work-experience programs that are not limited to just one career area, such as marketing.
- **Newspaper ads.** Reading the Help Wanted advertisements in your local papers will provide a source of job leads, as well as teach you about the local job market.
- **Employment agencies.** Most cities have two types of employment agencies, public and private. These employment agencies match workers with jobs. Some private agencies may charge a fee, so be sure to know who is expected to pay the fee and what the fee is.
- **Company personnel offices.** Large and medium-sized companies have personnel offices to handle employment matters, including the hiring of new workers. You can check on job openings by contacting the office by telephone or by scheduling a personal visit.
- **Searching the Internet.** Cyberspace offers multiple opportunities for your job search. Web sites, such as Hotjobs.com or Monster.com, provide lists of companies offering employment. There are tens of thousands of career-related Web sites, so the challenge is finding those that have jobs that interest you and that are up-to-date in their listings. Companies that interest you may have a Web site, which will provide valuable information on their benefits and opportunities for employment.

Applying for a Job

When you have contacted the sources of job leads and found some jobs that interest you, the next step is to apply for them. You will need to complete application forms, write letters of application, and prepare your own résumé. Before you apply for a job, you will need to have a work permit if you are under the age of 18 in most states. Some state and federal labor laws designate certain jobs

917

as too dangerous for young workers. Laws also limit the number of hours of work allowed during a day, a week, or the school year. You will also need to have proper documentation, such as a green card if you are not a U.S. citizen.

Job Application

You can obtain the job application form directly at the place of business, by requesting it in writing, or over the Internet. It is best if you can fill the form out at home, but some businesses require that you fill it out at the place of work.

Fill out the job application forms neatly and accurately, using standard English, the formal style of speaking and writing you learned in school. You must be truthful and pay attention to detail in filling out the form.

Personal Fact Sheet

To be sure that the answers you write on a job application form are accurate, make a personal fact sheet before filling out the application:

- Your name, home address, and phone number
- Your Social Security number
- The job you are applying for
- The date you can begin work
- The days and hours you can work
- The pay you want
- Whether or not you have been convicted of a crime
- Your education
- Your previous work experience
- Your birth date
- Your driver's license number if you have one
- Your interests and hobbies, and awards you have won
- Your previous work experience, including dates
- Schools you have attended
- Places you have lived
- Accommodations you may need from the employer
- A list of references—people who will tell an employer that you will do a good job, such as relatives, students, former employers, and the like

Letters of Recommendation

Letters of recommendation are helpful. You can request teachers, counselors, relatives, and other acquaintances who know you well to write these letters. They should be short, to the point, and give a brief overview of your assets. A brief description of any of your important accomplishments or projects should follow. The letter should end with a brief description of your character and work ethic.

Letter of Application

Some employees prefer a letter of application, rather than an application form. This letter is like writing a sales pitch about yourself. You need to tell why you are the best person for the job, what special qualifications you have, and include all the information usually found on an application form. Write the letter in standard English, making certain that it is neat, accurate, and correct.

Résumé

The purpose of a résumé is to make an employer want to interview you. A résumé tells prospective employers what you are like and what you can do for them. A good résumé summarizes you in a one- or two-page outline. It should include the following information:

1. **Identification.** Include your name, address, telephone number, and e-mail address.
2. **Objective.** Indicate the type of job you are looking for.
3. **Experience.** List experience related to the specific job for which you are applying. List other work if you have not worked in a related field.
4. **Education.** List schools attended from high school on, dates of attendance, and diplomas or degrees earned. You may also include courses related to the job you are applying for.
5. **References.** Include up to three references or indicate that they are available. Always ask people ahead of time if they are willing to be listed as references for you.

A résumé that you put online or send by e-mail is called an *electronic résumé*. Some Web sites allow you to post them on their sites without charge. Employers access these sites to find new employees. Your electronic résumé should follow the guidelines for a regular one. It needs to be accurate. Stress your skills and sell yourself to prospective employers.

Cover Letter

If you are going to get the job you want, you need to write a great cover letter to accompany your résumé. Think of a cover letter as an introduction: a piece of paper that conveys a smile, a confident hello, and a nice, firm handshake. The cover letter is the first thing a potential employer sees, and it can make a powerful impression. The following are some tips for creating a cover letter that is professional and gets the attention you want:

- **Keep it short.** Your cover letter should be one page, no more.
- **Make it look professional.** These days, you need to type your letter on a computer and print it on a laser printer. Do not use an inkjet printer unless it produces extremely crisp type. Use white or buff-colored paper; anything else will draw the wrong kind of attention. Type your name, address, phone number, and e-mail address at the top of the page.
- **Explain why you are writing.** Start your letter with one sentence describing where you heard of the opening. "Joan Wright suggested I contact you regarding a position in your marketing department," or "I am writing to apply for the position you advertised in the Sun City Journal."
- **Introduce yourself.** Give a short description of your professional abilities and background. Refer to your attached résumé: "As you will see in the attached résumé, I am an experienced editor with a background in newspapers, magazines, and textbooks." Then highlight one or two specific accomplishments.
- **Sell yourself.** Your cover letter should leave the reader thinking, "This person is exactly what we are looking for." Focus on what you can do for the company. Relate your skills to the skills and responsibilities mentioned in the job listing. If the ad mentions solving problems, relate a problem you solved at school or work. If the ad mentions specific skills or knowledge required, mention your mastery of these in your letter. (Also be sure these skills are included on your résumé.)
- **Provide all requested information.** If an ad asks for "salary requirements" or "salary history," include this information in your cover letter. However, you do not have to give specific numbers. It is okay to say, "My wage is in the range of $10 to $15 per hour." If the employer does not ask for this information, do not offer it.

- **Ask for an interview.** You have sold yourself, now wrap it up. Be confident, but not pushy. "If you agree that I would be an asset to your company, please call me at [insert your phone number]. I am available for an interview at your convenience." Finally, thank the person. "Thank you for your consideration. I look forward to hearing from you soon." Always close with a "Sincerely," followed by your full name and signature.
- **Check for errors.** Read and re-read your letter to make sure each sentence is correctly worded and there are no errors in spelling, punctuation, or grammar. Do not rely on your computer's spell checker or grammar checker. A spell check will not detect if you typed "tot he" instead of "to the." It is a good idea to have someone else read your letter, too. He or she might notice an error you overlooked.

 Interview

Understanding how to best prepare for and follow up on interviews is critical to your career success. At different times in your life, you may interview with a teacher or professor, a prospective employer, a supervisor, or a promotion or tenure committee. Just as having an excellent résumé is vital for opening the door, interview skills are critical for putting your best foot forward and seizing the opportunity to clearly articulate why you are the best person for the job.

Research the Company

Your ability to convince an employer that you understand and are interested in the field you are interviewing to enter is important. Show that you have knowledge about the company and the industry. What products or services does the company offer? How is it doing? What is the competition? Use your research to demonstrate your understanding of the company.

Prepare Questions for the Interviewer

Prepare interview questions to ask the interviewer. Some examples include:

- "What would my responsibilities be?"
- "Could you describe my work environment?"
- "What are the chances to move up in the company?"
- "Do you offer training?"
- "What can you tell me about the people who work here?"

Dress Appropriately

You will never get a second chance to make a good first impression. Nonverbal communication is 90 percent of communication, so dressing appropriately is of the utmost importance. Every job is different, and you should wear clothing that is appropriate for the job for which you are applying. In most situations, you will be safe if you wear clean, pressed, conservative business clothes in neutral colors. Pay special attention to grooming. Keep makeup light and wear very little jewelry. Make certain your nails and hair are clean, trimmed, and neat. Do not carry a large purse, backpack, books, or coat. Simply carry a pad of paper, a pen, and extra copies of your résumé and letters of reference in a small folder.

Exhibit Good Behavior

Conduct yourself properly during an interview. Go alone; be courteous and polite to everyone you meet. Relax and focus on your purpose: to make the best possible impression.

- Be on time.
- Be poised and relaxed.
- Avoid nervous habits.
- Avoid littering your speech with verbal clutter such as "you know," "um," and "like."
- Look your interviewer in the eye and speak with confidence.
- Use nonverbal techniques to reinforce your confidence, such as a firm handshake and poised demeanor.
- Convey maturity by exhibiting the ability to tolerate differences of opinion.
- Never call anyone by a first name unless you are asked to do so.
- Know the name, title, and the pronunciation of the interviewer's name.
- Do not sit down until the interviewer does.
- Do not talk too much about your personal life.
- Never bad-mouth your former employers.

Be Prepared for Common Interview Questions

You can never be sure exactly what will happen at an interview, but you can be prepared for common interview questions. There are some interview questions that are illegal. Interviewers should not ask you about your age, gender, color, race, or religion. Employers should not ask whether you are married or pregnant, or question your health or disabilities.

Take time to think about your answers now. You might even write them down to clarify your thinking. The key to all interview questions is to be honest, and to be positive. Focus your answers on skills and abilities that apply to the job you are seeking. Practice answering the following questions with a friend:

- "Tell me about yourself."
- "Why do you want to work at this company?"
- "What did you like/dislike about your last job?"
- "What is your biggest accomplishment?"
- "What is your greatest strength?"
- "What is your greatest weakness?"
- "Do you prefer to work with others or on your own?"
- "What are your career goals?" or "Where do you see yourself in five years?"
- "Tell me about a time that you had a lot of work to do in a short time. How did you manage the situation?"
- "Have you ever had to work closely with a person you didn't get along with? How did you handle the situation?"

After the Interview

Be sure to thank the interviewer after the interview for his or her time and effort. Do not forget to follow up after the interview. Ask, "What is the next step?" If you are told to call in a few days, wait two or three days before calling back.

If the interview went well, the employer may call you to offer you the job. Find out the terms of the job offer, including job title and pay. Decide whether you want the job. If you decide not to accept the job, write a letter of rejection. Be courteous and thank the person for the opportunity and the offer. You may wish to give a brief general reason for not accepting the job. Leave the door open for possible employment in the future.

Follow Up With a Letter

Write a thank-you letter as soon as the interview is over. This shows your good manners, interest, and enthusiasm for the job. It also shows that you are organized. Make the letter neat and courteous. Thank the interviewer. Sell yourself again.

Accepting a New Job

If you decide to take the job, write a letter of acceptance. The letter should include some words of appreciation for the opportunity, written acceptance of the job offer, the terms of employment (salary, hours, benefits), and the starting date. Make sure the letter is neat and correct.

Starting a New Job

Your first day of work will be busy. Determine what the dress code is and dress appropriately. Learn to do each task assigned properly. Ask for help when you need it. Learn the rules and regulations of the workplace.

You will do some paperwork on your first day. Bring your personal fact sheet with you. You will need to fill out some forms. Form W-4 tells your employer how much money to withhold for taxes. You may also need to fill out Form I-9. This shows that you are allowed to work in the United States. You will need your Social Security number and proof that you are allowed to work in the United States. You can bring your U.S. passport, your Certificate of Naturalization, or your Certificate of U.S. Citizenship. If you are not a permanent resident of the United States, bring your green card. If you are a resident of the United States, you will need to bring your work permit on your first day. If you are under the age of 16 in some states, you need a different kind of work permit.

You might be requested to take a drug test as a requirement for employment in some states. This could be for the safety of you and your coworkers, especially when working with machinery or other equipment.

Important Skills and Qualities

You will not work alone on a job. You will need to learn skills for getting along and being a team player. There are many good qualities necessary to get along in the workplace. They include being positive, showing sympathy, taking an interest in others, tolerating differences, laughing a little, and showing respect. Your employer may promote you or give you a raise if you show good employability skills. You must also communicate with your employer. For example, if you will be sick or late to work, you should call your employer as soon as possible.

There are several qualities necessary to be a good employee and get ahead in your job:

- be cooperative
- possess good character
- be responsible
- finish what you start

- work fast but do a good job
- have a strong work ethic
- work well without supervision
- work well with others
- possess initiative
- show enthusiasm for what you do
- be on time
- make the best of your time
- obey company laws and rules
- be honest
- be loyal
- exhibit good health habits

Leaving a Job

If you are considering leaving your job or are being laid off, you are facing one of the most difficult aspects in your career. The first step in resigning is to prepare a short resignation letter to offer your supervisor at the conclusion of the meeting you set up with him or her. Keep the letter short and to the point. Express your appreciation for the opportunity you had with the company. Do not try to list all that was wrong with the job.

You want to leave on good terms. Do not forget to ask for a reference. Do not talk about your employer or any of your coworkers. Do not talk negatively about your employer when you apply for a new job.

If you are being laid off or face downsizing, it can make you feel angry or depressed. Try to view it as a career-change opportunity. If possible, negotiate a good severance package. Find out about any benefits you may be entitled to. Perhaps the company will offer job-search services or consultation for finding new employment.

Take Action!

It is time for action. Remember the networking and contact lists you created when you searched for this job. Reach out for support from friends, family, and other acquaintances. Consider joining a job-search club. Assess your skills. Upgrade them if necessary. Examine your attitude and your vocational choices. Decide the direction you wish to take and move on!

Number and Operations

▶ *Understand numbers, ways of representing numbers, relationships among numbers, and number systems*

Fraction, Decimal, and Percent

A percent is a ratio that compares a number to 100. To write a percent as a fraction, drop the percent sign, and use the number as the numerator in a fraction with a denominator of 100. Simplify, if possible. For example, $76\% = \frac{76}{100}$, or $\frac{19}{25}$. To write a fraction as a percent, convert it to an equivalent fraction with a denominator of 100. For example, $\frac{3}{4} = \frac{75}{100}$, or 75%. A fraction can be expressed as a percent by first converting the fraction to a decimal (divide the numerator by the denominator) and then converting the decimal to a percent by moving the decimal point two places to the right.

Comparing Numbers on a Number Line

In order to compare and understand the relationship between real numbers in various forms, it is helpful to use a number line. The zero point on a number line is called the origin; the points to the left of the origin are negative, and those to the right are positive. The number line below shows how numbers in fraction, decimal, percent, and integer form can be compared.

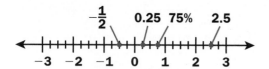

Percents Greater Than 100 and Less Than 1

Percents greater than 100% represent values greater than 1. For example, if the weight of an object is 250% of another, it is 2.5, or $2\frac{1}{2}$, times the weight.

Percents less than 1 represent values less than $\frac{1}{100}$. In other words, 0.1% is one tenth of one percent, which can also be represented in decimal form as 0.001, or in fraction form as $\frac{1}{1,000}$. Similarly, 0.01% is one hundredth of one percent or 0.0001 or $\frac{1}{10,000}$.

Ratio, Rate, and Proportion

A ratio is a comparison of two numbers using division. If a basketball player makes 8 out of 10 free throws, the ratio is written as 8 to 10, 8:10, or $\frac{8}{10}$. Ratios are usually written in simplest form. In simplest form, the ratio "8 out of 10" is 4 to 5, 4:5, or $\frac{4}{5}$. A rate is a ratio of two measurements having different kinds of units—cups per gallon, or miles per hour, for example. When a rate is simplified so that it has a denominator of 1, it is called a unit rate. An example of a unit rate is 9 miles per hour. A proportion is an equation stating that two ratios are equal. $\frac{3}{18} = \frac{13}{78}$ is an example of a proportion. The cross products of a proportion are also equal. $\frac{3}{18} = \frac{13}{78}$ and $3 \times 78 = 18 \times 13$.

Representing Large and Small Numbers

In order to represent large and small numbers, it is important to understand the number system. Our number system is based on 10, and the value of each place is 10 times the value of the place to its right.

The value of a digit is the product of a digit and its place value. For instance, in the number 6,400, the 6 has a value of six thousands and the 4 has a value of four hundreds. A place value chart can help you read numbers. In the chart, each group of three digits is called a period. Commas separate the periods: the ones period, the thousands period, the millions period, and so on. Values to the right of the ones period are decimals. By understanding place value you can write very large numbers like 5 billion and more, and very small numbers that are less than 1, like one-tenth.

Scientific Notation

When dealing with very large numbers like 1,500,000, or very small numbers like 0.000015, it is helpful to keep track of their value by writing the numbers in scientific notation. Powers of 10 with positive exponents are used with a decimal between 1 and 10 to express large numbers. The exponent represents the number of places the decimal point is moved to the right. So, 528,000 is written in scientific notation as 5.28×10^5. Powers of 10 with negative exponents are used with a decimal between 1 and 10 to express small numbers. The exponent represents the number of places the decimal point is moved to the left. The number 0.00047 is expressed as 4.7×10^{-4}.

Factor, Multiple, and Prime Factorization

Two or more numbers that are multiplied to form a product are called factors. Divisibility rules can be used to determine whether 2, 3, 4, 5, 6, 8, 9, or 10 are factors of a given number. Multiples are the products of a given number and various integers.

For example, 8 is a multiple of 4 because $4 \times 2 = 8$. A prime number is a whole number that has exactly two factors: 1 and itself. A composite number is a whole number that has more than two factors. Zero and 1 are neither prime nor composite. A composite number can be expressed as the product of its prime factors. The prime factorization of 40 is $2 \times 2 \times 2 \times 5$, or $2^3 \times 5$. The numbers 2 and 5 are prime numbers.

Integers

A negative number is a number less than zero. Negative numbers like –8, positive numbers like +6, and zero are members of the set of integers. Integers can be represented as points on a number line. A set of integers can be written {…, –3, –2, –1, 0, 1, 2, 3, …} where … means "continues indefinitely."

Real, Rational, and Irrational Numbers

The real number system is made up of the sets of rational and irrational numbers. Rational numbers are numbers that can be written in the form a/b where a and b are integers and $b \neq 0$. Examples are 0.45, $\frac{1}{2}$, and $\sqrt{36}$. Irrational numbers are non-repeating, non-terminating decimals. Examples are $\sqrt{71}$, π, and 0.020020002….

Complex and Imaginary Numbers

A complex number is a mathematical expression with a real number element and an imaginary number element. Imaginary numbers are multiples of i, the "imaginary" square root of –1. Complex numbers are represented by $a + bi$, where a and b are real numbers and i represents the imaginary element. When a quadratic equation does not have a real number solution, the solution can be represented by a complex number. Like real numbers, complex numbers can be added, subtracted, multiplied, and divided.

Vectors and Matrices

A matrix is a set of numbers or elements arranged in rows and columns to form a rectangle. The number of rows is represented by m and the number of columns is represented by n. To describe the number of rows and columns in a matrix, list the number of rows first using the format $m \times n$. Matrix A below is a 3×3 matrix because it has 3 rows and 3 columns. To name an element of a matrix, the letter i is used to denote the row and j is used to denote the column, and the element is labeled in the form $a_{i,j}$. In matrix A below, $a_{3,2}$ is 4.

$$\text{Matrix A} = \begin{pmatrix} 1 & 3 & 5 \\ 0 & 6 & 8 \\ 3 & 4 & 5 \end{pmatrix}$$

A vector is a matrix with only one column or row of elements. A transposed column vector, or a column vector turned on its side, is a row vector. In the example below, row vector b' is the transpose of column vector b.

$$b = \begin{pmatrix} 1 \\ 2 \\ 3 \\ 4 \end{pmatrix}$$

$$b' = \begin{pmatrix} 1 & 2 & 3 & 4 \end{pmatrix}$$

▶ Understand meanings of operations and how they relate to one another

Properties of Addition and Multiplication

Properties are statements that are true for any numbers. For example, $3 + 8$ is the same as $8 + 3$ because each expression equals 11. This illustrates the Commutative Property of Addition. Likewise, $3 \times 8 = 8 \times 3$ illustrates the Commutative Property of Multiplication.

When evaluating expressions, it is often helpful to group or associate the numbers. The Associative Property says that the way in which numbers are grouped when added or multiplied does not change the sum or product. The following properties are also true:

- **Additive Identity Property:** When 0 is added to any number, the sum is the number.

- **Multiplicative Identity Property:** When any number is multiplied by 1, the product is the number.

- **Multiplicative Property of Zero:** When any number is multiplied by 0, the product is 0.

Rational Numbers

A number that can be written as a fraction is called a rational number. Terminating and repeating decimals are rational numbers because both can be written as fractions.

Decimals that are neither terminating nor repeating are called irrational numbers because they cannot be written as fractions. Terminating decimals can be converted to fractions by placing the number (without the decimal point) in the numerator. Count the number of places to the right of the decimal point, and in the denominator, place a 1 followed by a number of zeros equal to the number of places that you counted. The fraction can then be reduced to its simplest form.

Writing a Fraction as a Decimal

Any fraction $\frac{a}{b}$, where $b \neq 0$, can be written as a decimal by dividing the numerator by the denominator. So, $\frac{a}{b} = a \div b$. If the division ends, or terminates, when the remainder is zero, the decimal is a terminating decimal. Not all fractions can be written as terminating decimals. Some have a repeating decimal. A bar indicates that the decimal repeats forever. For example, the fraction $\frac{4}{9}$ can be converted to a repeating decimal, $0.\overline{4}$

Adding and Subtracting Like Fractions

Fractions with the same denominator are called like fractions. To add like fractions, add the numerators and write the sum over the denominator. To add mixed numbers with like fractions, add the whole numbers and fractions separately, adding the numerators of the fractions, then simplifying if necessary. The rule for subtracting fractions with like denominators is similar to the rule for adding. The numerators can be sub-

tracted and the difference written over the denominator. Mixed numbers are written as improper fractions before subtracting. These same rules apply to adding or subtracting like algebraic fractions. An algebraic fraction is a fraction that contains one or more variables in the numerator or denominator.

Adding and Subtracting Unlike Fractions

Fractions with different denominators are called unlike fractions. The least common multiple of the denominators is used to rename the fractions with a common denominator. After a common denominator is found, the numerators can then be added or subtracted. To add mixed numbers with unlike fractions, rename the mixed numbers as improper fractions. Then find a common denominator, add the numerators, and simplify the answer.

Multiplying Rational Numbers

To multiply fractions, multiply the numerators and multiply the denominators. If the numerators and denominators have common factors, they can be simplified before multiplication. If the fractions have different signs, then the product will be negative. Mixed numbers can be multiplied in the same manner, after first renaming them as improper fractions. Algebraic fractions may be multiplied using the same method described above.

Dividing Rational Numbers

To divide a number by a rational number (a fraction, for example), multiply the first number by the multiplicative inverse of the second. Two numbers whose product is 1 are called multiplicative inverses, or reciprocals. $\frac{7}{4} \times \frac{4}{7} = 1$. When dividing by a mixed number, first rename it as an improper fraction, and then multiply by its multiplicative inverse. This process of multiplying by a number's reciprocal can also be used when dividing algebraic fractions.

Adding Integers

To add integers with the same sign, add their absolute values. The sum takes the same sign as the addends. An addend is a number that is added to another number (the augend). The equation $-5 + (-2) = -7$ is an example of adding two integers with the same sign. To add integers with different signs, subtract their absolute values. The sum takes the same sign as the addend with the greater absolute value.

Subtracting Integers

The rules for adding integers are extended to the subtraction of integers. To subtract an integer, add its additive inverse. For example, to find the difference $2 - 5$, add the additive inverse of 5 to 2: $2 + (-5) = -3$. The rule for subtracting integers can be used to solve real-world problems and to evaluate algebraic expressions.

Additive Inverse Property

Two numbers with the same absolute value but different signs are called opposites. For example, -4 and 4 are opposites. An integer and its opposite are also called additive inverses. The Additive Inverse Property says that the sum of any number and its additive inverse is zero. The Commutative, Associative, and Identity Properties also apply to integers. These properties help when adding more than two integers.

Absolute Value

In mathematics, when two integers on a number line are on opposite sides of zero, and they are the same distance from zero, they have the same absolute value. The symbol for absolute value is two vertical bars on either side of the number. For example, $|-5| = 5$.

Multiplying Integers

Since multiplication is repeated addition, $3(-7)$ means that -7 is used as an addend 3 times. By the Commutative Property of Multiplication, $3(-7) = -7(3)$. The product of two integers with different signs is always negative. The product of two integers with the same sign is always positive.

Dividing Integers

The quotient of two integers can be found by dividing the numbers using their absolute values. The quotient of two integers with the same sign is positive, and the quotient of two integers with a different sign is negative. $-12 \div (-4) = 3$ and $12 \div (-4) = -3$. The division of integers is used in statistics to find the average, or mean, of a set of data. When finding the mean of a set of numbers, find the sum of the numbers, and then divide by the number in the set.

Adding and Multiplying Vectors and Matrices

In order to add two matrices together, they must have the same number of rows and columns. In matrix addition, the corresponding elements are added to each other. In other words $(a + b)_{ij} = a_{ij} + b_{ij}$. For example,

$$\begin{pmatrix} 1 & 2 \\ 2 & 1 \end{pmatrix} + \begin{pmatrix} 3 & 6 \\ 0 & 1 \end{pmatrix} = \begin{pmatrix} 1+3 & 2+6 \\ 2+0 & 1+1 \end{pmatrix} = \begin{pmatrix} 4 & 8 \\ 2 & 2 \end{pmatrix}$$

Matrix multiplication requires that the number of elements in each row in the first matrix is equal to the number of elements in each column in the second. The elements of the first row of the first matrix are multiplied by the corresponding elements of the first column of the second matrix and then added together to get the first element of the product matrix. To get the second element, the elements in the first row of the first matrix are multiplied by the corresponding elements in the second column of the second matrix then added, and so on, until every row of the first matrix is multiplied by every column of the second. See the example below.

$$\begin{pmatrix} 1 & 2 \\ 3 & 4 \end{pmatrix} \times \begin{pmatrix} 3 & 6 \\ 0 & 1 \end{pmatrix} = \begin{pmatrix} (1\times3)+(2\times0) & (1\times6)+(2\times1) \\ (3\times3)+(4\times0) & (3\times6)+(4\times1) \end{pmatrix} = \begin{pmatrix} 3 & 8 \\ 9 & 22 \end{pmatrix}$$

Vector addition and multiplication are performed in the same way, but there is only one column and one row.

Permutations and Combinations

Permutations and combinations are used to determine the number of possible outcomes in different situations. An arrangement, listing, or pattern in which order is important is called a permutation. The symbol P(6, 3) represents the number of permutations of 6 things taken 3 at a time. For P(6, 3), there are $6 \times 5 \times 4$ or 120 possible outcomes. An arrangement or listing where order is not important is called a combination. The symbol C(10, 5) represents the number of combinations of 10 things taken 5 at a time. For C(10, 5), there are $(10 \times 9 \times 8 \times 7 \times 6) \div (5 \times 4 \times 3 \times 2 \times 1)$ or 252 possible outcomes.

Powers and Exponents

An expression such as $3 \times 3 \times 3 \times 3$ can be written as a power. A power has two parts, a base and an exponent. $3 \times 3 \times 3 \times 3 = 3^4$. The base is the number that is multiplied (3). The exponent tells how many times the base is used as a factor (4 times). Numbers and variables can be written using exponents. For example, $8 \times 8 \times 8 \times m \times m \times m \times m \times m$ can be expressed $8^3 m^5$. Exponents also can be used with place value to express numbers in expanded form. Using this method, 1,462 can be written as $(1 \times 10^3) + (4 \times 10^2) + (6 \times 10^1) + (2 \times 10^0)$.

Squares and Square Roots

The square root of a number is one of two equal factors of a number. Every positive number has both a positive and a negative square root. For example, since $8 \times 8 = 64$, 8 is a square root of 64. Since $(-8) \times (-8) = 64$, -8 is also a square root of 64. The notation $\sqrt{}$ indicates the positive square root, $-\sqrt{}$ indicates the negative square root, and $\pm\sqrt{}$ indicates both square roots. For example, $\sqrt{81} = 9$, $-\sqrt{49} = -7$, and $\pm\sqrt{4} = \pm2$. The square root of a negative number is an imaginary number because any two factors of a negative number must have different signs, and are therefore not equivalent.

Math Skills Handbook

Logarithm

A logarithm is the inverse of exponentiation. The logarithm of a number x in base b is equal to the number n. Therefore, $b^n = x$ and $\log_b x = n$. For example, $\log_4(64) = 3$ because $4^3 = 64$. The most commonly used bases for logarithms are 10, the common logarithm; 2, the binary logarithm; and the constant e, the natural logarithm (also called $ln(x)$ instead of $\log_e(x)$). Below is a list of some of the rules of logarithms that are important to understand if you are going to use them.

$$\log_b(xy) = \log_b(x) + \log_b(y)$$
$$\log_b(x/y) = \log_b(x) - \log_b(y)$$
$$\log_b(1/x) = -\log_b(x)$$
$$\log_b(x)y = y\log_b(x)$$

▶ *Compute fluently and make reasonable estimates*

Estimation by Rounding

When rounding numbers, look at the digit to the right of the place to which you are rounding. If the digit is 5 or greater, round up. If it is less than 5, round down. For example, to round 65,137 to the nearest hundred, look at the number in the tens place. Since 3 is less than 5, round down to 65,100. To round the same number to the nearest ten thousandth, look at the number in the thousandths place. Since it is 5, round up to 70,000.

Finding Equivalent Ratios

Equivalent ratios have the same meaning. Just like finding equivalent fractions, to find an equivalent ratio, multiply or divide both sides by the same number. For example, you can multiply 7 by both sides of the ratio 6:8 to get 42:56. Instead, you can also divide both sides of the same ratio by 2 to get 3:4. Find the simplest form of a ratio by dividing to find equivalent ratios until you can't go any further without going into decimals. So, 160:240 in simplest form is 2:3. To write a ratio in the form *1:n*, divide both sides by the left-hand number. In other words, to change 8:20 to *1:n*, divide both sides by 8 to get 1:2.5.

Front-End Estimation

Front-end estimation can be used to quickly estimate sums and differences before adding or subtracting. To use this technique, add or subtract just the digits of the two highest place values, and replace the other place values with zero. This will give you an estimation of the solution of a problem. For example, 93,471 − 22,825 can be changed to 93,000 − 22,000 or 71,000. This estimate can be compared to your final answer to judge its correctness.

Judging Reasonableness

When solving an equation, it is important to check your work by considering how reasonable your answer is. For example, consider the equation $9\frac{3}{4} \times 4\frac{1}{3}$. Since $9\frac{3}{4}$ is between 9 and 10 and $4\frac{1}{3}$ is between 4 and 5, only values that are between 9×4 or 36 and 10×5 or 50 will be reasonable. You can also use front-end estimation, or you can round and estimate a reasonable answer. In the equation 73×25, you can round and solve to estimate a reasonable answer to be near 70×30 or 2,100.

Math Skills Handbook

Algebra

▶ Understand patterns, relations, and functions

Relation
A relation is a generalization comparing sets of ordered pairs for an equation or inequality such as $x = y + 1$ or $x > y$. The first element in each pair, the x values, forms the domain. The second element in each pair, the y values, forms the range.

Function
A function is a special relation in which each member of the domain is paired with exactly one member in the range. Functions may be represented using ordered pairs, tables, or graphs. One way to determine whether a relation is a function is to use the vertical line test. Using an object to represent a vertical line, move the object from left to right across the graph. If, for each value of x in the domain, the object passes through no more than one point on the graph, then the graph represents a function.

Linear and Nonlinear Functions
Linear functions have graphs that are straight lines. These graphs represent constant rates of change. In other words, the slope between any two pairs of points on the graph is the same. Nonlinear functions do not have constant rates of change. The slope changes along these graphs. Therefore, the graphs of nonlinear functions are *not* straight lines. Graphs of curves represent nonlinear functions. The equation for a linear function can be written in the form $y = mx + b$, where m represents the constant rate of change, or the slope. Therefore, you can determine whether a function is linear by looking at the equation. For example, the equation $y = \frac{3}{x}$ is nonlinear because x is in the denominator and the equation cannot be written in the form $y = mx + b$. A nonlinear function does not increase or decrease at a constant rate. You can check this by using a table and finding the increase or decrease in y for each regular increase in x. For example, if for each increase in x by 2, y does not increase or decrease the same amount each time, the function is nonlinear.

Linear Equations in Two Variables
In a linear equation with two variables, such as $y = x - 3$, the variables appear in separate terms and neither variable contains an exponent other than 1. The graphs of all linear equations are straight lines. All points on a line are solutions of the equation that is graphed.

Quadratic and Cubic Functions
A quadratic function is a polynomial equation of the second degree, generally expressed as $ax^2 + bx + c = 0$, where a, b, and c are real numbers and a is not equal to zero. Similarly, a cubic function is a polynomial equation of the third degree, usually expressed as $ax^3 + bx^2 + cx + d = 0$. Quadratic functions can be graphed using an equation or a table of values. For example, to graph $y = 3x^2 + 1$, substitute the values −1, −0.5, 0, 0.5, and 1 for x to yield the point coordinates (−1, 4), (−0.5, 1.75), (0, 1), (0.5, 1.75), and (1, 4).

Plot these points on a coordinate grid and connect the points in the form of a parabola. Cubic functions also can be graphed by making a table of values. The points of a cubic function from a curve. There is one point at which the curve changes from opening upward to opening downward, or vice versa, called the point of inflection.

Slope

Slope is the ratio of the rise, or vertical change, to the run, or horizontal change of a line: slope = rise/run. Slope (m) is the same for any two points on a straight line and can be found by using the coordinates of any two points on the line:

$$m = \frac{y_2 - y_1}{x_2 - x_1}, \text{ where } x_2 \neq x_1$$

Asymptotes

An asymptote is a straight line that a curve approaches but never actually meets or crosses. Theoretically, the asymptote meets the curve at infinity. For example, in the function $f(x) = \frac{1}{x}$, two asymptotes are being approached: the line $y = 0$ and $x = 0$. See the graph of the function below.

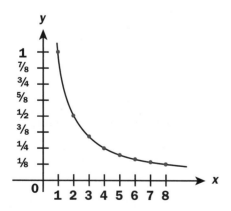

▶ Represent and analyze mathematical situations and structures using algebraic symbols

Variables and Expressions

Algebra is a language of symbols. A variable is a placeholder for a changing value. Any letter, such as x, can be used as a variable. Expressions such as $x + 2$ and $4x$ are algebraic expressions because they represent sums and/or products of variables and numbers. Usually, mathematicians avoid the use of i and e for variables because they have other mathematical meanings ($i = \sqrt{-1}$ and e is used with natural logarithms). To evaluate an algebraic expression, replace the variable or variables with known values, and then solve using order of operations. Translate verbal phrases into algebraic expressions by first defining a variable: Choose a variable and a quantity for the variable to represent. In this way, algebraic expressions can be used to represent real-world situations.

Constant and Coefficient

A constant is a fixed value unlike a variable, which can change. Constants are usually represented by numbers, but they can also be represented by symbols. For example, π is a symbolic representation of the value 3.1415…. A coefficient is a constant by which a variable or other object is multiplied. For example, in the expression $7x^2 + 5x + 9$, the coefficient of x^2 is 7 and the coefficient of x is 5. The number 9 is a constant and not a coefficient.

Monomial and Polynomial

A monomial is a number, a variable, or a product of numbers and/or variables such as 3×4. An algebraic expression that contains one or more monomials is called a polynomial. In a polynomial, there are no terms with variables in the denominator and no terms with variables under a radical sign. Polynomials can be classified by the number of terms contained in the expression. Therefore, a polynomial with two terms is called a binomial $(z^2 - 1)$, and a polynomial with three terms is called a trinomial $(2y^3 + 4y^2 - y)$. Polynomials also can be classified by their degrees. The degree of a monomial is the sum of the exponents of its variables. The degree of a nonzero constant such as 6 or 10 is 0. The constant 0 has no degree. For example, the monomial $4b^5c^2$ had a degree of 7. The degree of a polynomial is the same as that of the term with the greatest degree. For example, the polynomial $3x^4 - 2y^3 + 4y^2 - y$ has a degree of 4.

Equation

An equation is a mathematical sentence that states that two expressions are equal. The two expressions in an equation are always separated by an equal sign. When solving for a variable in an equation, you must perform the same operations on both sides of the equation in order for the mathematical sentence to remain true.

Solving Equations with Variables

To solve equations with variables on both sides, use the Addition or Subtraction Property of Equality to write an equivalent equation with the variables on the same side. For example, to solve $5x - 8 = 3x$, subtract $3x$ from each side to get $2x - 8 = 0$. Then add 8 to each side to get $2x = 8$. Finally, divide each side by 2 to find that $x = 4$.

Solving Equations with Grouping Symbols

Equations often contain grouping symbols such as parentheses or brackets. The first step in solving these equations is to use the Distributive Property to remove the grouping symbols. For example $5(x + 2) = 25$ can be changed to $5x + 10 = 25$, and then solved to find that $x = 3$.

Some equations have no solution. That is, there is no value of the variable that results in a true sentence. For such an equation, the solution set is called the null or empty set, and is represented by the symbol $\varnothing$ or {}. Other equations may have every number as the solution. An equation that is true for every value of the variable is called the identity.

Inequality

A mathematical sentence that contains the symbols < (less than), > (greater than), ≤ (less than or equal to), or ≥ (greater than or equal to) is called an inequality. For example, the statement that it is legal to drive 55 miles per hour or slower on a stretch of the highway can be shown by the sentence $s \leq 55$. Inequalities with variables are called open sentences. When a variable is replaced with a number, the inequality may be true or false.

Solving Inequalities

Solving an inequality means finding values for the variable that make the inequality true. Just as with equations, when you add or subtract the same number from each side of an inequality, the inequality remains true. For example, if you add 5 to each side of the inequality $3x < 6$, the resulting inequality $3x + 5 < 11$ is also true. Adding or subtracting the same number from each side of an inequality does not affect the inequality sign. When multiplying or dividing each side of an inequality by the same positive number, the inequality remains true. In such cases, the inequality symbol does not change. When multiplying or dividing each side of an inequality by a negative number, the inequality symbol must be reversed. For example, when dividing each side of the inequality $-4x \geq -8$ by -2, the inequality sign must be changed to $\leq$ for the resulting inequality, $2x \leq 4$, to be true. Since the solutions to an inequality include all rational numbers satisfying it, inequalities have an infinite number of solutions.

Representing Inequalities on a Number Line

The solutions of inequalities can be graphed on a number line. For example, if the solution of an inequality is $x < 5$, start an arrow at 5 on the number line, and continue the arrow to the left to show all values less than 5 as the solution. Put an open circle at 5 to show that the point 5 is *not* included in the graph. Use a closed circle when graphing solutions that are greater than or equal to, or less than or equal to, a number.

Order of Operations

Solving a problem may involve using more than one operation. The answer can depend on the order in which you do the operations. To make sure that there is just one answer to a series of computations, mathematicians have agreed upon an order in which to do the operations. First simplify within the parentheses, often called graphing symbols, and then evaluate any exponents. Then multiply and divide from left to

right, and finally add and subtract from left to right.

Parametric Equations

Given an equation with more than one unknown, a statistician can draw conclusions about those unknown quantities through the use of parameters, independent variables that the statistician already knows something about. For example, you can find the velocity of an object if you make some assumptions about distance and time parameters.

Recursive Equations

In recursive equations, every value is determined by the previous value. You must first plug an initial value into the equation to get the first value, and then you can use the first value to determine the next one, and so on. For example, in order to determine what the population of pigeons will be in New York City in three years, you can use an equation with the birth, death, immigration, and emigration rates of the birds. Input the current population size into the equation to determine next year's population size, then repeat until you have calculated the value for which you are looking.

▶ *Use mathematical models to represent and understand quantitative relationships*

Solving Systems of Equations

Two or more equations together are called a system of equations. A system of equations can have one solution, no solution, or infinitely many solutions. One method for solving a system of equations is to graph the equations on the same coordinate plane. The coordinates of the point where the graphs intersect is the solution. In other words, the solution of a system is the ordered pair that is a solution of all equations. A more accurate way to solve a system of two equations is by using a method called substitution. Write both equations in terms of y. Replace y in the first equation with the right side of the second equation. Check the solution by graphing. You can solve a system of three equations using matrix algebra.

Graphing Inequalities
To graph an inequality, first graph the related equation, which is the boundary. All points in the shaded region are solutions of the inequality. If an inequality contains the symbol $\leq$ or $\geq$, then use a solid line to indicate that the boundary is included in the graph. If an inequality contains the symbol $<$ or $>$, then use a dashed line to indicate that the boundary is not included in the graph.

▶ *Analyze change in various contexts*

Rate of Change
A change in one quantity with respect to another quantity is called the rate of change. Rates of change can be described using slope:

$$\text{slope} = \frac{\text{change in } y}{\text{change in } x}$$

You can find rates of change from an equation, a table, or a graph. A special type of linear equation that describes rate of change is called a direct variation. The graph of a direct variation always passes through the origin and represents a proportional situation. In the equation $y = kx$, k is called the constant of variation. It is the slope, or rate of change. As x increases in value, y increases or decreases at a constant rate k, or y varies directly with x. Another way to say this is that y is directly proportional to x. The direct variation $y = kx$ also can be written as $k = \frac{y}{x}$. In this form, you can see that the ratio of y to x is the same for any corresponding values of y and x.

Slope-Intercept Form
Equations written as $y = mx + b$, where m is the slope and b is the y-intercept, are linear equations in slope-intercept form. For example, the graph of $y = 5x - 6$ is a line that has a slope of 5 and crosses the y-axis at $(0, -6)$. Sometimes you must first write an equation in slope-intercept form before finding the slope and y-intercept. For example, the equation $2x + 3y = 15$ can be expressed in slope-intercept form by subtracting $2x$ from each side and then dividing by 3: $y = -\frac{2}{3}x + 5$, revealing a slope of $-\frac{2}{3}$ and a y-intercept of 5. You can use the slope-intercept form of an equation to graph a line easily. Graph the y-intercept and use the slope to find another point on the line, then connect the two points with a line.

Geometry

▶ *Analyze characteristics and properties of two- and three-dimensional geometric shapes and develop mathematical arguments about geometric relationships*

Angles

Two rays that have the same endpoint form an angle. The common endpoint is called the vertex, and the two rays that make up the angle are called the sides of the angle. The most common unit of measure for angles is the degree. Protractors can be used to measure angles or to draw an angle of a given measure. Angles can be classified by their degree measure. Acute angles have measures less than 90° but greater than 0°. Obtuse angles have measures greater than 90° but less than 180°. Right angles have measures of 90°.

Triangles

A triangle is a figure formed by three line segments that intersect only at their endpoints. The sum of the measures of the angles of a triangle is 180°. Triangles can be classified by their angles. An acute triangle contains all acute angles. An obtuse triangle has one obtuse angle. A right triangle has one right angle. Triangles can also be classified by their sides. A scalene triangle has no congruent sides. An isosceles triangle has at least two congruent sides. In an equilateral triangle all sides are congruent.

Quadrilaterals

A quadrilateral is a closed figure with four sides and four vertices. The segments of a quadrilateral intersect only at their endpoints. Quadrilaterals can be separated into two triangles. Since the sum of the interior angles of all triangles totals 180°, the measures of the interior angles of a quadrilateral equal 360°. Quadrilaterals are classified according to their characteristics, and include trapezoids, parallelograms, rectangles, squares, and rhombuses.

Two-Dimensional Figures

A two-dimensional figure exists within a plane and has only the dimensions of length and width. Examples of two-dimensional figures include circles and polygons. Polygons are figures that have three or more angles, including triangles, quadrilaterals, pentagons, hexagons, and many more. The sum of the angles of any polygon totals at least 180° (triangle), and each additional side adds 180° to the measure of the first three angles. The sum of the angles of a quadrilateral, for example, is 360°. The sum of the angles of a pentagon is 540°.

Three-Dimensional Figures

A plane is a two-dimensional flat surface that extends in all directions. Intersecting planes can form the edges and vertices of three-dimensional figures or solids. A polyhedron is a solid with flat surfaces that are polygons.

Polyhedrons are composed of faces, edges, and vertices and are differentiated by their shape and by their number of bases. Skew lines are lines that lie in different planes. They are neither intersecting nor parallel.

Congruence

Figures that have the same size and shape are congruent. The parts of congruent triangles that match are called corresponding parts. Congruence statements are used to identify corresponding parts of congruent triangles. When writing a congruence statement, the letters must be written so that corresponding vertices appear in the same order. Corresponding parts can be used to find the measures of angles and sides in a figure that is congruent to a figure with known measures.

Similarity

If two figures have the same shape but not the same size they are called similar figures. For example, the triangles below are similar, so angles A, B, and C have the same measurements as angles D, E, and F, respectively. However, segments AB, BC, and CA do not have the same measurements as segments DE, EF, and FD, but the measures of the sides are proportional.

For example, $\dfrac{\overline{AB}}{\overline{DE}} = \dfrac{\overline{BC}}{\overline{EF}} = \dfrac{\overline{CA}}{\overline{FD}}$.

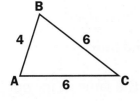

Solid figures are considered to be similar if they have the same shape and their corresponding linear measures are proportional. As with two-dimensional figures, they can be tested for similarity by comparing corresponding measures. If the compared ratios are proportional, then the figures are similar solids. Missing measures of similar solids can also be determined by using proportions.

The Pythagorean Theorem

The sides that are adjacent to a right angle are called legs. The side opposite the right angle is the hypotenuse.

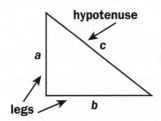

The Pythagorean Theorem describes the relationship between the lengths of the legs a and b and the hypotenuse c. It states that if a triangle is a right triangle, then the square of the length of the hypotenuse is equal to the sum of the squares of the lengths of the legs. In symbols, $c^2 = a^2 + b^2$.

Sine, Cosine, and Tangent Ratios

Trigonometry is the study of the properties of triangles. A trigonometric ratio is a ratio of the lengths of two sides of a right triangle. The most common trigonometric ratios are the sine, cosine, and tangent ratios. These ratios are abbreviated as *sin*, *cos*, and *tan*, respectively.

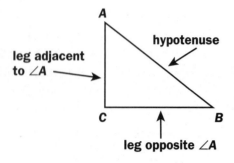

If ∠A is an acute angle of a right triangle, then

$$\sin \angle A = \frac{\text{measure of leg opposite } \angle A}{\text{measure of hypotenuse}},$$

$$\cos \angle A = \frac{\text{measure of leg adjacent to } \angle A}{\text{measure of hypotenuse}}, \text{ and}$$

$$\tan \angle A = \frac{\text{measure of leg opposite } \angle A}{\text{measure of leg adjacent to } \angle A}.$$

▶ *Specify locations and describe spatial relationships using coordinate geometry and other representational systems*

Polygons

A polygon is a simple, closed figure formed by three or more line segments. The line segments meet only at their endpoints. The points of intersection are called vertices, and the line segments are called sides. Polygons are classified by the number of sides they have. The diagonals of a polygon divide the polygon into triangles. The number of triangles formed is two less than the number of sides. To find the sum of the measures of the interior angles of any polygon, multiply the number of triangles within the polygon by 180. That is, if *n* equals the number of sides, then (*n* − 2) 180 gives the sum of the measures of the polygon's interior angles.

Cartesian Coordinates

In the Cartesian coordinate system, the *y*-axis extends above and below the origin and the *x*-axis extends to the right and left of the origin, which is the point at which the *x*- and *y*-axes intersect. Numbers below and to the left of the origin are negative. A point graphed on the coordinate grid is said to have an *x*-coordinate and a *y*-coordinate. For example, the point (1,−2) has as its *x*-coordinate the number 1, and has as its *y*-coordinate the number −2. This point is graphed by locating the position on the grid that is 1 unit to the right of the origin and 2 units below the origin.

The *x*-axis and the *y*-axis separate the coordinate plane into four regions, called quadrants. The axes and points located on the axes themselves are not located in any of the quadrants. The quadrants are labeled I to IV, starting in the upper right and proceeding counterclockwise. In quadrant I, both coordinates are positive. In quadrant II, the *x*-coordinate is negative and the *y*-coordinate is positive. In quadrant III, both coordinates are negative. In quadrant IV, the *x*-coordinate is positive and the *y*-coordinate is negative. A coordinate graph can be used to show algebraic relationships among numbers.

▶ *Apply transformations and use symmetry to analyze mathematical situations*

Similar Triangles and Indirect Measurement

Triangles that have the same shape but not necessarily the same dimensions are called similar triangles. Similar triangles have corresponding angles and corresponding sides. Arcs are used to show congruent angles. If two triangles are similar, then the corresponding angles have the same measure, and the corresponding sides are proportional. Therefore, to determine the measures of the sides of similar triangles when some measures are known, proportions can be used.

Transformations

A transformation is a movement of a geometric figure. There are several types of transformations. In a translation, also called a slide, a figure is slid from one position to another without turning it. Every point of the original figure is moved the same distance and in the same direction. In a reflection, also called a flip, a figure is flipped over a line to form a mirror image. Every point of the original figure has a corresponding point on the other side of the line of symmetry. In a rotation, also called a turn, a figure is turned around a fixed point. A figure can be rotated 0°–360° clockwise or counterclockwise. A dilation transforms each line to a parallel line whose length is a fixed multiple of the length of the original line to create a similar figure that will be either larger or smaller.

▶ *Use visualizations, spatial reasoning, and geometric modeling to solve problems*

Two-Dimensional Representations of Three-Dimensional Objects

Three-dimensional objects can be represented in a two-dimensional drawing in order to more easily determine properties such as surface area and volume. When you look at the triangular prism, you can see the orientation of its three dimensions,

length, width, and height. Using the drawing and the formulas for surface area and volume, you can easily calculate these properties.

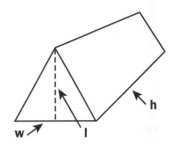

Another way to represent a three-dimensional object in a two-dimensional plane is by using a net, which is the unfolded representation. Imagine cutting the vertices of a box until it is flat then drawing an outline of it. That's a net. Most objects have more than one net, but any one can be measured to determine surface area. Below is a cube and one of its nets.

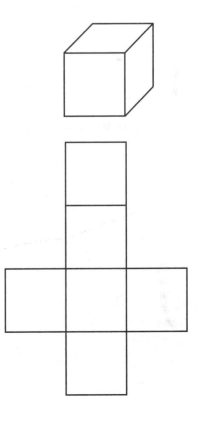

Measurement

▶ *Understand measurable attributes of objects and the units, systems, and processes of measurement*

Customary System

The customary system is the system of weights and measures used in the United States. The main units of weight are ounces, pounds (1 equal to 16 ounces), and tons (1 equal to 2,000 pounds). Length is typically measured in inches, feet (1 equal to 12 inches), yards (1 equal to 3 feet), and miles (1 equal to 5,280 feet), while area is measured in square feet and acres (1 equal to 43,560 square feet). Liquid is measured in cups, pints (1 equal to 2 cups), quarts (1 equal to 2 pints), and gallons (1 equal to 4 quarts). Finally, temperature is measured in degrees Fahrenheit.

Metric System

The metric system is a decimal system of weights and measurements in which the prefixes of the words for the units of measure indicate the relationships between the different measurements. In this system, the main units of weight, or mass, are grams and kilograms. Length is measured in millimeters, centimeters, meters, and kilometers, and the units of area are square millimeters, centimeters, meters, and kilometers. Liquid is typically measured in milliliters and liters, while temperature is in degrees Celsius.

Selecting Units of Measure

When measuring something, it is important to select the appropriate type and size of unit. For example, in the United States it would be appropriate when describing someone's height to use feet and inches. These units of height or length are good to use because they are in the customary system, and they are of appropriate size. In the customary system, use inches, feet, and miles for lengths and perimeters; square inches, feet, and miles for area and surface area; and cups, pints, quarts, gallons or cubic inches and feet (and less commonly miles) for volume. In the metric system use millimeters, centimeters, meters, and kilometers for lengths and perimeters; square units millimeters, centimeters, meters, and kilometers for area and surface area; and milliliters and liters for volume. Finally, always use degrees to measure angles.

▶ *Apply appropriate techniques, tools, and formulas to determine measurements*

Precision and Significant Digits

The precision of measurement is the exactness to which a measurement is made. Precision depends on the smallest unit of measure being used, or the precision unit. One way to record a measure is to estimate to the nearest precision unit. A more precise method is to include all of the digits that are actually measured, plus one estimated digit. The digits recorded, called significant digits, indicate the precision of the measurement. There are special rules for determining significant digits. If a number contains a decimal point, the number of significant digits is found by counting from left to right, starting with the first nonzero digit.

If the number does not contain a decimal point, the number of significant digits is found by counting the digits from left to right, starting with the first digit and ending with the last nonzero digit.

Surface Area

The amount of material needed to cover the surface of a figure is called the surface area. It can be calculated by finding the area of each face and adding them together. To find the surface area of a rectangular prism, for example, the formula $S = 2lw + 2lh + 2wh$ applies. A cylinder, on the other hand, may be unrolled to reveal two circles and a rectangle. Its surface area can be determined by finding the area of the two circles, $2\pi r^2$, and adding it to the area of the rectangle, $2\pi rh$ (the length of the rectangle is the circumference of one of the circles), or $S = 2\pi r^2 + 2\pi rh$. The surface area of a pyramid is measured in a slightly different way because the sides of a pyramid are triangles that intersect at the vertex. These sides are called lateral faces and the height of each is called the slant height. The sum of their areas is the lateral area of a pyramid. The surface area of a square pyramid is the lateral area $\frac{1}{2}bh$ (area of a lateral face) times 4 (number of lateral faces), plus the area of the base. The surface area of a cone is the area of its circular base (πr^2) plus its lateral area (πrl, where l is the slant height).

Volume

Volume is the measure of space occupied by a solid region. To find the volume of a prism, the area of the base is multiplied by the measure of the height, $V = Bh$. A solid containing several prisms can be broken down into its component prisms. Then the volume of each component can be found and the volumes added. The volume of a cylinder can be determined by finding the area of its circular base, πr^2, and then multiplying by the height of the cylinder. A pyramid has one-third the volume of a prism with the same base and height. To find the volume of a pyramid, multiply the area of the base by the pyramid's height, and then divide by 3. Simply stated, the formula for the volume of a pyramid is $V = \frac{1}{3}bh$. A cone is a three-dimensional figure with one circular base and a curved surface connecting the base and the vertex. The volume of a cone is one-third the volume of a cylinder with the same base area and height. Like a pyramid, the formula for the volume of a cone is $V = \frac{1}{3}bh$. More specifically, the formula is $V = \frac{1}{3}\pi r^2 h$.

Upper and Lower Bounds

Upper and lower bounds have to do with the accuracy of a measurement. When a measurement is given, the degree of accuracy is also stated to tell you what the upper and lower bounds of the measurement are. The upper bound is the largest possible value that a measurement could have had before being rounded down, and the lower bound is the lowest possible value it could have had before being rounded up.

Data Analysis and Probability

▶ *Formulate questions that can be addressed with data and collect, organize, and display relevant data to answer them*

Histograms

A histogram displays numerical data that have been organized into equal intervals using bars that have the same width and no space between them. While a histogram does not give exact data points, its shape shows the distribution of the data. Histograms also can be used to compare data.

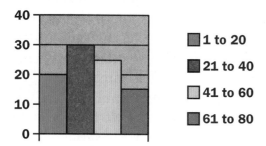

- ■ 1 to 20
- ■ 21 to 40
- □ 41 to 60
- ■ 61 to 80

Box-and-Whisker Plot

A box-and-whisker plot displays the measures of central tendency and variation. A box is drawn around the quartile values, and whiskers extend from each quartile to the extreme data points. To make a box plot for a set of data, draw a number line that covers the range of data. Find the median, the extremes, and the upper and lower quartiles. Mark these points on the number line with bullets, then draw a box and the whiskers. The length of a whisker or box shows whether the values of the data in that part are concentrated or spread out.

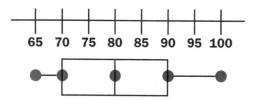

Scatter Plots

A scatter plot is a graph that shows the relationship between two sets of data. In a scatter plot, two sets of data are graphed as ordered pairs on a coordinate system. Two sets of data can have a positive correlation (as x increases, y increases), a negative correlation (as x increases, y decreases), or no correlation (no obvious pattern is shown). Scatter plots can be used to spot trends, draw conclusions, and make predictions about data.

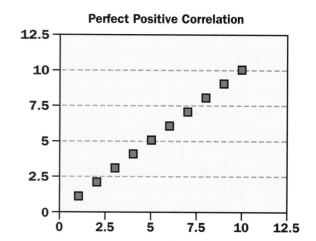

Randomization

The idea of randomization is a very important principle of statistics and the design of experiments. Data must be selected randomly to prevent bias from influencing the results. For example, you want to know the average income of people in your town but you can only use a sample of 100 individuals to make determinations about everyone. If you select 100 individuals who are all doctors, you will have a biased sample. However, if you chose a random sample of 100 people out of the phone book, you are much more likely to accurately represent average income in the town.

Statistics and Parameters

Statistics is a science that involves collecting, analyzing, and presenting data. The data can be collected in various ways—for example through a census or by making physical measurements. The data can then be analyzed by creating summary statistics, which have to do with the distribution of the data sample, including the mean, range, and standard error. They can also be illustrated in tables and graphs, like box-plots, scatter plots, and histograms. The presentation of the data typically involves describing the strength or validity of the data and what they show. For example, an analysis of ancestry of people in a city might tell you something about immigration patterns, unless the data set is very small or biased in some way, in which case it is not likely to be very accurate or useful.

Categorical and Measurement Data

When analyzing data, it is important to understand if the data is qualitative or quantitative. Categorical data is qualitative and measurement, or numerical, data is quantitative. Categorical data describes a quality of something and can be placed into different categories. For example, if you are analyzing the number of students in different grades in a school, each grade is a category. On the other hand, measurement data is continuous, like height, weight, or any other measurable variable. Measurement data can be converted into categorical data if you decide to group the data. Using height as an example, you can group the continuous data set into categories like under 5 feet, 5 feet to 5 feet 5 inches, over 5 feet five inches to 6 feet, and so on.

Univariate and Bivariate Data

In data analysis, a researcher can analyze one variable at a time or look at how multiple variables behave together. Univariate data involves only one variable, for example height in humans. You can measure the height in a population of people then plot the results in a histogram to look at how height is distributed in humans. To summarize univariate data, you can use statistics like the mean, mode, median, range, and standard deviation, which is a measure of variation. When looking at more than one variable at once, you use multivariate data. Bivariate data involves two variables. For example, you can look at height and age in humans together by gathering information on both variables from individuals in a population. You can then plot both variables in a scatter plot, look at how the variables behave in relation to each other, and create an equation that represents the relationship, also called a regression. These equations could help answer questions such as, for example, does height increase with age in humans?

▶ Select and use appropriate statistical methods to analyze data

Measures of Central Tendency

When you have a list of numerical data, it is often helpful to use one or more numbers to represent the whole set. These numbers are called measures of central tendency. Three measures of central tendency are mean, median, and mode. The mean is the sum of the data divided by the number of items in the data set. The median is the middle number of the ordered data (or the mean of the two middle numbers). The mode is the number or numbers that occur most often. These measures of central tendency allow data to be analyzed and better understood.

Measures of Spread

In statistics, measures of spread or variation are used to describe how data are distributed. The range of a set of data is the difference between the greatest and the least values of the data set. The quartiles are the values that divide the data into four equal parts. The median of data separates the set in half. Similarly, the median of the lower half of a set of data is the lower quartile. The median of the upper half of a set of data is the upper quartile. The interquartile range is the difference between the upper quartile and the lower quartile.

Line of Best Fit

When real-life data are collected, the points graphed usually do not form a straight line, but they may approximate a linear relationship. A line of best fit is a line that lies very close to most of the data points. It can be used to predict data. You also can use the equation of the best-fit line to make predictions.

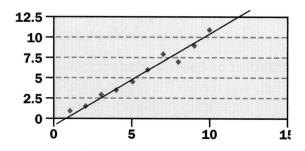

Stem and Leaf Plots

In a stem and leaf plot, numerical data are listed in ascending or descending order. The greatest place value of the data is used for the stems. The next greatest place value forms the leaves. For example, if the least number in a

set of data is 8 and the greatest number is 95, draw a vertical line and write the stems from 0 to 9 to the left of the line. Write the leaves from to the right of the line, with the corresponding stem. Next, rearrange the leaves so they are ordered from least to greatest. Then include a key or explanation, such as 1|3 = 13. Notice that the stem-and-leaf plot below is like a histogram turned on its side.

```
0|8
1|3 6
2|5 6 9
3|0 2 7 8
4|0 1 4 7 9
5|1 4 5 8
6|1 3 7
7|5 8
8|2 6
9|5
```

Key: **1|3 = 13**

▶ Develop and evaluate inferences and predictions that are based on data

Sampling Distribution

The sampling distribution of a population is the distribution that would result if you could take an infinite number of samples from the population, average each, and then average the averages. The more normal the distribution of the population, that is, how closely the distribution follows a bell curve, the more likely the sampling distribution will also follow a normal distribution. Furthermore, the larger the sample, the more likely it will accurately represent the entire population. For instance, you are more likely to gain more representative results from a population of 1,000 with a sample of 100 than with a sample of 2.

Validity

In statistics, validity refers to acquiring results that accurately reflect that which is being measured. In other words, it is important when performing statistical analyses, to ensure that the data are valid in that the sample being analyzed represents the population to the best extent possible. Randomization of data and using appropriate sample sizes are two important aspects of making valid inferences about a population.

▶ *Understand and apply basic concepts of probability*

Complementary, Mutually Exclusive Events

To understand probability theory, it is important to know if two events are mutually exclusive, or complementary: the occurrence of one event automatically implies the non-occurrence of the other. That is, two complementary events cannot both occur. If you roll a pair of dice, the event of rolling 6 and rolling doubles have an outcome in common (3, 3), so they are not mutually exclusive. If you roll (3, 3), you also roll doubles. However, the events of rolling a 9 and rolling doubles are mutually exclusive because they have no outcomes in common. If you roll a 9, you will not also roll doubles.

Independent and Dependent Events

Determining the probability of a series of events requires that you know whether the events are independent or dependent. An independent event has no influence on the occurrence of subsequent events, whereas, a dependent event does influence subsequent events. The chances that a woman's first child will be a girl are $\frac{1}{2}$,
and the chances that her second child will be a girl are also $\frac{1}{2}$ because the two events are independent of each other. However, if there are 7 red marbles in a bag of 15 marbles, the chances that the first marble you pick will be red are $\frac{7}{15}$ and if you indeed pick a red marble and remove it, you have reduced the chances of picking another red marble to $\frac{6}{14}$.

Sample Space

The sample space is the group of all possible outcomes for an event. For example, if you are tossing a single six-sided die, the sample space is {1, 2, 3, 4, 5, 6}. Similarly, you can determine the sample space for the possible outcomes of two events. If you are going to toss a coin twice, the sample space is {(heads, heads), (heads, tails), (tails, heads), (tails, tails)}.

Computing the Probability of a Compound Event

If two events are independent, the outcome of one event does not influence the outcome of the second. For example, if a bag contains 2 blue and 3 red marbles, then the probability of selecting a blue marble, replacing it, and then selecting a red marble is $P(A) \times P(B) = \frac{2}{5} \times \frac{3}{5}$ or $\frac{6}{25}$.

If two events are dependent, the outcome of one event affects the outcome of the second. For example, if a bag contains 2 blue and 3 red marbles, then the probability of selecting a blue and then a red marble without replacing the first marble is $P(A) \times P(B \text{ following } A) = \frac{2}{5} \times \frac{3}{4}$ or $\frac{3}{10}$. Two events that cannot happen at the same time are mutually exclusive. For example, when you roll two number cubes, you cannot roll a sum that is both 5 and even. So, $P(A \text{ or } B) = \frac{4}{36} + \frac{18}{36}$ or $\frac{11}{18}$.

Glossary

How To Use This Glossary

- Content vocabulary terms in this glossary are words that relate to this book's content. They are **highlighted yellow** in your text.
- Words in this glossary that have an asterisk (*) are academic vocabulary terms. These words help you with your understanding in all your school subjects and are often used on tests. They are **boldfaced black** in your text.

A

accounting The discipline that keeps track of a company's financial situation. (p. 128)

accounting program A program that can store and retrieve financial records and process all business transactions automatically. (p. 214)

* **accurate** Conforming exactly or almost exactly to fact or a standard; characterized by perfect conformity to fact or truth. (p. 691)

* **achieve** To gain with effort. (p. 245)

Ad Council A nonprofit organization that helps produce public service advertising campaigns for government agencies and other qualifying groups. (p. 148)

ad layout A sketch that shows the general arrangement and appearance of a finished ad. (p. 477)

* **adaptation** A company's use of an existing product or promotion from which changes are made to better suit the characteristics of a country or region. (p. 99)

* **adequate** Enough to meet a purpose; acceptable. (p. 757)

adjacent colors Those that are located next to each other on the color wheel and share the same undertones; also called analogous colors. (p. 430)

* **administration** The persons (or committees or departments etc.) who make up a body for the purpose of tending to or supervising something. (p. 137)

advertising A form of nonpersonal promotion in which companies pay to promote ideas, goods, or services in a variety of media outlets. (pp. 396, 441)

advertising agency An independent business that specializes in developing ad campaigns and crafting the ads for clients. (p. 468)

advertising campaign A group of advertisements, commercials, and related promotional materials and activities that are designed as part of a coordinated advertising plan to meet the specific goals of a company. (p. 467)

advertising proof A presentation of an ad that shows exactly how it will appear in print. (p. 481)

agent One who acts as an intermediary by bringing buyers and sellers together. (p. 495)

agreement A specific commitment that each member of a team makes to the group. (p. 243)

* **allocate** Distribute according to a plan or set apart for a special purpose. (p. 606)

allowance Partial return of a sale price for merchandise the customer has kept, for example if there is a defect. (p. 370)

* **analyze** Consider in detail in order to discover essential features or meaning. (p. 214)

* **anticipate** Act in advance of; deal with ahead of time. (p. 664)

* **appreciate** To recognize with gratitude; be grateful for. (p. 349)

* **approach** Ideas or actions intended to deal with a problem or situation. (p. 61)

aptitude An ability or natural talent, or the potential to learn a certain skill. (p. 874)

* **area** A part of a structure having some specific characteristic or function. (p. 369)

Articles of Incorporation Identifies the name and address of a new corporation, its purpose, the names of the initial directors, and the amount of stock that will be issued to each director. (p. 790)

aseptic packaging Packaging that utilizes a technology that keeps foods fresh without refrigeration for extended periods. (p. 741)

assertiveness Acting in a bold or self-confident manner. (p. 235)

* **assess** Place a value on; judge the worth of something. (p. 845)

asset Anything of monetary value that a person owns, such as cash, checking and savings accounts, real estate, or stocks. (p. 843)

* **associate** Make a logical or causal connection. (p. 666)

* **assure** To inform positively or to reinforce with certainty and confidence. (p. 753)

* **astute** Marked by practical intelligence. (p. 310)

* **attitude** A complex mental state involving beliefs and feelings and values and dispositions to act in certain ways. (p. 47)

attitude research Also known as opinion research; designed to obtain information on how people feel about certain products, services, companies, or ideas. (p. 663)

audience The number of homes or people exposed to an ad. (p. 453)

* **authority** The power to make decisions and tell others what to do. (p. 830)

* **authorize** To give or delegate power or authority. (p. 568)

* **automatic** Acting or operating in a manner essentially independent of external influence or control. (p. 494)

* **automatically** In a mechanical manner; by a mechanism. (p. 373)
* **awareness** Having knowledge of. (p. 717)

B

balance of trade The difference in value between exports and imports of a nation. (p. 87)

balance sheet A summary of a business's assets, liabilities, and owner's equity. (p. 858)

bar graph A drawing made up of parallel bars whose lengths correspond to what is being measured. (p. 180)

barrier An obstacle that interferes with the understanding of a message. (p. 191)

basic stock list A stock list used for staple items that should always be in stock. (p. 572)

* **benefits** Those things that aid or promote well-being. (p. 13)

Better Business Bureau (BBB) Nonprofit organization that set up self-regulation among businesses. Business members must "agree to follow the highest principles of business ethics and voluntary self-regulation, and have a proven record of marketplace honesty and integrity." (p. 150)

blind check method A method of checking whereby the receiver writes the description of the merchandise, counts the quantities received, and lists them on a blank form or dummy invoice. The list is then compared to the actual invoice after the blind check is made. (p. 559)

blisterpack A package with a preformed plastic mold surrounding individual items arranged on a backing. (p. 740)

blog Personal Web site where an individual shares thoughts, pictures, and comments with visitors. (p. 449)

bonded warehouse A public or private warehouse that stores products requiring payment of a federal tax. (p. 528)

boomerang method A method of answering objections by bringing the objection back to the customer as a selling point. (p. 331)

brand A name, term, design, symbol, or combination of these elements that identifies a business, product, or service, and sets it apart from its competitors. (p. 731)

brand extension A branding strategy that uses an existing brand name to promote a new or improved product in a company's product line. (p. 736)

brand label The information tag on a product or package that gives the brand name, trademark, or logo. (p. 742)

brand licensing A legal authorization by a brand owner to allow another company (the licensee) to use its brand, brand mark, or trade character for a fee. (p. 736)

brand mark Incorporates a unique symbol, coloring, lettering, or design element that is easily visible. (p. 732)

brand name A word, group of words, letters, or numbers that represents a product or service. (p. 731)

break-even point The point at which sales revenue equals the costs and expenses of making and distributing a product. (p. 592)

brick-and-mortar retailer A traditional retailer who sells goods to customers from a physical store. (p. 494)

broadcast media Radio and television. (p. 446)

budget account A credit account that allows for the payment of a purchased item over a certain time period without a finance charge. (p. 764)

bundle pricing Pricing method in which a company offers several complementary, or corresponding, products in a package that is sold at a single price. (p. 613)

business cycle Recurring changes in economic activity. (p. 75)

business philosophy A company's stated beliefs on how its business should be run. (p. 821)

business plan A proposal that outlines a strategy to turn a business idea into a reality. (p. 819)

business risk The potential for financial gain, loss, or failure. (pp. 117, 799)

buying behavior The process that individuals use to decide what they will buy, where they will buy it, and from whom they will buy it. (p. 825)

buying motive A reason a customer buys a product. (p. 302)

buying signals Things customers say or do to indicate a readiness to buy. (p. 341)

C

call report A written report that documents a sales representative's visit with a customer, including the purpose and outcome of the visit. (p. 280)

career outlook The number and types of jobs available in any field. (p. 876)

carload Minimum number of pounds of freight needed to fill a boxcar. (p. 519)

cash flow statement A monthly plan that tracks when cash is expected to come into the business and when it is expected to be paid out. (p. 859)

cash-on-delivery (COD) sale A transaction that occurs when a customer pays for merchandise at the time of delivery. (p. 369)

category management A process that involves managing product categories as individual business units. (p. 721)

cause packaging Packaging that promotes social and political causes. (p. 742)

centralized buying The buying process for all branches in a chain-store operation done in a central location. (p. 542)

* **challenge** A demanding or stimulating situation. (p. 876)

channel of distribution The path a product takes from its producer or manufacturer to the final user. (p. 493)

channels/media The avenues through which messages are delivered. (p. 191)

circle graph A pie-shaped figure that shows the relative sizes of the parts of a whole. (p. 181)

clip art Inexpensive or free images, stock drawings, and photographs. (p. 474)

closing the sale Obtaining positive agreement from a customer to buy. (p. 341)

co-branding A strategy that combines one or more brands in the manufacture of a product or in the delivery of a service. (p. 737)

cold call A sales visit without an appointment. (p. 285)

cold canvassing The process of locating as many potential customers as possible without checking leads beforehand. (p. 304)

* **collate** To assemble in proper sequence. (p. 323)

collateral Something of value that you pledge as payment for a loan in case of default. (p. 834)

color wheel Illustrates the relationships among colors. (p. 430)

command economy A system in which a country's government makes all economic decisions regarding what, how, and for whom. (p. 64)

* **commission** A fee for services rendered based on a percentage of an amount received or collected or agreed to be paid (as distinguished from a salary). (p. 493)

* **commit** To give entirely to a specific activity or cause. (p. 342)

common carrier Trucking company that provides transportation services to any business in their operating area for a fee. (p. 517)

communication The process of exchanging messages between a sender and a receiver. (p. 191)

communications program A computer program that enables users to communicate with other users through their computers. (p. 216)

* **community** A district where people live; occupied primarily by private residences. (p. 785)

* **comparable** Conforming in most respects; able to be compared. (p. 709)

* **compensate** To make up for shortcomings or a feeling of inferiority by exaggerating good qualities. (p. 332)

competition A business relation in which parties compete to gain customers. (p. 115)

complementary colors Colors that are opposite each other on the color wheel and create high contrast. (p. 430)

* **complex** Complicated in structure; consisting of interconnected parts. (p. 566)

* **component** Something determined in relation to something that includes it. (p. 731)

* **concentrate** To direct one's attention on something. (p. 378)

* **concept** An abstract or general idea inferred or derived from specific instances. (p. 419)

* **conduct** To direct or take part in the operation or management of something. (p. 8)

* **conflict** A disagreement or argument about something important. (p. 245)

consensus A decision about which all members of a team approve. (p. 243)

consignment buying A buying process in which goods are paid for only after the final customer purchases them. (p. 547)

* **consist** Be composed or made up of. (p. 219)

* **constant** Continually recurring or continuing without interruption. (p. 591)

consumer market Consumers who purchase goods and services for personal use. (p. 17)

consumer price index (CPI) Measures the change in price over a period of time of 400 specific retail goods and services used by the average urban household. (p. 73)

Consumer Product Safety Commission (CPSC) Responsible for overseeing the safety of products such as toys, electronics, and household furniture. (p. 140)

consumer promotions Sales strategies that encourage customers and prospects to buy a product or service. (p. 406)

* **contact** To be in or establish communication with. (p. 893)

contract carrier A for-hire trucking company that provides equipment and drivers for specific routes, per agreements between the carrier and the shipper. (p. 518)

contract manufacturing Hiring a foreign manufacturer to make your products according to your specifications. (p. 94)

* **control** The power to direct or determine. (p. 503)

controlling The process of setting standards and evaluating performance. (p. 257)

* **convert** Change from one system to another or to a new plan or policy. (p. 633)

* **convince** Make someone agree, understand, or realize the truth or validity of something. (p. 901)

copy The selling message of a written advertisement. (p. 473)

copyright Anything that is authored by an individual, such as writings (books, magazine articles, etc.), music, and artwork. (p. 115)

* **corporate** Of or belonging to a corporation, a business firm whose articles of incorporation have been approved in some state. (p. 97)

corporation A legal entity created by either a state or federal statute, authorizing individuals to operate an enterprise. (p. 789)

cost per thousand (CPM) The media-measurement cost of exposing 1,000 readers or viewers to an advertising impression. (p. 453)

coupon A certificate that entitles a customer to a cash discount on goods or services. (p. 406)

cover letter A letter written by a job applicant to introduce the applicant to an employer in the hopes of convincing the employer to read the résumé. (p. 901)

* **create** To make or cause to be or to become. (p. 7)

credit Loaned money in exchange for the promise to pay later. (p. 761)

credit union A cooperative association formed by groups of employees to serve as a financial organization and offer lower rates for the benefit of its members. (p. 834)

cross-training Preparing to do many different activities, such as for tasks on a team. (p. 243)

* **crucial** Of the greatest importance. (p. 454)

customer benefit Advantage or personal satisfaction a customer will get from a good or service. (p. 301)

customer profile Information about the target market, such as age, gender, income level, marital status, ethnic background, geographic residence, attitudes, lifestyle, and behavior. (p. 20)

customer relationship management (CRM) A system that involves finding customers and keeping them satisfied. (p. 277)

customization Creating specially designed products or promotions for certain countries or regions. (p. 101)

cycle count An inventory system involving a small portion of the inventory each day that is counted by stockkeeping units so that the entire inventory is accounted for on a regular basis. (p. 568)

D

data analysis The process of compiling, analyzing, and interpreting the results of primary and secondary data collection. (p. 686)

database A collection of related information about a specific topic. (p. 658)

database marketing Also known as customer relationship management (CRM); a process of designing, creating, and managing customer lists. (p. 658)

database program An application that stores and organizes information, like a filing cabinet. (p. 213)

DBA (Doing Business As) The registration by which the county government officially recognizes that a new proprietorship or partnership exists. (p. 790)

debt capital Borrowed funds, from sources such as banks, friends, and suppliers, that must be repaid. (p. 832)

decentralized buying The buying process in which local store managers or designated buyers are authorized to make special purchases for their individual stores. (p. 542)

decimal number Another way to write a fraction or mixed number whose denominator is a power of 10. (p. 167)

demand Consumer willingness and ability to buy products. The law of demand is the economic principle that price and demand move in opposite directions. (p. 119)

demand elasticity The degree to which demand for a product is affected by its price. (p. 592)

demographics Statistics that describe a population in terms of personal characteristics, such as age, gender, income, marital status, and ethnic background. (p. 44)

* **demonstrate** To show by one's behavior, attitude, or external attributes. (p. 233)

denominator The bottom number of a fraction, which represents how many parts in a whole. (p. 166)

depression A period of prolonged recession. (p. 76)

derived demand Demand in the organizational market that is based on, or derived from, the demand for consumer goods and services. (p. 125)

descriptive label A label that gives information about the product's use, construction, care, performance, and other features. (p. 742)

desktop publishing program A computer program that enables users to edit and manipulate both text and graphics in one document. (p. 215)

* **determine** Decide upon or fix definitely. (p. 681)

* **device** A machine or piece of equipment that does a particular job. (p. 807)

digits The ten basic symbols in our numbering system: 0, 1, 2, 3, 4, 5, 6, 7, 8, and 9. Each digit represents a number and can be combined to represent larger numbers. (p. 165)

direct check method A method of checking in which the merchandise is checked directly against the actual invoice or purchase order. (p. 560)

direct close A method in which the salesperson asks for the sale, when the buying signal is very strong. (p. 344)

direct distribution A channel of distribution that occurs when the producer sells goods or services directly to the customer with no intermediaries. (p. 495)

direct marketing A type of advertising that sends a promotional message to a targeted group of prospects and customers rather than to a mass audience. (p. 396)

disclaimer A statement that contains exceptions to and exclusions from a warranty. (p. 755)

discretionary income The money left after paying for basic living necessities, such as food, shelter, and clothing. (p. 45)

display The visual and artistic aspects of presenting a product or service to a target group of customers to encourage a purchase. (p. 419)

disposable income The money left after taking out taxes. (p. 45)

* **distinct** Serving to distinguish or identify a species or group. (p. 731)

distraction Something that competes with the message for the listener's attention. (p. 195)

* **distribution** The commercial activity of transporting and selling goods from a producer to a consumer. (p. 406)

distribution center A warehouse designed to speed delivery of goods and to minimize storage costs. (p. 526)

dollar control Represents the planning and monitoring of the total inventory investment made by a business during a stated period of time. (p. 570)

* **domestic** Produced in a particular country; of concern to or concerning the internal affairs of a nation. (p. 783)

domestic business A business that sells its products only in its own country. (p. 123)

drop shipper One who owns the goods he or she sells, but does not physically handle the actual products. (p. 494)

E

economic risk A risk that results from changes in overall business conditions. (p. 799)

economy The organized way a nation provides for the needs and wants of its population. (p. 61)

* **edit** Prepare for publication or presentation by correcting, revising, or adapting. (p. 215)

* **element** An important basic part of something complicated, for example, a system or plan. (p. 21)

e-marketplace An online shopping outlet. (p. 505)

embargo A total ban on specific goods coming into or leaving a country. (p. 89)

emotional barrier A bias against a sender's opinions that prevent a listener from understanding. (p. 195)

emotional motive A feeling expressed by a customer through association with a product. (p. 302)

empathy An understanding of a person's situation or frame of mind. (p. 239)

* **emphasis** Special importance or attention that is given to one thing. (p. 480)

employee discount A discount offered to workers by their employers. (p. 639)

empowerment Encouraging team members to contribute to and take responsibility for the management process. (p. 254)

* **enable** To make capable or able for some task. (p. 764)

endless chain method When salespeople ask previous customers for names of potential customers. (p. 303)

* **enhance** To increase; to make better or more attractive. (p. 199)

* **ensure** To make certain of something. (p. 525)

enterprise resource planning (ERP) Software used to integrate all parts of a company's business management, including planning, manufacturing, sales, marketing, invoicing, payroll, inventory control, order tracking, customer service, finance, and human resources. (p. 220)

entrepreneur Someone who creates, launches, organizes, and manages a new business and takes the risk of business ownership. (p. 779)

entrepreneurship The skills of people who are willing to invest their time and money to run a business; the process of starting and operating your own business. (pp. 62, 779)

enumeration A listing of items in order. (p. 200)

Environmental Protection Agency (EPA) Protects human health and our environment. Its responsibilities include monitoring and reducing air and water pollution and overseeing recycling and hazardous waste disposal. (p. 142)

Equal Employment Opportunity Commission (EEOC) Responsible for the fair and equitable treatment of employees with regard to hiring, firing, and promotions. (p. 141)

* **equate** Make equal, uniform, corresponding, or matching. (p. 593)

* **equip** To provide with something, usually for a specific purpose. (p. 427)

equity Equal rights and opportunities for everyone. (p. 237)

equity capital Money raised from within a company or from selling part of an owner's share. (p. 831)

* **error** A wrong action attributable to bad judgment or ignorance or inattention. (p. 560)

* **estimate** Judge tentatively or judge to be probable. (p. 175)

e-tailing Online retailing that involves retailers selling products over the Internet to customers. (p. 494)

ethics Guidelines for good behavior; the basic values and moral principles that guide the behavior of individuals and groups. (pp. 150, 236)

European Union (EU) Europe's trading bloc. (p. 90)

* **evaluate** To judge the worth or value of something. (p. 545)

everyday low prices (EDLP) Low prices set on a consistent basis with no intention of raising them or offering discounts in the future. (p. 616)

* **exceed** To be or do something to a greater extent; go beyond. (p. 761)

exclusive distribution Distribution that involves distributing a product in protected territories in a given geographic area. (p. 504)

excuse A reason given when a customer has no intention of buying in retail-sales situations. (p. 327)

executive summary A brief overview of the entire marketing plan. (p. 37)

exempt carrier A trucking company that is free from direct regulation of rates and operating procedures. (p. 518)

exit interview An opportunity for an employee and a manager to obtain valuable feedback when an employee leaves the company. (p. 265)

* **expand** To make something become larger in size and fill more space. (p. 819)

* **expansion** A time when the economy is expanding. (p. 75)

experimental method A research technique in which a researcher observes the results of changing one or more marketing variables while keeping all the other variables constant under controlled conditions. (p. 685)

* **expert** A person with special knowledge or ability who performs skillfully. (p. 468)

exports Goods and services sold to other countries. (p. 8)

express warranty A warranty clearly stated in writing or offered verbally to encourage a customer to make a purchase. (p. 754)

extended coverage A property insurance endorsement that provides protection against types of loss that may not be covered under a basic property insurance policy. (p. 808)

extended product feature Intangible attribute related to the sale of a product that customers find important. (p. 301)

extensive decision making A type of customer decision making used when there has been little or no previous experience with an item offered for sale. (p. 287)

F

* **factor** Anything that contributes causally to a result. (p. 31)

factors of production Resources that are comprised of land, labor, capital, and entrepreneurship. (p. 61)

feature-benefit selling Matching the characteristics of a product to a customer's needs and wants. (p. 299)

Federal Trade Commission (FTC) Enforces the principles of a private-enterprise system and protects consumers from unfair or deceptive business practices. (p. 143)

feedback A receiver's response to a message. (p. 191)

fidelity bond A bond that provides insurance that protects a business from employee dishonesty. (p. 810)

finance The function of business that involves money management. (p. 128)

firewall A hardware and software checkpoint for all requests for or inputs of data, incoming and outgoing. (p. 223)

fixtures Permanent or movable store furnishings that hold and display merchandise. (p. 423)

flexibility The ability to adapt to changing circumstances. (p. 235)

flexible-price policy A policy in which customers pay different prices for the same type or amount of merchandise. (p. 608)

flextime A system that allows workers to choose their work hours. (p. 147)

focal point An area in a display that attracts attention first. (p. 431)

Food and Drug Administration (FDA) Regulates the labeling and safety of food, drugs, and cosmetics sold throughout the United States. (p. 140)

forced-choice question A question that asks respondents to choose an answer from possibilities given on a questionnaire. (p. 689)

foreign corporation One that is incorporated under the laws of a state that differs from the one in which it does business. (p. 790)

foreign direct investment (FDI) The establishment of a business in a foreign country. (p. 95)

formal balance Created in a display by placing large items with large items and small items with small items. (p. 431)

* **formula** A group of symbols that make a mathematical statement. (p. 172)

for-profit business A business that seeks to make a profit from its operations. (p.124)

fraction Number used to describe or compare parts of a whole. (p. 166)

franchise A legal agreement to sell a parent company's product or services in a designated geographic area. (p. 785)

free on board (FOB) A delivery arrangement that means the price for goods includes delivery at the seller's expense to a specified point and no farther. (p. 383)

free trade Commercial exchange between nations that is conducted on free market principles, without regulations. (p. 88)

freight forwarder A private company that combines less-than-carload or less-than-truckload shipments from several businesses and delivers them to their destinations. (p. 523)

frequency The number of times an audience sees or hears an advertisement. (p. 453)

full warranty A written guarantee that if a product is found to be defective within the warranty period, it will be repaired or replaced at no cost to the purchaser. (p. 754)

* **funding** Money provided for a specific purpose, such as capital to finance the operation of a business. (p. 831)

G

gauge To form a judgment of something uncertain or variable. (p. 336)

general partnership A type of business ownership in which each partner shares in the profits and losses. (p. 787)

generalization A statement that is accepted as true by most people. (p. 200)

* **generate** To bring into existence; produce. (p. 124)

generic brand A product that does not carry a company identity. (p. 735)

geographical pricing Price adjustments required because of different shipping agreements. (p. 614)

geographics Segmentation of the market based on where people live. (p. 46)

global business A business that sells its products in more than one country. (p. 123)

globalization Selling the same product and using the same promotion methods in all countries. (p. 99)

goods Tangible items that have monetary value and satisfy one's needs and wants. (p. 7)

grade label A label that states the quality of the product, such as eggs. (p. 743)

graphics and design program Software application for creating and modifying images. (p. 215)

green marketing When companies engage in the production and promotion of environmentally safe products. (p. 148)

greeting approach A retail approach method in which the salesperson welcomes the customer to the store. (p. 308)

gross domestic product (GDP) The output of goods and services produced by labor and property located within a country. (p. 72)

gross national product (GNP) The total dollar value of goods and services produced by a nation, including goods and services produced abroad by U.S. citizens and companies. (p. 72)

gross profit The difference between sales revenue and the cost of goods sold. (p. 627)

gross sales The total of all sales for a given period of time. (p. 852)

* **guarantee** A pledge that something will happen or that something is true. (p. 719)

H

headline The phrase or sentence in an advertisement that captures the readers' attention, generates interest, and entices them to read the rest of the ad. (p. 471)

home page The entry point for a Web site, giving general information to introduce the company, person, or product. (p. 216)

horizontal organization A type of management style in which top management shares decision making with self-managing teams of workers who set their own goals and make their own decisions. (p. 254)

human risk Risk caused by employee dishonesty, errors, mistakes, and omissions, as well as the unpredictability of customers or the workplace. (p. 801)

hypertext markup language (HTML) The specific, detailed, and complicated code used to create a Web page. (p. 216)

hypertext transfer protocol (HTTP) The technology that links documents together on the Web. (p. 222)

I
---

* **identify** To ascertain the origin, nature, or definitive characteristics of. (p. 257)

illustration The photograph, drawing, or other graphic element that is used in an advertisement. (p. 473)

* **impact** A strong effect or influence. (p. 13)

implied warranty A warranty that takes effect automatically by state law whenever a purchase is made. (p. 755)

imports Goods and services purchased from other countries. (p. 85)

impression A single exposure to an advertising message. (p. 453)

incentive A higher-priced product, award, or gift card that is earned and given away through contests, sweepstakes, special offers, and rebates. (p. 408)

income statement A summary of income and expenses during a specific period such as a month or year. (p. 851)

* **indicate** To make a sign that something will happen, is true, or exists. (p. 781)

indirect distribution A channel of distribution that involves one or more intermediaries. (p. 495)

* **individual** A single human being as contrasted with a social group or institution. (p. 255)

industry A group of establishments primarily engaged in producing or handling the same product or group of products or in rendering the same services. (p. 125)

inflation Rising prices. (p. 73)

informal balance Achieved in a display by placing several small items with one large item within the display. (p. 431)

infrastructure The physical development of a country, such as roads, ports, and utilities. (pp. 61, 85)

initiative Taking action and doing what needs to be done without being asked. (p. 233)

installment account A time-payment plan that allows for payment over a period of time. (p. 764)

institutional advertising Advertising designed to create a favorable image for a company and foster goodwill in the marketplace. (p. 441)

institutional promotion A promotional method used to create a favorable image for a business, help it advocate for change, or take a stand on trade or community issues. (p. 395)

insurance policy A contract between a business and an insurance company to cover a specific business risk. (p. 807)

* **integral** Forming an essential part of something and needed to make it complete. (p. 739)

integrated distribution A type of distribution in which manufacturers own and run their own retail operations, acting as wholesaler and retailer for their own products. (p. 505)

intensive distribution Distribution that involves the use of all suitable outlets to sell a product. (p. 505)

* **interact** To act together or toward others or with others. (p. 116)

interactive kiosk An interactive point-of-purchase display that is a free-standing, full-service retail location. (p. 425)

interest The money paid for the use of money borrowed or invested. (p. 856)

* **interface** To join by means of a computer and any other entity, such as a printer or human operator. (p. 279)

intermediary Middleman business involved in sales transactions that move products from the manufacturer to the final user. (p. 493)

* **internal** Occurring within an institution or community. (p. 803)

international trade The exchange of goods and services among nations. (p. 85)

Internet An electronic communications network that connects computer networks and organizational computer facilities around the world. (p. 222)

Internet advertising The form of advertising that uses either e-mail or the World Wide Web. (p. 448)

internship Direct work in a job that allows the person to get experience, either with or without pay. (p. 876)

inventory Amount of merchandise on hand at any particular time, including raw materials, parts from suppliers, manufactured subassemblies, work-in-process, packing materials, or finished goods. (p. 565)

inventory management The process of buying and storing materials and products while controlling costs for ordering, shipping, handling, and storage. (p. 565)

inventory turnover The number of times the average inventory has been sold and replaced in a given period of time. (p. 571)

invest To commit (money or capital) in order to gain a financial return. (p. 75)

invoice Itemized list of goods that include prices, terms of sale, total, taxes and fees, and amount due. (p. 382)

J
---

jargon A specialized vocabulary used by members of a particular group. (p. 196)

job description A written statement listing the requirements of a particular job and the skills needed to fulfill those requirements. (p. 829)

job lead Information about a job opening, perhaps providing some indication about the type of work and who to contact. (p. 893)

joint venture A business enterprise that a domestic company and a foreign company undertake together. (p. 94)

* **journal** A ledger in which transactions have been recorded as they occurred. (p. 546)

just-in-time (JIT) inventory system A system that controls and coordinates the flow of parts and materials into assembly and manufacturing plants so that suppliers deliver parts and raw materials just before they are needed for use. (p. 565)

K

kiosk A point-of-purchase display that is a stand-alone structure. (p. 411)

L

label An information tag, wrapper, seal, or imprinted message that is attached to a product or its package. (p. 742)

labor Productive work (especially physical work done for wages). (p. 585)

law of diminishing marginal utility An economic law that states that consumers will buy only so much of a given product, even if the price is low. (p. 592)

layaway Removing merchandise from stock and keeping it in a separate area until the customer pays for it. (p. 369)

layman's terms Words that the average customer can understand. (p. 322)

liability A debt owed to others, such as a car payment, credit card debt, or taxes. (p. 843)

licensing Letting another company, or licensee, use a trademark, patent, special formula, company name, or some other intellectual property for a fee or royalty. (p. 93)

lifestyle The type of life you would like to live. (p. 873)

limited decision making Used when a person buys goods and services that he or she has purchased before but not regularly. (p. 287)

limited liability A type of investment in which the personal assets of the owners cannot be taken if a company does not meet its financial obligations or if it gets into legal trouble. (p. 789)

limited liability company (LLC) A relatively new form of business organization that is a hybrid of a partnership and a corporation. (p. 790)

limited partnership A type of business ownership in which each limited partner is liable for any debts only up to the amount of his or her investment in the company. (p. 789)

limited warranty A written guarantee that may exclude certain parts of the product from coverage or require the customer to bear some of the expense for repairs resulting from defects. (p. 755)

line graph A line (or lines) that joins points representing changes in a quantity over a specific period of time. (p. 180)

* **link** An instruction that connects one part of a program or an element on a list to another program or list. (p. 222)

* **logotype** A graphic symbol for a company, brand, or organization; logo. (p. 469)

* **longevity** Having a long life or existence. (p. 299)

loss leader An item priced at or below cost to draw customers into a store. (p. 596)

loyalty marketing program A marketing program that rewards customers by offering incentives for repeat purchases, such as a frequent flyer. (p. 410)

M

maintain To keep in a certain state, position, or activity. (p. 504)

maintained markup The difference between an item's final sale price and its cost. (p. 635)

major Significant; of considerable importance. (p. 180)

management The process of achieving company goals by effective use of resources through planning, organizing, and controlling. (pp. 128, 253)

market All people who share similar needs and wants and who have the ability to purchase a given product. (p. 17)

market economy An economic system in which there is no government involvement in economic decisions. (p. 63)

market intelligence Also known as market research; concerned with the size and location of a market, the competition, and segmentation within the market for a particular product. (p. 664)

market position The relative standing a competitor has in a given market in comparison to its other competitors. (p. 588)

market segmentation The process of classifying people who form a given market into even smaller groups. (p. 43)

market share A company's percentage of the total sales volume generated by all companies that compete in a given market (pp. 18, 588)

marketing The activity, set of institutions, and processes for creating, communicating, delivering, and exchanging offerings that have value for customers, clients, partners, and society at large. (p. 7)

marketing concept The idea that a business should strive to satisfy customers' needs and wants while generating a profit for the business. (p. 10)

marketing information system A set of procedures and methods that regularly generates, stores, analyzes, and distributes information for making marketing and other business decisions. (p. 658)

marketing mix The four basic marketing strategies called the four P's: product, place, price, and promotion. (p. 20)

marketing plan A formal, written document that directs a company's activities for a specific period of time. (p. 37)

marketing research The process and methods used to gather information, analyze it, and report findings related to marketing goods and services. (p. 655)

marketing strategy Identifies target markets and sets marketing mix choices that focus on those markets. (p. 39)

markup The difference between an item's cost and sale price. (p. 605)

marquee A canopy that extends over a store's entrance. (p. 420)

mass marketing Using a single marketing strategy to reach all customers. (p. 49)

media The agencies, means, or instruments used to convey messages to the public. (p. 442)

media/channels The avenues through which messages are delivered. (p. 191)

media planning The process of selecting the appropriate advertising media and deciding the time or space in which ads should appear to accomplish a marketing objective. (p. 451)

media research Also known as advertising research; focuses on issues of media effectiveness, selection, frequency, and ratings. (p. 665)

memorandum buying The buying process in which the supplier agrees to take back any unsold goods by a pre-established date. (p. 547)

merchandise approach A retail-sales method, also called the theme approach, in which the salesperson makes a comment or asks a question about a product in which the customer shows an interest. (p. 309)

merchandising Coordinating sales and promotional plans with buying and pricing. (p. 298)

* **method** A way of doing something, especially a systematic way. (p. 71)

middle management The type of management that implements the decisions of top management and plans how the departments under them can work to reach top management's goals. (p. 253)

* **minimum** The smallest possible quantity. (p. 641)

mini-national A midsize or smaller company that has operations in foreign countries. (p. 95)

mission statement A description of the ultimate goals of a company. (p. 258)

mixed brand A strategy that offers a combination of manufacturer, private distributor, and generic brand to consumers. (p. 737)

mixed bundling Packaging two or more different goods or services in one package. (p. 739)

mixed number A whole number and a fraction. (p. 166)

model stock list A stock list that is used for fashionable merchandise. (p. 572)

* **monitor** To keep an eye on; keep under surveillance. (p. 883)

monopoly Exclusive control over a product or the means of producing it. (p. 117)

multinational A large corporation that has operations in several countries. (p. 95)

* **mutual** Concerning each of two or more things; especially given or done in return. (p. 690)

N

national brand Also known as producer brand, this is owned and initiated by a national manufacturer or by a company that provides services. (p. 734)

natural risk A risk that is caused by natural occurrences, such as floods, fires, and earthquakes. (p. 800)

negotiation The process of working with parties in conflict to find a resolution. (p. 238)

net income The amount left after total expenses are subtracted from gross profit. (p. 855)

net sales The amount left after gross sales have been adjusted for returns and allowances. (p. 852)

net worth The difference between assets and liabilities. (p. 844)

* **network** A communication system consisting of a group of broadcasting stations that all transmit the same program. (p. 446)

networking The art of building alliances. (p. 893)

never-out list A stock list used for best-selling products that make up a large percentage of sales volume. (p. 572)

news release An announcement sent to the appropriate media outlets. (p. 399)

nonprice competition When businesses choose to compete on the basis of factors that are not related to price, including the quality of the products, service, financing, business location, and reputation. (p. 116)

nonprofit organization A group that functions like a business but uses the money it makes to fund the cause identified in its charter. (p. 124)

nonverbal communication Expressing oneself without the use of works, such as with facial expressions, eye movement, and hand motions. (p. 310)

North American Free Trade Agreement (NAFTA) An international trade agreement among the United States, Canada, and Mexico. (p. 91)

numerator The top number of a fraction, which represents the number of parts being considered. (p. 166)

O

objection A concern, hesitation, doubt, complaint, or other reason a customer has for not making a purchase. (p. 327)

objection analysis sheet A document that lists common objections and possible responses to them. (p. 328)

objective The goal intended to be attained. (p. 458)

observation method A research technique in which the actions of people are watched and recorded, either by cameras or by observers. (p. 685)

* **obtain** Come into possession of. (p. 656)

occupational area A category of jobs that involve similar interests and skills. (p. 885)

Occupational Information Network (O∙NET) A database that is the primary source for occupational information in the United States; contains information on skills, abilities, knowledge, work activities, and interests associated with occupations. (p. 876)

Occupational Outlook Handbook (OOH) A publication available online and in libraries that describes what workers do, working conditions, the training and education required, earnings, and expected job prospects in a wide range of occupations. (p. 875)

Occupational Safety and Health Administration (OSHA) Sets guidelines for workplace safety and environmental concerns and enforces those regulations. (p. 142)

on-approval sale An agreement that allows a customer to take merchandise home for further consideration. (p. 369)

one-price policy A policy in which all customers are charged the same prices. (p. 608)

open-ended question A question that requires more than a "yes" or "no" answer and requires respondents to construct their own response. (pp. 313, 689)

opening cash fund A limited amount of money in the cash register at the beginning of business. (p. 376)

open-to-buy (OTB) The amount of money a retailer has left for buying goods after considering all purchases received, on order, and in transit. (p. 540)

* **option** The act of choosing or selecting. (p. 517)

organization chart A diagram of a company's departments and jobs with lines of authority clearly shown. (p. 830)

organizational buyer One who purchases goods for business purposes, usually in greater quantities than that of the average consumer. (p. 537)

organizational market Also known as business-to-business (B2B), this includes all businesses that buy products for use in their operations. (p. 17)

organizational selling Sales exchanges that occur between two or more companies or business groups. (p. 285)

organizing Establishing a time frame in which to achieve a goal, assigning employees to the project, and determining a method for approaching the work. (p. 257)

* **overall** Including everything; regarded as a whole; general. (p. 656)

* **overseas** In a foreign country. (p. 382)

P
---

package The physical container or wrapping for a product. (p. 739)

* **paraphrase** To express the same message in different words. (p. 330)

partnership A legal agreement between two or more people to be jointly responsible for the success or failure of a business. (p. 787)

patent A document granting an inventor sole rights to an item or an idea. (p. 114)

patronage motive A reason for remaining a loyal customer of a company. (p. 302)

penetration pricing Setting the price for a new product very low to encourage as many as possible to buy the product. (p. 610)

* **perceive** To become aware of through the senses. (p. 233)

* **percent** A proportion multiplied by 100. (p. 178)

percentage A number expressed as parts per 100. (p. 178)

performance bond Also called a surety bond, a bond that provides financial protection for losses that might occur when a construction project is not finished due to a contractor's impaired financial condition. (p. 810)

performance standard An expectation for performance that reflects the plan's objectives. (p. 40)

* **period** An amount of time during which something happens. (p. 741)

perpetual inventory system An inventory system that tracks the number of items in inventory on a constant basis; tracking sales and other transactions as they occur. (p. 567)

* **perquisite** An incidental benefit awarded for certain types of employment (especially if it is regarded as a right). (p. 289)

* **perseverance** The act of persisting; continuing or repeating behavior. (p. 346)

personal financial statement A summary of one's current personal financial condition listing assets and liabilities. (p. 843)

personal selling Any form of direct contact between a salesperson and a customer. (p. 285)

persuade To convince someone to change an opinion in order to get him or her to do what you want. (p. 199)

PEST analysis Scanning of outside influences on an organization. (p. 34)

physical distribution Activities for delivering the right amount of product to the right place at the right time. (p. 515)

physical feature Tangible attribute that helps explain how a product is constructed. (p. 301)

physical inventory system An inventory system in which stock is visually inspected or actually counted to determine the quantity on hand. (p. 568)

planning Setting goals and determining how to reach them. (p. 257)

planning goals Small steps taken to get from where you are to where you want to be in your career. (p. 879)

planogram A computer-developed diagram that shows retailers how and where products within a category should be displayed on a shelf at individual stores. (p. 721)

podcast Any brief digital broadcast that includes audio, images, and video delivered separately or in combination. (p. 448)

point-of-purchase display (POP) A standalone structure that serves as a customer sales promotion device. (p. 424)

point-of-sale research Powerful form of research that combines natural observation with personal interviews to explain buying behavior. (p. 685)

point-of-sale system A combination of a cash register with a computer, making it possible to capture information about the transaction at the time of sale and apply it to different functions. (p. 374)

* **policy** A plan or course of action, as of a business, intended to influence and determine decisions, actions, and other matters. (p. 147)

* **potential** Expected to become or be; in prospect. (p. 85)

* **predict** To state, tell about, or make known in advance, especially on the basis of special knowledge. (p. 537)

premium Low cost item given to consumers at a discount or for free. (p. 407)

preretailing marking method A method of marking in which the pricing information is marked in advance on the purchase order, then entered into the buyer's computer system, and prices are available for marking as soon as merchandise is received. (p. 562)

presentation software Computer software that produces slide shows or multimedia presentations. (p. 215)

* **pre-sold** Refers to sales that are due to promotional efforts before a customer comes to a store. (p. 285)

prestige pricing Higher-than-average prices to suggest status and high quality to the customer. (p. 616)

price The value in money or its equivalent placed on a good or service. (p. 585)

price bundling When two or more similar products are placed on sale for one package price. (p. 739)

price competition A focus on the sale price of a product. The assumption is that, all other things being equal, consumers will buy the products that are lowest in price. (p. 116)

price discrimination When a firm charges different prices to similar customers in similar situations. (p. 595)

price fixing A situation that occurs when competitors agree on certain price ranges within which they set their own prices. (p. 595)

price gouging Pricing products unreasonably high when the need is great or when consumers do not have other choices. (p. 151)

price lining A pricing technique that sets a limited number of prices for specific groups or lines of merchandise. (p. 613)

primary data Data obtained for the first time and used specifically for the particular problem or issue under study. (p. 681)

principal The amount of money needed to start a business. (p. 856)

* **principle** A basic generalization that is accepted as true and that can be used as a basis for reasoning or conduct. (p. 429)

print media Advertising in newspapers, magazines, direct mail, signs, and billboards. (p. 442)

private carrier A trucking company that transports goods for an individual business. (p. 518)

private distributor brand Known as private brand, store brand, dealer brand, or private label, this is developed and owned by wholesalers and retailers. (p. 734)

private employment agency An employment agency not supported by taxes that must earn a profit to stay in business; it charges a fee for its services, paid either by the job applicant or the employer. (p. 894)

private enterprise Business ownership by ordinary people, not the government. (p. 113)

private sector Businesses not associated with government agencies. (p. 124)

private warehouse A storage facility designed to meet the specific needs of its owner. (p. 525)

problem definition Occurs when a business clearly identifies a problem and what is needed to solve it. (p. 679)

* **process** A particular course of action intended to achieve a result. (p. 191)

producer price index (PPI) Measures wholesale price levels in the economy. (p. 73)

product depth The number of items offered within each product line. (p. 708)

product feature Basic, physical, or extended attribute of a product or purchase. (p. 299)

product item A specific model, brand, or size of a product within a product line. (p. 708)

product life cycle The stages that a product goes through during its life. (p. 717)

product line A group of closely related products manufactured or sold by a business. (p. 708)

product mix All the different products that a company makes or sells. (p. 707)

product mix pricing strategy Adjusting prices to maximize the profitability for a group of products rather than for just one item. (p. 613)

product modification An alteration in a company's existing product. (p. 714)

product planning Making decisions about the features and services of a product or idea that will help sell the product. (p. 707)

product positioning The efforts a business makes to identify, place, and sell its products in the marketplace. (p. 720)

product promotion A promotional method used by businesses to convince prospects to select their goods or services instead of a competitor's brands. (p. 395)

product research Research that centers on evaluating product design, package design, product usage, and consumer acceptance of new and existing products. (p. 668)

product width The number of items offered within each product line. (p. 708)

production The process of creating, growing, manufacturing, or improving on goods and services. (p.127)

productivity Output per worker hour that is measured over a defined period time. (p. 71)

profit The money earned from conducting business after all costs and expenses have been paid. (p. 118)

* **project** To put or send forth. (p. 419)

promotion Decisions about advertising, personal selling, sales promotion, and public relations used to attract customers. (p. 395)

promotional advertising Advertising designed to increase sales. (p. 441)

promotional mix A cost-effective combination of advertising, selling, sales promotion, direct marketing, and public relations strategies used to reach company goals. (p. 396)

promotional pricing Used in conjunction with sales promotions when prices are reduced for a short period of time. (p. 616)

promotional tie-in Activity that involves sales promotions between one or more retailers or manufacturers; also called cross-promotion or cross-selling. (p. 409)

proportion The relationship between and among objects in a display. (p. 431)

* **proprietary** Made or produced or distributed by one having exclusive rights. (p. 94)

props Properties that are items or physical objects that hold the merchandise on display or support the display setting. (p. 428)

prospect A sales lead; a potential customer. (p. 303)

prospecting Looking for new customers. (p. 303)

protectionism A government's establishment of economic policies that systematically restrict imports in order to protect domestic industries. (p. 89)

prototype A model of a new product, usually made before the product is manufactured. (p. 713)

psychographics Grouping people with similar attitudes, interests, and opinions, as well as lifestyles and shared values. (p. 47)

psychological pricing Pricing techniques that create an illusion for customers. (p. 615)

public employment agency An employment agency supported by state or federal taxes that offers free services to both job applicants and employers. (p. 894)

public relations Activities that help an organization to influence a target audience. (p. 397)

public sector Government-financed agencies, such as the Environmental Protection Agency. (p. 124)

public warehouse A storage and handling facility offered to any individual or company that will pay for its use. (p. 526)

* **publication** A copy of a printed word offered for distribution. (p. 876)

publicity Bringing news or newsworthy information about an organization to the public's attention. (p. 399)

pull policy A type of promotion by manufacturers that directs promotional activities toward consumers. (p. 403)

* **purchase** To acquire by means of a financial transaction. (p. 113)

purchase order (PO) A legal contract between a buyer and seller that lists the quantity, price, and description of the products ordered, along with the terms of payment and delivery. (p. 381)

* **purpose** What something is used for. (p. 849)

* **pursue** To carry further or go in search of. (p. 894)

push policy A type of promotion in which manufacturers use a mix of advertising, personal selling, and trade discounts with partners in the distribution channel to "push" the product through to the retailer. (p. 403)

Q

qualitative research Marketing research that focuses on smaller numbers of people and tries to answer questions that begin with "why" or "how." (p. 663)

quality check method A checking method that inspects workmanship and general characteristics of the received merchandise. (p. 560)

quantitative research Marketing research that answers questions that begin with "how many" or "how much." (p. 663)

quota A limit on either the quantity or the monetary value of a product that may be imported. (p. 88)

R

rack jobber One who manages inventory and merchandising for retailers by counting stock, filling the shelves when needed, and maintaining store displays. (p. 493)

* **range** An amount or extent of variation; complete group that is included between two points on a scale of measurement or quality. (p. 44)

* **rapport** A feeling of sympathetic and mutual understanding. (p. 307)

* **ratio** A relationship between the sizes of two numbers or amounts. (p. 858)

rational motive A conscious, logical reason for a purchase. (p. 302)

realistic goal A goal that you have a reasonable chance of achieving. (p. 880)

real-time inventory system A system that uses Internet technology that connects applications, data, and users in real time. (p. 573)

receiving record Information recorded by businesses about they goods they receive. (p. 558)

recession A period of economic slowdown that lasts for at least two quarters, or six months. (p. 75)

recovery The term that signifies a period of renewed economic growth following a recession or depression. (p. 76)

reference Someone who knows your work habits and personal traits and will recommend you for a job. (p. 901)

referral A recommendation of another person who might buy the product being sold. (p. 303)

* **region** An area; place; space. Often refers to a geographic area. (p. 443)

* **register** To record in writing or enroll. (p. 408)

* **regulate** To bring into conformity with rules or principles. (p. 517)

* **relation** A logical or natural association between two or more things; relevance of one to another; connection (p. 605)

reliability When a research technique produces nearly identical results in repeated trials; the trait of being dependable. (p. 689)

remedial action A means of encouraging appropriate workplace behavior in order to improve employee performance. (p. 264)

* **require** Consider as obligatory, useful, just, or proper. (p. 258)

resources All the things used in producing goods and services; a source of aid or support that may be drawn upon when needed. (pp. 61, 253)

* **respond** To reply or show a response or a reaction to something. (p. 192)

* **restrict** To place limits on. (p. 528)

résumé A brief summary of personal information, education, skills, work experience, activities, and interests. (p. 902)

retailer A business that buys goods from whole-salers or directly from manufacturers and resells them to consumers. (pp. 126, 494)

return on investment (ROI) A financial calculation that is used to determine the relative profitability of a product. (p. 587)

reverse auction An auction in which companies post online what they want to buy, and suppliers bid for the contract. (p. 549)

revolving account A charge account offered by a retailer that sets the credit limit and payment terms. (p. 764)

risk management The systematic process of managing an organization's risks to achieve objectives in a manner consistent with public interest, human safety, environmental needs, and the law. (p. 799)

* **role** The actions and activities assigned to or required or expected of a person or group. (p. 147)

routine decision making A type of customer decision making used when a person needs little information about a product he or she is buying. (p. 288)

* **routing** Sending via a specific route. (p. 559)

RPN A reverse-entry method used in calculators, in which the operators follow the operands. (p. 175)

S

---

sales check A written record of a sales transaction that includes such information as the date, items purchased, prices, sales tax, and total amount due. (p. 365)

sales forecast The projection of probable, future sales in units or dollars. (p. 40)

sales promotion All marketing activities, other than personal selling, advertising, and public relations, that are directed at business or retail customers to boost sales. (p. 397)

sales promotions Incentives that encourage customers to buy products or services. (p. 405)

sales quota A dollar or unit sales goal set for the sales staff to achieve in a specified period of time. (p. 281)

sales tax A percentage fee levied by the government on the sale of goods and services. (p. 370)

sample Part of a target population that represents the entire population. (p. 684)

scarcity The difference between wants and needs and available resources. (p. 62)

secondary data Data already collected for some purpose other than the current study. (p. 681)

Securities and Exchange Commission (SEC) Regulator of the sale of securities (stocks and bonds). It is responsible for issuing licenses to brokerage firms and financial advisers and investigates any actions among corporations that affect the value of stocks. (p. 142)

segmented pricing strategy A strategy that uses two or more different prices for a product, though there is no difference in the item's cost. (p. 614)

selective distribution Distribution in which a limited number of outlets in a given geographic area sell a manufacturer's product. (p. 505)

self-esteem How you perceive your worth or value as a person. (p. 233)

selling point The function of a product feature and its benefit to a customer. (p. 301)

* **sequence** An order of steps; serial arrangement in which things follow in logical order or a recurrent pattern. (p. 200)

* **series** Similar things placed in order or happening one after another. (p. 641)

service approach A retail-selling method in which salespeople ask customers if they need assistance. (p. 309)

service close A closing method in sales in which services that overcome obstacles or problems are explained. (p. 345)

services Intangible items that have monetary value and satisfy your needs and wants. (p. 7)

setting Where communication takes place, including place, time, sights, and sounds. (p. 191)

* **shadowing** Spending time in the workplace with someone as he or she goes through a normal workday. (p. 297)

signature The name of the advertiser or logotype that is the distinctive identification symbol for a business. (p. 474)

* **significant** Of great importance. (p. 856)

* **similar** Having the same or some of the same characteristics. (p. 17)

site map An outline of what can be found on each page within a Web site. (p. 223)

situation analysis The study of the internal and external factors that affect marketing strategies. (p. 37)

six-month merchandise plan The budget that estimates planned purchases for a six-month period. (p. 538)

skimming pricing A pricing policy that sets a very high price for a new product. (p. 609)

slogan A catchy phrase or words that identify a product or company. (p. 475)

social media Electronic media that allows people with similar interests to participate in a social network. (p. 397)

sole proprietorship A business that is owned and operated by one person. (p. 786)

* **solidify** To make strong or united. (p. 278)

* **source** A person, plan, or thing that provides something needed. (p. 821)

source marking Method used by sellers or manufacturers to mark the price before delivering the merchandise to the retailer. (p. 561)

specialty media Relatively inexpensive useful items featuring an advertiser's name or logo; also called giveaways or advertising specialties. (p. 449)

* **specific** Stated explicitly or in detail. (p. 683)

specific goal A goal stated in exact terms and including some details. (p. 880)

spot check method A random checking method of one carton in a shipment for quantity, and one item in the carton is inspected for quality; if the item is as stated on invoice, remaining cartons are assumed to be in the same condition. (p. 560)

spreadsheet program A computer program that organizes, calculates, and analyzes numerical data. (p. 214)

staffing/temporary agency An employment agency not supported by taxes that must earn a profit to stay in business; it charges a fee for its services, paid either by the job applicant or the employer. (p. 894)

standard English The formal style of writing and speaking learned in school. (p. 899)

standing-room-only close A closing method in sales used when a product is in short supply or when the price will be going up. (p. 344)

start-up costs Projections of how much money a new business owner needs for the business's first year of operation. (p. 845)

* **statistic** A number that represents facts or that describes a situation. (p. 473)

stockholder An owner of a corporation with limited liability. (p. 789)

stockkeeping unit (SKU) A unit or group of related items. (p. 568)

storage The holding of goods until they are sold. (p. 525)

store layout Ways that stores use floor space to facilitate and promote sales and serve customers. (p. 421)

storefront A business's exterior, including the sign, marquee, outdoor lighting, banners, awnings, windows, and exterior design of the building. (p. 420)

* **strategy** An elaborate and systematic plan of action. (p. 586)

* **stress** To single out as important. (p. 802)

* **structure** An organization or system that is made up of many parts that work together. (p. 136)

* **subordinate** Having less power or authority than someone else. (p. 883)

substitution method Recommending a different product that would still satisfy the customer's needs. (p. 331)

suggestion selling Selling additional goods or services to the customer. (p. 359)

superior-point method A technique of overcoming objections by permitting the salesperson to acknowledge objections as valid, yet still offset them with other features and benefits. (p. 332)

supervisory-level management Type of management in which managers supervise the employees who carry out the tasks determined by middle and top management. (p. 253)

supply The amount of goods producers are willing to make and sell. (p. 119)

* **survey** A gathering of a sample of data or opinions considered to be representative of a whole. (p. 166)

survey method A research technique in which information is gathered from people through the use of surveys and questionnaires. (p. 684)

* **swatch** A sample piece of fabric. (p. 323)

SWOT analysis An assessment that lists and analyzes the company's strengths and weaknesses. SWOT is an acronym for strengths, weaknesses, opportunities, and threats. (p. 31)

T

* **target** Something or someone to be affected by an action or development. (p. 401)

target market The group of people most likely to become customers, identified for a specific marketing program. (p. 18)

tariff A tax on imports. (p. 88)

teamwork Work done by a group of people to achieve a common goal. (p. 243)

* **technical** Of or relating to proficiency in a practical skill. (p. 537)

* **technique** A method of doing something using a special skill. (p. 478)

* **technology** The practical application of science to commerce or industry or practical problems. (p. 31)

telecommuting Working at home, usually on a computer. Employees can send completed tasks by e-mail or mail-in disk. (p. 147)

telemarketing Telephone solicitation to make a sale. (p. 286)

terms for delivery The final delivery arrangement made between the buyer and seller. (p. 382)

* **theory** A belief; an abstract thought or idea. (p. 65)

third-party method A technique that involves using another customer or neutral person who can give a testimonial about the product. (p. 333)

30-day account A regular charge account that enables customers to charge purchases during a month and pay the balance in full within 30 days after they are billed. (p. 764)

till The cash drawer of a cash register. (p. 375)

time management Budgeting your time to accomplish tasks on a certain schedule. (p. 234)

ton-mile Movement of one ton (2,000 pounds) of freight one mile. (p. 519)

top management Those who make decisions that affect the whole company. (p. 253)

trade character A specific type of brand mark, one with human form or characteristics. (p. 732)

trade name Corporate brand; identifies and promotes a company or division of a particular corporation. (p. 731)

trade promotions Sales promotions designed to get support for a product from manufacturers, wholesalers, and retailers. (p. 405)

trademark A word, name, symbol, sound, brand name, brand mark, trade name, trade character, color, or a combination of these elements that identifies a good or service and cannot be used by anyone but the owner because it is registered with the federal government and has legal protection. (pp. 114, 732)

trading area The geographical area from which a business draws its customers. (p. 823)

* **tradition** A specific practice of long standing. (p. 382)

traditional economy An economic system in which habits, traditions, and rituals answer the basic questions of what, how, and for whom. (p. 63)

* **transfer** To move from one place to another. (p. 368)

transit advertising Advertisement seen on public transportation. (p. 445)

* **transmit** To send from one person or place to another. (p. 902)

transportation The marketing function of moving a product from the place it's made to where it is sold. (p. 516)

* **trend** A general direction in which something tends to move; current style or inclination. (p. 123)

triadic colors Three colors equally spaced on the color wheel, such as red, yellow, and blue. (p. 430)

trial close An initial effort to close a sale. (p. 342)

U

* **ultimate** Furthest or highest in degree or order; utmost or extreme. (p. 618)

* **undergo** To experience something, often unpleasant. (p. 805)

uniform resource locator (URL) The protocol used to identify and locate Web pages on the Internet; Web address. (p. 222)

* **unique** Radically distinctive and without equal. (p. 708)

unit control A stock control method that measures the amounts of merchandise a business handles during a stated period of time. (p. 570)

unit pricing A pricing method that allows consumers to compare prices in relation to a standard unit or measure. (p. 595)

Universal Product Code (UPC) A combination barcode and number used to identify a product and manufacturer that must be on every item sold by the manufacturer. (p. 374)

unlimited liability A type of investment in which the business owner's financial liability is not limited to investments in the business, but extends to his or her total ability to make payments. (p. 787)

utility An added value in economic terms; an attribute of goods or services that makes them capable of satisfying consumers' wants and needs. (p. 14)

V

* **validity** When the questions in a questionnaire measure what was intended to be measured; the quality of being logically valid or effective. (p. 689)

values Beliefs that guide the way we live. (p. 873)

* **vary** To be different; to change. (p. 790)

* **vehicle** A medium for the expression or achievement of something. (p. 618)

vertical organization A hierarchical, up-and-down structure in which the tasks and responsibilities of each level are clearly defined. (p. 253)

* **via** By way of. (p. 396)

* **visual** Able to be seen. (p. 634)

visual merchandising Coordinating all the physical elements in a place of business to project an image to customers. (p. 419)

* **volume** The property of something that is great in magnitude. (p. 349)

W

want slip Customer request for an item or items not carried in the store. (p. 545)

warranty A promise or guarantee given to a customer that a product will meet certain standards. (p. 753)

warranty of fitness for a particular purpose A warranty that is used when the seller advises a customer that a product is suitable for a particular use, and the customer acts on that advice. (p. 755)

warranty of merchantability A seller's promise that the product sold is fit for its intended purpose. (p. 755)

which close A closing method in sales that encourages a customer to make a decision between two items. (p. 344)

whistle-blowing Reporting an illegal action of one's employer. (p. 153)

wholesale and retail buyers Buyers who purchase goods for resale. (p. 538)

wholesaler A business that obtains goods from manufacturers and resells them to organizational users, other wholesalers, and retailers, also called distributors. (pp. 126, 493)

Wi-Fi Wireless fidelity; the technology that creates a wireless Internet connection with radio frequencies. (p. 217)

word-processing program An application that creates text documents that may contain a few graphics. (p. 213)

World Trade Organization (WTO) A global coalition of nations that makes the rules governing international trade. (p. 90)

World Wide Web A part of the Internet and a collection of interlinked electronic documents. (p. 222)

Index

Index

Index

Index

Index

Index

Top-heavy ad layouts, 478
Toshiba, 707
Total expenses, 855
Total quality management (TQM), 670
Total sales, 852
Touch-screens, 220, 221
Toyota, 86
Toys 'R' Us, 96, 420, 588
Trade agreements and alliances, 90–91
Trade associations, 657, 683, 821, 876
Trade barriers, 88–89
Trade characters, 732
Trade deficit, 87–88
Trade discounts, 617, 641
Trade names, 731
Trade promotions, 405–406
Trade regulations and laws, 96
Trade restrictions, 35
Trade shows, 406
Trade-in allowances, 617
Trademarks, 115, 732
Trading area, 823
Trading area analysis, 823–824
Traditional economies, 63
Traffic builders, 407
Training, 243, 263, 281, 297, 805
Transferring merchandise, 562–563
Transferring risk, 807–810
Transit advertising, 445–446
Transportation, as marketing function, 516
Transportation service companies, 522–523
Transportation systems, 516–521
Travel and entertainment cards, 762
Trial closes, 342
Tripadvisor.com, 125
Trucking, 517–519
Trustmarks, 8
Truth in Lending Act of 1968, 766
Turnover rates, 571 Twitter, 354, 449
Twitter, 11, 468
Tylenol, 714
Type sizes (print ads), 480
Typefaces (print ads), 479

U

Ultimate résumés, 903
Under Armour, 442
Unemployment, 35
Unemployment rate, 74
Unfair trade practices, 596
Uniform resource locators (URLs), 222
Unilever, 46, 95, 99
Unit control (stock), 570
Unit pricing, 595
United States-Chile Free Trade Agreement, 96
U.S. Congress, 138
U.S. Customs, 93

U.S. Department of Agriculture (USDA), 137, 138, 745
U.S. government, 137–145, 682
U.S. Postal Service (USPS), 382, 522, 787
Universal Product Code (UPC), 374, 547, 561, 573
Unlimited liability, 787
Unsecured loans, 764
Updating products, 719
UPS, 382, 518, 522
Up-selling, 350, 351
USF Holland, 517
uSocial, 615
Utilities, 14–15

V

Validity, of questionnaires, 689
VALS, 48
Value(s)
    in market segmentation, 48
    and price, 585
    in self-assessment, 873–874
Variable expenses, 854
Vending services, 495
Vendor services, 355
Vendors, discounts by, 640–642
Verizon, 138
Vertical organization, 253
Viacom, Inc., 95
Video ads, 448
Videoconferencing, 217
Violent crime, in the workplace, 807
Viral marketing, 443
Virtual ad agencies, 469
Visual control method (inventory), 568
Visual merchandisers, 419, 427
Visual merchandising, 419–425. See also Displays

W

Walk-in job applicants, 261
Walmart, 116, 547, 586, 588, 593
Warehouse Management Systems (WMS), 573
Warehouses, 525–527
Warranties, 753–756, 810
Warranties of fitness, 755
Warranties of merchantability, 755
W.E. Kellogg Institute for Food and Nutrition Research, 709
Web analytics, 667, 668
Web page design, 204
Web sites. See also Internet
    ads on, 468
    of companies, job leads from, 896
    development of, 223–224
    for job leads, 894
    sales support staff for, 286

selling via, 277–278
    as storefronts, 431
Web surveys, 694
Web-based software, 854
Web-page editors, 216
Wells Fargo, 655
Wendy's, 94, 376, 714
Which close, 344
Whistle-blowing, 152
Whole numbers, 165
Wholesale buyers, 538
Wholesalers, 126, 127, 493–494, 605
Wi-Fi (wireless fidelity), 217
Window displays, 421
Word of Mouth Productions, 480
Word-processing programs, 213
Work environment preferences, 874–875
Work experience programs, 894
Work permits, 901
Workers' compensation insurance, 810
Working environment risks, 802
Workplace ethics, 236–237
World Business Council for Sustainable Development (WBCSD), 149
World Trade Organization (WTO), 90
World Wide Web, 222–224. See also Internet
Wrigley, 422
Writing, 201–204

X

Xbox 360, 409
Xerox, 500

Y

Yahoo!, 97, 222, 661
Yellow Roadway, 517
Yes/no questions, 690
YouTube, 449

Z

Z ad layouts, 478

972